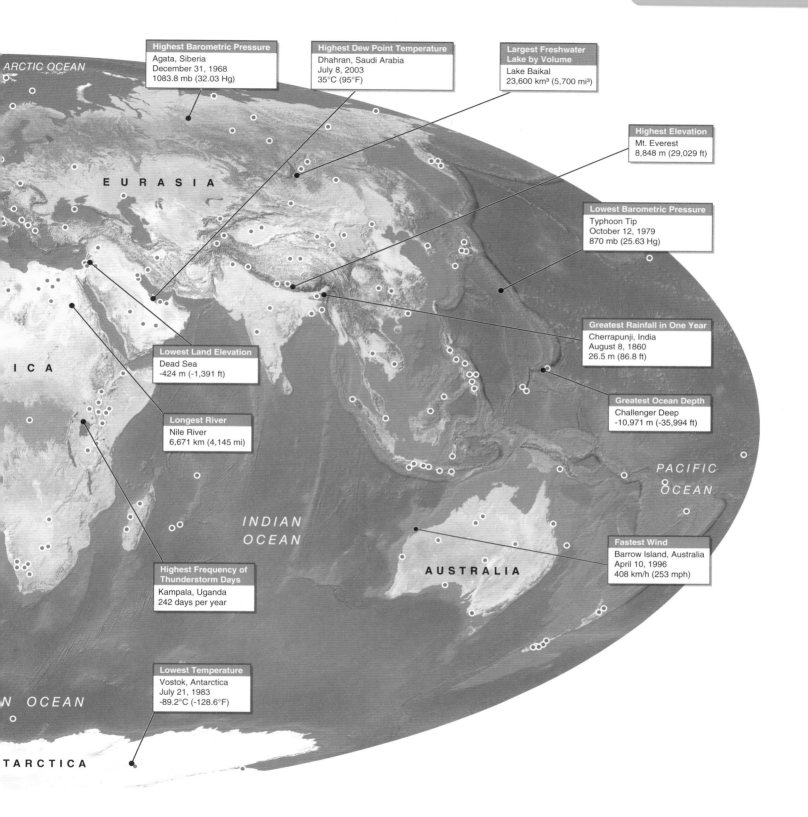

Highest Barometric Pressure
Agata, Siberia
December 31, 1968
1083.8 mb (32.03 Hg)

Highest Dew Point Temperature
Dhahran, Saudi Arabia
July 8, 2003
35°C (95°F)

Largest Freshwater Lake by Volume
Lake Baikal
23,600 km³ (5,700 mi³)

Highest Elevation
Mt. Everest
8,848 m (29,029 ft)

Lowest Barometric Pressure
Typhoon Tip
October 12, 1979
870 mb (25.63 Hg)

Greatest Rainfall in One Year
Cherrapunji, India
August 8, 1860
26.5 m (86.8 ft)

Lowest Land Elevation
Dead Sea
-424 m (-1,391 ft)

Greatest Ocean Depth
Challenger Deep
-10,971 m (-35,994 ft)

Longest River
Nile River
6,671 km (4,145 mi)

Fastest Wind
Barrow Island, Australia
April 10, 1996
408 km/h (253 mph)

Highest Frequency of Thunderstorm Days
Kampala, Uganda
242 days per year

Lowest Temperature
Vostok, Antarctica
July 21, 1983
-89.2°C (-128.6°F)

ARCTIC OCEAN

EURASIA

INDIAN OCEAN

PACIFIC OCEAN

AUSTRALIA

ICA

OCEAN

ARCTICA

Living Physical Geography

BRUCE GERVAIS

CALIFORNIA STATE UNIVERSITY, SACRAMENTO

 W. H. FREEMAN
& COMPANY

A Macmillan Education Imprint
New York

Vice President, Editorial: Charles Linsmeier
Associate Publisher: Steven Rigolosi
Marketing Manager: Taryn Burns
Developmental Editor: Donald Gecewicz
Media Editor: Lukia Kliossis
Market Development: Stephanie Ellis and Burrston House, Ltd.
Photo Editor: Sheena Goldstein
Photo Researcher: Jerry Marshall
Art Director: Diana Blume
Cover and Text Designer: Tom Carling, Carling Design Inc.
Project Editor: Enrico Bruno
Managing Editor: Lisa Kinne
Illustrations: Precision Graphics; Mapping Specialists
Art Manager: Matthew McAdams
Production Coordinator: Susan Wein
Composition: Tom Carling; codeMantra
Printing and Binding: Quad/Graphics
Cover Art: Tennessee Cove, Marin Headlands, © 2013 by Tom Killion

Library of Congress Control Number: 2014945391

ISBN-13: 978-1-4641-0664-4
ISBN-10: 1-4641-0664-9

W. H. Freeman and Company
41 Madison Avenue
New York, NY 10010
www.whfreeman.com

FSC
www.fsc.org
MIX
Paper from
responsible sources
FSC® C084269

For Nancy, Katherine, and Natalie

Brief Contents

Contents

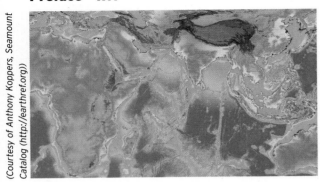

(Courtesy of Anthony Koppers, Seamount Catalog (http://earthref.org))

PART I
ATMOSPHERIC SYSTEMS: Weather and Climate

(© Andy Rouse/naturepl.com/NaturePL)

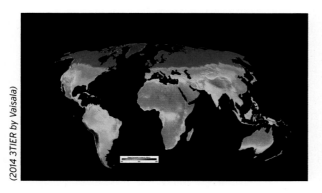

(2014 3TIER by Vaisala)

(Beyond/SuperStock)

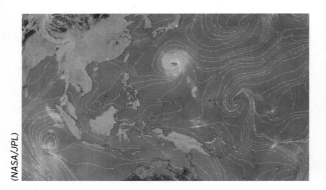

(NASA/JPL)

(© A. T. Willett/Alamy)

(© Ashley Cooper/Age Fotostock Inc.)

(© Philippe Michel/age fotostock)

(© Bill Bachmann/age fotostock)

(© Morales/age fotostock)

(© Design Pics Inc./Alamy)

(© Mannfred Gottschalk/Lonely Planet Images/Getty Images)

(© Last Refuge/Robert Harding Picture Library/Age Fotostock Inc.)

(EROS Center, U.S. Geological Survey)

(© Dr. Juerg Alean/Science Source)

(Per-Andre Hoffmann/Picture Press/Getty Images)

(Ben Pipe/Robert Harding World Imagery/Getty Images)

Preface

Living Physical Geography: The Big Picture

We are all living physical geography. Weather and climate strongly influence where we live and the types of crops farmers can grow. Almost half the world's population lives within 150 km (93 mi) of the coast, mostly in large cities situated in bays and estuaries at the mouths of major rivers. Floods and drought, cold snaps and heat waves, volcanic eruptions and earthquakes, soil development and landslides all influence human beings. Physical geography is now more relevant to society than ever. Changes in air quality and climate, losses of habitat and species, soil and water resource demands, and burgeoning renewable energy technologies are all topics that are in the news daily and are all central to the science of physical geography.

The idea for this book originated with my desire to highlight the relevance of physical geography to students' daily lives and to address the most pressing environmental and resource issues that people face today. *Living Physical Geography* is unique in that it emphasizes how people change, and are changed by, Earth's physical systems. This approach creates a student-friendly context in which to understand Earth systems science and reveals the connections between Earth and people.

Three major themes are woven throughout this book:

1. **Earth is composed of interacting physical systems.** The atmosphere, the biosphere, water, and Earth's crust are major physical systems that interact with and affect one another. Energy from the Sun and energy from Earth's interior change these systems.

2. **Earth is always changing.** The physical Earth is in a constant state of change on many different time scales. The weather changes within minutes, tides ebb and flow over hours, rivers shift their channels across centuries, and over millions of years species evolve, mountains grow and are worn down, and whole continents move.

3. **The influence of people is important.** Earth's land surface, atmosphere, life, and oceans are extensively changed by people. It is not possible to study modern physical geography without considering the influences of human activity.

There are other important themes that also provide the foundation for and enliven the study of physical geography in this book:

Spatial and temporal relationships underpin geographic thinking. Geographers often ask why things occur where they do and how they change through time. For example, why do deserts and rainforests occur where they do? How long have they been in their present locations? How are they changing now? *Living Physical Geography* examines Earth's physical features and processes through the lens of geographic space and time.

People depend on Earth's natural resources. From the energy we use, to the materials in the things we acquire, to the food we eat, people depend on natural resources from Earth's physical systems.

People are influenced by physical geography. Volcanic eruptions and earthquakes, the development of rich agricultural soils with river flooding, severe weather and climate change, storm protection of coastal cities by wetlands, freshwater supplies from groundwater and streams are a few examples of physical phenomena that influence the lives of people.

Science is driven by people. Scientific inquiry in the Earth sciences is driven by a fundamental curiosity about how the natural world works.

The Structure of *Living Physical Geography*

Living Physical Geography is divided into four main parts, focusing on the atmosphere, the biosphere, the building up of the lithosphere, and the wearing down of the lithosphere. Each part focuses on the flow and work of energy. Solar energy drives processes in the atmosphere, in the biosphere, and in the wearing down of the lithosphere. Earth's internal heat energy drives processes that build the lithosphere. Figure GT.11 (found on page 12), reprinted here, illustrates the book's organization.

PART I
Atmospheric Systems: Weather and Climate

Chapter 1 Portrait of the Atmosphere
Chapter 2 Seasons and Solar Energy
Chapter 3 Water in the Atmosphere
Chapter 4 Atmospheric Circulation and Wind Systems
Chapter 5 The Restless Sky: Storm Systems and El Niño
Chapter 6 The Changing Climate

PART II
The Biosphere and the Geography of Life

Chapter 7 Patterns of Life: Biogeography
Chapter 8 Climate and Life: Biomes
Chapter 9 Soil and Water Resources
Chapter 10 The Living Hydrosphere: Ocean Ecosystems

PART IV
Erosion and Deposition: Sculpting Earth's Surface

Chapter 15 Weathering and Mass Movement
Chapter 16 Flowing Water: Fluvial Systems
Chapter 17 The Work of Ice: The Cryosphere and Glacial Landforms
Chapter 18 Water, Wind, and Time: Desert Landforms
Chapter 19 The Work of Waves: Coastal Landforms

PART III
Tectonic Systems: Building the Lithosphere

Chapter 11 Earth History, Earth Interior
Chapter 12 Drifting Continents: Plate Tectonics
Chapter 13 Building the Crust with Rocks
Chapter 14 Geohazards: Volcanoes and Earthquakes

Part I: Atmospheric Systems: Weather and Climate

All meteorological phenomena are powered by the Sun. For example, wind is solar powered because it derives its energy from the unequal heating of Earth's surface by the Sun. Similarly, rainfall is the result of evaporation of water from the oceans by the Sun.

Part II: The Biosphere and the Geography of Life

Solar energy fuels the biosphere. Life on Earth obtains its energy from the Sun (with the exception of the organisms around some hydrothermal vents on land and in the deep ocean). Plants convert solar energy to chemical energy. When plants are eaten, their chemical energy flows into the organism consuming them.

Part III: Tectonic Systems: Building the Lithosphere

Earth's internal heat energy (geothermal energy) lifts, buckles, and breaks the crust. Earth's internal heat also creates new rocks and moves the plates of the lithosphere, forming mountains, valleys, volcanoes, and ocean basins.

Part IV: Erosion and Deposition: Sculpting Earth's Surface

Solar energy sculpts the lifted crust. Sunlight evaporates water into the atmosphere. That water subsequently falls to the ground as precipitation, then returns to the oceans through flowing streams and flowing glaciers. These streams and glaciers erode the crust, reducing its height and smoothing it.

Living Physical Geography features discussion of the hydrosphere throughout the text as it naturally occurs rather than treating it as a separate entity. For example, water runs through and influences nearly all of Earth's physical systems, including the atmosphere, ecosystems and biomes, fluvial and glacial systems, and the crust's groundwater. Additionally, *Living Physical Geography* devotes an entire chapter to the oceans by examining their physical structure and the geographic patterns of life found in them.

The contents of this book follow a logical sequence, but each instructor approaches the discipline in a different way and may present topics in a different order. For this reason, each chapter is largely self-contained and makes cross-references to key information in other chapters only when needed.

Living Physical Geography: Innovations

Living Physical Geography was written to help instructors teach physical geography more effectively. In addition to emphasizing the interactions between physical geography and people, *Living Physical Geography* offers the following structural innovations:

- Humidity is covered before atmospheric pressure and wind. The release of heat energy through condensation drives many atmospheric phenomena and the winds they produce. The wind generated by hurricanes, for example, is the result of condensation of water vapor into liquid water in the atmosphere. To understand why a hurricane's winds are so strong, it is necessary to first understand the role of water vapor's latent heat. In this book, atmospheric weather systems are arranged by their spatial scales, from localized mountain breezes to the continent-wide Asian monsoon.

- Köppen climate types are covered alongside biomes. In most physical geography textbooks, Köppen climate types and biomes are covered in two separate chapters. *Living Physical Geography* avoids this redundancy by combining these two compatible topics. In doing so, it establishes the natural link between climate and biomes and illustrates the interconnections of physical geography.

- The theory of plate tectonics undergirds all of Part III. Plate tectonics is covered before the topics of mountain building and rock formation, along with geohazards like earthquakes and eruptions, because all these geophysical phenomena are best contextualized within the paradigm of plate tectonics.

- Chapter 6, "The Changing Climate," is devoted to a scientific examination of climate change. Climate change is perhaps the fastest-moving topic in physical geography. The material presented in this book represents the most up-to-date examples, scientific research, and data on climate. Most students are deeply interested in climate change, and this chapter helps them to understand the current scientific consensus on this important topic and develop independent conclusions based on scientific data.

- Four chapters are devoted to the biosphere. The geography of the biosphere, including life in the oceans, receives extended coverage in *Living Physical Geography*. The theme of how people have changed the biosphere runs throughout Part II, "The Biosphere and the Geography of Life."

- A full chapter is devoted to the geography of life in the oceans. The physical and biological oceans are highly relevant to physical geography. Recent exploration and discoveries have improved scientific understanding of marine life, but scientists still know relatively little about the oceans. Chapter 10, "The Living Hydrosphere: Ocean Ecosystems," reflects recent advances in scientific knowledge of marine ecosystems and an awareness of the most pressing marine environmental issues.

Living Physical Geography Is Written for a Variety of Ways Students Learn

Living Physical Geography is written to engage students and hold their interest, especially those with little background in the Earth sciences. It uses a variety of learning tools to accommodate the different ways that students learn.

The art program and photography support the written text. Many figures illustrate processes in a step-by-step sequence. Basic geographic concepts, such as geographic scale and physical systems, are repeatedly developed throughout the book, reinforcing for students the major themes in physical geography.

Living Physical Geography Is an Integrated Textbook/ Media Learning Solution

Living Physical Geography is an integrated learning system that combines a textbook with digital media to enhance the teaching and learning of physical geography. The following media components are part of this integrated system:

Exploring with Google Earth
Google Earth is an important pedagogical tool in *Living Physical Geography*. An "Exploring with Google Earth" activity appears at the end of each chapter. The .kml files required to complete these activities are available on LaunchPad.

Students benefit from using Google Earth because it familiarizes them with the spatial relationships of physical and cultural features of Earth, vividly illustrating the spatial perspective that is essential to geography. Using these exercises, students will be able to quickly navigate to and interpret physical phenomena such as Mount Fuji, the Grand Canyon, the fjords of Greenland, the sand seas of Algeria, and the glaciers of New Zealand. (Answers to the Exploring with Google Earth questions are available in the Instructor's Manual.)

Animations and Videos

Animations are available for key figures throughout the book. The animations show the movement and development of select physical geography phenomena. For example, the formation of a stratovolcano as it grows by adding layers of ash and lava flows is animated to enhance student learning of this process.

These animations are accessible through LaunchPad, where they are accompanied by questions that assess students' understanding of the concepts. The animations are also available for immediate access with a smartphone using QR (Quick Response) codes that appear next to the relevant figures.

A library of short videos is also available. This collection is designed to support and further develop selected topics in each chapter. Select videos are conveniently accessible through QR codes in each chapter. The complete collection is also available, along with assessment questions, on LaunchPad.

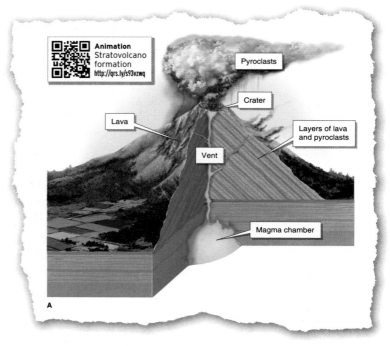

Animation
Stratovolcano formation
http://qrs.ly/s93vzwq

Pyroclasts

Crater

Lava

Layers of lava and pyroclasts

Vent

Magma chamber

A

Learning Tools

The learning tools in *Living Physical Geography* have been carefully designed to provide a multimedia, multimodal approach to the teaching and learning of physical geography.

Chapter Opener with Chapter Outline

Each chapter begins with a two-page image or photo that relates to the contents of the chapter. Each image is briefly described, and reference to the appropriate section within the chapter is provided to stimulate students to seek further information about the image. A brief chapter outline allows the reader to preview the chapter's contents.

1 Portrait of the Atmosphere

Chapter Outline

1.1 Composition of the Atmosphere

1.2 The Weight of Air: Atmospheric Pressure

1.3 The Layered Atmosphere

1.4 Air Pollution

1.5 Geographic Perspectives: Refrigerators and Life on Earth

"Living Physical Geography" Questions

The chapter opener also includes a set of "Living Physical Geography" questions. This feature is designed to stimulate interest in the chapter material by asking questions that students may already have. Each question is repeated at the place in the chapter where students will find the answer. Brief versions of the answers to each question are provided at the end of the chapter.

> **LIVING PHYSICAL GEOGRAPHY**
> ➤ What causes seasons?
> ➤ Does it snow in Hawai'i?
> ➤ Why are the sky blue and grass green?
> ➤ Why does the wind blow?

The Big Picture

At the beginning of each chapter, a brief description in a color band orients students to the chapter's main themes in one or two sentences.

THE BIG PICTURE *Earth's hot interior and its moving crust create volcanoes and earthquakes. These phenomena shape the surface of the crust and present hazards for people.*

Learning Goals

At the start of each chapter, a list of learning goals is provided. Each numbered section of the chapter begins with a repetition of the relevant learning goal. These learning goals break each chapter down into manageable units while helping instructors focus on the learning outcomes that are important to them.

LEARNING GOALS *After reading this chapter, you will be able to:*

2.1 ◎ Explain what causes seasons and give the major characteristics of the four seasons.
2.2 ◎ Understand the difference between temperature and heat.
2.3 ◎ Describe Earth's surface temperature patterns and explain what causes them.
2.4 ◎ Describe solar energy and its different wavelengths.
2.5 ◎ Explain Earth's energy budget and why the atmosphere circulates.
2.6 ◎ Assess the role of sunlight as a clean energy source.

The Human Sphere

Each chapter opens with a section titled "The Human Sphere." This opening story briefly explores the relationship between people and a physical phenomenon or process. The key goals of this feature are to illustrate the importance of people to physical geography and to demonstrate the relevance of physical geography to students' daily lives. Some examples of the Human Sphere topics include air pollution in Wyoming, Asian dust storms, EF5 tornadoes, non-native species, tsunamis, weathering on Mount Rushmore, and collecting mammoth remains from thawing permafrost.

THE HUMAN SPHERE: Exotic Invaders

FIGURE 7.1 **A Nile perch.** *The non-native Nile perch has inflicted serious ecological damage in Lake Victoria. It preys on the lake's native cichlid fish and has driven about 300 cichlid species to extinction or near-extinction. Nile perch grow to nearly 2 m (6.5 ft) and can weigh 200 kg (440 lb).* (© Walter Astrada/AFP/Getty Images)

NON-NATIVE (or exotic) organisms are those that have been moved outside their original geographic range by people. Some non-native organisms cause ecological damage by preying on or taking resources in their new ranges from native organisms (those that were there originally). In many areas where non-natives are successful, their natural predators are missing. For example, the Nile perch (*Lates niloticus*) (Figure 7.1), which was intentionally brought into Lake Victoria in eastern Africa in the 1950s as a food resource for local communities, has had significant negative effects on native fish species in the lake.

Today, non-native species are implicated in extinctions worldwide. About 50,000 non-native species have been introduced into the United States (although not all of them are harmful). Among the U.S. states, Hawai'i has a particularly serious problem with non-native organisms. Hawai'i has no native reptiles (such as snakes and lizards), no native amphibians (such as frogs), no native parrots, no native ants, and only one native mammal—a bat. Today, Hawai'i has many non-native organisms introduced by people, including escaped garden plants, wild pigs, piranhas, game, bass, trout, chickens, rats,

GEOGRAPHIC PERSPECTIVES
7.6 Journey of the Coconut

◎ Assess the relationship between people and the coconut palm and apply that knowledge to other organisms used by people.

Geographic Perspectives

Each chapter concludes with a section titled "Geographic Perspectives." These sections are mini-case studies that show students how to think like geographers. Some topics explored in the Geographic Perspectives sections are renewable wind and solar energy, the functional value of plant dispersal, strategies to address climate change, the pros and cons of fracking for natural gas, the pros and cons of dams on rivers, the consequences of rising sea level, and the importance of soils. Geographic Perspectives encourage critical thought and assessment in four ways:

1. By providing context for and developing a broader understanding of the material presented in the chapter

2. By illustrating the connections among seemingly disparate topics within a chapter and across chapters

3. By providing instructors with self-contained, manageable units that they can use to facilitate their teaching and stimulate classroom discussion

4. By presenting a balanced view of contemporary environmental issues to encourage critical discussion, reflection, and independent conclusions

Scientific Inquiry

Each chapter has a feature titled "Scientific Inquiry" that reveals why scientists do what they do, how they assess what they know, and how they collect and interpret scientific data. The goal of this feature is to dispel the percep-

FIGURE 7.4 **SCIENTIFIC INQUIRY: How do scientists track animal movement?** *Different animals require different means of tracking. GPS is important in many, but not all, tracking methods. (Butterfly, © Will & Deni McIntyre/Photo Researchers/Getty Images; fish, Eric Orbesen/NOAA Fisheries; goose, © FLPA/Mark Newman/age fotostock; wolf, Oregon Dept. of Fish & Wildlife.)*

GPS technology is too heavy for insects. This simple plastic tag is 2% of this monarch butterfly's (*Danaus plexippus*) weight. Scientists rely on people who find the tagged butterfly to return the tag by mail to the address shown on the tag, indicating where and when the butterfly was captured.

Birds and small fish can be fitted with GPS archival tags that record data for a year or more. These tags record data such as changing light levels and day length. For birds, the tag is glued to the feathers and will fall off when the bird molts (replaces its feathers). These archival tags do not transmit information, so the animal must be recaptured and the tag must be removed.

Pop-Up Satellite Archival Tags (PSATS) are used on large marine migratory animals such as sea turtles, seals, whales, and fish. After a set time, the tag detaches from the animal, floats to the surface, and transmits the data it has recorded to an orbiting satellite.

Radio collars used on large mammals transmit the GPS coordinates of the moving animals to satellites continuously. In December 2011, the male offspring of this female gray wolf (*Canis lupus*), also radio-collared, was tracked as he entered California to become the first known wolf in that state since 1924.

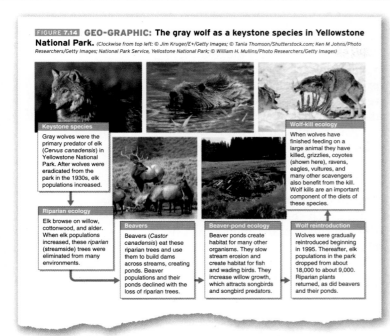

FIGURE 7.14 GEO-GRAPHIC: The gray wolf as a keystone species in Yellowstone National Park. (Clockwise from top left: © Jim Kruger/E+/Getty Images; © Tania Thomson/Shutterstock.com; Ken M Johns/Photo Researchers/Getty Images; National Park Service, Yellowstone National Park; © William H. Mullins/Photo Researchers/Getty Images)

Keystone species

Gray wolves were the primary predator of elk (*Cervus canadensis*) in Yellowstone National Park. After wolves were eradicated from the park in the 1930s, elk populations increased.

Wolf-kill ecology

When wolves have finished feeding on a large animal they have killed (shown here), ravens, eagles, vultures, and many other scavengers also benefit from the kill. Wolf kills are an important component of the diets of these species.

Riparian ecology

Elk browse on willow, cottonwood, and alder. When elk populations increased, these *riparian* (streamside) trees were eliminated from many environments.

Beavers

Beavers (*Castor canadensis*) eat these riparian trees and use them to build dams across streams, creating ponds. Beaver populations and their ponds declined with the loss of riparian trees.

Beaver-pond ecology

Beaver ponds create habitat for many other organisms. They slow stream erosion and create habitat for fish and wading birds. They increase willow growth, which attracts songbirds and songbird predators.

Wolf reintroduction

Wolves were gradually reintroduced beginning in 1995. Thereafter, elk populations in the park dropped from about 18,000 to about 9,000. Riparian plants returned, as did beavers and their ponds.

tion of science as something disconnected from students' daily lives or career options. Topics range from how stream gauges work and why they are important, to how data are collected from marine buoys and weather balloons to forecast hurricane threats, to how data are collected from ice cores for research into ancient atmospheric chemistry.

Geo-Graphics

The Geo-Graphic feature is a pedagogical tool that combines imagery with narrative. Geo-Graphics develop the text narrative without repeating information from the main text. A key goal of this feature is to provide an image-based avenue of learning for students who learn visually. Clear labels guide students through each Geo-Graphic in a logical sequence.

Picture This

In each chapter, the Picture This feature delivers pertinent and intriguing content that supplements the main text and illustrates a relevant principle. The wettest place on Earth, extreme climate events, coal mining, and collapse sinkholes are examples of topics visited in this feature. Each Picture This includes two or three Consider This questions that students can answer by reading supporting text within the feature or the text just preceding it. (Answers to the Consider This questions are available in the Instructor's Manual.)

Picture This

(© Randy Olson/National Geographic/Getty Images)   (© WaterFrame/Alamy)

Wolf Creek Crater — AUSTRALIA

O'ahu, Hawai'i — PACIFIC OCEAN

Which Is the Caldera?

One of these photos shows a volcanic caldera, and one shows an impact crater formed when a meteor struck Earth long ago. Based on the visual evidence from these photos, it is challenging to tell which is the impact crater and which is the caldera. More information is needed. One useful form of evidence is *shatter cone* rock. Meteors hit the planet with such force that the impact energy produces metamorphic shatter cones. Shatter cones are produced only at meteor impact sites. They are not visible in either of these photos.

Consider This

1. If you found a large crater-like landform in volcanic rock, could you be 100% certain that it is a caldera? Explain.

2. Note the geographic settings (see locator maps) for each landform. Based on your reading in this chapter and in Section 12.4, is there geographic information that could help you decide which landform is the caldera?

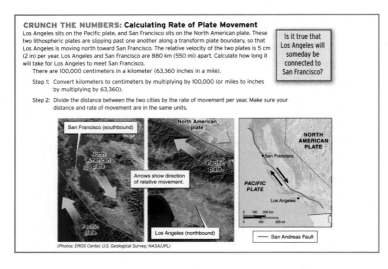

CRUNCH THE NUMBERS: Calculating Rate of Plate Movement

Los Angeles sits on the Pacific plate, and San Francisco sits on the North American plate. These two lithospheric plates are slipping past one another along a transform plate boundary, so that Los Angeles is moving north toward San Francisco. The relative velocity of the two plates is 5 cm (2 in) per year. Los Angeles and San Francisco are 880 km (550 mi) apart. Calculate how long it will take for Los Angeles to meet San Francisco.

There are 100,000 centimeters in a kilometer (63,360 inches in a mile).

Step 1: Convert kilometers to centimeters by multiplying by 100,000 (or miles to inches by multiplying by 63,360).

Step 2: Divide the distance between the two cities by the rate of movement per year. Make sure your distance and rate of movement are in the same units.

Is it true that Los Angeles will someday be connected to San Francisco?

(Photos: EROS Center, U.S. Geological Survey; NASA/JPL)

Crunch the Numbers

A feature titled "Crunch the Numbers" appears in each chapter at an appropriate point. These short quantitative reasoning exercises ask students to think about how the science of physical geography can be expressed in numbers as well as in words. (Answers to the Crunch the Numbers exercises are available in the Instructor's Manual.)

Key Information in Blue

Within each chapter, sentences with key information are emphasized in blue. Collectively, these highlights provide a snapshot of the most essential ideas in the chapter.

Chapter Study Guide

Each chapter concludes with a comprehensive study guide. Included are an Exploring with Google Earth question set, Focus Points that summarize the chapter text, a Key Terms list with page references, Concept Review questions, Critical-Thinking questions, a 10-question Test Yourself quiz, a visual Picture This: Your Turn exercise, a brief Further Reading list, and the answers to the "Living Physical Geography" questions (from the chapter opener). Answers to the study guide questions are provided in the Instructor's Manual.

Locator Maps and Places Visited Index

All photos whose subjects are located in real geographic space are accompanied by a locator map. The purpose of these locator maps is to emphasize and familiarize students with the locations and spatial relationships of places visited in the book. All places visited are listed in the Places Visited Index at the back of the book. The locations of the places visited are also shown on the world map on the inside front cover.

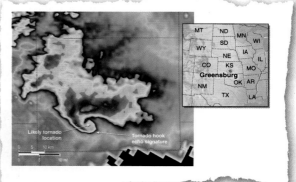

(National Weather Service, Dodge City, KS)

Consistent Use of the Mollweide Map Projection

The Mollweide map projection is used for most world maps in the text. This projection was chosen because it is an equal-area projection that preserves the true relative sizes of the continents. This quality is necessary so that the geographic extent of mapped features, such as regions of atmospheric warming or types of vegetation, can be meaningfully compared across different geographic regions. A consistent map projection fosters a more accurate understanding of spatial dimensions and relationships and greater geographic literacy.

Temperature anomaly

| -1 | -0.5 | -0.2 | 0.2 | 0.5 | 1 | 2 | 4 °C | No data |
| -1.8 | -0.9 | -0.36 | 0.36 | 0.9 | 1.8 | 3.6 | 7.2°F | |

(NASA)

LaunchPad: Resources for Students and Instructors

www.macmillanhighered.com/launchpad/gervais1e

Our new course space, LaunchPad, combines an interactive e-Book with high-quality multimedia content and ready-made assessment options, including LearningCurve adaptive quizzing. Pre-built, curated units are easy to assign or adapt with your own material, such as readings, videos, quizzes, discussion groups, and more. LaunchPad also provides access to a gradebook that provides a clear window on performance for your whole class, for individual students, and for individual assignments. The following resources are available on LaunchPad:

For Students

LearningCurve LearningCurve is an intuitive, fun, and highly effective formative assessment tool that is based on extensive educational research. Students can use LearningCurve to test their knowledge in a low-stakes environment that helps them improve their mastery of key concepts and prepare for classroom discussion, lectures, and exams. Each LearningCurve question provides hints and feedback, along with links to relevant reading in the integrated e-Book. A personalized study plan summarizes each student's results, pointing to the areas mastered, those still to be learned, and relevant sections of the e-Book that students should read. Because LearningCurve is adaptive, it moves students from basic knowledge through critical thinking and synthesis skills as they master content at each level.

e-Book. A complete e-Book is provided within LaunchPad. The e-Book offers powerful study tools for students and easily customizable features for instructors. Embedded resources within the e-Book include animations, videos, and Exploring with Google Earth Activities.

Animations and Videos. Each animation and video (see page xx) is accompanied by a multiple-choice assessment quiz. Results are reported directly to the instructor's gradebook.

Exploring with Google Earth Activities and .kml Files. These activities are online versions of the "Exploring with Google Earth" activities found at the end of each chapter. Here, students can access the .kml files required to complete these activities. Instructors can assign these activities online; results are reported directly to the instructor's gradebook. A tour of select figures in the text is also provided for more in-depth learning of the featured location.

For Instructors

The following resources are available exclusively to instructors on LaunchPad:

Test Bank and **Instructor's Manual**, by Bruce Gervais. The test bank contains approximately 2,500 multiple-choice and true or false questions. Each question is tied to the chapter's learning objectives. The Instructor's Manual includes teaching tips for each chapter, along with the answers or solutions to all the exercises found in the textbook. The author's intimate familiarity with the text material maximizes the effectiveness of the Test Bank's questions and provides useful insight for teaching tips in the Instructor's Manual.

PowerPoint Classroom Presentations, by Nicole C. James. A ready-made PowerPoint presentation is available for each chapter in the textbook. These presentations concisely summarize the key concepts in the chapters.

Textbook Image PowerPoint Presentations. All images from each chapter are provided in PowerPoint format for easy customization.

Textbook Photos and Images. All images and photos from the textbook are available as high-quality electronic files.

Living Physical Geography in the Laboratory: Lab Manual to Accompany *Living Physical Geography*

Theodore Erski, McHenry County College

For schools that offer a physical geography laboratory, *Living Physical Geography in the Laboratory* is the ideal lab manual to accompany *Living Physical Geography*. The manual contains 30 lab activities, each broken down into four problem-solving modules, thus permitting lab instructors to customize the manual to fit the amount of time they have for their lab period. Each lab activity contains the following:

- Recommended textbook reading before the laboratory activities
- Goals of the laboratory activities
- Key terms and concepts (from the textbook)
- Equipment required. Recognizing that many labs do not have access to expensive equipment, the manual focuses on activities that require only the most basic tools or equipment. Some problem-solving activities require more sophisticated equipment. Those activities are clearly separated into discrete modules so that instructors can skip them if the necessary equipment is not available.
- Four problem-solving modules
- Summary of key terms and concepts for each lab

The activities in *Living Physical Geography in the Laboratory* require critical thinking, map and image analysis, data analysis, and occasionally math.

Focus Group Participants

Monika Bachmann, Prince George's Community College; Leonhard Blesius, San Francisco State University; Karen Blevins, Mesa Community College; Caroline Bour, Blinn College; John Conley, Saddleback College; Heather Davis, Southwestern College; Bryant Evans, Houston Community College; Michael Farrell, Los Angeles City College; Leslie Fay, Rock Valley College; David Fox, Park University; Marc Garrett, Bridgewater State University; Mario Giraldo, California State University, Northridge; Brett Goforth, California State University, San Bernardino; Dafna Golden, Mount San Antonio College; Arleen Hill, University of Memphis; Miriam Helen Hill, Jacksonville State University; April Hiscox, University of South Carolina-Columbia; David Holt, University of Southern Mississippi; Michael Hopps, Central Lakes College; Mary Korte, Concordia University; Steve LaDochy, California State University, Los Angeles; George Leddy, Los Angeles Valley College; Liang Liang, University of Kentucky; Andrew Miller, Saginaw Valley State University; Richard Miller, Florida State University; Ricardo Nogueira, Georgia State University; David Pepper, California State University, Long Beach; James Powers, Pasadena City College; Matthew Purtill, West Virginia University; Baishali Ray, Young Harris College; Bradley Rundquist, University of North Dakota; Erinanne Saffell, Mesa Community College; Thomas Saladyga, Concord University; Anne Saxe, MiraCosta College - Oceanside Campus; Steven Smith, Sierra College; Marilyn Smulyan, San Francisco State University; Brian Steinberg, Northern Virginia Community College - Alexandria Campus; Ray Sumner, Long Beach City College; Chelsea Teale, Humboldt State University; Daniel Waktola, Los Angeles Mission College; John Ward, University of Wisconsin–Parkside

Acknowledgments

I am particularly grateful to the following people for their significant contributions to the book:

David Call (Ball State University)
Janice Hayden (Dixie State College of Utah)
Ingrid Luffman (East Tennessee State University)

I also express most sincere appreciation to the reviewers who contributed their knowledge, expertise, and time to *Living Physical Geography*:

Victoria Alapo, Metropolitan Community College—Fort Omaha
Faran Ali, Simon Fraser University
Jake Armour, University of North Carolina—Charlotte
Tamara Biegas, University of Texas at San Antonio
Wayne Brew, Montgomery County Community College
Robin Buckallew, Central Community College
Michaela Buenemann, New Mexico State University
Ke Chen, East Tennessee State University
Sam Copeland, State University of New York—Buffalo North Campus
Richard Crooker, Kutztown University
Daryl Dagesse, Brock University
Carolyn Damato, Salem State University
Jeremy Dillon, University of Nebraska at Kearney
Taly Drezner, York University
Josh Durkee, Western Kentucky University
Robert Edsall, Carthage College
Tracy Edwards, Frostburg State University
William Garcia, University of North Carolina—Charlotte
Colleen Garrity, State University of New York at Geneseo
Greg Gaston, University of North Alabama
Christopher Gentry, Austin Peay State University
Dusty Girard, Brookhaven College
J. Scott Greene, University of Oklahoma
Michael Grossman, Southern Illinois University Edwardsville
Hillary Hamann, University of Denver
William Hansen, Worcester University
Paul Hanson, University of Nebraska—Lincoln
Megan Harlow, Orange Coast College
Mark Hecht, Mount Royal University
Delia Heck, Ferrum College
Patricia Heiser, Carroll College
Chasidy Hobbs, University of West Florida
Margaret Holzer, Rutgers University
Chris Houser, Texas A&M University
Solomon Isiorho, Indiana University—Purdue University Fort Wayne
Renee Jacobsen, California State University, San Bernardino
Brian Jones, University of Alberta
Don Jonsson, Austin Community College

Ranbir S. Kang, Western Illinois University
Wilberg Karigomba, Northwest Area Community College
Ryan Kelly, Bluegrass Community & Technical College
William Kelvey, Carroll Community College
John Keyantash, California State University, Dominguez Hills
Thomas Krabacher, California State University, Sacramento
Barry Kronenfeld, Eastern Illinois University
Michael Lewis, University of North Carolina at Greensboro
Karl Lillquist, Central Washington University
Bruce Lindquist, Leeward Community College
Jennifer Lipton, Central Washington University
Taylor Mack, Louisiana Tech University
Steven Marsh, University of the Fraser Valley
Yvonne Martin, University of Calgary
Larry McGlinn, State University of New York at New Paltz
Armando Mendoza, Cypress College
Andrew Mercer, Mississippi State University
Peter Meserve, Fresno City College
Robert Milligan, Northern Virginia Community College—Woodbridge
Peter Muller, University of Miami
Steve Namikas, Louisiana State University
Elsa Nickl, University of Delaware
Abby Norton-Krane, Cuyahoga Community College
Thomas Orf, Las Positas College
Barry Perlmutter, College of Southern Nevada
Arliss S. Perry, Wright State University
Abdullah F. Rahman, Indiana University
Max W. Reams, Olivet Nazarene University
Ronald Reynolds, Bridgewater State University
Shouraseni Sen Roy, University of Miami
Ruth Ruud, Cleveland State University
David Sallee, University of North Texas/Tarrant County College
Ginger Schmid, Minnesota State University
David Shankman, University of Alabama
Andrew Shears, Kent State University
Erica A. H. Smithwick, Pennsylvania State University
Jane Southworth, University of Florida
Susanna Tong, University of Cincinnati
Cornelis J. van der Veen, University of Kansas
Scott Walker, Northwest Vista College
Megan Walsh, Central Washington University
James Wanket, California State University, Sacramento
Brad Watkins, University of Central Oklahoma
Theresa Watson, Central New Mexico Community College
Forrest Wilkerson, Minnesota State University
Sonja Yow, Eastern Kentucky University
Danlin Yu, Montclair State University

I am deeply grateful for the bedrock support provided by my family while I was writing this book. Thank you, Nancy, for being an inspiration while I was working through and forming many ideas. Thank you, Katherine and Natalie, for your patience while dad was out in the "shed" writing, and thanks for helping me with photo selections. I am immensely grateful for my family's love of nature and enjoyment of visiting wild places.

It was an honor to work with the staff at W. H. Freeman. I was so impressed by their friendly and professional demeanor and their generous support. My sincerest thanks to Steven Rigolosi for believing in my idea when I first presented it to him and for his guidance every step of the way. Steve provided many of the innovative ideas that have helped strengthen the book, and he has been a colleague and friend throughout. For that I am deeply appreciative. Thank you to Charles Linsmeier for his direction in the latter stages of the book.

Thanks to project editor Enrico Bruno and managing editor Lisa Kinne for their meticulous attention to all details great and small. I am thankful to Diana Blume, design manager, who did page makeup and helped assemble the pages in their final form, as well as to Matt McAdams, art manager, who oversaw the creation of the figures and illustrations. The assistance of Lukia Kliossis with assembling the animations and videos, as well as all the rich content in LaunchPad, is greatly appreciated. Thanks to Sheena Goldstein for guiding the manuscript through photo research and permissions. Thank you to Stephanie Ellis in market development, Taryn Burns in marketing, and to their colleagues in the field who have advocated for the value of this student-centered approach to living physical geography.

It was a great pleasure to work with development editor Donald Gecewicz. Don brought new ideas to the book and provided invaluable help in seeing both the big picture and the smallest of details. My thanks also to copyeditor Norma Sims Roche for her outstanding work on polishing the manuscript's text and fine-tuning the logical flow of ideas. Tom Carling with Carling Design created the beautiful and effective layout of the book. Thanks, Tom, for your hard work in arranging the art to fit into the space available. I am deeply grateful to Tom Killion for allowing me to use his beautiful work, *Tennessee Cove, Marin Headlands*, for the book's cover. Thank you to artist Rachel Rogge and Precision Graphics for their exquisite renderings and for their patience with me through the meticulous process of art revisions. Thanks to Beth Robertson and Mapping Specialists for their cartographic expertise and skill. Freelance photo researcher Jerry Marshall worked tirelessly to acquire the photographs used throughout the book, and I am grateful for his efforts.

I thank my colleagues in the Geography Department at California State University, Sacramento, James Wanket and Thomas Krabacher, for their assistance and feedback in developing the manuscript. I appreciate the support provided by the Department of Geography and the College of Natural Sciences and Mathematics at California State University, Sacramento. I am in debt to Ted Erski from McHenry County College for the hard work and long hours he put into writing *Living Physical Geography in the Laboratory*, the outstanding laboratory manual that accompanies this book. I am deeply appreciative of the input of the professional reviewers, my colleagues in the discipline, for combing through the early draft manuscripts and helping me hone the material. I have also benefited greatly from my experiences in the classroom and the field. Without my students, this book would not have been written. Thank you.

About the Author

Bruce Gervais is a professor of geography at California State University, Sacramento. He holds a B.A. in geography from San Francisco State University, a master's in geography from the University of California at Davis, and a doctorate in geography from the University of California at Los Angeles. Bruce's research focus is in paleoclimatology. For his doctoral research at UCLA, he studied ancient climates by using tree rings and fossil pollen preserved in lake sediments on the Kola Peninsula in northwestern Russia. He has published 12 peer-reviewed research papers detailing his work in Russia and California. Bruce enjoys spending his free time mountaineering, backpacking, and with his family. He welcomes your comments and can be reached at gervais@csus.edu.

(Bruce Gervais)

The author and his wife, Nancy, and their two daughters, Katherine and Natalie, at Mono Lake in eastern California. Katherine holds an air-filled volcanic rock called pumice that is light enough to float on water. Turn to Section 14.1 to find out more about pumice and other volcanic features.

About the Book Team

The Cover Artist

(Max James Fallon)

Tom Killion grew up in Marin County, California, where the rugged landscape inspired him to create Japanese-style woodblock prints. Tom studied history at the University of California at Santa Cruz, and holds a doctorate in African history from Stanford University. He has taught at Bowdoin College, San Francisco State University, and as a Fulbright Professor at Asmara University in Eritrea. In 1975, he produced his first book of woodcut prints, *28 Views of Mount Tamalpais*. In 1977, he founded Quail Press, where he has printed five handmade art books and over 400 relief prints. In 2000, he published *The High Sierra* of California in collaboration with Pulitzer Prize–winning poet Gary Snyder. Tom is currently working on his third collaboration with Snyder, *California's Wild Edge*, and lives with his family in Point Reyes, California.

The Illustrators

Precision Graphics

(W. Andrew Recher)

Rachel Rogge studied art history, biology, and science illustration at Humboldt State University in Northern California. In 2003, she completed the science communication graduate program in science illustration at the University of California, Santa Cruz, followed by internships at the Ruth Bancroft Garden in Walnut Creek, California, and the American Museum of Natural History in New York City. Rachel has illustrated two children's books, and her illustrations have appeared in science and natural history periodicals. She currently resides in Illinois, and has been creating art for science textbooks for over 8 years at Precision Graphics/Lachina.

Mapping Specialists

(Peter Robertson)

Beth Robertson is a Senior Cartographer at Mapping Specialists, Ltd., a Madison, Wisconsin-based company that since 1984 has been leading the way in providing custom cartography for educational, trade, and travel publishers, as well as many other types of cartography and graphics for both print products and Web resources. Beth studied environmental geography at the University of Wisconsin–Milwaukee where her love of maps drew her toward a career in cartography. She has produced thousands of maps for clients such as the National Geographic Society, Bedford/Freeman/Worth, National Park Service, and dozens of other companies. In recent years, Beth has been continually expanding her knowledge of html (and previously Flash) to produce animated and interactive graphics. She is currently enrolled in the Penn State World Campus post-baccalaureate certificate in geographic information systems. When she is not making maps, Beth enjoys bicycling and spending time with her husband and young son.

The Designer

(Tom Carling)

Tom Carling is the principal of Carling Design, a New York-based editorial design firm specializing in magazines, books, and custom-content publications. In recent years, Tom has designed numerous college-level titles for Macmillan Education in both the sciences and humanities. His approach to college textbook design is informed by his roots in trade magazines for clients such as *Sports Illustrated* and Lucasfilm as well as extensive experience in children's/young adult, non-fiction book design for DK Books, Scholastic, and many others. Several of his children's books have been recommended by the American Library Association for reluctant readers. Tom holds a BFA in art history from Syracuse University.

GT The Geographer's Toolkit

Chapter Outline

This map is centered on the Indian Ocean. It shows the depth of the oceans (dark purple regions are deepest), and the height of the land surfaces (brown areas are highest). The data used to make this map were acquired by remote sensing technology, which provides invaluable information about the physical Earth. *(Courtesy of Anthony Koppers, Seamount Catalog (http://earthref.org))*

LIVING PHYSICAL GEOGRAPHY

> Where do tornadoes get their energy?

> How do my car and phone know where I am?

> How do we know mountains are hidden deep in the ocean?

> Who built the massive statues on Easter Island and how?

To learn more about the remote sensing techniques that were used to make this map, go to Section GT.4.

THE BIG PICTURE *Physical geography studies how Earth's natural systems function, how they change naturally through space and time, and how people change them.*

LEARNING GOALS *After reading this chapter, you will be able to:*

GT.1 ◎ Define physical geography and explain different scales of geographic inquiry.

GT.2 ◎ Describe Earth's major physical systems and their characteristics.

GT.3 ◎ Use the geographic grid coordinate system to identify locations on Earth's surface and distinguish among different types of maps often employed in physical geography.

GT.4 ◎ Discuss how technologies such as satellite sensors and radar are used to study and portray Earth systems and processes.

GT.5 ◎ Apply the scientific method to Easter Island to study its history of human settlement.

GT.1 Welcome to Physical Geography!

◎ Define physical geography and explain different scales of geographic inquiry.

Have you ever wondered why deserts are barren and dry and tropical rainforests are lush and wet? Why Hawai'i has such delightfully pleasant winters but Alaska's are brutally cold? Why there is winter and summer? How millions of tons of water can be held aloft in a thunderstorm, then fall to the ground as rain? Why tornadoes form? Whether humans are causing climate change? Why there are no polar bears in the Southern Hemisphere or penguins in the Northern Hemisphere? Why mountains form and how they are worn down? The causes of volcanoes and earthquakes? These questions all stem from a fundamental curiosity about the natural world around us. They are all questions about Earth's physical geography, and they are all questions explored in this book.

What Is Physical Geography?

Physical geography is more than knowing the names of locations and places. **Physical geography** is the study of Earth's living and nonliving physical systems and how they change naturally through space and time or are changed by human activity. A **system** is a set of interacting parts or processes that function as a unit. Physical geography explores how Earth's natural physical landscapes have changed in the past and how they may change in the future.

Physical geography is nested within the larger discipline of **geography**: the study of the spatial relationships among Earth's physical and cultural features and how they develop and change through time. **Geography emphasizes the role of spatial relationships between people and the physical world to gain insight into cultural and physical phenomena. Geography has several other subdisciplines.** The counterpart to physical geography is *human geography*, which focuses on human phenomena, such as political voting patterns, human migration, transportation issues, and urban planning and development.

Often, physical geography and human geography overlap. In this book, for example, the role of people is never far from any topic. It is difficult to find regions or systems that are not at least in part **anthropogenic**: created or influenced by people. People modify Earth's physical landscapes to meet their needs, and in so doing, they are an active force of change. Earth's surface, its atmosphere, its oceans, and its organisms have been transformed in many ways by people in just the last few hundred years **(Figure GT.1)**.

All of our material goods are connected to natural resources derived from Earth's physical systems. The materials that meet our basic needs, such as our food, homes, cars, phones, computers, and clothing, were all once raw natural resources found in Earth's physical systems. In growing or manufacturing these materials, people modify Earth's natural environments.

People are also influenced by, and are a product of, Earth's physical systems and processes.

physical geography
The study of Earth's living and nonliving physical systems and how they change naturally through space and time or are changed by human activity.

system
A set of interacting parts or processes that function as a unit.

geography
The study of the spatial relationships among Earth's physical and cultural features and how they develop and change through time.

anthropogenic
Created or influenced by people.

A

FIGURE GT.1   **Anthropogenic landscapes.**
(A) Although wheat fields in Canada and the city of New York may not look alike, each has been completely transformed by people. The wheat fields of Saskatchewan, Canada, were once prairie grassland composed of a rich diversity of plant and animal species. (Note that locator maps, shown here, are used throughout this book to illustrate the geographic settings of photographs.) (B) Manhattan, New York, was once deciduous forest and coastal estuaries. (C) This composite image of night lights in North America was assembled from satellite data collected in April and October of 2012. Multiple images were combined to avoid cloudy skies. Night lights indicate where people live. The eastern United States and southern Canada are brighter and more populated than the arid western United States and mountainous Canadian provinces. Note that some lights are not related to populated centers, such as natural gas flares in North Dakota. (A. Dave Reede/All CanadaPhotos/Getty Images; B. Michael S. Yamashita/NationalGeographic/Getty Images; C. NASA)

B

C

Our evolutionary history is a result of Earth's changing land surface, ocean currents, and climate patterns. Changing climate and interactions with other organisms led to the evolution of bipedalism (walking upright) about 4 million years ago in eastern Africa. Through time, human intelligence has increased, as has our technological sophistication.

Physical geography explores the human transformation of Earth's physical landscapes through science. Science is fundamental to the discipline of physical geography and to all aspects of this book. Later in this chapter, Geographic Perspectives (Section GT.5) explores the fallen civilization of Easter Island to illustrate the process of science.

 GEOGRAPHIC PERSPECTIVES   The health and well-being of the human species are intertwined with Earth's natural and anthropo-genic environments. This book is a journey through the physical geography of Earth and the place humans now occupy there.

Scales of Inquiry

There are two types of scale that geographers often employ: spatial scale and temporal scale. Different spatial and temporal scales provide varied perspectives on physical phenomena. **Spatial scale** refers to the physical size, length, distance, or area of an object such as a cloud or a rainforest. Spatial scale also pertains to the physical space occupied by a process such as migration of a species or movement of sand along a coastline. (A *process* is a stepwise progression of events.) **Temporal scale** refers to the window of time used to examine phenomena and processes as well as the length of time over which they develop or change.

spatial scale
The physical size, length, distance, or area of an object or the physical space occupied by a process.

temporal scale
The window of time used to examine phenomena and processes or the length of time over which they develop or change.

FIGURE GT.2 **Spatial scale.** *Our perspective on the Namib Desert in southwestern Africa changes as spatial scale changes. Different spatial scales reveal different geographic patterns and processes and stimulate different kinds of questions. Images 3 and 4 are both developed from satellites.* (1. Johnny Haglund/ Lonely PlanetImages/Getty Images; 2. imagebroker.net/SuperStock; 3. NASA; 4. NASA)

Video
Spatial scale
http://qrs.ly/es3wdr1

Large scale   **SPATIAL SCALE**   Small scale

  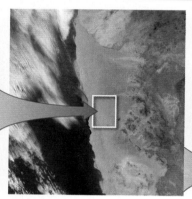 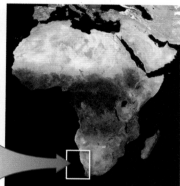

1 Do sand dunes move? How deep is this sand dune? Why is there no vegetation on the dunes?

2 How does the wind form these dune patterns? Where did the sand come from? Are sand dunes found only in deserts?

3 Why does this desert occur near the ocean? Why is southwestern Africa arid?

4 Why is desert found north and south of central Africa but not in central Africa, which is green and fertile? Does this pattern occur on other continents?

The study of space and time underpins the study of physical geography. Together, spatial and temporal scales reveal important information about Earth's physical systems. Using the two scales together provides a unique perspective.

Spatial Scale: Perspective in Space

Imagine your college campus or your neighborhood. You are probably thinking on a local spatial scale. On a more regional spatial scale, imagine the city where you live, or the state, or even the entire country or continent. These are all examples of different spatial scales. Thinking on local spatial scales involves more detail, such as what building a classroom is in or where a house in a neighborhood is found. On broader spatial scales, there is less local detail, but more geographic space is cov-

ered with a clearer view of the bigger picture and of context.

A **map** is a flat two-dimensional representation of Earth's surface. A map can be drawn at any spatial scale. **Large-scale** perspectives make geographic features large to show more detail. **Small-scale** perspectives make geographic features small to cover broad regions. A map at a local scale, such as a college campus map that shows individual buildings, is a large-scale map. A small-scale map includes a large area of Earth's surface, such as a continent or a hemisphere. **Figure GT.2** shows how different spatial scales lead to different perspectives and different levels of inquiry.

It is easy to know what a thing is at a large spatial scale (such as a sand dune), but seeing the small-scale patterns and processes that produced

map
A flat two-dimensional representation of Earth's surface.

large scale
A geographic scale that pertains to a geographically restricted area and makes geographic features large to show more detail.

small scale
A geographic scale that makes geographic features small to cover a large area of Earth's surface.

FIGURE GT.3 **Spatial scales used in geography.** *The phenomena studied in physical geography occur across a wide range of spatial scales. Large-scale features, such as a cliff face, occupy little geographic space, and small-scale features, such as a continent, occupy immense spaces. Use of different spatial scales to gain different perspectives underpins the study of physical geography.*

Spatial Scales of Physical Geography

Meters	Kilometers	Tens of kilometers	Thousands of kilometers	Tens of thousands of kilometers
Cliff face	Mountain	Mountain range	Continent	Earth

it is difficult from that perspective. At a small spatial scale, a geographic pattern begins to emerge: The Namib Desert is part of a broader pattern of aridity around the world. Global atmospheric flow results in this geographic pattern.

This shift in spatial scale provides a way of seeing how phenomena or processes are situated in relation to one another. Physical geography focuses on phenomena that range in size from meters to the entire planet (Figure GT.3).

Temporal Scale: Time as a Perspective

It is difficult to see clouds moving in the sky unless you keep your eyes fixed on them. Time-lapse video, however, shows clouds as roiling and billowing rapidly across the sky. Earth's physical landscapes today are merely one frame in a continuing landscape of change. On human time scales, most landscapes appear to be *static* (unchanging). On longer time scales, such as hundreds to thousands or millions of years, landscapes change and evolve. Mountains are lifted up, then eroded away; continents split apart as new ocean basins form. Natural climate cooling creates massive ice sheets that cover whole continents, and once-vegetated regions turn to barren desert. Most of the Sahara, for example, is barren today, without surface water and vegetation. Some 7,000 years ago, however, that desert was a *savanna* woodland (see Section 8.2) with many large lakes and was home to many animals, including crocodiles, hippos, giraffes, lions, and humans (Figure GT.4).

The temporal scale is particularly relevant to anthropogenic changes in Earth's environments. Rapid changes in Brazil's tropical rainforests, for example, have been well documented by satellite imagery through time, and that imagery has been crucial in monitoring losses of Amazon rainforest in South America. Figure GT.5 provides two different satellite images that reveal the rapid changes in the Amazon rainforest.

Physical geography explores phenomena and processes across temporal scales that range from minutes to millions of years. As Figure GT.6 on the next page shows, some phenomena, such as earthquakes, occur in minutes, while others, such as the development of mountain ranges, take millions of years. Some phenomena can occur over many time scales. Climate change, for example, occurs over decades to millions of years.

About the Metric System

You will notice as you use this book that two units of measurement are given. The *metric system* unit is provided first, and then the *U.S. customary*

FIGURE GT.4   **Green Sahara.** *This 7,000- to 9,000-year-old giraffe petroglyph (rock engraving) is in the Sahara Desert in Niger, Africa, where today it is very dry. Giraffes require woodlands, so the petroglyph's presence indicates that the climate was once much wetter. This petroglyph illustrates how temporal scale can provide a greater understanding of how environments change over long time spans.* (© Frans Lemmens/Lithium/age fotostock)

FIGURE GT.5   **Rondônia deforestation.** *These satellite images show deforestation in Rondônia, Brazil, between 1975 (left) and 2012 (right). The two images show the same location. Dark green areas are covered by forest. Light green and purple areas in the 2012 image have been cleared. Logging, agriculture, and cattle ranching are driving deforestation in the Amazon rainforest. Both spatial and temporal scales are evident in this image. In only 37 years (the temporal scale), large expanses (the spatial scale) of tropical rainforest habitat have been lost. The distance across each image is about 40 km (25 mi).* (EROS Data Center/Landsat/NASA)

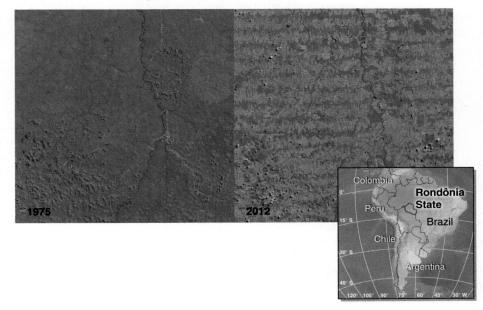

FIGURE GT.6 **Temporal scales used in physical geography.** *Different physical phenomena or processes occur on different temporal scales.*

Temporal Scales of Physical Geography

Minutes	Days	Years	Decades	Hundreds of years	Thousands of years	Millions of years
Earthquakes	Hurricanes	El Niño	Climate change	Soil development	Forest migration	Mountain building

unit is provided in parentheses. Inches, feet, and miles are part of the U.S. customary system of weights and measurements, which also includes pounds, gallons, and degrees Fahrenheit. Centimeters, meters, and kilometers are metric system units of distance, and this system also includes kilograms, liters, and degrees Celsius.

The United States is the only industrialized country that still has a customary system in widespread use. The metric system is used in all formal scientific research in all countries, including the United States, and by the public in most of the rest of the world. The metric system is favored because of the ease of conversion between different units, as shown in **Table GT.1**.

TABLE GT.1	AT A GLANCE: The Metric System
10 millimeters = 1 centimeter	
100 centimeters = 1 meter	
1,000 meters = 1 kilometer	
1 cubic centimeter = 1 milliliter = 1 gram of water	
1 calorie raises 1 gram of water 1°C	
At sea level, water freezes at 0°C and boils at 100°C	

GT.2 The Physical Earth

◎ Describe Earth's major physical systems and their characteristics.

Earth is a large system, and it is therefore necessary to divide it into smaller systems to understand how it works. In this section, we examine the interaction between matter and energy, Earth's physical shape, and Earth's major physical systems.

Matter and Energy

The flow of energy through Earth's physical systems is central to most topics in physical geography. **Energy** is the capacity to do work on or to change

the state of matter. **Matter** is any material that possesses mass and occupies space. Matter can exist in three states: solid, liquid, or gas. To change the state of matter (such as water), energy must be added to or removed from it **(Figure GT.7)**.

Several forms of energy influence Earth systems. **Radiant energy** is the energy of electromagnetic waves, such as light or X-rays. The Sun emits radiant energy that passes through Earth's atmosphere. A portion of that energy is absorbed by Earth's atmosphere and surface. When that radiant energy is absorbed, it is converted to heat. **Photosynthesis** is a process by which plants, algae, and some bacteria convert the Sun's radiant energy to stored chemical energy. **Chemical energy** is energy in a substance that can be released through a chemical reaction. All living organisms use chemical energy to move and to carry out metabolic functions. Gasoline is also a form of chemical energy. When burned, that energy works to move a car. **Geothermal energy** (heat from Earth's interior) moves entire continents and heaves and buckles mountain ranges. Lightning produced within a thunderstorm is *electrical energy*.

Two other important categories of energy in physical geography are *potential energy* and *kinetic energy* (both types of *mechanical energy*). Potential energy is stored in an object or material. A boulder perched over a cliff about to fall is an example of potential energy. Kinetic energy is the energy of movement. A boulder that is falling down a cliff and smashing into other rocks is an example of kinetic energy.

As energy flows through Earth's physical systems, it moves matter, and it changes its form in the process. **Figure GT.8** examines how the Sun's radiant energy changes from one form to another in Earth's physical systems.

Earth's Shape

From space, Earth looks like a perfect sphere, equal in all dimensions and perfectly smooth. Yet Earth is not a perfect sphere. Earth's true shape results from distortion by Earth's rotation, the vertical irregularities of Earth's surface, and gravitational

energy
The capacity to do work on or to change the state of matter.

matter
Any material that occupies space and possesses mass.

radiant energy
The energy of electromagnetic waves.

photosynthesis
The process by which plants, algae, and some bacteria convert the radiant energy of sunlight to chemical energy.

chemical energy
Energy in a substance that can be released through a chemical reaction.

geothermal energy
Heat from Earth's interior.

FIGURE **GT.7** **States of matter.** *Mount Robson (elevation 3,954 m or 12,972 ft), in British Columbia, is the highest peak in the Canadian Rockies. Berg Glacier flows down the mountain and into Berg Lake. Here, water exists in its three phases: solid ice in Berg Glacier, liquid water in Berg Lake, and water vapor (a gas) that is invisible in the atmosphere. To change the state of water from solid ice to liquid water to water vapor, energy must be added to the water. To change its state from gas to liquid to solid, energy must be removed from water.* (Jason Puddifoot/First Light/GettyImages)

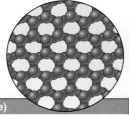

1. Solid (ice)

In a solid, molecules are bonded together to form a rigid structure. If heat energy is added to the water molecules, the ice will melt into liquid.

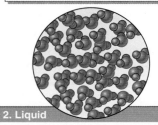

2. Liquid

In a liquid, molecular bonds continually form and break. If heat energy is added, the water will evaporate into a gas.

Mount Robson

Berg Glacier

Berg Lake

3. Gas

In a gas, molecules are not bonded together. Instead, they dart freely about.

Canada

Mount Robson, British Columbia

U.S.A.

FIGURE **GT.8** **GEO-GRAPHIC: A day in the life of solar energy.** *This graphic follows the path of solar radiant energy as it changes form and works on matter.* (1. Evan Kafka/Getty Images; 2. Marco Brivio/age fotostock/GettyImages; 3. U.S. Dept. of the Interior-Bureau of Reclamation; 4. REBECCA COOK/Reuters/Newscom)

1 The sun's radiant energy excites water molecules, causing them to *evaporate* into the atmosphere. When the evaporated water *condenses* to liquid, clouds form.

2 Rain from the clouds falls to Earth. The rain collects in a stream channel and forms a flowing river with kinetic energy that can erode canyons over time.

3 A dam creates a *reservoir* of water with potential energy. The reservoir's potential energy is converted to electrical energy when water is released from the base of the dam, causing turbines there to spin and generate electricity.

4 Electricity from the dam is used to charge the battery in this electric vehicle. A portion of the electrical energy is converted to the kinetic energy of motion and heat by car movement. The car's headlights convert the electrical energy to radiant energy.

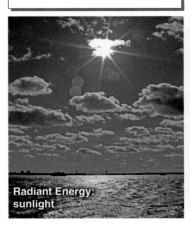

Radiant Energy: sunlight

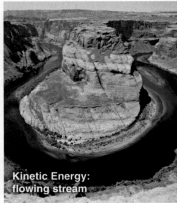

Kinetic Energy: flowing stream

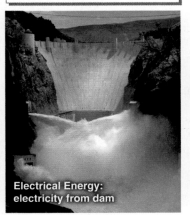

Electrical Energy: electricity from dam

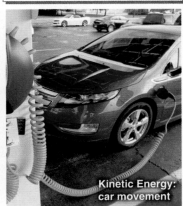

Kinetic Energy: car movement

Energy flow

FIGURE GT.9 **Earth's diameter.** *The diameter of the planet is 42 km (26 mi) greater between two equatorial points than between the poles.*

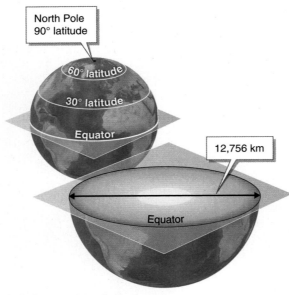

A. A diameter through the equator

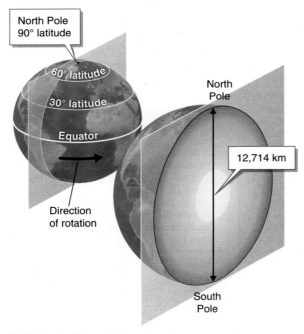

B. A diameter through the poles

relief
The difference in elevation between two or more points on Earth's surface.

crust
The rigid outermost portion of Earth's surface.

atmosphere
The layer of gases surrounding Earth.

EARTH'S ROTATION SPEED

LATITUDE	KM/H	MPH
0°	1,670	1,037
30°	1,447	899
60°	837	520
90°	0	0

anomalies. As a result of these three factors, Earth is actually an *oblate spheroid*, a slightly flattened sphere with an uneven surface. For simplicity, however, Earth will be referred to simply as a sphere throughout this book.

Rotation

Earth rotates on an imaginary axis that runs through both poles. Due to its decreasing circumference from the equator to the poles, Earth's rotation is fastest at the equator. Because the surface at the equator moves fastest, it bulges out more than other latitudes, and the planet flattens slightly at the poles **(Figure GT.9)**.

Relief and Gravitation

Earth's surface is folded and crumpled by geologic forces. From space, these folds and crumples are practically invisible. From the point of view of a human being on the ground, however, these surface features are dramatic. **Relief** is the difference in elevation between two or more points on Earth's surface. **(Figure GT.10)**.

Earth's shape sags and bulges as a result of its relief and as a result of differences in the thickness and mass of its **crust**, the rigid outermost portion of Earth's surface. This unevenness causes different gravity fields across the surface. Mountains, for example, have more mass than valleys. As a result, gravity is stronger beneath most mountains than beneath most adjacent valleys. These irregularities of gravity change the elevation of Earth's surface in relation to sea level by up to 100 m (330 ft) worldwide.

Earth Systems

One of the most important models in physical geography is the concept of physical systems. As we have seen, a system is a set of interacting parts or processes that function as a unit. A leaf, a tree, and a forest are each systems. The entire planet constitutes a system.

Energy and matter flow through Earth's systems. Energy from the Sun and Earth's internal geothermal energy do work on Earth's systems and change matter within them. **There are four main physical Earth systems: the atmosphere, the biosphere, the lithosphere, and the hydrosphere.**

The Atmosphere

The **atmosphere** is the layer of gases surrounding Earth. It is composed of *molecules* and *atoms* that extend outward from the surface of Earth for hundreds of kilometers. It contains over a dozen different gases, but consists mainly of molecules of nitrogen (N_2) and oxygen (O_2). The atmosphere

FIGURE GT.10 **Earth's relief.** *Mount Everest and the Dead Sea are the two most extreme vertical points on Earth's land surface. (A) Climbers attempt to reach the summit of Mount Everest. The mountain, on the border between Nepal and Tibet, is the highest point on the planet at 8,848 m (29,029 ft). (B) The Dead Sea's shoreline in Israel is 427 m (1,401 ft) below sea level. It is Earth's lowest land elevation. (A. AP Photo/Alpenglow Expeditions, Adrian Ballinger; B. SEUX Paule/Getty Images/Hemis.fr)*

performs many functions crucial to life, which include providing oxygen for life and gases that block harmful rays from the Sun. The atmosphere also moderates temperatures on Earth's surface, making life on land possible.

The Biosphere

The **biosphere** is all of life on Earth. Humans are part of the biosphere. The biosphere extends from deep within the crust to high in the atmosphere. Far below ground in Earth's crust live bacteria that are adapted to extreme pressure and heat. At 16 km (10 mi) above Earth's surface, tiny fern spores and microscopic bacteria and pollen float on air currents above the continents and oceans. Most of the biosphere, however, can be found on the land's surface and within the first few hundred meters of the surface of the oceans.

The Lithosphere

We walk on, build our homes on, and grow our food on the lithosphere. The **lithosphere** is Earth's rigid crust plus the heated layer beneath it down to about 100 km (62 mi). The lithosphere is fractured into 14 large *plates* (pieces) that slowly move, creating volcanoes, mountains, and earthquakes. The lithosphere also regulates and determines the atmosphere's chemistry over time scales of millions of years through volcanic eruptions and the weathering of rocks.

The Hydrosphere

Compared with other planets, one unique characteristic of Earth is the quantity of its liquid water. Earth has immense liquid oceans, which cover 71% of the planet's surface and are a little over 4 km (2.5 mi) deep on average. The **hydrosphere** encompasses all of Earth's water in its three states: solid, liquid, and gas. It includes water in the oceans, in the ground, in organisms, and in the atmosphere as **water vapor**: water in its gaseous state. Water is also present in the atmosphere as clouds, which are composed mostly of liquid water. Water is present in, and plays roles in, the other three systems, so henceforth we will not treat the hydrosphere as a separate system.

The Structure of *Living Physical Geography*

The material in this book is arranged in four parts, which focus on the work of solar and geothermal energy in the atmosphere, biosphere, and lithosphere. In Part I and Part II, we will see how solar radiant energy flows through the atmosphere and biosphere, transferring energy to the atmosphere and living organisms. In Part III, we will see how geothermal energy builds up the lithosphere. In Part IV, we will see how solar energy and gravity tear the lithosphere down through the work of flowing water (such as streams and coastal waves), ice, and wind (mainly in

biosphere
All life on Earth.

lithosphere
The rigid outer layer of Earth, called the crust, and the heated layer beneath it down to about 100 km (62 mi).

hydrosphere
All of Earth's water in its three phases: solid, liquid, and gas.

water vapor
Water in a gaseous state.

weather
The state of the atmosphere at any given moment.

deserts). **Figure GT.11** provides a visual diagram of the structure of this book.

Part I: Atmospheric Systems: Weather and Climate

The Sun's radiant energy flows through and does work on Earth's physical systems. The Sun gener- ates immense amounts of radiant energy. Some of this energy is intercepted by Earth.

Solar energy interacts with and warms Earth's atmosphere, land surface, and oceans. It sets the atmosphere in motion, creating weather and climate systems. **Weather** is the state of the atmosphere at any given moment and is made up of ever-changing

FIGURE **GT.11** *Living Physical Geography's* **structure.** *This book is organized around Earth's major physical systems. Its four parts focus on the atmosphere, the biosphere, the building of the lithosphere through plate tectonics, and the wearing down of the lithosphere by the Sun's radiant energy and by gravity. The chapters in each part are arranged in a sequence that shows the development of topics within each system. The hydrosphere plays a role within each system and is not treated as a separate system.*

PART I
Atmospheric Systems: Weather and Climate

Chapter 1 Portrait of the Atmosphere
Chapter 2 Seasons and Solar Energy
Chapter 3 Water in the Atmosphere
Chapter 4 Atmospheric Circulation and Wind Systems
Chapter 5 The Restless Sky: Storm Systems and El Niño
Chapter 6 The Changing Climate

PART II
The Biosphere and the Geography of Life

Chapter 7 Patterns of Life: Biogeography
Chapter 8 Climate and Life: Biomes
Chapter 9 Soil and Water Resources
Chapter 10 The Living Hydrosphere: Ocean Ecosystems

PART IV
Erosion and Deposition: Sculpting Earth's Surface

Chapter 15 Weathering and Mass Movement
Chapter 16 Flowing Water: Fluvial Systems
Chapter 17 The Work of Ice: The Cryosphere and Glacial Landforms
Chapter 18 Water, Wind, and Time: Desert Landforms
Chapter 19 The Work of Waves: Coastal Landforms

PART III
Tectonic Systems: Building the Lithosphere

Chapter 11 Earth History, Earth Interior
Chapter 12 Drifting Continents: Plate Tectonics
Chapter 13 Building the Crust with Rocks
Chapter 14 Geohazards: Volcanoes and Earthquakes

FIGURE GT.12 **Solar energy in the atmosphere.** *Differences in solar heating across Earth's surface set the atmosphere in motion, and evaporation of water by the Sun moves water vapor into the atmosphere. In this way, the Sun's radiant energy is transformed into the deadly kinetic energy of thunderstorms (such as this one in east-central Oklahoma) and tornadoes (such as this one is in Manchester, South Dakota).* (Top, David McGlynn/Getty Images; left, Robert Harding; right, Gene Rhoden/Weatherpix/GettyImages)

events on time scales ranging from minutes to weeks. **Climate**, on the other hand, is the long-term average of weather and the average frequency of extreme weather events. All atmospheric phenomena, ranging from gentle breezes to deadly tornadoes, are driven by solar energy. **Figure GT.12** portrays the link between the Sun's energy and Earth's weather.

> Where do tornadoes get their energy?*

Part II: The Biosphere and the Geography of Life

Almost all life on Earth is a physical manifestation of solar energy. Solar energy enters the biosphere through photosynthesis. Energy created during photosynthesis is then transferred to all other living organisms through their food, as shown in **Figure GT.13**.

Part III: Tectonic Systems: Building the Lithosphere

The highest mountains and the deepest ocean trenches were built by Earth's geothermal energy. Through the process of *plate tectonics* (see Chapter 11), geothermal energy grinds the plates of the lithosphere against one another, lifting and buckling mountains in the process and creating Earth's surface relief. Plate movement also creates

FIGURE GT.13 **Solar energy in the biosphere.** *Plants convert radiant energy from the Sun to chemical energy, which they use for growth. The keel-billed toucan (Ramphastos sulfuratus), whose range is from southern Mexico to Venezuela (inset map), will acquire chemical energy directly from the plant in the form of berries or indirectly as it eats insects that eat the plants.* (Left, David McGlynn/Getty Images; center, Bruce Gervais; right, Sue Flood/Getty Images)

Range of the keel-billed toucan

climate
The long-term average of weather and the average frequency of extreme weather events.

FIGURE GT.14 **Geothermal energy and the lithosphere.** *Earth's internal heat energy moves and breaks Earth's crust through the process of plate tectonics, creating surface features such as the Alps of Switzerland (left) and volcanoes in Iceland (right). (Left, Svetoslava Slavova/FlickrOpen/Getty Images; right, © Michel Detay/ Flickr Open/GettyImages)*

deep-sea trenches, triggers earthquakes, and fuels volcanoes **(Figure GT.14)**.

Part IV: Erosion and Deposition: Sculpting Earth's Surface

As geothermal energy builds Earth's relief, solar energy works to reduce relief and flatten Earth's surface through erosion. Erosion is the process of transporting rock fragments via flowing water in streams and in coastal areas, in flowing ice in glaciers, and in blowing air in desert environments. *Deposition* is the process in which sediments that are transported through erosion accumulate on Earth's surface.

Evaporation is the process of turning liquid water to water vapor. Through evaporation, solar energy heats and lifts water from the ocean's surface and moves it into the atmosphere. Through **condensation** (the process by which water vapor turns to liquid), the water returns to the conti-

FIGURE GT.15 **Solar energy and erosion.** *The erosive forces of flowing water and flowing ice, both parts of the hydrosphere, are a manifestation of solar energy. Streams and ice in glaciers flow downslope and erode the land surface. Left: Water cuts into and flows over a plateau, creating Angel Falls in Venezuela (the highest waterfall in the world). Right: One of the many glaciers in Glacier Bay, Alaska, has created a valley through erosion. (Sun, David McGlynn/Getty Images; waterfall, FabioFilzi/Vetta/Getty Images; glacier, Jim Wark)*

erosion
The process of transporting rock fragments via moving water, ice, or air.

evaporation
The process of changing liquid water to water vapor.

condensation
The process of changing water vapor to liquid.

Picture This

(Bruce Gervais)

A The atmosphere envelops Earth with a layer of gases, mostly nitrogen and oxygen. Solar energy streams through the atmosphere, warming it and evaporating water from the oceans. The clouds seen here are composed of tiny drops of liquid water that condensed from water vapor. If the liquid cloud droplets grow large enough, rain may fall from the clouds. These clouds are part of the hydrosphere.

B Plants in the biosphere convert the Sun's radiant energy to chemical energy. They also use the water precipitated by the clouds. The chemical energy of the plants streams through and fuels the chemical processes required by living organisms. The people will eat this converted solar energy in the form of peanut butter sandwiches and potato chips for lunch. All living organisms require water and in large part consist of water from the hydrosphere.

C The rocks of the lithosphere in the Grand Canyon were formed from layers of sediments. These sediments were deposited over many hundreds of millions of years in the shallow lakes and seas that once existed in the southwestern United States. Over time, these sediments were compressed and cemented into stone. Geothermal energy lifted the region, creating the Colorado Plateau. As the plateau was lifted higher, the Colorado River and other streams (the hydrosphere) cut into it through the process of erosion and exposed the many layers of rock.

Living Physical Geography

This photo shows two vacationers overlooking the Grand Canyon in Arizona from the canyon's North Rim. In most outdoor settings such as this, Earth's physical systems are readily visible.

Consider This

1. Give an example of how Earth's physical systems overlap and interact with one another.

2. Why is the hydrosphere so important to erosion of the lithosphere?

3. Explain the following statement: "Animals (including people) are solar powered."

---

nents as precipitation. **Precipitation** is falling rain, snow, sleet, or hail (see Section 3.5). Precipitation forms streams and glaciers that cut into the crust through erosion **(Figure GT.15)**.

Over geologic time, rivers may carve deep canyons into plateaus that were uplifted by geothermal energy. Glaciers of flowing ice gouge and grind deep valleys (see Section 17.3). As long as the Sun is shining to evaporate water from the oceans, these erosive forces will be at work flattening out what geothermal energy works to build **(Picture This)**.

GT.3 Mapping Earth

◎ Use the geographic grid coordinate system to identify locations on Earth's surface and distinguish among different types of maps often employed in physical geography.

Maps and mapping technology visually represent the physical world. To be effective, maps must be precisely fixed in real geographic space. The geographic grid coordinate system is one of the systems that can be used to accomplish this.

precipitation
Falling rain, snow, sleet, or hail.

Animation
Latitude
http://qrs.ly/wb3wdqs

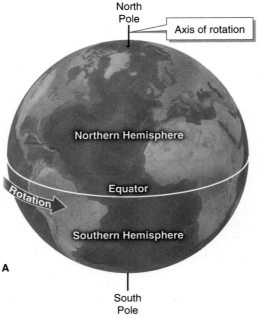

North Pole

Axis of rotation

Northern Hemisphere

Rotation

Equator

Southern Hemisphere

A

South Pole

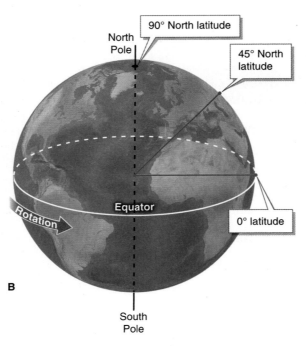

90° North latitude

North Pole

45° North latitude

Rotation

Equator

0° latitude

B

South Pole

FIGURE GT.16 **Earth rotation and latitude.**
(A) The equator is halfway between the poles. It divides Earth into the Northern Hemisphere and the Southern Hemisphere. (B) Latitudes are measured as the angle away from the equator. The latitude 45 degrees north marks the halfway point between the equator and the North Pole. The equator is at 0 degrees latitude, and the poles are at 90 degrees latitude north and south. Latitudes do not exceed 90 degrees.

geographic grid
The coordinate system that uses latitude and longitude to identify locations on Earth's surface.

latitude
The angular distance as measured from Earth's center to a point north or south of the equator.

equator
The line of latitude that divides Earth into two equal halves. The equator is exactly perpendicular to Earth's axis of rotation.

parallel
A line that forms a circle on the globe by connecting points of the same latitude.

tropics
The geographic region located between 23.5 degrees north and south latitude.

longitude
The angular distance as measured from Earth's center to a point east or west of the prime meridian.

prime meridian
Zero degrees longitude; the line of longitude that passes through Greenwich, England, and serves as the starting point from which all other lines of longitude are determined.

The Geographic Grid

Try telling someone how to get to your house without using street names and addresses. It would not be easy. It would be just as difficult to communicate where things are on Earth's surface without the geographic grid. The **geographic grid** is a coordinate system that uses latitude and longitude to identify locations on Earth's surface. Like a home address, the geographic grid pinpoints any location on Earth's surface.

Latitude

As we have seen, Earth rotates on an imaginary axis that runs through both poles. With the North Pole up, Earth rotates eastward parallel to lines of latitude. **Latitude** is the angular distance as measured from Earth's center to a point north or south of the equator. The **equator** is the line of latitude that divides Earth into two equal halves. The equator is exactly perpendicular to Earth's axis of rotation, and it creates the Northern Hemisphere and the Southern Hemisphere **(Figure GT.16)**.

Points of the same latitude connected together form a line called a **parallel**. *Latitude* is the name of the angle; *parallel* is the name of the line. Parallels are imaginary circles that run parallel to the equator and are named for their latitude; for example, a parallel at 40 degrees north is called the 40th north parallel **(Figure GT.17)**.

Latitude is given in degrees (°), minutes ('), and seconds ("). Each degree is divided into 60 minutes. Each minute is divided into 60 seconds. Degrees of latitude are approximately 111 km (69 mi) apart, minutes are 1.9 km (1.2 mi) apart, and seconds are 31 m (102 ft) apart.

Latitudes are often divided into three major zones: the tropics, midlatitudes, and high latitudes. The **tropics** are the geographic region located between 23.5 degrees north and south latitude. Midlatitudes and high latitudes are less well defined, but generally are divided at the 55th parallel. Besides these three major zones of latitude, geographers often use two subzones—subtropical and polar—as well **(Figure GT.18)**.

Longitude

Longitude is the angular distance as measured from Earth's center to a point east or west of the prime meridian. The **prime meridian** is the counterpart to the equator—it is the 0 degree starting point from which all other lines of longitude are determined. Unlike the equator, the prime meridian is not based on a natural plane of reference such as Earth's rotation. Its precise location

FIGURE GT.17

Latitude and parallels. *(A) Latitude is the measured angle in relation to the equator. (B) Parallels are points of latitude connected together to form a line and are named by their latitude.*

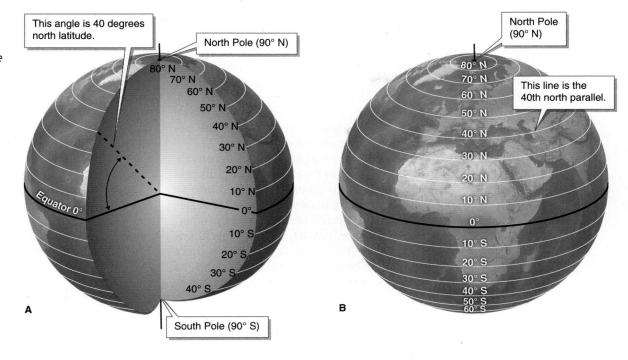

FIGURE GT.18 **Zones of latitude.** *This world map shows satellite measurements of the ocean surface temperature for July 2, 2013. Surface ocean temperature roughly corresponds with the major zones of latitude. Orange shows areas with surface water temperatures up to 32°C (90°F). Violet indicates surface water near freezing (0°C or 32°F). Surface seawater temperature is high in the tropics. Around the 55th parallel, at the boundary of the midlatitudes and high latitudes, the water quickly transitions to near-freezing temperatures. At high latitudes, seawater is always at temperatures near freezing.*

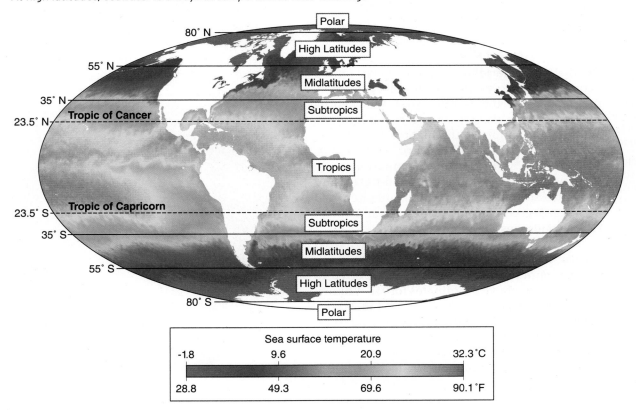

meridian
A line on the globe that runs from the North Pole to the South Pole and connects points of the same longitude.

was chosen arbitrarily in 1884 to pass directly through the Royal Observatory in Greenwich, England.

As with latitude and parallels, meridians are the counterpart to longitude. A **meridian** is a line that runs from the North Pole to the South Pole and connects points of the same longitude, as shown in **Figure GT.19**. Meridians are central to the development of world time zones.

Like latitude, longitude is given in degrees (°), minutes ('), and seconds ("). Each degree is divided into 60 minutes. Each minute is divided into 60 seconds. The distance between longitudes varies depending on the latitude. Meridians on the equator are 111 km (69 mi) apart. Because meridians all converge at a single point at the poles, there is zero distance between them at the poles, as shown in the quick-reference "At a Glance" **Table GT.2**.

TABLE GT.2 AT A GLANCE: Distances between Meridians from the Equator to the Poles		
LATITUDE	**DISTANCE (KM)**	**DISTANCE (MI)**
0°	111	69
30°	96	60
60°	56	35
90°	0	0

Using the Geographic Grid

Parallels and meridians together make up the geographic grid system. Geographic grid coordinates always give latitude first, followed by longitude. As an example, the coordinates for Mt. Whitney in California, the highest point in the continental United States, are 36°34'42" N, 118°17'32" W. This set of coordinates reads: "Thirty-six degrees, thirty-four minutes, and forty-two seconds north latitude; one hundred eighteen degrees, seventeen minutes, and thirty-two seconds west longitude."

Alternatively, *decimal degrees* are often used instead of minutes and seconds. With this approach, minutes and seconds are converted to decimals. The above coordinates for Mt. Whitney in decimal degrees are 36.57857°, –118.29225°. The Northern Hemisphere and Eastern Hemisphere are given in positive numbers; the Southern Hemisphere and Western Hemisphere are given in negative numbers. A decimal degree value of five decimal places, as given in the example above, is accurate to about 1 m (3.3 ft).

FIGURE GT.19　Longitude and meridians.
(A) Longitude is determined by the angular distance from the prime meridian, which runs through Greenwich, England. Traveling east from the prime meridian, we pass through the Eastern Hemisphere, which ends at 180 degrees. Traveling west from the prime meridian, we pass through the Western Hemisphere, which also ends at 180 degrees.
(B) Meridians are lines created by connecting points of longitude. The prime meridian (0 degrees longitude) and a portion of the 180th meridian (180 degrees longitude) are shown. All meridians terminate at the poles.

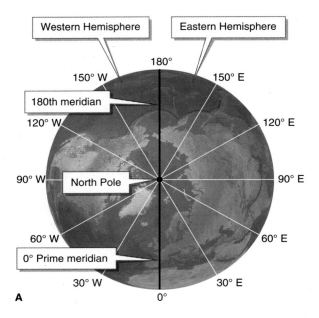

A

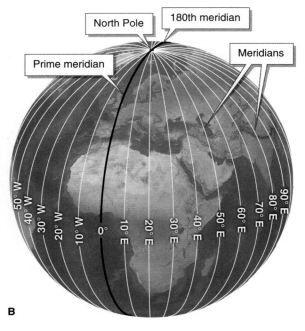

B

The Global Positioning System

Not long ago, if we got lost while driving, our options were to use a paper map or ask somebody for directions to get our bearings. Now there are navigation systems that pinpoint our location and provide directions as we are driving. These systems use the **Global Positioning System (GPS)**, a global navigation system that uses satellites and ground-based receivers to determine the geographic coordinates of any location. Each satellite uses radio waves to transmit its presence to ground receivers such as those found in our cars and smartphones. When signals from three or more satellites are received, a ground receiver can pinpoint its location on Earth. In physical geography, common applications of GPS include precisely locating satellite images on Earth's surface and tracking the movements of animals for conservation efforts. GPS has also been used to track the movement of Earth's lithospheric plates and to monitor active volcanoes for ground movement and potential eruptions. It also has many applications in weather forecasting and monitoring.

> How do my car and phone know where I am?

Picture This

(ODD ANDERSEN/AFP/Getty Images)

Global Positioning System (GPS)
A global navigation system that uses satellites and ground-based receivers to determine the geographic coordinates of any location.

Consider This

1. How does the geographic grid relate to GPS?

2. When was the last time you used GPS? What did you use it for?

FIGURE GT.20 **Using the geographic grid.**
This illustration shows both latitude and longitude. To find 50° N by 20° W, from the origin, first go north 50 degrees, then go west 20 degrees.

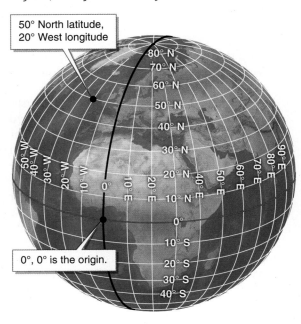

50° North latitude, 20° West longitude

0°, 0° is the origin.

When finding your way on the geographic grid, start on the *origin* (at 0°, 0°). From the origin, first find the latitude, then find the longitude **(Figure GT.20)**.

The latitudes and longitudes together create an *x–y* coordinate system that can be used to locate any point on the planet precisely. The GPS system is what enables our cars and phones to identify our location on Earth **(Picture This)**.

Maps

Cartography is the science and art of map making. **Maps are the most efficient means of communicating spatial information, and they are central to geographic inquiry.** Maps used in physical geography portray spatial relationships among objects, geographic regions, or physical phenomena such as rainfall or earthquakes. All maps reduce the size of geographic space onto the map's surface.

All maps have a purpose. Early maps were often used as an aid to navigation, as shown on the next page in **Figure GT.21**. Modern maps continue to

cartography
The science and art of map making.

Magellan's route. *This map was made in 1544 by Italian mapmaker Battista Agnese. The map shows the route of Ferdinand Magellan's fleet, the first to circumnavigate the globe.* (Library of Congress)

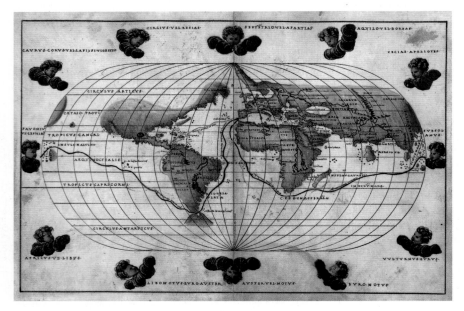

portray Earth's features, but they also have far more complex functions. Rather than being limited to showing the shapes and features of Earth's physical surface, physical geography maps portray the current and future state of Earth's physical systems to the best of our scientific understanding.

Maps are now widely available to the public with the advent of GPS technology in cars and digital maps available through online services such as Google Maps. Maps are traditionally printed on a flat surface such as paper, but spatial information can also be represented on computer screens, in spoken description, or in Braille.

Maps also provide factual information. Statistical and quantitative information, such as population numbers, temperature averages, atmospheric pressure differences across a region, or tornado frequency in the midwestern United States, can be effectively portrayed on maps.

The term *map* is also applied to concepts such as the "map of the human genome" or a "computer network map." These are not maps in a geographic sense, however, because they lack a relationship to geographic space.

It is important to keep in mind that Earth's surface is curved, but maps are flat. Depicting the curved surface of Earth on the flat surface of a map creates distortions of the shape and area of continents. Many different map *projections* are used to correct for this problem. Map projections are explored further in Appendix 2.

Cartographic distortion on a world map becomes obvious when routes of long-distance travel, such as that of an airplane, are plotted. For efficiency, airplanes follow straight lines called great circle routes whenever possible. A **great circle** is a continuous line that bisects the globe into two equal halves, such as the equator. It represents the shortest distance between two points on Earth. Great circle routes often do not appear as straight lines on world maps because of map distortion, as illustrated in **Figure GT.22**.

Small circle routes are not straight lines, and they do not bisect the globe into two equal halves. A small circle is a continuous line that forms a circle smaller than the equator. All parallels other than the equator form small circles on the globe. The equator is the only great circle parallel. All meridians are half of a great circle, and when two opposing meridians are combined, they create a great circle.

Map Scale: How Far Is It?

Maps always shrink real-world distances. It is usually helpful to know how much the real world has been reduced on a map. A map scale performs this function. A map scale specifies how much the real world has been reduced. For example, imagine you are new to a college campus and you notice on the campus map that a river runs nearby. You decide to walk on your lunch break to see the river. After about 20 minutes of walking, you still cannot find the river. Frustrated, you turn around and race back to campus for your next class **(Figure GT.23)**.

Types of Map Scales

There are three different types of map scales: bar scale, verbal scale, and representative fraction scale.

Bar scale (or *graphic map scale*): A bar scale uses a simple line segment to depict real-world distances. The scale used in Figure GT.23 is a bar scale. Bar scales are intuitive to use. The length of the line indicates distances on the map. The bar scale is the only scale type that remains accurate when the map is printed or photocopied in smaller or larger sizes. The reason is that when the map's size is changed, the bar scale line changes along with it. This makes the bar scale handy for online maps because they are often displayed on phones or computers and printed at different sizes.

great circle
A continuous line that bisects the globe into two equal halves, such as the equator; it is the shortest distance between two points on Earth.

map scale
A means of specifying how much the real world has been reduced on a map.

Animation
Great circle routes
http://qrs.ly/ul3wdqt

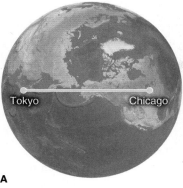

A

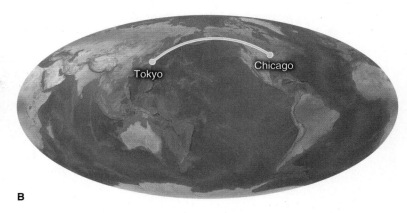

B

FIGURE GT.22 **Great circle routes.** *(A) Here a great circle route between Tokyo, Japan, and Chicago, Illinois, is plotted on the globe. When a great circle is continued all the way around the globe, it will always bisect Earth into two equal halves. (Note that this is not a world map because we can see only one half of the globe.) (B) The same route plotted on a world map. Great circle routes on many world maps appear curved and inefficient because of the distortion resulting when the full globe is projected onto a flat surface. (C) This great circle route is the longest possible straight line over water. It runs from Karachi, Pakistan, to the Kamchatka Peninsula, Russia, and is approximately 32,000 km (20,000 mi) long. On a world map, the straight line is curved because of map distortion.*

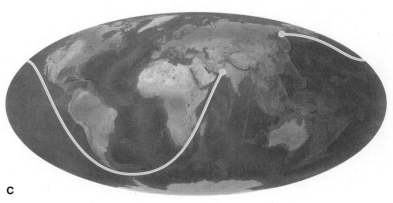

C

FIGURE GT.23 **Map scale.** *The campus map on the left shows the general layout of campus and the nearby river. There is no way to know what the real-world distances on this map are. On the right, this same map includes a map scale showing real-world distances on the map. In this map, it is clear that, although it looks close to campus, the river is several kilometers away and more than a short walk.*

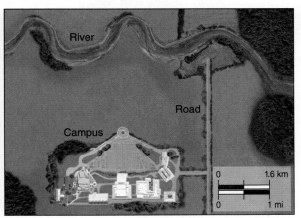

Verbal scale: Verbal map scales are also intuitive to use. A verbal scale works through a written statement such as "one inch represents one mile." It is easy to measure or estimate an inch on a map.

Representative fraction scale: A representative fraction scale uses real-world ground distances in fractional form. For example, a common fractional scale is written as 1/24,000 or 1:24,000. This means that 1 unit on the map represents 24,000 units in the real world. The unit can be any linear distance, but both sides of the equation must have the same units. In this example, one inch represents 24,000 inches in

Picture This

NORTH AMERICA

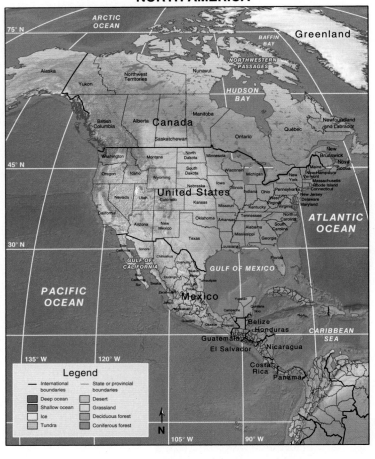

Map Elements

All maps should have several basic elements. Looking at the map at left, find the following elements:

1. *Title*: The map title summarizes the thematic content of the map. "Vegetation of California," "Arctic Sea Ice, September 2014" would be examples of map titles.

2. *Map scale*: Map scale is required for understanding real-world distances on a map.

3. *Legend*: Maps often use symbols and colors to represent data. This information must be clarified in a map's legend so the reader can accurately interpret the data. The colors in this map represent elevation, and the legend at the lower left specifies the elevation represented by each color.

4. *Direction*: North is usually "up" on a map, but not always. A large-scale map of an unfamiliar location should have a *north arrow*, or it should have the lines of the geographic grid. This is particularly important when north is not at the top of the map. These elements allow the readers to orient themselves.

5. *Date*: The date when the map was published, or when the data used in the map were generated, is required for knowing whether the map is current and for identifying updates. For example, a map of Arctic sea ice would be meaningless without a date because the extent of ice changes seasonally and year by year.

Consider This

1. What is the title of this map?

2. Are all of the map elements listed here found on this map? If not, which ones could you not find?

---

the real world, but it would be incorrect to say that one inch represents 24,000 centimeters, because centimeters are not the same unit as inches.

For a map to be effective, it should have a map scale. **Maps should also have several other elements that increase their effectiveness and reliability, such as a title, legend, direction arrow, and date (Picture This).**

Lines on the Map: Contour Lines

Topography, the shape and physical character of Earth's surface, is one kind of information that is often portrayed on maps. A common method of representing topography on a *topographic map* is by using **contour lines**, which are lines of equal elevation in relation to sea level. The increment

between contour lines is called the *contour interval*. **Figure GT.24** provides an example of the use of contour lines.

Very few topographic features are as symmetrical as the mountain in Figure GT.24. Most landscapes have more complex and irregular shapes. When uneven topographies appear on a topographic map, the spacing between contour lines reflects the steepness and irregularities of the terrain, as portrayed in **Figure GT.25**.

Contour lines always connect back to themselves, forming a closed loop. Topographic maps often do not show this, however, because the lines are cut off by the edges of the map. Anywhere on Earth, if you walked on the ground along a contour line, you would eventually wind up where you started. Contour lines converge only on vertical cliffs, and they never cross each other.

topography
The shape and physical character of Earth's surface.

contour lines
Lines of equal elevation in relation to sea level used on a topographic map.

FIGURE GT.24
GEO-GRAPHIC:

Contour lines. *The base of Mayon Volcano in the Philippines is approximately 500 m (1,640 ft) above sea level. The peak is 2,462 m (8,677 ft) in elevation. In this example, the contour interval is 500 m.* (© Rolly Pedrina/Oriental Touch/Robert Harding)

FIGURE GT.25 GEO-GRAPHIC:

Contour lines on a steep slope.

The base of Lembert Dome, in Yosemite National Park, is 2,600 m (8,528 ft) above sea level. The contour lines get closest together on its steepest slope. If you used the topographic map to plan a hike to the top of this mountain, you might decide that the side where the contour lines are farthest apart would be the easiest approach to the peak. (© Nicholas Pavloff/Lonely PlanetImages/Getty Images)

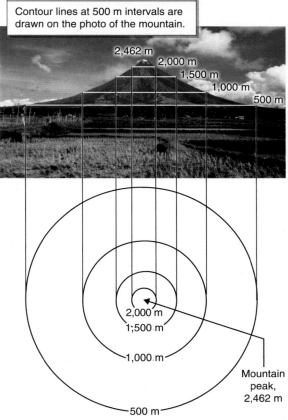

1. Profile (side) view
Contour lines at 500 m intervals are drawn on the photo of the mountain.

2,462 m
2,000 m
1,500 m
1,000 m
500 m

2,000 m
1,500 m
1,000 m
500 m

Mountain peak, 2,462 m

2. Map (top) view
Contour lines show changes in elevation. Note that if the peak of the mountain were 2,500 m, a new contour line would have to be drawn.

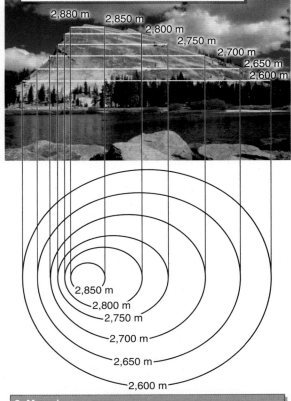

1. Profile view
The contour interval is 50 meters. The peak of this mountain is offset to the left (west).

2,880 m
2,850 m
2,800 m
2,750 m
2,700 m
2,650 m
2,600 m

2,850 m
2,800 m
2,750 m
2,700 m
2,650 m
2,600 m

2. Map view
Because the peak is offset, the contour lines get closer together where the side of the mountain is steep and farther apart where the mountain is gently sloped.

GT.4 Imaging Earth

◎ Discuss how technologies such as satellite sensors and radar are used to study and portray Earth systems and processes.

Remote sensing technologies, such as satellites and radar, collect data from a distance. Remote sensing is an important means of acquiring data to study the physical Earth. *Passive remote sensing* refers to the process of receiving information from Earth's surface using sensors, much as our eyes receive information about our surroundings. In *active remote sensing*, a signal is sent using a transmitter. The signal bounces off a surface and returns to the sender, where a receiver detects the reflected signal.

Satellite Imagery

Satellite remote sensing is one of the most important means of acquiring data used to monitor Earth's physical systems. Satellites have revolutionized our ability to monitor Earth's rapidly changing surface. No other generation has had so

remote sensing
Data collection from a distance.

FIGURE GT.26 **Satellite remote sensing.** *Satellite remote sensing is allowing scientists to monitor and study Earth's physical systems in new ways. (A) This image shows the unusual weather in an eight-day period during March 2012. Summerlike ground surface temperatures replaced normally cold weather for much of the United States and Canada, and temperature records were broken at over 1,000 locations. Temperatures are given as anomalies above or below the average for the same eight-day period of March between 2000 and 2011. (B) This image shows dense smoke from fires pouring from the Yucatán Peninsula, Mexico, and into the Gulf of Mexico, April 24, 2000.* (A. NASA; B. SeaWiFS/DigitalGlobe/NASA/Goddard Space Flight Center, and Digital Globe™)

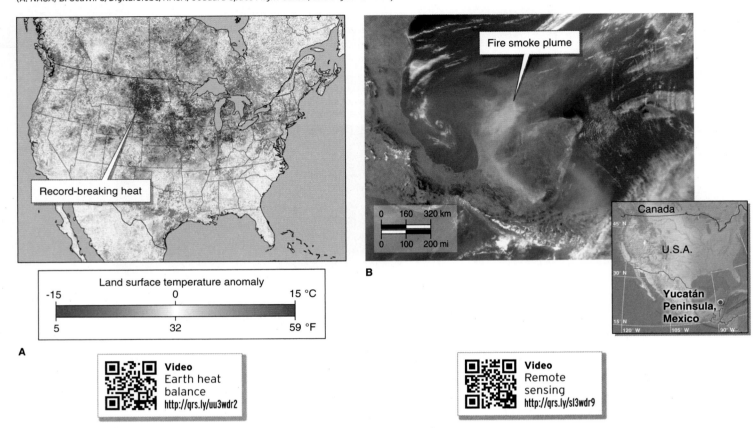

Video
Earth heat balance
http://qrs.ly/uu3wdr2

Video
Remote sensing
http://qrs.ly/sl3wdr9

FIGURE GT.27

Doppler radar.

(A) Doppler radar works by beaming microwaves, which reflect off falling precipitation (rain, snow, hail, and sleet) in the sky. An image is developed based on the reflected energy. (B) Hurricane Irene's spiral structure is clearly visible in this August 27, 2011, Doppler radar image of the U.S. East Coast centered on Virginia and North Carolina. Reds and yellows indicate heavy rainfall; greens and blues show regions of relatively less rainfall. (B. National Weather Service)

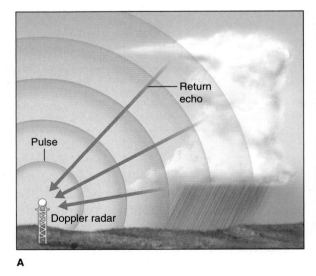

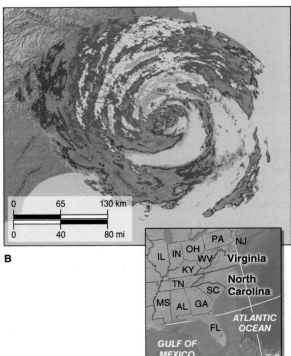

FIGURE GT.28

Sonar mapping. *The world's ocean basins have been mapped with sonar, revealing the world's longest mountain ranges and deepest valleys hidden beneath the sea. Transmitters aboard ships send and receive sonar pulses to create an image (inset). This image shows details of the underwater topography of the Hawaiian Islands. Purple and blue areas are over 5,000 m (16,400 ft) deep. Contour lines are also shown for elevation both above and below sea level.* (Left, Courtesy of Anthony Koppers, Seamount Catalog, http://earthref.org)

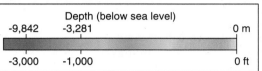

much Earth science data so freely available, and satellite remote sensing is largely the reason.

Just as a digital camera creates images using electronic sensors rather than photographic film, satellites often use passive electronic sensors to create digital images of Earth's surface. The sensors on satellites, however, are far more advanced in their capabilities. Personal digital cameras can sense only visible light, which is light that we can see with our eyes. Sensors on orbiting satellites are also able to sense other forms of energy that are invisible to us, such as heat radiation from Earth's surface. Satellite remote sensing provides many of the images used in this book. **Figure GT.26** provides examples of some of the applications of satellite remote sensing.

Radar and Sonar

Radar (short for *radio detection and ranging*) is an important active remote sensing technology. **Doppler radar** is an active remote sensing technology widely used in the study of the atmosphere. Doppler radar uses *microwave* energy to measure the velocity and direction of movement of particles of precipitation within a cloud. **Figure GT.27** provides a Doppler radar image of Hurricane Irene (2011) as an example.

Radar is also used to image the surface of Earth. Radar technology provides detailed images of surface relief that cannot be easily detected using photography or satellite imagery. Radar transmitters mounted on airplanes send a pulse of radio waves at an angle and receive the return signal reflecting off Earth's surface. *LIDAR* (*light detection and ranging*) is a relatively new type of remote sensing that uses light, rather than radio waves or microwaves, to image Earth's surface.

Another active remote sensing technique is *sonar* (*sound navigation and ranging*). Sonar has been invaluable in mapping features of the seafloor.

> **How do we know mountains are hidden deep in the ocean?**

Sonar works by sending a pulse of sound from a transmitter aboard a ship. The sound pulse reflects off the seafloor and back to a receiver on the ship. The reflected echoes are received and used to create a map of the seafloor **(Figure GT.28)**.

The remote sensing technologies described above can be used to create a **digital elevation model (DEM)**. A DEM is a digital representation of land surface or underwater topography. DEMs are particularly effective at portraying Earth's surface relief **(Figure GT.29)**.

Doppler radar
An active remote sensing technology that uses microwave energy to measure the velocity and direction of movement of particles of precipitation within a cloud.

digital elevation model (DEM)
A digital representation of land surface or underwater topography.

FIGURE GT.29 **A digital elevation model.** *This global digital elevation model was made from many different types of remotely sensed data. It effectively shows Earth's surface topography. Red areas are regions with the highest elevation; green and blue areas have the lowest elevation. Earth's highest regions are the Tibetan Plateau, the Andes, and the Antarctic ice sheet.* (U.S. Geological Survey)

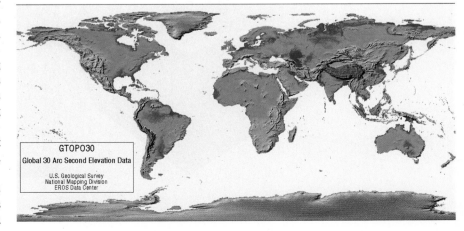

geographic information system (GIS)
A system that uses computers to capture, store, analyze, and display spatial data.

Geographic Information Systems

Once spatial data are acquired through remote sensing or other means, they can be manipulated using a **geographic information system (GIS)**. A GIS uses computers to capture, store, analyze, and display spatial data. Unlike traditional maps, which display all layers of information at once and are static (unchanging) once they are made, GIS maps are interactive, and layers of information can be chosen for display. Map users can interact with the spatial data within the database and can continually refine the map to explore different questions. Like maps, a GIS provides visual tools to help users gain a better understanding of the spatial relationships among various phenomena.

Unlike maps, a GIS integrates stacked layers of spatial data into a single dynamic unit. Each layer has a specific purpose and makes a specific contribution to helping the analyst achieve his or her goals. As new data become available, map layers can be updated or substituted, which will change the final GIS product.

California is prone to many natural hazards, particularly fires. The areas at greatest risk of fire can be precisely located using a GIS by spatially relating factors such as soil moisture, vegetation, and degree of urbanization (Figure GT.30).

Once these areas are identified, homeowners, forest managers, and restoration ecologists, for example, can identify high-risk areas and use this information to guide decisions. As new data become available, map layers can be updated or substituted, which will change the final GIS product.

GIS is one of the fastest growing fields in geography, and the field of GIS is rapidly developing in many public and private sectors of society as well. Landscape management, species conservation, water quality monitoring, fire management, and natural hazard zoning are just a few of the many applications of GIS. Many students who study geography and gain GIS skills are well prepared to go on to a career in GIS.

FIGURE GT.30 **Fire map from GIS.** *This fire threat map of California is useful for fire management and prevention. Areas shown in orange and red are at high risk of fire.* (Department of Forestry and FireProtection)

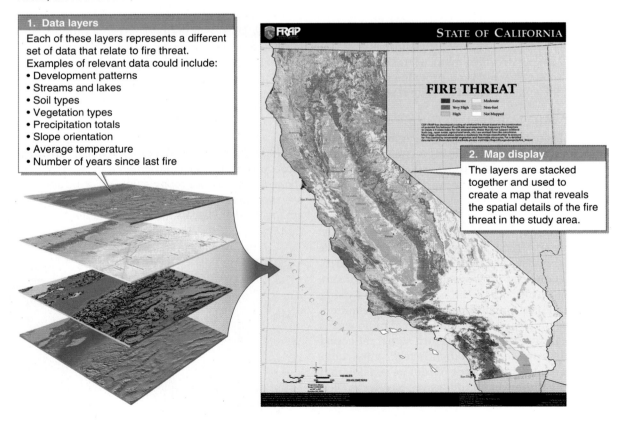

1.   Data layers

Each of these layers represents a different set of data that relate to fire threat. Examples of relevant data could include:
• Development patterns
• Streams and lakes
• Soil types
• Vegetation types
• Precipitation totals
• Slope orientation
• Average temperature
• Number of years since last fire

STATE OF CALIFORNIA

FIRE THREAT

Extreme   Moderate
Very High   Non-fuel
High   Not Mapped

2.   Map display

The layers are stacked together and used to create a map that reveals the spatial details of the fire threat in the study area.

GEOGRAPHIC PERSPECTIVES
GT.5 The Scientific Method and Easter Island

◎ Apply the scientific method to Easter Island to study its history of human settlement.

Most people are drawn by the beauty of nature and are curious about what it is and how it works. Scientists are no exception. In most cases, scientists are driven by their interest in the world. **Scientists follow the scientific method to answer questions about the world in a way that is based on rational thought and repeatable observations and conclusions.** The scientific method loosely follows this sequence:

1. *Observations*: You observe something that interests you or that you do not fully understand. Your observations must be repeatable; that is, others must be able to observe the same phenomenon.

2. *Questions*: You might ask why a thing is present or absent, why it behaves the way it does, how old it is, or where it came from.

3. *Develop a hypothesis*: The information you collect stimulates a *hypothesis*, which is a well-thought-out, testable idea that poses an answer to your original question. Hypotheses can be developed before, during, or after data collection.

4. *Collect data*: You collect data (often in the form of measurements) to learn more or to test your hypothesis.

5. *Test the hypothesis*: Scientific hypotheses must be testable. For example, a hypothesis about a tree's age is testable by counting the number of annual rings in the tree's trunk, but a hypothesis about whether a tree feels pain is not testable. Your hypothesis may be supported by all available information. However, the information you gathered may not support your hypothesis. In that case, you must either modify your hypothesis or throw it out and develop a new one.

6. *Further inquiry*: Whether your original hypothesis was supported by the data or not, new information and new questions often lead to new ideas and further inquiry.

Easter Island:
The Scientific Method Applied

Exploring the unusual history of Easter Island illustrates the sequence of observations, ideas, hypotheses, data collection, and hypothesis testing in the scientific method.

1. Observation: Stone Statues

Easter Island is a small, 166 km^2 (64 mi^2) volcanic island in the South Pacific Ocean. A person can walk around the entire island in half a day. The closest human neighbors are about 2,000 km (1,240 mi) to the west in the Pitcairn Islands **(Figure GT.31)**.

On Easter, 1722, the Dutch explorer Jacob Roggeveen was the first European to visit Easter Island. Roggeveen found a small population of people who had no boats and no wood, and who were locked in state of warfare. The hundreds of

FIGURE **GT.31** **Easter Island.** *Easter Island is about 2,000 km (1,240 mi) from the nearest inhabited islands, the Pitcairn Islands, and 3,610 km (2,250 mi) from Chile. Easter Island is called Rapa Nui in the local Polynesian language. (NASA image created by Jesse Allen, Earth Observatory, using data obtained from the University of Maryland's Global Land Cover Facility)*

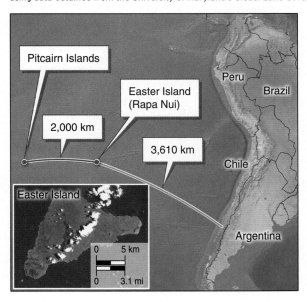

FIGURE GT.32 **Easter Island moai.** *When Jacob Roggeveen first reached Easter Island in 1722, islanders could not tell him who had made the hundreds of giant statues and the massive stone platforms that support them. The stone carvings weigh about 13 metric tons on average and stand about 4 m (13 ft) tall. Some are much larger.* (Art Wolfe/Getty Images)

large stone statues on the island, called *moai*, perplexed him **(Figure GT.32)**.

When asked, islanders said the statues "walked" to their present locations. They did not know how the statues were moved to their current positions from the stone quarries where they were carved, which are located far away from where the statues stand on the island today. Roggeveen never solved the mystery.

2. Question: How Were the Statues Moved across the Island?

> Who built the massive statues on Easter Island and how?

A person could claim the statues were once alive and walked to their present positions. This claim is not a scientific hypothesis, however, because it is easy to declare false—statues do not walk. Scientists had no doubt that people had carved the statues in stone quarries and somehow moved them across the island. But how? The islanders had no modern machinery, rope, or even wood. The question can be posed as follows: "How did the early inhabitants of Easter Island move enormous statues from stone quarries across the island to their current locations with no machinery, rope, or wood?"

3. Collect Data: Pollen

Without data, scientific inquiry is impossible. In 1977, British geographer J. R. Flenley was one of the first scientists to study the ecological history of Easter Island. His research team took cores of sediments from the marshes on the island and analyzed the pollen in the cores. Pollen from plants had been trapped in the marshes and preserved. The upper layers of the marshes reflect modern vegetation. The deeper sediments come from further back in time and contain ancient pollen from long ago. Changes in pollen types through time reveal the island's dynamic ecological history.

When Jacob Roggeveen reached the island, it was grassy and windswept, with almost no trees, as it largely is today. Flenley and his colleagues suspected that conditions were different in the past. As they analyzed the pollen data, they found, much to their amazement, that the island was once covered with some 23 species of trees. They also saw a decline in tree pollen that began around 800 CE. By 1550, very little tree pollen was preserved in the sediments, indicating that Easter Island's forests were gone by that time.

4. Hypothesis: Log Rollers

Hypotheses are testable ideas. They are statements that can be refuted. The pollen data provided enough information for researchers to develop a hypothesis about the transportation of the stone figures. Having discovered that the islands were once heavily forested, the scientists concluded that the statues were transported across the island using trees somehow. This conclusion led to a new hypothesis: Extensive track and roller systems made out of tree logs were used to move the statues.

5. Test the Hypothesis: Log Rollers Do Work

Is it possible to move the massive statues using logs as rollers? To test this idea, researchers later returned to Easter Island and attempted to move the statues using only those materials that would have been available to the original inhabitants. Although their efforts gave mixed results, they were able to move and right a statue after much labor using this technique. Other techniques using timber and twine made from trees met with mixed success.

A recent technique of "walking" the statues by lassoing them around the head with ropes and carefully balancing and rocking them back and forth to move them has also been tried with success on a 4.5-metric-ton replica statue. If this method was used, perhaps it explains why the islanders referred to the statues as having "walked" to their present locations around the island.

6. Further Inquiry: Collapse of Society

One of the hallmarks of the scientific process is that scientists follow the data to an outcome, rather than having an outcome in mind first and seeking support for it. There is no place for personal bias or desires in the scientific process. The researcher follows the data wherever they lead, as long as the data are legitimate and are analyzed logically and rationally.

Scientists studying Easter Island examined the preserved garbage mounds left by its early inhabitants to study what they ate. The earliest material at the bottom of the garbage heaps was about 1,200 years old, although this earliest date is still being debated. That is about when the first Polynesians colonized the island, and that is when the pollen data show the forest decline beginning. The earliest garbage consisted in large part of bones from dolphins (porpoises), sea turtles, seals, shellfish, and fish.

The Polynesian settlers also brought rats with them to Easter Island. Rat bones were found throughout the garbage mounds. These rats were probably a food source for the colonizers, and they probably caused significant ecological harm to the island's birds and trees by eating seeds and bird eggs.

Aside from shellfish, seafood can be acquired only with the use of boats. Yet scientists found fewer and fewer remains of seafood as time went on. The tops of the garbage mounds had no seafood whatsoever.

In some cases, scientists found cracked human bones in the garbage mounds, but only in the most recent parts of the piles. This evidence indicates that cannibalism began around 1600 on the island. Scientists hypothesize that when the forests were gone, the islanders could no longer build boats to fish. Famine, population collapse, and cannibalism followed.

How Is a Hypothesis Different from a Theory?

As the story of Easter Island started to unfold, scientists concluded that its inhabitants destroyed their forests, perhaps in large part to move statues. The statues are thought to have been a display of political power. It is thought that powerful chiefs competed to build the biggest and the most statues, at the expense of the well-being of the island's people and forests. Each piece of factual evidence from Easter Island supports the broader theory that the island suffered ecological and population collapse because of overexploitation of the forests.

A scientific hypothesis is a specific testable idea. *Theories* are constructed from many hypotheses that are all tested and supported by the available evidence. **Successful theories hold up as new evidence becomes available through time. Any theory can fail if new data contradict it.** When this happens, either the theory must be adjusted or it must be thrown out altogether.

Some theories are called *unifying theories* because they explain a wide range of seemingly unrelated phenomena. The theory of plate tectonics (see Chapter 11), for example, is a unifying theory that explains a wide range of physical phenomena, such as volcanoes, earthquakes, and mountain building.

In some cases, theories are so strong that no one reasonably thinks that new facts will ever refute them. In such a case, the theory is elevated to a scientific *law*. The law of gravity is an example. If apples or anything else were ever to fall upward, the law of gravity would have to be modified, or even abandoned.

THE GEOGRAPHER'S TOOLKIT **Study Guide**

Focus Points

GT.1 Welcome to Physical Geography!

Geography: Geography emphasizes spatial relationships to gain insight into cultural and physical phenomena.

Physical geography: Physical geography employs a range of spatial and temporal scales to explore Earth's physical systems and human influences on those systems.

Scale: Different spatial and temporal scales provide varied perspectives on physical phenomena.

GT.2 The Physical Earth

Earth systems: Earth's four major physical systems are the atmosphere, biosphere, lithosphere, and hydrosphere.

Solar energy: Solar energy flows through the atmosphere and biosphere. The Sun evaporates water, which precipitates on land and erodes the land surface as it flows.

Geothermal energy: Geothermal energy builds Earth's surface relief through the process of plate tectonics.

GT.3 Mapping Earth

Latitude zones: The major zones of latitude are the tropics, midlatitudes, and high latitudes.

Maps and map scale: Maps portray spatial information efficiently. How much Earth's surface has been reduced on a map is shown by the map scale.

Map elements: Maps should have a title, scale, legend, north arrow, and the date of publication.

GT.4 Imaging Earth

Remote sensing: Remote sensing provides important information about Earth's changing physical systems. Satellite sensors, Doppler radar, and sonar are important remote sensing technologies.

GT.5 Geographic Perspectives: The Scientific Method and Easter Island

Scientific method: The scientific method is a procedural framework that improves our understanding of the natural world.

Theory: A theory is constructed from many hypotheses that have been tested and supported by data.

Key Terms

anthropogenic, 4
atmosphere, 10
biosphere, 11
cartography, 19
chemical energy, 8
climate, 13
condensation, 14
contour line, 22
crust, 10
digital elevation model (DEM), 24
Doppler radar, 24
energy, 8
equator, 16
erosion, 14
evaporation, 14
geographic grid, 16
geographic information system (GIS), 26
geography, 4
geothermal energy, 8
Global Positioning System (GPS), 19
great circle, 20
hydrosphere, 11

large scale, 6
latitude, 16
lithosphere, 11
longitude, 16
map, 6
map scale, 20
matter, 8
meridian, 18
parallel, 16
photosynthesis, 8
physical geography, 4
precipitation, 15
prime meridian, 16
radiant energy, 8
relief, 10
remote sensing, 23
small scale, 6
spatial scale, 5
system, 4
temporal scale, 5
topography, 22
tropics, 16
water vapor, 11
weather, 12

Concept Review

GT.1 Welcome to Physical Geography!

1. Define physical geography.

2. What does "anthropogenic" mean?

3. Compare spatial scale to temporal scale. How is each used in geography?

4. Compare a large scale to a small scale. Which makes surface features appear larger on a map?

5. How does a change in scale lead to a change in perspective and in the types of questions that can be asked?

6. What are the two major systems of weights and measures? Which of these does the United States use? Which does most of the world use? What do scientists use?

GT.2 The Physical Earth

7. What is matter? In what three states does it occur? Give examples.

8. How is the term *energy* defined?

9. What type of energy gives motion to the atmosphere?

10. What factors cause Earth's shape to be an imperfect sphere?

11. Define the terms *atmosphere, biosphere, lithosphere,* and *hydrosphere.*

12. What two types of energy are emphasized in physical geography?

13. Life is a physical manifestation of solar energy. Explain.

14. Where does the energy come from to build up Earth's landscapes?

15. Where does the energy come from to erode Earth's surface?

GT.3 Mapping Earth

16. What is the geographic grid? How are angular measurements used to form it?

17. What are parallels and meridians? Give examples.

18. What and where are the three major global zones that are based on latitude? Briefly describe each of these zones.

19. What are the two subzones based on latitude?

20. What does GPS stand for? Describe what GPS is used for.

21. What is a map? Are all maps printed on paper?

22. Compare a great circle route with a small circle route. Which is used in long-distance flights by aircraft?

23. Compare a large-scale map with a small-scale map. Which would a map of a single mountain be?

24. What are five important elements most maps have?

25. What are contour lines? Provide examples of their use.

GT.4 Imaging Earth

26. What is remote sensing? Compare passive to active remote sensing.

27. Give three examples of remote sensing technologies in wide use today.

28. What is a digital elevation model (DEM)?

29. What is GIS and what is it used for?

30. What does it mean when we say that a map is interactive? Why is interactivity a desirable trait in maps?

GT.5 Geographic Perspectives: The Scientific Method and Easter Island

31. What is a scientific hypothesis? Why must a hypothesis be testable, and what is used to test one?

32. What is a scientific theory? Can one ever be "proved"? Explain.

33. How were pollen data used to shed light on how Easter Island's statues were moved?

34. What role did natural resources, particularly forests, play in the health and well-being of the Easter islanders?

Critical-Thinking Questions

1. Look around where you are right now. How many of the three states of water can be found within eyeshot? Where is each found?

2. Which of the three types of map scales will be accurate when you view a street map on your smartphone? Why?

3. Many cell phones allow authorities to monitor the owner's movement. Do you think this an acceptable use of GPS technology? Explain.

4. "There is no connection between heat waves and the frequency of earthquakes." Is this a testable scientific hypothesis? Explain.

5. Can you think of any parallels between Easter Island and today's global society with regard to the loss of natural resources?

Test Yourself

Take this quiz to test your chapter knowledge.

1. True or false? A world map is an example of a large-scale map.

2. True or false? Earth is not a perfect sphere due to its rotation, surface relief, and gravitational anomalies.

3. True or false? Water enters the atmosphere through evaporation.

4. True or false? Matter and energy flow through Earth's systems.

5. True or false? The highest angle of longitude is 90 degrees.

6. Multiple choice: A storm derives its energy from
   a. geothermal energy.
   b. chemical energy.
   c. solar energy.
   d. electrical energy.

7. Multiple choice: The equator is an example of
   a. latitude.
   b. longitude.
   c. a meridian.
   d. a small circle.

8. Multiple choice: Which of the following would be useful in determining the rate of rainfall in a storm?
   a. LIDAR
   b. sonar
   c. Doppler radar
   d. satellite visible image

9. Fill in the blank: Only when you are standing at _____ degrees latitude is Earth's rotational speed zero.

10. Fill in the blank: _____ specifies the relationship between distance in the real world and distance on a map.

Picture This. YOUR TURN

The Geographic Grid

The geographic grid is shown on this world map. The equator and the prime meridian are labeled. Latitudes and longitudes are 15 degrees apart. Using the origin (at 0°, 0°) as a starting point, identify the following locations on the map below. Only degrees (not minutes and seconds) are given for each location:

The Dead Sea, Israel	31° N, 35° E
The Himalayas, Nepal, and Tibet	30° N, 79° E
Iceland	64° N, 18° W
Madagascar	19° S, 46° E
Mt. Whitney, California	36° N, 118° W
Patagonia, Argentina	41° S, 69° W

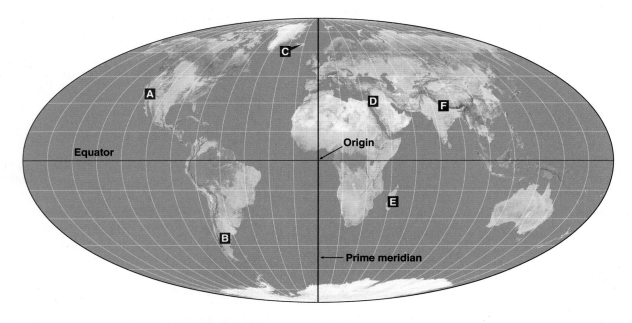

Equator
Origin
Prime meridian

Further Reading

1. de Blij, Harm. *Why Geography Matters: More Than Ever*. New York: Oxford University Press, 2012.

2. Jacobs, Frank. *Strange Maps: An Atlas of Cartographic Curiosities*. New York: Viking Studio, 2009.

3. Monmonier, Mark. *How to Lie with Maps*. 2nd ed. Chicago: University of Chicago Press, 1996.

Answers to Living Physical Geography Questions

1. **Where do tornadoes get their energy?** A tornado's energy comes from the Sun's heating of the atmosphere and from water that has been evaporated.

2. **How do my car and phone know where I am?** Cars and smartphones know where on Earth we are because their built-in GPS receivers sense coordinate data from satellites orbiting overhead.

3. **How do we know mountains are hidden deep in the ocean?** Sonar mapping allows scientists to image the seafloor by sensing reflected sound waves.

4. **Who built the massive statues on Easter Island and how?** Evidence indicates that Easter Islanders began building the large statues over 1,000 years ago and may have transported them across the island using a system of ropes and log rollers.

PART I
ATMOSPHERIC SYSTEMS:
Weather and Climate

The Sun's heating of Earth's surface and water vapor in the atmosphere give rise to gentle breezes and gale-force winds, sunny afternoons and torrential downpours. Part I explores the work of solar energy and water in creating atmospheric systems, and it explores the changing climate system.

CHAPTER 1
Portrait of the Atmosphere

An envelope of gases surrounds Earth, makes weather possible, and makes Earth habitable.

CHAPTER 2
Seasons and Solar Energy

Solar energy and seasons create temperature differences and atmospheric motion.

CHAPTER 3
Water in the Atmosphere

Solar energy evaporates water into the atmosphere, forming water vapor and precipitation.

CHAPTER 4
Atmospheric Circulation and Wind Systems

The Sun's energy drives global wind and precipitation patterns.

CHAPTER 5
THE RESTLESS SKY:
Storm Systems and El Niño

Atmospheric motion organizes into different systems, from gentle sea breezes to deadly storms.

CHAPTER 6
The Changing Climate

Earth's climate system changes naturally and from human activity.

(Chapter 1: © Andy Rouse/naturepl.com/NaturePL; Chapter 2: 2014 3TIER by Vaisala; Chapter 3: Beyond/SuperStock; Chapter 4: NASA/JPL; Chapter 5: © A. T. Willett/Alamy; Chapter 6: © Ashley Cooper/Age Fotostock Inc.)

PART

ATMOSPHERIC SYSTEMS: Weather and Climate

1 Portrait of the Atmosphere

SOUTH
AMERICA
45° S

SOUTH ATLANTIC OCEAN

South
Georgia

60° S

ANTARCTICA
75° W   60° W   45° W

This photo shows lenticular clouds that have formed over the mountains in South Georgia, a British overseas territory in the South Atlantic Ocean. The atmosphere's clouds and precipitation occur almost exclusively within the lowest layer of the atmosphere. *(© Andy Rouse/ naturepl.com/NaturePL.)*

LIVING PHYSICAL GEOGRAPHY

➤ What are clouds made of?

➤ How high does the atmosphere go?

➤ What are northern lights?

➤ Why are skin cancer rates increasing worldwide?

To learn more about the structure of the atmosphere, turn to Section 1.3.

THE BIG PICTURE *The atmosphere is composed of gases and has a layered structure. It shields us from the Sun's harmful rays, but human activity has changed the atmosphere's protective shield.*

LEARNING GOALS *After reading this chapter, you will be able to:*

1.1 ◎ Describe the gases and other materials that make up the atmosphere.

1.2 ◎ Explain what causes air pressure and how air pressure changes vertically within the atmosphere.

1.3 ◎ Name and describe the atmosphere's layers.

1.4 ◎ Identify major atmospheric pollutant types and discuss their effects on human health.

1.5 ◎ Assess the effects of anthropogenic pollutants in the ozonosphere and the anticipated condition of the ozonosphere in the coming decades.

THE HUMAN SPHERE: Wyoming's Air Pollution Problem

FIGURE **1.1** **Natural gas wells.** *Extraction of natural gas has brought economic prosperity and jobs to Wyoming, but it has also brought poor air quality. Excess natural gas that escapes from the ground is wasted as it is burned (or flared) off at this drilling rig in the Jonah Field near Pinedale, Wyoming.* (Joel Sartore/NationalGeographic/Getty Images)

FOR MANY, WYOMING BRINGS to mind clean skies as far as the eye can see. But lately, western Wyoming's ground-level ozone pollution has at times rivaled that found in Los Angeles or Houston, two of the smoggiest cities in the nation.

The United States is currently experiencing a boom in drilling for natural gas. Wyoming and many other states have both prospered from and suffered the consequences of a rush to extract natural gas from the ground (Figure 1.1).

Extracting natural gas from the ground is energy intensive and requires diesel-fueled machinery that pollutes the air. In addition, natural gas leaks from the wells. A 2012 study found that up to 9% of the gas extracted may leak directly into the atmosphere. This leakage, along with the exhaust from machinery, is resulting in significant ground-level pollution, including ozone pollution. The wells are also suspected of causing contamination of drinking water in the ground.

This chapter explores the composition of the atmosphere, air pressure in the atmosphere, the layered structure of the atmosphere, and air pollution. The protective role of the atmosphere is also examined in light of the effects of CFCs (chlorofluorocarbons), gases released into the atmosphere by human activities.

1.1 Composition of the Atmosphere

◎ Describe the gases and other materials that make up the atmosphere.

No other known planet has an atmosphere that is as supportive of life as Earth's. The atmosphere (or *air*) is the envelope of gases that surrounds the planet. If Earth were the size of a basketball, most of the atmosphere would be only about the thickness of a single piece of paper. As **Figure 1.2** shows, the atmosphere's thinness can be seen from the vantage point of space.

Gases in the Atmosphere

There are two groups of gases in the atmosphere: *permanent gases* and *variable gases* (or *trace gases*). Proportions of the permanent gases fluctuate only a little. Just over 99% of the atmosphere is composed of only two permanent gases: nitrogen (N_2) and oxygen (O_2). **Table 1.1** shows their proportions in the atmosphere and lists other permanent gases that occur in minute amounts.

Variable gases exist in extremely small quantities and do change in their proportions. There are many variable gases, but only those that absorb and emit thermal energy, called **greenhouse gases**, are included in this discussion. **Table 1.2** lists six prominent greenhouse gases and their concentrations in the atmosphere.

As we will see in Section 2.5, greenhouse gases create Earth's natural *greenhouse effect*. They absorb and radiate heat in the atmosphere. Without greenhouse gases, Earth's atmosphere would be very cold.

FIGURE 1.2 **Earth's atmosphere.** *The edge of Earth's atmosphere can be seen in this photo taken by astronauts aboard the International Space Station. The thin blue shell seen here edge-on is all that separates life on Earth from the inhospitable conditions of space. Although it looks like the atmosphere ends abruptly in this photo, it fades gradually with altitude.* (NASA)

TABLE 1.2 AT A GLANCE: **Variable Gases that Act as Greenhouse Gases**

VARIABLE GAS NAME	PERCENTAGE BY VOLUME	PPM*
Water vapor (H_2O)	0 to 4	
Carbon dioxide (CO_2)	0.0396	398
Methane (CH_4)	0.00017	1.7
Nitrous oxide (N_2O)	0.00003	0.3
Ozone (O_3)	0.000004	0.04
CFCs and HFCs**	0.00000002	0.0002

*ppm = parts per million. For example, 398 ppm carbon dioxide means that for every 1 million molecules of air, 398 are carbon dioxide molecules.
**Chlorofluorocarbons (CFCs) and hydrofluorocarbons (HFCs). CFCs and HFCs are manufactured by people and do not form naturally.

TABLE 1.1 AT A GLANCE: **Permanent Gases**

PERMANENT GAS NAME	PERCENTAGE BY VOLUME
Nitrogen (N)	78.08
Oxygen (O)	20.95
Argon (Ar)	0.93
Neon (Ne)	0.0018
Helium (He)	0.0005
Hydrogen (H)	0.00005
Xenon (Xe)	0.000009

Gas Sources and Sinks

Scientists use the terms *sources* and *sinks* to describe how gases enter and exit the atmosphere or are changed into different gases. Like water that enters a kitchen sink from the faucet (the *source*) and exits down the drain (the *sink*), gases enter the atmosphere through a source, and they leave the atmosphere through a sink. Sinks can be either physical environments (such as a lake or wetland) or processes (such as a chemical reaction), or both. Gas sources can be both natural and **anthropogenic** (created or influenced by people). **Table 1.3**, shown on the next page, details sources and sinks for the major gases in the atmosphere.

greenhouse gas
A gas that can absorb and emit thermal energy.

anthropogenic
Created or influenced by people.

TABLE 1.3 **Sources and Sinks for Atmospheric Gases**

GAS	SOURCE(S)	SINK(S)
Nitrogen (N_2)	Decaying and burning organic matter, volcanic eruptions, weathering of rocks	Enters soil and water with rain and biological activity
Oxygen (O_2)	Photosynthesis	Decomposition and weathering of rocks absorb O_2 from the atmosphere
Water vapor (H_2O)	Evaporation from oceans, plant photosynthesis, volcanic eruptions	Condensation and deposition convert H_2O to liquid and solid (ice) states
Carbon dioxide (CO_2)	Volcanic eruptions, decay of living matter, respiration, humans' burning of coal, oil, and natural gas for energy	Plants, oceans, and chemical reactions with rocks absorb CO_2
Methane (CH_4)	Anaerobic (oxygen-free) bacterial decomposition	Breakdown by ultraviolet radiation from the Sun
Nitrous oxide (N_2O)	Soil bacterial processes, human activities	Breakdown by ultraviolet radiation from the Sun
Ozone (O_3)	Ultraviolet radiation, burning fossil fuels	Breakdown by ultraviolet radiation from the Sun
CFCs and HFCs	Anthropogenic	Breakdown by ultraviolet radiation from the Sun

Aerosols in the Atmosphere

What are clouds made of?*

Aerosols are another important component of the atmosphere. **Aerosols** are microscopic solid or liquid particles suspended in the atmosphere. They are not gases because they are made up of matter in a solid or liquid, rather than a gaseous, state. Clouds are composed of aerosols because they are made up of cloud droplets and tiny ice crystals. **Cloud droplets** are microscopic drops of liquid water found in clouds.

Other common aerosols in the atmosphere include windblown dust, pollen, spores, bacteria, emissions from human activities such as farming and industrial pollutants, salt particles from the oceans, volcanic ash, and smoke.

Solid aerosols play an important role in the atmosphere as *condensation nuclei* in cloud formation processes. This topic is covered further in Section 3.5.

1.2 The Weight of Air: Atmospheric Pressure

◎ **Explain what causes air pressure and how air pressure changes vertically within the atmosphere.**

aerosols
Microscopic solid or liquid particles suspended in the atmosphere.

cloud droplets
Microscopic drops of liquid water found in clouds.

Gravity keeps molecules in the atmosphere and the oceans pinned to the planet, giving them weight. The gaseous atmosphere and the liquid ocean are both *fluids*, which means that they flow. But the molecules in the oceans are mostly water and are more closely packed together in a relatively dense liquid form. The molecules in the atmosphere, which are mostly nitrogen and oxygen, are farther apart from one another in their less dense, gaseous state. Nonetheless, the atmosphere has mass. Indeed, the total weight of the atmosphere is estimated to be 5 quadrillion metric tons!

How high does the atmosphere go?

If you were to travel straight up, how far would you have to travel to get to the top of the atmosphere? It turns out that the answer is not straightforward, because the atmosphere does not end abruptly; instead, it gradually fades. Ninety-nine percent of the atmosphere is found from Earth's surface up to about 32 km (20 mi). At some point above 10,000 km (6,000 mi), there are no more air molecules (see Figure 1.2).

Air Pressure

Molecules in a gaseous state move quickly. They constantly collide with and bounce off one another. At sea level, a single air molecule collides with some 10 billion other molecules each second. It also collides with any other object it comes in contact with, such as trees, the ground, birds, water, and people. Each time a molecule in the air hits any surface, it pushes ever so slightly against it.

FIGURE 1.3 **Air pressure.** *(A) The weight of water is greater above a person at the bottom of the deep end of a swimming pool than at the bottom of the shallow end. There is more water pressure in the deep end. (B) Similarly, the depth of the atmosphere and, therefore, the weight of air are greater for a person at sea level than high up in the mountains. Air pressure is always less at higher elevations.*

Animation
Air pressure
http://qrs.ly/ew41c2q

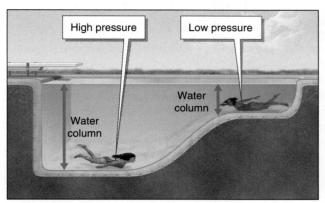

A. Swimming pool

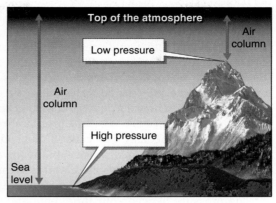

B. The atmosphere

The collective force (push) of air molecules creates pressure. **Air pressure** is the force exerted by molecules of air against a surface.

Except for a few locations below sea level (such as the Dead Sea, with an elevation of −427 m [−1,401 ft]), air pressure is greatest at sea level, and it decreases with increasing elevation. To illustrate this point, Figure 1.3 makes the comparison between pressure in a swimming pool and pressure in the atmosphere.

Air Density and Pressure

Because molecules in a gas are far apart, their density can increase as they are compressed. At most times, the density of air is greatest near sea level because the weight of the atmosphere above compresses the air (Figure 1.4).

Increased air density contributes to air pressure because in denser air, there are more molecules to exert force against objects, creating air pressure. This increased air density is the result of the weight of the overlying mass of air. (Note that, unlike molecules in air, molecules of water in a liquid are already close together and cannot be compressed further.)

Measuring Air Pressure

One way to express air pressure is in kilograms per square centimeter (kg/cm^2) or in pounds per square inch (lb/in^2 or *PSI*). At sea level, there is approximately 1 kg pressing on every square centimeter of all objects (or 14.7 lb pressing on every square inch). Put a different way, a column of air that is 1 cm^2 in area and extends from sea level all the way up to the top of the atmosphere would, on average,

FIGURE 1.4 **Air density, pressure, and height.** *Air density and pressure are greatest near sea level, where air molecules are most tightly compressed. At higher altitudes, air molecules are less compressed, so air has lower density and lower pressure. If a 1-cubic-meter (1 m^3) box (inset diagrams) were filled with air at sea level and another one higher in the atmosphere, the air in the sea-level box would have a higher molecular density and more air pressure.*

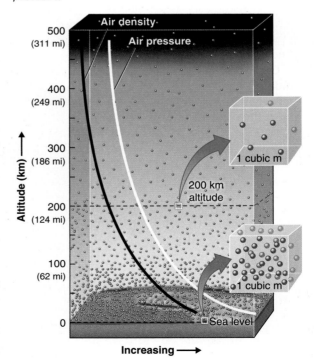

air pressure
The force exerted by molecules of air against a surface.

troposphere
The lowest layer of the atmosphere, extending from Earth's surface up to about 12 km (7.5 mi), where all weather occurs.

weigh 1 kg (or 14.7 lb for a 1 in² column of air). (See Section 4.2 for a discussion of air pressure in the context of weather systems.)

Because the atmosphere is weighing down on our bodies, you might wonder why we are not crushed by its weight, much like being crushed beneath the weight of a large boulder. The answer is that a large boulder is a solid and would press against us only from above. Air and water, on the other hand, are fluids. They flow around (and inside) our bodies. As a result, the atmosphere (and water, when we are swimming) pushes down, sideways, and up against our bodies. We experience the same pressure from all angles simultaneously. The cells in our bodies exert outward pressure in balance with the inward pressure exerted by the atmosphere, and as a result, we cannot feel the pressure of the atmosphere.

The pressure between our inner ears and the atmosphere is normally in equilibrium. When the outside pressure is changed by driving in mountainous areas or flying, this equilibrium is temporarily disrupted until our ears adjust to the change

of pressure. These pressure differences push on the eardrum and can be quite uncomfortable.

1.3 The Layered Atmosphere

◎ Name and describe the atmosphere's layers.

As we will see throughout this book, many of Earth's physical systems are composed of layers. In the lithosphere, layers make up Earth's internal structure. In the hydrosphere, the oceans have layers distinguished by light penetration, temperature, and life. In tropical rainforests, vegetation forms many different canopy and understory layers.

The atmosphere, too, is structured in layers. The *homosphere* and the *heterosphere* layers of the atmosphere can be distinguished based on concentrations of gases. These layers, however, play a minor role in Earth's physical systems. Layers based on changing trends in temperature with altitude, however, have important effects on Earth's physical systems.

Layers Based on Temperature
You may be familiar with the way the temperature of the atmosphere changes with altitude. If you have ever been high in the mountains, you probably noticed that the air is cooler there than at lower elevations. But if you kept climbing higher in the atmosphere, you might be surprised to find that high above the highest mountains, the atmosphere gets warmer again.

There are four main *thermal divisions* of the atmosphere based on changes in temperature with altitude: The **troposphere** extends from Earth's sur-

Layers of the Atmosphere

LAYER	ALTITUDE (KM)	ALTITUDE (MI)	MAJOR FEATURES
Thermosphere	80-600	50-370	Auroras (northern and southern lights) occur here
Mesosphere	50-80	30-50	Meteors burn up here
Stratosphere	12-50	7.5-30	Ozone gas absorbs harmful solar rays here
Troposphere	0-12	0-7.5	All weather occurs here

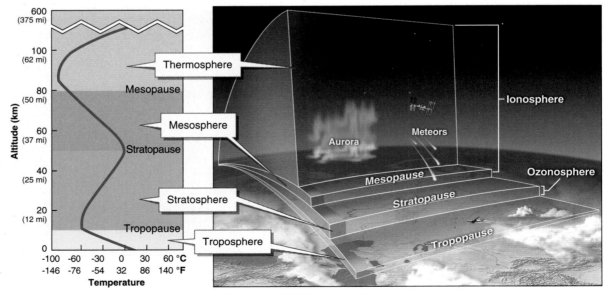

FIGURE 1.5 Layers of the atmosphere.
The atmosphere is divided into four layers based on changes of temperature as altitude changes. The red line on the diagram at left shows how temperature changes within each layer. The diagram at right portrays the relative thickness of each layer and the locations of the ozonosphere and ionosphere.

Early manned balloon flight

James Glaisher and Henry Coxwell were among the first to accurately measure temperature and humidity in the upper atmosphere. Reaching about 10 km (6 mi), they broke the world record for altitude in 1862. On that trip, they fainted due to a lack of oxygen, but they survived the expedition.

Radiosondes

Today, instrument packages called radiosondes are attached to unmanned weather balloons and are used to measure conditions in the upper atmosphere. Worldwide, about 900 stations release radiosondes. About 75,000 are launched each year in the United States, usually twice per day from about 100 cities. They record altitude, geographic location, temperature, pressure, humidity, and wind speed and direction.

FIGURE **1.6** **SCIENTIFIC INQUIRY:**
How do scientists study the upper atmosphere?

Understanding how the atmosphere is structured, how it is changing, and how weather can be accurately forecast requires careful and precise measurements. Radiosondes (weather balloons) and satellites are two essential means of taking scientific measurements of the atmosphere. (Top left, © Chronicle/Alamy; bottom left, © SCOTT AUDETTE/Reuters/Corbis; bottom right, NASA)

Satellites

Satellites provide invaluable data on changing conditions in Earth's upper atmosphere. They carry state-of-the-art instruments that measure a range of atmospheric phenomena, including temperature, humidity, airflow, clouds, and precipitation. This image is from the GOES (Geostationary Operational Environmental Satellite). The U.S. National Weather Service uses GOES imaging to monitor weather in the Western Hemisphere.

stratosphere
The atmospheric layer above the troposphere, which extends between about 12 and 50 km (7.5 and 30 mi) above Earth's surface and has a permanent temperature inversion.

temperature inversion
A layer of the atmosphere in which air temperature increases with increased height.

mesosphere
The layer of the atmosphere between 50 and 80 km (30 and 50 mi) above the surface.

thermosphere
The atmospheric layer located from 80 to 600 km (50 to 370 mi) above the surface.

environmental lapse rate
The rate of cooling with increasing altitude in the troposphere. The average environmental lapse rate is 6.5°C per 1,000 m or 3.6°F per 1,000 ft.

face up to about 12 km (7.5 mi), on average. It is the lowest layer of the atmosphere, in which all weather occurs. The next layer up, the **stratosphere**, is found between 12 and 50 km (7.5 and 30 mi) above Earth's surface. The stratosphere contains a permanent temperature inversion because it is heated as it absorbs radiation from the Sun. A **temperature inversion** is a layer of the atmosphere in which air temperature increases with increased height (see also Section 1.4). Above the stratosphere, the **mesosphere** lies between 50 and 80 km (30 and 50 mi) above Earth's surface. The **thermosphere** is located from 80 to 600 km (50 to 370 mi) above Earth's surface. **Figure 1.5** illustrates these divisions and their main characteristics.

Our knowledge of the atmosphere's structure is less than a century old. Much of what scientists know about the atmosphere comes from two main sources of information: weather balloons and orbiting satellites. The development of this knowledge is sketched in **Figure 1.6**.

The Weather Layer: The Troposphere

The troposphere is warmed from the bottom up by Earth's surface, which is warmed by sunlight. As one moves higher in the troposphere, air temperature generally decreases. The **environmental lapse rate** is the rate of cooling with increasing altitude in the troposphere. The average environmental lapse rate is 6.5°C per 1,000 m or 3.6°F per 1,000 ft. Keep in mind that this is an average rate, and that the atmosphere may cool much faster or slower, depending on the time and the location.

CRUNCH THE NUMBERS:
Calculating Temperature Changes

Imagine you are driving from the beach (at sea level) to the top of a mountain 3,000 m (9,840 ft) tall near the coast. Calculate the temperature of the troposphere at the mountaintop using the environmental lapse rates given. Notice that the environmental lapse rate changes with each example; it can change as a result of local conditions at any given time. Steeper environmental lapse rates lead to colder temperatures at high altitudes. The first example is done for you.

Ground Temperature (°C)	Environmental Lapse Rate	Height (m)	Temperature at This Height (°C)
30	4°C/1,000 m	3,000	18

Answer: The height change between sea level and the mountaintop is 3,000 m. (4°C/1,000 m) × 3,000 m = 12° of cooling. 30° − 12° = 18°

Ground Temperature (°C)	Environmental Lapse Rate	Height (m)	Temperature at This Height (°C)
30	6.5°C/1,000 m	3,000	
30	8°C/1,000 m	3,000	

Ground Temperature (°F)	Environmental Lapse Rate	Height Change (ft)	Temperature at This Height (°F)
86	2.2°F/1,000 ft	9,840	
86	3.6°F/1,000 ft	9,840	
86	4.4°F/1,000 ft	9,840	

In the **Crunch the Numbers** feature above, you will use the environmental lapse rate to calculate the temperature you can expect on a mountaintop.

In the lower troposphere, temperature inversions sometimes develop. There are many ways in which temperature inversions may form. They often develop in valleys, where a cold, dense mass of air may form close to the ground. Above this cold air mass, the temperature increases. Temperature inversions in the troposphere are usually no more than a few hundred meters thick, and a little higher up, the normal cooling trend resumes.

Temperature inversions in the atmosphere are significant in several ways. The temperature inversion in the stratosphere limits almost all clouds to the troposphere, as we'll see later in this section. Temperature inversions in the troposphere can trap pollutants near the ground surface (see Section 1.4). They also can create sleet and freezing rain during winter storms.

Roughly 80% of the mass of the atmosphere is in the troposphere, and it is where Earth's weather occurs. **Almost all clouds, and all storms and precipitation, are limited to the troposphere.** The troposphere experiences strong vertical mixing: The Greek word *tropos* means to turn over, or *convect*. The troposphere ends, and the stratosphere begins, at the **tropopause**. Almost all cloud tops end at the tropopause, where the atmosphere begins to warm due to the temperature inversion in the stratosphere. The temperature inversion prevents clouds from rising, as discussed in the **Picture This** feature below.

As we have seen, the average height of the tropopause is about 12 km (7.5 mi). At the equator, the tropopause is 18 km (11 mi) above Earth's surface. At midlatitudes, it is about 12 km (7.5 mi) above Earth's surface, and in the polar regions it occurs at about 8 km (5 mi) in altitude **(Figure 1.7)**.

Why is the tropopause roughly twice as high over the equator as over the poles? There are two reasons. First, solar heating of the atmosphere expands air and causes it to occupy more space.

tropopause
The boundary between the troposphere and the stratosphere.

Senegal-Mali border

Picture This

This portion of the cloud is protruding into the stratosphere.

The anvil structure stops at the tropospause.

(Image courtesy of the Earth Science and Remote Sensing Unit, NASA Johnson Space Center)

FIGURE 1.7 Tropopause height.

The equatorial tropopause is 10 km (6 mi) higher in altitude than the polar tropopause. (The thickness of the atmosphere in this diagram is greatly exaggerated.)

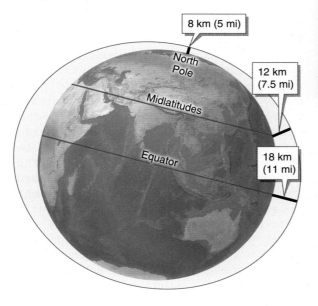

8 km (5 mi)

North Pole

Midlatitudes

12 km (7.5 mi)

Equator

18 km (11 mi)

FIGURE 1.8 Tropopause and stratosphere. *This photograph shows the space shuttle* Endeavor *against the backdrop of two layers of the atmosphere, seen edge-on. From this perspective, the nose tip of the shuttle appears to be touching the tropopause, but the space shuttle is far above the tropopause. The clear air of the stratosphere appears blue. Suspended aerosols and pollutants give the troposphere its reddish-brown color.* (NASA)

A Protective Shield: The Stratosphere

Above the tropopause is the stratosphere. There are very few clouds in the stratosphere, and the air is mostly free of atmospheric aerosols. As **Figure 1.8** shows, the contrast between the two layers can be vivid.

As a result of its permanent temperature inversion, there is little vertical mixing in the stratosphere—air flows in horizontal sheets instead—and storms and clouds usually do not enter the stratosphere from below. The temperature inversion in the stratosphere is caused by the absorption of ultraviolet radiation by stratospheric

Heating is greatest near the equator, in the tropics. Second, Earth rotates faster at the equator than in polar regions (see Section GT.2). Therefore, the atmosphere near the equator bulges outward more than that at higher latitudes, increasing its depth. The height of the tropopause also increases in summer and decreases in winter due to changing temperatures in the atmosphere.

The Tropopause

This towering cumulonimbus cloud has grown from Earth's surface up to the base of the stratosphere. Most of the cloud has not entered the stratosphere. Instead, it is splaying out horizontally at the base of the tropopause, creating a flattened anvil structure. The cloud cannot rise into the stratosphere because the cloud's relatively cold air is denser and heavier than the relatively warm air of the stratosphere. This photo was taken by an astronaut in the International Space Station while it was over the Senegal-Mali border on February 5, 2008. Note that the air is thick with aerosols that obscure Earth's surface.

Consider This

1. The anvil of this cumulonimbus cloud occurs at what boundary line?

2. Given the latitude of this cloud, how high does it extend in kilometers?

3. In the context of the relative densities of air and water, explain why a bubble of air rises in water. Relate your explanation to why this cumulonimbus cloud rises high in the troposphere and stops at the stratosphere.

ultraviolet (UV) radiation
Solar radiation that is shorter than visible wavelengths.

ozonosphere
(pronounced oh-ZO-no-sphere) A region of the stratosphere with high concentrations of ozone molecules that block ultraviolet radiation.

ionosphere
A region of the upper mesosphere and the thermosphere between about 80 and 500 km (50 to 310 mi) where gases are ionized by solar energy.

aurora borealis/australis
Displays of light (also called northern and southern lights) caused by energized molecules in the ionosphere.

ozone in the ozonosphere. **Ultraviolet (UV) radiation** is solar radiation that has shorter wavelengths than visible light. It can cause skin cancer and cataracts in people. The **ozonosphere** is a region of the stratosphere with high concentrations of ozone molecules that block UV radiation. The critical role of the ozonosphere is explored further in the Geographic Perspectives at the end of this

 GEOGRAPHIC PERSPECTIVES

chapter. The top of the stratosphere, the *stratopause*, occurs at about 50 km (30 mi) in altitude.

The Mesosphere and Thermosphere

The mesosphere lies above the stratosphere. Although air density (and pressure) in the mesosphere is extremely low, meteors (sometimes called shooting stars) heat up and vaporize as they encounter friction with the air molecules in the mesosphere. As in the troposphere, temperature decreases with height in the mesosphere, until it reaches about –90°C (–130°F) at about 85 km (53 mi) above Earth's surface.

Above the *mesopause* lies the thermosphere. As in the stratosphere, there is a permanent temperature inversion in the thermosphere, caused by absorption of the Sun's radiation by gas molecules. Temperatures in the thermosphere rise as high as 1,200°C (2,200°F). What would the thermosphere feel like to a person? The air would feel cold because it is extremely thin (air molecules are exceedingly far apart). As a result, very little heat would be transferred to your body.

The top of the thermosphere (the *thermopause*) is 600 km (370 mi) above Earth's surface. Here, the air is so thin that molecules move some 10 km (6 mi), on average, before colliding with another molecule. In the troposphere, where molecular density is much greater, molecules move only a millionth of a centimeter, on average, before colliding. At the

top of the thermosphere some molecules reach escape velocity, meaning that they can overcome Earth's gravitational pull and enter the depths of space forever. The region where molecules are free of Earth's gravity is the *exosphere*.

The Ionosphere: Nature's Light Show

The last atmospheric layer we will examine, the ionosphere, is distinguished by its electrical properties. The **ionosphere** is a region of the upper mesosphere and the thermosphere between roughly 80 and 600 km (50 to 373 mi) in altitude where nitrogen and oxygen are *ionized* by solar energy. The ionosphere interacts with and absorbs UV, X-ray, and gamma radiation from the Sun, all of which can harm life on Earth. The ionosphere also allows radio waves transmitted from Earth's surface to travel long distances through the atmosphere and is therefore important to radio communications.

> What are northern lights?

Nature's most impressive light shows, the **aurora borealis** (northern lights) and the **aurora australis** (southern lights), occur in the ionosphere. Auroras are caused by energized gas molecules in the ionosphere. The molecules are energized by charged particles (called the *solar wind*) from the Sun, creating beautiful displays of light. The colors of the aurora depend on the types of gases that are energized by the solar wind and the altitude at which they are energized. Auroras are found mostly near the poles because that is where Earth's magnetic field concentrates the solar wind's particles.

Aurora displays coincide with solar flare activity on the Sun. Although auroras are occasionally seen at latitudes as low as the southern United States, the best place to see them is at high latitudes during the dark winter months **(Figure 1.9)**.

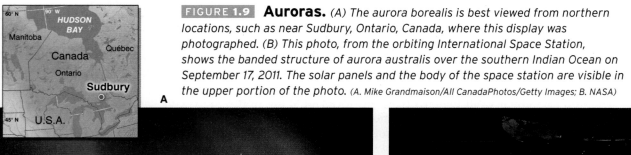

FIGURE 1.9   **Auroras.** *(A) The aurora borealis is best viewed from northern locations, such as near Sudbury, Ontario, Canada, where this display was photographed. (B) This photo, from the orbiting International Space Station, shows the banded structure of aurora australis over the southern Indian Ocean on September 17, 2011. The solar panels and the body of the space station are visible in the upper portion of the photo. (A. Mike Grandmaison/All CanadaPhotos/Getty Images; B. NASA)*

FIGURE **1.10** **Anthropogenic carbon monoxide emissions.** *These false-color maps show CO concentrations, averaged over a four-year period (from January 2000 through June 2004), for (A) late winter and (B) late spring. Concentrations are given in parts per billion by volume (ppbv): blue areas have little or no CO, and red areas have the highest CO concentrations. High concentrations result mostly from either burning of fossil fuels in industrialized regions (such as the United States and southern Canada, Europe, and much of East Asia) or burning of agricultural waste or forests in developing regions (such as northern South America, central Africa, and Southeast Asia). Note that the Northern Hemisphere's CO emissions are constant, while those in the Southern Hemisphere, which are mainly a result of seasonal burning of vegetation, vary more by season.*

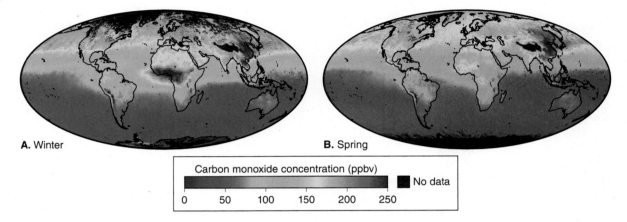

A. Winter   **B.** Spring

Carbon monoxide concentration (ppbv)   ■ No data

0   50   100   150   200   250

1.4 Air Pollution

◎ Identify major atmospheric pollutant types and discuss their effects on human health.

Air pollution is defined as harmful concentrations of gases or aerosols in the atmosphere. Air pollution is often called *smog*. This term comes from combining "smoke" and "fog," but fog has nothing to do with air pollution. Air pollutants originate from many different sources, natural as well as anthropogenic. Wildfires, for example, produce carbon monoxide, a toxic gas, and volcanoes release sulfur compounds.

This section focuses on anthropogenic pollutants, the majority of which come from the burning of fossil fuels. **Fossil fuels** are the ancient remains of plants preserved in the lithosphere in the form of coal, oil, and natural gas. When they are burned, greenhouse gases and toxic compounds are produced and released to the atmosphere.

There are two main categories of anthropogenic air pollutants: primary pollutants and secondary pollutants. A **primary pollutant** enters the air or water directly from its source, such as a car's tailpipe or a factory smokestack. Examples of primary pollutants are carbon monoxide (CO), sulfur dioxide (SO_2), nitrogen dioxide (NO_2), and anthropogenic volatile organic compounds (VOCs). A **secondary pollutant** is not emitted directly from

a source, but forms in the air or water through chemical reactions among primary pollutants.

Primary Pollutants

Carbon Monoxide

Carbon monoxide (CO) is a toxic odorless and invisible gas. When breathed in large amounts, CO reduces oxygen concentrations in the blood. Symptoms of CO poisoning include slowed reflexes and drowsiness. Death can happen within 1 to 3 minutes of exposure to high concentrations of CO gas.

There are many natural sources of CO, including volcanic eruptions, forest fires, and bacterial processes as well as natural chemical reactions in the troposphere. These natural emissions far exceed anthropogenic emissions, but the natural emissions are not concentrated locally. Instead, they form low *background* concentrations that are mixed and dispersed in the troposphere. As a result, they present little threat to people.

Anthropogenic carbon monoxide is formed mostly by the incomplete burning of carbon fuels (such as wood, gasoline, or coal). In urban areas in the United States, automobiles are the main source of CO emissions, producing up to 95% of the CO in the air. Clearing and burning of tropical rainforests also produces significant CO emissions in remote areas, particularly in the Southern Hemisphere, as **Figure 1.10** shows.

air pollution
Harmful concentrations of gases or aerosols in the atmosphere.

fossil fuels
The ancient remains of plants preserved in the lithosphere in the form of coal, oil, and natural gas.

primary pollutant
A pollutant that enters the air or water directly from its source.

secondary pollutant
A pollutant that is not directly emitted from a source, but forms through chemical reactions among primary pollutants in air or water.

carbon monoxide (CO)
A toxic odorless and invisible gas.

FIGURE 1.11 **Anthropogenic acid rain damage.** *(A) The pH scale ranges from 0 to 14. A pH value of 7 is neutral. Values above 7 are basic, or alkaline, and values below 7 are acidic. Extremely acidic rain can have a pH value as low as 2.0, close to that of lemon juice. (B) This weathered stone lion is outside the Leeds City Hall in Leeds, in the United Kingdom. It has been dissolved by acid rain caused by the long history of burning coal in the region. (C) Anthropogenic acid rain weakened these Fraser fir* (Abies fraseri) *and red spruce* (Picea rubens) *trees in Mt. Mitchell State Park, North Carolina. Once trees are weakened by acid rain, insects can more easily attack them, causing additional forest damage. (B. © Ryan McGinnis/Alamy; C. Will & Deni Mcintyre/PhotoResearchers/Getty Images)*

Battery acid	Lemon juice		Acid rain	Black coffee		Pure water	Baking soda		Soapy water		Drain cleaner
Acidic						**Neutral**					**Basic**
0	1	2	3	4	5	6	7	8	9	10	11	12	13	14

A

Sulfur Dioxide

Sulfur compounds (often denoted SO_x) are emitted from both natural and anthropogenic sources. **Sulfur dioxide (SO_2)** is produced by volcanic eruptions as well as by burning of fossil fuels. In high concentrations, it is a pungent gas that causes human health problems, including irritated lung tissue and the worsening of respiratory illnesses such as bronchitis and asthma.

Sulfur dioxide is the most prevalent sulfur compound produced by human activities. Over 80% of anthropogenic SO_2 emissions originate from the burning of coal to generate electricity. Sulfur dioxide combined with nitrogen compounds, such as nitrogen dioxide, forms droplets of *sulfuric acid* (H_2SO_4). These droplets can then precipitate and fall to Earth as **acid rain**: rainfall that has a lowered pH because it has mixed with sulfur compounds. Naturally acidic rain occurs downwind of volcanic eruptions. Anthropogenic acid rain occurs mostly near industrial areas. Over time, it dissolves certain types of rock, such as limestone and marble, that are often used in building construction and statues. It also can change soil and water chemistry, causing extensive ecosystem damage **(Figure 1.11)**.

In the United States, the acid rain problem has been much improved by passage of the Clean Air Act in 1963. In recent years, life has begun returning to formerly sterile lakes due to significant improvements in air quality and the resulting decrease in acid rain. In the last decade, however, Asia's increasing economic activity and coal burning have produced considerable acid rain problems there. Roughly a third of China has been hard hit by acid rain in the last decade, but the problem is improving. From 2006 to 2010. China's SO_2 emissions decreased by about 13% due to stronger rules governing those emissions.

Nitrogen Dioxide

In the United States, nitrogen compounds (often denoted NO_x) enter the atmosphere mainly through combustion of gasoline in cars and the burning of coal to generate electricity. An important nitrogen compound is **nitrogen dioxide (NO_2)**, a toxic reddish-brown gas produced mainly by vehicle tailpipe emissions. Exposure to NO_2 irritates lung tissue and, with chronic exposure, can lead to serious respiratory problems. In the United States, metropolitan regions with traffic congestion account for

sulfur dioxide (SO_2)
A pungent gas, produced by volcanic eruptions and by the burning of fossil fuels, that causes human health problems and acid rain.

acid rain
Rainfall that has a lowered pH because it has mixed with sulfur compounds.

nitrogen dioxide (NO_2)
A toxic reddish-brown gas produced mainly by vehicle tailpipe emissions.

almost 60% of NO_2 emissions. Coal burning accounts for 32% of U.S. emissions.

Volatile Organic Compounds

Volatile organic compounds (VOCs) (also called *hydrocarbons*) are toxic compounds of hydrogen and carbon. Examples of VOCs include methane, butane, propane, and octane. The methane that leaks from natural gas wells, discussed in the Human Sphere section at the start of this chapter, is a VOC. This group of chemicals may irritate the eyes, nose, and throat. They can also lead to liver, kidney, and central nervous system damage. Anthropogenic emissions come mostly from industrial processes and from automobiles, when gasoline is burned incompletely and when gasoline evaporates at gas stations. Natural bacterial decomposition of organic material such as vegetation and animal waste also contributes dispersed low concentrations of methane to the atmosphere. VOCs react with other compounds in the air, creating toxic secondary pollutants.

Secondary Pollutants

As we have seen, some secondary pollutants are a result of chemical reactions in the atmosphere. **Photochemical smog** is air pollution formed by the action of sunlight on tailpipe emissions. In this section, we will cover only one component of photochemical smog: ground-level ozone.

Ozone (O_3) is a molecule that is a pollutant in the lower atmosphere. In the stratosphere, however, it blocks harmful solar UV radiation. Without *stratospheric ozone*, these harmful rays would be deadly to organisms living on land. This topic is

 GEOGRAPHIC PERSPECTIVES explored further in the Geographic Perspectives at the end of the chapter.

Where ozone forms near the land surface, it is called *ground-level ozone*. Ground-level ozone forms when sunlight breaks down nitrogen dioxide (NO_2) into NO + O. Oxygen in the atmosphere (O_2) then combines with the atomic oxygen (O) made available when NO_2 breaks apart, resulting in ozone (O_3). Ultraviolet radiation breaks ozone apart within hours after it has formed. Therefore, ground-level ozone is typically highest in urbanized areas during the afternoon rush-hour traffic in summer, when sunlight is most direct and there is plenty of NO_2 available from tailpipe emissions.

Ozone irritates the eyes and nose, scars lung tissue, and can worsen respiratory ailments such as bronchitis, emphysema, and asthma. In many urban areas, local authorities declare summer "Ozone Action Days" or "Clean Air Alerts" to warn residents to restrict their outdoor activity during high-ozone periods.

TABLE 1.4	AT A GLANCE: The Air Quality Index
AIR QUALITY INDEX (AQI) VALUES	**LEVELS OF HEALTH CONCERN**
0 to 50	Good
51 to 100	Moderate
101 to 150	Unhealthy for sensitive groups
151 to 200	Unhealthy
201 to 300	Very unhealthy
301 to 500	Hazardous

In the United States, the Environmental Protection Agency (EPA) has created the Air Quality Index (or AQI). Canada uses a similar system, called the Air Quality Health Index. The AQI system ranks daily air quality in all major metropolitan regions from 0 to 500. These rankings are based on a number of pollutants in addition to ozone. An AQI of 151 or greater is considered unhealthy for all people **(Table 1.4)**.

Ozone corrodes rubber and plastics unless they are specially treated. Ground-level ozone can also reduce photosynthesis in plants by up to 10%, thus interfering with agricultural production.

Particulate Matter

Particulate matter (PM) consists of liquid and solid particles (aerosols) suspended in the atmosphere. Particulate matter can be either a primary pollutant or a secondary pollutant, depending on whether it was directly emitted from a source or whether it resulted from a chemical reaction. Particulates can be natural or anthropogenic; they include volcanic dust and sulfuric acid droplets, pollen, fire smoke, and dust. Black carbon soot is a type of particulate matter that results from the burning of fossil fuels, vegetation, and animal dung (an important source of cooking fuel in many developing nations). Particulate matter emissions in the United States come mainly from coal burning (about 40%), industrial processes (about 23%), and transportation (about 20%).

Particulate matter size is typically given in micrometers (μm; 1 μm = 1 millionth of a meter). The smaller the particle, the more harmful it is to human health. $PM_{2.5}$ is particulate matter of 2.5 μm diameter or less. PM_{10} is particulate matter of 10 μm diameter. For a sense of scale, a human hair is about 70 μm in diameter. Any inhaled particles smaller than 10 μm may move deep into the lungs and then into the bloodstream, where they

volatile organic compound (VOC)
A toxic compound of hydrogen and carbon; also called a *hydrocarbon*.

photochemical smog
Air pollution formed by the action of sunlight on tailpipe emissions.

ozone (O_3)
A molecule that is a pollutant in the lower atmosphere, but blocks harmful solar UV radiation in the stratosphere.

particulate matter (PM)
Liquid and solid particles (aerosols) suspended in the atmosphere.

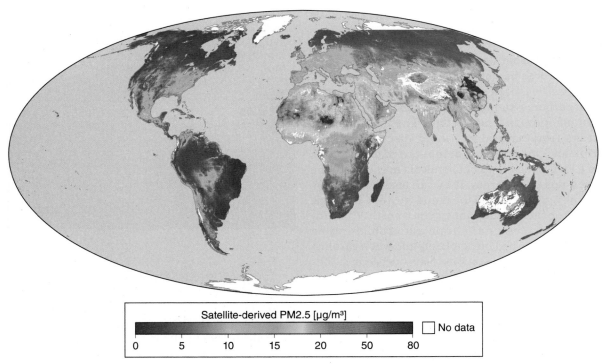

FIGURE 1.12 **Global particulate matter.** *This false-color satellite image shows global concentrations of PM$_{2.5}$ in micrograms per cubic meter ($\mu g/m^3$) averaged over five years (2001 to 2006). In the Sahara, the Arabian Desert, and interior Eurasia, particulate matter arises mostly from windblown dust. In the eastern United States, Europe, eastern China, and northern India, particulate matter arises from industrial emissions.*

Satellite-derived PM2.5 [$\mu g/m^3$]

☐ No data

0   5   10   15   20   50   80

can cause or worsen physical ailments, including bronchitis, asthma, various cancers, and heart disease.

Particulate matter enters the atmosphere by means of natural dust storms in desert areas, where there is little vegetation to anchor blowing soils, and in industrial areas, as the satellite image in Figure 1.12 illustrates.

Particulate matter is removed from the atmosphere as it settles out by gravity. It is also removed as falling rain and snow carry them to Earth's surface.

Factors That Affect Air Pollutant Concentrations

Once pollutants enter or form in the atmosphere, three factors concentrate them or carry them to other regions: topography, temperature inversions, and wind.

Topography: Valleys surrounded by mountains provide a natural basin in which air pollutants often concentrate. Many large cities are situated in flat valleys surrounded by mountains.

Temperature inversions: Temperature inversions often form in valleys as cold, dense air sits near the ground. These inversions can prevent air near the ground from rising higher. When pollutants are emitted into such an environment, they become concentrated

near the ground. Figure 1.13 shows this process happening in Salt Lake City, Utah, where temperature inversions are particularly common.

Wind: Wind typically reduces air pollution in regions where pollutants are formed or emitted by dispersing them more widely. However, wind sometimes removes pollutants from one region and concentrates them in others. North American pollution, for example, is carried by wind across the Atlantic Ocean to Europe. Similarly, particulate pollutants from industrial activity in China mix with dust storms that originate in the Gobi Desert in China and Mongolia and are then carried by wind across the Pacific to North America. The U.S. EPA has estimated that on some days, up to 25% of the particulate matter in Los Angeles originates in China. Figure 1.14 tracks a plume of pollution that moved from Asia to North America in 2001.

The Clean Air Act

Imagine that you were given the choice between fixing a minor toothache today or ignoring the problem indefinitely. You could save money by ignoring the problem and living with a little dull pain. But over time, the pain would worsen and a major dental issue would develop. Either way, the problem would have to be addressed because it

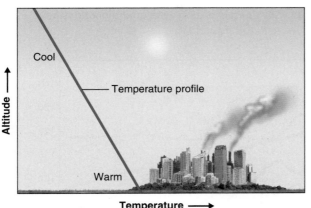

A. Normal temperature profile

FIGURE **1.13** **Temperature inversion and smog.**
(A) This normal temperature profile of the atmosphere shows decreasing temperature with altitude. This profile allows pollutants to rise and be dispersed by winds. (B) In a temperature inversion, a layer of air warms as altitude increases. This profile prevents air from rising and allowing winds to carry pollutants away. The air quality in Salt Lake City in winter is often poor due to persistent temperature inversions caused by cold, dense air that settles in the valley in which the city is located. During peak inversion times, temperatures can be some 20°C warmer at 2,000 m altitude (40°F at 6,500 ft) than at ground level. Pollution levels in Salt Lake City often exceed the federal standards. (Photo, C. Roland Li)

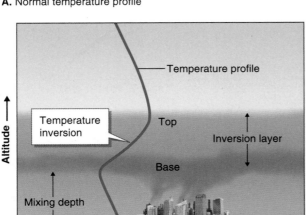

B. Temperature inversion

would not go away, and ignoring the pain would only allow it to worsen. This is what air pollution is like. Ignoring air pollution allows it to worsen as populations grow, as people drive more cars, and as more fossil fuels are burned to meet growing energy demands.

Faced with this choice, the U.S. Congress passed the Clean Air Act in 1970. It was amended in 1977

FIGURE **1.14**   **Wind carries pollution across the Pacific.** *The rapid economic development of China in the last few decades has relied in large part on burning coal to generate electricity. Coal combustion produces a wide range of dangerous pollutants, including particulate matter. The bike riders shown in the inset are suffering through industrial emissions in Beijing, China. The satellite image shows the migration of a plume of industrial emissions mixed with naturally occurring dust from the interior of China and Mongolia to North America between April 4 and April 16, 2001. Red and yellow areas show highest pollution concentrations. (Photo, PETER PARKS/AFP/Getty Images; map, NASA)*

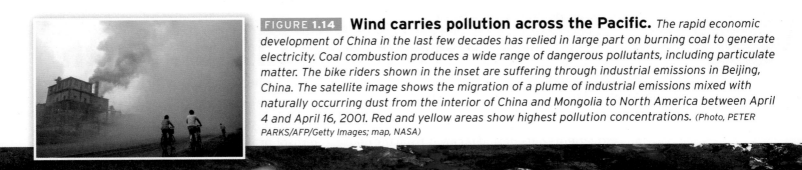

FIGURE **1.15** **Air pollution trends, 1990-2012.** *Emissions of five major air pollutants have decreased in the United States as a result of the Clean Air Act.* (*Data from U.S. EPA*)

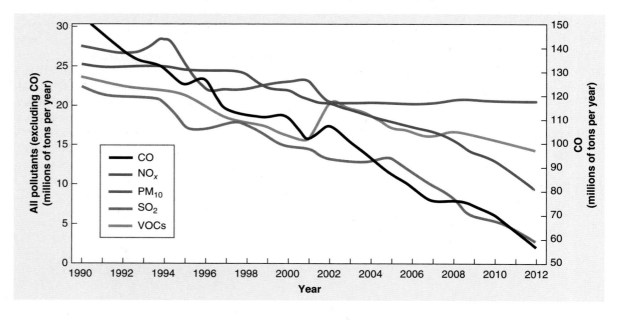

and again in 1990. The Clean Air Act imposed strict regulations on emissions of air pollutants. **The Clean Air Act has been effective at reducing air pollution in the United States, saving lives, and reducing national health care–related costs.** Figure 1.15 shows the declining trends in emissions of five major pollutants between 1990 and 2012.

Critics of the Clean Air Act argue that the technology necessary to reduce emissions is expensive and that implementing the law hurts the economy. They argue that enforcing clean air regulations moves jobs overseas, where it is cheaper to manufacture goods because pollution regulations are less stringent.

Proponents argue that, in the long run, clean air is cheaper than dirty air. According to the U.S. EPA, the United States will spend $65 billion to enforce the Clean Air Act for the period 1970–2020. These measures, however, will save the United States $2 trillion in health care–related costs for the same period. Furthermore, the lives saved and the improvements in the quality of life resulting from the law cannot easily be assigned a monetary value.

GEOGRAPHIC PERSPECTIVES
1.5 Refrigerators and Life on Earth

◎ Assess the effects of anthropogenic pollutants in the ozonosphere and the anticipated condition of the ozonosphere in the coming decades.

CFCs (chlorofluorocarbons)
A class of ozone-degrading compounds used mainly as refrigerants, aerosol propellants, and fire retardants.

Before the 1930s, it was a wise practice to keep refrigerators outside and far away from the house because they occasionally blew up. Refrigerator coolants consisted of a mix of volatile and explosive chemicals, which sometimes leaked and detonated. The safety of refrigeration increased with an invention that would change the world: **CFCs (chlorofluorocarbons)**, which are a class of ozone-degrading compounds used mainly as refrigerants, aerosol propellants, and fire retardants.

In 1930, General Motors and Du Pont held the patent on a new chlorofluorocarbon molecule, to which they gave the trademark name Freon. CFCs were nontoxic, cheap to make, and not explosive. Within five years of their introduction, refrigerators using Freon were the standard.

CFC molecules are *synthetic*, meaning that they do not form naturally. Before the 1920s, there were no CFC molecules in the atmosphere. By the early 1970s, it was known that CFCs were accumulating in the atmosphere, but scientists were not much concerned because these molecules are *inert*, meaning that they are not chemically reactive in the lower atmosphere. Because they are inert, they have a long *atmospheric lifetime*. After a CFC molecule is produced, it can last in the atmosphere for 60 years, 200 years, or even more than 1,000 years, depending on the type of CFC it is. This is where the problem began.

A Landmark Paper and an International Protocol

In 1974, Mario Molina and Sherwood Rowland, both at the University of California, Irvine, published a landmark paper. They announced that CFCs linger in the troposphere for decades. Furthermore, because they are less dense than oxygen and nitrogen, they slowly migrate upward toward the stratosphere. (Molina and Rowland would later receive the Nobel Prize for their work.) **Once in the stratosphere, CFCs are broken down by sunlight, and one of their components, chlorine, reacts with ozone, breaking it into oxygen atoms** and molecules. **Figure 1.16** illustrates the process of natural ozone formation and breakdown in the stratosphere as well as the role of CFCs in ozone destruction.

Chlorine from CFCs destroys ozone in the ozonosphere. **Without the protective layer of ozone, life on land would be burned by ultraviolet rays from the Sun.** Molina and Rowland recognized that in a span of only decades, CFCs had compromised Earth's UV shield that had protected the biosphere for over 2 billion years. With that single paper published in 1974, scientists and citizens realized that there were millions of tons of CFCs in the lower troposphere working their way up to the stratosphere, breaking apart to form chlorine, and destroying ozone molecules.

Satellite and ground-based measurements have provided key data about the response of the ozonosphere to these chemicals. These data show that the ozonosphere has thinned most dramatically over Antarctica, shown in **Figure 1.17** on the next page. The thinning is greatest over Antarctica because polar stratospheric clouds called *nacreous clouds*, so named for their shimmering mother-of-pearl quality, form in the cold air during the Antarctic spring (September) and assist in the process of chlorine reactions with ozone. Thinning

FIGURE 1.16 **Ozone formation and destruction.** *(A) Ozone forms naturally when ultraviolet (UV) radiation from the Sun breaks apart an oxygen molecule (O_2) into two atoms of oxygen (O). One of these atoms combines with a different oxygen molecule, forming ozone (O_3). (B) Ozone breaks down naturally when UV radiation breaks ozone molecules back down to oxygen. (C) Ultraviolet radiation breaks CFCs apart into separate atoms of chlorine, fluorine, and carbon. Chlorine then reacts with and breaks apart ozone. A single chlorine atom can convert several hundred thousand ozone molecules to oxygen.*

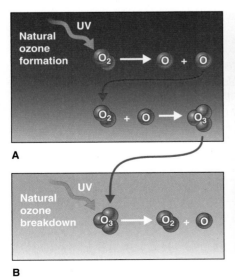
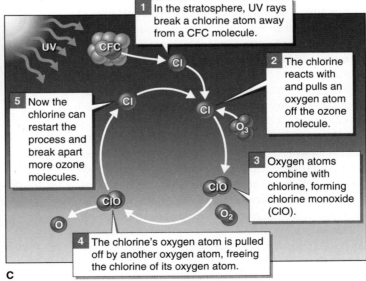

FIGURE **1.17**   **Thinning of the ozonosphere over Antarctica.** *Dobson units (DU) measure the concentration of ozone in the ozonosphere. Blues and purples show where there is the least ozone, and greens, yellows, and reds show a healthy ozonosphere. (A) This image was created on September 9, 2000, showing the largest ozone "hole" ever recorded for a single day: 29.9 million km² (11.5 million mi²). (B) This September 16, 2013 image shows that thinning over Antarctica has become slightly less extensive since September 2000. The area of ozonosphere thinning peaked at 24 million km² (9.3 million mi²) on this date. (A. NASA Ozone Watch; B. NASA Ozone Watch)*

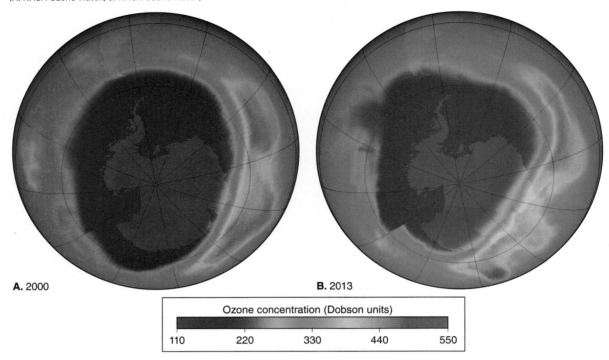

A. 2000   **B.** 2013

Ozone concentration (Dobson units)

110   220   330   440   550

is less severe over the North Pole because the stratosphere there is not as cold, so polar stratospheric clouds do not form there as easily.

In response to this problem, the Montreal Protocol, an international agreement banning further production of CFCs, was ratified in 1987, and in 1989 it went into effect. The protocol banned CFC production outright in some countries and mandated phaseouts in other countries. Concentrations of chlorine (from CFCs) in the stratosphere over Antarctica peaked in the early 1990s and have been on the decline ever since. By about 2040, they are expected to be down to 1980 levels **(Figure 1.18)**.

Although CFC production has been mostly phased out, the long residence time of CFCs in the troposphere means that they will continue to drift upward into the stratosphere for several more human generations. As long as there are CFCs in the atmosphere, the ozonosphere will remain vulnerable to thinning. Fortunately, stratospheric ozone is produced naturally. As the CFCs slowly disappear, the ozonosphere will repair itself.

Effects of a Thinning Ozonosphere

Without the protective ozonosphere, life on land would be impossible. Living organisms would have

to retreat permanently out of the Sun. There are many problems associated with increased exposure to UV radiation.

Human Health

Skin cancer: The cause of most cases of skin cancer is UV radiation exposure. All types of

FIGURE **1.18**   **Stratospheric chlorine concentrations over time.** *Measured and projected chlorine concentrations over Antarctica, in parts per trillion (ppt), between 1970 and 2090 show the effect of the Montreal Protocol.*

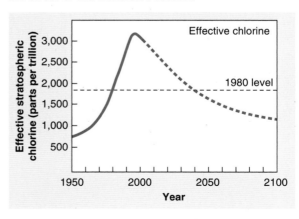

FIGURE 1.19 **Thinning of global ozonosphere avoided.** *These images show the results of a computer modeling study based on the assumption that CFCs would continue to be manufactured. The 2010 globe on the left shows modeled stratospheric ozone concentrations (in light blue and green) at midlatitudes and the tropics. To the right, the globes show increasingly lower ozone concentrations (in dark blue) over time. If the manufacture of CFCs had continued, ozone concentrations could have dropped to zero just after the middle of the twenty-first century, as shown by the image in blue on the far right. (NSA/SVS/GSFC Ozone Watch/NASA)*

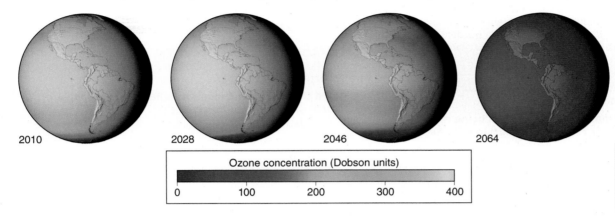

Video
Ozone layer
http://qrs.ly/il41c2x

skin cancer have been on the increase since the 1970s, although the increase in cases is partly a result of increased awareness and diagnosis. In the United States, melanoma (the most serious form of skin cancer) increased 800% among women and 400% among men from 1970 to 2009.

> Why are skin cancer rates increasing worldwide?

Reduced immunity: The skin is an important barrier that prevents pathogens in the environment, such as harmful viruses and bacteria, from entering our bodies. When exposure to UV radiation makes our skin less healthy, these pathogens can more easily invade our bodies and make us sick.

Cataracts: Cumulative exposure to UV radiation can cause a condition called cataracts, in which the lenses of the eyes become an opaque milky white. Vision is severely impaired by cataracts.

Plants

Agriculture: Plants are stressed by, and grow more slowly when they are exposed to increased levels of UV radiation. The result is reduced agricultural production. Scientists are working to increase tolerance for UV radiation in staple crops such as rice, wheat, corn, and soybeans.

Natural ecosystems: Almost all life on Earth depends on photosynthetic organisms such as plants to convert radiant energy from the Sun to the chemical energy that fuels the biosphere. If plants grow more slowly, this chain of connectivity will be affected.

A Crisis Averted

Antarctic ozonosphere thinning peaked in 2000 and is showing a gradual trend of improvement. Had the Montreal Protocol not been enacted, and had we continued producing CFCs, the world's ozonosphere could have disappeared by a little after the middle of the twenty-first century, as Figure 1.19 shows.

The Montreal Protocol is a good example of the international community working together to solve a problem that affects everyone. **Because of the Montreal Protocol, industry has largely replaced CFCs with HFCs (hydrofluorocarbons).** Unfortunately, HFCs are potent greenhouse gases: Molecule for molecule, they absorb up to twelve thousand times more energy than carbon dioxide. In a sense, we have traded the ozone-thinning problem for another equally serious problem: climate change. We will explore climate change further in the coming chapters.

CHAPTER 1 Exploring with ◎ Google Earth

To complete these problems, first read the chapter. When you are finished, go to LaunchPad and open the Exploring with Google Earth file for this chapter. Click on the "Workbook Problems" folder to "fly" to each of the problems listed below and answer the questions. Be sure to keep your "Borders and Labels" layer activated. Refer to Appendix 4 if you need help using Google Earth.

PROBLEM 1.1 This placemark highlights India. The surface of Earth is hidden by an opaque layer of pollution.

1. **Given how much atmospheric visibility is being reduced, what is the most likely type of air pollution seen here?**
   a. Ground-level ozone
   b. VOCs
   c. Particulate matter
   d. Sulfur dioxide

PROBLEM 1.2 This placemark highlights Puncak Jaya, the highest peak on the island of New Guinea.

1. **What is Puncak Jaya's elevation in feet?**
   a. 9,805 b. 13,903 c. 16,023 d. 17,500

2. **How far in miles is the mountain from the coast?**
   a. 60 b. 80 c. 100 d. 120

3. **Based on the average environmental lapse rate in the troposphere (see also Crunch the Numbers), about how much colder (in degrees Fahrenheit) is the peak of Puncak Jaya than the coast at sea level?**
   a. 30 b. 40 c. 50 d. 60

4. **In what country is Puncak Jaya located?**
   a. Papua New Guinea
   b. Indonesia
   c. Brunei
   d. Malaysia

PROBLEM 1.3 This placemark shows a photograph of tall thunderstorms near the Paraná River in southern Brazil. The photo was taken in 1984 by an astronaut aboard a space shuttle.

1. **In what layer of the atmosphere do these clouds occur?**
   a. The troposphere
   b. The stratosphere
   c. The ozonosphere
   d. The mesosphere

2. **At what part of the atmosphere do the flat tops of the clouds most likely stop?**
   a. The tropopause
   b. The stratopause
   c. The mesopause
   d. The thermopause

3. **What is the altitude of these cloud tops? (Note that this location is in the tropics.)**
   a. About 5 miles
   b. About 7 miles
   c. About 10 miles
   d. About 20 miles

PROBLEM 1.4 This placemark features satellite data showing high carbon monoxide concentrations (in reds and oranges) over Africa during February 2004.

1. **Given the geographic location, what is the probable source of this carbon monoxide?**
   a. Industrial pollutants and vehicles
   b. Natural oceanic sources
   c. Forest and agricultural waste burning
   d. Natural forest sources

2. **Why does the carbon monoxide also occur over the oceans?**
   a. Because the winds transport it there.
   b. Because the oceans emit it.

PROBLEM 1.5 This placemark shows high carbon monoxide concentrations (in reds and oranges) in South Asia. The data were collected in March 2007.

1. **Given the geographic location, what is the probable source of this carbon monoxide?**
   a. Industrial pollutants and vehicles
   b. Natural oceanic sources
   c. Forest and agricultural waste burning
   d. Natural forest sources

PROBLEM 1.6 This placemark features the remote Galápagos Islands in the eastern Pacific Ocean.

1. **Given the remoteness of the Galápagos, what is the probable source of this sulfur dioxide plume?**
   a. Industrial pollutants
   b. Soil bacteria
   c. Forest and agricultural waste burning
   d. Volcanoes

2. **What is the approximate length of the plume (east to west) in miles?**
   a. 100 b. 500 c. 1,000 d. 1,500

3. **Zoom in to the source of the plume. You will be able to see a green mountain symbol marking the feature that is producing the sulfur dioxide. (Make sure your Borders and Labels layer is activated.) What is the name of this surface feature?**
   a. Volcán La Cumbre
   b. Volcán Wolf
   c. Alcedo Volcano
   d. Volcán Cerro Azul

PROBLEM 1.7 This placemark shows particulate matter air pollution in eastern China just south and west of Beijing.

1. **Given the geographic location, what is the probable source of this particulate matter?**
   a. Industrial pollutants
   b. Soil bacteria
   c. Forest and agricultural waste burning
   d. Volcanoes

2. **What is the approximate elevation at the placemark?**
   a. 500 ft b. 700 ft c. 1,000 ft d. 1,400 ft

3. **What is the approximate elevation 60 miles to the west of the placemark?**
   a. 500 ft b. 1,200 ft c. 3,400 ft d. 5,000 ft

4. **Given your answers to the previous two questions, which factor probably plays a role in concentrating the air pollution at the placemark?**
   a. Wind
   b. Topography
   c. Temperature inversions
   d. All the above

CHAPTER 1 **Study Guide**

Focus Points

1.1 Composition of the Atmosphere

Types of gases: Gases in the atmosphere can be grouped into permanent gases and variable gases (or trace gases).

Greenhouse gases: Greenhouse gases, which absorb and emit thermal energy, play a crucial role in Earth's climate system.

Sources and sinks: Gases enter and exit the atmosphere through natural and anthropogenic sources and sinks.

1.2 The Weight of Air: Atmospheric Pressure

Air pressure: Because it has mass, the atmosphere is held down against the planet's surface by gravity, which gives it weight and creates pressure.

Air density: Air density and pressure are greatest near sea level because the weight of the atmosphere above compresses the air, increasing its density.

1.3 The Layered Atmosphere

Thermal divisions: The atmosphere can be divided into four layers based on changes in temperature with altitude: the troposphere, stratosphere, mesosphere, and thermosphere.

Troposphere: The troposphere gets colder with increasing altitude, and there is strong vertical mixing there. Earth's weather occurs in the troposphere.

Stratosphere: Storms and most clouds do not enter the stratosphere, and there is little vertical mixing there. Ozone molecules in the stratosphere block ultraviolet radiation.

1.4 Air Pollution

Categories of pollution: Anthropogenic air pollutants are grouped into two categories: primary pollutants and secondary pollutants.

Concentration of air pollution: Air pollution is concentrated in valleys, by temperature inversions, and by wind.

The Clean Air Act: Emissions of air pollutants in the United States have been reduced since the passage of the Clean Air Act in 1963.

1.5 Geographic Perspectives: Refrigerators and Life on Earth

The ozonosphere: Without the ozonosphere, life on land would be burned by ultraviolet radiation.

CFCs: Chlorine atoms from CFCs break down ozone molecules in the stratosphere.

Montreal Protocol: After the enactment of the Montreal Protocol, the manufacture of CFCs was mostly phased out.

Key Terms

acid rain, 46
aerosols, 38
air pollution, 45
air pressure, 39
anthropogenic, 37
aurora borealis/australis, 44
carbon monoxide (CO), 45
CFCs (chlorofluorocarbons), 50
cloud droplets, 38
environmental lapse rate, 41
fossil fuels, 45
greenhouse gas, 37
ionosphere, 44
mesosphere, 41
nitrogen dioxide (NO_2), 46

ozone (O_3), 47
ozonosphere, 44
particulate matter (PM), 47
photochemical smog, 47
primary pollutant, 45
secondary pollutant, 45
stratosphere, 41
sulfur dioxide (SO_2), 46
temperature inversion, 41
thermosphere, 41
tropopause, 42
troposphere, 40
ultraviolet (UV) radiation, 44
volatile organic compound (VOC), 47

Concept Review

The Human Sphere: Wyoming's Air Pollution Problem

1. Why does rural western Wyoming have poor air quality?

1.1 Composition of the Atmosphere

2. What are the two major permanent gases in the atmosphere, and what are some of the variable gases?

3. What are sources and sinks for gases? Give examples.

4. What are aerosols? Give examples of them.

1.2 The Weight of Air: Atmospheric Pressure

5. What is air pressure, and how much is there at sea level in kilograms per square centimeter? In PSI?

6. Why is air pressure greater near Earth's surface than higher up?

1.3 The Layered Atmosphere

7. List the four layers of the atmosphere that are based on changes in temperature with altitude.

8. What are the major characteristics of the troposphere? How do its temperature and pressure change with altitude?

9. What is the tropopause? What is its altitude at midlatitudes? What is its altitude at the equator and at the poles?

10. How high is the stratosphere? How does temperature change with altitude in the stratosphere?

11. Compare airflow in the stratosphere with that in the troposphere. How are they different?

12. What are auroras? Where do they occur on the planet and in what portions of the atmosphere? What causes them?

1.4 Air Pollution

13. What energy source do most anthropogenic atmospheric pollutants come from?

14. Give examples of primary pollutants, their sources, and their effects on human health.

15. What are secondary pollutants? Which one is used as an example in this chapter?

16. How is the ozone molecule both beneficial and harmful to people? Explain.

17. Why is particulate matter hazardous to human health?

18. What three physical factors make air pollution worse?

19. Why is it expensive for industry to pollute less?

20. What is the U.S. Clean Air Act? When was it enacted? Has it been successful? How?

1.5 Geographic Perspectives: Refrigerators and Life on Earth

21. What are CFCs and what are they used for?

22. How long do CFCs last in the troposphere? What happens when they reach the stratosphere?

23. What is the ozonosphere, how is it important, and how do CFCs affect it?

24. What are the projected trends in stratospheric chlorine concentrations for the next century?

25. What are nacreous clouds and how are they related to ozonosphere thinning over Antarctica? Why has there been less ozonosphere loss over the Arctic?

26. What are the connections between CFC production and human and ecological health?

Critical-Thinking Questions

1. Why is air pollution in the United States decreasing even though the numbers of cars and coal-burning power plants are increasing?

2. What is the general air quality where you live? How would you find out if you do not know the answer?

3. Acid rain is naturally produced by volcanoes. Given that acid rain is natural, why is acid rain caused by humans seen as a hazard?

4. Construct an argument between critics and supporters of the Clean Air Act, with one side stating it is too costly to enact, and the other side stating it is too costly not to enact. With which side do you identify more?

5. Can you think of other pressing global environmental problems like ozonosphere thinning that the world currently faces? Explain.

Test Yourself

Take this quiz to test your chapter knowledge.

1. **True or false?** The atmosphere is composed mostly of nitrogen.

2. **True or false?** Aerosols are gases in the atmosphere.

3. **True or false?** Air density and air pressure decrease as altitude increases.

4. **True or false?** In the stratosphere, temperature decreases with an increase in altitude.

5. **True or false?** Stratospheric chlorine concentrations peaked in the 1970s and have since been declining.

6. **Multiple choice:** Which of the following pollutants is most associated with acid rain?
   a. Ozone
   b. Carbon monoxide
   c. Sulfur dioxide
   d. Particulate matter

7. **Multiple choice:** In which of the following atmospheric layers is most ultraviolet radiation from the Sun absorbed?
   a. The troposphere
   b. The stratosphere
   c. The mesosphere
   d. The thermosphere

8. **Multiple choice:** Which of the following is not among the factors cited in this chapter as concentrating pollutants?
   a. Temperature inversions   b. Topography
   c. Wind   d. Vegetation

9. **Fill in the blank:** The _____ mandated the phaseout of CFCs by all industrialized countries.

10. **Fill in the blank:** The _____ is the region of the atmosphere where the aurora borealis and aurora australis occur.

Picture This. YOUR TURN

The Atmosphere's Thermal Divisions

Fill in the blanks on the diagram below using each of the following terms only once. In addition, indicate, using the boxes below, whether the temperature is increasing or decreasing with altitude.

1. Mesopause
2. Mesosphere
3. Stratopause
4. Stratosphere
5. Thermopause
6. Thermosphere
7. Tropopause
8. Troposphere

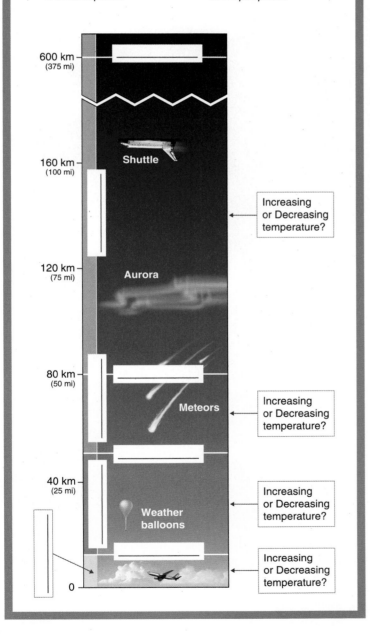

Further Reading

1. Molina, Mario, and Sherwood Rowland. "Stratospheric Sink for Chlorofluoromethanes: Chlorine Atom-Catalysed Destruction of Ozone." *Nature* 249 (1974): 810–812.

2. National Oceanic and Atmospheric Administration (NOAA). *Stratospheric Ozone Monitoring and Research in NOAA.* http://www.ozonelayer.noaa.gov/.

3. Pasachoff, Jay, and Vincent Schaefer. *A Field Guide to the Atmosphere.* Peterson Field Guides. Boston: Houghton Mifflin Harcourt, 1998.

Answers to Living Physical Geography Questions

1. **What are clouds made of?** Clouds are made of microscopic droplets of liquid water and ice crystals.

2. **How high does the atmosphere go?** Ninety-nine percent of the atmosphere is less than 32 km (20 mi) high.

3. **What are northern lights?** Northern lights result when the Sun's energy energizes gas molecules in the ionosphere, causing them to emit light.

4. **Why are skin cancer rates increasing worldwide?** Increased exposure to ultraviolet rays as a result of a diminished ozonosphere has caused skin cancer rates to rise. Increased awareness and vigilance have increased reported rates of skin cancer.

2 Seasons and Solar Energy

Chapter Outline

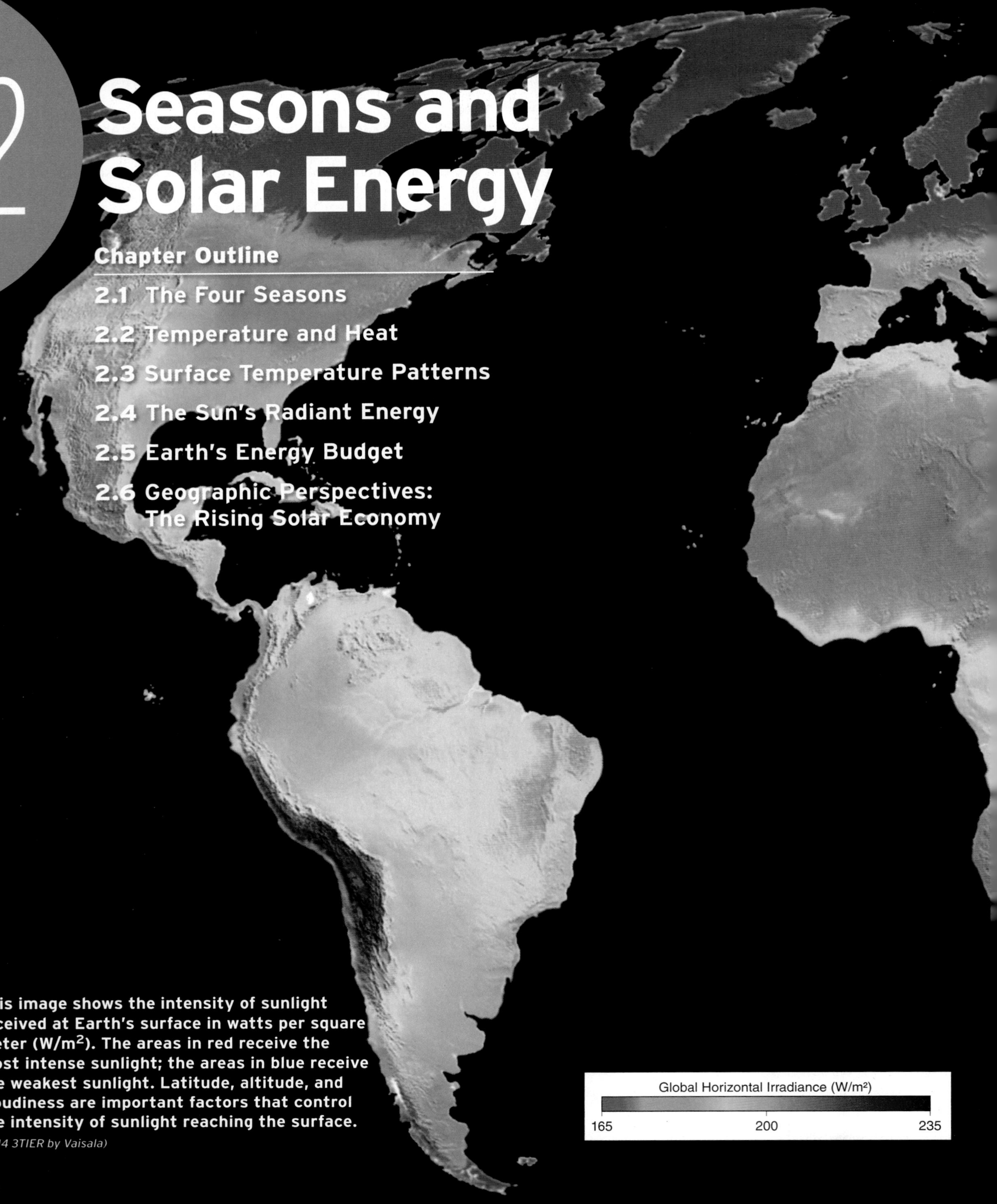

This image shows the intensity of sunlight received at Earth's surface in watts per square meter (W/m^2). The areas in red receive the most intense sunlight; the areas in blue receive the weakest sunlight. Latitude, altitude, and cloudiness are important factors that control the intensity of sunlight reaching the surface.

(2014 3TIER by Vaisala)

Global Horizontal Irradiance (W/m^2)

165   200   235

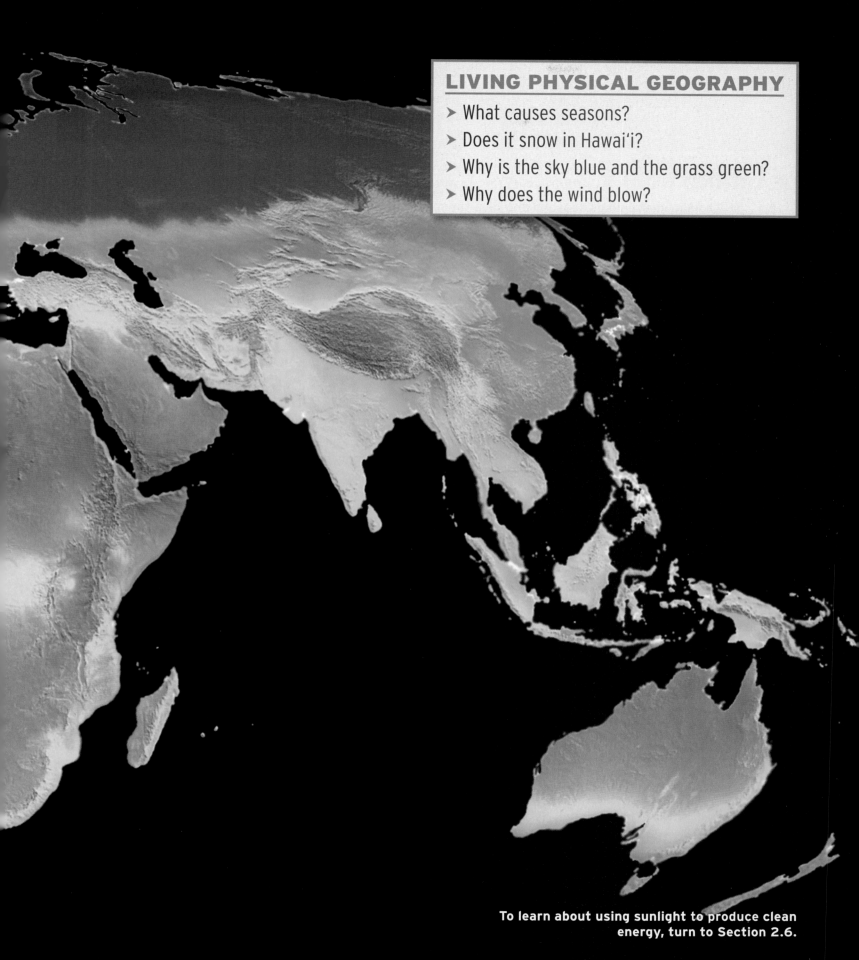

LIVING PHYSICAL GEOGRAPHY

> ➤ What causes seasons?
> ➤ Does it snow in Hawai'i?
> ➤ Why is the sky blue and the grass green?
> ➤ Why does the wind blow?

To learn about using sunlight to produce clean
energy, turn to Section 2.6.

THE BIG PICTURE *The Sun's unequal heating of Earth's surface causes seasonal and regional temperature differences and global atmospheric movement. Sunlight provides a promising source of clean energy.*

LEARNING GOALS *After reading this chapter, you will be able to:*

2.1 ◎ Explain what causes seasons and give the major characteristics of the four seasons.

2.2 ◎ Understand the difference between temperature and heat.

2.3 ◎ Describe Earth's surface temperature patterns and explain what causes them.

2.4 ◎ Describe solar energy and its different wavelengths.

2.5 ◎ Explain Earth's energy budget and why the atmosphere circulates.

2.6 ◎ Assess the role of sunlight as a clean energy source.

THE HUMAN SPHERE: **People and the Seasons**

FIGURE **2.1** **Stonehenge.** *Stonehenge, on Salisbury Plain, England, was built between 3000 and 2000 BCE. The exact purpose of Stonehenge is uncertain, but its stones are aligned to mark the changing position of the Sun across the year, so it most likely was used for observation of the astronomical seasons. (© David Nunuk/All Canada Photos/Getty Images)*

SEASONS MARK THE RHYTHMS OF LIFE. For many, spring and summer are a time of rebirth and growth, while fall and the harvest are times of maturity, achievement, and the reward for hard work. Winter brings a conclusion and rest, and the cycle begins again come spring.

The seasonal rhythm of the planet runs deep in many cultures at middle and high latitudes. Many of our activities and holidays mark seasonal events. Harvest times and periods of significance in many religious festivals are closely linked with seasons. Are there any connections you can trace between your cultural upbringing and Earth's seasons?

Most locations on Earth's surface are affected by *meteorological seasons,* the changes in temperature or precipitation over the year. Some regions on the planet, such as northern North America and Eurasia, experience extreme seasonality. Other regions, such as the lowland tropics, experience subtle and almost imperceptible changes over the course of the year in temperature and rainfall.

All locations on Earth experience *astronomical seasons*, changes in the positions of the Sun and stars in the sky through the year. The Gregorian calendar is used internationally and coincides closely with the changing position of the Sun. As shown in Figure 2.1, some ancient cultures built lasting monuments that served as calendars to mark key events of the astronomical seasons.

In this chapter we first explore the cause of seasons. We then examine solar energy, Earth's energy budget, and global surface temperature patterns. The Geographic **GEOGRAPHIC PERSPECTIVES** Perspectives at the end of the chapter explores the role of sunlight as a means of addressing climate change.

2.1 The Four Seasons

◎ Explain what causes seasons and give the major characteristics of the four seasons.

The idea of seasons means different things to different people. For many regions in the tropics, winter is warm and dry and summer brings soaking thunderstorms. At high-latitude locations, winter can bring bitter cold and weeks when the Sun does not rise above the horizon. Why does Earth experience seasons?

What Causes Seasons?

Earth and all the other planets of the solar system orbit (revolve around) the Sun in an *ellipse* rather than a true circle. The **plane of the ecliptic** is the flat plane that the orbital paths of the planets in the solar system trace. Because its orbital path is elliptical, Earth is closer to the Sun in January (at a point called the *perihelion*) than it is in July (at a point called the *aphelion*) by about 5 million km (3 million mi) **(Figure 2.2)**. The average distance between Earth and the Sun is called an *astronomical unit*, or *AU* (1 AU = 149.6 million km or 92.96 million mi). The changing distance between Earth and the Sun does not cause the seasons, however. If it did, it would be warmest in the Northern Hemisphere when Earth is closest to the Sun in January.

| What causes seasons?* | The seasons are caused by the tilt of Earth's axis. Four components of Earth's movement and position are necessary to |

understand how its tilt causes seasons:

1. *Earth's revolution and the plane of the ecliptic*: Earth's revolution around the Sun follows the flat plane of the ecliptic. Earth does not stray above or below this plane. Each revolu-

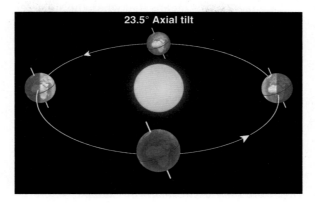

FIGURE 2.3 **Axial tilt.** *Earth's axis is tilted 23.5 degrees away from vertical in relation to the plane of the ecliptic.*

23.5° Axial tilt

tion takes 365 days, 5 hours, 48 minutes, and 46 seconds (or 365.25 days) to complete.

2. *Axial tilt*: Earth's *axis* is tilted 23.5 degrees in relation to the flat plane of the ecliptic **(Figure 2.3)**. If the axis were pointed straight "up," perpendicular to the plane of the ecliptic, the angle of its tilt would be zero.

3. *Parallel axis*: The North Pole points to *Polaris* (the North Star). As Earth orbits the Sun, the position of Polaris does not seem to move, just as the position of the Sun, Moon, or a distant mountain appears fixed as you drive in a car. Earth's axis is always parallel to itself in all locations along its orbital path (see Figure 2.3).

4. *Subsolar point*: Because Earth's surface is curved, the Sun's rays are exactly perpendicular (directly overhead) to Earth's horizontal surface at only one point at or near noon. This point is called the **subsolar point**.

FIGURE 2.2 **Aphelion and perihelion.** *Earth's orbit around the Sun follows an ellipse rather than a circle. Because Earth is closest to the Sun (at the perihelion) about January 3, sunlight at that time is about 7% stronger than when Earth is farthest from the Sun on July 4 (at the aphelion).*

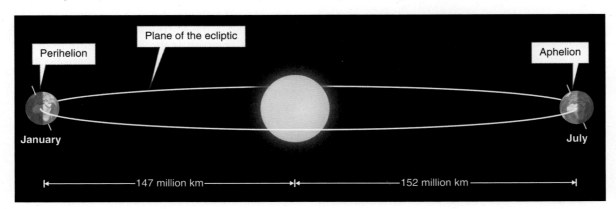

Perihelion
Plane of the ecliptic
Aphelion
January
July
|←——147 million km——→|←——152 million km——→|

plane of the ecliptic
The flat plane traced by the orbital paths of the planets in the solar system.

subsolar point
The single point at which the Sun's rays are perpendicular to Earth's surface at or near noon; restricted to between 23.5° north and south latitude.

Tropic of Cancer
The 23.5° north parallel; the maximum latitude of the subsolar point in the Northern Hemisphere.

Tropic of Capricorn
The 23.5° south parallel; the maximum latitude of the subsolar point in the Southern Hemisphere.

circle of illumination
The line separating night from day, where sunrise and sunset are occurring.

solar altitude
The altitude of the Sun above the horizon in degrees.

December solstice
A seasonal marker that occurs when the subsolar point is at 23.5° south, on about December 21.

March equinox
A seasonal marker that occurs when the subsolar point is over the equator about March 20.

As Earth rotates, the subsolar point moves along a constant line of latitude. As we saw in Section GT.3, Earth rotates 1,670 km/h (1,037 mph) at the equator. This means that when the subsolar point is at the equator, it is moving 1,670 km/h. In other words, if you wanted to keep up with the subsolar point, keeping the Sun straight overhead, you would have to travel 1,670 km/h westward along the equator.

The subsolar point moves gradually north and south over the year as a result of the tilt of Earth's axis. It never moves farther north than 23.5° north latitude (a parallel called the **Tropic of Cancer**) or farther south than 23.5° south latitude (a parallel called the **Tropic of Capricorn**). The latitude of the subsolar point is called the *solar declination*. For example, when the subsolar point is at the equator, the solar declination is 0 degrees. When the subsolar point is at 10° north latitude, the solar declination is 10 degrees north, and so on. As **Figure 2.4** shows, the latitude of the subsolar point is always 90 degrees away from the **circle of illumination**, the line separating night from day, where sunrise and sunset are occurring.

The subsolar point determines the **solar altitude**, the angle of the Sun above the horizon in degrees. Sunlight on the horizon is at zero degrees, and sunlight that is straight overhead is at 90 degrees. In Figure 2.4, only for person C is the solar altitude 90 degrees.

The solar altitude determines the intensity of the noontime Sun. Only in the tropics can the solar altitude be 90 degrees. The noontime solar altitude

FIGURE 2.4 **The subsolar point.** *The Sun's rays are parallel to one another when they reach Earth. Because Earth is spherical, they are exactly perpendicular to Earth's horizontal surface at only one point. Only person C, who is standing on the equator at noon, is standing on the subsolar point.*

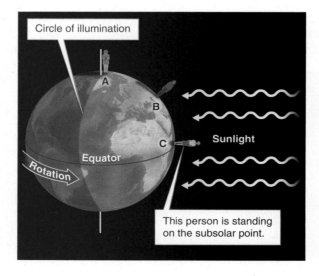

FIGURE 2.5 **Latitude and sunlight intensity.** *Sunlight enters the atmosphere perpendicular to Earth's surface only in the tropics. At higher latitudes, where the solar altitude is lower, the same amount of solar energy is distributed across a greater surface area, creating more diffuse sunlight. At higher latitudes sunlight also passes through a greater distance of atmosphere compared to lower latitudes, further reducing the intensity of sunlight.*

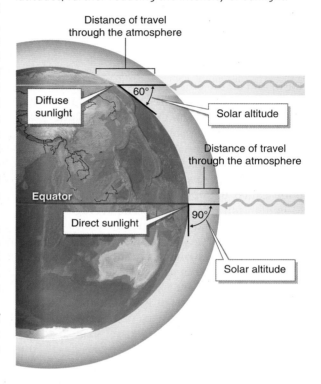

decreases (the Sun gets closer to the horizon) as one travels to higher latitudes, causing sunlight to become more diffuse (spread out) **(Figure 2.5)**.

Migration of the Subsolar Point

The subsolar point moves from the Tropic of Cancer to the Tropic of Capricorn, then back again, over a 12-month period. The Tropic of Cancer is the highest latitude at which the subsolar point will be found in the Northern Hemisphere, and the Tropic of Capricorn is the highest latitude of the subsolar point in the Southern Hemisphere. Because the latitude of the subsolar point changes, from our perspective on the ground, the Sun's path across the sky changes with the time of year **(Figure 2.6)**.

The **December solstice** occurs about December 21 each year when the subsolar point arrives at the Tropic of Capricorn. This seasonal event or marker is also called the *winter solstice* in the Northern Hemisphere. Following this, the subsolar point migrates northward. The **March equinox** (also called

FIGURE 2.6 **Topanga sunsets.** *These photos, all looking west, show the changing location of the setting Sun from Topanga Canyon in Southern California (at 34° north latitude), for December 21, March 21, and June 21.* (© David Lynch)

the *spring equinox* or *vernal equinox* in the Northern Hemisphere) occurs when the subsolar point crosses the equator about March 20. About June 21, the subsolar point arrives at the Tropic of Cancer, marking the **June solstice** (or *summer solstice* in the Northern Hemisphere). From there the subsolar point migrates back south. Three months later,

about September 22, it crosses the equator again, marking the **September equinox** (or *fall equinox* in the Northern Hemisphere). These seasonal markers are illustrated in **Figure 2.7**.

The importance of the tilt of Earth's axis to seasons is revealed when we imagine what would happen if that tilt were changed significantly

FIGURE 2.7 **Seasonal markers.** *Because Earth's axial tilt is 23.5 degrees from vertical, the subsolar point (shown as a dot and not visible at point 3 in the diagram) migrates between the Tropic of Cancer and the Tropic of Capricorn, across 47 degrees of latitude, in a six-month period.*

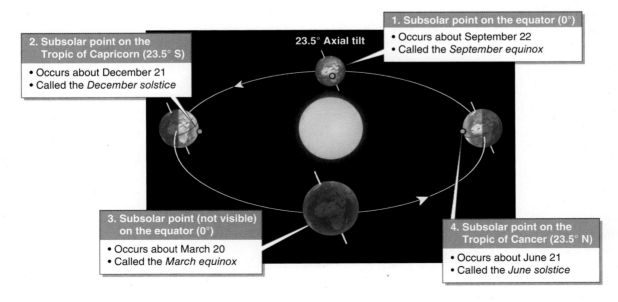

2. Subsolar point on the Tropic of Capricorn (23.5° S)
• Occurs about December 21
• Called the *December solstice*

23.5° Axial tilt

1. Subsolar point on the equator (0°)
• Occurs about September 22
• Called the *September equinox*

3. Subsolar point (not visible) on the equator (0°)
• Occurs about March 20
• Called the *March equinox*

4. Subsolar point on the Tropic of Cancer (23.5° N)
• Occurs about June 21
• Called the *June solstice*

June solstice
A seasonal marker that occurs when the subsolar point is 23.5° north latitude, about June 21.

September equinox
A seasonal marker that occurs when the subsolar point is over the equator about September 22.

FIGURE 2.8 **GEO-GRAPHIC** Tilt and seasonality.

No tilt

If Earth's axis had no tilt, the subsolar point (shown as a dot and not visible on the nearest globe) would always be on the equator, no matter what month it was. There would always be 12 hours of daylight and 12 hours of darkness for all locations.

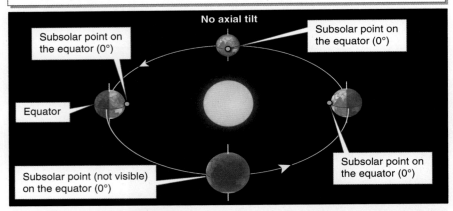

No axial tilt

Subsolar point on the equator (0°)
Subsolar point on the equator (0°)
Equator
Subsolar point (not visible) on the equator (0°)
Subsolar point on the equator (0°)

90-Degree tilt

If Earth's axis were tilted 90 degrees, the subsolar point (shown as a dot and not visible on the nearest globe) would migrate from the South Pole to the North Pole, then back to the South Pole, within the period of a year. This would produce extreme seasonal change.

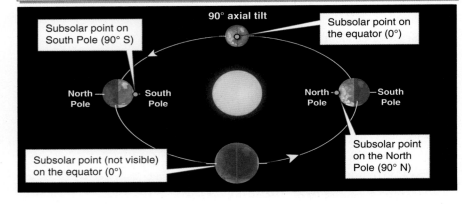

90° axial tilt

Subsolar point on South Pole (90° S)
Subsolar point on the equator (0°)
North Pole — South Pole
North Pole — South Pole
Subsolar point (not visible) on the equator (0°)
Subsolar point on the North Pole (90° N)

(Figure 2.8). If Earth's axis had no tilt, the subsolar point would always be on the equator, and there would be no seasonal change. If the tilt of Earth's axis were 90 degrees, the subsolar point would shift from the South Pole to the North Pole and back within a year, and seasonal changes would be much more extreme than they are.

How Does Earth's Tilt Affect Day Length?

Just as Earth's axial tilt causes the subsolar point to move across latitudes, it also causes the number of daylight hours to change. To illustrate, we will first look at what happens to day length on the equinoxes.

Day Length on an Equinox

On an equinox, all locations on Earth (except the poles) receive 12 hours of daylight and 12 hours of darkness. At these times, all locations on Earth rotate through equal day and night sides of the planet, as shown in **Figure 2.9**.

Day Length on the December Solstice

The situation is quite different on the December solstice, when the North Pole is pointed away from the Sun and the subsolar point is directly over the Tropic of Capricorn, at 23.5° south latitude. The equator always receives 12 hours of day and night, but the rest of the planet's day length varies, and the way it varies depends on the hemisphere.

Day length decreases northward on the December solstice. At the **Arctic Circle** (at 66.5° north latitude) and northward, there are 24 hours of darkness. Similarly, at the **Antarctic Circle** (at 66.5° south latitude) and southward, there are 24 hours of daylight **(Figure 2.10)**.

FIGURE 2.9 **Equinox day length.** *On the equinoxes, the subsolar point is at the equator, so the circle of illumination (which, as we have seen, is always 90° from the latitude of the subsolar point) passes through the poles. This position makes the length of the daylight side of the planet equal to the length of the night side of the planet. Therefore, any point on Earth, except the poles, will take 12 hours to rotate through the daylight side and 12 hours to rotate through the night side. At the poles, the half-disk of the Sun will trace the line of the horizon where the horizon is flat, such as over the North Pole's sea ice.*

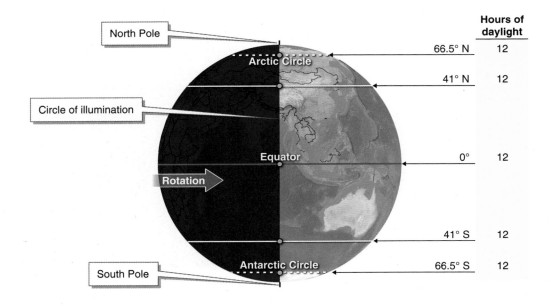

	Hours of daylight
North Pole	
Arctic Circle 66.5° N	12
41° N	12
Circle of illumination	
Equator 0°	12
Rotation	
41° S	12
Antarctic Circle 66.5° S	12
South Pole	

FIGURE 2.10 **December solstice day length.** *Imagine you are standing at 66.5° south, on the Antarctic Circle. At that location, you will never cross the circle of illumination as Earth rotates, and the Sun will not set at your location. Now imagine standing at 41° south latitude. Here you will rotate into the night side of the planet, but you will be on the daylight side much longer than you are on the night side. Day length is 15 hours and night length is 9 hours. On the equator, day and night are equal. At 41° north latitude, day length becomes 9 hours and night length is 15 hours. At 66.5° north latitude, on the Arctic Circle, you will receive no direct sunlight because that location does not cross the circle of illumination into the lighted side of the globe as Earth rotates. Locations just north of the Arctic Circle experience twilight for several hours as the Sun approaches, but it does not rise above the horizon.*

Arctic Circle
The 66.5° north parallel.

Antarctic Circle
The 66.5° south parallel.

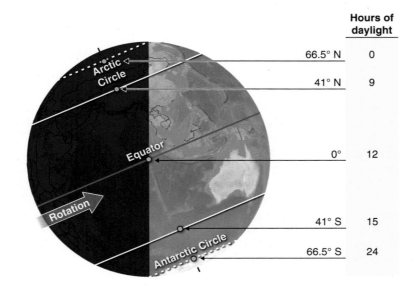

	Hours of daylight
66.5° N	0
41° N	9
0°	12
41° S	15
66.5° S	24

Day Length on the June Solstice

On the June solstice, day length increases north-ward. On June 21 at the Arctic Circle and northward, the Sun never sets. That is why the high Arctic in summer is often called "land of the midnight Sun" **(Figure 2.11)**.

If you were to stand on the equator for one year, you would see the solar altitude at noon range between 66.5° north (in June) and 66.5° south (in December). In other words, in the tropics, the noon Sun is always high in the sky, and seasonality is negligible. On the other hand, if

FIGURE 2.11 **June solstice day length.** *On the June solstice, the situation is reversed relative to the December solstice. As you travel north, daylight increases until you reach the Arctic Circle at 66.5° north. Locations within the Arctic Circle do not cross the circle of illumination into the night side of the globe, and as a result, day length is 24 hours. Traveling southward, day length decreases. Anywhere within the Antarctic Circle, 66.5° south, the night is 24 hours long.*

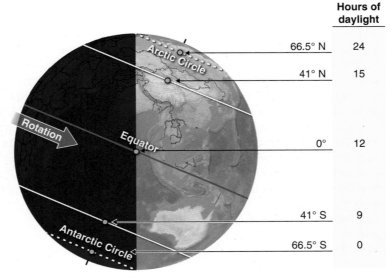

	Hours of daylight
66.5° N	24
41° N	15
0°	12
41° S	9
66.5° S	0

you were to stand on the North Pole for one year, you would see the noon solar altitude range from 23.5 degrees to the south (in June) to 0 degrees on the horizon (on the September equinox). After the September equinox, the Sun would be below the horizon for six months (until the March equinox). In short, the poles receive six months of continuous darkness, followed by six months of continuous daylight, as if there were one six-month-long day, followed by one six-month-long night.

Together, the changing solar altitude and the changing length of daylight hours produce Earth's seasonality.

2.2 Temperature and Heat

◎ Understand the difference between temperature and heat.

The human body's perception of air temperature and the actual measured air temperature are not the same. A cold day feels colder when it is windy, creating the *wind chill temperature*. A hot day feels hotter when it is humid, creating the **heat-index temperature** (see Appendix 5). It is not colder or hotter in either of these situations—it only feels so to people.

What Is Temperature?

So what exactly is temperature, and how do we measure it objectively? **Temperature** is defined as the average speed of molecular movement (or level of excitation) within a substance or object, and it is measured with a *thermometer*. Molecular movement is a form of kinetic energy. (Matter is made of molecules and atoms, but the term *molecules* will be used in this discussion as a generalization.)

Molecules move quickly in objects with high temperatures and relatively slowly in objects with low temperatures. If we were to somehow lower the temperature of an object to the point at which the molecules no longer moved, we would reach a point of 0 *kelvins*, or *absolute zero*. The Kelvin scale was developed by the British scientist Lord Kelvin (1824–1907), and is abbreviated K. Scientists sometimes prefer the Kelvin scale because it has no negative numbers, which facilitates calculations. The public uses the *Fahrenheit* and *Celsius* scales **(Figure 2.12)**.

In the early 1700s, the German scientist Daniel Gabriel Fahrenheit developed the Fahrenheit scale (abbreviated F). A few years afterward, the

heat-index temperature
The temperature perceived by people as a result of high atmospheric humidity coupled with high air temperatures.

temperature
The average kinetic movement of atoms and molecules of a substance.

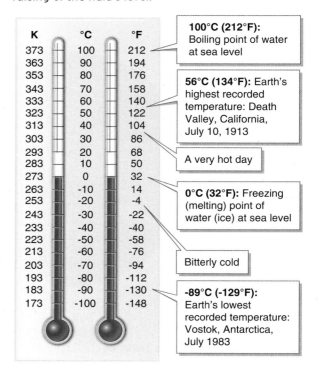

FIGURE 2.12 **The Kelvin, Celsius, and Fahrenheit scales.** *The thermometer at the right reads "0 degrees Celsius" or "32 degrees Fahrenheit." That same temperature is "273 kelvins," as shown on the thermometer at the left. A fluid (mercury or red-colored alcohol) in the glass tube of a thermometer expands and contracts as its temperature changes, resulting in a lowering or raising of the fluid's level.*

K	°C	°F
373	100	212
363	90	194
353	80	176
343	70	158
333	60	140
323	50	122
313	40	104
303	30	86
293	20	68
283	10	50
273	0	32
263	-10	14
253	-20	-4
243	-30	-22
233	-40	-40
223	-50	-58
213	-60	-76
203	-70	-94
193	-80	-112
183	-90	-130
173	-100	-148

100°C (212°F): Boiling point of water at sea level

56°C (134°F): Earth's highest recorded temperature: Death Valley, California, July 10, 1913

A very hot day

0°C (32°F): Freezing (melting) point of water (ice) at sea level

Bitterly cold

-89°C (-129°F): Earth's lowest recorded temperature: Vostok, Antarctica, July 1983

Swedish astronomer Anders Celsius introduced the Celsius scale (abbreviated C). Water freezes at 0°C (32°F) and boils at 100°C (212°F). Most countries use the Celsius scale, which is part of the metric system of weights and measures (see Section GT.1). The public in the United States is generally most familiar with the U.S. customary system, which uses the Fahrenheit scale. Students in the United States will therefore find it helpful to be able to convert the temperature scales back and forth. Each Celsius degree is 1.8 times larger than a Fahrenheit degree. A formula for converting °C to °F is

$$°F = (1.8 \times °C) + 32$$

A formula for converting °F to °C is

$$°C = (°F - 32)/1.8$$

The **Crunch the Numbers** feature provides conversion practice.

FIGURE 2.13 **Heat transfer.** *A cup of hot coffee immersed in ice water quickly loses its energy out the sides of the cup to the cooler water through conduction. This heat transfer also occurs when the hot cup is in the air, but less quickly.*

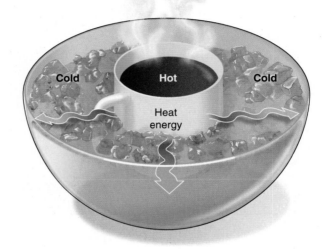

What Is Heat?

Temperature and heat are not the same. Temperature, as we have seen, is the average speed of molecular movement in a substance. **Heat** is the internal energy transferred between materials or systems due to their temperature differences. Molecules are too small to see, but the kinetic energy of their movement can be felt as heat. With a temperature increase, objects feel hotter because heat flows from objects of high temperature to objects of low temperature.

To illustrate this, let's imagine two identical ceramic mugs half full of hot coffee of the same temperature. Because each has the same temperature and the same amount of coffee, each has the same amount of internal energy.

Now imagine pouring all the coffee from one mug into the other so that one mug is full and the other is empty. The temperature of the full mug of coffee did not change, but its amount of internal energy doubled because it now has twice as much mass (or coffee).

Now imagine carefully setting the mug of hot coffee in a bowl of ice water, making sure no water spills into the coffee. Heat will flow out directly from the surface of the coffee into the surrounding air. The heat will *also* move out of the cup of coffee into the surrounding water and warm that water, and the coffee's temperature will decrease **(Figure 2.13)**.

How Heat Moves

Heat is transferred through space and Earth's physical systems in three ways: by conduction, convection, and radiation.

Conduction is the process by which energy is transferred through a substance or between objects in direct contact. When the coffee was poured into the ceramic mug, the temperature of the mug increased as the coffee's heat was transferred to the molecules in the mug. **In conduction, heat always flows from objects of higher temperature to objects of lower temperature.** Heat transfers faster when the temperature difference is greater and when the material through which it is traveling is a good *conductor* of heat **(Table 2.1)**. Metals are good

TABLE 2.1	AT A GLANCE: **Heat Conductivities of Familiar Materials**
MATERIAL	**HEAT CONDUCTIVITY***
Copper	0.99
Glass	0.0025
Dry sand	0.0013
Water at 20°C	0.0014
Wool felt	0.0001
Air at 0°C	0.000057

*Heat conductivity is defined as the quantity of heat in calories (c) that would flow through a square centimeter of the above materials in 1 second, given a temperature gradient of 1°C per centimeter.

heat
The internal energy transferred between materials or systems due to their temperature differences.

conduction
The process by which energy is transferred through a substance or between objects in direct contact.

convection
The transfer of heat through movement of mass within a fluid (liquid or gas).

radiation
The process by which wave energy travels through the vacuum of space or through a physical medium such as air or water.

FIGURE 2.14 **Hot air rising.** *This image shows the development of a rising parcel of warm air (called a* thermal*) over the period of about 30 minutes. The rising air transfers heat from Earth's surface to high levels in the troposphere through convection.*

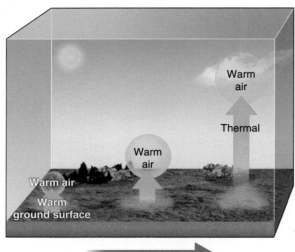

30 minutes

heat conductors, but still air is not. Air is an *insulator* (any material that inhibits energy from transferring through it). That is why warm jackets and the fur of animals in cold climates are thickly padded with air.

Convection is the transfer of heat through movement of mass within a fluid (a gas or liquid). Gases and liquids move and flow easily in response to differences in heating. For example, when the ground is warmed by sunlight, it heats the air above it. This heated warm air expands and becomes less dense, then rises, as shown in **Figure 2.14**.

Radiation is the process by which wave energy travels through the vacuum of space or through a physical medium such as air or water. Sunlight is an example of radiation. Radiation and electromagnetic energy are discussed in more detail in Section 2.4.

2.3 Surface Temperature Patterns

◎ **Describe Earth's surface temperature patterns and explain what causes them.**

What controls the overall air temperature regime of any given location on Earth? Death Valley, California, is always hot in summer; in fact, it holds the record for the highest air temperature ever officially recorded on Earth: 56°C (134°F) on July 10, 1913, in the shade! Earth's lowest official air temperature, −89°C (−129°F), was recorded in Vostok Station, Antarctica, at a scientific research base in July 1983. Why is Death Valley so hot? Why is Antarctica so cold?

Recording air temperatures gives us critical data for answering these questions as well as for monitoring climate change. Temperature data are compiled by the Global Historical Climatology Network (GHCN) and are recorded daily at over 75,000 meteorological stations in 180 countries and territories **(Figure 2.15)**. For each station, an average daily temperature is calculated from maximum and minimum daily temperature measurements. Average monthly and average annual temperatures are then derived from these calculations.

The difference between the average maximum and average minimum temperatures over a year at a location is its *annual temperature range*, or seasonality. Earth's maximum temperature range (the difference between the highest temperature in Death Valley and the lowest temperature in Antarctica) is therefore 145°C (265°F). In this section we use the average annual temperature and the annual temperature range to explore geographic patterns of temperature.

FIGURE 2.15 **Map of global temperature stations.** *This world map shows the locations of official GHCN meteorological stations that record air temperatures. Station density decreases in remote areas and in less economically developed countries. Ships and aircraft supplement the temperature data for sparsely covered regions. (Global Historical Climatology Network, NOAA/NESDIS/NCDC)*

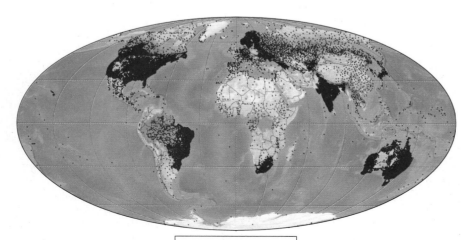

• Global temperature stations

Average Annual Temperature Patterns

The average annual temperature at any given location is controlled mainly by elevation and latitude. **The average annual temperature is lower at higher elevations and higher latitudes.**

Elevation: Colder in the Mountains

Does it snow in Hawai'i?

The troposphere is heated mostly by Earth's surface. In the troposphere, temperature decreases with altitude. In Section 1.3, we learned that there is an average environmental lapse rate of 6.5°C per 1,000 m (or 3.6°F per 1,000 ft). Mountains that protrude high into the troposphere are always cooler than surrounding lowland regions. High mountains are often snowcapped in summer, even in tropical locations, such as Hawai'i, where adjacent areas of low elevation are warm. **Figure 2.16** illustrates this point with a satellite thermal image.

Latitude: Colder near the Poles

Because Earth is spherical, temperature generally decreases away from the equator as sunlight becomes more diffuse (see Figure 2.5). Sunlight is increasingly diffuse outside the tropics, resulting in lower surface temperatures at higher latitudes **(Figure 2.17)**.

Patterns of Seasonality

Imagine you live in a city where the average January temperature is −47°C (−53°F). It is so cold that you must leave your car running all day and all night during the winter months to avoid an engine seized up through freezing. On a cold day, boiling water thrown into the air comes down as ice crystals, and if your house were not heated, there

FIGURE 2.16 **Land surface temperature and elevation.** *This satellite thermal infrared image shows average January land surface temperatures for South Asia during the period 2001-2010. Reds and oranges, which depict warm temperatures, are found mainly at low elevations, and blues, which show cold temperatures, are found mainly in mountainous regions.* (NASA)

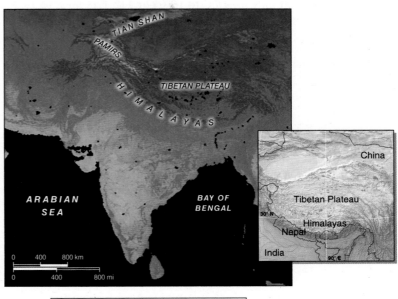

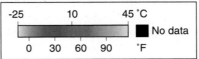

FIGURE 2.17 **Latitude-temperature relationship.** *(A) For every 145 km traveled poleward, the average surface temperature (averaged here across both hemispheres) decreases 1°C (1°F per 50 mi) (red dashed line) between 20 and 80 degrees latitude. The effects of elevation have been removed from this graph. The gray areas show the potential variation around the observed average temperature (black line). (B) As a general rule, average annual temperatures are highest near the equator and decrease toward higher latitudes. Antarctica is colder than the Arctic because of ocean currents and the high elevation of the Antarctic ice sheet. Notice too that in mountainous areas at low latitudes, the effect of elevation prevails, lowering temperatures even on the equator. In some areas, such as the Sahara in northern Africa, temperatures increase away from the equator because the persistently cloudless skies at slightly higher latitudes result in intense sunlight.*

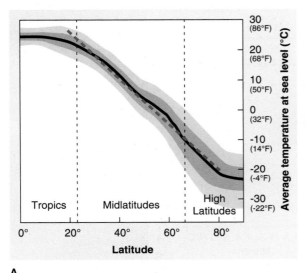

A

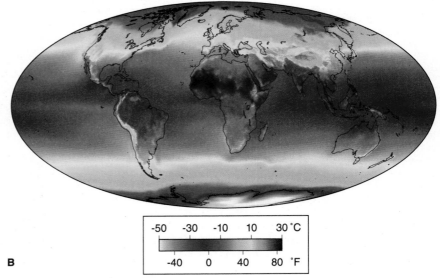

B

continental effect
The increase in seasonality with distance from the oceans.

would be no liquid water in it. Food containing water would be frozen solid. Come summer, the average temperature at the same location is roughly 15°C (59°F), and past heat waves have reached the upper thirties (Celsius; nineties Fahrenheit). Such is life for the 1,400 citizens of Verkhoyansk, Russia. The city has an average annual temperature range of 62°C (−47°C to 15°C) or 112°F (−53°F to 59°F).

Figure 2.18 gives a quick visual summary of the temperature ranges of two contrasting places, Verkhoyansk (67° north latitude), and Singapore (1° north latitude). The difference in seasonality between Verkhoyansk and Singapore can be explained by two factors: latitude and proximity to the oceans.

As a general rule, high latitudes have a greater annual temperature range than low latitudes. In addition, *continental* (inland) locations have a greater annual temperature range than *maritime* (ocean-influenced) locations. This increase in seasonality with distance from the oceans is called the **continental effect**.

As a general pattern, locations near the coast have *maritime climates*, with a relatively low annual

temperature range. In contrast, locations far inland have *continental climates*, with a relatively high annual temperature range. The relationship among latitude, continentality, and annual temperature range is illustrated in **Figure 2.19**.

What Causes the Continental Effect?

Why do inland regions have greater seasonality than coastal regions? There are four main factors that cause the continental effect: (1) the specific heat of water, (2) the evaporation of water, (3) the mixing of water, and (4) the transparency of water.

You may have noticed at the beach that the sand becomes warm in the afternoon sunlight, but the water does not—it is still cool and refreshing. If you were to go to that same beach early in the morning before sunrise, you might find that the sand is cooler than the water. The water hardly changes temperature over a 24-hour period, but the sand varies from warm during the day to cool at night. Land is quick to heat up and quick to cool down, but seawater's temperature changes much less. In addition, compared with the seasonal swings of temperature on land, the temperature of water changes relatively

FIGURE 2.18 **Seasonality in Verkhoyansk and Singapore.** *(A) Verkhoyansk, Russia, has among the highest annual temperature ranges of any city on the planet, as this climate diagram shows. This person (inset) in Verkhoyansk has thrown boiling water into −47°C (−53°F) air. The water has crystallized into ice before reaching the ground. (B) In contrast to Verkhoyansk, Singapore's average monthly temperatures vary by only a few degrees. Every month brings warm tropical temperatures.* (Bryan and Cherry Alexander/Science Source)

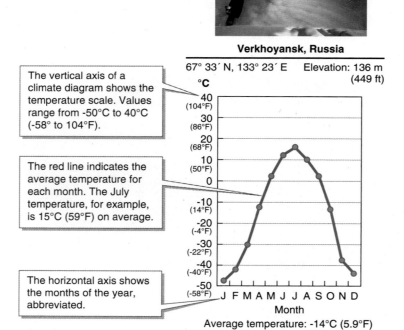

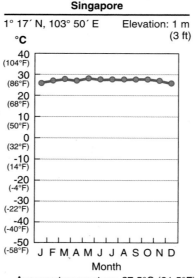

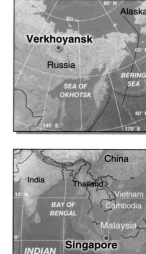

FIGURE 2.19 GEO-GRAPHIC Latitude and continentality influence seasonality. *This map shows average January ground surface temperatures during the period 2001–2010. The data were collected by NASA's satellite Terra.*

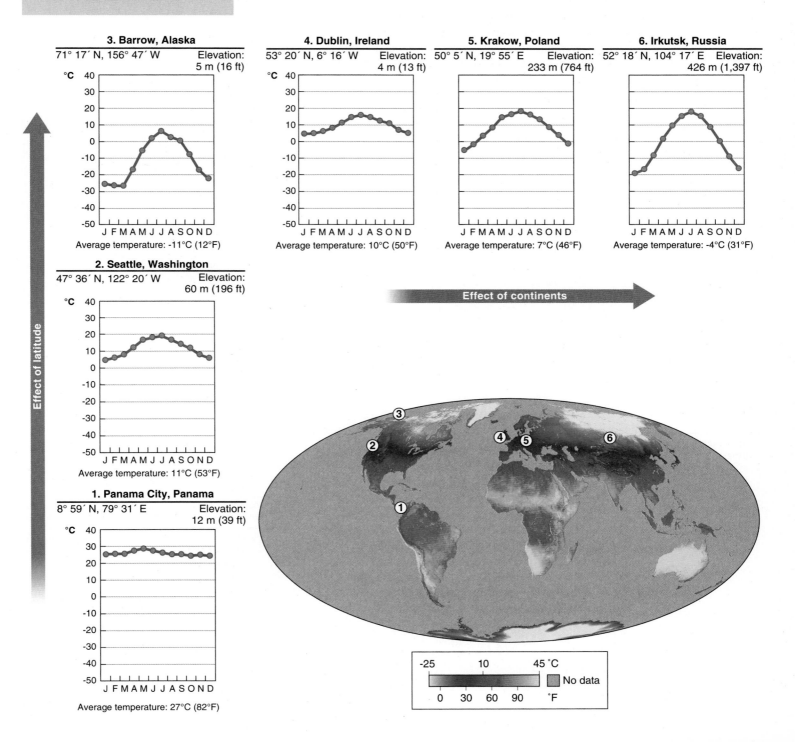

Effect of latitude

The annual temperature range increases as latitude increases. These three cities are all at sea level on the coast, but at different latitudes. Barrow has a much greater annual temperature range than Seattle, and Panama City has almost no annual temperature range. Note also that the average maximum temperature for all months decreases northward.

Continental effect

The annual temperature range increases inland due to the continental effect. These three cities are all at about the same latitude and elevation, but Dublin is coastal and Irkutsk is far inland. Krakow is inland, but not so far from the sea as Irkutsk. Notice that the maximum summer temperatures are similar at all three locations, but winter temperatures are much lower for inland regions.

3. Barrow, Alaska
71° 17′ N, 156° 47′ W   Elevation: 5 m (16 ft)
Average temperature: -11°C (12°F)

2. Seattle, Washington
47° 36′ N, 122° 20′ W   Elevation: 60 m (196 ft)
Average temperature: 11°C (53°F)

1. Panama City, Panama
8° 59′ N, 79° 31′ E   Elevation: 12 m (39 ft)
Average temperature: 27°C (82°F)

4. Dublin, Ireland
53° 20′ N, 6° 16′ W   Elevation: 4 m (13 ft)
Average temperature: 10°C (50°F)

5. Krakow, Poland
50° 5′ N, 19° 55′ E   Elevation: 233 m (764 ft)
Average temperature: 7°C (46°F)

6. Irkutsk, Russia
52° 18′ N, 104° 17′ E   Elevation: 426 m (1,397 ft)
Average temperature: -4°C (31°F)

Effect of latitude

Effect of continents

specific heat
The heat required to raise the temperature of any object or material by a given amount.

little between summer and winter. **Figure 2.20** shows the differences in daytime heating between land and water using satellite thermal imagery.

As a general pattern, continents become warmer in summer than oceans at the same latitude. In winter, continents become colder than oceans. **Figure 2.21** illustrates this phenomenon using *isotherms*, lines of equal temperature.

The cause of these temperature differences between land and water is the difference in their heat capacities. *Heat capacity* is the amount of heat that must be absorbed to change the temperature of an object. **Specific heat**, which is the heat required to raise the temperature of any object or material by a given amount, is a measure of heat capacity. Water's specific heat is higher than those of most materials that make up landmasses, and the continental effect results mainly from this difference.

Different materials have different specific heat values, as shown in **Table 2.2** on the next page. For example, it takes 1 calorie of energy to raise the temperature of 1 g of water 1°C. Therefore, water has a specific heat of 1. However, it takes only about one-fifth of a calorie to raise 1 g of dry sand 1°C. Dry sand, therefore, has a specific heat of approximately 0.2, one-fifth that of water. If we added 1 calorie to 1 g of sand, its temperature would increase by about 5°C. In other words, water can absorb five times more energy than dry sand. Thus, when the same amount of heat is applied, land heats up more than water.

Evaporation, water transparency, and water mixing are also important in moderating the temperature of water. Evaporation cools water and prevents it from becoming warmer than it would otherwise become. Because land has relatively little water to evaporate, land heats up more in sunlight than oceans do.

FIGURE **2.20** **Land and water heating.**
Land and surface water temperatures stand in sharp contrast in this thermal infrared image, made during a heat wave in the western United States on May 2, 2004. The land has heated up quickly, but the water has not. Notice that the inland mountains in California and in eastern Nevada (far right) have remained cooler because they are at higher elevations. (NASA)

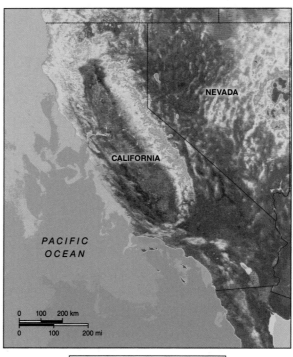

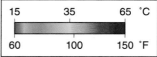

FIGURE **2.21** **Seasonal temperature patterns.** *(A) In summer, large landmasses heat up, causing isotherms to bend toward the poles. Locations 1 and 3, which are over water, are between 10°C and 15°C (50°F and 59°F). At the same latitude over land (location 2), the temperature is up to 10°C warmer. (B) In winter, isotherms bend toward the equator because landmasses are relatively cold. Location 2 (over land) is 10°C to 15°C colder than locations 1 and 3 (over water) at the same latitude.*

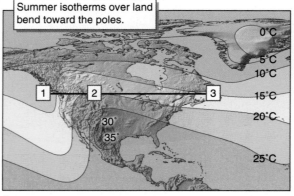

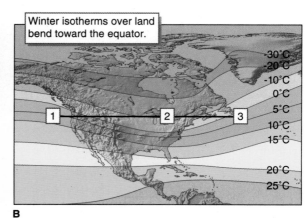

A

B

TABLE 2.2	AT A GLANCE: Specific Heat Properties of Different Materials	
SUBSTANCE	**SPECIFIC HEAT (Cal/g × °C)**	
Pure water	1	
Wet mud	0.6	
Dry sandy clay	0.33	
Dry quartz sand	0.19	

Transparency is also important. Because water is transparent, sunlight can pass through several hundred meters of water and warm it. Land is opaque, and sunlight does not penetrate it. Similarly, convection mixes the water warmed by sunlight with cooler water at greater depths. Land is rigid and cannot mix, so the land surface heats up faster and to a higher temperature.

Ocean Currents and Seasonality

Warm ocean currents originating in the tropics carry immense amounts of heat toward the poles. When warm ocean currents reach high latitudes, some of their heat is transferred to the atmosphere. A good example of such an *ocean-atmosphere heat transfer* in the Northern Hemisphere is the Gulf Stream, which flows from the tip of Florida along the coast of eastern North America and into the North Atlantic Ocean. The warm water transfers its heat to the atmosphere in the North Atlantic, warming regions downwind.

The Gulf Stream transports more water than all the rivers of the world combined. Some 30 million m³ (1 billion ft³) of water pass by Florida each second. This amount increases to some 150 million m³ (5.3 billion ft³) per second by the time the current reaches Nova Scotia, Canada. As a comparison, the Amazon River, the largest river in the world, has an average flow of about 200,000 m³ (7.1 million ft³) per second.

Warm ocean currents raise the average annual temperature and reduce the annual temperature range. Cold currents influence temperatures less. The Gulf Stream's effect on annual temperature ranges can be seen when coastal stations at the same latitude are graphed and compared **(Figure 2.22)**.

Because it transports so much heat, the Gulf Stream has many effects on physical geography, from hurricane formation to the behavior of the global climate system. We will examine the important effects of ocean currents and sea surface temperatures on storms in North America in Section 5.1.

Prevailing Wind and Seasonality

New York, New York, and Crescent City, California, are both coastal cities located at 40° north latitude. We might expect, therefore, that both would have maritime climates, but they do not. Although the average annual temperature for both cities is about 12°C (53°F), these two cities have very different

FIGURE 2.22 **Ocean currents influence average annual temperatures.** *The Gulf Stream warms northern Europe as it delivers its tropical heat to the North Atlantic Ocean and then to the atmosphere. The ocean current off the coast of Alaska is much colder than the Gulf Stream. Tromsø, Norway, and Barrow, Alaska, are at the same latitude (roughly 71° north latitude) and are both coastal towns at sea level. Tromsø's winters are less severe than Barrow's because of the heat delivered to the atmosphere by the Gulf Stream. This satellite thermal infrared image was made December 13, 2013. Light gray shows areas with no data. (Data from NASA)*

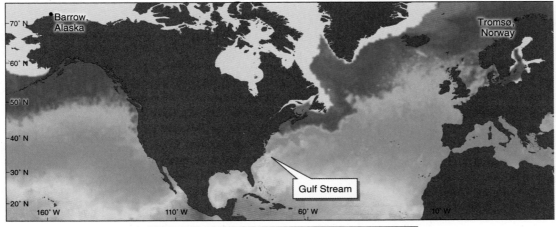
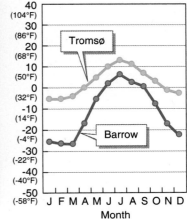
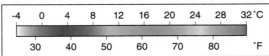

FIGURE 2.23 **Effect of prevailing winds on seasonality.** *New York, New York, is dominated by prevailing winds that originate in the interior of the North American continent. Although New York is coastal, the air masses it receives and, consequently, its annual temperature range are continental. Crescent City, California, in contrast, is dominated by prevailing winds that originate over the Pacific Ocean and, consequently, it has a maritime climate. The background map shows average January temperatures during the period 2001–2010. (NASA)*

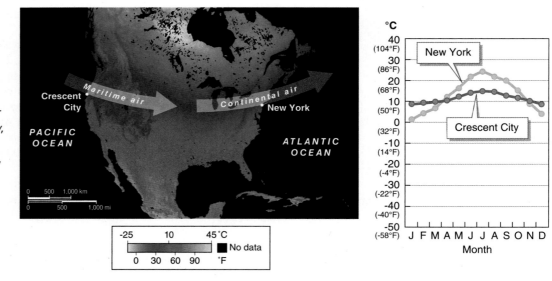

FIGURE 2.24 **Global annual temperature range map.** *When we sum up the factors that control seasonality, the geographic pattern that emerges is controlled by latitude, the continental effect, ocean currents, and prevailing winds.*

The greatest annual temperature ranges in North America occur in northern Canada due to the continental effect and latitude.

At equivalent latitudes, western North America has a lower annual temperature range than eastern North America due to prevailing winds.

Even though it is a high-latitude location, the North Atlantic Ocean has a low annual temperature range because of the warm Gulf Stream.

The greatest annual temperature range in the world occurs in northeastern Eurasia due to the continental effect and latitude.

The tropics have a very low annual temperature range due to the influence of latitude and the ocean.

Overall, the Southern Hemisphere has a lower annual temperature range than the Northern Hemisphere because there is less land.

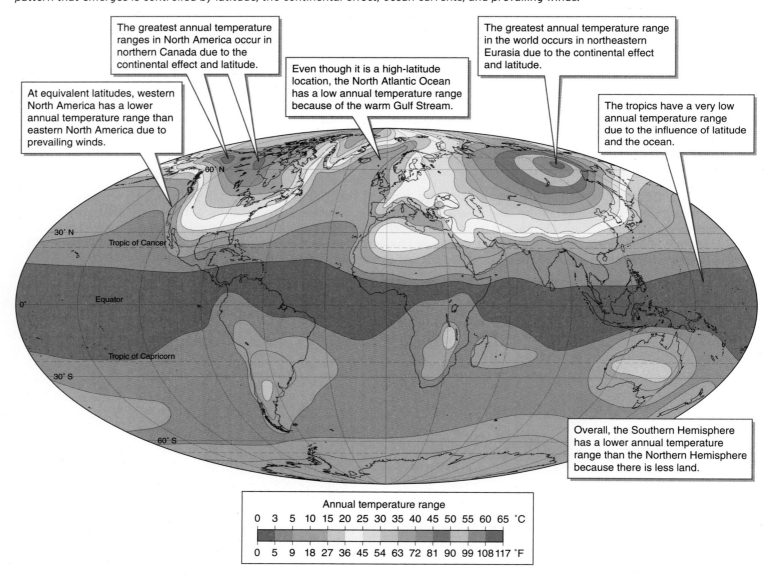

annual temperature ranges. New York, on the east coast, has a continental climate. Crescent City, in California, has a maritime climate. As shown in **Figure 2.23**, the direction of the *prevailing winds* causes this pattern.

Generally, because the prevailing wind direction is from the west, west coasts have maritime climates and east coasts have continental climates. This pattern is strongest at midlatitudes. It is weakened or nonexistent in the Southern Hemisphere (because landmasses there are small), polar regions (because the water is very cold), and in the tropics (because both land and sea are warm).

Many factors combine to control temperatures at any given location on the planet, but some play a larger role than others, depending on the geographic location. **Figure 2.24** shows the global patterns of Earth's annual temperature ranges and summarizes the main factors determining those patterns.

2.4 The Sun's Radiant Energy

◎ Describe solar energy and its different wavelengths.

Warm sunlight on your face is an example of the Sun's radiant energy. **Radiant energy**, or *radiation*, is energy that is propagated in the form of electromagnetic waves, including visible light and heat. All forms of radiation have both electrical and magnetic properties, and for that reason, they are referred to as *electromagnetic energy*. Light is only a small portion of the electromagnetic radiation emitted by the Sun.

Electromagnetic waves travel at *light speed*, 300,000 km (186,000 mi) per second. The Sun is, on average, 149.6 million km (92.96 million mi) away from Earth, so sunlight takes 8.5 minutes to reach Earth. Other objects in the night sky, such as stars and galaxies, are much farther away, and the light they emitted has taken thousands or millions of years (or longer) to reach Earth.

Photons and Wavelengths

All matter emits *photons* (packets of energy) of electromagnetic radiation. You and this book emit photons of electromagnetic radiation, as do light bulbs, computer screens, trees, rocks, and water—everything.

Photons travel in waves, and the distance between the peaks of two waves is the *wavelength*. Longer wavelengths have less energy than shorter wavelengths. The **electromagnetic spectrum (EMS)** is the full range of wavelengths of radiant energy, as shown in **Figure 2.25**. The Sun emits radiation in wavelengths across most of the EMS.

radiant energy
(or *radiation*)
Energy propagated in the form of electromagnetic waves, including visible light and heat.

electromagnetic spectrum (EMS)
The full range of wavelengths of radiant energy.

FIGURE 2.25   **The electromagnetic spectrum.** *Electromagnetic radiation travels in waves. Shorter wavelengths, shown on the left, include cosmic rays, gamma rays, X-rays, and ultraviolet rays. (Cosmic rays originate in distant exploded stars in space rather than the Sun.) Only visible wavelengths can be seen with our eyes. In the visible portion of the spectrum (shown in the inset), violet has the shortest wavelengths, at 0.4 μm, and red has the longest wavelengths, at 0.7 μm. Longer-than-visible wavelengths, shown on the right, include infrared radiation, microwaves, and TV and radio waves.*

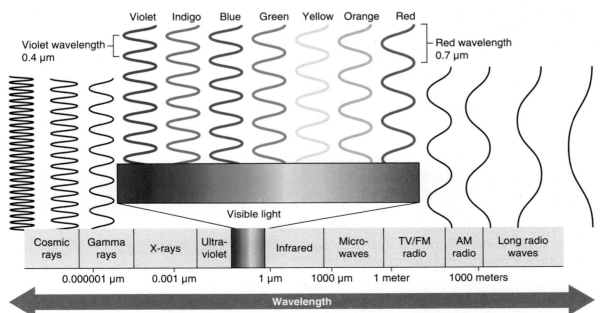

FIGURE 2.26 **Solar and terrestrial radiation.** *Most of the Sun's electromagnetic radiation ranges from ultraviolet waves to short infrared waves. The amount of energy the Sun emits is greatest in the visible portions of the spectrum, centered on 0.5 μm wavelengths, the wavelengths we see as green. Radiation emitted from Earth peaks at 10 μm wavelengths.*

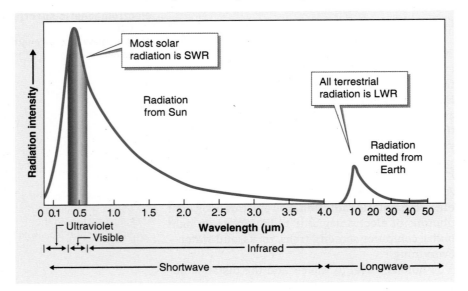

important to physical geography because they provide light, heat the planet's atmosphere and oceans, and fuel the biosphere.

Ultraviolet Radiation

As we learned in Section 1.5, most of the Sun's ultraviolet (UV) radiation is absorbed by ozone molecules high in the stratosphere. Clouds and aerosols also play important roles in determining how much UV radiation reaches Earth's surface. Thick clouds can absorb almost all UV radiation, and other atmospheric aerosols also scatter and absorb it. Generally, higher elevations receive more UV radiation because there are few molecules to scatter UV rays, resulting in more intense UV exposure. In mountains, UV radiation exposure is further increased when a cover of bright snow blankets the ground. Clean snow can reflect up to 95% of UV radiation.

UV radiation is subdivided into three categories depending on its wavelength: UV-A, UV-B, and UV-C (**Figure 2.27**). UV-A is both beneficial and harmful to living organisms. It is beneficial to people because our bodies use it to make vitamin D, but it is harmful to us because it causes sunburns and cataracts in the eyes. The shorter wavelengths of UV-B and UV-C can break apart DNA and cause cell mutations and cancers, but the atmosphere naturally protects us from them.

Objects with higher temperatures emit photons at shorter wavelengths than objects with lower temperatures. In addition, objects with higher temperatures emit photons at a higher rate than objects with lower temperatures. The Sun, for example, with a surface temperature of 5,800°C (10,500°F), emits energy with wavelengths centered on 0.5 μm (the visible portion of the EMS). Earth's lower atmosphere and surface, with an average temperature of 14.6°C (58.3°F), are far cooler than the Sun and emit electromagnetic radiation with wavelengths centered on 10 μm (the infrared portion of the EMS). Being cooler, Earth also emits energy at a lower rate than the Sun.

All radiation emitted by Earth (called *terrestrial radiation*) is **longwave radiation (LWR)**. LWR is defined as having wavelengths greater than 4 μm. Most solar radiation is **shortwave radiation (SWR)**. SWR has wavelengths less than 4 μm (**Figure 2.26**).

longwave radiation (LWR)
Radiation with wavelengths longer than 4 μm.

shortwave radiation (SWR)
Solar radiation with wavelengths shorter than 4 μm; includes visible sunlight.

visible radiation (or *light*)
The portion of the electromagnetic spectrum that people can see.

Visible Radiation: Light

Visible radiation (or *light*) has wavelengths between 0.40 and 0.75 μm (see Figure 2.25). Visible radiation is the portion of the electromagnetic spectrum that we can see. Forty-four percent of the Sun's radiation is concentrated in the visible wavelengths. When all visible light colors are combined, they blend into white.

FIGURE 2.27 **Ultraviolet radiation.**
Ultraviolet (UV) radiation encompasses wavelengths between 0.01 and 0.4 μm. It is subdivided into three categories: UV-A, UV-B, and UV-C.

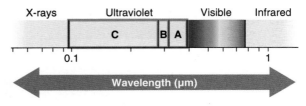

Earth's Important Wavelengths: Ultraviolet, Visible, and Infrared

Ninety-nine percent of the Sun's energy emissions are in three wavelength categories: ultraviolet radiation, visible radiation, and infrared radiation. These three wavelength categories are the most

Infrared Radiation

Infrared radiation (IR) has wavelengths longer than visible radiation; a portion of this radiation is heat. Infrared wavelengths range between 0.75 and 1,000 µm. Earth absorbs shortwave solar radiation and re-emits it as infrared radiation. This conversion from shortwave radiation to longwave radiation is exceedingly important in Earth's physical systems, as we will see next.

2.5 Earth's Energy Budget

◎ Explain Earth's energy budget and why the atmosphere circulates.

The fraction of the Sun's energy that Earth intercepts is called **insolation**, or *incoming solar radiation*. According to satellite measurements, 1,367 W/m^2 of solar energy reaches the top of the atmosphere. Insolation is transmitted, scattered, reflected, and absorbed in Earth's physical systems as it travels through the atmosphere to Earth's surface.

Transmission is the unimpeded movement of electromagnetic energy through a medium such as air, water, or glass. Ocean water transmits sunlight to limited depths. Some materials transmit only certain wavelengths of electromagnetic radiation. The atmosphere, for example, absorbs ultraviolet and infrared wavelengths but transmits visible wavelengths. Glass, on the other hand, transmits visible light but absorbs ultraviolet wavelengths.

Scattering is the process of redirecting solar radiation in random directions as it strikes physical matter, such as aerosols, gases, or the planet's surface. This process creates *diffuse light*. When light is scattered, its electromagnetic wavelength does not change; only its direction of travel changes **(Figure 2.28)**.

Reflection, like scattering, does not alter the wavelength of electromagnetic radiation. **Reflection** is the process of returning a portion of the radiation striking a surface in the general direction from which it came. If, for example, a UV photon is reflected off snow, it goes back into the atmosphere as a UV photon, unchanged.

infrared radiation (IR)
Electromagnetic radiation that has wavelengths longer than visible radiation.

insolation
(or *incoming solar radiation*) Solar radiation that reaches Earth.

transmission
The unimpeded movement of electromagnetic energy through a medium such as air, water, or glass.

scattering
The process of redirecting solar radiation in random directions as it strikes physical matter.

reflection
The process of returning a portion of the radiation striking a surface in the general direction from which it came.

FIGURE **2.28** **Diffuse light.** *The pink and orange glow we see before the Sun rises or sets is a result of light scattering in the atmosphere. When the solar altitude is low (see Section 2.1), sunlight interacts with more molecules and aerosols because it is passing through more atmosphere (see Figure 2.5). These materials scatter long wavelengths of pink and orange, allowing us to perceive them. In mountainous regions, diffuse light is called* alpenglow. *This photo, taken before sunrise, shows Mont Blanc Massive and Lac Blanc in France.*
(© K. Irlmeier/Blickwinkel/Age Fotostock)

Picture This

1. **Blue sky:** Nitrogen molecules in the atmosphere are small enough to scatter blue portions of the electromagnetic spectrum. This phenomenon, called *Rayleigh scattering*, produces the blue color of the sky. We perceive blue because it has been scattered from the EMS.

2. **White clouds:** Clouds are composed of liquid water droplets that are much larger than the individual wavelengths of visible light. All wavelengths of visible light are therefore equally reflected by the droplets, creating white.

Why is the sky blue and the grass green?

3. **Rainbow:** Rainbows form when visible light passes through raindrops in the atmosphere. As light enters a raindrop, it is slowed down and its direction changed through refraction. *Refraction* separates the different wavelengths of visible light, allowing our eyes to see them.

4. **Green vegetation:** Vegetation is green because chlorophyll in plant leaves absorbs all visible colors except green, which it reflects.

5. **Blue water:** The color of the oceans is not related to the color of the sky. Instead, like a filter, ocean water absorbs the longer wavelengths of reds and yellows before the shorter wavelengths of blues, leaving blue wavelengths for us to perceive.

(L. Valencia/Flickr Open/Getty Images)

Colors

This aerial photograph of Huahine, part of the Society Islands in French Polynesia, shows a world awash in tropical sunlight and color. Colors are produced when visible light is reflected, refracted, scattered, or absorbed.

Consider This

1. If the Sun burned hotter, what effect (if any) do you think this would have on colors? Explain your reasoning.

2. We learned in this chapter that the Sun's peak energy output is centered on green wavelengths in the visible spectrum. Why, then, is the Sun not colored green?

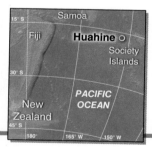

The colors our eyes perceive are the result of reflection, refraction, scattering, and absorption of visible wavelengths **(Picture This)**.

Albedo is the reflectivity of a surface, given as the percentage of incoming radiation that it reflects. Lighter-colored surfaces, such as snow, have a higher albedo than darker surfaces, such as vegetation. A perfectly reflective mirror would have an albedo of 100%. A perfectly absorptive surface (called a radiation *blackbody*) would have an albedo of 0%. In nature, surfaces have albedo values lying between those two extremes.

The albedo of Earth, taken as a whole, is 30%. The 70% of insolation not reflected back to space is absorbed. The planet's surface albedo, however, varies considerably from region to region. Surfaces with a low albedo absorb more insolation than do objects with a high albedo. For example, clean snow absorbs about 10% of insolation and reflects the remaining 90%. Older and dirtier snow is less reflective. **Figure 2.29** on the next page illustrates the different albedos of various surfaces.

Except in the case of incandescent lava or bioluminescent organisms, Earth does not emit light—it only reflects it. Earth is visible from space only because it is reflecting visible sunlight. **Figure 2.30** on the next page explains how scientists measure Earth's reflectivity.

albedo
The reflectivity of a surface, given as the percentage of incoming radiation that it reflects.

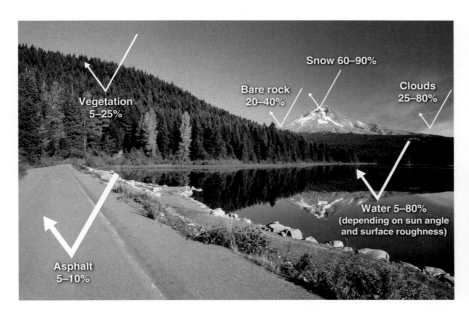

Snow 60–90%

Vegetation
5–25%

Bare rock
20–40%

Clouds
25–80%

Water 5–80%
(depending on sun angle
and surface roughness)

Asphalt
5–10%

FIGURE 2.29 **Albedo.** *Of the surfaces in this photo, the clean snow has the highest albedo, and the road surface and forest vegetation have the lowest. Water's albedo has a wide range because it depends on the choppiness of the water and the angle of the Sun. The albedo of clouds varies as well, depending on the type of clouds present. Oregon's Mount Hood is visible in the background. (© Craig Tuttle/Design Pics/Corbis)*

FIGURE 2.30 **SCIENTIFIC INQUIRY: How is Earth's reflectivity measured?**

Monitoring Earth's albedo is essential to climate studies. For example, decreasing snow cover due to global warming is decreasing Earth's albedo, allowing the surface to absorb and be warmed by sunlight rather than reflecting it and remaining cool. Scientists monitor planetary albedo from the ground and from orbiting satellites. (A. © Martin Shields/Photo Researchers/Getty Images; B. NASA)

(A) Ground-based *radiometers* are used to measure the amount of reflected shortwave radiation at Earth's surface. From these measurements, albedo can be determined for different types of surfaces.

(B) Satellites provide a more comprehensive portrait of Earth's albedo than ground-based radiometers. They can measure shortwave radiation reflected from cloud tops using a variety of sophisticated radiation sensors on board the satellite. An artist's rendering of the *Terra* satellite is shown here.

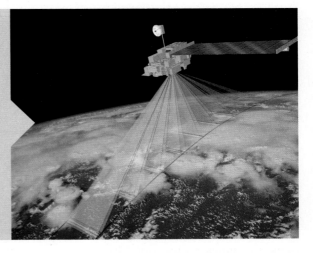

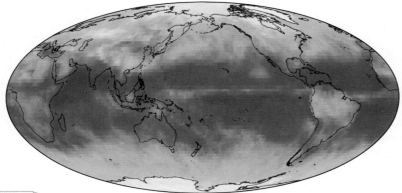

(C) This image shows reflection of shortwave radiation by Earth's surface and atmosphere. It was compiled from *Terra* for March 2005 as measured by Clouds and Earth's Radiant Energy System (CERES) instrumentation. High latitudes with extensive snow, ice, and cloud cover are the most reflective areas of the planet. The equatorial band of reflectivity is caused by persistent cloudiness. The dark oceans absorb a large proportion of incoming solar energy.

Video
Albedo
feedback
http://qrs.ly/du434bx

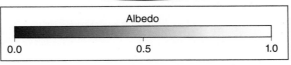

Albedo

0.0   0.5   1.0

FIGURE 2.31 **Urban heat island.** *(A) This generalized temperature profile (red line) shows the typical rise in temperature over an urbanized region in contrast to less developed rural areas. The urban heat island effect is most noticeable at night on calm, clear nights. (B) This nighttime thermal infrared map shows the city of Paris, France, during a record-breaking heat wave in early August 2003. The inner city is some 5°C (9°F) warmer than the surrounding farmlands.* (All rights reserved - copyright VITO Planetek © 2013)

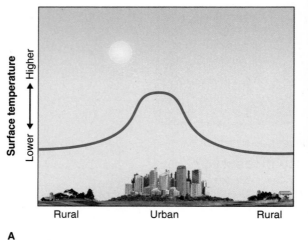

A

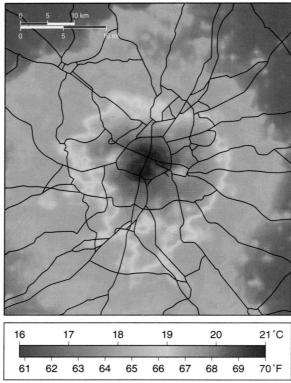

B

Once a photon is absorbed, it ceases to exist in its original state. It is instead converted to another form of energy. The solar energy absorbed by plants is converted to chemical energy. Solar panels absorb solar energy and convert it to electrical energy (see Geographic Perspectives at the end of this chapter).

GEOGRAPHIC PERSPECTIVES

Picture This

The Tuareg

The Tuareg are a group of nomadic Berber people who inhabit the Sahara of northern Africa. The Tuareg have occupied this desert region for at least 1,500 years, making a living by transporting goods with camels between sub-Saharan Africa and Europe. Today, Range Rovers, trains, and airplanes have replaced their camel caravans, but they still follow well-established trade routes through the desert (inset).

Traditional Tuareg dress often consists of loose-fitting cloth of various shades of dark brown and blue to protect its wearers from the hot Saharan sun and reflective sand. From a practical standpoint, the dark clothing does not seem to make sense. The low-albedo dark cloth absorbs sunlight and converts it to heat. Lighter, more reflective colors should be cooler.

(© McPHOTO/Age Fotostock)

Most objects convert absorbed solar energy to longwave radiation (heat), which raises the temperature of the object that absorbed it.

In general, the more shortwave energy an object can absorb (or the lower its albedo), the more longwave energy it can radiate. How much shortwave radiation an object can absorb depends on its heat capacity and its albedo. For example, an urbanized region may become significantly warmer than surrounding rural areas, forming an **urban heat island** (Figure 2.31).

Urban heat islands result from three main factors. First, cities have low albedos which allows them to absorb solar radiation. Second, cities are composed of materials such as asphalt, concrete, and bricks, which retain the absorbed heat energy and radiate it. Third, because evaporation cools the surrounding environment (see Section 3.1), the lack of water available for evaporation in cities also contributes to the urban heat island effect.

In a different example of a relationship between albedo and human comfort, the Tuareg people who inhabit the hot Sahara wear dark clothing, seemingly against common sense (Picture This).

The Great Balancing Act

Earth's surface temperature increases as Earth absorbs energy from the Sun, and it decreases as Earth radiates heat to the atmosphere and to space. Internal geothermal energy does warm Earth's surface, but not as much as the Sun's

energy does. If the Sun were to stop shining, the temperature of Earth's surface would plunge as it quickly radiated away its heat. Each night, the Sun effectively does stop shining, and the surface temperature drops because Earth loses more energy than it absorbs. Each day, the Sun rises again, and Earth's surface warms again because it absorbs more energy than it radiates (Figure 2.32). The atmosphere also warms and cools over a 24-hour period, just as Earth's surface does.

FIGURE 2.32 **Energy budget of a rock.** *The temperature of a rock or Earth's surface is a result of the balance between incoming energy and outgoing energy. (A) During the day, sunlight warms the rock. Incoming shortwave radiation is greater than outgoing longwave radiation, so the rock's temperature (T) increases. (B) At night there is no incoming SWR, but LWR continues to radiate from the rock, causing its temperature to decrease.*

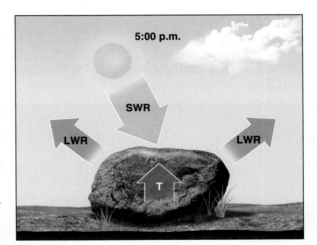

A

B

urban heat island
An urbanized region that is significantly warmer than surrounding rural areas.

Cultural reasons come into play in the choice of clothing color. However, from a physical standpoint, dark colors do make practical sense. Studies have shown that white clothing reflects heat back toward the body, while dark clothing better absorbs the body's heat (as well as the Sun's). As long as there is some wind to carry the excess heat away, dark, loose-fitting clothing can more effectively draw heat away from the body through absorption than lighter clothing.

Consider This

1. Would dark, tight-fitting clothing be an advantage in hot places? Explain.

2. Have you ever noticed that the albedo of your clothing affects your body temperature, particularly in the context of playing sports? Explain.

radiative equilibrium temperature
The temperature of an object resulting from the balance between incoming and outgoing energy.

greenhouse effect
The process by which the atmosphere is warmed as greenhouse gases (such as water vapor, carbon dioxide, and methane) and clouds absorb and counterradiate heat.

Just as a bank account's balance is the result of deposits and withdrawals, the temperature of Earth's surface and atmosphere is the result of a balance between incoming and outgoing energy. As long as the amount of energy absorbed is equal to the amount of energy radiated, the temperature will be stable, as illustrated in Figure 2.33. That stable temperature is called the **radiative equilibrium temperature**.

Although incoming solar SWR and outgoing terrestrial LWR are balanced, some complex and important interactions are involved, as illustrated in Figure 2.34. One of the most important aspects of Earth's radiation budget is the greenhouse effect, which delays the radiation of heat absorbed by Earth's surface to space. The **greenhouse effect** is the process by which the atmosphere is warmed as greenhouse gases, such as water vapor, carbon dioxide, and methane (see Section 1.1). Clouds absorb some of the heat emitted by Earth's surface, then *counterradiate* (or reradiate) that heat.

FIGURE 2.33 **Earth's balanced energy budget.** *The amount of solar energy that Earth intercepts is equal to the amount of solar energy that Earth reflects (30%) plus the amount of solar energy that Earth absorbs and then emits back to space (70%). The resulting radiative equilibrium temperature (measured in the lower atmosphere) is 14.6°C (58.3°F).*

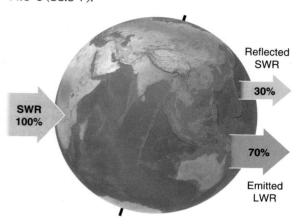

SWR 100%

Reflected SWR
30%

70%

Emitted LWR

Animation
Greenhouse effect
http://qrs.ly/qt434b5

FIGURE 2.34 **Geo-Graphic: Earth's energy budget.** *The same amount of energy that is absorbed by Earth is emitted by Earth.*

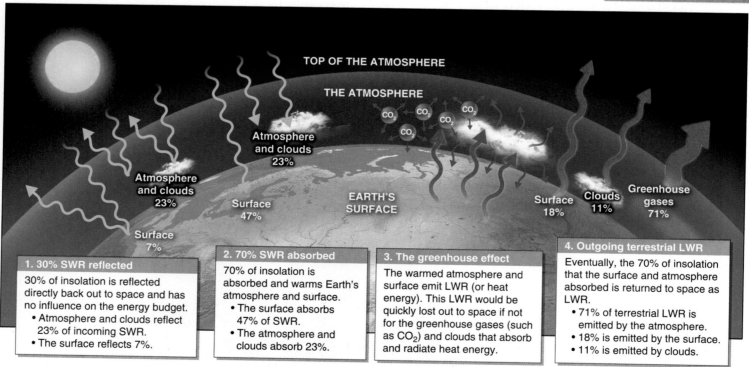

TOP OF THE ATMOSPHERE

THE ATMOSPHERE

CO_2 CO_2 CO_2 CO_2 CO_2

Atmosphere and clouds 23%

Atmosphere and clouds 23%

Surface 47%

EARTH'S SURFACE

Surface 18%

Clouds 11%

Greenhouse gases 71%

Surface 7%

1. 30% SWR reflected
30% of insolation is reflected directly back out to space and has no influence on the energy budget.
• Atmosphere and clouds reflect 23% of incoming SWR.
• The surface reflects 7%.

2. 70% SWR absorbed
70% of insolation is absorbed and warms Earth's atmosphere and surface.
• The surface absorbs 47% of SWR.
• The atmosphere and clouds absorb 23%.

3. The greenhouse effect
The warmed atmosphere and surface emit LWR (or heat energy). This LWR would be quickly lost out to space if not for the greenhouse gases (such as CO_2) and clouds that absorb and radiate heat energy.

4. Outgoing terrestrial LWR
Eventually, the 70% of insolation that the surface and atmosphere absorbed is returned to space as LWR.
• 71% of terrestrial LWR is emitted by the atmosphere.
• 18% is emitted by the surface.
• 11% is emitted by clouds.

FIGURE 2.35 **Annual energy balance by latitude.** *On average, only near 37° latitude does the amount of solar energy absorbed by Earth equal the amount of heat radiated by Earth. Equatorward of 37°, Earth absorbs more energy than it radiates. Poleward of 37°, Earth radiates more energy than it absorbs.*

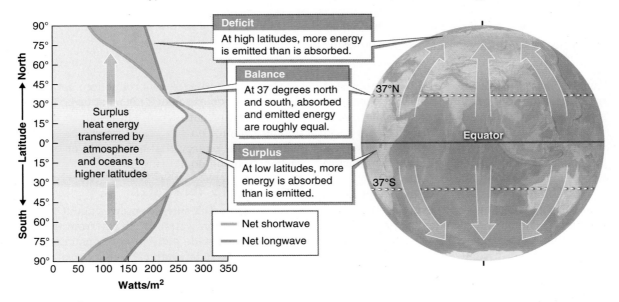

The Global Heat Engine

Heat is not "trapped" through the greenhouse effect. That would mean that it never radiates back to space. If heat were trapped, Earth's atmosphere would have long ago become extremely hot and inhospitable for life. Conversely, if it were not for the presence of greenhouse gases in the atmosphere, the greenhouse effect would not occur. The lower atmosphere would be, on average, some 30°C (54°F) colder than it is, cold enough to freeze the oceans. Humans have modified the greenhouse effect by adding greenhouse gases to the atmosphere; this important topic will be discussed in Section 6.3.

The Global Heat Engine

For the planet as a whole, incoming SWR and outgoing terrestrial LWR are balanced. But across most of Earth's surface, incoming and outgoing energy are not balanced. At most latitudes, there is either a surplus or a deficit of heat (**Figure 2.35**).

Between 37° north and south, Earth absorbs more energy than it radiates. Earth should therefore be heating up at a constant rate there, but it is not. The tropics are warm, but they are not growing warmer. Likewise, because Earth radiates more heat than it absorbs poleward of 37°, it should be growing ever colder at high latitudes,

but it is not. Instead, heat from tropical latitudes is *advected* (moved) poleward by the atmosphere and the oceans.

Heat is also imbalanced between the lower and upper atmosphere. Air near Earth's surface is usually warmer than air at higher altitudes because Earth's surface absorbs more solar energy than the atmosphere does. Heat is transferred to the atmosphere through radiation.

Earth's atmosphere and oceans flow mainly because of unequal heating across Earth's surface. The atmosphere moves about 60% of excess tropical heat to higher latitudes, and the oceans move about 40%. The movement of heat from low to high latitudes and low to high altitudes as a result of heating differences is called the **global heat engine**.

Almost all atmospheric movement, from gentle breezes to tornadoes, is the result of heating inequalities across latitude and altitude. Together, local convection and the global heat engine transport immense amounts of heat, both higher in latitude and higher in altitude. Water vapor, as we will see in Chapter 3, also plays a vitally important role in the global heat engine. The global heat engine underpins all the atmospheric processes explored in the remainder of Part I (Chapters 3 to 6).

Why does the wind blow?

global heat engine
The movement of heat from low to high latitudes and low to high altitudes as a result of heating differences.

GEOGRAPHIC PERSPECTIVES
2.6 The Rising Solar Economy

◎ Assess the role of sunlight as a clean energy source.

Imagine how difficult life would be without electricity, gas stoves, or gasoline. How would we get to school or work? Use computers and cell phones? What would we eat? How would food be harvested from the field, transported to the supermarket, and kept in refrigerators? How would we manufacture items like clothes and houses?

Just about every aspect of our lives requires the use of energy. The growth and development of world economic systems and societies are driven by the consumption of energy.

Where do we currently get our energy? Mostly from fossil fuels, which have driven the world economy since the middle of the 1800s. The global economy today relies on fossil fuels for about 85% of its energy needs. But our energy sources are changing, and the coming generations, beginning with ours today, will be part of a movement away from fossil fuels to renewable energy. **Renewable energy** comes from sources that are not depleted when used, such as sunlight or wind. Most renewable energy sources do not release greenhouse gases into the atmosphere, so they are also referred to as *carbon-free energy*. According to the International Energy Agency, by 2018, renewable energy could make up 25% of the energy the world consumes. By 2050, perhaps up to 80% of the world's energy will come from renewable sources.

Fossil fuels have served us well in many respects. Coal is widely used to generate electricity. Petroleum (oil) is used in the transportation sector. Natural gas has a wide range of uses, including heating of homes and water. But there are two serious problems with fossil fuels. First, they pollute the air, so they can jeopardize human health (see Section 1.4) and can contribute to climate change (see Section 6.3). Second, they are finite and will eventually run out—that is, they are *nonrenewable*.

According to the U.S. Department of Energy, the world consumed 90 million barrels of petroleum per day in 2013—the equivalent of 14.3 billion liters, or 3.8 billion gallons. In the same year, petroleum production was 89.9 million barrels per day. Because demand will continue to rise, but petroleum production cannot, consumption will eventually exceed production by a much greater amount. The time frame for this is uncertain, but generally, experts think it will occur within the next several decades.

Once demand exceeds production, petroleum will become too expensive for most uses. The increased cost of petroleum will result in a much greater reliance on sources of renewable energy, such as solar energy, that are mostly or entirely carbon-free and do not run out.

The Goal: 15 Terawatts

On average, Earth's surface receives about 101,000 terawatts (trillion watts) of energy from the Sun each day. Worldwide daily power consumption is approximately 15 terawatts. But that consumption is not spread evenly across the globe (Figure 2.36).

The global energy requirement of 15 terawatts could be more than met if only a small fraction of the total amount of sunlight reaching Earth were captured. There are other sources of renewable energy besides the Sun, some of which are listed in Table 2.3.

Because the Sun's energy output is so great, solar energy will certainly play a prominent role in the future energy mix. Sunlight is everywhere and seemingly free. All we have to do is collect it and use it. It sounds simple enough, except for two details: First, the radiant solar energy must be converted to electrical energy by solar panels, and solar panels take up space. Second, the energy must be transported to and stored where it is needed. We have the technology to meet these two challenges. The difficulty is doing so on a sufficiently large scale to meet global energy demand.

Unless we find a more efficient collection mechanism than solar panels, replacing even a small

renewable energy
Energy that comes from sources that are not depleted when used, such as sunlight or wind.

TABLE **2.3** AT A GLANCE: **Renewable Energy Capacity**	
RENEWABLE ENERGY TYPE*	**TOTAL THEORETICAL MAXIMUM CAPACITY (IN TERAWATTS)**
Solar	101,000
Wind	190
Biomass	92
Geothermal	42
Hydroelectric	4.7

Biomass energy is generated by the burning of organic material, such as agricultural wastes or plant oils. *Geothermal* energy comes from Earth's internal heat. *Hydroelectric* energy is generated by the flow of rivers by means of turbines on dams.

Night lighting reveals patterns of energy consumption. *This image, which shows night lighting worldwide, is a composite of many satellite images developed over several weeks in April and October 2012, to avoid cloud cover, and stitched together. Areas with dense populations and high levels of economic development (eastern North America, western Europe, northern India, South Korea, eastern China, and Japan, for example) consume the most energy. The Northern Hemisphere consumes more energy than the Southern Hemisphere. There are places, such as sub-Saharan Africa, where the population is large, but there are few lights because of low levels of economic development. Similarly, there are places where lights are caused by natural-gas flaring, not large populations. (NASA)*

fraction of our global 15-terawatt energy demand with solar energy will require considerable surface space devoted to collecting sunlight. Solar energy may be plentiful, but there is not much available space to capture and convert it. There are two approaches to capturing sunlight: decentralized and centralized solar energy production. **Decentralized solar energy production spreads solar energy production out over wide regions, while centralized production concentrates it geographically into large industrial facilities.**

The Decentralized Approach

Rooftops provide many opportunities to capture sunlight. In an idealized decentralized solar energy production approach, every household, apartment complex, and business would generate its own electricity. If too much were generated, it could be traded or sold. One way of generating electricity from the Sun is to use photovoltaic (PV) panels. The materials in PV panels, such as silicon, absorb photons of light and release electrons, creating an electric current. In addition to PV panels, there are paints and flexible plastic films that can convert sunlight to electricity. Imagine covering our houses, buildings, and cars with these materials. Even our clothes could be made of photovoltaic cloth that could power our cell phones and other personal electronic devices.

Solar roadways are another example of the decentralized approach. There are almost 9 million km (6 million mi) of roadways in the United States and 500,000 km (300,000 mi) in Canada. Roads occupy enormous amounts of space and are often exposed to full sun. Corridors of PV panels are already being placed along highways in several U.S. states. Solar panels in parking lots are also now providing the dual purpose of shading parked cars and generating clean electricity.

One problem with decentralized solar energy production, however, is that in many cases it is not yet cost-effective. Homeowners and businesses can receive grants and discounts from power companies and governments promoting conversion to solar energy. But for most, affordable and efficient rooftop PV panels are still years off.

The Centralized Approach

In centralized solar power production, solar farms generate power at an industrial facility and send it to where it is needed. Many centralized solar facilities in the United States are located in its southwestern deserts. As **Figure 2.37** on the next page shows, solar energy is more intense at lower latitudes worldwide, particularly in arid regions where cloud cover is scarce much of the year.

Although Figure 2.37 may suggest that solar energy production is effective only in deserts, this

FIGURE 2.37 **Solar intensity map.** *This map shows the intensity of solar radiation (in W/m²) striking the ground. The Sun's intensity on the ground depends on latitude and the persistence of cloud cover. Low latitudes that are cloud free most of the time receive the most intense sunlight. Examples of such areas are the Sahara and the Kalahari Desert in Africa, the U.S. Southwest, and northern Australia. Midlatitude locations at high elevations that are cloud free, particularly the Andes and the Tibetan Plateau, also receive abundant solar energy.* (2014 3TIER by Vaisala)

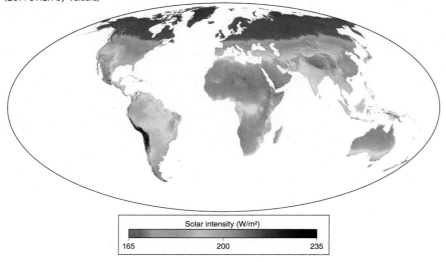

Solar intensity (W/m²)

165   200   235

is not the case. One of the largest-capacity solar energy facilities in the world is the Sarnia Solar Project in Ontario, Canada, which generates 97 megawatts, enough electricity to meet the needs of 12,000 homes.

Various companies are rushing to file applications to build solar PV farms on hundreds of thousands of acres in the U.S. Southwest **(Figure 2.38A)**. As an alternative to PV panels, concentrated solar power, or CSP, is also being developed in centralized solar industrial facilities **(Figure 2.38B)**.

Many proposed solar facilities have met stiff opposition in the United States. Why? Because there is no "empty" land to use. What appears to be a barren desert to many can be prime habitat for many different species, such as the endangered California desert tortoise (*Gopherus agassizii*), which is protected by federal law. Many solar farm projects have been bogged down in litigation because they take habitat from rare or endangered plants and animals. Proposals for solar farm projects that degrade the natural habitat of threatened species rarely win these court battles.

Where, then, can we build centralized solar power facilities? Many believe the best solution to this conflict is to build on already degraded desert land (such as old parking lots) rather than in relatively pristine wilderness. Others believe we should simply not build centralized solar farms at all. Instead, we should focus our efforts and dollars on the decentralized approach to solar power development. These are problems with no easy answers. Given our need for clean energy, however, transitioning to renewable energies such as solar is only a matter of time, regardless of the hurdles.

FIGURE 2.38 **Centralized solar energy.** *(A) Nellis Solar Power Plant in Clark County, Nevada, near Las Vegas, has a 14-megawatt capacity, enough to meet 25% of the power needs of the Nellis Air Force Base, for which it was built. Its 70,000 solar panels occupy 57 ha (140 acres). (B) This concentrated solar power project is located near Las Vegas, Nevada. Thousands of mirrors precisely track the Sun so that each reflects sunlight to heat a fluid (molten salt) within the three towers. The hot fluid is then used to boil water to create steam that drives a turbine to generate electricity.* (A. David Nunuk/Science Source; B. Jim West imageBROKER/Newscom)

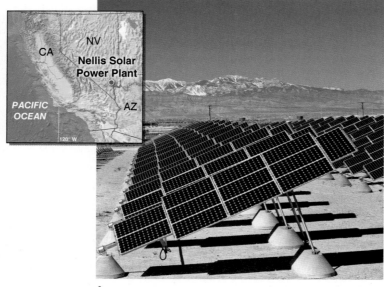

A

B

CHAPTER 2 Exploring with ⦿ Google Earth

To complete these problems, first read the chapter. When you are finished, go to LaunchPad and open the Exploring with Google Earth file for this chapter. Click on the "Workbook Problems" folder to "fly" to each of the problems listed below and answer the questions. Be sure to keep your "Borders and Labels" layer activated. Refer to Appendix 4 if you need help using Google Earth.

PROBLEM 2.1 Activate both overlays in the Problem 2.1 folder. You can toggle between them by selecting or deselecting one or both of them. The overlays in this problem show planetary albedo for June and December 2012. Lighter yellow and white indicate a higher albedo surface. Dark blues indicate a low-albedo surface.

1. **Which of the two overlays shows Earth's June albedo? (Hint: Note how the polar albedo changes between the overlays.)**
   a. Overlay A   b. Overlay B

2. **What information reveals this?**
   a. Albedo increases at all locations in Overlay A.
   b. Albedo increases at all locations in Overlay B.
   c. Albedo decreases at the North Pole in Overlay B.
   d. Albedo increases at the North Pole in Overlay B.

3. **In both overlays, there is a narrow band of high albedo near the equator. What is causing this reflective band?**
   a. Pollution   c. Warm ocean currents
   b. Cloudiness   d. Snowy mountains

4. **In what country is this placemark found?**
   a. Morocco   c. Tunisia
   b. Algeria   d. Mali

5. **Activate Overlay B (deactivate overlay A). Then deactivate the overlay, zoom in, and examine Earth's surface. Why is there a high albedo at this location?**
   a. Snow cover   c. Urban areas
   b. Persistent cloudiness   d. Extensive sand

PROBLEM 2.2 Deactivate any overlays that may already be activated. Then activate both overlays in the Problem 2.2 folder. You can toggle between them by selecting or deselecting one or both of them. The overlays in this problem show land surface temperatures for June and December 2012. A color key is provided at the top of the screen.

1. **Activate Overlay A (deactivate Overlay B). What is the approximate temperature for the location shown by the placemark?**
   a. Less than −25°C   c. 10°C to 45°C
   b. −25°C to 10°C   d. Greater than 45°C

2. **Now activate Overlay B (deactivate Overlay A). What is the approximate temperature for the location shown by the placemark?**
   a. Less than −25°C   c. 10°C to 45°C
   b. −25°C to 10°C   d. Greater than 45°C

3. **Which of these two overlays shows temperatures for June?**
   a. Overlay A   b. Overlay B

4. **Why is this placemark's location so different from the surrounding areas in either overlay?**
   a. It is in a deep valley.   c. It is at a high latitude.
   b. It is on high mountains.   d. It is near the ocean.

PROBLEM 2.3 Keep both overlays from Problem 2.2 activated. Toggle between them by selecting or deselecting one or both of them. These overlays show land surface temperatures for June and December 2012. A color key is provided at the top of the screen.

1. **Toggle between both overlays to get a sense of how temperature changes between them. What is the temperature range for this location?**
   a. −25°C to 10°C
   b. 10°C to 45°C
   c. −25°C to 45°C
   d. There is no significant temperature range.

2. **Which of the following factors best explains this temperature range?**
   a. Continentality
   b. Latitude
   c. Elevation
   d. Continentality and elevation

3. **In what country is this placemark found?**
   a. Cameroon   c. Nigeria
   b. Gabon   d. Equatorial Guinea

PROBLEM 2.4 Keep both overlays from Problem 2.2 activated. Toggle between them by selecting or deselecting one or both of them. These overlays show land surface temperatures for June and December 2012. A color key is provided at the top of the screen.

1. **Toggle between both overlays to get a sense of how temperature changes between them. What is the temperature range for this location?**
   a. −25°C to 10°C
   b. 10°C to 45°C
   c. −25°C to 45°C
   d. There is no significant temperature range.

PROBLEM 2.5 Deactivate all previous overlays and activate the overlay in the Problem 2.5 folder. This overlay shows the surface temperature for Buffalo, New York, for August 3, 2002. Whites and yellows show warm surfaces, and blues and purples show relatively cool surfaces.

1. **Is the city of Buffalo warmer or cooler than the surrounding region?**
   a. Warmer   b. Cooler

2. **What factors contribute to this temperature pattern?**
   a. Albedo   c. Convection
   b. Scattering   d. Greenhouse effect

3. **Based on your reading, what is the name of this phenomenon?**
   a. Urban heat island   c. Rayleigh scattering
   b. Specific heat   d. Insolation

PROBLEM 2.6 Deactivate all previous overlays and activate both overlays in the Problem 2.6 folder. Toggle between them by selecting or deselecting the top Night Lights overlay. The other overlay shows human populations in number of persons per square kilometer. Reds show high populations.

This placemark lands in Haiti. Activate the Night Lights overlay and notice how dark Haiti is. The island of Puerto Rico is visible 350 mi to the east. Note that Puerto Rico (a U.S. territory) is illuminated in night lights.

1. **Activate the population overlay and compare the populations of the two countries. Which statement best summarizes the populations of both islands?**
   a. Haiti has fewer people than Puerto Rico.
   b. Haiti has more people than Puerto Rico.
   c. Both Haiti and Puerto Rico have about the same populations.

2. **Based on the Night Lights overlay, which of the two countries uses more energy?**
   a. Haiti
   b. Puerto Rico
   c. Both use about the same amount of energy.

CHAPTER 2 **Study Guide**

Focus Points

2.1 The Four Seasons

Cause of seasons: The tilt of Earth's axis causes the subsolar point to migrate between the Tropic of Cancer and the Tropic of Capricorn, causing seasons.

Solar altitude: The solar altitude determines the intensity of sunlight.

Equinox day length: On the equinoxes, all locations on Earth experience 12 hours of day and 12 hours of night.

Solstice day length: On the June solstice, day length increases northward and decreases southward. The reverse is true for the December solstice.

2.2 Temperature and Heat

Heat transfer: Heat is transferred through conduction, convection, and radiation.

Heat: In conduction, heat always travels from objects of higher temperature to objects of lower temperature.

2.3 Surface Temperature Patterns

Average annual temperature: The average annual temperature decreases at higher elevations and at higher latitudes.

Annual temperature range: The annual temperature range increases at high latitudes and interior continental locations.

Ocean currents: Warm ocean currents from low latitudes raise the average annual temperature and reduce the annual temperature range.

Midlatitude coastal patterns: At midlatitude locations, the west coasts of continents have maritime climates, and the east coasts of continents have continental climates.

2.4 The Sun's Radiant Energy

Electromagnetic radiation: Electromagnetic radiation is emitted by all objects, and it travels in waves.

The Sun's emissions: Because of its high temperature, the Sun emits mostly shortwave radiation, most of it in visible wavelengths.

Earth's emissions: Earth mainly emits longwave infrared radiation because of the planet's relatively low temperature.

2.5 Earth's Energy Budget

Insolation: Incoming solar radiation can be transmitted, scattered, reflected, or absorbed.

Albedo: The albedo of Earth as a whole is 30%. Seventy percent of insolation is absorbed.

Absorption: Most absorbed solar radiation is converted to heat and warms Earth's surface and atmosphere.

Radiative equilibrium temperature: Earth's radiative equilibrium temperature is a result of the balance between incoming solar and outgoing terrestrial radiation.

Greenhouse effect: The greenhouse effect warms the atmosphere.

Global heat engine: There is a net surplus of heat between 37° latitude north and south, and a net deficit of heat at higher latitudes. These heating inequalities drive Earth's global climate engine.

2.6 Geographic Perspectives: The Rising Solar Economy

The Sun as an energy resource: The Sun provides Earth with enormous amounts of renewable energy.

Approaches to capturing sunlight: Capturing sunlight and converting it to electricity can be done by decentralized and centralized means.

Key Terms

albedo, 78
Antarctic Circle, 65
Arctic Circle, 65
circle of illumination, 62
conduction, 67
continental effect, 70
convection, 68
December solstice, 62
electromagnetic spectrum
   (EMS), 75

global heat engine, 83
greenhouse effect, 82
heat, 67
heat-index temperature, 66
infrared radiation (IR), 77
insolation, 77
June solstice, 63
longwave radiation (LWR), 76
March equinox, 62
plane of the ecliptic, 61

radiant energy, 75
radiation, 68
radiative equilibrium
   temperature, 82
reflection, 77
renewable energy, 84
scattering, 77
September equinox, 63
shortwave radiation
   (SWR), 76

solar altitude, 62
specific heat, 72
subsolar point, 61
temperature, 66
transmission, 77
Tropic of Cancer, 62
Tropic of Capricorn, 62
urban heat island, 81
visible radiation
   (light), 76

Concept Review

The Human Sphere: People and the Seasons

1. How are seasons important to people?

2.1 The Four Seasons

2. What are aphelion and perihelion and when do they occur?

3. What is axial tilt and why is it the single most important factor causing seasons?

4. What is the subsolar point? What would happen to it if there were no axial tilt? What would happens to it if axial tilt were 90°?

5. What happens to seasonality when axial tilt is increased?

6. In relation to the subsolar point, how are the tropics defined?

7. Describe day length and the position of the subsolar point for each of the four seasonal markers:

   June solstice   December solstice

   September equinox   March equinox

8. Why is one "day" six months long at the poles?

2.2 Temperature and Heat

9. Without using a calculator, convert 10°C to Fahrenheit. Convert 100°F to Celsius.

10. What is the difference between temperature and heat?

11. In what three ways is energy transferred? Give real-world examples of each.

2.3 Surface Temperature Patterns

12. Describe the relationship between average annual temperature and changes in elevation and latitude.

13. How do latitude and the continental effect influence the annual temperature range?

14. What factors cause seasonality to increase farther inland?

15. Why does the Southern Hemisphere have smaller average seasonal fluctuations (on average) than the Northern Hemisphere?

16. How is seasonality affected in regions under the influence of warm ocean currents?

17. Compare the general pattern of annual temperature ranges at midlatitudes on west coasts and on east coasts. Which has a higher temperature range, and why?

2.4 The Sun's Radiant Energy

18. What is electromagnetic radiation? Does a rock or tree emit electromagnetic energy? Explain.

19. Which radiates longer wavelengths of electromagnetic energy, the Sun or Earth? Explain why.

20. Which type of radiation has shorter wavelengths, infrared radiation or visible light?

21. When the visible portion of the EMS is blended together, what color do we perceive?

22. In the context of reflection, refraction, scattering, and absorption, explain the coloration of each of the following: blue sky, green grass, white clouds, blue water, and rainbows.

2.5 Earth's Energy Budget

23. Describe what happens to insolation (incoming solar radiation) when it is transmitted, scattered, reflected, and absorbed.

24. What is albedo? Give examples of surfaces and objects with high and low albedos. What is Earth's overall albedo?

25. What is an urban heat island? What causes it?

26. What does it mean that Earth's energy budget is balanced?

27. What is a radiative equilibrium temperature? What would happen to it if more energy came into Earth's atmosphere than left the atmosphere?

28. What is the greenhouse effect? Describe how it works in relation to Earth's energy budget.

29. Where on the planet is there a surplus of heat and where is there a deficit of heat?

30. Why is the lower atmosphere near Earth's surface warmer than the upper atmosphere? How does this temperature difference affect airflow?

31. What is the global heat engine? What causes it?

2.6 Geographic Perspectives: The Rising Solar Economy

32. Compare renewable energy with nonrenewable energy. Give examples of each.

33. What are two major problems with fossil fuels?

34. Why is solar energy important to society's future energy needs?

35. Compare photovoltaic panels with concentrated solar power plants in terms of how they generate electricity from sunlight.

36. Compare centralized to decentralized solar energy production. What are some pros and cons of each approach?

37. What is the connection between desert tortoises and solar energy in California?

Critical-Thinking Questions

1. What aspects of your life depend on the seasons or somehow relate to them?

2. With regard to melting snow and ice, how could climate warming change Earth's albedo? What would happen to the planetary radiative equilibrium temperature as a result?

3. At the latitude where you live, is there a net heat surplus or a net heat deficit?

4. What is the annual temperature range where you live? Is the climate influenced more by oceans or by the continental effect? How does latitude factor into your location's seasonality?

5. Would you put PV solar panels on your rooftop if you had financial assistance from a local government program? What would motivate you to do so or not to do so?

Test Yourself

Take this quiz to test your chapter knowledge.

1. True or false? Seasonality increases as axial tilt decreases.

2. True or false? The highest latitude the subsolar point can reach is 23.5° north and south.

3. True or false? Temperature and heat are the same phenomenon.

4. True or false? The greenhouse effect keeps Earth's atmosphere warm and habitable.

5. Multiple choice: On June 21, the subsolar point is
  a. on the equator.   c. over the Tropic of Capricorn.
  b. at 23.5° north.   d. at 23.5° south.

6. Multiple choice: Which of the following absorbs most SWR from the Sun?
  a. The continents   c. The atmosphere
  b. Clouds   d. The oceans

7. Multiple choice: Which of the following locations would have the lowest average annual temperature?
  a. At sea level in the tropics
  b. In the mountains in the tropics
  c. At sea level at high latitudes
  d. In the mountains at high latitudes

8. Multiple choice: Which of the following locations would have the highest annual temperature range?
  a. Inland low latitudes
  b. Coastal low latitudes
  c. Inland high latitudes
  d. Coastal high latitudes

9. Fill in the blank: _____ causes the sky to be blue.

10. Fill in the blank: Energy transfer by _____ occurs when a fluid such as the atmosphere or oceans circulate and mix.

Further Reading

1. Schiermeier, Quirin, Jeff Tollefson, Tony Scully, Alexandra Witze, and Oliver Morton. "Energy Alternatives: Electricity without Carbon." *Nature* 454 (2008): 816-823.

2. Wines, Michael. "A Push Away from Burning Coal as an Energy Source." *New York Times*, November 14, 2013.

3. Yergin, Daniel. *The Quest: Energy, Security, and the Remaking of the Modern World.* New York: Penguin, 2011.

Answers to Living Physical Geography Questions

1. What causes seasons? The tilt of Earth's axis causes seasons.

2. Does it snow in Hawai'i? It often snows in Hawai'i at the highest elevations (over 3,000 m or 10,000 ft), where it is always very cold. Hawai'i's lowest recorded temperature is −11°C (12°F).

3. Why is the sky blue and the grass green? The sky is blue because nitrogen in the atmosphere scatters blue sunlight. The grass is green because green light is reflected and all other colors are absorbed by the chlorophyll contained in grass.

4. Why does the wind blow? Wind is the result of heating inequalities across latitude and altitude. Together, local convection and the global heat engine cause the atmospheric movement we perceive as wind.

Picture This. YOUR TURN

Seasonality

Using what you have learned from reading this chapter, match the climate diagrams with the locations given on the map. Each diagram shows temperatures for every month of the year. Hint: If temperature drops during Northern Hemisphere summer months (May through August), it is a Southern Hemisphere location. Use each climate diagram only once.

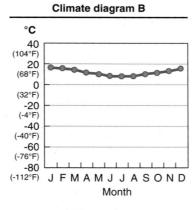

Climate diagram A

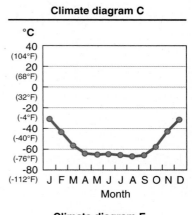

Climate diagram B

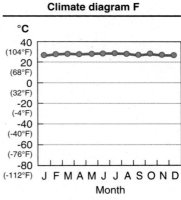

Climate diagram C

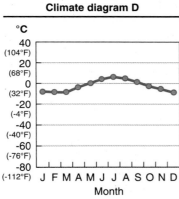

Climate diagram D

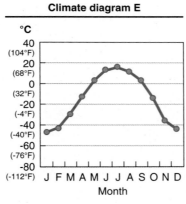

Climate diagram E

Climate diagram F

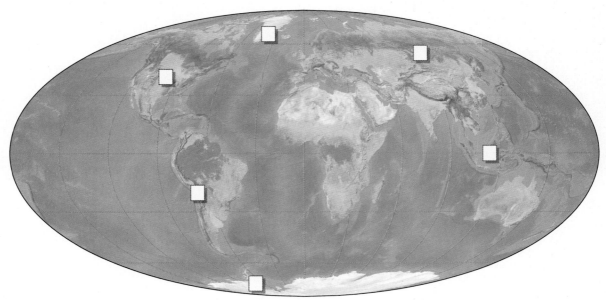

3 Water in the Atmosphere

Chapter Outline

Heavy rain falls from this cloud over the Black Sea just south of the Crimean Mountains on the Crimean Peninsula. *(Beyond/SuperStock)*

> How do hurricanes weigh trillions of tons yet remain suspended in the air?
> Why does water form on the outside of a glass containing a cold drink?
> What is fog?
> How big can hailstones get?

To learn about how precipitation forms within clouds, turn to Section 3.5.

THE BIG PICTURE *Evaporation of water from the oceans creates atmospheric humidity, clouds, and precipitation. Clouds in the atmosphere are intimately tied to Earth's climate system.*

LEARNING GOALS   *After reading this chapter, you will be able to:*

3.1 ◎ Explain what the hydrologic cycle is and why it is important.

3.2 ◎ Distinguish between the different ways of expressing atmospheric humidity and explain how each works.

3.3 ◎ Describe the role of atmospheric instability in cloud formation.

3.4 ◎ Identify and describe the major cloud types.

3.5 ◎ Name the different kinds of precipitation and explain how each forms.

3.6 ◎ Assess the interaction between cloud feedbacks and climate.

THE HUMAN SPHERE: Evaporation and the Great Lakes

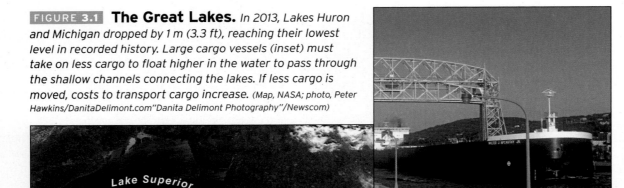

FIGURE 3.1 **The Great Lakes.** *In 2013, Lakes Huron and Michigan dropped by 1 m (3.3 ft), reaching their lowest level in recorded history. Large cargo vessels (inset) must take on less cargo to float higher in the water to pass through the shallow channels connecting the lakes. If less cargo is moved, costs to transport cargo increase.* (Map, NASA; photo, Peter Hawkins/DanitaDelimont.com"Danita Delimont Photography"/Newscom)

THE GREAT LAKES straddle the border of the United States and Canada. They hold roughly 18% of the world's surface freshwater and together form the largest system of freshwater lakes in the world. About 10% of the population of the United States and 25% of the population of Canada live in the watershed of the lakes. The Great Lakes and the St. Lawrence River (which connects the lakes to the Atlantic Ocean) support a $34 billion shipping industry. The level of the lakes remained stable over the last century—until 1998. Since then, the levels of Lake Huron and Lake Michigan have been dropping, potentially threatening the region's economy **(Figure 3.1).**

Why are the water levels of the Great Lakes dropping? The single most important factor is increased evaporation from the lakes. The lake levels represent a balance between evaporation on one hand and precipitation and resulting stream inflow on the other. If evaporation increases but precipitation and stream inflow do not, the lake levels will drop.

Ice cover is also important. According to the National Oceanic and Atmospheric Administration (NOAA), in the last 40 years, ice cover on Lake Superior has been reduced by 70% as a result of warmer water. A cover of ice decreases evaporation. With less ice, there is more evaporation. Similarly, with warmer water, there is more evaporation.

Scientists do not know if the level of the Great Lakes will continue to fall. The current drop might be part of a long-term trend reflecting climate change or a temporary fluctuation. For now, hydrologists expect the water level of the lakes to remain below the historical average into the foreseeable future as lake ice decreases and atmospheric temperatures increase.

We begin this chapter by exploring evaporation of water into the atmosphere. We then examine the different units used to express atmospheric humidity, and we explore the conditions necessary to produce clouds and precipitation. Next we describe cloud groups and precipitation types. Finally, we explore the interaction between cloud feedbacks and climate.

3.1 The Hydrologic Cycle and Water

◎ Explain what the hydrologic cycle is and why it is important.

Liquid water is heavy: it weighs 1 kg/L (8.3 lb/gal). A single small cumulus cloud, made of microscopic liquid cloud droplets, can contain millions of liters of water and weigh several hundred metric tons. Hurricanes are much larger and weigh trillions of metric tons. How does such weight defy gravity and remain suspended in the atmosphere? The answer to this question lies in the ability of water to shift between the three states, or phases, of matter: solid, liquid, and gas at temperatures found on Earth's surface.

> How do hurricanes weigh trillions of tons yet remain suspended in the air?*

States of Water: Solid, Liquid, and Gas

Water shifts between solid, liquid, and gaseous states through melting, evaporation, condensation, and freezing. **Evaporation** is the change in the state of water from liquid to water vapor (a gas), and **condensation** is the change in state from water vapor to liquid water **(Figure 3.2)**. When liquid water evaporates, it is mixed into the atmosphere as water vapor. Through evaporation, the Sun's energy lifts trillions of tons of water into the atmosphere, water molecule by water molecule. That

water vapor condenses into liquid cloud droplets, which are kept suspended in the atmosphere by updrafts of air. The resulting liquid water then falls back to Earth as precipitation. **Precipitation** is solid or liquid water that falls from the atmosphere to the ground.

Two additional state changes, which skip the liquid state of water entirely, are possible. During *sublimation*, ice shifts directly to water vapor. During *deposition*, water vapor forms ice directly.

FIGURE 3.2 **State changes in water.**

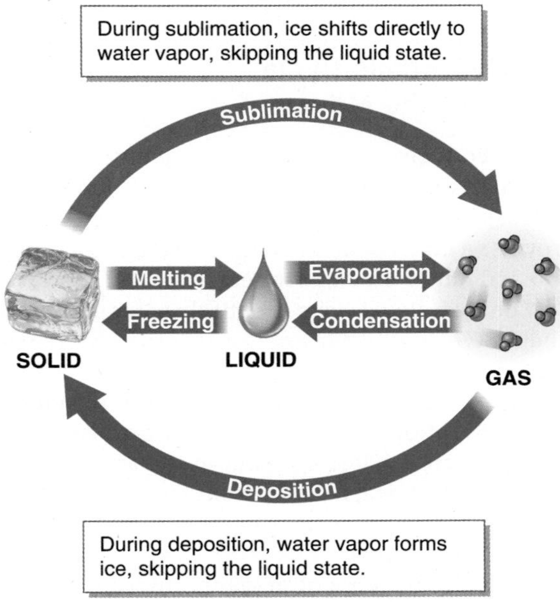

During sublimation, ice shifts directly to water vapor, skipping the liquid state.

Sublimation

Melting   Evaporation

Freezing   Condensation

SOLID   LIQUID   GAS

Deposition

During deposition, water vapor forms ice, skipping the liquid state.

evaporation
A change in the state of water from liquid to gas.

condensation
A change in the state of water from gas to liquid.

precipitation
Solid or liquid water that falls from the atmosphere to the ground.

*Answers to the Living Physical Geography questions are found on page 123.

FIGURE 3.3 **GEO-GRAPHIC:** **The hydrologic cycle.** *Water cycles between solid, liquid, and gaseous states and among all of Earth's physical systems through the hydrologic cycle.*

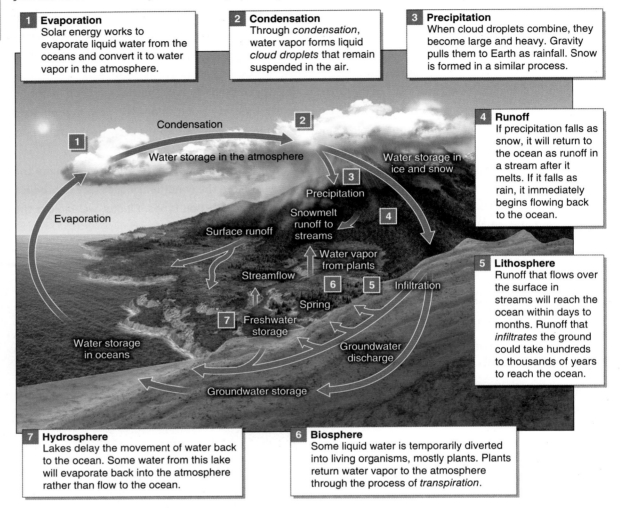

1 Evaporation
Solar energy works to evaporate liquid water from the oceans and convert it to water vapor in the atmosphere.

2 Condensation
Through *condensation*, water vapor forms liquid *cloud droplets* that remain suspended in the air.

3 Precipitation
When cloud droplets combine, they become large and heavy. Gravity pulls them to Earth as rainfall. Snow is formed in a similar process.

4 Runoff
If precipitation falls as snow, it will return to the ocean as runoff in a stream after it melts. If it falls as rain, it immediately begins flowing back to the ocean.

5 Lithosphere
Runoff that flows over the surface in streams will reach the ocean within days to months. Runoff that *infiltrates* the ground could take hundreds to thousands of years to reach the ocean.

7 Hydrosphere
Lakes delay the movement of water back to the ocean. Some water from this lake will evaporate back into the atmosphere rather than flow to the ocean.

6 Biosphere
Some liquid water is temporarily diverted into living organisms, mostly plants. Plants return water vapor to the atmosphere through the process of *transpiration*.

hydrologic cycle
The movement of water within the atmosphere, biosphere, lithosphere, and hydrosphere.

transpiration
The loss of water to the atmosphere by plants.

hydrogen bond
The bond between water molecules that results from the attraction between one water molecule's positive end and another's negative end.

FIGURE 3.4

A water molecule.

A water molecule consists of two hydrogen atoms covalently bonded to one oxygen atom. The oxygen side of the molecule has a weak negative charge, while the hydrogen side has a weak positive charge. These electrical charges create polarity for the water molecule.

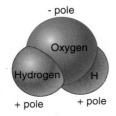

The Hydrologic Cycle: Water on the Move

The **hydrologic cycle** is the movement of water within the atmosphere, biosphere, lithosphere, and hydrosphere **(Figure 3.3)**. The hydrologic cycle provides a larger context for the movement of water into and out of the atmosphere.

The hydrologic cycle is entirely solar powered. About 30% of all solar energy absorbed by Earth goes to work in evaporating water from Earth's surface. **Evaporation from the oceans provides about 85% of the water vapor in the atmosphere. Transpiration**, the loss of water to the atmosphere by plants, and evaporation from surface streams and lakes account for the remaining 15% of atmospheric water vapor.

Globally, the amount of water entering the atmosphere is equal to the amount leaving it. Over land, however, precipitation exceeds evaporation.

Conversely, across most of the surface of the oceans, evaporation exceeds precipitation. The water removed from the oceans through evaporation is returned to the oceans by stream runoff from the continents or by rainfall directly on the oceans.

Properties of Water

Water readily shifts between its three states or phases at temperatures commonly found in the lower atmosphere. What are the properties of water that allow it to do this?

Water molecules are formed by the *covalent* bonding of hydrogen and oxygen atoms, as illustrated in **Figure 3.4**. Individual water molecules attach to one another because of their electrical *polarity*: The hydrogen end of a water molecule has a weak positive charge, and its oxygen end has a weak negative charge. One water molecule's positive end attaches to another water molecule's negative end, forming a **hydrogen bond**. The covalent bonds holding the atoms together to form a water molecule are far stronger than the hydrogen bonds that join water molecules.

The state of water depends on the number of hydrogen bonds in it. Ice has more hydrogen bonds than liquid water or water vapor. The hydrogen bonds in ice create a six-sided hexagonal lattice, in which each molecule is locked firmly to its neighbor. The hydrogen bonds in liquid water are weaker, and they continually form and break. Water vapor has few or no hydrogen bonds, and the water molecules move freely about (see Figure GT.7).

Water molecules join to other water molecules through *cohesion* (by means of hydrogen bonds), and water molecules join to other objects through *adhesion*. Cohesion is only one of the properties of water that are central to its roles in so many physical processes on Earth (Figure 3.5).

Latent Heat of Water: Portable Solar Energy

Water changes its state when energy is either added to or removed from water molecules. We learned in Section 2.2 that 1 calorie of energy raises 1 g of liquid water 1°C. So it makes sense that if we had 1 g of water (1 cm³ or 1 ml), and we added 1 calorie to it, the temperature of the water would rise from 98°C to 99°C. We could add one more calorie, and the temperature would rise to 100°C (212°F, water's boiling temperature at sea level). The water would begin boiling and vaporizing.

Logically, our next calorie of energy should raise the temperature of our gram of boiling water to 101°C. But that is not what happens. When we add one more calorie, the temperature of the water remains at

---

FIGURE 3.5 **GEO-GRAPHIC: Properties of water.** *(Ice, Copyright by kajophotography.com/Flickr RF/ Getty Images; map, NASA/JPL; rivers, Jim Wark; leaves, Don Johnston/Getty Images)*

Density
In most materials, the solid state is denser than the liquid state. When water freezes to a solid, however, it is less dense than liquid water. As a result, ice floats. If ice became more dense than liquid water, it would sink in liquid water and melt more slowly. As a result, bodies of water in cold regions would be perpetually frozen solid.

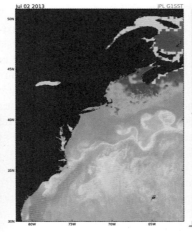

Specific Heat
Water has a high specific heat, meaning that it retains a large amount of heat compared with most other materials (see Section 2.3). The oceans strongly moderate coastal temperatures and the global climate system because of their specific heat properties.

The Universal Solvent
Water is known as the universal solvent. Almost anything can dissolve in it. Shown here is the confluence of the Milk and Missouri rivers in Montana. The Milk River carries high concentrations of dissolved and suspended materials. This property of water is essential for weathering and for carrying nutrients to plants.

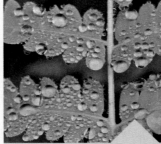

Cohesion
Water is attracted to itself through cohesion because of its electrical polarity. The wax on this leaf has no electrical charge, so water is able to form a bead as it "sticks" to itself rather than to the leaf. Water's cohesive and capillary (wicking) properties are necessary for the formation of precipitation. Cohesion allows plants on land to take up water through their tissues against the pull of gravity.

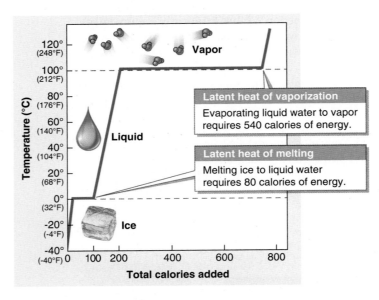

FIGURE 3.6 **Latent heat changes the state of water.** *The red line shows the number of calories that must be added to 1 g of water to change its state.*

100°C. If we continue to add calories, the water temperature still remains at 100°C. These calories absorbed by the water are referred to as latent heat. **Latent heat** is the energy that is absorbed or released during a change in the state of a substance, such as the evaporation or condensation of water.

In all, the state change of liquid water at 100°C to water vapor at 101°C requires 541 calories of energy. Five hundred and forty calories are required to vaporize the water, and 1 calorie is required to raise the water vapor temperature from 100° to 101°C. Those 540 calories work to break the hydrogen bonds in liquid water—to change its state—rather than to raise its temperature. The 1 calorie added that causes a change in temperature is referred to as *sensible heat*. Sensible heat changes the rate of kinetic molecular movement; latent heat does not.

The energy used to melt ice is called the *latent heat of melting*. Only 0.5 calorie of sensible heat is required to raise the temperature of ice 1°C because ice has a lower specific heat than liquid water. The energy used to vaporize liquid is called the *latent heat of vaporization* **(Figure 3.6)**. Similarly, as water vapor condenses, it must release its stored latent heat as *latent heat of condensation*.

Yet water's temperature does not have to be raised to 100°C for it to evaporate. We can prove

latent heat
Energy that is absorbed or released during a change in the state of a substance, such as during evaporation or condensation of water.

this by spraying a warm summer sidewalk with a garden hose. The water will not boil, but it will quickly evaporate. Even after winter rainstorms when it is cold outside, puddles on the streets and sidewalks evaporate.

When a photon of solar energy is absorbed by an individual water molecule at the surface of a body of water, the molecule may obtain enough energy to break the hydrogen bonds with its neighbors and evaporate. The energy involved in this process is called the *latent heat of evaporation*. This evaporation process occurs in natural outdoor settings with temperatures well under 100°C. Boiling, in contrast, occurs when the water temperature is 100°C, as in a pot of water on the stove or a natural hot spring.

Depending on the temperature of the water, the amount of energy required to evaporate it varies from about 540 calories to 600 calories per gram of water. In other words, it takes more calories to evaporate water at temperatures below 100°C **(Figure 3.7)**.

Evaporation is a cooling process. As we have just seen, up to 600 calories per gram of water are absorbed from the environment during the process of evaporation. Thus the temperature of the surrounding environment drops as heat is absorbed by water molecules. Your body feels cooler when your sweat evaporates on a hot summer day because it takes up to 600 calories of heat to evaporate 1 g of sweat. Many, but not all, of those calories come

FIGURE 3.7 **Water's states and calories.**
State changes in water require the addition or removal of latent heat. When water changes its state, heat is either absorbed or released to the environment.

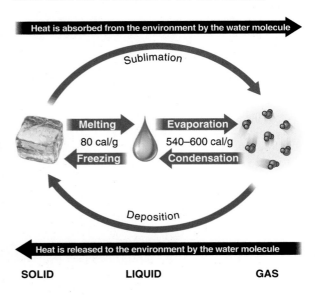

from your body. (Note that the calories we are using for these measurements are not the same as the calories used to measure the energy content of food, which are given in *kilocalories* or *kcal*. One kilocalorie is equal to 1,000 calories.)

Condensation is a warming process. About 600 calories of latent heat per gram of water are released to the surrounding environment as water vapor becomes liquid water.

Evaporation and condensation are always occurring at the same time in Earth's lower atmosphere and surface waters. When evaporation exceeds condensation, *net evaporation* is occurring, and the air is cloud free. When condensation exceeds evaporation, *net condensation* is occurring, and clouds form. Net condensation occurs when air has reached **saturation**: that is, the point at which the air's water vapor content is equal to the air's water vapor capacity.

3.2 Atmospheric Humidity

◎ Distinguish between the different ways of expressing atmospheric humidity and explain how each works.

Humidity is the amount of water vapor in the atmosphere. Only water vapor contributes to humidity. Condensation and precipitation lower humidity because they remove water vapor from the atmosphere.

As we have seen, evaporation from the oceans accounts for most of the water vapor in the atmosphere. The most humid air is found in the tropics near warm oceans, where evaporation rates are high **(Figure 3.8)**. In tropical rainforests, however, most of the humidity comes from transpiration by plants, not evaporation. Together, evaporation and transpiration create a single process of moving water to the atmosphere, called **evapotranspiration**.

Hygrometers of several types are used to measure humidity. *Sling psychrometers*, for example, are large, hand-held instruments that measure humidity using thermometers. Human hair is also used to measure humidity. Humidity changes the length of a hair, and its length can be calibrated to give a precise humidity value. Electronic sensors measure humidity by measuring electrical conductivity across a metal plate. They are used in radiosondes (weather balloons) because they are small, light, and can track rapid changes in humidity. Radiosondes transmit these data in real time to a ground-based receiving station. Finally, satellites remotely sense humidity in the atmosphere from high above Earth. They have the advantage of providing continuous and hemispheric coverage.

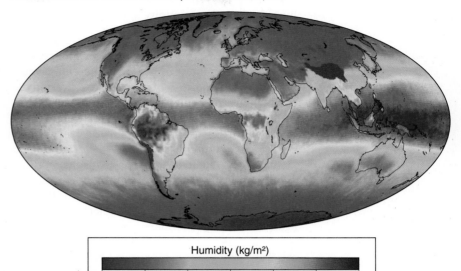

FIGURE 3.8 **Global pattern of humidity.** *This map shows the average water vapor content of the atmosphere for 2009, in weight of water (in kg) for a 1 m² column of air extending from Earth's surface to the top of the atmosphere. The tropics are most humid. Polar regions and deserts, such as the Sahara, have the lowest humidity.* (ESA DUE GlobVapour)

Humidity (kg/m²)

0   10   20   30   40   50   60

The Heat-Index Temperature

As the saying goes, "It's not the heat, it's the humidity." Heat waves are usually associated only with high temperatures, but high humidity also plays an important role in the effects of heat waves on people. As we saw in Section 2.2, the *heat-index temperature* is the temperature perceived by people as a result of atmospheric humidity coupled with air temperature (see also Appendix 5). When sweat evaporates from our bodies, it carries body heat away and provides cooling relief. High atmospheric humidity slows evaporation, sometimes causing our bodies to overheat.

Heat waves are the number one meteorological killer in the United States: Each year, about 400 people lose their lives because of heat waves. When a heat wave gripped the Chicago and Milwaukee areas in 1995, over 750 people died. In August 2003, as many as 70,000 people died in Europe as a result of exceptionally high heat-index temperatures there. In France nearly 15,000 people died as heat-index temperatures reached as high as 41°C (104°F). Again in 2010 and 2012, record-setting heat gripped the United States and Europe. According to the Intergovernmental Panel on Climate Change, heat waves caused by high temperatures and high humidity may become more frequent as the average temperature of the atmosphere continues to rise (see Section 6.4).

saturation
The point at which an air parcel's water vapor content is equal to its water vapor capacity.

humidity
The amount of water vapor in the atmosphere.

evapotranspiration
The combined processes of evaporation and transpiration.

hygrometer
An instrument used to measure humidity.

The Many Names for Humidity

Many different units of measure are used to express humidity. All measures of humidity gauge how much water vapor is in the air. Here we will examine four of these measures: vapor pressure, specific humidity, relative humidity, and the dew point.

Vapor Pressure

Vapor pressure expresses the water vapor content of air by the amount of pressure it creates. **Vapor pressure** is the portion of air pressure exerted exclusively by molecules of water vapor.

In Section 1.2, we learned that the weight of the atmosphere exerts 1 kg of pressure on every square centimeter (1 kg/cm² or 14.7 lb/in²) of all objects at sea level. A **millibar (mb)** is a measure of atmospheric pressure that is conceptually identical to kilograms per square centimeter. Both units refer to the force exerted by air molecules as they push against a surface. Millibars are commonly used by meteorologists and other scientists because they are finer units that can express small changes in atmospheric pressure. (A *hectopascal* or *hPa* is the metric equivalent of a millibar.)

The average weight of the atmosphere at sea level exerts 1013.25 mb of pressure, and a portion of this pressure is caused by molecules of water vapor. Imagine stuffing a water bottle into a backpack already filled with books. The extra "pressure" exerted by the water bottle in addition to the pressure exerted by the books and other items in the backpack would be equivalent to vapor pressure.

Evaporation and condensation occur continuously throughout the atmosphere, but net condensation occurs only when air is saturated. The vapor pressure at which saturation occurs, called the **saturation vapor pressure**, varies with air temperature. As shown in **Figure 3.9**, for every 10°C increase in air temperature, saturation vapor pressure approximately doubles. In other words, as air temperature increases, more water vapor must be added for saturation to occur.

Specific Humidity

Another measure of humidity evaluates the water vapor content of an air sample by mass. **Specific humidity** is the water vapor content of the atmosphere, expressed in grams of water per kilogram of air (g/kg):

$$\text{specific humidity} = \frac{\text{mass of water vapor}}{\text{mass of an air sample}}$$

If, for example, there are 10 g of water vapor in a kilogram of air, then the specific humidity is 10 g/kg. Specific humidity changes only when water vapor is added to or removed from the atmosphere. Condensation lowers specific humidity, and evaporation raises it.

vapor pressure
The portion of air pressure exerted exclusively by molecules of water vapor.

millibar (mb)
A measure of atmospheric pressure; average sea level pressure is 1013.25 mb.

saturation vapor pressure
The vapor pressure at which saturation occurs.

specific humidity
The water vapor content of the atmosphere, expressed in grams of water per kilogram of air (g/kg).

relative humidity (RH)
The ratio of water vapor content to water vapor capacity, expressed as a percentage.

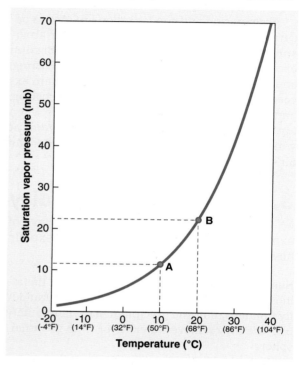

FIGURE 3.9 **Saturation vapor pressure varies with air temperature.** *The blue line shows how much water vapor must be in the air at a given temperature for saturation to occur. As the temperature increases, more water vapor must be added for saturation to occur. For example, at 10°C, the saturation vapor pressure is about 12 mb (point A), and at 20°C, the saturation vapor pressure is 24 mb (point B).*

Relative Humidity

Relative humidity is a common way of expressing humidity that you may already be familiar with. **Relative humidity (RH)** is defined as the ratio of water vapor content to water vapor capacity, expressed as a percentage.

Temperature and relative humidity are inversely related (they change in opposite directions). Warm air has a greater water vapor capacity than cold air. Therefore, if the air temperature rises, the water vapor capacity of the air also rises. In terms of its water vapor capacity, the air will have proportionally less water vapor as the temperature increases (as long as no water vapor is evaporated into the air so the level of water vapor remains constant). It may sound right to say that warm air can "hold" more water vapor than cold air—but the air is not "holding" water vapor because water vapor *is* the air. Instead, it is more accurate to say that warm air has a higher water vapor capacity.

If the temperature of air is lowered, the water vapor capacity of the air decreases. As cooling continues, the air will eventually become saturated. When air is saturated, the relative humidity is

100%. When the relative humidity is 100%, clouds and precipitation may form. **Figure 3.10** summarizes the general relationship between temperature and relative humidity graphically.

The following examples use water vapor content (expressed as vapor pressure) to illustrate quantitatively how relative humidity changes. First, we can express relative humidity using this formula:

$$\text{relative humidity} = \frac{\text{vapor pressure}}{\text{saturation vapor pressure}} \times 100$$

We will apply this relative humidity formula to an **air parcel**, defined as a body of air with uniform humidity and temperature.

Imagine a parcel of air at 30°C with a vapor pressure of 22 mb. At this temperature, the saturation vapor pressure is 42 mb (refer back to Figure 3.9). With these numbers, we can calculate the relative humidity (RH) of the air parcel:

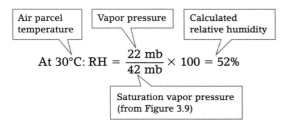

At 30°C: $\text{RH} = \dfrac{22\ \text{mb}}{42\ \text{mb}} \times 100 = 52\%$

Saturation vapor pressure (from Figure 3.9)

If we lower the temperature of the air parcel to 25°C, the relative humidity will increase:

At 25°C: $\text{RH} = \dfrac{22\ \text{mb}}{31\ \text{mb}} \times 100 = 71\%$

The saturation vapor pressure has dropped because the air parcel temperature has dropped.

At 19°C: $\text{RH} = \dfrac{22\ \text{mb}}{22\ \text{mb}} \times 100 = 100\%$

Notice that the 22 mb vapor pressure in the air parcel did not change because we did not add or remove water vapor from the atmosphere. Only the air temperature changed. **Crunch the Numbers** further explores how temperature changes the relative humidity of air.

FIGURE 3.10 **Relative humidity and temperature.** *(A) Changes in relative humidity are caused mostly by temperature changes in the atmosphere. This example illustrates how relative humidity changes from late afternoon to early morning. (B) Relative humidity is highest just as the Sun rises in the morning, when the air temperature is lowest. Note that in this example the water vapor content of the air is not changing. Only the air's capacity for water vapor is changing.*

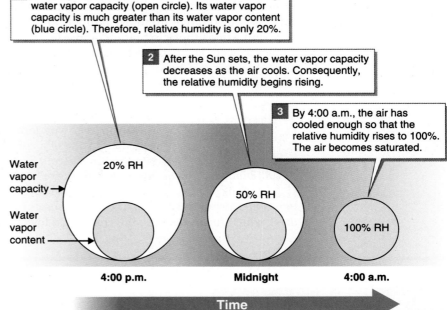

1 At 4:00 p.m., the afternoon air is warm and has a high water vapor capacity (open circle). Its water vapor capacity is much greater than its water vapor content (blue circle). Therefore, relative humidity is only 20%.

2 After the Sun sets, the water vapor capacity decreases as the air cools. Consequently, the relative humidity begins rising.

3 By 4:00 a.m., the air has cooled enough so that the relative humidity rises to 100%. The air becomes saturated.

A

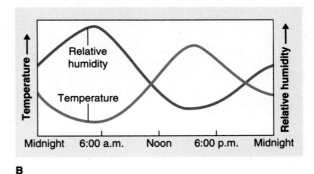

B

air parcel
A body of air of uniform humidity and temperature.

CRUNCH THE NUMBERS: Calculating Humidity

Read the description of relative humidity on pages 100-101 and use it as a guide as you work through these problems. Assume that vapor pressure does not change.

1. Calculate the relative humidity for a 20°C air parcel with a vapor pressure of 10 mb. (Hint: First use Figure 3.9 to find the saturation vapor pressure for 20°C air.)

2. Calculate the new relative humidity for that same parcel of air when the temperature rises to 30°C.

3. If the air temperature were lowered to 9°C, what would the new relative humidity be?

Polar air often has high relative humidity because it is cold. Warm tropical air also has high relative humidity because immense amounts of water are evaporated from warm tropical oceans. The high vapor pressure of tropical air creates high relative humidity even when the temperature is high, as shown in **Figure 3.11**.

Changes in vapor pressure also affect relative humidity. Increases in evaporation resulting in increases in relative humidity happen in many different atmospheric situations outside of the tropics as well. The two examples in **Picture This** show how air can become saturated by raising the vapor pressure.

> Why does water form on the outside of a glass containing a cold drink?

The Dew Point

Have you ever wondered why the outside of a container of an ice-cold beverage becomes wet? The water on the outside of the container is *condensate* (or *dew*), which forms because the cold liquid lowers

FIGURE 3.11 **Relative humidity and latitude.** *High relative humidity does not necessarily indicate humid air. It indicates, instead, how close to saturation the air is. Even very dry but very cold air can have high relative humidity.*

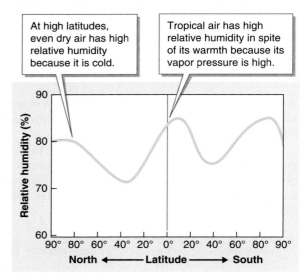

At high latitudes, even dry air has high relative humidity because it is cold.

Tropical air has high relative humidity in spite of its warmth because its vapor pressure is high.

Picture This

❶ *Evaporation fog is rising from this stream in the Sierra Nevada in California. Because the stream is warmer than the chilly early morning air, water is evaporating from the stream's surface and raising the vapor pressure to the saturation vapor pressure, resulting in condensation and visible liquid cloud droplets. (Bruce Gervais)*

❷ The same phenomenon happens on cold days when we exert ourselves physically and evaporate sweat into cold air. Evaporated water (sweat) raises the vapor pressure to the saturation vapor pressure, and a cloud forms. We are seeing liquid cloud droplets here, not water vapor. (AP Photo/Alex Brandon, File)

Saturation by Raising Vapor Pressure

Relative humidity can be increased to 100% by a rise in the vapor pressure so that it equals the saturation vapor pressure. This happens more readily when the air is cold and has a low saturation vapor pressure. Remember, water vapor is invisible. The "steam" (condensation) seen in the photos above is a cloud composed of liquid cloud droplets.

Consider This

1. Would evaporation fog continue to form if the water temperature of the stream decreased? Explain.

2. Could the cloud over the athlete's head have formed if the air were warm? Explain.

FIGURE **3.12** **Condensation and frost.** *(A) The cold water in this glass lowered the air temperature around the glass to the dew point. Consequently, liquid water condensed out of the air as a thin film of saturated air formed on the surface of the glass. (B) When the dew point is at or below freezing, deposition forms crystals of ice called hoarfrost or frost. These needles of frost accumulated on hawthorn berries in Bearsden, Scotland. They are about 1 cm (0.5 in) in length and formed in temperatures of about −5°C (23°F). (A. Bruce Gervais; B. © By Ian Miles-Flashpoint Pictures/Alamy)*

dew point
(or *dew-point temperature*)
The temperature at which air becomes saturated.

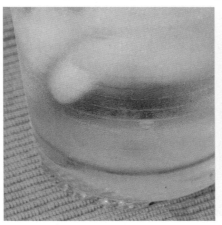

A   B

FIGURE **3.13** **North American dew points.** *This map shows lines of equal dew point in degrees Fahrenheit for May 1, 2013. It represents a common pattern of dew points for the United States and southern Canada for much of the year. The highest dew points are usually in the southeastern United States. The western interior states and provinces have lower dew points because the air is much drier.*

the temperature of the air surrounding the container to the **dew point** (or *dew-point temperature*): the temperature at which air becomes saturated (Figure 3.12).

On page 101, the air parcel we considered became saturated when its temperature was lowered to 19°C. For that parcel of air, therefore, the dew point was 19°C. The dew point is a reliable indicator of humidity because in unsaturated air, the dew point does not change as air temperature changes.

Dry air has a low dew point, and humid air has a high dew point. Once dew points are above about 20°C (70°F), the humidity becomes uncomfortable for people. Figure 3.13 shows the geographic pattern of humidity in the United States using dew points.

3.3 Lifting Air: Atmospheric Stability

◎ Describe the role of atmospheric instability in cloud formation.

As we saw in Section 1.3, the troposphere experiences strong vertical mixing. That mixing is a result of unstable air that moves higher in the atmosphere. Atmospheric instability is fundamental to many meteorological processes, and we will return to it later in this section.

Unstable air forms where warm air parcels rise on their own because they are less dense than the air surrounding them (see Figure 2.14).

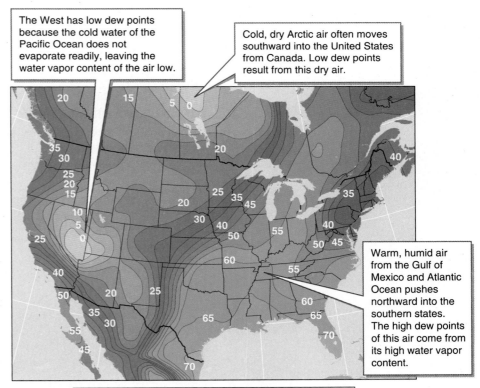

The West has low dew points because the cold water of the Pacific Ocean does not evaporate readily, leaving the water vapor content of the air low.

Cold, dry Arctic air often moves southward into the United States from Canada. Low dew points result from this dry air.

Warm, humid air from the Gulf of Mexico and Atlantic Ocean pushes northward into the southern states. The high dew points of this air come from its high water vapor content.

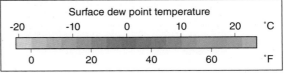

Surface dew point temperature

| -20 | -10 | 0 | 10 | 20 | °C |

| 0 | 20 | 40 | 60 | °F |

FIGURE 3.14 **A hot-air balloon festival in Albuquerque, New Mexico.** *Heating of the air inside these balloons makes it less dense than the air outside. The balloons therefore become buoyant and rise.* *(© Greg Meland/Alamy)*

Hot-air balloonists use the buoyancy of warm air to lift their balloons **(Figure 3.14)**. Uneven heating of Earth's surface by the Sun creates warm, relatively less dense parcels of air that are un-stable, like a hot-air balloon. An air parcel, how-ever, is much larger than a hot-air balloon. Unstable parcels do not mix with the surrounding air at first. Instead, they are maintained as cohesive units.

FIGURE 3.15 **Air pressure on a sealed bag.** *This sealed bag of potato chips expanded because atmospheric pressure decreased around it as it was taken from sea level to 2,130 m (7,000 ft) in elevation.* *(Bruce Gervais)*

Rising Air is Cooling Air: The Adiabatic Process

While driving upward into the mountains, you may have noticed that sealed bags of chips or flexible plastic bottles expand at higher elevations **(Figure 3.15)**. The same process that causes the air in these containers to expand acts on rising air parcels in the atmosphere.

As air parcels rise, they expand, and as they expand, they cool. In the atmosphere, air pressure decreases with height (see Section 1.2). As an air parcel rises, the air pressure outside of it decreases, and the air molecules inside of it push the parcel outward, causing it to expand. This expansion uses energy, and as a result, the temperature inside the parcel decreases. Conversely, when an air parcel descends in the atmosphere, it is compressed into a smaller volume. When an air parcel is compressed, the air temperature within it increases.

Temperature changes within air parcels result-ing from changes in their volume are called *adiabatic*

FIGURE 3.16 **Adiabatic temperature change.** *As air parcels move vertically in the atmosphere, they cool or warm because of changes in their volume. This unsaturated parcel is cooling and warming at the dry adiabatic rate of 10°C per 1,000 m.*

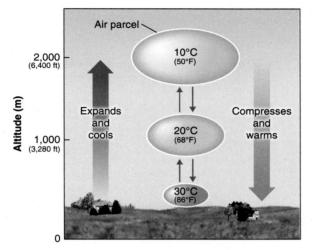

temperature changes. **Adiabatic cooling** is the cooling of an air parcel through expansion. **Adiabatic warming** is the warming of an air parcel through compression.

At what rate does the temperature of an air parcel change? The **dry adiabatic rate** is the rate of temperature change in an unsaturated parcel of air. The air temperature changes 10°C per 1,000 m (or 5.5°F per 1,000 ft) of change in altitude. That is, it will cool 10°C for every 1,000 m it rises, and it will warm 10°C for every 1,000 m it descends. Temperature changes at the dry adiabatic rate are illustrated in **Figure 3.16**.

Recall that the *environmental lapse rate*, described in Section 1.3, refers to the decrease in air temperature *outside* the air parcel as altitude increases. The average environmental lapse rate is 6.5°C per 1,000 m (or 3.6°F per 1,000 ft), but this rate varies considerably for any given location at any given time.

Forming Clouds: The Lifting Condensation Level

Net condensation in the atmosphere is almost always caused by air that is lifted and cooled to its dew point. In Section 3.2, we learned that as air temperature drops, the relative humidity increases. It follows that if an air parcel rises and cools, its relative humidity will rise. If the parcel's temperature decreases to the dew point, its relative humidity will become 100%. The air inside

the parcel will become saturated, and cloud formation will follow. The altitude at which the temperature inside the air parcel reaches the dew point is called the **lifting condensation level (LCL)**. Most clouds have flat bases because the LCL occurs at a constant altitude above Earth's surface, as shown in **Figure 3.17**.

Above the LCL, water vapor condenses into liquid cloud droplets. In Section 3.2, we learned that whenever water undergoes a change in its state, heat is either absorbed from the surrounding environment (during evaporation) or released to the surrounding environment (during condensation). Above the LCL, condensation releases latent heat, which slows the rate of adiabatic cooling to the moist adiabatic rate. The **moist adiabatic rate** is the rate of cooling in a saturated air parcel. It is usually about 6°C per 1,000 m (3.3°F per 1,000 ft). The air parcel continues to cool as it lifts and expands above the LCL, but it cools less quickly due to the release of latent heat. The moist adiabatic rate is always less than the dry adiabatic rate. How much less depends on how much condensation is occurring within the cloud and, subsequently, how much latent

adiabatic cooling
The cooling of an air parcel through expansion.

adiabatic warming
The warming of an air parcel through compression.

dry adiabatic rate
The rate of temperature change in an unsaturated parcel of air; 10°C/1,000 m (5.5°F/1,000 ft).

lifting condensation level (LCL)
The altitude at which an air parcel becomes saturated.

moist adiabatic rate
The rate of cooling in a saturated air parcel; usually about 6°C/1,000 m (3.3°F/1,000 ft).

FIGURE 3.17 **Lifting condensation level.**
Blocking of horizontal airflow and heating of air over Tinakula Island, in the Solomon Islands, creates an unstable parcel of air that rises, expands, and cools to the dew point. Air flows into the resulting cloud from its base, as shown by the orange arrow. (Michael McCoy/PhotoResearchers/Getty Images)

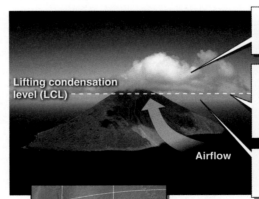

Above the LCL, air within the cloud is saturated. The air temperature is equal to the dew point.

At the LCL, the air temperature has just reached the dew point. The air has become saturated, and liquid droplets form from water vapor.

Below the LCL, air is not saturated. The air temperature is above the dew point.

stable atmosphere
A condition in which air parcels are cooler and denser than the surrounding air and will not rise unless forced to do so.

unstable atmosphere
A condition in which air parcels rise on their own because they are warmer and less dense than the surrounding air.

rain shadow
The dry, leeward side of a mountain range.

convective uplift
The rising of an air parcel that is warmer and less dense than the surrounding air.

orographic uplift
The rising of air over mountains.

heat is being released. **Figure 3.18** illustrates this shift in adiabatic rates.

Three Scenarios for Atmospheric Stability

In a **stable atmosphere**, the interior of air parcels is cooler and denser than the surrounding air. As a result, they will not rise unless forced to do so. A *conditionally unstable atmosphere* occurs where air parcels are stable while unsaturated near the ground and unstable when saturated higher up. In an **unstable atmosphere** air parcels are warmer and less dense than the surrounding air and rise on their own. These three stability scenarios are illustrated for three different air parcels in **Figure 3.19**.

In Figure 3.19, at location A, the air parcel cools at the dry adiabatic rate. The parcel is always warmer than the surrounding air and is therefore unstable. At location B, if the air parcel were to rise, it would always be cooler than the surrounding air and would be stable at all altitudes. Therefore, it will not rise higher unless it is somehow forced to do so (such as when moving over a mountain range).

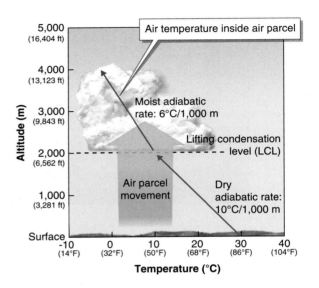

FIGURE 3.18 **Adiabatic rates.** *Starting on the ground, an unstable air parcel at 30°C rises, expands, and cools at the dry adiabatic rate of 10°C per 1,000 m. The parcel's dew point of 10°C is reached at 2,000 m (the LCL). Above 2,000 m, the air parcel is saturated and cools at a moist adiabatic rate of 6°C per 1,000 m.*

FIGURE 3.19 **GEO-GRAPHIC: Stability scenarios.** *Three air parcels at three different locations are shown here. Each parcel starts out at 30°C on the ground. The three locations have been given different environmental lapse rates to illustrate the importance of the environmental lapse rate to air parcel stability.*

Animation
Atmospheric stability
http://qrs.ly/py434cx

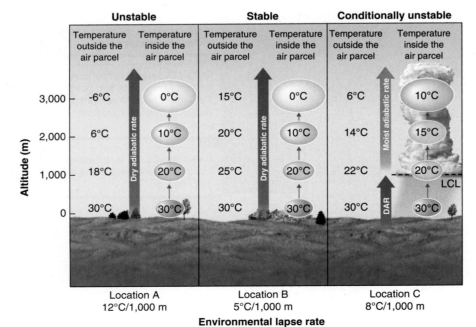

At location C, the air parcel is cooler than the surrounding air below 1,000 m and is stable. At 1,000 m, it cools to its dew point of 20°C and becomes saturated. Above 1,000 m, it cools at a moist adiabatic rate of 6°C per 1,000 m. As a result, it becomes warmer than the surrounding air and unstable at 2,000 m. This air parcel is conditionally unstable. It became unstable only when condensation released latent heat that decreased its rate of adiabatic cooling.

Just as adiabatic cooling results as an air parcel expands, adiabatic warming follows when an air parcel is compressed. As moving air meets the *windward* side of a mountain range (the side facing the prevailing wind), it is forced upward and cools adiabatically. As it flows back down the *leeward* side of the mountain (the side sheltered from the prevailing wind), it warms adiabatically. **Figure 3.20** on the facing page illustrates this process.

The leeward side of a mountain range is often warmer and drier than the windward side, because as air moves down the leeward side it compresses and warms. The leeward side of a mountain is often called a **rain shadow** due to the significantly reduced precipitation that falls there (see Figure 3.20). Arid regions can be found wherever tall mountains create a rain shadow. Hawai'i, for example, is seldom associated with aridity, but much of the island chain experiences rain-shadow aridity, as shown in **Figure 3.21** on the facing page.

FIGURE 3.20 **GEO-GRAPHIC: Latent heat release over mountain ranges.** *A parcel of air undergoes adiabatic temperature changes as it flows over a mountain range. 1. At the base of the mountain range, this air parcel's temperature is 22°C. As the parcel ascends the windward side, it expands and cools at the dry adiabatic rate (10°C/1,000 m). 2. At 1,000 m altitude, the air parcel has cooled to its dew point of 12°C. Above 1,000 m, it cools at a moist adiabatic rate of 6°C/1,000 m. 3. The parcel's temperature decreases to 0°C as it reaches the mountain peak. 4. On the leeward side, the descending parcel is compressed and warms at the dry adiabatic rate of 10°C/1,000 m. As the temperature increases, the relative humidity decreases, so the leeward side of the range is dry. 5. On the windward side, the parcel's temperature began at 22°C. At the same elevation on the leeward side, the parcel's temperature has increased to 30°C due to the release of latent heat.*

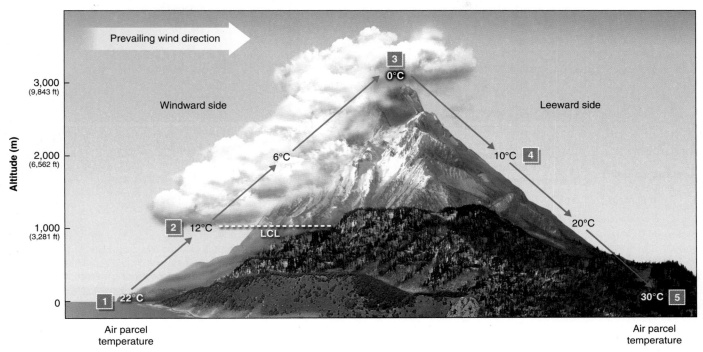

Four Ways to Lift Air and Form Clouds

As we have just seen, the lifting of air is fundamental to air saturation and cloud formation because rising air cools. **There are four ways in which air can be lifted higher in the atmosphere and cooled: convective uplift, orographic uplift, frontal uplift, and convergent uplift (Figure 3.22).**

Convective Uplift

As we saw in Section 2.5, the Sun heats Earth's surface unevenly, and Earth's surface warms the atmosphere unevenly in turn. Warmed air forms unstable air parcels, which rise (see Figure 2.14). This process is called **convective uplift**.

Orographic Uplift

Orographic uplift is the lifting of air over mountains (see Figure 3.20). Clouds formed by air moving up the windward side of mountains are called *orographic clouds*.

Frontal Uplift

In Earth's atmosphere, geographically extensive and homogeneous regions of air called *air masses*

FIGURE 3.21 **Hawai'i rain shadows.** *Most of the Hawaiian Islands experience a rain-shadow effect, as can be seen in this map of 2011 annual rainfall totals.* (Giambelluca, T.W., Q. Chen, A.G. Frazier, J.P.Price, Y.-L. Chen, P.-S. Chu, J.K. Eischeid, and D.M.Delparte, 2013: Online Rainfall Atlas of Hawai'i. Bull.Amer. Meteor. Soc. 94, 313-316, doi: 10.1175/BAMS-D-11-00228.1)

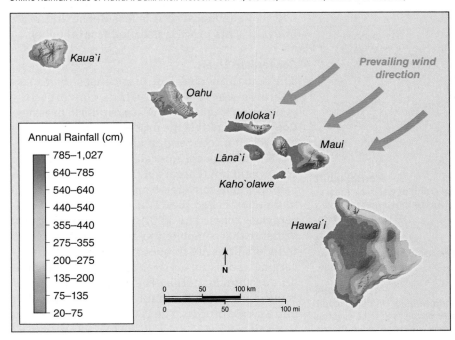

FIGURE **3.22** **Four ways to lift air.** *Air is lifted in the atmosphere through (A) convective uplift, (B) orographic uplift, (C) frontal uplift, and (D) convergent uplift.*

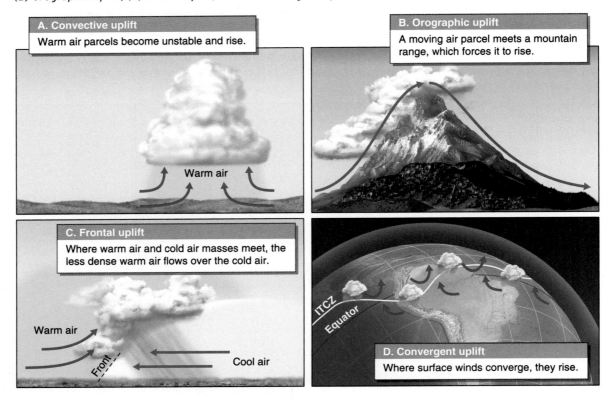

A. Convective uplift
Warm air parcels become unstable and rise.

Warm air

B. Orographic uplift
A moving air parcel meets a mountain range, which forces it to rise.

C. Frontal uplift
Where warm air and cold air masses meet, the less dense warm air flows over the cold air.

Warm air

Front

Cool air

ITCZ

Equator

D. Convergent uplift
Where surface winds converge, they rise.

(much larger than air parcels) form (see Section 5.1). Warm and cold air masses come into contact at midlatitudes, forming a transition zone, or *front*, between cold polar air and warm subtropical air. When warm and cold air masses meet, they do not mix. Instead, warm air flows over cold air because it is less dense and more buoyant. This process is called **frontal uplift**.

Convergent Uplift

The fourth mechanism that causes air to rise operates where surface winds converge in a geographic region of low atmospheric pressure. **Convergent uplift** is the process by which air rises as a result of converging airflow.

The most geographically widespread area of convergent uplift occurs in the tropics, where prevailing winds converge from the north and south in a region called the *ITCZ* (or *intertropical convergence zone*). The ITCZ forms a band of low pressure that completely encircles Earth, in which thunderstorms are frequent. Along the ITCZ, converging and rising air strengthens convective uplift and thunderstorms. Therefore, in the tropics, convective and convergent uplift blend together into a single process. The ITCZ is explored further in Section 4.3.

frontal uplift
The rising of warm air masses where they meet relatively cold air masses.

convergent uplift
The rising of air as a result of converging airflow.

cloud
An aggregation of microscopic water droplets and ice crystals suspended in the air.

3.4 Cloud Types

◎ **Identify and describe the major cloud types.**

Clouds are a wonderful addition to the beauty of nature. They delight the eye in ever-changing images of differing colors, textures, and shapes. You do not have to travel to exotic places to see clouds; they are overhead everywhere. From downtown urban areas to the most remote places on the globe, even in the most arid locations, clouds can be seen.

Cloud formation is important for many reasons. Clouds delivers freshwater to the continents in the form of precipitation, and they play other crucial roles in Earth's climate system as well. The Geographic

GEOGRAPHIC
PERSPECTIVES

Perspectives at the end of this chapter explores the relationship between clouds and climate further.

Clouds are composed of individual microscopic water droplets and ice crystals that are visible only when they are grouped together in large numbers. These particles are so light that they remain suspended by updrafts (vertical airflow).

Cloud Classification

The cloud classification scheme used today was developed in 1803 by Luke Howard, an English naturalist. The World Meteorological Organization published the *International Cloud Atlas* in 1956 based on Howard's classification scheme.

Following the system that is used to name living organisms, Howard employed Latin words to create three different groups of clouds based on their appearance: *cirrus* (wispy, feathered), *cumulus* (heaped, puffy), and *stratus* (layered). A later addition was the *alto* group, which, in the context of cloud names, means "middle." **Cirrus** clouds are high clouds with a feathery appearance that are composed of ice crystals. **Cumulus** clouds are dome-shaped, bunched clouds, with a flat base and billowy upper portions that often rise high in the troposphere; that is, they show strong vertical development. **Stratus** clouds are low, flat sheets of clouds.

Nimbus (rain) is included in a cloud type name if the cloud produces precipitation. Later, Howard's system was modified to include height categories. Cloud *form* categories are also used to describe and categorize clouds. **Clouds take three basic forms: cirriform, stratiform, and cumuliform.** All clouds can be described and categorized using these terms.

Nimbostratus clouds, for example, are low-level, rain-producing sheets of clouds. **Cumulonimbus** clouds are heaped-up rain clouds capable of strong vertical development and of producing severe weather. Nimbostratus and cumulonimbus clouds produce most of the precipitation that reaches the ground. **Figure 3.23** illustrates the eleven common cloud types found within the four major cloud groups.

cirrus
A high cloud with a feathery appearance that is composed of ice crystals.

cumulus
A dome-shaped, bunched cloud, with a flat base and billowy upper portions.

stratus
A cloud type characterized by low, flat sheets of clouds.

nimbostratus
Rain-producing low-level sheets of clouds.

cumulonimbus
A cloud that extends high into the atmosphere and is capable of strong vertical development and of producing severe weather.

Cirrus

Alto

Stratus

FIGURE 3.23

GEO-GRAPHIC:
Cloud categories.
(Cirrus, © Philip & Karen Smith/ The ImageBank/Getty Images; alto, No Photo, No Life!/Flickr/ Getty Images; stratus, Mark A. Schneider/Science Source)

CLOUD GROUP	ALTITUDE	CLOUD TYPE	CLOUD FORM	DESCRIPTION
Cirrus	Above 7,000 m (23,000 ft)	Cirrus	Cirriform	Wispy, thin
		Cirrocumulus	Cirriform	Thin, bunched layer
		Cirrostratus	Cirriform	Thin sheet, produces Sun or Moon halo
		Jet contrail	Cirriform	Linear clouds produced by jet engine exhaust
Alto	2,000 to 7,000 m (6,500 to 23,000 ft)	Altocumulus	Cumuliform	Middle-level, bunched
		Altostratus	Stratiform	Sheeted, Sun is slightly visible
Stratus	Up to 2,000 m (6,500 ft)	Stratus	Stratiform	Whole sky gray, Sun obscured
		Stratocumulus	Stratiform	Low, bunched
		Nimbostratus	Stratiform	Whole sky gray, precipitating
Cumulus	2,000 to 23,000 m (6,500 to 75,000 ft)	Cumulus	Cumuliform	Fair weather, puffy
		Cumulonimbus	Cumuliform	Severe weather, heavy rain

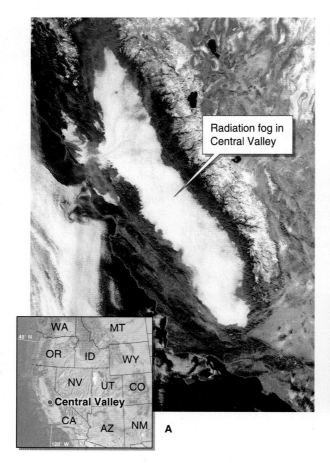

Radiation fog in
Central Valley

A

FIGURE 3.24 **Radiation fog.** *(A) This satellite image shows the Central Valley of California under an extensive blanket of radiation fog that developed as the cold valley air became saturated. Radiation fog in this region often results in car accidents on freeways due to poor visibility. (B) This radiation fog developed in Alhandra, Portugal, along the Tagus River valley. Alhandra's central church protrudes above the fog. The photo was taken at 8:00 a.m. before the warm sunlight began evaporating the fog. (A. NASA/ GSFC; B. © António Ferreira Pinto)*

B

FIGURE 3.25 **Advection fog.** *Advection fog often forms off the California coast near San Francisco as humid air moves over the cold California Current. As air moves over cold water, it is cooled to its dew point and becomes saturated, forming fog. Note that the fog hugs the ocean's surface because the cold air in which it formed is relatively dense. (Rob Kroenert/Flickr/Getty Images)*

Fog

Have you ever wondered what it would be like to walk inside a cloud? Perhaps you already have. **Fog** is a stratus cloud on or near the ground that restricts visibility to less than 1 km (0.62 mi).

| What is fog? | **All types of fog form where air at Earth's surface is cooled to the dew point.** There are many |

kinds of fog, including *orographic fog*, *freezing fog*, and *evaporation fog* (see Picture This on page 102). The two most common types are radiation fog and advection fog.

Radiation fog (or *valley fog*) is fog that results as the ground radiates its heat away at night. The cooled ground cools the air above it. If the air temperature near the ground is lowered to the dew point, net condensation (and fog) will occur **(Figure 3.24)**.

Unlike radiation fog, **advection fog** forms as moist air moves over a cold surface, such as a lake or a cold ocean current, and the air temperature is lowered to the dew point. Fog over the ocean is always advection fog. There is perhaps no better example of advection fog than that in San Francisco **(Figure 3.25)**.

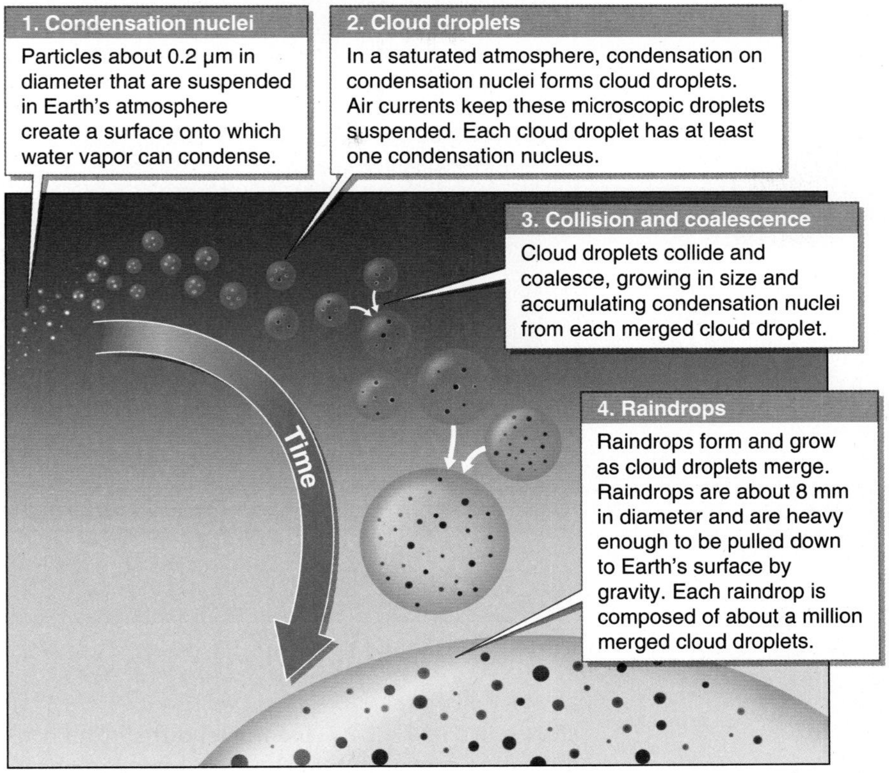

3.5 Precipitation: What Goes Up . . .

◎ **Name the different kinds of precipitation and explain how each forms.**

One of the most important aspects of clouds is their ability to bring water to Earth's continents. Without this water, life would exist only in the oceans. How does rain form and fall out of clouds?

Making Rain: Collision and Coalescence

The rain-making process starts with **condensation nuclei**: small particles, roughly 0.2 μm in diameter, that provide a surface on which water vapor can condense. Tiny bits of dust, bacteria, salt, smoke, pollen, volcanic ash, industrial pollution—all of these aerosols can act as condensation nuclei. **In saturated air, water vapor condenses onto condensation nuclei to form cloud droplets.**

Collision and coalescence, the process by which cloud droplets merge to make raindrops **(Figure 3.26)**, occurs in clouds at air temperatures of about −15°C (5°F) and warmer. When the raindrops become heavy enough, they fall to Earth. Referring back to Figure 3.5, without water's cohesive property, cloud droplets would not form or merge, and there would be no rainfall.

FIGURE 3.26 **GEO-GRAPHIC: The collision-and-coalescence process.** *A single raindrop forms from the collision and coalescence of many cloud droplets.*

1. Condensation nuclei
Particles about 0.2 μm in diameter that are suspended in Earth's atmosphere create a surface onto which water vapor can condense.

2. Cloud droplets
In a saturated atmosphere, condensation on condensation nuclei forms cloud droplets. Air currents keep these microscopic droplets suspended. Each cloud droplet has at least one condensation nucleus.

3. Collision and coalescence
Cloud droplets collide and coalesce, growing in size and accumulating condensation nuclei from each merged cloud droplet.

4. Raindrops
Raindrops form and grow as cloud droplets merge. Raindrops are about 8 mm in diameter and are heavy enough to be pulled down to Earth's surface by gravity. Each raindrop is composed of about a million merged cloud droplets.

Normally, water freezes at 0°C (32°F), but the microscopic size of a cloud droplet allows it to enter a *supercooled* state rather than freezing at 0°C. In a supercooled state, water freezes quickly as it comes into contact with a solid object on the ground. Below about −10°C (14°F), a mixture of ice crystals and supercooled droplets occurs. Below about −40°C (or −40°F), all cloud droplets freeze. Supercooled cloud droplets are essential in the process of forming snow.

Making Snow: The Ice-Crystal Process

The **ice-crystal process** (or *Bergeron process*) forms snow in clouds in which the temperature is 0°C or below. Most winter precipitation at middle and high latitudes, where clouds are typically well below freezing, results from the ice-crystal process.

The ice-crystal process is somewhat more complex and less well understood than the collision-and-coalescence process that forms raindrops. In general, there are two ways in which ice crystals grow to form snow. First, snow forms from water vapor as it is deposited directly on *ice nuclei*, as

fog
A cloud at or near ground level that reduces visibility to less than 1 km (0.62 mi).

radiation fog
(or *valley fog*) Fog that results when the ground radiates its heat away at night, cooling the air above it to the dew point.

advection fog
Fog that results from moist air moving over a cold surface, such as a lake or a cold ocean current, that lowers its temperature to the dew point.

condensation nucleus
A small particle in the atmosphere, about 0.2 μm in diameter, on which water vapor condenses.

collision and coalescence
The process by which cloud droplets merge to form raindrops.

ice-crystal process
(or *Bergeron process*) The process by which ice crystals grow within a cloud to form snow.

FIGURE **3.27** **Snow formation through deposition.** *(A) Snowflakes grow when water vapor, evaporated from supercooled cloud droplets, is deposited directly on an ice crystal, causing it to grow. (B) Snowflakes always grow as hexagons, reflecting the six-sided structure of the hydrogen bonds between water molecules (see Figure GT.7). (B. Robin Treadwell/Science Source)*

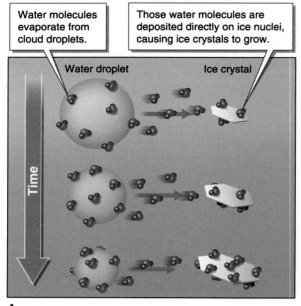

Water molecules evaporate from cloud droplets.

Those water molecules are deposited directly on ice nuclei, causing ice crystals to grow.

Water droplet   Ice crystal

Time

A

B

shown in **Figure 3.27**. Ice nuclei differ from condensation nuclei in that they are platelike or angular in shape. Salt crystals, some bacteria, and clay minerals are among the particles that can act as ice nuclei. In cold clouds, the saturation vapor pressure is slightly lower around ice crystals than it is around cloud droplets. Therefore, water vapor is deposited on an ice crystal more readily than it

condenses on a cloud droplet. The second way snow forms is through *contact freezing*, shown in **Figure 3.28**.

In *warm clouds*, the temperature is above 0°C, and the collision-and-coalescence process dominates. In *cold clouds*, the temperature is below 0°C throughout, and the ice-crystal process dominates. Clouds with a range of temperatures, and

FIGURE **3.28** **GEO-GRAPHIC: Snow formation through contact freezing.**

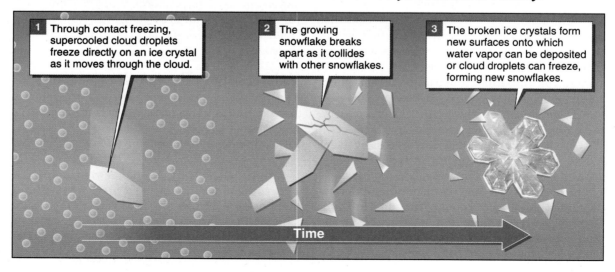

1 Through contact freezing, supercooled cloud droplets freeze directly on an ice crystal as it moves through the cloud.

2 The growing snowflake breaks apart as it collides with other snowflakes.

3 The broken ice crystals form new surfaces onto which water vapor can be deposited or cloud droplets can freeze, forming new snowflakes.

Time

in which both processes occur, are called *mixed clouds* (Figure 3.29).

Four Types of Precipitation

With the exception of hail, all types of precipitation are produced either through the collision-and-coalescence process or the ice-crystal process. Whether precipitation takes the form of rain, snow, sleet, or freezing rain depends on the *temperature profile* of the atmosphere—that is, the pattern of temperature change with altitude, as illustrated in Figure 3.30.

The world record for greatest snowfall in a single season was set on Mount Baker, in Washington State, which received 28.96 m (95 ft) in the 1998–1999 season. How was that snow depth measured? There is an established protocol for measuring snow and rain. Some of the techniques used are outlined in Figure 3.31 on page 114.

Hail Formation

Hail is formed in cumulonimbus clouds with strong vertical airflow. **Hail** consists of hard, rounded pellets of ice, called *hailstones*, that precipitate out of cumulonimbus clouds. Hailstones start as small pellets of ice called *graupel*, which form as super-cooled droplets of water freeze directly on snow

| FIGURE 3.29 | **Warm, cold, and mixed clouds.**

Cumulus clouds are warm clouds. Cirrus clouds are cold clouds. Cumulonimbus clouds are mixed clouds.

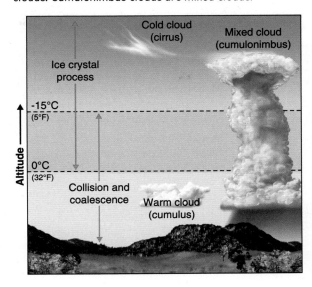

crystals. As graupel is transported through the upper parts of a cumulonimbus cloud, where the temperature is below freezing. Raindrops and cloud droplets freeze onto it and add to its mass. Updrafts keep hailstones suspended in the cloud. The longer the growing hailstone remains aloft in the cloud, the larger and heavier it will grow. Therefore, the

| FIGURE 3.30 | **Temperature profiles and precipitation.**

These four different temperature profiles at different geographic locations result in four different types of precipitation.

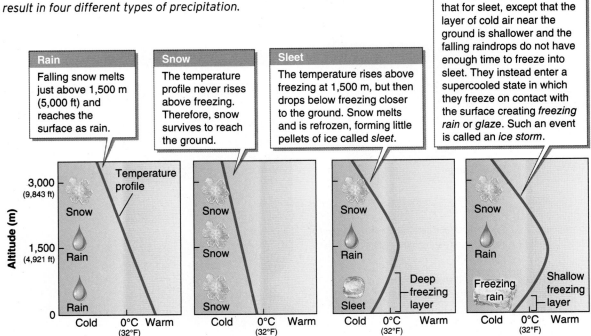

Rain
Falling snow melts just above 1,500 m (5,000 ft) and reaches the surface as rain.

Snow
The temperature profile never rises above freezing. Therefore, snow survives to reach the ground.

Sleet
The temperature rises above freezing at 1,500 m, but then drops below freezing closer to the ground. Snow melts and is refrozen, forming little pellets of ice called *sleet*.

Freezing rain
This scenario is the same as that for sleet, except that the layer of cold air near the ground is shallower and the falling raindrops do not have enough time to freeze into sleet. They instead enter a supercooled state in which they freeze on contact with the surface creating *freezing rain* or *glaze*. Such an event is called an *ice storm*.

hail
Hard, rounded pellets of ice that precipitate from cumulonimbus clouds with strong vertical airflow.

FIGURE 3.31 **SCIENTIFIC INQUIRY** How is precipitation **measured?** *Water managers must measure precipitation amounts to prepare for potential droughts or floods. Precipitation measurements are also central to understanding how climate change may be affecting precipitation. (Clockwise from top left: Photo by Ray Martin; National Weather Service Portland; AP Photo/Rich Pedroncelli; NASA/GSFC)*

Rain Gauge

How It Works
Rainfall is measured with a rain gauge. Rain falls into the cylinder, which is marked in centimeters and inches. If 1 cm of rain falls, it would cover the ground to a depth of 1 cm if it did not flow into the soil or downslope.

Automatic rain gauges use a similar principle, but weigh the amount of water rather than measuring its height. They can transmit data to receivers automatically.

Potential Problems
Rain gauges can be inaccurate in heavy wind or if they are too close to obstructions, such as buildings or trees.

How It Works
Like a rain gauge, a snow gauge captures snowfall from the air. After the snow has fallen, the chamber is heated and the melted water is measured.

Typically, the snow-water ratio is 10:1; this means that 10 cm of snow will melt into 1 cm of liquid water. But the ratio varies depending on the water content of the snow.

Potential Problems
Snow gauges suffer from inaccuracies as snow blows around and into and out of the gauge. Snow is more difficult to measure accurately and automatically than rain.

Snow Gauge

Snow Stick

How It Works
A hollow coring tube can be used to measure snow depth and take samples for analysis of water content.

Potential Problems
This technique is labor intensive. The threat of avalanches can pose a danger to field workers.

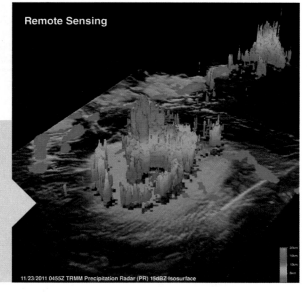

Remote Sensing

How It Works
Remote sensing techniques such as ground-based Doppler radar and satellite-based radar do not measure precipitation directly. Instead, they create precipitation estimates by examining return echoes and cloud-top temperatures.

This image shows Hurricane Kenneth on November 23, 2011, in the eastern Pacific. It is a composite image made with data from surface radar and infrared satellite sensors. The red regions show precipitation of up to 5 cm (2 in) per hour.

Potential Problems
Remote sensing precipitation estimates are less accurate than direct measurements.

11/23/2011 0455Z TRMM Precipitation Radar (PR) 15dBZ Isosurface

FIGURE 3.32 **Cumulonimbus clouds and hail.** *(A) Strong updrafts keep hailstones suspended in the cloud, allowing them to accumulate more ice. (B) This thunderstorm in the Black Rock Desert in Nevada is producing a deluge of heavy rain and hail. The hail is visible as the white curtain descending from the base of the cumulonimbus cloud. (B. George Post/Science Source)*

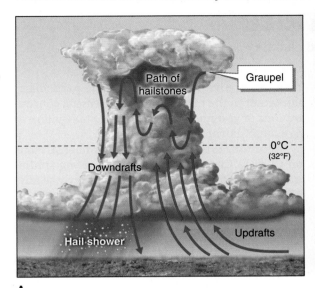

A

B

size of hailstones is related to the strength of updrafts in the cumulonimbus cloud (**Figure 3.32**).

> How big can hailstones get?

Most hailstones are less than 2 cm (0.75 in) in diameter. Sometimes, however, they are much larger. In the late afternoon of July 23, 2010, in Vivian, South Dakota, the world's largest officially recorded hailstone fell to Earth in a farm field (**Figure 3.33**). As recorded by a National Oceanic and Atmospheric Administration (NOAA) official, it measured 21.9 cm (8.63 in) in diameter—about the size of a bowling ball—and weighed 0.88 kg (1.94 lb).

Hail destroys crops and property, costing taxpayers more than a billion dollars per year. Most of this damage comes as hail pits fruits and disfigures them, making them worthless on the market, or damages young plants. Large hailstones can be deadly. Hailstones the size of tennis balls or larger fall to Earth at about 160 km/h (100 mph).

FIGURE 3.33 **World's largest hailstone.** *The world's largest officially recorded hailstone, which fell in Vivian, South Dakota, on July 23, 2010, weighed nearly 1 kg (2 lb). (NOAA)*

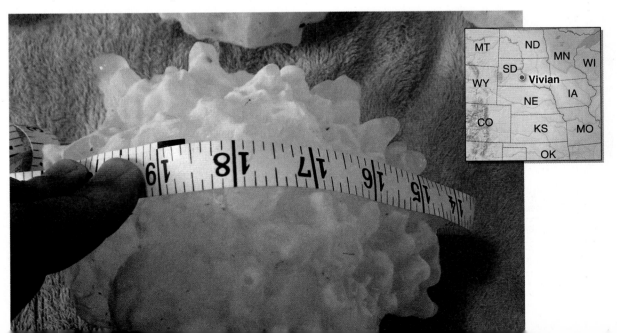

GEOGRAPHIC PERSPECTIVES
3.6 Clouds and Climate

◎ Assess the interaction between cloud feedbacks and climate.

How will Earth's climate change during our lifetimes? This is the question *climatologists*—scientists who study climate—are trying to gain a better understanding of. The better scientists understand how the climate system works, the more accurately they can predict its behavior. This is particularly important in the context of the increasing concentrations of greenhouse gases in the atmosphere as a result of burning fossil fuels.

According to the IPCC (Intergovernmental Panel on Climate Change), computer modeling studies indicate that the global temperature may rise anywhere between 2°C and 6°C (3.6°F to 10.8°F) by 2100 (see Section 6.4). These estimates represent a large range of uncertainty. Although many factors will be important in determining how much the temperature increases, the leading factors behind this uncertainty are how much CO_2 will be emitted to the atmosphere by human activity and how clouds will respond to atmospheric warming.

FIGURE 3.34 **Clouds as reflectors.** *(A) White arrows depict shortwave solar energy interacting with the cloud top. Some shortwave energy is scattered as it passes through the cloud, but most is reflected and scattered back to space. (B) This satellite image shows the albedo of the sky for the month of June 2013. A value of 100 in the color key indicates a reflectivity of 100%. Cloud-free skies, such as those over the Sahara in northern Africa, are dark blue and have low albedo values. Light blue and white areas show cloudy, reflective skies. The tropics and midlatitudes are particularly cloudy and reflective.* (A. David R. Frazier/Science Source)

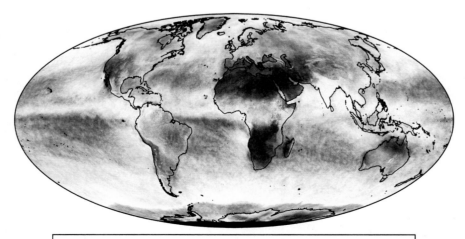

A

Clouds and Temperature

We learned in this chapter that as air temperature increases, evaporation is enhanced. Enhanced evaporation will put more water vapor into the atmosphere, and the atmosphere could become cloudier as a result. Whether or not a warmer world will be a cloudier world is uncertain, however. Higher temperatures do not always make more clouds. Both atmospheric water vapor and unstable air are necessary for cloud formation. Summer is not necessarily cloudier than winter, even though it is warmer and the specific humidity is often higher.

Temperature can change cloudiness, and cloudiness can change temperature. Clouds cool Earth's surface and atmosphere as their high-albedo surfaces reflect incoming shortwave radiation back to space. Scientists call this cooling effect *cloud albedo forcing*, meaning that reflection of insolation by clouds "forces" the temperature down. Cloud albedo forcing causes cooling, or *negative forcing* (Figure 3.34).

Clouds also warm the atmosphere by absorbing longwave energy emitted from Earth's surface. This terrestrial heat is delayed on its way back to space because it is absorbed by clouds (and by greenhouse gases) in the atmosphere, then radiated back to Earth's surface. Scientists call this effect *cloud greenhouse forcing* (Figure 3.35). Cloud greenhouse forcing causes warming, or *positive forcing*.

All clouds cause both negative forcing (cooling) and positive forcing (warming) simultaneously. How, then, would a changing climate influence cloud forcing? Scientists have not yet found the answer, but it lies somewhere in *cloud feedbacks*.

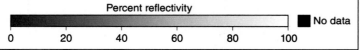

Percent reflectivity ⬛ No data

0   20   40   60   80   100

B

FIGURE 3.35 **Cloud greenhouse forcing.** *This satellite image shows outgoing longwave terrestrial radiation in watts per square meter (W/m²), averaged for March 2000. The equatorial regions shown in blue and purple are blanketed by thick clouds that reduce heat loss. Mid- and high latitudes have less heat to lose than the tropics and subtropics. (NASA image courtesy Takmeng Wongand the CERES Science Team at NASA LangleyResearch Center)*

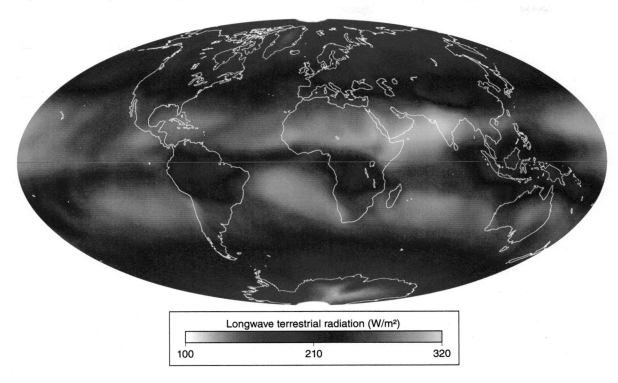

Longwave terrestrial radiation (W/m²)

| 100 | 210 | 320 |

Cloud Feedbacks

Whether clouds will accelerate the current warming trend or slow it down depends on whether they produce stabilizing or destabilizing feedbacks. *Feedbacks* are changes that cause other changes, or a cause-and-effect chain of reactions, within a system. Feedbacks are either negative or positive. A **negative feedback** is a process by which interacting parts in a system stabilize the system. A **positive feedback** is a process by which interacting parts in a system destabilize the system. Negative and positive cloud feedbacks can be summarized as follows:

Cloud Negative Feedback

1. Atmospheric warming increases the air's water vapor capacity and cloudiness.	2. Clouds reflect sunlight back to space.	3. The atmosphere cools.

Cloud negative feedbacks keep the temperature stable. Cloud positive feedbacks change the temperature. In the example given below, a cloud positive feedback causes a warming trend:

Cloud Positive Feedback

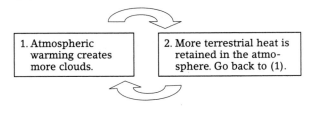

1. Atmospheric warming creates more clouds.	2. More terrestrial heat is retained in the atmosphere. Go back to (1).

Stratus Clouds

There are potentially dozens of cloud feedbacks. For example, clouds form multiple layers, ranging from low-altitude stratus to high-altitude cirrus. Each of these layers interacts differently with sunlight and heat radiating from Earth's surface.

Stratus clouds usually either produce negative forcing (cooling) or are neutral. Where they produce negative forcing, their absence can allow the Sun to heat the ground more intensely, thereby warming the air above the ground as heat is radiated off Earth's surface. In some geographic regions, stratus clouds may decrease as the temperature in the lower atmosphere increases, leading to this feedback:

negative feedback
A process in which interacting parts in a system stabilize the system.

positive feedback
A process in which interacting parts in a system destabilize the system.

**Stratus Cloud Positive Feedback—
Causes Warming Trend**

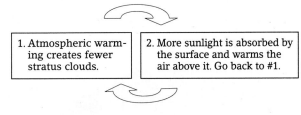

| 1. Atmospheric warming creates fewer stratus clouds. | 2. More sunlight is absorbed by the surface and warms the air above it. Go back to #1. |

Cirrus Clouds

Higher up, cirrus clouds are mostly transparent to shortwave solar energy and allow it to pass through to Earth's surface. However, they absorb longwave radiation from Earth's surface efficiently. Some research indicates that high-level cirrus clouds may increase outside the tropics in the coming decades, resulting in a positive feedback:

**Cirrus Cloud Positive Feedback—
Causes Warming Trend**

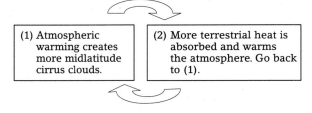

| (1) Atmospheric warming creates more midlatitude cirrus clouds. | (2) More terrestrial heat is absorbed and warms the atmosphere. Go back to (1). |

In contrast, other studies suggest that there will be fewer cirrus clouds within the tropics as the atmosphere warms. Therefore, the tropics could experience negative forcing (cooling) from cirrus clouds:

**Cirrus Cloud Negative Feedback—
Keeps Temperature in Check**

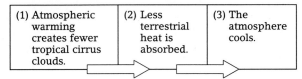

| (1) Atmospheric warming creates fewer tropical cirrus clouds. | (2) Less terrestrial heat is absorbed. | (3) The atmosphere cools. |

Currently, taken as a whole, cloud feedbacks are causing net cooling worldwide. Some scientists think that cloud negative feedbacks could significantly slow anthropogenic atmospheric warming and buy time to reduce our carbon emissions (see Section 6.4). The scientific consensus, however, is that while negative cloud feedbacks could slow anthropogenic climate change, they will not stop it. Other factors could accelerate atmospheric warming trends and lead to a destabilizing positive feedback. Given all these different possible outcomes, understanding how clouds and their feedbacks will respond to climate change is among the highest priorities and greatest challenges for climatologists.

CHAPTER 3 Exploring with ⊚ Google Earth

To complete these problems, first read the chapter. When you are finished, go to LaunchPad and open the Exploring with Google Earth file for this chapter. Click on the "Workbook Problems" folder to "fly" to each of the problems listed below and answer the questions. Be sure to keep your "Borders and Labels" layer activated. Refer to Appendix 4 if you need help using Google Earth.

PROBLEM 3.1 Activate the overlay in this folder. Florida is featured. The placemark points to a large cloud.

1. **What type of cloud is found at the placemark?**
   a. Cumulus   c. Nimbostratus
   b. Cumulonimbus   d. Altocumulus

2. **There are also many smaller clouds forming over the Florida peninsula. What type of clouds are those?**
   a. Cumulus   c. Nimbostratus
   b. Cumulonimbus   d. Altocumulus

3. **The land temperature is warming and creating warm air parcels. What type of lifting is creating these clouds?**
   a. Convective lifting
   c. Convergent lifting
   b. Frontal lifting
   d. Orographic lifting

4. **Although the information is not specifically provided, at what time of day was this image most likely captured?**
   a. Early morning after sunrise
   b. Early afternoon
   c. Late afternoon
   d. Late evening after sunset

PROBLEM 3.2 Deactivate all previous overlays and activate the overlay in this folder. This problem features the water vapor content of the atmosphere for the month of October 2012. Dark blue regions have the highest water vapor content. The dark blotches are areas of no data due to persistent cloud cover.

1. **With regard to latitude, what is the global pattern of water vapor content that you see in this overlay?**
   a. Water vapor decreases as latitude increases.
   b. Water vapor increases as latitude increases.
   c. There is no relationship between water vapor and latitude.

2. **With regard to elevation, what is the global pattern of water vapor content that you see in this overlay?**
   a. Water vapor decreases as elevation increases.
   b. Water vapor increases as elevation increases.
   c. There is no relationship between water vapor and elevation.

3. **Note that water vapor is high over central South America at the location of the placemark. What process contributes most of the water vapor at this location far away from the oceans?**
   a. Evaporation   c. Condensation
   b. Transpiration   d. Precipitation

PROBLEM 3.3 Keep the water vapor overlay from the previous problem activated. This placemark shows another area with high atmospheric water vapor content.

1. **What process contributes most of the water vapor at this location?**
   a. Evaporation   c. Condensation
   b. Transpiration   d. Precipitation

2. **What is the name of this country?**
   a. India   c. Burma
   b. Bangladesh   d. Bhutan

3. **Just a few hundred miles to the north, the air becomes much drier. What physical feature causes this change?**
   a. The Himalayas   c. The Indian Ocean
   b. The Tibetan Plateau d. The Gobi Desert

4. **Why is the water vapor content so low just a few hundred miles to the north of the placemark?**
   a. The air is colder there.   b. The air is warmer there.

PROBLEM 3.4 Deactivate all previous overlays and activate the overlay in this folder. This placemark shows a pattern of linear clouds that crisscross the image.

1. **Which cloud group do these clouds belong to?**
   a. Stratus   b. Alto   c. Cirrus   d. Cumulus

2. **How were these clouds formed?**
   a. They were formed behind mountains.
   b. They were formed by aircraft.
   c. They were formed as the ground cooled.
   d. They were formed along a front.

3. **What is the name of this specific cloud type?**
   a. Stratocumulus clouds   c. Cumulonimbus clouds
   b. Jet contrails   d. Fog

4. **What are these clouds composed of?**
   a. Water vapor
   b. Liquid cloud droplets
   c. Ice crystals
   d. A mixture of liquid and ice

5. **What is the approximate altitude of these clouds in feet?**
   a. About 6,000 feet or lower
   b. About 10,000 feet
   c. About 15,000 feet
   d. About 20,000 feet or higher

PROBLEM 3.5 Deactivate all previous overlays and activate the overlay in this folder. The placemark points to Lake Baikal in central Russia. It is the deepest (1,642 m or 5,387 ft), oldest (25 million years), and largest lake by volume in the world (holding 20% of all liquid surface freshwater). Because of its northern location, great volume, and great depth, it is a cold lake. Notice that the lake is covered with clouds in this image.

1. **What type of clouds have formed over the lake?**
   a. Fog   c. Cirrus
   b. Alto   d. Cumulus

2. Why do these clouds occur only over Lake Baikal?
a. The cold lake water has lowered the relative humidity.
b. The cold lake water has caused the air to become undersaturated.
c. The cold lake water has chilled the air to the dew point.
d. The lake is in a deep basin where evaporation exceeds precipitation.

PROBLEM 3.6 Deactivate all previous overlays and activate the overlay in this folder. This placemark is in the Yellow Sea between South Korea and China.

1. What type of clouds do you see?
a. Fog
b. Alto
c. Cirrus
d. Cumulus

2. What is another name for these clouds?
a. Nimbostratus clouds
b. Advection fog
c. Altostratus clouds
d. Radiation fog

3. Why do the clouds abruptly terminate over the Korean Peninsula?
a. The land is colder than the ocean and net condensation occurs on land.
b. The land is warmer than the ocean and net evaporation occurs on land.
c. High coastal mountains block the clouds from flowing onto the land.
d. The water becomes cold near the coast.

PROBLEM 3.7 Deactivate all previous overlays and activate the overlay in this folder. This image shows the Rio Negro in Brazil near where it enters the Amazon River in the Amazon rainforest.

1. What type of clouds are in this image?
a. Cumulus
b. Cumulonimbus
c. Stratus
d. Cirrus

2. Where did most of the water vapor at this location originate?
a. From evaporation from the oceans
b. From plant transpiration
c. From the Andes
d. From the Amazon River

CHAPTER 3 **Study Guide**

Focus Points

3.1 The Hydrologic Cycle and Water

Water in the atmosphere: About 85% of water vapor in the atmosphere originates from evaporation from the oceans. The remaining 15% comes from plant transpiration.

State changes of water: Water changes its state (solid, liquid, gas) when energy is added to or removed from water molecules. When water changes its state, hydrogen bonds linking water molecules are either formed or broken, depending on the state shift.

Evaporation and condensation: Evaporation is a cooling process because it absorbs heat from the environment. Condensation is a warming process because it releases latent heat to the environment.

Net condensation: Clouds form in environments of net condensation.

3.2 Atmospheric Humidity

Relative humidity: Changes in relative humidity happen mainly because of air temperature changes. As air cools, relative humidity rises. Saturated air has a relative humidity of 100%.

Humidity indicators: High vapor pressure, specific humidity, and dew point all indicate a high atmospheric water vapor content. Relative humidity does not reliably indicate the water vapor content of the atmosphere.

3.3 Lifting Air: Atmospheric Stability

Atmospheric stability: Lifting and cooling of air is the most common way an air parcel becomes saturated.

Lifting condensation level: Above the lifting condensation level, condensation releases latent heat and slows the rate of adiabatic cooling to the moist adiabatic rate.

Adiabatic heating and mountains: The leeward side of a mountain range is often warmer and drier than the windward side due to the release of latent heat through condensation.

Four ways to lift air: The four ways in which air is lifted are convective uplift, orographic uplift, frontal uplift, and convergent uplift.

3.4 Cloud Types

Cloud composition: Clouds are composed of suspended microscopic liquid cloud droplets and ice crystals.

Cloud forms: All clouds take one of three forms: cirriform, stratiform, or cumuliform.

Clouds that bring precipitation: Nimbostratus and cumulonimbus clouds bring precipitation. Cumulonimbus clouds can produce severe weather.

Fog: Fog forms where surface air has been cooled to the dew point. Most fog is either radiation fog or advection fog.

3.5 Precipitation: What Goes Up . . .

Condensation nuclei: Cloud droplets form around condensation nuclei (such as dust, pollen, or particulate pollution) suspended in the atmosphere.

Rain and snow: Rain is formed through collision and coalescence of cloud droplets in warm clouds. Snow is formed through the ice-crystal process in cold clouds.

Types of precipitation: The temperature profile of the atmosphere determines which form of precipitation occurs. Falling snow may become rain, sleet, or freezing rain as it falls from a cloud to the ground. Hail forms in cumulonimbus clouds.

3.6 Geographic Perspectives: Clouds and Climate Change

Clouds and temperature: Clouds affect atmospheric temperature through cloud forcings, and they are affected by atmospheric temperature in turn.

Cloud feedbacks: Clouds modify Earth's climate through numerous positive and negative feedbacks.

Key Terms

adiabatic cooling, 105
adiabatic warming, 105
advection fog, 111
air parcel, 101
cirrus, 109
cloud, 108
collision and coalescence, 111
condensation, 95
condensation nucleus, 111
convective uplift, 107
convergent uplift, 108
cumulonimbus, 109
cumulus, 109
dew point, 103
dry adiabatic rate, 105
evaporation, 95
evapotranspiration, 99
fog, 111
frontal uplift, 108
hail, 113
humidity, 99
hydrogen bond, 96
hydrologic cycle, 96

hygrometer, 99
ice-crystal process, 111
latent heat, 98
lifting condensation level (LCL), 105
millibar (mb), 100
moist adiabatic rate, 105
negative feedback, 117
nimbostratus, 109
orographic uplift, 107
positive feedback, 117
precipitation, 95
radiation fog, 111
rain shadow, 106
relative humidity, 100
saturation, 99
saturation vapor pressure, 100
specific humidity, 100
stable atmosphere, 106
stratus, 109
transpiration, 96
unstable atmosphere, 106
vapor pressure, 100

Concept Review

The Human Sphere: Evaporation and the Great Lakes

1. Why is the water level of the Great Lakes dropping, and how is this change a problem?

3.1 The Hydrologic Cycle and Water

2. What is the hydrologic cycle? Describe how water moves through it.

3. Explain how the hydrologic cycle is "solar powered."

4. In what three states does water occur? What are hydrogen bonds and how do they influence the state of water?

5. What must be added or removed from water to break or form hydrogen bonds?

6. What does it mean that water vapor has the highest internal energy state of water's states? What is the source of that energy?

7. Why is evaporation a cooling process? What is being cooled?

8. Why is condensation a warming process? What is being warmed?

9. What is atmospheric saturation? What causes air to become saturated?

3.2 Atmospheric Humidity

10. What is the heat-index temperature? How does humidity make the air feel warmer?

11. Compare specific humidity, vapor pressure, and the dew point in terms of what units each measure uses and how each can be increased or decreased.

12. What is saturation vapor pressure? How can it be increased or decreased?

13. What is relative humidity? How can it be increased or decreased?

14. Does a high relative humidity always mean that the air has a high water vapor content? Explain.

3.3 Lifting Air: Atmospheric Stability

15. What are adiabatic temperature changes and what causes them? Compare them with temperature changes caused by the environmental lapse rate.

16. Compare an unstable air parcel with a stable air parcel. What determines their stability?

17. Compare the dry adiabatic rate of cooling with the moist adiabatic rate. Why does adiabatic cooling occur at two different rates? Explain why the moist rate of cooling is less than the dry rate.

18. What is the lifting condensation level? Where is it, and what forms there?

19. Compare the windward and leeward sides of mountain ranges in terms of adiabatic temperature changes and precipitation amounts. What is a rain shadow? Why does a rain shadow form?

20. What are the four major ways air is lifted and cooled adiabatically to the dew point? Describe how each works.

21. Where, geographically, does convergent uplift mainly take place?

3.4 Cloud Types

22. What are clouds composed of? Give the four major cloud categories.

23. Which cloud type creates a thickly overcast sky with no precipitation?

24. Which clouds are composed of ice crystals? Why are they composed of ice?

25. What are jet contrails? What forms them, and where do they form?

26. Which types of clouds bring precipitation? Which types bring severe weather?

27. How do radiation fog and advection fog form? Which is more dangerous and why?

3.5 Precipitation: What Goes Up . . .

28. What are condensation nuclei and ice nuclei? For what processes are each required?

29. Compare and contrast how rain and snow form through the collision-and-coalescence and ice-crystal processes.

30. How are warm clouds, cold clouds, and mixed clouds defined? Which precipitation-forming processes occur in each?

31. What instruments are used to measure rain and snow?

32. Compare the temperature profile in the atmosphere necessary to form rain, snow, sleet, and freezing rain.

33. Which type of cloud produces hail? Explain how hail forms in this cloud.

34. What is the size of the largest hailstone ever found, and where did it fall?

3.6 Geographic Perspectives: Clouds and Climate

35. Why are clouds important to understanding how climate will change in the future?

36. How does temperature change cloudiness? How does cloudiness change temperature?

37. What is cloud greenhouse forcing? What overall effect does it have on the temperature of the lower atmosphere?

38. What is a negative feedback? Why is it a stabilizing force?

39. What is a positive feedback? Why is it a destabilizing force?

40. What is a cloud negative feedback? How does it relate to the term "negative forcing"?

41. What is a cloud positive feedback? How does it relate to the term "positive forcing"?

42. Currently, is the global cloud cover causing net positive forcing or net negative forcing?

Critical-Thinking Questions

1. If the hydrologic cycle is solar powered, does it "turn off" at night after the Sun has set?

2. Which of the four types of uplift occur where you live? What kinds of information do you need to answer this question?

3. Explain why "steam" fills the air in the bathroom during a hot shower on a cold day. What is that steam, and why does it form?

4. How can warm, humid tropical air have a lower relative humidity than cold, dry polar air?

5. Explain how fog can form over a cold pond in warm air and over a warm pond in cold air. Describe the relative temperatures of the water and air. Use any of the humidity variables you have learned in this chapter.

Test Yourself

Take this quiz to test your chapter knowledge.

1. **True or false?** When temperature goes up, relative humidity goes down.

2. **True or false?** Water cannot move through the hydrologic cycle as a gas.

3. **True or false?** Evaporation is a warming process.

4. **True or false?** When an air parcel is cooler than the surrounding air, the parcel is stable.

5. **True or false?** A positive feedback destabilizes a system.

6. **Multiple choice:** Which of the following is true when relative humidity is 100%?
   a. The air temperature and the dew point temperature are the same.
   b. Clouds and fog are likely.
   c. Vapor pressure = saturation vapor pressure.
   d. All of the above are true.

7. **Multiple choice:** Which of the following is likely to form when rain falls through a very shallow layer of freezing air near the ground?
   a. Rain   b. Hail   c. Freezing rain   d. Sleet

8. **Multiple choice:** Which of the following will not change if the water vapor content increases? (Assume that temperature does not change.)
   a. Specific humidity
   b. Dew point
   c. Relative humidity
   d. Saturation vapor pressure

9. **Fill in the blank:** The _____ process occurs in cold clouds and results in snow.

10. **Fill in the blank:** A _____ occurs on the leeward side of a mountain range and results in arid conditions there.

Picture This. YOUR TURN

Explain This Cloud

1. Which of water's three states is represented by the cloud seen here?
2. Why do we breathe out clouds on cold days?
3. What is the relative humidity inside this cloud?
4. What evidence is there that net evaporation is happening outside the cloud?

(© Enigma/Alamy)

Further Reading

1. Burt, Christopher. *Extreme Weather: A Guide and Record Book*. New York: Norton, 2007.

2. Fasullo, John T., and Kevin E. Trenberth. "A Less Cloudy Future: The Role of Subtropical Subsidence in Climate Sensitivity." *Science* 9 (2012): 792–794.

3. World Meteorological Organization. *International Cloud Atlas: Manual on the Observation of Clouds and Other Meteors*. Geneva: World Meteorological Organization, 1975.

Answers to Living Physical Geography Questions

1. **How do hurricanes weigh trillions of tons yet remain suspended in the air?** Trillions of tons of water can be suspended in the atmosphere because it exists as microscopic droplets of water and ice crystals, which individually are nearly weightless.

2. **Why does water form on the outside of a glass containing a cold drink?** The cold drink has lowered the air temperature near the container's surface to the dew point, resulting in condensation.

3. **What is fog?** Fog is a cloud with a base that touches or is close to the ground.

4. **How big can hailstones get?** The world's largest hailstone was nearly the size of a bowling ball. It fell in South Dakota in 2010.

4 Atmospheric Circulation and Wind Systems

Chapter Outline

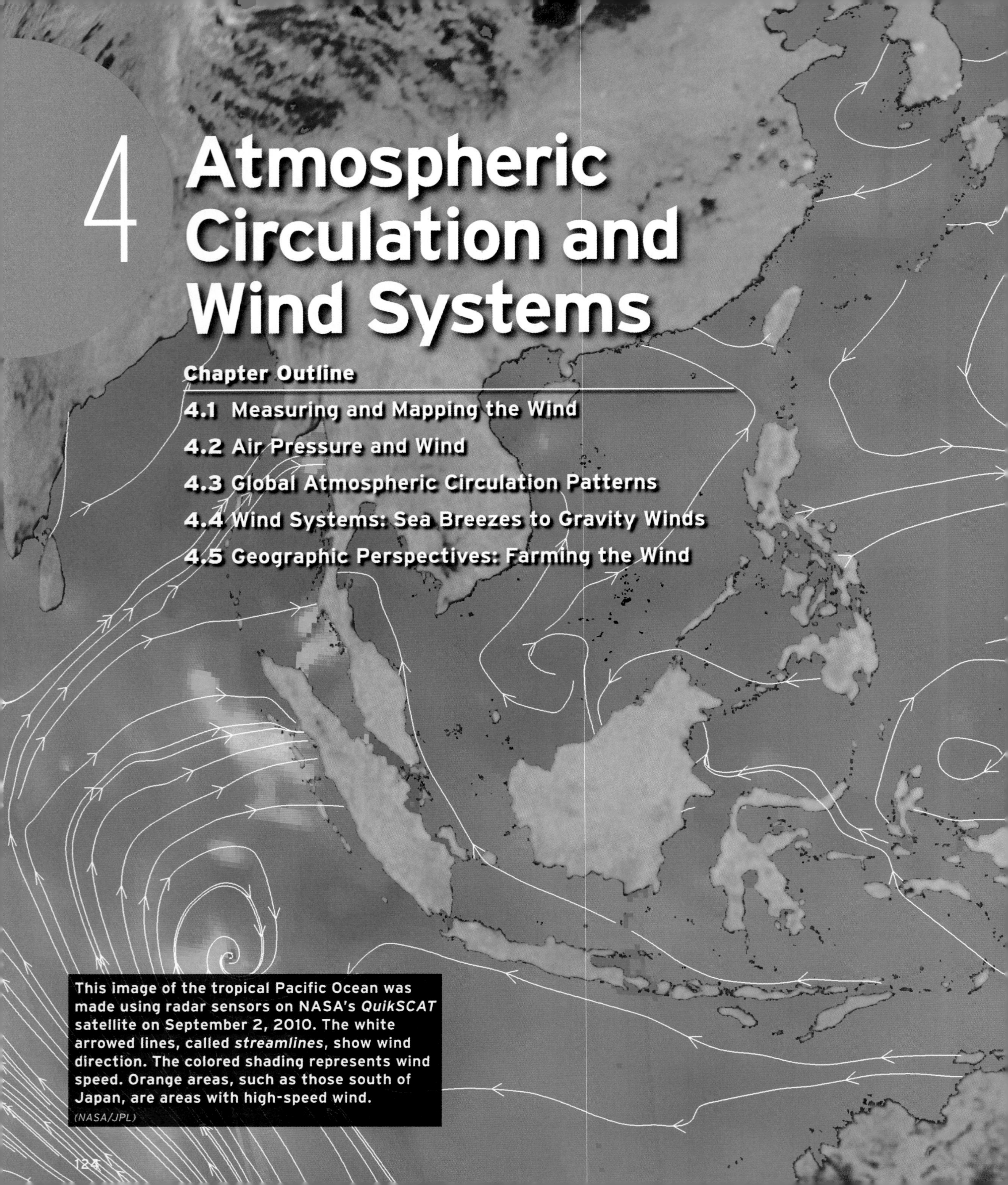

This image of the tropical Pacific Ocean was made using radar sensors on NASA's *QuikSCAT* satellite on September 2, 2010. The white arrowed lines, called *streamlines*, show wind direction. The colored shading represents wind speed. Orange areas, such as those south of Japan, are areas with high-speed wind.

(NASA/JPL)

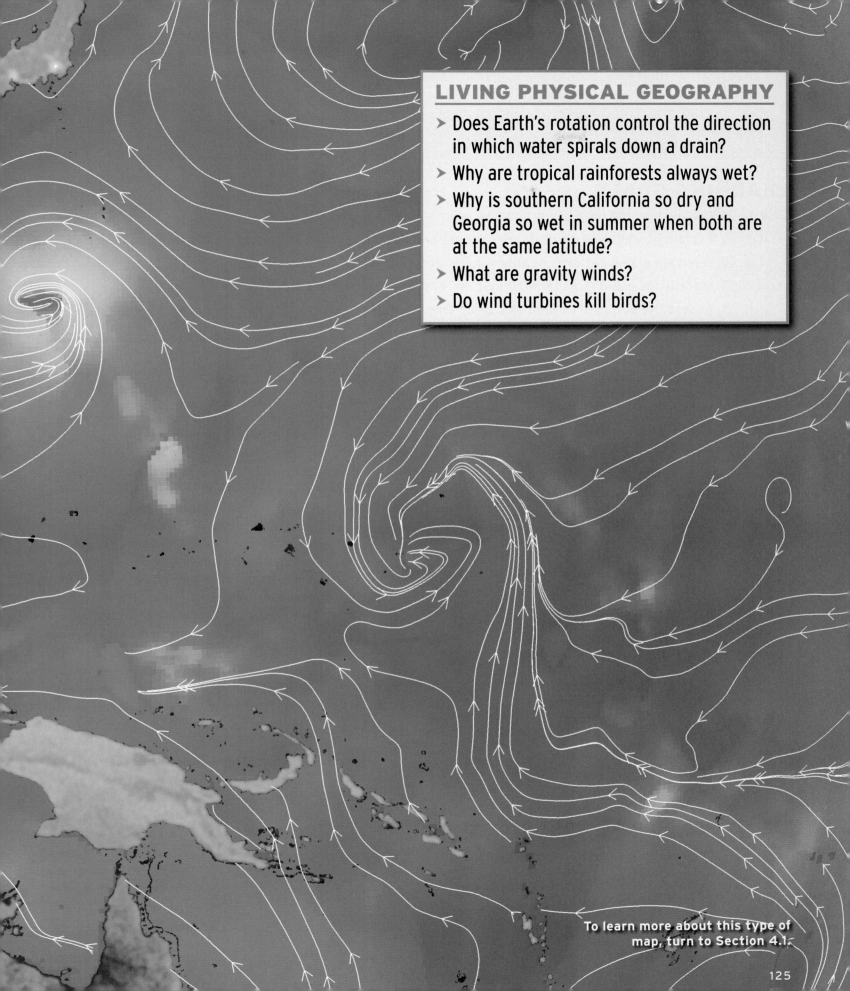

LIVING PHYSICAL GEOGRAPHY

> Does Earth's rotation control the direction in which water spirals down a drain?

> Why are tropical rainforests always wet?

> Why is southern California so dry and Georgia so wet in summer when both are at the same latitude?

> What are gravity winds?

> Do wind turbines kill birds?

To learn more about this type of map, turn to Section 4.1.

THE BIG PICTURE *The unequal heating of Earth's surface and Earth's rotation drive global wind patterns. The wind is increasingly used as a renewable energy source.*

LEARNING GOALS *After reading this chapter, you will be able to:*

4.1 ◎ Explain why the wind blows and how wind is measured and mapped.

4.2 ◎ Explain how surface air pressure changes and describe three controls on wind speed and direction.

4.3 ◎ Illustrate global patterns of atmospheric pressure, winds, and precipitation.

4.4 ◎ Identify local and regional wind systems and explain how they form.

4.5 ◎ Assess the potential of wind as a clean energy source.

THE HUMAN SPHERE: China's Dust Storms

FIGURE 4.1 **Dust storm.** *This May 2010 dust storm is approaching the town of Golmud in Qinghai Province, western China. It traveled about 1.6 km/h (1 mph) and reduced visibility to near zero, creating midnight-like conditions. (Xu Bo/ChinaFotoPress/ZUMAPRESS.com/Newscom)*

WINDBLOWN DUST is a growing problem for eastern Asia, particularly western China (Figure 4.1). About two dozen major dust storms develop each year in the western interior of China.

Chinese scientists estimate that dust storms have increased sixfold in the last four decades. Dust storms have always occurred in China, but human activity may be increasing their frequency. The process of desertification plays an important role in their formation. **Desertification** is the transformation of fertile land to desert, usually as a result of overgrazing, deforestation, or natural drought. Excessive plowing of arid lands, overgrazing by sheep and goats, and an increasing number of droughts are to blame for desertification, and thus for the growing number of dust storms, in western China.

Each year, several dust storms grow large enough to travel across the North Pacific Ocean to North America. In 2007, strong winds suspended an estimated 800,000 metric tons of dust in the air in China's Taklamakan Desert. Dust from that storm circulated twice around the Northern Hemisphere.

In this chapter, we explore how air pressure differences across Earth's surface create wind and global atmospheric circulation patterns. In the Geographic Perspectives at the end of this chapter, we assess the potential of wind to provide clean energy for the future.

Mongolia

China

Golmud, Qinghai Province

India   Myanmar (Burma)

15° N

90° E

4.1 Measuring and Mapping the Wind

◎ Explain why the wind blows and how wind is measured and mapped.

Why does the wind blow? **Wind is caused by air pressure differences that result from unequal heating of Earth's surface and from the release of latent heat in clouds.** As we learned in Chapter 2, the Sun's energy heats Earth's surface and atmosphere unequally. The tropics are heated more than the middle and high latitudes, and these differences in heating cause differences in air pressure. The outcome is the global heat engine (see Section 2.5) and atmospheric flow.

Latent heat is also an important cause of wind. As air parcels rise and cool to their dew point, water vapor condenses and releases latent heat (see Section 3.3). That latent heat warms the atmosphere and enhances atmospheric instability. As warm air rises, more air is pulled in along the ground, creating wind. Thunderstorms and hurricanes, for example, create wind in this manner.

Measuring the Wind

Wind speed is measured with an **anemometer**. Most anemometers are either cup anemometers or propeller anemometers. Both measure wind speed by the number of revolutions around a shaft per unit of time. Faster winds cause faster rotation of the shaft, which is calibrated to kilometers per hour (km/h), miles per hour (mph), meters per second (mps), or knots (kts). (A *knot* is equal to 1 nautical mile per hour, 1.86 km/h or 1.15 mph.) A **wind vane** (or *weather vane*) measures wind direction with a fin mounted on a vertical rod. The wind pushes the fin such that it always aligns with the wind. As shown in Figure 4.2, wind vanes and anemometers are often combined into a single instrument, an **aerovane**.

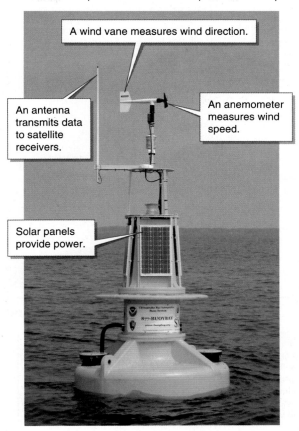

FIGURE 4.2 **Aerovane.** *This aerovane is mounted on an ocean buoy. Ocean buoys collect wind data (as well as many other types of data) with an aerovane and feed the data automatically to satellite receivers. The satellites then relay the data to land-based computers for weather reports and analysis.* (NOAA)

A wind vane measures wind direction.

An antenna transmits data to satellite receivers.

An anemometer measures wind speed.

Solar panels provide power.

The *Beaufort wind force scale* (or *Beaufort scale*) has long been used to rank wind speeds. The Beaufort scale is based on wind's observed effects on objects, rather than on directly measured wind speeds (Table 4.1).

desertification
The transformation of fertile land to desert, usually by overgrazing of livestock, deforestation, or natural drought.

anemometer
(pronounced an-eh-MOM-eter) An instrument used to measure wind speed.

wind vane
(or *weather vane*) An instrument used to measure wind direction.

aerovane
A combination of an anemometer and a wind vane; measures wind speed and direction.

TABLE 4.1	The Beaufort Wind Force Scale				
WIND FORCE	**DESCRIPTION**	**WIND'S EFFECT**	**WIND SPEED IN KM/H (MPH)**		
0-1	Calm	Smoke rises straight up	0-5.5	(0-3)
2-3	Light breeze	Leaves rustle and wind vane moves slightly	5.6-19	(4-12)
4-5	Moderate breeze	Loose paper blows around	20-38	(13-24)
6-7	Strong breeze	Open umbrellas are hard to hold and flip over	39-61	(25-38)
8-9	Gale	Walking against the wind is extremely difficult	62-88	(39-54)
10-11	Storm (whole gale)	Trees are uprooted	89-117	(55-73)
≥ 12	Hurricane force	Widespread damage	> 117	(> 73)

FIGURE 4.3 **GEO-GRAPHIC: Naming and mapping winds.** *(A) There are three basic categories of wind names: (1) names using compass or degree headings, (2) names in relation to water and land in coastal areas, and (3) names based on the prevailing direction of wind. (B) Wind barbs, wind vectors, and streamlines show the wind's speed and direction on a map. (Part A photo, Bruce Gervais; Part B photo, Remote Sensing Systems; maps, NASA/JPL)*

A. Naming the wind

Compass and degree headings

Winds are named by the direction they blow from. A south wind can also be called a 180° wind. Zero degrees represents calm conditions.

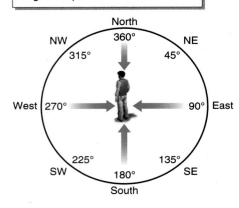

Onshore and offshore winds

Coastal winds are named by their direction in relation to sea and land.

Onshore winds blow from the sea onto the shore.

Offshore winds blow from the shore onto the sea.

The prevailing wind

The prevailing wind comes most frequently from a certain direction over a defined period.

A wind rose displays prevailing wind direction using a compass heading. This wind rose shows the prevailing wind direction is from the northwest.

These pines are flagged (windswept) by the prevailing wind.

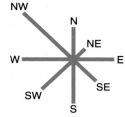

B. Mapping the wind

Wind barbs

The lengths and shapes of the flags on wind barbs specify wind speed. These barbs are also color-coded to portray wind speed. This map shows Hurricane Rita passing between Florida and Cuba in September 2005. The fastest wind speeds, shown in red and orange, were near the center of the storm.

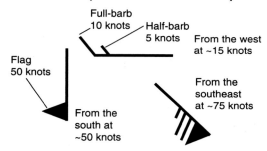

Wind barb description in the Northern Hemisphere

Full-barb 10 knots
Half-barb 5 knots
From the west at ~15 knots

Flag 50 knots
From the south at ~50 knots

From the southeast at ~75 knots

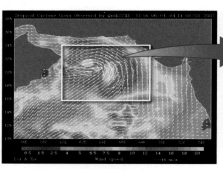

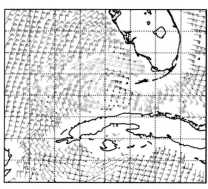

Wind vectors

Wind vectors are disconnected arrows that show the direction and speed of the wind. The wind vector length and background color indicate wind speed. This map shows Cyclone Gonu in the Indian Ocean in September 2007.

Streamlines

Streamlines use continuous lines with arrows indicating wind direction. Wind speed is shown by background coloration. Yellow and orange areas have the highest wind speeds.

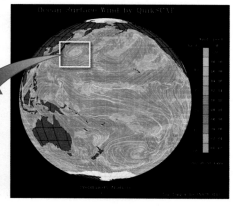

Mapping the Wind

Once wind measurements have been taken, the data can be portrayed in several ways. Winds are named by their direction of flow. For example, a **prevailing wind** is the direction the wind blows most frequently during a specified window of time. An **onshore wind** is a coastal wind that flows from sea to land. In contrast, an **offshore wind** is a coastal wind that flows from land to sea, as illustrated in Figure 4.3.

4.2 Air Pressure and Wind

◎ **Explain how surface air pressure changes and describe three controls on wind speed and direction.**

In Section 1.2, we learned that the higher a person travels in elevation, the less atmospheric pressure there is. Mountain climbers refer to pressures below 356 mb (found at about 8,000 m or 26,000 ft elevation) as the "death zone" because oxygen levels are too low for human survival. **Barometers** are instruments used to measure air pressure. For that reason, air pressure is also called *barometric pressure*. For extreme mountain climbers, having an accurate barometer can be a matter of life or death. As shown in Figure 4.4, there are two types of barometers: mercury barometers and aneroid barometers.

In this section, we examine differences in air pressure across geographic space. These horizontal differences in pressure are much more subtle than vertical differences. They are important, however, because even the slightest horizontal differences cause the wind to blow. Meteorologists identify two types of air pressure, categorized by the cause of pressure change: thermal pressure and dynamic pressure.

Thermal Pressure

Thermal pressure is air pressure caused by temperature. Warm air is associated with low pressure, and cold air is associated with high pressure. When the temperature of air is increased, its kinetic energy (rate of molecular movement) increases. Therefore, the air expands, which gives it a lower molecular density and lowers atmospheric pressure. Conversely, when the temperature of air is decreased, molecular movement decreases. As a result, the density of air molecules increases, and so does the air pressure.

prevailing wind
The direction the wind blows most frequently during a specified window of time.

onshore wind
A coastal wind flowing from sea to land.

offshore wind
A coastal wind flowing from land to sea.

barometer
An instrument used to measure air pressure.

thermal pressure
Air pressure resulting from changes in temperature.

FIGURE 4.4 SCIENTIFIC INQUIRY:

How is air pressure measured?

Meteorological reports and forecasting rely on measurements of air pressure. Generally, high pressure is associated with fair weather, and low pressure is associated with stormy weather.

How It Works

1. Mercury is poured into a glass tube with one open end. The tube is tipped into a *cistern*, where some of the mercury collects. The weight of the mercury creates a partial vacuum in the tube.

2. Air pressure exerts force downward (and in all other directions), pushing the mercury up into the tube.

3. The tube is marked in centimeters and inches. As pressure changes, the height of the mercury column changes accordingly. At sea level, the mercury will be pushed 76 cm (29.92 in) up the glass tube, on average.

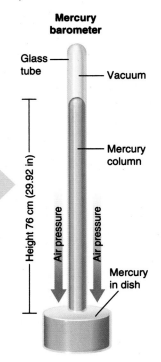

How It Works

1. Air is partially removed from a sealed, expandable metal chamber (called an *aneroid cell*).

2. When pressure is high, the chamber contracts. When pressure is low, the chamber expands.

3. The needle attached to the chamber is calibrated to provide accurate readings of the volume changes in the chamber. Aneroid barometers usually give pressure in millibars. Average pressure at sea level is 1,013.25 mb (or 1 kg/cm^2 or 14.7 lb/in^2; see Section 1.2).

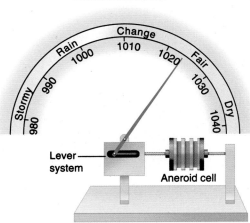

Air molecules can be compared to a crowd of people standing together. With their arms at their sides, they can stand close together, and many people can fit into a given space (a situation comparable to cool, dense air and thermal high pressure). When the people are active (doing jumping jacks or some other physical movement), they must stand farther apart, and they require more space (a situation comparable to warmer, less dense air and thermal low pressure).

Dynamic Pressure

Dynamic pressure is pressure caused by air movement. **The relationship between air temperature and air pressure is not constant because dynamic pressure can override thermal pressure.** Air flows in Earth's atmosphere because of thermal pressure gradients. Yet once the air is set in motion, dynamic pressure changes happen. Where air piles up on itself and compresses, it creates high pressure. Likewise, where airflow accelerates, the air "stretches," its molecular density decreases, and it creates low pressure. These changes in pressure occur mainly where air flows vertically in the atmosphere, as well as upwind and downwind of mountain ranges.

Wind Speed and Direction

Whether thermal or dynamic, air pressure differences across geographic space drive the wind. But why are some winds hurricane-force, while others are gentle breezes? Why do some winds spiral, while other travel in straight lines? **There are three forces that control wind speed and direction: pressure-gradient force, Coriolis force, and friction force.**

Pressure-Gradient Force

When horizontal differences in pressure occur across a region, a **pressure-gradient force** is created. The *pressure gradient* is the change in air pressure across Earth's surface. **The pressure gradient is the most important factor in setting the atmosphere in motion and determining wind speed and direction.** Without a pressure gradient, there is no wind.

Figure 4.5 illustrates the pressure-gradient concept using bicycle tires as an example. **Air flows from regions of high pressure to regions of low pressure.** The greater the pressure gradient between the bicycle tire and the outside air—the more the tube is inflated—the faster air will flow out of the tube. As long as the nozzle is open, the air will keep moving out of the tube until there is no more pressure gradient between the tube and the outside air.

Although horizontal pressure changes on Earth's surface are far more subtle, we can similarly envision the atmosphere's molecular density as higher in some regions and lower in others **(Figure 4.6)**. As in the bicycle tire, air will flow from regions of relatively high molecular density and high pressure into regions of relatively low molecular density and

FIGURE 4.5 **Bicycle tire air pressure.** *In a bicycle tire's inner tube, air molecules are packed together at a high density, and the air pressure inside the tube is high. When the tube's nozzle is opened or the tube is punctured, air molecules rush out of this high-pressure environment into the low-pressure environment of the surrounding air.*

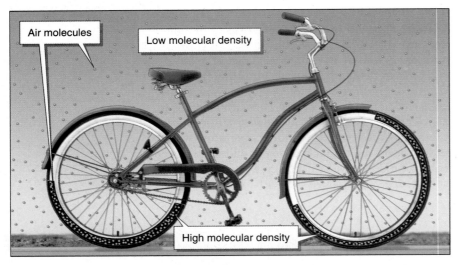

Air molecules
Low molecular density
High molecular density

FIGURE 4.6 **How a pressure gradient creates wind.** *(A) The molecules of air in this geographic region are distributed uniformly. No pressure gradient exists. Therefore, there is no wind. (B) The air molecules decrease in density across this geographic region from left to right. The horizontal pressure gradient runs from areas of high density to areas of low density. The air molecules will move down this pressure gradient, creating wind.*

Uniform pressure

• Uniform air pressure
• No pressure gradient
• No wind

A

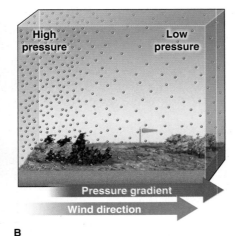

High pressure
Low pressure

Pressure gradient
Wind direction

B

low pressure. The greater the pressure difference between regions (the steeper the pressure gradient), the faster the air will flow between them. In regions where little pressure change occurs (a shallow pressure gradient), the air will move slowly.

Visualizing the Pressure Gradient: Isobars

Air pressure decreases rapidly as elevation increases. Near Earth's surface, it drops about 10 mb with each 100 m increase in elevation. Meteorologists must adjust for elevation differences when comparing surface pressures between geographic regions. *Station pressure* is barometric pressure that has not been adjusted to sea level. **Sea-level pressure** is barometric pressure that has been adjusted to sea level. The weather maps we see almost always show sea-level pressure. **Figure 4.7** illustrates how station pressure is adjusted to sea-level pressure.

FIGURE 4.8 **Visualizing isobars.**

(A) In this scenario, atmospheric pressure (molecular density) decreases across a region from left to right. Air pressure is quantified using a barometer, and a partition is drawn for every four millibars of pressure change. (B) When the top three-dimensional image is transferred onto a flat two-dimensional map, the partitions become lines of equal pressure, or isobars. Air pressure at location 1 is between the 1016 mb and 1020 mb isobars. Location 2 is on the 1012 mb isobar. Therefore, the pressure gradient runs from location 1 to location 2.

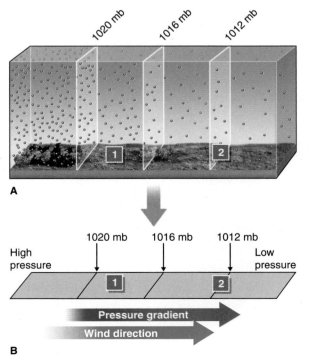

A

1020 mb   1016 mb   1012 mb

High pressure

1020 mb   1016 mb   1012 mb

Low pressure

1   2

Pressure gradient

Wind direction

B

FIGURE 4.7 **Station pressure and sea-level pressure.** *When the effects of elevation are factored in for these two stations, they have the same sea-level pressure, and there is no pressure gradient between them.*

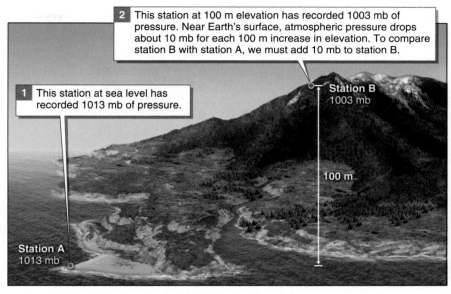

2 This station at 100 m elevation has recorded 1003 mb of pressure. Near Earth's surface, atmospheric pressure drops about 10 mb for each 100 m increase in elevation. To compare station B with station A, we must add 10 mb to station B.

1 This station at sea level has recorded 1013 mb of pressure.

Station B
1003 mb

100 m

Station A
1013 mb

Pressure reading = 1013 mb
Correction =   0 mb
_____
Corrected value = 1013 mb

Pressure reading = 1003 mb
Correction =   +10 mb
_____
Corrected value = 1013 mb

Once station pressure readings have been converted to sea-level pressure, sea-level pressure gradients can be mapped using isobars. An **isobar** is a line drawn on a map connecting points of equal pressure. Isobars are quantitative representations of the changing molecular density of the air over a geographic region **(Figure 4.8)**. The **Crunch the Numbers** feature asks you to calculate the average air pressure for high-elevation cities such as Denver, Colorado.

CRUNCH THE NUMBERS:
Calculate Denver's Station Pressure

Using the rate of decreasing barometric pressure given above (10 mb per 100 m), calculate the approximate average station pressure in millibars for Denver, Colorado, located at 1,609 m. To do this, first divide the elevation in meters by 100. Then convert the product to millibars by multiplying by 10. Once you have that number, subtract your answer from the average sea-level pressure, 1013 mb, to get Denver's average station pressure. Round to the nearest whole number.

dynamic pressure
Air pressure caused by air movement.

pressure-gradient force
The force resulting from changes in barometric pressure across Earth's surface.

sea-level pressure
Air pressure that has been adjusted to sea level.

isobar
A line drawn on a map connecting points of equal pressure. Isobars are quantitative representations of the changing molecular density of the air over a geographic region.

FIGURE 4.9 **Effects of pressure-gradient force on wind direction and speed.** *The wind blows in a direction perpendicular to the isobars, from areas of high pressure to areas of low pressure. Widely spaced isobars show a weak pressure gradient and slow wind (left arrow). Closely spaced isobars show a steep pressure gradient and fast wind (right arrow).*

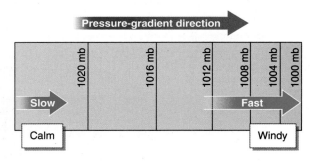

Isobars are the most important means of mapping horizontal pressure differences in Earth's atmosphere. There are two key points to remember about isobars **(Figure 4.9)**: (1) The pressure gradient runs perpendicular (90 degrees) to isobars. (2) Where isobars are close together, the wind blows fast because the pressure gradient is steep. Where isobars are far apart, there is little or no wind because the pressure gradient is shallow.

Coriolis Force

Earth's rotation creates Coriolis force, which causes objects that travel great distances to follow curved paths rather than straight lines.

Animation
Coriolis force
http://qrs.ly/7i434ed

FIGURE 4.10 **Coriolis force.** *The arrow traces the path of a flying object. (A) On a non-rotating Earth, objects would travel in straight lines over Earth's surface. (B) On a rotating Earth, objects still travel in straight lines, but Earth rotates beneath them.*

Coriolis force
(or *Coriolis effect*) The perceived deflection of moving objects in relation to Earth's surface.

boundary layer
The layer of the atmosphere where wind is slowed by friction with Earth's surface; extends about 1 km (3,280 ft) above the surface.

cyclone
A meteorological system in which air flows toward a low-pressure region, creating counterclockwise circulation in the Northern Hemisphere and clockwise circulation in the Southern Hemisphere.

anticyclone
A meteorological system in which air flows away from a high-pressure region, creating clockwise circulation in the Northern Hemisphere and counterclockwise circulation in the Southern Hemisphere.

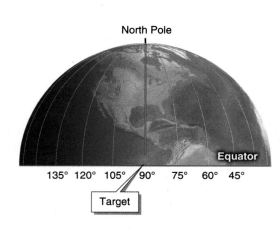
A. Non-rotating Earth

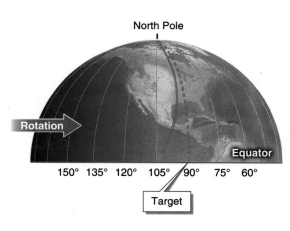
B. Rotating Earth

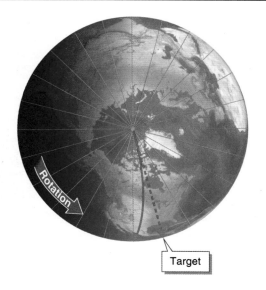

Coriolis force (or *Coriolis effect*) is the perceived deflection of moving objects in relation to Earth's surface. This deflecting effect is named after the French scientist Gaspard-Gustave de Coriolis (1792–1843). It causes a perceived deflection in the direction of flowing fluids, such as wind and ocean currents, and of flying objects traveling long distances, such as airplanes and missiles, relative to Earth's surface (Figure 4.10).

In the Northern Hemisphere, moving objects veer to the right because of Coriolis force. In the Southern Hemisphere, they veer to the left. The direction of travel does not affect the direction of deflection. Coriolis force is greatest at high latitudes, less at middle latitudes, and absent within about 5° north and south of the equator. Figure 4.11 illustrates the effect of Coriolis force on wind direction in relation to isobars.

> Does Earth's rotation control the direction in which water spirals down a drain?*

Large geographic distances are required for Coriolis force to have a significant effect. So water spiraling down the drain in a sink is not deflected by Coriolis force, because the distance of only centimeters is insufficient for deflection to occur.

Friction Force

As air flows down a pressure gradient, it is slowed by frictional drag near Earth's uneven surface. As friction slows the wind, Coriolis force deflects the wind less. Mountains, forests, buildings, and even ocean waves all slow the wind.

The **boundary layer**—the area of the atmosphere where wind is slowed by friction with Earth's surface—generally extends about 1,000 m (3,280 ft) above the surface. Above the boundary layer, the wind moves more quickly. The height of the boundary layer varies across Earth's surface. For example, the oceans have a relatively smooth surface, and the boundary layer extends only a few hundred meters above the water.

Cyclones and Anticyclones

Together, the three controls on wind speed and direction—pressure-gradient force, Coriolis force, and friction force—create rotating meteorological systems called cyclones and anticyclones. A **cyclone** is a system in which air flows toward a low-pressure region of the atmosphere, creating counterclockwise circulation in the Northern Hemisphere and clockwise circulation in the Southern Hemisphere. An **anticyclone** is a system in which air flows away from a high-pressure region, creating clockwise circulation in the Northern Hemisphere and counterclockwise circulation in the Southern Hemisphere. These systems are shown in detail in Figure 4.12.

FIGURE 4.11 **Effects of Coriolis force on wind direction.**
As wind flows down the pressure gradient, Coriolis force deflects it to the right in the Northern Hemisphere.
Arrows show the wind direction resulting from the pressure-gradient force and Coriolis force. Slow winds (left arrow) are deflected to the right less than fast winds (right arrow).

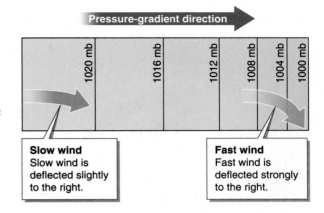

Pressure-gradient direction

1020 mb | 1016 mb | 1012 mb | 1008 mb | 1004 mb | 1000 mb

Slow wind
Slow wind is deflected slightly to the right.

Fast wind
Fast wind is deflected strongly to the right.

FIGURE 4.12 **GEO-GRAPHIC: Cyclones and anticyclones.**
Together, the three controls on wind speed and direction create rotating meteorological systems.

1. Wind direction without Coriolis force

The isobars show the pressure gradient. The red arrows show the direction in which the wind would blow if there were no Coriolis force.

Low

High

2. Wind direction with Coriolis force

The Coriolis force (green arrows) deflects the wind to the right of the pressure gradient (red arrows). The heavy blue lines show the direction of the wind as a result of the pressure gradient and the Coriolis force acting together.

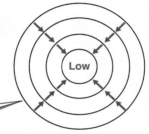

Coriolis force

Pressure gradient

Low
1004 mb
1008 mb
1012 mb

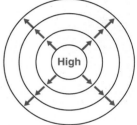

Coriolis force

Pressure gradient

High
1020 mb
1016 mb
1012 mb

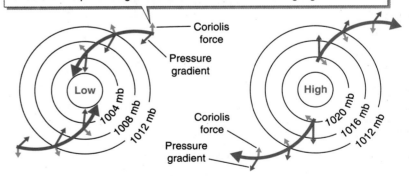

Divergence | Convergence

Rising air | Sinking air

Convergence | Divergence

L | H

Cyclone | **Anticyclone**

3. Cyclones and anticyclones in the Northern Hemisphere

Cyclones and anticyclones are three-dimensional systems. In a cyclone, air flows into the center, then rises in a central column and diverges higher up. In an anticyclone, air sinks in a central column, then diverges at Earth's surface.

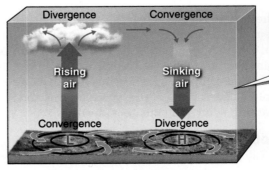

FIGURE 4.13 **Cyclones.** *Midlatitude cyclones and tropical cyclones (or hurricanes) both develop counterclockwise rotation in the Northern Hemisphere as air flows toward an area of low pressure (as shown by the arrows). (A) A satellite image of a midlatitude cyclone over Lake Michigan on September 26, 2011. (B) On August 25, 2011, Hurricane Irene was a tropical cyclone just off the coast of Florida. It later struck several states to the north, including North Carolina and New York. (NASA)*

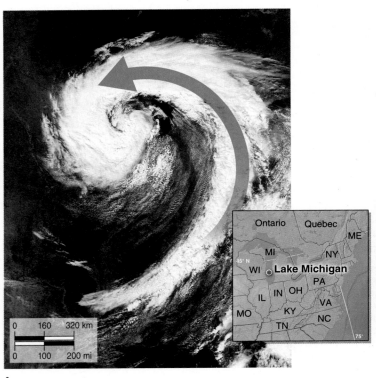

A

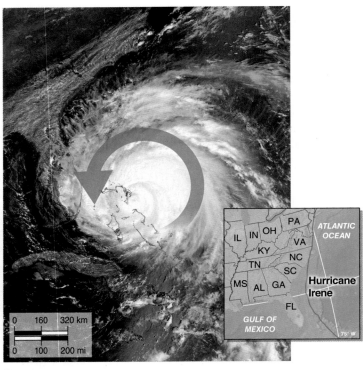

B

Cyclones are particularly important meteorological systems because most storms are cyclonic systems and they are sometimes destructive **(Figure 4.13)**. Storms are covered in greater detail in Chapter 5.

4.3 Global Atmospheric Circulation Patterns

◎ **Illustrate global patterns of atmospheric pressure, winds, and precipitation.**

When Earth is viewed from space, there does not seem to be a geographic pattern to the distribution of clouds and cloud-free skies. But on careful examination, a global geographic pattern of cloudiness and aridity begins to emerge. This section explores Earth's major pressure patterns and the resulting wind and climate patterns.

Global Pressure Systems

Earth's global pressure systems are the ITCZ, the subtropical high, the subpolar low, and the polar high. In the tropics, intense sunlight heats land and ocean surfaces during the day. As we saw in Section 2.1, that heating is strongest at the subsolar point. The heated surfaces, in turn, heat the air above them, creating a global band of unstable, buoyant air parcels that roughly tracks the migration of the subsolar point. This band, which is called the **ITCZ**, or *intertropical convergence zone*, results in thunderstorms and heavy precipitation (see Section 3.3).

The unstable air of the ITCZ rises as far as the tropopause (the base of the stratosphere). Because of the temperature inversion in the stratosphere, rising air parcels become stable at about 16,000 m (52,500 ft) in altitude as they encounter warm air at the tropopause (see Section 1.3). Thus the ascending air begins moving poleward because it cannot move into the stratosphere.

As the air moves poleward, Coriolis force causes the air to deflect eastward. This causes the wind to slow down and pile up. As a result, some of the air is redirected downward to Earth's surface at about 30° latitude.

As the air descends at 30° latitude, it is compressed and warmed adiabatically (see Section 3.3). This compression creates an area of high dynamic

ITCZ
(or *intertropical convergence zone*) A global band of unstable, buoyant air parcels that tracks the migration of the subsolar point.

subtropical high
A discontinuous belt of aridity and high pressure made up of anticyclones roughly centered on 30° north and south latitude.

subpolar low
A belt of low pressure roughly centered on 60° north and south and made up of cyclonic systems that bring frequent precipitation.

polar high
An area of cold, dense air at each pole that forms a zone of thermal high pressure.

pressure called the **subtropical high**, a discontinuous zone of high pressure and aridity made up of anticyclones roughly centered on 30° north and south latitude.

The **subpolar low** is a discontinuous band of low pressure, centered on 60° north and south, made up of cyclonic systems that bring frequent precipitation due to frontal lifting (see Section 3.3). The cold and dense air at each pole forms an area of thermal high pressure called the **polar high**. The dry air of the polar high creates polar deserts. This global pattern of pressure systems is illustrated in **Figure 4.14**.

FIGURE 4.14 GEO-GRAPHIC: Idealized pressure systems. *This illustration shows an idealized portrait of Earth's global pressure systems. The effects of Coriolis force are excluded to simplify the diagram. Pressure systems in the Southern Hemisphere mirror those of the Northern Hemisphere shown here. Only the subtropical high of the Southern Hemisphere is visible in this view.*

Animation
Global Pressure
http://qrs.ly/dz434ef

3. Subpolar low
• At about 60° north and south, warm surface winds from midlatitudes (*the westerlies*) encounter cold winds from the poles (*the polar easterlies*).
• In the process of frontal lifting, the warm air moves over the cold air, stretching the air and creating dynamic low pressure.
• The rising air cools and condenses, forming precipitation.

4. Polar high
• Bitter cold air forms thermal high pressure at the poles.
• The air is dense and heavy. It moves equatorward toward the subpolar low.
• Cold air has low humidity, so precipitation is low.

2. Subtropical high
• Heated air from the ITCZ travels poleward and descends at about 30° latitude.
• As it sinks, it compresses, forming dynamic high pressure.
• As it sinks, it also warms adiabatically. Its relative humidity decreases as it warms.
• Relative humidity is low and rainfall is low in the subtropical high.

1. ITCZ
• Near the equator, air is heated and rises. The rising air forms thermal low pressure.
• The rising air cools and condenses, creating heavy rainfall.

Polar high
Subpolar low
Subtropical high
ITCZ
Subtropical high

PRESSURE ZONE	TYPE OF PRESSURE	APPROX. LOCATION	CLIMATE
1. ITCZ	Thermal low	Tropical	Warm and rainy
2. Subtropical high	Dynamic high	30° north and south	Warm and dry
3. Subpolar low	Dynamic low	60° north and south	Cold and snowy
4. Polar high	Thermal high	90° north and south	Very cold and dry

Global Surface Wind Patterns

trade winds
Easterly surface winds found between the ITCZ and the subtropical high, between 0° and 30° north and south latitude.

doldrums
A low-wind region near the equator, associated with the ITCZ.

horse latitudes
The low-wind regions centered on 30° north and south.

Earth's major surface wind patterns result from the pressure systems we have just described. Coriolis force also plays a key role in the direction surface winds travel. **The trade winds are the most geographically extensive and consistent winds on Earth's surface.** Trade winds form because Coriolis force deflects air flowing from the subtropics to the equator westward, as shown in **Figure 4.15**. Trade winds are easterly surface winds found between the ITCZ and the subtropical high. Early trade between Europe and Africa and the Americas was made possible by these winds, and their name

is derived from this history. In the Northern Hemisphere, they are called the *northeasterly trade winds*. In the Southern Hemisphere, they are the *southeasterly trade winds*. As the trade winds travel to the equator from the subtropical high, they form a circulation loop called a *Hadley cell*.

The **doldrums** are a low-wind region near the equator associated with the ITCZ, where the trade winds meet. This region is generally not windy because air is rising upward rather than flowing horizontally. "The doldrums" is a reference to the lack of useful wind to move sailing ships to their destinations. The **horse latitudes** are a low-wind

Picture This

(© George Steinmetz/Corbis)

The Empty Quarter

The Empty Quarter, or *Rub' al Khali*, of the southeastern Arabian Peninsula, is located between 16° and 23° north latitude. It is Earth's largest sand desert. It covers nearly 650,000 km² (250,000 mi²) and stretches from Saudi Arabia into Yemen, Oman, and the United Arab Emirates. Some sand dunes rise 250 m (820 ft) above the surrounding desert floor. (Notice the Range Rover in the middle right foreground for scale.) The sand dunes are estimated to have been active for over a million years. Between 9,000 and 6,000 years ago, the climate of the region was wetter, and many permanent lakes formed. Large amounts of sand were deposited in these lakes. Subsequently, increased aridity due to natural climate change dried the lakes, and the sand in them was freed, forming the migrating dunes that we see today.

Consider This

1. Based on what you have learned in this chapter up to this point, explain why the Empty Quarter is so arid.

2. What do you think happened to the strength and position of the subtropical high in this region about 9,000 to 6,000 years ago? Explain.

FIGURE 4.15 **GEO-GRAPHIC: Global wind patterns.** *The global pattern of winds is determined by the global pressure systems and Coriolis force. Winds in the Southern Hemisphere mirror those of the Northern Hemisphere. Only the southeasterly trade winds are shown here for the Southern Hemisphere.*

Animation
Global wind
http://qrs.ly/ik434ej

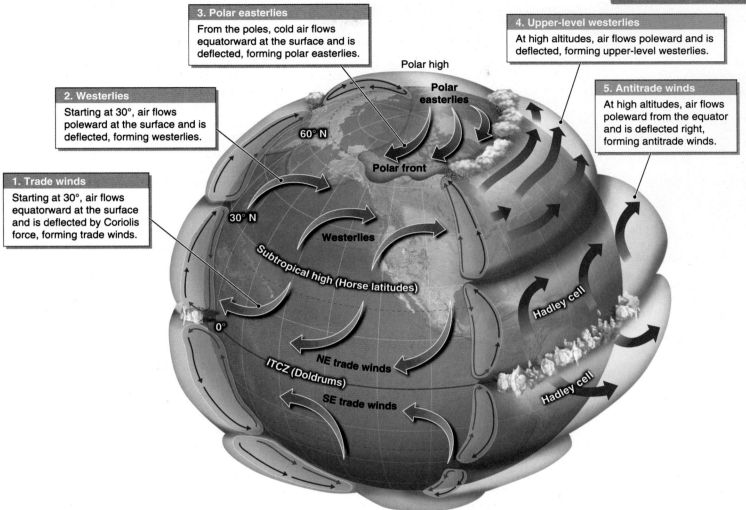

3. Polar easterlies
From the poles, cold air flows equatorward at the surface and is deflected, forming polar easterlies.

2. Westerlies
Starting at 30°, air flows poleward at the surface and is deflected, forming westerlies.

1. Trade winds
Starting at 30°, air flows equatorward at the surface and is deflected by Coriolis force, forming trade winds.

4. Upper-level westerlies
At high altitudes, air flows poleward and is deflected, forming upper-level westerlies.

5. Antitrade winds
At high altitudes, air flows poleward from the equator and is deflected right, forming antitrade winds.

Polar high
Polar easterlies
60° N
Polar front
30° N
Westerlies
Subtropical high (Horse latitudes)
0°
NE trade winds
ITCZ (Doldrums)
SE trade winds
Hadley cell
Hadley cell

region centered on 30° north and south, associated with the subtropical high, which is an area of gently subsiding air with little horizontal flow. As **Picture This** illustrates, the horse latitudes over land can be extremely arid.

The **westerlies** are surface winds, found in both hemispheres between the subtropical high and the subpolar low, that blow from the west. They form as the descending air of the subtropical high flows poleward along the surface and is deflected by the Coriolis force. In a similar manner, the polar high exports cold, dense air equatorward. Coriolis deflection creates **polar easterlies** that are cold and dry.

The trade winds and westerlies will have an important role to play in the growing technology of wind power because they occur where there are large human populations in need of energy. The Geographic Perspectives in Section 4.5 explores

GEOGRAPHIC PERSPECTIVES

Global Wind Patterns in Both Hemispheres

LATITUDE RANGE	SURFACE WINDS	UPPER-LEVEL WINDS
0° to 30°	Trade winds	Antitrade winds
30° to 60°	Westerlies	Upper-level westerlies
60° to 90°	Polar easterlies	

the role of wind power production in addressing human energy needs.

Upper-Level Winds

Upper-level winds, or *winds aloft,* are above the boundary layer and flow faster than surface winds due to the lack of friction. Coriolis force deflects these fast upper-level winds more than it does the relatively slow surface winds. As a result, upper-level winds flow mostly parallel to isobars. Upper-level winds that do not cross isobars due to strong Coriolis force deflection are called *geostrophic winds.* The

westerlies
Surface winds that come from the west and are found in both hemispheres between the subpolar low and the subtropical high.

polar easterlies
Cold, dry winds originating near both poles and flowing south and east.

FIGURE 4.16 **The polar jet stream.** *This image shows the polar jet stream at an altitude of about 15,000 m (49,200 ft). The fastest winds are areas of orange and red and are up to 360 km/h (224 mph). (NASA's Goddard Space Flight Center)*

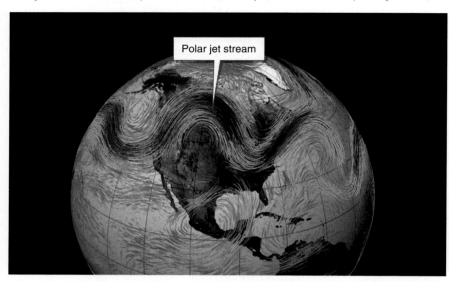

Video
Polar jetstream
http://qrs.ly/sy434eo

storms by increasing instability within them (see Section 5.4).

The subtropical jet stream can also play an important role in storm strength and moisture transport. The subtropical jet stream is situated over the subtropical high, at approximately 30° north and south. The direction of flow of both the polar jet stream and the subtropical jet stream follows **Rossby waves** (also called *longwaves*), large north–south undulations in the upper-level westerlies (Figure 4.17).

There are always three to six Rossby waves in the Northern Hemisphere polar jet stream. They are seldom stationary, but continually change their geographic position and depth. Rossby waves are also part of the global heat engine discussed in Section 2.5. As they bend north and south, Rossby waves provide meridional heat transport from the equator to the poles. In so doing, they export surplus heat from the tropics and deliver it to higher latitudes. Figure 4.18 illustrates how *cold outbreaks* occasionally occur as a Rossby wave trough deepens, is pinched off, and moves southward.

upper-level westerlies and antitrade winds, shown in Figure 4.15, are examples of geostrophic winds.

An intermittent fast band of wind called the *subtropical jet stream* is centered on 30° latitude in both hemispheres. Similarly, a high-velocity ribbon of geostrophic winds is embedded in the upper-level westerlies from fall through spring (Figure 4.16). This ribbon of winds, called the **polar jet stream**, is a discontinuous narrow band of fast-flowing air found between 30° and 60° north and south latitude. It is strongest between 7,000 to 12,000 m (23,000 to 39,000 ft) above sea level, and it is usually less than 5 km (3 mi) thick. Wind speeds in the polar jet stream can exceed 400 km/h (250 mph). Over the United States and Canada, commercial aircraft may fight the polar jet stream when traveling east to west or enjoy its gas- and time-saving benefits when traveling west to east.

polar jet stream
A discontinuous narrow band of fast-flowing air found at high altitudes between 30° and 60° latitude in the Northern Hemisphere.

Rossby wave
(or *longwave*) A large undulation in the upper-level westerlies.

The sharp temperature contrast that occurs near 60° latitude (at the subpolar low) causes a sharp north–south pressure gradient, and this in turn creates the polar jet stream. During winter, the temperature contrast between polar regions and midlatitude regions is greater than in summer. As a result, the polar jet stream flows fastest in winter. It plays a crucial role in midlatitude meteorology because it can strengthen midlatitude

FIGURE 4.17 **Rossby waves.** *Rossby waves are curves in the geostrophic winds. The polar and subtropical jet streams follow the curves in the Rossby waves. A trough occurs where Rossby waves bend equatorward, and a ridge forms where Rossby waves bend poleward. Rossby wave ridges often cause above-average temperatures on the ground and generally bring fair weather. Rossby wave troughs bring below-average temperatures and potentially stormy weather.*

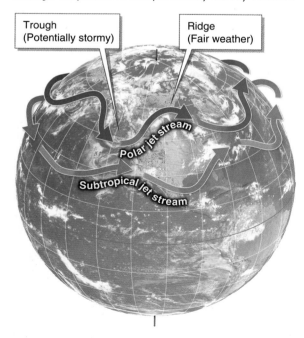

Trough (Potentially stormy)

Ridge (Fair weather)

Polar jet stream

Subtropical jet stream

Seasonal Shifts of Global Pressure

Seasons have an important influence on the global pattern of pressure systems and winds. We have referred to global pressure systems as being centered and fixed on key lines of latitude. For instance, the ITCZ was portrayed in Figure 4.14 as lying on the equator. However, the ITCZ shifts its latitude as it tracks the subsolar point (see Section 2.1). **Generally, the latitude of the ITCZ shifts with the latitude of the subsolar point (Figure 4.19), and the other global pressure systems shift with it.**

In the Northern Hemisphere, as the ITCZ moves northward in summer, it brings heavy precipitation to Central America and into Mexico. As one travels farther north in Mexico and leaves the influence of the ITCZ, the climate becomes progressively more arid. The subtropical high and the subpolar low also move north and south with the ITCZ's movement. Therefore, the mid-latitudes experience a marked seasonal contrast in weather patterns: They are affected by the subtropical high in summer and by the subpolar low in winter.

Global precipitation and, consequently, vegetation patterns are mainly controlled by the global pressure systems (see Section 8.1). As one moves outside the tropics, the general pattern of summer rainfall from the ITCZ is gradually replaced by winter precipitation from the subpolar low, as shown in **Figure 4.20** on the following page.

Why are tropical rainforests always wet?

The precipitation pattern shown in Figure 4.20 generally holds true for much of the world, but there are many exceptions. The windward sides of mountain ranges, for instance, are typically much wetter than surrounding lowlands, regardless of their latitude, due to precipitation resulting from orographic lifting (see Section 3.3). Their leeward rain-shadow sides are typically much drier than surrounding locations. Another exception that breaks this tidy latitudinal pattern is the influence of landmasses.

The Influence of Landmasses

Continental landmasses play an important role in global atmospheric circulation and precipitation. As you may recall from Section 2.3, land has a lower specific heat than seawater. Therefore, relative to the oceans, continental landmasses become hotter during the summer months and colder during the winter months.

This seasonal heating and cooling creates thermal low-pressure regions over land in summer and thermal high-pressure regions over land in winter (**Figure 4.21** on the following page). Because

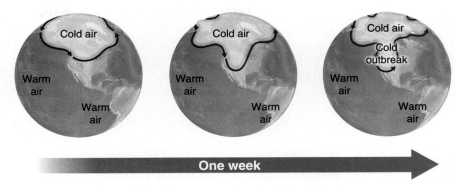

FIGURE 4.18 **Changing of position of Rossby waves.**
Rossby waves change their position and depth through time. The blue line represents the polar jet stream. A deep trough, and then a cold outbreak, develops over the Great Plains in this time sequence of one week.

Cold air / Warm air / Warm air

Cold air / Warm air / Warm air

Cold air / Cold outbreak / Warm air / Warm air

One week

FIGURE 4.19 **Seasonal migration of the ITCZ.**
The ITCZ tracks the subsolar point. It reaches its northernmost extent in July at 25° north latitude, passing over Southeast Asia. It reaches its southernmost extent in January at about 20° south latitude, passing over northern Australia.

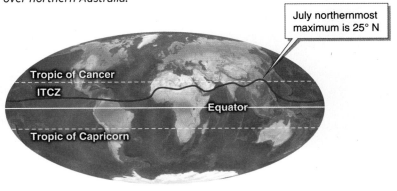

July northernmost maximum is 25° N

Tropic of Cancer
ITCZ
Equator
Tropic of Capricorn

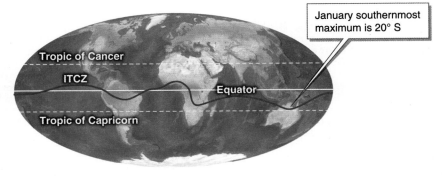

January southernmost maximum is 20° S

Tropic of Cancer
ITCZ
Equator
Tropic of Capricorn

these pressure systems are seasonal and do not last all year, they are called *semipermanent pressure systems*.

At a larger spatial scale, we can examine North America in more detail. **In summer, the East Coast of the United States is humid, but the West Coast is relatively arid. This pattern is due to the influence of the *Bermuda high* and the *Pacific high*.**

FIGURE 4.20 **GEO-GRAPHIC: Global precipitation pattern.** *The background image is from NASA's Blue Marble Next Generation series. Land colors are true color and show what the land surface would look like to a person in space if there were no clouds or atmosphere. Darker green areas are vegetated and have wet climates. Lighter tan areas are sparsely vegetated and arid.* (NASA)

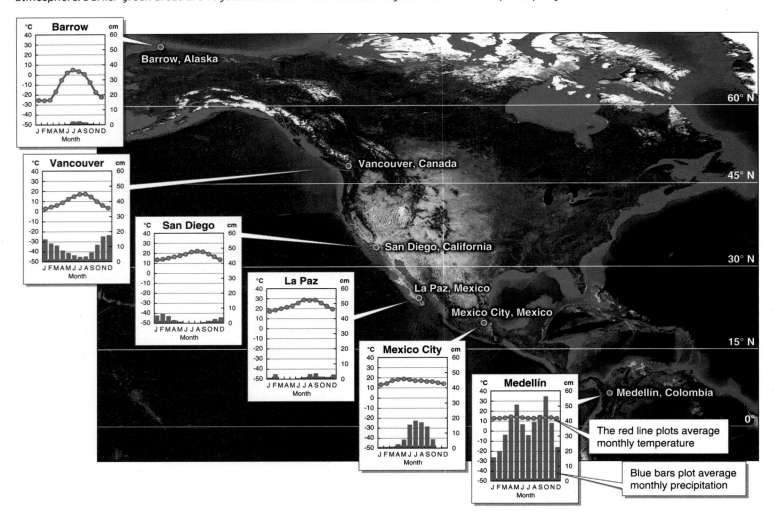

Climate Diagram Information

Barrow, Alaska: 71° N; sea level	Barrow is dominated by the polar high. During summer, a weakened subpolar low brings some precipitation.
Vancouver, Canada: 49° N; sea level	Vancouver is dominated by the subpolar low for most of the year. The subpolar-low rainfall diminishes during summer as the subtropical high moves north.
San Diego, California: 32° N; sea level	San Diego is mainly influenced by subtropical-high aridity, but it is far enough north that the polar jet stream can bring some rainfall during the winter months.
La Paz, Mexico: 24° N; 27 m (89 ft) elevation	La Paz is dominated year-round by the subtropical high. Some infrequent ITCZ-assisted thunderstorms reach this far north during late summer.
Mexico City, Mexico: 19° N; 2,421 m (7,943 ft) elevation	The ITCZ is near Mexico City from about May to August. In the winter, it moves south of the equator, and the subtropical high brings aridity.
Medellín, Colombia: 6° N; 1,495 m (4,905 ft) elevation	Medellín receives heavy rainfall in all months from the ITCZ. The ITCZ passes over Medellín twice a year, approximately May and November.

FIGURE 4.21 **Semipermanent pressure systems.** *Isobars are used to show the average global sea-level pressure in* (A) *January and* (B) *July.*

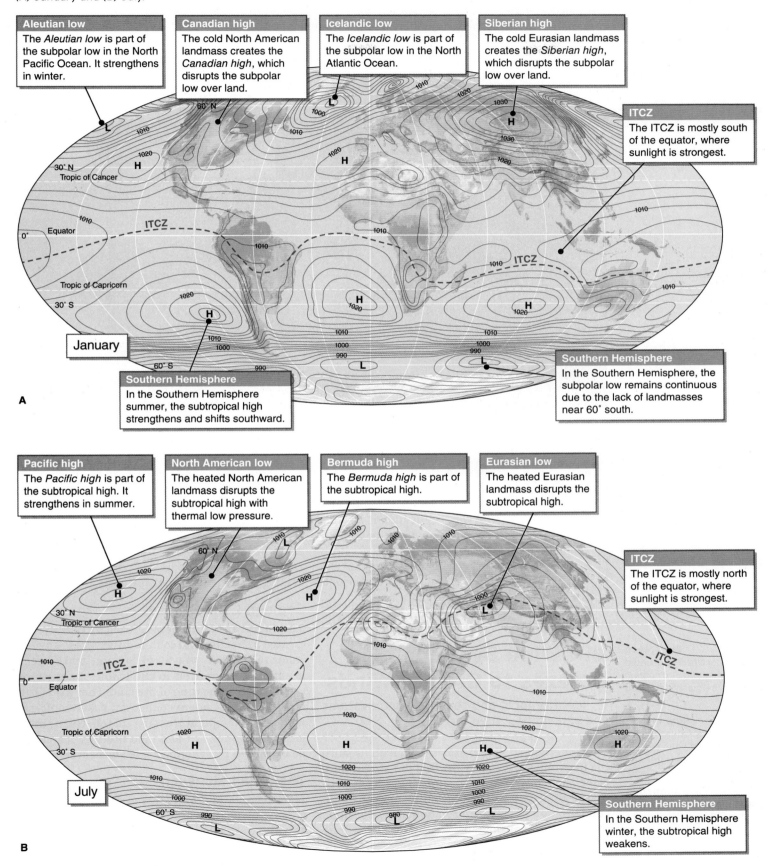

Aleutian low
The *Aleutian low* is part of the subpolar low in the North Pacific Ocean. It strengthens in winter.

Canadian high
The cold North American landmass creates the *Canadian high*, which disrupts the subpolar low over land.

Icelandic low
The *Icelandic low* is part of the subpolar low in the North Atlantic Ocean.

Siberian high
The cold Eurasian landmass creates the *Siberian high*, which disrupts the subpolar low over land.

ITCZ
The ITCZ is mostly south of the equator, where sunlight is strongest.

Southern Hemisphere
In the Southern Hemisphere summer, the subtropical high strengthens and shifts southward.

Southern Hemisphere
In the Southern Hemisphere, the subpolar low remains continuous due to the lack of landmasses near 60° south.

Pacific high
The *Pacific high* is part of the subtropical high. It strengthens in summer.

North American low
The heated North American landmass disrupts the subtropical high with thermal low pressure.

Bermuda high
The *Bermuda high* is part of the subtropical high.

Eurasian low
The heated Eurasian landmass disrupts the subtropical high.

ITCZ
The ITCZ is mostly north of the equator, where sunlight is strongest.

Southern Hemisphere
In the Southern Hemisphere winter, the subtropical high weakens.

FIGURE 4.22 **Pacific high and Bermuda high.** *The Bermuda high brings humid air up from the Gulf of Mexico and into the eastern half of North America. Western North America, in contrast, receives relatively cold and dry air from the Gulf of Alaska. Los Angeles and Atlanta are both at the same latitude and elevation, but these differences bring them very different summer weather. (NASA)*

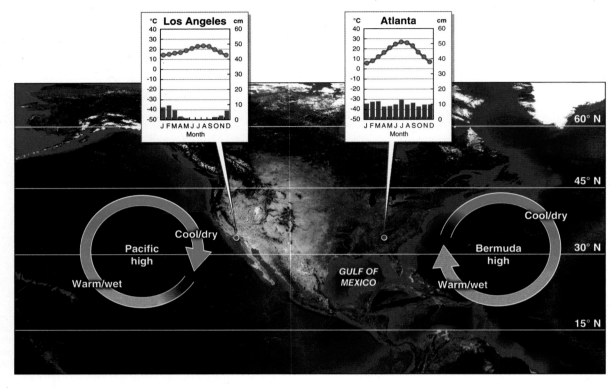

> Why is Southern California so dry and Georgia so wet in summer when both are at the same latitude?

The Bermuda high is a semipermanent anticyclone in the western Atlantic, and the Pacific high is a semi-permanent anticyclone in the eastern Pacific. Both systems are part of the sub-tropical high pressure belt **(Figure 4.22)**.

mosphere. These wind systems can be arranged by their geographic and temporal scales, as summarized in **Figure 4.23**.

All the wind systems described in this section can locally override global wind patterns. The first two wind systems we explore, sea and land breezes and the Asian monsoon, are created by unequal heating of land and ocean surfaces.

Sea and Land Breezes

Sea breezes and **land breezes** are microscale breezes created by heating and cooling differences between water and land **(Figure 4.24)**. Sea and land breezes are most pronounced in the tropics because of strong daytime heating of the land. They also form at midlatitudes, where cold ocean water contrasts with warm temperatures just inland. Given their localized nature, sea and land breezes can easily be disrupted by synoptic-scale storm systems.

The Asian Monsoon

Like sea and land breezes, the Asian monsoon is created by heating differences between land and sea. The word *monsoon* is derived from the Arabic *mausim*, which means "season." A **monsoon** is a

sea breeze
A local onshore breeze created by heating and cooling differences between water and land.

land breeze
A local offshore breeze created by heating and cooling differences between water and land.

monsoon
A seasonal reversal of winds, characterized by summer onshore airflow and winter offshore airflow.

4.4 Wind Systems: Sea Breezes to Gravity Winds

◎ Identify local and regional wind systems and explain how they form.

The underlying theme that has been with us since the beginning of Chapter 1 is that the atmosphere is set in motion by uneven heating of Earth's surface by the Sun. The release of latent heat through condensation and Earth's rotation also determine the direction of airflow. In this section, we examine major local and regional wind systems in the at-

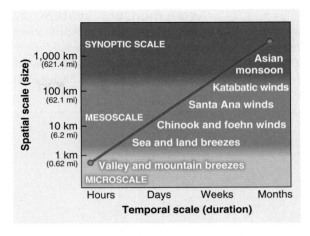

FIGURE 4.23 **Geographic scale of wind systems.** *Microscale systems, such as local breezes, last hours and cover up to 2 kilometers. Mesoscale systems, such as Santa Ana winds, are up to several hundred kilometers in extent and last for weeks. Synoptic-scale systems, such as the Asian monsoon, last months and span a thousand kilometers or more.*

METEOROLOGICAL SCALE	APPROXIMATE SIZE
Microscale	Up to 2 km (1.2 mi)
Mesoscale	Up to several hundred kilometers
Synoptic scale	1,000 km (620 mi) or larger

seasonal reversal of winds, characterized by summer onshore airflow and winter offshore airflow. About half the world's population experiences the influence of a monsoon system and knows only two seasons: a warm and rainy summer and a slightly cooler but dry winter. The Asian monsoon is the largest monsoon system in the world, and in summer it brings heavy rains, and sometimes flooding, to South Asia.

The Asian monsoon is separated into the *South Asian monsoon*, which affects India, and the *East Asian monsoon*, which affects Indonesia, northern Australia, southern China, Korea, and Japan. All monsoons consist of a *summer monsoon*, a warm and moist onshore airflow, and a relatively cool (but still warm) *winter monsoon*, an offshore flow of dry air originating in the continental interior.

In summer, Asian monsoon rains do not necessarily fall every day. Dry *break periods* can last a few weeks to more than a month. When these break periods are prolonged, drought and crop failures can result. Too little rain brings food shortages and potential famine for millions. When the break periods are short, too much rain results, and flooding, soil erosion, and waterborne disease outbreaks sometimes occur.

FIGURE 4.24 **GEO-GRAPHIC: Sea and land breezes.**

1. Sea breeze

By day, the land becomes warmer than the ocean, creating thermal low pressure over land and drawing air inland. Air flows from sea to land, creating an onshore sea breeze.

2. Land breeze

By night, the land cools more than the oceans, creating thermal high pressure and sinking air over land. Air flows offshore from the land out to sea, creating a land breeze.

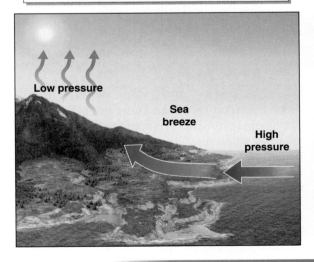

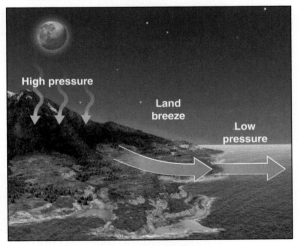

12 hours

FIGURE **4.25** **Asian monsoon system.** *(A) In summer, the ITCZ draws air north (shown with red arrows) from the Indian Ocean. This humid onshore airflow brings summer rains. (B) In winter, air flows away from the Siberian high over central Eurasia. As a result, dry offshore winds develop. The timing and strength of the summer monsoon rains depend on three factors: onshore airflow, orographic uplift, and the ITCZ.*

Animation
Asian
monsoon
http://qrs.ly/3b434ek

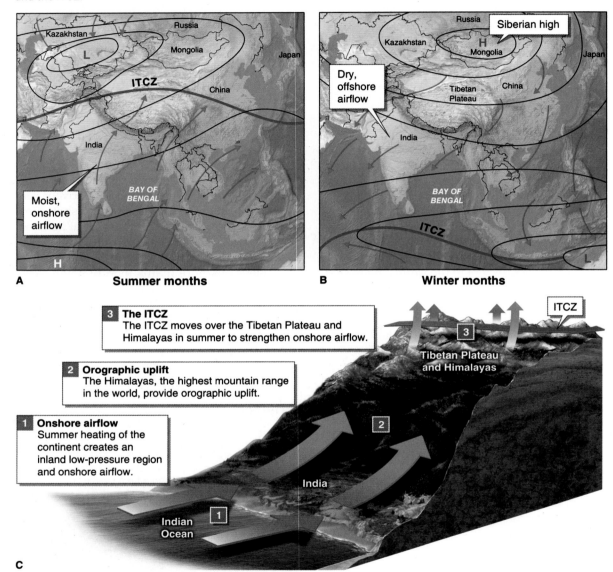

The Asian monsoon system is complex, and climatologists still cannot predict with accuracy how it will behave from one year to the next. **There are three synoptic-scale controls on the South Asian monsoon: (1) onshore airflow created by summer landmass heating, (2) orographic lifting by the Himalayas, and (3) movement of the ITCZ over the Himalayas and Tibetan Plateau (Figure 4.25).**

Onshore airflow, orographic uplift, and the ITCZ affect one another and overlap in their influence on the strength, duration, and timing of the South

Asian monsoon, creating an unpredictable system. For example, the high Tibetan Plateau acts like a chimney when the ITCZ forms over it and causes heated air to be injected high into the troposphere, further strengthening onshore airflow and precipitation. Extensive snow cover on the plateau can reduce the strength of this chimney effect by cooling the air and making it more stable. This diminishes the strength of the summer monsoon. As **Picture This** shows, the Asian monsoon brings significant amounts of rainfall to many regions in South Asia.

During the winter monsoon in Asia, the winds reverse and flow from land to sea. The cold interior of the Eurasian landmass develops the semipermanent Siberian high, from which dry air flows outward across Asia and out to sea.

The southwestern United States and northern Mexico also have a monsoon system. During summer, heating over the mountains and the resulting thermal low pressure create a pressure gradient that draws air inland from the warm Gulf of California and the Gulf of Mexico, resulting in summer thunderstorms.

The remaining four wind systems we will describe are all caused by sloped terrain. We will explore them in order of their spatial extent, starting with the most localized winds in mountains.

Picture This

(© DINODIA/Age Fotostock Inc.)

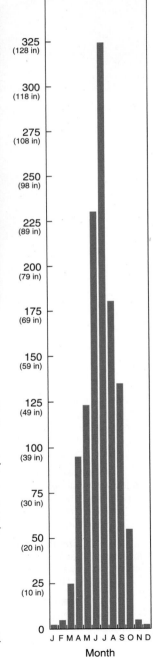

The Wettest Places on Earth

Mawsynram, India, has the distinction of being recognized by Guinness World Records as the wettest place on Earth. Each year it receives an average of 1,187 cm (467.4 in or 38.9 ft) of rainfall (shown with climate diagram at right). It is located in the Khasi Hills in Meghalaya State at about 1,400 m (4,560 ft) elevation. The nearby Nohakali Kai Falls, in Cherrapunji, are shown in this photo.

There are probably wetter locations, but they are not officially recognized. Lloró, Colombia, for example, claims an average yearly rainfall amount of 1,329 cm (523 in or 43.6 ft). Just 11 km (7 mi) to the east of Mawsynram, the town of Cherrapunji also claims to have the world's highest average annual rainfall. Cherrapunji does hold the official record for the greatest 12-month precipitation total. Between August 1, 1860, and July 31, 1861, Cherrapunji recorded 2,646.1 cm (1,041.77 in or 86.8 ft) of rainfall. Interestingly, Mawsynram and Cherrapunji (25° north latitude) are located at nearly the same latitude as the Empty Quarter (see Section 4.3), one of the most arid regions on Earth.

Consider This

1. Why might we expect Mawsynram to be arid? Given what you know about the Asian monsoon, explain the three factors that converge to make Mawsynram so wet.

2. What incentive(s) would compel a town to claim to be the wettest location on Earth? How could this incentive affect accurate and truthful measurements of rainfall?

FIGURE 4.26 **Valley and mountain breezes.**

> **1. Valley breeze**
>
> Daytime heating warms the Sun-facing slopes, creating unstable air parcels and low pressure. Air flows from valleys upslope as a result of the pressure gradient. If the rising air parcels cool to the dew point, clouds or thunderstorms may develop.

> **2. Mountain breeze**
>
> At night, the upper slopes cool, and the cold, heavy air sinks downslope, forming cool mountain breezes.

 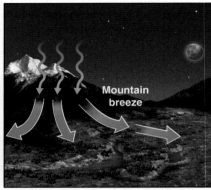

Time

Valley and Mountain Breezes

Valley and mountain breezes are local breezes produced by heating and cooling differences in mountainous areas. In summer, mountain slopes that face toward the afternoon Sun are heated and form warm, buoyant parcels of air. As this warmed air rises, it creates a pressure gradient that draws in air from adjacent valley floors, resulting in a **valley breeze**. As the air parcels rise, they expand and cool adiabatically. If there is sufficient vapor pressure in the rising air parcels, their temperature may drop to the dew point, and condensation will follow. Clouds such as cumulus and cumulonimbus formed from this condensation often produce afternoon summer thunderstorms in mountainous regions as valley breezes develop.

This situation is reversed after the Sun sets, as upper elevations cool faster than lower elevations. Cold, dense, and heavy **mountain breezes** flow downslope through canyons, finding the lowest valleys. Mountain breezes are strongest in winter when air is coldest **(Figure 4.26)**.

Chinook and Foehn Winds

Downslope winds on the leeward side of the Rocky Mountains are called **chinook winds**. **Foehn winds** are the same phenomenon in the European Alps, and there are other local names for this type of wind. As we saw in Section 3.3, the leeward side of a mountain range is typically warmer and drier than the windward side. This difference is due to the release of latent heat and precipitation on the windward side and adiabatic heating as air flows down the leeward side **(Figure 4.27)**.

Chinook winds are warm, dry winds that often come in sharp contrast to cold winter conditions. With the arrival of chinook winds, temperatures can rise 20°C (36°F) or more within a matter of minutes. These winds quickly melt and sublimate snow.

FIGURE 4.27 **Chinook and foehn winds.** *Warm chinook and foehn winds form as air flows up, over, and back down the leeward side of a mountain range.*

valley breeze
A local upslope breeze produced by heating and cooling differences in mountainous areas.

mountain breeze
A local downslope breeze produced by heating and cooling differences in mountainous areas.

chinook wind
A local downslope wind that forms on the leeward side of the Rocky Mountains.

foehn wind
(pronounced FEH-rn)
A downslope wind that forms on the leeward size of the European Alps.

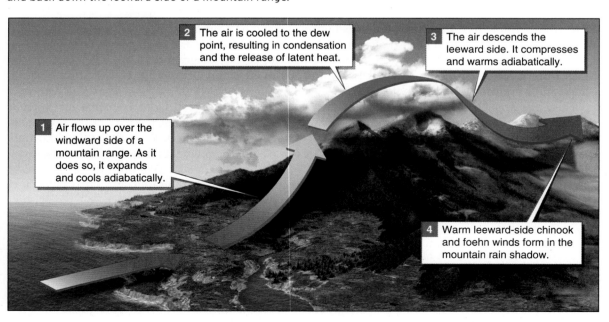

> **2** The air is cooled to the dew point, resulting in condensation and the release of latent heat.

> **3** The air descends the leeward side. It compresses and warms adiabatically.

> **1** Air flows up over the windward side of a mountain range. As it does so, it expands and cools adiabatically.

> **4** Warm leeward-side chinook and foehn winds form in the mountain rain shadow.

FIGURE 4.28 **Santa Ana winds.** *Santa Ana winds occur when high pressure occupies the Great Basin desert and relatively low pressure occurs off the Southern California coast.*

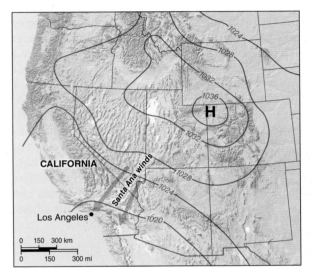

Santa Ana Winds

Santa Ana winds sometimes create a major fire hazard for parts of southern California and northern Baja California, Mexico. Santa Ana winds originate in the high desert of the Great Basin and flow to coastal California **(Figure 4.28)**.

Santa Ana winds form as high pressure develops in the Great Basin and cool air flows downslope toward coastal southern California. This flow is the result not only of the pressure gradient, but also of gravity, because the cool, relatively dense and heavy air sinks and flows downslope. As the air descends in elevation, it is compressed and warmed adiabatically. Because it originates in the desert, it is dry. Thus the temperature of Santa Ana winds approaches 32°C (90°F), and the relative humidity of these winds is often in the single digits.

Santa Ana winds occur from fall through spring and usually peak in December. **Santa Ana wind speeds can exceed 100 km/h (62 mph) in constricted valleys. Wildfires sometimes burn out of control in these hot, dry winds. As Figure 4.29** shows, rural residences can be vulnerable to Santa Ana wildfires.

Santa Ana winds
Winds that originate in the Great Basin and are heated adiabatically as they descend to sea level on the southern California coast and northern Baja California; often associated with major wildfires.

FIGURE 4.29 **October 2003 Santa Ana fires.** *(A) Outlined in red, fires burning in many areas from southern California to northern Baja California can be seen in this satellite image taken October 26, 2003. The strong offshore airflow is apparent as fire smoke blows over the Pacific Ocean. About 3,000 km² (1,150 mi²) burned, 3,000 homes were destroyed, and 26 people were killed in the 2003 fires. The cost totaled $2.5 billion. (B) The Cedar fire, shown here, burned in San Diego County in 2003 and was a result of Santa Ana winds. The fire burned 1,134 km² (438 mi²) and was the largest fire in California history. (A. NASA; B. David Hume Kennerly/Getty Images)*

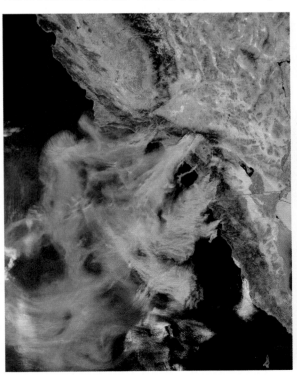

A

B

Katabatic winds. *The winds flowing into Terra Nova Bay, Antarctica, are pushing sea ice into long lines. Arrows show the direction of the wind. (NASA)*

Katabatic Winds

Katabatic winds, or *gravity winds* (*katabatikos* is Greek for "downhill movement"), form mainly over ice sheets or glaciers when intensely cold, dense, and heavy air spills downslope by the force of gravity. Katabatic winds are similar to mountain breezes and Santa Ana winds, but they are stronger, cover greater geographic distances, and are far colder. Where airflow is constricted and focused in valleys, the wind speeds can exceed those of hurricanes. Greenland and Antarctica experience katabatic winds commonly, but they can occur wherever high, cold plateaus are found. The effects of katabatic winds can be seen in the satellite image in **Figure 4.30**.

> **What are gravity winds?**

GEOGRAPHIC PERSPECTIVES
4.5 Farming the Wind

◎ **Assess the potential of wind as a clean energy source.**

Renewable energy sources such as the Sun and wind are inexhaustible and carbon-free. They do not add CO_2 to the atmosphere. For the most part, they have a relatively small environmental impact (although they are not impact-free). Like solar power, wind power is front and center in the renewable energy movement (also see the Geographic Perspectives in Chapter 2). Wind power, which is electricity that is derived from wind turbines, is one of the fastest-growing renewable energy technologies in the world **(Figure 4.31)**.

In 2013, 3.5% of the world's electricity supply came from wind. By 2020, it is estimated that this proportion will be nearer to 10%. The United States generated about 4% of its electricity needs from wind in 2013, and the U.S. Department of Energy has set the goal of generating 20% of all U.S. power from wind energy by the year 2030. This will require that the United States build about 100,000 new wind turbines. Can the United States meet the challenge?

katabatic wind (or gravity wind) Wind that forms mainly over ice sheets or glaciers when intensely cold, dense, and heavy air spills downslope by the force of gravity.

There is certainly enough wind energy available for the task. By some estimates, the total wind energy in the Dakotas alone is equivalent to 60% of U.S. electrical demand. But there are several hurdles that must be overcome:

1. Wind energy must be converted to electricity.

2. Electrical energy must be moved from where it is generated to where it is in demand.

3. The electricity must be made available during times of peak demand.

4. Environmental problems remain to be solved.

Converting the Wind to Electricity

Several different designs and approaches are used to harness the wind's energy potential. All wind

FIGURE 4.31 **Wind power statistics.**

(A) Top 10 countries by wind power capacity in 2013. China tops the list, and the United States is second. (B) Total world wind power generation in 2013 was 318 gigawatts (GW), roughly the equivalent of 67 nuclear power plants.

Top 10 Countries in Wind Power (2013)	
COUNTRY	**TOTAL INSTALLED CAPACITY (GW)**
China	80.8
United States	60
Germany	32.4
Spain	22.9
India	19.5
United Kingdom	9.6
Italy	8.4
France	7.8
Canada	6.6
Denmark	4.6

A

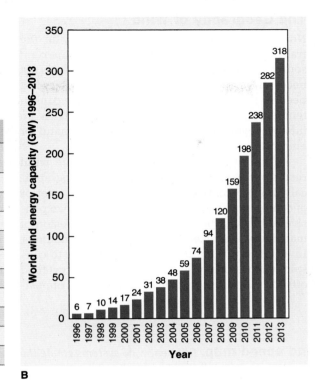

B

power designs use turbines, or spinning rotors, which convert the kinetic energy of a moving fluid such as water or air to electrical energy. The wind flows around and moves the rotor blades, causing them to turn a driveshaft to generate electricity **(Figure 4.32)**. The turbines are typically placed atop tall towers to catch the wind.

FIGURE 4.32 **GEO-GRAPHIC: Wind turbine schematic.**

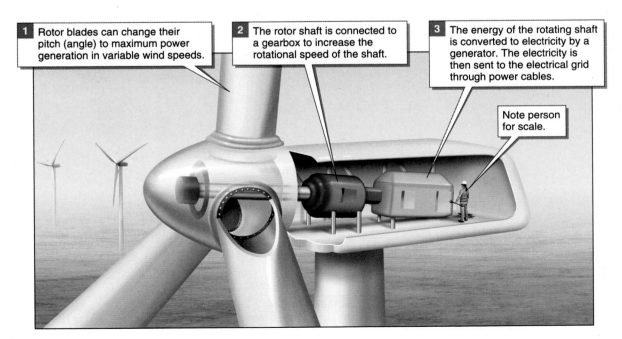

1 Rotor blades can change their pitch (angle) to maximum power generation in variable wind speeds.

2 The rotor shaft is connected to a gearbox to increase the rotational speed of the shaft.

3 The energy of the rotating shaft is converted to electricity by a generator. The electricity is then sent to the electrical grid through power cables.

Note person for scale.

The Geography of Wind

Not all places are equally windy. Worldwide, the trade winds and westerlies provide an important source of energy (Figure 4.33). The wind does not necessarily blow most strongly where power is most needed, however. In the United States, the consistently fastest winds occur in the Great Plains, an interior region where populations and demand for energy are low.

Offshore coastal areas have abundant wind resources. However, coastal winds are geographically limited compared with winds in the interior of continents, and offshore winds are more expensive to harness because of saltwater corrosion of machinery and adverse marine weather conditions. In addition, frequent political opposition to conspicuous wind power development has curtailed offshore wind projects. Given that political opposi-

tion, for the United States to meet its 20% wind capacity goal, most of that wind power will have to be generated from wind farms on the Great Plains because that is where the wind is strongest.

Given its geographic distance from population centers, Great Plains wind power will have to be transported over long distances, which can result in considerable power losses along transmission lines. This problem is being addressed by the modernizing of the U.S. power grid. Once the nation's grid is improved, moving electricity long distances will likely become increasingly efficient and economically viable.

Storing Wind Power

How can renewable energy sources such as wind meet daily spikes in energy demand in the morn-

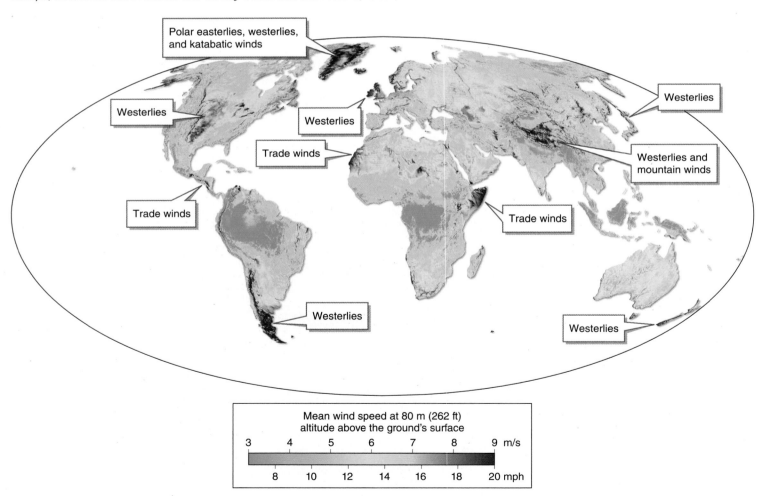

FIGURE 4.33 **World wind speed map.** *Different wind systems create the windiest regions of the world. North America, northern Europe, and China have reliable and strong westerlies.* *(2014 3TIER by Vaisala)*

Polar easterlies, westerlies, and katabatic winds

Westerlies

Westerlies

Westerlies

Trade winds

Westerlies and mountain winds

Trade winds

Trade winds

Westerlies

Westerlies

Mean wind speed at 80 m (262 ft) altitude above the ground's surface

3   4   5   6   7   8   9 m/s

8   10   12   14   16   18   20 mph

TABLE 4.2 Annual Bird Kill Estimates	
CAUSE	YEARLY FATALITIES
Building window collisions	100,000 to 1 billion
Domestic cats	365 million to 1 billion
Power line electrocutions and collisions	100,000 to 175 million
Agricultural pesticides	67 million to 90 million
Automobiles	60 million to 80 million
Communications towers	5 million to 6.8 million
Wind turbines	100,000 to 440,000

Source: *Nature* 486 (2012): 310-311. *Note:* These estimates for yearly bird kills are given as a range because actual numbers of bird kills are unknown.

ing and afternoon? **Wind farms that generate power when the wind is blowing must then store it for use when demand is high.** This significant hurdle is being dealt with through a variety of techniques and developing technologies.

Hydrogen Storage

When pure hydrogen is combined with oxygen, water is formed, and in the process, usable electricity is produced. Pure hydrogen can be made by separating hydrogen atoms from oxygen atoms in water through a process called *electrolysis*. Electrolysis uses electricity. The electricity can come from a wind farm.

Hydrogen could be made and transported in its pure gas form from wind farms to populated areas through existing natural gas pipelines that have been converted for hydrogen transport. In all, about 700 miles of pipeline have been converted in the United States.

Hydrogen can also be stored in hydrogen fuel cells, in which pure hydrogen is recombined with oxygen, releasing electricity in the process. This electricity can be used for personal laptops, cell phones, and hydrogen fuel cell cars.

Underground and Reservoir Storage

Underground caverns and mines or large metal tanks can be filled with air using air compressors or pumps. On a windy night, when people are sleeping and wind turbines are generating electricity, air pumps can use electricity to fill these reservoirs with compressed air. The compressed air can then be released at hours of peak energy demand. As the air rushes out of the reservoir through a narrow pipe, it can spin turbines to generate electricity.

Similarly, at night during off-peak hours, water can be pumped uphill into a large reservoir by electrical pumps running on wind power. During peak demand, the water can be released from the reservoir, and gravity will pull it back downhill, spinning turbines and generating electricity. One problem with these storage techniques, however, is that they are geographically limited—subterranean caverns and surface reservoirs are not available in many areas.

Environmental Impacts of Wind Power

Two factors that have sometimes stood in the way of wind power development have been the potential of turbines to kill birds and bats and concerns about the effects of wind farms on people who live nearby.

Birds and Bats

> Do wind turbines kill birds?

Rotating wind turbines kill bats, migratory songbirds, and large birds of prey such as hawks. Most bird kills occur through direct collision with the spinning rotor blades. Supporters of wind power argue, however, that these bird kills, while unwelcome, pale in comparison to the birds killed by domestic cats, windows (which birds accidentally fly into), and the other factors summarized in Table 4.2.

Bat kills by wind turbines are also a problem. According to studies by the National Wind Coordinating Committee, bird kills, on average, are 0.6 to 7.7 per turbine per season nationwide. For bats, the number is 3.4 to 47.5 per turbine. A single wind farm in West Virginia was killing an estimated 4,000 bats each year during the fall migration.

Given the importance of these animals in eco-systems, declines in the numbers of insect-eating songbirds, bats, and large raptors could be a serious concern. Slowing or shutting down the turbines during peak migratory periods, or on low-wind nights when bats are most active, could be a solution. Such efforts have documented an 80% reduction in bat kills.

Wumps and NIMBYs

People who live near large wind farms commonly complain of strange, deep rhythmic pulses, or "wumps." These complaints have been somewhat successfully addressed with new variable-pitch (angle) rotor blades, which can be adjusted to minimize such noises as they arise.

Many people want clean, renewable energy, but at the same time, they do not want 130-meter-tall wind turbines dominating the horizon. Wind farms can divide communities. Wind towers are large and conspicuous and diminish the natural beauty of a region. Offshore wind development in the United States, in particular, has been stymied by these NIMBY ("not in my back yard") views in some areas.

The Cape Wind Project, for example, has been waiting for more than 10 years to develop an offshore wind farm in sight of Martha's Vineyard in Nantucket Sound, off Cape Cod. Its construction was approved in 2013. The $2.5 billion project proposes to develop 130 wind turbines, each 137 m (440 ft) tall from the water's surface to blade tip. Many wealthy landowners have been opponents of the project. Although they favor renewable energy development, they do not want it marring their views of the ocean.

The Energy Mix

Renewable energy sources such as wind and solar power are dependent on weather, and weather is undependable. All renewable energy sources face this problem of intermittency. The solution lies in a diverse *energy mix*. By not relying on only one type of energy, but rather creating power from many different renewable sources, we could always have power from one source or another available. Energy from the wind will likely play an increasingly important role in meeting people's energy needs in the coming decades.

CHAPTER 4 Exploring with ⊚ Google Earth

To complete these problems, first read the chapter. When you are finished, go to LaunchPad and open the Exploring with Google Earth file for this chapter. Click on the "Workbook Problems" folder to "fly" to each of the problems listed below and answer the questions. Be sure to keep your "Borders and Labels" layer activated. Refer to Appendix 4 if you need help using Google Earth.

PROBLEM 4.1 Here, clouds in the equatorial eastern Pacific Ocean are shown.

1. **What is the approximate latitude of this band of cloudiness?**
   a. 0°
   b. 7° north
   c. 7° south
   d. 15° north

2. **What is the name of this band of cloudiness?**
   a. The ITCZ
   b. The subtropical high
   c. The subpolar low
   d. The polar high

3. **What lifting mechanism is responsible for this cloudiness?**
   a. Convective and convergent lifting
   b. Frontal lifting
   c. Orographic lifting

PROBLEM 4.2 Activate the overlay for this folder. This overlay shows the wind pattern of Hurricane Dean on August 20, 2007.

1. **What kinds of symbols are used to portray wind speed?**
   a. Wind vectors
   b. Wind barbs
   c. Wind arrows
   d. Streamlines

2. **What is the approximate wind speed at the location of the placemark? (Note: Use the text to decipher the symbols.)**
   a. 20 to 30 mph
   b. 30 to 40 mph
   c. 40 to 50 mph
   d. 50 mph or greater

3. **What is the name of the wind at the placemark?**
   a. North wind
   b. East wind
   c. 270° wind
   d. 180° wind

PROBLEM 4.3 This problem features two atmospheric systems occurring at the same time in the Bering Sea and in the Gulf of Alaska. Two markers are used in this problem, marker 1 and marker 2.

1. **Marker 1 is pinned to sea ice. Note that the wind direction is toward the south, away from the marker. The yellow placemark is pinned to the center of an atmospheric system. Based on the direction of rotation, as evidenced by the cloud patterns around the yellow placemark and marker 1, what kind of atmospheric system is this?**
   a. A cyclone
   b. An anticyclone
   c. Polar easterlies
   d. Westerlies

2. **Will air be ascending or descending at the yellow placemark?**
   a. Ascending
   b. Descending
   c. It is not possible to tell.

3. **Based on your observation of the cloud patterns at marker 2, what kind of system is this?**
   a. A cyclone
   b. An anticyclone
   c. Trade winds
   d. Westerlies

4. **Will air be ascending or descending at marker 2?**
   a. Ascending
   b. Descending
   c. It is not possible to tell.

PROBLEM 4.4 Deactivate the overlay from the previous problem and activate the overlay in this folder. This placemark falls west of the island of Hawai'i. Note the volcanic fog—or *vog*—that can be seen as a bluish haze at the placemark. This is a plume of sulfur dioxide resulting from the eruption of Kilauea.

1. **Given the direction in which the vog is moving away from the island, what kind of winds are these?**
   a. West winds
   b. East winds
   c. North winds
   d. South winds

2. **Given the latitude of Hawai'i, what is the general name for these winds on a global scale?**
   a. Trade winds
   b. Westerlies
   c. Polar easterlies
   d. Antitrade winds

PROBLEM 4.5 Activate the overlay for this folder. This problem features winds blowing smoke from the WH Complex fire in southern Montana, as photographed by an astronaut aboard the International Space Station on August 13, 2007.

1. **At a local scale, what is the name of these winds?**
   a. West winds
   b. East winds
   c. North winds
   d. South winds

2. **At what latitude does this placemark occur?**
   a. 10° north latitude
   b. 23° north latitude
   c. 45° north latitude
   d. 60° north latitude

3. **What is the general name for these winds on a global scale?**
   a. Trade winds
   b. Westerlies
   c. Polar easterlies
   d. Antitrade winds

PROBLEM 4.6 Deactivate any open overlays and activate the overlay for this placemark. This overlay shows the amount of vegetation as measured by the surface area of leaves (or *leaf area index*). Dark green areas are thickly vegetated because there is ample precipitation. Light green and brown areas are lightly vegetated because there is little precipitation.

1. **In what country is this placemark found?**
   a. Malaysia
   b. Indonesia
   c. New Zealand
   d. Australia

2. **What is the latitude of the placemark?**
   a. 24° north
   b. 24° south
   c. 38° south
   d. 50° south

3. **What global pressure belt is controlling climate here?**
   a. ITCZ
   b. Subtropical high
   c. Subpolar low
   d. Polar high

4. Which of the following best describes this climate?
a. Wet and warm
c. Wet and cold
b. Dry and warm
d. Dry and cold

PROBLEM 4.7 Keep the overlay from the previous problem activated.

1. What is the latitude of the placemark?
a. 9° north
c. 20° north
b. 9° south
d. 30° south

2. What global pressure belt is controlling climate here?
a. ITCZ
c. Subpolar low
b. Subtropical high
d. Polar high

3. Which of the following best describes this climate?
a. Wet and warm
c. Wet and cold
b. Dry and warm
d. Dry and cold

PROBLEM 4.8 Keep the overlay from the previous problem activated. This placemark falls on the Great Plains in the United States.

1. Compare the vegetation to the east of the placemark with the vegetation to the west of the placemark. Where is there more precipitation?
a. To the east of the placemark
b. To the west of the placemark

2. Which of the following causes this pattern of aridity and precipitation? (Refer to Figure 4.21 for help.)
a. Influence of the Bermuda high and Pacific high
b. Influence of the trade winds
c. Moisture carried by the westerlies
d. The position of the ITCZ

PROBLEM 4.9 Deactivate any open overlays. Activate the image overlay folder for this problem. This placemark features India and Bangladesh. The colors of the overlay represent rainfall totals between July 5 and 12 in 2004. Dark red areas received over 30 cm (12 in) of rain.

1. What atmospheric system produced this heavy rainfall in such a short time?
a. A hurricane
b. A midlatitude cyclone
c. The Asian monsoon
d. A thunderstorm

2. Is this rainfall associated with onshore flow or offshore flow?
a. Onshore flow
b. Offshore flow

3. Why does the heaviest rainfall occur in the foothills of the Himalayas?
a. Because of convective uplift
b. Because of orographic uplift
c. Because of convergent uplift
d. Because of frontal uplift

PROBLEM 4.10 Deactivate any open overlays, and then open the overlay in this folder. This placemark falls on a valley in the Chugach Mountains in southern Alaska. Strong winds are transporting dust in the valley out to sea.

1. Are these offshore winds or onshore winds?
a. Onshore winds
b. Offshore winds

2. Zoom in closer to the placemark. What is the approximate elevation of the mountains near the placemark?
a. 90 m
c. 1,500 m
b. 200 m
d. 5,000 m

3. What will happen to the temperature of these winds as they descend to sea level?
a. They will warm adiabatically.
b. They will cool adiabatically.
c. No change will occur.

4. What kind of winds are these?
a. Chinook winds
c. Sea breezes
b. Santa Ana winds
d. Monsoon

CHAPTER 4 Study Guide

Focus Points

4.1 Measuring and Mapping the Wind

Cause of the wind: Wind is caused by unequal heating of Earth's surface and the release of latent heat within clouds.

Wind names: Most winds are named for the direction from which they blow.

4.2 Air Pressure and Wind

Causes of pressure: Warm air is associated with low pressure, and cold air is associated with high pressure, but dynamic pressure can override thermal pressure.

Wind controls: Pressure-gradient force, Coriolis force, and friction force control wind speed and direction near Earth's surface. Air always flows from areas of high pressure to areas of low pressure.

Cyclones and anticyclones: Cyclones and anticyclones are important meteorological systems created by deflected flowing wind.

4.3 Global Atmospheric Circulation Patterns

Pressure systems: The four global pressure systems are the ITCZ, the subtropical high, the subpolar low, and the polar high.

Surface winds: The trade winds, the westerlies, and the polar easterlies are the major global surface winds.

Effect of seasons: The strength and latitude of the global pressure systems are strongly affected by the seasonal shift of the subsolar point and by landmasses. In the Northern Hemisphere, all the systems move north in June and south in December.

Semipermanent pressure: The Bermuda high is a semipermanent pressure system that brings summer precipitation to the East Coast of the United States. The Pacific high brings aridity to the West Coast.

4.4 Wind Systems: Sea Breezes to Gravity Winds

Wind systems: Earth's local and regional wind systems are set in motion by energy from the Sun. These wind systems range from microscale valley breezes to the synoptic-scale Asian monsoon system.

Land and sea winds: Sea and land breezes and the Asian monsoon result mainly from heating differences between the ocean and the land. The ITCZ, orographic uplift by the Himalayas, and heating of the Indian landmass generate the Asian monsoon.

Winds in sloped terrain: Valley and mountain breezes, chinook and foehn winds, Santa Ana winds, and katabatic winds form in sloped terrain and experience adiabatic temperature changes.

4.5 Geographic Perspectives: Farming the Wind

Wind energy: Wind is a clean and renewable energy source that is being rapidly developed.

Wind energy hurdles: There are many hurdles to wind energy development, including storage and transport of the generated energy, bird and bat kills, and the "wumps" and NIMBY problems.

Key Terms

aerovane, 127
anemometer, 127
anticyclone, 132
barometer, 129
boundary layer, 132
chinook wind, 146
Coriolis force, 132
cyclone, 132
desertification, 127
doldrums, 136
dynamic pressure, 131
foehn wind, 146
horse latitudes, 136
isobar, 131
ITCZ (intertropical convergence zone), 134
katabatic wind, 148
land breeze, 142
monsoon, 142
mountain breeze, 146

offshore wind, 129
onshore wind, 129
polar easterlies, 137
polar high, 134
polar jet stream, 138
pressure-gradient force, 131
prevailing wind, 129
Rossby wave (longwave), 138
Santa Ana winds, 147
sea breeze, 142
sea-level pressure, 131
subpolar low, 134
subtropical high, 134
thermal pressure, 129
trade winds, 136
valley breeze, 146
westerlies, 137
wind vane, 127

Concept Review

The Human Sphere: China's Dust Storms

1. What is desertification? How does it relate to dust storms?

4.1 Measuring and Mapping the Wind

2. What instrumentation is used to measure wind speed and direction?

3. What does the Beaufort scale categorize? On what does it base each category?

4. How are winds named? What is a prevailing wind?

5. What are three ways to portray wind on a map?

4.2 Air Pressure and Wind

6. How is air pressure measured?

7. How do thermal pressure and dynamic pressure create differences in air pressure? Explain each.

8. What are isobars and what do they represent?

9. Compare station pressure with sea-level pressure. Why must station pressure always be adjusted to sea-level pressure on surface pressure maps?

10. What are the three controls on wind speed and direction? How does each work?

11. Describe the circulation systems of cyclones and anticyclones. In which direction does air rotate in each of these systems in the Northern Hemisphere?

4.3 Global Atmospheric Circulation Patterns

12. What are the four global pressure systems? Describe the atmospheric circulation that results in these systems.

13. What causes the ITCZ? Why is it always near the equator?

14. Describe the moisture and temperature characteristics of each global pressure system, as well as where it is found geographically.

15. Describe the prevailing surface winds: the trade winds, the westerlies, and the polar easterlies. Where does each occur? Explain why they occur where they do.

16. What and where are the doldrums? What and where are the horse latitudes? What causes them?

17. Where is the polar jet stream?

18. What are Rossby waves? Of what significance are their ridges and troughs to the weather?

19. What happens to the four global pressure systems as the seasons change? What do they do in July? What do they do in January?

20. How do landmasses affect global pressure systems in winter? In summer? In this regard, why does the East Coast of the United States receive summer rainfall while the West Coast does not?

4.4 Wind Systems: Sea Breezes to Gravity Winds

21. What is the relationship between the geographic scale and the duration of wind systems? Give examples.

22. Review the major wind systems. Where is each found, and what causes each?

23. What is a monsoon? What three factors create the Asian monsoon? Describe the summer and winter weather of the Asian monsoon. Explain why they are different.

24. What hazards do Santa Ana winds present?

4.5 Geographic Perspectives: Farming the Wind

25. How is wind kinetic energy converted to electrical energy?

26. Where is it windiest in the United States? What is the inherent problem with this region as a source of wind power?

27. Why is storing and transporting wind energy so important to the growing wind energy market?

28. What methods are available to store wind energy?

29. How are birds and bats killed by wind turbines? Are there solutions to this problem?

30. What does NIMBY stand for? How does that term apply to wind power?

31. Generating power from wind energy is a response to what larger problem? Does wind energy completely solve that problem?

Critical-Thinking Questions

1. Look at Figure 4.5, showing the molecular density of the air in bicycle tires. If one of the tires goes flat from being punctured, what would happen to the pressure gradient between the inside and outside of the inner tube?

2. Which global pressure belt is most influential where you live?

3. Explain the precipitation and temperature pattern where you live in the context of Figure 4.21. Draw a climate diagram for your location.

4. Landmasses can get warmer as global temperatures rise. How could this change the strength of the Asian monsoon during summer? How might it affect precipitation from the monsoon?

5. If you owned a home overlooking the ocean, would you oppose or support a commercial-scale offshore wind turbine project that you could see from your house? Explain.

Test Yourself

Take this quiz to test your chapter knowledge.

1. **True or false?** An anemometer measures wind speed.

2. **True or false?** Cyclones rotate clockwise in the Northern Hemisphere.

3. **True or false?** A sea breeze is an onshore breeze.

4. **True or false?** Chinook winds experience adiabatic heating.

5. **True or false?** The Asian monsoon brings rainfall during winter.

6. **Multiple choice:** Which of the following is not one of the three controls on wind speed and direction covered in this chapter?
   a. Friction
   b. Pressure-gradient force
   c. Latitude
   d. Coriolis force

7. **Multiple choice:** Which of the following surface winds is found in midlatitude locations, such as the United States?
   a. Trade winds
   b. Westerlies
   c. Polar easterlies
   d. Antitrade winds

8. **Multiple choice:** Excluding coastal areas, where is there the most wind energy in the United States?
   a. The Great Plains
   b. The Great Basin
   c. The Northeast
   d. The Northwest

9. **Fill in the blank:** _____ is an instrument used to measure wind direction.

10. **Fill in the blank:** _____ are used to show changing pressure on a map.

Picture This. YOUR TURN

Global Pressure and Wind Systems

Below is a satellite image of the Western Hemisphere for October 13, 2013. Indicate where on the globe the following wind belts and pressure belts are found. The red arrows are surface winds. Use each term only once. *(NASA)*

Doldrums	Southeasterly trade winds
Horse latitudes	Subpolar low
ITCZ	Subtropical high
Northeasterly trade winds	Westerlies

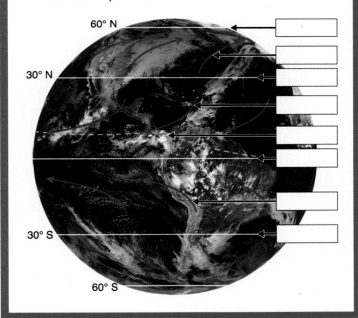

Further Reading

1. Burton, Tony et al. *The Wind Energy Handbook*. 2nd ed. Chichester: Wiley, 2011.

2. Makani Power. Airborne Wind Energy. http://www.google.com/makani/.

3. Marvel, Kate, and Ken Caldeira. "Geophysical Limits to Global Wind Power." *Nature Climate Change* 3 (2013): 118-121.

Answers to Living Physical Geography Questions

1. **Does Earth's rotation control the direction in which water spirals down a drain?** No, the distance within a sink is too short for Coriolis force to influence the water's direction of flow. The direction in which water spirals down a drain is determined by movement in the water and the shape of the sink basin.

2. **Why are tropical rainforests always wet?** It is rainy in the tropics because the ITCZ brings frequent rainfall.

3. **Why is southern California so dry and Georgia so wet in summer when both are at the same latitude?** The Bermuda high brings warm and humid air to Florida from the south during summer. The Pacific high brings cool and dry air from the north to southern California during summer.

4. **What are gravity winds?** Gravity winds are also called katabatic winds. They are winds that flow rapidly downslope because they are cold and heavy.

5. **Do wind turbines kill birds?** Each year up to half a million birds are killed by wind turbines.

5 THE RESTLESS SKY: Storm Systems and El Niño

Chapter Outline

Tornadoes are violently rotating columns of air that extend downward from the base of a severe thunderstorm. No two tornadoes are exactly alike. This long and ropy tornado was photographed in the Texas panhandle near Amarillo. A cloud of debris has formed where the tornado touches the ground.

(© A. T. Willett/Alamy)

To learn more about tornadoes, turn to Section 5.2.

THE BIG PICTURE *Atmospheric systems range in size and strength from afternoon thunderstorms to large and intense hurricanes. Atlantic hurricanes may become stronger in the coming decades.*

LEARNING GOALS *After reading this chapter, you will be able to:*

5.1 ◎ Distinguish among three types of thunderstorms and describe the weather associated with each.

5.2 ◎ Discuss how lightning and tornadoes form and the hazards that each presents.

5.3 ◎ Explain how hurricanes develop, where they occur, and what makes them dangerous.

5.4 ◎ Review the major characteristics and stages of development of a midlatitude cyclone.

5.5 ◎ Discuss how El Niño forms and describe its global effects.

5.6 ◎ Assess the current and potential vulnerability of the United States to major hurricanes.

THE HUMAN SPHERE: The EF5 Tornado

FIGURE 5.1 Tornado damage.
This aerial photo shows the damage done by the EF5 tornado that struck Moore, Oklahoma, on May 20, 2013. A tornado warning system alerted people to find safety before the tornado struck and kept the death toll to 23. (Jocelyn Augustino/FEMA)

THE LARGEST and most locally intense storm on the planet is the *EF5 tornado* (as rated on the enhanced Fujita scale; see Section 5.2). An EF5 tornado has wind speeds of more than 322 km/h (200 mph). There have been approximately 60 EF5 tornadoes in the United States over the last six decades, an average of one per year. In some years, there are none, and in other years, several develop during a single tornado outbreak over the course of a few days. Canada, the country with the second highest tornado activity after the United States, has seen only one EF5 tornado in its recorded history.

Winds in an EF5 tornado can destroy most human-built structures and cause a significant human death toll. One of the more recent EF5 tornadoes was the tornado that struck Moore, Oklahoma, on May 20, 2013, killing 23 people and injuring almost 400 others. It had a diameter of 2.1 km (1.3 mi), and its peak wind speeds were about 340 km/h (210 mph). **Figure 5.1** shows some of the damage done by this tornado.

This chapter highlights storm systems in the atmosphere. We start with thunderstorms and the phenomena they produce, such as lightning and tornadoes. We then move to the smaller-scale phenomena of hurricanes and midlatitude cyclones. Finally, we examine El Niño, an atmospheric system that is not a storm but has a global influence on Earth's storm systems. In the Geographic Perspectives, we will look at the influence of climate change on Atlantic hurricanes.

5.1 Thunderstorms

◎ Distinguish among three types of thunderstorms and describe the weather associated with each.

Storm systems derive their energy from solar heating of Earth's surface and the condensation of water vapor in the atmosphere. In this section we discuss the most localized storm systems, thunderstorms. Subsequent sections examine more geographically extensive storm systems, hurricanes and midlatitude cyclones. Later in the chapter we will explore changes in the global climate system brought on by El Niño. There is a direct relationship between the size and the duration of these atmospheric systems, as **Figure 5.2** shows.

Thunderstorms are cumulonimbus clouds that produce lightning and thunder. We explore thunderstorms as isolated systems here to understand how they function. It is important to keep in mind, however, that most thunderstorms do not occur in isolation. They are embedded within larger synoptic-scale systems, such as hurricanes and midlatitude cyclones.

Each day, there are about 40,000 thunderstorms worldwide. At any given time, some 2,000 thunderstorms are in progress somewhere in the world. The southeastern United States, particularly Florida, has the highest frequency of thunderstorms in the country as a result of warm and moist air masses that move north from the Gulf of Mexico **(Figure 5.3)**.

FIGURE 5.2 **Spatial and temporal relationships of atmospheric systems.**
At one end of the scale, single-cell thunderstorms are short-lived and occupy little geographic space. At the other end of the scale, El Niño (with its counterpart, La Niña), persists more than a year and has global effects.

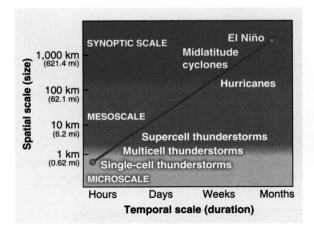

FIGURE 5.3 **Thunderstorm frequency maps.** *(A) Lightning indicates thunderstorm activity. This lightning-flash frequency map shows the average annual number of lightning flashes for the period 1995-2002. About 70% of all thunderstorms occur over land in the tropics. (B) This map shows the average number of thunderstorm days each year in the United States. On average, more than 80 thunderstorm days occur in the orange and red areas of South Florida.* (A. NASA image by Marit Jentoft-Nilsen, based on data provided by the Global Hydrology and Climate Center Lightning Team; B. Data from National Weather Service)

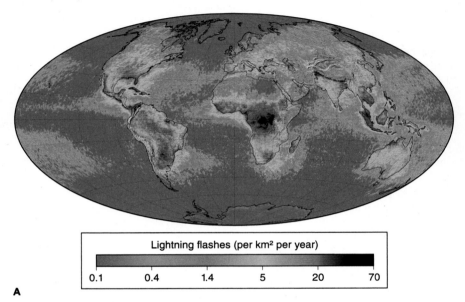

Lightning flashes (per km² per year)

| 0.1 | 0.4 | 1.4 | 5 | 20 | 70 |

A

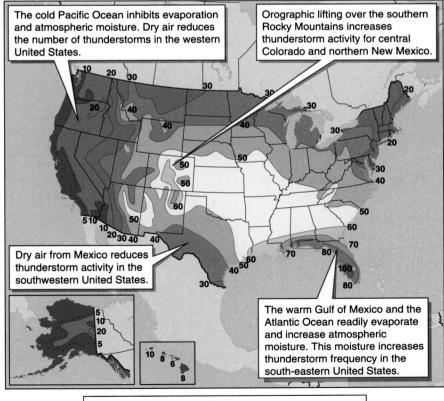

The cold Pacific Ocean inhibits evaporation and atmospheric moisture. Dry air reduces the number of thunderstorms in the western United States.

Orographic lifting over the southern Rocky Mountains increases thunderstorm activity for central Colorado and northern New Mexico.

Dry air from Mexico reduces thunderstorm activity in the southwestern United States.

The warm Gulf of Mexico and the Atlantic Ocean readily evaporate and increase atmospheric moisture. This moisture increases thunderstorm frequency in the south-eastern United States.

Annual thunderstorm days

| 0 | 10 | 20 | 30 | 40 | 50 | 60 | 70 | 80 | 100 | 120 |

B

thunderstorm
A cumulonimbus cloud that produces lightning and thunder.

air mass
A large region of air that is uniform in temperature and humidity.

wind shear
Changes in wind speed and direction with altitude.

single-cell thunderstorm
A type of thunderstorm that is short-lived and rarely severe.

multicell thunderstorm
A type of thunderstorm that forms under conditions of moderate wind shear, is organized in squall lines or clusters, and often produces severe weather.

severe thunderstorm
A thunderstorm that produces either hail sized 2.54 cm (1 in) in diameter, a tornado, or wind gusts of 93 km/h (58 mph) or greater.

squall line
A line of multicell thunderstorm cells that typically forms along a cold front.

Air masses are necessary components of many meteorological processes, particularly thunderstorms. An **air mass** is a large region of air, extending over thousands of kilometers, that is uniform in temperature and humidity. When air remains over a region for weeks or longer, it absorbs the characteristics of that region. For example, air over a warm desert will become warm and dry.

FIGURE 5.4 **Air mass types and source regions.** *Much of the United States receives several different air mass types from surrounding source regions.*

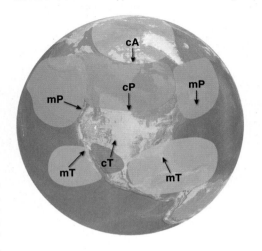

Air Mass Types	
AIR MASS TYPE (ABREVIATION)	**SOURCE REGION/ DESCRIPTION**
continental Arctic (cA)	The polar high/ Very cold and dry
continental Polar (cP)	The polar high/ Cold, dry (forms in winter)
maritime Polar (mP)	The polar high and subpolar low/ Cold, humid
continental Tropical (cT)	The subtropical high/ Hot, dry (forms only in summer)
maritime Tropical (mT)	The ITCZ and the subtropical high/ Warm, humid

FIGURE 5.5 **GEO-GRAPHIC: The three stages of a single-cell thunderstorm.**

1. Cumulus stage
A cumulonimbus cloud forms in warm, upward-flowing currents of air called *updrafts* (shown with red arrows). Air in updrafts rises and cools to its dew point. As condensation occurs, latent heat is released into the cloud, warming the interior and causing it to rise more vigorously.

2. Mature stage
Strong updrafts develop, and rain drags air downward as it falls, forming *downdrafts* (shown with blue arrows). The upper regions of the clouds are so cold that the liquid cloud droplets become *glaciated* and freeze into ice. At this stage, lightning, thunder, heavy rain, and hail are possible.

3. Dissipating stage
Following the mature stage, downdrafts and net evaporation cause the storm to weaken. The falling downdrafts block the updrafts that feed moisture to the cloud. Once updrafts are weakened, the cloud quickly evaporates.

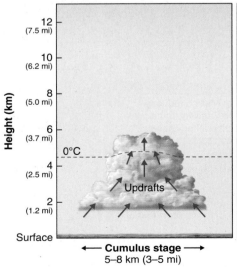
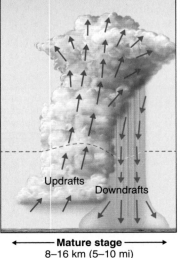
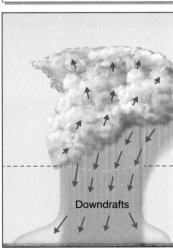

Height (km)

12 (7.5 mi)
10 (6.2 mi)
8 (5.0 mi)
6 (3.7 mi)
0°C
4 (2.5 mi)
2 (1.2 mi)
Surface

Updrafts

Updrafts   Downdrafts

Downdrafts

◄── Cumulus stage ──►
5–8 km (3–5 mi)

◄── Mature stage ──►
8–16 km (5–10 mi)

◄── Dissipating stage ──►
8–11 km (5–7 mi)

1 hour

Air over a warm ocean will become warm and humid.

Air mass types are referred to using abbreviations. Humidity characteristics come first, followed by temperature characteristics (Figure 5.4). For example, "mT" refers to a maritime-tropical air mass, meaning that it formed over an ocean in the tropics and is humid and warm. An mT air mass is essential for thunderstorm development.

There are three types of thunderstorms: single-cell thunderstorms, multicell thunderstorms, and supercell thunderstorms. The two most important factors that determine thunderstorm type are atmospheric humidity and **wind shear** (changes in wind speed and direction with altitude).

Single-Cell Thunderstorms

Single-cell thunderstorms are almost always relatively mild, short-lived thunderstorms that last up to an hour. They form within mT air masses where wind shear is weak. They develop in the late afternoon as unequal heating of the ground creates unstable air parcels (see Section 3.3). As these air parcels rise, they cool to the dew point, which results in condensation and cumulonimbus cloud formation. Single-cell thunderstorms typically experience a predictable sequence of growth, maturation, and dissipation (Figure 5.5).

Multicell Thunderstorms

Multicell thunderstorms form under conditions of moderate wind shear with wind speeds of about 40 to 65 km/h or 23 to 40 mph. These mesoscale systems consist of thunderstorm cells organized in long lines or clusters. Multicell thunderstorms often produce severe weather. They differ from single-cell thunderstorms in that they persist longer and form mainly along boundaries between air masses (called *fronts*) rather than within air masses.

Multicell thunderstorms are sometimes severe and typically last several hours. A **severe thunderstorm** is defined as one that produces either hail 2.54 cm (1 in) in diameter, a tornado, or wind gusts of 93 km/h (58 mph) or greater. Only about 10% (10,000) of the 100,000 thunderstorms that form in the United States each year are classified as severe.

Individual cells within a multicell thunderstorm persist for only about an hour (like single-cell thunderstorms), but as a whole, the system persists for many hours. Multicell thunderstorm systems are arranged in clusters called *mesoscale convective systems* or linearly in squall lines. A **squall line** is a line of multicell thunderstorm cells that typically forms along a cold front on a midlatitude cyclone (see Section 5.4). Squall lines can extend for hundreds of kilometers, persist for hours, and bring severe weather (Figure 5.6).

FIGURE 5.6 GEO-GRAPHIC: Anatomy of a squall line.

(A) This image shows a cross-section of a multicell thunderstorm organized along a squall line. The inset figure shows the squall line in a top view. The movement of the system is from left to right. As the system moves forward, warm air rising over the gust front gives rise to new cells (labeled Cell A and Cell B). Over the course of about 30 minutes, these cells will grow and replace cell C. A derecho originating from the downdrafts can be as damaging as hurricane or tornado winds. (B) This squall line moved over Washington, D.C., on July 25, 2010. It did significant damage to trees and power lines, causing extensive power outages. (B. NOAA-NASA GOES Project)

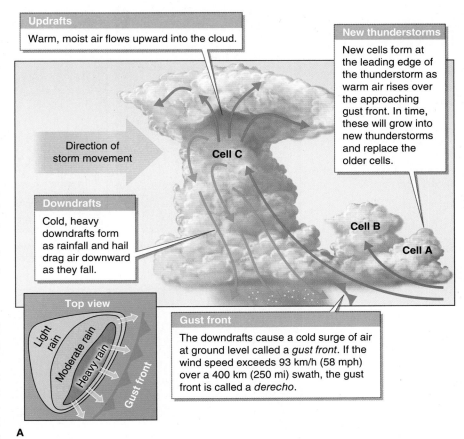

Updrafts
Warm, moist air flows upward into the cloud.

New thunderstorms
New cells form at the leading edge of the thunderstorm as warm air rises over the approaching gust front. In time, these will grow into new thunderstorms and replace the older cells.

Direction of storm movement

Cell C

Cell B

Cell A

Downdrafts
Cold, heavy downdrafts form as rainfall and hail drag air downward as they fall.

Top view
Light rain
Moderate rain
Heavy rain
Gust front

Gust front
The downdrafts cause a cold surge of air at ground level called a *gust front*. If the wind speed exceeds 93 km/h (58 mph) over a 400 km (250 mi) swath, the gust front is called a *derecho*.

A

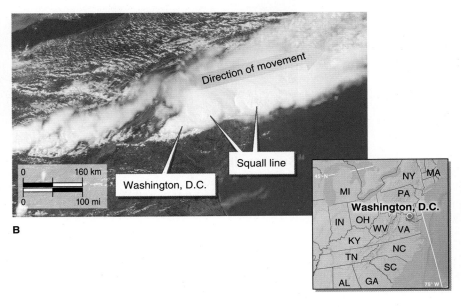

Direction of movement

Squall line

Washington, D.C.

0   160 km
0   100 mi

B

NY MA
MI   PA
Washington, D.C.
IN OH WV VA
KY   NC
TN   SC
AL GA

FIGURE **5.7** **Supercell thunderstorm formation.** *(A) A mesocyclone forms when a horizontal cylinder of rotating air is tilted vertically by strong updrafts. (B) The rounded striations (lines) seen here indicate rotation in a supercell thunderstorm. This supercell was photographed near Kadoka, South Dakota. (B. © Mike Hollingshead/Corbis)*

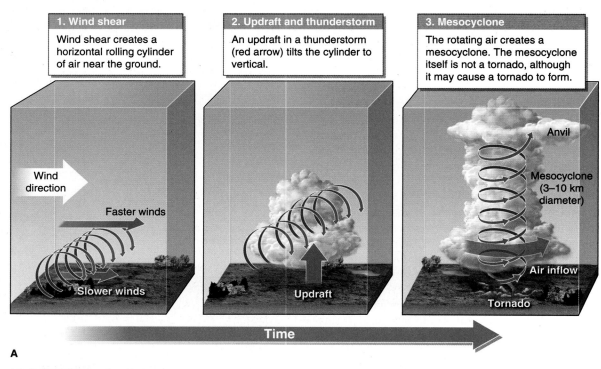

1. Wind shear
Wind shear creates a horizontal rolling cylinder of air near the ground.

2. Updraft and thunderstorm
An updraft in a thunderstorm (red arrow) tilts the cylinder to vertical.

3. Mesocyclone
The rotating air creates a mesocyclone. The mesocyclone itself is not a tornado, although it may cause a tornado to form.

Wind direction
Faster winds
Slower winds

Updraft

Anvil
Mesocyclone (3–10 km diameter)
Air inflow
Tornado

Time

A

MT | ND
SD | MN | WI
WY | ⊙ Kadoka
NE | IA
CO | KS | MO
OK

B

Supercell Thunderstorms

The least common but most powerful thunderstorm type is the **supercell thunderstorm,** which contains a rotating cylindrical updraft. Supercell thunderstorms usually produce severe weather. Almost all powerful tornadoes are produced by supercell thunderstorms.

Supercell thunderstorms form over land where there is humid air and strong wind shear. These

| Why do some thunderstorms rotate?* |

conditions frequently occur in spring in North America over the southern Great Plains in Kansas and Oklahoma. The term *supercell* refers to the thunderstorm as a whole, and the term **mesocyclone** refers to the rotating cylindrical updraft within the supercell. **Figure 5.7** outlines how a mesocyclone develops within a thunderstorm.

supercell thunderstorm
A thunderstorm with a rotating cylindrical updraft that usually produces severe weather.

mesocyclone
The rotating cylindrical updraft within a supercell thunderstorm.

*Answers to the Living Physical Geography questions are found on page 189.

5.2 Thunderstorm Hazards: Lightning and Tornadoes

◎ Discuss how lightning and tornadoes form and the hazards that each presents.

All thunderstorms are potentially dangerous. The two particularly hazardous phenomena produced by thunderstorms are lightning and tornadoes.

Lightning

Lightning is one of nature's most awe-inspiring displays. **Lightning** is an electrical discharge that all thunderstorms produce. Recent satellite data indicate that there are about 35 lightning flashes per second and over 3 million flashes per day worldwide. Lightning may discharge between cumulonimbus clouds (called *cloud-to-cloud* lightning), within a single cumulonimbus cloud, or between a cumulonimbus cloud and the ground (called *cloud-to-ground* lightning) **(Figure 5.8)**.

> **How wide is a bolt of lightning?**

A bolt of lightning is about 2.5 cm (1 in) in diameter and about 5 times hotter than the surface of the Sun (30,000°C or 54,000°F). **The air around a lightning bolt becomes superheated and expands explosively, creating an acoustic shock wave called thunder.**

FIGURE 5.9 **A fulgurite.** *Fulgurites are produced when heat melts sand into glass as lightning travels through the ground. This fulgurite is about 35 cm (14 in) long. (© Stan Celestian)*

When lightning strikes the ground, it follows channels of least resistance, particularly through objects with a high water content, such as wet soil or tree roots. Its path can be seen when the heat of lightning fuses silica in sand into a glassy hollow tube called a **fulgurite**, as shown in **Figure 5.9**.

What Causes Lightning?

Lightning is formed as cumulonimbus clouds develop a separation of electrical charges. As rain, ice crystals, and hail within the cloud collide, friction creates negative and positive charges within these particles. Larger particles become negatively charged

lightning
An electrical discharge produced by thunderstorms.

thunder
An acoustic shock wave produced when lightning rapidly heats and expands the air around it.

fulgurite
A glassy hollow tube formed where lightning strikes sand.

FIGURE 5.8 **Lightning.** *This 20-second exposure of a lightning storm in Athens, Greece, shows both cloud-to-cloud and cloud-to-ground lightning bolts. Only about 25% of all lightning discharges are cloud-to-ground. (© Christos Kotsiopoulos)*

wall cloud
A cylindrical cloud that protrudes from the base of a supercell thunderstorm.

tornado
A violently rotating column of air that descends from a cumulonimbus cloud and touches ground.

enhanced Fujita scale (EF Scale)
A system used to rank tornado strength based on damage done to the landscape.

FIGURE 5.10 **Electrical charges in a cloud.** *Lightning results as opposite electrical charges develop in different regions of a cloud and on the ground.*

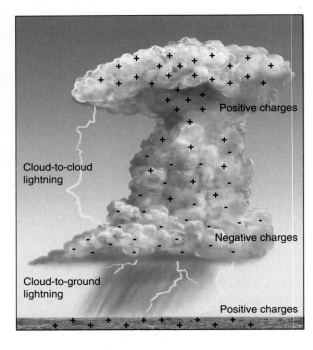

and smaller particles become positively charged. With the assistance of air turbulence, lighter ice crystals with a positive charge migrate upward in the cloud, and heavier particles, such as rain and hail, with a negative charge migrate to the lower parts of the cloud **(Figure 5.10)**.

Normally, Earth's surface has a negative charge, and the upper atmosphere has a positive charge. Because of the negative charge at the base of the thunderstorm, a positive charge follows along the ground beneath a thunderstorm like a shadow. Objects that protrude above the ground, such as buildings and trees, develop the strongest positive charge.

Air is an insulator and inhibits the flow of electricity. As a result, the opposite electrical charges between the cloud and ground, or within the cloud, build up to tens of millions of volts. Eventually, two oppositely charged regions develop an electrical connection, and a bolt of lightning is discharged. This discharge equalizes the electrical charges for a short while. Soon, however, another pair of opposite charges builds up and results in another lightning discharge.

Staying Safe in Lightning

Being caught outside in lightning is an unforgettable and potentially deadly experience. About 500 people are struck by lightning each year in the United States, mostly in Florida. Only about 10% of lightning-strike victims are killed. The rest suffer injuries ranging from minor burns to permanent disabilities. To stay safe, retreat indoors during thunderstorms if at all possible. **Figure 5.11** provides the basic guidelines to staying safe in a thunderstorm.

Light travels at a speed of 300,000 km (186,000 mi) per second. Thus, the light from a flash of lightning reaches our eyes almost instantly. The speed of sound is much slower, however, and depends on characteristics of the atmosphere. At sea level, sound travels at about 343 m (or 1,120 ft) per second. Because of the time lag between the lightning discharge and the sound of thunder, it is possible to calculate the distance of a bolt of lightning **(Crunch the Numbers)**.

The 30/30 rule of lightning safety states that it is not safe to go outdoors if lightning is within 10 km (6 mi) of your location (30 seconds between lightning and thunder) and that it is best to wait until 30 minutes after the storm has passed to go back outside. In some cases, lightning is too distant for thunder to be heard, resulting in silent flashes of what is often called *heat lightning*.

Tornado!

Most tornadoes form in supercell thunderstorms, but tornadoes can also form in hurricanes and cold fronts. Meteorologists do not yet understand why only

FIGURE 5.11 **Lightning safety.** *When outdoors, avoid being near the highest point on the landscape, such as on a mountain pass (1), in a boat on flat water, on a golf course (2) or soccer field, or under a single tall tree (3). When indoors, avoid materials that conduct electricity, such as landline phones, electrical appliances, computers (4), and running water. If caught outdoors in a forest, seek shelter among the lowest trees (5). Remaining in a car is relatively safe (6), as lightning is likely to be conducted safely through the metal exterior and down into the ground.*

CRUNCH THE NUMBERS:
Calculating Lightning Distance

After you see a flash of lightning, begin counting in seconds until you hear the sound of thunder. Using the speed of sound at sea level given in the text, determine how far away the lightning is by the length of time it took the sound to travel between the lightning and your position. (To convert meters to kilometers, divide by 1,000. To convert feet to miles, divide by 5,280.) If you count 15 seconds, how many kilometers (or miles) away is the lightning?

FIGURE 5.12 **Tornadic supercell.** *(A) A supercell thunderstorm contains a powerful rotating updraft called a mesocyclone. Tornadoes often descend from wall clouds at the base of the mesocyclone. (B) A tornado has formed from this supercell thunderstorm over Campo, Colorado. (B. © Mike Theiss/National Geographic Creative/Getty Images)*

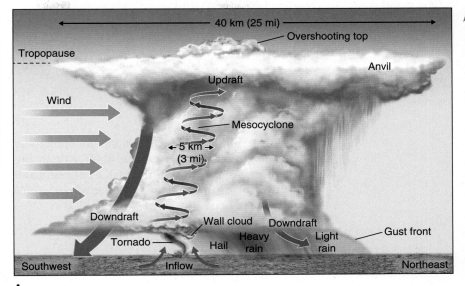

A

B

about 25% of supercell thunderstorms produce tornadoes. If a tornado does form, it usually descends from a **wall cloud**, a cylindrical cloud that protrudes from the base of the mesocyclone **(Figure 5.12)**. Scientists still do not know how tornadoes form in a supercell thunderstorm.

A **tornado** is a violently rotating column of air that descends from a cumulonimbus cloud and touches the ground. A *funnel cloud* is a rotating column that descends from a cumulonimbus cloud but is not in contact with the ground. Tornadoes are ranked using the **enhanced Fujita scale (EF scale)** **(Figure 5.13A)**. Tornado strength is estimated by the damage done to the landscape. As with many natural phenomena, the frequency and intensity of tornadoes are inversely related: There are many low-intensity (weak) tornadoes but very few high-intensity (strong) tornadoes **(Figure 5.13B)**.

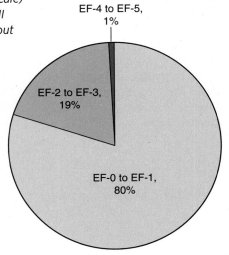

FIGURE 5.13 **Tornado intensity and frequency.** *(A) The enhanced Fujita scale (EF scale) uses six tornado strength categories. (B) Eighty percent of tornadoes are EF0 to EF1. Only 1% of all tornadoes in the United States are EF4 and EF5; however, those EF4 and EF5 tornadoes cause about two-thirds of tornado-related deaths.*

The Enhanced Fujita Scale

EF SCALE	WIND SPEED, KM/H (MPH)	TYPICAL DAMAGE
EF0	105-137 (68-85)	Light damage. Some roof tiles peeled off. Tree branches broken.
EF1	138-177 (86-110)	Moderate damage. Roof tiles stripped. Windows broken.
EF2	178-217 (111-135)	Considerable damage. Frame houses shifted from foundations. Large trees snapped or uprooted.
EF3	218-266 (136-165)	Severe damage. Trains overturned. Cars lifted off the ground.
EF4	267-322 (166-200)	Devastating damage. Houses disintegrate. Cars thrown and small missiles generated.
EF5	Over 322 (Over 200)	Incredible damage. Cars fly through the air more than 100 m.

A

B

CHARACTERISTIC	TYPICAL	UNUSUAL
TABLE **5.1** AT A GLANCE: U.S. Tornado Characteristics		
Time of year	April–July	Winter
Time of day	4:00 to 6:00 p.m.	Early morning
Diameter	50 m (160 ft)	1.5 km (1 mi)
Forward movement speed	48 km/h (30 mph)	113 km/h (70 mph)
Length of ground path	3 km (2 mi)	480 km (300 mi)
Duration	5 minutes	Up to 6 hours

Most tornadoes in the United States cause only light to moderate damage, and they stay on the ground no longer than 5 minutes. The months of April through July are the most active period for tornadoes **(Table 5.1)**.

Tornado Geography

> Do tornadoes ever strike the same place twice?

Tornadoes do strike the same place twice. Despite very low odds, Codell, Kansas (current population about 2,700), was struck by tornadoes three years in a row—1916, 1917, and 1918—all on May 20!

The United States has the highest frequency of tornadoes and the strongest tornadoes in the world (Figure 5.14A). The United States experiences about 1,200 tornadoes each year, the highest number of any country. Canada ranks second in tornado frequency for any country, with about 100 per year on average.

Because Florida experiences the most thunderstorm days per year, it also experiences the most tornadoes (4.7 per 10,000 km^2 or 3,860 mi^2). The majority of these are EF0 and EF1 tornadoes.

FIGURE **5.14**

Tornado geography.

(A) As this tornado risk map shows, tornadoes occur on every continent except Antarctica. (B) The region of the Great Plains that extends roughly from northern Texas to South Dakota is often called Tornado Alley. Warm maritime tropical (mT) air from the Gulf of Mexico, dry continental tropical (cT) air from the interior deserts, and cold continental polar (cP) air from the north frequently meet over the Great Plains. These air masses often stack on top of one another and together provide high humidity, strong instability, and wind shear. These conditions give rise to supercell thunderstorms.

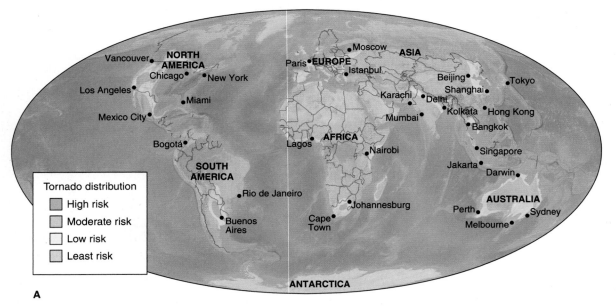

Tornado distribution
- High risk
- Moderate risk
- Low risk
- Least risk

A

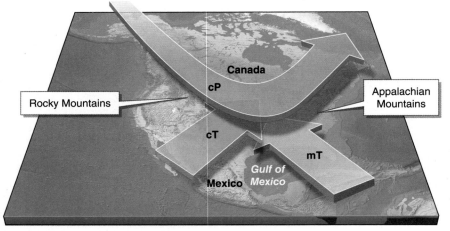

B

Kansas, on the Great Plains, experiences the second highest frequency of tornadoes (4.5 per 10,000 km²). Because the Great Plains are relatively flat, warm and humid mT air masses from the south interact there with dry and cold air masses from the west and north. In most other parts of the world, mountain ranges keep these air masses separate. Most EF4 and EF5 tornadoes in the United States occur between the Rocky Mountains and the Appalachian Mountains as far north as the Dakotas (Figure 5.14B).

Warning the Public, Saving Lives

When a tornado touches ground in the United States, the National Weather Service issues an alert. Tornado sirens sound the alarm, and all media channels, including TV, radio, and the Internet, broadcast the alert. These alerts have saved many thousands of lives since they were first implemented in the mid-1950s.

A **tornado watch** is issued hours in advance of a possible storm to help people prepare. Watches are issued when conditions are favorable for tornadic thunderstorms. A **tornado warning** is issued when a tornado or funnel cloud has been seen and called in to local authorities or when a strong near-surface rotation pattern (called a *hook echo signature*) is detected by Doppler radar (Figure 5.15).

The most important element in staying safe during a tornado is early warning. Those living where powerful tornadoes are possible should always have a two-day (or more) stock of food and water stored away. Table 5.2 provides the basic guidelines of tornado safety.

FIGURE 5.15 **A hook echo signature.** *This Doppler radar reflectivity image shows the hook echo signature produced by the Greensburg, Kansas, tornado of May 4, 2007. The heaviest precipitation is shown in orange and red. Pink indicates large hail. The overall hook echo pattern reflects rotation of the mesocyclone. Usually the tornado itself cannot be detected by radar because it is too small.* (National Weather Service, Dodge City, KS)

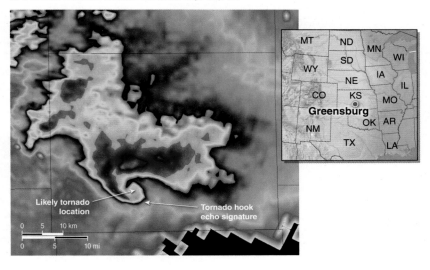

5.3 Nature's Deadliest Storms: Hurricanes

◎ Explain how hurricanes develop, where they occur, and what makes them dangerous.

The fastest wind ever officially recorded was produced by the release of latent heat in tropical cyclone Olivia. The storm produced a wind gust of 408 km/h (252 mph), measured on April 10, 1996, on Barrow Island, Australia.

Hurricane is the North American name for a tropical cyclone with sustained winds of 119 km/h (74 mph) or greater. Hurricanes are capable of producing meters of rainfall, heavy flooding, and damaging high winds. A single storm can devastate extensive coastal regions and cause hundreds of thousands of fatalities. To make matters worse, tornadoes often form in the severe thunderstorms that precede hurricanes.

What Is a Hurricane?

What does the word *hurricane* mean?

The word *hurricane* is derived from *Huracán/Juracán*, meaning "god of storms" in the Taino language of the Lesser Antilles islands in the Caribbean Sea. Hurricanes are deep low-pressure systems occurring in the tropics. Like all cyclonic storm systems, hurricanes rotate counterclockwise (in the Northern Hemisphere) around a region of low barometric pressure. Meteorologists refer to hurricanes as tropical cyclones. A **tropical cyclone**

TABLE 5.2	AT A GLANCE: Tornado Safety	
WHAT TO DO	**WHAT TO AVOID**
Indoors	
Retreat to a basement or interior room or hallway.	Windows, which are easily shattered into dangerous glass shards.
Retreat to the lowest floor.	Heavy objects such as refrigerators, which can fall on a person.
Crouch in a bathtub.	Exterior walls, which can fail in high winds.
Cover yourself with a mattress or sleeping bag.	Mobile homes, even those with anchored foundations, are unsafe in a tornado.
Outdoors	
Find low ground and lie facedown with arms over head.	Cars. If caught in a car, park on the side of road. Keep seat belt on, and put head down below the windows.
	Bridges. Wind speed increases under bridges.

tornado watch
An alert issued by the National Weather service when conditions are favorable for tornadic thunderstorms.

tornado warning
A warning issued by the National Weather Service after a tornado has been seen and called in to local authorities or when one is suggested by a Doppler radar hook echo signature.

hurricane
The North American name for a tropical cyclone with sustained winds of 119 km/h (74 mph) or greater.

tropical cyclone
A tropical cyclonic storm with sustained winds of 119 km/h (74 mph) or greater.

typhoon
A name used for tropical cyclones in Southeast Asia.

is a cyclonic storm with sustained winds of 119 km/h (74 mph) or greater.

Tropical cyclones go by many names depending on the geographic region in which they occur. North America and Central America use *hurricane*, southeastern Asia uses **typhoon**, and countries bordering the Indian Ocean use *cyclone*, except Australia, which uses *tropical cyclone*.

In addition, individual tropical cyclones are given identifying names, such as Hurricane Sandy or Typhoon Jelawat (which means "carp"). Naming systems are different for each of the ocean basins

FIGURE 5.16 **Tropical cyclone anatomy.** *This image shows Typhoon Haiyan on November 7, 2013. This storm was notable for being the strongest tropical cyclone ever to strike land. Arrows show the direction of rotation within the storm. Haiyan formed a well-defined eye, eyewall, and rain-band structure. It had maximum 1-minute sustained wind speeds of 315 km/h (195 mph). Haiyan took over 6,200 lives, mostly in the Philippines. The inset map shows Haiyan's path over the Philippines, then mainland Southeast Asia.* (NASA)

Eyewall
The eyewall is a region of tightly rotating air. Airflow spirals upward vertically to the tropopause. The fastest winds and the heaviest rain of the storm are found in the eyewall.

Eye
The eye has the lowest pressure of the storm. Within the center of the eye, air gently sinks.

Rain bands
Rain bands are regions of uplift that wrap around the storm and spiral inward to the storm's eye.

0   160 km
0   100 mi

PACIFIC OCEAN
SOUTH CHINA SEA
Philippines
Haiyan's path

FIGURE 5.17 **GEO-GRAPHIC: Hurricane latent heat positive feedback.**

Hurricanes derive their high wind speeds from latent heat positive feedback.

Animation
Hurricane
positive feedback
http://qrs.ly/vs434g3

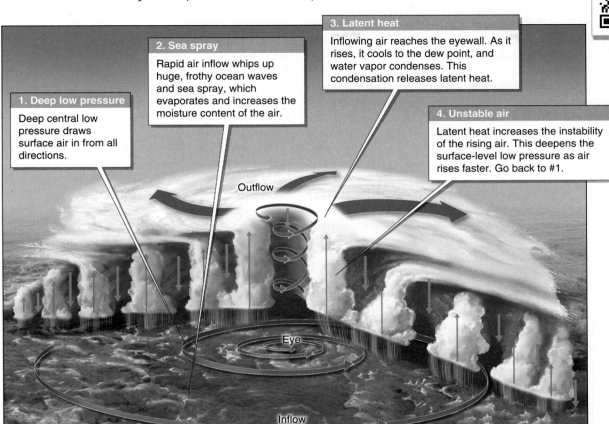

1. Deep low pressure

Deep central low pressure draws surface air in from all directions.

2. Sea spray

Rapid air inflow whips up huge, frothy ocean waves and sea spray, which evaporates and increases the moisture content of the air.

3. Latent heat

Inflowing air reaches the eyewall. As it rises, it cools to the dew point, and water vapor condenses. This condensation releases latent heat.

4. Unstable air

Latent heat increases the instability of the rising air. This deepens the surface-level low pressure as air rises faster. Go back to #1.

Outflow

Eye

Inflow

where tropical cyclones occur. Atlantic Ocean hurricanes are named according to an alphabetical list of common first names in English, French, and Spanish. The names of destructive hurricanes, like Hurricane Sandy and Hurricane Katrina, are taken off the list and replaced by other names starting with the same letter. The names of Pacific typhoons west of the 180th meridian describe a range of phenomena, including food, star constellations, plants, and wildlife.

Why Are Hurricane Winds So Fast?

Hurricane winds are among the fastest and most sustained on the planet. Air rapidly flows in toward the low-pressure center of a hurricane, and Coriolis force causes that airflow to be deflected, creating a rotating pinwheel structure (Figure 5.16).

Like that of a thunderstorm, the strength of a hurricane depends on how much water vapor condenses to liquid. Condensation is important because it releases latent heat into the storm (see Section 3.1). As the rotating airflow grows faster, it pulls in more moisture, which releases latent heat and further strengthens the storm, creating a positive feedback (Figure 5.17).

The latent heat positive feedback in hurricanes results in high winds and, sometimes, extraordinary amounts of precipitation. Rainfall amounts, however, are more often a function of the hurricane's forward speed than its strength. Cyclone Gamede moved slowly over the island of Réunion in the Indian Ocean in 2007. The storm brought 3.93 m (12.9 ft) of rain in a three-day period. After six days of continuous rainfall, precipitation totals came to 5.51 m (18.1 ft), setting world records for rainfall totals during a single storm.

tropical storm
A tropical cyclonic storm with sustained winds between 63 and 118 km/h (39 to 73 mph).

Saffir-Simpson scale
A hurricane ranking system based on measured wind speeds.

Stages of Hurricane Development

We learned in Section 4.3 that the trade winds of the tropics flow from east to west. As these winds flow across northern Africa, they develop ripples called *tropical waves*. Some tropical waves are generated by the Ethiopian Highlands in eastern Africa and the Atlas Mountains of northwestern Africa. Land-sea temperature contrasts between the Sahara and the Atlantic Ocean can also form tropical waves from which a hurricane may later develop. The ITCZ provides the instability that allows a hurricane to develop and persist. **Figure 5.18A** shows the stages of hurricane development from tropical disturbance to tropical storm. **Tropical storms** are cyclonic systems that have sustained winds between 63 and 118 km/h (39 to 73 mph).

Once a hurricane has formed, it may strengthen if conditions are favorable. Meteorologists use the **Saffir-Simpson scale**, a hurricane ranking system based on measured wind speeds, to describe five categories of hurricane intensity (Figure 5.18B).

FIGURE 5.18 **Hurricane development.** *(A) A tropical disturbance may develop into a hurricane if conditions are right. This image shows the progression of a single tropical disturbance into a hurricane as it crosses the Atlantic Ocean. Not all Atlantic hurricanes form off the west coast of northern Africa, however; hurricanes also form within the Caribbean Sea and the Gulf of Mexico. (B) The Saffir-Simpson scale of hurricane intensity.*

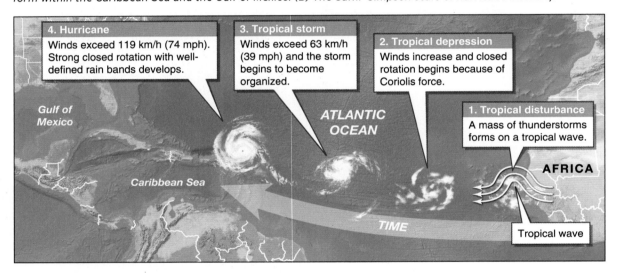

Stages of Hurricane Development

STAGE	WIND SPEEDS	OTHER CHARACTERISTICS
Tropical disturbance	Light	A mass of thunderstorms with no rotation
Tropical depression	<61 km/h (<38 mph)	Closed rotation begins
Tropical storm	63-118 km/h (39-73 mph)	Stronger rotation, heavy rainfall
Hurricane	>119 km/h (>73 mph)	Strong circulation, heavy rain. Identifiable eye, eyewall, and rain bands often evident.

A

The Saffir-Simpson Scale

CATEGORY	WIND SPEED (KM/H)	WIND SPEED (MPH)	PRESSURE (MB)	DAMAGE
1	119-153	74-95	> 980	Minimal
2	154-177	96-110	965-979	Moderate
3	178-209	111-130	945-964	Extensive
4	210-249	131-155	920-944	Extreme
5	> 250	> 155	< 920	Catastrophic

B

FIGURE 5.19 SCIENTIFIC INQUIRY: How do meteorologists monitor hurricanes?

Knowing where and when a hurricane will strike, as well as its likely strength, is essential to efforts to save lives. Decisions to evacuate coastal areas are based on close monitoring of these storms by NASA, NOAA, and the National Weather Service. (NOAA PMEL Carbon Group and the University of Georgia; http://www.pmel.noaa.gov/co2/)

Satellites

Satellites such as NASA's *Terra* provide early detection and tracking of hurricanes. But they cannot provide enough detail to develop accurate forecasts and warnings.

Aircraft reconnaissance and dropsondes

As hurricanes approach U.S. shores, aircraft drop small instrument platforms called *dropsondes* into the storms. These devices provide measurements of wind speed, pressure, humidity, and air temperature. These data are radioed back to the plane by the dropsonde as it descends through the storm.

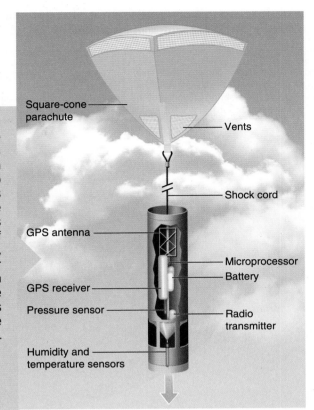

Square-cone parachute
Vents
Shock cord
GPS antenna
Microprocessor
Battery
GPS receiver
Pressure sensor
Radio transmitter
Humidity and temperature sensors

Marine buoys

Buoys are floating meteorological stations anchored to the seafloor. They record seawater temperature at the surface and at depth. They also record meteorological conditions just above the water.

Doppler radar

When a hurricane comes within 320 km (200 mi) of shore, Doppler radar can begin imaging it, providing detailed information on wind strength, rainfall intensity, and direction of movement. Meteorologists use these data to develop wind speed and precipitation forecasts as the storm comes ashore.

Video
Hurricane monitoring
http://qrs.ly/t8434gb

For a hurricane to persist and strengthen, it must have an ample supply of warm seawater that readily evaporates. Warm seawater is the main fuel for hurricanes. Generally, water temperature must be about 26°C (80°F). Cooler water reduces the moisture supply to hurricanes because it does not evaporate as quickly. The high waves stirred up by the storm will mix deeper, cooler seawater with the surface water, so the warm water must extend to about 60 m (200 ft) in depth. There must also be little to no wind shear, which tears hurricanes apart.

As hurricanes approach populated areas, meteorologists monitor them closely to forecast where they will make landfall and how strong they will be when they do (Figure 5.19).

FIGURE 5.20 **GEO-GRAPHIC: The geography of hurricanes.** *This map shows the paths of all hurricanes, tropical storms, and tropical depressions in recorded history. TD = tropical depression. TS = tropical storm.* (Robert Rohde/globalwarmingart.com)

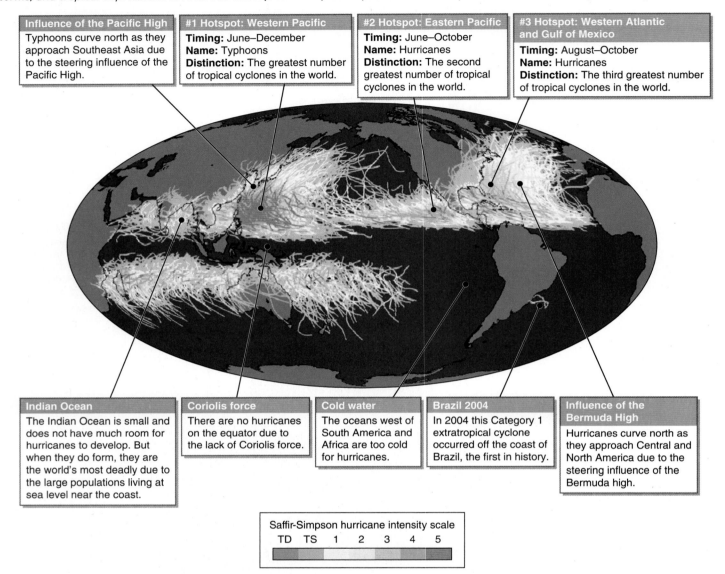

Influence of the Pacific High
Typhoons curve north as they approach Southeast Asia due to the steering influence of the Pacific High.

#1 Hotspot: Western Pacific
Timing: June–December
Name: Typhoons
Distinction: The greatest number of tropical cyclones in the world.

#2 Hotspot: Eastern Pacific
Timing: June–October
Name: Hurricanes
Distinction: The second greatest number of tropical cyclones in the world.

#3 Hotspot: Western Atlantic and Gulf of Mexico
Timing: August–October
Name: Hurricanes
Distinction: The third greatest number of tropical cyclones in the world.

Indian Ocean
The Indian Ocean is small and does not have much room for hurricanes to develop. But when they do form, they are the world's most deadly due to the large populations living at sea level near the coast.

Coriolis force
There are no hurricanes on the equator due to the lack of Coriolis force.

Cold water
The oceans west of South America and Africa are too cold for hurricanes.

Brazil 2004
In 2004 this Category 1 extratropical cyclone occurred off the coast of Brazil, the first in history.

Influence of the Bermuda High
Hurricanes curve north as they approach Central and North America due to the steering influence of the Bermuda high.

Saffir-Simpson hurricane intensity scale
TD TS 1 2 3 4 5

Hurricane Geography

Subtropical highs guide hurricanes in all ocean basins. Where hurricanes make *landfall* (move onshore) in the eastern United States (assuming they do make landfall) depends on the steering influence of the Bermuda high, which is part of the subtropical high-pressure belt (see Section 4.3). **Figure 5.20** summarizes the factors that control the paths of hurricanes and the resulting geographic extent of hurricanes worldwide.

storm surge
A rise in sea level caused by the strong winds and low atmospheric pressure of a hurricane.

Why Are Hurricanes Dangerous?

Hurricanes present two basic hazards: flooding and sustained high winds. Hurricanes bring two types of flooding, inland flooding from rivers over-flowing their banks and coastal flooding from storm surges.

Coastal flooding is the most dangerous aspect of hurricanes. The strong winds and low atmospheric pressure of a hurricane cause a rise in sea level called a **storm surge (Figure 5.21).** Low-lying coastal areas are inundated by seawater as a storm surge comes ashore. The storm's high winds also create large waves that break on top of the storm surge. The storm surge is typically about 80 to 160 km (50 to 100 mi) wide.

High winds do not cause as many human fatalities as flooding, but if people are caught outside in high winds, they are at risk of being struck by flying debris. High winds also cause much property damage.

TABLE 5.3 The 10 Deadliest Hurricanes Worldwide

RANK	APPROXIMATE DEATHS	LOCATION	DATE
1	500,000	West Bengal/ Bangladesh	1970
2	300,000	Hooghly River, Bengal, India	1737
3	300,000	Haiphong, Vietnam	1881
4	300,000	Coringa, southern India	1839
5	200,000	Bengal	1584 or 1582
6	200,000	China	1975
7	200,000	Calcutta, Bengal, India	1876
8	140,000	Burma	2008
9	140,000	Bangladesh	1991
10	100,000	Arabian Sea, western India	1882

Inland flooding from hurricanes does sometimes cause considerable loss of life. For instance, Hurricane Mitch struck Honduras and Nicaragua in 1998 and caused rivers there to overflow their banks and cut into steep cliff faces. This created a dangerous mix of mudslides and flooding. In all, some 11,000 people died in that storm as a result of inland flooding, and 1.5 million people were left homeless.

Worldwide, hurricanes are the main meteorological killer. The losses of life they inflict can be staggering (Table 5.3). With satellite technology, hurricanes can no longer catch us by surprise, but this fact does not always prevent the loss of human lives. Some particularly deadly hurricanes have occurred in recent times. The most recent devastating hurricane was in 2008 in Burma.

All but two of the disasters listed in Table 5.3 occurred in countries bordering the Indian Ocean. Burma, Bangladesh, and India have suffered the greatest losses of life. Presumably, such large death tolls could have been avoided by getting people out of harm's way. Yet large populations live at sea level near the coast where there is no high ground. Dire poverty also makes it impossible to evacuate everyone.

As Table 5.4 shows, the United States also experiences deadly hurricanes, but loss of life is far less there because of better warning systems and better ability to evacuate people in coastal areas to higher ground.

Hurricane Katrina occurred in recent times, yet caused the third most fatalities. New Orleans

FIGURE 5.21 **Storm surge.** *A dome of seawater causes sea level to rise as a hurricane comes ashore. About 95% of the raised sea level is the result of strong winds that pile up the seawater. Decreased atmospheric pressure, which allows the sea to expand upward, contributes to about 5% of the storm surge.*

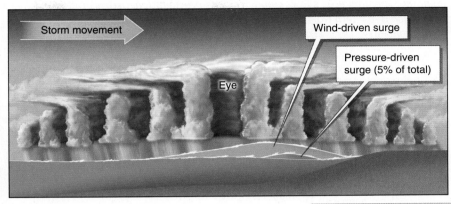

Storm movement

Wind-driven surge

Pressure-driven surge (5% of total)

Eye

Video
Storm surge protectors
http://qrs.ly/vm434gf

lies in a topographic bowl that is below sea level and easily flooded. When the hurricane struck the city, some of the protective walls surrounding it failed, and much of the bowl filled with water. Poverty and inability or unwillingness to evacuate were also important factors in that disaster. The Geographic Perspectives at the end of this chapter explores the threat posed to New Orleans and other U.S. cities by hurricanes.

GEOGRAPHIC PERSPECTIVES

TABLE 5.4 The 10 Deadliest Hurricanes in the United States

RANK	APPROXIMATE DEATHS	LOCATION	DATE
1	8,000	Galveston, Texas	1900
2	2,500	Lake Okeechobee, Florida	1928
3	1,836	Hurricane Katrina, New Orleans	2005
4	1,800–2,000	Louisiana and Mississippi	1893
5	1,000–2,500	South Carolina and Georgia	1893
6	700	Georgia and South Carolina	1881
7	638	New England	1938
8	600	Florida	1919
9	500	Georgia and South Carolina	1804
10	450	Corpus Christi, Texas	1919

FIGURE 5.22 **GEO-GRAPHIC: Midlatitude cyclone.** *(A) This weather map of North America shows how a typical warm front and cold front integrate to form a midlatitude cyclone. Pressure decreases toward the center of the system, as shown by the isobars; the lowest pressure, at the center, is labeled L for "low." Notice the changing air temperature and dew point ahead of and behind both fronts. After a warm front moves through, the air temperature and dew point rise. After a cold front moves through, the air temperature and dew point fall. The gray area shows cloudiness and precipitation. (B) This October 26, 2010, satellite image shows a midlatitude cyclone spanning much of eastern North America. It is labeled with the features illustrated in part A. (B. NASA Earth Observatory imagery created by Jesse Allen, using imagery provided courtesy of the NASA GOES Project Science Office)*

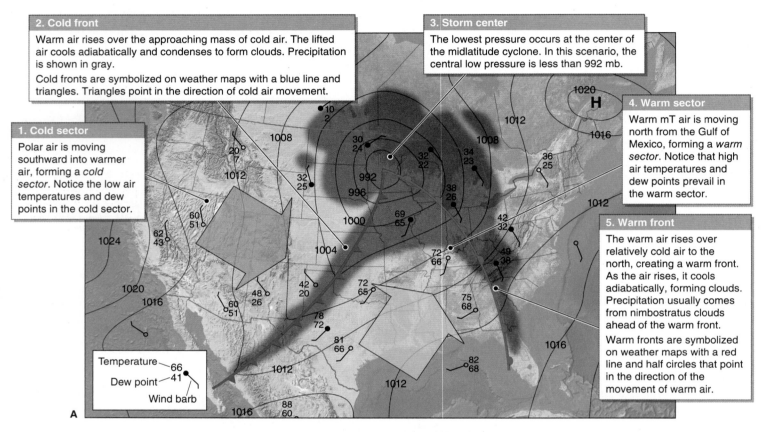

2. Cold front

Warm air rises over the approaching mass of cold air. The lifted air cools adiabatically and condenses to form clouds. Precipitation is shown in gray.

Cold fronts are symbolized on weather maps with a blue line and triangles. Triangles point in the direction of cold air movement.

1. Cold sector

Polar air is moving southward into warmer air, forming a *cold sector*. Notice the low air temperatures and dew points in the cold sector.

3. Storm center

The lowest pressure occurs at the center of the midlatitude cyclone. In this scenario, the central low pressure is less than 992 mb.

4. Warm sector

Warm mT air is moving north from the Gulf of Mexico, forming a *warm sector*. Notice that high air temperatures and dew points prevail in the warm sector.

5. Warm front

The warm air rises over relatively cold air to the north, creating a warm front. As the air rises, it cools adiabatically, forming clouds. Precipitation usually comes from nimbostratus clouds ahead of the warm front.

Warm fronts are symbolized on weather maps with a red line and half circles that point in the direction of the movement of warm air.

Temperature — 66
Dew point — 41
Wind barb

A

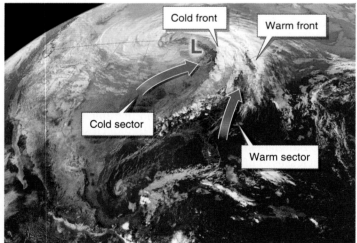

B

5.4 Midlatitude Cyclones

◎ Review the major characteristics and stages of development of a midlatitude cyclone.

In Section 4.2, we learned that a *cyclone* is any meteorological system that rotates counterclockwise (in the Northern Hemisphere) around a low-pressure center. When large cyclonic systems occur at midlatitudes, they are called **midlatitude cyclones** (or *extratropical cyclones*). They are also called *depressions, lows,* or *low-pressure systems,* names reflecting the fact that they are geographically extensive regions of low barometric pressure. In contrast to hurricanes, which are fueled by the release of latent heat, midlatitude cyclones form as a result of temperature contrasts between air masses.

Midlatitude cyclones bring storms from fall through spring between approximately 30° and 70° latitude in both hemispheres. In the Northern Hemisphere, the United States, most of Canada, Europe, and Asia are influenced by these large storm systems, which move from west to east with the westerlies. Some 10 to 20 midlatitude cyclones are in progress at any given time worldwide. They are the largest storm systems on the planet, having a diameter of 1,600 km (1,000 mi) or more. In some cases, they become as strong as hurricanes at sea level. In mountainous regions, they commonly produce hurricane-force winds.

Anatomy of a Midlatitude Cyclone

There are many different permutations of midlatitude cyclones, depending on the types of air masses that are interacting and the characteristics of geostrophic winds aloft. **Most midlatitude cyclones are composed of a warm front and a cold front. A warm front** is produced when warm air advances on and flows over cooler, denser air. Warm fronts may bring precipitation, but they are rarely associated with severe weather. A **cold front** is a region where cold, dense air advances on relatively warm and less dense air. Cold fronts are sometimes associated with severe weather. The different densities of warm and cold air prevent air masses from mixing together as they converge. Without this characteristic, frontal systems would not form. **Figure 5.22** illustrates how fronts may combine to form a midlatitude cyclone.

Effects of Midlatitude Cyclones on Weather

As a midlatitude cyclone moves over a region, the weather experienced in that region will reflect the type of front moving through. In most cases, a warm front moves through the region first and is followed by a cold front. **Warm fronts are usually associated with nimbostratus clouds that bring steady precipitation. Cold fronts are usually associated with cumulonimbus clouds that bring short bursts of rainfall and potentially severe weather. Figure 5.23** on page 178 diagrams the typical characteristics and weather patterns of frontal systems.

Life Cycle of a Midlatitude Cyclone

Like a single-cell thunderstorm or a hurricane, a midlatitude cyclone experiences stages of growth, maturation, and dissipation over a period of about one to two weeks (**Figure 5.24A** on page 179). Although midlatitude cyclones do not all look and behave alike, temperature gradients and, therefore, pressure gradients give rise to all of them. In addition, they must have *upper-level support* to persist. In other words, they do not form unless geostrophic winds are lifting air.

Most midlatitude cyclones begin as waves in the subpolar low. If an upper-level Rossby wave trough is present (see Section 4.3), the low pressure at Earth's surface will deepen (decrease) and the cyclonic system will strengthen (**Figure 5.24B** on page 179). Upper-level troughs maintain surface-level low pressure by pulling air from the surface to higher altitudes.

One particularly important type of midlatitude cyclone is called a **nor'easter**. These powerful storms bring blizzard-like conditions from the Mid-Atlantic states north to New England (see Figure 5.28 on page 183). Nor'easters form where mT air from the Gulf of Mexico meets cold air from the Great Plains. Their name derives from the direction of the wind (from the northeast) that they bring to the regions where their precipitation falls.

After midlatitude cyclones move over the Great Lakes, the cold air behind them often creates lake-effect snow. **Lake-effect snow** is heavy snowfall that results as cold air moves over large, relatively warm bodies of water, such as the Great Lakes. Heavy snows downwind of the lakes sometimes bury towns in snow. The warm water readily evaporates and increases the atmospheric humidity. **Picture This** on page 180 explores this phenomenon further.

midlatitude cyclone
(or *extratropical cyclone*)
A large cyclonic storm at midlatitudes.

warm front
A region where warm air advances on and flows over cooler, heavier air; not associated with severe weather.

cold front
A region where cold air advances on relatively warm air; sometimes associated with severe weather.

nor'easter
A type of midlatitude cyclone that brings blizzard-like conditions to the Mid-Atlantic states and New England.

lake-effect snow
Heavy snowfall that results as cold air moves over large, relatively warm bodies of water, such as the Great Lakes.

FIGURE 5.23 **GEO-GRAPHIC: Cold and warm fronts and their weather patterns.**

(A) Warm front characteristics. (B) Cold front characteristics. (C) Warm and cold fronts compared.

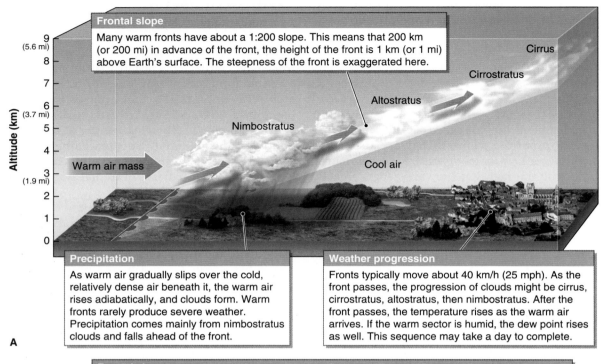

Frontal slope

Many warm fronts have about a 1:200 slope. This means that 200 km (or 200 mi) in advance of the front, the height of the front is 1 km (or 1 mi) above Earth's surface. The steepness of the front is exaggerated here.

Precipitation

As warm air gradually slips over the cold, relatively dense air beneath it, the warm air rises adiabatically, and clouds form. Warm fronts rarely produce severe weather. Precipitation comes mainly from nimbostratus clouds and falls ahead of the front.

Weather progression

Fronts typically move about 40 km/h (25 mph). As the front passes, the progression of clouds might be cirrus, cirrostratus, altostratus, then nimbostratus. After the front passes, the temperature rises as the warm air arrives. If the warm sector is humid, the dew point rises as well. This sequence may take a day to complete.

A

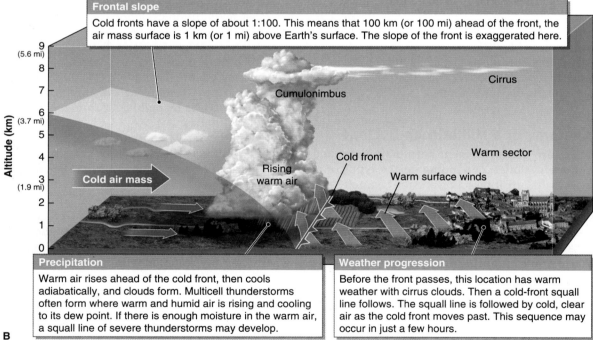

Frontal slope

Cold fronts have a slope of about 1:100. This means that 100 km (or 100 mi) ahead of the front, the air mass surface is 1 km (or 1 mi) above Earth's surface. The slope of the front is exaggerated here.

Precipitation

Warm air rises ahead of the cold front, then cools adiabatically, and clouds form. Multicell thunderstorms often form where warm and humid air is rising and cooling to its dew point. If there is enough moisture in the warm air, a squall line of severe thunderstorms may develop.

Weather progression

Before the front passes, this location has warm weather with cirrus clouds. Then a cold-front squall line follows. The squall line is followed by cold, clear air as the cold front moves past. This sequence may occur in just a few hours.

B

	WARM FRONT	COLD FRONT
Map symbol		
Frontal slope	Shallow	Steep
Progression of clouds	Cirrus–alto–stratus	Cirrus–cumulonimbus
Likely weather	Steady rain, snow, or ice	Intense showers, potentially severe weather
Duration of precipitation	A day or more	A few hours
Speed of movement	Relatively slow	Relatively fast

C

FIGURE 5.24 GEO-GRAPHIC: Development of a midlatitude cyclone.

(A) A typical midlatitude cyclone undergoes several stages of development. (B) Rossby wave troughs provide essential upper-level support for midlatitude cyclones.

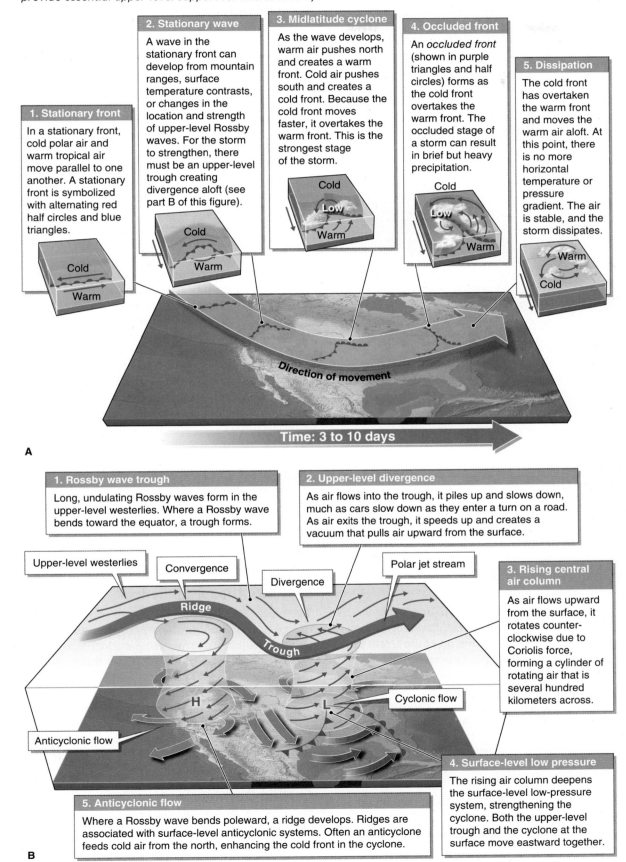

2. Stationary wave

A wave in the stationary front can develop from mountain ranges, surface temperature contrasts, or changes in the location and strength of upper-level Rossby waves. For the storm to strengthen, there must be an upper-level trough creating divergence aloft (see part B of this figure).

3. Midlatitude cyclone

As the wave develops, warm air pushes north and creates a warm front. Cold air pushes south and creates a cold front. Because the cold front moves faster, it overtakes the warm front. This is the strongest stage of the storm.

4. Occluded front

An *occluded front* (shown in purple triangles and half circles) forms as the cold front overtakes the warm front. The occluded stage of a storm can result in brief but heavy precipitation.

5. Dissipation

The cold front has overtaken the warm front and moves the warm air aloft. At this point, there is no more horizontal temperature or pressure gradient. The air is stable, and the storm dissipates.

1. Stationary front

In a stationary front, cold polar air and warm tropical air move parallel to one another. A stationary front is symbolized with alternating red half circles and blue triangles.

Direction of movement

Time: 3 to 10 days

A

1. Rossby wave trough

Long, undulating Rossby waves form in the upper-level westerlies. Where a Rossby wave bends toward the equator, a trough forms.

2. Upper-level divergence

As air flows into the trough, it piles up and slows down, much as cars slow down as they enter a turn on a road. As air exits the trough, it speeds up and creates a vacuum that pulls air upward from the surface.

Upper-level westerlies

Convergence

Divergence

Polar jet stream

Ridge

Trough

3. Rising central air column

As air flows upward from the surface, it rotates counter-clockwise due to Coriolis force, forming a cylinder of rotating air that is several hundred kilometers across.

Cyclonic flow

H

L

Anticyclonic flow

4. Surface-level low pressure

The rising air column deepens the surface-level low-pressure system, strengthening the cyclone. Both the upper-level trough and the cyclone at the surface move eastward together.

5. Anticyclonic flow

Where a Rossby wave bends poleward, a ridge develops. Ridges are associated with surface-level anticyclonic systems. Often an anticyclone feeds cold air from the north, enhancing the cold front in the cyclone.

B

Picture This

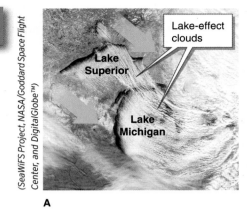

(SeaWiFS Project, NASA/Goddard Space Flight Center, and DigitalGlobe™)

Lake Superior

Lake Michigan

Lake-effect clouds

A

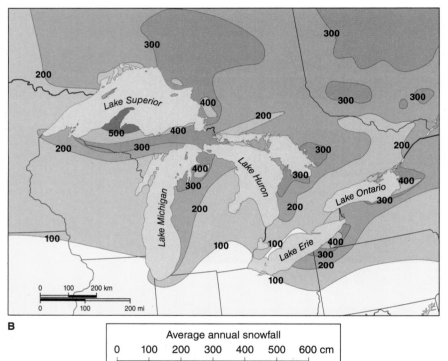

B

Average annual snowfall

0	100	200	300	400	500	600 cm
0	40	80	120	160	200	240 in

Lake-Effect Snow

The satellite image on the left shows wind direction (with arrows) over Lake Superior and Lake Michigan and downwind lake-effect clouds. The map on the right shows average annual snowfall totals downwind of the Great Lakes. The Upper Peninsula of Michigan, bordering Lake Superior, receives up to 500 cm (200 in) per year, on average. Although it is particularly pronounced in the Great Lakes region, lake-effect snow occurs wherever cold Arctic air masses move over large, relatively warm bodies of water. The highest snow totals in the world occur on the island of Hokkaido, Japan, after cold air from Asia moves over the Sea of Japan.

Consider This

1. Why do large lakes produce more lake-effect snows than small lakes?
2. If the water temperature decreased in the Great Lakes, would lake-effect snows increase or decrease? Explain.

5.5 El Niño's Wide Reach

◎ Discuss how El Niño forms and describe its global effects.

For generations, fisherman in Peru have reaped the bounty of the sea. Commonly around Christmastime, their catches decrease as cold, nutrient-rich coastal surface water disappears and is replaced by nutrient-poor warm water from the equatorial regions. In other seasons, cold water *upwells* (moves from the seafloor to the surface), bringing nutrients from the seafloor to the sunlit surface of the ocean, supporting high marine productivity and one of the world's largest anchovy fisheries. This upwelling stops, however, when the warm water arrives. The warm water normally lingers a few weeks to a few months, and then the cold water returns, and the upwelling and fishing resume. Given the timing of this event, it was named "*El Niño*" after the Christ child.

El Niño is not a storm system. It is a periodic shift in the state of Earth's climate caused by the temporary slackening and reversing of the Pacific equatorial trade winds and increased surface temperatures in the seas off coastal Peru. Normally, El Niño lasts only a few weeks and does not go beyond the coast of western South America. During some El Niños, however, the cold waters do not immediately return. Instead, the warm surface water persists and gets warmer. This warm water affects climates around the world within a few months, creating a global *El Niño event* that can influence all the storm systems discussed thus far in this chapter.

El Niño events occur randomly, about every 3 to 7 years on average. They develop in March through June and reach peak intensity between December and April, when equatorial sea surface temperatures are highest. By July, they usually dissipate, although some weak El Niños have lasted as long as four years.

El Niño's Global Influence

The global influence of El Niño events illustrates the connections among the oceans, the atmosphere, and climate patterns around the world. For instance, during El Niño years, hurricane activity usually decreases in the Atlantic Ocean and increases in the Pacific Ocean. Tornadoes in North America increase. The Asian monsoon often weakens, resulting in dangerous drought and potential food shortages for millions. El Niño alters air temperature and precipitation patterns worldwide, usually in the pattern shown in Figure 5.25.

El Niño Development

Figure 5.26 shows the typical sequence of events in the tropical Pacific Ocean that lead up to an El

FIGURE 5.25 **El Niño's global influence.** *Strong El Niño events reach around the globe, from Australia, where they bring drought and wildfires, all the way to the southeastern United States, where severe weather typically increases.*

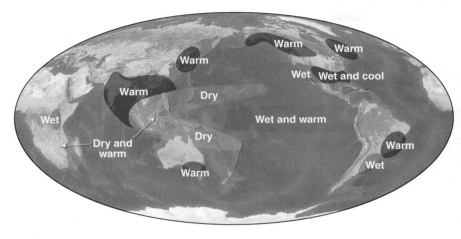

El Niño's Wide Reach

IF YOU LIVE IN	YOU MIGHT EXPECT
Southwestern United States	Wet and stormy weather
Great Plains and south-eastern United States	More tornadoes
Northwestern United States, western and central Canada	Dry and warm weather
Northeastern United States, eastern Canada	Dry and warm weather
U.S. East Coast	Fewer hurricanes
Southeastern Asia	More typhoons
Australia, Indonesia	Drought and fires
India	Warmer temperatures
Peru and Ecuador	Flooding rains

Animation
El Niño development
http://qrs.ly/t9434g5

FIGURE 5.26 **GEO-GRAPHIC: Normal and El Niño ocean-atmosphere patterns.**
(A) Normal ocean-atmosphere conditions. (B) El Niño ocean-atmosphere conditions.

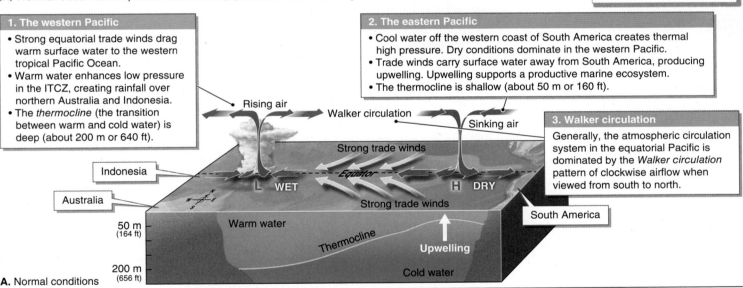

1. The western Pacific
- Strong equatorial trade winds drag warm surface water to the western tropical Pacific Ocean.
- Warm water enhances low pressure in the ITCZ, creating rainfall over northern Australia and Indonesia.
- The *thermocline* (the transition between warm and cold water) is deep (about 200 m or 640 ft).

2. The eastern Pacific
- Cool water off the western coast of South America creates thermal high pressure. Dry conditions dominate in the western Pacific.
- Trade winds carry surface water away from South America, producing upwelling. Upwelling supports a productive marine ecosystem.
- The thermocline is shallow (about 50 m or 160 ft).

3. Walker circulation
Generally, the atmospheric circulation system in the equatorial Pacific is dominated by the *Walker circulation* pattern of clockwise airflow when viewed from south to north.

Rising air   Walker circulation   Sinking air
Strong trade winds
Indonesia   *Equator*   L WET   H DRY
Australia   Strong trade winds   South America
50 m (164 ft)   Warm water
200 m (656 ft)   Thermocline   Upwelling   Cold water
A. Normal conditions

1. Trade wind reversal
The trade winds slacken or reverse direction.

2. Reversed pressure pattern
The pressure systems reverse, with high pressure over Indonesia and low pressure over coastal South America. These changes reverse the direction of the Walker circulation to flow counterclockwise.

5. Drought
High pressure dominates the western Pacific, and Indonesia and Australia suffer from drought.

Rising air
Sinking air   Strong countercurrent   WET
Atmospheric pressure rises   Atmospheric pressure falls
DRY

3. Flooding
Western South America receives flooding rains.

50 m (164 ft)   Warm water
Thermocline
4. Thermocline depth
The slope of the thermocline reverses. It becomes shallower near Indonesia and deeper near Peru.

200 m (656 ft)   Cold water
B. El Niño conditions

El Niño
A periodic change in the state of Earth's climate caused by the slackening and temporary reversal of the Pacific equatorial trade winds and increased sea surface temperatures off coastal Peru.

Niño event. Slackening and reversal of the trade winds in the Pacific is one of the most prominent changes that lead up to an El Niño event.

Toward the end of an El Niño event, the pattern of atmospheric pressure returns to normal. After some El Niño events, the pressure pattern returns to an "enhanced normal," a phenomenon called *La Niña*. During La Niña, the low pressure over Indonesia is deeper than normal and the high pressure near western South America is higher than normal. La Niña does not always follow El Niño, but when it does occur, it typically lasts about 9 months to a year.

El Niño and La Niña events and the changes they cause in the climate system are collectively referred to as *ENSO* (the *El Niño-Southern Oscillation*). **Figure 5.27** shows the history of El Niños and La Niñas since 1965.

FIGURE 5.27 **El Niño and La Niña events.** *(A) Sea surface temperature anomalies in the equatorial Pacific Ocean during El Niño and La Niña events stand in stark contrast. El Niño's most prominent feature is the migration of warm water to the eastern end of the Pacific basin. During La Niña, this warm water is replaced by unusually cold water. (B) Sea surface temperature anomalies since 1965 are plotted for the eastern equatorial Pacific Ocean. Temperatures are given in relation to the long-term average. Temperatures 0.5°C above the long-term average are El Niño events, and temperatures 0.5°C below the long-term average are La Niña events. (A. Data from NOAA)*

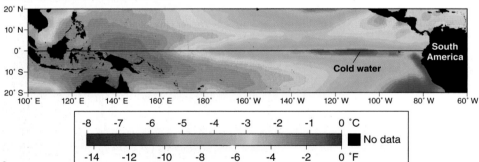

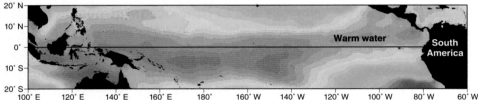

El Niño conditions, December 1997

La Niña conditions, December 1998

A

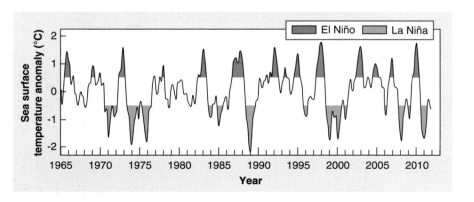

B

Scientists still do not know what triggers El Niño, and they cannot reliably predict El Niño events more than 6 months in advance. During the last 50 years, El Niños and La Niñas occurred about half of the time (in a total of about 25 years). The other half of the time, ocean conditions were near normal. Given how often these patterns develop, many scientists question whether "normal" conditions are simply transitional states and the ENSO system is normal. Furthermore, recent research on corals indicates that El Niño intensity has been greater in the last several decades than at any other time in the last 7,000 years, and perhaps much longer. These data are leading scientists to question the potential influence of anthropogenic climate change on El Niño.

GEOGRAPHIC PERSPECTIVES
5.6 Are Atlantic Hurricanes a Growing Threat?

◎ Assess the current and potential vulnerability of the United States to major hurricanes.

The vulnerability of the United States to hurricanes was made clear in 2005, when Hurricane Katrina struck and flooded New Orleans. Because of natural settling and compaction of the sediments on which New Orleans was built, much of the city is slowly sinking and is now below sea level. Three hundred and fifty miles of seawalls and river levees are all that keep the ocean and the Mississippi River out of the city.

The 6 m (20 ft) storm surge generated by Hurricane Katrina caused many of the levees protecting New Orleans to be overtopped by water or collapse as water flowed under them. Within hours, 80% of New Orleans was under water, in some places 25 feet deep. The cost was more than 1,800 human lives and some $128 billion in structural damage. More recently, in 2012, Superstorm Sandy, in which a hurricane combined with a nor'easter, inflicted significant damage in the New Jersey and New York coastal areas (Figure 5.28).

Hurricane Activity

About 300 hurricanes have struck the United States since record keeping began, and more than 100 have struck since 1950. Almost all coastal regions in the Gulf of Mexico, in the southeastern United States, and up the eastern coast of North America have been struck by hurricanes (Figure 5.29).

Except for New Orleans, Miami is the largest metropolitan region in the United States most at risk of flooding and wind damage by a major hurricane. The last time Miami was struck by a hurricane was in 1950, when Hurricane King made a direct hit on downtown. In all, King caused 3 deaths and about 50 injuries. Although

FIGURE 5.28 **Superstorm Sandy, 2012.** *This satellite image of the East Coast of the United States captures the storm's extent on the afternoon of October 28, 2012. The storm took over 286 lives, and its financial toll was some $68 billion. Because Hurricane Sandy combined with a nor'easter, the result was a particularly powerful storm.* *(NASA Earth Observatory image by Robert Simmon with data courtesy of the NASA/NOAA GOES Project Science team)*

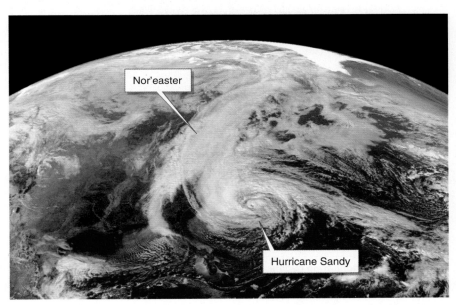

Nor'easter

Hurricane Sandy

FIGURE 5.29 **U.S. hurricane activity.** *Each colored dot gives the hurricane return period—the number of years, on average, between major hurricanes (category 3 or higher)—for its stretch of coast since records have been kept. The dots are spaced about 100 km (60 mi) apart. The lower the return period, the more vulnerable a stretch of coastline is. On the southern tip of Florida, for example, category 3 hurricanes have struck about every 19 years.*

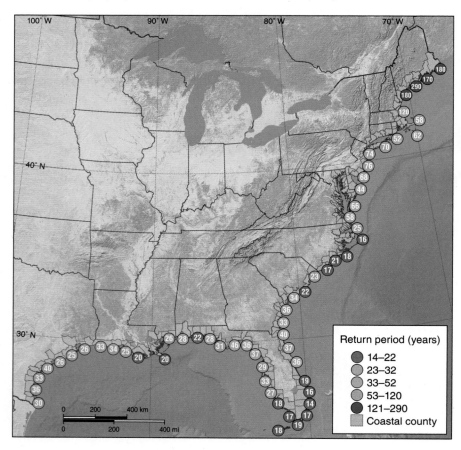

FIGURE 5.30 **Atlantic hurricane activity, 1851-2013.** *This chronology shows all detected hurricanes (872 in total, 308 category 3 and above) that formed in the Atlantic Ocean from 1851 to 2013. Before satellite monitoring, which began in 1966, the record is less reliable. The black line shows long-term trends. Data are from the National Atmospheric and Oceanic Administration (NOAA) Atlantic Hurricane Database (http://www.aoml.noaa.gov/hrd/tcfaq/E11.html).*

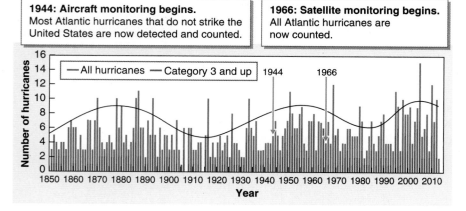

damage was considerable, there was little loss of life because fewer than half a million people lived in the Miami metropolitan region at the time. Miami has not suffered a direct strike by a hurricane since, although Hurricane Andrew struck Homestead, a southern suburb, in 1992.

Since 1950, however, the population of South Florida has grown significantly, and it is projected to be one of the fastest-growing regions in the country for the next several decades. Development now covers much of the coastal area. Some 5.5 million people live in Miami and the surrounding area. Scientists estimate that if a category 4 hurricane were to strike Miami today, it could cause some $90 billion in damage and bring significant loss of human life.

Climate Change and Hurricanes

Atmospheric warming has caused a sea-level rise of about 20 cm (8 in) in the last century. This fact alone makes all coastal cities more vulnerable to the storm surges of hurricanes. But are hurricanes growing stronger because of global warming? Are there more hurricanes because of global warming? Because the air and oceans are warming, hurricanes might be expected to become more frequent and stronger. So far, however, this has not been the case.

There is a natural cyclical pattern of hurricane activity. The 1950s and 1960s was an active period for hurricanes. In the 1970s and 1980s, hurricane activity decreased. Then, in the 1990s, it began to increase again, as shown in **Figure 5.30**.

Taken as a whole, there has been little to no change in the average number or strength of Atlantic hurricanes during the past century. The atmosphere's temperature began increasing about 100 years ago, but long-term hurricane activity does not reflect this trend. Nor do other ocean basins in which hurricanes form show any significant trend in increasing frequency or intensity of hurricanes.

Earth's climate is exceedingly complex. There are many factors besides the temperature of the oceans and atmosphere that influence hurricane activity. El Niño, for example, decreases the number of Atlantic hurricanes by causing increased wind shear, which tears hurricanes apart. La Niña, on the other hand, favors Atlantic hurricane development. Similarly, a 2011 study published in the journal *Science* finds that that wind and wave heights over the oceans have increased by up to 7% in the last two decades worldwide. Windiness and associated wind shear may suppress hurricane formation. Because of these and other complicating factors, scientists are uncertain how climate change will influence hurricanes in the coming decades.

CHAPTER 5 **Exploring with ◎ Google Earth**

To complete these problems, first read the chapter. When you are finished, go to LaunchPad and open the Exploring with Google Earth file for this chapter. Click on the "Workbook Problems" folder to "fly" to each of the problems listed below and answer the questions. Be sure to keep your "Borders and Labels" layer activated. Refer to Appendix 4 if you need help using Google Earth.

PROBLEM 5.1 Deactivate any open overlays and activate the overlay in this folder. This placemark highlights a storm system off the southern coast of Louisiana. Arrows show wind direction. The fastest winds are shown in red.

1. **Based on the wind pattern seen here, what kind of storm is this?**
   a. Midlatitude cyclone
   b. Tornado
   c. Hurricane
   d. Mesocyclone

PROBLEM 5.2 Activate the image overlay folder for this problem if it is not already activated. This placemark highlights a storm system in the northern Philippines.

1. **At approximately what latitude is this storm system found?**
   a. 10° south
   b. 0°
   c. 17° north
   d. 35° north

2. **What kind of storm system is this?**
   a. Midlatitude cyclone
   b. Tornado
   c. Hurricane
   d. Mesocyclone

3. **What is the diameter of this system?**
   a. 200 km
   b. 550 km
   c. 830 km
   d. 1,200 km

4. **Zoom in closer to the placemark. What is the circular feature shown here?**
   a. The eye
   b. A squall line
   c. A warm front
   d. A gust front

5. **What is this feature's diameter?**
   a. 10 km
   b. 40 km
   c. 70 km
   d. 200 km

PROBLEM 5.3 Deactivate all previous overlays and activate the image overlay in this folder if it is not already activated. This placemark lands on the midwestern United States. A large storm system is visible in this satellite image.

1. **What kind of storm is this?**
   a. Midlatitude cyclone
   b. Tornado
   c. Hurricane
   d. Mesocyclone

2. **What is the approximate length of this system from north to south?**
   a. 100 mi
   b. 500 mi
   c. 1,000 mi
   d. 1,500 mi

PROBLEM 5.4 Keep the overlay from the previous problem activated.

1. **What portion of the storm does this placemark fall on?**
   a. The cold sector
   b. The eye
   c. The cold front
   d. Rain band

2. **What kind of weather would you expect to find here?**
   a. Showers and potentially severe weather
   b. Fair weather
   c. Steady precipitation but no severe weather
   d. Above-average temperatures

3. **What would you expect the temperature to do in the next few hours at this location?**
   a. Increase
   b. Decrease
   c. Remain the same

PROBLEM 5.5 Deactivate all previous overlays and activate the overlay in this folder.

1. **This placemark falls on a linear track on the ground. Based on your reading of the chapter and your examination of the figures featured in Google Earth for this chapter, what type of severe weather would produce such a track?**
   a. Midlatitude cyclone
   b. Tornado
   c. Hurricane
   d. Single-cell thunderstorm

2. **Zoom in close to the placemark. About how wide is the feature?**
   a. 300 ft
   b. 1,100 ft
   c. 2,300 ft
   d. 5,000 ft

3. **Zoom out until you can see the entire overlay. About how long is the feature?**
   a. 10 mi
   b. 20 mi
   c. 40 mi
   d. 100 mi

PROBLEM 5.6 Deactivate any open overlays and activate the overlay in this folder.

1. **This placemark pins to a tornado-forming type of thunderstorm in northwestern Wisconsin. What type of system is this?**
   a. Single-cell thunderstorm
   b. Multicell thunderstorm
   c. Supercell thunderstorm
   d. Hurricane

2. **In the center of the system, portions of the cloud protrude higher and cast shadows. This is particularly evident on the systems to the south. What is the name of these protrusions?**
   a. The eyewall
   b. Overshooting top
   c. Cold front
   d. Gust front

3. **How high do these features rise?**
   a. To the tropopause
   b. A little past the tropopause
   c. To the top of the stratosphere
   d. Into the mesosphere

4. **Measuring from northwest to southeast, about how many kilometers in diameter is the placemarked system?**
   a. 50 km
   c. 160 km
   b. 100 km
   d. 240 km

PROBLEM 5.7 Deactivate all previous overlays and activate the overlay in this folder. This placemark falls on the Yucatán Peninsula in Mexico.

1. **The yellow placemark points to a thunderstorm cluster. What type of thunderstorm is this most likely to be? (Hint: There is no frontal boundary.)**
   a. Single-cell thunderstorm
   b. Multicell thunderstorm
   c. Supercell thunderstorm

2. **Why are most of the cumulus clouds and thunderstorms seen here forming over the peninsula rather than over water?**
   a. The land is warmer than the water.
   b. The land is cooler than the water.
   c. The land is more humid than the water.
   d. The land is less humid than the water.

3. **Is the air stable or unstable over the land?**
   a. Stable
   b. Unstable

4. **What kind of lifting is causing the clouds to form?**
   a. Orographic lifting
   c. Convective lifting
   b. Convergent lifting
   d. Frontal lifting

PROBLEM 5.8 Deactivate all previous overlays and activate the overlay in this folder. The year 2005 was a record year for Atlantic hurricanes, in terms of both numbers and strength. This overlay shows all 2005 Atlantic hurricanes. Sea surface temperatures for the same time period are also shown in this overlay. The warmest water is shown in orange.

1. **Why do Atlantic hurricanes generally travel from east to west across the tropical Atlantic Ocean? What is guiding their movement?**
   a. The westerlies
   c. Geostrophic winds
   b. The trade winds
   d. The doldrums

2. **Why do most hurricane paths hook to the north as they approach the United States?**
   a. Because of the influence of the Bermuda high
   b. Because the trade winds steer them northward
   c. Because geostrophic winds guide them
   d. Because of ocean currents

3. **Hurricane intensity is shown using line width and shades of purple. Where storms are more intense, a wide line colored dark purple is used. Why does hurricane intensity rapidly decrease in all cases after the storms make landfall?**
   a. The evaporation rate drops.
   b. The land blocks the wind.
   c. Hurricanes require deep water.
   d. It is warmer over land.

CHAPTER 5 **Study Guide**

Focus Points

5.1 Thunderstorms

Spatial and temporal scales: Microscale atmospheric systems last hours, and synoptic and global atmospheric systems last weeks to months.

Air masses: Warm and humid mT air masses are essential for thunderstorm development.

Thunderstorm geography: Thunderstorms are most frequent in the tropics over land.

Thunderstorm types: There are three types of thunderstorms: single-cell, multicell, and supercell thunderstorms. Multicell and supercell thunderstorms may bring severe weather.

5.2 Thunderstorm Hazards: Lightning and Tornadoes

Lightning and thunder: Lightning is a discharge of electricity within a thunderstorm. Thunder is created as air is heated by lightning and rapidly expands.

Tornadoes: Tornadoes form in thunderstorms, hurricanes, and cold fronts. The United States has the most frequent and strongest tornadoes in the world.

5.3 Nature's Deadliest Storms: Hurricanes

Hurricane structure: Hurricanes consist of a calm eye, an eyewall of heavy wind and rain, and rain bands.

Hurricane strength: Hurricanes must have warm seawater to persist. They derive their strength from the latent heat positive feedback.

Stages of growth: Hurricanes go through a series of stages of formation, from tropical wave, to tropical disturbance, to tropical depression, to tropical storm, to tropical cyclone.

Hurricane geography: Worldwide, hurricanes are restricted to tropical oceans. They do not occur within about 5° latitude of the equator due to the lack of Coriolis force there.

Hurricane hazards: The coastal storm surge is the most dangerous aspect of a hurricane, particularly in the Indian Ocean.

5.4 Midlatitude Cyclones

Midlatitude cyclone effects: Midlatitude cyclones bring storms to midlatitude regions, such as the United States and Canada, from fall through spring.

Warm and cold fronts: Most midlatitude cyclones are composed of warm fronts that bring steady precipitation and cold fronts that bring bursts of short-lived showers.

Stages of development: A midlatitude cyclone undergoes a sequence of growth, maturation, and dissipation over the span of days to weeks.

5.5 El Niño's Wide Reach

El Niño impacts: El Niño rearranges moisture and weather patterns for many regions, causing drought and flooding for many parts of the world. El Niño brings fewer hurricanes for the Atlantic Ocean, and it often weakens the Asian monsoon.

La Niña: La Niña often follows El Niño and creates "enhanced normal" meteorological conditions for affected areas.

5.6 Geographic Perspectives: Are Atlantic Hurricanes a Growing Threat?

U.S. cities at risk: Except for New Orleans, Miami is the largest metropolitan area most at risk for a hurricane disaster.

Long-term trend: Climate change could result in more and stronger hurricanes, but so far no such trend has been observed.

Key Terms

air mass, 162
cold front, 177
enhanced Fujita scale
  (EF scale), 166
fulgurite, 165
hurricane, 169
lake-effect snow, 177
lightning, 165
mesocyclone, 164
midlatitude cyclone, 177
multicell thunderstorm, 162
El Niño, 180
nor'easter, 177
Saffir-Simpson Scale, 172
severe thunderstorm, 162

single-cell thunderstorm, 162
squall line, 162
storm surge, 174
supercell thunderstorm, 164
thunder, 165
thunderstorm, 162
tornado, 166
tornado warning, 169
tornado watch, 169
tropical cyclone, 169
tropical storm, 172
typhoon, 170
wall cloud, 166
warm front, 177
wind shear, 162

Concept Review

5.1 Thunderstorms

1. Describe the relationship between the duration of an atmospheric system and its spatial scale.

2. What is an air mass? Describe the characteristics of an mT air mass. Where does it form?

3. What is a thunderstorm? What kind of cloud produces a thunderstorm? What are the three types of thunderstorms?

4. Describe the global geographic pattern of thunderstorms. Where are they most and least frequent, and why?

5. Describe the life cycle of single-cell thunderstorms. How long do they last, and what causes them to dissipate?

6. How are multicell thunderstorms different from single-cell thunderstorms in terms of where they form and their longevity?

7. What is a squall line, and how does it relate to multicell thunderstorms?

8. What is a supercell thunderstorm? How does it relate to a mesocyclone?

9. Are all supercell thunderstorms classified as severe? What makes a thunderstorm severe?

10. Explain how a supercell thunderstorm begins rotating and describe the general anatomy of this type of storm.

5.2 Thunderstorm Hazards: Lightning and Tornadoes

11. What is lightning? What kind of cloud produces it?

12. What is thunder? What causes it?

13. What is a fulgurite?

14. Review outdoor lightning safety. Is it safe to be in a car during a lightning storm? Is everywhere indoors safe from lightning?

15. How does lightning form?

16. What is a tornado? What system is used to rank tornado strength, and on what evidence is it based?

17. Describe the typical characteristics of tornadoes.

18. Where in the world are tornadoes most powerful and most frequent?

19. Describe the specific air masses that converge in the Great Plains to create tornadoes.

20. Compare a tornado watch with a tornado warning. Under what conditions is each issued?

5.3 Nature's Deadliest Storms: Hurricanes

21. What is the minimum wind speed required for a storm to be classified as a hurricane?

22. What are the four major stages of hurricane development?

23. What system is used to rank hurricane strength? What are the rankings based on?

24. Draw and label the anatomy of a hurricane. Where are winds fastest? Where are they slowest? Describe air movement direction in a hurricane.

25. Explain the role of the hurricane positive feedback in maintaining high wind speeds. Why is sea spray so important to this feedback?

26. Describe and explain the global geographic pattern of hurricanes.

27. What aspects of hurricanes are the most dangerous?

28. What ocean basin has the most dangerous hurricanes? What makes this area so dangerous?

5.4 Midlatitude Cyclones

29. What is a midlatitude cyclone? Where do midlatitude cyclones occur? How do cold fronts and warm fronts relate to them?

30. Compare a cold front with a warm front in terms of how they form and the weather that is typically associated with each.

31. Describe the life cycle of a midlatitude cyclone, beginning with a stationary front and ending with an occluded front.

5.5 El Niño's Wide Reach

32. What influences does El Niño have on global climate and weather?

33. What is an El Niño event? Compare and contrast the ocean-atmosphere system in the equatorial Pacific in a normal year and in an El Niño year.

34. What is the El Niño-Southern Oscillation (ENSO)?

5.6 Geographic Perspectives: Are Atlantic Hurricanes a Growing Threat?

35. Which coastal states in the United States have the shortest hurricane return period?

36. Except for New Orleans, which large U.S. metropolitan area is most vulnerable to hurricanes?

37. In the context of climate change, why might a person reasonably expect that hurricanes should be getting more frequent and stronger?

38. How would you characterize Atlantic hurricane activity since 1944?

39. Are scientists certain how hurricane activity will change in the coming decades?

Critical-Thinking Questions

1. Based on your reading of this chapter, what, if any, atmospheric hazards occur where you live?

2. Do you think it would be possible to reduce the vulnerability of the Great Plains to tornadoes? What would need to be done to accomplish this?

3. What steps could be taken to reduce the vulnerability of the United States to hurricanes? How would these steps be different from those taken to address the threat from tornadoes?

4. What kinds of changes would be needed to reduce the vulnerability of countries bordering the Indian Ocean to hurricanes?

5. How does El Niño influence the weather where you live?

Test Yourself

Take this quiz to test your chapter knowledge.

1. **True or false?** El Niño occurs randomly about every 3 to 7 years.

2. **True or false?** Warm fronts usually bring steady rain, but not severe weather.

3. **True or false?** Colorado has fewer thunderstorm days than California.

4. **True or false?** Most lightning moves between cloud and ground.

5. **True or false?** Hurricanes usually do not catch populated areas by surprise.

6. **Multiple choice:** Which of the following can produce a fulgurite?
   a. A valley or mountain breeze
   b. A tornado
   c. A bolt of lightning
   d. A hurricane

7. **Multiple choice:** Which of the following locations is the safest in a lightning storm?
   a. At a park under tall trees
   b. On a golf course
   c. Indoors
   d. In a boat on a lake

8. **Multiple choice:** Which of the following is not a criterion used to categorize a thunderstorm as severe?
   a. Tornado generation
   b. Hail 2.5 cm (1 in) in diameter
   c. Wind gusts of 93 km/h (58 mph) or greater
   d. Frequency of lightning

9. **Fill in the blank:** A _____ is a line of multicell thunderstorms.

10. **Fill in the blank:** The coastal sea-level rise caused by a hurricane is called a _____.

Picture This. YOUR TURN

Name That Storm

In this satellite image for September 23, 2004, Hurricane Jeanne (labeled) and two well-organized midlatitude cyclones can be seen. There is also one tropical disturbance visible in the image. Find and label these systems. Can you find Jeanne's eye and rain bands? Can you also find the cold sectors of the midlatitude cyclones? Fill in the boxes with the terms given here. Some terms will be used more than once. *(NOAA)*

Midlatitude cyclone	Tropical disturbance
Rain bands	Eye
Cold sector	

Hurricane Jeanne

Further Reading

1. Cullen, Heidi. *The Weather of the Future: Heat Waves, Extreme Storms, and Other Scenes from a Climate-Changed Planet.* New York: Harper, 2010.

2. Irfan, Umair. "El Niño Climate Pattern May Influence Disease Outbreaks Globally." *Scientific American*, January 30, 2012.

3. Yancheva, Gergana, et al. "Influence of the Intertropical Convergence Zone on the East Asian Monsoon." *Nature* 445 (2007): 74–77.

Answers to Living Physical Geography Questions

1. **Why do some thunderstorms rotate?** Wind shear sometimes causes updrafts in thunderstorms to rotate.

2. **How wide is a bolt of lightning?** A bolt of lightning is about 2.5 cm (1 in) in diameter.

3. **Do tornadoes ever strike the same place twice?** Codell, Kansas, was struck by tornadoes three years in a row, in 1916, 1917, and 1918, all on May 20.

4. **What does the word *hurricane* mean?** Hurricane means "god of storms" in the Taino language.

6 The Changing Climate

Chapter Outline

AK
Kenai Fjords
○ National Park
*GULF OF
ALASKA*
Canada

45° N *PACIFIC OCEAN*
150° W   135° W   WA

The lower edge of the Exit Glacier (visible in the background) in Kenai Fjords National Park, Alaska, was located at the base of this sign in 1978. It has retreated 3.2 km (2 mi) in the last 200 years.

(© Ashley Cooper/Age Fotostock Inc.)

LIVING PHYSICAL GEOGRAPHY

> What factors cause Earth's climate to change?

> Was Superstorm Sandy a result of anthropogenic climate change?

> How do scientists reconstruct Earth's ancient climates?

> Are people causing climate change?

78

To learn more about climate change and the retreat of glaciers worldwide, go to Section 6.4.

THE BIG PICTURE *Earth's climate system changes naturally, but it is also changed by human activities. Addressing anthropogenic climate change is a challenging and ongoing task.*

LEARNING GOALS *After reading this chapter, you will be able to:*

6.1 ◎ Identify the major parts of the climate system and distinguish between climate forcing factors and climate feedbacks.

6.2 ◎ Discuss the reasons why climate changes and list the factors that cause it to change.

6.3 ◎ Compare the long-term and short-term carbon cycles and describe the role of human activity in changing those cycles.

6.4 ◎ Weigh the evidence of an anthropogenic greenhouse effect in the atmosphere and describe its consequences.

6.5 ◎ Assess different approaches to tackling climate change.

THE HUMAN SPHERE: **The Greenland Norse**

THE SCANDINAVIAN NORSE (or Vikings) settled coastal southern Greenland in the 980s CE and developed a thriving society based on livestock rearing and trade. Perhaps between 3,000 and 5,000 Norse lived on Greenland at the peak of the settlement period. Active trade went on among Greenland, Iceland, and mainland Europe until the late 1300s. Greenland was always too cold to grow grain crops, so settlers relied on grain imports from mainland Europe. The Greenland Norse traded polar bear hides, walrus ivory, butter, and wool for grain and other commodities from northern Europe that they could not make or grow, such as nails and wood.

For four centuries, the Norse thrived in Greenland. They colonized Greenland during the **Medieval Warm Period**, a naturally warm period that extended from about 950 to 1250 CE and was felt mostly in the Northern Hemisphere. Unfortunately for the Greenland Norse, the **Little Ice Age** soon followed, and conditions in Greenland rapidly deteriorated. The Little Ice Age, a natural cooling period that extended from about 1350 to 1850, was also felt mostly in the Northern Hemisphere.

FIGURE 6.1 **An abandoned Greenland church.**
The church of Hvalsey, in southeastern coastal Greenland, is one of the remains of the Greenland Norse society. (© Danita Delimont/Gallo Images/Getty Images)

Soon sea ice made it difficult to travel by boat to trade with Europe. Worse, it became too cold for the Norse to grow food for themselves or for their livestock. The last written record of the Greenland Norse was a marriage document created in 1408. After that time, the Norse abandoned the Greenland settlements. They probably left for Iceland and mainland Europe, leaving behind gravesites and stone ruins **(Figure 6.1)**.

In this chapter, we explore Earth's climate system and the factors that cause it to change naturally. Then we explore patterns of climate change on time scales ranging from millions of years to decades. Finally, we examine the role of human activity in modifying the chemistry of the atmosphere, the resulting climate changes, and what can be done to address them.

6.1 The Climate System

◎ Identify the major parts of the climate system and distinguish between climate forcing factors and climate feedbacks.

There is a saying, "Climate is what you expect, but weather is what you get." **Climate** is the long-term average of weather and the average frequency of extreme weather events. **Weather** is the state of the atmosphere at any given moment and comprises ever-changing events on time scales ranging from minutes to weeks. Sunshine, rain showers, heat waves, thunderstorms, and clouds all are aspects of weather.

Table 6.1 summarizes events that represent weather and climate. These events occur along a time continuum ranging from hours to tens of millions of years.

Weather observations such as temperature, precipitation, wind, and humidity are averaged to represent the climate of a given region. Simple annual averages of temperature and precipitation, however, do not fully describe the climate of a region. Take, for example, the average annual temperature and precipitation for San Diego, California, and Tucson, Arizona (Figure 6.2). Judging by their annual averages, these two cities appear to have similar climates—but they do not. Remember that climate also includes the frequency of extreme events. For example, much of Tucson's rainfall comes from thunderstorms in July and August, but San Diego gets winter precipitation from midlatitude cyclones and almost no summer rain. Tucson has a greater annual temperature range, with colder winters and hotter summers, than San Diego. Hard freezes and snow in winter are extremely rare in San Diego, but below-freez-

FIGURE 6.2 **Climate diagrams for San Diego and Tucson.**
Although average annual temperatures and amounts of precipitation for these two cities are similar, the climate diagrams, which show average monthly temperature (red line) and precipitation (blue bars), reveal that their climates are quite different.

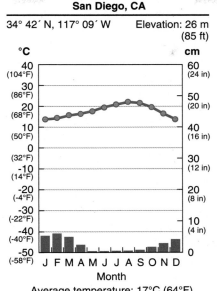

San Diego, CA
34° 42′ N, 117° 09′ W   Elevation: 26 m (85 ft)
Average temperature: 17°C (64°F)
Average precipitation: 26 cm (10.3 in)

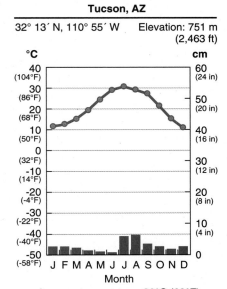

Tucson, AZ
32° 13′ N, 110° 55′ W   Elevation: 751 m (2,463 ft)
Average temperature: 20°C (69°F)
Average precipitation: 29 cm (11.6 in)

ing winter temperatures do sometimes occur in Tucson.

Geographers have identified and named many different types of climates, ranging from wet equatorial rainforest climates to dry interior desert climates. Several different classification systems are used to identify and classify Earth's many types of climates. The one used in this book is called the *Köppen climate classification system*. The emphasis in this chapter, however, is on the average state of Earth's climate as a whole, rather than on climate

Medieval Warm Period
A naturally warm period from about 950 to 1250 CE; felt mostly in the Northern Hemisphere.

Little Ice Age
A natural cooling period from about 1350 to 1850 CE; felt mostly in the Northern Hemisphere.

climate
The long-term average of weather and the average frequency of extreme weather events.

weather
The state of the atmosphere at any given moment, comprising ever-changing events on time scales ranging from minutes to weeks.

TABLE 6.1 **Weather and Climate**		
PHENOMENA	**TEMPORAL SCALE**	**WEATHER OR CLIMATE?**
Cloudiness, rain shower, rainbow, sea breeze, tornado	Hours	Weather
Night-and-day temperature difference	Days	Weather
Hurricane, midlatitude cyclone	Weeks	Weather
Winter, hurricane season, drought	Months	Climate
Asian monsoon	One year	Climate
El Niño and La Niña	Years to decades	Climate
Younger Dryas*	1,000 to 10,000 years	Climate
Quaternary* glacial and interglacial cycles	10,000 to 1,000,000 years	Climate
Cenozoic* cooling	Millions of years	Climate

*These terms will be defined in Section 6.2.

cryosphere
The frozen portion of the hydrosphere.

types in different geographic regions. The Köppen system is presented in Section 8.1 in the context of global vegetation patterns.

Climate is a result of the interaction between Earth's major systems: the atmosphere, biosphere, lithosphere, hydrosphere, and cryosphere. Energy and matter move through these systems and form the climate system. The first four systems were introduced in Section GT.2. The **cryosphere** is the frozen portion of the hydrosphere, which includes glaciers and sea ice. We live in the atmosphere and are affected by it in a direct way, but the other systems are equally important in determining how Earth's climate functions.

In addition, the climate system involves long-distance connections between different geographic regions. El Niño (see Section 5.5) is a good example of the role of such long-distance connections, called *climate teleconnections*. We will examine all of these aspects of the climate system later in this chapter.

Climate Change

The subject of anthropogenic climate change is often in the news. Weather stations, orbiting satellites, and ocean buoys have recorded a gradual creeping upward of temperatures in the troposphere. **Since 1880, the average temperature of the lower atmosphere has increased 0.83°C (1.5°F).** The surface of the oceans has warmed by about 0.56°C (1°F) in the last century as well. These temperature trends are climate change.

Climate change occurs when the long-term average of any given meteorological variable, such as temperature or precipitation, changes. Individual extreme weather events do not change the long-term average. Think of putting a single drop of water in a glass half filled with water. One drop does not change the water level. If enough drops are added, however, the water level will gradually rise.

One question that frequently comes up is whether a single extreme event, such as a single heat wave or storm, was caused by climate change. Scientists

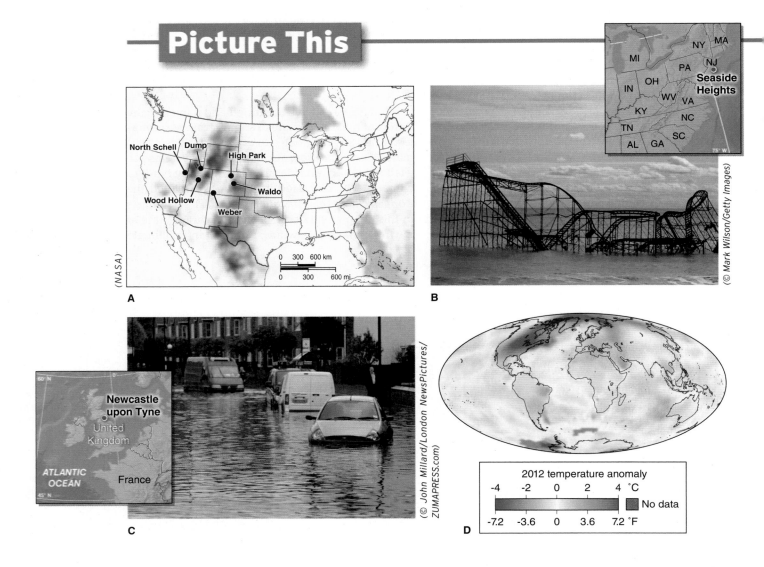

Picture This

(NASA)

North Schell   Dump

High Park

Wood Hollow

Weber   Waldo

A

B

(© Mark Wilson/Getty Images)

NY   MA
MI   PA   NJ
IN   OH   WV   Seaside Heights
KY   VA
TN   NC
AL   GA   SC
75° W

Newcastle upon Tyne
United Kingdom
ATLANTIC OCEAN   France
60° N
45° N

(© John Millard/London NewsPictures/ ZUMAPRESS.com)

C

D

2012 temperature anomaly
-4   -2   0   2   4   °C
No data
-7.2   -3.6   0   3.6   7.2   °F

do know that the long-term average number of heat waves worldwide is increasing. The "extra" heat waves are a result of Earth's changing atmosphere. Yet separating the heat waves or storm events that would have occurred naturally from those that were caused by increased atmospheric temperatures is scientifically challenging. Picture This explores this topic further.

Climate Forcing and Feedbacks

What factors cause Earth's climate to change?*

The behavior of Earth's climate is controlled by forces that are unaffected by the climate system, called **climate forcing factors**. Earth's climate is also controlled by factors that arise within the climate system and are changed by the climate system, called climate feedbacks. A *climate feedback* enhances or diminishes climate change that has already been set in motion (see Section 3.6).

*Answers to the Living Physical Geography questions are found on page 220.

As an example of a climate forcing factor, the Sun, if it were to shine more intensely, would force climate into a warmer state through *solar forcing*. Similarly, *volcanic forcing* occurs when volcanoes erupt aerosols into the stratosphere, where they reflect sunlight and cool the planet's surface.

Unlike climate forcings, climate feedbacks involve interacting parts of the climate system that affect one another. We learned in Section 3.6 that negative feedbacks maintain a system's stability and that positive feedbacks destabilize a system. There are many feedbacks in the climate system, some of which can support climate stability and others that can destabilize the climate system and cause climate change.

An example of a destabilizing positive feedback in the climate system is the **ice-albedo positive feedback**. When the temperature of the atmosphere increases, more snow and ice are melted. Bare ground and ice-free water absorb more solar energy

climate forcing factor
A force that can change climate and is unaffected by the climate system.

ice-albedo positive feedback
A destabilizing positive feedback in the climate system in which the melting of ice and snow expose bare ground and ice-free water, which absorb more solar energy and cause more warming.

Extreme Events and Climate Change

The year 2012 was a year of extreme events. (A) The United States experienced a series of record heat waves in June 2012. In the same month, the western United States saw record-breaking wildfires. This satellite image shows smoke aerosols on June 26, 2012. (B) In October, Superstorm Sandy, which had the lowest barometric pressure (940 mb) ever recorded in the North Atlantic Ocean, brought the highest storm surge New York City had ever experienced. Here, a Seaside Heights, New Jersey, roller coaster lies stranded in the sea after Sandy. (C) In March, the United Kingdom experienced its fifth worst drought, followed immediately by its wettest April on record. (D) As a whole, the year 2012 stood as the ninth warmest in recorded history and the warmest ever for the United States. This map shows 2012 surface temperatures measured by satellite, above or below the annual average for the period 1951–1980.

Scientists want to know which, if any, of these extreme events were caused by climate change. In September 2013, a study published in the *Bulletin of the American Meteorological Society* took significant steps toward answering this question. Seventy-eight researchers from the National Oceanic and Atmospheric Administration (NOAA) and the British Met Office found that half (6 of 12) of the extreme weather events that occurred in 2012 could be statistically linked to the increased average global temperature. For example, they found that the extreme rainfall in April 2012 in the United Kingdom was caused by natural climate variation. On the other hand, the record flooding from Superstorm Sandy and the June 2012 U.S. heat waves were attributed to human-caused climate change. This study does not say that Superstorm Sandy and the heat waves would not have occurred without climate change. It finds, instead, that they would not have been as intense if not for anthropogenic climate change.

Was Superstorm Sandy a result of anthropogenic climate change?

Consider This

1. Can scientists say with certainty whether any single extreme event was caused by climate change?

2. Can scientists say with certainty whether the intensity of any single extreme event was caused by climate change?

Cenozoic era
The last 66 million years of Earth history, marked by a persistent global cooling trend that began about 55 million years ago.

Quaternary period
The last 2.6 million years of Earth history; an ice age.

glacial period
A cold interval within the Quaternary ice age.

interglacial period
A warm interval that occurs between glacial periods.

Holocene epoch
The current interglacial period of warm and stable climate; the last 10,000 years of Earth history.

Milankovitch cycles
Small changes in Earth-Sun orbital geometry that resulted in Quaternary glacial-interglacial cycles.

than snow and ice and cause more warming, creating a positive feedback loop:

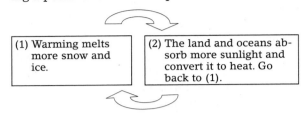

| (1) Warming melts more snow and ice. | (2) The land and oceans absorb more sunlight and convert it to heat. Go back to (1). |

The ice-albedo positive feedback destabilizes the climate system and causes climate change by enhancing the warming trend that was already taking place. But the ice-albedo positive feedback can cause cooling as well. If, for whatever reason, there were a cooling trend in Earth's atmosphere, the ice-albedo positive feedback would enhance that cooling trend:

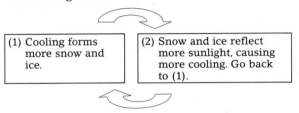

| (1) Cooling forms more snow and ice. | (2) Snow and ice reflect more sunlight, causing more cooling. Go back to (1). |

In this positive feedback loop, it would get colder as more snow and ice reflected sunlight. But positive climate feedbacks do not go on forever. They are kept in check by negative feedbacks that function to stabilize a changing system. We will return to the important role of climate forcing factors and feedbacks as we move through the remainder of this chapter.

FIGURE 6.3 **Cenozoic cooling trend.** *The atmospheric temperature has dropped steadily since the early Cenozoic era. Temperatures are given as anomalies above or below today's average, defined as 0°C. The cooling trend began when India began colliding with Asia and forming the Himalayas and Tibetan Plateau.*

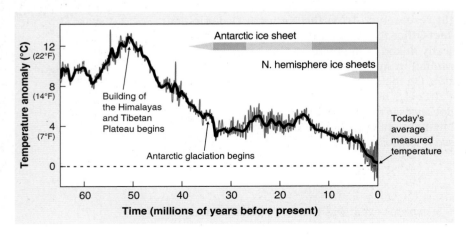

6.2 Trends, Cycles, and Anomalies

◎ **Discuss the reasons why climate changes and list the factors that cause it to change.**

Throughout geologic time, Earth's climate has always changed. The climate that we are experiencing today has been around for only about 10,000 years, a mere snapshot in Earth's history. Earth has experienced climates so cold that nearly the entire planet was covered in ice and snow, as well as climates so warm that there was no polar ice. **Earth's climate history can be reduced to three natural modes of change: long-term trends, repeating cycles, and random anomalies.**

Climate Trends: A Long, Slow Cooling

The **Cenozoic era** began about 66 million years ago. Early in that era, about 55 million years ago, the average global temperature was about 12°C (22°F) warmer than it is today. There was no ice at either of the poles. Atmospheric CO_2 concentrations were above 1,000 ppm, far higher than the present concentration of roughly 400 ppm (see Section 1.1). About 55 million years ago, a long, slow cooling trend began **(Figure 6.3)**.

The building and uplift of the Tibetan Plateau and the Himalayas are the leading explanation for the Cenozoic cooling trend. Gradual weathering and erosion of the uplifting mountain range caused CO_2 in the atmosphere to bond with other minerals that became dissolved in rivers. These minerals were then stored away as sediments and rocks on the ocean floor. As CO_2 was drawn out of the atmosphere and transferred to the lithosphere, a persistent cooling trend developed.

Climate Cycles: A Climate Roller Coaster

During the ice age of the last 2.6 million years, which geologists call the **Quaternary period**, the climate has experienced a series of swings like a roller coaster, cycling back and forth between cold glacial periods and warm interglacial periods some 22 times.

Glacial and Interglacial Periods

A **glacial period** (or *glacial*) is an interval of cold climate within the Quaternary ice age. An **interglacial period** (or *interglacial*) is an interval of warm climate that occurs between glacial periods. Between about 2.6 million and 1 million years ago, swings between warm and cool climates occurred on a 41,000-year cycle. Since about 1 million years ago, glacial periods have lasted about 90,000 years, followed by interglacial periods that have lasted about 10,000 years before the climate cools once again (Figure 6.4). Scientists think that this change to a longer cycle was the result of the lowering elevation of the ice sheets as their weight pushed into the crust.

We are currently in an interglacial called the **Holocene epoch** (or the Holocene). **The Holocene, which began about 10,000 years ago and continues today, is Earth's most recent interglacial.** Within the Quaternary as a whole, the Holocene has been a period of unusually stable climate. Given that the average length of warm periods over the past million years is 10,000 years, we are nearing the end of the Holocene. Following this same cyclical pattern, in the next few thousand years Earth's climate should enter a glacial cooling trend that will last some 90,000 years.

Why has climate cycled back and forth between warm interglacials and cold glacials about 22 times during the last 2.6 million years? The first person to contribute to our understanding of this phenomenon was the largely self-educated Scottish scientist James Croll (1821–1890). Interestingly, Croll worked as a janitor while he was developing his climate theory. He first developed the idea that changes in Earth's orbit around the Sun could produce cold glacial periods. This idea was further developed and mathematically refined by the Serbian astrophysicist Milutin Milankovitch (1879–1958).

Milankovitch Cycles

Milankovitch identified three periodic changes in Earth's orbital relationship to the Sun that led to changes in the timing and distribution of solar heating across Earth's surface (Figure 6.5). He argued that these small changes in Earth-Sun orbital geometry, now called **Milankovitch cycles**, resulted in Quaternary glacial and interglacial cycles. Milankovitch developed a mathematical model that predicted climate cycles about every 100,000 years. His work went unrecognized for about 50 years, until the middle 1970s, when new data from marine sediments led the scientific community to embrace his important theory.

Internal feedbacks are important in amplifying the climate changes forced by Milankovitch cycles. Changing Earth-Sun orbital geometry is a process that operates outside of, and is unaffected by, the climate system. Milankovitch cycles, therefore, constitute a climate forcing factor, referred to as *orbital forcing*.

FIGURE 6.4 **Quaternary temperature cycles.** *Climate swings occurred on a 41,000-year cycle before about 1 million years ago, then transitioned to a 100,000-year cycle after that.*

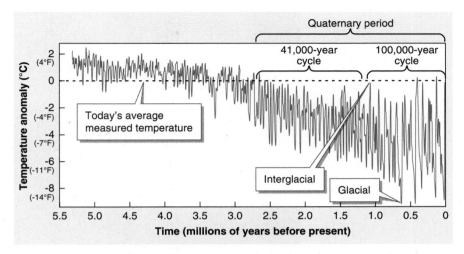

FIGURE 6.5 **GEO-GRAPHIC:**

Milankovitch cycles. *Milankovitch cycles create glacial and interglacial periods.*

Animation
Milankovitch cycles
http://qrs.ly/he43dc2

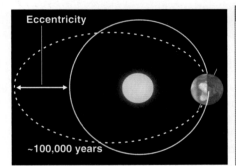

1. Orbital eccentricity

The shape of Earth's orbit around the Sun changes from circular to relatively elliptical. The diameter of the ellipse changes by about 18 million km (11 million mi). It takes about 100,000 years for this change to take place. When Earth moves closer to the Sun along its orbital path, the solar energy it receives is stronger than when it is farther away. Note that the shape of the ellipse is greatly exaggerated here.

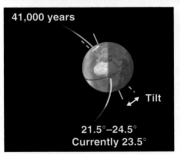

2. Tilt

The angle of Earth's axial tilt changes with respect to the plane of the ecliptic (see Section 2.1). The tilt shifts between 21.5 and 24.5 degrees from vertical over a period of about 41,000 years. Currently, the tilt is 23.5 degrees from vertical. Greater axial tilt increases seasonal contrasts in the middle and high latitudes.

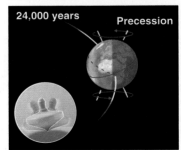

3. Precession

As Earth rotates on its axis, it wobbles like a spinning top. This wobble, called *precession*, operates on a cycle of roughly 24,000 years. Precession changes the timing of the seasons in relation to the elliptical orbit. For example, the Northern Hemisphere is currently pointed away from the Sun at the perihelion, when Earth is closest to the Sun in January. At other times, the Northern Hemisphere points toward the Sun at the perihelion.

Picture This

Mount Pinatubo

In June 1991, Mount Pinatubo, in the Philippines, erupted and sent 10 km³ (2.4 mi³) of pulverized rock and ash into the upper atmosphere. Its eruption column was 32 km (20 mi) in vertical height. The veil of aerosols (ash and sulfuric acid droplets) ejected by the volcano spread around the world within weeks and remained suspended in the stratosphere for over five years. The aerosols caused about 1.3°C (2.3°F) of cooling in some regions.

Only the largest volcanic eruptions cause climate cooling. To cause cooling, aerosols must enter the stratosphere, where rainfall will not wash them out of the atmosphere.

Consider This

1. How do volcanoes cause climate cooling?

2. Why is it that large volcanic eruptions cool the climate, but small ones do not?

Milankovitch cycles alter the intensity of sunlight over the seasons, but the Sun's energy output does not change. The most important aspect of orbital forcing is that it cools the Northern Hemisphere in summer so that snow and ice do not melt. Therefore, snow accumulates and forms continental ice sheets. As the ice sheets grow, the ice-albedo positive feedback causes further cooling. Glacial periods occur when the orbital distance from the Sun is greatest in the Northern Hemisphere summer and axial tilt is at a minimum.

Climate Anomalies: Random Events

The pattern of climate change is like a layer cake. The bottom layer is the long-term Cenozoic cooling trend. On top of that are the Milankovitch cycles and feedbacks. And on top of that layer are climate anomalies. **Anomalous climate events occur randomly through time and are caused by climate forcings and feedbacks different from those that drive longer-term climate patterns.** Changes in the Sun's output and volcanic eruptions are two examples of climate anomalies.

Changes in the Sun's Output

If the Sun's total energy output were to increase, Earth would warm. If it decreased, Earth would cool. The amount of solar energy reaching Earth, or **solar irradiance**, has been measured precisely since 1978 by satellites orbiting above the distorting effects of Earth's atmosphere. During that time, only small variations in the intensity of the Sun's output have been detected.

Sunspots are dark and relatively cool regions that migrate across the surface of the Sun. About every 11 years, sunspot activity peaks. Dark sunspots are surrounded by regions of unusually high temperatures. As a result, increased sunspot numbers are correlated with a very slight overall increase of energy from the Sun reaching Earth. Ultraviolet radiation increases significantly during high sunspot activity. Fewer sunspots could cool Earth, and more sunspots could warm it.

Although sunspots occur in cycles, not all of them have a discernible effect on Earth's climate. Instead, these cycles produce random climate events. For example, low sunspot activity may have triggered periodic episodes of cooling, such as the Little Ice Age. High sunspot activity may have triggered periods of warming, such as the Medieval Warm Period (see "The Human Sphere" on page 192).

Volcanic Eruptions

Volcanoes are climate wild cards. Nobody knows when a large volcanic eruption capable of causing climate change will happen. When volcanoes erupt, they inject ash and sulfur dioxide into the stratosphere. Sulfur dioxide combines with water to form reflective sulfuric acid droplets. These aerosols may remain suspended in the stratosphere for up to five years, where they reflect incoming sunlight, cooling Earth's surface. Volcanoes can also cause long-term warming when they emit large quantities of CO_2 over time spans of thousands to millions of years. Picture This explores this topic using the example of Mount Pinatubo.

The eruption of Mount Tambora, in Indonesia, in 1815 was among the largest historical volcanic eruptions. It led to cold summers and failed crops in many regions of the world. In many locations in northern Europe, 1816 was "the year without a summer." This event is explored further in the Geographic Perspectives in Chapter 14.

Changes in the Ocean Conveyor Belt

Before the 1980s, scientists thought that climate changed from one state to another smoothly and too slowly for humans to perceive. In the 1980s, however, new data indicated that climate can change in a matter of decades or less. Like a precariously balanced bucket that sometimes tips over, the climate system reaches "tipping points," after which it may change quickly.

Rapid climate change can be caused by positive climate feedbacks that are triggered by climate forcing factors. The resulting behavior of the climate system is referred to as *nonlinear* because the initial changes within the system are slow at first, then accelerate as positive feedbacks take over and destabilize the system rapidly.

One example of nonlinear climate change was the **Younger Dryas** cold period (named after a cold-loving plant called *Dryas octopetala*), which occurred between 12,900 and 11,600 years ago. Within a few decades or less, much of the Northern Hemisphere plunged into deep cold, some places more than others. Ice cores retrieved from the summit of the Greenland ice sheet show that the average temperature there dropped about 15°C (27°F) and stayed low for about 1,300 years. **Figure 6.6** compares the Younger Dryas event with the relatively stable Holocene climate of the last 10,000 years.

What happened almost 13,000 years ago to cause temperatures to plunge so quickly? The answer probably lies in the North Atlantic Ocean. At grocery stores, we often see conveyor belts that transport our groceries from the cart to the cashier. Scientists think that an important part of Earth's climate system behaves like a conveyor belt. The **ocean conveyor belt** is the global system of surface and deep ocean currents that transfers heat toward the poles. Its flow depends on differences in the buoyancy of ocean water caused by differences in its temperature and salinity. Colder, saltier water sinks to the depths and warmer,

solar irradiance
The amount of solar energy that reaches Earth.

Younger Dryas
A cold period that occurred 12,900 to 11,600 years ago.

ocean conveyor belt
The global system of surface and deep ocean currents that transfers heat toward the poles.

FIGURE 6.6 **The Younger Dryas.** *The Younger Dryas cold period came and went abruptly. For comparison, the Medieval Warm Period and the Little Ice Age are also shown. Compared with the Younger Dryas, climate change in those events was insignificant.*

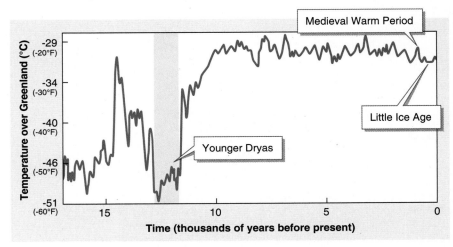

FIGURE 6.7 GEO-GRAPHIC:

The ocean conveyor belt system.

A global system of currents moves heat from the tropics to higher latitudes. The ocean conveyor belt starts in the tropical Atlantic Ocean, where trade winds push the Gulf Stream up the east coast of North America. The Gulf Stream transports 25% of all global heat moving to higher latitudes. The faster it flows, the more heat it delivers to the North Atlantic Ocean and to the atmosphere in the Northern Hemisphere. (Map by Robert Simmon, adapted from the IPCC 2001 and Rahmstorf 2002)

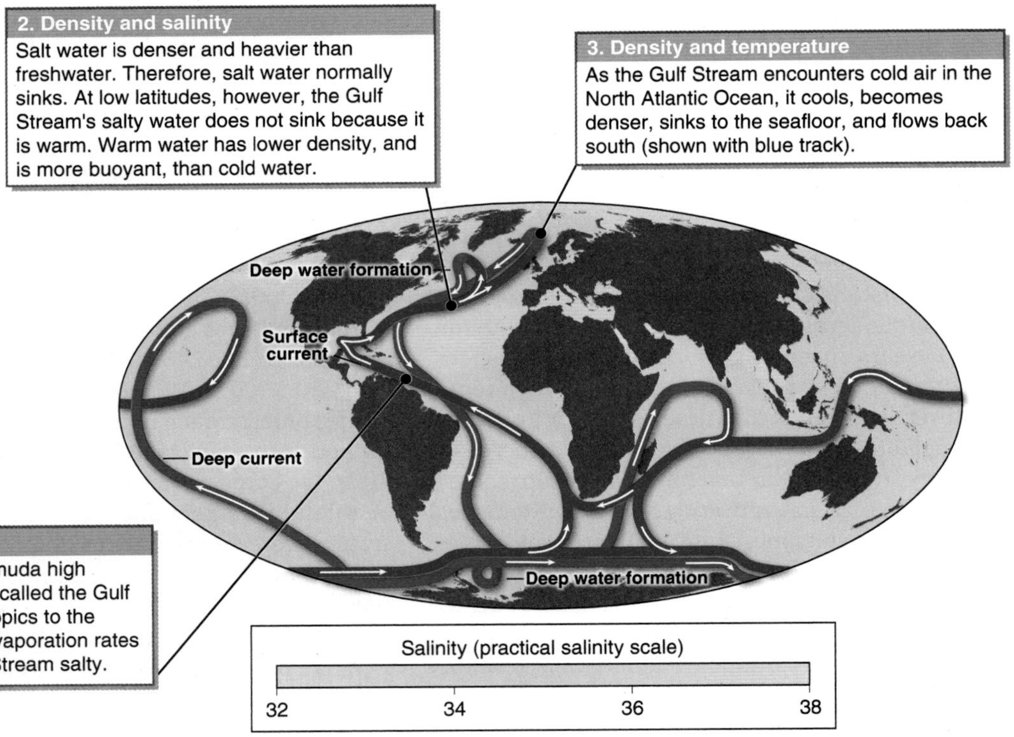

2. Density and salinity

Salt water is denser and heavier than freshwater. Therefore, salt water normally sinks. At low latitudes, however, the Gulf Stream's salty water does not sink because it is warm. Warm water has lower density, and is more buoyant, than cold water.

3. Density and temperature

As the Gulf Stream encounters cold air in the North Atlantic Ocean, it cools, becomes denser, sinks to the seafloor, and flows back south (shown with blue track).

Deep water formation

Surface current

Deep current

Deep water formation

1. Gulf Stream

The trade winds and the Bermuda high create a warm ocean current called the Gulf Stream that flows from the tropics to the North Atlantic Ocean. High evaporation rates in the tropics make the Gulf Stream salty.

Salinity (practical salinity scale)

32   34   36   38

FIGURE 6.8 Laurentide ice sheet.

At its maximum extent 20,000 years ago, the Laurentide ice sheet covered much of Canada. As it melted in response to Milankovitch forcing, the meltwater flowed out the St. Lawrence River, the Mississippi River, and the Mackenzie River, adding fresh water to the oceans into which it flowed. At times during the melting process, ice dams created huge inland lakes (such as those shown here). Scientists hypothesize that ice dams broke repeatedly over time and released massive pulses of fresh water into the North Atlantic Ocean. These pulses slowed or stopped the ocean conveyor belt system and caused cooling events such as the Younger Dryas.

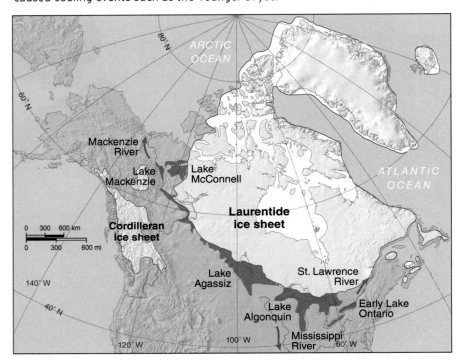

fresher water rises to the surface. **Figure 6.7** explains how this system works.

Scientists think that if the ocean conveyor belt system slows down or stops, the Northern Hemisphere gets colder. Scientists have found evidence that about 12,900 years ago, the ocean conveyor belt system greatly slowed or shut down entirely, plunging most of the Northern Hemisphere into 1,300 years of frigid Younger Dryas climate.

Why would the ocean conveyer belt system slow or shut down? Scientists believe that a massive influx of fresh water into either the North Atlantic Ocean or the Arctic Ocean forced the system to shut down. Why would fresh water shut the system down? Fresh water is more buoyant than salt water. If the Gulf Stream were freshened, it would become more buoyant and would no longer sink in the North Atlantic Ocean as shown in Figure 6.7. If the water did not sink, the current would slow down or stop flowing altogether.

It would take a lot of fresh water to slow the ocean conveyor belt system. Where would such a massive influx of fresh water come from? As **Figure 6.8** shows, that water probably came from the melting of the **Laurentide ice sheet**, the large ice sheet that covered much of North America during the most recent glacial period until about 20,000 years ago.

Reading the Past: Paleoclimatology

How do scientists know what Earth's climate was like so many thousands of years ago?

> How do scientists reconstruct Earth's ancient climates?

Earth's climate history is recorded in various natural archives, such as growth rings in trees, glaciers, and ocean sediments.

Scientists who study Earth's ancient climates, or **paleoclimates**, are called *paleoclimatologists*. They analyze natural Earth materials that record environmental changes in layers that have been left undisturbed. By analyzing these materials, they can reconstruct ancient environments **(Figure 6.9)**.

Laurentide ice sheet
The large ice sheet that covered much of North America 20,000 years ago.

paleoclimate
Ancient climate.

FIGURE 6.9   SCIENTIFIC INQUIRY: How do paleoclimatologists reconstruct ancient climates?

Natural archives of information about Earth's past can be found in a wide range of environments. In each of the settings shown here, layers are formed that record the changing environmental conditions. Layers can be formed through biological growth, as in tree rings and corals; through the settling of material by gravity, as in lake sediments, marine sediments, and glaciers; or through nonliving growth, such as mineral deposits in caves. Scientists extract cores of these materials and analyze the layers to gain an understanding of past environments and how they change through time. (From top left to bottom right: Bruce Gervais; Hickerson/FGBNMS/NOAA; © Auscape/UIG/Getty Images; © Rod Benson; Lonnie G. Thompson, Byrd Polar Research Center, Ohio State University; IODP/TAMU; John Beck, IODP/TAMU)

Tree rings

Corals

Temporal Resolution and Extent of Paleoclimate Records

MATERIAL	HOW FAR BACK IN YEARS?	TEMPORAL RESOLUTION
Tree rings	Thousands	Annual
Corals	Tens of thousands	Annual
Glaciers	Hundreds of thousands	Annual
Cave deposits	Hundreds of thousands	Decades
Lake sediments	Hundreds of thousands	Decades
Marine sediments	Millions	Centuries

Cave Deposits

Lake sediments

Natural materials vary in how far back in time their records reach and in their *temporal resolution:* how focused in time the information is. Tree rings provide information for each year (annual resolution), while marine sediments provide information for increments of about 100 years or longer (centennial resolution).

Ice cores

Marine sediments

carbon cycle
The movement of carbon through Earth's physical systems.

6.3 Carbon and Climate

◎ Compare the long-term and short-term carbon cycles and describe the role of human activity in changing those cycles.

Earth's climate system is strongly influenced by greenhouse gases in the atmosphere, particularly water vapor and carbon dioxide (see Table 1.2). Carbon dioxide has a particularly important influence today because human activities emit more of it, and its anthropogenic emissions are growing faster than any other greenhouse gas. The remainder of this chapter will focus on the role of carbon and carbon dioxide in changing Earth's climate.

Carbon atoms move among Earth's physical systems through the **carbon cycle**. When a covalent bond forms between a carbon atom and two oxygen atoms, a carbon dioxide molecule (CO_2) is formed. When this bond is broken, the carbon atom is freed from the oxygen atom. In this section, we will consider both carbon atoms and carbon dioxide molecules as they move through the carbon cycle.

The carbon cycle can be divided into a *long-term carbon cycle* and a *short-term carbon cycle*.

The long-term carbon cycle involves the movement of carbon into and out of the lithosphere and takes millions of years to unfold. The short-term carbon cycle involves the movement of carbon among the oceans, the atmosphere, and the biosphere over spans of time from minutes to a few thousand years. (Section 7.5 includes a more detailed description of the carbon cycle.)

The Long-Term Carbon Cycle

About 99.9% of Earth's carbon (65,500 billion metric tons) is stored in the lithosphere, where it is bonded with other elements to form different materials, including many types of rocks and fossil fuels (coal, oil, and natural gas). The other 0.1% of Earth's carbon is found in the oceans, atmosphere, and biosphere. Carbon is moved from the atmosphere, oceans, and biosphere into the lithosphere through weathering and erosion and through the burial and preservation of photosynthetic organisms on land and in the oceans. Carbon leaves the lithosphere through volcanic eruptions and through the burning of fossil fuels.

The Role of Weathering and Erosion

Carbon dioxide in the atmosphere combines with rainwater to form a weak acid called *carbonic acid* (H_2CO_3). Carbonic acid in rainwater slowly dissolves the rocks over which it flows through the process of *chemical weathering*. This process releases calcium ions that rivers carry to the oceans. *Ions* are atoms or molecules with electrical charges that readily react with other particles. Calcium ions combine with bicarbonate ions (HCO_3^-) in seawater to create chalky white *calcium carbonate* ($CaCO_3$) sediments, which are similar to the deposits that accumulate on faucets in homes with hard, mineral-rich water. Organisms such as corals and clams build their shells from calcium carbonate ions, pulling carbon from seawater in the process. When they die, their shells form layers of sediments as well. Over time, these sediments and remnants of shells, cemented together, form *carbonate rocks* such as limestone, locking away immense reserves of carbon in long-term storage in the lithosphere **(Figure 6.10)**.

The Role of Photosynthesis

The second way that carbon enters long-term storage in the lithosphere is through photosynthetic organisms, which include plants, algae, and certain types of bacteria (see Section GT.2). These organisms convert the Sun's radiant energy to chemical energy through the process of photosynthesis. During photosynthesis, they absorb carbon dioxide from the atmosphere, split the oxygen from it, and store the resulting carbon in their tissues.

FIGURE 6.10 **GEO-GRAPHIC: The transfer of carbon from the atmosphere to the lithosphere.**

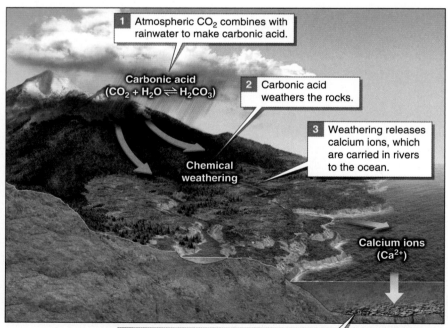

1 Atmospheric CO_2 combines with rainwater to make carbonic acid.

Carbonic acid
($CO_2 + H_2O \rightleftharpoons H_2CO_3$)

2 Carbonic acid weathers the rocks.

3 Weathering releases calcium ions, which are carried in rivers to the ocean.

Chemical weathering

Calcium ions
(Ca^{2+})

4 Calcium ions combine with bicarbonate ions in seawater to form calcium carbonate. Calcium carbonate is eventually converted to carbonate rocks, such as limestone, on the seafloor.

Normally, after these photosynthetic organisms die, they soon decompose. The carbon in their tissues recombines with oxygen in the atmosphere to make carbon dioxide again. Under certain *anaerobic* (oxygen-free) conditions, however, these organisms and the carbon in their tissues will be preserved rather than decompose.

Several hundred million years ago, microscopic photosynthetic marine algae and bacteria (called *phytoplankton*) and terrestrial forests grew, died, and did not decompose. At that time, Earth was much warmer, and climate favored their preservation. Their remains accumulated and were preserved in marine sediments or in peat wetlands on land. Over millions of years, the preservation of these organisms gradually transferred carbon from the atmosphere and oceans into long-term storage in the lithosphere. Today people use the remains of these organisms as fossil fuels.

The Short-Term Carbon Cycle

The short-term carbon cycle involves the movement of carbon among the oceans, the atmosphere, and the biosphere on time scales ranging from minutes to thousands of years. The oceans absorb large amounts of CO_2 from the atmosphere. As **Figure 6.11** shows, most carbon in the short-term cycle resides in the oceans.

Carbon does not take long to move between the biosphere, atmosphere, and oceans. For example, each breath you take moves carbon from the atmosphere to the biosphere (in the form of your body). Whenever an organism dies and decomposes, bacteria recycle the carbon in its body back into the atmosphere and the soil, where it is available to other organisms.

FIGURE 6.11 **Carbon in the short-term carbon cycle.** *Almost all of the carbon (91%) involved in the short-term carbon cycle resides in the oceans.*

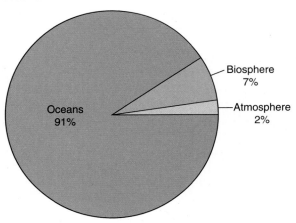

Oceans 91%

Biosphere 7%

Atmosphere 2%

FIGURE 6.12 **Natural transfer of carbon dioxide between the lithosphere and the atmosphere.** *Natural atmospheric CO_2 concentrations changed little in the last 800,000 years because the same amount of carbon that entered the atmosphere through volcanoes left the atmosphere through weathering of rocks.*

1. Volcanoes
Each year volcanoes move about 130 to 440 million metric tons of carbon dioxide into the atmosphere.

Atmosphere

130–440 million metric tons CO_2 per year

Volcanic eruption

130–440 million metric tons CO_2 per year

Ocean sediments

2. Chemical weathering
Chemical weathering of rocks moves about the same amount of carbon dioxide out of the atmosphere back into the lithosphere.

Human Modification of the Carbon Cycle

Once in the lithosphere, carbon cycles back to the atmosphere when volcanoes erupt and when people burn fossil fuels for energy. **People have greatly accelerated the transfer of carbon from the lithosphere to the atmosphere by burning fossil fuels.** Before the Industrial Revolution, when people first began burning large amounts of fossil fuels, there was an equilibrium between carbon entering the atmosphere through volcanic eruptions and carbon leaving the atmosphere through chemical weathering and sedimentation on the ocean floor **(Figure 6.12)**.

Now people move about 100 to 300 times more CO_2 into the atmosphere than all the world's volcanoes combined. By burning fossil fuels, people are effectively transferring carbon from long-term storage to the short-term carbon cycle. As

FIGURE 6.13 **Anthropogenic transfers of carbon dioxide to the atmosphere.** *Human activity adds about 35 billion metric tons (2010 rates) of CO_2 to the atmosphere each year, according to the 2014 Intergovernmental panel on Climate Change (IPCC) report. In about 4 days, human activity emits an entire average year's worth of volcanic CO_2 emissions.*

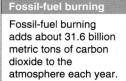

Animation
Carbon cycles
http://qrs.ly/qx43dc0

Deforestation

When forests are cut down and burned, their stored carbon enters the atmosphere. Each year, about 3.4 billion metric tons of carbon dioxide enter the atmosphere by forest loss and land-use changes.

Fossil-fuel burning

Fossil-fuel burning adds about 31.6 billion metric tons of carbon dioxide to the atmosphere each year.

Atmosphere

3.4 billion metric tons CO_2 per year

31.6 billion metric tons CO_2 per year

Deforestation

Fossil-fuel burning

Figure 6.13 illustrates, fossil fuel burning is the main human activity that adds CO_2 to the atmosphere, but deforestation also plays a role.

6.4 Climate at the Crossroads

◎ Weigh the evidence of an anthropogenic greenhouse effect in the atmosphere and describe its consequences.

The transfer of carbon from long-term storage to the short-term carbon cycle has important implications for the climate system. Carbon dioxide in the atmosphere is a greenhouse gas and a climate forcing factor. It absorbs heat and increases the temperature of the atmosphere (see Section 2.5).

Human activity is increasing atmospheric CO_2 concentrations by 2.5 parts per million (ppm) per year. Precise measurements of atmospheric CO_2 were begun by Charles Keeling in 1958 at Mauna Loa Observatory in Hawai'i. The observatory is far away from the effects of cities and pollution, and the measurements are taken upwind of any volcanic emissions. The **Keeling curve** is a graph showing the change in atmospheric CO_2 concentrations since 1958 **(Figure 6.14)**.

But what were atmospheric CO_2 concentrations before 1958, when Keeling and other scientists began measuring them? To find out, scientists have analyzed air bubbles in ancient ice from the

FIGURE 6.14 **Atmospheric carbon dioxide concentrations are increasing.**
(A) The Keeling curve shows concentrations of CO_2 in the atmosphere. The green line shows actual CO_2 measurements, which fluctuate with the seasons. In summer, values drop as plants grow and pull CO_2 from the atmosphere. In winter, values rise as plants lose their leaves, which decay and release stored carbon back into the atmosphere. The black line is the annual average. (B) The rate of increase of atmospheric CO_2 concentrations. The black bars show the average annual rate of increase by decade. In the 1960s, CO_2 rose a little less than 1 ppm per year. By 2000–2010, the average annual rate of increase had doubled to 2 ppm per year. (Data from NOAA)

Keeling curve
A graph showing the change in atmospheric CO_2 concentrations since 1958.

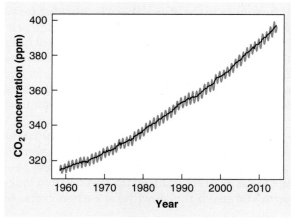

A. Atmospheric CO_2 concentrations

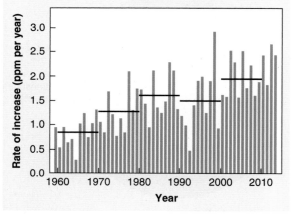

B. Rate of increase in atmospheric CO_2 concentrations

Greenland and Antarctic ice sheets (Figure 6.15). They found that before 1800, CO$_2$ concentrations were much lower than they are today. Atmospheric CO$_2$ increased after societies began burning fossil fuels in large quantities.

As we have seen, Milankovitch cycles are largely driving the shifts between glacial and interglacial periods. **During the past 800,000 years, atmospheric temperatures and CO$_2$ concentrations have changed together, as illustrated in Figure 6.16.** During glacial periods, carbon is stored in the oceans, and during interglacial periods, large amounts of carbon are transferred from the oceans to the atmosphere. Photosynthetic plants and algae cause these changes as they grow and absorb CO$_2$ from the atmosphere and as they die and release the carbon they absorbed back to the atmosphere.

The Warming Atmosphere

During the last 800,000 years, natural atmospheric CO$_2$ concentrations never exceeded 300 ppm, but today's concentrations have risen to about 400 ppm. This increase is a result of the addition of CO$_2$ to the atmosphere by human activities. **Human emissions of CO$_2$ and other greenhouse gases into the atmosphere are creating an anthropogenic greenhouse effect: an enhancement of the natural greenhouse effect that is warming the planet.** The Geographic Perspectives at the end of this chapter explores how we can reduce our CO$_2$ emissions to address this problem.

FIGURE 6.15 **Atmospheric CO$_2$ concentrations since 1000 CE.**
(A) Scientists take ice cores from the Greenland and Antarctic ice sheets in segments (shown here). When the segments are placed end to end, the cores are up to 3 km (2 mi) long. Scientists then carefully analyze ancient gas bubbles preserved in the ice. (B) Ancient air from ice cores provides a basis for comparison with the chemistry of today's atmosphere. (Left, © Reto Stoeckli; right, © British Antarctic Survey/Science Source)

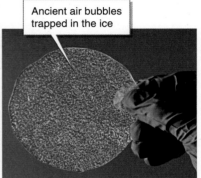

Greenland ice core

Ancient air bubbles trapped in the ice

A

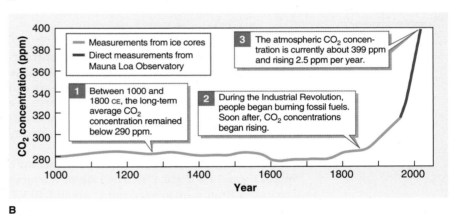

1 Between 1000 and 1800 CE, the long-term average CO$_2$ concentration remained below 290 ppm.

2 During the Industrial Revolution, people began burning fossil fuels. Soon after, CO$_2$ concentrations began rising.

3 The atmospheric CO$_2$ concentration is currently about 399 ppm and rising 2.5 ppm per year.

B

FIGURE 6.16 **Carbon dioxide concentrations and temperatures have changed together.**
Atmospheric carbon dioxide concentrations (top) and temperatures (bottom) during the last 800,000 years are recorded in ice cores from Antarctica. Natural CO$_2$ concentrations (top) never surpassed 300 ppm.

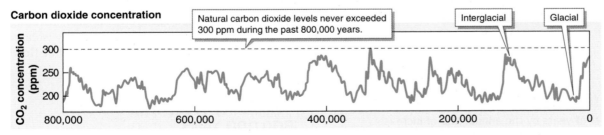

Carbon dioxide concentration

Natural carbon dioxide levels never exceeded 300 ppm during the past 800,000 years.

Interglacial

Glacial

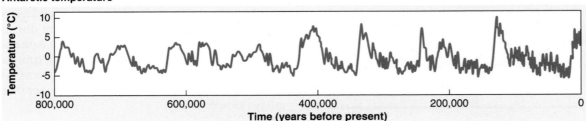

Antarctic temperature

Time (years before present)

FIGURE 6.17 **Earth's average temperature, 1880–2013.** *This graph shows global average temperatures from 1880 to 2013, given as anomalies above or below the 1951–1980 average, defined as 0°C. Since the beginning of the twenty-first century, Earth's average temperature has been 0.6°C (1.08°F) above the 1951–1980 average. The last below-average year was 1976. After that, all years have seen an above-average global temperature. Each passing decade since 1976 has been warmer than the preceding decade. The year 2012 was the warmest year for the United States, and the tenth warmest year for the planet as a whole, since 1880. The year 2013 was the seventh warmest year globally.*

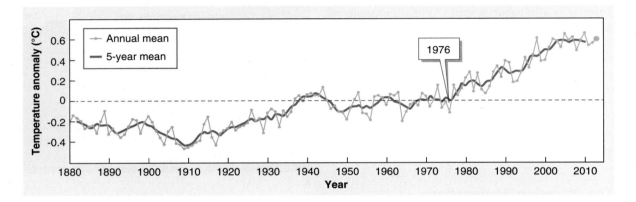

Carbon dioxide is the most important contributor to the anthropogenic greenhouse effect. Because CO_2 concentrations and temperatures increase and decrease together, atmospheric temperatures are expected to rise to match the rising CO_2 concentrations, and as **Figure 6.17** shows, that is already happening.

According to NASA, Earth's average temperature in 2013 was 14.6°C (58.3°F). The rate of warming fluctuates from year to year, but is about 0.013°C (0.023°F) per year on average. **Crunch the Numbers** uses these data to calculate a rough estimate of Earth's average temperature by the year 2050.

Your results in Crunch the Numbers are likely to be an underestimate because the rate of warming is not expected to remain constant. Nonlinear positive feedbacks, such as the ice-albedo positive feedback (see Section 6.1), may increase the rate of warming as the warming continues.

The ice-albedo positive feedback is already well under way in the Arctic, which is warming at about twice the global rate (Figure 6.18). Recent studies also indicate that dark *soot*, black dust from fossil fuel combustion at lower latitudes, could be responsible for up to 75% of the warming in the Arctic. As soot settles on ice, it darkens the white surface and lowers the albedo of the ice. As a result, the ice absorbs more solar radiation, which in turn causes more warming.

Given its accelerated rate of warming, the Arctic will continue to experience the greatest temperature shifts on the planet. Antarctica is also warming, but not as quickly, because it is relatively isolated by the *Antarctic circumpolar current* that flows around it.

Comparing Today with the Last 800,000 Years

Research on ice cores from Antarctica and Greenland has given scientists a firm understanding of atmospheric chemistry and temperature during the last 800,000 years. **Earth's average atmospheric temperature is higher now than at any time in the last 1,500 years.** But within the context of the last 800,000 years, there were periods warmer than today **(Figure 6.19)**.

CRUNCH THE NUMBERS:
Earth's Temperature in the Year 2050

Calculate Earth's average temperature for 2050, assuming that the current rate of warming remains constant.

In degrees Celsius:

1. Calculate how many years to 2050: _____

2. Multiply the number of years by the annual rate of increase: _____

3. Add the temperature increase to the current average: _____

In degrees Fahrenheit:

1. Calculate how many years to 2050: _____

2. Multiply the number of years by the annual rate of increase: _____

3. Add the temperature increase to the current average: _____

The most recent of those warm periods was the *Eemian* (also called the *Sangamonian*) *interglacial*, during which temperatures were 3°C to 4°C (5°F to 7°F) above today's average. Eemian sea level was about 4 to 6 m (13 to 20 ft) higher than today's due to the melting of glaciers at high latitudes. Although temperatures during the Eemian were warmer than today's, atmospheric CO_2 concentrations never rose above 300 ppm. Because CO_2 and temperature are coupled (see Figure 6.16), it stands to reason that the atmosphere will get warmer in the next century than it was in the Eemian because atmospheric CO_2 concentrations are already higher and are quickly rising.

Is the Warming Trend Natural?

Given the evidence, the current warming trend can be explained only by the current increase in atmospheric CO_2 concentrations caused by human activities. There is no known natural

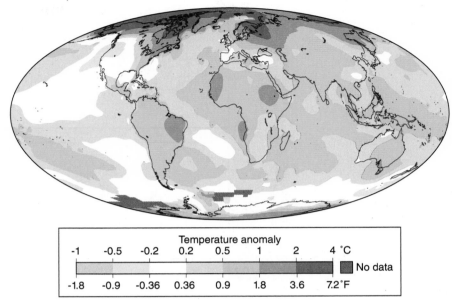

FIGURE 6.18 **Arctic warming.** *This map shows temperatures averaged for December 2003–December 2013, given as anomalies above or below the 1951–1980 global average, defined as 0°C. The Arctic is warming fastest due to the ice-albedo positive feedback. (NASA)*

FIGURE 6.19 **Atmospheric temperature reconstructions.** *Temperatures are given as anomalies above or below the average for the instrumental record-keeping period (1951 to 1980), which is defined as 0°C. (A) The current global average annual temperature is warmer than any other over the last 1,500 years. This temperature reconstruction is based mainly on data derived from tree rings and pollen in lake sediments. (B) This 800,000-year temperature reconstruction is based on ice-core data from Antarctica. Four interglacials were as warm as, or warmer than, today, the most recent of which was the Eemian, 125,000 years ago.*

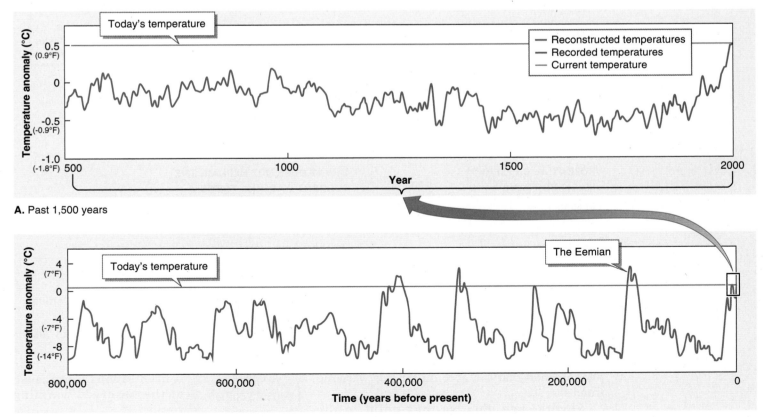

A. Past 1,500 years

B. Past 800,000 years

FIGURE 6.20 **GEO-GRAPHIC: Possible causes of the current warming trend.** *Climate scientists do not believe that natural climate forcing factors, such as El Niño (described in Section 5.5) or the factors discussed in Section 6.2, have produced the warming trend of the last 100 years. The graphs show the departure from the average temperature (from 1951-1980 and defined as 0°C) caused by each of these factors.*

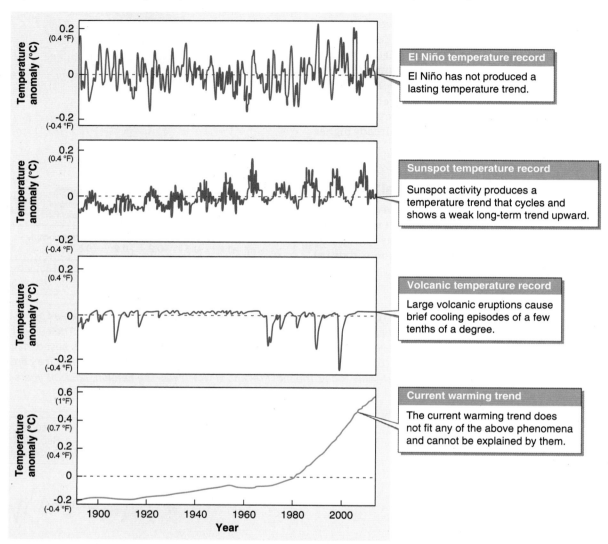

El Niño temperature record
El Niño has not produced a lasting temperature trend.

Sunspot temperature record
Sunspot activity produces a temperature trend that cycles and shows a weak long-term trend upward.

Volcanic temperature record
Large volcanic eruptions cause brief cooling episodes of a few tenths of a degree.

Current warming trend
The current warming trend does not fit any of the above phenomena and cannot be explained by them.

POTENTIAL CAUSE OF WARMING TREND	WHY IT DOES NOT EXPLAIN THE CURRENT WARMING TREND
El Niño	El Niño does not last decades.
Solar irradiance changes	The Sun's energy output is not increasing.
Volcanic eruptions	On short time scales, volcanic eruptions cause cooling.
Ocean conveyor belt	The speed of ocean conveyor belt circulation has not increased.
Milankovitch cycles	The warming is far too rapid, and current changes in orbital geometry should be cooling, not warming, the planet.
Mountain uplift and erosion	Uplift and erosion operate on time scales of millions of years.

phenomenon that can account for this warming trend **(Figure 6.20)**.

Several key observations point to the anthropogenic increase in atmospheric CO_2

Are people causing climate change?

concentrations as the cause of the observed warming trend:

1. The rapid pace of atmospheric warming mirrors the rapid pace of CO_2 increase in the atmosphere.

2. The nights are warming faster than the days. Greenhouse gases absorb outgoing terrestrial heat both day and night. The warming is most pronounced at night, however, when Earth is losing the heat it absorbed during the day.

3. The lower stratosphere is cooling. This cooling trend in the stratosphere is caused mainly by increased heat retention in the lower troposphere due to the increase of greenhouse gases.

A Strange New World

One question about climate change that often arises is this: "Climate change has happened before. Why should people be concerned?" **Whether natural or anthropogenic, any kind of climate change can be destabilizing for human societies.** There are 7 billion people living today, and the population may reach 9 billion by 2050. Complex societies are vulnerable to small changes in climate, which could result in major demographic, economic, and environmental shifts. Human societies have developed during 10,000 years of stable Holocene climate. Any change to the climate system, natural or anthropogenic, will challenge modern societies.

Positive Changes

A warming world will have positive aspects for some societies. Some countries may benefit agriculturally. Canada, for example, may improve its agricultural output and may even switch to growing corn in the near term. England is at the northernmost limit of wine-grape growing, but that is quickly changing, and many growers are switching to grapes in anticipation of a wine industry.

A new Arctic economy based on shipping, fishing, tourism, and petroleum and natural gas exploration is already opening up. According to the USGS, the Arctic could provide some 30% of the world's natural gas in the coming years. Arctic shipping routes have been blocked by ice year-round until recently, but Arctic ice cover is rapidly diminishing, and these sea routes are now open for part of the year **(Figure 6.21)**.

Shifting Physical Systems

Benefits such as these are minor, however, compared with the detrimental effects of a warming world. With each passing year, evidence mounts that rapid shifts in Earth's physical systems are underway. These shifts raise serious concerns for human populations in the coming decades. **Figure 6.22** presents some of the changes currently happening in Earth's physical systems. In the next 50 years, these changes are almost certain to continue.

FIGURE 6.21 **GEO-GRAPHIC: New Arctic shipping routes.** *The Northwest Passage and the Northern Sea Route can offer a considerably shorter, faster, and less costly route for shipping traffic between the Atlantic and Pacific oceans. Before 2010, these routes were mostly covered with sea ice in summer. As the Arctic sea ice melts, however, these routes are opening up to shipping traffic.*

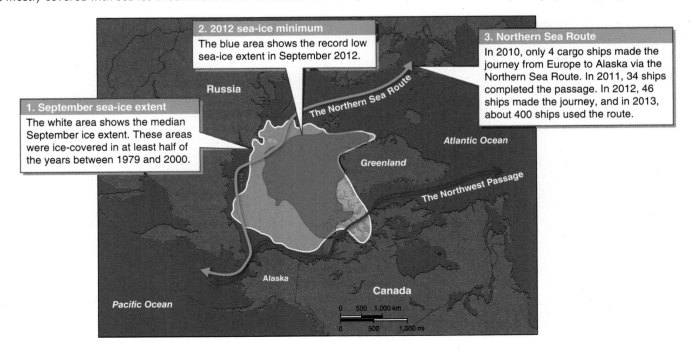

2. 2012 sea-ice minimum
The blue area shows the record low sea-ice extent in September 2012.

3. Northern Sea Route
In 2010, only 4 cargo ships made the journey from Europe to Alaska via the Northern Sea Route. In 2011, 34 ships completed the passage. In 2012, 46 ships made the journey, and in 2013, about 400 ships used the route.

1. September sea-ice extent
The white area shows the median September ice extent. These areas were ice-covered in at least half of the years between 1979 and 2000.

Russia

The Northern Sea Route

Atlantic Ocean

Greenland

The Northwest Passage

Alaska

Canada

Pacific Ocean

0   500   1,000 km

0   500   1,000 mi

Changes in the Cryosphere

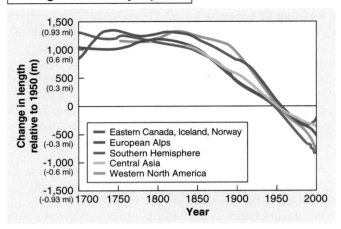

FIGURE 6.22 **Shifting physical systems.** *Many of Earth's physical systems are responding to changing atmospheric CO$_2$ concentrations and temperatures. (Muir Glacier photos: Field, William Osgood. 1941/Image/photo courtesy of Molnia, Bruce F. 2004/USGS and the National Snow and Ice Data Center, University of Colorado, Boulder. Muir Glacier: From the Glacier Photograph Collection. Boulder, Colorado USA: National Snow and Ice Data Center/World Data Center for Glaciology. Digital media.)*

Glacial retreat by region   This graph shows the change in the length of glaciers as they retreat upslope in meters. Since 1950, glaciers worldwide have retreated an average of 500 m (1,600 ft).

1941   Present

Glacial retreat, Muir Glacier   Muir Glacier, Glacier Bay National Park and Preserve, Alaska (shown here) has retreated 12 km (7 mi) since 1941, an average of 200 m (650 ft) per year.

Snowpack   This map shows April snowpack trends for western North America between 1950 and 2000. Large red circles show the greatest loss of snowpack, while blue circles show areas where snowpack increased. Winter snowpack in most western U.S. states is decreasing. In some places, snowpack has decreased by up to 80% over the last 50 years. *(EPA, Society and Ecosystems)*

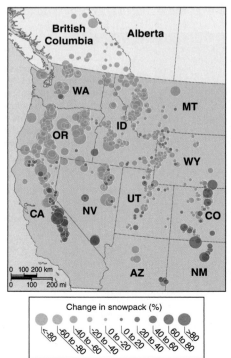

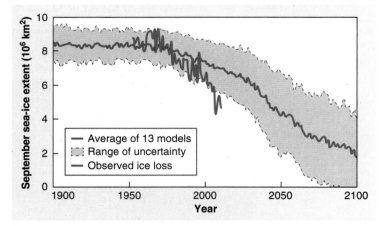

Arctic sea ice   Arctic sea ice in summer 2012 was the lowest on record. Observed loss of Arctic sea ice (red line) exceeds computer-based forecasts of ice loss (blue line). At the present rate of loss, there will be no summer sea ice by the middle of this century.

Changes in the Biosphere

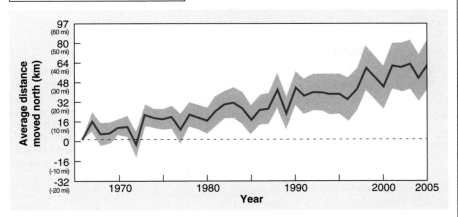

Bird abundance   This graph portrays population movements in 305 different bird species in the United States. These populations shifted north by an average of about 56 km (35 mi) over 40 years. Many plants and animals are shifting northward and upslope in response to warming.

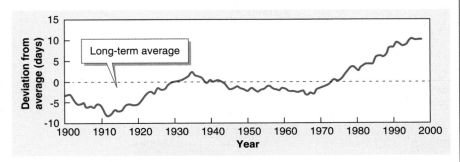

Growing season   This graph shows changes in the growing season in the continental United States since 1900. The growing season is 15 days longer, on average, than it was in 1900. On average, spring is arriving sooner and fall is lasting longer.

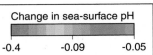

Sea level   Global sea level has risen about 200 mm (8 in) since 1880, about 3.2 mm per year. Sea level is rising due to the expansion of seawater as it warms and the loss of ice in mountain glaciers and ice sheets.

Changes in the Hydrosphere

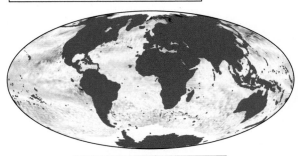

Sea surface temperature   This map shows sea surface temperature anomalies for September 2011. Between 1880 and 2010, the average sea surface temperature increased by 0.56°C (1°F). Higher water temperatures extend to a depth of 3,000 m (9,800 ft). As a result of reduced sea ice, some northern regions have water temperatures 5°C (9°F) above normal. (*NASA*)

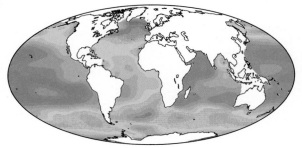

pH   This map shows changes in the acidity of seawater at the ocean surface from the 1700s to the 1990s (lower pH = more acidic). The oceans have absorbed about 30% of the CO_2 emitted by human activities into the atmosphere. As CO_2 dissolves in seawater, the water's pH decreases. The pH of seawater has dropped from approximately 8.25 to 8.14 since 1850. This rate of pH change in the oceans is the fastest in over 21 million years.

FIGURE 6.23 **Projections of carbon dioxide concentrations and surface temperatures by 2100.** *(A) Projections of atmospheric CO_2 concentrations by 2100 range from 550 ppm to 900 ppm. This wide range of values results from uncertainties regarding future rates of anthropogenic CO_2 emissions. (B) These four modeled emissions scenarios range from "low growth," in which the rate of anthropogenic CO_2 emissions grows slowly, to "high growth," in which anthropogenic emissions increase greatly. The "no growth" scenario shows the warming that would result if anthropogenic CO_2 emissions were completely stopped as of 2007. Some warming would continue to happen due to lags in the climate system. (C) IPCC temperature forecasts for North America by the 2090s under the two different emissions growth scenarios (low and high). Darker reds indicate warmer temperatures. (C. Adapted from from Climate Change 2007: The Physical Science Basis. Working Group I Contribution to the Fourth Assessment Report of the Intergovernmental Panel on Climate Change, Figure SPM.5.)*

Animation
Carbon dioxide projections
http://qrs.ly/8d43dc8

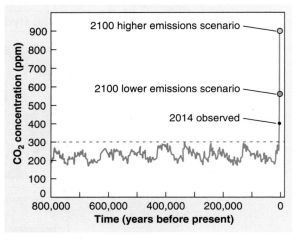

A

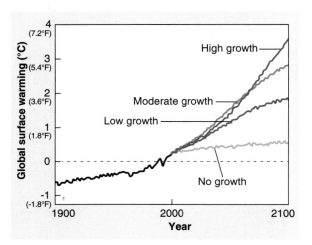

B

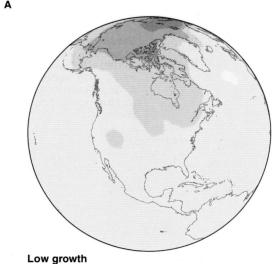

Low growth

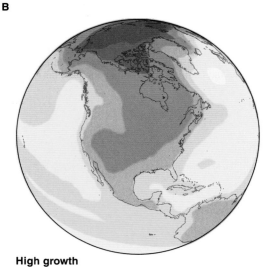

High growth

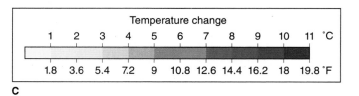

C

The following is a brief summary of some of the major anticipated changes to Earth's systems:

Sea level: The Intergovernmental Panel on Climate Change (IPCC) projects that by 2100, sea level is likely to rise up to 1.2 m (46 in, or nearly 4 ft). Additionally, new research published in May 2014 in *Science* found that as the west Antarctic ice sheet thins and flows into the ocean, even more sea level rise is inevitable.

Extreme weather: The combination of rising temperatures and, in certain regions, increasing evaporation due to warmer temperatures is now leading to both more drought and more flooding rains. Satellite data show that between 1987 and 2006, average annual global precipitation amounts increased 7.4% as a result of fewer but more intense storms, not more storms.

Atmospheric circulation: Climate models project that the downward limbs of the Hadley cells (see Section 4.3) could migrate poleward as the equator-to-pole temperature gradient lessens. Such a shift would change wind and precipitation patterns at midlatitudes worldwide.

Extinctions: Many species are now moving upslope and to higher and cooler latitudes in response to warming temperatures (see Figure 6.22). As species continue this migration response, cities, highways, farms, and other human-built landscapes will impede their movement. For this reason, biologists anticipate that many species will go extinct as they attempt to find suitable habitat.

Computers and Climate Projections

Climatologists use Earth system models to develop predictions about how climate might respond to greenhouse gas forcing. An **Earth system model** is a mathematical simulation of the behavior of the atmosphere, oceans, and biosphere that can be used to create long-term climate projections. Because of the complexity of the climate system, these models run some 80 million calculations per hour and billions of calculations over weeks and months, requiring the world's fastest supercomputers.

According to the Intergovernmental Panel on Climate Change, most models project a temperature increase in the lower atmosphere ranging from 2°C to 6°C (3.6°F to 10.8°F) by the end of this century.

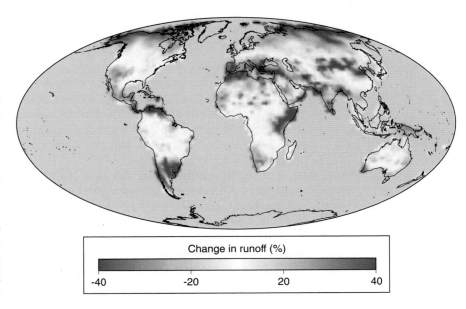

FIGURE 6.24 **Forecast stream runoff changes.** *This map shows forecast stream runoff patterns for the end of the century. Changing precipitation and temperatures are predicted to reduce stream runoff in some regions and increase it in other regions. The southwestern United States is expected to experience stream reductions of up to 40% by 2100. (Map by Robert Simmon, using data from Chris Milly, NOAA Geophysical Fluid Dynamics Laboratory)*

Change in runoff (%)

-40   -20   20   40

This range of uncertainty results from various factors. For example, there is uncertainty as to how much CO_2 will be emitted by human activities in the coming years **(Figure 6.23)**. There are also many complicating factors, such as cloud feedbacks (see Section 3.6), that affect the climate system.

Climate change is expected to change precipitation patterns. Much of Canada and the northeastern United States are expected to receive increased precipitation. The southwestern United States and the Mediterranean are expected to become drier. For many regions, changes in precipitation coupled with changes in temperature are projected to alter stream runoff significantly **(Figure 6.24)**, and these changes will alter the availability of surface water for human use.

More than a half century of evidence and over 50,000 published scientific papers fact-checked by other experts indicate that Earth's climate is changing in response to the anthropogenic greenhouse effect. That people are causing climate change is not in dispute among scientists. How to address the problem is the subject of the next section.

Earth system model
A mathematical simulation of the behavior of the atmosphere, oceans, and biosphere; used to create long-term climate projections.

GEOGRAPHIC PERSPECTIVES
6.5 Stabilizing Climate

◎ **Assess different approaches to tackling climate change.**

On May 9, 2013, the atmosphere's CO_2 concentration reached 400 ppm at Mauna Loa Observatory in Hawai'i. As the summer progressed, it was drawn back down naturally to the high 390s. At the current rate of increase, atmospheric CO_2 concentrations will reach 400 ppm in 2015. It will not drop below that for at least 1,000 years, and probably much longer.

The last time atmospheric CO_2 was at 400 ppm was about 3 million years ago, before the Quaternary ice age began (see Section 6.2). At that time, temperatures were 2°C to 3°C (3.6°F to 5.4°F) higher than today. Global sea level was about 25 m (82 ft) higher than today as a result of less glacier ice.

If anthropogenic CO_2 emissions continue to grow at current rates, CO_2 concentrations will reach 900 ppm by the end of this century (see Figure 6.23A), a concentration that last occurred about 35 million years ago. If CO_2 reaches this concentration, we will face a world that is very different from the world we live in today. How can we avoid this scenario?

Twenty-Five Billion Metric Tons

One goal set by climate scientists is to reduce CO_2 emissions so that atmospheric CO_2 concentrations do not exceed 500 ppm. Doing so could keep future warming within 2°C (3.6°F). **On a global scale, yearly CO_2 emissions would have to be reduced about 80% from current levels, by about 25 billion metric tons, within the next two decades to keep atmospheric CO_2 under 500 ppm.**

Reducing the flow of CO_2 to the atmosphere by 80% within two decades is a daunting but technologically achievable goal. Accomplishing it will involve a significant restructuring of the way people produce energy and the way people use fossil fuels. Table 6.2 suggests six specific steps we can take to accomplish this goal. If these six actions were fully implemented, CO_2 emissions would stabilize by 2050 at about 500 ppm. This table is a small sampling of the many actions that can be taken to reduce global carbon emissions.

Addressing the Problem

There is a growing movement to tackle the problem of climate change on a variety of fronts, from the level of the national government to the individual. Environmentally friendly green economies are quickly growing in many countries. A **green economy** is a sustainable economic system that

green economy
A sustainable economic system that has a small environmental impact and is based on renewable energy sources.

TABLE **6.2** Cutting CO_2 Emissions by 80%	
ACTION	**HOW TO DO IT**
1 **Cars:** Double the fuel efficiency of all cars worldwide and halve the number of miles traveled by cars each year.	Improve technology in vehicles. Phase out inefficient vehicles. Improve city design and mass transit.
2 **Buildings:** Reduce energy use in all buildings 25%.	Improve insulation and building design. Improve efficiency of heating and cooling, lighting, and appliances.
3 **Coal efficiency:** Improve coal power plant efficiency from the current 40% to 60%.	Improve technology for burning coal and converting it to electricity.
4 **Solar energy:** Increase photovoltaic solar power capacity.	Increase today's photovoltaic capacity by 700 times. This would require 2 million hectares of land (see Section 2.6).
5 **Wind energy:** Increase wind power capacity.	Increase today's wind capacity by about 40 times. This would require 30 million hectares (74 million acres) of land (see Section 4.5).
6 **Deforestation:** Reverse deforestation in the tropics.	Provide economic alternatives to cutting forests for developing countries. Reduce demand for forest products in developed countries by supporting recycling and more efficient manufacturing.

FIGURE 6.25 **Greenhouse gas reduction targets for major cities.** *(A) The cities included here are a small sample of cities worldwide that have set goals for reducing their greenhouse gas emissions (relative to 1990 levels). Toronto, Canada, for example, has the goal of reducing its carbon emissions by 80% by the year 2050. (B) Chicago is a leader among American cities reducing carbon emissions. Planted rooftops, for example, reduce electricity use by cooling buildings in summer and warming them in winter. This planted rooftop on Chicago's City Hall building was the first on a municipal building in the United States. (B. © AP Photo/Chicago Department of Environment, Mark Farina)*

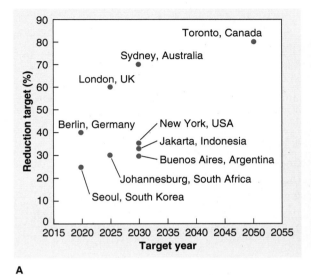

A

B

has a small environmental impact and is based on renewable energy sources.

Coping with increased droughts, floods, disease, sea-level rise, and shifting agricultural zones as a result of changing climate would be far more costly than taking early steps to curb greenhouse gas emissions and preventing serious climate change. Approaches to dealing with the climate problem can be divided into international, local, and individual responses.

International Response

There has been much talk among nations about limiting greenhouse gas emissions. The United Nations Copenhagen Accord in 2009 and the climate change conference in Durban, South Africa, in 2011 were two recent meetings at which the problem was addressed. This work continues with the 2015 climate conference in Paris, where participating nations will agree to legal obligations to cut their carbon emissions. Some 55 nations, which account for 87% of global CO_2 emissions, registered an informal commitment to reduce their greenhouse gas emissions. Canada and the United States, for example, have committed to lowering their CO_2 emissions by 17% from their 2005 emission levels by the year 2020.

National Response

Carbon taxes are seen by many as the most important legislation at the national level to reduce carbon emissions quickly and efficiently. Carbon emissions beyond a predetermined level could be taxed. This would provide an incentive to produce less carbon.

In a similar scheme, carbon *cap-and-trade* systems allocate carbon "credits" to carbon producers, such as manufacturing companies. A company may purchase more carbon credits from other companies that have carbon credits to sell. Because the overall number of carbon credits is limited, the total carbon emissions of a country would be reduced.

Carbon taxes are politically unpopular. Voluntary reductions and cap-and-trade schemes have thus far been largely ineffective, as evidenced by the upward march of CO_2 concentrations in the atmosphere. One important goal of the next generation will be to establish enforceable and effective legislation to promote greenhouse gas reductions.

Local Response

Half the people in the world live in urban areas, and this percentage is growing. Cities contribute up to 40% of global CO_2 emissions. Over 2,800 cities worldwide have formally committed to reducing their CO_2 emissions. The C40 Cities Climate Leadership Group is a coalition of major cities committed to reducing their greenhouse gas emissions under specific deadlines (Figure 6.25).

Many states have also initiated emissions reduction goals that are voluntary. California, New

TABLE 6.3	**Reducing One's Carbon Footprint**
ACTIVITY	**HOW TO REDUCE THE CARBON FOOTPRINT**
Reduce, reuse, recycle	Generating less waste and recycling reduce the amount of greenhouse gases emitted by resource extraction, manufacturing, transport, and disposal of materials.
Driving	Living closer to work, biking, walking, using public transportation, carpooling, and combining errands for fewer trips reduce the amount of fuel burned.
Home energy use	Insulating the attic and outside walls, LED lighting, and efficient appliances reduce energy use.
Water use	Purifying and distributing water require energy. Using less water consumes less energy.
Renewable energy use	Using solar and wind energy decreases reliance on fossil fuels. Many local power companies allow users to select whether their power comes from conventional or renewable sources.
Diet	Raising livestock for meat is more carbon-intensive than growing plants for direct human consumption. Eating organic food reduces the use of fossil-fuel fertilizers. Eating locally produced food reduces the need to transport food long distances.
Flying	Flying is a carbon-intensive activity. Flying less reduces fuel use.
Political engagement	Climate-friendly legislation can be an effective way to manage greenhouse gas emissions.
Carbon offsets	Carbon offsets are investments in renewable, carbon-free energy sources such as wind energy and solar energy. These projects can reduce carbon emissions from conventional energy sources such as coal or oil.

York, Michigan, Connecticut, and Florida, for example, have set an ambitious goal of reducing greenhouse gas emissions by 80% (relative to 1990 levels) by the year 2050.

Individual Response

The challenge of coping with climate change can seem overwhelming to an individual. Almost all of our daily activities rely on energy from fossil fuels and emit CO_2 into the atmosphere. The average car emits about 5.5 metric tons of CO_2 each year. Heating, cooling, and electricity use in the average house in the United States produce about 11 metric tons of CO_2 each year.

One approach to the problem is to understand your personal carbon footprint. A **carbon footprint** is the amount of greenhouse gases (particularly CO_2) that any activity generates. There is much literature available on living a low-carbon lifestyle, but the main goal is to reduce greenhouse gas emissions. Many of the steps required to reduce one's personal carbon footprint call for lifestyle changes (Table 6.3). There are many online "carbon calculators" that allow you to estimate your CO_2 emissions and consider ways to reduce your carbon footprint.

Since the year 1976, every decade has been warmer than the previous one (see Figure 6.17). Atmospheric CO_2 concentrations and temperatures continue to rise. At the same time, green economies and active reduction of carbon emissions are developing a growing momentum. At present, no one yet knows how this planetary-scale unintended experiment will play out.

carbon footprint
The amount of greenhouse gases (particularly carbon dioxide) any activity generates.

CHAPTER 6 **Exploring with ⊚Google Earth**

To complete these problems, first read the chapter. When you are finished, go to LaunchPad and open the Exploring with Google Earth file for this chapter. Click on the "Workbook Problems" folder to "fly" to each of the problems listed below and answer the questions. Be sure to keep your "Borders and Labels" layer activated. Refer to Appendix 4 if you need help using Google Earth.

PROBLEM 6.1 This placemark is pinned to the terminus (end point) of the Franz Josef Glacier in New Zealand. Activate the two red pins in this folder if they are not already activated. One pin marks the terminus of the glacier in 1948, and the other shows the terminus of the glacier in 2006.

1. **How far has the glacier retreated between 1948 and 2006?**
   a. 570 m   c. 2,480 m
   b. 1,060 m   d. 3,500 m

2. **What is the average rate of retreat of the glacier in meters per year? (Divide the number of meters of retreat by the number of years.)**
   a. 11 m   c. 26 m
   b. 18 m   d. 43 m

PROBLEM 6.2 The placemark features the Antler Glacier in Alaska. Activate the two red pins in this folder if they are not already activated. One pin shows the terminus (end point) of the glacier in 2005, and another one shows it in 1948.

1. **How far has the glacier retreated between 1948 and 2005?**
   a. 5,000 m   c. 6,000 m
   b. 5,550 m   d. 6,500 m

2. **What is the average rate of retreat of the glacier in meters per year? (Divide the number of meters of retreat by the number of years.)**
   a. 97 m   c. 131 m
   b. 102 m   d. 321 m

PROBLEM 6.3 Activate the Northwest Passage and the Northern Sea Route overlays in this problem's folder and answer the following questions.

1. **Using the measuring tool's "path" option, measure the distance a ship would travel between Lisbon, Portugal, and Tokyo, Japan, in miles. Use the route that takes the ship through the Suez Canal. (You can locate the Suez Canal in the sidebar search function.) What is this distance?**
   a. 10,000 mi   c. 14,000 mi
   b. 12,000 mi   d. 16,000 mi

2. **Now measure the path between the same two cities using the Northern Sea Route. About how much shorter is this route than the Suez Canal route?**
   a. 1,000 mi shorter   c. 3,000 mi shorter
   b. 2,000 mi shorter   d. 5,000 mi shorter

PROBLEM 6.4 Activate the IPCC Temperature Projections "Medium Emissions Scenario" overlay in this problem's folder to answer the following questions.

1. **This placemark falls on Chicago. By the 2090s, what is the average temperature change that Chicago and much of the Midwest, the Great Plains, and the western interior of the United States are predicted to experience under the medium emissions scenario?**
   a. 3°C to 4°C warmer   c. 5°C to 6°C warmer
   b. 4°C to 5°C warmer   d. 6°C to 7°C warmer

2. **What region of the world is predicted to experience the greatest temperature increase?**
   a. The tropics   c. The Arctic
   b. The midlatitudes   d. The Antarctic

3. **How much warmer is temperature predicted to be there?**
   a. Up to 8°C warmer   c. Up to 10°C warmer
   b. Up to 9°C warmer   d. Up to 11°C warmer

CHAPTER 6 **Study Guide**

Focus Points

6.1 The Climate System

The climate system: The climate system is composed of Earth's physical systems, mainly the atmosphere, biosphere, lithosphere, hydrosphere, and cryosphere.

Temperature increase: The average global atmospheric temperature has risen by 0.83°C (1.5°F) since 1880.

Climate change: Climate change occurs when the long-term trend of meteorological variables or weather extremes, such as the average temperature or the number of heat waves, changes.

Extreme events: The occurrence of extreme events cannot be scientifically attributed to climate change, but the intensity of those events can.

The ice-albedo positive feedback: The ice-albedo positive feedback destabilizes the climate system and causes climate change by enhancing whatever trend is already taking place.

6.2 Trends, Cycles, and Anomalies

Modes of climate change: Climate change occurs through long-term trends, repeating cycles, and random anomalies. These changes are caused by climate forcing factors and climate feedbacks.

The Holocene: The Holocene (the last 10,000 years) is Earth's most recent interglacial. Climate has been unusually stable during the Holocene.

Rapid climate change: Climate can rapidly switch between different states on a time scale of decades.

Reconstructing past climates: Earth's past climates are recorded in various natural materials, including tree rings, glaciers, cave deposits, and ocean sediments.

6.3 Carbon and Climate

Carbon cycles: Carbon is removed from the atmosphere, oceans, and biosphere and stored for many millions of years in the lithosphere in the long-term carbon cycle. Carbon moves relatively quickly among the atmosphere, biosphere, and oceans in the short-term carbon cycle.

Human activity and carbon cycling: Each year, burning of fossil fuels and deforestation are moving about 35 billion metric tons of carbon from the lithosphere and biosphere into the atmosphere.

6.4 Climate at the Crossroads

Anthropogenic greenhouse effect: Natural atmospheric CO_2 concentrations have not exceeded 300 ppm over the last 800,000 years. Because of human activities, atmospheric CO_2 concentrations are now 400 ppm and rising 2.5 ppm per year. As a result, atmospheric temperatures are rising.

Carbon dioxide and temperature: Atmospheric CO_2 concentrations and temperatures have risen and fallen together during the last 800,000 years.

The Arctic: The ice-albedo positive feedback is warming the Arctic at about twice the rate of the rest of the world.

Causes of the current warming trend: No known natural climate forcing factor, such as volcanic activity or sunspot activity, can explain the current warming trend.

Effects of warming: The negative aspects of warming far outweigh any positive aspects.

Changes in Earth's physical systems: Earth's physical systems are changing because of atmospheric warming.

Climate projections: Climate projections based on computer modeling vary depending on assumptions about how much CO_2 will be emitted into the atmosphere.

6.5 Geographic Perspectives: Stabilizing Climate

500 ppm goal: Most climate scientists conclude that limiting atmospheric CO_2 concentrations to less than 500 ppm could avoid significant climate change. To meet this goal, annual global CO_2 emissions must be cut by about 25 billion metric tons, or 80%, in the next few decades.

How to reduce carbon: Doubling the efficiency of cars, increased use of carbon-free energy, carbon taxes, and personal choices are some of the options available to address climate change.

Key Terms

carbon cycle, 202
carbon footprint, 215
Cenozoic era, 196
climate, 193
climate forcing factor, 195
cryosphere, 194
Earth system model, 213
glacial period, 196
green economy, 214
Holocene epoch, 196
ice-albedo positive
   feedback, 195

interglacial period, 196
Keeling curve, 204
Laurentide ice sheet, 201
Little Ice Age, 193
Medieval Warm Period, 193
Milankovitch cycles, 196
ocean conveyor belt, 199
paleoclimate, 201
Quaternary Period, 196
solar irradiance, 199
weather, 193
Younger Dryas, 199

Concept Review

The Human Sphere: The Greenland Norse

1. When did the Medieval Warm Period occur? When did the Little Ice Age occur? What impacts on human societies did they have?

6.1 The Climate System

2. What is the difference between weather and climate?

3. How is climate defined?

4. Compare the definitions of weather and climate. Is one day of record heat an example of weather or climate? What about one warmer-than-average year? A decade of warmer-than-average years?

5. Besides the atmosphere, what are the other parts of the climate system?

6. What happened to temperatures in the Northern Hemisphere during the Younger Dryas?

7. By how much has the average temperature of the lower atmosphere increased over the last 100 years?

8. Is the temperature increase over the last 100 years an example of weather or climate change? Explain.

9. If a severe storm strikes, can scientists definitely say it was caused by climate change? Explain.

10. What are climate forcing factors? How are they different from climate feedbacks? Give examples of each.

11. Explain how ice cover at high latitudes can function as a positive feedback that destabilizes climate or as a negative feedback that stabilizes climate.

6.2 Trends, Cycles, and Anomalies

12. What caused the Cenozoic cooling trend?

13. Describe the Quaternary ice age in terms of its timing and repeated climate cycles. Describe the climate of the Holocene epoch.

14. What are Milankovitch cycles? With what kind of climate change pattern are they associated?

15. What are glacials and interglacials? About how long, on average, has each lasted during the last million years? What caused them, climate forcing or climate feedbacks?

16. Provide an example of a climate anomaly. Do climate forcings or climate feedbacks cause anomalies?

17. What natural archives do paleoclimatologists examine to reconstruct ancient climates and environments?

6.3 Carbon and Climate

18. Where is most carbon on Earth stored? How does carbon enter and leave this long-term storage?

19. Compare and contrast the long-term carbon cycle with the short-term carbon cycle. Explain how carbon moves within each.

20. What two main types of human activity are transferring carbon to the atmosphere? How many billion metric tons are transferred to the atmosphere each year?

6.4 Climate at the Crossroads

21. What is the current rate of increase of CO_2 concentrations in the atmosphere each year in parts per million?

22. What is the Keeling curve? What does it show?

23. How do we know what prehistoric CO_2 concentrations were? Compare current CO_2 concentrations in the atmosphere with those over the last 800,000 years.

24. What concentration (in ppm) did natural atmospheric CO_2 not exceed over the last 800,000 years?

25. What is the current atmospheric CO_2 concentration (in ppm)? Where is this "extra" carbon coming from?

26. Describe the relationship between CO_2 and global atmospheric temperature.

27. Geographically, where is most of the current warming trend happening? Why is it happening there?

28. Are there any natural climate forcing factors that can explain the current warming trend?

29. What are some of the responses of Earth's physical systems to the current warming trend? What changes in Earth's physical systems are anticipated in this century?

30. What is a climate model? Why do climate models make such a wide range of climate projections?

6.5 Geographic Perspectives: Stabilizing Climate

31. What actions must be taken to address the problem of climate change?

32. To avoid significant climate change, what is the atmospheric CO_2 concentration that most scientists think must not be exceeded?

33. By what percentage should global anthropogenic CO_2 emissions be cut to achieve that concentration?

34. How, specifically, can individuals reduce their CO_2 emissions?

35. Give an example of how a single individual is linked to Earth's climate system.

Critical-Thinking Questions

1. What differences and what similarities can you think of between the Greenland Norse and modern societies in the context of vulnerability to climate change?

2. Has reading this chapter altered your view on climate change? Explain.

3. Do you or anyone you know (such as your parents or grandparents) have personal anecdotal information and experiences (such as stories or memories) about climate change?

4. The topic of climate change has been politically controversial. Why do you think that is? What views might people with different interests take on this topic?

5. Read through Table 6.3 again. Do you find these individual approaches to addressing climate change agreeable or disagreeable? Specifically, do you think altering one's diet or plane travel is a reasonable response to the problem? Explain.

Test Yourself

Take this quiz to test your chapter knowledge.

1. **True or false?** A single year of record-breaking heat is a definite sign of climate change.

2. **True or false?** Modern human emissions of CO_2 are about equal to natural emissions from volcanoes.

3. **True or false?** Most of Earth's carbon is stored in the lithosphere.

4. **True or false?** To stabilize CO_2 concentrations in the atmosphere, human carbon emissions must be cut by about 80% in the next few decades.

5. **True or false?** Worldwide, most mountain glaciers are receding upslope in response to anthropogenic climate change.

6. **Multiple choice:** During the last 800,000 years, natural atmospheric CO_2 concentrations did not rise above
   a. 100 ppm.   c. 300 ppm.
   b. 200 ppm.   d. 400 ppm.

7. **Multiple choice:** Today's atmospheric CO_2 concentration is about
   a. 100 ppm.   c. 300 ppm.
   b. 200 ppm.   d. 400 ppm.

8. **Multiple choice:** Why are the oceans becoming more acidic?
   a. Because they are warming
   b. Because of ocean currents
   c. Because organic activity is causing acidification
   d. Because they are absorbing CO_2 from the atmosphere

9. **Fill in the blank:** The _____ is a graph of measurements that show increasing CO_2 concentrations in the atmosphere.

10. **Fill in the blank:** The study of ancient climate is called _____.

Picture This. YOUR TURN

Annual Carbon Dioxide Increase

The graph shows atmospheric concentrations of CO_2 measured at the Mauna Loa Observatory. The green line shows seasonal variation around the annual average (black line). Use what you have learned in this chapter to answer the following questions.

1. Why does the global atmospheric CO_2 concentration fluctuate seasonally?

2. Why is the average global CO_2 concentration rising with each passing year? Where is that carbon coming from?

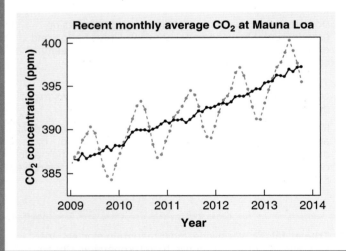

Further Reading

1. Diamond, Jared. *Collapse: How Societies Choose to Fail or Succeed.* New York: Viking Press, 2005.

2. Riser, Stephen, and M. Susan Lozier. "Rethinking the Gulf Stream." *Scientific American* 308 (February 2013): 50-55.

3. Zachos, James, et al. "Trends, Rhythms, and Aberrations in Global Climate 65 Ma to Present." *Science* 292 (2001): 886-993.

Answers to Living Physical Geography Questions

1. **Was Superstorm Sandy a result of anthropogenic climate change?** No single weather event can be definitively attributed to climate change. Scientists do know that the intensity of this storm would have been less had it not been for climate change.

2. **What factors cause Earth's climate to change?** Climate changes in response to climate forcing factors from outside the climate system and climate feedbacks within the climate system.

3. **How do scientists reconstruct Earth's ancient climates?** Scientists use tree rings, lake sediments, corals, glacial ice, and other natural materials to reconstruct Earth's ancient climates.

4. **Are people causing climate change?** All available evidence points to human activities as the primary cause of Earth's warming atmosphere.

PART II
THE BIOSPHERE AND THE GEOGRAPHY OF LIFE

Sunlight powers the biosphere. Almost all living organisms depend on solar energy. Part II explores the global geographic patterns of life on land and in the oceans, soil and water resources, and the human transformation of the biosphere.

CHAPTER 7
PATTERNS OF LIFE:
Biogeography

Geographic patterns of life are determined by natural factors and by human activities.

CHAPTER 8
CLIMATE AND LIFE:
Biomes

Climate and human activity determine vegetation types across Earth's surface.

CHAPTER 9
SOIL AND WATER RESOURCES

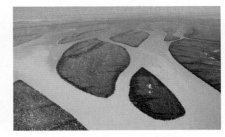

Soil and water resources are essential for human well being.

CHAPTER 10
THE LIVING HYDROSPHERE:
Ocean Ecosystems

Ocean ecosystems are patterned geographically and changed by people.

THE BIOSPHERE AND THE GEOGRAPHY OF LIFE

(Chapter 7: © Philippe Michel/age fotostock; Chapter 8: © Bill Bachmann/age fotostock; Chapter 9: © Morales/age fotostock; Chapter 10: © Reinhard Dirscherl/WaterFrame/Getty Images)

7 PATTERNS OF LIFE: Biogeography

Chapter Outline

The Avenue of the Baobabs, near the town of Morondava in Madagascar. Baobab trees (*Adansonia grandidieri*) are often called "upside-down" trees because their branches look like roots.

(© Philippe Michel/age fotostock)

LIVING PHYSICAL GEOGRAPHY

> Why do animals migrate?
> Why do cacti have spines?
> How are wolves important to ecosystems?
> Why do coconuts float?

To learn more about these trees and why they grow in such an unusual form, turn to page 234.

THE BIG PICTURE *Geographic patterns of life are determined by natural factors and by human activities. The biosphere can be organized by flows of energy and matter, by genetic similarities among organisms, and by ecological units of life.*

LEARNING GOALS *After reading this chapter, you will be able to:*

7.1 ◎ Identify and explain major geographic patterns of life on Earth.

7.2 ◎ Discuss factors that limit the geographic ranges of organisms.

7.3 ◎ Explain how organisms expand their geographic ranges.

7.4 ◎ Discuss the role of ecological disturbance and the return of life following disturbance.

7.5 ◎ Describe three approaches to organizing the biosphere.

7.6 ◎ Assess the relationship between people and the coconut palm and apply that knowledge to other organisms used by people.

THE HUMAN SPHERE: Exotic Invaders

FIGURE 7.1 **A Nile perch.** *The non-native Nile perch has inflicted serious ecological damage in Lake Victoria. It preys on the lake's native cichlid fish and has driven about 300 cichlid species to extinction or near-extinction. Nile perch grow to nearly 2 m (6.5 ft) and can weigh 200 kg (440 lb). (© Walter Astrada/AFP/Getty Images)*

NON-NATIVE (or *exotic*) organisms are those that have been moved outside their original geographic range by people. Some non-native organisms cause ecological damage by preying on or taking resources in their new ranges from native organisms (those that were there originally). In many areas where non-natives are successful, their natural predators are missing. For example, the Nile perch (*Lates niloticus*) **(Figure 7.1)**, which was intentionally brought into Lake Victoria in eastern Africa in the 1950s as a food resource for local communities, has had significant negative effects on native fish species in the lake.

Today, non-native species are implicated in extinctions worldwide. About 50,000 non-native species have been introduced into the United States (although not all of them are harmful). Among the U.S. states, Hawai'i has a particularly serious problem with non-native organisms. Hawai'i has no native reptiles (such as snakes and lizards), no native amphibians (such as frogs), no native parrots, no native ants, and only one native mammal—a bat. Today, Hawai'i has many non-native organisms introduced by people, including escaped garden plants, wild pigs, piranhas, game, bass, trout, chickens, rats, mongooses, cats, snails, frogs, insects, cattle, deer, boa constrictors, and goats, among others. Many of these non-natives are threatening the islands' native organisms. Hawai'i incurs about a half billion dollars a year in crop losses, property damage (from non-native termites and rooting wild pigs), and costs to fight the invaders.

However, some non-native organisms are vital to the economy. Hawaiian crops such as cattle, sugarcane, pineapple, and banana are not native to the islands. Without these non-native organisms, the Hawaiian economy would be relatively limited.

This chapter highlights major geographic patterns of life on Earth and focuses on the processes that shaped these patterns. It explores the movements of organisms across Earth's surface and the roles of fire and other forms of ecological disturbance. It also develops three approaches that allow us to categorize and organize the biosphere. Finally, the Geographic Perspectives at the end of the chapter examines the history of the coconut palm through the eye of a geographer.

7.1 Biogeographic Patterns

◎ Identify and explain major geographic patterns of life on Earth.

Earth is covered by a continuous mantle of life. Everywhere, living creatures are rooting, swimming, drifting, flying, walking, crawling, climbing, and burrowing. Fern spores ride stratospheric winds. Bacteria reside in the depths of the oceans and kilometers deep within Earth's crust. A single handful of healthy soil can hold hundreds of millions of beneficial soil microbes. Yet **biodiversity** (the number of living species in a specified region) is not arranged haphazardly across Earth's surface. Patterns of life result from conditions that exist now and existed in the past.

Every species has a story to tell. Why it lives where it lives, what is currently preventing it from moving to other places, and what transpired in the past to bring it to its current geographic locations all are part of the story that biogeographers try to piece together. **Biogeography** is the study of the geography of life and how it changes through space and time. **Biogeographers seek to understand why organisms live where they do. This information provides insight into the workings of Earth's physical systems and a better understanding of Earth's natural and human history.** The roots of modern biogeography are often traced to the German explorer Alexander von Humboldt (1769–1859) and the English naturalist Alfred Russel Wallace (1823–1913), who published *The Geographical Distribution of Animals* in 1876.

Here are some questions a biogeographer might ask:

•   Why are there no penguins in the Northern Hemisphere and no polar bears in the Southern Hemisphere?

•   Why are the tropics rich with species while biodiversity gradually decreases at higher latitudes?

•   Why are some species geographically widespread and others restricted to small areas?

•   How do terrestrial species like sunflowers reach remote places such as Hawai'i?

•   How do people affect the geographic ranges of species?

•   How are new species formed, and what causes species to go extinct?

•   How do organisms respond to climate change?

The discipline of biogeography is closely tied to **ecology**, the study of the interactions between organisms and their environment. The **ecosystem** is a fundamental unit of ecology that includes both living organisms within a community and the nonliving components of the environment in which they live, such as energy, minerals, gases, and water.

Global Patterns of Biodiversity

Biodiversity is often measured by numbers of **species**: groups of individuals that naturally interact and can breed and produce fertile offspring. Why is it that some locations, such as the tropics, have many more species than others?

non-native
(or *exotic*) An organism that has been brought outside its original geographic range by people.

biodiversity
The number of living species in a specified region.

biogeography
The study of the geography of life and how it changes through space and time.

ecology
The study of the interactions between organisms and their environment.

ecosystem
The living organisms within a community and the nonliving components of the environment in which they live.

species
A group of individuals that naturally interact and can breed and produce fertile offspring.

FIGURE 7.2 **The latitudinal biodiversity gradient among plant species.** *The number of plant species per 10,000 km² (3,860 mi²) is shown by the colors on the map. Generally speaking, tropical and subtropical regions have the highest biodiversity, although the Mediterranean region lies outside of the subtropics (see Figure GT.18) and is an exception to this pattern.*

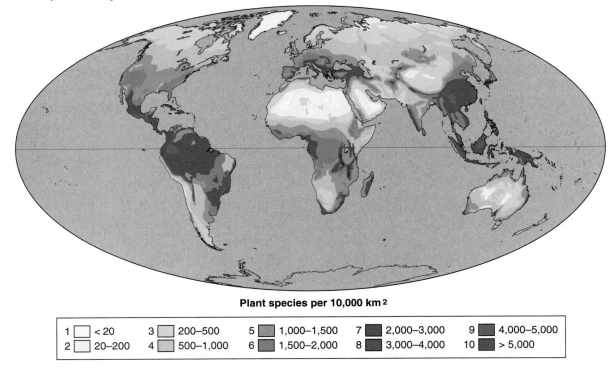

Plant species per 10,000 km²

1	< 20	3	200–500	5	1,000–1,500	7	2,000–3,000	9	4,000–5,000
2	20–200	4	500–1,000	6	1,500–2,000	8	3,000–4,000	10	> 5,000

The Latitudinal Biodiversity Gradient

Compared with higher latitudes, the tropics are bursting with species. **Biodiversity is highest in the tropics and decreases toward the poles (Figure 7.2).** This *latitudinal biodiversity gradient* is Earth's most prominent small-scale biogeographic pattern.

Scientists do not know why most of the tropics and subtropics are more biodiverse than the mid- and high latitudes. Evidence from fossils indicates that this pattern has been in place for at least 300 million years. After many decades of research, scientists have not found a single overriding cause of the latitudinal biodiversity gradient. More than 20 hypotheses have been put forward to explain the pattern, but none by itself adequately accounts for it.

The most significant factor in the latitudinal biodiversity gradient appears to be the rate of plant growth. In other words, areas with abundant sunlight and water (such as the tropics) have both high plant growth rates and high biodiversity.

FIGURE 7.3 **Large islands have more biodiversity than small islands.** *Cuba is the largest island in the Caribbean and has the greatest number of reptile species. Most larger Caribbean islands have more reptile species than smaller Caribbean islands. Note that the graph axes are plotted on a logarithmic scale to emphasize this trend.*

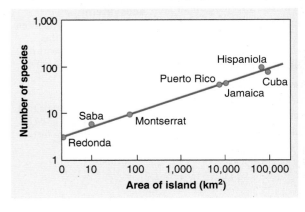

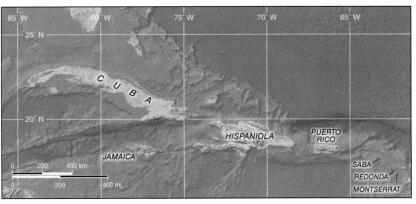

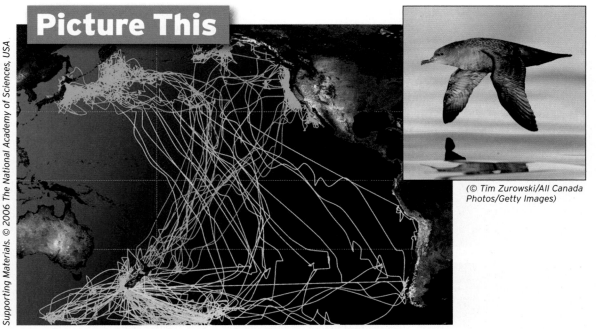

Reprinted from: Migratory shearwaters integrate oceanic resources across the Pacific Ocean in an endless summer, Scott A. Shaffer et al, Proceedings of the National Academy of Sciences 103: 12799-12802 (2006) Figure 1A of Supporting Materials. © 2006 The National Academy of Sciences, USA

Picture This

(© Tim Zurowski/All Canada Photos/Getty Images)

Sooty Shearwater Migration

The sooty shearwater (*Puffinus griseus*) never experiences winter. This seabird's long-distance migration enables it to remain in the summer hemisphere year-round. Using GPS, scientists have tracked sooty shearwaters migrating up to 64,000 km (40,000 mi) per year and traveling up to 500 km (310 mi) per day. This map shows the tracks of 19 birds. Blue lines show flight tracks during breeding periods; orange and yellow lines show migration for food resources.

Consider This

1. How do you think the sooty shearwater knows where it is in such vast geographic space? What "map" is the bird using?

2. What specific "push-pull" factors can you think of that would compel the sooty shearwater to migrate such great distances?

Biogeographic Patterns among Islands

Another major spatial biogeographic pattern is found among islands: **Larger islands tend to have more species than smaller islands (Figure 7.3)**. Islands are immensely interesting from a biogeographer's perspective, and island biogeography is an important subdiscipline within biogeography.

In biogeography, the term *island* can refer to any habitat that is surrounded by an inhospitable environment. For instance, a freshwater pond that is surrounded by land can be a biogeographic island. Cold, isolated mountaintops surrounded by hot lowland desert are also biogeographic islands.

Migration

Biodiversity also changes across Earth's surface over time as species migrate. Migration is the seasonal movement of organisms from one place to

> Why do animals migrate?*

another, usually for feeding or breeding. Many species migrate *latitudinally* (north and south) and *altitudinally* (upslope and downslope) in response to changes in resource availability over time. Migration is a result of the "push" of dwindling resources in one region and the "pull" of increasing resources in another. As the organisms follow their resources, they create moving fronts of biodiversity. For example, many species of birds migrate to the Arctic to take advantage of the brief bounty of insects and plants in the Arctic summer. Thus, Arctic biodiversity increases between June and August. After the birds leave in fall, Arctic biodiversity decreases. Picture This shows the journey of one such bird, the sooty shearwater.

Scientists make great efforts to track the movements of animals to understand their ecological

migration
The seasonal movement of populations from one place to another, usually for feeding or breeding.

*Answers to the Living Physical Geography questions are found on page 253.

FIGURE 7.4 **SCIENTIFIC INQUIRY: How do scientists track animal movement?** *Different animals require different means of tracking. GPS is important in many, but not all, tracking methods. (Butterfly, © Will & Deni McIntyre/Photo Researchers/Getty Images; fish, Eric Orbesen/NOAA Fisheries; goose, © FLPA/Mark Newman/age fotostock; wolf, Oregon Dept. of Fish & Wildife.)*

GPS technology is too heavy for insects. This simple plastic tag is 2% of this monarch butterfly's (*Danaus plexippus*) weight. Scientists rely on people who find the tagged butterfly to return the tag by mail to the address shown on the tag, indicating where and when the butterfly was captured.

Birds and small fish can be fitted with GPS archival tags that record data for a year or more. These tags record data such as changing light levels and day length. For birds, the tag is glued to the feathers and will fall off when the bird molts (replaces its feathers). These archival tags do not transmit information, so the animal must be recaptured and the tag must be removed.

Pop-Up Satellite Archival Tags (PSATS) are used on large marine migratory animals such as sea turtles, seals, whales, and fish. After a set time, the tag detaches from the animal, floats to the surface, and transmits the data it has recorded to an orbiting satellite.

Radio collars used on large mammals transmit the GPS coordinates of the moving animals to satellites continuously. In December 2011, the male offspring of this female gray wolf (*Canis lupus*), also radio-collared, was tracked as he entered California to become the first known wolf in that state since 1924.

requirements. Before the development of GPS technology, the migration patterns of many animals were poorly understood or unknown. **Figure 7.4** details applications of GPS and other techniques used in tracking animal movement today.

Patterns of Biodiversity Resulting from Evolution

Many interesting biogeographic patterns reveal the underlying process of evolution at work. **Evolution** is the process of genetically driven change in a population caused by selection pressures in the environment. A **population** is a group of organisms that interact and interbreed in the same geographic area. Through time, as genetic changes accrue, speciation will result. **Speciation** is the creation of new species through evolution. All organisms on Earth originated through the process of evolution and resulting speciation.

Ideas about evolution were first developed by Charles Darwin (1809–1882), who observed biogeographic patterns among the finches of the Galápagos Islands, and by Alfred Russel Wallace, who observed birds in Malaysia and Indonesia. In 1859, Darwin and Wallace proposed what would become known as the *theory of evolution*.

Observations That Support the Theory of Evolution

The theory of evolution is based on three observations:

• First, in nature, **more offspring are produced than the environment can support.** Because of resource limitations, the environment cannot support an unlimited number of individuals within a population.

> *Example:* A single adult salmon can lay some 7,000 eggs. If all these eggs grew into adult fish and reproduced, the population of salmon would overwhelm the resources available after only a few generations.

• Second, populations are composed of genetically unique individuals. Most organisms result from *sexual reproduction*, in which half the genes of each parent are combined to create a genetically unique

evolution
The process of genetically driven change in a population caused by selection pressures in the environment.

population
A group of organisms that interact and interbreed in the same geographic area.

speciation
The creation of new species through evolution.

offspring. Populations are therefore composed of individuals with varying genetic traits.

Example: Most salmon are intolerant of warm water. Combinations of genes that confer a slightly higher tolerance for warm water could occur randomly in a few individuals within a population of salmon.

• Third, some of these genetic traits may be better than others at allowing an individual to cope with environmental stress. Through *natural selection,* those individuals with beneficial genetic traits are more likely to reproduce and pass on those traits to the next generation. In this way, the beneficial traits become more common in the population.

Example: As seawater warms, the warmth-tolerant salmon are better adapted to the changing conditions. They produce more offspring than the warmth-intolerant salmon. Through time, the population becomes increasingly composed of salmon that are slightly more tolerant of warmer water.

Patterns of Convergence

Some unrelated organisms look strikingly similar. **Convergent evolution** is a process by which two or more unrelated organisms that experience similar environmental conditions evolve similar adaptations. All subtropical deserts, for example, impose similar selection pressures: intense sunlight, sparse vegetation cover, and persistent and severe moisture deficits. Because these environments select for the same traits, unrelated organisms in geographically isolated but similar desert environments may begin to look alike **(Figure 7.5)**.

convergent evolution
An evolutionary process in which two or more unrelated organisms that experience similar environmental conditions evolve similar adaptations.

FIGURE 7.5 **Evolutionary convergence.** *(A) Hopping, tufted tails, and nocturnal activity evolved in all three of these unrelated, geographically isolated mammals in response to their subtropical desert environments. Hopping is more efficient in sand than running; a flagged tail confuses predators, such as snakes; and nocturnal activity conserves water and helps the animals to evade bird predators. (B) New World cacti and Old World euphorbs are genetically unrelated plants. They look alike because they have both evolved for life in the desert. Spines, photosynthetic stems rather than leaves, and a fluted body are all adaptations to severe water deficits (see Section 7.2). (Clockwise from top left: © Bob and Clara Calhoun/Photoshot; © Matthijs Kuijpers/Alamy; © Werner Bollmann/age fotostock/Alamy; © Forest & Kim Starr, www.starrenvironmental.com; © ANT Photo Library/Science Source)*

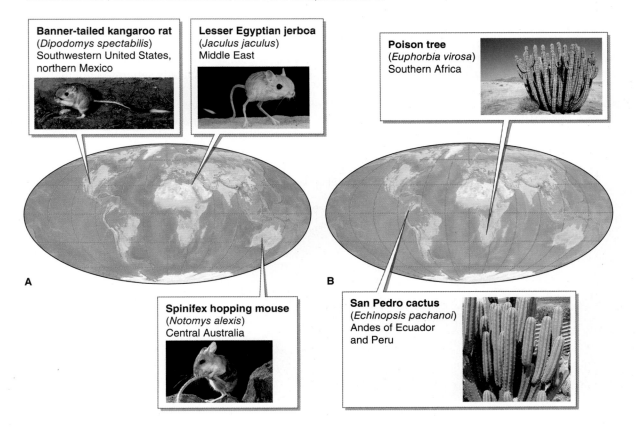

Banner-tailed kangaroo rat (*Dipodomys spectabilis*) Southwestern United States, northern Mexico

Lesser Egyptian jerboa (*Jaculus jaculus*) Middle East

Poison tree (*Euphorbia virosa*) Southern Africa

A

B

Spinifex hopping mouse (*Notomys alexis*) Central Australia

San Pedro cactus (*Echinopsis pachanoi*) Andes of Ecuador and Peru

dispersal
The movement of an organism away from where it originated.

divergent evolution
An evolutionary process by which individuals in one reproductively isolated population evolve adaptations different from those of closely related individuals in another population.

biogeographic region
A continental-scale region that contains genetically similar groups of plants and animals.

niche
The resources and environmental conditions that a species requires.

habitat
The physical environment in which an organism lives.

endemic
Restricted to one geographic area.

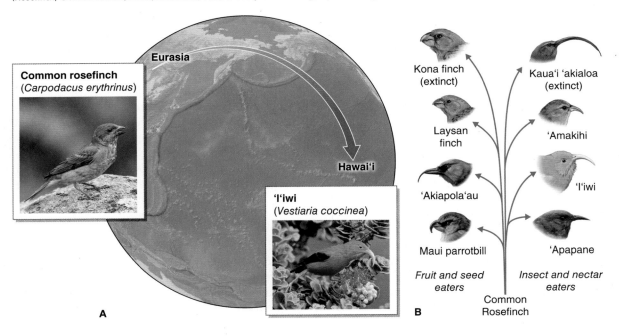

FIGURE 7.6 **Divergent evolution in Hawai'i.** *(A) Genetic evidence indicates that about 5 million to 7 million years ago, a group of common rosefinches crossed 6,000 km (3,700 mi) of Pacific Ocean and colonized Hawai'i. (B) About 50 species of Hawaiian honeycreepers (of which 8 are shown here) evolved from a single ancestral species of common rosefinch. The beak shapes and sizes evolved as the birds began to occupy different niches. Those on the left eat fruit and seeds. Those on the right eat insects and flower nectar. (Rosefinch, © Niko Pekonen/NHPA/Photoshot; 'I'iwi, © Cathy & Gordon Illg/Jaynes Gallery/DanitaDelimont.com/Newscom)*

Patterns of Divergence

Another interesting biogeographic pattern seen on oceanic islands such as those of Hawai'i is that of dispersal and divergent evolution. **Dispersal** is the movement of an organism away from where it originated. Hawai'i, for example, is exceedingly remote from the mainland and was never connected to it. Therefore, native land organisms first colonized Hawai'i by dispersing across the Pacific Ocean. Organisms that managed to reach Hawai'i from the mainland became cut off from the mainland population from which they came. In a biological context, such isolation, called *reproductive isolation*, means that the two geographically separated populations

FIGURE 7.7 **Biogeographic regions.** *At a global scale, physical barriers isolate groups of organisms in one region from groups in another region. Over time, this isolation has resulted in eight biogeographic regions. Each biogeographic region is somewhat geographically isolated from the adjacent one by deserts, oceans, mountain ranges, or deepwater channels.*

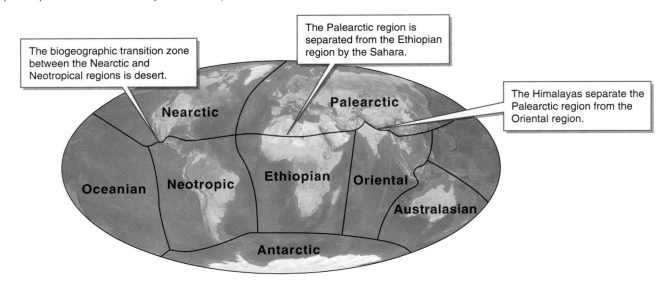

are no longer interacting and that *gene flow* between them has stopped.

When populations become reproductively isolated, individuals within one population begin to diverge genetically from those in the other population through a process called **divergent evolution**. Those species that did disperse to Hawai'i long ago diverged genetically from their mainland ancestors for two main reasons. First, they no longer interbred with and shared genes with those ancestors, and second, there were unique selection pressures on each of the islands that were not found on the mainland. **Figure 7.6** uses Hawaiian honeycreepers to illustrate the concept of divergent evolution.

Biogeographic Regions

Evolutionary divergence acts on smaller (broader) spatial scales as well. **Biogeographic regions** are continental-scale regions that contain genetically similar groups of plants and animals. They result from the isolation of large continental regions from one another by physical barriers. **Figure 7.7** shows the names and locations of the world's eight biogeographic regions.

The edges of the biogeographic regions, called *biogeographic transition zones*, are found in areas such as deserts, mountains, and oceans that restrict movement of species and gene flow between regions, resulting in evolutionary divergence. The North American biogeographic region is called the *Nearctic*. Most plants and animals there are genetically distinct from those of the *Neotropic* biogeographic region to the south. The biogeographic transition zone between the Nearctic and Neotropic regions is desert.

7.2 Setting the Boundaries: Limiting Factors

◎ Discuss factors that limit the geographic ranges of organisms.

Aside from humans, no single species lives everywhere, and for good reason: No single species can adapt to the wide range of environmental extremes found across Earth's surface. All species have an ecological **niche**, which consists of the resources and environmental conditions that the species requires. A niche can be thought of as a species' job or way of obtaining food. Niches exist within **habitat**, the physical environment in which a species lives.

Species with narrow ecological niches are called *specialists*. Species with broad niches are called *generalists*. The peregrine falcon (*Falco peregrines*), for example, is a generalist found on every continent

(**Figure 7.8A**). It is therefore said to have a *cosmopolitan* geographic range. The yellow-eared parrot (*Ognorhynchus icterotis*), on the other hand, is a specialist with a geographic range restricted to the Colombian Andes (**Figure 7.8B**). The yellow-eared parrot is an **endemic** species: a species that is restricted to one geographic area.

Why is it that the peregrine falcon is found worldwide, but the yellow-eared parrot is endemic to the Colombian Andes? **Species that have narrow ecological niches are usually geographically restricted, and species with broad niches are more likely to be geographically widespread.**

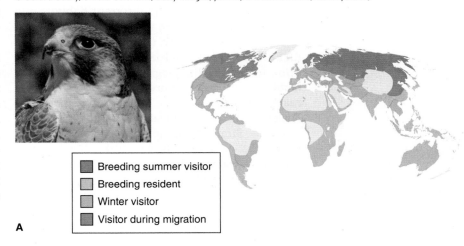

FIGURE 7.8 **Geographic range maps for the peregrine falcon and yellow-eared parrot.** *(A) The peregrine falcon can be found on every continent due to its migration between summer and winter areas. (B) The yellow-eared parrot is found only in the Colombian Andes at the localities shown. (Falcon, © Gerard Soury/Oxford Scientific/Getty Images; parrot, © Roland Seitre/naturepl.com)*

■ Breeding summer visitor
□ Breeding resident
□ Winter visitor
■ Visitor during migration

A

B

limiting factor
Any factor that prevents an organism from reaching its reproductive or geographic potential.

extinction
The permanent and global loss of a species.

TABLE 7.1 AT A GLANCE: Limiting Factors for Plants and Animals	
PHYSICAL LIMITING FACTORS	**BIOLOGICAL LIMITING FACTORS**
Light	Predation
Temperature	Competition
Water	Mutualism

The geographically restricted yellow-eared parrot has a narrow niche. It requires wax palm trees (*Ceroxylon* spp.) which grow in cloud forests (forests perpetually shrouded in clouds) of the Colombian Andes. The parrot eats the fruit of the palms and nests in their canopies. It can live only where the tree lives. In contrast, the geographically widespread peregrine falcon has a broad niche: It preys mostly on medium-sized birds, grabbing them out of the air, and builds nests in a variety of settings. As a result, it can live in many different habitats and climates as long as there are birds there to eat.

Generally speaking, the narrower a species' niche is, the more limiting factors will be operating to restrict its geographic range. A **limiting factor** is any factor that prevents an organism from reaching its reproductive or geographic potential. For example, too little water can limit the growth of plants. Similarly, too much water can limit the growth of, or even kill, drought-tolerant cacti. Therefore, water (either too little or too much of it) can function as a limiting factor.

Limiting factors result in stress for an organism and lower reproductive success. Reproductive success is important because it is the foundation of any species' long-term success. If a species does not reproduce, its fate will be **extinction**: the permanent and global loss of the species.

Physical Limiting Factors

Limiting factors can be divided into two groups, *physical* limiting factors and *biological* limiting factors. Six major limiting factors are shown in Table 7.1, but many others exist that are not discussed here.

Light

Some plants cannot grow in full sunlight or full shade, while others can tolerate a wide range of light conditions. Many plants can be categorized as either light-loving *heliophytes* or shade-loving *sciophytes*. Heliophytes are intolerant of shade. Their leaves tend to be small and may have a thick waxy coating that reduces moisture loss in intense sunlight. Many heliophytes also have a whitish or silvery appearance due to small hairs that reflect sunlight. Some heliophyte leaves are oriented edge-on to the noontime sunlight to reduce its intensity (Figure 7.9A). In contrast, sciophytes maximize their capture of dimmed light such as that found on a forest floor by having large, flat, dark leaves (Figure 7.9B).

Temperature

Temperature strongly controls the geographic ranges of plants. Extreme high or low temperatures

FIGURE 7.9 **Heliophytes and sciophytes.** *(A) This manzanita (Manzanita spp.) displays many of the characteristics of heliophytes, including small leaves that are oriented edge-on to the Sun. (Note the hummingbird in the foreground for scale.) (B) The giant rhubarb (Gunnera manicata) has one of the largest leaves of any plant. Its leaves are up to 3 m (11 ft) across. Giant rhubarb's leaves have many sciophyte characteristics, including their large size and dark green color, that maximize their absorption of sunlight. (Left, Used with permission of www. laspilitas.com; right, Dr Morley Read/Science Source)*

A   B

lead to reduced photosynthesis and mortality in plants. Animals are also limited by temperature (Figure 7.10).

Many animals, such as amphibians, insects, and most fishes and reptiles, are *poikilotherms* (or *cold-blooded*). This means that their body temperature is the same as the temperature of the environment. *Endothermic* (or *warm-blooded*) organisms, such as birds and mammals, maintain a constant core body temperature that is usually much higher than the environmental temperature. The core body temperature of a warm-blooded organism is kept nearly constant by a regulatory process called *homeostasis*.

Dormancy (a period of inactivity) is a common response of poikilotherms to low temperatures. Frogs and insects often hide from low winter temperatures by going underground into mud or burrows. Many endothermic animals enter a state of *hibernation* (winter dormancy) in a protected environment during the winter. During hibernation, their metabolic rate decreases to conserve energy. Endothermic animals that remain active in cold winter temperatures increase their metabolic rate and develop thick insulating layers of fat, fur, or feathers.

Many mammals living in cold environments have shorter appendages (such as legs, ears, and tails) than their counterparts in warm regions (Figure 7.11). This evolutionary pattern is called *Allen's rule*.

Water

All organisms need liquid water to carry out their metabolic processes. Plants can be grouped into three categories based on their water requirements:

1. *Hydrophytes* are plants that require submersion in water. A water lily is an example of a hydrophyte.

2. *Mesophytes* are plants that can tolerate a broad range of soil moistures, but are generally intolerant of prolonged drought. Most plants are mesophytes.

3. *Xerophytes* are plants that are adapted to environments with little available moisture. Cacti are xerophytes.

Plants have two main types of adaptations for coping with a lack of water: They *escape* water stress or they *reduce* water stress. *Annual* plants (plants that go to seed, then die, each year) escape water stress. Their seeds can remain dormant in the soil as a *seed bank* during long periods of drought, then germinate when conditions improve. Some seeds from the Sahara have germinated after 100 years of dormancy in the soil.

FIGURE 7.10 **Temperature as a limiting factor.** *The geographic range of the eastern phoebe (Sayornis phoebe) in winter (blue and purple areas) coincides with areas where the average January temperature is −4°C (25°F) or warmer (south of the black line). North of this line, winter temperatures are too cold for the eastern phoebe. The bird moves north into the brown range during summer. (© Don Johnson/All Canada Photo/Getty Images)*

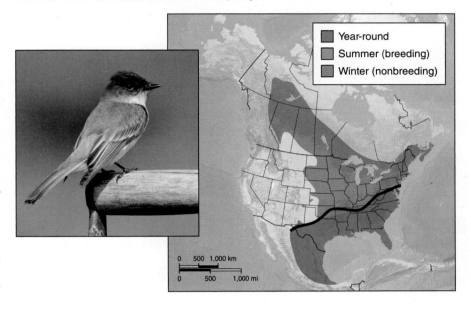

Year-round
Summer (breeding)
Winter (nonbreeding)

0   500 1,000 km
0   500   1,000 mi

FIGURE 7.11 **Allen's rule.** *Allen's rule states that appendage length in mammals decreases as latitude increases. This anatomical variation helps animals to maintain suitable body temperatures in these different climates. Among hares and rabbits in North America, the southernmost species have long appendages as a means to radiate body heat for cooling. Appendage length decreases to the north as a means of conserving heat. Fur length and thickness in these animals also increases northward.*

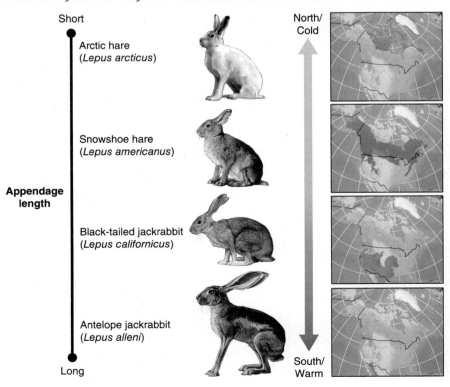

Short

Arctic hare
(*Lepus arcticus*)

Snowshoe hare
(*Lepus americanus*)

Appendage length

Black-tailed jackrabbit
(*Lepus californicus*)

Antelope jackrabbit
(*Lepus alleni*)

Long

North/Cold

South/Warm

FIGURE 7.12 GEO-GRAPHIC: The barrel cactus has many adaptations for conserving water in its Sonoran Desert environment. *(© Craig K Lorenz/Photo Researchers/Getty Images)*

CAM photosynthesis

Cacti and some other plants use crassulacean acid metabolism (CAM), a specialized photosynthetic process whereby plants open their pores at night for photosynthesis. Opening pores during the day, as most plants do, would result in costly water loss.

Waxy stem

The body of this cactus is its stem. Cactus stems have a thick waxy coating to prevent water loss.

Green stem

The leaves of the cactus have been reduced to spines. The stem of the plant carries out photosynthesis.

Reduced leaves

Large leaves would lose water rapidly. The leaves of cacti have evolved into spines, which also serve the purpose of warding off animals seeking water.

Expandable stem

The stem of the cactus is ribbed to allow it to swell and store water.

Shallow root mat

Cacti have a shallow mat of fibrous roots (not visible here) that absorb rainwater quickly before it drains away into the porous sandy soil.

Why do cacti have spines?

Perennial plants (plants that live longer than one year) must reduce water stress because they cannot escape it. The barrel cactus (*Ferocactus wislizeni*) is a xerophytic perennial that reduces water stress by a variety of adaptations **(Figure 7.12)**. Other perennial plants have a long *taproot* that reaches moisture deep in the ground. Taproots of mesquite (*Prosopis* spp.) have been measured at more than 50 m (160 ft) long, although the aboveground portion of this desert plant is no more than 3 m (10 ft) tall. The baobabs of Africa and Madagascar reduce water stress by developing unusually thick trunks in which water is stored. A large baobab tree, like those shown in the opening photo for this chapter, can store up to 120,000 L (31,500 gal) of water.

predation
The consumption of one organism by another.

Like plants, animals either escape water stress or reduce water loss while they are active. Because animals are mobile, many of them escape dry conditions through migration. There are many examples of animals that undertake seasonal migrations in response to changes in water availability. Large herds of animals throughout sub-Saharan Africa, such as wildebeests and zebras, follow the rainfall of the ITCZ and the plant growth (food) that comes with it.

Other animals have adaptations for reducing water stress. The kangaroo rats of the southwestern United States and northern Mexico (see Figure 7.5), for example, live in extremely arid desert climates. These animals never drink liquid water; instead, they derive water from the dry foods they eat. Water is produced as the compounds in their food react and combine with oxygen in their bodies. Their other water-conserving adaptations include producing urine with high concentrations of *urea* relative to its water content, producing dry feces, and never sweating. Like many desert animals, they are also nocturnal, hiding away in their cool burrows during the day to avoid heat and predators.

Biological Limiting Factors

Just as physical limiting factors such as light, temperature, and water influence the geographic range of a species, so too do the biological limiting factors of predation, competition, and mutualism.

Predation

Predation—the consumption of one organism by another—is one limiting factor that nearly all organisms must cope with. A mountain lion that kills and eats a deer is a predator. Another form of predation that may be less obvious is *herbivory*: An insect that eats a plant is also a predator.

The geographic ranges of many species are determined by where their food sources live. Many insects have a narrow or specialized dietary range and eat only one or a few species of plants. The monarch butterfly, for example, can live only where its *host plant*, milkweed (*Asclepias* spp.), lives, as shown in **Figure 7.13**.

Most mammals are generalists and have a broad dietary range. Humans are a good example of a generalist mammal. Specialist mammals, with a narrow dietary range, are far less common. Two examples are the giant panda (*Ailuropoda melanoleuca*), which eats only bamboo, and the koala (*Phascolarctos cinereus*), which eats only leaves from eucalyptus trees.

Native predators are unlikely to hunt their prey to extinction. Instead, a predator may reduce the population of a prey species to the point that the predator must find a new source of food because that prey species becomes too difficult to find. This process is called *prey switching*. As a mountain lion reduces a deer population, for example, deer become too difficult for the mountain lion to find, and it will focus on another prey species. Or the mountain lion may simply hunt in a different area where deer are more abundant.

Non-native predators, however, do hunt prey to extinction. The Nile perch, for example, has caused almost 300 native species of cichlids to go extinct in Lake Victoria since it was introduced there (see "The Human Sphere").

> **How are wolves important to ecosystems?**

Native predators sometimes function as **keystone species**, species whose effects indirectly support many other species within an ecosystem. Keystone species play a crucial role in maintaining healthy ecosystems. The gray wolf, for example, is a keystone species in Yellowstone National Park, but no one understood its importance to other species until wolves, which had been eradicated from the park, were reintroduced in 1995 (Figure 7.14).

FIGURE 7.13 Monarchs and milkweed.
The caterpillars of monarch butterflies (see Figure 7.4) eat only plants in the milkweed family. The northern edge of the milkweed's geographic range is limited by low winter temperatures in Canada. The northern edge of the monarch's range is therefore bounded by the northern limit of milkweed.

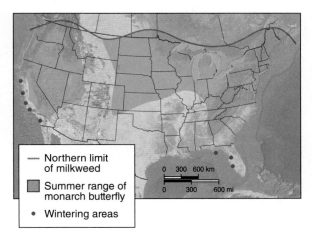

— Northern limit of milkweed
▨ Summer range of monarch butterfly
• Wintering areas

0 300 600 km
0 300 600 mi

keystone species
A species whose effects support many other species within an ecosystem.

FIGURE 7.14 GEO-GRAPHIC: The gray wolf as a keystone species in Yellowstone National Park. *(Clockwise from top left: © Jim Kruger/E+/Getty Images; © Tania Thomson/Shutterstock.com; Ken M Johns/Photo Researchers/Getty Images; National Park Service, Yellowstone National Park; © William H. Mullins/Photo Researchers/Getty Images)*

Keystone species
Gray wolves were the primary predator of elk (*Cervus canadensis*) in Yellowstone National Park. After wolves were eradicated from the park in the 1930s, elk populations increased.

Riparian ecology
Elk browse on willow, cottonwood, and alder. When elk populations increased, these *riparian* (streamside) trees were eliminated from many environments.

Beavers
Beavers (*Castor canadensis*) eat these riparian trees and use them to build dams across streams, creating ponds. Beaver populations and their ponds declined with the loss of riparian trees.

Beaver-pond ecology
Beaver ponds create habitat for many other organisms. They slow stream erosion and create habitat for fish and wading birds. They increase willow growth, which attracts songbirds and songbird predators.

Wolf reintroduction
Wolves were gradually reintroduced beginning in 1995. Thereafter, elk populations in the park dropped from about 18,000 to about 9,000. Riparian plants returned, as did beavers and their ponds.

Wolf-kill ecology
When wolves have finished feeding on a large animal they have killed, grizzlies, coyotes (shown here), ravens, eagles, vultures, and many other scavengers also benefit from the kill. Wolf kills are an important component of the diets of these species.

FIGURE **7.15** **Examples of mutualism.** *(A) The hummingbird benefits from the concentrated energy provided by flower nectar. The flowering plant benefits from pollination by the hummingbird. (B) Insects such as this bumblebee (Bombus spp.) visit flowers for meals of pollen and nectar. Flowers receive pollination from the visiting insects. (C) A clownfish escapes its predators by living in the stinging tentacles of a sea anemone. It also finds food scraps from the anemone's fish meals. The anemone is kept free of parasites, and is fed nutrient-rich feces, by the clownfish. The clownfish is an obligate mutualist because it needs the anemone to survive. The anemone, on the other hand, is a facultative mutualist: It does better with clownfish mutualists, but can survive without them.* (A. © Rolf Nussbaumer/RF/Getty Images; B. © Cosmin Manci/Shutterstock.com; C. © Richard Whitcombe/Shutterstock.com)

A **B** **C**

Competition

Competition is an interaction between organisms that require the same resources. A *resource* is anything that an organism needs, including food, territory, and mates. All organisms must compete with other organisms for resources. Competition between individuals of the same species is called *intraspecific competition*, and competition between different species is called *interspecific competition*.

Plant species living in the same habitat compete with one another if their niches overlap. Hydrophytes do not compete with xerophytes because each occupies very different niches and habitats. However, xerophytes compete with other xerophytes when they occupy the same physical space. Plants compete in three main ways:

1. Plants shade one another as they compete for light.

2. Plants often employ chemicals that inhibit seed germination or growth in other plants. Such chemical competition is called *allelopathy*.

3. Plant roots compete for available nutrients and water beneath the ground.

The degree of competition among organisms depends on how similar their niches are. Individuals of the same species have identical niches and compete for exactly the same resources. Very different species, such as wolves and beavers, can share the same habitat, but they do not compete with one another for resources because they have different niches. Wolves and coyotes, on the other hand, live in the same habitat and have similar niches. As a result, they compete for many of the same resources. Wolves, for example, chase coyotes away from carcasses and are occasionally seen killing coyotes.

Animals may also compete indirectly. For example, the house cat (*Felis catus*) and the barn owl (*Tyto alba*) are competitors although they rarely interact directly. The barn owl eats small rodents and hunts on the wing, mostly at night. House cats hunt small rodents from the ground day and night. Although the two predators rarely meet, they are exploiting the same resource.

Mutualism

The old saying that nature is "red in tooth and claw" suggests that predation and competition are the most common types of biological interactions. Yet there are just as many examples of benign interactions between species. A relationship between two species that benefits both of them is called **mutualism** (Figure 7.15A). Mutualism can be a limiting factor because species are unlikely to reach their full reproductive potential without their mutualistic partners.

Mutualism occurs in most ecological settings. In cases of *obligate mutualism*, neither party can survive without its partner. In *facultative mutualism*, both parties benefit from the relationship, but they do not need it to survive. In some cases of mutualism, one party is an obligate mutualist while the other is a facultative mutualist (Figure 7.15C).

competition
An interaction between organisms that require the same resources.

mutualism
A relationship between two species from which both species benefit.

7.3 Moving Around: Dispersal

◎ **Explain how organisms expand their geographic ranges.**

Dispersal allows organisms to reduce competition, to obtain more resources, and to respond to environmental change. Nearly all organisms are able to disperse, some farther than others. It takes about 100 years for earthworms to disperse (unaided by people) 1 km (0.6 mi), while some birds, such as sooty shearwaters and Arctic terns (*Sterna paradisaea*), can fly over 500 km (300 mi) in a single day.

Intra-range dispersal occurs when an organism disperses within its current geographic range. *Extra-range dispersal* occurs when an organism disperses outside its current geographic range. In most cases, extra-range dispersal is lethal to the disperser because the ecological conditions found outside the current geographic range are unfavorable. Otherwise, the species would probably already occupy those regions. Successful extra-range dispersal followed by reproduction results in geographic range expansion, as we saw in Section 7.1.

Only a propagule can establish an extra-range population. A **propagule** is any material that is able to establish a new reproducing population, such as a seed, a mating pair, or a rooting branch. A single male is not a propagule because it cannot start a new population.

Modes of dispersal can be grouped into two categories. Organisms dispersing under their own power, such as by flying, are *active dispersers*. Most animals are active dispersers. Organisms that move about using outside forces, such as wind or ocean currents, or by hitching a ride on other organisms are *passive dispersers*. Except in the rare cases in which seeds are forcefully ejected from their fruits once they dry, all plants are passive dispersers; some of their dispersal strategies are shown in **Figure 7.16**.

Barriers to Dispersal

There are many barriers to dispersal that affect the geographic ranges of species. A *barrier to dispersal* is any object or factor that restricts the dispersal of an organism. Species living on small, remote islands are surrounded by the formidable barrier of the ocean. Similarly, species living high on mountains in the Great Basin are in virtual islands of suitable habitat that are surrounded by a barrier of inhospitable desert.

Biogeographic *corridors*, which allow unrestricted movement between habitats, are the opposite of barriers. The terms *barrier* and *corridor* are relative because what is an impassable barrier for one organism can be a corridor for another. For example, great white sharks (*Carcharodon carcharias*) frequently travel between California and Hawai'i. Seawater is a corridor to a shark; for a freshwater fish that is intolerant of salt water, however, that seawater is an impassable barrier.

propagule
Any material that is able to establish a new population.

FIGURE 7.16 **GEO-GRAPHIC:**
Dispersal strategies of plants. *(From left to right: © Walter Meayers Edwards/National Geographic/Getty Images; Steve & Dave Maslowski/Photo Researchers/Getty Images; © Yuris/ Shutterstock.com; © M Swiet Productions/Flickr/Getty Images)*

MODE OF DISPERSAL	DISPERSAL TERM
By wind	*Anemochore*
By water	*Hydrochore*
By animals	*Zoochore*

Wind dispersal – anemochory	Animal dispersal – zoochory	Animal dispersal – zoochory	Water dispersal – hydrochory
Tumbleweeds (*Kali tragus*) detach from their roots and shake out seeds like a salt shaker as they roll across open fields. A single plant can release 50,000 seeds.	Acorns are cached by squirrels, jays, and other animals. Many cached nuts are forgotten and successfully germinate. Blue jays (*Cyanocitta cristata*) have been recorded as caching some 4,500 acorns in a single season.	Colorful and nutritious fruit and seeds are eaten and passed through the digestive systems of animals. As the animals move about, they pass and disperse the seeds.	Coconuts (*Cocos nucifera*) float for months at sea. When they wash up on an island beach, freshwater rains trigger germination.

FIGURE 7.17 **Degrees of barriers.** *Levels of resistance to dispersal vary depending on distance from the source of dispersing species and the severity of the barrier. Here, a continental mainland represents the source of species. The species on island 1 are filtered by the ocean: Some species from the mainland reach island 1, but not all. The distance to island 2 filters most dispersers. Reaching Island 3 directly from the mainland through sweepstakes dispersal is exceedingly unlikely. Using the islands as stepping-stones, however, increases the chances a species can reach the remote island.*

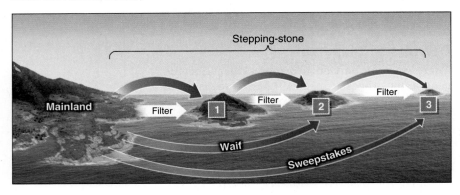

Species are found where they are as a result of many factors, among the most important of which are *biogeographic filters* (barriers that allow certain types of organisms to disperse across them and not others). These barriers include *climatic filters*, such as deserts or ice caps. Predation, competition, or a lack of mutualistic partners may act as *biological filters*. The oaks and pines of the Northern Hemisphere, for example, have never been able to cross the equator to the Southern Hemisphere because of the se-

sweepstakes dispersal
Dispersal across an extensive region of inhospitable space.

stepping-stone
An island in an island chain that aids in the dispersal of organisms.

verity of the competition (a biological filter) and the warmth in the tropics (a climatic filter). Likewise, only one bear species has successfully crossed the equator. The spectacled bear (*Tremarctos ornatus*) inhabits forests of the Andes as far south as northern Chile. All other true bears live north of the equator.

Islands far away from the mainland can be difficult for dispersers to reach. Successful dispersal to remote islands is called *waif dispersal* (or *accidental dispersal*) because the organism that reached them was presumably lost (*waif* means "abandoned") and far out of its normal range. Waif dispersal is an unlikely event with a low chance of success. Dispersal to extremely remote islands (such as the rosefinch's dispersal to Hawai'i; see Figure 7.6), is so unlikely that it is like winning a lottery or a sweepstakes. Such long-distance dispersal to remote islands is called **sweepstakes dispersal**. Conversely, island chains that aid in the dispersal of organisms are called **stepping-stones** because they allow organisms to colonize remote islands by "stepping" from one island to another (as the rosefinch did once it had reached the Hawaiian Islands). These concepts are illustrated in **Figure 7.17**.

Colonization and Invasion

The cattle egret (*Bubulcus ibis*) is found throughout much of North America, Europe, Africa, and Asia. It is a generalist and is often found feeding on insects associated with cattle. It first dispersed across the Atlantic Ocean to northern South America, perhaps as early as the 1870s. As far as is known, this bird crossed the Atlantic Ocean without the help of people. Its crossing of the Atlantic is therefore considered a natural event. The bird then quickly spread throughout the Western Hemisphere, as shown in **Figure 7.18**.

Most biogeographers consider the cattle egret's dispersal across the Atlantic Ocean to be a colonization event. **Colonization** is the successful establishment of a population in a new geographic region without the help of people. Some biogeographers, however, think the cattle egret is an example of **invasion**: the successful and unwanted establishment of a species in a new geographic area as a result of human activity. They argue that the cattle egret would probably have crossed the Atlantic Ocean long ago if it were capable of doing so unaided. Instead, its crossing coincides with the increased movement of people across the Atlantic Ocean in the early 1900s, strongly suggesting that people intentionally or accidentally transported the bird across the ocean. Furthermore, its successful range expansion is made possible by the expansion of the cattle pasture habitat that the bird uses. For these reasons, they argue that the cattle egret should be considered an exotic species.

Many organisms are dispersed around the world by people. Some are completely dependent on

FIGURE 7.18

The cattle egret.

The cattle egret spread throughout the Americas after it dispersed across the Atlantic Ocean.
(© Peter Chadwick/Gallo Images/Getty Images)

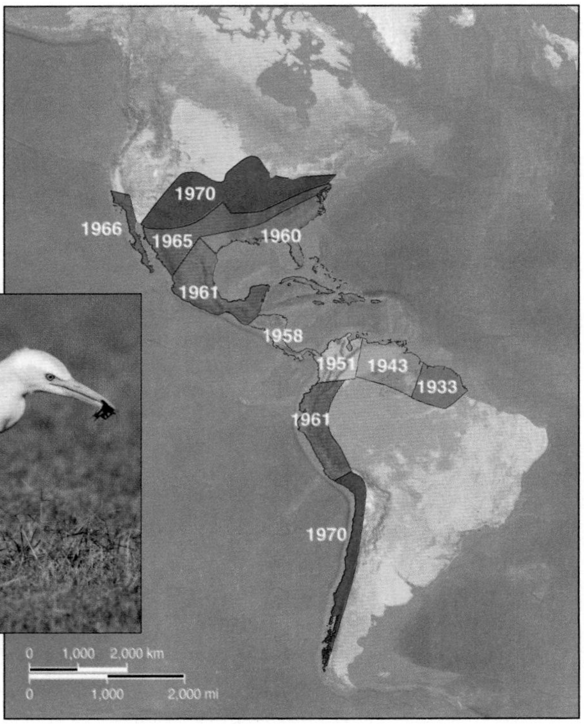

humans not only for their dispersal, but also for their very existence. Our food crops, such as wheat, corn, and rice, are largely or completely incapable of reproducing and dispersing without human help. These organisms are now dispersed throughout the world. The Geographic Perspectives at the end of this chapter explores this topic further.

7.4 Starting Anew: Ecological Disturbance and Succession

◎ Discuss the role of ecological disturbance and the return of life following disturbance.

We tend to think that balance and equilibrium exist in nature. More often, ecosystems are in a constant state of disequilibrium and change as they adjust to ecological disturbances through the process of ecological succession. An **ecological disturbance** is a sudden event that disrupts an ecosystem. **Ecological succession** is the step-by-step series of changes in an ecosystem that follows an ecological disturbance.

Ecological Disturbance

Ecological disturbances can range from local fires that burn vegetation to massive volcanic eruptions that create an extensive barren landscape. **Both *biotic* (living) forces and *abiotic* (nonliving) forces can create ecological disturbances.** The removal of wolves from Yellowstone by people (see Figure 7.14) was a biotic disturbance, as was the introduction of the non-native Nile perch into Lake Victoria (see Figure 7.1).

Table 7.2 gives some examples of different types and severities of ecological disturbances. In this section, we take a more detailed look at the role of one type of disturbance—fire—in the landscapes of western North America.

Fire is a widespread, common, and important disturbance in most vegetated regions. In many ecosystems, fire is as important as water, light, or soil nutrients. Many plant communities are dependent on fire. Wherever there is enough precipitation for vegetation to grow and a dry and warm season, fire will occur. Before wildfires were suppressed by people, many North American ecosystems had natural *fire-return intervals* of less than 35 years (Figure 7.19A). **Many plants have adaptations to survive and even thrive in fire** (Figure 7.19B).

Fire suppression has a long history in North America. In the 1930s, to save property and trees with commercial value, the U.S. Forest Service began a "10:00 a.m." fire policy. Its aim was to have any given wildfire contained by ten o'clock the morning

TABLE 7.2	AT A GLANCE: Types of Ecological Disturbances	
	TYPE OF ECOLOGICAL DISTURBANCE	SEVERITY
ABIOTIC	Volcanic eruption	Moderate to severe
	Wildfire	Moderate to severe
	Wind	Moderate
	Flooding	Moderate
	Avalanche	Moderate
BIOTIC	Insect outbreak	Moderate to severe
	Anthropogenic forces (such as logging or farming)	Moderate to severe
	Introduction of non-native species	Moderate

FIGURE 7.19 **Fire frequency and plant adaptations.** *(A) Before wildfires were suppressed, many areas in North America had frequent fires. This map shows natural fire-return intervals for the United States. (B) Plants have many adaptations for surviving wildfires. Intense fires, however, can kill even the most fire-adapted plants and seeds in soil. (Photos from left to right: Steve Norman, US Forest Service; © Paul Tomlins/Flower/age fotostock)*

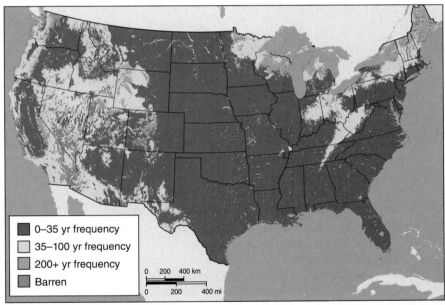

0–35 yr frequency
35–100 yr frequency
200+ yr frequency
Barren

0   200   400 km
0   200   400 mi

A

Crown sprouting	Serotinous cones	Deep roots and seeds
Crown sprouting allows a tree to sprout from the surviving root and trunk. These redwoods (*Sequoia sempervirens*) are crown sprouting after being burned.	Serotinous cones stay closed until heated by a fire. After the fire, they slowly open and release their seeds. These knobcone pines (*Pinus attenuata*) have serotinous cones.	Many plants of the North American prairies survive by sprouting from deep roots that are unharmed by fire and by germinating from seeds that survive in the soil.

1.5 m (5 ft)

3.0 m (10 ft)

B

colonization
The successful establishment of a population in a new geographic region without the help of people.

invasion
The successful and unwanted establishment of a species in a new geographic area as a result of human activity.

ecological disturbance
A sudden event that disrupts an ecosystem.

ecological succession
The step-by-step series of changes in an ecosystem that follows a disturbance.

FIGURE 7.20 **Fire intensity.** *(A) When fires are frequent, fuel loads remain low, and fires burn as gentle surface fires, such as this one in the Sequoia and Kings Canyon national parks in California. (B) The Waldo Canyon fire near Colorado Springs, Colorado, became an intense canopy fire that burned 74 km² (29 mi²) in Pike National Forest in June 2012. As a result of a century of fire suppression in the area, it was the most destructive fire in Colorado history up to that time, forcing some 32,000 people out of their homes and destroying 346 homes. (A. Eric Knapp, US Forest Service; B. © RJ Sangosti/The Denver Post via Getty Images)*

A

B

after it was first reported. Before the policy of fire suppression, *surface fires* (fires that burn gently on the forest floor and kill few trees) were a common occurrence (Figure 7.20A). But these fires were extinguished by the Forest Service.

Fire suppression led to a buildup of dead and living vegetation, and these high fuel loads resulted in catastrophic canopy fires that could be impossible to extinguish. A *canopy fire* (or *crown fire*) burns in the forest canopy (the uppermost layer of branches) and usually kills the trees (Figure 7.20B).

In the past few decades, the essential ecological role of fire has been increasingly recognized. In an attempt to address the problem of fuel buildup in western U.S. forests caused by a century of fire suppression, *prescribed burns* and *mechanical thinning* operations (in which vegetation is removed by manual cutting) are sometimes employed to reduce fuel loads.

Ecological Succession: The Return of Life

Given enough time, life returns following fire or any other disturbance (Figure 7.21). There are two types of ecological succession, depending on the severity of the disturbance. *Primary succession* occurs when life is completely removed from a landscape. Large volcanic eruptions and large landslides are examples of disturbances that can trigger primary succession. In most cases, however, some life survives the disturbance, and ecosystems rebuild through the process of *secondary succession*.

Ecological succession takes place in stages and may require decades or centuries to complete. A **sere** is a stage of ecological succession that follows a disturbance. A typical sequence of seres that would occur in the eastern United States is illustrated in Figure 7.22. The return of the former ecosystem can take years to centuries, depending on the severity of the disturbance and the responsiveness of the ecosystem. In the past, scientists used the *climax community* model, which assumed that a community would persist indefinitely in the

FIGURE 7.21 **Disturbance and ecological succession.** *(A) In 1988, numerous fires burned 793,880 acres of Yellowstone National Park. This photo shows an area just after it was burned. (B) Twenty years later, lodgepole pine (Pinus contorta) is returning to these burned areas. (A. National Park Service, Yellowstone National Park; B. © Katie LaSalle-Lowery)*

NATURALLY RESEEDED BY WILDFIRE IN 1988

20 years

A. 1988   B. 2008

FIGURE **7.22** **A model of ecological succession.** *The return of life following ecological disturbance follows a sequence of seres. Given enough time, on the order of centuries, after the initial disturbance (left), bare ground will eventually be covered by the vegetation that existed before the disturbance—in this example, oak-hickory forest.*

Animation
Ecological
succession
http://qrs.ly/7b43dd4

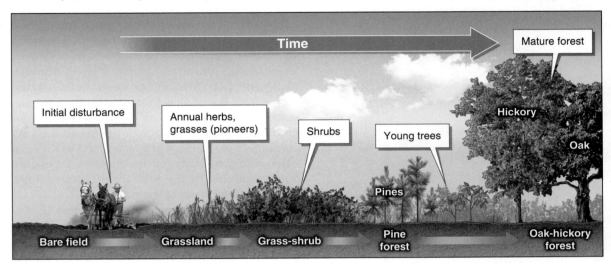

absence of any further disturbance. In the example in Figure 7.22, the oak-hickory forest would be the climax community.

The climax community model has been replaced by a view that change and disturbance go on continually. Fire, volcanic eruptions, climate change, non-native species, and human transformation of ecosystems create an ongoing process of disturbance in almost all ecosystems. Scientists now view communities as mosaics, each in different stages of ecological succession, each continually being reset by new disturbances.

7.5 Three Ways to Organize the Biosphere

◎ Describe three approaches to organizing the biosphere.

The biosphere is the most complex of Earth's physical systems. This section explores three major approaches to organizing the biosphere that also reveal how it functions. **There are three main ways of categorizing life on Earth: the trophic hierarchy, the taxonomic hierarchy, and the spatial hierarchy.**

The Trophic Hierarchy

The first approach to organizing the biosphere is based on the movement of energy and matter through it, beginning with solar energy. Photosynthesis is

the gateway through which solar energy enters the biosphere. The process of photosynthesis converts solar radiant energy to chemical energy that is stored as sugars, as shown in **Figure 7.23**.

A **primary producer** is any organism that is able to convert sunlight to chemical energy through photosynthesis. On land, most primary producers are plants. In freshwater bodies and in the oceans,

FIGURE **7.23** **GEO-GRAPHIC:**
The process of photosynthesis.

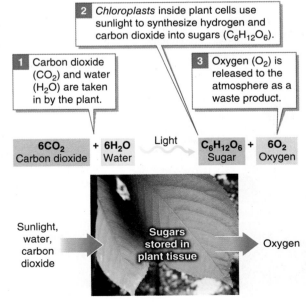

2 *Chloroplasts* inside plant cells use sunlight to synthesize hydrogen and carbon dioxide into sugars ($C_6H_{12}O_6$).

1 Carbon dioxide (CO_2) and water (H_2O) are taken in by the plant.

3 Oxygen (O_2) is released to the atmosphere as a waste product.

$$6CO_2 + 6H_2O \xrightarrow{\text{Light}} C_6H_{12}O_6 + 6O_2$$
Carbon dioxide   Water   Sugar   Oxygen

Sunlight, water, carbon dioxide → Sugars stored in plant tissue → Oxygen

sere
A stage of ecological succession that follows ecological disturbance.

primary producer
An organism that can convert sunlight into chemical energy through photosynthesis.

FIGURE 7.24 **Food chains.** *Energy (red arrow) flows through food chains from one organism to the next. Nutrients are recycled (green arrows) by scavengers, detritivores, and decomposers at all levels.*

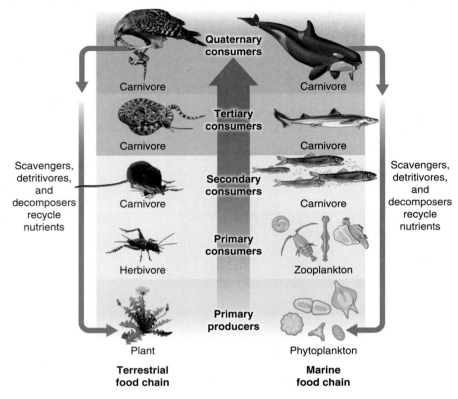

FIGURE 7.25 **Food webs and the 10% rule.** *Flows of energy and matter in trophic systems form interconnected webs. Energy flows to successively higher trophic levels. Because of the 10% rule, the owl can obtain only about 0.1% of the original energy fixed by the plants.*

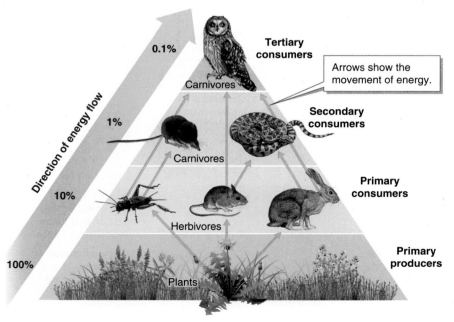

the primary producers are microscopic algae and plantlike bacteria called *cyanobacteria*. **Phytoplankton** are microscopic bacteria and algae that are suspended in the sunlit portions of water and photosynthesize.

Photosynthesis does not truly produce energy. Instead, it converts energy from one form (radiant energy) to another (chemical energy). Of the total solar energy falling on a photosynthetic organism, less than 5% is converted to chemical energy through photosynthesis. This chemical energy is then transferred from the photosynthetic organisms to consumers. A **consumer** is any organism that cannot produce its own food through photosynthesis. As consumers eat primary producers, and as they are eaten in turn by other consumers, the solar energy made available by the primary producers flows through a *food chain* **(Figure 7.24)**.

Food chains are composed of **herbivores**, organisms that eat only primary producers; *carnivores*, organisms that eat only other consumers; and **omnivores**, organisms that eat both primary producers and other consumers. Herbivores such as grasshoppers are called *primary consumers* because they eat plants directly. A mouse that eats a grasshopper is a *secondary consumer*, a snake that eats the mouse is a *tertiary consumer*, and so on.

When an organism dies, its tissues are recycled by scavengers, detritivores, and decomposers. The biosphere would have long ago run out of organic material to metabolize if not for the work of these organisms. *Scavengers* are animals such as coyotes and vultures that feed on *carrion* (dead animals). Many animals are at least part-time opportunistic scavengers. *Detritivores*, such as earthworms or fly larvae (maggots), feed only on *detritus* (decomposing plant or animal remains). **Decomposers**, such as fungi and bacteria, are organisms that break organic material down into simple compounds that reenter the trophic system through plants.

The food chain concept is a good starting point, but in nature, energy and matter do not flow in straight paths. Instead, the movements of energy and matter through the biosphere form complex systems of ecological interconnections called **food webs**. The different levels of an ecosystem through which energy and matter flow are called **trophic levels**.

Plants form the base of terrestrial trophic levels. Their chemical energy passes to consumers at higher trophic levels. **With each higher trophic level, only about 10% of available energy is passed on.** The remainder either is not absorbed by the consumer's body or is lost as heat. This phenomenon of energy loss is approximated as the *10% rule* **(Figure 7.25)**.

The 10% rule can apply to **biomass** (the dried weight of living material) as well as to energy. Because of this loss of energy at successive trophic levels, there is a rapid diminishment in biomass with each trophic level. **Populations of top predators (such as wolves and owls) typically have very low total biomass compared with the trophic levels below them.** In Crunch the Numbers, you will calculate how much biomass at the primary producer level is necessary to support one owl that weighs 0.5 kg (1.1 lb).

Many organisms occupy more than one trophic level. Bears, for example, can be scavengers when they eat carrion, herbivores when they eat berries, and carnivores when they eat insects. This makes them omnivores. Picture This shows an organism that defies conventional trophic categorization.

The Taxonomic Hierarchy

The second way of organizing the biosphere is based on the genetic relationships among organisms. **Taxonomy** is the classification and naming of organisms based on their genetic similarities. Taxonomy has two main goals: (1) to assign a unique name to every known species, and (2) to reveal genetic relationships among organisms.

How Scientific Names Work

You may have noticed in this chapter that when a specific organism is named, its common name and its scientific name are given. The scientific name is given in parentheses. Scientists give every known species on Earth a unique scientific name that consists of a genus name and a species name.

Humans, for example, are *Homo sapiens*. *Homo* in Latin means "person," and *sapiens* means "wise." *Homo* is the genus name and *sapiens* is the name for our species. It might help to think of the genus as a car make, such as "Honda." Just as there can be many car models within a car make (such as "Honda Civic," "Honda Accord," and so on), there can be many species within a genus. This naming system, which was first developed by the Swedish naturalist Carl Linnaeus (1707–1778), is called the *Linnaean binomial* (two-name) *classification*

Picture This

(© Nicholas Curtis)

A Photosynthetic Slug: Plant or Animal?

The eastern emerald elysia (*Elysia chlorotica*) is a sea slug that is about 3 cm (1.2 in) long. It does something animals do not normally do—it converts sunlight to food through photosynthesis. It is a solar-powered slug. The elysia is found on the east coast of the United States in shallow salt marshes and tidal pools such as those in the Chesapeake Bay. As the slug feeds on algae, it takes their chloroplasts and incorporates them into its own cells. It then uses the chloroplasts to make sugars directly from sunlight, just as plants do. The elysia can go without eating algae for months, using energy from sunlight instead. The elysia has incorporated the algal genes into its own genetic makeup. Natural fusion of genes across such distantly related life forms is extremely unusual.

Consider This

1. What trophic level(s) does the eastern emerald elysia occupy?

2. How would photosynthesis be an advantage to this animal?

phytoplankton
Microscopic bacteria and algae that are suspended in the sunlit portions of water and photosynthesize.

consumer
An organism that cannot produce its own food through photosynthesis.

herbivore
An organism that eats only plants.

omnivore
An organism that eats both plants and animals.

decomposer
An organism that breaks organic material down into simple compounds.

food web
The ecological interconnections among organisms occupying different trophic levels.

trophic level
One of the levels of an ecosystem through which energy and matter flow.

biomass
The dried weight of living material.

taxonomy
The classification and naming of organisms based on their genetic similarities.

CRUNCH THE NUMBERS: Calculating Biomass

Calculate the primary producer biomass necessary to support a 0.5 kg (1.1 lb) owl.

1. Determine how many trophic levels the owl is above the primary producer level (see Figure 7.25), and what percentage of the original energy is available at the owl's trophic level.

2. Convert the percentage of energy captured at the owl's trophic level to a decimal (by dividing it by 100).

3. Divide the owl's biomass (0.5 kg) by the decimal you obtained in step 2.

FIGURE 7.26 **The taxonomic hierarchy.** *Humans, bonobos (similar to chimpanzees and the closest living relative to humans), and bottlenose dolphins are in the same domain, kingdom, phylum, and class. At the level of orders, they diverge. Dolphins belong to the order Cetacea, whose members are mammals adapted to marine environments. Humans and bonobos are both in the family Hominidae, but they are not in the same genus. Note that only the genus and species are italicized.*

Eukarya is one of the three domains of life. It includes all organisms whose cells contain a nucleus.

Animalia is one of the five kingdoms of life. It includes all animals.

Chordates are animals with a spinal nerve cord.

All mammals have hair and lactate.

Units of life	All life		
Domain	Eukarya	Eukarya	Eukarya
Kingdom	Animalia	Animalia	Animalia
Phylum/ Division	Chordata	Chordata	Chordata
Class	Mammalia	Mammalia	Mammalia
Order	Primates	Primates	Cetacea
Family	Hominidae	Hominidae	Delphinidae
Genus	*Homo*	*Pan*	*Tursiops*
Species	*Homo sapiens* (humans)	*Pan paniscus* (bonobo)	*Tursiops truncatus* (bottlenose dolphin)

FIGURE 7.27 **Analogous traits.** *Birds (A) and bats (B) superficially look alike (they both have wings) and behave alike (they both fly), but they are only distantly related genetically. Birds are in the class Aves and bats are in the class Mammalia.*
(A. © Tony Campbell/Shutterstock.com; B. © Kevin Schafer/ Photographers Choice/Getty Images)

A **B**

system. Note that the genus name is capitalized and the species name is not. The genus name (or its abbreviation) always accompanies the species name.

The taxonomic hierarchy consists of a series of nested groups. Each group belongs to another, larger group, in the same way folders are nested within one another in a computer or cell phone operating environment **(Figure 7.26)**. Each family has at least one genus, and each genus has at least one species.

The taxonomic system uses *homologous traits* to group organisms that are genetically related to one another because they share a close common ancestor. For example, all birds have feathers, a characteristic that is unique to the class *Aves.* From ostriches to parrots to hawks—if it has feathers, it is a bird and is a member of *Aves.*

Many related organisms do not look alike. For example, a cow, a bat, and a whale do not look alike, but they are genetically similar. They all have hair, and they all feed their young milk from mammary glands. Only mammals have these features.

Through convergent evolution (see Section 7.1), organisms sometimes look deceptively alike but have no close genetic ties. Such superficial resemblances between organisms are called *analogous traits* **(Figure 7.27)**. Analogous traits do not reflect genetic similarities and are never used in taxonomic groupings. It would be misleading to group such organisms together because such a grouping would not reveal genetic relationships, one of the goals of taxonomy.

Common Names and Scientific Names

Common names and scientific names have different uses. A common name is a local name for an organism. Common names are useful because they are familiar. A problem with them is that there is often more than one common name per species. The "black bear," for instance, is also called "North American black bear," "American black bear," and "cinnamon bear," depending on where in North America you live. The Linnaean system assigns only one scientific name to each species. The scientific name for the black bear is *Ursus americanus. Ursus* means "bear" in Latin and *americanus* describes where it lives. There is only one *Ursus americanus.*

The Spatial Hierarchy

The third way of organizing the biosphere is based on the ecological units of life. **The spatial hierarchy identifies units of life that range from the individual to the entire biosphere.** The individual organism is the most localized unit of the spatial hierarchy. The whole biosphere is the larg-

FIGURE 7.28 **The spatial hierarchy.** *The spatial hierarchy is scaled geographically from large-scale, localized phenomena, through small-scale, continent-wide phenomena, to the entire biosphere.*

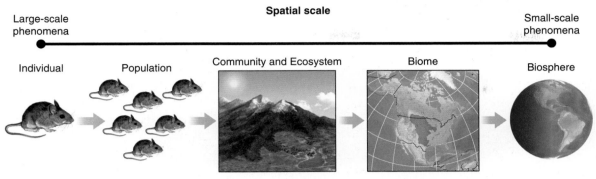

community
The populations of organisms interacting in a geographic area.

est unit in this categorization scheme, as shown in **Figure 7.28**.

Individuals make up populations of organisms, and populations form communities. A **community** consists of the populations of organisms interacting in a geographic area. Communities are named after their most conspicuous feature, by their geographic setting, or by the niche of the most prominent organisms living in them (**Figure 7.29**).

As we have seen, a community and its physical environment constitute an ecosystem. The ecosystem concept emphasizes the interconnectivity and interdependence of all facets of a landscape, both living and nonliving, including chemicals and nutrients. Many chemicals that are essential components of living organisms cycle through ecosystems. Oxygen, water, phosphorus, and potassium are just a few. **Figure 7.30**, on the next page, traces the nitrogen cycle and the carbon cycle to illustrate how these chemicals move through ecosystems.

The last category of the spatial hierarchy is the biome. Earth's biomes are geographically extensive. Only the biosphere is greater in spatial extent. *Biomes* are extensive expanses of vegetation types that are determined by climate. They will be the focus of the next chapter.

FIGURE 7.29 **Communities.** *(A) Populations of wildebeest, zebra, and antelope compose the grazing community on the grasslands in the Maasai Mara National Reserve in Kenya. This community is identified by the grazing niche of the large animals that dominate this landscape. (B) Sea urchins and sea stars make up this tide pool community along the rocky coast in Gwaii Haanas National Park, British Columbia. This community is identified by its geographic setting. (A. © James Warwick/The Image Bank/Getty Images; B. © David Nunuk/All Canada Photos/Getty)*

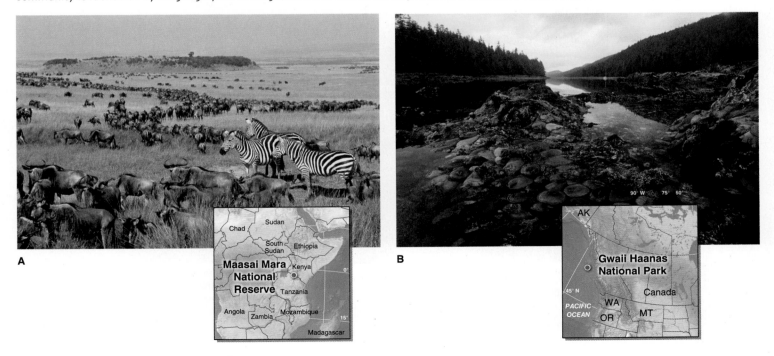

FIGURE 7.30 **GEO-GRAPHIC: Chemical elements cycle through ecosystems.**

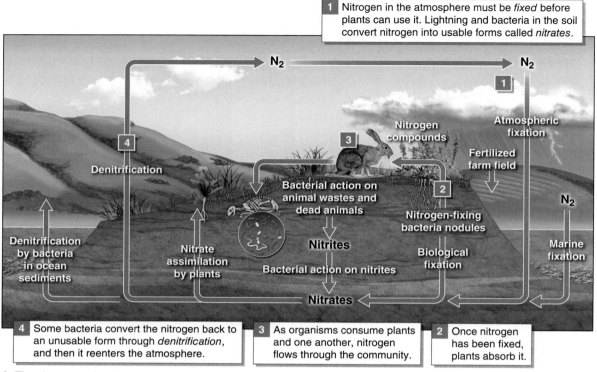

1 Nitrogen in the atmosphere must be *fixed* before plants can use it. Lightning and bacteria in the soil convert nitrogen into usable forms called *nitrates*.

4 Some bacteria convert the nitrogen back to an unusable form through *denitrification*, and then it reenters the atmosphere.

3 As organisms consume plants and one another, nitrogen flows through the community.

2 Once nitrogen has been fixed, plants absorb it.

A. The nitrogen cycle

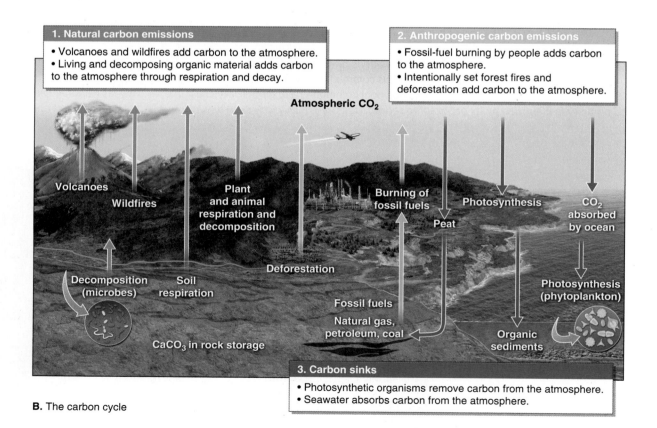

1. Natural carbon emissions

- Volcanoes and wildfires add carbon to the atmosphere.
- Living and decomposing organic material adds carbon to the atmosphere through respiration and decay.

2. Anthropogenic carbon emissions

- Fossil-fuel burning by people adds carbon to the atmosphere.
- Intentionally set forest fires and deforestation add carbon to the atmosphere.

3. Carbon sinks

- Photosynthetic organisms remove carbon from the atmosphere.
- Seawater absorbs carbon from the atmosphere.

B. The carbon cycle

GEOGRAPHIC PERSPECTIVES
7.6 Journey of the Coconut

◎ Assess the relationship between people and the coconut palm and apply that knowledge to other organisms used by people.

Many people associate the coconut (*Cocos nucifera*) with food or with a tropical vacation getaway. The coconut is certainly an important food, and it is an icon of tropical paradise. But it also illuminates many fascinating principles of biogeography.

Geographers are interested in where things are and why they are where they are. No one knows for certain where the coconut palm originated. Today, the tree has a *pantropical* distribution, meaning that it is found throughout all coastal tropical regions. But where did it first evolve? How did it come to be spread across the tropics?

Genetic evidence suggests that the coconut palm arose some 11 million years ago in the vicinity of the Malay Peninsula, Indonesia, the Philippines, and New Guinea. Wild coconuts were *domesticated* by people as they began to grow it as a food source; that is, it was genetically modified by its interactions with people. Today there are two major varieties of the coconut palm, indicating that it was domesticated in two different areas: once near India, producing the *Indian variety*, and once near Indonesia, producing the *Pacific variety* (Figure 7.31).

Coconut Dispersal

Why do coconuts float?

But how did the coconut disperse across the tropical oceans from where it first arose? As we have learned in this chapter, plants disperse in a variety of ways, from being blown on the wind, to being transported in the digestive tracts of animals, to floating in water. As shown in **Figure 7.32**, coconuts are hydrochores and are well adapted to disperse by floating in water.

FIGURE 7.31 **Coconut range map.** *The Pacific variety of coconut palm probably originated somewhere in southeastern Asia and spread throughout the tropical Pacific and Indian oceans. The Indian variety probably originated in India and spread throughout the Indian and Atlantic oceans.*

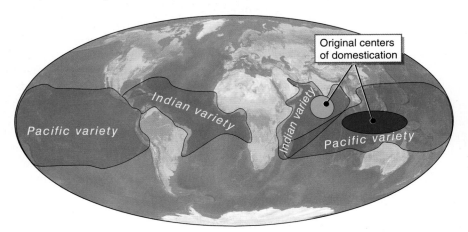

FIGURE 7.32 **The coconut seed.** *(A) The coconut seed is surrounded by layers of waterproof barriers: an outer skin, a fibrous husk, and a shell. The inner endosperm, or "meat," contains sweet freshwater. (B) Coconuts can float in salt water for months and still germinate if washed up on a distant beach.*
(© Darryl Torckler/The Image Bank/Getty Images)

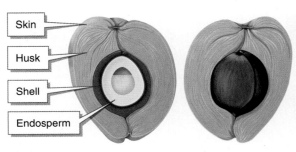

A

B

If a coconut seed disperses north or south of about 26 degrees latitude, it cannot successfully establish a new population because of the limiting factors of low winter temperatures and dry air. The coconut is restricted to humid tropical regions and mostly to coastal regions.

Human Migration and Coconut Dispersal

As it turns out, the same traits that allow the coconut seed to survive long-distance travel on ocean currents also allowed it to survive long-distance travel in outrigger canoes. The endosperm supports a young coconut palm as it first germinates and grows. The meat, oil, and water of the endosperm are also nourishing for people. During a 2,000-year period, people dispersed across the tropical Pacific Ocean from Taiwan to Papua New Guinea. Using the Pacific islands as stepping-stones, they dispersed all the way to Easter Island and the Hawaiian Islands. **Figure 7.33** provides a map of this remarkable migration event.

The coconut's stores of freshwater and nutrition made it an ideal food and source of water for ocean travelers. Archeologists know that migrating people brought the coconut with them be-cause people and the coconut appear on remote Pacific islands at the same time. The Hawaiian Islands, for example, were colonized about 1,100 years ago. The earliest garbage dumps in Hawai'i have coconut shells preserved in them. Before that time, there is no evidence of humans ever having set foot in Hawai'i and that no coconut had ever grown on the islands naturally. The same is true for Easter Island (see Section GT.5).

When the first Europeans sailed to the western shores of tropical South America in the early 1500s, they found mature coconut palm groves there. Somehow, the coconut palm had dispersed to western South America. Whether Austronesian voyagers brought it there or the coconut drifted there on its own is still a mystery.

Europeans also dispersed the coconut palm across the tropics. After 1500, Europeans began dispersing coconuts to regions where the plant already grew as well as to new regions **(Figure 7.34)**.

Artificial Selection

The relationship between people and the coconut illustrates not only dispersal but also the important process of *artificial selection*. Long ago, people began

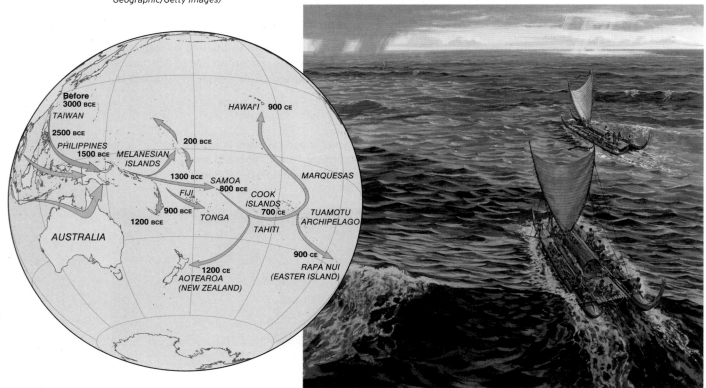

FIGURE 7.33 **Austronesian dispersal.** *Austronesians dispersed eastward across the Pacific Ocean in outrigger canoes (inset). The earliest dates of their arrival on Pacific islands are given. They brought with them several different types of plants and animals, including the coconut.* (© Herbert Kawainui Kane/National Geographic/Getty Images)

FIGURE **7.34** **Coconut dispersal by Europeans.**

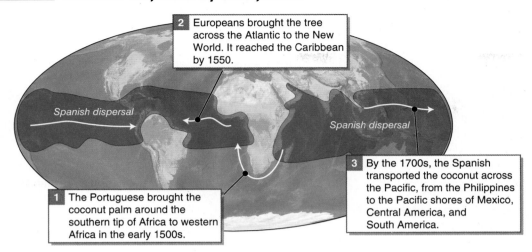

2 Europeans brought the tree across the Atlantic to the New World. It reached the Caribbean by 1550.

Spanish dispersal

Spanish dispersal

3 By the 1700s, the Spanish transported the coconut across the Pacific, from the Philippines to the Pacific shores of Mexico, Central America, and South America.

1 The Portuguese brought the coconut palm around the southern tip of Africa to western Africa in the early 1500s.

selecting individual coconut palms with useful traits, such as those with the sweetest and most nutritious meat and oil, those that did not grow too tall, and those with the best fiber. They then cultivated trees with those traits over many plant generations. Through time, this selection process created the 80 kinds of coconut palms we see today **(Figure 7.35)**.

Like the coconut, most domesticated plants and animals familiar to us today are the result of artificial selection. The fruits and vegetables in the grocery store are examples of organisms changed by people. Artificial selection works through many generations as small changes add up through time. In one familiar example, all modern dog breeds, including chihuahuas and poodles, are descended from the gray wolf.

Humans and many organisms, including the coconut palm, share a relationship of mutualism. Not only do we benefit from these organisms, but they also benefit from us. The coconut's journey reveals a fascinating story of dispersal, human migration history, plant-human mutualism, and the importance of organisms shaped by artificial selection.

FIGURE **7.35** **Coconut diversity.** *The many varieties of coconut palms have been bred for different height and seed characteristics. Only a few varieties are shown here. All coconut varieties are descended from the two major Indian and Pacific varieties.*

Solomon Islands tall

Rennell Island tall

Malaysian tall

Hybrid

Malaysian dwarf

Fiji dwarf

Tree

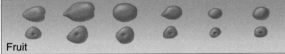

Fruit

CHAPTER 7 Exploring with ◎ Google Earth

To complete these problems, first read the chapter. When you are finished, go to LaunchPad and open the Exploring with Google Earth file for this chapter. Click on the "Workbook Problems" folder to "fly" to each of the problems listed below and answer the questions. Be sure to keep your "Borders and Labels" layer activated. Refer to Appendix 4 if you need help using Google Earth.

PROBLEM 7.1 This placemark highlights a November 2012 eruption of Tolbachik volcano on the Kamchatka Peninsula. Activate the folder for this problem to answer the questions below.

1. **What kind of ecological succession will follow this eruption?**
   a. Primary succession   b. Secondary succession

2. **How long is this lava flow?**
   a. 2 km   b. 11 km   c. 18 km   d. 25 km

3. **Zoom out. Where is this eruption occurring?**
   a. Japan   b. Alaska   c. Russia   d. North Korea

PROBLEM 7.2 This placemark highlights the Ponderosa fire, which burned 15,000 acres in Northern California in August 2012. Activate the folder for this problem to see a natural color satellite image of the smoke from the Ponderosa fire burning on August 19. The red outlines show hot spots where fires were still burning. If you zoom out, you will see the smoke column from the Chips fire to the south and east.

1. **Based on the photo accompanying this placemark, what kind of fire was this at the location of the placemark?**
   a. A surface fire   b. A canopy fire

2. **What kind of ecological succession will occur after this fire?**
   a. Primary succession   b. Secondary succession

3. **What is the length of the burning area shown within the red outline?**
   a. 7 km   b. 13 km   c. 20 km   d. 100 km

4. **Deactivate the fires layer by clicking the folder for this problem and zooming in to the placemark. This image was made before the fire, so no burn scar is visible. You can see a number of bare patches made by clear-cut logging of the forest here. What kind of ecological succession will take place in these patches?**
   a. Primary succession   b. Secondary succession

PROBLEM 7.3 This placemark visits the Aleutian Islands of Alaska in the North Pacific Ocean.

1. **What kind of biological dispersal do island chains such as this provide?**
   a. Stepping-stone dispersal   c. Sweepstakes dispersal
   b. Waif dispersal

PROBLEM 7.4 This placemark visits Ascension Island.

1. **How far is this island from the nearest continent?**
   a. 500 mi   b. 900 mi   c. 1,400 mi   d. 2,000 mi

2. **How did native terrestrial organisms reach Ascension?**
   a. Stepping-stone dispersal   c. Sweepstakes dispersal
   b. Waif dispersal

PROBLEM 7.5 Southern California's Channel Islands are featured here.

1. **About how far from the mainland is the island nearest to the mainland?**
   a. 2 mi   b. 19 mi   c. 45 mi   d. 90 mi

2. **Which of the Channel Islands would you expect to have the highest plant and animal diversity?**
   a. San Nicolas   c. San Miguel
   b. San Clemente   d. Santa Cruz

3. **The Channel Island fox (*Urocyon littoralis*) dispersed to the islands about 16,000 years ago. By what means did it reach the islands?**
   a. Stepping-stone dispersal   c. Sweepstakes dispersal
   b. Waif dispersal

4. **The fox is found on six of the islands. Assuming the fox reached the Channel Islands only once, by what means did it disperse to the other five islands?**
   a. Stepping-stone dispersal   c. Sweepstakes dispersal
   b. Waif dispersal

5. **There are six subspecies of the Channel Island fox, none of which look like the ancestral gray fox on the mainland. What process produced these changes?**
   a. Convergent evolution   c. Ecological succession
   b. Divergent evolution   d. Ecological disturbance

CHAPTER 7 Study Guide

Focus Points

The Human Sphere: Exotic Invaders

Non-native organisms: Organisms that are moved outside their natural geographic range by people can cause ecological problems.

7.1 Biogeographic Patterns

Biogeography: Biogeographers study the geographic patterns of life to learn about Earth's physical systems and Earth's natural and human history.

Biodiversity patterns: The tropics are the most biodiverse region on Earth. Large islands are more biodiverse than small islands. Biodiversity changes seasonally as animals migrate.

Patterns resulting from evolution: Biogeographic patterns of convergence and divergence result from the process of evolution.

7.2 Setting the Boundaries: Limiting Factors

Niches: Species with narrow ecological niches usually have restricted geographic ranges. Species with broad niches are usually geographically widespread.

Limiting factors: Geographic ranges of species are determined by physical and biological limiting factors.

Keystone species: Keystone species play crucial roles in the functioning of ecosystems.

Competition: The degree of competition among organisms depends on the similarity of their niches.

7.3 Moving Around: Dispersal

Dispersal: Dispersal allows organisms to reduce limiting factors such as competition, to obtain more resources, and to respond to environmental change.

Range expansion: Geographic ranges expand when organisms successfully disperse outside the boundaries of their current range.

Dispersal modes: Organisms may disperse under their own power (called active dispersal) or with the help of wind, water, or other organisms (called passive dispersal).

7.4 Starting Anew: Ecological Disturbance and Succession

Ecological disturbance: Ecological disturbance is caused by both biotic and abiotic factors.

Fire suppression: In North America, fires have been intentionally suppressed by people, resulting in an accumulation of fuel and subsequent catastrophic fires.

Reducing fuel buildup: Prescribed burns and mechanical thinning reduce fuel buildup in forests caused by fire suppression.

Ecological succession: After a disturbance event, life returns to an area through ecological succession.

7.5 Three Ways to Organize the Biosphere

Approaches to organizing the biosphere: The biosphere can be organized on the basis of flows of energy and matter, genetic similarities, and the spatial dimensions of ecological units of life.

The trophic hierarchy: The trophic hierarchy is based on energy flow. Higher trophic levels have less available energy and biomass.

The taxonomic hierarchy: The taxonomic hierarchy places organisms in nested groups according to their shared genetic relationships.

The spatial hierarchy: Ecological units of life range from the individual to the entire biosphere.

7.6 Geographic Perspectives: Journey of the Coconut

Coconut dispersal: The coconut seed is well adapted to disperse by floating on seawater as well as for dispersal by people.

Artificial selection: The coconut palm illustrates the influences that people and their domesticated organisms have on one another.

Key Terms

biodiversity, 225
biogeographic regions, 230
biogeography, 225
biomass, 244
colonization, 240
community, 245
competition, 236
consumer, 243
convergent evolution, 229
decomposer, 244
dispersal, 230
divergent evolution, 230
ecological disturbance, 240
ecological succession, 240
ecology, 225
ecosystem, 225
endemic, 230
evolution, 228
extinction, 232

food web, 244
habitat, 230
herbivore, 244
invasion, 240
keystone species, 235
limiting factor, 232
migration, 227
mutualism, 236
niche, 230
non-native (or *exotic*), 225
omnivore, 244
phytoplankton, 243
population, 228
predation, 234
primary producer, 241
propagule, 237
sere, 241
speciation, 228
species, 225
stepping-stone, 238
sweepstakes dispersal, 238
taxonomy, 245
trophic level, 244

Concept Review

The Human Sphere: Exotic Invaders

1. What is the difference between a native species and a non-native species?

2. Why are non-native species sometimes destructive in their new habitats? What is missing in those new habitats that was in their old habitats?

3. Can exotic species also be beneficial to people? If so, give examples.

7.1 Biogeographic Patterns

4. Define biogeography and biodiversity.

5. What is a species?

6. Describe the generalized spatial and temporal patterns of biodiversity with respect to latitude, island size, and seasons.

7. What is evolution? Describe the basic steps of the process and explain how it works.

8. What is a population? Provide biogeographic examples that result from evolution once populations are geographically isolated.

9. What is convergent evolution?

10. What is divergent evolution?

11. What are biogeographic regions and how do they form?

7.2 Setting the Boundaries: Limiting Factors

12. Compare the terms *niche* and *habitat*. Why do species with a narrow niche usually have limited geographic ranges?

13. What does it mean to say that an organism is endemic to a place? What factors would cause an organism to be endemic?

14. What is a limiting factor? Give examples of physical and biological limiting factors. Explain how each acts to limit the range of a species.

15. What is Allen's rule? How does it relate to limiting factors?

16. What adaptations do many cacti have to cope with life in the desert?

17. What is a keystone species? Give an example. How does the concept of a keystone species relate to limiting factors?

18. What is mutualism? Give examples of it. How can it be a limiting factor for a given organism?

7.3 Moving Around: Dispersal

19. In the context of biogeography, what is dispersal? Why do organisms disperse?

20. By what means do plants and animals disperse?

21. What barriers present resistance to dispersal? Compare the relative ease or difficultly of dispersing to islands close to the mainland and far away from it.

22. Compare colonization and invasion. How does the cattle egret exemplify both concepts?

7.4 Starting Anew: Ecological Disturbance and Succession

23. What is ecological disturbance? What causes it?

24. Review the importance of fire to western North American forests. What problem has developed? What is being done to address it?

25. What is ecological succession? What causes it? What are seres?

26. What is a climax community? Is this model always accurate?

7.5 Three Ways to Organize the Biosphere

27. What three hierarchies are used to organize the biosphere? Explain what each is based on.

28. What are trophic levels? Where do producers and consumers fit in? What is a tertiary consumer?

29. Compare a food chain with a food web. Which is more representative of the real world?

30. What is the 10% rule in relation to trophic levels?

31. What types of consumers recycle dead organisms?

32. What are homologous traits? How are they used to create taxonomic groups?

33. Compare common names and scientific names. On what is each based? How is each type of name useful?

34. What is a community? How is the term defined? Give examples of a few communities.

35. What is the carbon cycle? What is the nitrogen cycle? How do they work? Why are they important?

7.6 Geographic Perspectives: Journey of the Coconut

36. Is *Cocos* the genus or the species name for the coconut palm?

37. What are the two basic varieties of coconut palm and where did each originate?

38. The coconut uses two main modes of dispersal. What are they?

39. Where did Austronesians disperse the coconut? Where did Europeans disperse it?

40. What are the two primary limiting factors controlling the coconut's geographic range?

41. What is artificial selection? How does it relate to domestication? How does the coconut illustrate the process of artificial selection?

42. Describe the ecological relationship between humans and the coconut.

Critical-Thinking Questions

1. The theory of evolution has been a source of controversy between scientists and some religious groups since it was first developed. Do you find it controversial? Explain.

2. What trophic level(s) do you occupy? Why is it more efficient for people to eat as primary consumers rather than as secondary consumers?

3. By definition, when people move an organism to a new place, that organism is non-native. People brought the coconut to Hawai'i over a thousand years ago. Because that was so long ago, do you think enough time has passed that we can consider this plant native to Hawai'i now? Explain.

4. Does evolutionary convergence (Section 7.1) result from analogous traits or homologous traits (Section 7.5)? Explain.

5. Compare natural selection (Section 7.1) with artificial selection (Section 7.6). How are they the same and how are they different?

Test Yourself

Take this quiz to test your chapter knowledge.

1. **True or false?** When a species disperses on its own to a new location outside its geographic range, it is considered a native species.

2. **True or false?** Allen's rule states that there are more species in the tropics than at higher latitudes.

3. **True or false?** After ecological disturbance, ecosystems do not always return to the same climax community that existed prior to the disturbance.

4. **True or false?** Many species have more than one common name.

5. **Multiple choice:** What an organism does to obtain food is called its
   a. niche.   c. prey.
   b. habitat.   d. community.

6. **Multiple choice:** Which of the following is not an evolutionary adaptation to fire by plants?
   a. Serotinous cones   c. Deep roots
   b. Crown sprouting   d. Fire-proof leaves

7. **Multiple choice:** Which of the following does fire suppression often cause?
   a. A small fire   c. A surface fire
   b. A crown fire   d. A prescribed burn

8. **Multiple choice:** Which of the following is not an example of a limiting factor?
   a. Temperature   c. Predation
   b. Light   d. A scavenger

9. **Fill in the blank:** A _____ is a stage of ecological succession following ecological disturbance.

10. **Fill in the blank:** _____ is the term used to describe an interaction between two species from which both species benefit.

Picture This. YOUR TURN

Trophic-Level Feeding

These copper sharks (*Carcharhinus brachyurus*) are feeding on schooling sardines (*Sardinops sagax*) off the coast of South Africa. Sardines eat small animals called zooplankton (see Figure 7.24). The zooplankton eat microscopic plants called phytoplankton. Based on this information, answer the following questions. (Hint: Draw out this food chain with the phytoplankton at the primary producer level.) *(© Alexander Safonov/Flickr/GettyImages)*

1. What trophic level do the copper sharks occupy?

2. Given the 10% rule, how much energy from the primary producers do they receive?

Further Reading

1. Hulme, Philip E. "Invasive Species Unchecked by Climate." *Science* 335 (2012): 538-539.

2. MacDonald, Glen. *Biogeography: Introduction to Space, Time and Life*. New York: Wiley, 2003.

3. Quammen, David. *The Boilerplate Rhino: Nature in the Eye of the Beholder*. New York: Scribner, 2001.

Answers to Living Physical Geography Questions

1. **Why do animals migrate?** Animals migrate from areas where resources are in short supply to areas where they are more abundant.

2. **Why do cacti have spines?** Cacti have spines to ward off animals trying to take their stores of water.

3. **How are wolves important to ecosystems?** Wolves function as keystone species in ecosystems, and many unrelated species benefit from their presence.

4. **Why do coconuts float?** Coconuts float because they have evolved to disperse long distances on ocean currents.

8 CLIMATE AND LIFE: Biomes

This African male elephant moves across a sea of grass in the Maasai Mara National Reserve in Kenya, with monsoon clouds in the backdrop.

(© Bill Bachmann/age fotostock)

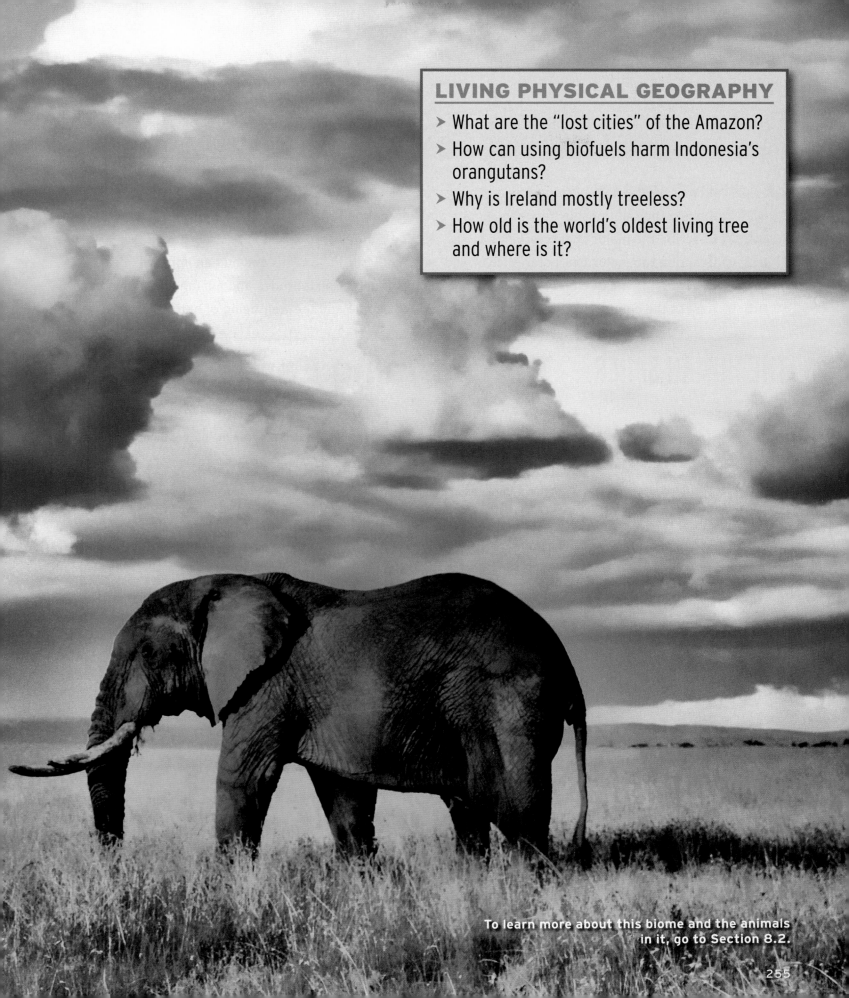

LIVING PHYSICAL GEOGRAPHY

> What are the "lost cities" of the Amazon?

> How can using biofuels harm Indonesia's orangutans?

> Why is Ireland mostly treeless?

> How old is the world's oldest living tree and where is it?

To learn more about this biome and the animals in it, go to Section 8.2.

THE BIG PICTURE *The broad geographic patterns of vegetation are determined mostly by climate. Humans are rapidly transforming these patterns.*

LEARNING GOALS *After reading this chapter, you will be able to:*

8.1 ◎ Explain the relationship between climate and vegetation structure.

8.2 ◎ Describe the major characteristics of low-latitude biomes and human impacts in each.

8.3 ◎ Describe the major characteristics of mid- and high-latitude biomes and human impacts in each.

8.4 ◎ Describe the major characteristics of the biomes found at all latitudes and human impacts in each.

8.5 ◎ Assess the connection between the well-being of people and the well-being of nature.

THE HUMAN SPHERE: **Terraforming Earth**

FIGURE 8.1 **Great Plains farmland.** *In this satellite image of southwestern Kansas, agricultural fields watered by center-pivot irrigation are visible as circular green areas. The larger fields are about 1.6 km (1 mi) in diameter.* (NASA/GSFC/METI/ERSDAC/JAROS, and U.S./Japan ASTER Science Team)

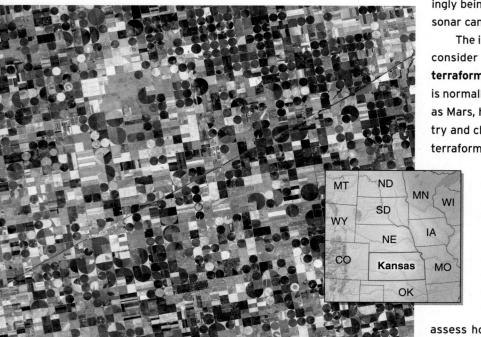

THESE ARE INTERESTING TIMES for Planet Earth. They are the best of times and the worst of times, to quote the English novelist Charles Dickens. Human technological innovation is more advanced than ever and has improved conditions for humanity. Technology is being used to obtain natural resources more efficiently and to feed more people now than ever before. About 40% of Earth's ice-free land surface is under agricultural production or in use as rangelands for livestock grazing. As **Figure 8.1** shows, much of the Great Plains of North America, which was once grassland, is now fields of wheat, soybeans, and corn.

But technology has allowed people to exploit natural resources too well. Wild places are increasingly being converted to cropland and rangeland. Fishing boats using sonar can find and catch fish that were once beyond human reach.

The impact of human technology is so large that some scientists consider it a form of planetary engineering, or "terraforming." To **terraform** a planet is to transform it to suit human needs. The term is normally used in the context of making an inhospitable world, such as Mars, hospitable for human colonization by changing the chemistry and character of its surface and atmosphere. Earth is now being terraformed to better meet humanity's needs. But this transformation comes with a price: The growing human population is placing increasing demands on Earth's natural resources. Wild places are increasingly fragmented, and natural ecosystems are quickly being converted to human-modified systems.

In this chapter, we explore Earth's terrestrial (land) biomes and human impacts (the human "footprint") in each biome, starting with those found at low latitudes, then moving to those at midlatitudes and high latitudes. We then explore biomes found at all latitudes. Lastly, we assess how Earth's biomes have changed and the importance of natural systems to people.

8.1 Climates and Biomes

◎ Explain the relationship between climate and vegetation structure.

The type of native vegetation found in any given area mainly reflects three physical limiting factors: temperature, water, and light. At a local level, other factors may be important too, such as soil types and biological limiting factors like herbivory and nutrient supplies. In mountain ranges, slope steepness, slope *aspect* (the direction the slope is facing), and *microclimates* (the distinct climates of restricted areas) also determine the types of plants that will grow.

When viewed from a small-scale perspective, Earth's land surface is covered by biomes. A **biome** is an extensive geographic region with relatively uniform vegetation structure. *Vegetation structure* refers to the type of vegetation that dominates a region, such as closed forest or open grassland. Biomes are the second-largest units in the ecological hierarchy; Only the biosphere is larger (see Section 7.5). **Biome classifications are based on vegetation structure, which is determined mostly by climate. Table 8.1** summarizes the terms describing vegetation structure that will be used in this chapter.

Within each biome, plants take on a variety of *growth forms*, detailed from largest to smallest in **Table 8.2**. In addition to the names of these plant growth forms, this chapter will use a number of *botanical* (plant-related) terms that describe characteristics of plant growth and plant adaptations **(Table 8.3)**.

Because of the spatial correspondence between climates and biomes, classifying and categorizing climate types is fundamental to this discussion of biomes. One of the most widely used climate classification systems is the **Köppen climate classification system**, first published by Wladimir Köppen in 1884. The Köppen system categorizes climates based on the temperature and precipitation characteristics of a region. (Appendix 6 provides further detail on the Köppen climate classification system.)

Because of the strong correspondence between vegetation structure and climate, the Köppen climate categories were originally based on the type of natural vegetation growing in an area. There are six major Köppen climate groups containing 25 climate zones. The climate zones and Earth's biomes are mapped in **Figure 8.2**.

Biomes can be portrayed graphically by plotting temperature and precipitation. As shown in **Figure 8.3**, each biome occupies a different climatological space on the graph.

TABLE 8.2 AT A GLANCE: Plant Growth Forms

GROWTH FORM	DESCRIPTION
Tree	Tall, upright woody growth
Liana	Woody, climbing vine
Shrub	Many woody stems
Forb	Low, nonwoody plant other than grass
Epiphyte	Grows on surfaces of trees, not parasitic
Bryophyte	Member of the division that includes mosses

TABLE 8.3 AT A GLANCE: Botanical Terms

TERM	DESCRIPTION
Broad-leaved	Has wide, flat leaves; usually deciduous
Coniferous	Bears cones; usually needle-leaved and evergreen
Deciduous	Loses all leaves in one season, usually winter
Evergreen	Loses leaves gradually so it always has leaves
Herbaceous	Lacking woody tissue
Needle-leaved	Has narrow, needle-like leaves; usually evergreen
Sclerophyllous	Has hard, leathery, and waxy leaves
Woody	Grows rigid trunks and stems

TABLE 8.1 AT A GLANCE: Vegetation Structure

STRUCTURE	DESCRIPTION
Forest	Dominated by trees with a closed canopy
Woodland	Widely spaced trees with a grass understory
Shrubland	Continuous cover of shrubs
Grassland	Continuous cover of grasses
Scrubland	Widely spaced, drought-adapted shrubs
Desert	Sparse plant cover

terraform
To transform a planet to suit human needs.

biome
An extensive geographic region with relatively uniform vegetation structure.

Köppen climate classification system
(pronounced KUHR-pen)
A system used to classify climate types by temperature and precipitation.

FIGURE 8.2 **GEO-GRAPHIC: Climate zone and biome maps.** *A comparison of the spatial distributions of (A) Köppen climate zones and (B) biomes shows that the two correspond roughly in space. Extreme events such as droughts and disturbances such as fire can also determine the spatial distribution of vegetation. For this reason, biomes and Köppen climate zones do not overlap precisely.*

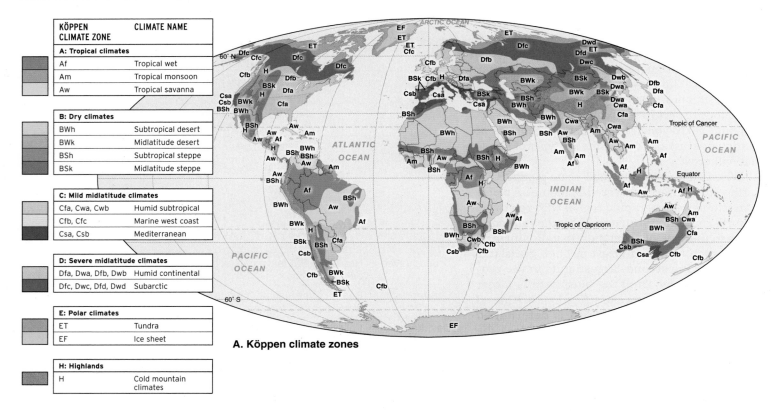

KÖPPEN CLIMATE ZONE	CLIMATE NAME
A: Tropical climates	
Af	Tropical wet
Am	Tropical monsoon
Aw	Tropical savanna
B: Dry climates	
BWh	Subtropical desert
BWk	Midlatitude desert
BSh	Subtropical steppe
BSk	Midlatitude steppe
C: Mild midlatitude climates	
Cfa, Cwa, Cwb	Humid subtropical
Cfb, Cfc	Marine west coast
Csa, Csb	Mediterranean
D: Severe midlatitude climates	
Dfa, Dwa, Dfb, Dwb	Humid continental
Dfc, Dwc, Dfd, Dwd	Subarctic
E: Polar climates	
ET	Tundra
EF	Ice sheet
H: Highlands	
H	Cold mountain climates

A. Köppen climate zones

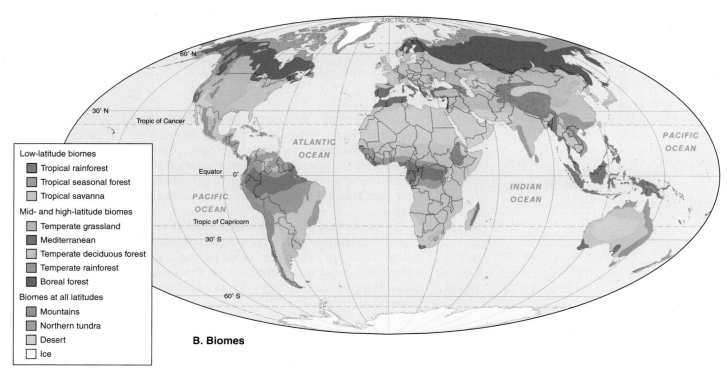

Low-latitude biomes
- ■ Tropical rainforest
- ■ Tropical seasonal forest
- ■ Tropical savanna

Mid- and high-latitude biomes
- ■ Temperate grassland
- ■ Mediterranean
- ■ Temperate deciduous forest
- ■ Temperate rainforest
- ■ Boreal forest

Biomes at all latitudes
- ■ Mountains
- ■ Northern tundra
- ■ Desert
- □ Ice

B. Biomes

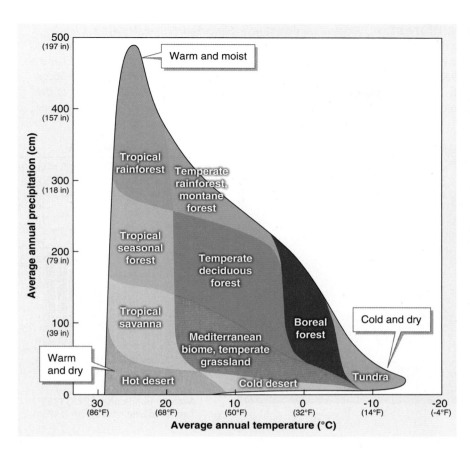

FIGURE 8.3 **Biome and climate diagram.**
This modified Whittaker diagram *portrays the relationship between biomes and climates graphically. Tropical rainforests occupy the climates with the highest precipitation and temperature, represented by the space at the top left. Tundra occupies the climates with the lowest precipitation and temperature, at the lower right, and subtropical desert occupies warm and dry climates, at the lower left.*

Animation
Biome and
climate diagram
http://qrs.ly/fw44otx

8.2 Low-Latitude Biomes

◎ Describe the major characteristics of low-latitude biomes and human impacts in each.

Low-latitude biomes are found almost entirely between 30 degrees north and south latitude. Excluding mountainous regions, low-latitude biomes lack any significant cold period. **There are three low-latitude biomes: tropical rainforest, tropical seasonal forest, and tropical savanna.**

Tropical Rainforest

The tropical rainforest biome, found in the humid lowland tropics, has the highest primary productivity, the highest biomass, and the highest biodiversity of any biome (Figure 8.4). It occupies some 13% of Earth's land surface and accounts for about 40% of the world's biodiversity. A great variety of organisms in many different groups, including insects, birds, mammals, and amphibians, live in this biome. Worldwide, for example, there are about 250 species of *primates*, such as humans, gorillas, lemurs, and monkeys. All primates are mammals, and all have nails instead of claws, flexible hands and feet,

good eyesight, and high intelligence. With the exception of humans, all primates live in tropical or subtropical areas. Most of them live in the tropical rainforests.

In the tropical rainforest biome, water is available in every month, and competition for light is a major limiting factor. As a result, the tropical rainforest biome develops a complex vertical structure. Its vegetation consists of multiple layers of broad-leaved evergreen plants **(Figure 8.5)**. The topmost layer, called the *emergent layer*, consists of trees that protrude above the canopy. The shaded *forest floor* may receive as little as 1% of the sunlight that the canopy and emergent layers do. As a result, the forest floor is dark and damp. Fungi (mushrooms and molds) are common, and they rapidly decompose and recycle fallen plants.

The strong vertical structure of the rainforest biome is driven by competition among the plants to reach sunlight. Many tropical rainforest trees have buttress roots to support tall growth to reach the light **(Figure 8.6A)**. **Lianas**, which are woody climbing vines, are well adapted to tropical rainforest habitat. They grow quickly up trees to reach light in the canopy (see Figure 8.4A). Lianas also provide routes of travel for arboreal (tree-dwelling)

tropical rainforest
A forest biome in the humid lowland tropics; characterized by a multi-layered forest structure and high biodiversity.

liana
A woody climbing vine.

FIGURE 8.4   **Tropical rainforest.** *(A) Tropical rainforest near Sandakan, Sabah, Malaysia. Lianas are seen here growing up the trunks of tall trees to reach the light above. (B) Climate diagram for Sandakan. Tropical rainforests are found where the average annual temperature does not drop below 18°C (64°F) and an average of at least 250 cm (98 in) of precipitation falls each year. (C) Although tropical rainforest can occur within about 25 degrees north and south of the equator, this biome is found mainly within 10 degrees of the equator. About half of all tropical rainforest is found in the Amazon Basin in South America. (A. © Mattias Klum/ National Geographic/Getty Images)*

A

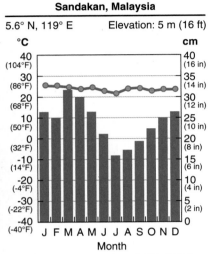

Sandakan, Malaysia

5.6° N, 119° E   Elevation: 5 m (16 ft)

Average temperature: 24°C (75°F)
Total precipitation: 285 cm (112 in)

B

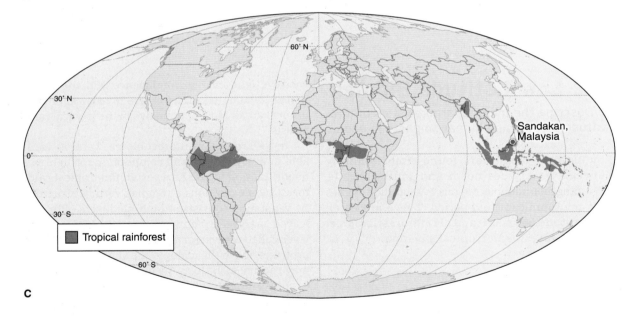

Tropical rainforest

C

Tropical Rainforest	
Köppen climate zone	Tropical wet: Af
Vegetation	Broad-leaved evergreen trees, lianas, epiphytes
Notable features	ITCZ-dominated, no dry or cold season; layered forest structure and competition for light; high biodiversity
Human footprint	Logging, burning, cattle ranching, agriculture

epiphyte
A plant that grows on the surface of another plant but does not take nutrients from that plant.

animals such as monkeys. **Epiphytes** are plants that grow on the surfaces of other plants for access to light but do not take nutrients from those plants (Figure 8.6B).

The "crowded jungle" perception of the tropical rainforest is misleading. A walk through the shaded floor of a healthy tropical rainforest would be clear and unobstructed by plants in many places. Crowded plant growth occurs only where there are high light levels, such as in the canopy above, in light gaps created where large trees have fallen, or along stream banks.

Mutualism (see Section 7.2) between plants and animals is common in the tropical rainforest biome. At midlatitudes, many plants rely on the persistent westerlies (see Section 4.3) to disperse their pollen, seeds, and fruits. In contrast, equatorial tropical rainforests are dominated by the windless doldrums. Instead of the wind, bats, birds, fish, and mammals pollinate flowers and disperse seeds and fruit. Many

FIGURE 8.5 **Tropical rainforest structure.** *Four layers of vegetation can be identified in many tropical rainforests: the emergent layer, the canopy, the understory, and the forest floor.*

FIGURE 8.6 **Plant adaptations to reach light.** *(A) Buttress roots in Gunung Mulu National Park, Borneo, Sarawak, Malaysia. These roots keep tall and top-heavy tropical rainforest trees from falling over. (B) Epiphytes growing on trees in Rio Frio, Cano Negro Nature Reserve, Costa Rica. Epiphytes have no contact with the ground. They derive all their nutrients and water from rainwater that collects in their leaves and in the crooks of the tree limbs. (A. Anders Blomqvist/Lonely Planet Images/Getty Images; B. © Oliver Gerhard/Imagebroker RF Getty Images)*

Picture This

Geoglyphs

(© Sanna Saunaluoma)

Lost Cities of the Amazon

More than 200 mysterious trench systems in the ground, called *geoglyphs*, have been found in recent years throughout the Amazon rainforest as trees have been cleared away. Many more are likely to be discovered as deforestation continues. The geoglyphs were built some 2,000 years ago, but it is not clear why they were built. They indicate that large permanent settlements, or "lost cities," may have once existed in the rainforest.

> **What are the "lost cities" of the Amazon?***

Amazon rainforest soils are typically nutrient-poor and reddish in color (see Section 9.1). In the lost cities, the soil, called *terra preta*, or "black earth," is uncharacteristically rich with organic matter and dark in color. The inhabitants of these ancient settlements built up the soil with charcoal, their own waste, animal bones, and food scraps. These modifications would have made the soil more suitable for growing crops to feed large populations. Most scientists in the past had assumed that there were few permanent human settlements in the Amazon. Based on these archaeological sites, some scientists now estimate that populations in the Amazon could have been as high as 10 million.

Consider This

1. Is *terra preta* an anthropogenic soil? Explain.

2. Do people modify soils today? If so, how?

tropical plants produce nutritious and brightly colored fruits and seeds to attract animal dispersers. In some tropical rainforests, up to 90% of plant species are pollinated by animals.

Where there is volcanic activity, such as throughout Indonesia, tropical rainforest soils are young and nutrient-rich because they are continually replenished by volcanic ash. However, most tropical rainforest soils (called *oxisols*, see Section 9.1) are poor in nutrients. *Soil weathering* (chemical disintegration) in the warm, humid climate and *leaching* by heavy rainfall move nutrients deep into the soil out of the reach of plant roots. Decaying organic material is quickly taken up by the shallow root systems of the forest vegetation, rather than entering the soils.

Soils in the Amazon rainforest are particularly nutrient-poor due to leaching. People living in the Amazon long ago modified the soils to support farming. Those modified soils are still being discovered today, as **Picture This** above discusses.

Human Footprint

Natural resources are like large bank accounts: Spend all the money in one shopping spree, and it disappears. Carefully manage it, live off the interest, and it can last generations. The same is true of rainforests and other natural resources. Currently, undisturbed tropical rainforest is quickly being lost through deforestation. **Figure 8.7** shows the typical sequence of events that cause deforestation in the Amazon rainforest. The important issue of habitat loss and fragmentation is further explored in the Geographic Perspectives at the end of this chapter.

Each geographic region has unique factors that drive rainforest loss. While hardwood logging, cattle ranching, and soybean and sugarcane cultivation are driving rainforest loss in the Amazon, Indonesia is losing its rainforests to the production of palm oil. **Picture This** on the facing page explores the Indonesian palm oil industry as a force of deforestation.

*Answers to the Living Physical Geography questions are found on page 293.

FIGURE 8.7 **GEO-GRAPHIC: Economic development of the Amazon.** *Deforestation in the Amazon rainforest often follows the sequence outlined here. Increasingly, the slash-and-burn step is being skipped, as commercial logging is followed directly by commercial-scale cattle ranching and agriculture. Between 2000 and 2006, an average of approximately 21,000 km² (8,100 mi²) of Brazilian rainforest was lost each year. (1. © Stuart Wilson/Photo Researchers RM/Getty Images; 2. © Colin Jones/Impact/HIP/The Image Works; 3. © Guido van der Werf, Vrije Universiteit, Amsterdam)*

1. Roads and logging

Logging companies or local political bodies build roads into remote, untouched forested regions. Valuable hardwood trees, such as teak and mahogany, are selectively removed from the forest.

2. Subsistence slash-and-burn agriculture

Logging roads make the forest accessible to poverty-stricken, small-scale, *subsistence* farmers who cut the forests down (or *slash* them), burn the vegetation, and then plant crops. The nutrient-poor soils require them to move on after 3 to 4 years to another plot, where they must burn and plant again in a continuing *slash-and-burn* cycle.

3. Commercial ranching and agriculture

About 90% of all deforested areas in the Amazon are currently being grazed by cattle. Beef and leather are exported mainly to Asian, North American, and European markets. Soybeans and sugarcane are grown for export and to make *biofuels* for vehicles in Brazil.

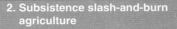

Picture This

Orangutans and Palm Oil

Orangutans (*Pongo pygmaeus* and *Pongo abelii*) are among the most intelligent land animals, and they are one of the closest living relatives of humans. Their name comes from the Malay words *orang hutan*, which mean "man of the forest." They live only in the rainforests of Sumatra and Borneo. They have lost over 80% of their original habitat, and their populations have been halved in the last few decades, dropping to about 60,000 individuals. If the current rates of deforestation continue, most scientists believe orangutans will be extinct in the wild within two decades.

> How can using biofuels harm Indonesia's orangutans?

A new and powerful driver of deforestation and habitat loss has been the international demand for palm oil. About 85% of the world's palm oil comes from Malaysia and Indonesia. Palm oil is made from the seeds of the African oil palm (*Elaeis guineensis*), which is grown on large plantations, often on cleared rainforest land (center photo). The tree is native to western Africa. Palm oil has a wide range of uses, from cosmetics to foods to lubricants and, increasingly, biofuels for cars and trucks. Palm oil is used in about 50% of the packaged products in a typical grocery store. It can be difficult to detect because it is often processed into palm-oil derivatives or labeled as "vegetable oil." *(Top, © Guenter Guni/E+/Getty Images; center, © Michael Thirnbeck/FlickrVision/Getty Images)*

Consider This

1. How does the biodiversity of the original orangutan habitat compare with the biodiversity of a palm-oil plantation?

2. Trace the connection between the future of orangutans in the wild and a box of cookies in the grocery store.

The tropical rainforest biome is home to approximately 40% of all species on Earth. So this biome is central to efforts to estimate the global extinction rate. The global extinction rate is in large part a reflection of the rate of deforestation in this biome. A recent assessment published in *Science* in 2013 states that there are anywhere from 5 million to 8 million species worldwide. About 1% to 5% of those species are lost each decade, mostly because of habitat loss, and mostly in tropical rainforests. **Crunch the Numbers** asks you to use these figures to estimate about how many species are being lost each year.

Consumers of many of the products that are driving rainforest loss—such as palm oil, soybeans, beef, and hardwood lumber—are becoming increasingly aware of the connection between these products and the forests from which they come. For example, a growing number of governments and companies require that imports of palm oil are sourced from growers that meet stringent sustainability requirements, including the use of farming methods that do not cause deforestation. Roughly 45 million metric tons of palm oil are produced each year, and about 13% (6 million metric tons) is certified as sustainable. This percentage, though small, is growing.

Tropical Seasonal Forest

The **tropical seasonal forest** biome is less well known than the tropical rainforest. In the summer wet season, it is often mistaken for tropical rainforest, but it is distinguished from that biome by its winter dry season. The tropical seasonal forest biome is found in the warm lowland tropics, where it borders tropical rainforest **(Figure 8.8)**. The tropical seasonal forest is sometimes considered an *ecotone* (a transition between two biomes) for the tropical rainforest and the tropical savanna. Many trees in this biome are broad-leaved and deciduous. A *deciduous* tree or shrub sheds its leaves, leaving bare branches. In the tropical seasonal forest biome, many trees shed their leaves in response to winter drought.

The most distinctive characteristic that separates the tropical seasonal forest from the tropical rainforest is a dry season in the winter that lasts weeks to months. Throughout South Asia, summer precipitation in the tropical seasonal forest comes from the summer monsoon. There are only three dominant layers in most tropical seasonal forests: canopy, shrubs, and forest floor. The canopy is lower and more open than that of the tropical rainforest, so more light reaches the forest floor. The diversity of insects, birds, mammals, reptiles, and amphibians is, in many cases, nearly as high as that of the tropical rainforest.

Human Footprint

As a result of the dry season, the tropical seasonal forest is extremely vulnerable to fire. It is easy to burn the forest during the dry season. Increasing pressure from growing human populations, coupled with poverty, force people into the forest for subsistence farming. The soils of the tropical seasonal dry forest are better suited for crops and grazing than the soils of tropical rainforests.

Tropical Savanna

Tropical seasonal forest grades into tropical savanna, which is centered at about 25 degrees north and south latitude **(Figure 8.9** on page 266). **Tropical savanna** is characterized by wet summers and dry winters. Tropical savanna is a woodland biome, characterized by widely spaced trees with a continuous cover of grass. The winter dry period lasts much longer in tropical savanna than in tropical seasonal forest, as long as seven months in some locations. In the drier portions of tropical savanna, where the winter dry season lasts for six months or more, a type of tropical savanna called *thorn woodland* is found. In thorn woodland, the vegetation is dominated by shrubs and small trees that are tough and thorny. This growth form is a response to frequent fires, grazing by animals, and prolonged drought.

The tropical savanna has low biomass and low biodiversity. Three factors strongly influence its vegetation structure:

1. *Seasonally intense rainfall:* The rainfall arrives with the ITCZ in summer, all within a few months, and often as intense thunderstorms. Deciduous plants grow during the rainy season and go dormant during the dry season.

---

tropical seasonal forest
A biome in the warm lowland tropics, characterized by high biodiversity and trees that are deciduous in response to winter drought.

tropical savanna
A woodland biome with a wet summer and dry winter climate pattern, characterized by widely spaced trees with a grass understory.

> ### CRUNCH THE NUMBERS:
> ## Estimating the Global Rate of Species Extinction
>
> Assuming the global extinction rate is 3% of species per decade, calculate the range of annual species loss worldwide. First, assume that there are 5 million species. Then do the same calculation, but with the assumption there are 8 million species.
>
> 1. Calculate species loss per decade by multiplying 3% by the estimated number of species.
>
> 2. Divide your answer by 10 to get the annual rate of species loss.

FIGURE 8.8 **Tropical seasonal forest.** *(A) Tropical seasonal forest near Ho Chi Minh City, Vietnam. (B) Climate diagram for Ho Chi Minh City. Average annual temperatures in this biome are similar to those of the tropical rainforest biome, never dropping below 18°C (64°F). Precipitation averages 150 to 250 cm (60 to 98 in) per year. (C) Most of the tropical seasonal forest lies within the tropics. In India, however, it was once found as far north as 30 degrees latitude (but has been converted to agriculture). (A. mathess/iStock/360/Getty Images)*

A

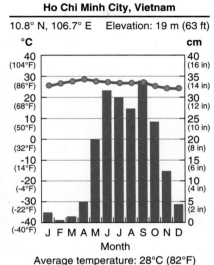

B

Ho Chi Minh City, Vietnam

10.8° N, 106.7° E   Elevation: 19 m (63 ft)

Average temperature: 28°C (82°F)
Total precipitation: 193 cm (76 in)

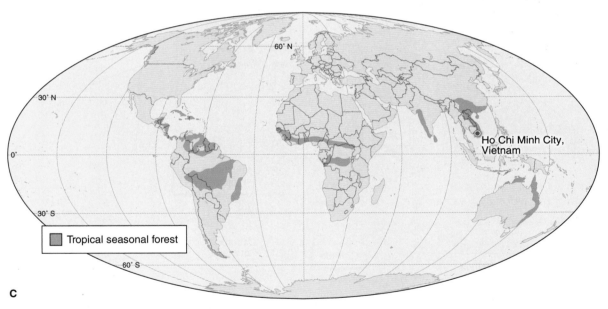

C

Tropical seasonal forest

Tropical Seasonal Forest	
Köppen climate zone	Tropical monsoon: Am
Vegetation	Broad-leaved deciduous trees, shrubs
Notable features	ITCZ-dominated, some water stress in winter; winter fires are common; high biodiversity
Human footprint	Mostly converted to agriculture

FIGURE 8.9 **Tropical savanna.** *(A) An African bull elephant (Loxodonta africana) in tropical savanna near the Okavango Delta, Botswana. (B) Climate diagram for Gaborone, Botswana. (Note that Gaborone is in the Southern Hemisphere, so the summer rainy season occurs in November through March.) In tropical savanna, average annual temperatures range from 15°C to 30°C (59°F to 86°F). Winters are warm. Annual average rainfall ranges from 40 to 175 cm (16 to 68 in). Thorn woodland may receive as little as 30 cm (12 in) of rainfall per year. (C) Tropical savanna has many local names, as labeled here. Half of all tropical savanna is found in Africa, where the biome covers about 65% of the continent. (A. © AfriPics.com/Alamy)*

A

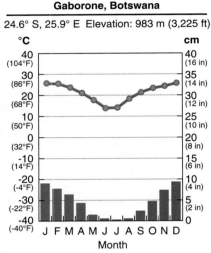

B

Gaborone, Botswana

24.6° S, 25.9° E Elevation: 983 m (3,225 ft)

Average temperature: 21°C (70°F)
Total precipitation: 53 cm (21 in)

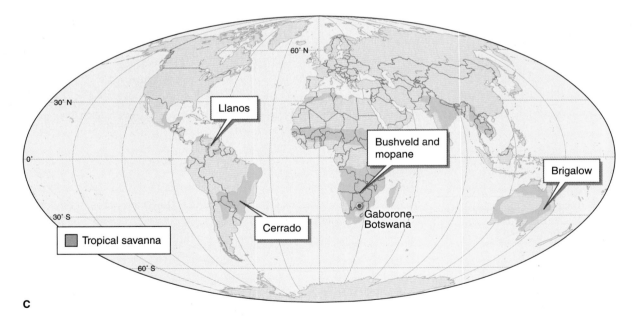

C

Tropical Savanna	
Köppen climate zones	Tropical savanna: Aw; Subtropical steppe: BSh
Vegetation	Broad-leaved deciduous trees, woody and thorny shrubs, grass and forb understory
Notable features	Water stress in winter, summer rain from the ITCZ; frequent fires and plant adaptations to drought and fire are common; large grazing animals (in Africa); low biomass
Human footprint	Overgrazing by livestock leading to desertification; hunting and poaching of large animals

FIGURE 8.10 **GEO-GRAPHIC:** **African savanna grazing sequence.** *Different herbivorous mammals eat different parts of plants at different times. This variation allows large populations of many species to coexist in the same region without exhausting the resources. As the monsoon rains diminish and the vegetation dries, the animals migrate to a different area with new growth. This diagram shows a common progression of animals that takes places over weeks and months on the savanna.* *(1. © James Hager/Robert Harding World Imagery/Getty Images; 2. © Jim Richardson/National Geographic/Getty Images; 3. © Vadim Petrakov/Shutterstock.com; 4. © Martin Harvey/ Photolibrary/Getty Images)*

1. Water buffalo

After monsoon rains, water buffalo (*Bubalus bubalis*) arrive first, eat leaves and tall river grasses, then move on.

2. Zebras

The plains zebra (*Equus quagga*) follow the water buffalo. They eat the shortened grasses and new grass growth stimulated by the trampling and grazing of water buffalo.

3. Wildebeests

Wildebeests (*Connochaetes gnou* and *C. taurinus*) eat taller grasses that zebras do not eat.

4. Topi

Topi (*Damaliscus korrigum*), eland (*Taurotragus oryx*), and Thompson's gazelles (*Eudorcas thomsonii*) eat herb and grass growth stimulated by earlier animal activity.

Time

2. *Fire:* During the warm winter dry season, abundant fuel and dry conditions favor frequent fires. Many savanna plants are adapted to survive fires.

3. *Grazing pressure:* More than 90 species of grazing ungulates (hoofed mammals) roam the African tropical savanna. Although the tropical savanna has low overall biomass, it is able to support the world's largest and densest grazing animal community because the animals do not all graze at the same time (**Figure 8.10**).

Human Footprint

One prevalent threat to the tropical savanna biome is overgrazing by livestock, particularly cattle, sheep, and goats. Increased burning by people to stimulate grass growth for livestock is also degrading savanna woodlands and threatening the habitat of native

FIGURE 8.11 **Saving large animals.** *(A) Hunting pressures have reduced the once-widespread populations of the black rhino (Diceros bicornis) in Kenya. In 2011, a subspecies of the black rhino, called the western black rhino, was officially declared extinct. The remaining black rhino populations are critically endangered. (B) Wildlife wardens are armed to protect the animals from poachers.* *(A. Martin Harvey/Gallo Images/Getty Images; B. © Raffaele Meucci/age fotostock)*

A

B

FIGURE 8.12 **SCIENTIFIC INQUIRY: Managing elephant populations.** *To reduce conflicts between elephants and people, scientists have used two main means of managing elephants within national parks: translocation and contraception. (Left, © AfriPics. com/Alamy; right, © Carl de Souza/AFP/Getty Images)*

Translocation
Elephants can be transported from areas of high population densities to areas of low population densities. This method is difficult, dangerous, and costly, and there is no guarantee that the elephant will not return to the place from which it was moved. This photo shows a sedated elephant being hoisted by crane onto a flatbed truck for relocation.

Contraception
Vasectomies are sometimes performed to permanently sterilize male bull elephants, but more often, females are injected with a nonhormonal form of birth control from the safety of a helicopter. This method is effective at managing elephant population numbers, and it is safer, faster, and less costly than male vasectomies, which are permanent. One drawback is that the treatment lasts only one year and must be repeated annually.

grazing ungulates. In addition, populations of these large animals have declined greatly because of hunting for trophies, elephant ivory, and rhinoceros horn (Figure 8.11). An international boycott of ivory has helped to protect elephants from illegal poaching. Many large game preserves and parks have been established throughout Africa to protect its large animals. These parks are also generating significant revenue from travelers called *ecotourists*, who seek to visit natural places (see Section 10.2).

Increasingly, conflicts between African elephants and people have arisen in parts of Africa. In some cases, wildlife conservation measures have allowed elephant populations to increase. More often, however, as a result of human population growth, people have expanded their farms and villages into elephant habitat, escalating the conflicts. As a result, it is sometimes necessary to manage the elephant populations and control their numbers, as detailed in Figure 8.12.

8.3 Midlatitude and High-Latitude Biomes

◎ Describe the major characteristics of mid- and high-latitude biomes and human impacts in each.

temperate grassland
A grass-dominated biome characterized by significant moisture deficits, natural fires, and grazing herbivores.

In this section, we continue traveling higher in latitude as we survey Earth's biomes. Midlatitudes, or *temperate* latitudes, are the transitional regions between warm subtropical air and cold polar air. Temperate biomes experience a large annual temperature range if they are far from the moderating effects of the oceans, but have a smaller annual temperature range if they are near the coast. The five biomes found at middle and high latitudes are temperate grassland, the Mediterranean biome, temperate deciduous forest, temperate rainforest, and boreal forest.

Temperate Grassland

The **temperate grassland** biome is largely dominated by grasses. It is characterized by significant moisture deficits for most of the year, natural fires, and grazing herbivores, all of which keep trees from becoming established. Temperate grasslands are found mostly between 30 and 60 degrees latitude in continental interiors. They go by several local names: *prairie* in North America, *pampas* in South America, *steppe* in Eurasia, and *veldt* in South Africa (Figure 8.13).

About 90% of the plant biomass in temperate grasslands is grasses, but grasses comprise only about 20% of the species diversity. *Forbs* (non-grass herbs) such as milkweed (*Asclepias* spp.), purple coneflower (*Echinacea purpurea*), and black-eyed susan (*Rudbeckia* spp.) greatly increase the plant biodiversity in grasslands in North America. Most of the grassland biomass is found in the roots of grasses, which may have a biomass some three times greater than the aboveground portions of the plant. Generally, taller grasses have deeper and more extensive root systems than shorter grasses.

Before its conversion to agriculture, the temperate grassland of North America was dominated by

FIGURE 8.13 **Temperate grassland.** *(A) The pampas grassland biome near Córdoba, Argentina. (B) Climate diagram for Córdoba. (Note that Córdoba is in the Southern Hemisphere, so the temperature is coolest in June through August.) Most temperate grassland regions have a large annual temperature range, with warm summers and cold winters. Average annual temperatures vary from 18°C (64°F) in South Africa to 2°C (35°F) or less in Canada and Eurasia. Precipitation in grasslands ranges from 30 to 100 cm (12 to 40 in). (C) Temperate grasslands occur extensively in interior North America, Eurasia, southern South America, and southern Africa. There are also scattered temperate grasslands in Madagascar, New Zealand, California, and Australia. Grasslands go by many local names, as shown on this map. (A. © Eduardo Pucheta Photo/Alamy)*

A

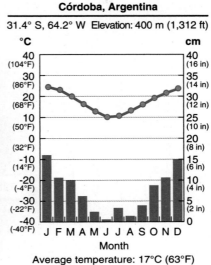

Córdoba, Argentina

31.4° S, 64.2° W Elevation: 400 m (1,312 ft)

Month

Average temperature: 17°C (63°F)

Total precipitation: 87 cm (34 in)

B

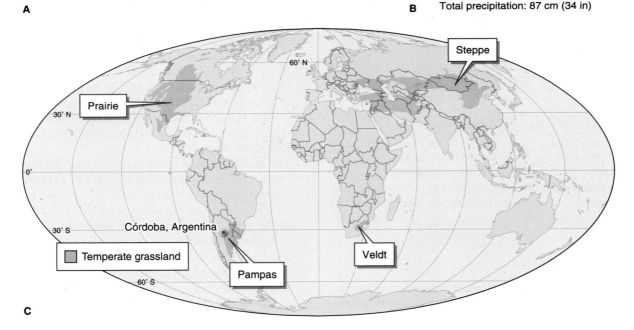

C

Temperate Grassland	
Köppen climate zones	Subtropical steppe: BSh; Midlatitude steppe: BSk
Vegetation	Continuous cover of grasses and forbs
Notable features	Aridity caused by interior locations and the subtropical high; strongly continental climate; moisture deficits in most or all months, too dry for trees; frequent fires; low biomass
Human footprint	Mostly converted to agriculture and rangeland

FIGURE **8.14** **Map of prairie types of North America.** *The height of grasses decreases westward, reflecting the increasing aridity in interior North America. The grassland-desert ecotone lies on the the western margin of the short-grass prairie.*

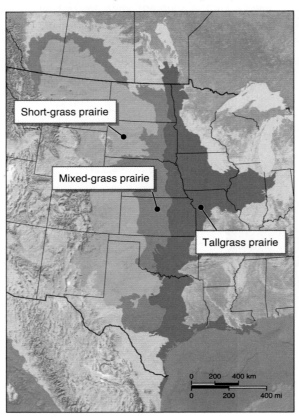

PRAIRIE TYPE	DOMINANT SPECIES
Tallgrass	Big bluestem (*Andropogon gerardii*) and switchgrass (*Panicum virgatum*)
Mixed-grass	Little bluestem (*Schizachyrium scoparium*)
Short-grass	Buffalo grass (*Buchloe dactyloides*)

Mediterranean biome
A biome characterized by hot, dry summers and winter rainfall, with vegetation adapted to drought and fire.

sclerophyllous
Having stiff, leathery, and waxy leaves adapted to reduce water loss and herbivory.

three prairie types: *tallgrass prairie* in the eastern Great Plains, *mixed-grass prairie* in the central Great Plains, and *short-grass prairie* in the western Great Plains **(Figure 8.14)**.

Human Footprint
The temperate grassland biome has been greatly reduced in its geographic extent. This biome is a desirable place for people to live, farm, and raise livestock. Roughly 80% of the original North American prairie is now either developed or being used for commercial agriculture and cattle ranching. The North American grassland ecosystem had many animal species whose populations collapsed with the loss of these grasslands during the early twentieth century. Prairie dogs (*Cynomys* spp.) were important keystone species and are explored further in **Figure 8.15**.

Where temperate grassland has not been converted to agriculture, extensive grazing by cattle has altered this biome. Cattle grazing has changed nearly all of the North American short-grass prairie by allowing non-native plant species to establish themselves and become dominant. Where cattle are grazed intensively, as many as 90% of the plant species are non-native weeds. Moderate cattle grazing, however, can simulate the effects of grazing by the now-scarce bison, to which grasses are adapted, and may therefore be beneficial for the prairie ecosystem. Grassland restoration managers are increasingly seeing the value of cattle as a stand-in for native grazers.

The Mediterranean Biome
The smallest and perhaps most unusual climate zone is that found in the Mediterranean biome. The **Mediterranean biome** is characterized by hot, dry summers and winter rainfall. **Three physical factors control the vegetation structure of the Mediterranean biome: (1) extended summer drought lasting five months or longer, (2) frequent fires, and (3) low soil nutrients and soil organic matter.** Many of its plants are adapted to drought and fire. About half the world's area of this biome is found in the Mediterranean region of southern Europe and northern Africa **(Figure 8.16** on page 272).

The Mediterranean biome has high biodiversity and high endemism, meaning that many species are geographically restricted to it. The fynbos of South Africa and the chaparral of California, for example, each have about 6,000 different plant species. The Mediterranean region has more than 7,000. About half of all plant species in the Mediterranen biome are annuals. A few perennials are summer deciduous. Many plants of this biome have **sclerophyllous** leaves, which are hard, leathery, waxy leaves adapted to reduce water loss and herbivory.

Many plants of the Mediterranean biome display fire-adapted traits, such as serotinous cones, crown sprouting, and thick bark (see Section 7.4). The ecological health of the Mediterranean biome is dependent on fire. Fires cycle nutrients back into the soil and stimulate germination of seeds and vegetation regrowth.

FIGURE 8.15 **GEO-GRAPHIC: Prairie dogs and their partners.** *Prairie dogs are keystone species in North American temperate grasslands. They are mutualistic partners of many grassland organisms, including bison and pronghorn. In addition, prairie dog burrowing improves plant growth in grasslands by aerating the soil and allowing water to better infiltrate the ground. The animals also add nitrogen to the soil with their fecal pellets.* (Left, © Merilee Phillips/Flickr Open/Getty Images; center, © Werner & Kerstin Layer Naturfoto/Picture Press/ Getty Images; right, © Danita Delimont/Gallo Images/Getty Images)

Bison

Bison (*Bison bison*) prefer to forage near prairie dog colonies or "towns," where the prairie dogs' activities improve plant growth. Bison keep the grass around prairie dog colonies short, which gives the prairie dogs a clear view of approaching predators such as birds of prey, foxes, and ferrets.

Prairie dogs

There are five species of prairie dogs in North America. All of them provide habitat or food for many other species including:
• Black-footed ferret (*Mustela nigripes*)
• Burrowing owl (*Athene cunicularia*)
• Ferruginous hawk (*Buteo regalis*)
• Golden eagle (*Aquila chrysaetos*)
• Swift fox (*Vulpes velox*)
• Grasshopper mouse (*Onychomys leucogaster*)

Pronghorn

Pronghorn (*Antilocapra americana*) feed on forbs in preference to grasses, which provide less nutritional benefit. Like bison, they find good forage near prairie dog colonies and help to keep vegetation near the colonies short.

Mutualism   Mutualism

Conservation status

Between 10 million and 75 million bison originally occupied the grasslands of North America. By 1884, the bison was almost extinct because of exploitation by European immigrants. Due to conservation efforts, there are about 15,000 wild-ranging bison in North America today. About 500,000 are raised in captivity for food.

Conservation status

There were originally several billion prairie dogs in North America. Farming and intentional extermination reduced their numbers. By the turn of the twenty-first century, they were at a fraction of their former numbers, and currently all five species are at risk from human activities.

Conservation status

Pronghorn may originally have been more numerous than bison. By 1920, there were about 13,000 left. With careful management, they have increased to nearly 1 million.

Human Footprint

The main anthropogenic agents of change in the Mediterannean biome are agriculture and urban development, overgrazing of livestock (particularly by sheep and goats around the Mediterranean Sea), fire suppression, and non-native plants. California has been particularly hard hit in this last regard, as more than 1,000 non-native plants have established populations there. The native perennial grasses of California have been almost completely replaced by non-native annual species, mostly from the Mediterranean region. The Mediterranean region, in turn, has been invaded by plants from California.

Temperate Deciduous Forest

Temperate forests reflect the precipitation caused by the subpolar low at midlatitudes. There are two kinds of temperate forest: temperate deciduous forest and temperate rainforest.

The **temperate deciduous forest** biome is dominated by trees that shed their leaves in winter in response to low temperatures. Examples of such trees include oak (*Quercus*), maple (*Acer*), elm (*Ulmus*), and beech (*Fagus*). This biome occurs at midlatitudes where the annual temperature range is large and winters bring below-freezing temperatures. As the map in **Figure 8.17** on page 273 shows, this biome is found mainly in the Northern

temperate deciduous forest
A biome dominated by trees that shed their leaves in winter in response to low temperatures.

FIGURE 8.16 **The Mediterranean biome.** *(A) This photo near Tunis, Tunisia, shows the shrubland vegetation structure of the Mediterannean biome. The white strip on the hillside is a firebreak made by people that is designed to contain wildfires. (B) Climate diagram for Tunis. Average annual temperatures in the Mediterranean biome range from 5°C to 20°C (41°F to 68°F), and annual precipitation totals average 50 to 120 cm (19 to 47 in). (C) The Mediterranean biome is centered at about 35 degrees latitude, and it is geographically isolated on the western margins of five different continents. With the exception of the Mediterranean region itself, all of these locations have cold ocean currents offshore that inhibit evaporation of seawater and increase aridity. The Mediterranean biome goes by several different local names in these locations, as shown on this map. (A. © Bruno Barbier/Hemis/Alamy)*

A

B

Tunis, Tunisia

36.82° N, 10.17° E   Elevation: 40 m (131 ft)

Average temperature: 18°C (65°F)
Total precipitation: 46 cm (18 in)

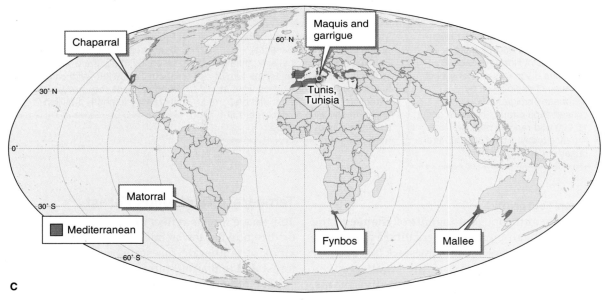

C

Mediterranean Biome	
Köppen climate zones	Mediterranean: Csa, Csb
Vegetation	Few trees; sclerophyllous shrubs; adapted to fire
Notable features	Aridity caused by the subtropical high and cold offshore ocean currents; mild winters, summer drought; frequent fires; high biodiversity
Human footprint	Agriculture, non-native species, human development, fire suppression

FIGURE 8.17 **Temperate deciduous forest.** *(A) Temperate deciduous forest in Cherokee National Forest, near Chattanooga, Tennessee. (B) Climate diagram for Chattanooga. Average annual temperatures in the temperate deciduous forest biome vary from 2°C to 20°C (35°F to 68°F). Average annual precipitation ranges from 50 to 250 cm (20 to 98 in). (C) Temperate deciduous forest is or was located mainly in eastern North America and western Europe, and it was formerly found in eastern Asia. To a lesser extent, it is also found at midlatitudes in South America, Australia, and New Zealand (not shown here). (A. © Raymond Gehman/ National Geographic/Getty Images)*

A

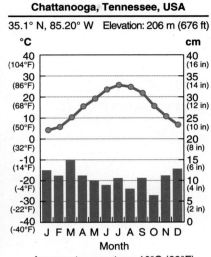

Chattanooga, Tennessee, USA

35.1° N, 85.20° W   Elevation: 206 m (676 ft)

Month

Average temperature: 16°C (60°F)
Total precipitation: 133 cm (52 in)

B

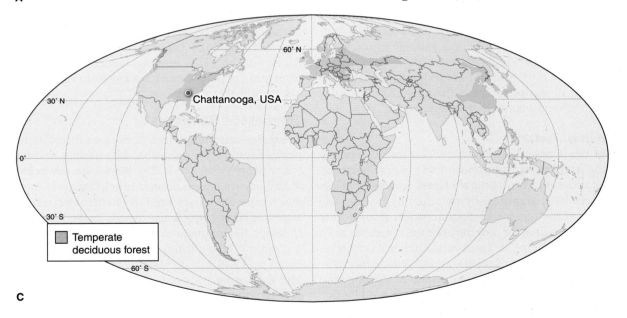

C

Temperate Deciduous Forests	
Köppen climate zones	Humid subtropical: Cfa, Cwa, Cwb; humid continental: Dfa, Dwa, Dfb, Dwb
Vegetation	Broad-leaved deciduous trees
Notable features	Winter storms caused by the subpolar low and summer thunderstorms; cold winters, warm summers; fall colors
Human footprint	Extensively converted to agriculture and urbanized settlement in China and Europe

FIGURE 8.18 **Agricultural fields in County Kerry, Ireland.** *Ireland, like most of northern Europe, has a climate that supports temperate deciduous forest. Throughout Europe, forests were cleared several thousand years ago for farming and livestock grazing. This entirely anthropogenic landscape is maintained by people. If left alone, it would develop into oak and pine forest through ecological succession over many centuries.* (© AIMSTOCK/E+/Getty Images)

Hemisphere because there is more land at mid-latitudes there than in the Southern Hemisphere.

The deciduous trees in these forests lose their leaves through *abscission*, a process triggered by change in light and moisture conditions in the fall. They often turn bright colors as they lose their green chlorophyll, revealing brighter-colored *anthocyanin* pigments beneath.

Human Footprint

In the temperate deciduous forest biome, much of the primary forest has been lost to agriculture and human settlement. **Primary forest** is forest that has never been significantly modified by people. The soils of the temperate deciduous forest are fertile and well suited for farming once the forest has been cleared. Logging for hardwood lumber has also reduced the extent of temperate deciduous forests.

Today, the British Isles, much of Europe, and eastern China have few forests. Instead, they support extensive agricultural systems. The forests in these areas were cleared beginning some 8,000 years ago. Human activities keep the land under agricultural production even though the climate is suitable for the return of forest **(Figure 8.18)**.

Forests that have been cleared or disturbed and regrown are called **secondary forests**. Secondary forests usually have lower biodiversity than primary forests. In some areas, the temperate deciduous forest has rebounded after having once been cut.

In eastern North America, for example, deciduous forests are more geographically extensive and less damaged by acid rain today than they were a century and a half ago. Legislation such as the Clean Air Act in the 1970s (see Section 1.4) and a long-term trend of people moving away from rural areas are responsible.

Temperate Rainforest

Compared with temperate deciduous forest, temperate rainforest is geographically limited, and far fewer people ever see it. The **temperate rainforest** biome occurs where annual precipitation is high and temperatures are mild. It is characterized by large trees that form a dense canopy. In the Northern Hemisphere dominant tree species include western red cedar (*Thuja plicata*), sitka spruce (*Picea sitchensis*), and western hemlock (*Tsuga heterophylla*). The California redwood (*Sequoia sempervirens*) dominates most coastal areas of California. A dense understory layer of vegetation lies beneath the trees. Many epiphytic species, such as ferns, lichens, and *bryophytes* (mosses and their relatives), thrive in the canopy.

Many temperate rainforests are located along the western coasts of continents, where abundant precipitation, fog, and high humidity occur. Evergreen needle-leaved trees dominate this biome in the Northern Hemisphere. In the Southern Hemisphere, evergreen broad-leaved trees, such as the southern beech (*Nothofagus*) and *Eucalyptus*, are more common. As the climate diagram in **Figure 8.19** shows,

> **Why is Ireland mostly treeless?**

primary forest
Forest that has never been significantly modified by people.

secondary forest
Forest that has regrown after being disturbed or cleared by people.

temperate rainforest
A forest biome found mostly on the west coasts of continents where annual precipitation is high; typically has large trees forming a dense canopy.

FIGURE 8.19 **Temperate rainforest.** *(A) Temperate rainforest near Vancouver, British Columbia, Canada. Because of the abundant precipitation and mild temperatures, immense trees dominate these forests if they have not been logged. (B) Climate diagram for Vancouver. Summers are cool and winters are mild. Average annual temperatures in the temperate rainforest biome range from about 3°C to 20°C (37°F to 68°F). Average annual rainfall ranges from 170 to 350 cm (67 to 138 in), and precipitation falls in all months. (C) The temperate rainforest biome is scattered throughout midlatitudes where precipitation is sufficient to support it. The largest intact temperate rainforests are along the coasts of western North America, southern Chile, and southeastern Australia. (A. © Steve Ogle/All Canada Photos/Getty Images)*

A

Vancouver, British Columbia, Canada

49.1° N, 122.6° W   Elevation: 100 m (328 ft)

B

Average temperature: 10°C (51°F)
Total precipitation: 119 cm (47 in)

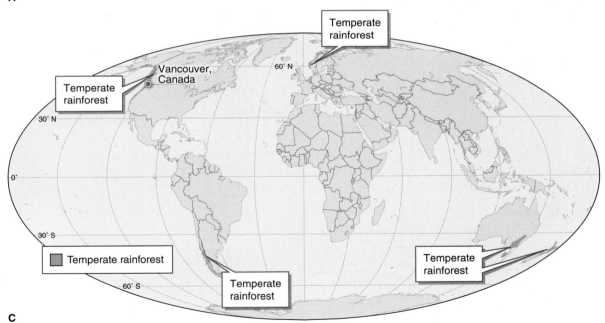

C

Temperate Rainforest	
Köppen climate zones	Marine west coast: Cfb, Cfc
Vegetation	Needle-leaved and broad-leaved evergreen trees and layered forest structure; epiphytes, bryophytes, and ferns are common
Notable features	Coastal locations and orographic precipitation; the subpolar low brings abundant precipitation; mild winters and cool summers
Human footprint	Logging

FIGURE 8.20 **Boreal forest.** (A) The boreal forest near Fort Smith, Northwest Territories, Canada. (B) Climate diagram for Fort Smith. Average annual temperatures in the boreal forest biome range from −5°C to 3°C (23°F to 37°F). Annual precipitation averages 40 to 200 cm (16 to 79 in). (C) The boreal forest, called taiga in Eurasia, extends across North America and Eurasia. It is centered at about 60 degrees north latitude. (A. © Garry Foote)

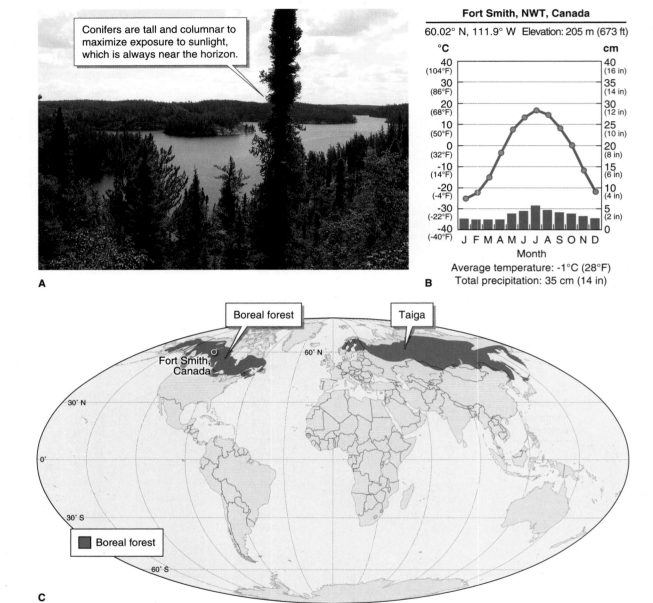

Boreal Forest	
Köppen climate zones	Subarctic: Dfc, Dwc, Dfd, Dwd
Vegetation	Needle-leaved evergreen trees
Notable features	Cold winters and a short summer growing season; found only in the Northern Hemisphere
Human footprint	Logging, oil and mineral extraction

the temperate rainforest receives more precipitation, and has a more moderate maritime climate, than the temperate deciduous forest.

Human Footprint

The future of the temperate rainforest biome has become a political issue, as different sides have fought either to use it for profit or to preserve it. California redwoods, for example, make prized outdoor decking and furniture because of the rot-resistant qualities of their wood. Logging that began in the late 1800s and continued through much of the twentieth century cleared large expanses of old-growth groves of redwoods. Today, only about 5% of the original temperate rainforest in California, Oregon, and Washington has remained unlogged. In British Columbia, about 50% remains, and Alaska has about 90% of its original temperate rainforest, most of it is found in the Tongass National Forest which has largely been protected from logging. Worldwide, about half of the temperate rainforest has been cut. In many areas, temperate rainforest is actively managed as a timber resource.

Boreal Forest

The **boreal forest** is a cold coniferous forest biome found in North America and Eurasia. The boreal forest is among the largest biomes, comprising about one-fourth of all forested land on Earth. This biome occurs in continental interiors where there are low winter temperatures and a short summer growing season. As **Figure 8.20** shows, the boreal forest is not found in the Southern Hemisphere due to the lack of interior continental climates there. Its vegetation is dominated by *coniferous*, or cone-bearing, trees, most of which are needle-leaved and evergreen. Dominant coniferous tree species of this biome include pine (*Pinus*), spruce (*Picea*), fir (*Abies*) and larch (*Larix*). An understory of mosses, lichens, and herbaceous plants lies beneath the canopy.

Fire can be an important factor in the boreal forest during the summer. The fire-return interval ranges from a few decades in the southern portions of the boreal forest to over a thousand years at the northern edge of the forest.

Human Footprint

The boreal forest is the most sparsely populated forested region on Earth. Vast tracts through Eurasia and North America have remained mostly unaltered by people. This is quickly changing, however, as world demand grows for forest products, such as paper and lumber, and minerals, such as petroleum. Recent open-pit mining in Alberta's tar sand deposits has generated considerable conflict between the energy industry's political representatives and those seeking cleaner fuels with fewer environmental impacts in the United States and Canada.

8.4 Biomes Found at All Latitudes

◎ Describe the major characteristics of the biomes found at all latitudes and human impacts in each.

Three biomes occur across a wide range of latitudes. We cover the biomes in this section using a moisture gradient, from wet to dry, rather than latitude. We start with the montane forest biome, then move into the relatively dry tundra, and then conclude with the desert biome.

Montane Forest

The **montane forest** biome occurs where orographic lifting increases precipitation on the windward side of a mountain range (see Section 3.3). The vegetation of the montane forest biome is needle-leaved in the Northern Hemisphere and broad-leaved in the Southern Hemisphere. Because it is found at many latitudes, the montane forest is one of the most climatologically diverse biomes **(Figure 8.21)**.

The montane forests of the Northern Hemisphere are dominated by tree species in the pine family, such as spruce, larch, pine, and fir. The pine family does not occur in the Southern Hemisphere, and montane forests there are dominated by different tree species depending on the location. Evergreen broad-leaved eucalyptus trees, for example, dominate Australia's montane forests. New Zealand's montane forests are dominated by evergreen broad-leaved southern beeches, as are Patagonia's in southern South America.

The world's oldest trees are also found in this biome. High elevations at midlatitudes have low temperatures for much of the year. These low temperatures and a short growing season cause many tree species to grow slowly and live for millennia **(Figure 8.22)**.

> How old is the world's oldest living tree and where is it?

Human Footprint

Commercial logging is a significant factor in montane forests. Many of these forests have been subjected to *clear-cutting*: removal of all trees over a large area. The results are clearly visible from space, as **Figure 8.23** shows.

boreal forest
A cold coniferous forest biome found in North America and Eurasia, with vegetation made up of needle-leaved evergreen trees and an understory of mosses, lichens, and herbaceous plants.

montane forest
A forest biome composed of needle-leaved trees in the Northern Hemisphere and broad-leaved trees in the Southern Hemisphere; found on windward sides of mountains with abundant precipitation.

FIGURE 8.21   **Montane forest.** *(A) Montane forest near Creel, Chihuahua, Mexico. (B) Climate diagram for Creel. Average annual temperatures vary greatly within the montane forest biome depending on elevation and latitude. Average annual precipitation also varies significantly by latitude, with some areas receiving over 250 cm (98 in). As a rule, precipitation is always sufficient to support trees. (C) Montane forest is found in North America from the highlands of Mexico to southern Alaska. Other significant montane forests are found in the Andes in South America, the eastern African highlands, the European Alps, and the mountains of Asia. (A. © Sebastian Rauprich)*

A

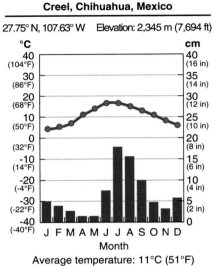

B

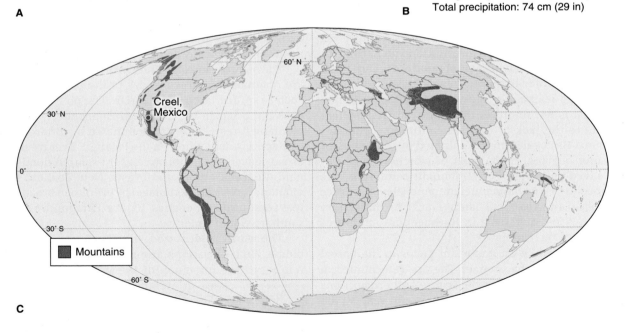

C

Montane Forest	
Köppen climate zone	Cold mountain climates: H
Vegetation	Needle-leaved evergreen trees in the Northern Hemisphere, broad-leaved evergreen trees in the Southern Hemisphere
Notable features	Cool temperatures; at midlatitudes, winters are cold; low seasonality in the tropics
Human footprint	Logging, fire suppression

FIGURE 8.22 **Montane forests are home to ancient trees.** *(A) The longest-lived tree species is the bristlecone pine (Pinus longaeva). The oldest known individual is 5,062 years old. (B) The oldest giant sequoias (Sequoiadendron giganteum) are over 3,000 years old. They are the heaviest single-stemmed trees on the planet. The General Sherman tree, shown here, is 31.3 m (102 ft) in circumference and 83.8 m (275 ft) tall. It weighs almost 2,000 metric tons. (Left, © Rob Blakers/Lonely Planet Images/Getty Images; right, Bruce Gervais)*

A

B

FIGURE 8.23 **Clear-cuts in the Pacific Northwest.** *The montane forests of western Washington and Oregon have few areas that have been spared clear-cutting practices. Clear-cuts are visible here in southern Washington as light patches. The distance across this image is approximately 23 km (14 mi). (NASA)*

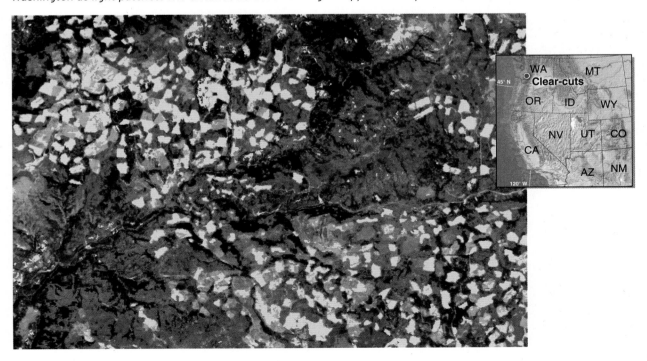

FIGURE 8.24   **Tundra.** *(A) Purple saxifrage (Saxifraga oppositifolia) is typical of the low-growing herbaceous plants in the tundra biome. This plant is in full bloom near Resolute, Nunavut, Canada. (B) Climate diagram for Resolute. Average annual temperatures in tundra range from –15°C to –5°C (–5°F to 23°F). Average annual precipitation varies considerably with latitude, but is generally less than 100 cm (39 in). (C) Most of the tundra biome is found at high northern latitudes. High mountain regions also support tundra. (A. © Wayne Lynch/All Canada Photos/Alamy)*

A

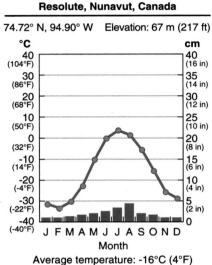

B

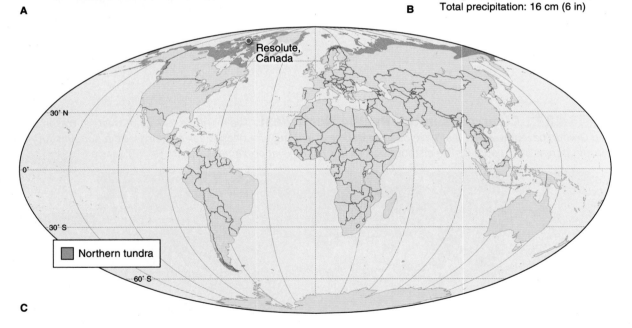

C

Tundra	
Köppen climate zone	Tundra and cold mountain climates: ET, H
Vegetation	Small shrubs and herbs, no trees
Notable features	Very cold winters, short summer growing season; too cold for trees; occurs at high latitudes and high elevations; soils often permanently frozen
Human footprint	Mineral extraction

FIGURE 8.25 **Alpine tree line, Alberta, Canada.** *An alpine tree line (marked by the dotted line) can be seen clearly in this photo in Banff National Park, Alberta. Harsh conditions stunt tree growth and inhibit trees above this line.* (© Daniel Mosquin)

Fire is also a powerful force in the montane forest biome, as we saw in Section 7.4, and many of its plants are adapted to fire. Anthropogenic fire suppression, and the resulting fuel buildup, can result in catastrophic fires that change the forest structure and species composition. To reverse this trend, forest managers are now using prescribed burns and selective cutting to reduce accumulations of fuel. Where these techniques are applied, they can be effective at addressing the problem.

Tundra

The **tundra** biome occurs at any latitude where it is too cold for trees to grow. There are two types of tundra: alpine tundra, found at high elevations, and northern tundra, found at high latitudes in the Northern Hemisphere. **Alpine tundra** is a cold, treeless high-elevation biome whose vegetation consists mainly of shrubs and herbaceous perennials. Alpine tundra occurs in high mountainous areas, including the Canadian Rockies, the Andes, and the Himalayas (see Figure 8.23C). **Northern tundra** is a cold, treeless high-latitude biome, also dominated by herbaceous perennials. It is found north of the boreal forest throughout northern Eurasia and North America **(Figure 8.24)**.

The ecotone between the boreal forest and the northern tundra is called the **northern tree line**. Similarly, the upper limit of trees in mountains,

defined by low temperatures, is called the **alpine tree line** (or *timberline*) **(Figure 8.25)**.

The northern tundra and alpine tundra at mid-latitudes have large annual temperature ranges. Alpine tundra within the tropics, called *tropical alpine scrubland*, has little annual temperature variation. Instead, it experiences diurnal temperature swings: Days are cool and nights below freezing every day of the year. Tropical alpine scrubland occurs above 3,300 m (10,560 ft) elevation and is found in Hawai'i, the Andes of South America, the mountains of East Africa, and in the New Guinea highlands. It is dominated by herbaceous perennials with rosette growth forms. The similarity of the plants in these widely separated locations is an example of ecological equivalence, as **Picture This** on page 282 explains.

Many northern tundra soils are *permafrost* soils, which are frozen just below the surface year-round (see Section 17.1). The vegetation structure of all tundra consists of a single layer of small shrubs and low herbs. Plants remain low to the ground, where it is warmer and where they can be covered by an insulating layer of snow in winter. There are few annual plants in the tundra because the growing season is too short and cold for most plants to complete their life cycle and set seed. The biomass of standing tundra vegetation is low, as is the diversity of species. Many of the same species grow throughout the tundra across broad geographic regions.

tundra
A biome that occurs at any latitude where it is too cold for trees to grow.

alpine tundra
A cold, high-elevation treeless biome with herbaceous perennials.

northern tundra
A cold, treeless high-latitude biome with vegetation consisting of shrubs and herbaceous perennials; found north of the boreal forest throughout northern Eurasia and North America

northern tree line
The northernmost limit of the boreal forest.

alpine tree line
The upper limit of trees in mountains, defined by low temperatures.

Picture This

A

B

C

Ecological Equivalance

All of Earth's biomes reflect the response of the biota to regional climate. Through evolution, different, unrelated groups of plants and animals within similar climates begin to resemble one another. Thus, widely separated but similar climates produce similar plant and animal adaptations. This biome-level resemblance is called *ecological equivalence*.

Although tropical alpine scrublands in different regions are structurally alike, their plant species are genetically unrelated. Different groups of plants have converged on the structure that works best in the Köppen H climate zone in the tropics. Tropical high-elevation settings receive intense ultraviolet radiation. Many tropical alpine plants are adapted to reduce the effects of UV exposure. Many have evolved parabolic *rosettes*, a growth form in which all the leaves emerge from one location on the plant. Reflective silver hairs, also common in tropical alpine plants, reflect UV radiation to protect the plant from its harmful effects. Shown here are the Haleakalā silversword (*Argyroxiphium sandwicense*) of Hawai'i (A), espeletia (*Espeletia pycnophylla*) of the Andes in Ecuador (B), and giant lobelia (*Lobelia deckenii*) on Mt. Kilimanjaro in Tanzania (C). *(A. © Rich Reid/NationalGeographic/Getty Images; B. © Christian Heeb/ Prisma BildagenturAG/Alamy; C. Photo © Marjn van den Brink)*

Consider This

1. Why do plants in two geographically separate areas with dissimilar climates not develop ecological equivalence?

2. How does ecological equivalence illustrate convergent evolution (see Section 7.1)?

An important feature of the northern tundra is the number of migratory animals it receives each summer. Although its summers are brief, they are productive because the daylight hours are very long. North of the Arctic Circle, the Sun does not set (see Section 2.1). As a result, biological productivity experiences a brief burst in summer. Many bird species use the northern tundra for summer breeding.

Human Footprint

Because of the tundra's remoteness and harsh conditions, the human footprint in this biome is limited. Human impacts are occurring mostly through road building and resource extraction. As shown in **Figure 8.26**, the northern tundra is increasingly being developed for its mineral resources, particularly petroleum and minerals.

Oil and gas exploration on the North Slope of Alaska has had an impact on the tundra. Large reserves of natural gas on the Yamal Peninsula of Russia have been developed as well. Metals such as nickel, tungsten, and platinum are extracted from many northern tundra sites, particularly in northern Russia.

Climate change is having a growing impact on tundra permafrost soils. The Arctic is the fastest-warming region on Earth, and tundra ecosystems are rapidly changing as their permafrost soils thaw. Permafrost soils are rich in carbon from organic remains. As they thaw, they emit methane and carbon to the atmosphere, contributing to the greenhouse effect (see Section 17.1).

Desert

Desert is a biome with chronic moisture deficits and sparse, drought-adapted vegetation. The largest of the biomes in area, desert covers nearly 30% of Earth's land surface and is found on every continent. Most deserts receive less than 25 cm (10 in) of annual precipitation. The single largest desert is the Sahara of northern Africa, covering almost 10 million km^2 (3.9 million mi^2) (**Figure 8.27** on page 284).

The three broad groups of deserts are hot deserts (which are located beneath the subtropical high), rain-shadow deserts (on the leeward sides of mountain ranges), and cold deserts (found at high latitudes and high elevations).

1. *Hot deserts*, such as the Namib Desert in Namibia and the Sahara in Northern Africa, are caused by the descending air of the subtropical high in the vicinity of 30 degrees latitude north and south.

2. *Rain-shadow deserts* form on the leeward sides of mountain ranges due to adiabatic heating (see Section 3.3). The Gobi Desert, for example, is found throughout Mongolia in the rain shadow of the Himalayas, the Pamirs, and the Altai ranges. Its location in the continental interior, and its high elevation and resulting low temperatures, also contribute to the Gobi's aridity.

3. *Cold deserts* are found at the poles and at high elevations. Polar regions are deserts because cold air has low water vapor content. The McMurdo dry valleys of Antarctica, for example, are exceedingly cold and arid.

In many deserts, a combination of factors causes aridity. For example, the Atacama Desert of Chile averages 0.4 cm (0.15 in) of precipitation per year and is among the driest locations on Earth. It lies in the rain shadow of the Andes and is under the influence of the subtropical high. In addition, a cold offshore current inhibits evaporation and rainfall from the Pacific Ocean.

In all deserts, plants and animals exhibit a wide range of physiological and behavioral responses to the scarcity of water, including deep roots to reach water and germination from seeds (see Section 7.2).

Human Footprint

Deserts are largely off-limits to permanent human settlement because of the lack of available water. As a result, human impacts have been relatively light in this biome. There are places, however, where large populations live in the desert biome. In the United States, for example, Las Vegas, Nevada, and Phoenix, Arizona, are located in deserts. These cities import water, mostly from the Colorado River, or pump it from the ground. This water use has reduced stream flow and influenced the ecology of many streams and riparian (streamside) areas significantly. Other rivers that flow through deserts include the Indus River, which flows through the deserts of eastern Pakistan and western India, and the Nile River, which flows through the easternmost Sahara. These rivers support large populations along their courses. People have lived sustainably in these desert areas for millennia.

desert
A biome with chronic moisture deficits and drought-adapted vegetation.

FIGURE 8.26 Ekati diamond mine, Yellowknife, Northwest Territories, Canada. *Canada is the second largest diamond producer in the world, after Russia. The Ekati Diamond Mine is North America's first commercial diamond mine and one of the largest diamond mines in the world. Open-pit mines such as this one permanently alter the landscape. These pits are about 0.75 km (0.5 mi) across and several hundred feet deep. (Jason Pineau/All Canada Photos/Getty Images)*

FIGURE **8.27**   **Desert.** *(A) The Sahara near Salah, Algeria. (B) Climate diagram for Salah. (C) The largest and driest deserts are found beneath the subtropical high, centered at about 30 degrees latitude north and south, but deserts are found at other latitudes as well. (A. © Raouf Djaiz)*

A

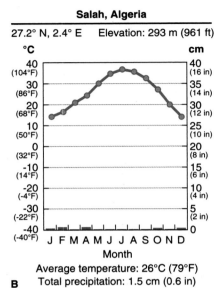

B

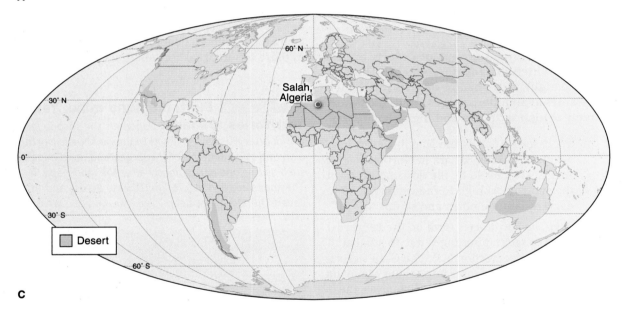

C

Desert	
Köppen climate zone	Subtropical desert: BWh; midlatitude desert: BWk; ice sheet: EF
Vegetation	Xerophytes
Notable features	Severe moisture deficits in most or all months; very low biomass
Human footprint	Water diversion from rivers, off-road vehicles, solar power facilities, livestock grazing

GEOGRAPHIC PERSPECTIVES
8.5 The Value of Nature

◎ Assess the connection between the well-being of people and the well-being of nature.

Human modification of the environment is one of the prevailing themes in our tour of biomes. All biomes have been modified by people, some more than others. The concept of natural biomes, as described in this chapter, provides a background for the current mosaic of human land uses, as shown in Figure 8.28.

Habitat fragmentation is the division and reduction of natural habitat into smaller pieces by human activity. In his book *Song of the Dodo*, David Quammen

habitat fragmentation
The division and reduction of natural habitat into smaller pieces by human activity.

FIGURE **8.28**   **Human land uses.** *A GIS was used to map the different types of human activities that are affecting natural biomes. In some regions, such as in India and eastern China, the original natural biomes no longer exist. In other regions, such as northern Canada, the natural biomes are intact.* (Erle C. Ellis, University of Maryland, Baltimore County http://ecotope. org/anthromes/v2)

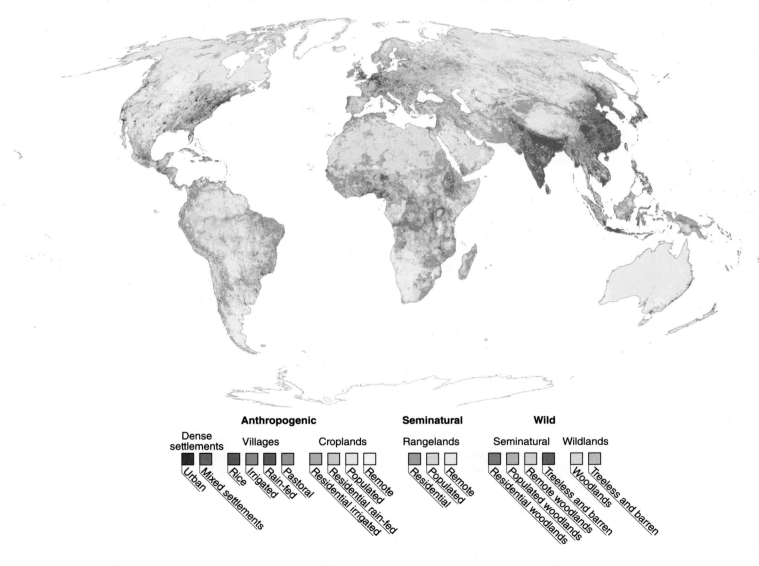

Anthropogenic

Dense settlements
- Urban
- Mixed settlements

Villages
- Rice
- Irrigated
- Rain-fed
- Pastoral

Croplands
- Residential irrigated
- Residential rain-fed
- Populated
- Remote

Seminatural

Rangelands
- Residential
- Populated
- Remote

Wild

Seminatural
- Residential woodlands
- Populated woodlands
- Remote woodlands
- Treeless and barren

Wildlands
- Woodlands
- Treeless and barren

FIGURE 8.29 **GEO-GRAPHIC: Historic and modern threats to habitat and species.** *(From left to right: © Jack Nevitt Photography/Flickr/Getty Images; © Hong Liu, Florida International University; © Thomas Kokta/Photolibrary/Getty Images; © Mark Carwardine/naturepl.com; U.S. Fish & Wildlife Service)*

Feathers and fur

The snowy egret (*Egretta thula*) nearly went extinct as it was killed for its feathers for Victorian fashion. Many fur-bearing animals, such as seals and mink, were hunted nearly to extinction.

Beauty

Plant collectors drive plants to rarity and extinction. This *Geodorum* orchid is sought after by collectors because it is exceedingly rare.

Bushmeat

Mountain gorillas (*Gorilla beringei*) are hunted for their meat (called *bushmeat*). Deforestation and human settlement are also reducing their numbers.

Pseudo-medicine

Animal body parts, such as rhino horns, are coveted for their supposed medicinal qualities. This rhino's horns have been intentionally removed so poachers will lose interest in it.

Non-native species

Introductions of exotic species can cause serious problems for native organisms. When avian malaria was introduced into Hawai'i, it decimated many native bird species, including the Hawaiian crow (*Corvus hawaiiensis*).

compares the process of habitat fragmentation to cutting up a Persian rug: A whole Persian rug functions exquisitely, but if the rug is cut into pieces, it becomes worthless. Our tour of biomes has revealed that habitat fragmentation is reducing Earth's natural biomes and ecosystems into ever-smaller pieces that are surrounded by anthropogenic landscapes.

India, Java, and much of eastern China are bright blue and purple in Figure 8.28, indicating villages with large human populations engaged in irrigated and rain-fed agriculture. The seasonal tropical forest and tropical savanna biomes that would occur naturally in India are completely gone, as are China's temperate deciduous forests. The slopes of the Himalayas, once montane forest, are now mainly rice-growing agricultural settlements and dense mixed settlements.

Food production accounts for a large proportion of human land use. The most widespread human land use is rangelands, where domesticated livestock graze. Rangelands are followed by *croplands*, the second most widespread human land use.

Habitat and Species Loss

Over the last 500 years, hunting pressure was responsible for over 90% of the extinctions of mammals and birds. **Today, habitat fragmentation, climate change, and competition from non-native species are the most significant factors causing species endangerment and extinction.** Figure 8.29 discusses examples of other factors that are or have been important in threatening species and their habitat.

Most of us do not hunt rhinos for their horns or orchids for our collections. But we all contribute to habitat fragmentation. The materials people use and the foods people eat come to us through a global network of trade. International trade, driven by consumer demand, accounts for 30% of the threats to species worldwide. Research published in the journal *Nature* in June 2012 details the relationships between international demand for goods and threats to species resulting from those demands. Many of the goods and materials North Americans and Europeans enjoy originate overseas, where their extraction or production takes an environmental toll. Coffee, for example, comes from Brazil, beef from Argentina, cacao (chocolate) from Central America, and palm oil from Indonesia. Figure 8.30 links these goods to the ecosystems from which they come.

The Value of Natural Biomes

Why should anyone care about the loss of a rare orchid, or a spider monkey in Central America? It is unfortunate that 21,000 km² (8,100 mi²) of Amazon rainforest are lost each year, and with it, probably several thousand species never before seen by people. But does it matter in a practical sense? Most people will never see a tropical rainforest. Fewer still will ever see a spider monkey outside a zoo.

Trade in coffee and chocolate is thriving. Is that not good? People matter, too. Why should we value orchids and spider monkeys? In a strictly self-serving sense, we should care about other species and their natural environments because they support people in many ways:

• *Material resources:* Think about the materials around you right now—the table, your phone, this book, your clothes and food, the materials in the building you are in. All of these materials, without exception, were at one point resources found in nature. Humans depend on nature for raw resources. When we degrade ecosystems we reduce their natural resources.

• *Ecosystem services:* Natural ecosystems and the species in them provide humans with clean air and drinking water, fertile soil, filtration of pollutants along coastal zones, buffers against hurricane storm surges, pollination of food crops, and potential new compounds for medicines. These benefits can all be viewed as services because people need them for their health and sustenance.

• *Aesthetic delight:* Without vibrant and healthy nature, the world would be gritty, boring, and monotonous. Ecosystems and their species do more than clean the air and water and fill our stomachs—they feed our spirits. Without the complete Persian rug of life, the world is less interesting and nurturing for people.

• *Ecotourism revenue:* Although not without controversy, ecotourism provides important revenue sources for many regions. People travel long distances to see wild places, and in so doing, they create a significant revenue source for people in the places they visit.

FIGURE **8.30** **Habitat loss.** *Unless they are locally produced or responsibly produced in the host country, many of the goods we use are connected to habitat degradation and species endangerment far away. (Left, © Alex Robinson/AWL Images/Getty Images; right, © happydancing/Shutterstock.com)*

Mexico, Central America

United States, Canada, Europe

The spider monkey (*Ateles geoffroyi*) is critically threatened in Mexico and Central America by expansion of coffee and cacao plantations.

Demand for coffee and chocolate in the United States, Canada, and Europe drives habitat loss in Mexico and Central America and threatens the spider monkey.

Video Economics lesson http://qrs.ly/la44ou6

• *Climate stabilization:* Saving species forestalls climate change. Saving the orangutan, for instance, requires saving the forests in which these animals live. Healthy forests absorb carbon dioxide from the atmosphere and slow the rate at which this greenhouse gas warms the planet (see Chapter 6). Deforestation releases the carbon stored in trees and the soil to the atmosphere.

Humans are connected to and supported by the biosphere. Saving species and their habitats maintains natural resources, preserves ecosystem services, generates revenue through ecotourism, and preserves a richer and more interesting world. Saving species also addresses the problem of climate change. So the answer to the question, "Do people matter?" is resoundingly yes. The health and well-being of people are inextricably connected to the health and well-being of the biosphere.

CHAPTER 8 Exploring with ☺ Google Earth

To complete these problems, first read the chapter. When you are finished, go to LaunchPad and open the Exploring with Google Earth file for this chapter. Click on the "Workbook Problems" folder to "fly" to each of the problems listed below and answer the questions. Be sure to keep your "Borders and Labels" layer activated. Refer to Appendix 4 if you need help using Google Earth.

PROBLEM 8.1 This placemark is located in Québec, Canada.

1. **What biome is found at this placemark?**
   a. Tundra
   b. Boreal forest
   c. Montane forest
   d. Temperate deciduous forest

2. **Zoom in and out. Pan around. Notice the forest's checkerboard pattern. What activity has caused this pattern?**
   a. Mining
   b. Urban development
   c. Logging
   d. Villages

PROBLEM 8.2 This placemark location is persistently rainy and many streams can be seen on the ground.

1. **What is the latitude of this location?**
   a. 0°
   b. 10° N
   c. 15° N
   d. 20° S

2. **What biome is found here?**
   a. Tropical rainforest
   b. Tropical savanna
   c. Desert
   d. Temperate rainforest

3. **What country is this?**
   a. Democratic Republic of the Congo
   b. Equatorial Guinea
   c. Cameroon
   d. Gabon

PROBLEM 8.3 Zoom out to about 800 km (500 mi) eye altitude. Then zoom back in to the placemark by double-clicking it again.

1. **What is the latitude of this location?**
   a. 0°
   b. 9° S
   c. 14° N
   d. 21° S

2. **What biome was once at this placemark?**
   a. Tropical rainforest
   b. Tropical savanna
   c. Desert
   d. Temperate rainforest

3. **What caused the open fields seen here?**
   a. Deforestation by people
   b. Natural processes
   c. Natural fires
   d. None of the above

4. **Zoom in until you can see the circular feature at the placemark. Based on your reading in this chapter, what is the placemarked circular feature?**
   a. A modern irrigation ditch
   b. A modern building foundation
   c. An ancient geoglyph
   d. Local art

5. **What is the diameter of this feature?**
   a. 130 m
   b. 210 m
   c. 500 m
   d. 1,020 m

PROBLEM 8.4 This placemark lands on two georeferenced photographs of dozens of hippopotamuses wallowing in a mud pool. Note that the photos are duplicates and that they are not accurately georeferenced, as they do not align with the river precisely.

1. **In what country is this placemark?**
   a. Burundi
   b. Tanzania
   c. Kenya
   d. Democratic Republic of the Congo

2. **Zoom in to the photos and survey the surrounding vegetation. Based on your assessment of the vegetation in this imagery and the location of this placemark, what is this biome? The hippos themselves provide a clue. You can also use the textbook's biome maps for help.**
   a. Tropical rainforest
   b. Tropical savanna
   c. Desert
   d. Temperate rainforest

PROBLEM 8.5 This placemark lands in the Southern Hemisphere in a thickly forested biome.

1. **In what country is this placemark?**
   a. Argentina
   b. Chile
   c. Uruguay
   d. Bolivia

2. **Based on your reading in this chapter and the text biome maps, what biome is this?**
   a. Temperate deciduous forest
   b. Tropical alpine scrubland
   c. Tropical rainforest
   d. Temperate rainforest

3. **What kinds of trees make up this forest?**
   a. Broad-leaved deciduous
   b. Broad-leaved evergreen
   c. Needle-leaved
   d. Needle-leaved and coniferous

PROBLEM 8.6 This placemark is located in a large desert in central Eurasia.

1. **In what country is this placemark?**
   a. China
   b. India
   c. Kyrgyzstan
   d. Mongolia

2. **What is the name of this desert?**
   a. Taklamakan
   b. Gobi
   c. Sahara
   d. Arabian

3. **What is the elevation at this placemark?**
   a. 1,190 m
   b. 2,050 m
   c. 3,500 m
   d. 4,280 m

4. **What kind of desert is this?**
   a. Hot desert
   b. Rain-shadow desert
   c. Cold desert
   d. A combination of b and c

PROBLEM 8.7 This placemark highlights a locally intense human impact on the environment.

1. **Based on your reading in the text, what is the purpose of this large pit?**
   a. Diamond mining
   b. Coal mining
   c. Logging
   d. Urban settlement

2. **What is the diameter of the pit?**
   a. 0.5 km (0.31 mi)
   b. 1.2 km (0.74 mi)
   c. 2.5 km (1.5 mi)
   d. 4.3 km (2.7 mi)

3. **What country is this?**
   a. Russia
   b. Mongolia
   c. China
   d. Kazakhstan

PROBLEM 8.8 Deactivate any open overlays and activate the Forest Canopy Heights overlay in this folder. This overlay shows the heights of existing forests worldwide, ranging from a few meters (light green) to 70 meters (darkest green areas). Activate your Borders and Labels layer, if it is not already activated, to help orient yourself.

1. **What biome is found at this placemark?**
   a. Temperate deciduous forest
   b. Desert
   c. Boreal forest
   d. Temperate rainforest

PROBLEM 8.9 Keep the Forest Canopy Heights overlay activated to answer this question.

1. **What kind of forest is found at this placemark?**
   a. Temperate deciduous forest
   b. Tropical rainforest
   c. Boreal forest
   d. Temperate rainforest

PROBLEM 8.10 Keep the Forest Canopy Heights overlay activated to answer these questions. This placemark falls in northern Eurasia.

1. **What is this placemark's latitude?**
   a. 40° N
   b. 50° N
   c. 65° N
   d. 75° N

2. **What biome is this?**
   a. Temperate deciduous forest
   b. Tropical rainforest
   c. Boreal forest
   d. Mediterranean

3. **What is the name for the limits of the forest here?**
   a. The alpine tree line
   b. The northern tree line

PROBLEM 8.11 Keep the Forest Canopy Heights overlay activated to answer these questions. This placemark falls in northern Eurasia.

1. **What is this placemark's approximate elevation?**
   a. 1,400 m
   b. 2,500 m
   c. 3,300 m
   d. 4,100 m

2. **What biome is this?**
   a. Montane forest
   b. Boreal forest
   c. Northern tundra
   d. Eastern deciduous forest

3. **What is the name for the limits of the forest here?**
   a. The alpine tree line
   b. The northern tree line

CHAPTER 8 Study Guide

Focus Points

8.1 Climates and Biomes

Biomes: Biomes are regions with a uniform vegetation structure. Their locations are determined mostly by climate.

Köppen climate classification system: The Köppen climate classification system is used to classify different climate types.

8.2 Low-Latitude Biomes

Three biomes: The three low-latitude biomes are tropical rainforest, tropical seasonal forest, and tropical savanna. Tropical rainforest is the most biodiverse of all biomes.

Climate: Low-latitude biomes have warm climates, and they are either wet all year (tropical rainforest) or have a winter dry season.

Vegetation: Plant adaptations in low-latitude biomes vary, from the complex layered structure of the tropical rainforest to the fire-adapted plants of tropical savanna.

Human footprint: Roads, logging, farming, and livestock ranching have had the greatest impacts in low-latitude biomes.

8.3 Midlatitude and High-Latitude Biomes

Five biomes: The five midlatitude and high-latitude biomes are temperate grassland, the Mediterranean biome, temperate deciduous forest, temperate rainforest, and boreal forest.

Climate: Winters are mild in the Mediterrean and temperate rainforest biomes, and they are cold in the other biomes at mid- and high latitudes. Precipitation is lowest in temperate grasslands and highest in temperate rainforests.

Vegetation: Vegetation structure at midlatitudes varies widely, from the dry Mediterranean biome to temperate rainforest, with the world's largest trees. Fire occurs in all midlatitude biomes.

Human footprint: Human impacts includes non-native species and logging in forested biomes and agriculture and livestock operations in grasslands.

8.4 Biomes Found at All Latitudes

Three biomes: Montane forest, tundra, and desert are found at all latitudes. Some montane forests support large trees. Alpine tundra occurs at high elevations, and northern tundra at high latitudes, where it is too cold for trees. Desert has low biomass and drought-adapted vegetation.

Climate: The climates of these biomes vary by latitude. The montane forest biome has sufficient moisture to support forests and is cool. Tundra is always cold. Deserts have perennial moisture deficits and may be hot or cold.

Vegetation: Vegetation in these three biomes ranges from thickly wooded montane forest to the shrubs and herbs of the treeless tundra to the sparsely vegetated open ground of desert.

Human footprint: Human impacts include logging in montane forest, mineral extraction in tundra, and water diversions from desert streams.

8.5 Geographic Perspectives: The Value of Nature

Habitat fragmentation: Habitat fragmentation is the most significant driver of species extinctions today.

International trade: International trade is a driving force in habitat fragmentation and degradation of natural biomes.

Value of natural biomes: Natural biomes provide humans with resources, services, aesthetic value, and climate stabilization.

Key Terms

alpine tree line, 281
alpine tundra, 281
biome, 257
boreal forest, 277
desert, 283
epiphyte, 260
habitat fragmentation, 285
Köppen climate classification system, 257
liana, 259
Mediterranean biome, 270
montane forest, 277
northern tree line, 281

northern tundra, 281
primary forest, 274
sclerophyllous, 270
secondary forest, 274
temperate deciduous forest, 271
temperate grassland, 268
temperate rainforest, 274
terraform, 257
tropical rainforest, 259
tropical savanna, 264
tropical seasonal forest, 264
tundra, 281

Concept Review

The Human Sphere: Terraforming Earth

1. What does the term *terraforming* mean? How does the term relate to human influence on Earth?

8.1 Climates and Biomes

2. What is a biome? What physical factors determine biome type?

3. What is vegetation structure? Plant growth form? Give examples of both.

4. Give examples of botanical terms used in this chapter.

5. Briefly describe the Köppen climate classification system. What are the six major climate types used in this system?

6. Describe the spatial relationship between biomes and climate.

7. For each biome in this chapter, describe where it occurs, the major physical characteristics in terms of biodiversity, its structure, climate, fire's prevalence, and important limiting factors.

8. For each biome, discuss the main human impacts.

8.2 Low-Latitude Biomes

9. Why is it that the Amazon tropical rainforest has poor soils, yet those of Indonesia are rich?

10. What percentage of Earth's species is estimated to live in the tropical rainforest biome? How many species are estimated to go extinct each year?

11. How do poor soils, farming, and deforestation relate to one another in the tropical rainforest?

12. Why is tropical seasonal forest particularly vulnerable to human activities?

13. What other regional names does the tropical savanna go by?

14. What are the three factors that largely shape the tropical savanna biome?

15. What is a grazing sequence, and how does it allow many large animals to use the same areas in the same season?

8.3 Midlatitude and High-Latitude Biomes

16. What other local names does the temperate grassland go by?

17. What three prairie types are found in the North America?

18. Describe the ecological role of the prairie dog. Specify its relationships with bison and pronghorn.

19. What other local names does the Mediterranean biome go by?

20. How does the Mediterranean biome's biodiversity compare with that of other temperate biomes?

21. What is unusual about the climate of the Mediterranean biome?

22. Why does fire often occur in the Mediterranean biome?

23. Define deciduous.

24. What is the most prominent human impact in the temperate deciduous forest biome?

25. What name does the boreal forest go by in Eurasia?

26. Describe the climate and vegetation of the boreal forest.

8.4 Biomes Found at All Latitudes

27. Why is it that forests occur on the windward slopes of mountains but are much less common on the leeward slopes?

28. What is the difference between northern tundra and alpine tundra?

29. What is an alpine tree line? What is a northern tree line?

30. What is tropical alpine scrubland and where is it found? How does it pertain to convergent evolution?

31. Compare the biomass of the desert with the biomass of a tropical rainforest.

32. What is the main limiting factor in deserts?

8.5 Geographic Perspectives: The Value of Nature

33. Give examples of the main types of human land uses that have modified natural biomes.

34. What is currently the main driver of species extinctions?

35. Why should we save a spider monkey species in a remote tropical seasonal forest in Mexico? Of what practical use is the spider monkey to people?

Critical-Thinking Questions

1. Using Figure 8.2, find the biome you live in. Using Figure 8.28, can you tell what its leading category of human land use is now?

2. Many people in Brazil claim that other countries such as the United States have no business telling Brazil not to cut its rainforests because most developed countries (such as the United States) cut their forests early in their histories. Do you agree or disagree with this argument? Explain.

3. Most tropical rainforest canopy trees have a flat, umbrella-like structure. Most boreal forest trees have a narrow, pole-like structure. In the context of solar altitude (see Section 2.1), explain the structure of these trees.

4. Non-native species are often most successful when they are transported to the same or a similar biome. They are less successful if they are transported to a different biome. For example, many invasive plants in California came from the Mediterranean region. Why do you think these plants have been able to successfully establish in California?

5. Besides helping people, can you think of other reasons to save habitat and species?

Test Yourself

Take this quiz to test your chapter knowledge.

1. **True or false?** The Amazon rainforest has nutrient-poor soils.

2. **True or false?** Trees in temperate rainforests and tropical rainforests are mostly evergreen.

3. **True or false?** The geographic distribution of the boreal forest, tundra, tropical alpine scrubland, and tropical savanna all are controlled by low temperatures.

4. **True or false?** Of all the biomes, deserts have the lowest biomass and tropical rainforests have the highest biomass.

5. **True or false?** At small spatial scales, climate is the most important determinant of vegetation structure.

6. **Multiple choice:** Which of the following biomes is characterized by summer drought, winter rain, and frequent fire?
   a. Mediterranean   c. Tropical rainforest
   b. Tundra   d. Tropical savanna

7. **Multiple choice:** Which of the following biomes is treeless due to chronic moisture deficits, grazing, and fire?
   a. Grassland
   b. Tundra
   c. Desert
   d. Tropical alpine scrubland

8. **Multiple choice:** Today, the most important agent of extinction is
   a. exotic species.
   b. hunting.
   c. habitat fragmentation.
   d. climate change.

9. **Fill in the blank:** _____ marks the uppermost elevations of trees in mountains.

10. **Fill in the blank:** An _____ is a plant that lives on other plants.

Picture This. YOUR TURN

Name That Biome

Match each of the following biomes to the photos. Use each biome name only once. Hints for each biome are provided.
(A. © John Warburton-Lee/AWL Images/Getty Images; B. © Micha Pawlitzki/Photographer's Choice/Getty Images; C. © Mark Cosslett/NationalGeographic/Getty Images; D. © Tetra Images/Getty Images)

Northern tundra   Temperate rainforest
Temperate grassland   Tropical savanna

BIOME	PRECIPITATION	TEMPERATURE
A	Summer wet, winter dry	Always warm
B	High year-round	Mild
C	Low, mostly in summer	Very low
D	Low	Hot summers, cold winters

A

B

C

D

Further Reading

1. Lenzen, M., et al. "International Trade Drives Biodiversity Threats in Developing Nations." *Nature* 486 (2012): 109-112.

2. Little, Jane Braxton. "Regrowing Borneo's Rainforest–Tree by Tree." *Scientific American*, December 2008.

3. Quammen, David. *The Song of the Dodo: Island Biogeography in an Age of Extinction.* New York: Scribner, 1997.

Answers to Living Physical Geography Questions

1. **What are the "lost cities" of the Amazon?** The remains of trench systems and modified soils indicate that portions of the Amazon rainforest may have supported large human populations about 2,000 years ago.

2. **How can using biofuels harm Indonesia's orangutans?** Orangutan rainforest habitat is cleared to make way for palm-oil plantations used to make biofuels.

3. **Why is Ireland mostly treeless?** Temperate deciduous forests in Ireland and most of northern Europe were cut by people long ago. If left to nature, the forests would return after centuries.

4. **How old is the world's oldest living tree and where is it?** The world's oldest living tree, a bristlecone pine, is estimated to be 5,062 years old. It is growing in California's White Mountains, at a location that is kept undisclosed to protect it from souvenir seekers.

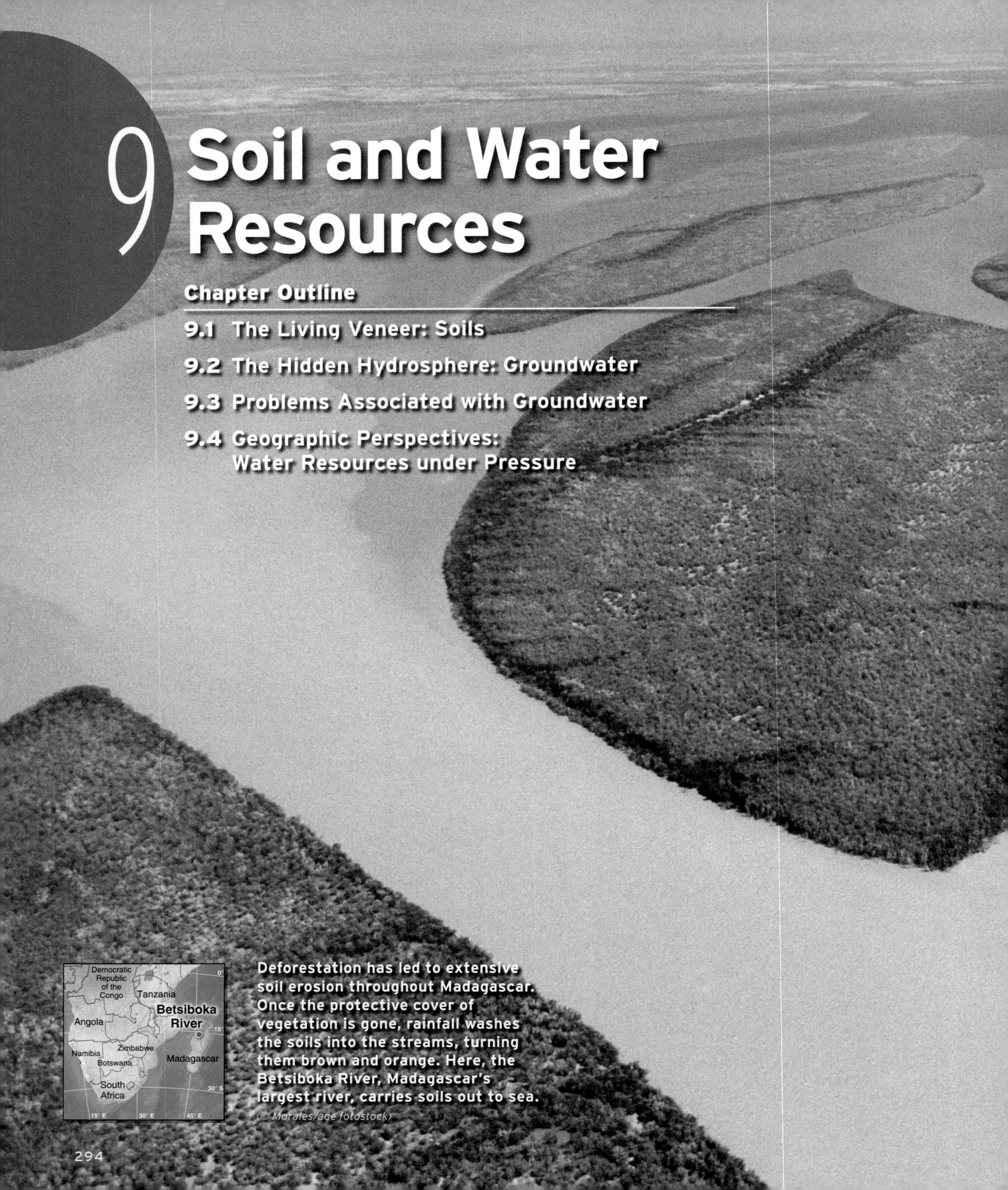

9 Soil and Water Resources

Chapter Outline

9.1 The Living Veneer: Soils

9.2 The Hidden Hydrosphere: Groundwater

9.3 Problems Associated with Groundwater

9.4 Geographic Perspectives: Water Resources under Pressure

Deforestation has led to extensive soil erosion throughout Madagascar. Once the protective cover of vegetation is gone, rainfall washes the soils into the streams, turning them brown and orange. Here, the Betsiboka River, Madagascar's largest river, carries soils out to sea. (© Morales/age fotostock)

LIVING PHYSICAL GEOGRAPHY

➤ What is the difference between dirt and soil?

➤ How long does it take for soils to form?

➤ Why does water in houses gush from the faucets?

➤ How much water is needed to produce 1 kg (2.2 lb) of beef?

To learn more about soil erosion, turn to Section 9.1.

THE BIG PICTURE *Many factors determine soil characteristics, including climate and bedrock. Porous rocks and sediments hold water in the ground. Soils and groundwater are both essential resources for people.*

LEARNING GOALS   *After reading this chapter, you will be able to:*

9.1 ◎ Describe how soils form and erode, and explain why soils are important to people.

9.2 ◎ Explain different features of aquifers and how water moves through the ground.

9.3 ◎ Describe problems with groundwater that result from human activities.

9.4 ◎ Assess the importance of water resources to human societies.

THE HUMAN SPHERE: The Collapse of the Maya

FIGURE 9.1 **A Mayan ruin.**
The Mask Temple in Lamanai, Belize, like most Mayan works, was carved out of limestone. Limestone bedrock probably played a central role in the collapse of the Maya. (© Alex Robinson/AWL Images/Getty Images)

THE COLLAPSE of the powerful Maya civilization is a reminder of the importance of soil and water resources to human societies. Maya society stretched from Mexico's Yucatán Peninsula as far south as southern Honduras and El Salvador (Figure 9.1). Altogether, their complex civilization existed for some 3,100 years, between approximately 2000 BC and 1100 CE. The Maya had one of the most technologically advanced and successful preindustrial civilizations in the world. But over a brief 80-year period (between 1020 and 1100 CE), their civilization disintegrated. Their populations collapsed, and their great inland cities were abandoned.

There have been many hypotheses attempting to explain what caused the demise of the Maya. Wasted natural resources, as a result of perpetual warfare between neighboring Mayan cities, and environmental change are most often cited. In 2012, a study published in the journal *Science* provided new insight. It definitively established that Mayan populations grew as the climate became wetter and shrank in times of drought. This finding suggests that water resources played a key role in the demise of the Maya.

The region in which the Maya lived is composed mostly of limestone bedrock. Water dissolves limestone, creating underground stream systems. There were few surface streams and little available surface water for the Maya. A series of droughts between 1020 and 1100 CE brought great hardship for them. Furthermore, the tropical soils of the Mayan region are low in fertility. Scientists think that drought and the resulting reduction of plant cover probably further reduced the fertility of these soils. A lack of soil and water resources, therefore, probably played a pivotal role in the disappearance of the Maya.

In this chapter, we examine soil and water resources in the context of their importance to modern societies. We first look at soil formation and soils as a natural resource for people. We then explore how water enters and moves through the ground. Finally, we examine water's role as a natural resource.

9.1 The Living Veneer: Soils

◎ **Describe how soils form and erode, and explain why soils are important to people.**

Soils are a fundamentally important natural resource. **Soil** is the layer of sediment closest to Earth's surface that has been modified by organisms and water, and it is the region of the lithosphere into which plant roots extend. The gateway for solar energy entering the terrestrial biosphere, as we have seen, is plant photosynthesis, and almost all land plants are rooted in soil. Without soil, there would be no plants and little life on land.

Even marine ecosystems are tied to soils. Marine phytoplankton (see Section 7.5) use nutrients derived from stream runoff and windblown dust from the continents as well as nutrients (or sediments) stirred up from the seafloor.

Pedogenesis, the process of soil formation, occurs through the weathering of rocks, the activities of organisms, the movement of rainwater, and time. Soils form as weathering breaks down bedrock into smaller fragments. **Bedrock** is rock that is structurally part of and connected to Earth's crust. Any loose Earth material that covers bedrock is called **regolith** (Figure 9.2).

Soil Characteristics

Most soils, when exposed in a *soil profile* (or cross section), have several distinct layers, or horizons. **Soil horizons** are horizontal zones within the soil that are identified by their different physical and chemical properties. Weathering and the activities of organisms create soil horizons. In addition, rainwater carries soil particles downward through the process of **eluviation**. Rainwater also carries dissolved nutrients downward through the process of **leaching**. In the process of *illuviation*, particles and minerals are deposited deeper in the soil. Both eluviation and leaching are important in the development of soil horizons, as shown in Figure 9.3 on page 298.

Most soils contain components from all four of Earth's major physical systems: rock fragments and minerals (lithosphere), water (hydrosphere), air (atmosphere), and organic material (biosphere). Although no two soils are alike, most soils are composed chiefly, by volume (but not by weight), of rock fragments, minerals, and air.

Soil is often described by its texture, which is determined by the relative amounts of sand, silt, and clay composing it. Sand, silt, and clay are inorganic

soil
The layer of sediment that has been modified by organisms and water; the region of the lithosphere into which plant roots extend.

pedogenesis
The process of soil formation.

bedrock
Rock that is structurally part of and connected to Earth's crust.

regolith
Any loose, fragmented Earth material that covers bedrock.

soil horizon
A horizontal zone within the soil identified by its chemical and physical properties.

eluviation
The process by which rainwater carries soil particles downward.

leaching
The process by which rainwater carries dissolved nutrients downward.

FIGURE 9.2 **Regolith.** *Regolith consists of all unconsolidated Earth material, from broken bedrock all the way up to the ground's surface. It is composed of fragments ranging from large rocks to tiny grains of sand, as well as organic material.*

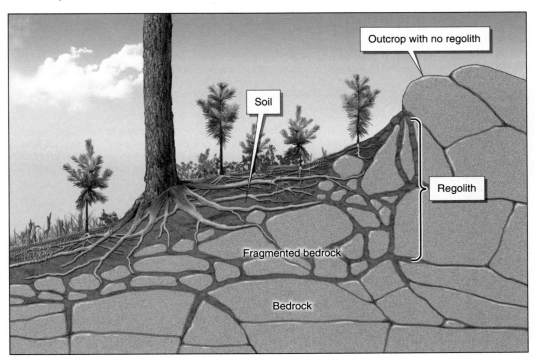

Outcrop with no regolith

Soil

Regolith

Fragmented bedrock

Bedrock

FIGURE 9.3 **GEO-GRAPHIC: Soil and soil horizon development.** *(A) Through weathering and biological activity, surfaces of bare bedrock form soils over time. (B) Eluviation and leaching lead to the formation of soil horizons. (C) There are six main categories of soil horizons, arranged vertically. Few soils have all six categories, and some soils have none. (A. Bruce Gervais)*

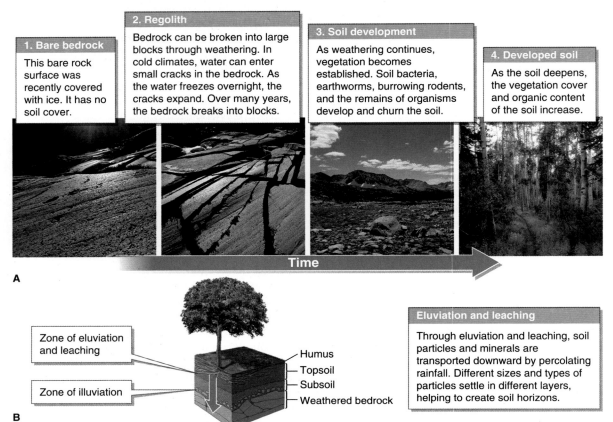

1. Bare bedrock

This bare rock surface was recently covered with ice. It has no soil cover.

2. Regolith

Bedrock can be broken into large blocks through weathering. In cold climates, water can enter small cracks in the bedrock. As the water freezes overnight, the cracks expand. Over many years, the bedrock breaks into blocks.

3. Soil development

As weathering continues, vegetation becomes established. Soil bacteria, earthworms, burrowing rodents, and the remains of organisms develop and churn the soil.

4. Developed soil

As the soil deepens, the vegetation cover and organic content of the soil increase.

Time

A

Zone of eluviation and leaching

Zone of illuviation

Humus
Topsoil
Subsoil
Weathered bedrock

Eluviation and leaching

Through eluviation and leaching, soil particles and minerals are transported downward by percolating rainfall. Different sizes and types of particles settle in different layers, helping to create soil horizons.

B

Soil horizon categories

Through the downward migration of particles and minerals, well-defined soil horizons can form. There are six categories of soil horizons, each a result of soil development, eluviation, leaching, and illuviation.

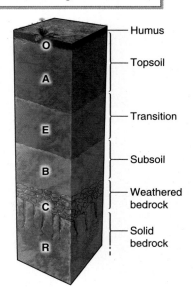

Humus
Topsoil
Transition
Subsoil
Weathered bedrock
Solid bedrock

C

O horizon

The "organic horizon" is the topmost layer, composed mainly of organic material (humus). The best farmlands have a well-developed O horizon.

A horizon

The A horizon (or topsoil) is also rich in organic matter. The activities and remains of organisms play an important part in forming this layer of soil. Most plant roots are restricted to the A horizon.

E horizon

The E horizon is formed by eluviation and leaching as rainwater moves dissolved chemicals and small clay particles deeper to the layers below. The E horizon is lighter in color than the topsoil above, and it represents a transition zone between the topsoil layers and the subsoil and bedrock below.

B horizon

Transported clays and dissolved chemicals are deposited through the process of illuviation in the B horizon, or subsoil. High concentrations of clay, aluminum, and iron are typically found in this horizon.

C horizon

The C horizon is composed of unconsolidated weathered rock sandwiched between the base of the soil horizons above and the bedrock below. There is little to no organic material in the C horizon.

R horizon

The R horizon (for rock) consists mostly of solid, unweathered bedrock.

FIGURE 9.4 **Sand, silt, and clay.**

The relative sizes of sand, silt, and clay particles are shown here. For comparison, human hair is about 0.1 mm or less in diameter.

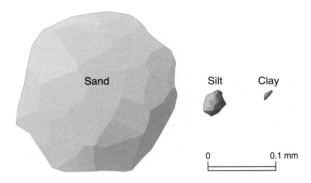

Sand   Silt   Clay

0   0.1 mm

Soil Particle Sizes	
	SIZE (MM)
Sand	0.05–1
Silt	0.002–0.05
Clay	<0.002

soil particles of three size classes **(Figure 9.4)**. Soil textures can be summarized graphically in a *soil texture triangle* **(Figure 9.5)**.

One soil type particularly important to people is loam. **Loam** has a mineral content of about 40% sand, 40% silt, and 20% clay and contains large amounts of organic material. Farmers value loam because it retains and transmits moisture and nutrients that are easily accessible to plants. *Sandy soils* and *rocky soils* are dominated by mineral particles and have low organic content. Large *pores* (or air spaces) between particles allow water to drain from sandy and rocky soils rapidly, and nutrients are quickly leached out of reach of plants. As a result, they make poor agricultural soils. The opposites of sandy and rocky soils are *clay soils* and *silt soils*. Clay and silt particles are extremely small and impede water flow, which makes these soils unsuitable for many plants. Loam is the ideal soil texture for growing crops.

Soil Formation Factors

Many different factors help to determine what types of soils will form in any given place and how fast they will form.

Climate

Temperature, rainfall, and even the types of organisms living in and affecting the soil are a function of climate. **Soil develops most quickly where chemical weathering (the chemical disintegration of rocks) predominates, such as in the lowland tropics, where it is always warm and moist.**

Soil develops more slowly in cold climates and in arid climates. As **Figure 9.6** on page 300 shows, soil types and soil development coincide with the broad latitudinal climate zones determined by global atmospheric pressure systems (see Section 4.3).

Parent Material

A soil's *parent material* is the rock and mineral matter that is weathered into particles of sand, silt, and clay. Parent material is composed of both the weathered bedrock beneath the soil and regolith that has been transported to the site by streams, glaciers, or wind. The type of parent material, which may be granite, basalt, sandstone, or even volcanic ash, plays a part in the chemical composition of the soil, the texture of the soil, and the rate at which soil can form (**Figure 9.7**, page 300).

> **What is the difference between dirt and soil?***

Organisms

"Dirt" is what we track into the house. Soil is the living medium in which we grow our food. **Healthy soil is a teeming metropolis of worms, insects, and microbes that churn and digest organic material.** Without the effects of biological activity, broken bedrock would simply be sterile regolith, composed of gravel and sand, like that found on the Moon or Mars.

The topmost layer of soil, the O horizon, is composed primarily of partially decomposed vegetation such as leaf litter. Just below the O horizon is the A horizon, also called *topsoil*. The A horizon is

loam
Soil that consists of approximately 40% sand, 40% silt, and 20% clay and has a high organic content.

FIGURE 9.5 **Soil texture triangle.** *Soil texture is determined by a soil's relative proportions of sand, silt, and clay.*

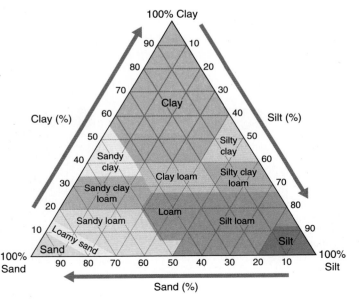

FIGURE 9.6 **Soils and climate zones.** *Generally, the character of soils parallels climate patterns.*

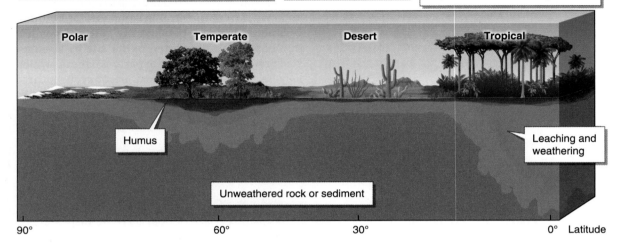

Polar high: Cold	Subpolar low: Cold and moist	Subtropical high: Warm and dry	ITCZ: Warm and wet
Soils are poorly developed or absent in polar regions. Ice cover and insufficient vegetation inhibit soil formation.	Temperate soils have rich and well-developed topsoil due to ample precipitation and biological activity.	Subtropical desert soils are poorly developed due to sparse vegetation and a lack of available moisture.	Tropical soils are deeply weathered due to large amounts of rainfall and warm temperatures that enhance chemical weathering. Rainwater leaches nutrients out of reach of plants. As a result, many tropical soils are nutrient-poor.

thin—its average depth worldwide ranges from about 5 to 20 cm (2 to 8 in).

Soil horizons O and A are strongly influenced by the activities of organisms (see Figure 9.3C). Seeds and plant roots are concentrated in these horizons. Microbes, nematodes, earthworms, beetles, and other insects all digest, *bioturbate* (mix), and build soil. Bioturbation redistributes nutrients and particles throughout the A horizon. Wastes from these organisms and from larger animals also contribute to the chemical and physical structure of these horizons. Soil organisms create **humus**, the brownish-black mixture of organic material that makes up the bulk of these horizons by volume.

On a local level, people can play an important role in soil development. There are many examples of organic-rich anthropogenic soils, including the *terra preta* that was developed by indigenous cultures in the Amazon rainforest (see Section 8.2), *plaggen soils* that were developed throughout Europe during medieval times, and many modern soils developed by composting **(Figure 9.8)**.

Topography and Moisture

The steepness of a slope is directly related to the depth of soil that can develop there. Less regolith accumulates on steeper slopes because gravity pulls it down to low-lying areas. Thick soil can form only where the ground is level. Steeper slopes have thinner soils **(Figure 9.9)**.

Within a climate zone, *aspect* (the direction in which a slope is facing) controls soil moisture. In the Northern Hemisphere, for example, south-facing slopes are usually relatively dry and warm, while those facing north are moister and cooler. Similarly, groundwater (water that flows underground) may rise to the surface as springs in some areas. Factors such as these influence soil structure, and moisture is a key determinant of the type of soil that will form in a given area.

FIGURE 9.7 **Soils and parent material.**
Bedrock that is resistant to weathering forms soils more slowly, and the resulting soils are thinner.

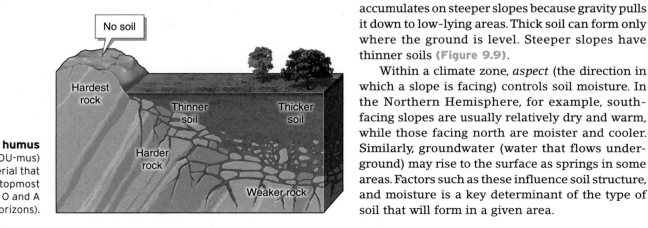

humus
(pronounced HYOU-mus)
Organic material that makes up the topmost layers of soil (the O and A horizons).

FIGURE 9.8 **Anthropogenic soil.** *The soil shown here is a result of San Francisco's mandatory composting ordinance. The city requires all residents and restaurants to compost food scraps and paper food wrappers. Since 1996, when the program was first implemented, over 1 million tons of topsoil have been made from this compost. Farmers often call this composted soil "black gold," referring to both its color and how well their crops grow in it.* (© Jose Luis Villegas/Sacramento Bee/ZUMAPRESS.com)

Time

> How long does it take for soils to form?

Inputs of new inorganic material and biological activity build and renew soils over time. The average thickness of Earth's soils is only about 1 m (3.3 ft). **Soils develop at a rate of 2.5 cm (1 in) per 200 to 1,000 years.** Anthropogenic soils, on the other hand, can be formed in less than a year.

As we have seen, soil formation takes longer in cold climates than in warm climates. In addition, it takes much longer to form soil from bare rock than from sediments such as sand. As **Figure 9.10** illustrates, older rock surfaces are generally covered by thicker soils.

Soil Erosion

The National Academy of Sciences estimates that, as a general trend, the world's croplands are losing soil at a rate 10 to 40 times faster than soil can form naturally. Worldwide, an area of cropland roughly the size of Indiana is significantly degraded

FIGURE 9.9 **Soil and slope.** *Gentle slopes develop thicker soils than steep slopes. Soils cannot form where topography is too steep.*

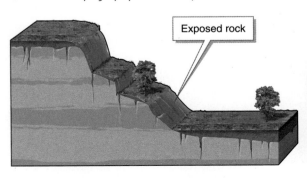

FIGURE 9.10 **Soil and time.** *Older exposures of bedrock have had more time to develop thicker soils than new rock exposures, such as those created by a relatively recent lava flow.*

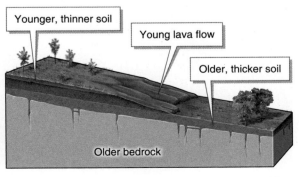

CRUNCH THE NUMBERS: Calculating Soil Loss

Parts of Iowa have experienced net rates of soil loss as fast as 0.1 cm (0.04 in) per year over the last 150 years.

To calculate total soil loss, multiply the annual rate of loss by years.

1. How much topsoil has been lost in the last century and a half in parts of Iowa?

2. If farmers slowed the rate of soil loss to half the rate above, how much soil would be lost in the next 100 years?

or lost every year (about 10 million ha, or 25 million acres). **The most important factor in soil loss and degradation is erosion by water run-off and wind.** Other causes of soil loss include poor agricultural practices, roads, settlements, and poisoning with pesticides and herbicides.

Valuable topsoil is the first to be eroded away because of its position at the soil surface. Erosion can also change soil texture. Finer particles, such as silt and clay, erode before heavier particles, such as sand. Loam, for example, can be become sandy soil if its silt and clay are blown away.

Soil erosion can occur rapidly in a single heavy downpour, or it can happen gradually and imperceptibly over long periods. Either way, soil will be lost if soil erosion exceeds the rate of soil formation. Crunch the Numbers asks you to calculate annual rates of soil loss in Iowa.

Two widespread factors contribute to soil erodibility: the removal of vegetation and poor agricultural practices. First, plant roots anchor soil. When plant cover is removed, the soil becomes prone to erosion by moving water and wind. Deforestation, overgrazing, fire, and plowing are a few of the factors that remove anchoring plant roots. Poor agricultural practices, such as leaving the soil unplanted and exposed to wind and flowing water, also lead to soil erosion **(Figure 9.11)**. Bare soils without protection by crops or crop residue are prone to erosion. In addition, *compaction* of soil layers by

FIGURE 9.11 **Soil erosion in Georgia.** *Western Georgia's Providence Canyon (also called Georgia's Little Grand Canyon) did not exist before 1800. The early settlers used poor farming practices, which triggered soil erosion that led to the formation of gullies, then deep ravines, and eventually canyons 50 m (160 ft) deep. The canyons are still deepening by erosion. Tourists are drawn to the area today to hike in the canyons.*
(Anita Patterson Peppers/Shutterstock)

FIGURE 9.12 **Agriculture on slopes.** *(A) Contour plowing in Montgomery County, Iowa. This farming method creates furrows that follow a line of equal elevation on a slope. It prevents water from collecting in small channels that run downslope and eroding the soil. The green strips of vegetation catch sediments and further reduce soil loss. (B) Banaue Rice Terraces, Philippines. Terracing is a farming method used on very steep slopes. For over 2,000 years, rice has been sustainably grown in the Philippines using this method. (C) Most of Haiti's hills are severely eroded due to farming on steep slopes without protective contouring or terracing. The hills shown here were once forested. The native vegetation was cleared for farming or cut for fuel. Erosion then washed away the soil, leaving the hills permanently damaged and largely without cover.*
(A. Photo by Tim McCabe, USDA Natural Resources Conservation Service; B. © Travel Ink/Gallo Images/Getty Images; C. © James P. Blair/National Geographic/Getty Images)

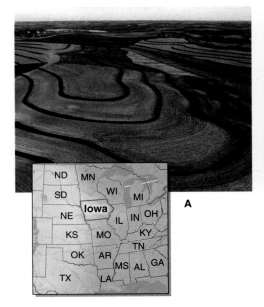

A

B

C

heavy machinery can decrease the pores in soil into which water can seep, leading to greater surface runoff and faster erosion.

When steep slopes are farmed, they can experience severe soil erosion. To reduce erosion, contour plowing and terracing can be employed **(Figure 9.12)**.

Naming Soils: Soil Taxonomy

Many localities are named after the color of their dominant soils: the Yellow River (Huang He) of China, the Red River between Oklahoma and Texas, the White Sands of New Mexico, the Painted Desert of Arizona, and the Kemet or "black soils" of the Nile Delta in Egypt.

Color and horizon development are used to classify and name soils. Soil color reveals the soil's history and the conditions under which it formed, as well as its composition. The *Munsell Soil Color Book*, shown in **Figure 9.13**, is widely used among soil scientists as a means to identify soil types based on their colors.

In biology, scientists use the Linnaean taxonomic system to name organisms. Similarly, the Köppen system classifies climates. Scientists use several different systems to classify soils. Canada, for example, uses a system called the *Canadian System*

FIGURE 9.13 **Identifying soils by color.** *The Munsell Soil Color Book is widely used to identify soils by their color. The table lists the biomes in which certain soil colors are often found. (© J. Kelley, SoilScience.info)*

Soil color	Characteristics	Biome
Black or dark brown	High organic content	Temperate grasslands
Brown	Iron oxides with high organic content	Temperate deciduous forest
Red or orange	Strong chemical weathering of iron and aluminum	Tropical rainforest
Blue/green-gray	Persistently saturated soils	Estuaries
Gray	Heavy leaching of iron	Boreal forest

FIGURE 9.14 **Soil taxonomy.** *(A) The soil taxonomy classification system recognizes 12 soil orders based on soil color, texture, and chemical makeup. The 12 soil orders display a wide range of colors and horizons as a result of the different processes from which they form. (B) Climate is often an important factor in determining the geographic distribution of soil orders. This soil map bears many similarities to the map of Köppen climate zones (see Figure 8.2). In many areas, however, there is no spatial correspondence between soils and climate zones because many other factors, such as parent material and topography, determine soil types. Andisols, for example, are a product more of their parent material (volcanic ash) than of climate. (All photos courtesy of USDA Natural Resources Conservation Service)*

Alfisols	Andisols	Aridisols	Entisols	Gelisols	Histosols
Soils that develop in humid climates. Found under forests. B horizon is grayish-brown, with clay accumulation. Little color change with depth.	Soils that develop from volcanic ash. Fertile and suitable for agriculture. Easily eroded if not protected by vegetation.	Desert soils with little organic matter and rapid drainage.	Poorly developed soils with no horizon development. Often found in new deposits from rivers, glaciers, or sand dunes.	Soils that show evidence of disturbance by frost. They occur where the ground is permanently frozen (permafrost).	Soils that form in wetlands or places with deep forest litter with very high organic content. No horizon development.

Inceptisols	Mollisols	Oxisols	Spodosols	Ultisols	Vertisols
Young soils with poorly developed horizons. Common in the northern tundra.	Humus-rich soils. Thick, dark A horizon with a soft texture. High nutrient content, among the most fertile soils in the world. Form within grasslands at midlatitudes. Well-developed horizons.	Heavily weathered soils rich in iron and aluminum minerals. Low nutrient content. Form in tropical regions with high rainfall. Found at tropical and subtropical latitudes.	Acidic, nutrient-poor soils. Often with bleached E horizon. Found under coniferous forests in snowy climates.	Old, deeply weathered soils. Low in nutrients, high in clays. Common in the southeastern United States.	Clay-dominated soils that shrink and crack when dry and swell when wet. Low organic content.

A

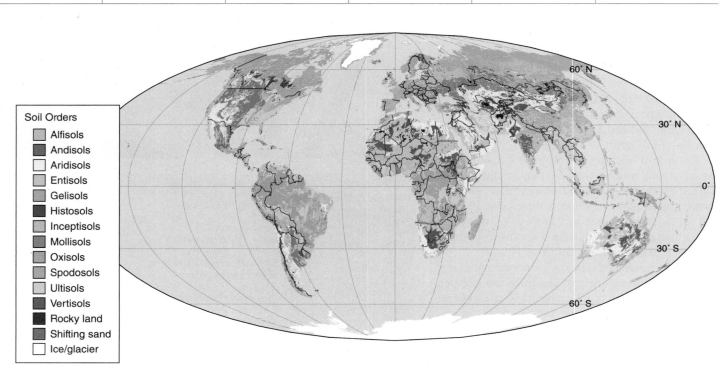

Soil Orders
- Alfisols
- Andisols
- Aridisols
- Entisols
- Gelisols
- Histosols
- Inceptisols
- Mollisols
- Oxisols
- Spodosols
- Ultisols
- Vertisols
- Rocky land
- Shifting sand
- Ice/glacier

B

of Soil Classification. One soil classification system that is widely used in the United States, called **soil taxonomy**, groups soils into 12 soil orders, as shown in Figure 9.14.

The Importance of Soils to People

Soils are essential to life, both on land and in the oceans. They are essential to humans as the medium in which we grow most of our food. This section explores some of the other ecosystem services that soils provide.

Medicines

Scientists have learned much from the chemicals that soil bacteria make. Among the first naturally occurring antibiotics used in the treatment of human diseases was tyrothricin (or gramicidin), which was isolated from soil bacteria in 1939. The Actinobacteria, a widespread group of soil bacteria, have been used to make more than 20 different antibiotic compounds. The antibiotics actinomycin, neomycin, and streptomycin are in widespread commercial use today and have saved countless human lives.

Mitigation of Climate Change

Soils contain enormous amounts of organic material and, therefore, large amounts of carbon. Terrestrial carbon stocks in the soil are greater than those in living biomass (plants). The boreal forest contains by far the greatest amount of carbon in its soils. Table 9.1 gives the global carbon stocks in various vegetation types, sorted by soil carbon amounts.

When carbon is exposed to the air, it oxidizes (reacts with oxygen) to form the greenhouse gases carbon dioxide and methane. Any changes in the vegetation cover that holds soil in place can result in oxidation of soil carbon, which forms carbon dioxide that enters the atmosphere. Deforestation and changes in land use that result in soil disturbance and loss are directly linked to oxidation of soil carbon. Such changes have contributed about 20% to the climate warming of the last century (see also Section 6.4).

Water Purification

Up until about the 1980s, New York City's water supply, located in the Catskill Mountains, was filtered by vegetation and soils. New York's water was nicknamed "the champagne of drinking water" in reference to its purity. The city's water supply began to be polluted in the 1980s, however, due to increasing construction of vacation homes near streams, building of new roads, and poor agricultural practices in the Catskills. Rather than constructing a costly water filtration plant to clean the water, the city took land in the Catskills through eminent domain. It allowed forest to return and soils to develop to filter the water in its reservoirs

TABLE 9.1	Soil Carbon Stocks		
VEGETATION TYPE	**SOIL CARBON (PG C)***	**PLANT CARBON (PG C)**	**TOTAL CARBON (PG C)**
Boreal forest	471	88	559
Temperate grasslands	295	9	304
Tropical savanna	264	66	330
Wetlands	225	15	240
Tropical rainforest	216	212	428
Desert	191	8	199
Cropland	128	3	131
Tundra	121	6	127
Temperate forest	100	59	159

Source: http://www.ipcc.ch/ipccreports/tar/wg1/pdf/TAR-03.PDF.
*1 Pg C (petagram of carbon) = 10^{15} g of carbon (2.2 trillion lb).

naturally, as they had the past (Figure 9.15). A water filtration plant would have cost up to $8 billion (plus $300 million in yearly maintenance costs) compared with the roughly $1.5 billion it cost the city to buy land. Some 830,000 ha (2 million acres) of temperate deciduous forest was allowed to return to the Catskills to filter and clean the water naturally.

soil taxonomy
A soil classification system that groups soils into 12 categories, or orders.

FIGURE 9.15 **New York City drinking water.** *The Ashokan Reservoir, in the Catskill Mountains of southeastern New York, provides the city of New York with drinking water. It is one of 19 reservoirs and 3 lakes that provide water for the city.* (© AP Photo/Mike Groll)

drought
A prolonged period of water shortage.

groundwater
Water found beneath Earth's surface in sediments and rocks.

9.2 The Hidden Hydrosphere: Groundwater

◎ Explain different features of aquifers and how water moves through the ground.

Soils and water are two closely tied natural resources that are essential to people. Soil is the medium that holds crop plants and natural vegetation, and water is required by all plants. This section begins by briefly exploring the connection between surface water and drought. It then examines water in the ground, both as a physical system and as a natural resource for people.

Every drop of water that we drink and every bite of food that we eat depends on the availability of freshwater. Most of Earth's water is in the oceans. Only a small proportion is available to people as freshwater, and only a small proportion of that freshwater is available at Earth's surface in streams and lakes (Table 9.2). Much of the water we rely on comes from underground.

Surface Water and Drought

The geographer Charles W. Thornthwaite (1899–1963) established a widely used method of determining water availability for the vegetation in a particular area. The Thornthwaite system considers

TABLE 9.2	AT A GLANCE: Reservoirs of Water		
All water		**All freshwater**	
Oceans	97.20%	Glaciers	2.15%
Freshwater	2.80%	Groundwater	0.62%
		Lakes	0.017%
		Soil water	0.005%
		Atmosphere	0.001%
		Streams	0.0001%

three key variables: (1) the amount of precipitation, (2) actual evapotranspiration (evaporation from surface water and soil and transpiration from plants; see Section 1.1), and (3) *potential evapotranspiration*, the amount of water that would evaporate and be transpired if it were available. Wherever potential evapotranspiration exceeds precipitation, there is a natural water deficit. Deserts, for example, have little vegetation cover and few permanent bodies of water. Thus, the potential for evapotranspiration is high in deserts, but actual evapotranspiration is low due to the lack of plants and surface water.

It is normal for deserts to have persistent water deficits. In other biomes, such as tropical deciduous forest or tropical savanna, water deficits are normal for only a few summer months of the year. When water deficits persist longer than normal as a result of a lack of precipitation, the result is a **drought**: a prolonged period of water shortage. The *Palmer Drought Severity Index* is a measure of dryness based mostly on potential evapotranspiration. This index is useful because it indicates the extent of drought occurring in an area (Figure 9.16).

What Flows Below: Groundwater

Surface water in streams and lakes is a vitally important resource, but its availability fluctuates over weeks or months. Groundwater, on the other hand, acts as a buffer in times of drought. Groundwater is slower to respond to drought than surface water, but after several back-to-back years of drought, groundwater supplies begin diminishing as well. **Groundwater** is water found beneath Earth's surface in sediments and rocks. Many cities located far from permanent sources of surface water, particularly those in arid regions, rely on groundwater for most or all of their needs. **About half of the water people use in the United States comes from the ground.** The Geographic Perspectives at the end of this chapter discusses the present and future status of water resources.

How does water get into the ground, and what happens to it once it is there? The rest of this section explores this and other questions about groundwater.

FIGURE 9.16 **Palmer Drought Severity Index.** *The Palmer Drought Severity Index uses 0 as a normal baseline value. Negative values indicate water deficits; positive values indicate water surpluses. This map shows the Palmer Drought Severity Index for January 2014. At this time, the western United States experienced moderate to extreme drought. For many parts of California, the drought was among the most extreme ever recorded. At the same time, the Dakotas and eastern Montana experienced extremely moist conditions.* (NOAA/NCDC)

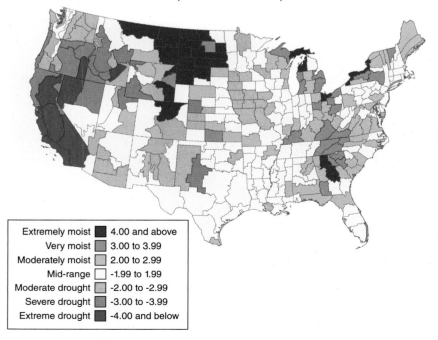

Extremely moist	4.00 and above
Very moist	3.00 to 3.99
Moderately moist	2.00 to 2.99
Mid-range	-1.99 to 1.99
Moderate drought	-2.00 to -2.99
Severe drought	-3.00 to -3.99
Extreme drought	-4.00 and below

Porosity and Permeability

When there is a water surplus, such as during a rainstorm or snowmelt, water moves through the soil through narrow, meandering channels by the process of **percolation**. Plants and evaporation pull some of this water out of the soil and return it to the atmosphere. Much of this water, however, migrates downward into the ground.

Groundwater flows into and through pores underground. **Porosity** is a measure of the available air space within soil, sediments, or rocks. Dry sand, for example, has high porosity. The porosity of the ground is expressed as a percentage. If half of a dry bucket of sand consists of open pores, then its porosity is 50%.

In most regions, significant stores of water do not exist much deeper than 0.8 km (0.5 mi) from the surface. At greater depths, the pressure from the weight of the ground compacts the pores, leaving little room for water.

The rate at which water flows through pores within the ground varies from several centimeters to several meters per day. The ease with which water can flow through soil, sediments, or rocks is called **permeability.** The permeability of a material depends on the size, number, and configuration of pores within it. Permeability is high where there are many adjacent pores, creating straight paths for water flow.

Sand is far more permeable than clay. Clay has many pores, but they are very narrow because clay particles are flat and platelike in shape. Like narrow streets in a city that restrict the flow of cars, the small and narrow connections between pores in clay restrict the flow of water. In other words, clay has high porosity (it can absorb water), but low permeability (water cannot pass easily through it). Different rock types have different porosities and permeabilities **(Figure 9.17)**. Many rocks have no porosity and no permeability and therefore contain no water.

Groundwater in Aquifers

An **aquifer** is any sediment or rock with pores that contain water. Aquifers store and transmit water, and they are an important water resource for people in many arid regions. An **aquiclude**, in contrast, is a sediment or rock layer that lacks pores and cannot contain water. Aquicludes have low or no porosity or permeability. They greatly limit or altogether prevent water movement.

Most aquifers are *unconfined aquifers*, meaning that rainwater can move into them directly from the surface. When an aquiclude separates an aquifer from the surface, the aquifer is a called a *confined aquifer* **(Figure 9.18)**.

What would happen if you were to go out into your backyard with a shovel and dig a deep hole

FIGURE 9.17 **Sandstone porosity and permeability.** *Two magnified thin sections (slices) of rock from two different sandstone formations in southern Utah's Zion National Park, on the Colorado Plateau, illustrate differences in porosity and permeability. The Navajo sandstone (A) is composed of larger particles and is therefore more porous and permeable than the Kayenta sandstone (B).*

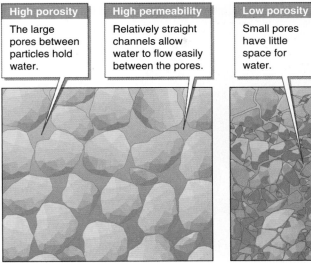

High porosity
The large pores between particles hold water.

High permeability
Relatively straight channels allow water to flow easily between the pores.

Low porosity
Small pores have little space for water.

Low permeability
Angular channels slow the flow of water between pores.

A. Navajo sandstone

B. Kayenta sandstone

FIGURE 9.18 **Confined and unconfined aquifers.** *Rainwater moves into an unconfined aquifer directly from Earth's surface. A confined aquifer is separated from the surface by a layer of impermeable rock or sediments (an aquiclude).*

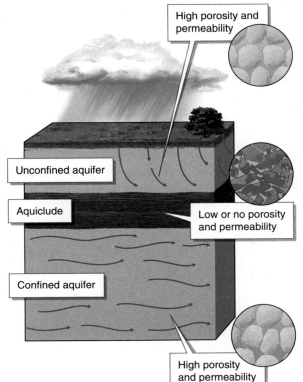

High porosity and permeability

Unconfined aquifer

Aquiclude

Low or no porosity and permeability

Confined aquifer

High porosity and permeability

percolation
The process by which rainwater moves through the soil through narrow, meandering channels.

porosity
The available air space within sediments or rocks.

permeability
The ease with which water can flow through soil, sediments, or rocks.

aquifer
A sediment or rock layer with pores that contain water.

aquiclude
A sediment or rock layer that lacks pores and cannot contain water.

FIGURE 9.19 **Groundwater zones.** *The water table lies at the top of the zone of saturation. The capillary fringe forms a gradual transition between the zone of aeration and the zone of saturation.*

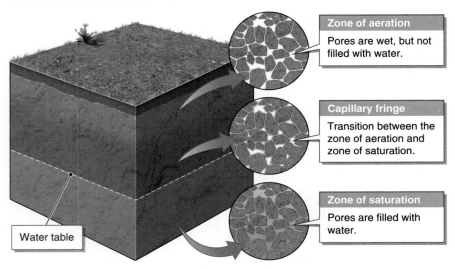

Zone of aeration
Pores are wet, but not filled with water.

Capillary fringe
Transition between the zone of aeration and zone of saturation.

Zone of saturation
Pores are filled with water.

Water table

zone of aeration
The layer of the ground not permanently saturated with water.

water table
The top surface of an aquifer's zone of saturation.

zone of saturation
The layer of the ground that is usually saturated with water.

capillary fringe
The region of transition between the zone of aeration and the zone of saturation.

infiltration
The process by which water seeps into the ground through the force of gravity.

groundwater recharge
The movement of water into an aquifer.

groundwater discharge
The movement of water out of an aquifer.

perched water table
A localized water table that lies above the regional water table.

spring
A naturally occurring discharge of groundwater that is pushed to the ground surface by hydraulic pressure.

to the aquifer below? You would first dig through the aquifer's **zone of aeration**, the layer of the ground that is not permanently saturated. If you kept digging, you would eventually reach the water table. The **water table** is the top surface of the aquifer's **zone of saturation**, the layer of the ground usually saturated with water. You would not reach the water table abruptly, however. Instead, the soil would gradually become wetter and wetter as you approached the zone of saturation. Eventually, the hole might fill with a mud slurry just above the water table.

This thought experiment demonstrates the structure of soil moisture above an aquifer. The ground becomes gradually wetter with digging because water

FIGURE 9.20 **Groundwater movement and hydraulic pressure.** *Within the aquifer in this diagram, water will flow from h_1 to h_2, and from P_1 to P_2. There is more hydraulic pressure at P_1 because it has a higher column of water above it than does P_2.*

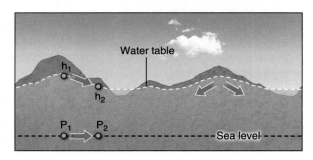

Water table

h_1

h_2

P_1 P_2

Sea level

is pulled up from the zone of saturation into the zone of aeration by capillary action and surface tension (both of which result from cohesion; see Section 3.1 on the properties of water). The gradual transition between the zone of aeration and the zone of saturation is called the **capillary fringe** (Figure 9.19).

Groundwater Movement

An unconfined aquifer's water table is seldom level. The water table roughly parallels the height of the ground surface (Figure 9.20). The contours of the water table determine differences in hydraulic pressure (water pressure), and thus the direction of water movement, in the aquifer.

Why does the water table follow surface topography instead of being level like the surface of a pond? The process by which rainwater seeps into the ground through the force of gravity is called **infiltration**. When rain falls on areas of high elevation, the infiltrating water has a farther distance to travel downward. If no more rain were ever to fall, gravity would eventually create a level water table.

Infiltration results in **groundwater recharge**, the entry of water into an aquifer. The movement of water out of an aquifer and onto the ground surface is called **groundwater discharge** (Figure 9.21).

The Height of the Water Table

How far below the ground surface is the water table? In most cases, bodies of surface water, such as ponds or streams, represent the height of the water table. The water table may lie at the ground surface and form a lake or stream, or it may lie hundreds of meters below the surface.

In arid regions, the water table typically lies far below the surface of the ground because of the lack of precipitation and infiltration to fill the pores. As a result, there are few permanent surface streams or water bodies in most arid regions. Streams in these regions are often *ephemeral* or *exotic*: They flow only after sudden heavy precipitation events add water to the stream channel faster than it can infiltrate the ground.

At any given location, the water table is not fixed. It fluctuates because of seasonal changes in precipitation, water withdrawals from aquifers by people, and long-term changes in climate (Figure 9.22).

Localized impermeable layers of rock or sediment, called *discontinuous aquicludes*, sometimes form perched water tables. A **perched water table** is a localized water table that lies above the *regional water table* (Figure 9.23, page 310).

Perched water tables sometimes create springs. A **spring** arises where hydraulic pressure pushes groundwater onto the surface. Springs may form along cliff faces and hillsides where water collects above a small, localized aquiclude, as shown in Figure 9.24 on page 310.

Hydraulic Pressure and the Potentiometric Surface

> Why does water in houses gush from the faucets?

Have you ever wondered why water forcefully gushes out of your home's faucets or garden hose? The hydraulic pressure pushing the water out is created by gravity. Our water supply is fed to our homes from a higher elevation, and the pull of gravity forces the water through the pipes that lead into our homes and faucets. In some places, the water supply flows from a reservoir located at an elevation higher than the buildings it supplies; in others, water is pumped mechanically into a water tower.

FIGURE 9.21 **Groundwater recharge and discharge.** *Groundwater recharge areas are usually higher in elevation than groundwater discharge areas.*

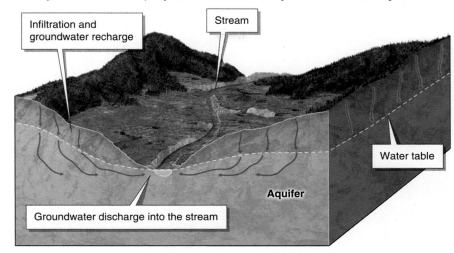

FIGURE 9.22 **The varying height of the water table.** *Permanent lakes and streams indicate the local height of the water table. (A) The Um El Ma Oasis in the Sahara, in southwestern Libya. Oases form where a depression in the sand dunes dips below the water table. Although almost no water falls from the sky, there is water stored in the aquifer just below the sand surface. (B) In humid regions, drought can lower the water table. Standing bodies of water can disappear if the water table drops. (A. © Frans Lemmens/The Image Bank/Getty Images)*

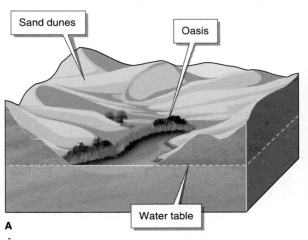

A

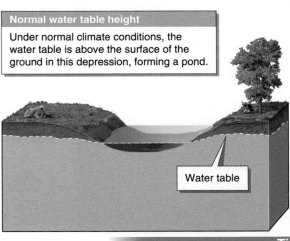

B

FIGURE 9.23 **Perched water table.** *Perched water tables form where discontinuous aquicludes prevent water from flowing downward to the regional water table.*

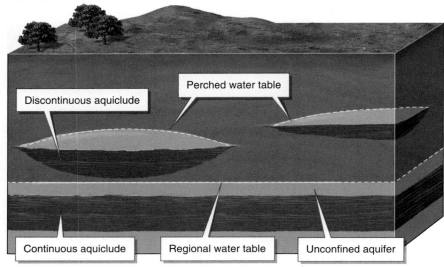

Water gushes from our faucets because our homes lie below the potentiometric surface created by the elevation of the water supply. The **potentiometric surface** is the elevation to which hydraulic pressure pushes water in pipes or wells. Any struc-

tures higher than the potentiometric surface will have no water pressure **(Figure 9.25)**.

Wells are holes dug or drilled by people to get water from the ground. When a well is drilled downward into the zone of saturation, it will fill with water up to the height of the water table. **The tops of most wells lie above the potentiometric surface of the aquifer, so pumps (or buckets) must be used to lift the water up out of the well.** A well drilled down only as far as the zone of aeration will not produce water unless the water table rises to the well during the rainy or snowmelt season.

An **artesian well** is a well that has been drilled through an aquiclude into a confined aquifer below. Water gushes out of some artesian wells with no pumping required because they are below the potentiometric surface of the recharge area of the aquifer. Artesian wells may form where sedimentary rocks (see Section 13.3) are tilted and permeable and impermeable layers of rock intersect the ground surface, forming a confined aquifer. Rainwater flows into the permeable layers where they are exposed at the surface. Because the recharge area is higher in elevation than the aquifer, the recharge area creates hydraulic pressure that pushes water through the aquifer, much as a water tower pushes water through the pipes of a building **(Figure 9.26)**.

FIGURE 9.24 **Grand Canyon spring.** *(A) Water infiltrates permeable sedimentary rocks and collects above a localized aquiclude, forming a perched water table. A spring results where the water emerges from the side of a cliff. (B) Vasey's Paradise is a spring that flows into the Colorado River in Coconino County, Arizona. The Grand Canyon has many such springs that form where localized aquicludes create perched water tables that abut canyon walls. (B. © Universal Images Group via Getty Images)*

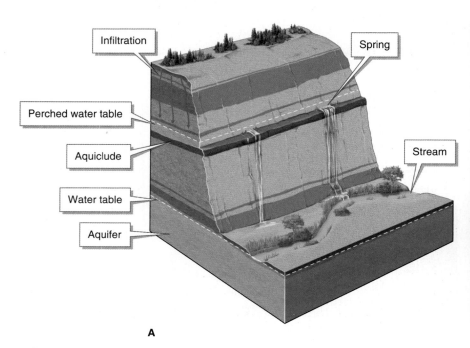

A

B

FIGURE **9.25** **The potentiometric surface.** *(A) The potentiometric surface can be visualized as a dome with a surface that drops in all directions with distance away from the water supply. The house farthest from this water tower will have poor water pressure because it is at the level of the potentiometric surface. (B) Water tanks in New York City provide water pressure for the buildings on which they sit. Modern skyscrapers use mechanical pumps, rather than water tanks, to provide water pressure to the building. (B. © John Cairns/Alamy)*

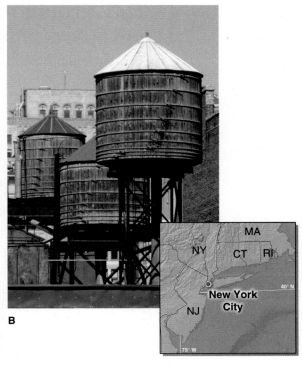

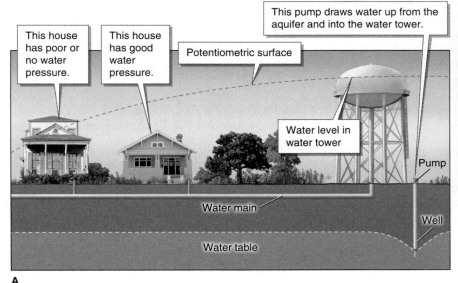

B

A

FIGURE **9.26** **Artesian wells.** *Water gushes from artesian wells that are located below the potentiometric surface of a groundwater recharge area. Water must be pumped up from an artesian well located above the potentiometric surface. Vendome Well (inset), in south-central Oklahoma, is an artesian well that gushes 9,500 L (2,500 gal) of naturally saline water each minute. (Courtesy of Butch Bridges, www. oklahomahistory.net)*

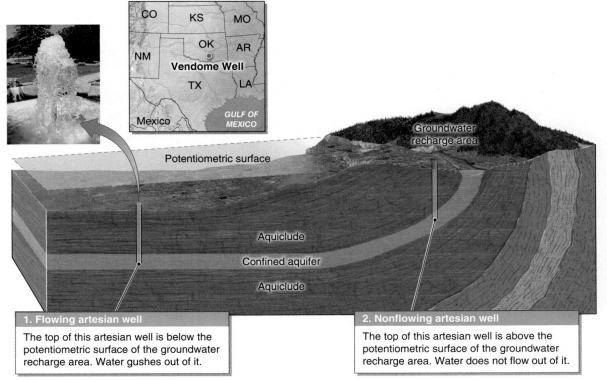

potentiometric surface
The elevation to which hydraulic pressure will push water in pipes or wells.

well
A hole dug or drilled by people to gain access to groundwater.

artesian well
A well that has been drilled through an aquiclude into a confined aquifer below and may gush water.

9.3 Problems Associated with Groundwater

◎ **Describe problems with groundwater that result from human activities.**

Groundwater is essential for human needs, particularly in arid regions, where most or all water used by people comes from the ground. Heavy reliance on groundwater can create conflict among neighboring communities drawing from the same aquifer. **There are two major problems associated with human use of groundwater resources: (1) withdrawal of groundwater faster than it is replenished and (2) pollution of groundwater.**

groundwater overdraft
Withdrawal of water from an aquifer faster than the aquifer is recharged at the site of a well.

cone of depression
The cone-shaped lowering of the water table resulting from groundwater overdraft.

Too Much Too Fast: Groundwater Overdraft and Mining

The height of the water table in an unconfined aquifer is the result of a balance between groundwater recharge (inputs) and groundwater discharge (outputs). Human activities can disrupt this hydrologic balance by groundwater overdraft and groundwater mining.

Groundwater Overdraft
Groundwater overdraft is the removal of water from an aquifer faster than the aquifer is recharged at the site of a well. Groundwater overdraft often forms a **cone of depression**: a cone-shaped lowering of the water table around the well from which water is being removed (**Figure 9.27**). Overdraft and the resulting cone of depression change the topography of the water table near the well. As a result, the pattern of hydraulic pressure and the direction of water movement in the aquifer can also change. Water can migrate toward the lowered water table at the cone of depression.

Groundwater overdraft can result in several additional problems, including a lowered water table at other wells, contamination of wells by salt water, and land subsidence.

1. *Lowered water table:* If neighboring wells are not deep, the cone of depression can lower the water table and cause them to go dry (see Figure 9.27).

2. *Saltwater intrusion:* In coastal regions, a freshwater aquifer may lie on top of salty ground-

---

FIGURE 9.27 **GEO-GRAPHIC: Groundwater overdraft may lower the water table.**
When water is withdrawn from an aquifer faster than the aquifer is recharged, the water table drops. In the example on the right side of the figure, water withdrawals from a well used by a large factory have lowered the water table out of the reach of a smaller well.

Animation
Lowered water table
http://qrs.ly/1a457cf

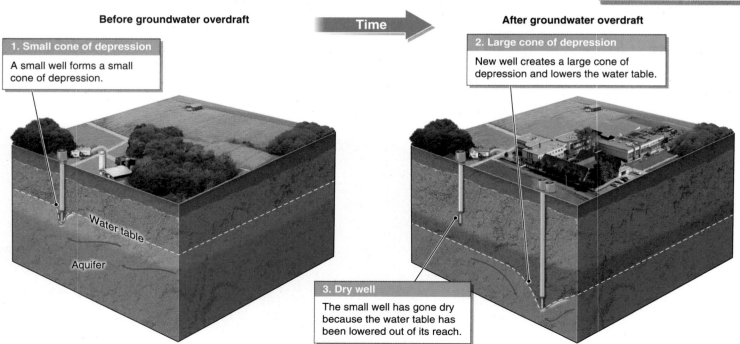

Before groundwater overdraft

Time

After groundwater overdraft

1. Small cone of depression
A small well forms a small cone of depression.

2. Large cone of depression
New well creates a large cone of depression and lowers the water table.

Water table

Aquifer

3. Dry well
The small well has gone dry because the water table has been lowered out of its reach.

FIGURE 9.28 **GEO-GRAPHIC: Saltwater intrusion.** *Hydraulic pressure exerted by the weight of ocean water forces salt water inland. A freshwater aquifer exerts pressure against the salt water, creating an equilibrium line between the two. Groundwater overdraft can reduce the hydraulic pressure of the freshwater and cause the equilibrium line to retreat inland, allowing salt water to contaminate the well.*

Animation
Saltwater
intrusion
http://qrs.ly/9w457cg

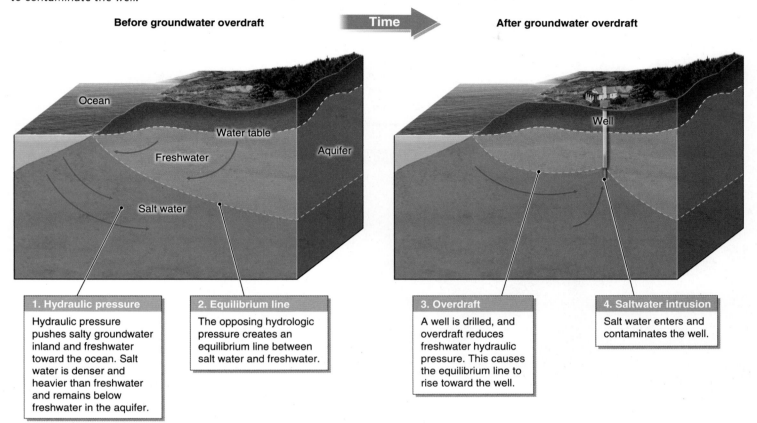

Before groundwater overdraft

Time

After groundwater overdraft

Ocean

Water table

Freshwater

Aquifer

Salt water

Well

1. Hydraulic pressure

Hydraulic pressure pushes salty groundwater inland and freshwater toward the ocean. Salt water is denser and heavier than freshwater and remains below freshwater in the aquifer.

2. Equilibrium line

The opposing hydrologic pressure creates an equilibrium line between salt water and freshwater.

3. Overdraft

A well is drilled, and overdraft reduces freshwater hydraulic pressure. This causes the equilibrium line to rise toward the well.

4. Saltwater intrusion

Salt water enters and contaminates the well.

water. Groundwater overdraft may cause the salty water to migrate higher in the aquifer and contaminate wells. This process is called **saltwater intrusion** (Figure 9.28). Saltwater contamination of a well is permanent and irreversible.

3. *Land subsidence:* The pressure of the water in the pores of sediments keeps sediment particles apart while the ground is saturated. When water is removed, these pores can collapse under the weight of the sediments. When this happens, the elevation of the land surface drops as the sediments are compacted (Figure 9.29A on page 314) In most cases, once the pores in the aquifer collapse, they can no longer hold water, and the aquifer is lost permanently. Near Mendota, in the San

Joaquin Valley, California, the land elevation has dropped more than 8.5 m (28 ft) due to groundwater overdraft. In some cases of land subsidence, large surface fissures (or cracks) can open up (Figure 9.29B).

Groundwater Mining

Groundwater mining is the process of extracting groundwater from areas where there is little to no groundwater recharge. In areas where there is no recharge, once groundwater has been mined, it is gone permanently.

North America's largest aquifer is the Ogallala Aquifer (also called the High Plains Aquifer), which lies beneath the Great Plains (Figure 9.30A on page 315). About 200,000 water wells tap into the Ogallala Aquifer. Most of them are connected to center-pivot irrigation systems used for agricultural fields

saltwater intrusion
The contamination of a well by salt water as a result of groundwater overdraft.

groundwater mining
The process of extracting groundwater where there is little to no groundwater recharge.

FIGURE 9.29 **GEO-GRAPHIC: Land subsidence.** *(A) The collapse of pores caused by groundwater overdraft results in land subsidence. (B) These large subsidence fissures have opened up in the town of Queen Creek, in southern Arizona. (B. Arizona Department of Water Resources)*

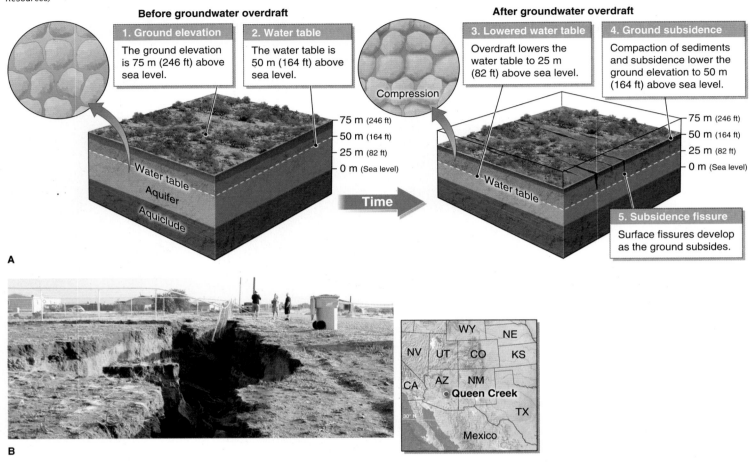

Before groundwater overdraft

1. Ground elevation
The ground elevation is 75 m (246 ft) above sea level.

2. Water table
The water table is 50 m (164 ft) above sea level.

After groundwater overdraft

3. Lowered water table
Overdraft lowers the water table to 25 m (82 ft) above sea level.

4. Ground subsidence
Compaction of sediments and subsidence lower the ground elevation to 50 m (164 ft) above sea level.

Compression

Water table
Aquifer
Aquiclude

Time

75 m (246 ft)
50 m (164 ft)
25 m (82 ft)
0 m (Sea level)

Water table

75 m (246 ft)
50 m (164 ft)
25 m (82 ft)
0 m (Sea level)

5. Subsidence fissure
Surface fissures develop as the ground subsides.

A

B

WY · NE · NV · UT · CO · KS · CA · AZ · NM · Queen Creek · TX · Mexico

(Figure 9.30B). Agriculture in the Great Plains generates some $20 billion in revenue each year, or about one-ninth of the total U.S. agricultural production.

The water in the Ogallala is **fossil groundwater**: water that entered the aquifer long ago and is no longer being replenished. Most of it came from the now-melted Laurentide ice sheet that covered much of North America during the most recent glacial period (see Section 6.2). In the southern portions of the Ogallala, the climate is too arid to recharge the aquifer. There, farmers and ranchers are mining the Ogallala's groundwater. As a result, the water table is dropping across the southern stretches of the aquifer, by more than 1.6 m (5 ft) each year in some places (Figure 9.31). The deeper the water table becomes, the more energy and expense is required to pump water because it has a longer way to go to reach the surface.

Aquifers in arid regions, where there are no permanent surface water bodies, are always com-

posed of fossil groundwater. Many countries face looming problems with the loss of groundwater, including China, India, Pakistan, and most countries in the Middle East. About one-fourth of India's food is grown using groundwater that is not being replaced. Saudi Arabia, in the hyperarid Arabian Desert, has developed an agricultural economy centered on mining fossil groundwater, as highlighted in **Picture This** on page 316.

Groundwater Pollution

Common sources of groundwater pollution include leaks from landfills (or dumps), septic systems, and gas station tanks; agricultural chemicals; animal sewage from factory farms; and mining activities. The process of mining natural gas from shale rock is also linked to groundwater pollution (see Section 13.5).

In some areas, toxic chemicals are (or were) intentionally dumped on the ground or injected into aquifers from wells to dispose of them cheaply.

fossil groundwater
Water that entered an aquifer long ago and is no longer being replenished.

FIGURE **9.30** **The Ogallala Aquifer.** *(A) The Ogallala Aquifer (as mapped in 2009) stretches from South Dakota to northern Texas. Its zone of saturation is thickest in Nebraska, where it is about 300 m (1,000 ft) thick. (B) This aerial photo shows the circular irrigation patterns produced by farms using the Ogallala Aquifer near the Texas Panhandle. (B. © Robert S. Ogilvie)*

FIGURE **9.31** **Water table changes in the Ogallala Aquifer.** *The water table has dropped more than 46 m (150 ft) in historic times in some areas, mostly in northern Texas.*

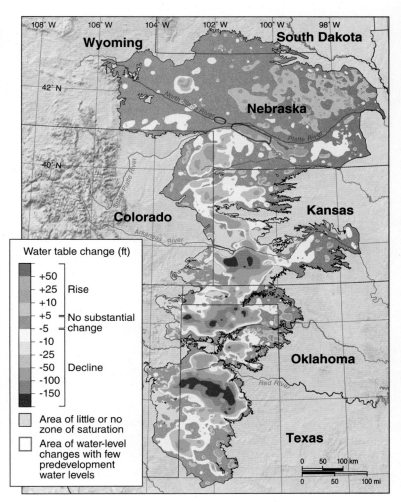

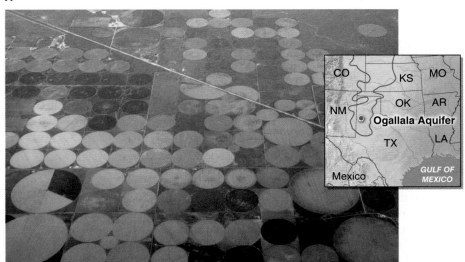

A

B

Picture This

(Map: NASA Earth Observatory image created by Robert Simmon and Jesse Allen, using Landsat data provided by the United States Geological Survey; photo, © Matt Green)

Groundwater Mining

This Landsat satellite image acquired in January 2012 shows center-pivot irrigation plots for grain, fruit, and vegetable farming in Saudi Arabia. This method of farming is increasingly used in arid regions where fossil groundwater is available. The fossil groundwater in Saudi Arabia is at least 10,000 years old. It entered the ground when the climate was wetter during the most recent glacial period (see Section 6.2).

The green agricultural fields visible in the desert indicate that groundwater is being mined. At the center of each green circle is a well pipe and a diesel pump that pulls water up from the aquifer below. Here, water is pumped from as deep as 1 km (0.6 mi) beneath the surface. The water moves through a tubular arm called a gantry that stretches across the circle's radius (inset). The gantry slowly sweeps around the field. The diameter of each circle is about 1 km (0. 6 mi).

Consider This

1. Why do circular agricultural fields always indicate that groundwater is being used?

2. Why is farming in the Arabian Desert unsustainable?

---

contaminant plume
The cloud of pollution that migrates through an aquifer away from its source.

groundwater remediation
The process of cleaning a contaminated aquifer.

In the 1950s and 1960s, the large utility company Pacific Gas and Electric (PG&E) dumped hexavalent chromium into a collecting pool. From there, the chemical seeped into the ground and migrated several miles through the aquifer. The wells in nearby Hinkley, California, gradually became contaminated, and rates of various types of cancers skyrocketed in the small town. Many of the residents became ill and died. Although PG&E denied wrongdoing, the company was held accountable in court because of the efforts of the environmental activist Erin Brockovich. Environmental regulations are now in place to stop (or at least reduce) such practices.

Once pollutants have entered an aquifer, they disperse as a **contaminant plume**: a cloud of pollution that migrates through the aquifer away from its source (Figure 9.32). Any pollutants, natural or anthropogenic, that enter the aquifer stay there for centuries or longer. Therefore, the loss of an aquifer through groundwater pollution is, in most cases, permanent.

Various techniques for cleaning up polluted groundwater have been tried. These techniques include the use of bacteria to digest the contaminants and the use of chemicals to react with the contaminants, changing them into other, less harmful chemicals. The process of cleaning a contaminated aquifer is called **groundwater remediation** (Figure 9.33). In most instances, however, the best option becomes closing contaminated wells and stopping the "upstream" sources of contaminants.

FIGURE **9.32** **Aquifer contaminant sources.** *Sources of groundwater contaminant plumes (in light orange) come from a variety of human activities. Contaminant plumes migrate in the direction of water flow within an aquifer.*

Video
Groundwater
contamination
http://qrs.ly/sq457cm

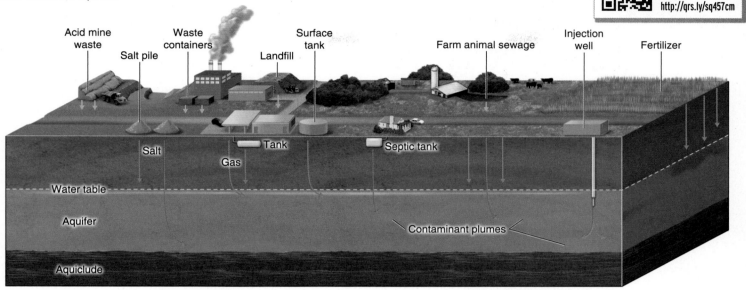

FIGURE **9.33** **SCIENTIFIC INQUIRY: How is contaminated groundwater cleaned?** *In 1980, the U.S. Environmental Protection Agency Superfund Program was established to clean up the nation's worst toxic contamination. Over 80% of EPA Superfund sites are areas of contaminated groundwater. The method of cleanup used depends on the type of contaminant, the physical circumstances at the site, and the cost. Generally, contaminated water is either pumped from the ground and treated, or it is treated while in the ground, a method called* in situ *remediation.*

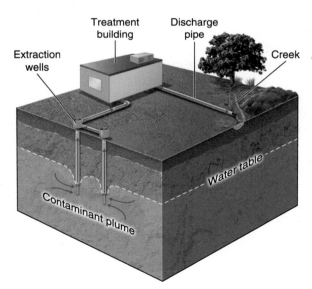

1. Pump and Treat
Extraction wells are placed in the path of the migrating contaminant plume, and the contaminated water is pumped from the aquifer. Once at the surface, the water is treated with filtration, chemical additives, or bacteria. A combination of all these methods may be used. Once cleaned, the treated water is discharged into the local watershed or sewer system.

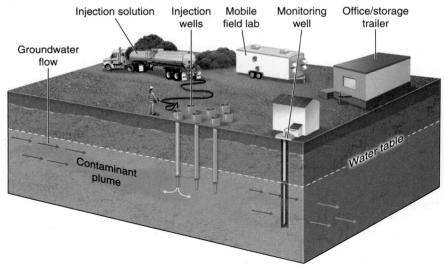

2. In Situ Remediation
In situ remediation involves the injection of chemicals, such as hydrogen peroxide (H_2O_2), or bacteria into the contaminated aquifer. The chemicals or bacteria break the contaminants down into safer compounds.

GEOGRAPHIC PERSPECTIVES
9.4 Water Resources under Pressure

◎ Assess the importance of water resources to human societies.

It is a paradox that even though 71% of Earth's surface is covered by water, and even though water is perpetually cleaned and freshened through the hydrologic cycle (see Section 3.1), freshwater is a resource that many people lack. There is a limit to how fast water is cleaned in the hydrologic cycle. As the global human population and its economic affluence grow, water, both on the surface and in the ground, is becoming an increasingly important and scarce resource.

> How much water is needed to produce 1 kg (2.2 lb) of beef?

Water Footprints

The **water footprint** is the amount of water required to produce a specific item, food, or service. Consider how much water is needed to produce some common foods (Table 9.3).

Why does a single kilogram of beef require 13,620 liters of water to produce? The food the cow ate during its lifetime—mainly corn, if it lived in North America—required water to grow, and the cow needed water to drink. In addition, water is used to process and prepare the meat for consumers. A lot of water goes into producing food, and

water footprint
The amount of water required to produce a specific item, food, or service.

virtual water
The unseen water required to produce a manufactured item or food.

TABLE 9.4 AT A GLANCE:
Water Footprints of Manufactured Items

ITEM PRODUCED	WATER FOOTPRINT	
	LITERS	GALLONS
1 empty 1-liter plastic water bottle	3	0.79
1 cotton T-shirt	2,700	713
500 sheets of binder paper	5,000	1,320
1 pair of (cow) leather shoes	7,580	2,002
1 car	147,810	39,047

typically, meat and dairy products consume more water than plant-based foods. But there are exceptions, such as chocolate.

When foods are grown in a suitable climate, much of the water used to grow or raise them falls directly from the sky. Chocolate, for example, comes from the seeds of the cacao tree (*Theobroma cacao*). Plantations of cacao trees are located in tropical regions where the climate naturally meets the plant's water needs. In contrast, some foods are grown or raised in semiarid or arid lands, such as beef in Texas. In this example, the water needed does not fall from the sky and must instead be pumped from the ground or diverted from streams.

Manufactured goods, such as computers, cars, and clothing, all take water to produce. Compared with foods, it is less easy to see why material goods require water, but many of them have substantial water footprints (Table 9.4).

Many services require water as well. Golf courses, for example, have an inordinately large water footprint. Their close-cut turfgrass stores little water and requires uninterrupted irrigation. There are over 16,000 golf courses in the United States. The average water consumption of all U.S. golf courses is 2.3 million acre-feet, or roughly 2.9 trillion L (766 billion gal) per year (Figure 9.34).

TABLE 9.3 AT A GLANCE:
Water Footprints of Foods

ITEM PRODUCED	WATER FOOTPRINT	
	LITERS	GALLONS
1 apple	70	18
1 L (0.26 gal) of coffee	876	231
1 kg (2.2 lb) of wheat	1,000	264
1 kg (2.2 lb) of rice	3,400	898
1 kg (2.2 lb) of chicken	3,546	937
1 kg (2.2 lb) of beef	13,620	3,598
1 kg (2.2 lb) of chocolate	24,000	6,340

Out of economic necessity, and to their credit, many golf course managers are adapting to the realities of increasing water scarcity. About 1,000 golf courses in the United States are now using, at least in part, recycled or reclaimed water (wastewater from the golf facility and treated sewage water). They are also planting more drought-tolerant varieties of turfgrass to reduce their water footprint.

The Global Reach of Virtual Water

Water resources have a borderless, global dimension. **Water consumption is not restricted by political borders because many of the goods people use and the foods people eat come from somewhere else, often far away.** Imported foods and goods are sometimes more common than domestic products. Chinese toys, New Zealand apples, Chilean grapes and wines, California almonds, Japanese electronics and cars, and Midwestern beef all exact a water toll on their country of origin.

The unseen water required to produce a manufactured item or food is called **virtual water**. As these goods move around the planet, their virtual water travels with them, as shown in **Figure 9.35**.

Between 1996 and 2005, the average annual global flow of virtual water was 908 trillion L (240 trillion gal). Of this, 92% was in the form of agricultural crops or products derived from crops (such as paper and cotton). **Figure 9.36** on page 320 shows the balance between water exports and imports for individual countries between 1996 and 2005.

Earth's physical systems, such as soils and water, and the people in them are interconnected. Countries that receive imports have an impact on the water resources and environments of the exporting country. For example, diversions of water from the Aral Sea are used to grow cotton in the desert of Uzbekistan. These diversions are causing the Aral Sea to shrink and its wetland ecosystems to disappear, leaving behind toxic dust that has poisoned local residents. The cotton grown in Uzbekistan using the diverted water is then exported somewhere else, such as China, to manufacture goods such as jeans and T-shirts. These items are then exported to world markets such as the United States, Canada, and Europe. Although virtual water is unseen, its effects link a simple cotton T-shirt with the loss of the entire inland ecosystem of the Aral Sea.

The Future of Water

The human population has just passed the 7 billion mark and continues to grow. This single statistic underpins all environmental issues today, but it is particularly relevant to the scarcity of water

FIGURE 9.34 **A desert golf course.** *The average golf course in the United States uses about 539,000 L (142,000 gal) of water per day. Desert golf courses, such as the one shown here in Palm Springs, California, use up to 378 million L (100 million gal) of water each day in summer.* (© Jennifer Photography Imaging/E+/Getty Images)

FIGURE 9.35 **Virtual water movement.** *Japan exports roughly 1.5 million automobiles each year to the United States. Meanwhile, the United States exports roughly 150,000 metric tons of rice to Japan each year. When these products are converted to virtual water, it is clear that more than just material goods are being exchanged. Not all of the virtual water used to produce these cars came from Japan, however. Many of the materials used to make an automobile, such as rubber and metals, were themselves imported to Japan from somewhere else. So water is only passing through Japan to the United States as virtual water in the form of automobile components.* (Left, © Ken Shimuzu/AFP/Getty Images; right, © Ken James/Bloomberg via Getty Images)

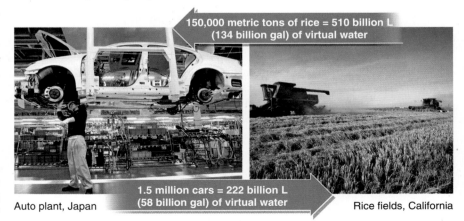

150,000 metric tons of rice = 510 billion L (134 billion gal) of virtual water

1.5 million cars = 222 billion L (58 billion gal) of virtual water

Auto plant, Japan

Rice fields, California

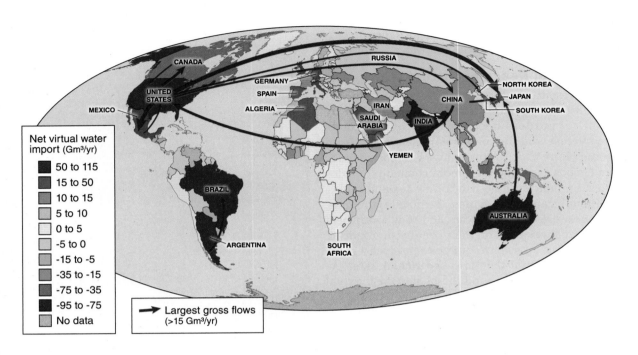

FIGURE 9.36 **Water balance.** *The balance between water exports and imports (or water balance) for individual countries between 1996 and 2005. Countries with negative water balances export more virtual water than they import. Countries with positive water balances import more virtual water than they export. The blue flow lines show exports of water over 15 Gm³ (billion cubic meters) per year.*

resources. Global population numbers are an important part of the story, but not the only part. Higher levels of economic development are usually associated with higher water demands, and unequal political power within a geographic region can also exacerbate water shortages for politically disadvantaged populations.

In economically developed nations, water shortages range from an inconvenience to causing serious economic and ecological harm. In developing countries, water resources are a matter of life and death. Consider these statistics from the United Nations:

- Worldwide, 884 million people do not have access to safe drinking water. About 40% of those people live in sub-Saharan Africa.

- Nearly 5,000 children in developing countries die each day (1.8 million per year) from waterborne diseases such as dysentery and cholera.

- By some estimates, half the world's hospital beds are filled with people who got sick from drinking contaminated water.

Economic development for poverty-stricken countries is absolutely a good thing. It improves access to clean drinking water, medicines, education, health, and a whole range of other social benefits. Economic development also creates more efficient use of water and possibilities for recycling water. However, affluence also increases demand for material goods. These material goods put more pressure on water resources because water is needed to make them.

Human population growth, economic development, and climate change are three converging global forces that will make freshwater an increasingly precious natural resource. As a result, conflict over water is likely to be the catalyst for serious environmental, geopolitical, and humanitarian issues in the coming decades.

CHAPTER 9 Exploring with ⦿ Google Earth

To complete these problems, first read the chapter. When you are finished, go to LaunchPad and open the Exploring with Google Earth file for this chapter. Click on the "Workbook Problems" folder to "fly" to each of the problems listed below and answer the questions. Be sure to keep your "Borders and Labels" layer activated. Refer to Appendix 4 if you need help using Google Earth.

PROBLEM 9.1 Wheat and lentils are widely grown in an area known as the Palouse, a region in the northwestern United States that includes southeastern Washington and northwestern Idaho.

1. **What is the name of the kind of plowing that follows a constant elevation along a hill?**
   a. Continuous plowing
   b. Terracing
   c. Hill plowing
   d. Contour plowing

2. **Why do farmers plow the land this way?**
   a. Because it saves gas
   b. To take advantage of groundwater
   c. To maximize sunlight
   d. To prevent soil erosion

PROBLEM 9.2 Rice is grown on very steep slopes in many parts of southeastern Asia. Zoom in closely and pan around to determine what kind of agriculture is being practiced here.

1. **What is this kind of agriculture called?**
   a. Terracing
   b. Contour plowing
   c. Denudation
   d. Jointing

2. **Would this farming technique work in an arid climate if no water were diverted from nearby streams?**
   a. Yes
   b. No

PROBLEM 9.3 This unusually wet environment in western Egypt is in one of the driest deserts on Earth. Shown here are four water bodies surrounded by a sea of sand dunes.

1. **Where did the water that fills these depressions come from?**
   a. Rainfall
   b. Snowmelt
   c. Groundwater
   d. Human activity

2. **What is the general name of this type of physical feature?**
   a. Erg
   b. Sinkhole
   c. Artesian well
   d. Oasis

3. **What does the surface level of these four water bodies reveal?**
   a. The height of the water table
   b. The depth of the depression
   c. The amount of rainfall
   d. The age of the basin

PROBLEM 9.4 Activate your 3D Buildings layer in the sidebar menu. You will see water towers in Kuwait City, Kuwait. Pan around to see the towers and the skyscrapers behind them.

1. **How do these water towers provide water pressure to neighboring portions of Kuwait City?**
   a. Gravity provides water pressure.
   b. Diesel pumps in the towers provide water pressure.
   c. A large water footprint from the towers provides water pressure.
   d. Groundwater discharge from the towers provides water pressure.

2. **What invisible surface do the tall skyscrapers in the background lie above?**
   a. The zone of saturation surface
   b. The water table surface
   c. The cone of depression surface
   d. The potentiometric surface

3. **Pan around so you can see the skyscrapers and the water towers together. Does the water pressure in the top floors of the skyscrapers come from the water towers?**
   a. Yes
   b. No
   c. It is impossible to tell.

4. **What country borders Kuwait to the northwest?**
   a. Iran
   b. Saudi Arabia
   c. Qatar
   d. Iraq

PROBLEM 9.5 The desert of Libya receives almost no rainfall, but crops are grown there, as evidenced by these circular agricultural fields.

1. **Where is the water coming from to grow these crops?**
   a. Stream diversions by people
   b. Natural rainfall
   c. Groundwater mining
   d. Water recycling

2. **Why is this type of agriculture unsustainable in the long term?**
   a. Because climate will change
   b. Because population growth will outstrip food supplies
   c. Because food tastes will change
   d. Because groundwater will run out

3. **What is the approximate diameter of these circles?**
   a. 0.5 km
   b. 1 km
   c. 1.5 km
   d. 2 km

PROBLEM 9.6 This location features a water-intensive activity discussed in Section 9.4, Geographic Perspectives. As you zoom out while answering the questions, take note of the three artificial islands that protrude into the sea.

1. **What land use do you see at this location?**
   a. Shopping center
   b. Golf course
   c. Park
   d. Forested land

2. **Zoom out and observe the vegetation structure in this area. Which biome do you think this area is part of?**
   a. Tropical rainforest
   b. Tropical savanna
   c. Tundra
   d. Desert

3. **In what city is this feature found?**
   a. Doha
   b. Abu Dhabi
   c. Muscat
   d. Dubai

CHAPTER 9 **Study Guide**

Focus Points

9.1 The Living Veneer: Soils

Soil composition: By volume, soils are composed mostly of weathered fragments of rocks and minerals. Healthy soils are filled with living organisms and their organic remains.

Soils and climate: Soils develop most quickly where it is warm and wet and most slowly where it is cold and dry. On a small (broad) geographic scale, climate is an important soil-forming factor.

Anthropogenic soils: People can form soils intentionally by composting.

Soils and time: In nature, a few centimeters of soil take centuries or more to form.

Soil erosion: Human activity is causing soil erosion to happen faster than soils form naturally.

Soil taxonomy: The soil taxonomy classification system groups soils into 12 orders, based mainly on horizon development and color.

Importance of soils: Soils provide food and other ecosystem services, such as new medicines, climate change mitigation, and water purification.

9.2 The Hidden Hydrosphere: Groundwater

Surface water: The Palmer Drought Severity Index provides a measure of water deficits.

Groundwater: About half the water used in the United States comes from the ground.

Permeability: Water flows through rocks or sediments at a rate of centimeters to meters per day, depending on the permeability of those materials.

Surface water: Bodies of surface water, such as lakes and streams, occur where the water table reaches Earth's surface.

Water table fluctuations: The water table fluctuates over time as a result of seasonal changes in precipitation, long-term climate change, and withdrawals of groundwater by people.

Wells: The tops of most wells lie above the potentiometric surface of the groundwater recharge area, and water must be pumped out of them. Water gushes out of some artesian wells.

9.3 Problems Associated with Groundwater

Groundwater overdraft and mining: Groundwater overdraft and groundwater mining withdraw water from aquifers more rapidly than it can be replenished.

Groundwater pollution: Contaminants that enter groundwater by infiltration come from a variety of sources, including gasoline tanks, sewage, and landfills.

9.4 Geographic Perspectives: Water Resources under Pressure

Water footprints: Food crops and material goods, such as computers and clothing, require water to produce.

Virtual water: Global virtual water flow exceeds 900 trillion L (237 trillion gal) each year.

Key Terms

aquiclude, 307
aquifer, 307
artesian well, 310
bedrock, 297
capillary fringe, 308
cone of depression, 312
contaminant plume, 316
drought, 306
eluviation, 297
fossil groundwater, 314
groundwater, 306
groundwater discharge, 308
groundwater mining, 313
groundwater overdraft, 312
groundwater recharge, 308
groundwater remediation, 316
humus, 300
infiltration, 308
leaching, 297

loam, 299
pedogenesis, 297
perched water table, 308
percolation, 307
permeability, 307
porosity, 307
potentiometric surface, 310
regolith, 297
saltwater intrusion, 313
soil, 297
soil horizon, 297
soil taxonomy, 305
spring, 308
virtual water, 319
water footprint, 318
water table, 308
well, 310
zone of aeration, 308
zone of saturation, 308

Concept Review

The Human Sphere: The Collapse of the Maya

1. When and where did the Maya civilization flourish?

2. Describe the link between the collapse of the Maya and their soil and water resources.

9.1 The Living Veneer: Soils

3. What is pedogenesis?

4. What are soil horizons? How do they form? How many are there? Do all soils have each of them?

5. Describe the major characteristics of each of the soil horizons.

6. What four major components do soils consist of?

7. On a small (broad) geographic scale, what is the single most important factor that determines what kinds of soils will form? Explain why it is important.

8. What other soil-forming factors are there? Briefly explain each.

9. What factors contribute to soil loss and soil degradation? Which of these is the most important?

10. Compare tropical soils, subtropical desert soils, and temperate soils with regard to degree of weathering and leaching as well as topsoil depth.

11. What is contour plowing? What is terracing? How do they reduce soil erosion?

12. What are the 12 soil orders, and what characteristics are used to identify them?

13. What overall information can be gained from the color of soil? For example, what does a blue-green soil signify?

14. What kinds of ecosystem services do soils provide?

15. Why did New York City choose to buy and preserve temperate deciduous forest land rather than build a water filtration plant?

16. How are soils linked to climate change?

9.2 The Hidden Hydrosphere: Groundwater

17. What is a drought?

18. What is the Palmer Drought Severity Index, and how does it determine the degree of drought for a given region?

19. How does water get into the ground?

20. Compare the terms *porosity* and *permeability*. What do they relate to, and how are they different? Discuss these terms in the context of sand and clay.

21. Compare the terms *aquiclude* and *aquifer*. Where does each of them occur, and how are they different?

22. Compare a confined aquifer with an unconfined aquifer. What confines an aquifer?

23. Compare the zone of aeration with the zone of saturation. What is the capillary fringe, and where does it occur in relation to the zones of aeration and saturation?

24. Compare the terms *infiltration* and *percolation*. How are they different?

25. How does water enter an aquifer? How does water leave an aquifer?

26. What does a lake or stream tell us about the depth of the water table?

27. What is a perched water table?

28. What is a spring and how does it form? Is it an area of recharge or discharge for an aquifer? Explain.

29. What is the potentiometric surface? If a building is above the potentiometric surface of its water supply, will water flow from its faucets? Explain.

30. What is a well? How do some artesian wells differ from other wells?

31. Using the concepts of the potentiometric surface and the area of groundwater recharge, explain how water can gush from an artesian well.

9.3 Problems Associated with Groundwater

32. In the context of recharge and discharge, what is groundwater overdraft?

33. What is groundwater mining?

34. Discuss the problems resulting from groundwater overdraft. What are they, and what processes cause each of them?

35. What is fossil groundwater? Can you relate this term to groundwater mining?

36. How do aquifers become polluted?

37. What is a contaminant plume? What cleanup options are available once contamination occurs?

9.4 Geographic Perspectives: Water Resources under Pressure

38. What is a water footprint? Why does one apple take 70 liters of water to produce?

39. Why do golf courses have unusually large water footprints?

40. What is virtual water? Give examples.

Critical-Thinking Questions

1. Examine the soil taxonomy map in Figure 9.14 and find where you live. What soil order(s) occurs where you live? What other methods could you use to determine the soil type where you live?

2. In Section 9.1, the ecosystem services provided by soils are outlined. Can you think of any additional services soils provide?

3. How does buying a cotton T-shirt potentially relate to environmental issues in other areas, such as the Aral Sea in Uzbekistan?

4. How does economic development affect water resources within a country?

5. Do you think luxury services such as golf courses are justifiable given their large water footprint? Does your answer depend on whether you golf or not? Are there other similar luxuries you could argue as being unjustifiable? If so, what are they?

Test Yourself

Take this quiz to test your chapter knowledge.

1. **True or false?** Loam is composed of about 40% sand, 40% silt, and 20% clay.

2. **True or false?** Aquifers form mainly in porous sediments or rocks.

3. **True or false?** Groundwater overdraft can increase the height of the water table.

4. **True or false?** The water footprint for a kilogram of wheat is greater than the water footprint for a kilogram of beef.

5. **Multiple choice:** Which of the following soils would most likely be found in a tropical rainforest?
   a. Alfisol
   b. Gelisol
   c. Oxisol
   d. Vertisol

6. **Multiple choice:** Which of the following biomes has the greatest stores of soil carbon?
   a. Tropical rainforest
   b. Boreal forest
   c. Temperate grassland
   d. Wetland

7. **Multiple choice:** Which of the following problems is not associated with groundwater overdraft?
   a. Subsidence
   b. Dry wells
   c. Surface fissures
   d. Lowered potentiometric surface

8. **Fill in the blank:** _____ occurs when a well becomes contaminated with salt water.

9. **Fill in the blank:** The unseen water used to make a product is called _____ .

10. **Fill in the blank:** The process of soil formation is called _____ .

Picture This. YOUR TURN

Groundwater Features

Use the following terms to fill in the boxes on the diagram. Use each term only once.

1. Aquiclude
2. Artesian well
3. Confined aquifer
4. Perched water table
5. Potentiometric surface
6. Recharge area
7. Unconfined aquifer
8. Water table

Further Reading

1. Huggins, David R., and John P. Reganold. "No-Till: How Farmers Are Saving the Soil by Parking Their Plows." *Scientific American*, July 2008.

2. Logan, William Bryant. *Dirt: The Ecstatic Skin of the Earth*. New York: W.W. Norton, 2007.

3. Reisner, Marc. *Cadillac Desert: The American Desert and Its Disappearing Water*. New York: Penguin Books, 1993.

Answers to Living Physical Geography Questions

1. **What is the difference between dirt and soil?** Dirt is what we track into the house on our shoes. Soil is the living medium in which we grow our food.

2. **How long does it take for soils to form?** People can compost food scraps into soils in a matter of months. Natural soil formation occurs at a rate of a few centimeters per century.

3. **Why does water in houses gush from the faucets?** Any house situated below the potentiometric surface of a nearby water source will have sufficient water pressure in the pipes to make the water gush from the faucets.

4. **How much water is needed to produce 1 kg (2.2 lb) of beef?** About 13,620 L (3,598 gal) of water are needed to produce 1 kg (2.2 lb) of beef.

10 THE LIVING HYDROSPHERE: Ocean Ecosystems

Chapter Outline

PACIFIC OCEAN

Philippines 15° N

Republic of Palau

120° E 135° E

These islands of green are in the Republic of Palau in the western equatorial Pacific. They are composed of ancient uplifted coral reefs. Coral sands and living coral reefs surround the islands.

(© Reinhard Dirscherl/WaterFrame/Getty Images)

LIVING PHYSICAL GEOGRAPHY

➤ How deep are the oceans?

➤ Why are the oceans salty?

➤ Why do most deep-sea organisms glow?

➤ What is the Great Pacific Garbage Patch?

To learn more about coral reefs, see Section 10.2

THE BIG PICTURE *Ocean ecosystems range from tropical coral reefs to dark and frigid deep-sea communities. All ocean ecosystems are influenced by people, and plastic pollution in the oceans is a growing problem.*

LEARNING GOALS *After reading this chapter, you will be able to:*

10.1 ◎ Discern the major physical features of the oceans.

10.2 ◎ Describe the ecosystems along continental margins and human influences on those ecosystems.

10.3 ◎ Explain how polar marine ecosystems function.

10.4 ◎ Describe the geographic patterns of life in the open ocean.

10.5 ◎ Assess the environmental impact of and remedies for plastic pollution in the oceans.

THE HUMAN SPHERE: Coastal Dead Zones

FIGURE 10.1 **Coastal dead zones.** *Red circles show the locations and sizes of coastal dead zones. The largest circles show dead zones 10,000 km² (3,860 mi²) in extent or greater. Dead zones of unknown size are shown with black dots. Note that there are fewer dead zones in the Southern Hemisphere because there is less agricultural activity there.*

COASTAL DEAD ZONES are areas in coastal waters where there is too little dissolved oxygen to support most forms of marine life. Coastal dead zones are a natural phenomenon, but human activity has increased both their numbers and their geographic extent in recent decades. Dead zones are now occurring in areas where they were not found before (Figure 10.1).

Anthropogenic dead zones are closely tied to agriculture. Dead zones form or increase in size as fertilizers, applied in excess to agricultural fields, are carried into streams by rainfall runoff. The streams carry the fertilizers to the coastal areas. There they fertilize phytoplankton (see page 344), creating explosive phytoplankton growth. After the phytoplankton die, they settle into deep water, where microbes decompose their remains. The process of decomposition removes dissolved oxygen from the water, creating a dead zone. Most marine life asphyxiates when it enters these anoxic (oxygen-free) dead zones. This chapter explores the oceans and emphasizes the human influences on them. We first examine the physical characteristics of the world's oceans. Next, we explore life along the continental margins, in polar waters, and in the open ocean. Finally, we examine the growing problem of plastic debris in the world's oceans.

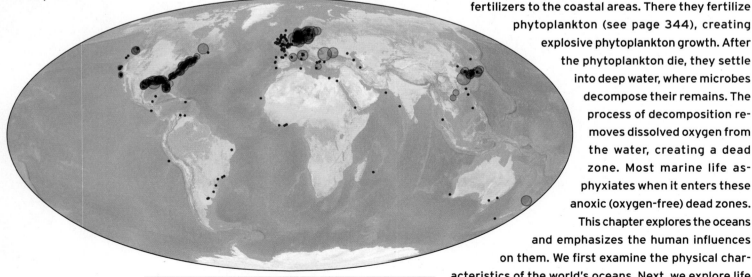

Dead zone size (km²)						
Unknown	0.1	1	10	100	1,000	10,000

10.1 The Physical Oceans

◎ Discern the major physical features of the oceans.

Physical geography explores all of Earth's physical systems. The oceans are a particularly important realm of physical geography. Consider these facts:

1. The oceans are large and deep. They cover 71% of Earth's surface, and they are 4 km (2.5 mi) deep, on average. If Earth's surface were a smooth sphere without valleys or mountains, seawater would cover the planet to a depth of 2,500 m (8,200 ft). **Table 10.1** provides some key statistics on the oceans.

2. Because of their size, the oceans regulate the atmosphere's chemical composition and modify Earth's climate and weather systems.

3. Seventy percent of the oxygen in the atmosphere comes from photosynthesis in the oceans.

4. There would be no life on Earth without the oceans.

5. Nearly half the world's population depends directly on the oceans as a main source of food.

The Five Oceans

The terms *sea*, *gulf*, *bay*, *sound*, and *strait* are used in reference to large bodies of salt water. **Figure 10.2** provides an example of each of these water bodies using the Gulf of Mexico region.

TABLE 10.1	Physical Characteristics of the Oceans	
CHARACTERISTIC	SIZE (METRIC)	SIZE (U.S. CUSTOMARY)
Total area	331,441,932 km^2	127,970,392 mi^2
Total volume	1,303,155,354 km^3	312,643,596 mi^3
Average depth	4 km	2.5 mi
Greatest depth	10,916 m	35,814 ft
Longest mountain range	16,000 km	9,920 mi

How deep are the oceans?*

FIGURE 10.2 **Names for large bodies of water.** *The most commonly used geographic names for ocean features are applied here to the Gulf of Mexico region.*

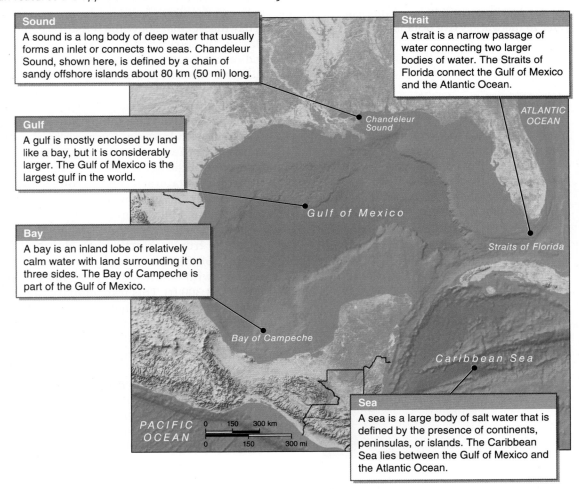

Sound
A sound is a long body of deep water that usually forms an inlet or connects two seas. Chandeleur Sound, shown here, is defined by a chain of sandy offshore islands about 80 km (50 mi) long.

Strait
A strait is a narrow passage of water connecting two larger bodies of water. The Straits of Florida connect the Gulf of Mexico and the Atlantic Ocean.

Gulf
A gulf is mostly enclosed by land like a bay, but it is considerably larger. The Gulf of Mexico is the largest gulf in the world.

Bay
A bay is an inland lobe of relatively calm water with land surrounding it on three sides. The Bay of Campeche is part of the Gulf of Mexico.

Sea
A sea is a large body of salt water that is defined by the presence of continents, peninsulas, or islands. The Caribbean Sea lies between the Gulf of Mexico and the Atlantic Ocean.

Chandeleur Sound
ATLANTIC OCEAN
Gulf of Mexico
Straits of Florida
Bay of Campeche
Caribbean Sea
PACIFIC OCEAN

0 150 300 km
0 150 300 mi

FIGURE 10.3 **The five ocean basins and their major characteristics.**

Pacific Ocean   Atlantic Ocean   Indian Ocean   Southern Ocean   Arctic Ocean

OCEAN BASIN	AREA (KM²)	AREA (MI²)	PERCENTAGE OF TOTAL OCEAN AREA	NOTABLE FEATURE
Pacific	152,617,159	58,925,790	46	The largest and oldest ocean basin
Atlantic	81,705,396	31,546,616	25	Has a submerged mountain range called the Mid-Atlantic Ridge
Indian	67,469,539	26,050,123	20	Found mostly in the Southern Hemisphere
Southern	20,973,318	8,097,840	6	Surrounds Antarctica
Arctic	8,676,520	3,350,021	3	Mostly ice-covered

The term *ocean* is used to refer to the five major water-filled basins on Earth's surface, shown in Figure 10.3. Throughout the remainder of this chapter, *sea* and *ocean* will be used interchangeably to refer to the world's five oceans.

FIGURE 10.4 **Depth of penetration of solar radiation.** *In the open ocean, in clear water, relatively long wavelengths of insolation, such as infrared, red, orange, and yellow, are absorbed in the first 50 m (160 ft) of water. Shortwave UV radiation is also absorbed near the water surface. Green and violet light penetrate just over 100 m (330 ft), and blue light penetrates as much as 250 m (820 ft).*

thermocline
The transitional zone between warm surface water and cold water at depth.

epipelagic zone
The sunlit surface of the ocean down to 200 m (650 ft).

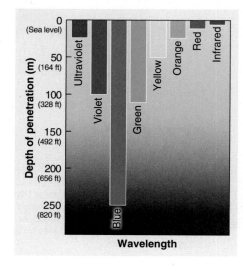

Layers of the Ocean

Only the ocean's surface layers absorb light and are heated directly by sunlight. The depth to which light can penetrate seawater depends on the time of day, the weather above the sea surface, and water clarity. In murky water containing suspended sediments, light barely penetrates 10 m (33 ft). Different wavelengths of light penetrate seawater to different depths. As Figure 10.4 shows, blue wavelengths of light penetrate deepest.

The ocean's surface temperatures vary considerably with latitude. **Because of the direct sunlight in the tropics and the largely cloud-free skies of the subtropical high, tropical and subtropical waters receive strong solar heating.** Higher-latitude waters receive far less solar heating and are much colder, as shown in Figure 10.5.

In the tropics, starting at a depth of about 100 m (330 ft), the water temperature quickly declines with depth until about 500 to 1,000 m (1,640 to 3,300 ft). This transitional zone of temperature decline is called the **thermocline**. The depth of the thermocline varies by latitude and by ocean (see Figure 10.5). Below 2,500 m at all latitudes, seawater temperatures stabilize to a uniform 2°C (35.6°F).

The oceans can be divided into five vertical layers or zones (Figure 10.6). These layers are distinguished by light penetration, water temperature, and seafloor features. The topmost layer, called the **epipelagic zone**, is the sunlit surface of the ocean. It extends down to 200 m (650 ft).

FIGURE 10.5 **Average annual sea surface temperatures.** *Latitudinal differences in sea surface temperature, like differences in air temperature, are a result of latitudinal differences in solar heating. The Arctic Ocean's surface is largely frozen throughout most of the year, but in the tropics, water temperatures can reach 30°C (86°F) or more. The three inset graphs show how water temperature changes with depth at different latitudes.*

High latitudes

At high latitudes, water temperature is nearly the same at all depths.

Tropics

In tropical waters, water temperature is higher near the surface.

Equatorial

Equatorial surface water is the warmest because it receives the most insolation.

Average annual sea surface temperature (°C)

0	5	10	15	20	25	30 °C
32	41	50	59	68	77	86 °F

FIGURE 10.6 **GEO-GRAPHIC: Vertical zones of the oceans.**

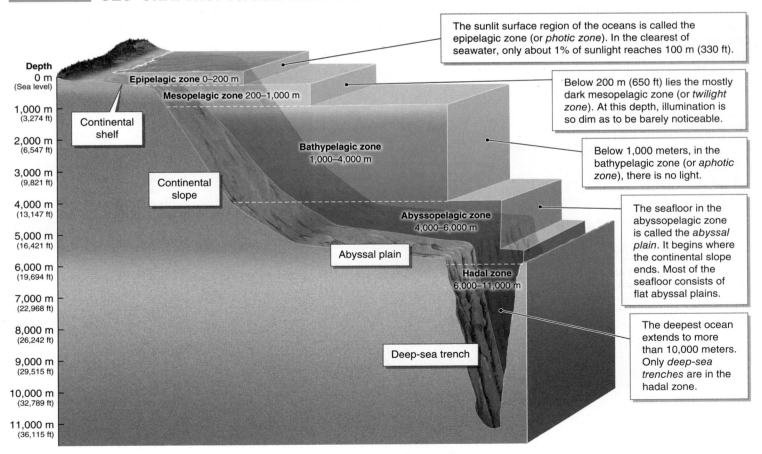

The sunlit surface region of the oceans is called the epipelagic zone (or *photic zone*). In the clearest of seawater, only about 1% of sunlight reaches 100 m (330 ft).

Below 200 m (650 ft) lies the mostly dark mesopelagic zone (or *twilight zone*). At this depth, illumination is so dim as to be barely noticeable.

Below 1,000 meters, in the bathypelagic zone (or *aphotic zone*), there is no light.

The seafloor in the abyssopelagic zone is called the *abyssal plain*. It begins where the continental slope ends. Most of the seafloor consists of flat abyssal plains.

The deepest ocean extends to more than 10,000 meters. Only *deep-sea trenches* are in the hadal zone.

Epipelagic zone 0–200 m
Mesopelagic zone 200–1,000 m
Continental shelf
Continental slope
Bathypelagic zone 1,000–4,000 m
Abyssopelagic zone 4,000–6,000 m
Abyssal plain
Hadal zone 6,000–11,000 m
Deep-sea trench

Depth
0 m (Sea level)
1,000 m (3,274 ft)
2,000 m (6,547 ft)
3,000 m (9,821 ft)
4,000 m (13,147 ft)
5,000 m (16,421 ft)
6,000 m (19,694 ft)
7,000 m (22,968 ft)
8,000 m (26,242 ft)
9,000 m (29,515 ft)
10,000 m (32,789 ft)
11,000 m (36,115 ft)

CRUNCH THE NUMBERS: Water Pressure in the Deep Ocean

Calculate water pressure in the deep ocean in kilograms per square centimeter or pounds per square inch.

Step 1: Calculate the number of bars by dividing the depth by 10 m (or 33 ft if you are working in U.S. customary units).

Step 2: Calculate kg/cm^2 by multiplying the number of bars by 1 (or by 14.7 to get psi).

Problem 1

Sperm whales dive to 2,000 m (6,580 ft) as they hunt giant squid. They have collapsible rib cages and lungs that allow them to withstand the great pressure at that depth. What is that pressure?

Problem 2

The Challenger Deep, in the Mariana Trench, is the deepest point in the ocean at 10,916 m (35,814 ft). What is the pressure at that depth?

Water Pressure

At the ocean's surface, there is no water pressure. Yet if you were to dive down to 10 m (33 ft), you would experience 1 kg/cm^2 (14.7 psi) of pressure. For every 10 m in depth, water pressure increases approximately one bar (or one atmosphere), which is 1 kg/cm^2 (see Section 1.2). The enormous pressures in the deep ocean create a formidable barrier to scientists attempting to explore life there. Crunch the Numbers shows how water pressure is calculated.

Seawater Chemistry

Salinity

Leonardo da Vinci thought that the oceans were salty because rivers ran past salt mines and deposited the salt in the oceans. His hypothesis was not

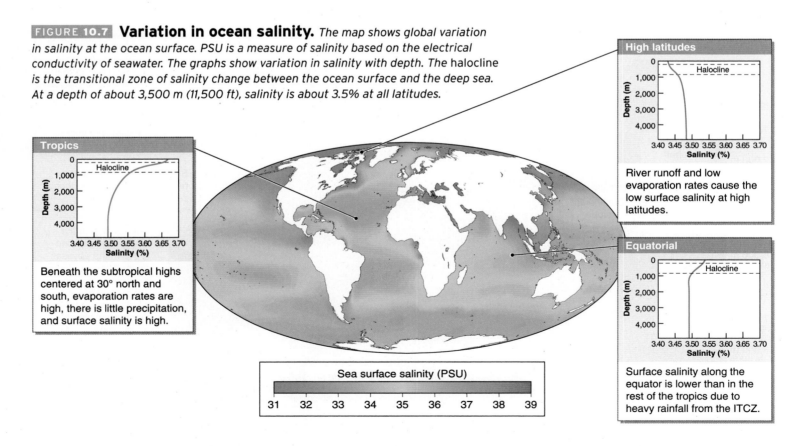

FIGURE 10.7 **Variation in ocean salinity.** *The map shows global variation in salinity at the ocean surface. PSU is a measure of salinity based on the electrical conductivity of seawater. The graphs show variation in salinity with depth. The halocline is the transitional zone of salinity change between the ocean surface and the deep sea. At a depth of about 3,500 m (11,500 ft), salinity is about 3.5% at all latitudes.*

Tropics

Beneath the subtropical highs centered at 30° north and south, evaporation rates are high, there is little precipitation, and surface salinity is high.

High latitudes

River runoff and low evaporation rates cause the low surface salinity at high latitudes.

Equatorial

Surface salinity along the equator is lower than in the rest of the tropics due to heavy rainfall from the ITCZ.

Sea surface salinity (PSU)

31   32   33   34   35   36   37   38   39

salinity
The concentration of dissolved minerals in seawater.

FIGURE 10.8 **Materials dissolved in seawater.** *Ocean water contains many dissolved materials. (The abbreviation "ppt" stands for "parts per trillion.")*

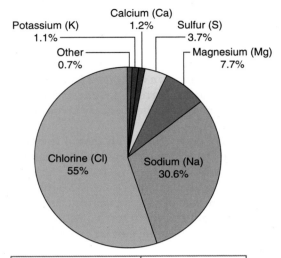

Materials dissolved in seawater	Amounts dissolved in seawater (ppt)
Chlorine (Cl)	18.98
Sodium (Na)	10.56
Magnesium (Mg)	1.27
Sulfur (S)	0.88
Calcium (Ca)	0.40
Potassium (K)	0.38
Other	0.70

is high, and (2) salinity decreases where rivers discharge their freshwater or where there are persistent heavy rains.

By volume, most of the material dissolved in ocean water is chlorine and sodium, but every element on Earth is found dissolved in ocean water in trace amounts **(Figure 10.8)**. When sodium is combined with chloride, the result is sodium chloride (NaCl), or salt.

Ocean Acidity

The oceans play an important part in the short-term carbon cycle. About one-third of all anthropogenic carbon emissions since the late 1800s have been absorbed by the oceans (see Section 6.3). **As atmospheric carbon dioxide is absorbed by seawater, the carbon dioxide forms carbonic acid (H_2CO_3), which makes seawater more acidic.** **Figure 10.9** shows recent decreases in the pH of seawater.

The chemistry of this ocean acidification is well understood. However, scientists do not understand how it will affect marine organisms in the coming decades. They are concerned that shell-building organisms, such as corals, mollusks, and microscopic plantlike organisms called *foraminifera*, will be affected by the increasing acidity of seawater. There are fewer available calcium ions in acidic

salinity
The concentration of dissolved minerals in seawater.

too far off the mark. Rivers do deposit salt and many other minerals in the oceans, but not because they run past salt mines.

Salinity is the concentration of dissolved minerals in seawater. As rivers flow over the continents, they dissolve minerals from the rocks and transport those dissolved minerals to the ocean. **Each year, rivers deposit about 2.5 billion tons of dissolved minerals, including salt, in the oceans.** The salinity of the oceans remains constant, however, because shell-building organisms, chemical reactions with rocks, chemical precipitation, and the recycling of Earth's crust deep into its interior through plate tectonics (see Section 12.2) remove salt from the oceans at the same rate that it is deposited by rivers.

> Why are the oceans salty?

The average ocean salinity is 3.5% by volume (35 g/L or 4.6 oz/gal). Ocean salinity varies geographically from about 1% to 4.1% **(Figure 10.7)**. There are two main reasons for this geographic variation: (1) salinity increases where evaporation

FIGURE 10.9 **Changes in ocean acidity.** *This map shows estimated changes in the pH of ocean surface water from the 1700s to the 1990s. Seawater pH has decreased in all ocean basins. Ocean surface pH varies geographically because of differences in the activities of organisms, the concentrations of atmospheric CO_2, and the effects of ocean currents, stream runoff, and precipitation amounts.*

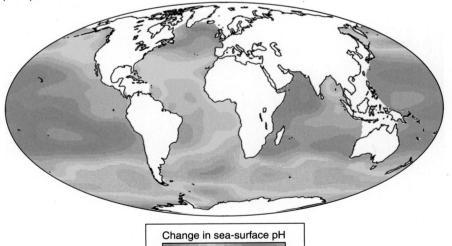

Change in sea-surface pH		
-0.4	-0.09	-0.05

FIGURE 10.10 **Surface ocean currents.**
Warm currents are shown with red arrows and cold currents with blue arrows. The five gyres and other major surface ocean currents are labeled.

Animation
Perpetual ocean
http://qrs.ly/of45sfl

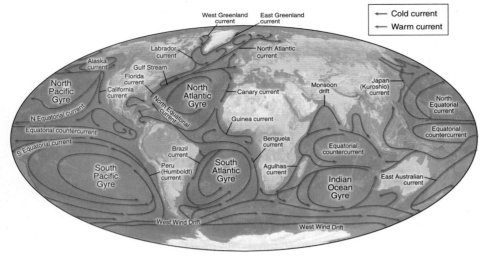

gyre
A large, circular ocean current.

bathymetry
Measurement of depth and topography beneath the surface of a body of water.

water, and a decrease in calcium ions could inhibit the ability of these animals to build their calcium carbonate shells.

Many scientists are concerned that the current rate of ocean acidification is faster than what has occurred naturally at any time during the last 300

FIGURE 10.11 **Bathymetry of the North Atlantic.** *The bathymetric features of the oceans include the shallow and sloping continental shelves, the continental slopes, the flat abyssal plains, mid-ocean ridges, and deep-sea trenches. The vertical scale of the ocean depths is greatly exaggerated here.*
(NOAA National Environmental Satellite and Information Service)

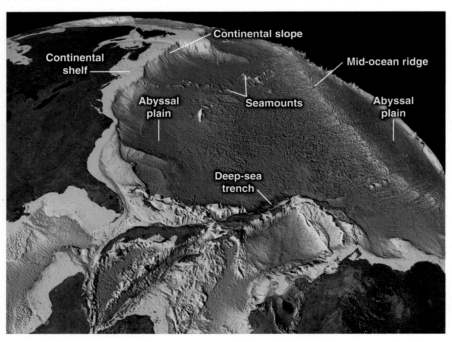

million years. Past ocean acidification has been linked to global mass extinctions of shell-building organisms.

Surface Ocean Currents

The atmosphere and the oceans are both fluids. Therefore, they flow, as wind in the atmosphere and as currents in the oceans. **There are two kinds of ocean currents: (1) surface ocean currents driven by wind and (2) deep ocean currents driven by differences in water density (see Section 6.2).** Surface ocean currents and deep ocean currents both redistribute heat energy across Earth's surface.

If you have ever blown air over a hot cup of coffee or tea, you may have noticed that the force of moving air pushes the surface to the far side of the cup. On a hemispheric scale, the wind blows across the surface of the oceans, and the friction between the air and the water's surface sets the water in motion, forming surface ocean currents. As we saw in Section 4.2, Coriolis force deflects wind to the right in the Northern Hemisphere and to the left in the Southern Hemisphere, creating anticyclonic systems. It deflects moving water in the same way, creating large circular ocean currents called **gyres (Figure 10.10)**.

One notable result of ocean gyres is that they corral plastic and other trash in the oceans, concentrating it into vast garbage patches. The

GEOGRAPHIC PERSPECTIVES

Geographic Perspectives at the end of this chapter explores this problem further.

Seafloor Topography

Imagine completely drying up the oceans. What would the exposed seafloor look like? **The features of the seafloor include major mountain ranges, extensive plains, and deep trench systems (Figure 10.11).** The measurement of depth and topographic features beneath the surface of a body of water is called **bathymetry** (see also Figure 10.6).

If the oceans were dried up, you would see **continental shelves** (the shallow, gently sloping areas of seafloor near continental margins). You would see steeper *continental slopes* forming the transition between the continental shelves and the endless flat stretches of the deep seafloor. The **abyssal plains** are large flat areas on the ocean floor at depths between 4,000 and 6,000 m (13,000 and 20,000 ft).

From these plains rise the world's longest mountain ranges, called **mid-ocean ridges**, which are submarine mountain systems stretching from pole to pole. Isolated **seamounts** rise from the seafloor. Many of these are flat-topped inactive volcanoes that once protruded above sea level. For example, islands like Hawai'i are enormous mountains protruding from the seafloor, with only their tops above the surface of the ocean. **Deep-sea trenches**: long narrow valleys on the seafloor that are the deepest parts of the oceans. Some of these trenches drop more than 6 vertical km (4 mi).

10.2 Life on the Continental Margins

◎ Describe the ecosystems along continental margins and human influences on those ecosystems.

Life in the oceans is not grouped into biomes, as it is on land. Marine biological interactions are instead referred to as ecosystems, and more locally, as communities of interacting organisms.

Our tour of life in the oceans begins at the margins of continents, where people interact intensively with marine ecosystems. Marine ecosystems on the margins of continents are readily accessible to be seen, enjoyed, used, and influenced by people. These ecosystems, in the order in which they are covered in this chapter, include coral reefs, mangrove forests, seagrass meadows, estuaries, kelp forests, and beaches and rocky shores.

Coral Reefs

Coral reefs, often called the rainforests of the sea, are one of nature's greatest displays of life. **Coral reefs are the most biodiverse marine ecosystems.** There are two broad types of corals: cold-water corals and warm-water corals. Cold-water corals live at all latitudes and at great depths in the ocean, but compared with warm-water corals, less is known about them.

This section will focus on warm-water corals. Warm-water corals live only near the sea surface in coastal regions at latitudes less than 30° north and south **(Figure 10.12)**.

Coral reefs occupy only 0.1% of the area near the ocean's surface, about 286,000 km² (110,000 mi²), but they are used by approximately one-third (4,000 species) of all known marine fishes. Scientists are still learning about coral reefs, and perhaps less than 10% of coral reef species have been identified.

Corals look like plants, but they are animals called *zooxanthellae*, which are related to jellyfishes. There are about 700 known species of corals. Most corals share an obligate mutualism with algae (see Section 7.2): The corals filter nutrients from seawater and make them available to photosynthetic algae living within the corals'

FIGURE 10.12 **Distribution of warm-water coral reefs.** *(A) Coral species diversity is greatest in Southeast Asia. The area of greatest coral diversity is called the* Coral Triangle. *(B) Royal gramma* (Gramma loreto) *swim among lettuce corals in this coral reef in the Phoenix Islands of the Republic of Kiribati. (B. © Paul Nicklen/National Geographic/Getty Images)*

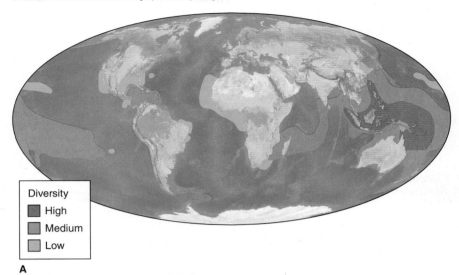

Diversity
- High
- Medium
- Low

A

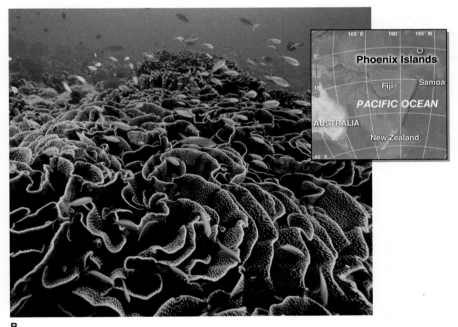

B

tissues. The algae, in turn, provide the corals with carbohydrates and fats.

Corals require clean, well-lighted, warm water between 18°C and 30°C (64°F and 86°F). They are intolerant of low salinity and low light levels. Therefore, they are absent at the mouths of large rivers, such the Amazon River or the great rivers of Southeast Asia, where the water is too fresh and suspended sediments diminish the light. Furthermore, corals cannot survive exposure to air above the low-tide line.

continental shelf
The shallow, sloping seafloor near continental margins.

abyssal plain
A flat plain on the ocean floor at depths between 4,000 and 6,000 m (13,000 and 20,000 ft).

mid-ocean ridge
A submarine mountain range.

seamount
A mountain rising from the seafloor, often a flat-topped inactive volcano.

deep-sea trench
A long narrow valley on the seafloor; deep-sea trenches are the deepest parts of the oceans.

fringing reef
A coral reef that forms near and parallel to a coastline.

barrier reef
A coral reef that runs parallel to the shoreline and forms a deep-water lagoon behind it.

atoll
A ring of coral reefs with an interior lagoon, formed around a sinking volcano.

lagoon
A fully or partly enclosed stretch of salt water formed by a coral reef or sand spit.

coral bleaching
The loss of coloration in corals caused by the absence of their mutualistic algae, which occurs when they have been stressed or have died.

FIGURE 10.13 GEO-GRAPHIC: Three kinds of coral reefs. *A fringing reef, a barrier reef, and an atoll may develop in sequence around a sinking volcanic island. Fringing reefs also form near mainland coasts. Barrier reefs form along mainland coasts as well, but are separated from the coast by open water.*
(Photos from left to right: © Chad Ehlers/Photographer's Choice/Getty Images; © Scott Winer/Oxford Scientific/Getty Images; NASA image created by Jesse Allen, using EO-1 ALI data provided courtesy of the NASA EO-1 Team)

Animation
Atoll formation
http://qrs.ly/of45sfl

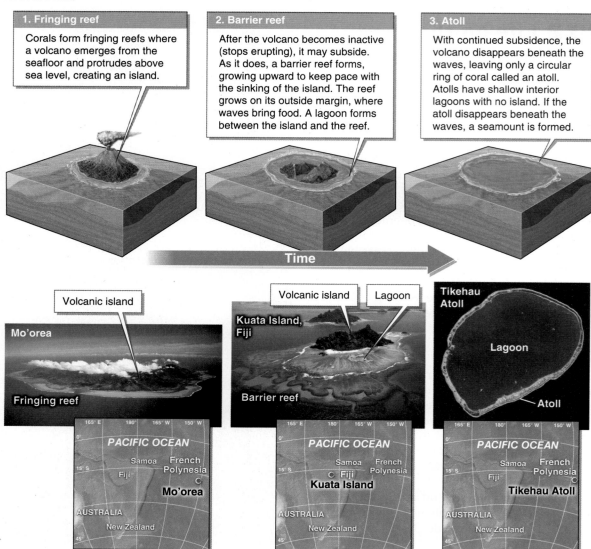

1. Fringing reef
Corals form fringing reefs where a volcano emerges from the seafloor and protrudes above sea level, creating an island.

2. Barrier reef
After the volcano becomes inactive (stops erupting), it may subside. As it does, a barrier reef forms, growing upward to keep pace with the sinking of the island. The reef grows on its outside margin, where waves bring food. A lagoon forms between the island and the reef.

3. Atoll
With continued subsidence, the volcano disappears beneath the waves, leaving only a circular ring of coral called an atoll. Atolls have shallow interior lagoons with no island. If the atoll disappears beneath the waves, a seamount is formed.

Reef-building corals create hard limestone shells that form rocklike reefs. Only the topmost layer of the reef is alive; each generation of corals builds on top of the preceding generation's shells. The hard skeletons build the reef through time.

There are three kinds of coral reefs: fringing reefs, barrier reefs, and atolls. A **fringing reef** forms near and parallel to a coastline. A **barrier reef** runs parallel to a coastline and forms a deep-water lagoon behind it. An **atoll** is a ring of coral reefs with an interior lagoon that forms around a sinking volcano. **Lagoons** are fully or partly enclosed stretches of salt water formed by a coral reef or sand spit. Charles Darwin (see Section 7.1) was the first to recognize that atolls develop as volcanoes gradually sink beneath the ocean's surface. All three reef types can develop during the sequence of atoll formation, as illustrated in **Figure 10.13**.

Threats to Coral Reefs

Worldwide, coral reefs are in decline, and their decline points to deeper, global-scale changes occurring in Earth's physical systems. Scientists estimate that 90% of coral reefs will be threatened by 2030, and by 2050, all reefs could be threatened. As **Figure 10.14** shows, fewer than half the world's coral reefs are currently in a healthy state.

The first sign of trouble for a reef is coral bleaching. **Coral bleaching** is the loss of coloration in corals that occurs when they have been stressed or have died. When corals become stressed, they expel the algae living within them. The corals then starve because they are unable to produce enough food. Most of the color of corals comes from their algal partners. Once the algae are gone, the corals appear white, as Figure 10.15 shows.

Coral bleaching events are increasing for a number of different reasons. Warm water associated with strong El Niños (see Section 5.5) brings widespread coral bleaching events. Many other factors also stress corals and trigger bleaching:

1. *Sea surface temperatures above 30°C (86°F).* Seawater temperatures are rising in many tropical regions as a result of rising atmospheric temperatures.

2. *Destructive fishing.* Fishermen often use cyanide and dynamite to kill and capture fish. These techniques also kill corals.

3. *Coastal development and pollution.* Polluted runoff from developed areas stresses corals.

4. *Coastal sedimentation.* Increased coastal development reduces soil-anchoring vegetation and increases erosion of sediments, which settle on and smother corals.

5. *Increased ocean acidity.* Oceans are absorbing increasing amounts of atmospheric CO_2, which is decreasing the pH of seawater.

FIGURE 10.14 **Coral reef status.** *At present, only 46% of the world's warm-water coral reefs are considered healthy.*

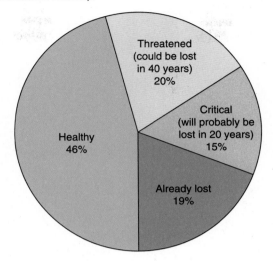

Threatened (could be lost in 40 years) 20%

Critical (will probably be lost in 20 years) 15%

Healthy 46%

Already lost 19%

6. *Diseases carried by viruses or bacteria.* Various pathogens (infectious agents like bacteria) are favored in warmer water, and the stressors already mentioned increase coral vulnerability to disease.

In April 2013, research published in the journal *Science* reported that many coral species have the ability to survive bleaching events and recover more quickly than previously known. Following bleaching events, corals and reef biodiversity are able to rebound within about a decade. This finding is good news because it suggests that, once stressors are

FIGURE 10.15 **Coral bleaching.** *Coral bleaching turns colorful reefs white and eventually kills the corals. The white portions of this coral in Cenderawasih Bay, Papua New Guinea, are bleached.* (© Reinhard Dirscherl/WaterFrame/Getty Images)

Picture This

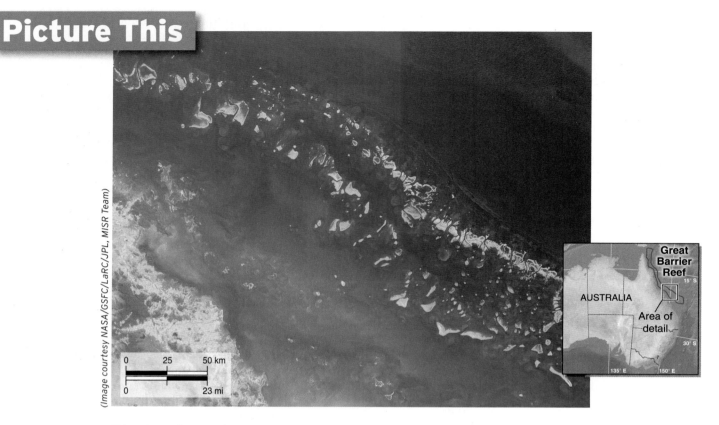

(Image courtesy NASA/GSFC/LaRC/JPL, MISR Team)

The Great Barrier Reef

The Great Barrier Reef in northeastern Australia is the largest coral reef system in the world. It is composed of a labyrinth of nearly 3,000 reef formations. The reef stretches more than 2,600 km (1,600 mi), is up to 60 km (40 mi) wide in some places, and covers some 350,000 km^2 (135,135 mi^2) in area (red area of the inset map). This satellite image shows only the southern portions of the reef off the central Queensland coast.

The Great Barrier Reef possesses some of Earth's richest biodiversity. It supports 350 to 400 species of corals, 1,500 fish species, 4,000 species of mollusks, some 240 species of birds, 30 whale species, and 6 sea turtle species.

In response to widespread declines in fish populations and poor reef health, the Great Barrier Reef Marine Park was established in 2004. Fishing was banned in 32% of the reef's area. Only two years after the protections were put in place, the reef's fish biomass doubled and the reefs recovered in the protected areas. About 2 million tourists visit the reef each year, and the park generates over $3.4 billion from ecotourism annually.

Consider This

1. Weigh the pros and cons of restricting or banning fishing (or hunting, or collecting) from a natural area to allow wildlife populations to recover.

2. Have you ever been an ecotourist? If so, where?

---

reduced, the decline of the world's coral reefs can be slowed or possibly reversed.

mangrove forest
A coastal marine ecosystem dominated by saltwater-tolerant shrubs and trees, found in the tropics and subtropics.

The Value of Coral Reefs
About a half billion people use coral reefs directly or rely on them for their food and economic livelihood. Compounds to fight cancer, HIV, and malaria have been discovered in coral reef species. International tourism in many tropical regions, such as the Caribbean Sea and Hawai'i, is centered on coral beaches and coral reefs. In the Caribbean Sea alone, coral reefs are estimated to provide roughly $5 billion yearly in the form of tourism, fishing, and food security. **Picture This** explores

FIGURE **10.16** **Mangrove forests.** *(A) Mangrove forests are found mostly between 30° north and south latitude along coastal shorelines. Mangrove tree species diversity is greatest in Southeast Asia. (B) Mangroves on Nusa Lembongan Island, near Bali, Indonesia. Mangrove trees are the only trees that can grow immersed in salt water. They have several adaptations to cope with high salinity, including the ability to exude salt from pores on their leaves. (A. Spalding, M., Kainuma, M., Collins, L. (2010a). World Atlas of Mangroves. A collaborative project of ITTO, ISME, FAO, UNEP-WCMC, UNESCO-MAB, UNU-INWEH and TNC. London (UK): Earthscan, London. 319 pp. Spalding, M., Kainuma, M., Collins, L. (2010b). Data layer from the World Atlas of Mangroves. In Supplement to: Spalding et al. (2010a). Cambridge (UK): UNEP World Conservation Monitoring Centre. URL: data.unep-wcmc. B. © Jason Edwards/National Geographic/Getty Images)*

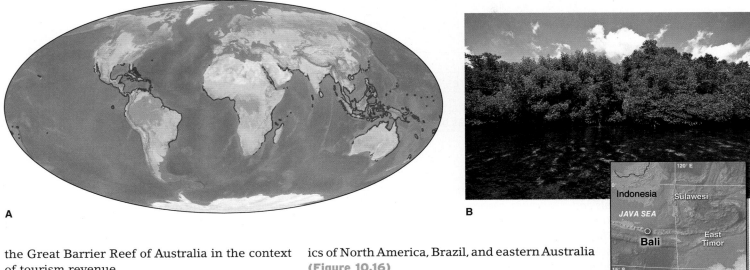

A

B

the Great Barrier Reef of Australia in the context of tourism revenue.

Mangrove Forests

Mangrove forests are ecosystems dominated by saltwater-tolerant coastal shrubs and trees. They are found in the tropics and subtropics. These unique halophytic (salt-tolerant) plants, called *mangroves*, occupy, or once occupied, nearly all tropical coastal waters. Where the water is warm enough, their range extends far into the subtrop-

ics of North America, Brazil, and eastern Australia **(Figure 10.16)**.

The mud in which mangrove roots grow is almost completely devoid of oxygen. In response, mangrove trees have evolved pneumatophore (air-breathing) roots **(Figure 10.17)**. These roots allow the plant to take in air through small tubes, called *lenticels*, when they are exposed at low tide.

Mangrove forests are important ecosystems because they function as nurseries for coral reef fishes as well as many commercial fish species.

FIGURE **10.17** **Mangrove roots.** *Mangroves have broad stilt-like roots that stand above low tide, provide support for the plants in loose sediments, and allow the plants to exchange gases with the atmosphere. Here, a juvenile lemon shark (Negaprion brevirostris) is swimming among mangrove roots in the Bimini Islands of the Bahamas. (© Brian J. Skerry/National Geographic/Getty Images)*

seagrass meadow
A shallow coastal ecosystem dominated by flowering plants that resemble grasses.

FIGURE 10.18 **Threats to mangrove forests.** *The table lists the factors that are detrimental to coastal mangrove forests. The pie chart shows where the remaining mangrove forests are found. Asia and Africa together have 63% of the world's remaining mangrove forests.*

Threats to Mangrove Forests
Large-scale conversion to shrimp aquaculture
Conversion for tourism
Coastal pollution
Clearance for agriculture
Urbanization
Natural disasters such as hurricanes

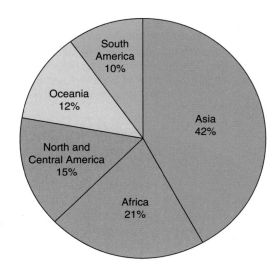

FIGURE 10.19 **Seagrass meadows.** *(A) Distribution of seagrass meadows. Like that of corals and mangroves, seagrass species richness is greatest in Southeast Asia and northern Australia. (B) A green sea turtle (Chelonia mydas) hovers over turtle grass (Thalassia testudinum) in Hol Chan Marine Reserve in Belize. A single acre of seagrass can support 40,000 fish and 50 million invertebrates such as clams, burrowing worms, sea stars, and conches.* (B. © Brian J. Skerry/National Geographic/Getty Images)

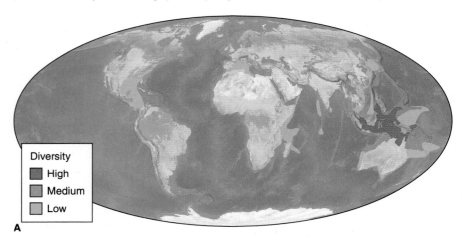

A

B

Marine invertebrates such as oysters, clams, mussels, barnacles, and anemones affix themselves to the roots of mangrove trees. The roots of mangroves trap and hold loose sediments that would otherwise be swept away by currents. The resulting mud in which mangroves grow provides habitat for crabs and sea worms, which in turn attract other organisms, such as predatory fish and birds.

As **Figure 10.18** details, there are many threats to mangrove forests. **The single most important force of degradation for mangrove forests is shrimp aquaculture (farming).** Between 1980 and 2000, more than 30% of the world's mangrove forests were converted to farms growing shrimp for export to North America, Europe, and Asia.

Half the world's original mangrove forests are now gone, and these ecosystems are estimated to have dropped from 32 million to 15 million ha (80 million to 37 million acres) as of 2007. About 1% of the remaining mangrove forest area, or 142,000 ha (350,000 acres), is lost each year. At this rate, mangrove forests outside of protected reserves will be gone by the end of the century.

Mangroves are a renewable economic resource for people, and they provide a defense against dangerous surges of water caused by hurricanes or tsunamis (see The Human Sphere in Chapter 14). Coastlines with healthy mangrove forests experience considerably less flooding and erosion compared with regions where the mangrove forests are gone. Protecting mangroves goes hand-in-hand with protecting the livelihoods of people and the habitats of species.

Seagrass Meadows

Seagrass meadows, like mangrove forests, are an often-overlooked marine ecosystem. **Seagrass meadows** are shallow coastal ecosystems dominated by

TABLE 10.2 AT A GLANCE: Threats to Seagrass Meadows
Coastal pollution
Dredging (deepening of ports and harbors)
Bottom trawling (dragging fishing nets along the seafloor)
Aquaculture
Beach development
Rising sea level

sheets in the Northern Hemisphere (see Section 6.2) began melting 15,000 years ago. The meltwater drained into the oceans and caused sea levels to rise about 85 m (280 ft). Coastal areas were flooded and river-carved coastlines were drowned, forming many estuaries. These partially flooded coastal rivers valleys are called *rias*. San Francisco Bay, Rio de la Plata, the mouth of the Amazon River, Puget Sound in Washington State, and the Chesapeake Bay are some of the largest estuaries (Figure 10.20).

estuary
A brackish-water ecosystem found at the mouth of a river that is influenced by tides.

flowering plants that resemble grasses. They are important natural fish nurseries. Although they are most common in tropical waters, seagrass meadows are found in temperate waters as well (Figure 10.19).

The plant species we call seagrasses are not true grasses. The seagrasses comprise about 60 different species within four families of flowering plants, all of which look like grasses, with flat and narrow leaf blades. Some common seagrasses are eelgrass (*Zostera* spp.), turtle grass (*Thalassia testudinum*), and manatee grass (*Syringodium filiforme*).

Seagrass meadows provide critical habitat for many species of marine life in their juvenile stages of development. Some animals, such as green sea turtles, as well as manatees (*Trichechus* spp.) and their relatives, dugongs (*Dugong dugong*), graze on seagrasses. The plants trap sediment, which reduces suspended sediments and improves coastal water quality. Their roots stabilize sediments in coastal areas, reducing coastal erosion.

Several anthropogenic forces, summarized in Table 10.2, are causing losses of seagrass meadows globally. Like coral reefs and mangrove forests, seagrass meadows contribute most to local economies when they are preserved rather than converted to another use. In the Mediterranean Sea and elsewhere, effective efforts to save and restore seagrass meadows have focused on stemming pollution from stream runoff in coastal areas (particularly phosphorus and nitrogen from agricultural fields), establishing protected areas, and replanting seagrass meadows that have diminished or have been lost.

Estuaries

An **estuary** is a brackish-water ecosystem at the mouth of a river that is influenced by tides. *Brackish water* forms where fresh river water and ocean water mix to produce water that is salty, but less salty than ocean water. Salinity in estuaries varies considerably, depending on river discharge and tidal levels.

Many large estuaries are about 10,000 years old. They were formed as the great continental ice

FIGURE 10.20 The Chesapeake Bay. *(A) Landsat image of the Chesapeake Bay. This estuary was a river valley when sea levels were lower about 15,000 years ago. (B) Most of the original wetlands of the Chesapeake Bay have been developed and are gone. Some, such as these wetlands in the Blackwater National Wildlife Refuge in Maryland, have been preserved. (A. NASA/Goddard Space Flight Center Scientific Visualization Studio; B. © Trevor Clark/Aurora/Getty Images)*

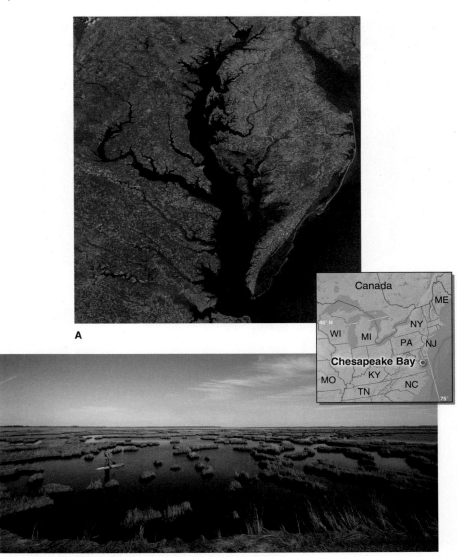

A

B

kelp forest
A coastal marine ecosystem dominated by kelp, found where ocean water is colder than 20°C (68°F).

TABLE **10.3**	AT A GLANCE: **Threats to Estuaries**
Heavy industry	
Dredging, infilling, and housing development	
Coastal pollution	
Seawalls	
Non-native species	

In the tropics, mangrove forests colonized these drowned river environments. At middle and high latitudes, a variety of salt-tolerant herbaceous plants dominate estuarine environments. Common estuary plants include cordgrass (*Spartina alterniflora*), pickleweed (*Salicornia* spp.), and needlerush (*Juncus roemerianus*).

FIGURE **10.21** **Kelp forests.** *(A) Distribution of kelp forests. (B) Many organisms use kelp forests. This sea lion (Zalophus californianus) swims in a kelp forest in Northern California. (B. © Photo Researchers/Getty Images)*

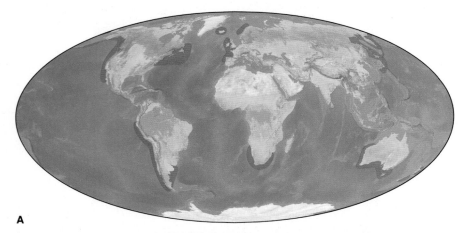

A

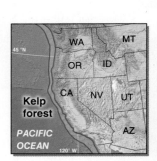

B

As rivers flow into estuaries, they bring in organic-rich clays and silts. These sediments are deposited and accumulate into *mudflats*, which are exposed twice daily during low tide. All estuaries have deep deposits of mud that are rich in organic material. Primary productivity is high in estuaries, as plant growth is fueled by the nutrient-rich sediments.

Estuaries are important habitats for many kinds of organisms, particularly for the juvenile stages of many fish species. Some 75% of the commercial fish catch in the United States consists of fish that depend on estuaries for at least part of their life cycle. Many bird and mammal species also rely on estuary habitat. Migratory birds use estuaries as rest and feeding stops on their long-distance migrations.

Because estuaries are flat and have calm waters, they make ideal locations for human settlement. Seventy percent of the world's largest cities, including London, Shanghai, Buenos Aires, Hong Kong, Boston, and New York City, are located on estuaries (or what were once estuaries). People expand settlements onto estuaries by first filling them in with debris, such as soil or even garbage, then expanding the cities onto the newly created surface.

Because of the heavy human influence on estuaries, they are the world's most endangered marine ecosystems. Table 10.3 summarizes the threats to estuaries.

Estuaries provide many economic benefits to people. They not only provide shelter for juvenile commercial fish species, but also enhance tourism, recreation (including recreational fishing), and production of shellfish (such as oysters and abalone). Estuaries also absorb wave energy from large storms, such as hurricanes, significantly reducing coastal erosion and property loss. Furthermore, they filter pollutants from rivers before they enter the sea, significantly improving coastal water quality.

Kelp Forests

Kelp forests are marine ecosystems found in temperate and polar waters where the water temperature does not exceed 20°C (68°F) (Figure 10.21). They are dominated by large algae called *kelp*. There are three groups of kelp: green kelp (*Chlorophyta*), tan kelp (*Phaeophyta*), and red kelp (*Rhodophyta*). Only tan kelp form kelp forests.

Limited to zones with adequate light, kelp forests grow only in water no deeper than 50 m (165 ft). The kelp rely on *holdfasts*, which resemble roots, but function only to anchor the algae to the rocks. Many kelp grow quickly—some tan kelp can grow 1 m (3.3 ft) per day.

Communities of fish, sea urchins, anemones, sea stars, mollusks, and lobsters inhabit kelp forests. Kelp employ toxins to deter many grazers. Sea

<table>
<tr><td colspan="1">TABLE 10.4 AT A GLANCE: Threats to Kelp Forests</td></tr>
</table>

TABLE 10.4 AT A GLANCE: **Threats to Kelp Forests**
Pollution and sediment runoff from streams
Ocean warming caused by climate change and El Niño
Removal of keystone species, such as sea otters
Non-native species, particularly sea urchins
Harvesting of kelp for food and other products

urchins, however, can eat kelp, and if their populations increase, kelp forests often suffer declines. **Figure 10.22** explores the Pacific sea otter's role as a keystone species in kelp forests.

Like other coastal ecosystems, kelp forests are vulnerable to threats posed by human activities **(Table 10.4)**. Fortunately, the rapid growth rates of kelp allow them to recover rapidly if degradation pressure stops.

Beaches and Rocky Shores

The coastal ecosystems most familiar to people may be beaches and rocky shores. Most of us have strolled along a beach barefoot or gazed at the horizon from a rocky shore. **Because they are exposed to the force of crashing waves and wind, beaches and rocky shores are high-energy environments.** As a result, many organisms in these environments are either anchored to the rocks (such as barnacles, sea urchins, and sea stars) or hidden within the sand (such as clams, periwinkles, and crabs). Rocky coastlines sometimes harbor communities that live in *tide pools*, still pools that form at low tide **(Figure 10.23)**.

In general, biodiversity is not particularly high in beach and rocky shore environments, but many organisms live only in these habitats or rely on them during at least part of their life cycle. Shorebirds such as gulls, sandpipers, terns, and pelicans are common on beaches and rocky shores. Marine mammals such as sea lions, seals, and sea otters are found in these environments as well. Sea turtles nest only on warm beaches in the tropics. Human settlement, pollution runoff, and erosion of sand are the most significant threats to beach and rocky shoreline ecosystems **(Table 10.5)**.

TABLE 10.5 AT A GLANCE: **Threats to Beaches and Rocky Shores**
Conversion to vacation resorts and construction
Pollution runoff
Fishing pressure
Erosion of sand
Non-native species

FIGURE 10.22 **GEO-GRAPHIC: The Pacific sea otter as a keystone species.** *(1. © Marc Shandro/Flickr/Getty Images; 2. Gulf of Maine Cod Project, NOAA National Marine Sanctuaries; Courtesy of National Archives; 3. © Mark Conlin/Oxford Scientific/Getty Images)*

1. Keystone species

Each day, a Pacific sea otter (*Enhydra lutris*) eats about 25% of its body weight in food. Much of its diet is purple sea urchins (*Strongylocentrotus* species).

2. Overhunting

In the 1800s, the Pacific sea otter disappeared throughout most of its range in the northern Pacific Ocean due to hunting for its fur. By 1900, it was nearly extinct. In 1911, it was legally protected.

3. Ecosystem changes

A *trophic cascade* occurs when a keystone species, such as the sea otter, is removed and other species are affected. Purple sea urchins (shown below) feed on kelp holdfasts, killing the whole kelp plant. When the sea otter was removed, sea urchin populations grew. As a result, kelp forests and the species that depend on them suffered.

4. Reintroduction

Pacific sea otter reintroductions (return to a former geographic range) have contributed to the recovery of many Pacific kelp forests. Although the Pacific sea otter has been returned to some of its former range, its population numbers are still low.

FIGURE 10.23 **Tide pools in southern Oregon.** *Tide pools harbor unique communities composed of sea anemones, crabs, octopuses, kelp, and many other organisms. Most tide pools are easy to reach and explore at low tide. (Bruce Gervais)*

FIGURE 10.24 **Phytoplankton.** *(A) Phytoplankton include bacteria and algae. All phytoplankton are microscopic; hence, these drawings do not represent the actual size of each organism. Scale bars are provided to give the approximate relative sizes of each. (B) This phytoplankton bloom, shown as light-blue water, is in the Barents Sea, off the northern coast of Norway. In a phytoplankton bloom, phytoplankton populations increase dramatically. An individual phytoplanktonic organism lives only a few days, but blooms last several weeks. (A. Sally Bensusen, NASA EOS Project Science Office; B. NASA image courtesy Jeff Schmaltz, MODIS Rapid Response Team at NASA GSFC)*

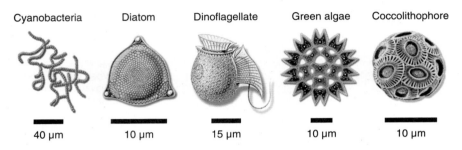

Cyanobacteria   Diatom   Dinoflagellate   Green algae   Coccolithophore

40 μm   10 μm   15 μm   10 μm   10 μm

A

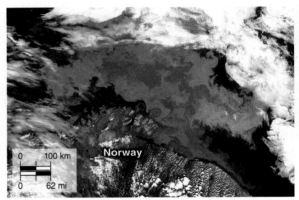

B

10.3 Life in Polar Waters

◎ Explain how polar marine ecosystems function.

All the marine ecosystems that we have described up to this point are close to shore and are heavily influenced by human activities. The polar waters are close to the edges of the continents as well, but far fewer people live near them and influence them. Compared with other continental margin environments, polar waters have remained relatively little affected by human activity.

The Importance of Phytoplankton

At the base of the food web in the polar oceans are microscopic photosynthetic algae and other microorganisms, collectively called *phytoplankton* (Figure 10.24). All oceans contain phytoplankton. Even though ocean phytoplankton account for only 1% of the world's photosynthetic biomass, they are very productive, and they produce 70% of the oxygen in Earth's atmosphere.

Marine ecosystems rely on phytoplankton to convert solar energy to the chemical energy that all other marine organisms require. (Hydrothermal and geothermal vent ecosystems are the exception, as we will see in Section 10.4.) The key to primary productivity in ocean water is **upwelling**: the circulation of water from the seafloor to the ocean surface. Upwelling brings nutrients from the seafloor sediments to the sunlit epipelagic zone where phytoplankton reside. The more upwelling that occurs, the better the phytoplankton will be fertilized and grow, and the more productive the ecosystem will be.

FIGURE 10.25 **Phytoplankton productivity.** *Phytoplankton blooms are shown in green, yellow, orange, and red over the oceans. Blue areas have the lowest phytoplankton activity, and red areas have the highest. Note the concentration of phytoplankton activity at high latitudes. (SeaWiFS Project, NASA/Goddard Space Flight Center, and DigitalGlobe™)*

upwelling
The circulation of nutrient-rich water from the seafloor to the ocean surface.

pelagic
Relating to the open sea.

Northern Hemisphere spring/early summer
(April through June)

Southern Hemisphere spring/early summer
(August through October)

Phytoplankton in Polar Waters

Polar waters are not thermally layered, meaning that the surface water is as cold as the water at depth (see Figure 10.5). As a result, deep, nutrient-rich cold water can readily circulate to the surface because it is not denser than the surface water. Where surface water is warm, the greater density of cold water often prevents it from moving to the surface. Thus, ocean currents created by the wind readily bring nutrients from the seafloor sediments to the surface in polar areas, but less so where surface waters are warm. **Because of the strong upwelling in polar waters, they are among the most biologically productive in the world (Figure 10.25).**

Compared with polar terrestrial ecosystems, polar marine ecosystems can respond rapidly to spring warming because phytoplankton, with a life span of a few days, grow as soon as temperature and light levels are suitable. Land plants at high latitudes, however, must wait for the snow to melt and ground temperatures to increase. Thus, there is far less available energy in polar terrestrial ecosystems and far less biomass on land. Antarctica, for instance, is barren and has little biomass, while the seas just offshore are teeming with life supported by phytoplankton blooms.

Many migratory birds, as well as mammals such as whales, make their way to the high latitudes each summer to gorge on the brief but bountiful productivity of the polar waters. During the dark polar winter, phytoplankton activity shuts down, and many species migrate to more productive latitudes. **Picture This** discusses the migration of the Arctic tern in the context of polar marine productivity.

10.4 Life in Open Waters

◎ **Describe the geographic patterns of life in the open ocean.**

Because the oceans are so large and so deep, open-ocean, or **pelagic**, ecosystems are the most geographically extensive ecosystems on the planet. The *open waters* (also called the *high seas*) cover about 50% of Earth's surface in total. Our knowledge of the open ocean, however, is still in its infancy. Scientists are working to understand what lives there, how pelagic ecosystems function, and how people are influencing them.

We begin with two geographic approaches to examining the open waters: (1) tracing the daily movements of organisms vertically through layers of the ocean and (2) following the periodic movements of organisms horizontally across the ocean's surface.

Picture This

(© Arctic-Images/The Image Bank/Getty Images)

Arctic Tern Migration

The Arctic tern (*Sterna paradisaea*) is one of the greatest long-distance voyagers in nature, and its journey illustrates the powerful draw of the productive polar waters. It migrates from pole to pole, always following the summer. It arrives in the Arctic in May or June just in time for the summer bounty. In August or September, it flies south to Antarctic waters to spend the summer there.

Tracking of Arctic terns has shown that they fly along routes that roughly skirt the edges of the continents, rather than in straight lines (inset map). Thus, these birds commonly travel some 80,000 km (50,000 mi) or more each year. During this journey, the birds may rest on land only once a year, while nesting. Arctic terns feed, mate, and even sleep while flying. Since this remarkable bird lives about 30 years, it can travel as much as 2.4 million km (1.5 million mi) during its lifetime.

Consider This

1. List the costs and benefits of long-distance migration such as that of the Arctic tern.

2. If there were strong upwelling in tropical waters, do you think the Arctic tern would migrate such a long distance? Explain.

bioluminescence
The production of light through chemical means by living organisms.

Layers of Light: Daily Vertical Migrations

Much of the open ocean's surface is a biological desert by day, but it is full of life at night, when organisms migrate upward from the safety of the dark depths to feed at the surface. **These daily vertical migrations, or "commutes," represent the largest synchronized animal movements on Earth.** All types of organisms rise to the surface each night, including zooplankton, jellyfish, fish, and squid. Some organisms, such as jellyfish, take hours to reach the surface, spending more time in migrating than in feeding.

Many other organisms make a "reverse commute" to feed. In other words, they live at the lighted ocean surface but dive into the depths for their food **(Figure 10.26)**.

Trans-Ocean Migrations

During the last decade, thanks to new GPS tagging and tracking technology, scientists have begun to piece together where pelagic migratory organisms go. Scientists are using a variety of electronic tagging techniques on migratory species to reveal where they migrate, when they migrate, and why they migrate. **Figure 10.27** traces the migrations of two species, the great white shark and the bluefin tuna.

Life in the Deep

No sunlight reaches below the mesopelagic zone, which ends at a depth of 1,000 m (3,280 ft) (see Figure 10.6). Most of the open ocean is therefore pitch black and perpetually just above freezing. Pressures at these depths are extremely high because of the immense weight of water above.

There is, however, light at these depths. **Ninety percent of organisms in the deep sea make their own light.** **Bioluminescence** is the production of light through chemical means by living organisms. Bioluminescence has evolved independently among

FIGURE **10.26** **Deep-diving organisms.** *(A) The strange-looking ocean sunfish (Mola mola) lives at the ocean surface and dives about 200 m (660 ft) deep to eat jellyfish. Note the GPS data recorder tag just behind the top fin of the fish. (B) Sperm whales (Physeter macrocephalus) dive as deep as 3,000 m (10,000 ft)—three vertical kilometers straight down—to feed on giant squid. Like dolphins and bats, they locate their prey in the dark using sound, or echolocation. (A. © Mike Johnson; B. © Jens Kuhfs/Photographers Choice/Getty Images)*

A

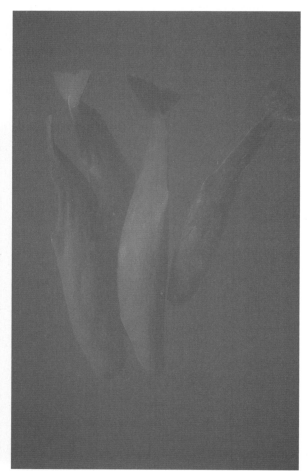

B

FIGURE 10.27 **Pelagic animal migrations.** *An understanding of the movement patterns of marine organisms is an important conservation tool for protecting their populations. (A) Great white sharks (Carcharodon carcharias) routinely travel between California and Hawai'i and congregate in between at a location scientists call the shark café, probably to find mates. The yellow dots represent the locations of several dozen tagged sharks over a period of a few years. (B) Bluefin tuna (Thunnus thynnus), like many pelagic organisms, routinely cross ocean basins. The dots represent the locations of a single 15 kg (33 lb) bluefin that crossed the North Pacific between California and Japan three times in less than two years. (A. Courtesy of Salvador Jorgensen, Monterey Bay Aquarium; Photos: Michael Patrick O'Neill/Science Source)*

A

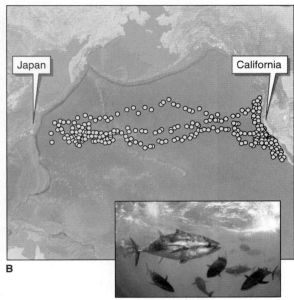

B

Why do most deep-sea organisms glow?

unrelated groups of deep-sea organisms at least 40 times. It is used to attract mates and prey and to hide and escape from predators **(Figure 10.28)**.

Scientific study of life in the deep ocean is a particularly challenging endeavor. The tremendous pressures of the deep have created a formidable barrier to scientific investigation, and staffed missions are very expensive. Robotic submersibles and trawls, which are far less costly, have been among the most important sources of scientific information on deep-ocean ecosystems **(Figure 10.29** on page 348).

Biological Islands: Seamounts and Hydrothermal Vents

The abyssal plains are relative biological deserts. Rising from these plains are biological islands in the form of seamounts and hydrothermal vents. Collectively, seamount ecosystems are larger in area than any terrestrial biome. Together, they make up an area approximately the same size as the continent of South America. These ecosystems, however, are largely

FIGURE 10.28 **Adaptations to the deep sea.** *The black-belly dragonfish (Stomias atriventer) has many traits that are common among deep-sea fishes: large eyes for detecting bioluminescence in extremely low-light conditions, a bioluminescent lure to attract prey, and a large jaw with cage-like teeth to trap prey. Silver scales reflect the faint light and reduce the fish's silhouette, lowering its visibility to predators and prey. (© Dave Wrobel)*

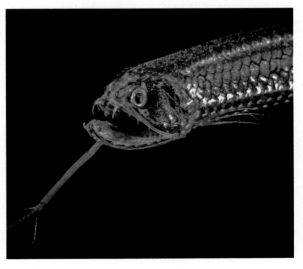

FIGURE 10.29 SCIENTIFIC INQUIRY: **How do scientists explore life in the deep?**
The deep oceans are the least understood of Earth's ecosystems, but evolving submersible technology is improving scientists' understanding of deep-sea ecosystems. Each approach to scientific exploration of the deep has advantages and disadvantages. (All photos: NOAA Ocean Explorer)

Trawl Sampling
Nets that are dragged along behind a vessel, called *trawls*, are the mainstay of research on life in the deep. *Benthic trawls* capture samples from the ocean floor. *Pelagic trawls* capture samples from the middle of the water column. *Plankton nets* collect plankton-sized organisms in a fine net with a mesh size of 335 μm (0.01 in).

Advantages: Samples large areas of the ocean.

Limitations: Some animals swim out and avoid capture. Soft-bodied animals such as jellyfish are damaged beyond recognition.

ROV Sampling
Remotely operated vehicles (ROVs) such as the *Hercules*, shown here, are equipped with instruments for exploration of the deep. *Slurp guns* vacuum up specimens. *Mechanical arms* reach out and grab samples from the seafloor.

Advantages: Targets specific habitats for study. Collects live specimens for study.

Limitations: Limited sampling area. More expensive to operate than trawls.

ROV Photo Documentation
Photos of organisms taken from ROVs are invaluable in documenting marine life in its natural ecological setting. This deep-water sea cucumber swims in total darkness and near-freezing temperatures at a depth of 3,200 m (10,500 ft).

Advantages: Photos of deep-sea organisms in their natural habitat provide an ecological context and show how they behave.

Limitations: Identification of unknown species can be difficult using photography alone. A physical specimen is necessary for genetic analysis.

---

inaccessible to scientific study and barely understood by scientists **(Figure 10.30)**.

Like winds around a high mountain, ocean currents flow over and around large seamounts. These currents may accelerate and become turbulent, stirring up nutrients from the seafloor and bringing them to the sunlit surface. The nutrients stimulate phytoplankton blooms, which support other organisms. Many migratory species seek out and congregate above seamounts, including sharks, tuna, whales, and seabirds.

Like seamounts, hydrothermal vent communities are rich biological islands on the seafloor.

hydrothermal vent community
A unique ecosystem found at volcanic hot springs that emit mineral-rich water onto the seafloor.

Hydrothermal vent communities are unique ecosystems found at hydrothermal vents, volcanic hot springs that emit mineral-rich water. Seawater circulates through fissures in the crust and becomes heated to over 400°C (750°F) before emerging from the seafloor. The water becomes a stew of acids, sulfides, methane, and carbon dioxide as the rocks dissolve in it. Specialized bacteria metabolize these chemicals by the process of *chemosynthesis*, and other organisms feed on those bacteria. These hydrothermal vent communities get their energy from geothermal energy rather than solar energy. If the Sun were to stop shining, these organisms would

FIGURE 10.30 **Seamounts.** *(A) Locations of some of the world's largest seamounts. (B) A sonar image of the Kawio Barat seamount in the Celebes Sea, south of the Philippines. The vertical heights of this seamount are color coded. From its base to its peak, it is about 3,000 m (10,000 ft) high. (B. Image courtesy of INDEX 2010: Indonesia-USA Deep-Sea Exploration of the Sangihe Talaud Region)*

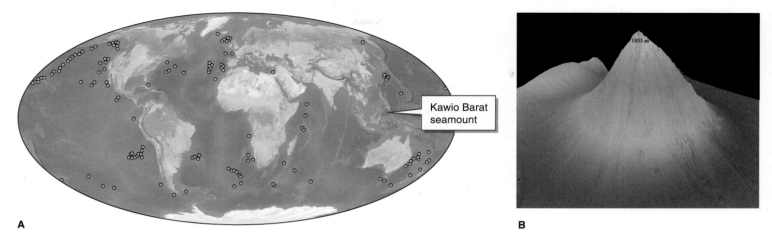

A

Kawio Barat seamount

1855 m

B

probably not be affected, while the rest of the biosphere would disappear. The locations of some hydrothermal vents are shown in **Figure 10.31**.

Reaping the Bounty: Industrial Fishing

All marine ecosystems, whether on the continental margins or in the open ocean, support fisheries of one type or another. A **fishery** is a region where fish are caught for human consumption. The livelihoods of about a half billion people, mostly in economically developing countries, are dependent on small-scale, local, and sustainable fishing. *Sustainable* fishing means that the amount of fish taken is equal to or less than the reproductive rate of the fish population.

Unsustainable fishing occurs when fish are taken out of a fishery faster than the population can reproduce, causing the fish population to decline. Due to unsustainable fishing, about 30% of the world's fisheries have *collapsed*, defined here as being reduced to 10% of their former fish populations.

A growing human population, coupled with advances in industrial fishing technology in the last five decades, is to blame for global fishery declines. The global fish catch peaked in 1989 at 90 million tons and has since leveled off or declined. The decline is not due to conservation efforts—there

fishery
A region where fish are caught for human consumption.

FIGURE 10.31 **Hydrothermal vents.** *(A) Hydrothermal vents occur in all five ocean basins. As mineral-rich water escapes from the seafloor, the minerals precipitate out, forming chimneys called* black smokers. *(B) This hydrothermal vent was photographed at a depth of 2,250 m (7,500 ft) near Vancouver, Canada, on the Juan de Fuca Ridge. More than 600 new animal species have been discovered at hydrothermal vents, including the deep-sea tube worms* (Riftia pachyptila) *seen here. (B. © Verena Tunnicliffe, University of Victoria)*

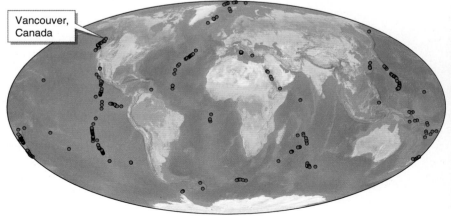

Vancouver, Canada

A

B

FIGURE 10.32 **GEO-GRAPHIC: Addressing industrial fishing bycatch.** *(Photo, C. Ortiz Rojas, NOAA)*

1. Drift net fishing (or gillnetting)

Huge factory ships locate fish with sonar and airplanes. Each ship then launches 20 to 50 small, fast boats to set out drift nets totaling thousands of miles in length. The nets are set out for several days. Fish are caught in the nets by their gills.

Addressing bycatch:
Drift nets can be outfitted with sonar devices that whales and dolphins can hear, allowing them to avoid the nets. Restricting drift nets to minimum distances from regions where birds breed can help minimize bird bycatch.

2. Trawling

Trawling nets can be as large as a football field. *Bottom trawling* drags nets on the seafloor, raking in seafloor organisms indiscriminately.

Addressing bycatch:
Turtle-excluding devices (TEDs) are small doorways that allow many sea turtles to escape the net while keeping desired fish. Bottom trawling has the highest bycatch of any fishing method and should be minimized or, many scientists believe, abolished.

3. Long-lining

Long-lining employs a central line up to 80 km (50 mi) long with thousands of baited hooks dangling from it. The depth of the central line can be set depending on the targeted fish species.

Addressing bycatch:
Setting the line at specific depths and using specially designed hooks reduces bycatch of sea turtles, albatross, and other unwanted species.

4. Seining

Seining employs a net that surrounds schooling fish. The net is drawn shut, and the fish are hauled in.

Addressing bycatch:
Seining has high dolphin bycatch, because dolphins are attracted to the schooling fish. Lowering the lip of the net so the dolphins can escape is one means employed to reduce dolphin kills.

  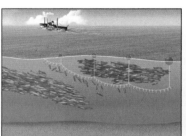 

FIGURE 10.33 **Drying shark fins.** *Thousands of shark fins have been laid out to dry on this rooftop in Hong Kong, the capital of the shark fin industry. In the past, the fins were dried mostly on sidewalks. In recent years, rooftops have become the preferred location to dry the fins to avoid increasing scrutiny of this destructive practice.* (© Antony Dickson/AFP/Getty Images)

drift net fishing
An industrial fishing method in which large nets are suspended in the upper reaches of the ocean.

trawling
An industrial fishing method in which nets are dragged through the water column or along the seafloor.

longline fishing
An industrial fishing method that employs thousands of baited hooks on lines up to 80 km (50 mi) in length.

seining
An industrial fishing method that uses a large net to surround and catch fish.

bycatch
Unwanted organisms caught by industrial fishing methods, which are usually thrown back to sea dead.

are now more fishing boats in the ocean than ever. Rather, it is due to the fact that there are fewer fish in the oceans now than in the past.

Drift net fishing, trawling, longline fishing, and seining are four methods commonly employed in industrial fishing. **Drift net fishing** suspends large nets in the upper reaches of the ocean. **Trawling** drags nets through the water column or along the seafloor. **Longline fishing** employs thousands of baited hooks on lines up to 80 km (50 mi) in length. **Seining** encircles fish and traps them in a large net. These fishing methods invariably kill other marine species **(Figure 10.32)**. **Bycatch** consists of unwanted organisms, such as birds and sea turtles, caught by industrial fishing methods. These organisms are usually thrown back to sea dead. Bycatch is a serious problem that threatens sea turtles, albatross, whales, dolphins, and many species of fish.

Approximately one-third of the world's open-water shark species (over 100 species) are considered endangered or critically endangered due to forces such as habitat degradation and unsustainable fishing. Because sharks are keystone species in many marine ecosystems, healthy functioning of those ecosystems is compromised when sharks are lost. Worldwide, an estimated 75 million sharks are killed every year only for their fins, which are used to make shark fin soup **(Figure 10.33)**.

GEOGRAPHIC PERSPECTIVES
10.5 The Problem with Plastic

◎ Assess the environmental impact of and remedies for plastic pollution in the oceans.

Plastic is cheaper than most natural materials, and it often performs better. Nearly everything we use is composed at least partly of plastic: electronics (cell phones and computers), packaging, facial scrubs, toothbrushes, credit cards, bags, bottles, car parts, combs and hairbrushes, clothing—modern society depends on plastic. So how is plastic relevant to physical geography or the oceans? The answer has to do with these statistics:

1. Each year, about 300 million metric tons of plastic are made. That is about 42 kg (92 lb) per year for each person on Earth.

2. More plastic has been made in the last 10 years than in all of the previous 100 years.

3. Only about 5%–10% of all plastic made is recycled.

4. Most plastic is not *biodegradable* (it cannot be broken down by decomposers). About 40% of plastic is disposed of in landfills, and the rest is either still in use or litters the continents and oceans.

What Happens to Plastic in the Oceans?

How does plastic get into the oceans? **Most of the plastic entering the oceans comes from streams flowing into the sea and from beaches.** Plastic trash in the streets of towns and cities is washed into storm drains, then into rivers, then into the oceans.

About 70% of all plastic that enters the oceans eventually sinks to the seafloor. There it is swept away by deep-ocean currents to accumulate in ocean basins. That plastic will persist for thousands to tens of thousands years or longer. Large accumulations of plastic presumably lie somewhere on the seafloor, but they have not yet been found.

> **What is the Great Pacific Garbage Patch?**

The 30% of plastic that remains suspended in the sunlit epipelagic zone is carried on the ocean gyres. **Eventually, that plastic collects in the** center of the gyre in what is often referred to as a *garbage patch* or *plastic vortex*. The **Great Pacific Garbage Patch**, a region of concentrated

FIGURE 10.34 **Suspended plastic.** *Charles Moore, one of the first discoverers of the plastic in the oceans, holds a jar containing small bits of plastic captured by a towed sieve. Note that the plastic is suspended in the water, not floating. (Courtesy of Algalita Marine Research Institute)*

plastic litter formed by the North Pacific Gyre, is the largest and best known of these collections. It is made up of an estimated 100 million metric tons of plastic trash, creating what many scientists now call the *plastisphere*. This suspended plastic ranges in size from massive clumps of fishing nets to minuscule bits of plastic invisible to the human eye. Most of the pieces are less than 1 cm (0.4 in) in length and cannot be seen from a boat. Towing a fine sieve (net) through the water catches them **(Figure 10.34)**.

The plastic in garbage patches is undetectable to satellites because most of it is suspended just beneath the water surface. Yet ocean current patterns are well known, and computer simulations

Great Pacific Garbage Patch
A region of concentrated plastic litter formed by the North Pacific Gyre.

FIGURE **10.35** **Locations of plastic in the ocean gyres.** *This map shows the probable locations of concentrated plastic debris in the oceans predicted by computer simulations of ocean current patterns. Each of the regions of plastic concentrated in the gyres covers an area roughly equivalent to the continental United States. Red areas show the greatest concentration of plastic particles. Light blue and white areas have the lowest plastic concentrations.* (Nikolai Maximenko, International Pacific Research Center, SOEST, University of Hawaii)

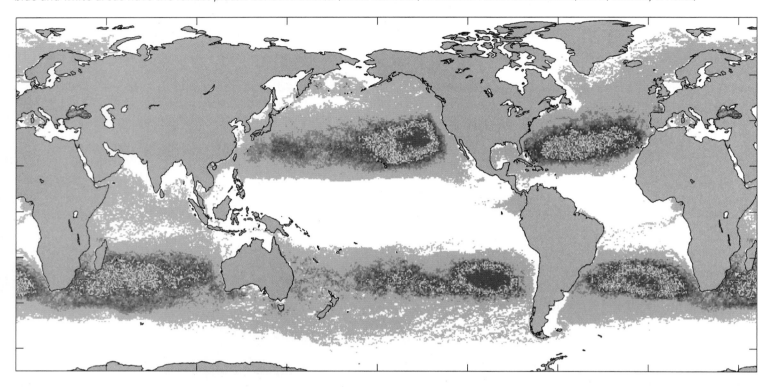

FIGURE **10.36** **Plastic trash on a remote beach.** *This beach is on tiny uninhabited Henderson Island that is 37.3 km² (14.4 mi²) in extent. Henderson Island is part of the remote Pitcairn Islands in the South Pacific. Most of this plastic originated from fishing boats and from Asia, some 11,000 km (7,000 mi) distant.* (© John Salmon)

FIGURE 10.37 **Plastic threatens marine animals.** *(A) This green sea turtle is dining on a jellyfish, a main food for sea turtles. To sea turtles, translucent plastic bags suspended in the water look like jellyfish. Ingested plastic can kill a sea turtle by blocking its digestive tract. (B) This adolescent Laysan albatross (Phoebastria immutabilis) from Kure Atoll probably died of starvation as its parents fed it a diet of plastic. Its stomach was filled with 340 g (12 oz) of trash. Plastic ingestion is a common cause of mortality for albatross nestlings on Hawai'i. Worldwide, seabird mortality from eating plastic is estimated to be about 1 million birds per year. Fish mortality related to plastic is unknown. (A. © Ai Angel Gentel/Flickr/Getty Images; B. © David Liittschwager/National Geographic/Getty Images)*

A   B

reveal where the plastic collects, as shown in **Figure 10.35**.

Transported by ocean currents, suspended plastic finds its way to the most remote areas. There, waves wash it onto beaches, where it collects and breaks down further **(Figure 10.36)**.

How Does Plastic in the Oceans Pose a Problem?

Small plastic particles provide a surface on which potentially harmful algae and bacteria can grow. For example, bacteria in the genus *Vibrio*, which cause cholera and other human health ailments, have been found on ocean plastic. Researchers suspect that such pathogens are able to persist longer and travel farther as they cling to plastic particles adrift in the ocean.

Suspended plastic particles in the oceans also attract and *adsorb* (bind to their surface) toxic chemicals that have entered ocean waters (such as *PCBs* and *DDEs* from industrial activity and pesticides from agricultural spraying). **Plastics have been found to carry concentrations of PCBs and DDEs 1 million times those of seawater.** The toxins may then enter organisms that eat the plastic. Scientists have documented ingestion of microscopic bits of plastic by organisms such as barnacles, krill (small shrimplike organisms), and fish that filter-feed on plankton. Toxins from the plastic particles could then work their way through almost all marine trophic levels and even into terrestrial trophic systems, eventually finding their way to our dinner plates. It is not yet known, however, whether these toxic chemicals are making their way through marine food webs.

Plastic does more obvious harm to marine life when animals eat it or become entangled in it **(Figure 10.37)**. Scientists estimate that 100,000 marine mammals and sea turtles are killed by plastic each year, mostly through entanglement.

Plastic debris is not limited to the oceans. In 2012, scientists found that the Great Lakes contain high concentrations of microscopic plastic particles. Most of them come from facial cleansers that contain tiny plastic beads.

Fixing the Problem

The problem with plastic in the oceans resembles other situations in which a pollutant released into the environment by people has led to problems in Earth's physical and biological systems later on. Toxic air pollutants (Section 1.4), CFCs in the ozonosphere (Section 1.5), and carbon in the atmosphere (Section 6.3) are three examples we have examined in this book.

As of 2014, a cumulative total of 29 billion metric tons of plastic had been made. At this rate, by the middle of this century, a total of roughly 40 billion metric tons of plastic will have been made,

FIGURE 10.38 **Plastic pollution awareness.** *This message about plastic pollution in the oceans captures the viewer's attention and conveys the information at a glance. Many major cities, such as Los Angeles, and even states, such as Hawai'i, have already implemented, or are considering, a ban on plastic bags in grocery stores. Such measures have passed because the public supports them. (© 2011 Ferdi Rizkiyanto)*

mostly in the United States, Europe, and China. There is too much plastic being made to clean it up after it has entered the environment, and doing away with plastic altogether is not practical.

What can society do? There is no single solution. An important step toward addressing this problem is making the problem widely known. As **Figure 10.38** demonstrates, a social media campaign to inform the public is under way.

What can an individual do? Reduce, reuse, and recycle. Many of the plastic items that enter the oceans are designed to be one-use items, such as water bottles, grocery bags, and utensils. These items are used for only a few days, hours, or even minutes. They then spend millennia in landfills or in the environment. About half of all plastic made is made to be disposed of immediately.

To address this issue, closed-loop systems need to be developed. In a *closed-loop* system, plastics

would be designed to be reused and recycled indefinitely. Many plastics made now (such as PVC, polyurethane, and polystyrene foam) have properties that make them difficult or impossible to recycle.

Another important step is to create plastics that biodegrade in the environment. Biodegradable vegetable-based plastics, made from plants such as corn, are becoming increasingly available. The more consumers demand them, the more they will be made available. Biologically based and reusable plastics are two important solutions to this problem.

Modern society needs plastic, and it needs healthy ecosystems. The two need not be mutually incompatible. The way plastic is perceived and manufactured will certainly change as more people become aware of this growing ecological problem.

CHAPTER 10 Exploring with ◎ Google Earth

To complete these problems, first read the chapter. When you are finished, go to LaunchPad and open the Exploring with Google Earth file for this chapter. Click on the "Workbook Problems" folder to "fly" to each of the problems listed below and answer the questions. Be sure to keep your "Borders and Labels" layer activated. Refer to Appendix 4 if you need help using Google Earth.

PROBLEM 10.1 This placemark falls on a long, linear mountain range.

1. **What is the name of this submarine feature?**
   a. Seamount   c. Deep-sea trench
   b. Abyssal plain   d. Mid-ocean ridge

PROBLEM 10.2 This placemark falls offshore of the continental margin.

1. **What is the name of this submarine feature?**
   a. Continental shelf   c. Abyssal plain
   b. Continental slope   d. Mid-ocean ridge

PROBLEM 10.3 This placemark is located on the flat expanse of the open-ocean seafloor.

1. **What is the name of this expanse of seafloor?**
   a. Continental shelf   c. Abyssal plain
   b. Continental slope   d. Mid-ocean ridge

PROBLEM 10.4 This placemark is located on the lowest point on Earth's crust, Challenger Deep.

1. **What is the name for a linear submarine feature such as the one shown here?**
   a. Seamount   c. Deep-sea trench
   b. Abyssal plain   d. Mid-ocean ridge

2. **What is the approximate water depth at this placemark?**
   a. 3,300 ft   c. 25,000 ft
   b. 18,000 ft   d. 30,000 ft

PROBLEM 10.5 This placemark is located in the tropical Pacific Ocean. When you are finished with the questions, zoom out and take note of the hundreds of these landforms that dot the ocean floor in this area.

1. **What is the name for this submarine landform? You can pan around beneath the water to get a better view of the feature.**
   a. Seamount   c. Deep-sea trench
   b. Abyssal plain   d. Mid-ocean ridge

2. **Measure the depth of the water directly over this landform. Then measure the depth of the water on the ocean floor. What is the total approximate vertical relief of this feature?**
   a. 4,000 ft   c. 10,000 ft
   b. 8,000 ft   d. 18,000 ft

3. **How would you characterize the biodiversity on this landform?**
   a. High   b. Medium   c. Low

PROBLEM 10.6 This placemark is located in the tropical Pacific Ocean.

1. **What is the name for these ring-shaped islands?**
   a. Barrier islands   c. Ringed islands
   b. Spits   d. Atolls

2. **What built these islands?**
   a. Lava flows   c. People
   b. Corals   d. Sand accumulations

3. **What were these islands long ago?**
   a. Part of a continent   c. Deep-sea trenches
   b. Volcanoes   d. Mid-ocean ridges

PROBLEM 10.7 This placemark is located in coastal waters of tropical South Asia.

1. **What type of ecosystem is shown here?**
   a. Tropical rainforest   c. Estuary
   b. Tropical savanna   d. Mangrove forest

2. **What country is this?**
   a. Bangladesh   c. Pakistan
   b. India   d. Thailand

PROBLEM 10.8 This placemark is located off the coast of Belize.

1. **What type of coral reef system is shown here? Zoom out to get a better view.**
   a. Fringing reef   c. Atoll
   b. Barrier reef

2. **What ocean basin is this?**
   a. Atlantic   c. Indian
   b. Pacific   d. Southern

PROBLEM 10.9 This placemark is in the Pacific Ocean between Hawai'i and California. It shows the recorded migration of a single great white shark.

1. **What is the name of this region where the great white shark is zigzagging about?**
   a. The shark café
   b. The shark grounds
   c. The shark park
   d. The shark congregation

2. **According to the text, what is the shark likely to be doing in this area?**
   a. Feeding   c. Rearing young
   b. Mating   d. Resting

PROBLEM 10.10 This placemark is located in the North Pacific Ocean. It shows the migration of four salmon sharks. Activate both folders in this problem to answer the question below.

1. **What range of water temperatures appears to mark the southern limit of salmon sharks?**
   a. 40°F–50°F   c. 60°F–70°F
   b. 50°F–60°F   d. 70°F–80°F

CHAPTER 10 **Study Guide**

Focus Points

10.1 The Physical Oceans

Five oceans: The Pacific Ocean is the largest and oldest of the five ocean basins.

Layers: The oceans can be divided into five vertical layers. Sunlight enters only the uppermost layer.

Surface ocean currents: Surface ocean currents are driven by wind. Coriolis force deflects the moving water, creating large circular ocean currents called gyres.

Seafloor features: Seafloor topography includes continental shelves, continental slopes, abyssal plains, major mountain ranges, and deep-sea trenches.

10.2 Life on the Continental Margins

Ecosystem types: Marine ecosystems along continental margins range from tropical coral reefs to kelp forests, rocky shorelines, and beaches.

Human footprint: All coastal marine ecosystems are influenced by human activity, particularly pollution, overfishing, habitat loss, and non-native species.

Fish nurseries: Mangroves, seagrass meadows, and estuaries provide important shelter for young fish.

Conservation: Coastal ecosystems provide long-term, sustainable benefits for people when they are preserved rather than converted to other uses.

10.3 Life in Polar Waters

Human footprint: Polar marine ecosystems are relatively little affected by people.

Food webs: Phytoplankton form the base of the food web in marine ecosystems.

Seasonal productivity: Polar waters are highly productive during spring and summer.

10.4 Life in Open Waters

Migration: Many marine organisms migrate vertically between ocean surface waters and deeper layers. Others migrate horizontally across ocean basins.

Bioluminescence: Many deep-water organisms produce light to find mates, capture prey, and avoid predators.

Biodiversity: Seamounts and hydrothermal vents support species-rich ecosystems on the deep seafloor.

Fishing: Industrial fishing employs drift nets, trawling, longlines, and seining to catch seafood.

10.5 Geographic Perspectives: The Problem with Plastic

Path to the oceans: Plastic enters the oceans mostly by stream runoff from towns and cities and from beaches.

Gyres and beaches: Marine plastic is concentrated in the centers of ocean gyres and deposited on beaches.

Problems: Marine plastic carries high concentrations of industrial pollutants absorbed from seawater. Wildlife may eat toxic plastic or become entangled in plastic.

Fixing the problem: Solving this problem requires changing the way we use and make plastic.

Key Terms

abyssal plain, 335
atoll, 336
barrier reef, 336
bathymetry, 334
bioluminescence, 346
bycatch, 350
continental shelf, 335
coral bleaching, 336
deep-sea trench, 336
drift net fishing, 350
epipelagic zone, 330
estuary, 341
fishery, 349
fringing reef, 336
Great Pacific Garbage
   Patch, 351

gyre, 334
hydrothermal vent
   community, 348
kelp forest, 342
lagoon, 336
longline fishing, 350
mangrove forest, 338
mid-ocean ridge, 335
pelagic, 344
salinity, 333
seagrass meadow, 340
seamount, 336
seining, 350
thermocline, 330
trawling, 350
upwelling, 344

Concept Review

The Human Sphere: Coastal Dead Zones

1. What is a coastal dead zone? How does it form? How have people influenced dead zones in recent decades?

10.1 The Physical Oceans

2. How many ocean basins are there? What are their names? Which is the largest and oldest?

3. How deep does light penetrate in the oceans? Which color goes deepest?

4. At what rate does pressure increase with depth in the oceans?

5. Compare the surface temperatures of tropical oceans with those of polar oceans. Compare the deep-water temperatures (below 2,500 m) of tropical and polar oceans.

6. Why is seawater salty? Describe the pattern of ocean

surface salinity from the equator to the poles, and explain why it changes.

7. What drives surface ocean currents? What are gyres? Why do they flow in large circular loops?

8. Review the major topographic features of the seafloor.

10.2 Life on the Continental Margins

9. What are the two major types of corals? Which type builds reefs in the tropics?

10. Describe the overall biodiversity of coral reefs.

11. Describe the mutualist relationship between corals and algae.

12. What are the three kinds of coral reefs? Use each to describe the process of atoll formation.

13. Which coral reef is the largest in the world? Where is it?

14. Why is it said that corals are "canaries in a coal mine"?

15. What are the major threats to corals today?

16. What is coral bleaching? What causes it? Is it permanent?

17. What is a mangrove forest? Where are mangrove forests found? Why are they important?

18. What is the most significant threat to mangrove forests?

19. What are seagrass meadows? Where are they found? Why are they important?

20. What are estuaries? How does brackish water relate to them?

21. How were many estuaries formed? Why are they important? Why are so many major cities located on estuaries?

22. What is a kelp forest? Where are kelp forests found? What are the threats to kelp forests?

10.3 Life in Polar Waters

23. What are phytoplankton? Why are they essential to nearly all marine ecosystems?

24. Why do so many organisms migrate to polar waters in spring and summer? Give examples of organisms that do this.

10.4 Life in Open Waters

25. Why do so many organisms undergo a daily vertical migration? Where do they migrate to and from?

26. What compels organisms to migrate across ocean basins?

27. What and where is the shark café? What species of shark goes there, and why?

28. What is bioluminescence? Where in the oceans is it used? What functions does it have?

29. How do scientists sample life from the deep sea?

30. What are seamounts, and why do they have high biodiversity?

31. What are hydrothermal vents? Describe the life found at them. What is extremely unusual about it?

32. What are the four types of industrial fishing in wide use? What is bycatch?

33. How does soup relate to the wasteful destruction of sharks?

10.5 Geographic Perspectives: The Problem with Plastic

34. How does plastic enter the oceans?

35. What is the relationship between ocean gyres and ocean garbage patches?

36. Why does plastic become more toxic the longer it resides in the ocean?

37. How does plastic pose a threat to marine life? To people?

38. What are some of the solutions to the problem of plastic in the oceans?

Critical-Thinking Questions

1. What is the connection between the burning of fossil fuels and ocean acidity? In this regard, how have the oceans acted to slow atmospheric warming?

2. What food served in a local seafood restaurant may be connected directly to the loss of mangrove forests in the tropics?

3. Trace the connection between upwelling and ocean productivity. Why does upwelling occur more readily in cold polar waters? Explain why tropical ocean water has low phytoplankton productivity.

4. The Monterey Bay Aquarium in California publishes a *Seafood Watch Pocket Guide* that details how consumers can protect marine ecosystems by avoiding seafood caught using ecologically destructive fishing techniques. In your region, what are the "Best Choices" of seafood species? What species should be avoided?

5. Can you think of any other solutions to the plastic problem not proposed in Geographic Perspectives?

Test Yourself

Take this quiz to test your chapter knowledge.

1. **True or false?** The wind creates ocean gyres.

2. **True or false?** Ocean salinity is greatest along the equator.

3. **True or false?** Trawls, longlines, drift nets, and seines are used in industrial fishing.

4. **True or false?** In the open ocean, many organisms migrate to the epipelagic zone at night.

5. **True or false?** Kelp forests occur at all latitudes in coastal areas.

6. **Multiple choice:** Which of the following is the most biodiverse ecosystem?
   a. Mangrove forest   c. Estuary
   b. Coral reef   d. Seagrass meadow

7. **Multiple choice:** Why do seamounts have high biodiversity?
   a. Because they are warm
   b. Because they are near the lighted surface
   c. Because there is nutrient upwelling around them
   d. Because of volcanic minerals in seawater near them

8. **Multiple choice:** If you live in a coastal city at midlatitudes, chances are that your city is sited on what was once
   a an estuary.
   b. a coral reef.
   c. a mangrove forest.
   d. a kelp forest.

9. **Fill in the blank:** Unwanted organisms, such as birds and turtles, caught by industrial fishing methods are called
   _____ .

10. **Fill in the blank:** The concentrated region of plastic in the subtropical Pacific Ocean is called the _____ .

Picture This. YOUR TURN

Marine Ecosystems

Nine marine ecosystems are marked on the globe. Use the hint given for each letter to identify the correct ecosystem. Choose from the following list of terms, using each term only once.

1. **Coral reef**
2. **Mangrove forest**
3. **Seagrass meadow**
4. **Estuary**
5. **Kelp forest**
6. **Polar waters**
7. **Open waters**
8. **Seamount**
9. **Hydrothermal vent**

Hints:

A Threatened by shrimp farming
B Most threatened ecosystem on Earth
C Dominated by algae
D Submerged atolls
E Daily vertical migrations
F Chemosynthetic ecosystems
G Most species-rich marine ecosystem
H Preferred by manatees and dugongs
I High seasonal primary productivity

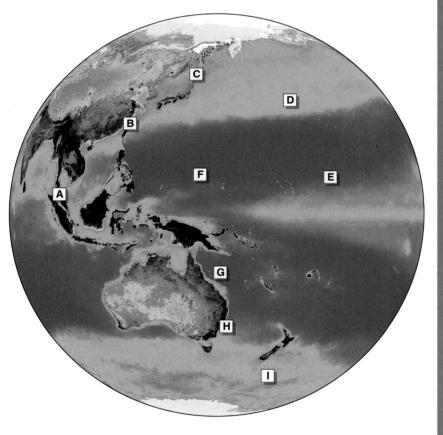

SeaWiFS Project, NASA/Goddard Space Flight Center, and DigitalGlobe™

Further Reading

1. Dean, Cornelia. "Study Finds Hope in Saving Saltwater Fish." *New York Times*, July 30, 2009.

2. Earle, Sylvia A., and Linda K. Glover. *Ocean: An Illustrated Atlas*. Washington, D.C.: National Geographic Society, 2008.

3. Worm, Brian, et al. "Impacts of Biodiversity Loss on Ocean Ecosystem Services." *Science* 314 (2006): 787-790.

Answers to Living Physical Geography Questions

1. **How deep are the oceans?** The oceans are 4 km (2.5 mi) deep on average and nearly 11 km (7 mi) at their deepest.

2. **Why are the oceans salty?** The oceans are salty because rivers carrying dissolved minerals, including salt, empty into them.

3. **Why do most deep-sea organisms glow?** Deep-sea organisms glow to attract resources such as mates and food or to hide from or confuse predators.

4. **What is the Great Pacific Garbage Patch?** The Great Pacific Garbage Patch is a concentration of plastic that has entered the ocean through storm drains and rivers in urban areas and collected in the North Pacific Gyre.

PART III
**TECTONIC
SYSTEMS:**
Building the
Lithosphere

Earth's internal heat energy moves entire continents, lifts mountains,
forms volcanoes, and generates powerful earthquakes. Part III explores
the role of plate tectonics in building and shaping Earth's surface.

CHAPTER 11

Earth History, Earth Interior

Earth and the solar system formed 4.6 billion
years ago. The planet's hot interior is structured
in layers.

CHAPTER 12

**DRIFTING CONTINENTS:
Plate Tectonics**

Earth's internal heat energy drives the
movement of lithospheric plates, creating
mountains, valleys, and other features.

CHAPTER 13

**Building the Crust
with Rocks**

Plate tectonics drives the rock cycle that
creates and transforms rocks.

CHAPTER 14

**GEOHAZARDS:
Volcanoes and Earthquakes**

Volcanoes and earthquakes shape the crust's
surface and are significant hazards for people.

11 Earth History, Earth Interior

Thick clouds of toxic steam rich with hydrochloric acid are produced as incandescent lava spills into the sea on Hawai'i.

(© Sami Sa... 'Photographe 's Choice RF/Getty Images)

LIVING PHYSICAL GEOGRAPHY

> How did Earth form?

> How did the atmosphere and oceans form?

> Why doesn't the hot interior of Earth melt the crust?

> How long would it take to drive to the center of Earth?

To learn more about the composition and structure of Earth's interior, turn to Section 11.3.

THE BIG PICTURE *Earth formed 4.6 billion years ago. The planet's hot interior is structured in layers. Heat energy moves Earth's hot interior and its outer crust.*

LEARNING GOALS *After reading this chapter, you will be able to:*

11.1 ◎ Explain the origin of Earth and its atmosphere and oceans.

11.2 ◎ Describe the major divisions of geologic time and explain how the age of ancient Earth material is determined.

11.3 ◎ Describe the planet's internal structure and understand the importance of lithospheric plate movement.

11.4 ◎ Assess the connection between Earth's internal heat and life on Earth.

THE HUMAN SPHERE: The Anthropocene

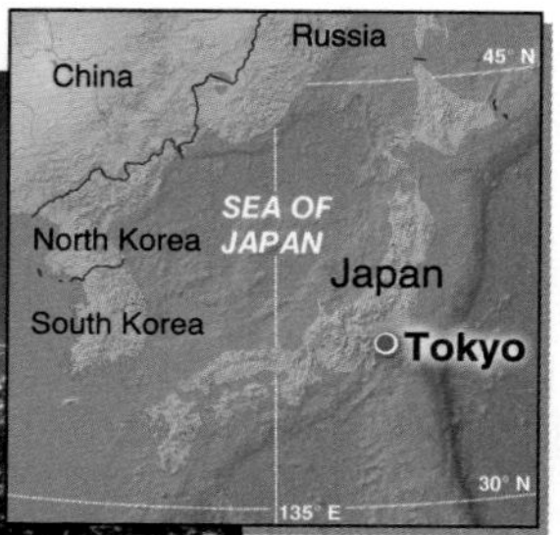

FIGURE 11.1 **Tokyo, Japan.**
Tokyo is the largest city in the world with a population of 13.2 million people. The surrounding metropolitan region has an additional 22 million people. Like many regions on Earth, this city and the area surrounding it have been completely transformed by people.
(© ngkaki/E+/Getty Images)

THERE ARE JUST OVER 7 BILLION PEOPLE ON EARTH TODAY, and by midcentury, there will likely be about 9 billion. No other single species in Earth's history has been such a pervasive force of change in Earth's physical systems as humans are now.

Many scientists believe that the extent of human environmental impacts is sufficient to warrant a new geologic epoch in Earth history. This new epoch, called the **Anthropocene**, or the "Age of Humans," is the age of human transformation of Earth's physical systems (Figure 11.1).

The beginning of the Industrial Revolution, around 1800, is often cited as the beginning of the Anthropocene. At that time, human activity began changing the chemistry of the atmosphere. Atmospheric carbon dioxide levels began rising as people burned coal, and then petroleum, for energy (see Section 6.3). The increased concentration of CO_2 in the atmosphere led to an anthropogenic greenhouse effect. Atmospheric warming has caused sea level to rise about 20 cm (8 in) in the last century as Earth's ice sheets and glaciers have melted and seas have warmed and expanded (as we will see in Section 17.5).

In addition, the oceans are becoming more acidic as they absorb CO_2 from the atmosphere (see Section 10.1).

Many of the world's major rivers have been dammed, and about half the world's freshwater runoff is used by people. Nearly 40% of Earth's land surface not covered by glaciers is used to grow food for people. Globally, people move more sediment and rock using bulldozers and other earth-moving equipment than is moved naturally by weathering and erosion. About 90% of all mammal biomass is made up of people and domesticated animals, such as cows and sheep. About 10,000 years ago, the proportion of mammal biomass made up of people and domesticated animals was only 0.1%.

The proposed Anthropocene is one of many divisions of geologic time that mark Earth's extensive history. This chapter investigates how Earth was formed, how scientists divide Earth's history into geologic time periods, and how Earth's interior is structured. This chapter also explores the connection between the planet's internal heat energy and the biosphere.

11.1 Earth Formation

◎ Explain the origin of Earth and its atmosphere and oceans.

Earth is one of eight planets in our solar system. Our solar system includes the Sun and all objects orbiting the Sun, including hundreds of thousands of rocky asteroids and icy comets as well as the eight planets. Earth's solar system is not the only solar system in existence, however. So far, astronomers have discovered nearly two thousand planets outside our own solar system, and nearly 800 other solar systems. About three new planets are discovered every week.

Solar systems are found in galaxies. The Milky Way galaxy is the galaxy in which Earth resides. Galaxies are organized, rotating masses of hundreds of billions of stars. Scientists estimate that there are some 100 billion to 400 billion stars in the Milky Way and about the same number of planets. When we are away from city lights and under clear skies, the Milky Way is visible to us as a band of stars in the night sky (Figure 11.2).

Galaxies are immensely large, and the distances between them are vast. The Milky Way, for example, is 120,000 *light-years* across; that is, it takes light 120,000 years to cross the galaxy from end to end. Light travels at 300,000 km (186,000 mi) per second. The Andromeda galaxy, the closest large galaxy to Earth, is 2.5 million light-years away. Some of the farthest galaxies from Earth are more than 13 billion light-years away. In other words, it took more than 13 billion years for their light to reach Earth. When we look up into the night sky, most of the objects that we see shining are so far away that the light they emit began traveling years ago, often long before we were born.

The Milky Way and Andromeda galaxies are two among many hundreds of billions of galaxies in the universe. Scientists' understanding of the universe is incomplete and evolving. Astronomers think that atoms (and molecules) that make up physical matter constitute only about 4% of the mass of the universe. The rest of its mass may be composed of *dark energy*, which may constitute 74% of the universe's mass, and *dark matter*, which may make up 22% of its mass.

The universe began about 13.8 billion years ago. This age estimate is based on astronomer Edwin Hubble's observation that galaxies and other objects are all moving away from Earth and from one another. From this observation, Hubble surmised that the universe is expanding, an idea

FIGURE **11.2** **The Milky Way.** *From the vantage point of Earth, the disk structure of the Milky Way galaxy is revealed in the cloudy band of stars we see at night if we are away from artificial lighting. This photo was taken near Bardenas, Spain.* (© Inigo Cia/Flickr/Getty Images)

called the *expanding universe theory*. From the rate of their movement, Hubble and other astronomers calculated that all the galaxies would have been at a single point about 13.8 billion years ago. At that time, that single point exploded in the *Big Bang*. Since then, the universe has been expanding.

Formation of Stars and Planets

A star is formed as a cloud of dust and gas in space, called a *nebula*, coalesces by mutual gravitational attraction and collapses. As the mass of this *protostar* increases, its internal pressure and temperature rise through gravitational compression. Eventually, as more and more material is accumulated, the object's interior temperature reaches about 10 million °C (18 million °F). At this temperature, hydrogen atoms fuse to form helium. Enormous amounts of heat and light are produced by this nuclear fusion.

Not all the dust and gas in a nebula coalesces into the growing star. It also coalesces into smaller bodies that are not massive enough to trigger nuclear fusion, resulting in the formation

> How did Earth form?*

Anthropocene
(pronounced an-THROP-a-seen) The age of human transformation of Earth's physical systems; generally seen as starting in 1800.

*Answers to the Living Physical Geography questions are found on page 383.

FIGURE 11.3 **GEO-GRAPHIC:**
Solar system and planet formation.
(© Mark Garlick/Science Source)

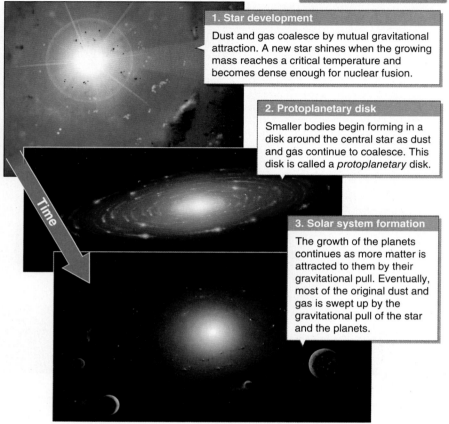

Time

1. Star development

Dust and gas coalesce by mutual gravitational attraction. A new star shines when the growing mass reaches a critical temperature and becomes dense enough for nuclear fusion.

2. Protoplanetary disk

Smaller bodies begin forming in a disk around the central star as dust and gas continue to coalesce. This disk is called a *protoplanetary* disk.

3. Solar system formation

The growth of the planets continues as more matter is attracted to them by their gravitational pull. Eventually, most of the original dust and gas is swept up by the gravitational pull of the star and the planets.

FIGURE 11.4 **The solar system.** *The solar system consists of the Sun and eight planets as well as many smaller objects. The planets and the Sun are scaled to their relative sizes in this illustration, but distances between planets are not to scale—they are much farther apart than shown here. The orbital paths that the planets take around the Sun are shown with white lines. (NASA/JPL-Caltech/T. Pyle (SSC))*

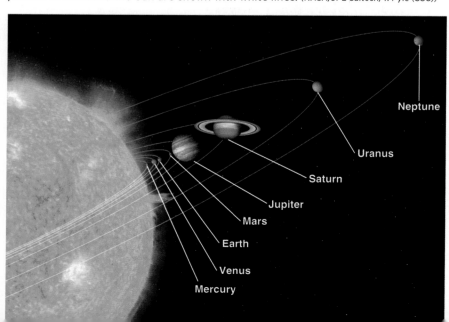

Neptune
Uranus
Saturn
Jupiter
Mars
Earth
Venus
Mercury

of planets, asteroids, and other objects **(Figure 11.3)**. Our solar system and everything in it, including Earth, is formed from the coalescence of dust and gas about 4.6 billion years ago.

The Sun is 333,000 times the mass of Earth, and about 1 million Earths would fit inside the volume of the Sun. The mass of the Sun exerts a strong gravitational pull that keeps the planets locked in their respective orbits along a flat plane **(Figure 11.4)**. Earth is the third closest planet to the Sun; Venus and Mars are its two nearest neighbors.

Most of the planets in the solar system have orbiting satellites, or moons. The leading hypothesis to account for the formation of Earth's Moon states that another planet in the solar system collided with Earth about 4.5 billion years ago. That other planet, called *Theia*, is thought to have been about two-thirds the size of Earth. Much of Theia was vaporized in the collision with Earth or melted into Earth. The impact was so violent that material from Earth and Theia was thrown out into space. Some of this material coalesced by gravitational attraction to create the Moon.

Earth has been pounded by large asteroids throughout its history. During the *Late Heavy Bombardment*, in the early history of the solar system, this type of collision was common. So many asteroids struck Earth that heat from the friction of their impacts kept Earth's surface molten for millions of years. Eventually, most objects in Earth's orbit were swept up by these collisions. Earth's molten surface then cooled and hardened into the rigid outermost portion of Earth, called the **crust**.

Now, about 15 metric tons of rock and dust from space enter Earth's atmosphere each year. Most debris particles entering Earth's atmosphere are no bigger than grains of sand. Occasionally, large objects do hit Earth and leave their mark in the form of an impact crater. Most impact craters on Earth are erased by erosion, but some remain **(Figure 11.5)**.

Formation of the Atmosphere and Oceans

Earth's atmosphere formed from gases emitted by volcanoes. A **volcano** is a mountain or hill

> How did the atmosphere and oceans form?

formed by eruptions of lava and rock fragments. As material from Earth's interior moves through the crust to reach the surface it forms volcanoes. While the crust was forming, extensive volcanic activity pumped huge quantities of gases such as hydrogen, water vapor, carbon dioxide, hydrogen sulfide, and nitrogen from Earth's interior to form the early atmosphere.

Where did the water in the oceans come from? **Over 4 billion years ago, water vapor from volcanic emissions condensed out of the atmosphere and collected in the low-lying areas of the crust, forming the oceans.** Icy comets from space also delivered water to Earth, but scientists now think that most of the water in the oceans came from volcanic outgassing.

There are two great reservoirs of water on Earth. The first is on Earth's surface, mostly in the form of oceans and ice sheets. Groundwater (described in Section 9.2) is also part of this reservoir of water. Experimental evidence, however, indicates that another reservoir of water some 100 times greater than groundwater exists deep within Earth's interior. The internal Earth is an environment of great heat and great pressure. Common rocks found near the surface, such as *olivine*, are dry. Deep inside the planet, however, olivine is heated to high temperatures and crushed under enormous pressures, which transform it into wadsleyite and ringwoodite. These rocks can incorporate 3% of their weight in water. Given the volume of Earth's interior, there is likely more water there than at the surface.

The early atmosphere was transformed after photosynthetic organisms appeared. Photosynthetic bacteria called **cyanobacteria** were among the first forms of life to evolve about 3.5 billion years ago. These bacteria began releasing oxygen as a waste product of photosynthesis. They are still found on Earth today, as Picture This on page 368 shows.

As early as 3 billion years ago, oxygen concentrations in the atmosphere began to rise. Oxygen concentrations increased significantly during a time called the *Great Oxidation Event* 2.4 billion years ago. After the Great Oxidation Event, oxygen levels were sufficient for the ozonosphere to form. The ozonosphere blocked the harmful UV rays of the Sun (see Section 1.5), making it possible for life to leave the protective cover of the oceans and move onto land.

Multicellular life (in the form of red algae) first arose about 1.2 billion years ago. Land plants evolved about 475 million years ago. Dinosaurs appeared in the fossil record roughly 240 million years ago, then went extinct 66 million years ago, probably because of a large asteroid impact. The earliest mammals appeared about 210 million years ago, but the mammals did not flourish until after the dinosaurs went extinct. The earliest evidence of modern humans dates back to about 200,000 years ago. In the next section, we will see how these dates are estimated and how they are used to divide geologic time.

FIGURE 11.5 **Impact craters.** *(A) The locations of the major surviving impact craters on Earth's surface are shown as red dots. Barringer Crater (or Meteor Crater) in Arizona and Manicouagan Crater in Quebec are highlighted. Manicouagan Crater is one of the oldest surviving impact craters. (B) The Willamette meteorite, displayed in the American Museum of Natural History in New York, is the largest meteorite ever found in the United States. It is 3.05 m (10 ft) tall. The 15.5-ton meteorite is composed of iron and nickel and is more than 1 billion years old. It entered the atmosphere over the Willamette Valley in Oregon at an estimated 64,400 km/h (40,000 mph). Intense heat caused by friction with the atmosphere pitted its surface.* (A. Manicouagan Crater, image courtesy of the Image Science & Analysis Laboratory, NASA Johnson Space Center; Barringer Crater, © Robert Llewellyn/Imagestate Media Partners Limited-Impact Photos/Alamy; B. Bruce Gervais)

Barringer Crater, Arizona
Age: 50,000 years
Diameter: 1.2 km (0.8 mi)

Manicouagan Crater, Québec, Canada
Age: 215 million years
Diameter: 100 km (62 mi)

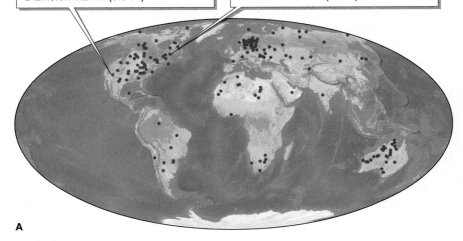

A

B

crust
The rigid outermost portion of Earth's surface.

volcano
A mountain or hill formed by eruptions of lava and rock fragments.

cyanobacteria
Photosynthetic bacteria that were among the first forms of life to evolve about 3.5 billion years ago.

Picture This

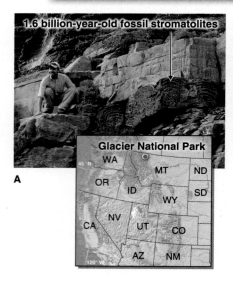

1.6 billion-year-old fossil stromatolites

A

Living stromatolites

B

Stromatolites

The black arrow in photo A points to a layer of fossilized cyanobacteria that lived in colonies called *stromatolites*. Stromatolite fossils are sometimes nicknamed "sliced cabbage" because of their appearance. The fossils shown here are found in the Helena Formation in Glacier National Park, Montana. They are about 1.6 billion years old. Stromatolites found in other locations date as far back as 3.5 billion years.

Stromatolites are among the earliest forms of life preserved in the fossil record, and they persist to this day. Living stromatolites can be found in Shark Bay, in Western Australia, as shown in photo B. The cyanobacteria secrete calcium carbonate that hardens into the colony structure. They also secrete a gelatinous mucus that protects them from the harmful ultraviolet rays of the Sun. *(A. © Charles Corrick; B. © L Newman & A Flowers/PhotoResearchers/Getty Images)*

Consider This

1. How did stromatolites make it possible for life to colonize land? (Hint: See Section 1.5.)

uniformitarianism
The principle that the same imperceptible gradual processes are operating now and have operated in the past.

relative age
The age of one object or event in relation to the age of another without regard to how old either is.

11.2 Deep History: Geologic Time

◎ Describe the major divisions of geologic time and explain how the age of ancient Earth material is determined.

Earth is 4.6 billion years old. This immense span of Earth history is divided and subdivided using the geologic time scale **(Figure 11.6A)**. The divisions of time are based on major geologic events, such as mass extinction events, where at least 75% of all species go extinct. The five mass extinctions in Earth's history were caused by many factors, including periods of intense volcanic activity, global climate change, and asteroid impacts. Episodes of rapid evolution of new species also provide a basis for defining new divisions of time. The immensity of geologic time is revealed if it is compressed into a single calendar year **(Figure 11.6B)**.

The Principle of Uniformitarianism

Uniformitarianism is the principle that the same gradual and nearly imperceptible processes are operating now and have operated in the past. **Most physical and biological systems that we see today are the result of small and gradual changes accumulating over long periods of time.** The term *uniformitarianism* can also be summarized in the phrase, "The present is the key to the past." The processes that shape Earth are similar to tree growth: It is nearly impossible to watch a tree grow, yet we know that even the largest trees grow from small seeds. Similarly, the Grand Canyon was formed by geologic uplift coupled with downcutting by the Colorado River. As the land slowly rose, the river carved into the rocks, sand grain by sand grain, eventually forming a mile-deep canyon. The same processes were active in the past as are active today, but they are usually too slow and gradual to perceive on human time scales.

Uniformitarianism underpins almost all the tectonic and erosional processes that we will describe in the rest of this book. This key concept is also central to understanding the process of biological evolution that resulted in Earth's biodiversity. Over 3.5 billion years, through the accumulation of gradual changes, the first single-celled photosynthetic cyanobacteria differentiated into the myriad species in the biosphere we see today.

Sudden catastrophic events also play an important role in Earth history, however. Collisions with asteroids, for example, have changed the course of history for the biosphere. After the removal of the dinosaurs, most likely by an asteroid impact, 66 million years ago, mammals evolved and filled their vacated niches. Catastrophic events occur intermittently, but uniformitarianism is constant.

How Do Scientists Date Earth Materials?

In Earth science, there are two ways to evaluate the age of an object. **Relative age** compares the age of one object or event with the age of another without specifying how old either is.

FIGURE 11.6 **Geologic time.**

(A) Earth's history is divided into eons, which are subdivided into eras, periods, and epochs. We live in the Holocene epoch, nested in the Quaternary period, in the Cenozoic era of the Phanerozoic eon. Note that the Hadean, Archaean, and Proterozoic eons are compressed and not to scale. Collectively they constitute 88% of Earth's history. The Phanerozoic, greatly elongated here, spans only 12% of Earth's history. Many of the major biological events of Earth history are labeled here. (B) In this graphic, Earth history is compressed into a single year of time and the four eons are shown. Earth and the solar system form on January 1. Each "month" on the calendar represents about 383 million years. Using this perspective, the immensity of geologic time becomes clearer.

Eon	Era	Period	Age estimates of boundaries in mega-annum (Ma) unless otherwise noted
Proterozoic (P)	Neoproterozoic (Z)	Ediacaran	630
		Cryogenian	850
		Tonian	1,000
	Mesoproterozoic (Y)	Stenian	1,200
		Ectasian	1,400
		Calymmian	1,600
	Paleoproterozoic (X)	Statherian	1,800
		Orosirian	2,050
		Rhyacian	2,300
		Siderian	2,500
Archaean (A)	Neoarchean		2,800
	Mesoarchean		3,200
	Paleoarchean		3,600
	Eoarchean		~4,000
Hadean (P_A)			

A

Eon	Era	Period	Epoch	Age estimates of boundaries in mega-annum (Ma) unless otherwise noted	Major events in the biosphere
Phanerozoic	Cenozoic (Cz)	Quaternary (Q)	Holocene	11,477 yr	First modern humans
			Pleistocene	1.806	
	Tertiary (T)	Neogene (N)	Pliocene	5.332	
			Miocene	23.03	
		Paleogene (R)	Oligocene	33.9	
			Eocene	55.8	
			Paleocene	66.0	
	Mesozoic (Mz)	Cretaceous (K)	Upper/Late	99.6	Extinction of dinosaurs and many other species
			Lower/Early	145.5	
		Jurassic (J)	Upper/Late	161.2	First flowering plants First birds
			Middle	175.6	
			Lower/Early	199.6	
		Triassic (TR)	Upper/Late	228.0	First mammals
			Middle	245.0	First dinosaurs
			Lower/Early	251.0	
	Paleozoic (Pz)	Permian (P)	Lopingian	260.4	
			Guadalupian	270.6	
			Cisuralian	299.0	
		Carboniferous (C) Pennsylvanian (P)	Upper/Late	306.5	
			Middle	311.7	
			Lower/Early	318.1	First reptiles
		Carboniferous (C) Mississippian (M)	Upper/Late	326.4	Extensive coal swamps
			Middle	345.3	
			Lower/Early	359.2	First amphibians
		Devonian (D)	Upper/Late	385.3	
			Middle	397.5	
			Lower/Early	416.0	First insects
		Silurian (S)	Pridoli	418.7	
			Ludlow	422.9	
			Wenlock	428.2	
			Llandovery	443.7	
		Ordovician (O)	Upper/Late	460.9	First land plants
			Middle	471.8	
			Lower/Early	488.3	
		Cambrian (C)	Upper/Late	501.0	
			Middle	513.0	First fishes
			Lower/Early	542.0	

Ka = *kilo-annum* or thousand years ago
Ma = *mega-annum* or million years ago
Ga = *giga-annum* or billion years ago

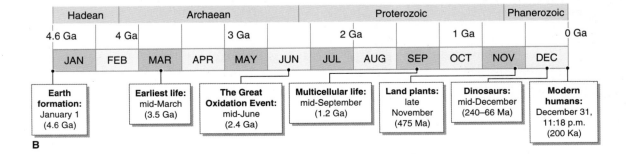

Hadean	Archaean	Proterozoic	Phanerozoic
4.6 Ga	4 Ga	3 Ga	2 Ga	1 Ga	0 Ga

| JAN | FEB | MAR | APR | MAY | JUN | JUL | AUG | SEP | OCT | NOV | DEC |

Earth formation: January 1 (4.6 Ga)

Earliest life: mid-March (3.5 Ga)

The Great Oxidation Event: mid-June (2.4 Ga)

Multicellular life: mid-September (1.2 Ga)

Land plants: late November (475 Ma)

Dinosaurs: mid-December (240–66 Ma)

Modern humans: December 31, 11:18 p.m. (200 Ka)

B

absolute age
An age that is specified in years before the present.

superposition
The principle that in a sequence of rock layers, the oldest rocks are always at the bottom and the youngest at the top.

Relative age and the principle of superposition. *(A) The layers of sand poured into this glass represent sedimentary rock layers that have formed from sand over time. The layer at the bottom was deposited first and is older than the top layer. (B) The Colorado River has cut the mile-deep Grand Canyon in northern Arizona, exposing rock layers that were first deposited 1.7 billion years ago. Rocks at the top of the canyon are younger than those below. (B. © Michael Runkel/Robert Harding World Imagery/Alamy)*

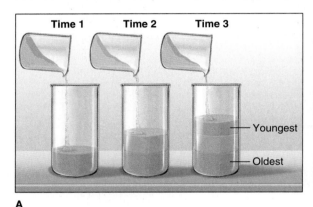

The topmost rocks are younger than those below them.

The oldest rocks are at the base of this series of rock layers.

A

B

Absolute age is an age that is specified in years before the present.

Relative age accounts for the order of events. For example, if two trees are growing side by side and one is smaller, we might reasonably conclude that the smaller tree is younger. We do not know how old it is in absolute terms. We know only that it is younger relative to the larger tree.

This concept can be applied to rock layers in Earth's crust. A sequence of rock layers forms as layers of sediments are deposited, one after another, and eventually harden into sedimentary rock (a process described in more detail in Section 13.3). The principle of **superposition** states that in such a sequence of rock layers, the oldest rocks are at the bottom and the youngest rocks are at the top (**Figure 11.7**).

Absolute age. *These ancient rocks near Hudson Bay, Canada (A), have an absolute age and a relative age far greater than the newly formed rocks encasing this road sign in Hawai'i (B). (A. Jonathan O'Neil, University of Ottawa; B. © G. Brad Lewis/America 24-7/Getty Images)*

Absolute age: about 4 billion years These ancient rocks in the Hudson Bay region of Canada are the oldest known rocks on Earth.

Absolute age: about one decade Hardened lava from a 2003 lava flow covers a road in Hawai'i Volcanoes National Park in Hawai'i.

A

B

Absolute age, which is given in actual numbers of years, is determined using various dating techniques. For example, tree-ring analysis (called *dendrochronology*) provides absolute ages of trees. Most trees create one new growth ring each year. Counting the growth rings in a cut tree allows an investigator to determine the absolute age of a tree.

Another way absolute ages can be determined is through **radiometric dating**, the technique of assigning ages to materials based on the radioactive decay of unstable elements in those materials. Radiometric dating methods, which have been in wide use since the 1950s, have provided a means by which the ages of ancient materials such as rocks and bones can be determined. These methods are based on the premise that unstable elements in some materials decay (convert) to a stable element at a constant rate through time. Young objects containing an unstable element have high proportions of that element because there has not been enough time for it to decay to the stable form. In very old objects, the unstable element is largely gone, having decayed to its stable form.

Radiocarbon dating is a radiometric dating technique that works on once-living organic material no older than about 60,000 years. *Uranium-lead dating* is used to assign absolute ages to Earth's oldest rocks. This technique measures the decay of unstable uranium isotopes to stable lead isotopes. It has been used to date the oldest rocks on Earth to about 4 billion years before the present. Those rocks are metamorphic rocks from northern Quebec, Canada, on the Hudson Bay coast **(Figure 11.8)**.

11.3 Anatomy of a Planet: Earth's Internal Structure

◎ Describe the planet's internal structure and understand the importance of lithospheric plate movement.

Generations have been intrigued by the mystery of what lies beneath Earth's surface. The nineteenth-century author Jules Verne imagined large chasms filled with oceans and huge crystals. In the *Divine Comedy*, Dante imagined Earth's interior as composed of nine concentric shells, each named after a human mortal sin, and a lake of ice at the center.

The modern scientific understanding of Earth's interior does not include mortal sin or a frozen core. Instead, Earth's interior is hot and under enormous pressure due to the weight of overlying rock. At Earth's center, the pressure is some 3,600,000 times greater than that found on the surface.

The temperature of Earth's interior increases with depth. This pattern is called the *geothermal gradient*. In deep gold mines in South Africa, temperatures reach almost 54°C (130°F) only 3.5 km (2 mi) below the surface. At 40 km (24 mi) below the surface, the temperature climbs to about 500°C (930°F). The temperature at the core of the planet is about 6,000°C (10,832°F)—nearly as hot as the Sun's surface.

Four factors have created and continue to create a hot Earth interior:

1. *Friction:* As we have seen, Earth formed through the coalescence of dust and gas. The denser elements, such as iron and nickel, sank toward the middle of the planet beneath the less dense materials, such as silicon and magnesium. This sorting of materials by density resulted in movement that generated friction and, therefore, heat.

2. *Asteroid bombardment:* The Late Heavy Bombardment of early Earth by asteroids also generated heat from friction and kept Earth's surface molten for several hundred million years.

3. *Tidal forces:* When the Moon first formed, it was only about 24,300 km (15,000 mi) away from Earth (compared with today's average distance of 384,399 km, or 238,854 mi). Because it was so close, the Moon's gravitational pull exerted enormous tidal forces, which distorted Earth's shape and created heat from the friction of the movement.

4. *Radioactivity:* The fourth source of Earth's internal heat is radioactive decay of unstable elements, mainly potassium, uranium, and thorium. These elements give off heat during the decay process.

How Do Scientists Know What Is Inside Earth?

The average density of Earth is about 5.5 g/cm^3, a figure calculated by dividing the mass of the planet by its volume. The average density of the crust's rocks, however, is less than this (about 2.92 g/cm^3), indicating that Earth's interior must be denser than its surface.

radiometric dating
A method of assigning absolute ages to Earth materials based on the radioactive decay of unstable elements in those materials.

FIGURE 11.9 **SCIENTIFIC INQUIRY: How do scientists study Earth's hidden interior?** *An understanding of Earth's internal composition and structure is essential to understanding geologic phenomena. Volcanic eruptions and earthquakes, for example, are directly related to the composition and movement of Earth's interior.* (Top right, Sarah Robinson/EarthScope National Office. EarthScope is supported by the US National Science Foundation; bottom left, U.S. Dept. of Interior, U.S. Geological Survey; bottom right, G. Glatzmaier, LANL/P. Roberts, UCLA/Science Source)

Seismic waves

A powerful earthquake sends out seismic waves that travel through the planet. As seismic waves pass through materials of differing densities in the planet's interior, they are bent and change their speed.

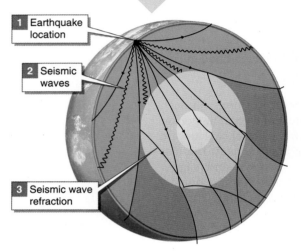

1 Earthquake location

2 Seismic waves

3 Seismic wave refraction

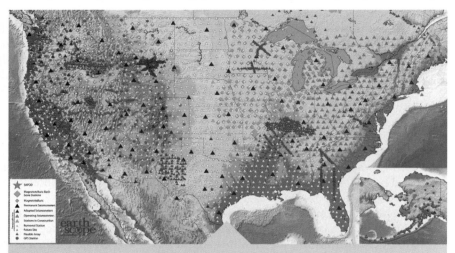

Measuring seismic waves

Gathering data about the paths of seismic waves helps scientists understand the composition of Earth's deep interior. The EarthScope Program, funded by the U.S. National Science Foundation, uses more than 400 *seismometers* (instruments that detect seismic waves) to obtain a detailed understanding of Earth's interior beneath the continental United States down to 90 km (56 mi). The EarthScope seismometer network is mapped here.

Volcanic rock samples

Scientists sample and analyze rocks that travel from Earth's interior to its surface through volcanoes. The chemistry of these rocks reflects the chemistry of Earth's interior.

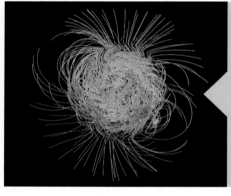

Earth's magnetic field

The presence of Earth's magnetic field indicates that the planet has a dynamic liquid metal core.

Most of what is known of Earth's deep interior has come from analysis of the behavior of **seismic waves**: energy released by earthquakes that travels through Earth's interior. An **earthquake** is a sudden shaking of the ground caused by movements of Earth's crust. There are also other lines of direct and indirect evidence relating to Earth's internal structure **(Figure 11.9)**.

Earth's Interior Layers

It is no coincidence that Earth's atmosphere, oceans, and interior are arranged in layers that decrease in density away from Earth's center. In fact, the atmosphere and oceans are a continuum with the solid Earth. Each layer is made of matter in solid, liquid, or gaseous states. As Earth coalesced from dust and gas during the formation of the solar system, the densest materials settled deepest, leaving the least dense materials at the top. The same thing happens when a glass of unfiltered orange juice is left undisturbed for several hours: The heavy pulp settles to the bottom. Similarly, the atmosphere's gas molecules are the least dense and lightest of Earth's materials, and they therefore rest on top of the denser and heavier liquid oceans and the solid Earth.

Earth's interior has three principal layers: the core, the mantle, and the lithosphere **(Figure 11.10)**.

earthquake
A sudden shaking of the ground caused by movements of Earth's crust.

seismic wave
Energy released by an earthquake that travels through Earth's interior as a wave.

FIGURE **11.10** **Earth's interior.** *The layers of Earth's interior are distinguished by the density of their rock material. The thickness of the crust varies; the depths shown here are average depths below sea level. To increase their visibility, the lithospheric mantle and the crust are not drawn to relative scales.*

Animation
Earth's interior
http://qrs.ly/25466kw

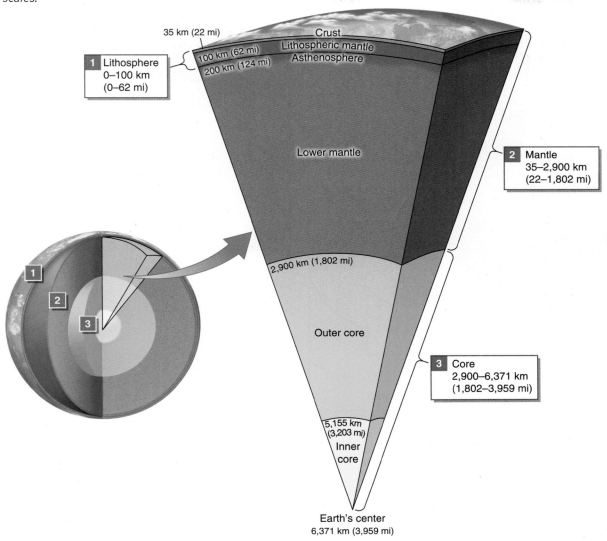

Crust

35 km (22 mi)

Lithospheric mantle

1 Lithosphere 0–100 km (0–62 mi)

100 km (62 mi)

Asthenosphere

200 km (124 mi)

Lower mantle

2 Mantle 35–2,900 km (22–1,802 mi)

2,900 km (1,802 mi)

Outer core

3 Core 2,900–6,371 km (1,802–3,959 mi)

5,155 km (3,203 mi)

Inner core

Earth's center 6,371 km (3,959 mi)

Here, we will examine Earth's interior layers, starting from the core and moving outward to the lithosphere.

The Core

The center of Earth is 6,371 km (3,959 mi) below sea level. The solid **inner core**, which extends from Earth's center to about 5,155 km (3,203 mi), is composed of a mixture of dense elements, mostly iron and nickel. Inner core temperatures reach up to 6,000°C. These temperatures would melt the inner core if not for the extreme high pressure found there that keeps the inner core solid.

The **outer core**, which surrounds the inner core, is composed of a liquid alloy of iron and nickel. Temperatures in the outer core are as low as 4,000°C (7,232°F) and increase toward the inner core. The outer core extends to about 2,900 km (1,802 mi) below the surface. The outer core is liquid because pressures within it are less than those of the inner core, allowing the outer core to melt and flow. This circulating liquid metal generates electrical currents and creates Earth's *magnetic field*.

A familiar use of Earth's magnetic field is as a navigational aid for people and migratory

inner core
The innermost layer of Earth, composed of solid iron and nickel.

outer core
The second innermost layer of Earth, composed of a liquid alloy of iron and nickel, which generates Earth's magnetic field.

FIGURE 11.11   **Geographic and magnetic north.** *(A) The geographic North Pole (or true north) and the magnetic North Pole occur in different positions in the Northern Hemisphere. (B) Although the geographic North Pole is permanently fixed, the magnetic North Pole moves about 55 km (34 mi) per year. In the last century, the location of the magnetic North Pole has migrated over 2,000 km (1,242 mi). Here, its position is tracked from 1600 to 2011. If the magnetic North Pole continues at its present trajectory and speed, it will be in northern Russia by the end of this century.*

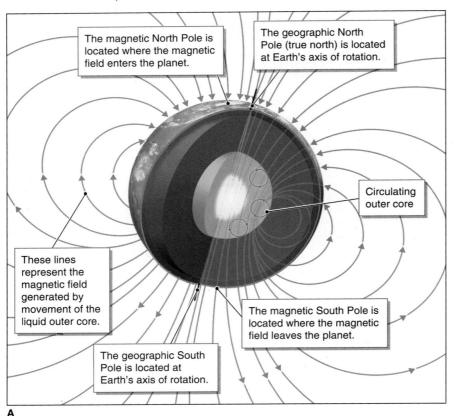

The magnetic North Pole is located where the magnetic field enters the planet.

The geographic North Pole (true north) is located at Earth's axis of rotation.

Circulating outer core

These lines represent the magnetic field generated by movement of the liquid outer core.

The magnetic South Pole is located where the magnetic field leaves the planet.

The geographic South Pole is located at Earth's axis of rotation.

A

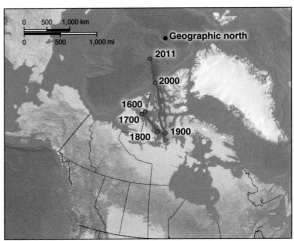

Geographic north

2011
2000
1600
1700
1800   1900

B

animals. As **Figure 11.11** illustrates, magnetic north and geographic north are not the same.

The magnetic field also forms the magnetosphere, which surrounds Earth and shields it from the *solar wind*, a stream of electrically charged particles emitted by the Sun (see Figure 11.15). This critical function is explored further in the Geographic Perspectives at the end of this chapter. Because the magnetic field is perpendicular to Earth's surface near the poles, it allows the solar wind to reach the uppermost atmosphere, causing it to light up, creating auroras, or northern and southern lights (see Section 1.3).

mantle
The layer of heated and slowly deforming solid rock between the base of the crust and the outer core.

The Mantle

The **mantle** is the layer of heated and slowly deforming solid rock that lies between the base of the crust and the outer core. The lower limit of the mantle lies 2,900 km (1,802 mi) below the surface, and it extends upward to approximately 35 km (22 mi) below the surface. Temperatures in the mantle range from about 4,000°C (7,232°F) near the outer core to about 900°C (1,652°F) near the crust.

The mantle has three layers: the lower mantle, the asthenosphere, and the *lithospheric mantle* (see Figure 11.10). Altogether, the mantle makes up about 84% of Earth's volume. It is composed of *silicate* rocks (made mostly of minerals that contain silica) that are rich in iron and magnesium. These rocks are heated to temperatures well above their melting point. Because they are under such great pressure, however, they remain solid.

Even though the lower mantle is solid rock, it is not rigid and unmovable. Instead, it slowly deforms and flows in great circular convection loops at a rate of about 15 cm (6 in) per year. When a solid is able to deform and flow, its behavior is described as *plastic*. Warm (but unmelted) candle wax or beeswax is plastic in that it can be squeezed and shaped with your fingers once it is warmed.

The **asthenosphere** (from the Greek for "weak") is the layer of the mantle found between depths of about 100 and 200 km (62 and 125 mi). There is considerably less pressure in the asthenosphere than in the rest of the mantle below. As a result, although the rocks here are still in a solid state, they are nearer to melting and are consequently weak and easily deformed. In contrast, the outermost portion of the mantle, the lithospheric mantle, is rigid and relatively brittle. The lithospheric mantle is discussed next in the context of the third major layer of Earth's interior, the lithosphere.

The Lithosphere

The **lithosphere** consists of Earth's rigid crust and the rigid lithospheric mantle beneath it, extending to a depth of about 100 km (62 mi) on average (see Figure 11.10). The lithosphere is not plastic and does not deform and flow. Instead, when subjected to stresses from the moving asthenosphere beneath, it cracks and breaks, forming lithospheric plates. These plates are important because their movement drives earthquake and volcanic activity, which we will explore in Chapter 12.

The outermost portion of the lithosphere, the crust, is the part of Earth we walk on and that the atmosphere and oceans rest on. The crust is not melted by Earth's internal heat because it is in contact with the atmosphere and oceans, which are relatively cold. Although Earth's crust makes up less than 1% of Earth's volume, it is very important to people. It is home. It is where we grow food, extract minerals and energy resources such as petroleum, and build our houses and cities.

> Why doesn't the hot interior of Earth melt the crust?

There are two types of crust: continental crust and oceanic crust. **Continental crust** makes up the continents. It is composed mainly of **granite**, a silica-rich rock made up of coarse grains. **Oceanic crust** lies beneath the oceans and is composed mainly of **basalt**, a dark, heavy, fine-grained volcanic rock.

Granite forms from magma that cools deep in the crust. **Magma** is melted rock that is below the surface of the crust. Chemically, granite is composed chiefly of silica, aluminum, potassium, calcium, and sodium. It is light in both weight (2.7 g/cm^3) and color compared with basalt, which weighs about 3 g/cm^3. But not all continental rocks are granite. Rocks found on the continents vary more in age and chemistry than do those in oceanic crust, and they come from different formative processes than the rocks found on the seafloor.

Basalt, on the other hand, is formed from lava. **Lava** is magma that spills onto the surface of the crust. Chemically, basalt is composed mostly of compounds of silica that are high in iron and magnesium. When melted, basalt has low *viscosity*, which means that it is runny and flows easily downhill.

But how thick is the crust? The Croatian scientist Andrija Mohorovičić (1857–1936) identified the crust-mantle boundary by examining seismic waves and finding a point where rock density rapidly increases. That point, named the *Mohorovičić discontinuity*, or the **Moho**, after Mohorovičić, who formalized the concept in 1909, is the boundary that separates the crust from the lithospheric mantle below. The depth of the Moho is about 35 km (22 mi) on average, but it varies depending on the type of crust it lies beneath.

The Moho is deepest beneath continental crust and shallowest beneath oceanic crust. Beneath oceanic crust, the Moho is found at about 7 km (4 mi) in depth. Beneath continental crust, it is found at about 70 km (40 mi) in depth, but that depth varies with continental topography. It is deepest beneath high mountains and much less deep in areas where the continental crust is being stretched by tectonic processes **(Figure 11.12)**. Overall, the thickness of Earth's crust is 0.01% to 1% of the radius of the planet, about the same as the thickness of an apple peel as a percentage of the rest of the apple.

FIGURE 11.12 **Depth of the Moho.** *The Moho follows the contours of the crustal surface in reverse.*

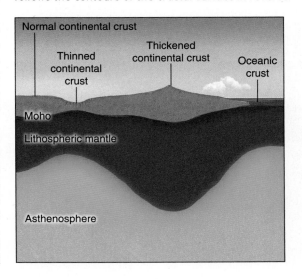

asthenosphere
The layer of the mantle, which deforms and flows, found between about 100 and 200 km (62 and 124 mi) in depth.

lithosphere
The layer of Earth that consists of the rigid crust and the rigid lithospheric mantle beneath it, extending to a depth of about 100 km (62 mi) on average.

continental crust
The crust that makes up the continents, composed mainly of granite.

granite
A silica-rich rock composed of coarse grains.

oceanic crust
The crust beneath the oceans, composed mainly of basalt.

basalt
A dark, heavy, fine-grained volcanic rock that constitutes oceanic crust.

magma
Melted rock that is below the surface of Earth's crust.

lava
Hot molten rock that spills onto the surface of Earth's crust.

Moho
The boundary that separates the crust from the lithospheric mantle, which lies about 35 km (22 mi) deep on average.

CRUNCH THE NUMBERS:
Calculating Travel Time to the Center of Earth

If you drove nonstop toward the center of Earth traveling at 100 km/h (62 mph), how long would it take to get to the upper surface of each of the following layers? For your calculations, divide the distance by travel speed. The first calculation is done for you. (See Figure 11.10 for the depths of each layer.)

1. The Moho:

Answer: *35 km/100 km/h = 0.35 hours; 0.35 × 60 minutes = 21 minutes.*

2. The asthenosphere:

3. The outer core:

4. Earth's center:

How long would it take to drive to the center of Earth?

As a thought experiment to get a sense of the thicknesses of Earth's interior layers, Crunch the Numbers asks you to calculate how long it would take to drive to Earth's center.

Plates of the Lithosphere

The lithosphere is broken into pieces, or *plates*, each of which moves over Earth's surface as the mantle beneath it slowly convects. There are 14 major lithospheric plates as well as several minor plates. As Figure 11.13 shows, the margins of these lithospheric plates are sometimes visible on land.

As the plates move, they buckle into mountains, bend and warp into hills, and break, causing earthquakes. If there were no *plate tectonics* (plate movement), Earth would become flat as weathering and erosion wore the surface down and sediments filled in valleys (a process called *gradation*). The plates of the lithosphere are also important in the context of heat loss from Earth's interior to space. Heat loss is not evenly distributed across Earth's surface, as shown in Picture This.

Arrows show relative plate movement direction.

North American plate

Pacific plate

Plate boundary

San Andreas Fault

South

FIGURE 11.13 **A lithospheric plate boundary.** *The San Andreas Fault, which runs down the length of western central and southern California, is the boundary between the North American plate and the Pacific plate. Relative to the North American plate, the Pacific plate is moving north. This photo was taken looking southeast near the Carrizo Plain National Monument from an altitude of about 1,680 m (5,500 ft).* (© David K. Lynch)

NV

CA

Carrizo Plain National Monument

AZ

San Andreas Fault

120° W

Picture This

Heat Flow from Earth to Space

This image displays losses of Earth's internal heat energy through the crust and out to space in watts per square meter. Heat loss is lowest where the crust is thickest, such as at point 1. At many plate boundaries, the crust is thin, and heat loss is high, as at point 2. (Compare this image with the map of lithospheric plate boundaries in Figure 12.7.)

Consider This

1. What is the relationship between Earth's heat loss and lithospheric plate boundaries?

2. Observe point 1, in the mountainous west of North America. Relative to the plate boundaries beneath the oceans, is heat loss in this mountainous area high or low?

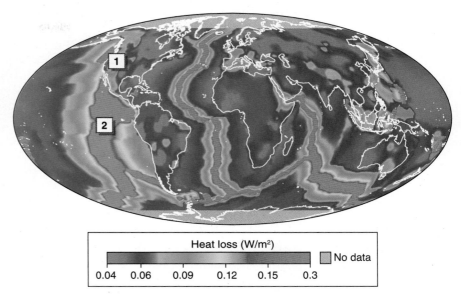

Heat loss (W/m²)						No data
0.04	0.06	0.09	0.12	0.15	0.3	

GEOGRAPHIC PERSPECTIVES
11.4 Earth's Heat and the Biosphere

◎ Assess the connection between Earth's internal heat and life on Earth.

What effect does Earth's internal heat have on the biosphere? What would happen if Earth's interior cooled? We cannot cool down Earth's interior to see what happens. We can, however, learn from other planets.

Lessons from Mars

Today, Mars is barren, bitter cold, and devoid of life, as far as we can tell. There is water on Mars, but it is permanently frozen at both poles and hidden deep within the Martian soils. The average temperature at midlatitudes is about −45°C (−50°F). Atmospheric pressure is only a hundredth of Earth's, so low that humans could not survive for a full minute without a pressurized suit. In fact, in terms of atmospheric pressure and temperature, a typical day on Mars might be similar to a typical day 120 km (75 mi) or so above Earth's surface—little breathable air, bitter cold, and an utterly inhospitable environment.

Earth stands in sharp contrast to Mars. Whereas Mars appears reddish-beige from space, Earth is blue and white, due to its immense liquid water oceans and the clouds in its oxygen-rich atmosphere (Figure 11.14 on page 378). But evidence suggests that Mars, too, once had oceans and a thicker atmosphere.

What caused Earth and Mars to take such very different paths early in the history of the solar system? Why did Mars lose its water and atmosphere, even as Earth's were retained? The answer lies just below our feet.

The Outer Core and Life

Our tour of the internal Earth in this chapter revealed the layered structure of the planet. We have seen that the outer core is made predominantly of iron and nickel, and that it generates a magnetic field as it circulates deep within Earth's interior. And we have seen that Earth's magnetic field forms a shell-like **magnetosphere** that

magnetosphere
The outer edge of the magnetic field that surrounds Earth and shields it from the solar wind.

FIGURE 11.14   **Earth and Mars.** *Earth and Mars are shown here in their relative sizes and true colors. Robotic missions to Mars and satellite imaging of the Martian surface have revealed evidence that the planet once had extensive liquid oceans and rivers like those of Earth. So different was ancient Mars from what we see today that scientists are even hopeful of finding evidence that life once existed there. (NASA/JPL)*

FIGURE 11.15   **The magnetosphere.** *The white lines represent the solar wind, which is deflected by Earth's magnetosphere, shown as a blue elongated bubble around Earth.*

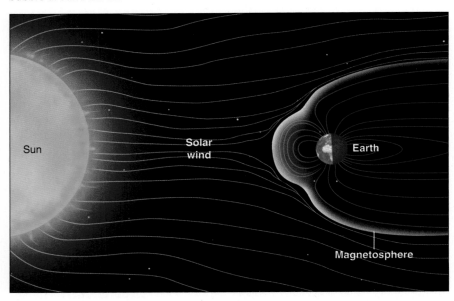

envelops the planet and protects it from the solar wind **(Figure 11.15)**.

Sudden increases in the solar wind create problems for people on Earth, including cancer, communications problems with satellites and cell phones, and drought. **Because of the solar wind's damaging effects on organisms, terrestrial life probably would not be possible without the magnetic field.** Life would reside only within the protective water of the oceans.

The magnetic field plays another important role in making Earth a habitable planet. Scientists know that Mars once had oceans and a thicker atmosphere. They also know that Mars once had a stronger magnetic field than it does today. Evidence for this conclusion lies in rocks found on Mars and on Earth that have become magnetized as they cooled directly from molten lava. Satellites with *magnetometers* (instruments that detect magnetism) orbiting Mars can detect this magnetism in surface rocks. On Earth, new rocks still become magnetized today. On Mars, only rocks several billion years old or older are magnetized; newer rocks are not. Several billion years ago, the rocks on Mars stopped becoming magnetized as they cooled.

For whatever reason, and scientists are not sure why, the strength of the Martian magnetic field diminished several billion years ago. One possibility is that the interior of Mars cooled enough that its liquid metal core stopped circulating and creating a magnetic field. Another possibility is that Mars was hit by a series of very large asteroids, which heated the surface, disrupting the core's ability to generate a magnetic field. Once the magnetic field of Mars was weakened, the atmosphere would have been exposed to the solar wind. Many scientists think that Mars's atmosphere and oceans were stripped away by the charged particles of the solar wind, leaving the planet the cold and sterile place it is today.

If Earth lost its magnetic field, its atmosphere and oceans would also be stripped away by the solar wind. Instead, Earth's internal heat generates the magnetic field that prevents this from happening.

Tectonism, Oceans, and Climate

Earth's internal heat also plays a critical role in moderating the chemistry of Earth's atmosphere through tectonism. As we have seen in this chapter, convection and flow in the lower mantle and the asthenosphere result in movement of the overlying lithospheric plates. And as the plates move, they create volcanic activity (as we will see in Section 12.3).

Volcanoes were instrumental in creating and modifying Earth's early atmosphere and oceans, and they continue to modify those physical systems today. In Section 2.5, we saw that carbon dioxide is an important greenhouse gas that modifies the average temperature of the atmosphere. As part of the long-term carbon cycle (see Section 6.3), weathering and erosion of rocks remove carbon dioxide from the atmosphere and store it as carbon in sediments and rocks on the seafloor. Over geologic time, the atmosphere could lose its carbon dioxide to the ocean basins through this process, and Earth's atmosphere could become colder through time.

This does not happen because carbon-rich seafloor sediments, and the lithospheric plates that carry them, are subducted (drawn down) beneath the continents and deep into the asthenosphere and lower mantle (see Section 12.3). Volcanism caused by this plate movement eventually returns the stored carbon to the atmosphere, where it recombines with oxygen to form carbon dioxide. **If the lithospheric plates did not move and form volcanoes that recycle carbon to the atmosphere, carbon dioxide concentrations would drop over time, and Earth could become much colder than it is now.**

Earth's internal heat generates the magnetic field that shields life from the harmful solar wind. It also drives the movement of the lithospheric plates and creates volcanoes. These phenomena provided water to create the oceans, and they modify Earth's atmosphere and make it suitable for life. The planet's internal heat is an essential part of its life-support system.

CHAPTER 11 Exploring with ⊚ Google Earth

To complete these problems, first read the chapter. When you are finished, go to LaunchPad and open the Exploring with Google Earth file for this chapter. Click on the "Workbook Problems" folder to "fly" to each of the problems listed below and answer the questions. Be sure to keep your "Borders and Labels" layer activated. Refer to Appendix 4 if you need help using Google Earth.

PROBLEM 11.1 This placemark visits coastal South America. Note both markers in this problem's folder. Make sure both are activated.

1. **What is the elevation at marker 1?**
   a. 5,000 ft   c. 17,000 ft
   b. 12,000 ft   d. 20,000 ft

2. **What is the elevation at marker 2?**
   a. –10,000 ft   c. –22,000 ft
   b. –15,000 ft   d. –27,000 ft

3. **At which marker is the crust thicker?**
   a. Marker 1   b. Marker 2

4. **What is the total vertical relief between these two marked locations?**
   a. 22,000 ft   c. 42,000 ft
   b. 34,000 ft   d. 47,000 ft

5. **In what country is this placemark?**
   a. Chile   c. Bolivia
   b. Peru   d. Argentina

PROBLEM 11.2 This placemark visits a large circular feature in North America that was formed 241 million years ago.

1. **Based on your reading in this chapter, what caused this circular feature?**
   a. A volcano
   b. A meteorite
   c. Heat from Earth's interior
   d. Erosion by streams

2. **What is the name of the lake at this feature?**
   a. Lac Manicouagan   c. Lac Mistassini
   b. Michikamau Lake   d. Lac à l'Eau Claire

3. **What is the diameter of this feature?**
   a. 1 km   c. 30 km
   b. 20 km   d. 60 km

4. **In what Canadian province is this feature located?**
   a. Alberta   c. Québec
   b. Manitoba   d. Nova Scotia

PROBLEM 11.3 This problem relates to the thickness of Earth's interior layers. Measure the distances between the cities provided to answer the questions.

1. **Which two cities are about the same distance apart as the average thickness of the crust?**
   a. San Francisco and Hayward, California
   b. San Francisco and San Jose, California
   c. San Francisco and Los Angeles, California

2. **Which two cities are about the same distance apart as the distance from the crust's surface to the base of the asthenosphere?**
   a. Toronto, Canada, and New York City
   b. Toronto and Rochester, New York
   c. Toronto and Cleveland, Ohio

3. **Which two cities are about the same distance apart as the distance from the crust's surface to Earth's center?**
   a. Mexico City and Vancouver, Canada
   b. Mexico City and Caracas, Venezuela
   c. Mexico City and Santiago, Chile

PROBLEM 11.4 This problem features Earth's magnetic field at the North Pole. Make sure the two markers in this folder are activated. In addition, activate the latitude-longitude grid from the View menu at the top of your screen. Marker 1 shows the position of the magnetic North Pole in 1850. Marker 2 shows the position of the magnetic North Pole in 2010.

1. **How many miles has the magnetic North Pole traveled since 1850?**
   a. 800 mi   c. 1,200 mi
   b. 1,000 mi   d. 2,000 mi

2. **How many miles per year, on average, has the magnetic North Pole shifted during this period? (Divide the distance traveled by the number of years it took to travel that distance.)**
   a. 4 mi per year   c. 12.3 mi per year
   b. 7.5 mi per year   d. 16 mi per year

3. **Currently, how far is the magnetic North Pole from the geographic North Pole?**
   a. 220 mi   b. 300 mi   c. 370 mi   d. 440 mi

PROBLEM 11.5 This problem features Earth's magnetic field at the South Pole. Make sure the two markers in this folder are activated. In addition, activate the latitude-longitude grid from the View menu at the top of your screen. Marker 1 shows the position of the magnetic South Pole in 1850. Marker 2 shows the position of the magnetic South Pole in 2010.

1. **How many miles has the magnetic South Pole traveled since 1850?**
   a. 330 mi   b. 410 mi   c. 560 mi   d. 730 mi

2. **How many miles per year, on average, has the magnetic South Pole shifted during this period? (Divide the distance traveled by the number of years it took to travel that distance.)**
   a. 4.6 mi per year   c. 6.3 mi per year
   b. 5 mi per year   d. 7.2 mi per year

3. **Currently, how far is the magnetic South Pole from the geographic South Pole?**
   a. 450 mi   b. 630 mi   c. 900 mi   d. 1,200 mi

4. **Based on your answers to Problem 11.4 and your answers to this problem, which of the following statements best summarizes the relationship between the magnetic North Pole and the magnetic South Pole?**
   a. The two magnetic poles have synchronous movement.
   b. The two magnetic poles move mostly independently of each other.

CHAPTER 11 Study Guide

Focus Points

11.1 Earth Formation

Formation of the solar system: The solar system, including Earth, was formed by the coalescence of dust and gas.

Formation of the atmosphere and oceans: Earth's atmosphere and oceans were formed from gases emitted by volcanoes early in Earth's history.

11.2 Deep History: Geologic Time

The geologic time scale: Earth is 4.6 billion years old. Its history is divided into epochs, periods, eras, and eons based on major geologic events that occurred in the past.

Uniformitarianism: Earth's physical systems operate mostly under gradual changes that accumulated over geologic time.

Absolute and relative age: Relative age accounts for the order of events. Absolute age provides the specific age of an object.

11.3 Anatomy of a Planet: Earth's Internal Structure

Earth's interior: Earth's interior is hot and under enormous pressure.

Earth's interior layers: Earth is composed of three main layers: the core, the mantle, and the lithosphere.

Thickness of the crust: The Moho, which marks the base of Earth's crust, is deepest beneath high mountains and shallowest beneath the oceans.

Lithospheric plate movement: Convection in the mantle drives the movement of lithospheric plates and creates surface topography.

11.4 Geographic Perspectives: Earth's Heat and the Biosphere

Earth's internal heat energy created and maintains Earth's life-support systems.

Key Terms

absolute age, 370
Anthropocene, 364
asthenosphere, 375
basalt, 375
continental crust, 375
crust, 366
cyanobacteria, 367
earthquake, 372
granite, 375
inner core, 373
lava, 375
lithosphere, 375

magma, 375
magnetosphere, 377
mantle, 374
Moho, 375
oceanic crust, 375
outer core, 373
radiometric dating, 371
relative age, 368
seismic wave, 372
superposition, 370
uniformitarianism, 368
volcano, 366

Concept Review

The Human Sphere: The Anthropocene

1. What is the Anthropocene? When did it start?

11.1 Earth Formation

2. What is a solar system? How many planets are in our solar system?

3. What is a galaxy? What are galaxies composed of? What is the name of our galaxy?

4. What units are used to measure the size of a galaxy? How big is our galaxy?

5. What is the universe? What was the Big Bang and when did it happen?

6. Describe the sequence of events that formed our solar system.

7. How did the Moon form? When did it form?

8. How did the atmosphere and oceans form?

9. When did life first evolve? What kind of life was it?

11.2 Deep History: Geologic Time

10. What is the geologic time scale? What marks the beginning or end of a division of time?

11. How old is Earth?

12. Review some of the major events that have occurred in Earth's history and when they occurred.

13. What is uniformitarianism? Use it to explain how a mountain range forms.

14. Compare and contrast relative ages with absolute ages. How is each determined?

11.3 Anatomy of a Planet: Earth's Internal Structure

15. Why is Earth's interior hot?

16. What evidence is used to determine Earth's internal structure?

17. List the layers of Earth's interior, starting from the core and moving outward to the crust.

18. What generates Earth's magnetic field? What does the magnetic field deflect?

19. What is the difference between the magnetic North Pole and the geographic North Pole?

20. What is the Moho?

21. What are the two kinds of crust, and where is each of them found?

22. Where on the planet is the crust thickest? Where is it thinnest?

23. Why is the lithosphere broken into plates?

11.4 Geographic Perspectives: Earth's Heat and the Biosphere

24. Explain the connection between the loss of the Martian magnetic field and the loss of that planet's early atmosphere and oceans.

25. Given what we know about Mars, how is Earth's internal heat essential for life?

26. What role do volcanoes have in forming Earth's atmosphere and oceans?

27. What role do volcanoes have in contributing to the greenhouse effect?

28. How are the oceans and the greenhouse effect important to life on Earth?

Critical-Thinking Questions

1. What observations would you need to make to determine whether the Moho was greater than or less than the average depth of 35 km where you live?

2. What physical features can you identify where you live that were formed under the principle of uniformitarianism?

3. In Figure 11.8B, how do we know whether lava or the road it covers is older? Refer to absolute ages and relative ages in your answer.

4. New evidence shows that most stars have orbiting planets and that planets are more common than stars. Do you think that there might be life on other planets besides Earth? What conditions would be necessary to support life? How, if at all, would the discovery of life on another planet change your perspective on Earth's life?

Test Yourself

Take this quiz to test your chapter knowledge.

1. True or false? Earth is 4.6 billion years old.

2. True or false? Deep drill holes reveal the internal structure of Earth.

3. True or false? Oceanic crust is composed of basalt and is heavier than continental crust.

4. True or false? Earth's atmosphere and oceans originated from volcanic gases.

5. True or false? The magnetic North Pole is also called true north.

6. Multiple choice: Which of the following generates Earth's magnetic field?
   a. The lithosphere
   b. The crust
   c. The outer core
   d. The inner core

7. Multiple choice: Which of the following is an example of the principle of superposition?
   a. Mountain building over long stretches of geologic time
   b. Earth's interior heat
   c. Layered sediments with the oldest layers at the bottom
   d. The process of plate movement

8. Multiple choice: Which of the following lists the interior layers of Earth in the correct order, from the surface downward?
   a. Lithosphere, asthenosphere, lower mantle, inner core
   b. Asthenosphere, lower mantle, lithosphere, inner core
   c. Crust, lithospheric mantle, lower mantle, asthenosphere
   d. Crust, lower mantle, asthenosphere, outer core

9. Fill in the blank: The principle of _____ is based on the accumulation of slow and gradual changes over geologic time.

10. Fill in the blank: Radiometric dating provides a(n) _____ for materials.

Picture This. YOUR TURN

Earth in Cross Section

Label each part of Earth's interior described in this chapter. Put one star next to layers that are plastic and deformable. Put two stars next to the layer that generates the magnetic field. You should use each of these terms only once:

1. Asthenosphere
2. Continental crust
3. Inner core
4. Lithosphere
5. Lower mantle
6. Moho
7. Oceanic crust
8. Outer core
9. Lithospheric mantle

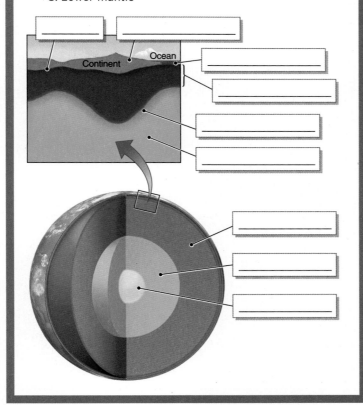

Continent   Ocean

Further Reading

1. Crutzen, Paul. "Geology of Mankind." *Nature* 415 (2002): 23.

2. Hazen, Robert. *The Story of Earth: The First 4.5 Billion Years, from Stardust to Living Planet.* New York: Viking, 2012.

3. Kolbert, Elizabeth. "The Lost World." *New Yorker*, December 23 and 30, 2013.

Answers to Living Physical Geography Questions

1. **How did Earth form?** Like the Sun and the other planets, Earth formed 4.6 billion years ago as dust and gas in space coalesced. All matter on Earth is derived from this dust and gas.

2. **How did the atmosphere and oceans form?** The atmosphere and oceans formed from gases emitted from Earth's interior by volcanoes.

3. **Why doesn't the hot interior of Earth melt the crust?** The atmosphere and oceans are cold and prevent Earth's hot interior from melting the crust.

4. **How long would it take to drive to the center of Earth?** It would take 2.7 days to drive to the center of Earth at highway speeds.

12 DRIFTING CONTINENTS: Plate Tectonics

Chapter Outline

Mount Assiniboine stands behind Sunburst Peak on the border of British Columbia and Alberta, Canada. The crust that forms these mountains was transported across the Pacific Ocean, then piled in crumpled heaps along the western edge of the continent.

(© Design Pics Inc./Alamy)

LIVING PHYSICAL GEOGRAPHY

> Why do the coastlines of Africa and South America fit together?

> How can whole continents move?

> Is it true that Los Angeles will someday be connected to San Francisco?

> How do mountains form?

To learn more about how plate movement forms mountains, turn to Section 12.3.

THE BIG PICTURE *The movements of lithospheric plates create mountains, ocean basins, and many other physical features of Earth. The Tibetan Plateau and its surrounding mountains provide food security.*

LEARNING GOALS *After reading this chapter, you will be able to:*

12.1 ◎ Compare the theory of continental drift with the theory of plate tectonics.

12.2 ◎ Describe the evidence used to develop the theory of plate tectonics and explain how lithospheric plates move.

12.3 ◎ Describe the three types of plate boundaries and the landforms resulting from each plate boundary type.

12.4 ◎ Describe landforms that result from tectonic processes away from plate boundaries.

12.5 ◎ Assess the relationship between food security in South Asia and the changing climate of the Tibetan Plateau.

THE HUMAN SPHERE: Life on Earth's Shifting Crust

FOR BETTER OR FOR WORSE, HUMANS ARE AFFECTED by the movements of Earth's lithospheric plates. For instance, earthquakes, which are a result of plate movement, range from minor annoyances to major disasters. Large earthquakes can reduce cities to rubble and generate enormous ocean waves, called tsunamis, that destroy coastal areas (see The Human Sphere in Chapter 14).

Moving plates also create volcanoes, which can be just as disruptive to the lives of people. In April and May of 2010, the eruption of Eyjafjallajökull volcano in Iceland caused the cancellation of some 100,000 airline flights. The next year, in 2011, Grímsvötn, another Icelandic volcano (Figure 12.1), grounded thousands more flights.

The movements of Earth's lithospheric plates are also beneficial to people. Ash from erupting volcanoes, for example, settles to the ground and creates some of the world's most fertile agricultural soils, called andisols (see Section 9.1). The moving plates also build the land on which we live. The land surface of many island nations, such as Japan, Indonesia, and much of New Zealand, was built by volcanoes. Plate movements even modify the

FIGURE 12.1 **Volcanic ash from Grímsvötn.** *On May 22, 2011, Grímsvötn sent plumes of ash into the air that traveled over northern Europe, causing the cancellation of thousands of flights. Aircraft engines fail when they take in volcanic ash, so planes must be grounded until the ash clears.* (© AFP/Getty Images)

Grímsvötn volcano
Iceland
60° N
Norway Finland
Sweden
U.K. Poland
Germany
45° N
France
Italy
15° E

chemistry of the atmosphere and its greenhouse effect by moving carbon from the atmosphere to the lithosphere and back again over millions of years (see Section 11.4).

This chapter explores Earth's dynamic lithosphere, first in the context of continental drift theory, then in the modern framework of plate tectonics theory. Next, it describes interactions between plates and the resulting topography. Finally, it explores the Tibetan Plateau's affect on climate and people.

12.1 Continental Drift: Wegener's Theory

◎ Compare the theory of continental drift with the theory of plate tectonics.

Some 300 million years ago, Earth would hardly have been recognizable to us from space. At that time, Earth had only one ocean and one *supercontinent*, called **Pangaea** (meaning "whole land"), formed by the fusion of all the continents into a single large landmass (Figure 12.2). The ocean that surrounded Pangaea, called the **Panthalassic Ocean**, was much larger than the Pacific Ocean is today.

FIGURE 12.2 **Pangaea.** *This map shows the configuration of continents as they looked 300 million years ago, when they were fused into one supercontinent called* Pangaea.

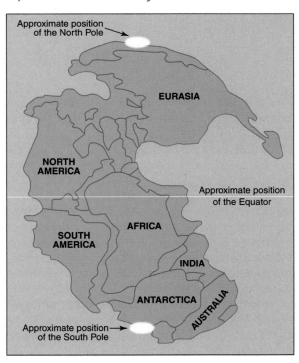

Pangaea was *rifted* (split apart) as a result of convection in the asthenosphere beneath it. **The transition from Pangaea to today's continental configuration occurred in two major steps: the opening of the Tethys Sea and, later, the opening of the Atlantic Ocean.** The opening of the Tethys Sea, which began about 200 million years ago, created two large landmasses: Laurasia to the north and Gondwana to the south. **Laurasia** consisted of the landmasses that would become North America, Greenland, and Eurasia. **Gondwana** consisted of the landmasses that would become South America, Australia, Africa, India, and Antarctica. The opening of the northern Atlantic Ocean started about 180 million years ago, and by 65 million years ago, the Atlantic was fully opened. As the Atlantic Ocean basin developed, the shapes of the continents began to take their modern form (Figure 12.3 on page 388).

Pangaea is only the most recent supercontinent. *Rodinia* formed about 750 million years before Pangaea (more than 1 billion years ago). There were other supercontinents before Rodinia, each of which broke apart and rearranged into a new supercontinent.

It took a long time and much scientific evidence for scientists to accept that continents move. As recently as the late 1950s, most scientists thought that the continents were fixed and immovable. How could entire continents made of solid rock move thousands of miles? As we will see, the growing body of evidence supporting the idea of a dynamic lithosphere eventually became indisputable.

The first person to propose a theory of continental movement was the German meteorologist Alfred Lothar Wegener (1880–1930; his name is pronounced VEGG-en-er). Wegener's theory of **continental drift** proposed that continents move slowly across Earth's surface. One piece of evidence that motivated Wegener to pursue his theory was the jigsaw-puzzle fit

Pangaea
The supercontinent formed about 300 million years ago by the fusion of all continents.

Panthalassic Ocean
The single large ocean that surrounded Pangaea 300 million years ago.

Laurasia
A landmass that resulted when Pangaea split about 200 million years ago, which consisted of modern-day North America, Greenland, and Eurasia.

Gondwana
A landmass that resulted when Pangaea split about 200 million years ago, which consisted of modern-day South America, Australia, Africa, India, and Antarctica.

continental drift
A theory proposed by Alfred Wegener stating that continents move slowly across Earth's surface.

> Why do the coastlines of Africa and South America fit together?*

*Answers to the Living Physical Geography questions are found on page 415.

FIGURE **12.3** **GEO-GRAPHIC:** **Breakup of Pangaea.**

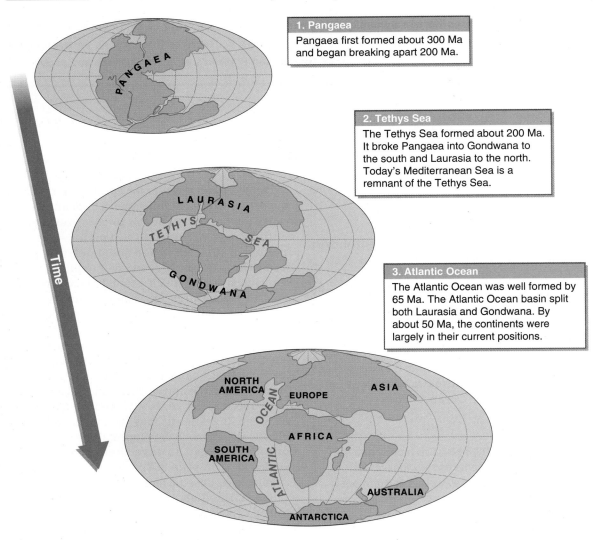

1. Pangaea
Pangaea first formed about 300 Ma
and began breaking apart 200 Ma.

2. Tethys Sea
The Tethys Sea formed about 200 Ma.
It broke Pangaea into Gondwana to
the south and Laurasia to the north.
Today's Mediterranean Sea is a
remnant of the Tethys Sea.

3. Atlantic Ocean
The Atlantic Ocean was well formed by
65 Ma. The Atlantic Ocean basin split
both Laurasia and Gondwana. By
about 50 Ma, the continents were
largely in their current positions.

between the east coast of South America and the west coast of Africa **(Figure 12.4)**.

Wegener was not the first to be struck by how the continental outlines fit together, but he was the first to assemble a formal theory proposing that the continents shift. **Wegener supported his theory using evidence from matching rock types on separated continents, deposits of glacial gravels, and fossil remains of organisms (Figure 12.5).**

Wegener formally proposed his theory in 1912 and published it in his book *The Origins of Continents and Oceans*. Wegener's theory was dismissed by his professional colleagues because no forces sufficiently powerful to move continents such great distances were known.

Wegener's biography reveals that the process of science and scientific revolutions are not neat and tidy. Established views are hard to change. Some scientists rejected Wegener's idea because it conflicted with their paradigm (conceptual model) of the crust being fixed and impossible to move. Wegener's theory was forgotten for five decades.

Scientific evidence supporting Wegener's theory would come later, decades after his death. With the discovery of that evidence, Wegener's theory was embraced by scientists and given a new name. **Plate tectonics** is the theory describing the origin, movement, and recycling of lithospheric plates and the resulting landforms.

Continental drift theory states that continents are moving. **Plate tectonics theory addresses how the lithospheric plates on which continents rest move and interact.**

plate tectonics
A theory addressing the origin, movement, and recycling of lithospheric plates and the landforms that result.

12.2 Plate Tectonics: An Ocean of Evidence

◎ Describe the evidence used to develop the theory of plate tectonics and explain how lithospheric plates move.

In 1912, when Wegener first proposed his theory of continental drift, almost nothing was known about seafloor bathymetry. Following World War II, emerging seafloor research methods using sonar provided new evidence that led to the development of the theory of plate tectonics.

One important research tool was the ship *Glomar Challenger*. The *Challenger* could drill 1.6 km (1 mi) long samples from seafloor rock in water 5 km (3 mi) deep. Researchers aboard this vessel sampled rock materials in the Atlantic Ocean along a *transect* (or line) that crossed the mid-ocean ridges (see Section 10.1). Scientific data were pouring in from the *Challenger* and other sources. Scientists could not make sense of this new information using the paradigm that the continents are fixed and unmoving.

Harry Hess is considered one of the founders of plate tectonics. In 1960, he formalized the theory of *seafloor spreading*, which eventually developed into the broader theory of plate tectonics. Hess used data on the ages of seafloor rocks and on patterns of magnetism in those rocks to propose that new oceanic crust forms at mid-ocean ridges and then moves apart. Hess's theory and additional scientific evidence (as illustrated in **Figure 12.6** on page 390)

FIGURE 12.4 **Evidence for continental drift: The fit of South America and Africa.** *If the Atlantic Ocean were closed, North America and South America would fit tightly against Europe, Greenland, and Africa.*

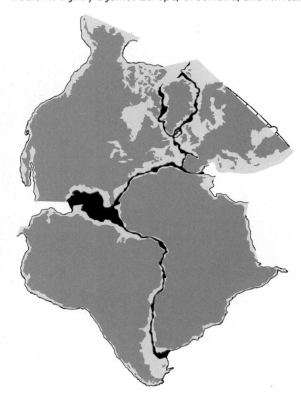

led not only to a consensus among scientists that the lithospheric plates are in motion, but also to a complex model showing how it is possible for them

FIGURE 12.5 **GEO-GRAPHIC: Evidence for continental drift: Rock types and fossils.**

1. Matching mountains and rock types

The Appalachian Mountains in the eastern United States are geologic counterparts of the Atlas Mountains in northwestern Africa. Eastern Greenland's rocks also match those found in Scotland and Norway. If the Atlantic Ocean were closed up, all of these rock types would match up.

2. Glacial gravels

Ancient *tillites* (rocks formed from glacial gravel deposits) in southern Africa, southern South America, India, southern Australia, and Antarctica suggest that those continents were once joined and covered with ice.

3. The geography of fossils

Geographically separated fossils of now-extinct organisms suggest formerly connected continents. The extinct *Mesosaurus*, shown here, lived in southern South America and in southern Africa. This reptile lived only in freshwater and could not have crossed the ocean. Its distribution suggests that the two continents were once connected.

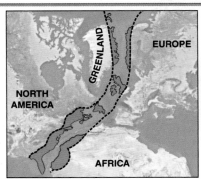

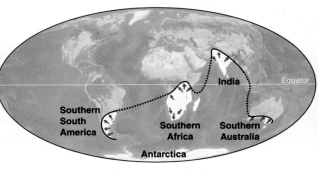

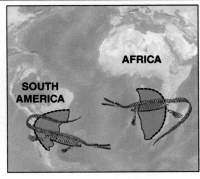

FIGURE 12.6 SCIENTIFIC INQUIRY: What is the evidence on which plate tectonics theory is based?

A wide range of data and observations, gathered from the ocean basins with many scientific tools, supports the theory of plate tectonics.
(Top left, © Dr. Ken MacDonald/Science Source; top center, Gulf of Alaska 2004. NOAA, WHOI, and the Alvin Group; top right, Woods Hole Science Center, U.S. Geological Survey; map, NOAA/NGDC)

Mid-ocean ridges

Bathymetric mapping with sonar in the 1950s revealed mid-ocean ridges. Sampling of rocks from these mountain ranges revealed that they are volcanic in origin.

Significance: These submerged volcanic mountain ranges occur where new oceanic crust is being formed.

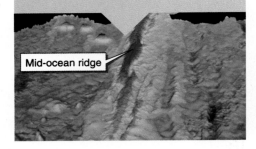

Mid-ocean ridge

Seamounts

Flat-topped, submerged mountains called seamounts were also discovered using sonar (see Section 10.4). Seamounts, too, were found to be predominantly volcanic in origin.

Significance: The flat tops of many seamounts indicate that they were once subject to erosion at the sea surface. Later, plate movements carried them into deep water.

Deep-sea trenches

Deep-sea trenches are located near some continental and island-chain margins (see Section 10.1). The Puerto Rico Trench is the deepest location in the Caribbean Sea. Florida can be seen at the upper right.

Significance: Deep-sea trenches reveal where oceanic crust dives deep into the mantle in the process of subduction.

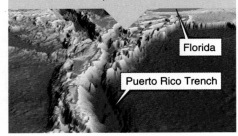

Florida

Puerto Rico Trench

Seafloor magnetic reversals

Every 200,000 years, on average, for unknown reasons, Earth's magnetic field flips: North becomes south and south becomes north. As lava hardens into rock, iron particles in the lava record the location of magnetic north like a compass. Samples of seafloor rocks reveal a matching pattern of magnetic reversals in rocks of equal distance from mid-ocean ridges.

Significance: These matching magnetic stripes on either side of the mid-ocean ridges can be explained only if oceanic crust is moving away from mid-ocean ridges through time.

Normal magnetism
At time 1 (T_1), new rocks cool from lava at a mid-ocean ridge and record the direction of magnetic north.

Normal polarity

T_1

Magma

Time

Reversed magnetism
At time 2 (T_2), new rocks record the new direction of magnetic north after a magnetic reversal.

Reversed polarity

T_1 T_2 T_1

Time

Normal magnetism
At time 3 (T_3), new rocks record the direction of magnetic north after another magnetic reversal.

Normal polarity

T_1 T_2 T_3 T_2 T_1

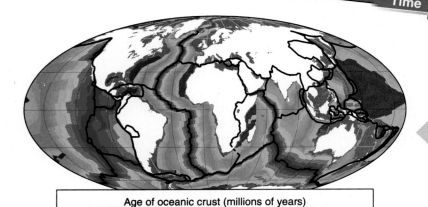

Ages of seafloor rocks

The age of the seafloor increases away from a mid-ocean ridge. Few seafloor rocks are older than 150 million years.

Significance: This pattern of older crust farther from mid-ocean ridges indicates that crust forms at mid-ocean ridges, then moves away from them.

Age of oceanic crust (millions of years)

0   20   40   60   80   100   120   140   160   180   280

to move. According to this model, **new lithosphere forms at mid-ocean ridges, and old lithosphere is recycled deep into the mantle through subduction,** a process in which oceanic lithosphere of one plate bends and dives into the mantle beneath another plate.

Plate Tectonics: The Current Model

According to the current model of plate tectonics, the lithosphere is broken into 14 major plates and many smaller fragments, all of which move independently of one another across the surface of the planet. These plates lie atop the convecting asthenosphere and are set in motion by it. The plates are not floating on a sea of molten rock. The rocks of the asthenosphere are hot, but they are under great pressure and, as a result, they do not melt. Instead, the asthenosphere is solid rock that is plastic and can deform and slowly flow, like warm (but not melted) wax (see Section 11.3).

The margins of the lithospheric plates are called **plate boundaries.** The large plates are called *primary plates* and smaller plates are called *secondary plates.* There are seven primary and seven secondary plates. The largest plate is the Pacific plate **(Figure 12.7).**

subduction
The process in which oceanic lithosphere bends and dives into the mantle beneath another lithospheric plate.

plate boundary
The margin of a lithospheric plate.

FIGURE **12.7** **Plates of the lithosphere.** *The 14 major lithospheric plates are shown here. Black triangles are used to show where one plate is moving toward another; the triangles point in the direction the plate is moving. For example, the Nazca plate is moving eastward toward the South American plate. Most lithospheric plates are composed of both continental and oceanic crust. At a transform boundary, plates move laterally past one another.*

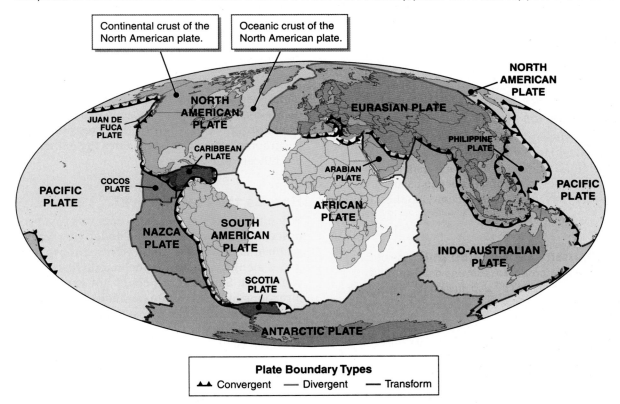

Plate Names	
PRIMARY PLATES	**SECONDARY PLATES**
African plate	Arabian plate
Antarctic plate	Caribbean plate
Eurasian plate	Cocos plate
Indo-Australian plate	Juan de Fuca plate
North American plate	Nazca plate
Pacific plate	Philippine plate
South American plate	Scotia plate

ridge push
The process by which magma rising along a mid-ocean ridge forces oceanic crust of two separate plates apart.

mantle drag
The dragging force between the asthenosphere and the overlying lithosphere.

slab pull
The process by which the weight of subducting oceanic lithosphere accelerates plate movement by pulling the plate deeper into the mantle.

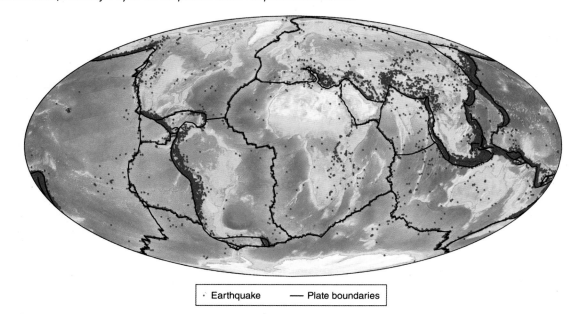

FIGURE 12.8 **Global earthquake patterns.** *This map shows the locations of nearly 360,000 earthquakes that occurred between 1963 and 1998. Although some earthquakes do occur far from plate boundaries, the majority of earthquakes occur on plate boundaries.*

· Earthquake — Plate boundaries

How Do We Know Where the Plate Boundaries Are?

The geographic pattern of earthquakes reveals where plate boundaries are. After World War II, scientists began placing extensive networks of seismometers around the ocean basins to measure and record earthquake activity. To their astonish-ment, they found that earthquakes were not randomly distributed, as they had anticipated. Instead, as shown in **Figure 12.8**, earthquakes occur in a geographic pattern that delineates the outlines of the lithospheric plates.

How Do the Plates Move?

When the theory of plate tectonics was first proposed, it was assumed that the underlying mantle grabbed and dragged the overlying lithospheric plates along by friction as the mantle flowed and convected. Such models could not explain the directions of plate movement, however, because it is impossible to arrange mantle convection patterns in a way that accounts for the direction of observed plate movements. For that reason, scientists modified the theory by concluding that there must be additional forces moving the lithospheric plates.

Plate movement is thought to be a result of three factors: ridge push, mantle drag, and slab pull **(Figure 12.9)**. **Ridge push** is the process by which magma rising along a mid-ocean ridge lifts oceanic lithosphere and forces it apart. Lateral flow of the asthenosphere beneath the plates creates **mantle drag** between the asthenosphere and the overlying lithosphere. In the process of **slab pull**, the weight of the subducting portion of a plate (a *slab*) accelerates plate movement by pulling the plate deeper into the mantle.

> How can whole continents move?

FIGURE 12.9 **Ridge push, mantle drag, slab pull.** *Computer analysis suggests that where oceanic lithosphere is sinking deep into the mantle, about 90% of plate movement may be caused by slab pull alone. Mantle drag is the least significant of the three forces in these subduction zones.*

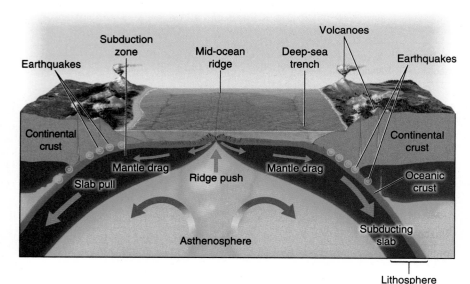

Subduction zone
Volcanoes
Mid-ocean ridge
Deep-sea trench
Earthquakes
Earthquakes
Continental crust
Continental crust
Mantle drag
Mantle drag
Oceanic crust
Slab pull
Ridge push
Subducting slab
Asthenosphere
Lithosphere

FIGURE 12.10 **Plate movement velocity.** *Each of the 14 lithospheric plates moves independently and at a different speed. Red arrows show absolute plate velocities; blue arrows show relative plate velocities. Longer arrows indicate faster movement. The numbers are distances traveled each year in centimeters. Symbols for different types of plate boundaries are given to the right of the map: Triangles show where plates converge. Red lines show where plates diverge. Thin black lines show where plates slip past one another sideways in transform movement.*

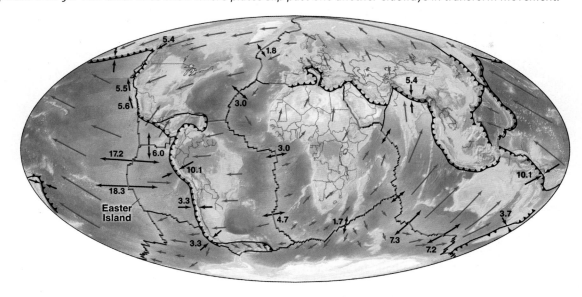

- ▲▲ Convergent plate boundary
- — Divergent plate boundary
- — Transform plate boundary
- → Absolute plate velocity
- → Relative plate velocity
- **7.2** Distance traveled per year in cm

How Fast Do the Plates Move?

Two kinds of plate velocity can be measured: relative and absolute. *Relative plate velocity* is the speed of a plate in relation to the speed of another plate, and *absolute plate velocity* is the speed of a plate in relation to a fixed object, such as the center of Earth.

Imagine riding your bike at 10 km/h (6 mph) past someone who is standing still on the sidewalk. Your speed, to that person, is 10 km/h. That is your *absolute* velocity. If another bicyclist passes you traveling 12 km/h (7.5 mph), that rider's absolute velocity is 12 km/h (to the person standing on the sidewalk). But from your perspective on your bicycle, that rider is traveling only 2 km/h. Two kilometers per hour is that rider's *relative* velocity.

Similarly, if two lithospheric plates each have an absolute velocity of 5 cm (2 in) per year, and they are both moving away from each other, their relative velocity is 10 cm (4 in). If they are traveling in the same direction, however, their relative velocity is 0 cm per year, because they are both moving in the same direction at the same speed, like two bicyclists traveling at the same speed together.

Today, plate movement can be measured with millimeter-level accuracy using orbiting satellites and GPS technologies. **Figure 12.10** shows the Pacific and Nazca plates near Easter Island are the fastest-moving plates, each moving at a relative velocity of about 18 cm (7 in) per year.

Why Is the Theory of Plate Tectonics Important?

Plate tectonics is one of the most important scientific theories developed in the twentieth century because it explains such a wide range of geophysical phenomena. **Plate tectonics is called a *unifying theory* because it gathers together seemingly unrelated phenomena and puts them together under the same umbrella of explanation.** The formation and geographic locations of volcanoes, earthquake patterns, rock types and ages, island formation, lake formation, undersea mountain ranges, deep-sea trenches, continental mountain ranges, the shapes and outlines of continents, and even the geographic ranges of plants and animals can all be explained by this one theory.

12.3 Plate Boundary Landforms

◎ Describe the three types of plate boundaries and the landforms resulting from each plate boundary type.

Most deformation of Earth's crust occurs at the margins of the lithospheric plates. The extent of deformation, and the resulting landforms, depend on the way the plates move in relation to one another. There are three types of plate boundaries: divergent plate boundaries, convergent plate boundaries, and transform plate boundaries **(Figure 12.11)**.

divergent plate boundary
A region where two lithospheric plates move apart.

convergent plate boundary
A region where two lithospheric plates move toward each other.

transform plate boundary
A plate boundary where one lithospheric plate slips laterally past another.

rift
A region where continental crust is stretching and splitting.

rift valley
A linear valley with volcanoes formed by rifting of continental crust, sometimes filled with freshwater to form a deep lake.

FIGURE 12.11 **Three types of plate boundaries.** *(A) A divergent plate boundary occurs where two plates move apart as new crust is formed. Here, two plates move apart as new oceanic crust is formed at a mid-ocean ridge. (B) A convergent plate boundary occurs where two plates move toward one another. Here, one plate subducts beneath another, forming a deep-sea trench. The subducting plate is recycled into the mantle. Magma rises up through the overriding plate, creating a chain of volcanoes. (C) A transform plate boundary is formed as two plates slide past each other.*

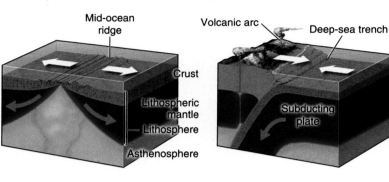
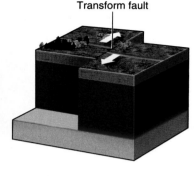

A. Divergent plate boundary

B. Convergent plate boundary

C. Transform plate boundary

A **divergent plate boundary** occurs where two plates move apart. A **convergent plate boundary** occurs where two plates move toward each other. A **transform plate boundary** occurs where one plate slips laterally past another.

Divergent Plate Boundaries

Mid-Ocean Ridges

Although they are hidden beneath the ocean, mid-ocean ridges are the most geographically extensive landforms on the planet. If we could see through the waters of the oceans, we would see the mountain ranges of the mid-ocean ridges running the length of the ocean basins **(Figure 12.12)**.

Along the mid-ocean ridges, the mantle flows upward to the base of the lithosphere. Pressure near the crust is much less than that found deep in the mantle. As mantle material migrates upward,

the pressure on it decreases. As the pressure decreases, the melting point of the rock is lowered, and the rock melts into magma.

Magma has a lower density, and is thus more buoyant, than the solid rock of the crust that surrounds it. As a result, magma rises upward. It may cool beneath the crust's surface. If it is *extruded* (pushed out) onto the seafloor, however, it forms submarine volcanoes.

This rising magma, and its formation of new oceanic crust, creates the ridge push that moves the plates at the mid-ocean ridge farther apart, allowing more magma to rise into the crust from below and continue the process. This process is called *seafloor spreading*. The seafloor spreading model explains why the youngest seafloor is always found along the mid-ocean ridges, where it has recently formed, and it explains how ocean basins grow and become wider **(Figure 12.13)**.

Rifting

A **rift** is a region where continental crust is stretching and splitting. At a rift, two portions of the crust are moving apart, as they do at a mid-ocean ridge, allowing mantle material to rise and melt into magma. The buoyant magma then rises up through the crust to create volcanoes. This process results in a **rift valley**: a long valley with volcanoes formed by rifting of continental crust. Rift valleys sometimes fill with freshwater to form very deep lakes. As rift valleys continue to open and deepen, they may be flooded with seawater, creating an inland sea and, with more time, a new ocean basin. **Figure 12.14A** illustrates the sequence of rifting and the formation of a rift valley and a new ocean basin.

Lake Tanganyika, in the East African Rift system **(Figure 12.14B)**, is 1,470 m (4,820 ft) deep. Because of its great depth, it is the world's second largest

FIGURE 12.12 **Mid-ocean ridges.** *Diverging plates create mid-ocean ridges (shown with a red line) that run nearly from pole to pole. These underwater mountain ranges are far larger than any mountain range on dry land.*

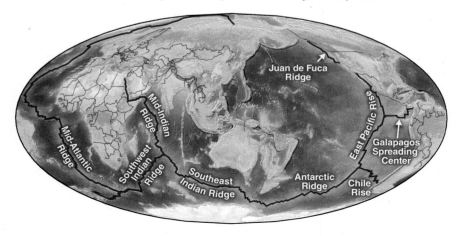

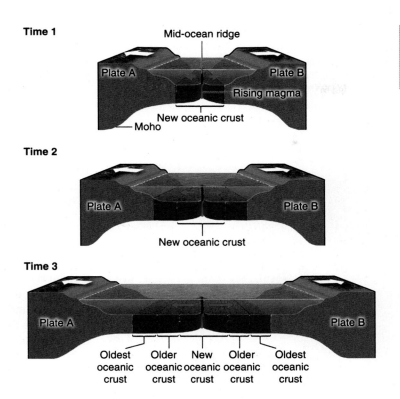

FIGURE **12.13** **Seafloor spreading.** *As two plates diverge, new oceanic crust is continually added at a mid-ocean ridge. Each of the two plates shown in this diagram is composed of both oceanic crust (colored gray) and continental crust (colored tan). As the two plates diverge, the ocean basin grows larger.*

Animation
Seafloor
spreading
http://qrs.ly/a83w0pv

FIGURE **12.14** **GEO-GRAPHIC: Rifting.** *(A) Rifting of a continent can eventually lead to the development of a new ocean basin. (B) The East African Rift system has been opening at a rate of about 3 mm (0.12 in) per year over the last 40 million years. The rifting started in the north, near the Red Sea, and has been working its way southward, like a big zipper unzipping the margin of the African continent. (B. NOAA/NGDC)*

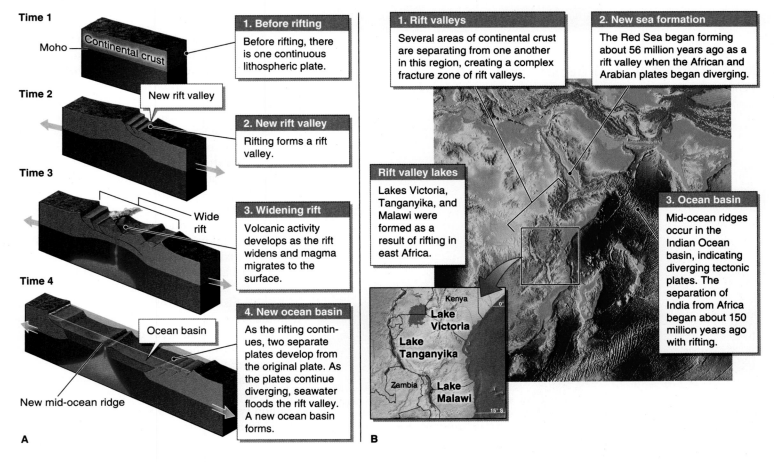

Time 1

Moho — Continental crust

1. Before rifting

Before rifting, there is one continuous lithospheric plate.

Time 2

New rift valley

2. New rift valley

Rifting forms a rift valley.

Time 3

Wide rift

3. Widening rift

Volcanic activity develops as the rift widens and magma migrates to the surface.

Time 4

Ocean basin

New mid-ocean ridge

4. New ocean basin

As the rifting continues, two separate plates develop from the original plate. As the plates continue diverging, seawater floods the rift valley. A new ocean basin forms.

A

1. Rift valleys

Several areas of continental crust are separating from one another in this region, creating a complex fracture zone of rift valleys.

2. New sea formation

The Red Sea began forming about 56 million years ago as a rift valley when the African and Arabian plates began diverging.

Rift valley lakes

Lakes Victoria, Tanganyika, and Malawi were formed as a result of rifting in east Africa.

3. Ocean basin

Mid-ocean ridges occur in the Indian Ocean basin, indicating diverging tectonic plates. The separation of India from Africa began about 150 million years ago with rifting.

Kenya
Lake Victoria
Lake Tanganyika
Zambia **Lake Malawi**
15° S

B

FIGURE **12.15** **Lake Baikal.** *Lake Baikal is a rift valley lake that has formed on the Eurasian plate. The bottom of the lake is 1,186 m (3,893 ft) below sea level. In time, if rifting continues and forms a valley connecting to the ocean, it will fill with seawater.* (© Planet Observer/Universal Images Group/Getty Images)

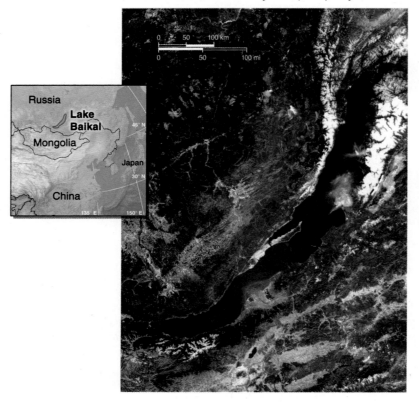

lake by volume of water (not by surface area). Lake Malawi is 706 m (2,316 ft) deep and is the world's sixth largest lake by volume. Also on the East African Rift system, Lake Victoria is the second largest lake in the world by surface area (68,800 km^2 or 26,600 mi^2).

The world's largest lake by volume is Lake Baikal, in Russia. It is 1,642 m (5,387 ft) deep and contains 20% of Earth's surface freshwater. It is thought to be the oldest lake in the world (at 25 million years old). It, too, is a result of rifting **(Figure 12.15)**.

Convergent Plate Boundaries

Subduction

We live on a planet with many natural hazards. Certainly among the most deadly of those natural hazards are the powerful and explosive volcanoes that form along convergent plate boundaries where subduction is occurring (see Figure 12.11B). The presence of a deep-sea trench shows where subduction is occurring.

As the plates grind against each other during subduction, they generate earthquakes, some of which are very powerful. An earthquake is caused when two plates are stuck together, then suddenly become unstuck, releasing energy that radiates out as seismic waves (see Section 14.3). The locations of these earthquakes follow the profile of the subducting plate. Thus, subduction zones produce a sloping pattern of increasingly deep earthquake *foci* (or centers) called a **Wadati-Benioff zone**. **Figure 12.16** illustrates why earthquakes become progressively deeper toward the east in western South America.

Oceanic lithosphere is consumed and recycled in the process of subduction. This process occurs at the same rate that new oceanic crust is formed at mid-ocean ridges. The mantle is sometimes referred to as the graveyard of oceanic crust. Almost all oceanic crust is younger than 150 million years because of subduction (see Figure 12.6).

Continental lithosphere, on the other hand, is not subducted because it is less dense than oceanic lithosphere and thus too buoyant. This property has kept the continents free of subduction for most of Earth's history. Therefore, the oldest and most tectonically stable portions of the lithosphere are found in continental areas called *shields*.

Shields form the stable nucleus of a continent. The crust of the continental shields is at least 570 million years old. The oldest shield is the Canadian Shield, which is estimated to have formed about 4 billion years ago, just after early Earth's surface cooled from a molten state (see Section 11.1).

FIGURE **12.16** **A Wadati-Benioff zone.** *The Nazca plate is subducting beneath the South American plate, creating a pattern of progressively deeper earthquakes toward the east.*

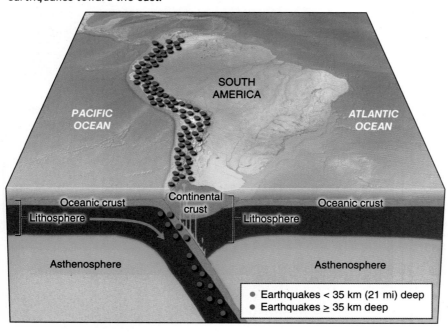

- Earthquakes < 35 km (21 mi) deep
- Earthquakes ≥ 35 km deep

FIGURE 12.17 **GEO-GRAPHIC: Continental-oceanic convergent plate boundary.** *(A) Continental volcanic arcs are formed along the margin of a continent where oceanic crust is being subducted. (B) The Cascade Range in the Pacific Northwest of the United States and southern Canada is a continental volcanic arc. It is the result of the Juan de Fuca plate subducting beneath the North American plate (the black line with triangles shows the plate boundary and the direction of plate movement). The mid-ocean ridge separating the Pacific plate from the Juan de Fuca plate is also shown in this map. Mount St. Helens (in the foreground of the photo) and Mount Rainier are among the 18 active volcanoes in the Cascades.* (photo, © Gary Braasch/Corbis)

Animation
Subduction
http://qrs.ly/uv47ll0

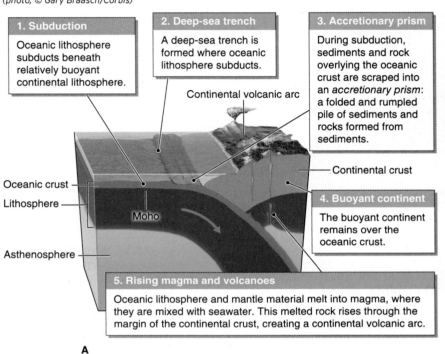

1. Subduction
Oceanic lithosphere subducts beneath relatively buoyant continental lithosphere.

2. Deep-sea trench
A deep-sea trench is formed where oceanic lithosphere subducts.

3. Accretionary prism
During subduction, sediments and rock overlying the oceanic crust are scraped into an *accretionary prism*: a folded and rumpled pile of sediments and rocks formed from sediments.

Continental volcanic arc

Continental crust

4. Buoyant continent
The buoyant continent remains over the oceanic crust.

Oceanic crust
Lithosphere
Moho
Asthenosphere

5. Rising magma and volcanoes
Oceanic lithosphere and mantle material melt into magma, where they are mixed with seawater. This melted rock rises through the margin of the continental crust, creating a continental volcanic arc.

A

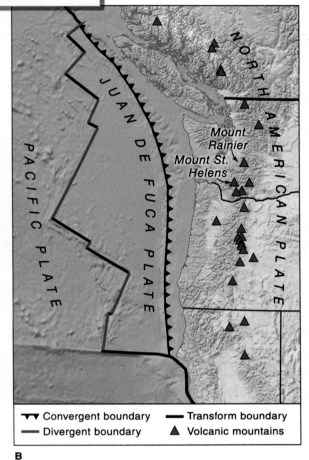

Mount Rainier
Mount St. Helens

▼▼ Convergent boundary   —— Transform boundary
—— Divergent boundary   ▲ Volcanic mountains

B

Mount Rainier

Mount St. Helens

Types of Subduction

When oceanic lithosphere is subducted beneath continental lithosphere, extensive regions of volcanic activity result. The subducting oceanic lithosphere brings large amounts of seawater with it into the lithospheric mantle. Water lowers the melting point of the mantle, and as a result, portions of the oceanic crust and the mantle melt into magma.

Because magma is less dense and more buoyant than the surrounding solid rock, it rises up, melting its way through the margin of the continental crust. As it does so, it incorporates continental crust material in a process called *partial melting*. The pressure exerted by the surrounding rock also squeezes the magma up to the surface. This process forms a **continental volcanic arc**: a long chain of volcanoes on the margin of a continent above a subducting plate **(Figure 12.17)**.

Subduction can also occur where the oceanic lithosphere of two separate plates converges. In this case, a similar sequence of events occurs: Oceanic lithosphere of one plate subducts beneath that of another plate, resulting in a chain of volcanoes. The difference, however, is that the region of subduction is submerged beneath the ocean, and the volcanoes form on the seafloor, where they may eventually rise above sea level to form islands. A **volcanic island arc** is a chain of islands formed

Wadati-Benioff zone
A sloping pattern of increasingly deep earthquake foci found in a subduction zone.

continental volcanic arc
A long chain of volcanoes formed on the margin of a continent above a subducting plate.

volcanic island arc
A chain of islands formed where oceanic lithosphere of one plate is subducting beneath oceanic lithosphere of another plate.

FIGURE 12.18 **Oceanic-oceanic convergent plate boundary.**
Volcanic island arcs are formed where the oceanic crust of one plate is subducted beneath the oceanic crust of another plate.

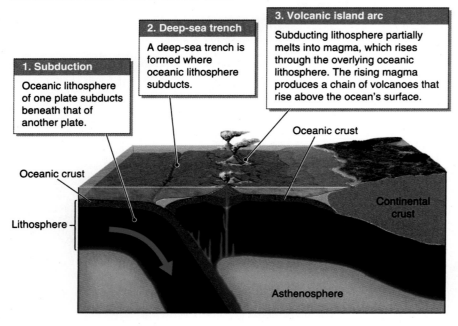

2. Deep-sea trench
A deep-sea trench is formed where oceanic lithosphere subducts.

1. Subduction
Oceanic lithosphere of one plate subducts beneath that of another plate.

3. Volcanic island arc
Subducting lithosphere partially melts into magma, which rises through the overlying oceanic lithosphere. The rising magma produces a chain of volcanoes that rise above the ocean's surface.

Oceanic crust

Oceanic crust

Continental crust

Lithosphere

Asthenosphere

Pacific Ring of Fire
A zone of volcanically active mountain chains resulting from subduction on the margins of the Pacific Ocean.

collision
Convergence of the continental crust of two different plates.

accreted terrane
A mass of crust that is transported by plate movement and fused onto the margin of a continent.

where oceanic lithosphere of one plate is subducting beneath that of another plate **(Figure 12.18)**. Examples of volcanic island arcs include Tonga, the western Aleutian Islands of Alaska, northeastern Japan, East Timor, the Philippines, and most of Indonesia.

Extensive chains of volcanoes, formed through both types of subduction, occur around the perimeter of the Pacific Ocean, from Chile to Mexico to California, north to Alaska, and south again to

FIGURE 12.19 **Pacific Ring of Fire.** *The Pacific Ring of Fire spans some 40,000 km (25,000 mi) and contains over 75% of the world's active volcanoes. With the exception of the Puerto Rico Trench and the South Sandwich Trench, all deep-sea trench systems are found in the Pacific Ring of Fire.*

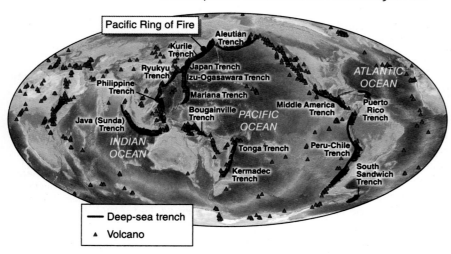

Pacific Ring of Fire

Aleutian Trench
Kurile Trench
Ryukyu Trench
Japan Trench
Izu-Ogasawara Trench
Philippine Trench
Mariana Trench
Bougainville Trench
Java (Sunda) Trench
Middle America Trench
Puerto Rico Trench
ATLANTIC OCEAN
PACIFIC OCEAN
INDIAN OCEAN
Tonga Trench
Peru-Chile Trench
Kermadec Trench
South Sandwich Trench

— Deep-sea trench
▲ Volcano

Japan, the Philippines, and Indonesia, all the way to Antarctica. Collectively, these volcanic mountain ranges make up the **Pacific Ring of Fire**: a zone of volcanically active mountain chains resulting from subduction on the margins of the Pacific Ocean **(Figure 12.19)**.

Collision
Eventually, if subduction continues, two continents will come together because oceanic crust is completely subducted and the following continent collides at the plate boundary. **Collision** occurs where the continental crust of two different plates converges. Because continental crust does not subduct, collision results in the formation of a mountain belt as the crust is heaved upward. As illustrated in **Figure 12.20**, collision can follow after the closing of an ocean basin.

Collision results in a jumble of rocks that have been crushed, broken, folded, and chemically transformed by the enormous heat and pressure it generates. **Nonvolcanic mountains form where the crust is thickened and buckled by collision.**

Collision sutures plates together. The Appalachian Mountains in the eastern United States were formed 280 million years ago as the continental crust of two different plates collided and fused to form the North American plate. The Himalayas are still being formed by collision between the Indo-Australian plate and the Eurasian plate **(Figure 12.21)**. This collision has created the world's highest plateau and mountain range. The Geographic Perspectives section at the end of this chapter explores the role this region plays in providing water and food for people. Eventually, the Indo-Australian plate will fuse with the GEOGRAPHIC PERSPECTIVES Eurasian plate in the region of the Himalayas and the growth of the Himalayas will stop.

Accreted Terranes
Why do some continents have a mosaic of mismatched crust types along their margins? An **accreted terrane** is a mass of crust that is transported by plate movement and fused onto the margin of a continent. Accreted terranes result from a combination of subduction of oceanic lithosphere and collision of landmasses that are smaller than continents. Terranes can travel thousands of miles across ocean basins before they encounter a continent. (Note that *terrane* refers to a piece of land added to continental crust, while *terrain* refers to the topography of a landscape.)

India is not considered an accreted terrane because the Indian landmass before it joined to Eurasia was considered a whole continent. However, as the Indo-Australian plate pushed northward into the Eurasian plate, it bulldozed several preexisting terranes ahead of it. Thus, the Himalayas are composed of mismatched pieces of accreted terranes and the Indian landmass.

FIGURE 12.20 **GEO-GRAPHIC:** **Continental-continental convergent plate boundary.**

1. Subduction and closing of ocean basin

In this diagram, two plates are converging. The oceanic lithosphere of plate A initially subducts beneath the continental lithosphere of plate B. A continental volcanic arc is produced on the margin of plate B. As the plates converge, the ocean basin closes.

2. Collision and suturing

After the oceanic lithosphere has been subducted and the ocean basin is closed, the continental crust of both plates collides and eventually joins through *suturing* into a single new plate. A new nonvolcanic mountain belt is formed at the suture. The oceanic lithosphere detaches and sinks into the mantle.

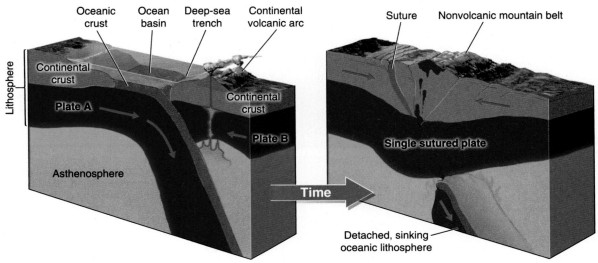

FIGURE 12.21 **The collision between India and Eurasia.** *The Indian landmass, once located south of the equator, moved north with the Indo-Australian plate and collided with the Eurasian landmass. The Indo-Australian plate moved north at an absolute rate of about 15 cm (6 in) per year. The Indo-Australian plate is pushing beneath the Eurasian plate and lifting it up to create the Himalayas and the Tibetan Plateau. These landforms are rising at a net rate of about 5 mm (0.2 in) every year, or 50 cm (1.6 ft) every century. The fastest rates of uplift are roughly 10 mm (0.39 in) per year in the western Himalayas in Pakistan. As a whole, the Himalayas are the fastest-rising mountain range in the world. The depth of the Moho (the base of the crust) is about 70 km (43 mi) beneath the Tibetan Plateau. Nowhere on Earth is the crust thicker than beneath the Himalayas and Tibetan Plateau.*

Animation
Collision
http://qrs.ly/8747ll1

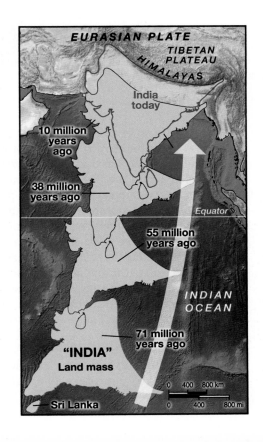

FIGURE **12.22**

Accreted terranes. *(A) Pieces of continental crust and volcanic island arcs are carried along on oceanic crust toward a continent. The oceanic crust subducts, forming active volcanoes, but the relatively buoyant terranes do not. Instead, they are scraped off and fused onto the continent's margin. (B) Through this process many different terranes have been added to the North American landmass at various times in the past. (B photos, from top: Andrew Greene, Hawaii Pacific University; © altrendo nature/ Stockbyte/Getty Images; David Lynch)*

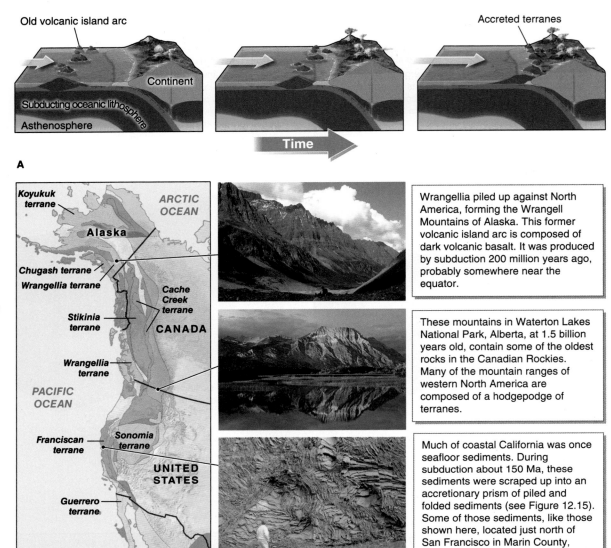

Wrangellia piled up against North America, forming the Wrangell Mountains of Alaska. This former volcanic island arc is composed of dark volcanic basalt. It was produced by subduction 200 million years ago, probably somewhere near the equator.

These mountains in Waterton Lakes National Park, Alberta, at 1.5 billion years old, contain some of the oldest rocks in the Canadian Rockies. Many of the mountain ranges of western North America are composed of a hodgepodge of terranes.

Much of coastal California was once seafloor sediments. During subduction about 150 Ma, these sediments were scraped up into an accretionary prism of piled and folded sediments (see Figure 12.15). Some of those sediments, like those shown here, located just north of San Francisco in Marin County, were transformed into *chert* rock.

Accreted terranes are found worldwide, but the largest accreted terrane group is in western North America. From Alaska to Mexico, terranes that have traveled across the Pacific Ocean basin have piled up on the western edge of the North American continent. As Figure 12.22 shows, these terranes have significantly increased the size of the continent.

Scientists can use their knowledge of plate movements to predict that certain landmasses that are currently isolated in the ocean will eventually become part of a continent. Picture This features the Seychelles, in the western Indian Ocean, as an example of a terrane that will one day join a continent.

Transform Plate Boundaries

Where two plates slip laterally past each other, a transform plate boundary is created (see Figure 12.11C). At transform plate boundaries, the crust is being sheared and torn, but no new crust is formed, and no old crust is recycled into the mantle. No mountains are built, and there are no volcanic eruptions.

Transform plate boundaries are most common on the seafloor at mid-ocean ridges, as illustrated in Figure 12.23. When on dry land, transform plate boundaries are conspicuous, and few are more conspicuous or notorious than California's San Andreas Fault (see Figure 11.13). The Pacific and North American plates grind past one another along this transform plate boundary, creating hundreds of earthquakes each day (most too small to be felt). Occasionally, this plate movement creates powerful and dangerous earthquakes.

Picture This

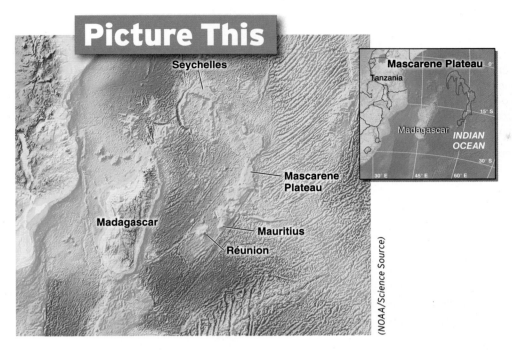

(NOAA/Science Source)

The Mascarene Plateau

The Seychelles, a chain of islands in the western Indian Ocean, form an independent country about 1,300 km (800 mi) east of mainland Africa. The Seychelles are part of the larger archipelago of 115 islands that sit on the Mascarene Plateau. The northern portion of the Mascarene Plateau, where the Seychelles are located, is composed of buoyant granitic continental crust. The southern portion is composed of volcanic rock, and the island of Réunion, found at the southern end of the plateau, is volcanically active. The island of Mauritius, near Réunion, is an extinct volcano.

The granitic crust of the Seychelles was last attached to India 65 million years ago. The islands lie on a piece of the Indo-Australian plate that detached as India moved northward and into Eurasia. Much or all of the Mascarene Plateau could be added to the Eurasian continent in the distant future as plate movement transports it northward across the ocean basin (see Figure 12.10).

Consider This

1. What kinds of evidence do you think would be necessary to support the theory that the northern Mascarene Plateau was once attached to India?

2. Why will the granitic portions of the Mascarene Plateau and the Seychelles never subduct into the mantle?

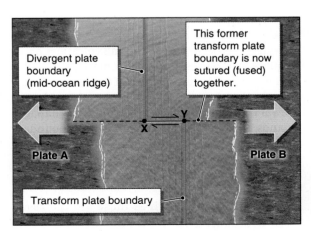

FIGURE 12.23 **Transform plate boundaries.** *Plate A is moving away from plate B along a mid-ocean ridge (red line). The region between points X and Y is a transform plate boundary (yellow line). The dotted line shows a scar formed by the former transform plate boundary.*

Animation
Transform
fault
http://qrs.ly/z547ll2

CRUNCH THE NUMBERS: Calculating Rate of Plate Movement

Los Angeles sits on the Pacific plate, and San Francisco sits on the North American plate. These two lithospheric plates are slipping past one another along a transform plate boundary, so that Los Angeles is moving north toward San Francisco. The relative velocity of the two plates is 5 cm (2 in) per year. Los Angeles and San Francisco are 880 km (550 mi) apart. Calculate how long it will take for Los Angeles to meet San Francisco.

> Is it true that Los Angeles will someday be connected to San Francisco?

There are 100,000 centimeters in a kilometer (63,360 inches in a mile).

Step 1: Convert kilometers to centimeters by multiplying by 100,000 (or miles to inches by multiplying by 63,360).

Step 2: Divide the distance between the two cities by the rate of movement per year. Make sure your distance and rate of movement are in the same units.

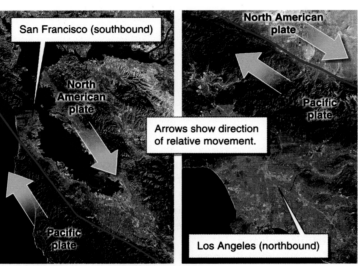

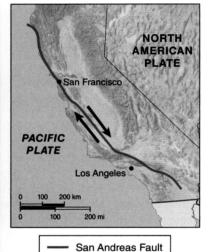

(Photos: EROS Center, U.S. Geological Survey; NASA/JPL)

Crunch the Numbers takes a mathematical approach to gauging the rate of movement of crust along this transform plate boundary.

Active and Passive Continental Margins

Notice in Figure 12.7 on page 391 that only some plate boundaries follow the outlines of continents. Geographers distinguish between active continental margins and passive continental margins **(Figure 12.24)**. An **active continental margin** is a plate boundary; in many cases, it consists of a deep-sea trench and a narrow continental shelf (see Section 10.1). A **passive continental margin** typically has a broad, sloping continental shelf and does not coincide with a plate boundary.

12.4 Hot Spots, Folding and Faulting, and Mountain Building

◎ **Describe landforms that result from tectonic processes away from plate boundaries.**

There are two tectonic processes that do not fit into the three types of plate boundary interactions discussed in the previous section, but are nevertheless important in building landforms: hot spots and folding and faulting. In this section we describe those processes, and we summarize the tectonic processes that result in mountain building.

Hot Spots

So far, the types of volcanoes that we have discussed all occur at plate margins where divergence or subduction is occurring. But not all volcanoes occur on plate boundaries. There are some 30,000 islands in the Pacific Ocean, and most of them are volcanic islands that formed far from plate boundaries. Hawai'i, Easter Island, Tahiti, and the Galápagos Islands are a few examples of non-plate boundary volcanic islands. In the Atlantic Ocean, the Canary Islands and the Cape Verde Islands are also volcanic in origin but are not found directly on plate boundaries.

Volcanic islands such as these are the result of geologic hot spots. A **hot spot** is a location at

---

active continental margin
A margin of a continent that follows a plate boundary, typically characterized by a deep-sea trench and a narrow continental shelf.

passive continental margin
A margin of a continent that does not coincide with a plate boundary, typically characterized by a broad, sloping continental shelf.

hot spot
A location at the base of the lithosphere where high temperatures cause the overlying crust to melt.

FIGURE 12.24 **Active and passive continental margins.** *(A) Active continental margins occur at the boundaries of two separate lithospheric plates. Passive continental margins occur where continental and oceanic crust are fused into a single plate. (B) The west coast of South America is an active continental margin. The east coast of the continent is a passive continental margin.*

Active continental margin	Passive continental margin
An active continental margin occurs where oceanic lithosphere of one plate is subducting beneath continental lithosphere of a separate plate. Deep-sea trenches are often found on active continental margins.	A passive continental margin occurs where oceanic lithosphere and continental lithosphere are fused together into a single plate and move as one. Broad, shallow continental shelves are found on passive continental margins.

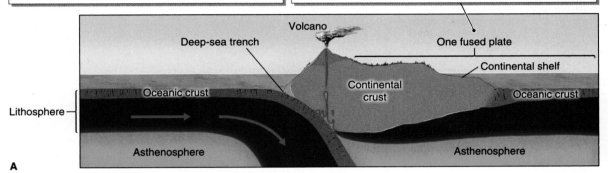

A

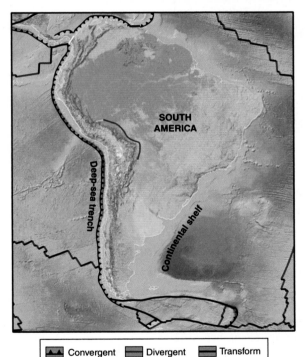

B

FIGURE 12.25 **A hot spot.** *A plume of hot solid rock anchored deep in the mantle slowly rises and melts the base of the lithosphere. The resulting magma then rises up through the crust. In oceanic crust, it creates submarine lava flows that build oceanic islands once they rise above sea level.*

4 Volcanic island

3 Submarine lava flows

2 Rising magma body

1 Rising mantle plume

mantle plume
A mostly stationary column of hot rock that extends from deep in the mantle up to the base of the lithosphere.

the base of the lithosphere where high temperatures cause the overlying crust to melt. A hot spot results from a **mantle plume**, a mostly stationary column of hot solid rock that extends from deep in the mantle up to the base of the lithosphere **(Figure 12.25)**.

Mantle plumes are incompletely understood. They are thought to be rooted in Earth's outer core, to remain mostly stationary, and to rise at a rate of several centimeters per year. The plumes are

FIGURE 12.26 **Island formation at a hot spot.** *(A) As the overlying plate moves over a stationary hot spot, it creates a chain of volcanoes. Old volcanoes that have moved off the hot spot become extinct and are eroded and diminished in size. Eventually, the inactive volcanoes are moved into deeper water, where they become flat-topped seamounts. (B) The Hawaiian Islands were formed by a stationary hot spot. As the Pacific plate moves over the hot spot, new islands are formed and old islands are moved into deeper water. The maximum ages of the islands are given in millions of years (Ma). A new island, named Lo'ihi, is forming and will rise above the sea in about 10,000 years.*

Animation
Hawai'i formation
http://qrs.ly/a83w0pv

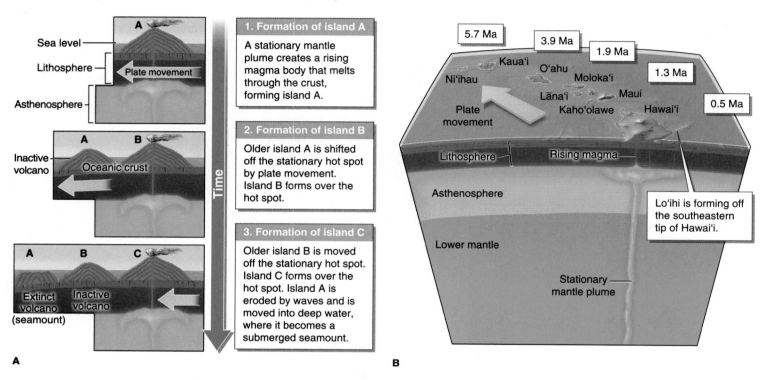

not liquid, but rather slowly deforming rock. As a hot spot approaches the lower lithosphere, a decrease in pressure lowers the rock's melting point and allows it to melt into magma. The buoyant magma melts its way through the overlying crust, where it forms a volcano. As a lithospheric plate moves over a hot spot, a line of volcanoes may be formed **(Figure 12.26)**.

If you look carefully at a bathymetric map of the world's ocean basins, you will find many linear ridges that look as if a giant knife had made long incisions in the crust. Volcanic islands and submerged seamounts are often associated with these linear ridges. Hot spots melt through the crust as the plates move over them, creating these lines of inactive volcanoes, called *hot spot tracks* **(Figure 12.27)**.

An active continental hot spot persists beneath the North American plate at the location of Yellowstone National Park. This hot spot has produced a number of volcanic eruptions, including one of Earth's largest known eruptions 640,000 years ago (see Section 14.2). It also produced a string of volcanic landforms called *calderas* (collapsed volcanoes) **(Figure 12.28)**. Some scientists

fold
A wrinkle in the crust resulting from deformation caused by geologic stress.

fault
A fracture in the crust where movement and earthquakes occur.

think that the magma body that resides just below Yellowstone National Park today could erupt again.

Bending and Breaking: Folding and Faulting

When hit with a hammer, rocks break into smaller fragments because they are brittle. When they are slowly compressed and heated, however, rocks in many cases are able to deform and fold (bend) before they fault (break). A **fold** is a wrinkle in the crust resulting from deformation caused by geologic stress, and a **fault** is a fracture in the crust where movement and earthquakes occur.

Folding and faulting can occur anywhere on Earth's surface. Generally, folding occurs most often where two plates are converging, particularly in regions of subduction and collision. Faulting, too, occurs most often near plate boundaries, but many regions far away from plate boundaries are also faulted. Folding and faulting are particularly important elements of lithospheric plate movement because each can produce prominent surface landforms.

FIGURE 12.27 **Hot spot tracks.** *Hot spot tracks are found throughout the world's ocean basins. Most of their volcanic mountains are no longer active and are submerged beneath the surface of the oceans. On this map hot spot tracks are shown in red. Red dots show the location of volcanoes that sit atop hot spots.*

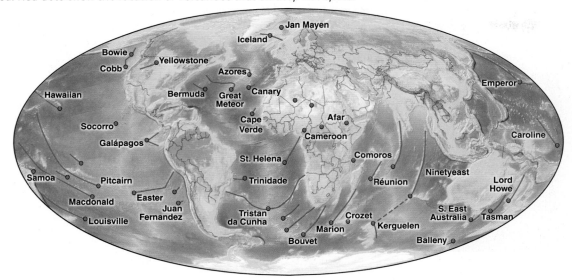

FIGURE 12.28 **Yellowstone hot spot.** *(A) Some 16 million years ago, the oldest of the extinct volcanoes on the Yellowstone hot spot track, McDermitt Caldera, was located over the hot spot. The southwestern direction of plate movement has transported McDermitt Caldera, and the other now-extinct volcanoes produced by the Yellowstone hot spot, to the southwest. The ages of the calderas are given in millions of years (Ma). Yellowstone's hot springs and geysers, such as the Grand Prismatic Spring (B) and Old Faithful (C), are the active result of the active magma body that resides beneath the park.* (B. © Justin Reznick/E+/Getty Images; C. U.S. Geological Survey)

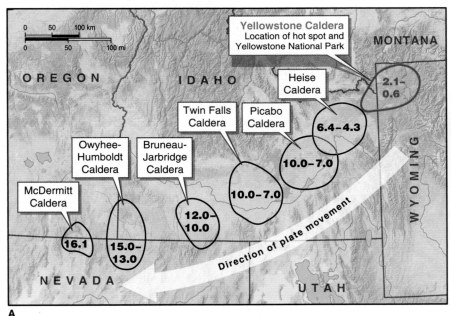

A

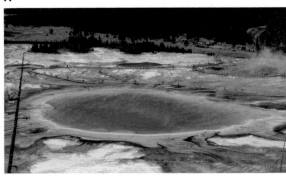

B

C

FIGURE 12.29 **Folding.** *(A) These folded volcanic rocks are located in Hamersley Gorge, Karijini National Park, Australia. The distance across this photo is only a few tens of meters. (B) A satellite image of kilometers-long folds in sedimentary rocks in the Béchar Basin, northwestern Algeria. These rocks were folded in a continental collision between the African and Eurasian plates beginning about 65 million years ago. The ground distance of this satellite image is approximately 100 km (60 mi) across.* (A. © Ignacio Palacios/Lonely Planet Images/Getty Images; B. Image courtesy of the Image Science & Analysis Laboratory, NASA Johnson Space Center)

A   B

FIGURE 12.30 **Anticlinal ridges and synclinal valleys.** *(A) Like a rug left rumpled on the floor when its two ends have been pushed toward each other, Earth's crust deforms into synclinal and anticlinal folds when it is compressed. (B) An anticlinal ridge and a synclinal valley are visible in this satellite image of the Zagros Mountains of western Iran. These folds are a result of collision between the Arabian and Eurasian plates.* (B. EROS Center, U.S. Geological Survey)

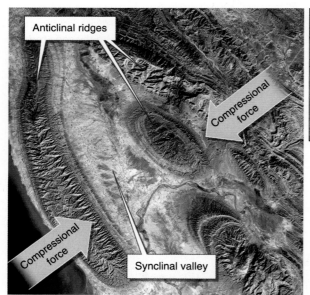

A

B

Folded Landforms

Many mountain ranges are the result of folding, which can occur anywhere compressional forces are pushing the crust together. Folds may also occur at just about any spatial scale, from centimeters to kilometers, and in nearly any rock type, as shown in **Figure 12.29**.

The two major types of folds are anticlines and synclines. An **anticline** is a fold in the crust with an archlike ridge, and a **syncline** is a fold in the crust with a U-shaped dip. Generally, when synclines and anticlines occur across a wide region, ridges form on the anticlines and valleys form on the synclines **(Figure 12.30)**.

When a folded surface is eroded by streams, softer rock is often removed more quickly than harder rock, leaving the more resistant rock to form a ridge. This process can result in an *inverted topography*, with synclinal ridges and anticlinal valleys **(Figure 12.31)**.

Block Landforms

Faulting results when rocks can deform no further by folding, and they break. When this happens, the energy stored in the rocks is released and travels through the crust as seismic waves that shake the ground in an earthquake. (Faulting and earthquakes are covered in greater detail in Section 14.3.)

FIGURE 12.31 **GEO-GRAPHIC: Inverted topography.** *(A) Erosion of anticlinal ridges can result in anticlinal valleys. Similarly, layers of sedimentary rock that are resistant to erosion may form synclinal ridges. (B) This roadcut exposes a synclinal ridge near Hancock, Maryland. (B. © Mark Burnett/Photo Researchers/Getty Images)*

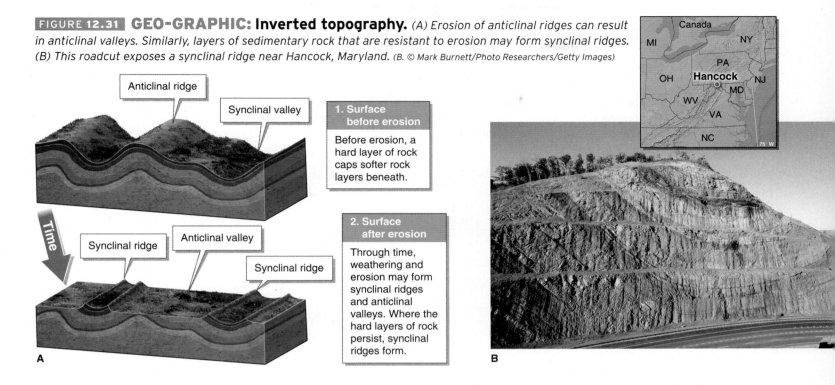

1. Surface before erosion

Before erosion, a hard layer of rock caps softer rock layers beneath.

2. Surface after erosion

Through time, weathering and erosion may form synclinal ridges and anticlinal valleys. Where the hard layers of rock persist, synclinal ridges form.

Anticlinal ridge

Synclinal valley

Time

Synclinal ridge

Anticlinal valley

Synclinal ridge

A

B

Through time, continued faulting can create blocks of crust that move vertically relative to each other. These blocks are called *fault blocks*. Like folds, fault blocks occur across many spatial scales and in a variety of tectonic settings. There are many fault-block mountain ranges in the world, some of which have dramatic relief **(Figure 12.32)**.

Orogenesis: Tectonic Settings of Mountains

The building of mountain ranges by any tectonic process is called **orogenesis** (from the Greek *oros*, "mountain," and *genesis*, "origin"). Most mountains are grouped together to form linear ranges. These ranges, called **orogenic belts**, form most commonly

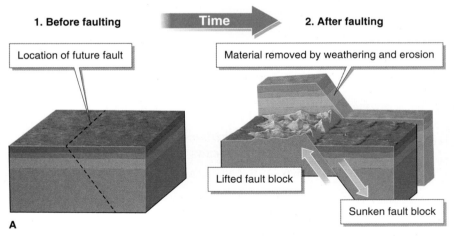

1. Before faulting   **Time**   **2. After faulting**

Location of future fault

Material removed by weathering and erosion

Lifted fault block

Sunken fault block

A

FIGURE 12.32 **The Teton Range, Wyoming.** *(A) This diagram illustrates the fault block system that formed the Teton Range. The range formed when a 65 km (40 mi) long fault block was lowered, beginning about 13 million years ago. Erosion by streams and glaciers subsequently cut into the higher block, removing most of the overlying rocks and creating the jagged mountain topography seen today. (B) Grand Teton, standing at 4,197 m (13,770 ft) and visible here, is the highest peak in the Teton Range. (B. © John Wang/Photodisc/Getty Images)*

Grand Teton →

Lifted fault block

Sunken fault block

B

anticline
A fold in the crust with an archlike ridge.

syncline
A fold in the crust with a U-shaped dip.

orogenesis
Mountain building.

orogenic belt
A linear mountain range.

along plate boundaries, particularly in areas of collision and subduction. Away from plate boundaries, isolated mountains and orogenic belts form in areas of rifting, hot spot tracks, and folding and faulting. **Figure 12.33** summarizes the tectonic settings and processes covered in this chapter and their roles in orogenesis.

How do mountains form?

FIGURE 12.33 **Mountain ranges.** *(A) This table summarizes the tectonic settings of mountain ranges and specifies whether the setting produces volcanically active mountains. (B) Earth's 10 longest terrestrial mountain ranges are labeled here. Red and orange areas show the highest surface elevations. The accompanying table orders the ranges by their length and indicates their tectonic setting.*

TECTONIC SETTING	VOLCANICALLY ACTIVE MOUNTAINS?
Divergent plate boundaries Seafloor spreading Rifting	Yes Yes
Convergent plate boundaries Subduction Collision Accretion of terranes	Yes No Sometimes (if subduction is still occurring)
Hot spots	Yes
Folding and faulting (these processes also occur on plate boundaries)	Sometimes (depending on the tectonic setting)

A

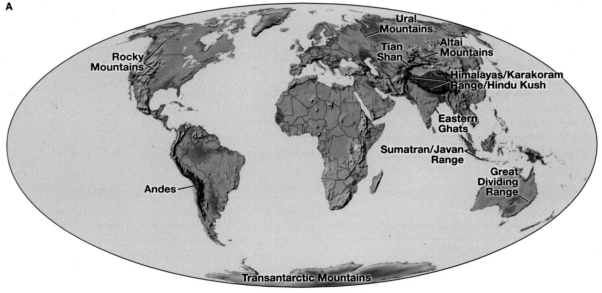

RANGE	LOCATION	LENGTH (KM)	LENGTH (MI)	TECTONIC PROCESS
Andes	South America	7,300	4,526	Subduction
Rocky Mountains	North America	6,000	3,720	Faulting
Himalayas/Karakoram Range/ Hindu Kush	Asia	4,000	2,480	Collision
Great Dividing Range	Australia	3,600	2,232	Collision
Transantarctic Mountains	Antarctica	3,500	2,170	Faulting
Sumatran/Javan Range	Sumatra, Java	2,900	1,798	Subduction
Tian Shan	China	2,300	1,426	Collision
Eastern Ghats	India	2,100	1,302	Collision
Altai Mountains	Asia	2,000	1,240	Collision
Ural Mountains	Russia	2,000	1,240	Collision

B

GEOGRAPHIC PERSPECTIVES
12.5 The Tibetan Plateau, Climate, and People

◎ **Assess the relationship between food security in South Asia and the changing climate of the Tibetan Plateau.**

The Tibetan Plateau and the Himalayas (Sanskrit for "abode of the snow") are often referred to as the roof the world. This region is a dramatic example of the effects of continental collision. The area has many geophysical superlatives:

- The average elevation of the plateau is about 4,500 m (14,800 ft), the highest on Earth.

- No other mountain range is rising as quickly as the Himalayas. The western portions are rising up to 10 mm (0.39 in) per year. (This is the net rate of uplift, after erosion.)

- The region contains the largest volume of ice outside the polar regions.

- The plateau and surrounding mountains cover some 2.9 million km^2 (1.1 million mi^2), or almost half the area of the continental United States.

- About 20% of the world's population (1.4 billion people) receive freshwater from the region. It is the source of seven of Earth's largest rivers.

Tectonically Driven Climate Change

Beginning about 55 million years ago, in the early Cenozoic era, a long global cooling trend began (see Section 6.2). This cooling trend coincided with the beginning of the collision between the Indian landmass and the Eurasian plate and the resulting uplift of the Tibetan Plateau and surrounding mountains..

The prevailing theory is that the uplift of the Tibetan Plateau was mainly responsible for the Cenozoic cooling trend. This uplift may have caused global cooling in three main ways:

1. *Blocking airflow:* The plateau and its mountains changed atmospheric circulation in the Northern Hemisphere. The uplifted region was so high that it diverted the westerlies and cold polar air masses farther south than they would otherwise go, as **Figure 12.34** shows.

2. *Changing atmospheric chemistry:* As the Tibetan Plateau rose, weathering and erosion of the uplifting mountain ranges transferred carbon from the atmosphere to long-term storage in seafloor sediments (see Section 6.3). Carbon dioxide levels dropped from about 1,000 ppm (parts per million) to the recent preindustrial levels of 300 ppm and lower. This reduction of atmospheric CO_2 is thought to have been the main factor behind the long, slow Cenozoic cooling trend.

3. *Reflecting sunlight:* As the plateau was lifted to higher and colder elevations, its vegetation cover was reduced to alpine tundra (see Section 8.4) or bare ground, exposing lighter-colored rocks. In addition,

FIGURE 12.34 **The Tibetan Plateau.**
The Tibetan Plateau and the surrounding mountain ranges—the Tian Shan, Pamirs, Karakoram Range, and Himalayas—influence airflow across South Asia. Cold polar air (blue arrows) is channeled south around these high ranges and the plateau.

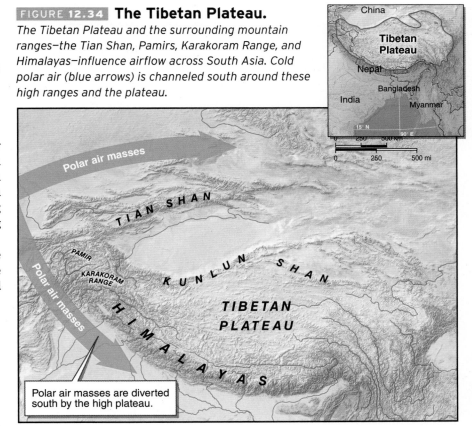

Polar air masses are diverted south by the high plateau.

it became covered in snow for much of the year, and permanent glaciers developed in the Himalayas. Bare rock, snow, and ice have high albedos. They reflect sunlight energy back out to space, rather than allowing it to warm the ground surface. Because the uplifted region was so geographically extensive, it reflected significant amounts of solar energy, resulting in cooling of the global atmosphere.

Anthropogenic Climate Change

As long as the plateau is being weathered, it will continue to pull carbon dioxide out of the atmosphere (see Section 6.3). But this transfer of carbon is a very slow process.

Over the last 150 years, people have been burning fossil fuels and releasing CO_2 to the atmosphere much faster than natural processes such as weathering (and the ocean waters and plants) can remove it from the atmosphere. Thus, fossil fuel combustion has resulted in a net increase of CO_2 in the atmosphere. Today, CO_2 concentrations are about 400 ppm and rising (see Section 6.4).

FIGURE 12.35 **Asian rivers.** *Eight major rivers originate on the Tibetan Plateau.*

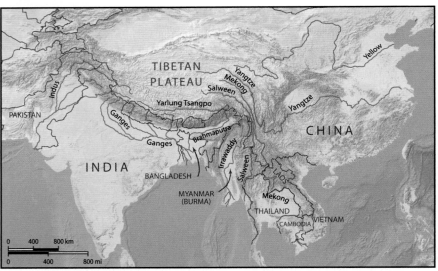

As atmospheric CO_2 concentrations increase, the atmosphere gets warmer. As the atmosphere gets warmer, mountain glaciers retreat upslope, where it is cooler. A 2012 study published in *Nature* examined over 7,000 glaciers in the Tibetan Plateau region. The researchers concluded that the glaciers of the Himalayas lost about 12 billion tons of ice per year between 2003 and 2008. Now, rather than the plateau driving climate change, climate change is changing the plateau and the surrounding mountain ranges. **Anthropogenic climate change is reversing the 55-million-year cooling trend brought on by the geologic uplift of the plateau.**

Glaciers and Food Security

There is a direct relationship between the glaciers of the Tibetan Plateau region and the food security of the human population. **About 1.4 billion people, approximately one-fifth of humanity, use water from these glaciers in some capacity as it melts and runs off into the region's rivers.**

Asia's large rivers are fed by summer monsoon rainfall (see Section 4.4) and by seasonal melting of snow and glaciers in the mountains. The eight major rivers that originate on the Tibetan Plateau are the Indus, Ganges, Brahmaputra/Yarlung Tsangpo, Irrawady, Salween, Mekong, Yangtze, and Yellow **(Figure 12.35)**. The Yangtze River is the longest river in Asia, at 6,300 km (3,915 mi), and the third longest river in the world. It flows through heavily populated areas of China, where it supports several hundred million people.

These rivers provide water for all aspects of human life, including household needs, fishing, navigation, hydroelectric power generation, and agriculture. The rivers are also tied to the global economy. For example, the water from these rivers supports about 75% of the world's rice exports.

Many scientists see South Asia as particularly vulnerable to climate change in the coming decades, given the connection between glaciers, rivers, and people in the region. In the short term, further loss of the Tibetan Plateau's glaciers could increase water supplies for South Asia as the ice melts. The long-term outlook, however, would change if the glaciers melted away and the volume of water flowing through the region's major rivers decreased.

CHAPTER 12 Exploring with ☺ Google Earth

To complete these problems, first read the chapter. When you are finished, go to LaunchPad and open the Exploring with Google Earth file for this chapter. Click on the "Workbook Problems" folder to "fly" to each of the problems listed below and answer the questions. Be sure to keep your "Borders and Labels" layer activated. Refer to Appendix 4 if you need help using Google Earth.

PROBLEM 12.1 This placemark falls in the Democratic Republic of the Congo. Note the string of long lakes north and south of the placemark.

1. Given this location, and given what you have read in this chapter, what tectonic setting formed these lakes?
   a. A continental volcanic arc
   b. A rift valley
   c. A collision zone
   d. A subduction zone

PROBLEM 12.2 Activate the Plate Boundaries overlay in this figure. This placemark highlights North America.

1. What kind of continental margin is the West Coast of North America?
   a. Passive continental margin
   b. Active continental margin
   c. It cannot be determined from the available information.

2. What kind of continental margin is the East Coast?
   a. Passive continental margin
   b. Active continental margin
   c. It cannot be determined from the available information.

PROBLEM 12.3 Keep the Plate Boundaries overlay activated to answer these questions.

1. What is the name of this island group?
   a. The Galápagos
   b. The Azores
   c. The Canary Islands
   d. Madeira

2. What type of plate boundary runs through the placemarked island?
   a. A divergent plate boundary
   b. A convergent plate boundary
   c. A transform plate boundary

3. Given this plate boundary type, would you expect this island to be volcanically active?
   a. Yes
   b. No

4. Normally, this type of plate boundary occurs where?
   a. On the margin of a continent
   b. On a continent
   c. In an ocean basin
   d. In a rift valley

PROBLEM 12.4 This placemark falls in the far east of Eurasia. Keep the Plate Boundaries overlay activated to answer these questions.

1. What is the name of region where the placemark is located? (Google Earth labels it to the north of the placemark.)
   a. Kamchatka Peninsula
   b. Korean Peninsula
   c. Sakhalinskaya Island
   d. The Hamgyong Mountains

2. What country is this?
   a. Russia
   b. North Korea
   c. China
   d. Japan

3. What type of plate boundary is found here?
   a. A convergent plate boundary
   b. A divergent plate boundary
   c. A transform plate boundary

4. What specific type of plate interaction is occurring here?
   a. Subduction
   b. Rifting
   c. Collision
   d. Hot spot

5. Given this plate boundary type, would you expect this peninsula to be volcanically active?
   a. Yes
   b. No

PROBLEM 12.5 Keep the Plate Boundaries overlay activated to answer these questions. You will also need to activate the Large Earthquake History overlay in this folder if it is not already activated. This placemark lands on the Pacific plate.

1. Based on your examination of the seafloor bathymetry and the plate boundary color from the Plate Boundaries overlay, what kind of plate boundary is this?
   a. A divergent plate boundary
   b. A convergent plate boundary
   c. A transform plate boundary

2. Which of the following statements best describes the pattern of earthquake depth westward from the placemark?
   a. Earthquakes are uniformly shallow.
   b. Earthquakes are uniformly deep.
   c. Earthquakes trend shallower farther west from the placemark.
   d. Earthquakes trend deeper farther west from the placemark.

3. What is the name for this earthquake pattern?
   a. A hot spot track
   b. A Wadati-Benioff zone
   c. A rift valley
   d. A collision

4. Given this plate boundary type, would you expect this area to be volcanically active?
   a. Yes
   b. No

PROBLEM 12.6 Keep the Plate Boundaries overlay activated to answer these questions. You will also need to activate the Volcanic Chains overlay in this folder if it is not already activated. This placemark lands on the Pacific Plate.

1. Note that the yellow pins show submerged features of increasing ages. Collectively, what is this submerged landform called?
   a. Hot spot track
   b. Orogenic belt
   c. Volcanic island arc
   d. Accreted terrane

2. What is the age of the oldest of these submarine landforms?
a. 10 million years
b. 30 million years
c. 50 million years
d. 80 million years

3. Measure the distance from the placemarked island to the farthest dated submarine landform to the east. What is the approximate distance?
a. 1,000 km
b. 1,600 km
c. 2,000 km
d. 2,600 km

4. What is the approximate average rate of plate movement per year for this area? (Divide the distance from question 3 by the oldest age of the seafloor near the coast. Multiply the result by 100,000 to get centimeters per year.)
a. 3.3 cm per year
b. 4.5 cm per year
c. 5 cm per year
d. 8.7 cm per year

5. Is this calculated rate of plate movement absolute velocity or relative velocity?
a. Absolute velocity
b. Relative velocity

PROBLEM 12.7 Keep the Volcanic Chains overlay from the previous problem active for this problem. This placemark falls on Midway, part of the Hawaiian Islands chain. Be sure to activate the two markers in the folder for this problem. (Note that the ages of the islands and seamounts are given in millions of years and that the error range of the radiometric dates is indicated by the ± symbol.)

1. What is the age of Midway?
a. 19.9 million years
b. 31 million years
c. 47.9 million years
d. 57.2 million years

2. Do the seamounts get older or younger as they trend to the west and north from Midway?
a. Older
b. Younger

3. Zoom out until you can see marker 2 to the northwest of the placemark. What is the maximum age of the seamounts at marker 2?
a. 15 million years
b. 81 million years
c. 160 million years
d. 241 million years

4. Note that the seamounts hook north at marker 1. Which of the following best explains the cause of this pattern?
a. A shift in plate movement direction
b. The formation of a mid-ocean ridge
c. The development of a fault block
d. An accreted terrane

5. Measure the distance between the island of Hawai'i and the location at marker 2. (Use the Path function in the measuring tool so you can measure the crook in the island chain.) What is the approximate average annual rate of plate movement for this portion of the Pacific plate? (Divide the distance traveled by the oldest age of the seafloor near the coast. Multiply this result by 100,000 to get centimeters per year.)
a. 1 cm per year
b. 4 cm per year
c. 7 cm per year
d. 11 cm per year

CHAPTER 12 **Study Guide**

Focus Points

12.1 Continental Drift: Wegener's Theory

Breakup of Pangaea: The supercontinent Pangaea split into Laurasia and Gondwana about 200 million years ago. The opening of the Atlantic Ocean led to the modern configuration of the contents.

Continental drift: Alfred Wegener was the first to formally propose the theory of continental drift, which states that continents move.

12.2 Plate Tectonics: An Ocean of Evidence

Plate tectonics theory: Plate tectonics theory addresses why and how lithospheric plates move.

Oceanographic evidence: Many forms of evidence from the ocean basins, including seafloor bathymetry, rock sample ages, and patterns of magnetization, led to the development and acceptance of the theory of plate tectonics.

Moving plates: Plate tectonics theory states that there are 14 major lithospheric plates that move independently of one another across the surface of the planet.

Plate boundaries: Earthquake activity reveals plate boundary locations.

How plates move: Ridge push, mantle drag, and slab pull move the lithospheric plates.

Plate velocity: The fastest relative plate movement is 18 cm (7 in) per year.

Unifying theory: Plate tectonics is a unifying theory that helps to explain many seemingly separate physical phenomena.

12.3 Plate Boundary Landforms

Plate boundaries: There are three types of plate boundaries: divergent plate boundaries, convergent plate boundaries, and transform plate boundaries.

Plate boundary landforms: Landforms created by plate movements include deep-sea trenches, volcanic island arcs, continental volcanic arcs, and nonvolcanic mountain ranges.

Rifting: Continental rifting splits a single continental landmass, creating a volcanic rift valley. Rifting can lead to new plate margins and a new ocean basin.

Plate recycling: Subduction recycles oceanic lithosphere into the mantle.

Buoyant continental crust: Continental lithosphere does not subduct. Because of this, Earth's oldest crust is continental crust.

Accreted terranes: Much of western North America is the result of the accumulation of accreted terranes.

12.4 Hot Spots, Folding and Faulting, and Mountain Building

Hot spots: Hot spots are created where stationary mantle plumes melt through the crust.

Folding and faulting: Earth's crust can be folded and faulted in response to tectonic stresses. Folding produces anticlines and synclines, and faulting produces earthquakes.

Orogenesis: Many mountain ranges form in orogenic belts along plate boundaries.

12.5 Geographic Perspectives: The Tibetan Plateau, Climate, and People

The Tibetan Plateau and people: About 20% of the human population relies on rivers that originate from glaciers and snowmelt on the Tibetan Plateau. Climate change threatens the food and water security of these populations.

Key Terms

accreted terrane, 398
active continental margin, 402
anticline, 407
collision, 398
continental drift, 387
continental volcanic arc, 397
convergent plate boundary, 394
divergent plate boundary, 394
fault, 404
fold, 404
Gondwana, 387
hot spot, 402
Laurasia, 387
mantle drag, 392
mantle plume, 403
orogenesis, 407

orogenic belt, 407
Pacific Ring of Fire, 398
Pangaea, 387
Panthalassic Ocean, 387
passive continental margin, 402
plate boundary, 391
plate tectonics, 388
ridge push, 392
rift, 394
rift valley, 394
slab pull, 392
subduction, 391
syncline, 407
transform plate boundary, 394
volcanic island arc, 397
Wadati-Benioff zone, 397

Concept Review

The Human Sphere: Life on Earth's Shifting Crust

1. How are plate movements harmful to people? How are they beneficial?

12.1 Continental Drift: Wegener's Theory

2. What was Pangaea and when did it exist?

3. Which of today's continents made up Laurasia and Gondwana?

4. What theory did Alfred Wegener develop? In what year? On what evidence did he base his theory?

5. Was Wegener's theory accepted by his colleagues during his lifetime? Why or why not?

12.2 Plate Tectonics: An Ocean of Evidence

6. What is plate tectonics theory? How is it the same as, and how is it different from, continental drift theory?

7. What geophysical evidence was used to develop plate tectonics theory?

8. What is a lithospheric plate, and how many are there?

9. How are the plate boundaries determined?

10. Why do the plates move?

11. Using relative velocity, how fast do the plates move?

12. What does it mean to say that plate tectonics is a unifying theory?

12.3 Plate Boundary Landforms

13. Describe the movements of lithospheric plates at divergent, convergent, and transform plate boundaries.

14. What is a mid-ocean ridge? Where do they form? How do they form?

15. What is rifting? Where does it occur? What happens to a continent when rifting occurs on it?

16. How does rifting relate to the formation of new oceanic crust and new ocean basins?

17. How does rifting create a new plate boundary?

18. What is subduction? At what type of plate boundary does it occur?

19. Describe the relative ages of oceanic crust and continental crust and explain why they are different.

20. What is a Wadati-Benioff zone, and how does it provide supporting evidence for subduction?

21. What is the Pacific Ring of Fire? What kinds of mountains form along the Pacific Ring of Fire?

22. What is collision? What kind of mountains results from collision? Give a real-world example.

23. What are accreted terranes? Where do they come from, and why do they pile up against continental margins? Why do they not subduct?

24. What is a transform plate boundary? What kind of landforms do transform plate boundaries produce?

25. Compare an active to a passive continental margin.

12.4 Hot Spots, Folding and Faulting, and Mountain Building

26. What is a hot spot? What physical features on Earth are produced by hot spots?

27. What is a hot spot track? Explain how they are formed.

28. How are rocks folded? What is the difference between folding and faulting?

29. Compare anticlines with synclines. What is an inverted topography and how does it form?

30. What is a fault block? What do fault blocks create?

31. What is orogenesis? Review the major mountain ranges of the world and the tectonic formation of each.

12.5 Geographic Perspectives: The Tibetan Plateau, Climate, and People

32. When and how did the Tibetan Plateau and its mountains form?

33. What does it mean that the Tibetan Plateau is a climate driver? In what three ways does the plateau modify climate?

34. What is happening currently to the plateau's glaciers? Why?

35. What are the connections among geologic uplift, glaciers, rivers, and feeding people?

Critical-Thinking Questions

1. What is the nearest plate boundary to where you live? What kind is it? Use figures 12.7 and 12.11 for help.

2. What do rift valley lakes, volcanoes, and earthquakes have in common?

3. The rate of crust formation at mid-ocean ridges must be exactly equal to the rate of crust recycling at subduction zones. Is this statement true or false? Explain.

4. Are there mountains near where you live? If so, how were they formed? If you do not know, what kind of questions would you ask to determine how they were formed? Use Figure 12.33 for help.

5. Most hot spot tracks are straight, but some curve sharply. How would you explain a curved hot spot track?

Test Yourself

Take this quiz to test your chapter knowledge.

1. **True or false?** Gondwana consisted of South America, North America, and Eurasia.

2. **True or false?** Continental crust does not subduct.

3. **True or false?** The Pacific Ring of Fire is a result of rifting.

4. **True or false?** The Andes were formed by diverging plates.

5. **True or false?** Earth's oldest crust is found on the ocean floor.

6. **Multiple choice:** Which of the following was formed by a hot spot?
   a. The Himalayas
   b. The Yellowstone Caldera
   c. The East African Rift system
   d. The Teton Range

7. **Multiple choice:** Which of the following is not related to the Tibetan Plateau and climate change?
   a. Changing volcanic activity
   b. Changing atmospheric CO_2 concentrations
   c. Changing flow patterns of the westerlies
   d. Changing midlatitude albedo

8. **Multiple choice:** Which of the following cannot occur when two plates converge?
   a. Earthquakes
   b. Volcanoes
   c. Rift valleys
   d. Mountains

9. **Fill in the blank:** A _____ forms when oceanic crust subducts beneath other oceanic crust.

10. **Fill in the blank:** _____ is thought to be responsible for most of the movement of subducting oceanic crust.

Further Reading

1. Hughes, Patrick. "Alfred Wegener (1880-1930): On the Shoulders of Giants." Earth Observatory, NASA, February 8, 2001. http://earthobservatory.nasa.gov/Features/Wegener/wegener.php.

2. Kääb, Andreas, Etienne Berthier, Christopher Nuth, Julie Gardelle, and Yves Arnaud. "Contrasting Patterns of Early Twenty-First-Century Glacier Mass Change in the Himalayas." *Nature* 488 (2012): 495-498.

3. Redfern, Ron. *Origins: The Evolution of Continents, Oceans and Life.* Norman: University of Oklahoma Press, 2001.

Answers to Living Physical Geography Questions

1. **Why do the coastlines of Africa and South America fit together?** Africa and South America fit together because they were part of a single continent, Gondwana, about 65 million years ago, before the Atlantic Ocean basin opened.

2. **How can whole continents move?** Convection in the hot material of Earth's mantle sets the plates in motion.

3. **Is it true that Los Angeles will someday be connected to San Francisco?** These two cities, which lie on opposite sides of a transform plate boundary, will be brought together by plate movement millions of years in the future.

4. **How do mountains form?** All of Earth's mountain ranges were formed by different types of plate movement, although some do not lie at plate boundaries.

Picture This. YOUR TURN

Tectonic Landforms and Features

Fill in the blanks on the diagram, using each of the following terms only once.

1. Active continental margin
2. Collision
3. Continental crust
4. Deep-sea trench
5. Mid-ocean ridge
6. Nonvolcanic mountains
7. Oceanic crust
8. Transform plate boundary
9. Rifting
10. Subducting oceanic lithosphere
11. Volcanic island arc

13 Building the Crust with Rocks

Chapter Outline

This sandstone formation is part of the Bungle Bungle Range in Purnululu National Park, Western Australia. The sandstone was formed from sediments deposited in layers by streams in a valley about 375 million years ago. Through time, the sediments were turned to rock, then erosion slowly exposed and rounded the rock into these domes.

(© Manfred Gottschalk/Lonely Planet Images/Getty Images)

Map labels: TIMOR SEA; 15° S; Purnululu National Park; AUSTRALIA; 30°; GREAT AUSTRALIAN BIGHT; 120° E; 135° E; 150° E

LIVING PHYSICAL GEOGRAPHY

> Why is ice classified as a mineral?

> How are rocks formed?

> What is coal?

> What is fracking and why is it controversial?

To learn more about how sedimentary rocks form, turn to Section 13.3.

THE BIG PICTURE *Plate tectonics drives the rock cycle that creates and transforms rocks. Natural gas deposits within layers of sedimentary rock are a controversial energy source.*

LEARNING GOALS *After reading this chapter, you will be able to:*

13.1 ◎ List the main mineral groups that make up rocks and discuss how rocks are formed, transformed, and recycled.

13.2 ◎ Describe the different types of igneous rocks and where they form.

13.3 ◎ Explain the three types of sedimentary rocks, where they form, and how they provide information about Earth's history.

13.4 ◎ Explain where metamorphic rocks form and how they are categorized.

13.5 ◎ Assess the pros and cons of extracting natural gas trapped in shale through hydraulic fracturing.

THE HUMAN SPHERE: **People and Rocks**

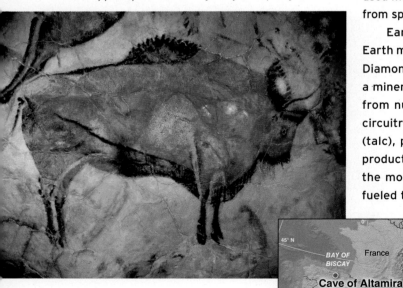

FIGURE 13.1 **Cave of Altamira.** *This painting of a now-extinct species of bison was found in the Cave of Altamira, located near Santander, Spain. Some of the images in this cave were made about 35,600 years ago and are among the earliest known cave paintings in Europe. Stone tools were used to grind various Earth materials, including iron oxides and ochre from rocks, to make the paints. These bison were hunted using stone-tipped spears. (© Heritage Images/Getty Images)*

OUR SUCCESS AS A SPECIES IS DIRECTLY LINKED TO EARTH'S ROCKS. About 2.6 million years ago in eastern Africa, our early hominid ancestors began chipping and grinding rocks into tools. Those tools were not used for hunting. Instead, they were used for cutting and scraping meat from animal carcasses and breaking the bones for their marrow.

Through time, as humans evolved, so did their use of rocks and an increasingly wide range of Earth materials. In more recent prehistoric times, Paleolithic humans used materials derived from Earth's crust in a wide range of applications, ranging from spear tips to pigments for cave murals like those in **Figure 13.1**.

Earth materials continue to be prominent in the lives of humans today. Earth materials such as copper and gold are used in electronics manufacturing. Diamonds and rubies are carefully cut and polished to make jewelry. Uranium, a mineral found in many rocks in Earth's crust, is used in applications ranging from nuclear energy to atomic weaponry. Pencil lead (graphite), electronic circuitry (silicon and quartz), wallboard and concrete (gypsum), baby powder (talc), plant fertilizer (sulfur), soap (borax), and toothpaste (calcite) are all products of minerals and rocks derived from the crust. Coal has been among the most economically important rocks for the last century and a half. Coal fueled the Industrial Revolution and continues to power a large portion of the modern global economy. Humans could not have followed the path of increasing technological advancement without rocks, and our modern economy would not exist without fossil fuels, such as coal, from the ground.

This chapter explores how rocks are formed, the major rock types in Earth's crust, and the tectonic context of rock formation. We also examine a growing controversy around a procedure that extracts natural gas from the ground.

13.1 Minerals and Rocks: Building Earth's Crust

◎ List the main mineral groups that make up rocks and discuss how rocks are formed, transformed, and recycled.

> **Why is ice classified as a mineral?***

Mineralogists—scientists who study minerals—have identified more than 4,600 types of minerals and discover dozens of new ones each year. But what exactly is a mineral? **Minerals** are naturally occurring, crystalline, solid chemical elements or compounds with a uniform chemical composition. Minerals are abiogenic (not made by organisms). Thus, naturally forming ice is a mineral.

Most types of minerals are very rare and form only where conditions are exactly right. Precious gemstones and metals, including diamond, gold, silver, ruby, opal, sapphire, and jasper, are minerals. But common table salt is also a mineral. Table sugar

FIGURE 13.3 **Elements of the crust.**
This pie chart shows the relative percentages of the main elements that make up Earth's crust.

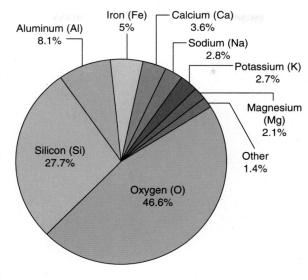

- Aluminum (Al) 8.1%
- Iron (Fe) 5%
- Calcium (Ca) 3.6%
- Sodium (Na) 2.8%
- Potassium (K) 2.7%
- Magnesium (Mg) 2.1%
- Other 1.4%
- Silicon (Si) 27.7%
- Oxygen (O) 46.6%

FIGURE 13.2 **Crystalline and noncrystalline materials.** *(A) Quartz is a mineral whose crystals have an orderly arrangement of atoms. The naturally formed flat edges (or faces) of quartz crystals reflect this atomic orderliness. (B) Obsidian is not a mineral, but is instead a type of volcanic rock that is referred to as* glassy *because of its lack of crystals. In noncrystalline rocks such as obsidian, the atoms are arranged randomly.*
(A. © De Agostini Picture Library/Getty Images; B. Bruce Gervais)

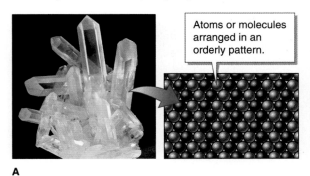

Atoms or molecules arranged in an orderly pattern.

A

Atoms or molecules arranged randomly.

B

is crystalline, but it is an organic compound made by living plants, and it is therefore not a mineral. Petroleum is not a mineral because it is liquid.

All minerals form through the process of **crystallization**, which occurs when atoms or molecules come together in an orderly patterned structure called a *crystal*. Although crystallization occurs on Earth's surface, as it does where salt forms, the process of crystallization is most common in subterranean cavities where water circulates and *precipitates* (deposits) minerals.

Mineral crystals have angular and flat surfaces. As **Figure 13.2** shows, the surfaces of crystals can reflect the arrangement of interlocking atoms and molecules that make up the mineral.

Mineral Classes in Rocks

Although there are thousands of minerals, just a few dozen of them make up most rocks in Earth's crust. Seventy-four percent of the crust is made up of just two elements: oxygen and silicon **(Figure 13.3)**.

There are four main rock-forming groups of minerals: silicates, oxides, sulfides and sulfates, and carbonates. Most rocks in Earth's crust are composed of minerals in these four mineral classes.

Silicates: Silicon (Si) and oxygen (O) combine with each other and with other elements to form *silicate minerals*. Ninety-five percent of the continental crust is formed from silicate minerals. Rocks formed from silicates are structurally strong and relatively resistant to weathering

mineral
A naturally occurring, crystalline, solid chemical element or compound with a uniform chemical composition.

crystallization
A process in which atoms or molecules come together in an orderly patterned structure.

*Answers to the Living Physical Geography questions are found on page 441.

FIGURE 13.4 **Gypsum crystals.** *These gypsum crystals in Mexico's Cueva de los Cristales ("Cave of Crystals") are some of the world's largest crystals. (Note the people in the photo for scale.) This cave was inundated with groundwater until a mining company pumped the water out, revealing the large crystals within. Because these crystals formed through precipitation in water, they will not grow as long as the cave is kept dry. (© Carsten Peter/Speleoresearch & Films/National Geographic/Getty Images)*

The *feldspars*, another class of silicate minerals, are the most common class of minerals in Earth's crust. Oceanic crust is the most extensive type of crust and it is composed largely of feldspars.

Oxides: Oxides are formed when other chemical elements combine with oxygen. Iron combined with oxygen, for example, forms the mineral *hematite*. Hematite gives many rocks a reddish coloration.

Sulfides and sulfates: Sulfides form as sulfur combines with other elements. *Sulfates* form as sulfur and oxygen combine with other materials. Many sulfide minerals are ores of metals such as lead, zinc, mercury, and copper. *Gypsum* ($CaSO_4 \cdot 2H_2O$) forms when sulfur and oxygen combine with calcium and other elements **(Figure 13.4)**.

Carbonates: Carbonates form when carbon combines with other elements, particularly oxygen. Carbonate minerals such as *calcite* commonly cement particles of sediment together to form sedimentary rocks. One of the most common carbonate rocks is limestone, composed mostly of calcium carbonate ($CaCO_3$).

and erosion. *Quartz*, a silicate mineral composed of silica (SiO_2), is the second most abundant mineral on Earth. Most of the sand in beaches and deserts is made of quartz grains, and quartz is found in abundance in granite and gneiss.

Rocks

Most rocks are composed of one or more minerals. A **rock** is a solid mass composed of minerals or volcanic glass. Some minerals, such as sodium

FIGURE 13.5 **Roadcut outcrops.** *A roadcut near Golden, Colorado, has created an outcrop that reveals layers of sedimentary rock. (© Francois Gohier/Science Source)*

chloride (NaCl), can form rocks on their own, such as rock salt (*halite*), but most rocks are an assemblage of many minerals cemented or interlocked together. Minerals can be bonded together with a natural cement. They can also interlock tightly into a coherent mass to from a *crystalline rock* (one possessing crystals).

The Geography of Outcrops

Earth's crust is composed of rocks and covered by sediments derived from rocks. **Sediments** are accumulations of small fragments of rock and organic material that are not cemented together. Rock fragments, or *clasts*, are formed by weathering of larger blocks of rock. Clasts are transported by flowing water, ice, or wind and deposited in layers of loose sediments. The sand on a beach, for example, is deposited by flowing rivers and the action of coastal waves. Over most of Earth's surface, sediments form a veneer that covers the underlying bedrock (rock that is still structurally part of Earth's crust).

Exposed areas of bedrock, or **outcrops**, dominate the landscape in tectonically and volcanically active mountainous regions, but there are few outcrops in the flat interior regions of continents,

such as the Great Plains of North America, where the bedrock in most places is buried beneath sediments that are hundreds of meters thick or more. Most outcrops are found in mountainous areas, in stream canyons, on rocky coastlines, and where roads have been cut into hills or mountains **(Figure 13.5)**.

The Rock Cycle

Rocks come in many types, from soft to hard, light to dark, and in all colors. Some look like human hair, and some are so light they float. The wide array of rock types can be grouped into three broad families: igneous rocks, sedimentary rocks, and metamorphic rocks. **Igneous rocks** cool from magma or lava. **Sedimentary rocks** are formed through cementation and compaction of sediments. **Metamorphic rocks** are formed by heat and pressure applied to preexisting rocks.

The **rock cycle** is a conceptual model that describes the formation and transformation of rocks in the crust. In the rock cycle, rocks are formed, transformed from one type to another, and recycled into the mantle **(Figure 13.6)**. Rocks first form when magma

How are rocks formed?

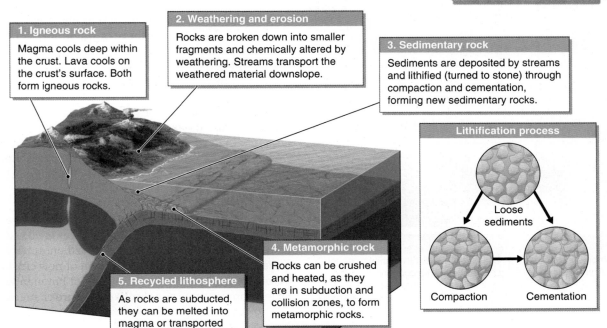

FIGURE 13.6 **GEO-GRAPHIC: The rock cycle.** *All rocks in Earth's crust are formed, transformed, and recycled in the rock cycle. Here, the rock cycle is shown in the setting of subduction and a continental volcanic arc.*

Animation
The rock cycle
http://qrs.ly/2b47n0o

1. Igneous rock
Magma cools deep within the crust. Lava cools on the crust's surface. Both form igneous rocks.

2. Weathering and erosion
Rocks are broken down into smaller fragments and chemically altered by weathering. Streams transport the weathered material downslope.

3. Sedimentary rock
Sediments are deposited by streams and lithified (turned to stone) through compaction and cementation, forming new sedimentary rocks.

4. Metamorphic rock
Rocks can be crushed and heated, as they are in subduction and collision zones, to form metamorphic rocks.

5. Recycled lithosphere
As rocks are subducted, they can be melted into magma or transported deep into the mantle.

Lithification process

Loose sediments

Compaction   Cementation

rock
A solid mass composed of minerals or volcanic glass.

sediment
An accumulation of small fragments of rock and organic material that is not cemented together.

outcrop
An exposed area of bedrock.

igneous rock
Rock that has cooled from magma or lava.

sedimentary rock
Rock formed from compacted and cemented sediments.

metamorphic rock
Rock formed by heat and pressure applied to preexisting rock.

rock cycle
A model of the processes by which rocks form, are transformed from one type to another, and are recycled into the mantle.

lithification
The formation of sedimentary rock through compaction and cementation of loose sediments.

cementation
A process in which minerals fill the spaces between loose particles and bind them together to form sedimentary rock.

decompression melting
The melting of hot mantle material into magma as a result of changes in pressure, which lower the melting point of the rock; occurs as mantle material rises to a shallow depth in the lithosphere.

cools and hardens (or *freezes*) into rock from a molten (liquid) state, either deep within Earth's crust or as lava extruded (pushed out) onto the crust's surface from a volcanic vent.

After rocks harden, they are subject to weathering, a process by which they are reduced to fragments of varying size or chemically broken down. The resulting fragments are transported downslope (mostly by flowing water) and deposited as sediments. Through the processes of compaction and cementation, loose sediments may experience **lithification** (transformed into rock). Compaction of the sediments occurs as they accumulate and their weight compresses the particles. **Cementation** is a process in which minerals fill the spaces between sediment particles and bind them together to form sedimentary rock. Most sedimentary rocks are formed through compaction and cementation (see Figure 13.6).

Next in the rock cycle, sedimentary rock can be buried deep in the crust through tectonic collision or subduction (see Section 12.3). There it can be compressed and heated under enormous pressure. Through compression and heating, any rock can become a new metamorphic rock. If a rock is heated enough, it can melt into magma. Thus, through the rock cycle, rocks may be transformed from igneous rock, to sedimentary rock, to metamorphic rock, and back to igneous rock.

This conceptual model of the rock cycle is a good start, but it falls short of capturing the complexity of the process of rock formation and transformation. Rock may take any of several transformational pathways, depending on the tectonic setting in which it is formed. In Figure 13.6, if the metamorphic rock were to be exposed at the crust's surface, it would be weathered and eroded into sediments. Those sediments could then lithify into sedimentary rock. In another example, seafloor igneous rocks form from cooled magma and lava at mid-ocean ridges, and are then transported across the ocean basin and recycled into the mantle by subduction (see Section 12.3), without ever undergoing weathering.

FIGURE 13.7 **Tectonic settings for igneous rock formation.** *Igneous rocks are formed through decompression melting or flux melting in four tectonic settings.*

Animation
Igneous rock formation
http://qrs.ly/1y47n0p

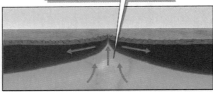

Decompression melting

1. Mid-ocean ridges
Diverging oceanic crust allows mantle material to rise, decompress, and melt into magma, creating mid-ocean ridges.

Decompression melting

2. Rift valleys
Continental rifting allows mantle material to rise, decompress, and form volcanoes at the surface.

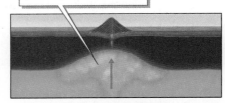

Decompression melting

3. Hot spots
Rising mantle plumes decompress and melt, resulting in hot spot volcanoes.

Flux melting

4. Subduction zones
Seawater mixes with mantle material where oceanic lithosphere subducts, causing it to melt into magma.

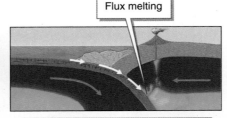

13.2 Cooling the Inferno: Igneous Rocks

◎ Describe the different types of igneous rocks and where they form.

Magma and lava are molten materials that originate from either the asthenosphere or the lithospheric mantle. Indeed, the word *igneous* is derived from the Latin word *ignis*, which means "fire."

As you might recall from Section 11.3, the asthenosphere is not in a molten state. Under surface conditions, it would be hot enough to melt, but because of the great pressures it is under, it does not melt. Instead, it is composed of solid rock that slowly deforms and flows. Where, then, does the magma that cools to form igneous rocks come from?

How Do Rocks Melt?

The asthenosphere melts in two settings: where pressure on it is reduced or where water is mixed with it. Decompression melting of the asthenosphere plays a prominent role in the creation of new crust. **Decompression melting** is the melting of hot mantle material into magma as a result of pressure changes.

FIGURE 13.8 **Igneous rock formations.** *Extrusive igneous rock forms from lava on Earth's surface. Intrusive igneous rock forms several types of features as it cools below the surface. These features remain buried unless erosion exposes them.*

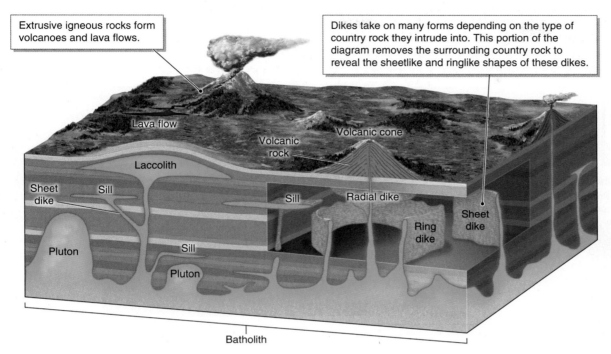

Extrusive igneous rocks form volcanoes and lava flows.

Dikes take on many forms depending on the type of country rock they intrude into. This portion of the diagram removes the surrounding country rock to reveal the sheetlike and ringlike shapes of these dikes.

Lava flow

Volcanic cone

Volcanic rock

Laccolith

Sheet dike

Sill

Sill

Radial dike

Sheet dike

Ring dike

Pluton

Sill

Pluton

Batholith

Igneous Rock Formations

As magma moves upward through the surrounding rock (called *country rock*) and solidifies, several types of features may form, including batholiths, plutons, sills, dikes, and laccoliths **(Figure 13.8)**. A **batholith** is a body of intrusive igneous rock hundreds of kilometers in extent and formed by the movement and fusion of numerous plutons. A **pluton**, like a batholith, is a dome-shaped igneous rock mass, but up to only a few tens of kilometers in diameter. A **sill** is a horizontal sheet of igneous rock that has cooled from magma injected between layers of preexisting rock. A **dike** is similar to a sill, but forms a vertical sheet of igneous rock. A **laccolith** is a shallow, dome-shaped igneous rock body.

Intrusive igneous rock formations are hidden beneath Earth's surface until they are exposed by **exhumation**: the removal of overlying rock and sediment to expose deeper rocks at the surface. This process takes millions of years and requires geologic uplift that exposes rocks to erosive forces. **Figure 13.9** illustrates the exhumation of a batholith, a laccolith, and a dike in the western United States.

It occurs as mantle material is brought to a shallow depth in the lithosphere, where the pressure on it decreases enough to allow it to melt. Decompression melting occurs in three tectonic settings: at mid-ocean ridges, in rift valleys, and at hot spots.

Mantle material also melts into magma in subduction zones. **Flux melting** is the process by which subducted water causes mantle material to melt by lowering its melting point.

Decompression melting and flux melting both result in the production of magma, which contributes to building the crust when it cools and hardens into new igneous rock. Figure 13.7 on the facing page summarizes the tectonic settings in which melting of mantle material into magma occurs (see Sections 12.3 and 12.4 for further details about these tectonic settings).

Once magma forms, it rises into the crust because it is less dense and more buoyant than the lithospheric mantle. Magma may cool either within the crust or on the crust's surface. Rock that has cooled from lava on the crust's surface is called **extrusive igneous rock** (or volcanic rock). **Intrusive igneous rock** cools from magma underground.

flux melting
The process by which subducted water lowers the melting point of mantle material and causes it to melt.

extrusive igneous rock
(or volcanic rock) Rock that has cooled from lava on the crust's surface.

intrusive igneous rock
Rock that has cooled from magma below the crust's surface.

batholith
A body of intrusive igneous rock hundreds of kilometers in extent and formed by the movement and fusion of numerous plutons.

pluton
A dome-shaped igneous rock mass of no more than a few tens of kilometers in diameter.

sill
A horizontal sheet of igneous rock that was injected between layers of preexisting rock.

dike
A sheetlike vertical igneous rock formation.

laccolith
A shallow, dome-shaped igneous rock body.

exhumation
The removal of overlying rock and sediment to expose deeper rocks at the surface.

FIGURE 13.9 **GEO-GRAPHIC: Exhumation of a batholith, a laccolith, and a dike.** *Weathering and erosion have removed overlying rocks to expose these intrusive igneous features. (A) The Sierra Nevada mountain range in California is an exhumed batholith. Many kilometers of sedimentary and volcanic rocks once covered the Sierra Nevada. These older rocks were removed by erosion as the batholith was uplifted. (B) Pine Valley Mountain in southern Utah is the one of the largest laccoliths in the United States, measuring about 35 km (20 mi) across. It is an igneous intrusion that formed between layers of sedimentary rock that have since been eroded away. Once the overlying sedimentary rock was removed, erosion by streams cut canyons into the laccolith. (C) Shiprock is a prominent landform found in northwestern New Mexico. A large volcano once existed there. After the volcano became extinct, its outer layers of rock were eroded away, exposing the relatively resistant volcanic neck and the dike. (A. Bruce Gervais; B. Utah Geological Society; C. © Universal Images Group/Getty Images)*

1. Batholith formation

A batholith forms beneath sedimentary and volcanic rocks and pushes up into them.

2. Exhumation

Geologic uplift (shown with arrows) lifts the batholith. Overlying rocks are removed through erosion, exposing the batholith.

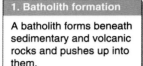

Preexisting rock

Batholith

Time

A

---

1. Sedimentary rock layers

Sedimentary rocks develop horizontal layers.

2. Laccolith formation

Magma intrudes through the sedimentary rock layers and separates a layer of rock near the surface, forming a laccolith.

3. Exhumation

Erosion removes the overlying sedimentary rocks and cuts into the laccolith, forming an exposed and eroded laccolith.

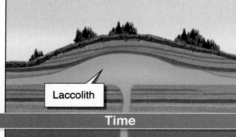

Exposed laccolith

Laccolith

Sedimentary rocks

Time

Laccolith

Sedimentary rocks

Pine Valley Mountain

B

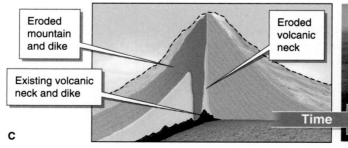

Eroded mountain and dike

Eroded volcanic neck

Existing volcanic neck and dike

Time

Shiprock

C

Igneous Rock Categories

The presence (or absence) of crystals and the resulting rock texture reveal much about the conditions under which an igneous rock formed. Magma deep within the crust cools slowly, over decades to millions of years, because the rocks that surround the magma insulate it and slow its heat loss. This long span of time gives mineral crystals time to develop as the magma solidifies into rock. These slowly cooled rocks often have visible crystals, which may be up to several centimeters across, and a rough texture. Such coarse-grained rocks, called *phaneritic* rocks, sparkle as large crystal faces reflect light.

Igneous rocks that cool more quickly closer to the surface have smaller crystals and are called *aphanitic* rocks. Their crystals cannot be seen without the aid of magnification.

In a third category, glassy rocks have no orderly crystalline arrangement of atoms because they cool rapidly at the surface. When a glassy rock is broken, the fresh surface often shines and reflects light just as glass does (see Figure 13.2B).

Plutons and batholiths (see Figure 13.8) cool slowly and are usually composed of phaneritic rock such as granite or diorite. Laccoliths and dikes, on the other hand, cool more rapidly nearer the surface and are typically composed of aphanitic rocks, such as rhyolite or andesite. Because lava cools at the surface very quickly, it may be composed of glassy rocks, such as obsidian or pumice.

The silica content of rocks, along with rock texture, is used to distinguish igneous rock categories **(Figure 13.10)**. The amount of silica in magma depends largely on the amount of country rock melted and incorporated into the magma as it rises through the crust. *Felsic* igneous rocks (also called *granitic* rocks; see Section 11.3) are composed of about 70% silica. They are light in color and contain high concentrations of silica, aluminum, potassium, and sodium. *Mafic* igneous rocks (also called *basaltic* rocks), in contrast, contain only about 50% silica. Mafic rocks are relatively high in magnesium, iron, and olivine.

13.3 Layers of Time: Sedimentary Rocks

◎ Explain the three types of sedimentary rocks, where they form, and how they provide information about Earth's history.

The desert in today's southwestern United States was once a large, shallow sea and series of large freshwater lakes that dried up and re-formed many times. Rivers carried dissolved and fragmented rock material into these water bodies and deposited it as sediments. Many of these sediments were rich

FIGURE 13.10 **Classifying igneous rocks.** *Igneous rocks can be organized by their texture, silica content, density, and color. Felsic rocks (such as granite), which have a high silica content, tend to be lighter in color, while mafic rocks (such as basalt), with less silica, are darker. (From top left: © C. Bevilacqua/De Agostini/Getty Images; © Joyce Photographics/Science Source; © Breck P. Kent; © Joel Arem/Photo Researchers/Getty Images; © Breck P. Kent; © Breck P. Kent)*

in hematite (or other iron oxides). Later, the sediments were lithified and then exposed through erosion, in many places forming dramatic and brightly colored scenery **(Figure 13.11)**.

FIGURE 13.11 **Layered sedimentary rock formations in Bryce Canyon, Utah.** *The sediments that formed these rocks were laid down beginning about 63 million years ago over a period of about 23 million years by a system of streams and freshwater lakes. The oldest sediments are at the bottom (according to the principle of superposition; see Section 11.2). Hematite gives the sediments their vibrant orange color. (Bruce Gervais)*

TABLE 13.1 **Sedimentary Rock Types**	
1. Clastic sedimentary rocks Composed of rock and mineral fragments	
ROCK TYPE	**FORMED FROM**
Claystone	Clay
Shale	Clay
Siltstone	Silt
Mudstone	Silt and clay
Sandstone	Sand
Conglomerate	Cobbles, sand, silt, and clay
2. Organic sedimentary rocks Composed of the remains of organisms	
ROCK TYPE	**FORMED FROM**
Fossiliferous limestone	Shell fragments from coral reefs
Chalk	Shell fragments of marine phytoplankton
Bituminous coal	Peat
3. Chemical sedimentary rocks Composed of precipitated and evaporated mineral deposits	
ROCK TYPE	**FORMED FROM**
Rock salt (halite)	Evaporated water
Gypsum	Evaporated seawater
Limestone and tufa	Precipitated calcium carbonate

Sedimentary Rock Categories

There are three types of sedimentary rock: clastic sedimentary rock, organic sedimentary rock, and chemical sedimentary rock. These three types are distinguished by the kinds of sediments of which they are composed, the environment in which they form, and the processes that form them (Table 13.1). **Clastic sedimentary rock** is composed of broken pieces of other rocks; the sizes of those pieces determine the kind of clastic sedimentary rock that forms (see Figure 9.4). **Organic sedimentary rock** is composed mostly of organic material derived from ancient organisms or their shells. **Chemical sedimentary rock** is formed as dissolved minerals are precipitated out of water.

Sedimentary rocks form only in *depositional environments*, which are places where sediments accumulate. The sedimentary rock formations we see in today's landscapes reflect the environments in which their sediments accumulated and lithified long ago. There are many depositional environments on Earth's surface. **Figure 13.12** shows some of the more geographically widespread environments in which sediments accumulate.

The processes that form sedimentary rocks operate under the principle of uniformitarianism (see Section 11.2). These slow and gradual processes

FIGURE 13.12   **GEO-GRAPHIC: Depositional environments.**

clastic sedimentary rock
Sedimentary rock composed of broken pieces of other rocks.

organic sedimentary rock
Sedimentary rock composed mostly of organic material and derived from ancient organisms.

chemical sedimentary rock
Sedimentary rock that forms as dissolved minerals are precipitated out of water.

shale
A clastic sedimentary rock formed from clay.

sandstone
A clastic sedimentary rock composed chiefly of quartz sand grains.

limestone
A chemical sedimentary rock composed mostly of calcite.

Deserts and coastal sand dunes
Sand accumulates in deserts and on coastal beaches, then lithifies into sandstone.

River floodplains
Rivers transporting silt, clay, and mud often overflow their banks and spill onto surrounding flat-lying regions, called floodplains. Through time, sediments on floodplains accumulate to great thickness. River sediments lithify into sandstone, siltstone, and shale.

Estuaries and lakes
In lakes, wetlands, and estuaries, thick layers of sediment lithify into shale, mudstone, and siltstone. Shallow, ephemeral lakes in inland arid environments form sediment deposits.

Coastal environments
Streams deposit their sediments where they reach the ocean. The coastal sediments lithify into siltstone, mudstone, claystone, and shale. Coral reefs are limestone-forming environments.

Offshore environments
Shells from microscopic marine organisms and sediments eroded from the continents and carried by rivers accumulate on the seafloor. These sediments lithify into mudstone, chalk, limestone, and siltstone.

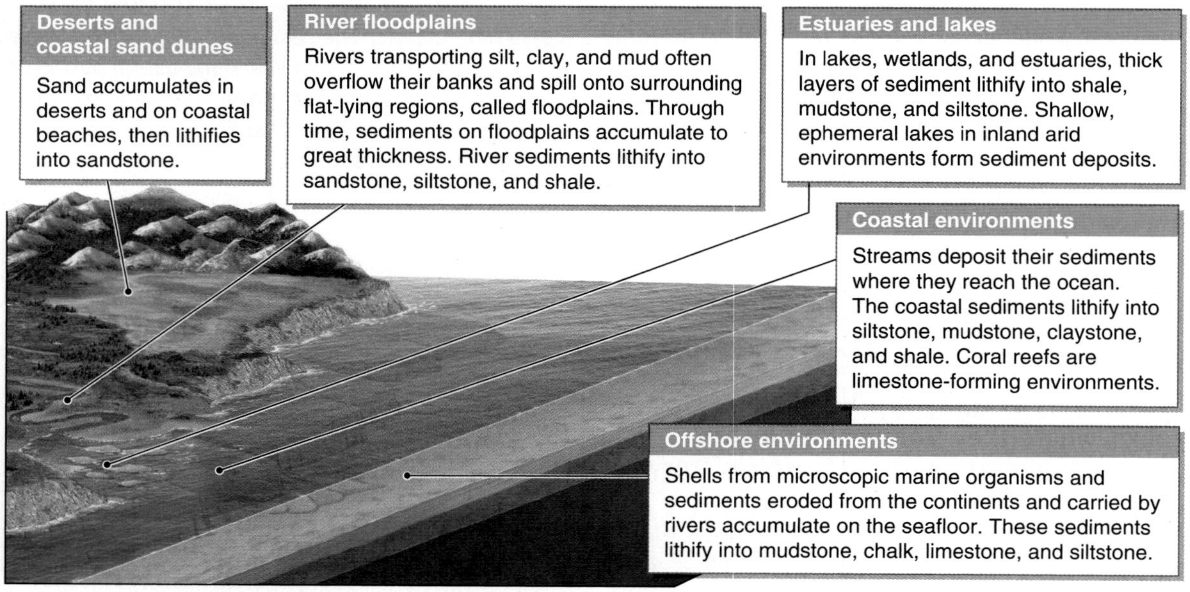

are difficult to observe on human time scales, but nonetheless operate in the world around us today. Crunch the Numbers asks you to calculate how long it takes for sediments on the seafloor to develop into sedimentary rock.

The Three Most Common Sedimentary Rocks

Although 96% of Earth's crust is composed of igneous and metamorphic rocks, most of the rocks exposed on the crust's surface are sedimentary rocks (Table 13.2). About 99% of those sedimentary rocks are shale, sandstone, or limestone. **Shale** is a clastic sedimentary rock formed from clay-sized particles. **Sandstone** is a clastic sedimentary rock composed chiefly of quartz sand grains. **Limestone** is a chemical sedimentary rock composed mostly of calcite. **Figure 13.13** shows the modern environments associated with these three types of sedimentary rock.

TABLE 13.2	AT A GLANCE: Rock Abundances and Exposures	
	PROPORTION OF THE CRUST	PROPORTION EXPOSED AT THE SURFACE
Igneous and metamorphic rocks	96%	25%
Sedimentary rocks	4%	75%

FIGURE 13.13 **Depositional environments of the most common sedimentary rocks.** *(A) Deposits of clay in estuaries, lakes, and on the seafloor lithify into shale. This shale, called Utica shale, near Fort Plain, New York, is 450 million years old. (B) Sand dunes form in desert and coastal beach environments. These lithified dunes, which formed about 170 million years ago, are part of the Navajo sandstone formation in Zion National Park, Utah. (C) There are many kinds of limestone, but all are at least 50% calcite. Most limestone is formed as minerals dissolved in water precipitate out as a solid. These limestone rocks, which formed about 260 million years ago, are part of the Kaibab Formation in the Grand Canyon in northern Arizona. (A. © Ron Erwin/All Canada Photos/ Getty Images; Michael C. Rygel via Wikimedia Commons; B. © Witold Skrypczak/Lonely Planet/Images Getty Images; Bruce Gervais; C. © Tobias Bernhard/Oxford Scientific/Getty Images; Bruce Gervais)*

	PROPORTION OF ALL SEDIMENTARY ROCKS
Shale	45%
Sandstone	32%
Limestone	22%
Other	1%

A

B

C

coal
An organic rock formed from the remains of terrestrial wetland forests and widely used today as a fuel source.

peat
A brownish-black, heavy soil found in wetlands, formed from the partially decomposed remains of plants.

Economically Significant Sedimentary Rocks

Human society is built on natural resources. Most natural resources must either be mined or grown. In the case of minerals and rocks, they must be mined. Among the sedimentary rocks, coal, shale, and some chemical sedimentary rocks are particularly important in this regard.

Buried Sunshine: Coal

What is coal?

The most economically valuable sedimentary rock is coal. **Coal** is an organic rock that is formed from the remains of terrestrial wetland forests. The two main types of coal are bituminous coal and anthracite coal. Bituminous coal is an organic sedimentary rock formed from peat, and anthracite coal is a metamorphic rock that forms as bituminous coal is subjected to great heat and pressure.

Coal forms from ancient deposits of **peat**, a brownish-black, heavy soil that forms in wetlands from the partially decomposed remains of plants. When peat is compacted and heated by being bur-

ied deeply beneath other sediments, it can lithify into coal (Figure 13.14).

Coal plays a central role in today's world economies, and about 36% of the energy consumed in the United States comes from coal. Unfortunately, many types of coal mining are environmentally destructive, particularly the widespread practice of coal mountaintop removal in West Virginia, described in **Picture This**.

Petroleum

Petroleum (or *oil*) is not a mineral or rock because it is a liquid. It deserves special mention here, however, because it is found in association with sedimentary rocks. In addition, it is an economically vital material resource for humanity today.

Petroleum is a *hydrocarbon*, meaning that it is composed of chains or rings of molecules made of hydrogen and carbon atoms. Like coal, it is derived from the organic remains of ancient organisms. Whereas coal is formed from ancient terrestrial wetland forests, petroleum is formed from the remains of ancient marine zooplankton and phytoplankton.

FIGURE 13.14 **GEO-GRAPHIC: Coal.** *Coal is often called "buried sunshine" because it is solar energy stored in plants that grew long ago. Ancient terrestrial forests that lived some 300 million years ago were partially decomposed to form peat and then lithified into coal. (A. © Science Source; B. © Corey Appleby)*

1. Plants in wetlands

Forests in ancient wetlands were preserved as peat rather than decomposed.

A

2. Coal

Over millions of years of deep burial and the resulting pressure and heating, peat was transformed into coal. This exposed coal seam in West Virginia is less than 1 m thick.

Coal seam

B

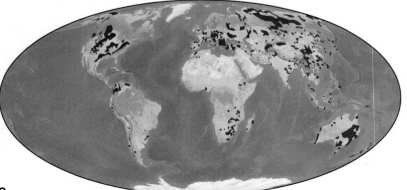

C

3. Worldwide coal distribution

Coal deposits represent the former locations of once-verdant terrestrial forest wetlands.

Picture This

(© Mandel Ngan/AFP/Getty Images)

Coal Mining by Mountaintop Removal

Coal is a relatively inexpensive energy source because it is easily mined and there are abundant supplies of it worldwide. Coal produces abundant energy. But mining (and burning) coal takes a toll on the environment.

In the United States, coal is readily accessible near the crust's surface throughout much of the Appalachian Mountains, particularly in West Virginia. *Mountaintop removal* is a technique of coal mining used when coal deposits are too close to the surface to be safely mined underground. Surface vegetation, soil, and rock are removed to extract the coal deposits beneath. In all, about 470 mountaintops have been leveled in Kentucky, West Virginia (shown in photo and inset map), Virginia, and Tennessee since the 1980s, and 4.9 million hectares (12 million acres) of temperate deciduous forest have been destroyed by coal mountaintop removal.

Mountaintop removal also causes significant water pollution. The removed soil and rock, or *overburden*, is deposited in adjacent valleys. More than 1,100 km (700 mi) of streams in the Appalachian Mountains now lie beneath overburden. The overburden leaches toxic trace elements such as selenium, lead, nickel, and cadmium. These elements enter stream systems, where they poison the organisms that live in the streams and the people who drink water from them. After the coal has been removed from the mining area, the mining companies are required to replant vegetation (a practice called *reclamation*), but the streams and their biodiversity are lost.

Consider This

1. How does coal burning affect air quality (see Section 1.4)?

2. How does coal burning affect climate (see Section 6.3)?

As much as modern society depends on coal, petroleum is equally or even more important to our everyday lives, accounting for about 25% of the U.S. energy supply. On average, each person in the United States uses about 70 L (20 gal) of petroleum each day.

Sedimentary rocks are often associated with deposits of petroleum and natural methane gas. Shale can form a porous reservoir, where natural gas and petroleum accumulate. On the other hand, if shale is nonporous, it can form a *cap rock*, trapping petroleum and natural gas beneath the ground.

evaporite

A deposit of one or more minerals resulting from the repeated evaporation of water from a basin.

Some porous shale can hold natural gas within its pore spaces. Such "shale gas" is playing an increasingly prominent role in the North American energy supply. **Shale gas currently provides about 35% of the natural gas supplies in the United States, and this figure is growing rapidly due to the current boom in shale gas extraction.** This controversial topic is explored in Geographic Perspectives at the end of this chapter.

Evaporites

Some chemical sedimentary rocks have significant economic value. One such group of chemical sedimentary rocks is the evaporites, which are used in many applications, ranging from lithium ion batteries (lithium) to construction materials (gypsum) to seasonings (table salt). An **evaporite** is a deposit of one or more minerals resulting from the repeated evaporation of water from a basin. **Figure 13.15** highlights one particularly important evaporite deposit, Salar de Uyuni in Bolivia.

FIGURE 13.15 **Salar de Uyuni.** *(A) Salar de Uyuni, in Bolivia, is the largest exposed evaporite deposit in the world, measuring 200 km (124 mi) across and some 10,500 km² (4,000 mi²) in area. The polygonal cracks (left photo) in the sediments were formed by repeated swelling and shrinking due to wetting and drying. Lithium, borax, and rock salt (or table salt) are some of the minerals mined and processed here (right photo). The deposit is estimated to contain 10 billion tons of salt as well as 42% of the world's lithium supply. (B) Evaporites form in arid environments as a shallow lake basin repeatedly fills with water, which then evaporates. Every time the basin floods and evaporates, a thin layer of evaporites is left behind. Through time, these layers accumulate into extensive deposits. (A. © Mike Theiss/National Geographic/Getty Images; B. © Christian Kober/ Robert Harding World Imagery/Getty Images)*

A

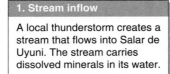

1. Stream inflow

A local thunderstorm creates a stream that flows into Salar de Uyuni. The stream carries dissolved minerals in its water.

2. Evaporite deposition

Because Salar de Uyuni is in a desert, the stream stops flowing once the storm has passed, and the water in the basin evaporates. The dissolved minerals in the water are left behind, forming evaporites.

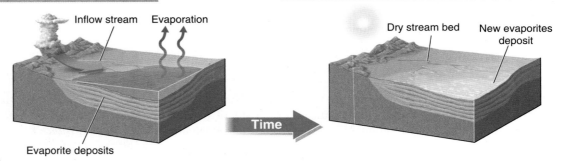

Inflow stream   Evaporation

Dry stream bed   New evaporites deposit

Time

Evaporite deposits

B

Windows to the Past: Fossils

Sedimentary rocks reveal much about Earth's ancient life and environments because it is in these rocks that fossils are preserved. **Fossils** are the remains or the impressions of organisms preserved in sedimentary rock. **Figure 13.16** explores the use of fossils to study Earth's ancient history.

fossil
The remains or the impression of an organism preserved in sedimentary rock.

FIGURE 13.16 **SCIENTIFIC INQUIRY: What information do fossils provide about the past?**

Fossils provide a wealth of scientific information about Earth's past. Much of what scientists know about Earth's ancient past has been learned by studying fossils. (Top right: © Universal Images Group/Getty Images; bottom center: © Christos Kotsiopoulos)

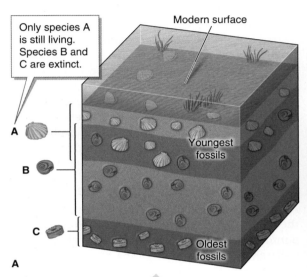

Only species A is still living. Species B and C are extinct.

Modern surface

A

B

C

Youngest fossils

Oldest fossils

A

Evolution and extinction
Fossils reveal that organisms change through time and form new species in the process of evolution. Undisturbed sedimentary rocks contain a progression from older to younger fossils from bottom to top. As different fossil types disappear and appear through time, the process of extinction and evolution is revealed.

Climate and environmental change
These 225-million-year-old fossilized tree trunks are in the Petrified Forest National Park in northern Arizona. After the trees fell, they were washed down a stream and buried in silt and volcanic ash. Over time, silica and other minerals replaced the wood, leading to their fossilization. The presence of these trees shows that the climate was much wetter and warmer when they were growing. Today northern Arizona is desert.

NV

NM

Arizona

Petrified Forest National Park

Mexico

Romania

Italy

45° N

Greece

Turkey

Ligourio

MEDITERRANEAN SEA

15° E

30° E

Libya

Relative and absolute ages of rocks
Index fossils provide stratigraphic markers that allow scientists to determine the ages of sedimentary rocks at a glance. These dated fossils are used as a quick reference to determine the ages of rocks. The fossils shown are extinct 240-million-year-old *ammonites* from Ligourio, Greece, on the Mediterranean Sea. Ammonites serve as index fossils worldwide because they are easy to identify and their absolute ages are already known.

protolith
The parent or original rock from which metamorphic rock was formed.

13.4 Pressure and Heat: Metamorphic Rocks

◎ Explain where metamorphic rocks form and how they are categorized.

Caterpillars undergo *metamorphosis* and become butterflies. Rocks undergo *metamorphism* and become new rocks. **All types of rocks can undergo the process of metamorphism.** Even metamorphic rocks can be metamorphosed more than once. The result of metamorphism is a physical, mineralogical, or chemical transformation of the **protolith**: the parent or original rock.

The process of metamorphism involves enormous pressures, high temperatures, or both. Metamorphism occurs while the rock is in a solid state. If the rock is heated too much, it will melt into magma and form igneous rock. The thermal range for metamorphism is roughly between 100°C and 900°C (200°F and 1,600°F).

There are many variables involved in metamorphism that determine the characteristics of the final rock. These variables include the degree of heating, the degree of compression, the length of time under these conditions, the original chemical constitution of protolith, and the presence or absence of chemically reactive fluids, such as water.

Tectonic Settings of Metamorphism

Very high temperatures can be found on the crust's surface in volcanic regions, where lava flows may cook surface rocks. High pressures and temperatures, however, are far more common deep within the crust. As a result, metamorphism is a process that normally takes place kilometers deep in the crust in regions of subduction and collision. Therefore, most metamorphic rocks are hidden away deep within the crust, and they are the least common of the three rock families on the crust's surface. Metamorphic rocks must be exhumed if they are to be exposed.

There are two broad categories of metamorphic processes: contact metamorphism and regional metamorphism. *Contact metamorphism* occurs when rock comes into contact with and is heated by magma. *Regional metamorphism* results from the great heat and pressure found at convergent plate boundaries. Contact metamorphism is more geographically localized than regional metamorphism. Contact metamorphism and regional metamorphism do not produce different kinds of metamorphic rocks. The type of metamorphic rock that forms depends on the protolith and the degree of heating and compression.

Metamorphic Rock Categories

All metamorphic rocks fit into two categories on the basis of their physical structure: foliated and nonfoliated (**Figure 13.17**). *Foliated* metamorphic rocks show flat or wavy banding patterns that may superficially resemble sedimentary layers, but are unrelated to them in how they were formed. Foliation is caused by shearing forces as pressure is applied

---

FIGURE 13.17 **Foliated and nonfoliated metamorphic rocks.** *(A) These metamorphic rocks near Geiranger, Norway, a type called* gneiss, *show a conspicuous banded foliation pattern. (B) Marble is a nonfoliated metamorphic rock that is prized by sculptors for its fine grain and ease of carving. Shown here is a detail of Michelangelo's* David, *carved from marble. (A. © Dr. Juerg Alean/Science Source; B. © The Bridgeman Art Library/Getty Images)*

A

B

to the rock from different directions. The foliated layers are formed by mineral grains that run parallel to one another and perpendicular to the direction of compression. *Nonfoliated* metamorphic rocks, which form where pressure and heat are uniform, have little or no structured grain pattern or mineral arrangement and usually lack any banded or layered appearance.

Foliated metamorphic rocks are classified by grain size. Nonfoliated metamorphic rocks are classified by their chemical composition. The metamorphic rocks shown in Table 13.3 represent only a small fraction of the types of metamorphic rocks found in nature, but they are among the most common metamorphic rocks exposed at the crust's surface.

| TABLE 13.3 | **Metamorphic Rock Classification** | | | | |

Foliated Metamorphic Rocks (Classified By Grain Size)

ROCK NAME	GRAIN SIZE	PROTOLITH	TEMPERATURE REQUIRED	DESCRIPTION
Slate	Small	Shale or mudstone	Low	Dark in color; mineral grains are too small to see with naked eye. Used in building materials such as roofing tiles.
Schist	Intermediate	Slate	Intermediate	Minerals are medium-grained and visible with naked eye. Used in outdoor paving or indoor flooring.
Gneiss	Large	Schist	High	Coarse-grained and typically banded or wavy, with dark and light layers of minerals. Used in flooring, building facades, and gravestones.

Nonfoliated Metamorphic Rocks (Classified By Chemical Composition)

ROCK NAME	PRIMARY MINERAL	PROTOLITH	DESCRIPTION
Marble	Calcite	Limestone or chalk	Hard rock that may be banded. Often used in sculpture, building facades, and kitchen countertops.
Quartzite	Quartz	Sandstone	Very hard rock, highly resistant to weathering. Commonly used in sandpaper and sandblasting.
Anthracite Coal	Carbon	Bituminous coal	Hard, black, and shiny, with a high carbon content.

(Top to bottom: © Tyler Boyes/Shutterstock.com; © Breck P. Kent; © Gary Ombler/Dorling Kindersley/Getty Images)

GEOGRAPHIC PERSPECTIVES
13.5 Fracking for Shale Gas

◎ Assess the pros and cons of extracting natural gas trapped in shale through hydraulic fracturing.

fracking
(or *hydraulic fracturing*) The procedure by which water is pumped under high pressure into a shale formation to extract natural gas and oil.

Fracking is short for *hydraulic fracturing*: a procedure in which water, sand, and chemicals are pumped under high pressure into shale bedrock to extract natural gas and oil trapped in the pores of the shale. This technique was first developed in the 1940s and has become common practice in many regions worldwide in the last decade.

As the prices of fossil fuels rise, it becomes economically profitable to develop reserves that are more difficult and more expensive to use, such as shale gas. In the United States, the number of oil and gas wells almost doubled between 1990 and 2009 to 493,000. As of 2012, there were 483,000 wells producing natural gas in the United States **(Figure 13.18)**.

Fracking is projected to take on an increasingly significant role in meeting U.S. energy needs in the coming decades. In 2000, shale gas provided only 1% of natural gas supplies in the United States. **By 2035, it is estimated that half of U.S. gas production will be made available through fracking.** Natural gas

provides about 30% of the energy consumed in the United States, but this number is rapidly growing because of fracking.

There are about 187 trillion m^3 (6.6 quadrillion ft^3) of natural gas locked in shale worldwide. China, Argentina, the United States, and Mexico have the largest shale gas reserves in the world. **Figure 13.19** shows where gas-bearing shale is found in North America.

How Fracking Works

Shale, as we saw in Section 13.3, is a fine-grained sedimentary rock formed from clay. Although the pore spaces within shale are small, they often contain natural gas. Conventional gas extraction techniques are ineffective in shale because the gas flows out of the formation too slowly to be of economic use.

To speed up the flow of gas from a well drilled in shale, water, sand, and a cocktail of nontoxic and

FIGURE 13.18 **A drilling rig in Pinedale, Wyoming.** *This natural gas drilling rig is being used to drill a well through which natural gas will be extracted by fracking from a shale formation deep below the surface.* (© Robert Nickelsberg/Getty Images)

toxic chemicals are injected at high pressures into the well to fracture the rock. Fracturing increases the permeability of the rock and lets oil and gas escape up the wellhead, where it can be captured and used. **Figure 13.20** diagrams the process of fracking.

This procedure sounds straightforward: We get more natural gas from shale by injecting water, sand, and chemicals into it. **Several potentially serious problems result from this method of gas extraction, including water pollution.**

> What is fracking and why is it controversial?

Fracking Fluid

Each fracking operation at each well requires about 26 million L (7 million gal) of water. Millions of liters of toxic and radioactive wastewater, called *fracking fluid*, are left over after a fracking operation is complete. This wastewater is collected at the fracking site and must be safely disposed of.

Why is the water toxic and radioactive? Chemicals such as benzene and xylene, two known carcinogens, are sometimes added to water during the fracking process to help bring out the gas. In addition, the water absorbs natural radium from the rock, becoming radioactive in the process.

The fracking industry has been grappling with how to dispose of the millions of gallons of toxic fracking fluid it produces. Fracking fluid has been

FIGURE 13.19 **Shale gas reserves in North America.**
The geographic extent of shale formations from which shale gas is potentially recoverable by fracking is shown in dark orange.

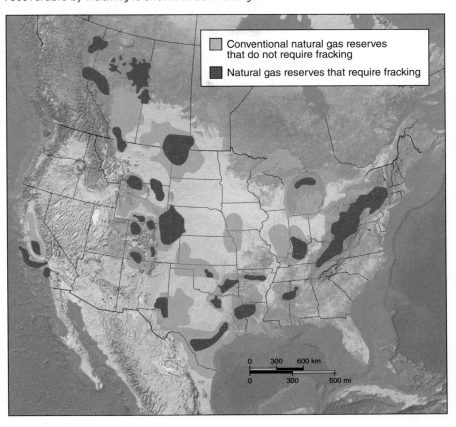

- Conventional natural gas reserves that do not require fracking
- Natural gas reserves that require fracking

FIGURE 13.20 **GEO-GRAPHIC: The fracking process.** *Hydraulic fracturing frees natural gas within shale by injecting water under high pressure and cracking the shale.*

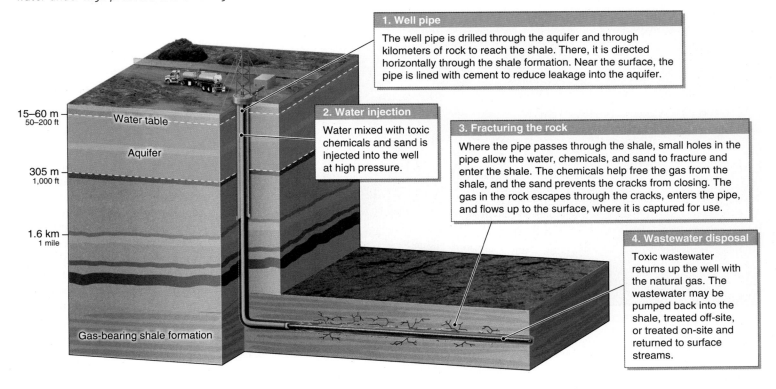

1. Well pipe
The well pipe is drilled through the aquifer and through kilometers of rock to reach the shale. There, it is directed horizontally through the shale formation. Near the surface, the pipe is lined with cement to reduce leakage into the aquifer.

2. Water injection
Water mixed with toxic chemicals and sand is injected into the well at high pressure.

3. Fracturing the rock
Where the pipe passes through the shale, small holes in the pipe allow the water, chemicals, and sand to fracture and enter the shale. The chemicals help free the gas from the shale, and the sand prevents the cracks from closing. The gas in the rock escapes through the cracks, enters the pipe, and flows up to the surface, where it is captured for use.

4. Wastewater disposal
Toxic wastewater returns up the well with the natural gas. The wastewater may be pumped back into the shale, treated off-site, or treated on-site and returned to surface streams.

15–60 m
50–200 ft — Water table

Aquifer

305 m
1,000 ft

1.6 km
1 mile

Gas-bearing shale formation

discharged into rivers and sent to wastewater treatment plants, neither of which can handle its volume and contaminants. So far, the best solution seems to be to inject it back underground under high pressure. Unfortunately, injecting fracking fluid back in the ground can trigger earthquakes. A study published in *Science* in July 2014 definitively linked disposing of fracking fluid in this way to increased earthquake activity in central Oklahoma. An even

FIGURE 13.21 **Water contamination by fracking.** *(A) Fracking fluid is stored on site in plastic-lined containment ponds like this one. (B) The groundwater in some areas near fracking operations has become so contaminated with methane that it is possible to set the water on fire as it comes out of the faucet. (A. © Mladen Antonov/AFP/Getty Images; B. © Melanie Stetson Freeman/The Christian Science Monitor/Getty Images)*

A

B

bigger problem, injecting fracking fluid back into the ground may contaminate groundwater supplies.

Drinking Water

Opponents of fracking claim that it contaminates drinking water supplies in two ways. First, the toxic fracking fluid finds its way to surface streams and drinking water supplies through accidental trucking spills or leaks from pipelines and containment ponds (Figure 13.21A). Opponents also argue that fracking threatens drinking water supplies with methane gas contamination (Figure 13.21B). Methane has contaminated drinking water in Colorado, Ohio, New York, Pennsylvania, Texas, and West Virginia. Samples from 60 water wells near fracking operations in northeastern Pennsylvania and upstate New York found methane concentrations 17 times higher than average in drinking water supplies. Where it occurs, methane contamination of water by fracking is most likely to be caused by failure of the cement casing placed around the well where it passes through groundwater (see Figure 13.20).

Air Pollution and Climate Change

Natural gas burns cleaner than coal, and it has been hailed by many environmentalists and the natural gas industry as a clean alternative to coal. A report published in *Nature* in 2013 challenged this view. The report found that up to 9% of the natural gas being extracted from fracking wells in Utah leaks directly into the atmosphere. Compared with carbon dioxide, molecule for molecule, methane is 21 times more potent as a greenhouse gas. If the Utah wells are representative of the industry as a whole (which is not yet known), then natural gas obtained through fracking is a more carbon-intensive fuel (causes more global warming) than coal. A comprehensive assessment of methane leakage rates at fracking wells is being conducted by NOAA and the U.S. EPA, and the results are pending.

Summing Up: The Pros and Cons

In some areas, the perceived risks of fracking outweigh its perceived benefits. Many U.S. states, counties, and cities have issued moratoriums on fracking or are considering legislation that would restrict fracking. For example, New Jersey, North Carolina, and New York, as well as the cities of Buffalo (New York) and Pittsburgh (Pennsylvania), have issued moratoriums on fracking within their jurisdictions. In 2012, Vermont banned all fracking. The Canadian province of Québec suspended fracking in 2012, and France banned fracking in 2011.

These jurisdictions are exceptions. Fracking proceeds apace in most of the United States and around the world. Some governments, such as South Africa's, have even lifted bans on fracking and are forging ahead with it. The pros and cons of fracking for the United States are summarized in Figure 13.22.

People need energy. From the standpoint of climate change, natural gas is a preferable option to relatively dirty coal. Unfortunately, all fossil fuels, natural gas included, contribute to climate change. Looking ahead several decades, it remains to be seen whether the current boom in natural gas development will provide a relatively clean source of energy while renewable energy sources are developed or whether it simply is a continuation of society's dependence on fossil fuels.

FIGURE 13.22 **Two sides to fracking.**

(Left, © Mladen Antonov/AFP/Getty Images; right, © Justin Sullivan/Getty Images)

Advocates: The oil and gas industry claims that fracking is moving the United States away from reliance on dirty coal and politically volatile foreign oil.

Opponents: Those who oppose fracking claim there are safer energy alternatives than shale gas. Here, protesters in Sacramento, California in 2012 fight to keep fracking out of the state.

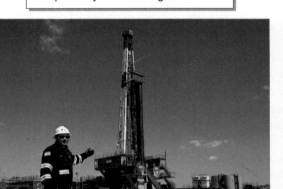

Fracking Pros and Cons

REASONS FOR	REASONS AGAINST
Buys time while renewable energy technologies are developed	Natural gas leaks and heavy machinery that runs on diesel put carbon dioxide into the atmosphere, contributing to climate change
Provides jobs, good for the economy	Causes surface water and groundwater pollution and earthquakes at some locations
Natural gas burns cleaner than coal and reduces use of coal	Releases, by accident and deliberately, large amounts of methane into the atmosphere
Reduces dependence on foreign oil	Creates air pollution around drilling sites

CHAPTER 13 Exploring with ⊚ Google Earth

To complete these problems, first read the chapter. When you are finished, go to LaunchPad and open the Exploring with Google Earth file for this chapter. Click on the "Workbook Problems" folder to "fly" to each of the problems listed below and answer the questions. Be sure to keep your "Borders and Labels" layer activated. Refer to Appendix 4 if you need help using Google Earth.

PROBLEM 13.1 This placemark highlights the Grand Canyon in northern Arizona.

1. **Judging by the structural details of the rocks provided by Google Earth, what type of rocks make up this location?**
   a. Intrusive igneous rocks   c. Sedimentary rocks
   b. Extrusive igneous rocks   d. Metamorphic rocks

PROBLEM 13.2 This placemark falls on the western coast of Central America. Activate the Plate Boundaries overlay in this folder to answer these questions. The pink boundary shown here is a region of subduction.

1. **What kind of mantle melting is occurring here?**
   a. The mantle is melting through flux melting because water is mixing with mantle material.
   b. The mantle is melting through decompression because this is a rift zone.
   c. The mantle is melting through decompression because plates are diverging here.
   d. The mantle is melting though decompression because this is a hot spot.

PROBLEM 13.3 Keep the Plate Boundaries overlay active to answer these questions. This placemark lands on western California.

1. **Is mantle material melting into magma at this location?**
   a. Yes   b. No

2. **Which of the following best describes this location?**
   a. Water is mixing with the subducting plate, causing flux melting.
   b. Mantle material is melting because it is decompressing.
   c. This area is not volcanically active.

PROBLEM 13.4 This placemark falls in southern Colorado on a linear landform.

1. **What is the name of this landform?**
   a. A dike   c. A batholith
   b. A sill   d. A laccolith

2. **How long is this feature?**
   a. 1 mi   c. 4 mi
   b. 2 mi   d. 8 mi

3. **Zoom out until you can see more of the mountain on which this feature occurs. Pan around. Note that there are many similar linear features. Which of the following best describes the geographic pattern of these features?**
   a. They radiate from a central point.
   b. They lie parallel to one another.
   c. They cross each other at right angles.
   d. They do not follow a pattern.

PROBLEM 13.5 This placemark falls in southern Colorado. Be sure the polygon in the folder for this problem is activated.

1. **Here you will see thousands of spots on the landscape. What type of resource extraction is occurring here?**
   a. Natural gas drilling and probably fracking
   b. Coal mining
   c. Salt mining
   d. Marble quarrying

2. **Double-click the polygon in this folder, or zoom out to 44 km eye altitude. You will see a polygon outlining the extent of this human activity. Take two measurements: First, measure the extent of this human activity from north to south, then from east to west. What is the approximate area in square miles that this land use occupies? (Multiply north-south distance by east-west distance to get square miles.)**
   a. 10 mi²   c. 500 mi²
   b. 100 mi²   d. 1,000 mi²

PROBLEM 13.6 This problem's placemark falls on an intensive type of mining.

1. **What natural resource is being extracted here?**
   a. Natural gas   c. Coal
   b. Salt   d. Fossils

2. **Based on your understanding of the rocks associated with this natural resource, what is the main rock type in this area?**
   a. Intrusive igneous rock   c. Sedimentary rock
   b. Extrusive igneous rock d. Metamorphic rock

PROBLEM 13.7 This problem's placemark falls on an intensive type of mining.

1. **What natural resource is being extracted here?**
   a. Natural gas   c. Coal
   b. Salt   d. Fossils

2. **About how long is this mine?**
   a. 1 mi   c. 8 mi
   b. 4 mi   d. 16 mi

PROBLEM 13.8 This placemark highlights the Makgadikgadi Pans, where water repeatedly fills a natural basin and evaporates.

1. **What type of sedimentary rock will form in this natural basin?**
   a. Clastic sedimentary rock
   b. Organic sedimentary rock
   c. Chemical sedimentary rock

2. **What type of mining would most likely be found here?**
   a. Natural gas extraction c. Coal mining
   b. Salt mining   d. Petroleum extraction

3. **What is the diameter of this feature?**
   a. 55 km   c. 160 km
   b. 100 km   d. 300 km

4. **Zoom out. What country is this?**
   a. Botswana   c. Swaziland
   b. South Africa   d. Namibia

CHAPTER 13 Study Guide

Focus Points

13.1 Minerals and Rocks: Building Earth's Crust

Composition of rocks: Almost all rocks are composed of one or more minerals.

Rock families: All rocks can be grouped into the igneous, sedimentary, and metamorphic rock families.

The rock cycle: Rocks are formed, transformed, and recycled into the mantle through the rock cycle.

13.2 Cooling the Inferno: Igneous Rocks

Melting: Mantle material melts into magma by means of decompression melting and flux melting.

Tectonic settings: Igneous rocks form in hot spots, mid-ocean ridges, rift valleys, and subduction zones.

Intrusive igneous rocks: Intrusive igneous rocks cool slowly, allowing time for the growth of crystals.

Extrusive igneous rocks: Extrusive igneous rocks cool relatively quickly and have smaller or no crystals.

13.3 Layers of Time: Sedimentary Rocks

Prevalence of sedimentary rocks: Sedimentary rocks cover 75% of the crust's surface, but they make up only 4% of the crust.

Sedimentary rock types: The three types of sedimentary rocks are clastic, organic, and chemical sedimentary rocks.

Coal: Coal is widely used as an energy source, but its mining can cause environmental problems.

Evaporites: Evaporites are an economically important type of chemical sedimentary rock.

Sedimentary rocks and Earth history: Fossils in sedimentary rock reveal ancient life and ancient environments on Earth.

13.4 Pressure and Heat: Metamorphic Rocks

Metamorphism: Rock of any type can experience metamorphism if it is heated, subjected to high pressures, or both.

Tectonic settings of metamorphism: Most metamorphism occurs at convergent plate boundaries.

13.5 Geographic Perspectives: Fracking for Shale Gas

Fracking and fuel supply: In 2000, shale gas provided about 1% of the U.S. natural gas supply. This number is expected to rise to 50% by 2035.

Pros and cons: The hydraulic fracturing (fracking) technique of extracting natural gas from shale has both positive and negative results.

Key Terms

batholith, 423
cementation, 422
chemical sedimentary
    rock, 426
clastic sedimentary rock, 426
coal, 428
crystallization, 419
decompression melting, 422
dike, 423
evaporite, 430
exhumation, 423
extrusive igneous rock, 423
flux melting, 423
fossil, 431
fracking, 434
igneous rock, 421
intrusive igneous rock, 423
laccolith, 423

limestone, 426
lithification, 422
metamorphic rock, 421
mineral, 419
organic sedimentary
    rock, 426
outcrop, 421
peat, 428
pluton, 423
protolith, 432
rock, 421
rock cycle, 421
sandstone, 426
sediment, 421
sedimentary rock, 421
shale, 426
sill, 423

Concept Review

The Human Sphere: People and Rocks

1. What roles have Earth materials played in human history?

13.1 Minerals and Rocks: Building Earth's Crust

2. What is a mineral?

3. What are the four mineral classes? Which is most common?

4. What are rocks composed of? In what two ways are rocks held together?

5. How is bedrock different from an outcrop? Where are outcrops found?

6. Within the context of the rock cycle, compare igneous, sedimentary, and metamorphic rocks.

7. Through what process are rocks recycled into the mantle?

8. Where does the energy needed to drive the rock cycle come from?

9. How does plate tectonics relate to the rock cycle?

13.2 Cooling the Inferno: Igneous Rocks

10. Describe the tectonic settings in which igneous rocks form.

11. In what two ways does mantle material melt into magma in the crust?

12. Give examples of igneous rock formations found beneath the surface. How are these subsurface features exposed at the surface through geologic time?

13. What is an igneous rock? How is an intrusive igneous rock different from an extrusive igneous rock?

14. Provide examples of igneous rock types.

15. Compare phaneritic igneous rocks with aphanitic igneous rocks with respect to where each forms. Give examples of each.

16. Compare felsic igneous rocks with mafic igneous rocks with respect to their silica content.

13.3 Layers of Time: Sedimentary Rocks

17. What is a sedimentary rock? How are sedimentary rocks formed?

18. What percentage of Earth's crust is sedimentary rock? What percentage of the exposed crust is sedimentary rock?

19. Compare clastic, organic, and chemical sedimentary rocks in terms of how each is formed.

20. Give examples of depositional environments where sedimentary rocks form.

21. Provide examples of sedimentary rock types.

22. What kind of rock is coal? Describe how it forms. Describe petroleum and natural gas in the context of their importance to people.

23. What is mountaintop removal mining? Where is it practiced? How is it environmentally destructive?

24. How is salt formed? What kind of sedimentary rock is salt?

25. What are fossils? What information do fossils give us about Earth's history and life?

13.4 Pressure and Heat: Metamorphic Rocks

26. What is metamorphism? Give two tectonic environments in which metamorphism occurs.

27. What are the two categories of metamorphic rocks? How do they differ in appearance?

28. What is a metamorphic rock protolith? Give examples.

29. Give several examples of metamorphic rocks.

13.5 Geographic Perspectives: Fracking for Shale Gas

30. What is fracking? What does this term stand for? Describe the steps in the technique of fracking.

31. What are the roles of water and chemicals in this procedure?

32. As of 2012, how many oil and gas wells were in use in the United States? What are the projected trends for use of shale gas in the coming decades?

33. What is fracking fluid, and why is it contaminated with toxins and radioactivity?

34. Give the pros and cons of fracking.

Critical-Thinking Questions

1. Using only your own knowledge, draw a mental map connecting your house or campus to the nearest outcrop of rock.

2. Do all rocks, those of the oceans and those of the continents, experience recycling in the rock cycle? Explain.

3. Without exhumation, would we be able to find metamorphic rocks at Earth's surface? Explain.

4. How do shale and coal relate to climate change?

5. Weigh the pros and cons of fracking. If it were proposed for the region where you live, do you think you would support it or oppose it? If it is already going on in your region, do you think it has had a positive or a negative influence on that region?

Test Yourself

Take this quiz to test your chapter knowledge.

1. True or false? An outcrop is exposed bedrock.

2. True or false? If Earth's interior were cold, there would be no rock cycle.

3. True or false? Most of Earth's crust is composed of sedimentary rocks.

4. True or false? Clay lithifies into shale.

5. True or false? Sandstone is an example of an organic sedimentary rock.

6. Multiple choice: Which of the following rocks requires great heating and compression to form?
a. Marble
b. Sandstone
c. Granite
d. Shale

7. Multiple choice: Which of the following is the most common sedimentary rock type?
a. Limestone
b. Sandstone
c. Shale
d. Coal

8. Multiple choice: Which of the following is not an intrusive igneous feature?
a. A batholith
b. A dike
c. A sill
d. A fossil

9. Fill in the blank: _____ is the removal of overlying material through erosion to expose igneous rock formations.

10. Fill in the blank: The process of turning sediments into rock is called _____.

Picture This. YOUR TURN

Rock Identification

Identify the major rock types pictured below. Write the answer in the space provided. Choose from the following list of terms and use each term only once.

1. Coal
2. Extrusive igneous rock
3. Gneiss
4. Granite
5. Marble
6. Sandstone

> This rock cools directly from lava.

> This rock forms under great heat and pressure and has a banded structure.

> This rock forms layers and is composed of cemented sediments.

> This rock cools deep within the ground directly from magma.

> This is an organic sedimentary rock.

> This rock has formed under great heat and pressure. Its protolith is limestone.

(From top left: © Stocktrek Images/Getty Images; © Siim Sepp/Alamy; Bruce Gervais; © Siim Sepp/Shutterstock.com; © Li Jingwang/E+/Getty Images; © Grant Faint/ Photographer's Choice RF/Getty Images)

Further Reading

1. Hughes, David. "Energy: A Reality Check on the Shale Revolution." *Nature* 494 (2013): 307-308.

2. iLoveMountains.org. *The Human Cost of Coal: Mountaintop Removal's Effect on Health and the Economy*. Accessed March 16, 2013. http://ilovemountains.org/the-human-cost.

3. Pellant, Chris. *Smithsonian Handbooks: Rocks and Minerals*. Washington, D.C.: Dorling Kindersley, 2002.

Answers to Living Physical Geography Questions

1. **Why is ice classified as a mineral?** Ice meets all the criteria for being a mineral: It is solid, crystalline, naturally occurring, and has a uniform chemical composition.

2. **How are rocks formed?** Rocks are formed from cooled magma or lava, from sediments that are cemented and compacted together, or from preexisting rocks that are heated and compressed under tremendous pressures.

3. **What is coal?** Coal is a rock formed from the remains of terrestrial forests that grew 300 million years ago or more.

4. **What is fracking and why is it controversial?** Fracking is a method used to extract natural gas from shale. Proponents argue that it produces clean energy, while opponents argue that it pollutes water and air.

14 GEOHAZARDS: Volcanoes and Earthquakes

Chapter Outline

Mount Nyiragongo is a volcano located in Virunga National Park in the Democratic Republic of the Congo. Mount Nyiragongo has a molten lake of lava in the crater of its summit, obscured here by steam. Nyiragongo's lava is unusually runny, flowing downslope at speeds up to 100 km/h (62 mph). The volcano has twice sent lava streams down into nearby villages and into the city of Goma. (© Last Refuge/Robert Harding Picture Library/Age Fotostock Inc.)

LIVING PHYSICAL GEOGRAPHY

> What is a tsunami?

> Why do some volcanoes explode violently?

> What causes earthquakes?

> What was the "Year without a Summer"?

To learn more about this type of volcano, turn to Section 14.1.

THE BIG PICTURE *Earth's hot interior and its moving crust create volcanoes and earthquakes. These phenomena shape the surface of the crust and present hazards for people.*

LEARNING GOALS *After reading this chapter, you will be able to:*

14.1 ◎ Describe three main types of volcanoes and major landforms associated with each.

14.2 ◎ Explain the hazards volcanoes pose and which geographic areas are most at risk.

14.3 ◎ Explain what causes earthquakes.

14.4 ◎ Describe the types of seismic waves produced by earthquakes, how earthquakes are ranked, and what can be done to reduce our vulnerability to earthquakes.

14.5 ◎ Assess the potential links between large volcanic eruptions, Earth's physical systems, and people.

THE HUMAN SPHERE: Deadly Ocean Waves

tsunami
A large ocean wave triggered by an earthquake or other natural disturbance.

geohazard
A hazard posed to people by the physical Earth.

JUST BEFORE 8:00 A.M. ON DECEMBER 26, 2004, the seafloor off the coast of the island of Sumatra, in Indonesia, was thrust upward 5 m (16 ft) in a magnitude 9.1 earthquake. This earthquake was the third strongest in recorded history. The movement of the seafloor heaved an estimated 30 km^3 (7.2 mi^3) of seawater upward, creating a series of waves that radiated across the Indian Ocean. Such large ocean waves triggered by an earthquake or other natural disturbance of the ocean floor are called **tsunamis**.

In the open ocean, the waves traveled at nearly the speed of a jetliner (800 km/h or 500 mph), but they went largely undetected because they had a wavelength (the distance between wave crests) of hundreds of kilometers. Thus, the thousands of boats in the Indian Ocean did not detect the waves as they passed underneath.

> What is a tsunami?*

As the waves approached shallow water, however, the wavelengths decreased and the height of the waves grew up to 15 m (50 ft) high in some regions. Some coastal areas even experienced 30 m (100 ft) waves. The waves devastated coastal areas along the Indian Ocean, particularly in regions nearest the earthquake. Most of the city of Banda Aceh, on Sumatra (Figure 14.1), was destroyed.

In response to this catastrophe, the Indian Ocean Tsunami Warning System, similar to one already active in the Pacific Ocean, was developed and activated in June of 2006. Cell-phone users can access a free app that is connected to the detection system and provides real-time data and warnings. It is hoped that with this system in place, another catastrophic loss of life can be avoided.

This chapter focuses on geologic hazards, or **geohazards**: hazards presented to people by the physical Earth. Examples of geohazards include volcanic eruptions, earthquakes, and tsunamis. We first examine volcano types as well as the behavior of volcanoes and the hazards they present. We next explore earthquakes and the dangers they pose for people. Finally, we take a look at the global reach of large volcanic eruptions and their effects on human societies.

FIGURE 14.1 **Banda Aceh.** *A French military helicopter surveys the destruction in Banda Aceh, Indonesia, on January 14, 2005. The 2004 tsunami surged across the crowded city at about 60 km/h (35 mph), far faster than a person can run. About 170,000 people died in Banda Aceh on the day of the tsunami. (© Joel Saget/ AFP/Getty Images)*

14.1 About Volcanoes

◎ **Describe three main types of volcanoes and major landforms associated with each.**

Volcanoes shape Earth's crust. They can pour cubic kilometers of lava onto Earth's surface to build new islands and landmasses. They form beautiful snow-capped peaks that have inspired humans for generations, and they provide nutrient-rich soils that plants thrive in. Volcanoes can also be extremely dangerous and cause catastrophic loss of human life.

Active volcanoes—those that have erupted in the last 10,000 years and could erupt again—pose the greatest danger to human life. Volcanoes that have not erupted for 10,000 years or more, but could awaken again, are considered *dormant* or *inactive*. An **extinct volcano** is one that has not erupted for tens of thousands of years and can never erupt again.

Three Types of Volcanoes

Volcanoes are surface landforms created by accumulations of the materials they emit over time. Although they take on many shapes and sizes, most volcanoes can be categorized as either stratovolcanoes, shield volcanoes, or cinder cones.

A **stratovolcano**, or *composite volcano*, is a large, potentially explosive, cone-shaped volcano composed of alternating layers of lava and pyroclasts. **Pyroclasts**, or *pyroclastic materials*, encompass any fragmented solid material that is ejected from a volcano. Pyroclasts range in size from **ash**—pulverized rock particles and solidified droplets of lava that form a fine powder—to large boulders. Stratovolcanoes are the most conspicuous type of volcano. Their cones can tower over landscapes, as shown in **Figure 14.2**.

A **shield volcano** is a broad, domed volcano formed from many layers of fluid basaltic lava

active volcano
A volcano that has erupted during the last 10,000 years and is likely to erupt again.

extinct volcano
A volcano that has not erupted for tens of thousands of years and can never erupt again.

stratovolcano
(or *composite volcano*) A large, potentially explosive cone-shaped volcano composed of alternating layers of lava and pyroclast.

pyroclast
(or *pyroclastic materials*) Any fragment of solid material that is ejected from a volcano, ranging in size from ash to large boulders.

ash (volcanic)
Fine volcanic powder consisting of pulverized rock particles and solidified droplets of lava.

shield volcano
A broad, domed volcano formed from many layers of basaltic lava.

FIGURE 14.2 **A stratovolcano: Mount Fuji.** *(A) The interior structure of a stratovolcano consists of a central vent, surrounded by alternating layers of lava flows and pyroclasts. The solidified lava holds the pyroclastic material together, allowing stratovolcanoes to develop steep slopes. Magma travels up from the reservoir (magma chamber) beneath the volcano through the vent, and to the summit crater. (B) Mount Fuji, an active stratovolcano, has a symmetrical conical profile typical of stratovolcanoes. It reaches a height of 3,775 m (12,387 ft). (B. © Takeshi.K/Flickr/Getty Images)*

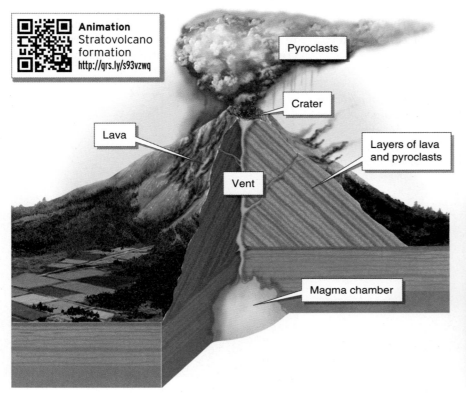

Animation
Stratovolcano formation
http://qrs.ly/s93vzwq

Pyroclasts

Crater

Lava

Layers of lava and pyroclasts

Vent

Magma chamber

A

Mongolia   Russia
China   SEA OF JAPAN
Mount Fuji, Japan
Taiwan

B

FIGURE 14.3 **Shield volcanoes: Hawai'i.** *(A) Shield volcanoes are built of layers of basaltic lava flows. There are no alternating layers of pyroclasts like those found in stratovolcanoes. (B) Mauna Kea, on Hawai'i, has a typical shield volcano profile. The island of Hawai'i, formed on a hot spot (see Section 12.4), is made up of five shield volcanoes that have joined together. Mauna Kea is the highest, standing at 4,207 m (13,803 ft). (B. © Peter French/Design Pics/Corbis)*

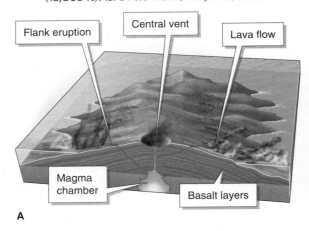

A   B

cinder cone
A small, cone-shaped volcano consisting of pyroclasts that settle at the angle of repose.

angle of repose
The steepest angle at which loose sediments can settle.

(Figure 14.3). Shield volcanoes are much larger than stratovolcanoes. In fact, they are so large that they can be difficult to identify as volcanoes from the ground. Instead, they look like a broad, gently sloped horizon.

Cinder cones are small, cone-shaped volcanoes consisting of pyroclasts that settle at the **angle of repose**: the steepest angle at which loose sediments can settle. The steepness of the slope of a cinder cone ranges from 25 to 35 degrees, depending on the size of the pyroclasts that were ejected during their formation. Cinder cones can form in any volcanic setting, but particularly on the flanks or at the bases of stratovolcanoes and shield volcanoes.

Most cinder cones are less than 400 m (1,300 ft) high, and are roughly symmetrical. Many cinder cones erupt for a few decades or less, then become extinct. Structurally, cinder cones are the simplest of the three types of volcanoes, as illustrated in **Figure 14.4**.

Cinder cones are the smallest type of volcano. **Figure 14.5** illustrates and compares the differences in the extents of the three volcano types.

What Do Volcanoes Make?

Active stratovolcanoes and shield volcanoes make and eject a variety of physical materials, ranging in size from fine ash to large boulders, and they create landforms from small volcanic craters to vast

FIGURE 14.4 **Cinder cone, Kenya.** *(A) Cinder cones consist of pyroclastic material that has settled out in a cone near a volcanic vent. The larger, heavier material settles close, and the smaller, lighter material settles farther away. (B) The southern end of Lake Turkana in Kenya has several cinder cones. This one is 1 km (0.6 mi) in diameter, 220 m (700 ft) tall, and has a 187 m (600 ft) deep crater. (B. © Gallo Images/Richard du Toit/Alamy)*

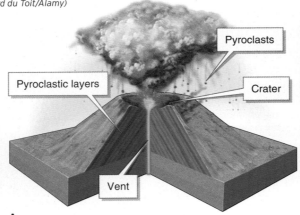

A   B

FIGURE 14.5 **Volcano sizes.** *A typical cinder cone, Mount Fuji, and the Big Island of Hawai'i (composed of five fused shield volcanoes) are drawn to scale to show their relative sizes. Much of Hawai'i is submerged beneath the ocean, so the immense size of its shield volcanoes is hidden.*

Sea level

Cinder cone   Fuji–stratovolcano   Hawai'i–shield volcano   No vertical exaggeration

0 5 10 km
0 5 10 mi

lava fields. Here we discuss three categories of volcanic products: lavas, pyroclasts and gases, and volcanic landforms.

Molten Rock: Lava

Lava is one of the most conspicuous products of volcanic activity. Lava comes only from volcanoes or volcanic *fissures* in the ground. Lava flows range from fast-moving sheets of basaltic lava to blocky, glowing boulders that slowly push and tumble across a landscape. Lava also forms cohesive masses of molten rock thick enough to plug a volcanic vent.

The thickness of a material is called its *viscosity*. The higher a material's viscosity, the more resistant it is to flowing. The viscosity of lava is controlled by many factors, including its temperature, gas content, crystal content, and silica (SiO_2) content. Silica plays an important role in determining lava viscosity because it forms long chains of molecules that bind the lava together.

Three types of lava can be classified according to their silica content and temperature: mafic, intermediate, and felsic. Mafic lava has a temperature of about 1,000°C to 1,200°C (1,800°F to 2,200°F), has a silica content of 50% or less, has a low viscosity, and flows easily. Mafic lava builds shield volcanoes. When mafic lava solidifies into smooth, billowy lobes over the surface, it is called **pāhoehoe (Figure 14.6A)**. When it takes on a blocky, rough surface, it is called **'a'ā**.

Intermediate lava has a temperature of about 800°C to 1,000°C (1,500°F to 1,800°F), a silica content between 50% and 70%, and a medium viscosity **(Figure 14.6B)**. Andesitic lava, often called *blocky* lava because of its blocky texture as it moves downslope, is one type of intermediate lava. Stratovolcanoes are composed mostly of intermediate lava and felsic lava.

Of the three lava types, *felsic lava* has the coolest temperature, at about 650°C to 800°C (1,200°F to 1,500°F), and the highest silica content, 70% or more. Its resulting high viscosity restricts its ability to flow. *Plug domes*, which may block volcanic vents, are composed of viscous felsic lava **(Figure 14.6C)**.

pāhoehoe
(pronounced pa-HOY-hoy) A lava flow with low viscosity and a smooth, glassy, or ropy surface.

'a'ā
(pronounced AH-ah) A mafic lava flow with a rough, blocky surface.

FIGURE 14.6 **Three types of lava.** *(A) Mafic lava has a low viscosity and flows in streams or sheets downslope. This volcanologist (a scientist who studies volcanoes) is sampling pāhoehoe in Hawai'i Volcanoes National Park, on the island of Hawai'i. (B) Intermediate lava is more viscous than mafic lava and resists movement. This photo shows the blocky consistency of intermediate lava on Mount Etna, Sicily. (C) Thick, felsic lava has formed a plug dome in the volcanic vent of Mount St. Helens.*
(Top, © David R. Frazier/Science Source; center, © Tom Pfeiffer/www.volcanodiscovery.com; bottom, USGS/photo by John S. Pallister)

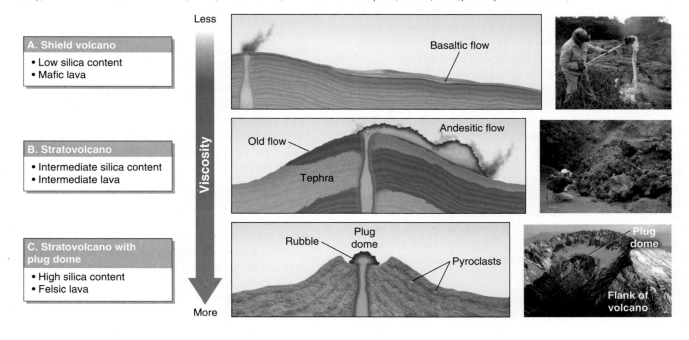

Less

Viscosity

More

A. Shield volcano
• Low silica content
• Mafic lava

B. Stratovolcano
• Intermediate silica content
• Intermediate lava

C. Stratovolcano with plug dome
• High silica content
• Felsic lava

Basaltic flow

Andesitic flow
Old flow
Tephra

Rubble   Plug dome
Pyroclasts

Plug dome
Flank of volcano

FIGURE 14.7 **Mafic lava formations.** *(A) This lava lake is on Erta Ale volcano, in the Danakil depression in Ethiopia, one of only five volcanoes in the world that have a persistent lava lake. (B) Mafic lava erupted beneath the ocean forms pillow lava. Seawater quickly cools the lava, and as a result, it takes a rounded form resembling pillows (illustrated in the inset). West Mata volcano, shown in the photo, was discovered in May 2009. It is about 1,200 m (4,000 ft) underwater, some 200 km (125 mi) southwest of Samoa in the Pacific Ocean. (A. © Dr. Juerg Alean/Science Source; B. NOAA/NSF)*

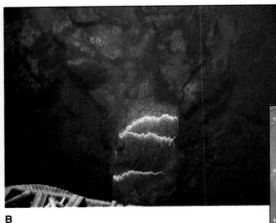

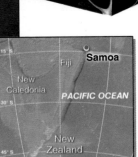

A   B

What determines the amount of silica in magma? Two main factors determine its silica content: the makeup of the solid mantle material from which the magma first melted and the type of rock the magma passes through on its way to the surface of the crust. For example, as magma migrates through granitic crust in a subduction zone, it will partially melt the surrounding granite through which it is passing (see Section 13.2). Granite is high in silica and will be mixed into the magma, creating a felsic magma. On the other hand, magma migrating up through basaltic oceanic crust, as it does at a hot spot, becomes mafic lava that spills from a volcano. Mafic lava forms many spectacular lava features, two of which are shown in **Figure 14.7**.

Mafic lava that erupts beneath the ocean forms rounded *pillow lava* (Figure 14.7B). Because most volcanic activity on Earth occurs at divergent plate boundaries along mid-ocean ridges, pillow lavas are the most geographically widespread but least seen lava formations. In time, pillow-lava accumulations can grow to considerable size and even form new islands. The formation of the Hawaiian Islands began with pillow lava.

Blown into the Air: Pyroclasts and Gases

Explosive volcanic eruptions produce pyroclasts with a wide range of sizes, shapes, and consistencies. Some common types of pyroclasts are described here.

Volcanic ash: Volcanic eruptions can spray droplets of lava high into the air, which solidify as they cool.

In powerful explosive eruptions, existing rock from the volcano can also be pulverized into a fine powder and ejected into the atmosphere. These materials constitute volcanic ash, which is very fine-grained and soft to the touch.

Lapilli and pumice: Two other types of pyroclasts are lapilli and pumice. Both are formed from intermediate and felsic lava. **Lapilli** are marble- to golf ball–sized cooled fragments of lava **(Figure 14.8A)**. **Pumice** is a lightweight, porous rock with at least 50% air content. It is formed from silica-rich lava that is frothy with gas bubbles. The air spaces that the bubbles occupied are preserved as the lava hardens. Pumice can be as small as lapilli or as large as boulders **(Figure 14.8B)**. It floats on water, and island volcanoes sometimes disgorge large amounts of pumice into the oceans, forming *pumice rafts*.

Volcanic bombs and blocks: A volcanic **bomb** is a streamlined fragment of lava ejected from a volcano that cooled and hardened as it was still moving through the air. A volcanic **block** is a fragment of rock from the volcano's cone that is ejected during an explosive eruption **(Figure 14.9)**.

Volcanic gases: By volume, about 8% of most magma is gas. Gas is not a pyroclastic material, but gas emissions produce pyroclasts. **As gas forcefully exits a volcano, it blasts lava and rock debris into the air, generating pyroclasts.** Gas in magma expands as the magma migrates toward the surface of the crust, where there is less pressure. At the surface, the gases in magma expand rapidly, creating an explosion.

lapilli
(pronounced la-PILL-eye)
Marble- to golf ball–sized cooled fragments of lava.

pumice
A lightweight, porous rock with at least 50% air content, formed from felsic lava.

bomb (volcanic)
A streamlined fragment of lava ejected from a volcano that cooled and hardened as it moved through the air.

block (volcanic)
A fragment of rock from the volcano's cone that is ejected during an explosive eruption.

FIGURE **14.8** **Lapilli and pumice.** *(A) These small pebbles, shown in the top photo, are lapilli formed by an eruption on the flank of Darwin Volcano on the Galápagos Islands. The lower photo shows a polished cross section of a lapillus. The rings were formed as the rock traveled through the air and molten debris stuck to it, much like a hailstone grows in a thunderstorm. (B) This man easily lifts a large, air-filled pumice boulder near Mono Lake, California. (A. © David K. Lynch; B. Courtesy of Richard Nolthenius, Cabrillo College)*

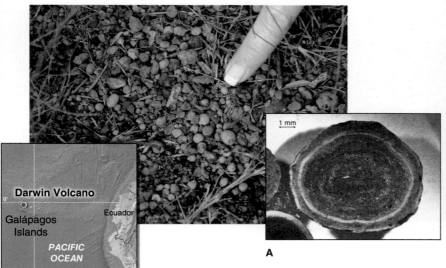

A

B

Aside from their role in generating pyroclasts, volcanic gases are not usually lethal to people. The main gases emitted by volcanoes are water vapor, carbon dioxide, sulfur dioxide, and hydrogen sulfide (H_2O, CO_2, SO_2, and H_2S). Where volcanic gases are concentrated, however, they can be lethal. An example of this occurred near Lake Nyos, in Cameroon, in western Africa, in 1986. Lake Nyos is located on an inactive volcano. A magma chamber below the lake leaks CO_2 into the lake. Occasionally, the CO_2 is released from the lake in a sudden *outgassing* event. In August 1986, the lake is thought to have emitted about 1.6 million tons of CO_2, suffocating 1,700 people and 3,500 head of livestock.

FIGURE **14.9** **Bombs and blocks.** *(A) This volcanic bomb was found in the Pinacate Volcanic Field in northwestern Sonora, Mexico. Its typical streamlined shape is the result of airflow around it as it cooled in flight. (B) The flanks of Licancabur volcano, near the town of San Pedro de Atacama in central Chile, are littered with blocks that once made up the volcano, but were torn from it during an eruption. (A. © Peter L. Kresan; B. © Paul Harris/AWL Images/Getty Images)*

A B

FIGURE 14.10 **Columnar jointing.** *This photo shows a small portion of the island of Staffa, in the Inner Hebrides of northwestern Scotland. Most of Staffa is composed of mafic lava that slowly cooled 55 million years ago, allowing time for columnar jointing to form. Here, the joints mainly sit perpendicular to the cooling surface.*
(© Photo by Lady of the Dawn/Flickr Open/Getty Images)

FIGURE 14.11 **Large igneous provinces.**

All of these large igneous provinces were formed where mantle plumes formed geologic hot spots. Most of the eruptions that formed them caused global climate change, and some even caused global mass extinction events when they rapidly elevated atmospheric CO_2 levels.
(Left, © Peter L. Kresan; center, © Serguei Fomine/Global Look/ Corbis; right, © Tony Waltham/ Robert Harding/Getty Images)

Columbia Plateau

The Columbia Plateau formed from flood basalts. It is 500 m (1,640 ft) thick in places and covers some 220,000 km² (85,000 mi²).

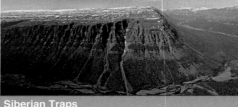

Siberian Traps

Flood basalts cover extensive areas of Siberia in central Eurasia. The word *trap* is derived from the Swedish word *trappa*, which means stairs, alluding to the stairlike appearance of flood basalts. The Siberian Traps are 250 million years old and cover about 2 million km² (770,000 mi²). They are 3,500 m (11,500 ft) thick in places.

Deccan Traps

Ellora Caves, in northwestern Maharashtra State, India, are a World Heritage Site. Ellora is one of hundreds of archaeological sites carved into the flood basalts of the Deccan Plateau of India, also called the Deccan Traps. The Deccan Traps cover 500,000 km² (200,000 mi²) and are more than 2,000 m (6,500 ft) thick. They were formed 68 million years ago.

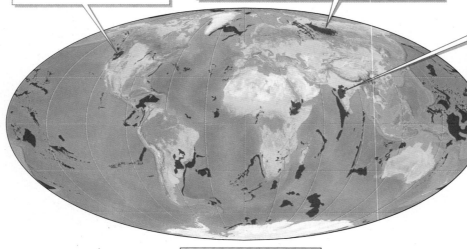

■ Large igneous province

FIGURE 14.12 **Quilotoa Caldera, Ecuador.** *(A) A caldera forms as a magma chamber empties and collapses. (B) A lake fills the caldera of Quilotoa in Ecuador. The caldera was formed about 8,000 years ago when a major volcanic eruption caused the collapse of the volcano's magma chamber. The caldera gradually filled with rainwater to form this caldera lake. The lake's greenish color is due to dissolved minerals in the water.* (B. © Hemis.fr/SuperStock)

Animation
Caldera formation
http://qrs.ly/zd3w00p

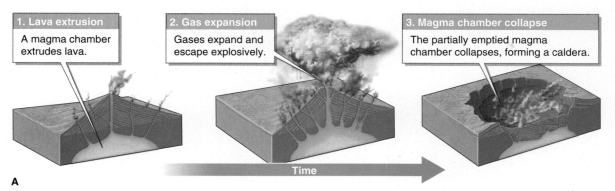

1. Lava extrusion
A magma chamber extrudes lava.

2. Gas expansion
Gases expand and escape explosively.

3. Magma chamber collapse
The partially emptied magma chamber collapses, forming a caldera.

Time

A

B

Honduras
Nicaragua
Panama
PACIFIC OCEAN
Colombia
Quilotoa Caldera, Ecuador

After the Lava Cools: Volcanic Landforms

Volcanic landforms are typically very conspicuous on Earth's surface. Some notable volcanic landforms, in addition to volcanic mountains, are columnar jointing, large igneous provinces, and calderas.

Columnar jointing: As basaltic lava cools and hardens into rock, cracks and weak planes in the rock, called **joints**, develop. A geometric jointing pattern called **columnar jointing**, shown in **Figure 14.10**, sometimes forms, in which angular columns result from joint formation in the lava during cooling.

Large igneous provinces: **Large igneous provinces (LIPs)** are accumulations of basaltic lava that cover extensive geographic areas. If you have ever driven through eastern Washington and Oregon, you drove over the Columbia Plateau. The rocks of the Columbia Plateau superficially resemble sedimentary rocks, but they are *flood basalts*, lava flows that poured onto the crust over several million years. The Columbia Plateau flows formed between 17 million and 6 million years ago and created a large igneous province. There are several dozen large igneous provinces around the world **(Figure 14.11)**.

Calderas: After an eruption, the emptied magma chamber can collapse, forming a large circular depression called a **caldera** (from the Spanish word for "cauldron"). The process of caldera formation is illustrated in **Figure 14.12**. Calderas can be many kilometers in diameter. They usually have flat bases and steep slopes. Calderas can be mistaken for meteor impact craters, but the two can be differentiated because each leaves different types of evidence **(Picture This**, page 452).

joint
A crack or weak plane in rock.

columnar jointing
A geometric pattern of angular columns that forms from joints in basaltic lava during cooling.

large igneous province (LIP)
An accumulation of flood basalts that covers an extensive geographic area.

caldera
A large depression that forms when a volcano's magma chamber empties and collapses after the volcano erupts.

Picture This

(© Randy Olson/National Geographic/Getty Images)

(© WaterFrame/Alamy)

O'ahu, Hawai'i

PACIFIC OCEAN

Wolf Creek Crater

AUSTRALIA

Which Is the Caldera?

One of these photos shows a volcanic caldera, and one shows an impact crater formed when a meteor struck Earth long ago. Based on the visual evidence from these photos, it is challenging to tell which is the impact crater and which is the caldera. More information is needed. One useful form of evidence is *shatter cone* rock. Meteors hit the planet with such force that the impact energy produces metamorphic shatter cones. Shatter cones are produced only at meteor impact sites. They are not visible in either of these photos.

Consider This

1. If you found a large crater-like landform in volcanic rock, could you be 100% certain that it is a caldera? Explain.

2. Note the geographic settings (see locator maps) for each landform. Based on your reading in this chapter and in Section 12.4, is there geographic information that could help you decide which landform is the caldera?

14.2 Pele's Power: Volcanic Hazards

◎ Explain the hazards volcanoes pose and which geographic areas are most at risk.

In Hawaiian myth, Pele is the volcano goddess. She is said to reside in the summit caldera of Kilauea on the island of Hawai'i. Pele embodies the many facets of volcanoes, ranging from life-sustaining benevolence to destructive malevolence. In this section, we turn to Pele's malevolent side and examine the main geohazards that volcanoes present.

Two Kinds of Eruptions: Effusive and Explosive

Shield volcanoes, such as those found on Hawai'i, present little threat to human life. Shield volcanoes have nonexplosive **effusive eruptions** that emit more lava than gases. Mafic lava from shield vol-

effusive eruption
A nonexplosive eruption that produces mostly lava.

canoes usually flows slowly downhill and can be avoided.

Stratovolcanoes, on the other hand, are potentially serious geohazards. Their eruptions are called *explosive eruptions*. An explosive eruption is violent and yields large amounts of pyroclasts. **Stratovolcanoes may produce effusive outpourings of mafic lava like shield volcanoes, but they are also capable of exploding violently with little warning.**

Explosive eruptions send rock, ash, and volcanic gases high into the troposphere, or even into the stratosphere. In the troposphere, rain washes the volcanic material out in a few days or weeks. There is no rainfall in the stratosphere, however, so once ash and sulfur gases enter the stratosphere, they can remain suspended there for five years or more. These materials can encircle the globe and cause climate cooling for a few years (see Section 6.2).

Large explosive eruptions result when gas-rich felsic magma migrates upward through the crust and encounters less pressure, which causes it to expand rapidly. Once the magma and gases begin expanding, the surrounding magma chamber is enlarged, allowing more gas to expand and further enlarge the magma chamber. This process can unfold over the course of minutes to hours and can result in a catastrophic explosive eruption.

> Why do some volcanoes explode violently?

Island volcanoes can become particularly explosive when seawater migrates into the magma chamber, as might occur after an earthquake. As water comes into contact with the intense heat, it turns to vapor and expands rapidly and explosively. Figure 14.13 shows an explosive volcanic eruption in which the force of the expanding gases and collapsing magma chamber sent ash billowing high into the atmosphere.

Ranking Volcanic Eruption Strength

The **volcanic explosivity index (VEI)** ranks volcanic eruption magnitude based on the amount of material a volcano ejects during an eruption. A VEI 5 eruption emits more than 1 km^3 (0.24 mi^3) of pyroclastic material into the atmosphere, and a VEI 6 eruption emits more than 10 km^3 (2.4 mi^3). During the last 10,000 years, there have been about 50 VEI 6 eruptions. The eruption of Tambora, described in Geographic Perspectives, was the only VEI 7 eruption in historic times. Figure 14.14 compares large historical eruptions to the colossal prehistoric eruption of the Yellowstone caldera, 640,000 years ago.

GEOGRAPHIC PERSPECTIVES

The Two Greatest Threats: Lahars and Pyroclastic Flows

Stratovolcanoes are among the most dangerous geohazards on the planet. Lava flows from these volcanoes are not their biggest threat because their lava usually flows slowly, so people can escape. The two greatest volcanic hazards are lahars and pyroclastic flows. Together, they account for about half of the volcano-related deaths in any given year.

Torrents of Mud: Lahars

A **lahar** (a Javanese word that means "mudflow" or "debris flow") is a mudflow that results when a snow-capped stratovolcano erupts. A lahar is a thick slurry of mud, ash, water, and other debris that moves rapidly down the volcano's flank. Lahars can travel tens of kilometers down the slopes of

FIGURE 14.13 Volcanic ash cloud. *This photo of the Soufrière Hills volcano on the island of Montserrat, in the Caribbean Sea, was taken on March 24, 2010, by a passenger on a commercial aircraft. The magma chamber of the volcano collapsed and sent ash 12,500 m (40,000 ft) into the atmosphere.* (© Mary Jo Penkala/Solent News & Photo/Sipa Press/Newscom)

FIGURE 14.14 The volcanic explosivity index. *The eruption of Mount St. Helens in 1980 emitted about 1 km³ of pulverized rock and volcanic ash into the atmosphere. In contrast, the most recent major Yellowstone eruption occurred about 640,000 years ago and ejected 1,000 times more material.*

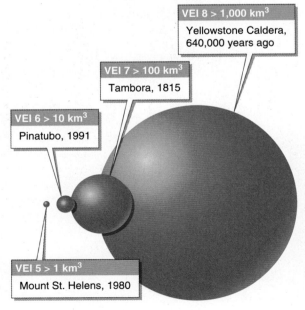

VEI 8 > 1,000 km³
Yellowstone Caldera, 640,000 years ago

VEI 7 > 100 km³
Tambora, 1815

VEI 6 > 10 km³
Pinatubo, 1991

VEI 5 > 1 km³
Mount St. Helens, 1980

volcanic explosivity index (VEI)
An index used to rank volcanic eruptions based on the amount of material a volcano ejects during an eruption.

lahar
A thick slurry of mud, ash, water, and other debris that flows rapidly down a snow-capped stratovolcano when it erupts.

pyroclastic flow
(or *nuée ardente*) A rapidly moving avalanche of searing hot gas and ash.

Soufrière Hills volcano, Montserrat

Volcanic vent

Hardened ash and mud

FIGURE 14.15 **A lahar.** *Plymouth, Montserrat, was destroyed by a lahar from the Soufrière Hills volcano in August 1997. This 2010 photo shows the town buried in 12 m (39 ft) of ash and mud, with the volcano steaming in the background. Plymouth was evacuated just before the 1997 eruption, then abandoned after it was buried. The Soufrière Hills volcano continues to be very active today, routinely forcing evacuations from the southern part of the island.*
(© Bernhard Edmaier/Science Source)

volcanoes and into the flatlands below, where people may reside. Lahars are not hot. Their danger lies in the fact that they move quickly and can engulf whole villages in minutes. **Figure 14.15** shows a lahar that engulfed Plymouth, the former capital city of Montserrat, an island in the Caribbean Sea.

Blazing Clouds: Pyroclastic Flows

Pyroclastic flows (also called *nuées ardentes*, meaning "blazing clouds") are rapidly moving avalanches of gas and ash. Pyroclastic flows are one of the greatest volcanic hazards because they can travel at speeds up to 700 km/h (450 mph) and they can be as hot as 500°C (930°F). At night, these avalanches can glow orange from their intense heat. The largest flows can travel hundreds of kilometers from the volcanic vent. **Figure 14.16** shows a pyroclastic flow on Mount Merapi in Indonesia.

Lahars and pyroclastic flows are by far the most significant geohazards volcanoes present, but they are not the only ones. Volcanoes can also produce large earthquakes, dangerous lava flows, and smothering ashfalls. **Picture This** explores an unusual and unfortunate volcanic event that happened in Italy many centuries ago.

FIGURE 14.16 **Pyroclastic flows.** *Mount Merapi, on the island of Java, is the most active volcano in Indonesia. A pyroclastic flow roils down the volcano in this relatively minor November 2, 2010, eruption.*
(© Beawiharta/Reuters/Landov)

Indonesia

Mount Merapi, Java

Picture This

(© Bettmann/CORBIS)

The Pompeii Disaster

In 79 CE, on the morning of August 24, a series of earthquakes shook the region near the Italian city of Pompeii. At about 1:00 p.m., a menacing black ash cloud billowed up 25 km (15 mi) and shrouded Pompeii (and the nearby city of Herculaneum) in blackness. Eruptions continued for a week. As many as 16,000 people may have died, crushed under the weight of ash as rooftops collapsed or asphyxiated as they were buried alive. The town was entombed beneath 6 m (18 ft) of ash.

In 1749, mysterious terra cotta roof tiles were found beneath farm fields where a canal was being dug, hinting at a lost city beneath. It was not until the late 1880s that archaeologists began to excavate the ash to reveal the ruins of Pompeii beneath. As they were digging, they found many mysterious cavities in the ash. When these cavities were injected with plaster, shapes of people were revealed.

Mount Vesuvius, which was responsible for the destruction of Pompeii, is still alive and active. It last erupted for a period of 31 years, from 1913 to 1944. Since then, it has been silent. Fully aware of the risk posed by the volcano, the Italian government has offered up to 30,000 euros (US$40,000) to each of the 500,000 people living in the "red zone" of the volcano (the area of greatest hazard) to move farther away. Most have declined this offer.

Consider This

1. When did Mount Vesuvius last erupt? How do you think the number of people living around the volcano then compares with the local population today?
2. If given the opportunity, would you live in the red zone of Vesuvius or another such risky zone? Explain.

Can Scientists Predict Volcanic Eruptions?

Because volcanoes can be such a serious geohazard, predicting their eruptions would save many lives. Scientists can sometimes predict an eruption within weeks or months if a volcano gives warning signs. The monitoring of Mount St. Helens, in Washington State, is a good example of the process of monitoring warning signs and successfully anticipating an eruption, as illustrated in **Figure 14.17**.

FIGURE 14.17 **SCIENTIFIC INQUIRY: Can scientists predict dangerous volcanic eruptions?** *Careful monitoring of Mount St. Helens allowed scientists to predict its eruption in 1980 and warn people to get out of harm's way. Changes in the gases emitted by a volcano, widening cracks, swelling of the volcano's surface, and increasing earthquake activity can all be signs that magma is moving upward through the magma chamber. Given the growing body of data that pointed to an impending eruption, scientists urged local authorities to close the mountain to the public before the eruption, saving thousands of lives.* (1. USGS, photo by Thomas Casadevall; 2. U.S. Geological Survey, photo by Lyn Topinka; 3. U.S. Geological Survey, photo by Lyn Topinka; 4. U. S. Geological Survey, photo by P. W. Lipman; 5. U.S. Geological Survey, Volcano Hazards Program, photo by Mike Doukas)

1. Scientists take gas samples to understand how magma is moving beneath the ground.

2. Surface cracks are measured. Widening of cracks could indicate that magma is rising up through the magma chamber.

3. Seismic stations on the volcano measure earthquake activity.

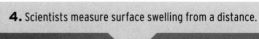

4. Scientists measure surface swelling from a distance.

5. The May 1980 eruption of Mount St. Helens was not a surprise. Scientists collected data and closely monitored the volcano before its eruption.

WA
Mount St. Helens
45° N
OR   ID   WY
NV   UT   CO
CA
AZ   NM
120° W

FIGURE 14.18 **Active stratovolcanoes in the Pacific Ring of Fire.** *The three stratovolcanoes shown here are a small sampling of the many active stratovolcanoes in the Pacific Ring of Fire. The eruption history of each volcano back to 1800 is shown with orange bars. The height of each bar represents that eruption's VEI category. Eruption data are provided by the Global Volcanism Program administered by the Smithsonian Institution. (Top, © Roger Ressmeyer/CORBIS; center, © Beawiharta/Reuters/Landov; bottom, © David Wall Photo/Lonely Planet/Getty Images)*

Volcán de Colima, Mexico

Volcán de Colima is one of Mexico's most active volcanoes. It generated a catastrophic VEI 5 eruption on January 17, 1913. Today, some 300,000 people live within about 40 km (25 mi) of the volcano, which puts them at risk in the event of another major eruption.

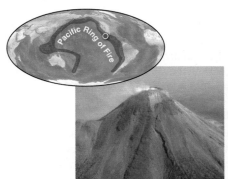

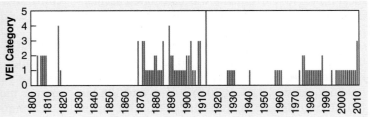

Mount Merapi, Indonesia

Mount Merapi is Indonesia's most active volcano. It has erupted almost continually over the last 450 years. Volcanic gases and steam can be seen at the summit almost every day of the year. Merapi produced a VEI 4 eruption in October 2010 that killed 150 people and displaced 320,000. A mandatory government evacuation order just before the eruption averted what would have been a catastrophic loss of life.

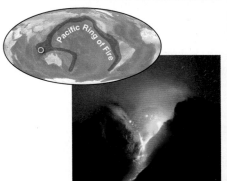

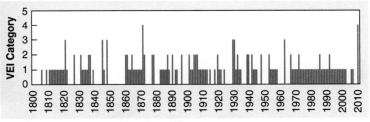

Whakaari/White Island, New Zealand

Whakaari/White Island is New Zealand's most active volcano. Seventy-five percent of the volcano lies submerged in the ocean; only the peak (standing at 321 m or 1,053 ft above sea level) can be seen.

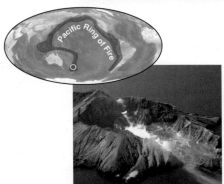

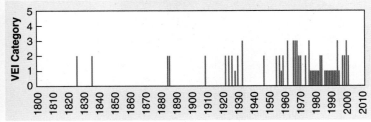

The Pacific Ring of Fire

Plate tectonic theory provides the framework to understand why volcanic landforms occur where they do. All volcanoes are found where the mantle is melted into magma, namely, at or near mid-ocean ridges (divergent plate boundaries), subduction zones (convergent plate boundaries), continental rifts, and hot spots (see Sections 12.3 and 12.4).

More than 60% of the Pacific Ocean's margins, totaling some 40,000 km (25,000 mi), are subduc-tion zones with active and dangerous stratovol-canoes. These volcanoes make up the Pacific Ring of Fire (see Section 12.3). **Although shield volcanoes are found in the Pacific Ring of Fire, explosive stratovolcanoes are the most common type of volcano there.** Many of them are dormant, but there are also many active and dangerous stratovolcanoes. **Figure 14.18** provides an eruption history for some of the more active stratovolcanoes in the Pacific Ring of Fire.

14.3 Tectonic Hazards: Faults and Earthquakes

◎ **Explain what causes earthquakes.**

On Friday, March 11, 2011, seismographs around the world began detecting one of the largest earthquakes in recorded history, now called the 2011 Tōhoku earthquake. The shaking began at 2:46 p.m. local time. The earthquake was calculated at magnitude 9.0, a colossal event. There are more than 1 million detectable earthquakes on the planet each year, and this single 9.0 event released more energy than all of the others combined. Only four other recorded earthquakes have been larger. The earthquake focus was 32 km (20 mi) deep and 128 km (80 mi) from Sendai, on the island of Honshu, Japan. The aftershocks that followed for weeks were as powerful as magnitude 7.2.

The damage caused by the earthquake and its aftershocks was made much worse by a tsunami that reduced the low-lying coastal regions in its path to ruins (see the Human Sphere section at the beginning of this chapter to learn about tsunamis). To make matters even worse, local nuclear power plants survived the shaking, but were not designed to be flooded by salt water. After they were flooded, they leaked radiation, which traveled across the Northern Hemisphere. Bringing the damaged nuclear plants under control and stopping radiation leaks have been among the greatest challenges brought by this earthquake. As of 2014, radiation continues to leak from the Fukushima Daiichi nuclear power plant into the Pacific Ocean.

Faulting and Earthquakes

Although usually less noticeable than volcanic hazards, earthquakes are as dangerous as volcanoes, or even more so. The 2011 Tōhoku earthquake, like all earthquakes, occurred when Earth's crust broke along a geologic fault, which is a fracture in the crust where movement and earthquakes occur (see Section 12.4).

Most earthquakes are too small to be felt by people. Only seismographs can detect them. Many

FIGURE **14.19**

Three fault types.

Faults occur where breakage and slippage happen in the crust. The direction of force and the resulting block movement determine the type of fault.

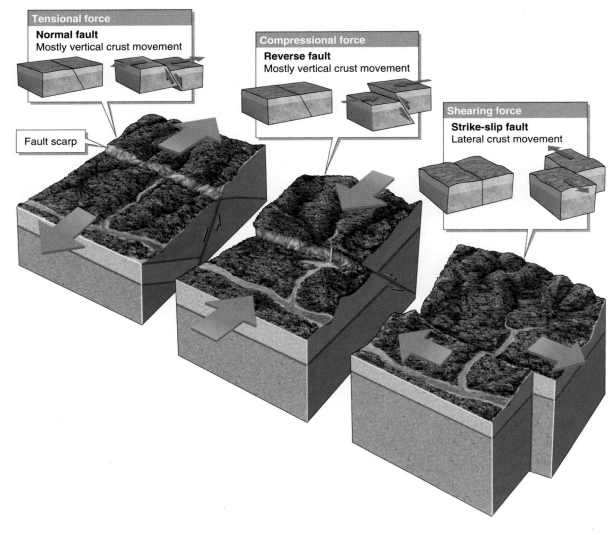

Tensional force
Normal fault
Mostly vertical crust movement

Fault scarp

Compressional force
Reverse fault
Mostly vertical crust movement

Shearing force
Strike-slip fault
Lateral crust movement

of those that do shake the ground strongly occur in remote areas, such as the deep seafloor, and are harmless to people. Very rarely, a massive earthquake, such as the Tōhoku earthquake, occurs near a populated region, causing catastrophic loss of life and structural damage to the built environment.

Three Types of Faults

There are three basic types of faults: normal faults, reverse faults, and strike-slip faults **(Figure 14.19)**. A **normal fault** is a result of *tensional force* (extension) as two pieces of Earth's crust, called *fault blocks*, are pulled apart. As a result, one fault block slips downward in relation to the other fault block. A **reverse fault** results from *compressional force*, which pushes one block upward in relation to another block. Under certain circumstances, reverse faults are also called *thrust faults*. A **strike-slip fault** occurs where one block moves horizontally in relation to another block as a result of *shearing* (lateral) *force*.

Reverse and normal faults create a **fault scarp**, or cliff face, that results from the vertical movement of the fault blocks. Strike-slip faults create little up or down block movement. Where strike-slip faults cross orchards, streams, roads, sidewalks, and other linear features, those features may be *offset* by fault movement. *Left-lateral* strike-slip faults occur when, from the perspective of either block, the opposite

FIGURE 14.20 **Right-lateral strike-slip fault.** *On September 4, 2010, the magnitude 7.1 Canterbury earthquake struck South Island, New Zealand. The tire tracks on this dirt road once connected. This fault is a right-lateral strike-slip fault because the opposite side moved to the right.* (© Kate Pedley Photography)

block moves to the left. *Right-lateral* strike-slip faults, as shown in **Figure 14.20**, occur when the opposite block moves to the right.

Fault scarps indicate that a normal or reverse fault is at work, and offset features indicate that a strike-slip fault is present. Like much of the western United States, California and Nevada have many fault systems with all three fault types, as shown in **Figure 14.21**.

normal fault
The result of tensional force as two fault blocks move apart, causing one fault block to slip downward in relation to the other fault block.

reverse fault
The result of compressional force as two fault blocks are pushed together, causing one block to move upward in relation to another block.

strike-slip fault
The result of shearing force as one block moves horizontally in relation to another block.

fault scarp
A cliff face resulting from the vertical movement of a reverse or normal fault.

FIGURE 14.21 **Fault map of California and Nevada.** *(A) The North American and Pacific plates are fractured by many fault systems in the western United States. (B) In the Great Basin Desert of Nevada, the crust is being rifted and stretched, creating a series of normal faults oriented north-south and resulting in horst and graben topography. The fault blocks have rotated slightly as the crust has been stretched. Portions of the blocks form grabens (valleys), and portions of them form horsts (mountain ranges), as illustrated here. The photograph shows Nevada's snow-capped Wheeler Peak, part of one of the many mountain ranges in Nevada produced by a rotated and tilted block.* (Bruce Gervais)

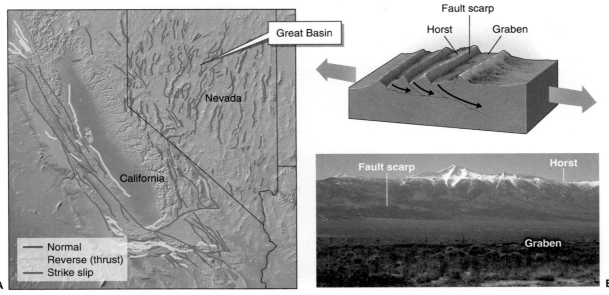

focus
The location of initial movement along a fault during an earthquake.

epicenter
The location on the ground's surface immediately above the focus of an earthquake, where earthquake intensity is usually greatest.

aftershock
A small earthquake that follows the main earthquake.

How Do Faults Generate Earthquakes?

When subjected to geologic stresses, fault blocks usually do not move smoothly past one another. Instead, friction between them causes them to stick together, and stress energy builds up in the crust. **Eventually, the geologic stress exceeds the friction, the crust breaks (either along a preexisting fault or along a new fault), and the blocks move. As each block moves, the built-up stress energy is released and travels through the crust as seismic waves, resulting in an earthquake.**

> **What causes earthquakes?**

Elastic-rebound theory describes how fault blocks bend, break, and rebound back to their original shape as they move in relation to one another. The blocks may become stuck again from friction, then slip again in this *stick-slip* process. The **focus** is the location of initial movement along a fault during an earthquake. The **epicenter** is the location on the ground's surface immediately above the focus of the earthquake and is usually the area of greatest shaking. These concepts are illustrated in **Figure 14.22**.

What Are Foreshocks and Aftershocks?

Small *foreshock* earthquakes sometimes precede large earthquakes. Foreshocks may be caused by smaller cracks developing as the deformed and stressed crust is about to fail. Going back to the bending stick analogy used in Figure 14.22, as the stick bends, small splinters of wood may form—these are the foreshocks. They may indicate that the stick is about to break—or that the rocks are about to fault. The breaking of the stick represents the main earthquake.

Very commonly, especially with large earthquake events, smaller earthquakes called **aftershocks** follow the main shock. Aftershocks occur because the blocks are settling into their new positions after they have been moved. Most aftershocks are much smaller than the main earthquake and occur on the same fault as the initial earthquake. Occasionally, aftershocks occur on different faults nearby.

Geographic Patterns of Earthquakes

Most earthquakes occur along plate boundaries in *seismic belts*. Plate boundaries give rise to earthquakes because of the interactions between moving plates that occur there. **Figure 14.23** explains some major characteristics of earthquakes at different types of plate boundaries.

Animation
Earthquake generation
http://qrs.ly/yy3w00y

FIGURE 14.22 **GEO-GRAPHIC: Earthquake generation.**

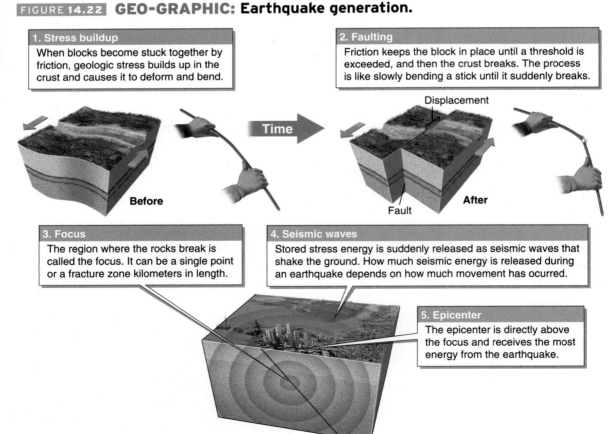

1. Stress buildup
When blocks become stuck together by friction, geologic stress builds up in the crust and causes it to deform and bend.

2. Faulting
Friction keeps the block in place until a threshold is exceeded, and then the crust breaks. The process is like slowly bending a stick until it suddenly breaks.

Displacement

Time

Before

After

Fault

3. Focus
The region where the rocks break is called the focus. It can be a single point or a fracture zone kilometers in length.

4. Seismic waves
Stored stress energy is suddenly released as seismic waves that shake the ground. How much seismic energy is released during an earthquake depends on how much movement has ocurred.

5. Epicenter
The epicenter is directly above the focus and receives the most energy from the earthquake.

FIGURE 14.23 **GEO-GRAPHIC: The tectonic settings of earthquakes.**

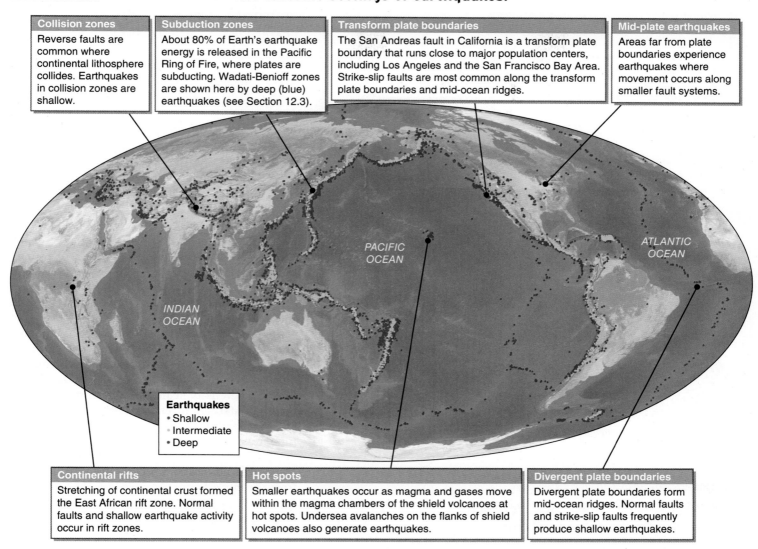

Collision zones
Reverse faults are common where continental lithosphere collides. Earthquakes in collision zones are shallow.

Subduction zones
About 80% of Earth's earthquake energy is released in the Pacific Ring of Fire, where plates are subducting. Wadati-Benioff zones are shown here by deep (blue) earthquakes (see Section 12.3).

Transform plate boundaries
The San Andreas fault in California is a transform plate boundary that runs close to major population centers, including Los Angeles and the San Francisco Bay Area. Strike-slip faults are most common along the transform plate boundaries and mid-ocean ridges.

Mid-plate earthquakes
Areas far from plate boundaries experience earthquakes where movement occurs along smaller fault systems.

PACIFIC OCEAN

ATLANTIC OCEAN

INDIAN OCEAN

Earthquakes
• Shallow
• Intermediate
• Deep

Continental rifts
Stretching of continental crust formed the East African rift zone. Normal faults and shallow earthquake activity occur in rift zones.

Hot spots
Smaller earthquakes occur as magma and gases move within the magma chambers of the shield volcanoes at hot spots. Undersea avalanches on the flanks of shield volcanoes also generate earthquakes.

Divergent plate boundaries
Divergent plate boundaries form mid-ocean ridges. Normal faults and strike-slip faults frequently produce shallow earthquakes.

14.4 Unstable Crust: Seismic Waves

◎ **Describe the types of seismic waves produced by earthquakes, how earthquakes are ranked, and what can be done to reduce our vulnerability to earthquakes.**

No two earthquakes are exactly alike. After people have been in an earthquake, they may describe "rolling" or "up-and-down" or "sideways" movement. Earthquakes generate several different types of seismic waves. The movements people experience depend on the dominant type of seismic waves passing through the ground beneath them and the type of ground underfoot. Seismic waves can be categorized by where they travel and how they move through the crust, as illustrated in **Figure 14.24**.

P waves are fast-traveling compressional waves that move through the body of Earth. They are always the first to arrive after an earthquake. They are soon followed by *S waves*, which move perpendicularly to the direction they travel through the body of Earth. *L waves* and *R waves*, which move through the crust at Earth's surface, arrive last and produce the greatest shaking **(Figure 14.25)**.

The seismic waves detected at the earthquake focus always reach the epicenter first and, normally, shake the ground there the most. Ground shaking usually decreases with distance from the epicenter because the crust absorbs seismic wave energy.

Detecting Earthquakes

The instruments used to detect, measure, and record ground shaking are called **seismographs** (or *seismometers*). Before the digital era, seismographs consisted of a swinging pendulum that recorded

seismograph
(or *seismometer*) An instrument used to detect, measure, and record ground shaking.

FIGURE 14.24 **Seismic waves.** *Seismic waves can be categorized in two ways: by where they travel and by how they move.*

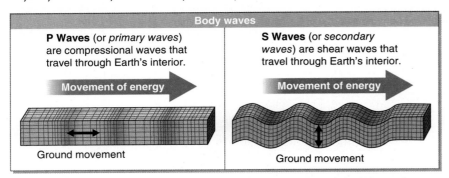

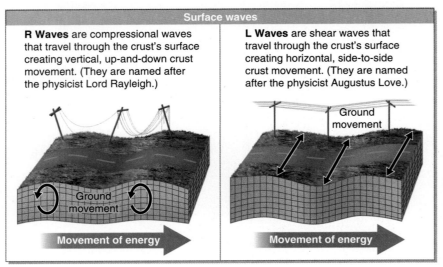

Categories of Seismic Waves

CATEGORIES BASED ON WHERE WAVES TRAVEL:

Body waves pass through the "body" of Earth.

Surface waves travel near the surface of the crust.

CATEGORIES BASED ON HOW WAVES MOVE:

Compressional waves produce movement that goes back and forth in a direction parallel to the direction of the traveling waves.

Shear waves move back and forth perpendicular to the direction the waves are traveling.

Animation
Seismic waves
http://qrs.ly/qk3w014

modified Mercalli intensity (MMI) scale
An earthquake ranking system based on the damage done to structures.

ground shaking (**Figure 14.26A** on the facing page). Modern electronic seismographs generate an electrical signal to measure ground shaking and are far more sensitive than traditional pendulum seismographs (**Figure 14.26B**).

Ranking of Earthquake Strength

The amount of ground shaking caused by an earthquake depends on the earthquake's magnitude, the distance from its focus, and the composition of the ground being shaken. Two measures are used to characterize an earthquake's strength: (1) *intensity* and (2) *magnitude*.

TABLE 14.1 **AT A GLANCE: Modified Mercalli Intensity Scale**

CATEGORY	DESCRIPTION
I-III: Slight	Not felt, barely noticeable movement.
IV-VI: Moderate to strong	Dishes can be broken. Easily felt by those near the epicenter.
VII-IX: Very strong to violent	Difficult to stand upright. Poorly built structures are badly damaged. Considerable damage to well-built structures may occur.
X-XII: Intense to cataclysmic	Poorly built structures collapse. All buildings may be destroyed, and rivers may be rerouted.

Earthquake Intensity

Earthquake intensity is determined by the amount of damage an earthquake causes to physical structures. The *Mercalli intensity scale* (or *Mercalli scale*) was developed in 1902 by the Italian scientist Giuseppe Mercalli as a means to estimate the intensity of shaking. No instruments are used to rank earthquakes on the Mercalli scale; instead, the scale is subjectively based on the observed damage done to structures. Later, the Mercalli intensity scale was developed into the **modified Mercalli intensity (MMI) scale**. In this system, earthquakes are ranked using Roman numerals, ranging from I to XII (**Table 14.1**).

There is no single MMI value for a given earthquake. Instead, locations progressively farther away from the epicenter experience less shaking as the seismic waves dissipate with distance, so each location is given its own MMI value. **Figure 14.27** provides a modified Mercalli intensity map of the 2010 Haiti earthquake.

The distance seismic waves travel through the crust depends in large part on the integrity of the crust. In the western United States, for example,

FIGURE 14.25 **Seismogram.** *This seismogram shows a typical sequence of seismic waves over 1-minute increments.*

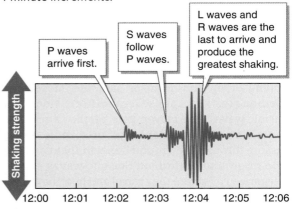

FIGURE 14.26 **Seismographs.** *Seismographs are anchored to the ground and record Earth movement on paper. The paper record is called a seismogram. (A) Traditional seismographs consist of a box attached to bedrock. Inside the box is a heavy pendulum with an ink pen attached to it. When the ground shakes, the pendulum remains stationary, recording the movement on a seismogram. (B) Modern electronic seismographs use a stationary magnet and a wire coil to generate an electronic signal. Greater Earth movement creates a stronger voltage that moves the needle more. (B. © Zephyr/Science Source)*

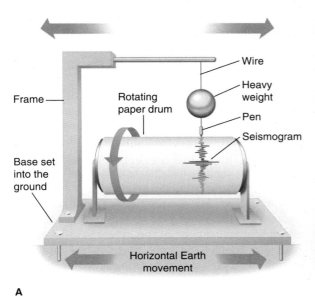

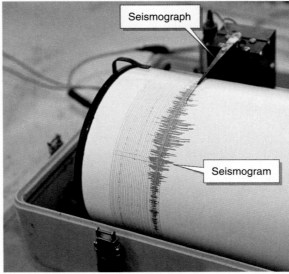

A

B

FIGURE 14.27 **Intensity rankings for the 2010 Haiti earthquake.** *Color is used in a continuous gradation to denote the intensity of ground shaking during the January 12, 2010, Haiti earthquake. Red areas experienced the greatest shaking. Port-au-Prince, which was close to the epicenter, experienced an intensity of VIII, "very strong to violent." Many structures there collapsed on people (inset photo). The death toll for this event is estimated by the USGS to be 100,000. (Left, U.S. Geological Survey, Earthquake Hazards Program; right, © Thony Belizaire/AFP/Getty Images)*

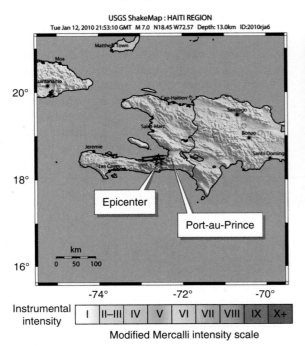

FIGURE 14.28 **Liquefaction.** *This building sank into soil that liquefied during the magnitude 7.4 Kocaeli (İzmit) earthquake in Turkey on August 17, 1999.* (© Ali Kabas/Hulton Archive/Getty Images)

many faults separate sections of the crust, and seismic waves do not travel as far as they would if the crust were not fractured. In the eastern United States, seismic waves tend to travel greater distances because there are fewer faults.

Another factor that influences the intensity of an earthquake is the composition of the ground. **Loose, wet sediments deposited by rivers or human-made landfills are susceptible to liquefaction.** **Liquefaction** is the transformation of solid sediments into an unstable slurry by ground shaking. Buildings resting on top of sediments may sink during liquefaction, as Figure 14.28 shows, unless their supporting piles are anchored in more stable ground, such as bedrock.

Earthquake Magnitude

Earthquake magnitude is determined from measurements of ground movement using seismographs. More ground movement creates higher-magnitude earthquakes. Each earthquake is given a single magnitude number that indicates the maximum shaking at the epicenter. Scientists can calculate earthquake magnitude from any seismograph on Earth if its distance from the epicenter is correctly established.

In 1935, the American geologist Charles Richter developed the *Richter scale* to quantify earthquake magnitudes using seismographic measurements. Richter's system had limitations that have been addressed by several newer scales. One of these is the **moment magnitude scale**, an earthquake ranking system based on the amount of ground movement produced.

The moment magnitude scale relies on seismographic data to quantify ground movement. The scale also uses other types of data, such as how much the fault slipped, the amplitude of the ground movement (its up-and-down and back-and-forth extent), and the physical characteristics of the rocks at the epicenter. It takes several weeks to collect data and calculate the moment magnitude scale because scientists have to go out and inspect the ground for indications of the extent of movement. Although there is no upper limit to the moment magnitude scale, no earthquake exceeding magnitude 10.0 has ever been recorded. The strongest earthquake ever recorded, which occurred in Chile in 1960, was a magnitude 9.5.

What Do Magnitude Numbers Mean?

Earthquake magnitude indicates both how much the ground shakes and how much energy is released:

1. *Ground shaking:* With each whole-number increase in magnitude, 10 times more ground movement occurs. A magnitude 5 earthquake shakes the ground 10 times more than a magnitude 4 earthquake and 100 times (10×10, or 10^2) more than a magnitude 3 earthquake.

2. *Energy released:* With each unit of increase in magnitude, about 32 times more energy is released. A magnitude 5 earthquake releases about 32 times more energy than a magnitude 4 earthquake and about 1,024 times (32×32, or 32^2) more energy than a magnitude 3 earthquake (Crunch the Numbers).

CRUNCH THE NUMBERS: Calculating Ground Shaking and Energy Released during an Earthquake

Compared with a magnitude 2 earthquake,

1. How much more ground shaking occurs during a magnitude 5 earthquake?
2. How much more energy is released during a magnitude 5 earthquake?
3. How much more ground shaking occurs during a magnitude 7 earthquake?
4. How much more energy is released during a magnitude 7 earthquake?

liquefaction
The transformation of solid sediments into an unstable slurry as a result of ground shaking during an earthquake.

moment magnitude scale
An earthquake ranking system based on the amount of ground movement produced.

The amount of energy released by a large earthquake is phenomenal. Comparing earthquake magnitude with familiar events, or kilograms of TNT, allows us to put the power of earthquakes into perspective (Figure 14.29).

Living with Earthquakes

When you think about it, earthquakes in and of themselves are not much to be feared. Imagine that you are picnicking in an open, grassy field when a strong earthquake occurs. What would happen? You would first experience up-and-down movement with the arrival of P waves, then you would experience side-to-side movement with the following S waves. Then the R waves and L waves would move the ground up and down and sideways. Your drinks would spill, and you might be tossed into the air. The sensation would be disorienting and exhilarating or terrifying, depending on your perspective. But you would probably not get hurt.

The same strong earthquake, occurring in a populated area, could bring death to thousands as structures collapse, bridges fail, bricks and glass rain down from above, and gas mains burst into flames. By itself, ground movement is not the problem—the structures that fail during ground movement create the hazard (Figure 14.30).

Earthquakes are as old as Earth's crust itself. As long as Earth's mantle moves the crust's plates, there will be earthquakes. So we have to learn to live with them. But what are our options?

FIGURE 14.29 **Energy equivalent of earthquake magnitude.** *The 1906 San Francisco earthquake released as much energy as the 1980 Mount St. Helens eruption (or 56 billion kg of TNT).*

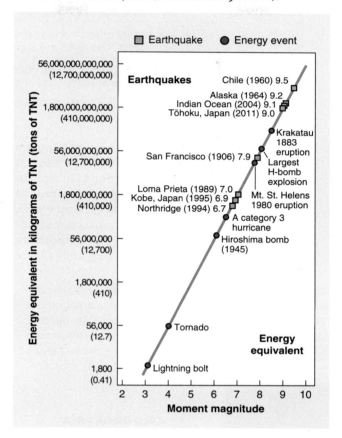

FIGURE 14.30 **Earthquake damage.** *(A) L-wave shearing caused this freeway overpass to collapse in Kobe, Japan, in 1995 during a magnitude 6.9 earthquake. (B) Intense R-wave shaking lasted 3 minutes in February 2010 during the 8.8 magnitude earthquake near Santiago, Chile. This overpass structure failed, overturning these cars. (A. © JIJI PRESS /AFP/Getty Images; B. © AP Photo/David Lillo)*

TABLE 14.2	AT A GLANCE: **Earthquake Preparedness**
HEAVY ITEMS	Secure unstable heavy items, such as bookshelves, to walls and check for other objects that could become a hazard during shaking.
SAFE PLACES	Identify safe places indoors and outdoors you can quickly get to.
SHUTOFFS	Learn and then teach other family members how to turn off gas, electricity, and water to your home. Gas leaks are a common source of fires after an earthquake has struck.
SURVIVAL KIT	Keep a survival kit in a safe place. It should include a flashlight, radio, batteries, first-aid kit, emergency food and water, nonelectric can opener, essential medicines, and shoes.

Saving Lives

Because many lives are lost when built structures fail during earthquakes, engineers have redesigned structures to better withstand ground shaking. In the United States, building codes require that engineers build structures in accordance with the seismic risk for the region, and older structures must be *retrofitted* with steel support to make them safer. These building codes have made earthquakes far less of a hazard than before. Unfortunately, many countries do not have such building codes, and their residents are at risk from the collapse of buildings in earthquakes.

Another effective means of saving lives is to give earthquake warnings. Electrons in copper wire travel far faster than seismic waves in Earth's crust. Thus, after an earthquake occurs, an automated system of alerts can be broadcast electronically. After the 2011 Tōhoku earthquake, for example, people living in Tokyo, 370 km (230 mi) from the epicenter, had 80 seconds to shut off gas mains, stop trains, and seek shelter. These actions saved many lives. The USGS is developing an earthquake warning system in Southern California. This system could give downtown Los Angeles 50 seconds of warning time if a major earthquake occurred along the nearby San Andreas Fault.

Responsibility for earthquake safety also rests with every individual who lives where earthquakes are common. Table 14.2 lists some of the important ways individuals can prepare themselves for an earthquake.

FIGURE 14.31 **Seismic probabilities for California.** *It is almost certain that a magnitude 6.7 earthquake will strike the dark orange areas on this map between the years 2009 (when the map was developed) and 2038. But it is not possible to predict exactly where within the red areas and exactly when such an earthquake will occur.* (U.S. Geological Survey, California Geological Survey, and the Southern California Earthquake Center)

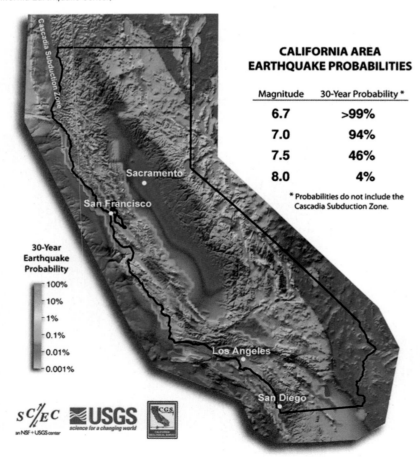

CALIFORNIA AREA EARTHQUAKE PROBABILITIES

Magnitude	30-Year Probability *
6.7	>99%
7.0	94%
7.5	46%
8.0	4%

* Probabilities do not include the Cascadia Subduction Zone.

30-Year Earthquake Probability

- 100%
- 10%
- 1%
- 0.1%
- 0.01%
- 0.001%

Predicting Earthquakes

Scientists cannot predict earthquakes. Many seismologists believe we will never be able to predict earthquakes because their precise timing and location are largely random. Seismologists are much better at determining long-term *seismic probabilities* than at making short-term predictions. For example, they know that a 6.7 earthquake has a 99% probability of happening in California within the next three decades, and they know where the probability of such an event is highest (Figure 14.31).

The *seismic risk* of an area is determined by considering many factors, including the seismic probability, the types of faults present, how active those faults have been in recorded history, and the number of people living near them. Picture This highlights a twist of events in which scientists were prosecuted for failing to adequately warn the public of an earthquake.

(© VINCENZO PINTO/AFP/Getty Images)

Faulting Scientists

At 3:32 a.m. on April 6, 2009, a magnitude 6.3 earthquake struck L'Aquila, Italy, destroying large portions of the city and killing 309 people. Most of Italy has a high seismic probability, and large earthquakes are certainly not unheard of there. The L'Aquila earthquake was unusual in one important way: Six scientists and a former government official were blamed for the disaster and charged with involuntary manslaughter.

There were many foreshocks before the main earthquake. The six government scientists assured the public that there was no imminent danger. Their reasoning, now known to be incorrect, was that with each little earthquake, the stress on the plates was gradually easing. Six days before the disaster, one of the scientists even told the town's residents, who were increasingly on edge from the foreshocks, to relax and have a glass of wine.

The prosecutors representing the families of the victims based their accusations on the failure of the scientists to evaluate the seismic risk and communicate it to the public. "They were obligated to evaluate the degree of risk given all these [foreshocks]," said a prosecutor, "and they did not." The defendants based their defense largely on the fact that scientists cannot predict earthquakes and argued that they should not be held accountable for acts of Mother Nature. They also claimed that the ruling would set a dangerous precedent. The defendants were found guilty and sentenced to six years in jail. Residents affected by the earthquake applauded the verdict. (Postscript: On November 10, 2014, a judge reversed the guilty verdict and cleared the scientists of all charges.)

Consider This

1. Do you agree that the scientists should have been held accountable for this disaster and prosecuted? Explain.

2. What other natural hazards might present a similar situation and similar liability for scientists?

3. If scientists were held legally liable for bad predictions of natural disasters, how might the future of their scientific fields be affected?

GEOGRAPHIC PERSPECTIVES
14.5 The World's Deadliest Volcano

◎ Assess the potential links between large volcanic eruptions, Earth's physical systems, and people.

The Gothic horror novel *Frankenstein* and physical geography are linked in a surprising way. The novel's author, Mary Shelley, was vacationing on Lake Geneva in Switzerland in the summer of 1816. The weather was uncharacteristically cold, gloomy, and stormy, so her vacation was spent confined indoors with her husband and friends. They held a contest writing ghost stories to see who could best express how they felt about their miserable situation. Shelley won, and *Frankenstein* was born. Little did Shelley know that her inspiration was due to the eruption of Tambora, a volcano 12,300 km (7,600 mi) away on the island of Sumbawa, east of Java, the year before.

Tambora (elevation 2,850 m or 9,350 ft) is part of the Sunda Arc, the volcanic island arc that makes up part of Indonesia. Subduction of the Indo-Australian plate beneath the Eurasian plate formed the Sunda Arc, which is the most volcanically active and dangerous section of the Pacific Ring of Fire. Three particularly notable volcanoes in the Sunda Arc are Krakatau, Toba, and Tambora **(Figure 14.32)**.

Krakatau's most recent big eruption was in 1883. It was a VEI 6 eruption that killed over 36,000 people. Toba's eruption about 73,000 years ago was one of the largest known volcanic eruptions in Earth's history. Scientists estimate that it had a magnitude of VEI 8 and believe that it caused significant climate change worldwide as ash veiled the Sun and cooled the planet for as much as several centuries. **Tambora's most recent big eruption, in 1815, holds the dubious distinction of causing the greatest known human death toll of any volcanic eruption.**

The Waking Giant

In 1812, after centuries of sleep, Tambora awoke with a series of blasts that could be heard over hundreds of miles. These massive detonations culminated in an 1815 eruption of colossal proportions.

At about 7:00 p.m. on April 10, 1815, a VEI 7 eruption occurred that could be heard as far away as South Asia, some 2,600 km (1,600 mi) away. Similar eruptions thundered during the night and into the next day. Mount Tambora was blown apart by the force of these blasts and was reduced in height by almost 1.5 km (1 mi). A column of ash punched into the stratosphere and reached an altitude of 43 km (27 mi), nearly to the base of the mesosphere. Thick ash rained down to the north **(Figure 14.33)**. Up to 100,000 people died in the immediate vicinity of Tambora, both directly in pyroclastic flows and indirectly in tsunamis, as well as from starvation resulting from crop failure.

Today, Tambora continues to show signs of life. In August 2011, the mountain erupted small amounts of ash into the atmosphere. Earthquakes are common, indicating shifting magma and gas in the magma chamber. Surprisingly, few of the 3,000 or

FIGURE 14.32 **Sunda Arc volcanoes.** *Krakatau and Tambora are two of Indonesia's approximately 150 active volcanoes (red triangles). Toba is considered extinct because it has not erupted in over 10,000 years. The caldera of Tambora (inset photo), which was formed in 1815, is 7 km (4.5 mi) across and approximately 1,240 m (3,970 ft) deep.*

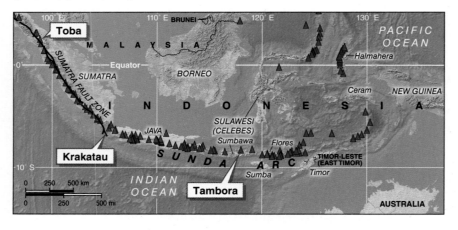

FIGURE 14.33 **Geographic extent of the Tambora ashfall.** *The ash that settled on the ground was 1 m (3.3 ft) deep as far from the volcano as 800 km (500 mi) away in southern Borneo.*

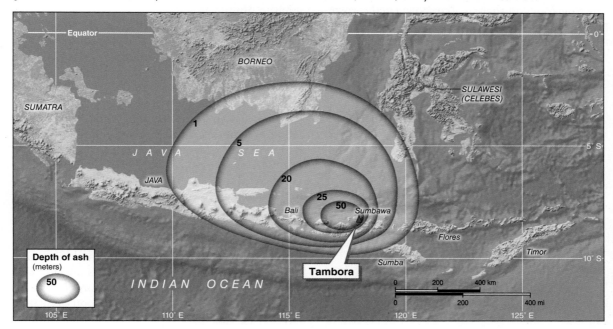

Tambora's Wide Reach

Stratovolcano eruptions ranked VEI 7 put more than 100 km³ (24 mi³) of ash, as well as an estimated 400 million tons of sulfur gases, into the atmosphere. When sulfur combines with water, it creates droplets of sulfuric acid. These droplets can remain suspended in the stratosphere for several years. The ash and sulfuric acid droplets reflect and absorb solar radiation in the stratosphere and cool Earth's surface (see Section 6.2). Climatologists have coined the term *volcanic winter* to describe the cooling effects of large volcanic eruptions.

The Year without a Summer

> What was the "Year without a Summer"?

The year 1816 was nicknamed the Year without a Summer or Eighteen-Hundred-and-Froze-to-Death because it was unusu-

so people living on the flanks of the volcano today even know about the 1815 eruption and the loss of life that occurred. Some 130 million people now live on the nearby island of Java. A similar eruption today would bring catastrophic loss of life. Scientists are carefully monitoring Tambora for signs of re-awakening.

ally cold in both eastern North America and northern Europe (**Figure 14.34**, page 470).

North America, Europe, Argentina, South Africa, India, and China all experienced unusually cold summers in 1816. The average summer temperature in the northeastern United States was about 3°C to 6°C (5°F to 10°F) below average. There was snow in New England in every month of the year in 1816.

Unfortunately, Tambora's effects on humanity were not limited to unseasonable snowstorms. Tambora triggered crop failure and disease outbreaks and changed rainfall patterns as well.

Crop Failure

Crop failure was widespread, leading to hunger and starvation in New England, the United Kingdom, Germany, and across much of Europe. There is almost no vintage 1816 wine from Europe because the grape harvests were destroyed by the low temperatures. New England experienced an unusual number of killing frosts and record low agricultural harvests during the summer of 1816.

Many European cities had already been shaken politically by the Napoleonic Wars, and the food shortages after the eruption of Tambora sparked social unrest, riots, arson, and looting. Britain

FIGURE **14.34** **Europe's Year without a Summer.** *This reconstruction of summer temperatures (in degrees Celsius departure from today's average) for Europe in 1816 comes mostly from tree ring analysis. The cooling in the Northern Hemisphere lagged the Tambora eruption by a year because it took several months for the volcanic aerosols to circulate in the upper atmosphere and cool Earth's surface.*

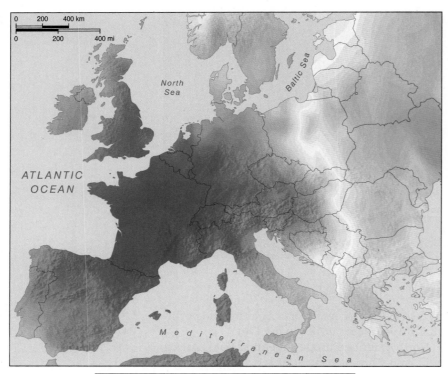

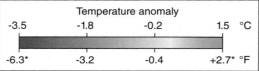

even stopped collecting income taxes in 1816 in response to food shortages and a hungry and volatile populace.

Typhus Outbreak

Tambora is blamed for a typhus epidemic between 1816 and 1819 in Europe. It is thought to have started in Ireland, spread to England, and then moved south into continental Europe. Some 65,000 people lost their lives in this epidemic. People were vulnerable to this disease because of the poor nutrition resulting from crop losses caused by the eruption.

Indian Monsoon

Tambora's aerosols in the upper atmosphere are thought to have changed the Asian monsoon rainfall pattern (see Section 4.4), causing widespread crop failures, severe hunger, and greater susceptibility to diseases. Cholera outbreaks and famine occurred in 1816 in the Bengal region of eastern India because rainfall from the monsoon came late and heavy, causing severe flooding. The cholera outbreak spread into parts of Europe, China, and Russia as people traveled between regions and transmitted the disease.

The atmosphere, biosphere and people, lithosphere, and hydrosphere are all connected in ways that are sometimes challenging to see until an event like Tambora reveals these connections.

CHAPTER 14 Exploring with ☺ Google Earth

To complete these problems, first read the chapter. When you are finished, go to LaunchPad and open the Exploring with Google Earth file for this chapter. Click on the "Workbook Problems" folder to "fly" to each of the problems listed below and answer the questions. Be sure to keep your "Borders and Labels" layer activated. Refer to Appendix 4 if you need help using Google Earth.

PROBLEM 14.1 This placemark lands on Volcán de Colima in Mexico. Pan around and carefully examine the summit crater.

1. **What kind of volcano is this?**
   a. Stratovolcano   c. Cinder cone
   b. Shield volcano   d. Plug dome

2. **Zoom in. What landform is visible in Colima's summit crater?**
   a. A plug dome   c. A cinder cone
   b. A lahar   d. A shield volcano

PROBLEM 14.2 This placemark highlights a volcanic landform.

1. **What is the name of this volcanic landform?**
   a. A plug dome   c. A cinder cone
   b. A lahar   d. A caldera

2. **Is it active?**
   a. Yes   b. No

3. **What kind of volcano can make such a landform?**
   a. A stratovolcano
   b. A shield volcano
   c. Both a stratovolcano and a shield volcano

4. **Zoom out. Where is this?**
   a. Iran   c. Greece
   b. Turkey   d. Italy

PROBLEM 14.3 This placemark is on a coastal location. Note that the historical imagery feature is activated in the upper portion of your screen. It shows an aerial photo for 07/22/2010. (If it is not activated, be sure to activate it.)

1. **Which of the following best describes the condition of the surface on 07/22/2010?**
   a. There is nothing unusual about the surface.
   b. The surface has been slightly disturbed by some natural event.
   c. The surface has been destroyed by some natural event.

2. **Now move the historical imagery slider to the right and stop when the date reads 03/31/2011. Wait while the aerial photo for this date loads. Which of the following best describes the situation on the ground on this date?**
   a. There is nothing unusual about the surface.
   b. The surface has been slightly disturbed by some natural event.
   c. The surface has been destroyed by some natural event.

3. **Zoom out. Where is this location?**
   a. Russia   c. Japan
   b. North Korea   d. China

4. **What natural disaster most likely occurred here, given this geographic setting, the pattern of damage, and what you have read in this chapter?**
   a. A volcanic explosion   c. An earthquake
   b. A tsunami   d. A fire

5. **Move the slider all the way to the right for the most recent photo. Has this area been rebuilt?**
   a. Yes   b. No

PROBLEM 14.4 This placemark highlights a large circular lake.

1. **Given the subject of this chapter, what process formed this lake?**
   a. A caldera formed after a magma chamber collapsed. Later, it filled with water.
   b. An asteroid created this crater, which filled with water.
   c. A large igneous province was eroded into a bowl, then filled with water.
   d. A cinder cone crater filled with water.

2. **Zoom in to the island in the lake. What is the name of the island landform found inside the lake?**
   a. A shield volcano   c. A cinder cone
   b. A stratovolcano   d. A plug dome

3. **Zoom out. Where is this lake?**
   a. Oregon   c. California
   b. Washington   d. Idaho

PROBLEM 14.5 This placemark lands on a large volcano in Mexico.

1. **What is the name of this volcano? (Make sure your Borders and Labels layer is activated.)**
   a. Popocatépetl   c. Mount Tlaloc
   b. Iztaccihuatl   d. La Malinche

2. **What kind of volcano is this?**
   a. Shield volcano   c. Cinder cone
   b. Stratovolcano   d. Plug dome

3. **Can this volcano produce explosive eruptions?**
   a. Yes   b. No

4. **There is a large city to the northwest. What city is it?**
   a. Veracruz   c. Zacatlán
   b. Puebla   d. Mexico City

5. **How many kilometers away is this city?**
   a. 70 km   c. 120 km
   b. 90 km   d. 200 km

PROBLEM 14.6 This placemark lands on a volcano in Iceland. Zoom out, tilt, and pan around to get a sense of this volcano's shape and dimensions.

1. **What kind of volcano is this?**
   a. Shield volcano   c. Cinder cone
   b. Stratovolcano   d. Plug dome

2. **Is this volcano likely to produce explosive eruptions?**
   a. Yes   b. No

PROBLEM 14.7 Activate the ShakeMap overlay in this folder. This problem features the 2010 Haiti earthquake.

1. **The placemark points to the epicenter. How strong was the shaking at the epicenter?**
   a. Weak
   b. Moderate
   c. Very strong
   d. Violent

2. **What was the potential damage at the epicenter?**
   a. Light
   b. Moderate
   c. Heavy

3. **Find Port-au-Prince to the east. How far in kilometers was Port-au-Prince from the epicenter?**
   a. 20 km
   b. 27 km
   c. 38 km
   d. 48 km

4. **How strong was the shaking in Port-au-Prince?**
   a. Light
   b. Moderate
   c. Very strong
   d. Extreme

5. **What was the potential damage level?**
   a. Light
   b. Moderate
   c. Heavy

PROBLEM 14.8 This placemark highlights a volcano that produced a VEI 6 eruption in 1991.

1. **Approximately how much material did this volcano eject during that eruption?**
   a. 1 km^3
   b. 10 km^3
   c. 100 km^3
   d. 1,000 km^3

2. **What is the name of this volcano?**
   a. Pinatubo
   b. Hekla
   c. Tambora
   d. Krakatau

3. **Which of the following best describes this volcano's activity level?**
   a. Active
   b. Dormant
   c. Extinct

4. **Double-click Marker 1 in this problem's folder. What is this marker highlighting?**
   a. Lapilli
   b. A lahar
   c. Liquefaction
   d. Ash

PROBLEM 14.9 Activate the ShakeMap overlay in this folder if it is not already activated. This problem features the 2011 Tōhoku earthquake in Japan.

1. **What earthquake ranking scale is provided in this overlay?**
   a. The moment magnitude scale
   b. The Richter scale
   c. The Mercalli intensity scale

2. **The placemark points to the epicenter of the earthquake. How far was the epicenter from Tokyo, the world's most populous city?**
   a. 100 km
   b. 175 km
   c. 375 km
   d. 450 km

3. **What was the approximate level of ground shaking in Tokyo?**
   a. Strong
   b. Very strong
   c. Severe
   d. Violent

4. **What kind of damage was potentially sustained in Tokyo?**
   a. Light
   b. Moderate
   c. Heavy

PROBLEM 14.10 Deactivate any open overlays. This placemark lands on Wallace Creek in California. The placemark points to the San Andreas Fault, running mostly east-west in this view. The stream runs roughly north to south on the screen. Note the change of direction of the stream where it crosses the San Andreas Fault.

1. **What kind of fault caused the stream to change direction?**
   a. Normal fault
   b. Reverse fault
   c. Strike-slip fault

2. **What pattern of deformation is seen in this stream?**
   a. Offset
   b. S wave
   c. Liquefaction
   d. Stick-slip

3. **Which of the following best describes this specific fault type?**
   a. Right-lateral fault
   b. Left-lateral fault
   c. Fault block

CHAPTER 14 **Study Guide**

Focus Points

14.1   About Volcanoes

Types of volcanoes: There are three main types of volcanoes: stratovolcanoes, shield volcanoes, and cinder cones.

Lava: Lava, the most conspicuous product of volcanic activity, ranges from runny mafic to thick felsic lava.

Pyroclasts: Volcanoes eject materials into the air ranging in size from fine ash to large blocks.

Gases: Gases, particularly carbon dioxide and water vapor, are a significant component of volcanic emissions.

Volcanic landforms: Landforms resulting from volcanism include columnar jointing, flood basalts, and calderas.

14.2   Pele's Power: Volcanic Hazards

Shield volcanoes: Shield volcanoes have gentle, effusive eruptions.

Stratovolcanoes: Stratovolcanoes erupt both effusively and explosively. Explosive eruptions occur when gas in the magma chamber expands rapidly.

Volcanic geohazards: Lahars and pyroclastic flows are the two greatest threats posed by stratovolcanoes.

Eruption prediction: Scientists can sometimes predict a volcanic eruption by monitoring gas emissions and earthquake activity.

Pacific Ring of Fire: The Pacific Ring of Fire has the greatest number of explosive stratovolcanoes on the planet.

14.3   Tectonic Hazards: Faults and Earthquakes

Fault types: Faults occur as normal faults, reverse faults, and strike-slip faults.

Fault indicators: Fault scarps indicate normal and reverse faults. Offset features indicate strike-slip faults.

Earthquakes: Earthquakes are caused when the crust suddenly breaks and releases built-up stress energy in the form of seismic waves.

Seismic belts: Earthquakes occur mainly in seismic belts that coincide with plate boundaries.

14.4   Unstable Crust: Seismic Waves

Intensity and magnitude: Earthquake intensity is determined by the amount of damage done to built structures, and earthquake magnitude is determined by the degree of measured ground shaking.

Earthquake prediction: Scientists cannot predict earthquakes.

Saving lives: Building codes and retrofitting greatly strengthen buildings and save human lives.

14.5   Geographic Perspectives: The World's Deadliest Volcano

Tambora: The 1815 eruption of Tambora was the strongest and deadliest volcanic eruption in recorded history.

Key Terms

'a'ā, 447
active volcano, 445
aftershock, 460
angle of repose, 446
ash (volcanic), 445
block (volcanic), 448
bomb (volcanic), 448
caldera, 451
cinder cone, 446
columnar jointing, 451
effusive eruption, 452
epicenter, 460
extinct volcano, 445
fault scarp, 459
focus, 460
geohazard, 444
joint, 451
lahar, 453
lapilli, 448

large igneous province
   (LIP), 451
liquefaction, 464
modified Mercalli intensity
   (MMI) scale, 462
moment magnitude scale, 464
normal fault, 459
pāhoehoe, 447
pumice, 448
pyroclast, 445
pyroclastic flow, 454
reverse fault, 459
seismograph, 461
shield volcano, 445
stratovolcano, 445
strike-slip fault, 459
tsunami, 444
Volcanic Explosivity Index
   (VEI), 453

Concept Review

The Human Sphere: Deadly Ocean Waves

1. What is a tsunami? How are tsunamis generated? Why are they geohazards?

14.1   About Volcanoes

2. What are the three kinds of volcanoes? Which is the smallest volcano type and which is the largest? Describe how each is built up.

3. What are the three types of lava? Explain how each behaves and what causes it to behave that way.

4. Give examples of the types of materials volcanoes produce. Briefly describe each.

5. What is a joint? What is columnar jointing? In which kind of lava can it be found?

6. What is a large igneous province? Give three examples of where they can be found.

7. What is a caldera and how does it form?

14.2   Pele's Power: Volcanic Hazards

8. What are the two types of volcanic eruptions, and what controls which type of eruption will occur?

9. What is the VEI?

10. What are the two most deadly products of volcanic eruptions? Explain why each is so hazardous.

11. Can scientists predict volcanic eruptions? Explain.

12. What is the Pacific Ring of Fire? Explain the kind of volcanoes found there and why they are deadly.

14.3 Tectonic Hazards: Faults and Earthquakes

13. Describe the three types of faults. What is the direction of force and the type of movement associated with each?

14. Explain how an earthquake forms using the terms *stress* and *friction*. What is elastic rebound theory in this context? What is the *stick-slip* process?

15. Define and briefly explain the following terms: focus, epicenter, and seismic waves.

16. What is a foreshock? What is an aftershock? What causes them?

17. Describe the geographic pattern of earthquakes worldwide. Where do most earthquakes occur?

14.4 Unstable Crust: Seismic Waves

18. Compare a body wave to a surface wave. Where does each travel?

19. Compare a compressional wave with a shear wave. What kind of movement does each produce?

20. What scientific instrumentation is used to measure ground shaking?

21. Compare P waves, S waves, L waves, and R waves in terms of the sequence of their arrival after an earthquake and the strength of the ground shaking they cause.

22. What does the Mercalli scale indicate about an earthquake? What evidence does it use to rank earthquakes?

23. What information about an earthquake does the moment magnitude scale provide?

24. What is liquefaction? On what kind of ground does it occur?

25. Can scientists predict earthquakes?

26. In what ways can people reduce their vulnerability to earthquakes?

14.5 Geographic Perspectives: The World's Deadliest Volcano

27. What kind of volcano is Tambora? In the context of plate tectonics, explain how Tambora was formed.

28. Given the VEI ranking of Tambora's 1815 eruption, how much pyroclastic material did it eject into the atmosphere?

29. When was the "Year without a Summer," and how does the term "volcanic winter" relate to it?

30. Outline the negative effects the Tambora eruption set in motion for various parts of the world.

Critical-Thinking Questions

1. Are you vulnerable to volcanic hazards where you live? If you are unsure, how would you find out?

2. Is there a risk of an earthquake occurring where you live? If you do not know, what kinds of questions could you ask to find out?

3. If a VEI 6 or greater eruption occurred today, what effects do you think it would have locally (where you live) and globally?

4. Do you think scientists will ever be able to predict accurately when a given region will be hit by an earthquake?

5. In Sri Lanka, many elephants ran to high ground minutes before the 2004 tsunami struck, even though their unknowing riders ordered them to stop. Similarly, there are many eyewitness accounts of animals such as horses and dogs acting strangely or panicking minutes before an earthquake strikes. What do you think animals may be sensing that humans and scientific instruments are not sensing? Do you think scientists should pursue further research into this area, or would it be a waste of money?

Test Yourself

Take this quiz to test your chapter knowledge.

1. **True or false?** Shield volcanoes produce effusive eruptions.

2. **True or false?** Lava viscosity is in large part the result of the silica content of the lava.

3. **True or false?** Lava is one of the most deadly hazards of volcanoes.

4. **True or false?** S waves travel fastest and are the first to arrive after an earthquake.

5. **Multiple choice:** Which of the following is not associated with explosive volcanic eruptions?
   a. Stratovolcano
   b. Felsic magma
   c. Caldera formation
   d. Large igneous province

6. **Multiple choice:** Which of the following types of seismic waves produces a rolling movement on the surface of Earth's crust?
   a. P waves   b. S wave   c. L waves   d. R waves

7. **Multiple choice:** About how much more ground shaking does a magnitude 8 earthquake create than a magnitude 5 earthquake?
   a. 100 times more   c. 10,000 times more
   b. 1,000 times more   d. 100,000 times more

8. **Multiple choice:** Which of the following is not a type of pyroclast?
   a. Bombs   b. Ash   c. Lapilli   d. Lava flows

9. **Fill in the blank.** A _____ is a slurry of mud created when a snow-capped volcano erupts.

10. **Fill in the blank.** The _____ is the point directly over an earthquake's focus.

Picture This. YOUR TURN

Name That Fault

These three photos show examples of the three fault types discussed in this chapter. Fill in the blank spaces above each photo with one of the following types of faults: **normal fault**, **reverse fault**, or **strike-slip fault**. You may use each more than once.
(Left, Courtesy of Rick Scott; center, © David K. Lynch; right, Russell L. Losco, Lanchester Soil Consultants, Inc.)

 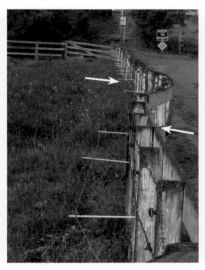 

Further Reading

1. Hall, Stephen. "Scientists on Trial: At Fault?" *Nature* 477 (2001), 264-269.

2. Klingaman, William. *The Year without Summer: 1816 and the Volcano That Darkened the World and Changed History.* New York: St. Martin's Press, 2013.

3. Revkin, Andrew. "With No Alert System, Indian Ocean Nations Were Vulnerable." *New York Times*, December 27, 2004.

Answers to Living Physical Geography Questions

1. **What is a tsunami?** A tsunami is a giant ocean wave triggered by a natural event, usually an earthquake. When these waves reach shallow coastal waters, they can grow to great heights and devastate coastal areas.

2. **Why do some volcanoes explode violently?** Volcanoes explode violently when gas in magma expands rapidly as the magma migrates upward toward the crust and experiences less pressure.

3. **What causes earthquakes?** When crust under stress suddenly breaks and moves, ripples of energy travel outward and shake the ground.

4. **What was the "Year without a Summer"?** The year 1816 was named the "Year without a Summer" in eastern North America because of the cooling effects of aerosols from the Tambora eruption in the stratosphere.

PART **IV**
EROSION AND DEPOSITION:
Sculpting Earth's Surface

The Sun evaporates water that precipitates back down on the continents, and gravity sets that water in motion. Part IV explores the work of weathering, erosion, and sediment deposition in sculpting Earth's surface. Through time, even the highest mountains are reduced to grains of sand by the action of streams, glaciers, wind, and coastal waves.

CHAPTER 15

Weathering and Mass Movement

Weathering breaks apart and dissolves rock. Weathered rock material moves downslope by the force of gravity.

CHAPTER 16

FLOWING WATER: Fluvial Systems

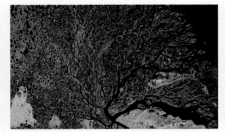

Flowing water transports weathered material downslope and deposits it. Most of Earth's surface has been shaped by streams.

CHAPTER 17

THE WORK OF ICE: The Cryosphere and Glacial Landforms

Glaciers flow downslope and gouge Earth's surface, creating unique landforms.

CHAPTER 18

WATER, WIND, AND TIME: Desert Landforms

Desert environments are sculpted by flowing water and wind.

CHAPTER 19

THE WORK OF WAVES: Coastal Landforms

Beaches and rocky shorelines are shaped by coastal wave energy.

15 Weathering and Mass Movement

Chapter Outline

The rock composing this rounded and weathered boulder is older than most rocks on Earth. It is part of an ancient mountain range in eastern Argentina called the Tandilia System. About 2.5 billion years ago, that mountain range was as high as the Himalayas, but weathering and erosion have reduced the once-mighty range to the low hills that are present today.

(c) Luis Argerich/National Geographic Society/Corbis

LIVING PHYSICAL GEOGRAPHY

➤ Where does beach sand come from?

➤ Why are homes sometimes swallowed by the ground?

➤ What is a disappearing stream?

➤ Where are the highest sea cliffs in the world?

To learn more about weathering and erosion, turn to Section 15.1.

THE BIG PICTURE *Weathering reduces rocks to fragments. Gravity moves weathered material downslope, sometimes with deadly speed.*

LEARNING GOALS *After reading this chapter, you will be able to:*

15.1 ◎ Distinguish between physical weathering and chemical weathering and provide examples of each.

15.2 ◎ Describe different kinds of karst landforms and explain how each forms.

15.3 ◎ Identify different types of mass movements and describe their behavior and causes.

15.4 ◎ Assess the threats to people from mass movements and explain how their vulnerability to those threats can be reduced.

THE HUMAN SPHERE: Weathering Mount Rushmore

FIGURE 15.1 **Mount Rushmore maintenance.** *Every year, rope climbers descend the Mount Rushmore National Memorial and caulk minute cracks with a silicone sealant. The sealant prevents water from entering the cracks, then freezing and widening them through the process of frost wedging. (Courtesy of NPS, Mount Rushmore National Memorial)*

THE MOUNT RUSHMORE NATIONAL MEMORIAL is carved from a body of granite in the Black Hills of South Dakota. Like any rock, the granite that makes up this monument is continually subject to the effects of weathering that break down rocks over time. The sculpted surface makes the rock more susceptible to weathering than it would otherwise be because there is a greater surface area on which weathering can act. To protect the monument from weathering, the U.S. National Park Service closely monitors and maintains its rock surface (Figure 15.1).

Scientists have also developed a system that identifies "rock blocks" that provide key support for large portions of the monument. If these blocks move, other portions of the monument would be more susceptible to movement as well. These key rock blocks are monitored by laser-based instruments that can measure movement to within 0.0003 cm (0.00001 in). These instruments take measurements four times each day. Thus far, monitoring of the blocks has revealed that they move very little and that the blocks are structurally sound.

We begin this chapter with a focus on the different kinds of weathering processes that act on rocks and the effects of these processes. We then turn our attention to mass movement events, which range from imperceptible ground movements to dangerous avalanches. Lastly, we examine the hazards posed to people by mass movements.

15.1 Weathering Rocks

◎ Distinguish between physical weathering and chemical weathering and provide examples of each.

They say nothing lasts forever. This adage is certainly true of Earth's physical surface. Even the mightiest and most massive mountains are ephemeral features in the great span of geologic time. In Part III, we examined the work of Earth's geothermal energy in building Earth's surface and creating vertical relief. In Part IV, we explore how these uplifted landforms are torn down. The Sun evaporates water that precipitates back down on the continents, and gravity sets that water in motion. The Sun also creates differences in atmospheric pressure, and these differences drive the wind and ocean waves. Streams, flowing glaciers, wind, and coastal waves carve into Earth's uplifted surface. Therefore, solar energy drives erosion of the crust's surface.

Tectonic forces act sporadically across Earth's surface, but the forces that reduce vertical relief are present nearly everywhere on land and never rest. **Weathering** is the process by which solid rock is dissolved and broken apart into smaller fragments. **Erosion** is the transportation of rock fragments by moving water, ice, or air. Weathering, erosion, and deposition of rock material are all processes of **denudation**: the lowering and wearing away of Earth's surface.

Denudation begins with the disintegration of rock into smaller and smaller fragments. The forces of weathering may physically break rocks apart or decompose them through chemical reactions with water. Unweathered, or "fresh," rock surfaces are either newly formed or newly exposed. Eventually, all rocks exposed at Earth's surface will weather, either through physical weathering or chemical weathering.

Physical Weathering

Physical weathering breaks rocks down into smaller pieces, or clasts—collectively called *debris*—without altering the chemical makeup of the rock. The processes of physical weathering have their greatest effect at high elevations and high latitudes.

Natural cracks in rock, called joints, provide surface areas on which physical weathering processes can act. Nearly all outcrops have joints. Tectonic stresses near geologic faults commonly fracture rocks and create jointing. Igneous rocks become jointed as the rock cools and changes shape slightly. Sedimentary rocks usually have horizontal joints at their *bedding planes* (the surfaces where their layers meet), but sedimentary rocks also form vertical jointing as a result of stresses on the rock, as shown in **Figure 15.2**.

Pressure-release jointing occurs when overlying rocks and sediments, or *overburden*, are removed from rocks that formed at great depths. After the overburden

FIGURE 15.2 **Rock jointing.** *Vertical and horizontal jointing occur in all types of rock. This sandstone in Zion National Park, Utah, shows both kinds of jointing. (Bruce Gervais)*

Vertical joints

Horizontal joints along bedding planes

Zion National Park

is removed, the enormous pressure associated with deep burial lessens, and the rock expands slightly, creating joints. Pressure-release jointing is most common in intrusive igneous rocks and metamorphic rocks.

Exfoliation, a type of pressure-release jointing, is a process in which joints form parallel to the rock surface, creating sheetlike slabs of rock resembling the layers of an onion. These slabs peel off through *sheeting*, creating broken horizontal slabs of rock that can slip off the rock face. Sheeting slabs can be a few millimeters thick or several meters thick. Exfoliation sometimes rounds the edges of large granite plutons, creating *exfoliation domes*, such as Half Dome in Yosemite National Park or Enchanted Rock in Texas, shown in **Figure 15.3**.

weathering
The process by which solid rock is dissolved and broken apart into smaller fragments.

erosion
The transport of rock fragments by moving water, ice, or air.

denudation
The lowering and wearing away of Earth's surface.

physical weathering
The breakdown of rocks into smaller pieces, or clasts, without altering the chemical makeup of the rock.

exfoliation
A physical weathering process in which joints form parallel to a rock surface, creating sheetlike slabs of rock.

FIGURE 15.3 **Exfoliation and sheeting.** *Exfoliation and sheeting have rounded the edges of Enchanted Rock near Fredericksburg, Texas, creating an exfoliation dome. (© Photo Researchers/Getty Images)*

Animation
Exfoliation
http://qrs.ly/tg49ecy

Sheeting slabs

Fredericksburg

FIGURE 15.4 **Frost wedging.** *This granite boulder (about 2 m, or 6.5 ft, across) in the Sierra Nevada, in California, has been cracked by frost wedging.* (Bruce Gervais)

Where temperatures routinely drop below freezing, frost wedging is the most important type of physical weathering. **Frost wedging** is the process by which water trapped in an opening in a rock freezes and expands, causing the opening to grow. When liquid water freezes to ice, it expands by almost 10%. If water freezes in a confined space, such as a water pipe in a house, a glass bottle in the freezer, or a joint in a rock, it applies considerable force as it expands against the material confining it. Repeated freezing and thawing of water in rock joints pries the rocks apart over time, as shown in **Figure 15.4**.

Salt wedging is a process in which salt crystals grow in pore spaces on a rock's surface and dislodge individual mineral grains within the rock. Salt wedging weakens rock so that wind and rain can further disintegrate it. Salt crystal growth requires that the rock surface be continually wetted, then dried. Salt wedging occurs mostly in arid climates where evaporation is high and in coastal areas where rocks are coated with salt spray from waves. **Tafoni** are rounded pits or cavities on the surface of a rock that form through salt wedging. They are most common in coastal regions **(Figure 15.5)**.

Biophysical weathering refers to weathering by any living organism. Animals from small rodents to massive elephants can physically break rock down into smaller pieces. **Root wedging** occurs when plant roots grow into joints seeking water. Many city residents have seen sidewalks buckled by tree roots as they push up from below. The same thing happens in natural settings: As roots grow, they force rocks apart **(Figure 15.6)**.

Chemical Weathering

Physical weathering breaks rock apart without altering its chemical structure. **Chemical weathering**, in contrast, changes the minerals in rock through chem-

FIGURE 15.5 **Tafoni.** *This sandstone in Shore Acres State Park, in southwestern Oregon, shows the peculiar pitted pattern of tafoni, the rounded surface cavities caused by salt wedging. This photo shows an area about 1 m (3.3 ft) across.* (Bruce Gervais)

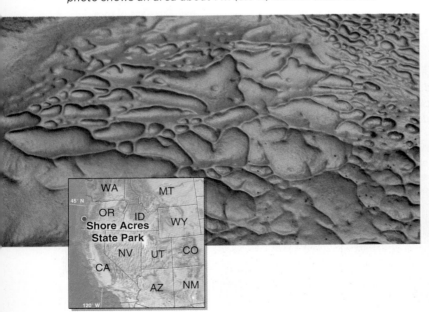

FIGURE 15.6 **Root wedging.** *This western juniper (Juniperus occidentalis) near South Lake Tahoe, California, is growing in a joint in granite and pushing the rock apart.* (Bruce Gervais)

FIGURE 15.7 Weathering and surface area.

The more fragmented rock becomes, the greater its surface area, and the more weathering can take place.

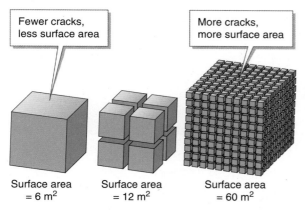

Fewer cracks, less surface area

More cracks, more surface area

Surface area = 6 m²

Surface area = 12 m²

Surface area = 60 m²

ical reactions involving water. **Physical and chemical weathering both occur at the same time and affect each other's rates.** For example, because chemical weathering occurs mainly on the surfaces of rocks, physical weathering assists in the process of chemical weathering by breaking rocks into smaller pieces and creating a greater surface area on which chemical weathering can act (Figure 15.7).

Chemical weathering is dominant where temperatures are above freezing and there is ample moisture. As a result, rocks in the lowland tropics are most altered by chemical weathering.

A number of chemical reactions can result in chemical weathering. One such reaction is *carbonation*, which results when carbon dioxide dissolves in water, forming carbonic acid (H_2CO_3). Carbonic acid reacts with carbonate rocks such as limestone. As limestone is weathered through carbonation, rainwater carries away the dissolved material in a carbonic acid solution. Section 15.2 describes some of the topographic results of this process.

Hydrolysis occurs when water reacts with and combines with minerals in rocks to form new minerals. Typically, the new minerals are softer and more easily eroded than the original minerals. Silicate minerals, such as those found in granite, are particularly susceptible to hydrolysis.

Similarly, during *hydration*, water is added onto minerals in rock or soil, causing the material to expand and weaken. Hydration changes the texture, composition, and volume of minerals in rocks. Clay, for instance, softens through hydration as it absorbs water. One type of clay, called bentonite, can increase in volume by 1,600% through hydration. Similarly, hydration of the mineral anhydrite forms gypsum.

In *oxidation*, oxygen atoms combine with the minerals in rocks and weaken them. Just as iron rusts, rock containing iron-based minerals, such as hematite, rusts into a softer, reddish-brown rock.

Biochemical weathering refers to chemical weathering resulting from the activities of living organisms. Many plant roots, bacteria, lichens, and fungi obtain nutrients by producing acids that break down minerals in rocks.

Differential Weathering

Weathering does not occur equally across the surface of a rock. Angular blocks, for example, experience the most weathering along their edges and corners. This pattern of weathering leads to the formation of rounded or spheroidal boulders, as illustrated in Figure 15.8.

frost wedging
A physical weathering process in which water trapped in an opening in a rock freezes and expands, causing the opening to grow.

salt wedging
A physical weathering process in which salt crystals grow in pore spaces on a rock's surface and dislodge individual mineral grains within the rock.

tafoni
Pits or cavities on the surface of a rock that form through salt wedging.

root wedging
A physical weathering process in which plant roots break rocks apart.

chemical weathering
A process that changes the minerals in a rock through chemical reactions involving water.

FIGURE 15.8 Spheroidal weathering.

(A) Sharp edges and corners weather more rapidly than flat surfaces. As a result, weathering rounds the edges of rocks over time. (B) These granite boulders in the Namib Desert, Namibia, have been rounded by weathering. (© Ruedi Walther)

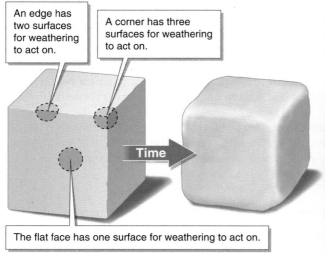

An edge has two surfaces for weathering to act on.

A corner has three surfaces for weathering to act on.

Time

The flat face has one surface for weathering to act on.

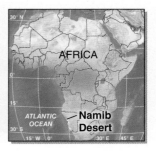

AFRICA

ATLANTIC OCEAN

Namib Desert

FIGURE 15.9 **Landforms created by differential weathering.** *(A) Devil's Tower, in Wyoming, is a resistant column of intrusive igneous rock that was once surrounded by sedimentary rock. The less resistant sedimentary rock has been weathered and eroded away, creating this monolith. (B) A natural arch forms, typically in sandstone, when weak joints and bedding planes are eroded fastest. Like all natural arches, this one near Ghayen, Iran, will eventually collapse with further weathering. (C) Hoodoos are tall, columnar rock formations, usually capped with a layer of rock that is resistant to erosion. The resistant cap protects the softer rocks beneath from erosion. These hoodoos are near Drumheller in Alberta, Canada.* (A. © Joel Sartore/National Geographic/ Getty Images; B. © Rene Mattes/hemis.fr/Getty Images; C. © Wayne Barrett & Anne MacKay/All Canada Photos/Getty Images)

A

B

C

Picture This

The Life of a Sand Grain

One of the minerals most resistant to weathering is quartz, a mineral found in many rocks. Many minerals in rocks are subject to chemical weathering, particularly oxidation and hydrolysis. Quartz, however, is extremely resistant to chemical weathering and may persist for millions of years as grains of quartz sand.

Many beaches of the world are made up in large part of quartz sand grains that were long ago weathered out of bedrock. An individual sand grain on the beach might have been weathered from granite high on a mountain range long ago. From there, it might have been transported to a beach, where the waves washed over it for millennia. This ancient beach sand could then have been lithified to form new sedimentary rock, only to be uplifted by geologic forces into a different mountain range, with our quartz grain in it. Eventually, weathering might have torn this mountain range down, too, creating a new beach many millions of years later. This process could have been repeated several times through hundreds of millions of years.

> Where does beach sand come from?*

Each grain of sand on a beach is a product of Earth's deep geologic history. In this sense, when we walk across a beach, such as this one on the shoreline of Point Reyes in northern California, we also walk across a portion of Earth's ancient history.

Consider This

1. How does differential weathering result in a beach composed of quartz sand?

2. How can quartz grains be older than the bedrock from which they come?

(Bruce Gervais)

*Answers to the Living Physical Geography questions are found on page 507.

Weathering that occurs at different rates across a rock surface is called **differential weathering**. As Figure 15.9 shows, differential weathering also results when rocks of different types occur within a body of rock, sometimes creating dramatic or unusual landforms.

Weathering also acts on weaker minerals within rocks more than on relatively resistant minerals. As a result, resistant minerals, such as quartz, persist through time, while weaker minerals are broken down. Many beaches are composed of resistant quartz grains that were once embedded within rocks, as Picture This discusses.

15.2 Dissolving Rocks: Karst Landforms

◎ Describe different kinds of karst landforms and explain how each forms.

In 1864, when Jules Verne's book *Journey to the Center of the Earth* was published, its readers were transported to enormous subterranean caverns lighted by bioluminescent bacteria living on the caverns' ceilings and filled with a deep subterranean ocean, on the shores of which were found giant mushrooms, petrified forests, and even living dinosaurs. Although these phenomena are not real, Verne's imagination no doubt was inspired at least in part by subterranean karst caverns.

Karst refers to an area dominated by the weathering of carbonate rocks, usually limestone. The term *karst* is the German form of the Slovenian term *kras*, which means "barren landscape." Groundwater plays a particularly important role in weathering limestone rocks and creating unusual surface landforms as well as subterranean cavern systems.

Karst Processes

Why do carbonate rocks dissolve in rainwater? As rain falls through the atmosphere, it absorbs a small amount of carbon dioxide from the air. Water also absorbs carbon dioxide as it flows through soil that is rich in organic substances. Once water has absorbed carbon dioxide, it forms carbonic acid. Through the process of carbonation, acidic water reacts with the calcite in limestone, causing *dissolution*, the process in which minerals are dissolved in water and carried away. The rock is dissolved most where it is weakest; namely, along joints in the rock (see Section 15.1).

In some cases, acids other than carbonic acid dissolve carbonate rocks. In the unusual case of Carlsbad Caverns and Lechuguilla Cave in New Mexico, for example, sulfuric acid that forms from natural oil deposits is dissolving the limestone bedrock.

Areas with limestone bedrock form the most widespread type of karst topography. All carbonate rocks, including marble, dolomite, gypsum, and chalk, are, however, subject to dissolution. Karst topography forms fastest in warm tropical regions. Although some Arctic regions have carbonate rocks, dissolution is greatly slowed there because water is frozen and chemically nonreactive for most of the year. Carbonate rocks susceptible to weathering by karst processes cover about 15% of Earth's land surface (Figure 15.10).

differential weathering
Unequal weathering across a rock surface.

karst
An area dominated by the weathering of carbonate rocks, usually limestone.

FIGURE 15.10 **Karst regions.** *This world map shows carbonate rocks exposed at the surface and subject to weathering by karst processes.*

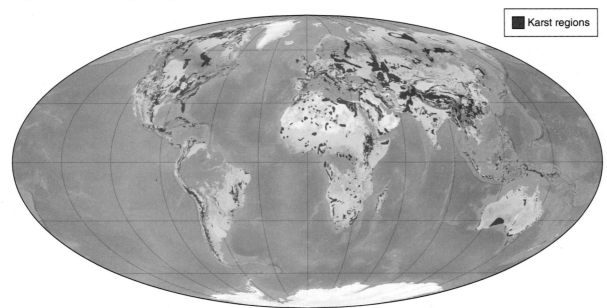

Karst regions

FIGURE 15.11 **Sinkholes.** *(A) Most sinkholes form gradually as limestone at Earth's surface dissolves and is carried away by water. Sinkholes can give way quickly, destroying structures built on them (inset photo). When the lowest elevation of a sinkhole is lower than the water table, a sinkhole lake forms. (B) This Landsat satellite image of Florida is centered on Orlando. The dark areas are surface waters. Most of the lakes visible here are sinkhole lakes. Some of them are as large as 15 km (9 mi) across. For scale, this image is about 200 km (124 mi) across. (Top right: © Red Huber/Orlando Sentinel/MCT via Getty Images; B. EROS Center, U.S. Geological Survey)*

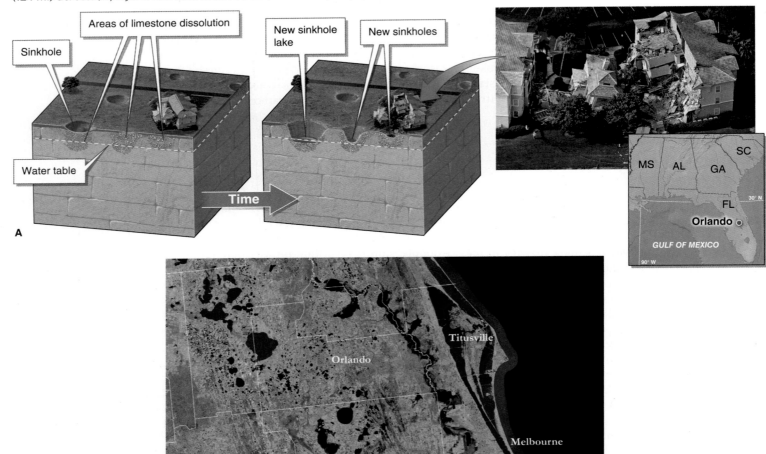

A Riddled Surface: Karst Topography

> Why are homes sometimes swallowed by the ground?

On August 12, 2013, a sinkhole opened up beneath a resort home near Orlando, Florida **(Figure 15.11A)**. Over a span of about 15 minutes half of the house had collapsed into the 60-foot diameter sinkhole, giving the occupants time to safely evacuate. Areas where karst processes prevail, such as Florida, are often referred to as having *karst topography*.

A **sinkhole** (or *doline*) is a depression in Earth's surface that results from the weathering of carbonate rock underground. In the United States, sinkholes are particularly common in Kentucky, Tennessee, and Michigan. Yet Florida has the greatest number of sinkholes. Between 2006 and 2010, Florida insurance companies paid out almost $2 billion for damage done by the state's sinkholes. Florida also has the greatest number of **sinkhole lakes**: sinkholes that are filled with water, as shown in **Figure 15.11B**.

Many limestone karst regions are riddled with steep-walled depressions called collapse sinkholes. A **collapse sinkhole** is formed where the ceiling of a subterranean cavern has collapsed. **Figure 15.12** illustrates the process of collapse sinkhole formation.

sinkhole
A depression in Earth's surface resulting from the weathering of carbonate rock underground.

sinkhole lake
A sinkhole that has filled with water.

collapse sinkhole
A sinkhole formed where the ceiling of a cavern has collapsed.

FIGURE 15.12 **Collapse sinkhole formation.** *(A) The process of limestone weathering that leads to a collapse sinkhole can take thousands of years or more, but the collapse event happens in a matter of minutes after the ceiling of a subterranean cavern gives way. (B) The world's largest collapse sinkhole, China's Xiaozhai Tiankeng, located in Chongqing municipality, is a double collapse sinkhole 662 m (2,172 ft) deep. The larger depression formed first. The interior sinkhole formed later.* (B. Courtesy of John Gunn, University of Birmingham)

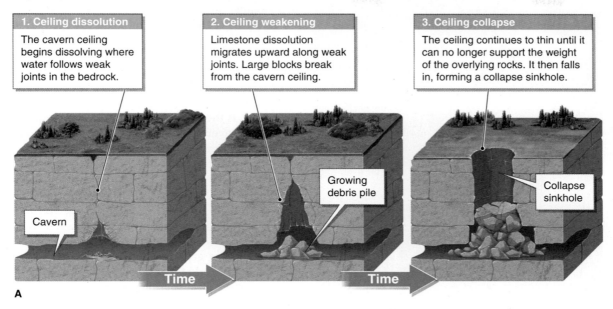

1. Ceiling dissolution
The cavern ceiling begins dissolving where water follows weak joints in the bedrock.

Cavern

2. Ceiling weakening
Limestone dissolution migrates upward along weak joints. Large blocks break from the cavern ceiling.

Growing debris pile

Time

3. Ceiling collapse
The ceiling continues to thin until it can no longer support the weight of the overlying rocks. It then falls in, forming a collapse sinkhole.

Collapse sinkhole

Time

A

China

30° N

Xiaozhai
Tiankeng

120° E

B

FIGURE 15.13 **Ik-Kil Cenote.** *This cenote on the Yucatán Peninsula is popular with swimmers. The edge of the cenote is draped with plant roots that reach all the way to the water below.* (© Pola Damonte/Flickr Open/Getty Images)

disappearing stream
A stream that leaves the ground surface and flows into subterranean channels.

When the lowest level of a collapse sinkhole lies below the water table, a *cenote* forms. Most of the Yucatán Peninsula of Mexico is composed of limestone, and it has many karst features, including cenotes (Figure 15.13). Another spectacular example of a collapse sinkhole is explored in Picture This.

In karst regions, flowing groundwater often excavates subterranean caverns. The fastest dissolution of limestone occurs just below the water table, where the groundwater acidity is highest. As a result, limestone caverns often run parallel to the ground surface, following bedding planes in the limestone. If the water table drops, a new series of horizontal caverns may start forming below the old series of caverns (Figure 15.14).

There are few surface streams in karst regions because water flows underground through cavern systems. The surface streams that are found there usually flow for only short stretches, then disappear into the ground. A stream that leaves the ground surface and flows into subterranean channels is called a **disappearing stream** (Figure 15.15).

> What is a disappearing stream?

Many unique landforms are associated with limestone karst topography. *Limestone pavement*, for example, is a type of bare surface consisting of deeply weathered limestone (Figure 15.16). It is found where exposed limestone bedrock has been dissolved by rainwater and an overlying cover of soil and vegetation is absent.

Picture This

The Great Blue Hole, Belize

The Great Blue Hole, in Belize, is a submarine collapse sinkhole that formed during the most recent glacial period, when sea levels were about 85 m (280 ft) lower than they are today. As the continental ice sheets melted about 10,000 years ago (see Section 6.2), sea level rose, and the collapse sinkhole was inundated with seawater. Coral reefs now fringe the sinkhole and support rich marine biodiversity. The Great Blue Hole, which is about 300 m (984 ft) across and 125 m (410 ft) deep, is among the largest sinkholes on Earth.
(© Greg Johnson/Lonely Planet Images/Getty Images)

Consider This

1. How did the Great Blue Hole form?

2. Why could this collapse sinkhole not have formed after sea level rose?

FIGURE 15.14 **GEO-GRAPHIC: Development of karst caverns and karst topography.** *Karst topography can form where cavern systems have been exposed at the ground surface.*

Animation
Karst topography
http://qrs.ly/pm49ecz

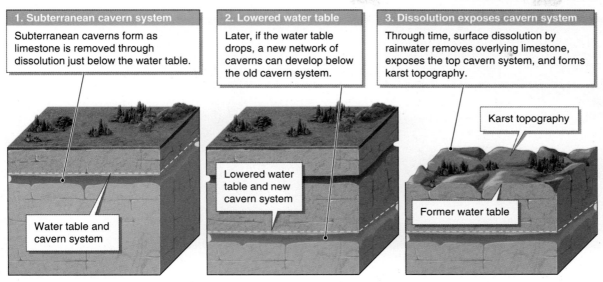

1. Subterranean cavern system
Subterranean caverns form as limestone is removed through dissolution just below the water table.

Water table and cavern system

2. Lowered water table
Later, if the water table drops, a new network of caverns can develop below the old cavern system.

Lowered water table and new cavern system

3. Dissolution exposes cavern system
Through time, surface dissolution by rainwater removes overlying limestone, exposes the top cavern system, and forms karst topography.

Karst topography

Former water table

FIGURE 15.15 **Disappearing stream.** *This small stream in West Virginia is spilling over a resistant shale cliff that is sandwiched between layers of limestone. Notice that the stream emerges from above the shale as a spring and flows back into a subterranean channel as a disappearing stream.* (© James Van Gundy)

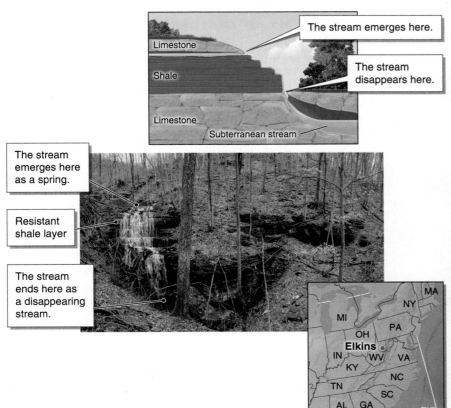

The stream emerges here.

Limestone

Shale

The stream disappears here.

Limestone

Subterranean stream

The stream emerges here as a spring.

Resistant shale layer

The stream ends here as a disappearing stream.

MA
NY
MI
OH
PA
IN
Elkins
WV
VA
KY
NC
TN
SC
AL
GA
75° W

FIGURE 15.16 **Limestone pavement.**
This limestone pavement near Malham, North Yorkshire, England, has weathered along relatively weak linear joints in the bedrock, giving it the appearance of having been built by people.
(© Adam Burton/Robert Harding World Imagery/Getty Images)

60° N   0°
Scotland   NORTH
SEA
Northern
Ireland
Ireland   Malham
United
Kingdom
ATLANTIC
OCEAN   France
15° W

FIGURE **15.17** **Cockpit karst and karst spires.** *(A) The Chocolate Hills, in Bohol Province in the Philippines, are a spectacular example of cockpit karst topography. (B) The Tsingy is a weathered limestone plateau in the Melaky region of western Madagascar that is composed of karst spires. The pattern of weathering was shaped by vertical jointing in the limestone bedrock, resulting in these sharp spires. Because of its unique landforms and the unique species found among them, the area is listed as a UNESCO World Heritage Site.* (A. © Per Andre Hoffman/Picture Press/Getty Images; B. © Inaki Caperochipi/age fotostock/Getty Images)

A

B

speleothem
A cavern formation that forms by precipitation of calcium carbonate.

stalactite
A speleothem that grows from the ceiling of a cavern downward.

stalagmite
A speleothem that grows from the floor of a cavern upward.

limestone column
A cylindrical speleothem resulting when a stalactite joins with a stalagmite.

mass movement
(or *mass wasting*) Downslope movement of rock, soil, snow, or ice caused by gravity.

FIGURE **15.18** **Tower karst.** *Southern China has extensive exposures of limestone and the world's best examples of tower karst. This 400 m (1,312 ft) high karst tower is in Zhangjiajie National Forest Park, near Zhangjiajie City in northern Hunan Province, China.* (© Feng Wei Photography/Flickr RF/Getty Images)

Cockpit karst is a limestone surface with a topography dramatically different from limestone pavement. Cockpit karst consists of vegetated rounded hills formed by limestone weathering **(Figure 15.17A)**.

In other cases, rather than rounded hills, karst processes create *karst spires*. In Madagascar, a "stone forest" called the Tsingy seemingly grows from the ground. Sharp pinnacles and pointed spires of limestone form a labyrinthine landscape that covers several thousand square kilometers and is almost completely inaccessible to people **(Figure 15.17B)**.

As a landscape's surface is lowered by karst processes, pinnacles of *tower karst* may form where weak vertical joints focus the dissolution of the rock along vertical planes **(Figure 15.18)**.

A Hidden World: Subterranean Karst

In regions with limestone bedrock, subterranean caverns are common. In the open air of karst caverns, water seeping from the ground surface outside enters through the cavern ceiling and drips and flows across the ceiling and down the walls. Minerals such as calcium carbonate are slowly precipitated out of the flowing and dripping water. These minerals accumulate into formations called **speleothems** (or *cavern formations*).

Dripstones are speleothems formed by precipitation of calcium carbonate by dripping water. *Flowstones* are sheetlike calcium carbonate deposits formed along the edges that water drops flow down before they drip. Dripstones and flowstones, which form extremely slowly, are commonly several hundred thousand years old. Among the most common dripstones are **stalactites**, formations that grow from the ceiling downward. Conversely, **stalagmites** grow from the cavern floor upward as water drips from stalactites. A **limestone column** is a cylindrical dripstone that results when a stalactite joins with a stalagmite. Stalactites often form a hollow structure called a *soda straw* when they first begin forming. Examples of these speleothems are shown in Figure 15.19.

When the climate is wetter, more water drips from speleothems, and calcium carbonate builds slightly faster than during dry periods. If, however, the water table rises enough to flood the cavern again, the speleothems will stop growing. Similarly, if water stops flowing into the cavern and the ceilings and walls become dry, speleothem growth will stop. For this reason, speleothems play an important role in paleoclimatology (see Section 6.2). They have been used to provide detailed climate reconstructions spanning several hundred thousand years. If the average rate of speleothem growth is known, the age of the speleothems can be estimated (Crunch the Numbers).

CRUNCH THE NUMBERS:
Calculating the Age of a Speleothem

Assume that speleothem growth occurs at a constant rate of 0.01 mm (0.000393 in) in radius per year. How old is a limestone column that is 1.5 m (4.92 ft) in radius? (Note that there are 1,000 millimeters in a meter and 12 inches in a foot.) For this calculation, divide the radius by the growth rate.

15.3 Unstable Ground: Mass Movement

◎ Identify different types of mass movements and describe their behavior and causes.

We have already explored many natural hazards in this book, including tornadoes, hurricanes, volcanoes, and earthquakes. Another significant hazard is posed by soil and rock sliding down a slope by the force of gravity. Landslides and other similar events are collectively called mass movement (or *mass wasting*) events. **Mass movement** is the movement of rock, soil, snow, or ice downslope by gravity.

Why Mass Movement Occurs

A slope is *stable* when it is unlikely to fail and *unstable* when it has failed (experienced mass movement) in the past or is likely to do so soon. Several factors, summarized in Table 15.1, create weak layers

---

FIGURE 15.19 **GEO-GRAPHIC: Dripstone development.**

(A) Dripstones form as water drips through the open air of a cavern and deposits calcium carbonate. (B) The Frasassi Caves, near the town of Genga, Italy, contain excellent examples of dripstones. The inset photo shows a polished cross-section of a stalactite and the hollow soda straw center that forms in the stalactite.
(B. left, © A. de Gregorio/DeAgostini/Getty Images; right, © David K. Lynch)

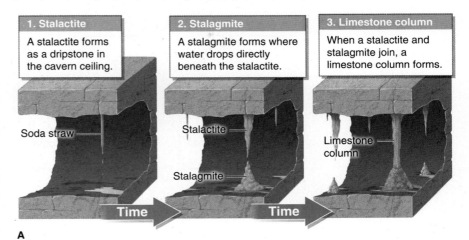

1. **Stalactite**
A stalactite forms as a dripstone in the cavern ceiling.
Soda straw

2. **Stalagmite**
A stalagmite forms where water drops directly beneath the stalactite.
Stalactite
Stalagmite

3. **Limestone column**
When a stalactite and stalagmite join, a limestone column forms.
Limestone column

Time   Time

A

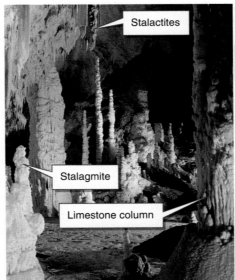
Stalactites
Stalagmite
Limestone column

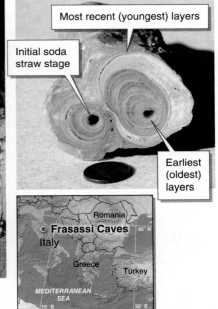
Most recent (youngest) layers
Initial soda straw stage
Earliest (oldest) layers

Romania
Frasassi Caves
Italy
Greece
Turkey
MEDITERRANEAN SEA
Libya

B

TABLE 15.1	AT A GLANCE: Factors That Make Slopes Unstable
Geologic faults	
Jointing in rocks	
Foliation planes in metamorphic rock	
Layers of saturated clay or sand	
Layers of ice between snow layers	

FIGURE 15.20 **Slope stability.** *(A) The angle of repose is the steepest slope a material can maintain while remaining stable. It is a result of the relationship between gravitation and friction among particles, and it varies depending on the shape, size, and wetness of those particles. (B) If the resistance force (F_r) is equal to or greater than the downslope force (F_d), the material will not move. If the resistance force is less than the downslope force, the material will move. In this example, the downslope force is increased by steepening of the slope, as might occur where a hillside is cut by a new road.*

A — Well-rounded sand grains have a small angle of repose. Irregularly shaped gravel has a large angle of repose.

B — $F_r \geq F_d$ Slope steepens $F_r < F_d$. Downslope force (F_d). Resistance force (F_r). Rock does not move. Rock moves.

within rocks, regolith, or snow and potentially create an unstable slope.

Conversely, several factors increase slope stability. Friction and electrical charges hold soil particles together. Soil moisture and plant roots also anchor regolith and keep it from moving. Vegetated regolith that is moist, but not saturated, is far more stable than dry and unvegetated regolith. The surface tension of water and the roots of plants both help bind particles together.

A material's angle of repose (see Section 14.1) is determined by the equilibrium between gravity pulling particles downward and friction holding particles in place. Larger particles have steeper angles of repose than smaller particles. Put another way, the stability of a slope depends on the relationship between *resistance force*, which keeps the material in place, and *downslope force* (or *gravitational force*), which induces the material to slip downhill **(Figure 15.20)**.

Mass movements can be caused by any factor that increases the downslope force or decreases the resistance force. The main factors that can change these forces and result in slope failure are summarized in Table 15.2.

Types of Mass Movements

There are many different types of mass movements, and they range in duration from hundreds of years to a few seconds. We will explore mass movement types, starting with the slowest and most gradual and working up to the fastest and most dangerous, in the sequence shown in Table 15.3.

TABLE 15.2 **Factors That Cause Mass Movements**

FACTOR	EFFECT ON DOWNSLOPE AND RESISTANCE FORCES
Earthquakes	Ground shaking can increase downslope force. Ground shaking can also separate particles of regolith and decrease the friction that holds them together.
Rivers and roadcuts	Steeper slopes are subject to greater downslope force. Rivers often undercut their banks and make them steeper. Roadcuts may make slopes steeper and more likely to fail.
Ground saturation	As soils become saturated, they become heavier, and the downslope force increases. Saturation moves soil particles farther apart, reducing friction between them. Mass movement commonly follows storms that bring heavy, soaking rains. Broken water pipes on steep slopes can also lead to mass movement.
Weathering	Increased weathering weakens the integrity and strength of rocks and regolith.
Removal of vegetation	Removal of vegetation and its anchoring roots weakens the ground and decreases the resistance force.

TABLE 15.3 **AT A GLANCE: Types of Mass Movements**

TYPE OF MASS MOVEMENT	RATE OF MOVEMENT
Soil creep	Slow
Slumps	↑
Flows and landslides	↕
Avalanches	
Rockfall	Fast

FIGURE 15.21 **Soil creep.** *(A) Soils work their way downslope as they expand and contract with the seasons. (B) Soil creep is fastest near the land surface and slows down nearer bedrock.*

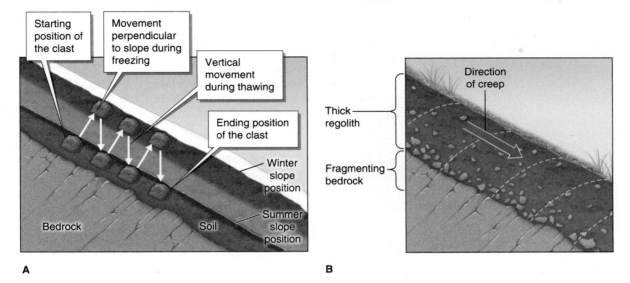

A

B

Soil Creep

Soil creep is the imperceptible downslope movement of soil and regolith as their volume changes in seasonal expansion-contraction cycles. Clay particles in soil expand when wetted or warmed and then, as the season changes, contract when dried or cooled. In addition, wet soils that freeze in winter can expand by about 10%. When thawed in spring, they contract by the same amount. As they expand, soils move outward perpendicularly away from the sloped surface. As they contract, they settle downward vertically. These movements result in soil creep **(Figure 15.21)**.

These small movements add up to significant downslope migration of soils after many years. Soil creep is like the tides: It is too slow to be seen in motion, but its effects are easy to see in a landscape **(Figure 15.22)**.

FIGURE 15.22 **Soil creep and its effects.** *Structures and vegetation on hillsides sometimes sag downslope because of soil creep. (Bruce Gervais)*

soil creep
The imperceptible downslope movement of soil and regolith as their volume changes in seasonal expansion-contraction cycles.

FIGURE 15.23 **Solifluction in the Tian Shan Mountains, Kyrgyzstan.** *(© Marli Miller)*

Soil is slowly flowing downhill in sheets

solifluction
A type of soil creep in which freeze-thaw cycles cause the soil to flow slowly downslope in overlapping sheets.

slump
A type of mass movement in which regolith detaches and slides downslope along a spoon-shaped failure surface and comes to rest more or less as a unit.

A special type of soil creep, called **solifluction**, occurs in northern and alpine tundra (see Section 8.4). Solifluction is a type of soil creep in which freeze-thaw, expansion-contraction cycles cause the soil to flow slowly downslope in overlapping sheets, as shown in **Figure 15.23**.

Another type of imperceptible soil movement is caused by the movements of livestock, particularly cattle, on the slopes of hills. This phenomenon is explored in **Picture This**.

Slumps

A **slump** is a type of mass movement in which regolith detaches and slides downslope along a spoon-shaped plane, called a *failure surface*, and comes to rest more or less as a unit. Slumps are often called *rotational slides* because they follow the concave failure surface over which regolith moves. The topmost point of detachment of the slump, and the resulting cliff, is called the *head scarp*. The base of the slump is called the *toe*, as shown in **Figure 15.24**.

Flows and Landslides

Flows and landslides are common occurrences in all mountainous regions. **Landslide** is a general term for the rapid movement of rock or debris down a steep slope. *Flows* are always mixed with large amounts of water, and overall, they move less quickly than landslides.

There are several different kinds of flows. Their surface areas vary from a few square meters to tens of square kilometers. Their rate of movement depends on the type of flow, the water content of the moving material, and the steepness of the slope. On gentle slopes, they may move at the rate of a slow walk, but on steeper slopes, it may be impossible to outrun them.

Mudflows are fast-moving flows composed mostly of mud. In **debris flows**, a fast-flowing

Picture This

(© Laura Alice Watt)

Cattle Terraces

These parallel ridges, called *cattle terraces* (or *livestock terraces*), are near Hollister, California. The terraces are trails that cattle have created as they walk along the hillside. There is nothing special about the soils where cattle terracing occurs. The terraces are formed because the slope is too steep for the cattle to walk straight up or down, so they must instead follow a line of equal elevation, or a *contour*. Cattle terraces are common on slopes of intermediate steepness where cattle are grazed in large numbers. If a slope is too gentle, cattle will not follow the contours, and terraces will not develop. Likewise, if a slope is too steep, cattle will not graze on it for fear of falling. Cattle terraces are a form of mass movement similar to soil creep or solifluction.

Consider This

1. Why do cattle follow the contour of the hillside rather than walking straight up or down the hill?

2. If you went to a new area and saw what looked like cattle terraces, what evidence would you look for to support the hypothesis that cattle made the terraces?

FIGURE 15.24 **Slumps.** *(A) Slumps can be triggered by earthquakes or heavy rains. Their downhill rate of movement ranges from millimeters per day or less to several meters per minute. They range in size from a few meters to a few kilometers across. (B) This slump occurred in Stone Canyon near Los Angeles. Heavy spring rains were blamed for the slump.* (Tom McHugh/Science Source)

Video
Landslide hazards
http://qrs.ly/8i49ed1

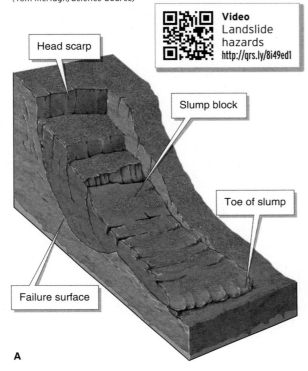

A

B

slurry of mud is mixed with large objects, such as rocks and vegetation. Volcanic eruptions often produce debris flows called lahars (see Section 14.2). One of the most deadly debris flows in history, however, occurred in northern Venezuela not because of a volcanic eruption, but because of heavy rains **(Figure 15.25)**.

All landslides occur in mountainous terrain where slopes are steep (but not vertical). They can move at rates of several hundred kilometers per hour and come to rest within minutes after the initial movement begins.

landslide
Rapid movement of rock or debris down a steep slope.

mudflow
A fast-moving flow composed mostly of mud.

debris flow
A fast-flowing slurry of mud mixed with large objects, such as rocks and vegetation.

FIGURE 15.25 **Caraballeda debris flow.** *(A) In December 1999, after heavy rains, a debris flow devastated Caraballeda, in the state of Vargas, Venezuela. Up to 30,000 people died, and 75,000 were displaced. The damage totaled up to $3 billion. (B) Boulders the size of small houses were transported in the debris flow.* (A. U.S. Geological Survey, photo by Matthew C. Larsen; B. U.S. Geological Survey, photo by Matthew C. Larsen)

A

B

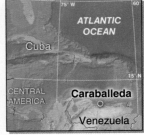

FIGURE 15.26 **SCIENTIFIC INQUIRY: Can scientists predict dangerous landslides?** *The key to developing an early warning system for deadly landslides is monitoring ground movement long before the slope fails. Heavy rains are more likely to trigger a mass movement event on slopes that have been moving before the rains. Long-term monitoring stations allow scientists to develop a history of slope movement for a given location. Scientists issue evacuation warnings if the slope shows signs of moving, although accurate predictions of the timing of slope failure are not possible. (Clockwise from top left: © 2014 Nicole Feidl and UNAVCO; © TUM, Forschungsgruppe alpEWAS; © TUM, Forschungsgruppe alpEWAS)*

GPS sensors

A network of sensors connected to the GPS (Global Positioning System) is installed on unstable slopes. Even the smallest movements of the soil are measurable using the GPS.

Laser measurements

Lasers located on unstable soil are beamed and reflected off an unmoving object nearby, such as an outcrop. Small changes in ground position can be detected by the reflected laser signal, providing extremely precise measurements of even small movements.

Borehole cables

Scientists drill deep boreholes through the ground and lower wire cables into the boreholes. If the ground begins slowly moving, the cables will be pinched and send a signal that the ground is shifting.

rock slide
A landslide that consists of rocks and broken rock fragments.

debris slide
A landslide that consists of a mixture of rocks, soil, and vegetation.

avalanche
A turbulent cloud of rock debris or snow that is mixed with air and races quickly down a steep slope.

A **rock slide** is a landslide that consists predominantly of rocks and broken rock fragments, and a **debris slide** (or *debris avalanche*) consists of regolith and other material, such as soil and trees. Heavy rains and earthquakes often trigger the slope failure that gives rise to landslides. At the end of this chapter, Geographic Perspectives discusses the hazards of landslides and the efforts of scientists to predict slope failure and save lives. **Figure 15.26** details the techniques scientists are using to monitor ground movement on unstable slopes.

GEOGRAPHIC PERSPECTIVES

Where are the highest sea cliffs in the world?

Landslides also occur on the seafloor where slopes are steep. Much of the coastline of the Hawaiian Islands, for example, is dominated by enormous head scarps formed by undersea debris slides that occurred before the islands were settled by people **(Figure 15.27)**.

Avalanches

National Geographic photographer and adventurer Jimmy Chin did what few people have ever done: He rode a snow avalanche 300 m (984 ft) down

FIGURE 15.27 **Undersea debris slides in the Hawaiian Islands.** *(A) The north coast of Moloka'i, shown here, has been shaped by large debris slides. These sea cliffs are the highest in the world. (B) The debris slides that shaped sea cliffs continued down the steep submarine slopes surrounding the Hawaiian Islands. The brown areas in this map show the extent of these submarine debris slides, most of which are larger than the islands themselves. The 2,000 m (6,560 ft) depth contour is shown. (A. © Richard J. Anderson)*

A

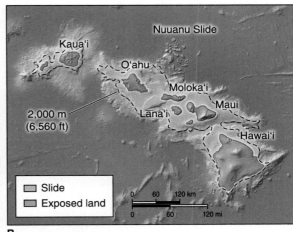

B

a mountain and survived. While Chin was on a photo shoot in the Grand Tetons of Wyoming, a "large, wet slab" cracked loose around him as he began a downhill ski run. As the churning cloud of snow consumed him, he struggled to stay on top. He knew that when it came to rest, the snow would compact and entomb him like cement and he would suffocate within minutes. He managed to work his way to the surface before the avalanche came to a rest. He was bruised and shaken, but alive.

Broadly defined, an **avalanche** is a turbulent cloud of rock debris or snow that is mixed with air and races quickly down a steep slope. *Snow avalanches* are composed mostly of snow. If the avalanche consists of rock, broken trees, and other material, it is called a *debris avalanche*. Avalanches are mixed with air and are therefore extremely turbulent. They gain such momentum that they are capable of knocking down trees and buildings in their path. Like slumps, they are triggered when a slip at a failure surface releases snow or debris. Snow avalanches often happen in the same area repeatedly, forming *avalanche chutes* through which snow and debris avalanches regularly move **(Figure 15.28)**.

FIGURE 15.28 **An avalanche chute.**

Avalanche chutes form where the topography of mountainous areas guides snow avalanches. This snow avalanche is moving down an avalanche chute in the Pamirs, a mountainous region in Tajikistan. (© Medford Taylor/National Geographic/Getty Images)

FIGURE 15.29 **Rockfall in Yosemite Valley.** *(A) This map shows the locations of rockfall events in Yosemite Valley over 150 years. The season is coded by color, and the amount of material that fell is indicated by the size of the colored circle. (B) This photo captured a major rockfall event as it occurred on October 11, 2010. (C) Large angular boulders dot Yosemite Valley's floor. Many of these boulders, which originated from prehistoric rockfall events, traveled far into the valley before they came to rest. (A. Greg Stock, Yosemite National Park, National Park Service; B. © Tom Evans, www.elcapreport.com; C. Steven M. Bumgardner, Yosemite National Park, National Park Service)*

A

B

C

FIGURE 15.30

Talus. *Talus accumulates to form a talus cone at the base of Kearsarge Pinnacles in the Sierra Nevada, in California. The talus has settled at its angle of repose. When two or more talus cones converge, as shown here, a talus apron is formed. (Bruce Gervais)*

Rockfall chute

Talus cone

Talus apron

Rockfall

Rockfall occurs when rocks tumble off a vertical or nearly vertical cliff face **(Figure 15.29)**. As rocks fall, they are broken apart into smaller fragments and dislodge other rocks as well. Rockfall is particularly common along roadcuts. Near rocky cliffs, the asphalt surface of roads is often pitted by earlier rockfall events.

Rockfall caused by frost wedging on steep mountain faces often creates piles of rock. The pieces of angular broken rock that accumulate at the base of a steep slope or vertical cliff are called **talus** (or *scree*). Repeated rockfall events in the same location can carve notches into the bedrock called *rockfall chutes*. Talus accumulates at the base of rockfall chutes in cone-shaped piles, or *talus cones*, as shown in **Figure 15.30**.

The agents of weathering and mass movement all act simultaneously and continuously to reduce the vertical relief that Earth's internal geothermal energy has built up. **Figure 15.31** reviews these processes in the context of the Grand Canyon.

rockfall
A type of mass movement in which rocks tumble off a vertical or nearly vertical cliff face.

talus
(or *scree*) Pieces of angular broken rock that accumulate at the base of a steep slope or vertical cliff.

FIGURE 15.31 **GEO-GRAPHIC: Carving the Grand Canyon.** *(© Gary Crabbe/age fotostock)*

Plate tectonics

Geologic uplift
Uplift of the Colorado Plateau gives the Colorado River a steeper slope and more energy to carry sediments away.

Mass movement

Rockfall
This boulder is perched precariously and will eventually fall in high wind, during an earthquake, or as weathering continues.

Rock slide
These lobes protruding into the river were formed by rock slides. They formed temporary dams until the river cut through them.

Talus and angle of repose
Frost wedging and other types of weathering break off blocks of rock that accumulate in talus cones at the angle of repose.

Weathering

Differential weathering
These layers of sedimentary rock are composed of different materials and have different resistances to weathering, creating the stair-step pattern seen here.

Jointing
Weathering occurs fastest along weak areas or cracks in the rock, called joints.

Chemical weathering
Iron minerals (such as hematite) in the rock are oxidizing (rusting). This chemical weathering process weakens the rock.

Physical weathering
Frost wedging widens cracks in the sandstone, breaking the rock apart.

Erosion

Stream erosion
(see chapter 16)
Like a conveyor belt, the Colorado River carries material that slides into it downslope toward the ocean. This process deepens and widens the canyon through time.

Vegetation
These dark areas are covered by streamside plants. At the river's edge, plant roots anchor sandy soil and reduce erosion. Plant roots can also cause physical weathering as they break rocks into smaller fragments.

WA
MT
45° N
OR   ID   WY
NV   UT   CO
CA   Grand Canyon
AZ   NM
120° W

GEOGRAPHIC PERSPECTIVES
15.4 Deadly Mass Movements

◎ Assess the threats to people from mass movements and explain how their vulnerability to those threats can be reduced.

Mass movement events are deadly hazards for people. According to the USGS, mass movement events are among the world's most deadly of natural disasters. It is estimated that $2 billion to $4 billion in damage and an average of 50 deaths are caused by mass movements in the United States annually. A study published in the journal *Geology* in 2012 found that between 2004 and 2010, there were 2,620 deadly mass movements worldwide, which killed about 32,300 people **(Figure 15.32)**.

Causes of Deadly Mass Movements

As we have seen, the factors that cause most mass movement events are the undercutting of steep slopes, the removal of vegetation, earthquakes, and heavy and prolonged rainfall. Many mass movement disasters have been preceded by deforestation and slope steepening through development, which weakens the slopes. An earthquake, or saturation of the ground by heavy rainfall, then triggers slope failure. Major mass wasting events causing 1,000 deaths or more have occurred, on average, about every 4.5 years in the last 50 years **(Figure 15.33)**.

A less obvious hazard is created by landslides when rivers are blocked by debris. River canyons are frequently sites of slides because stream erosion cuts steep walls that become unstable through time. These slides often settle across rivers, damming them and creating lakes behind the dam debris. The 2008 Sichuan earthquake created 66 new lakes as landslide debris dammed the streams. More than 40 of these debris dams had to be carefully removed

FIGURE **15.32** **Deadly mass movements.** *This map shows the locations of 2,620 mass movement events that took place between 2004 and 2010 and resulted in human deaths. Landslides that were triggered by earthquakes are not included. If they were included, this number would be considerably higher.*

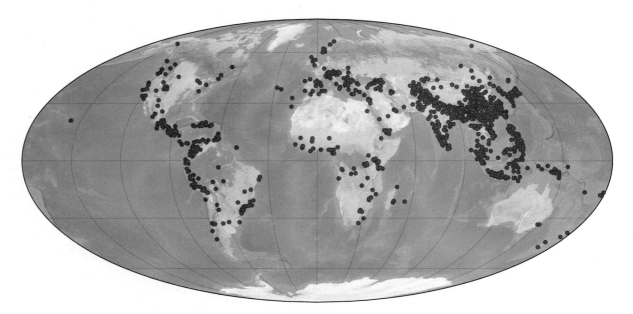

FIGURE 15.33 **Recent deadly mass movements.** *(A) On February 27, 2006, half the village of Guinsaugon, on Leyte Island, in the Philippines, was buried by this debris slide. The slide traveled quickly down the steep slopes over a distance of 3.8 km (2.3 mi) before coming to rest. Some 1,100 people died in this single slide. (B) This table lists recent mass movement disasters that took 10,000 lives or more. Note that in some cases, multiple mass movement events are grouped together under a single trigger event, such as the Sichuan earthquake in 2008 and Hurricane Mitch in 1998.* (AP Photo/Wally Santana)

A

YEAR	LOCATION	ESTIMATED FATALITIES	TRIGGER
1999	Vargas, Venezuela	30,000	Heavy rains
2005	Pakistan and India	25,500	Kashmir earthquake
1985	Colombia (Tolima)	23,000	Eruption of Nevado del Ruiz volcano
2008	China (Sichuan)	20,000	Sichuan earthquake
1970	Peru (Ancash)	18,000	Earthquake
1998	Honduras, Guatemala, Nicaragua, and El Salvador	10,000	Heavy rains from Hurricane Mitch

B

because scientists feared that the dams would suddenly break and the impounded water would submerge communities downstream.

Assessing the Risk

Many developing countries are particularly vulnerable to mass movement disasters. Factors that increase the possibility of a disaster include heavy rainfall brought by the summer monsoon (see Section 4.4) or by tropical cyclones (see Section 5.3), farming on steep slopes (see Section 9.1), *shantytown* (slum) settlements on steep hillsides, large populations, and poverty. In many large ur-

banized regions, such as Rio de Janeiro, Brazil, or Manila, in the Philippines, human population growth and economic marginalization have driven uncontrolled settlement expansion onto steep and unstable slopes, where mass movements are more likely to occur.

Mapping the spatial variation in mass movement risk is a relatively straightforward task. Using satellite data and a GIS (see Section GT.4), scientists have mapped areas of greatest mass movement susceptibility (**Figure 15.34** on page 502). But as useful as it is for identifying areas of risk, such maps do not provide real-time warnings as changes in weather elevate the risk of mass movements.

FIGURE **15.34** **Global landslide risk.** *This map of landslide risk, which includes all types of ground movement, was made using satellite data and a GIS. To make the map, scientists analyzed slope steepness (steeper slopes have a higher risk), land-use types (land with less vegetation has a higher risk), and soil types (coarse-grained soils have a higher risk). The black dots show areas where significant landslides occurred between 2003 and 2006.*

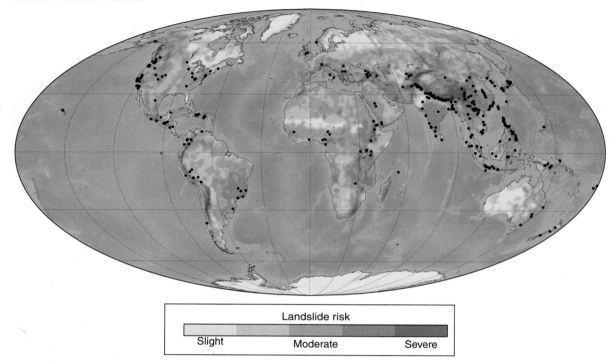

FIGURE **15.35** **TRMM map of potential landslide areas.** *This map shows landslide risks for South Asia for August 22, 2013. This map is based on 7-day average rainfall intensities and rainfall totals. Areas with increased landslide potential are circled in yellow. Areas that are likely or very likely to experience landslides are colored orange and red.* (Harold F. Pierce/NASA Goddard Space Flight Center)

To address this problem, scientists have developed a risk-assessment program that is based on rainfall rates and amounts. It is available in real time to anyone with an Internet connection. The TRMM (Tropical Rainfall Measuring Mission), run by NASA and the Japan Aerospace Exploration Agency (JAXA), evaluates landslide risk by using satellites to measure rainfall amounts and rainfall intensity for all tropical areas. These data are used in conjunction with the mass movement risk map above to provide real-time warnings **(Figure 15.35)**.

At a global scale, identifying broad regions most at risk of landslides is a relatively simple task. However, at a large geographic scale, identifying which specific slopes will fail, and which towns and villages are at risk, is difficult. Although monitoring techniques like those shown in Figure 15.26 can detect ground movements, there is not yet a warning system for mass movements analogous to the U.S. tornado warning system (see Section 5.2), which has proved so effective at giving people enough lead time to get out of harm's way. Scientists are trying to develop a similar system that gives residents warning of landslide hazards. These efforts could reduce our vulnerability to these natural disasters.

CHAPTER 15 Exploring with ◉ Google Earth

To complete these problems, first read the chapter. When you are finished, go to LaunchPad and open the Exploring with Google Earth file for this chapter. Click on the "Workbook Problems" folder to "fly" to each of the problems listed below and answer the questions. Be sure to keep your "Borders and Labels" layer activated. Refer to Appendix 4 if you need help using Google Earth.

PROBLEM 15.1 This geographically remote limestone plateau is in Bolívar State, in southeastern Venezuela. Note the large circular depressions in the land surface.

1. **What is the name for these sunken, circular landforms?**
   a. Sinkholes
   b. Collapse sinkholes
   c. Disappearing streams
   d. Wells

2. **What is the name of the process that created these landforms?**
   a. Groundwater overdraft
   b. Infiltration
   c. Erosion
   d. Carbonation

3. **Zoom out. Why are there no surface streams on this plateau, even though it has a tropical rainforest climate?**
   a. Because it is too arid
   b. Because it is the dry season
   c. Because streams run underground here
   d. Because human activity has diverted the streams

PROBLEM 15.2 Note that this placemark, near the placemark for the previous problem, pins to an exposed, blocky bedrock surface.

1. **What is the name of this type of bedrock surface?**
   a. Tower karst
   b. Cockpit karst
   c. Limestone pavement
   d. Collapse sinkhole

PROBLEM 15.3 This placemark lands on the Arecibo Observatory in Puerto Rico, the largest radio telescope in the world. The telescope is built in a natural, steep-sided depression in limestone bedrock. Pan around and zoom in and out to get a sense of the landscape's features.

1. **What is the name of the natural depression in which the telescope was built?**
   a. Sinkhole
   b. Sinkhole lake
   c. Cone of depression
   d. Aquifer

2. **Notice the rounded hills that compose this landscape. What is the name for this type of landscape?**
   a. Cockpit karst
   b. Limestone pavement
   c. Tower karst
   d. Kame-and-kettle topography

3. **What is the distance across the telescope?**
   a. 20 m
   b. 102 m
   c. 315 m
   d. 500 m

PROBLEM 15.4 Florida is composed of low-lying limestone bedrock that is pockmarked with many water-filled depressions, forming wetlands, ponds, and lakes. This placemark is pinned to Lake Louisa.

1. **What is the name of these natural depressions after they have filled with water?**
   a. Sinkholes
   b. Collapse sinkholes
   c. Sinkhole lakes
   d. Tower karst

2. **What natural features here indicate the elevation of the water table?**
   a. The elevation of the land
   b. The elevation of the lake surfaces
   c. The growth of vegetation
   d. The locations of cities and farms

3. **Compare the elevation of Lake Louisa with that of the larger Lake Apopka just to the northeast in this same view. (Measure near the shoreline, not the center of the lake.) Which is higher?**
   a. Lake Louisa
   b. Lake Apopka

4. **In what direction will groundwater flow in this area?**
   a. From Lake Louisa to Lake Apopka
   b. From Lake Apopka to Lake Louisa

PROBLEM 15.5 This mass movement occurred on October 9, 1963, in Italy, leaving a large open scar on the mountainside. The material slid into the reservoir and created a large wave that overtopped the dam. Some 2,000 people lost their lives in this mass movement event. In response to this catastrophe, the reservoir was drained. All that remains is Vajont Dam, visible in the foreground of this view. Turn on your 3D Buildings layer in the sidebar menu to better see the dam.

1. **What kind of mass movement was this?**
   a. Soil creep
   b. Mudflow
   c. Slump
   d. Debris flow

2. **The placemark is on what part of this mass movement?**
   a. The head scarp
   b. The toe
   c. The flow body
   d. The talus

PROBLEM 15.6 This placemark is pinned to a landform in the Karakoram Range of Pakistan.

1. **What is the name of this landform?**
   a. Talus cone
   b. Avalanche
   c. Debris flow
   d. Hoodoo

2. **What physical weathering process created this landform?**
   a. Carbonation
   b. Pedogenesis
   c. Frost wedging
   d. Biochemical weathering

PROBLEM 15.7 Lines following equal elevations on the hillside are seen at this placemark.

1. **What are these lines on the hillside called?**
   a. Soil creep
   b. Slumps
   c. Exfoliation
   d. Cattle terraces

2. **How were they formed?**
   a. By walking cattle
   b. Through solifluction
   c. By debris flows
   d. Through physical weathering

PROBLEM 15.8 Mount Bawakaraeng, in South Sulawesi, Indonesia, is a volcano. This mass movement event on the slopes of the mountain was triggered by the collapse of the wall of a caldera of the volcano, not a volcanic eruption.

1. **What kind of mass movement event was this?**
   a. Slump
   b. Soil creep
   c. Debris flow
   d. Rock slide

2. **Zoom out until you can see marker 1. (You may need to activate it if it is not already activated.) How many kilometers did the material travel from the top of the mountain down to marker 1?**

   a. 1 km

   b. 3 km

   c. 6 km

   d. 9 km

3. **What is the approximate elevation drop of the mass movement, from top to bottom?**

   a. 900 m

   b. 1,780 m

   c. 2,400 m

   d. 3,000 m

PROBLEM 15.9 This placemark marks the terminus of the accumulations of several enormous submarine landslides that occurred at different times in the past. The slides originated on Oʻahu and Molokaʻi islands.

1. **What is the length of the slide material between the placemark and the Molokaʻi coast?**

   a. 50 mi

   b. 100 mi

   c. 150 mi

   d. 250 mi

2. **What is the depth where the placemark is positioned at the terminus of the slide material?**

   a. 1,500 ft

   b. 4,500 ft

   c. 10,300 ft

   d. 14,800 ft

PROBLEM 15.10 This placemark is in Pasadena, California, at the foot of the San Gabriel Mountains. It marks one of hundreds of concrete dam-like structures built at the base of the San Gabriel Mountains in Los Angeles County (notice another one just to the east—or to the right). These structures are not designed to hold water. They are instead designed to constrain mass movements within a concrete channel. Zoom out and tilt to get a sense of these structures in the geographic context of the city and the San Gabriel Mountains.

1. **What type of mass movement are these structures designed to protect city residents and property from?**

   a. Avalanches

   b. Rockfall

   c. Debris flows

   d. Soil creep

2. **Zoom out a bit. Notice marker 1, located in a small canyon. Tilt your view so you can see its position in relation to the containment channel. Do mass movements pose a risk to the residents of homes along the street at marker 1?**

   a. Yes

   b. No

PROBLEM 15.11 This placemark, also in Southern California, pins to a road that suddenly terminates.

1. **What kind of mass movement destroyed this road?**

   a. Soil creep

   b. A slump

   c. Rockfall

   d. A lahar

2. **Pan to the south and west of the placemark. What evidence indicates that this mass movement destroyed homes, but that they have been rebuilt?**

   a. Houses are built at strange angles at the base of the debris compared with the rest of the neighborhood.

   b. Several neighborhood roads appear to be partially buried by debris.

   c. Both of these features indicate that the mass movement destroyed homes and they were subsequently rebuilt.

CHAPTER 15 **Study Guide**

Focus Points

15.1 Weathering Rocks

Physical weathering: Rates of physical weathering are greatest at high elevations and high latitudes.

Frost wedging: Frost wedging is the most important type of physical weathering where temperatures fall below freezing.

Chemical weathering: Chemical weathering is dominant where temperatures remain above freezing and there is plenty of moisture.

15.2 Dissolving Rocks: Karst Landforms

Karst processes: Carbonate rocks dissolve in naturally acidic rainwater, forming karst topography. Most karst topography is found in limestone bedrock.

Surface karst topography: Limestone pavement, sinkholes, collapse sinkholes, disappearing streams, cockpit karst, and tower karst are among the most prominent surface features in karst topography.

Subterranean karst: Subterranean landforms, such as caverns and speleothems, are common in karst regions.

15.3 Unstable Ground: Mass Movement

Causes of mass movement: When the downslope force exceeds the resistance force, a slope will fail, and mass movement will occur. Many factors, such as earthquakes, heavy rains, and roadcuts, can trigger mass movement events.

Mass movement speed: Material moves downslope at speeds ranging from slow soil creep to rapid and deadly avalanches and rockfall.

15.4 Geographic Perspectives: Deadly Mass Movements

Human toll: Many human fatalities caused by landslides occur because people live on steep and unstable slopes that have been weakened by heavy rains.

Key Terms

avalanche, 497
chemical weathering, 482
collapse sinkhole, 486
debris flow, 494
debris slide, 496
denudation, 481
differential weathering, 485
disappearing stream, 488

erosion, 481
exfoliation, 481
frost wedging, 482
karst, 485
landslide, 494
limestone column, 491
mass movement (or *mass wasting*), 491

mudflow, 494
physical weathering, 481
rockfall, 499
rock slide, 496
root wedging, 482
salt wedging, 482
sinkhole, 486
sinkhole lake, 486
slump, 494

soil creep, 493
solifluction, 494
speleothem, 490
stalactite, 491
stalagmite, 491
tafoni, 482
talus (or *scree*), 499
weathering, 481

Concept Review

The Human Sphere: Weathering Mount Rushmore

1. Why is weathering such a concern to the people responsible for maintaining the Mount Rushmore National Memorial?

15.1 Weathering Rocks

2. Geothermal energy builds vertical relief. Where does the energy that reduces vertical relief come from?

3. Compare and contrast the processes of weathering and erosion. What does weathering do to rocks? What does erosion do to rocks and rock fragments?

4. What is denudation? What processes denude Earth's surface?

5. What is physical weathering? Geographically, where is it most common? Give examples of physical weathering processes.

6. Why are joints important to the process of weathering?

7. What is exfoliation? Where does it occur?

8. What is frost wedging? Where does it take place?

9. Besides frost wedging, what two other types of physical weathering break rocks apart? Briefly explain each.

10. Describe chemical weathering and give examples of chemical reactions that cause it.

11. Geographically, where is chemical weathering the dominant weathering process?

12. What is differential weathering? How does it relate to jointing and bedding planes?

13. Give three examples of landforms created by differential weathering.

15.2 Dissolving Rocks: Karst Landforms

14. What is karst? What processes give rise to karst landforms?

15. In which type of bedrock is karst most commonly found?

16. What is a sinkhole and how does one form?

17. What is a collapse sinkhole and how does one form?

18. What is a sinkhole lake?

19. What is a karst cavern? Where do karst caverns form in relation to the water table?

20. Explain what a disappearing stream is and how it forms.

21. What is limestone pavement?

22. Explain how cockpit karst and tower karst form.

23. What are speleothems? Why do they form only when the water table drops below a karst cavern?

24. What are dripstones and flowstones?

25. Contrast stalactites, stalagmites, and limestone columns. How does each form?

15.3 Unstable Ground: Mass Movement

26. What is a mass movement event? What single factor do all kinds of mass movements share?

27. What are resistance and downslope forces in the context of mass movement events? Give examples of how each force can change.

28. What happens when the resistance force exceeds the downslope force? What happens when the downslope force exceeds the resistance force?

29. Review the different types of mass movements and the settings in which each occurs.

30. What are the differences between flows and landslides?

31. Define an avalanche. Are all avalanches composed of snow?

32. What is talus? What is a talus cone? How do rockfall chutes relate to talus cones?

15.4 Geographic Perspectives: Deadly Mass Movements

33. What natural and anthropogenic factors increase the chance of a mass movement event?

34. Can scientists predict landslides with accuracy?

35. Explain how scientific tools have helped reduce human vulnerability to mass movement disasters.

Critical-Thinking Questions

1. Chemical weathering occurs faster as temperatures warm and rainfall increases. On a global scale, how might human activities change the rate of chemical weathering?

2. In terms of geologic time, do you think that landforms resulting from differential weathering, such as natural arches and hoodoos, are short-lived or permanent features? Explain.

3. Are there subterranean caverns near where you live? If you do not know, how would you find out?

4. The process of weathering has been going on since Earth first formed and never stops, yet many rocks are still "fresh" and relatively unweathered. Why haven't all of Earth's rocks been weathered away long ago?

Test Yourself

Take this quiz to test your chapter knowledge.

1. **True or false?** Frost wedging is a type of physical weathering.

2. **True or false?** Chemical weathering occurs mostly at high latitudes.

3. **True or false?** Debris flows move slowly and are rarely fatal.

4. **True or false?** A snow avalanche is a type of mass movement.

5. **True or false?** Only limestone rock forms karst topography.

6. **True or false?** Dripstones and flowstones are two common types of speleothems.

7. **Multiple choice:** Which of the following increases the resistance force on a slope?
   a. A roadcut   c. Vegetation growth
   b. An earthquake   d. Heavy rains

8. **Multiple choice:** Which of the following requires vertical joints to form?
   a. A collapse sinkhole   c. Tower karst
   b. Limestone pavement   d. Cockpit karst

9. **Fill in the blank:** Natural arches are the result of

   _____.

10. **Fill in the blank:** A pitted surface caused by weathering in a coastal area is most likely _____.

Picture This. YOUR TURN

Mass Movement

Fill in the blanks on the diagram, using each of the following terms only once.

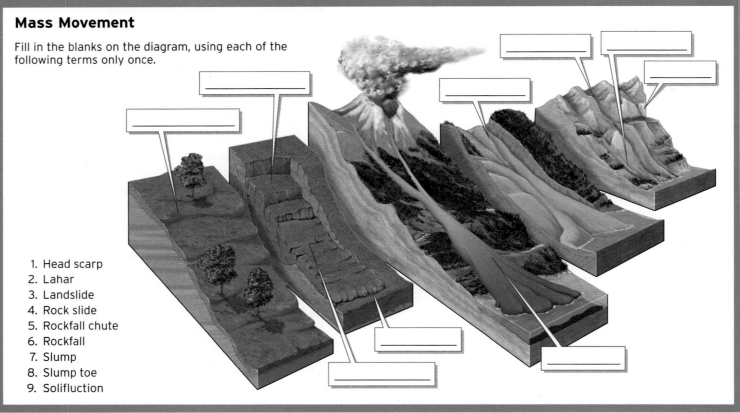

1. Head scarp
2. Lahar
3. Landslide
4. Rock slide
5. Rockfall chute
6. Rockfall
7. Slump
8. Slump toe
9. Solifluction

Further Reading

1. Larsen, Isaac J., and David R. Montgomery. "Landslide Erosion Coupled to Tectonics and River Incision." *Nature Geoscience* 5 (2012): 468–473.

2. Turner, Keith, and Robert Schuster. *Landslides: Investigation and Mitigation*. Washington, D.C.: Transportation Research Board, 1996.

3. Perkins, Sid. "Death Toll from Landslides Vastly Underestimated." *Nature*, August 8, 2012. doi:10.1038/nature.2012.11140.

Answers to Living Physical Geography Questions

1. **Where does beach sand come from?** The sand grains that make up most beaches are the weathered and eroded remnants of bedrock that once formed mountains.

2. **Why are homes sometimes swallowed by the ground?** Sinkholes are depressions that form when carbonate rocks dissolve. Any unlucky structures sitting over a forming sinkhole can be pulled into them.

3. **What is a disappearing stream?** A disappearing stream is a stream that leaves the ground surface and flows into a hidden subterranean cavern system.

4. **Where are the highest sea cliffs in the world?** The north coast of Moloka'i, in the Hawaiian Islands, has sea cliffs that are the highest in the world.

16

FLOWING WATER: Fluvial Systems

Chapter Outline

Lena River Delta

Russia

Mongolia China Japan

This satellite image shows where the Lena River meets the Arctic Ocean in northeastern Russia. Here, the river forms a delta as it splits into a fine network of streams, resembling the pattern of branches on a tree.

(EROS Center, U.S. Geological Survey)

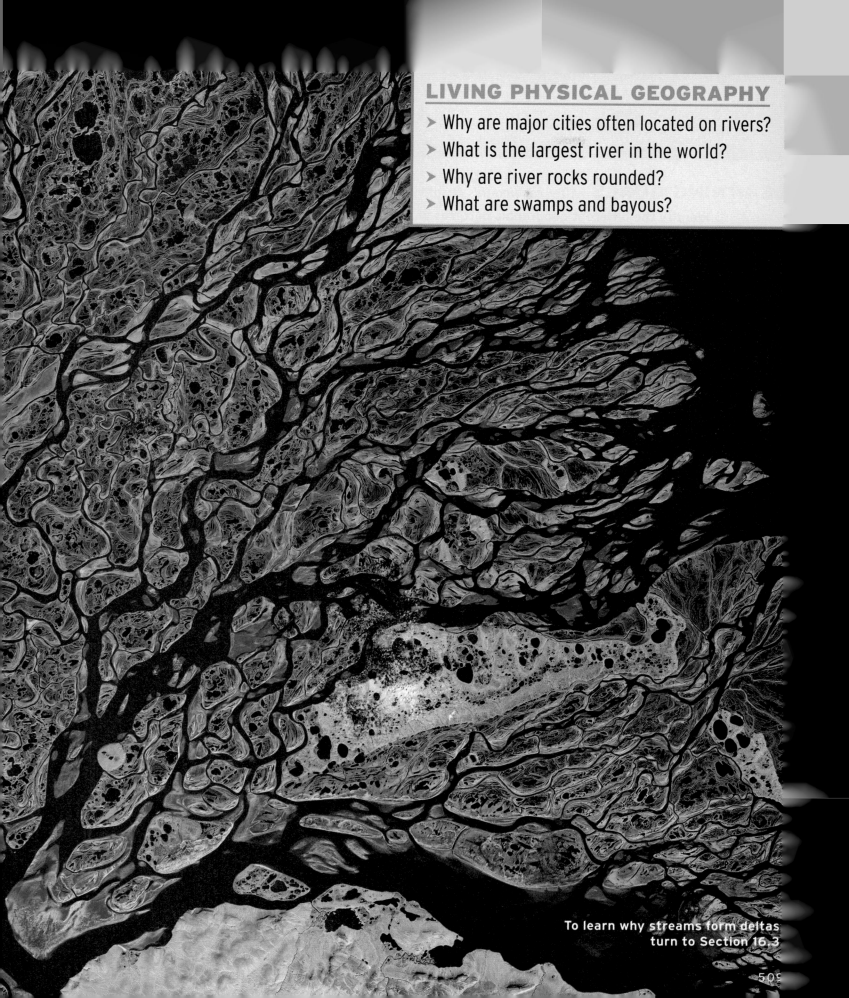

LIVING PHYSICAL GEOGRAPHY

> Why are major cities often located on rivers?
> What is the largest river in the world?
> Why are river rocks rounded?
> What are swamps and bayous?

To learn why streams form deltas turn to Section 16.3

THE BIG PICTURE *Flowing water is the most important agent of erosion. Streams erode Earth's surface and also build it up by depositing the sediments they transport.*

LEARNING GOALS *After reading this chapter, you will be able to:*

16.1 ◎ Identify the different geographic patterns of stream systems.

16.2 ◎ Explain how streams evolve through time as they erode Earth's surface.

16.3 ◎ Discuss landforms resulting from the deposition of sediment by streams.

16.4 ◎ Describe two modes of stream flooding and explain how people reduce their vulnerability to flooding.

16.5 ◎ Assess the benefits and drawbacks of dams.

THE HUMAN SPHERE: **People and Floodplains**

FIGURE 16.1 **The Fertile Crescent.**
The first permanent human settlements, the development of agriculture, and animal domestication began on the corridor of land extending from the lower Nile River to the Tigris and Euphrates rivers (shaded area).

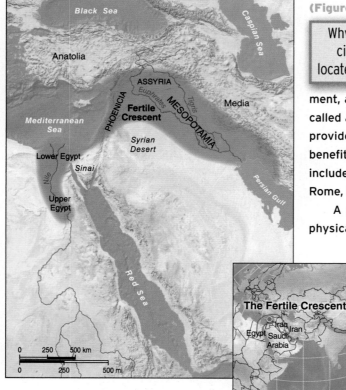

PEOPLE HAVE ALWAYS LIVED near large rivers. Early subsistence agriculture and the first sedentary (nonmigratory) human societies began over 10,000 years ago on the crescent of land called the *Fertile Crescent* formed by the lower Nile River and the Tigris and Euphrates rivers in ancient Mesopotamia. Today, this area spans Iraq, western Iran, southern Turkey, Syria, Lebanon, Israel, and Egypt (Figure 16.1).

> Why are major cities often located on rivers?*

The land in the floodplains along most large rivers is flat and desirable for settlement. **Floodplains** are the areas of flat land near a stream that experience flooding on a regular basis. They are composed of deep layers of sediment, as we will see in Section 16.3. The soils deposited by occasional flooding, called *alluvial soils*, or entisols (see Section 9.1), are rich and fertile. Rivers also provide corridors for transportation inland from the ocean. Because of these benefits, many major cities have been established along rivers: Familiar examples include Buenos Aires, Cairo, Jakarta, London, Madrid, Paris, Portland (Oregon), Rome, Shanghai, Tokyo, and Washington, D.C.

A problem arises, however, when rivers overflow their banks. Like many physical geographic phenomena, rivers are spatially and temporally dynamic systems. Their flat floodplains were built as they spilled out of their channels many times in the past and deposited the sediments they carried.

In this chapter, we explore the influence of rivers in shaping Earth's surface and in shaping people's lives. We first examine the surface geographic patterns formed by stream channels and see how streams cut into and erode Earth's surface. Next, we look at landforms built as streams deposit their sediments. Finally, we explore the benefits and costs of blocking streams with dams.

*Answers to the Living Physical Geography questions are found on page 542.

16.1 Stream Patterns

◎ Identify the different geographic patterns of stream systems.

Water is one of the most important compounds on Earth. In the hydrologic cycle, water evaporates from the oceans, enters the atmosphere, condenses into clouds, and precipitates over land (see Section 3.1). The resulting surface runoff flows back to the oceans in streams. A **stream** is a channel in which water flows downhill by the force of gravity. The term *stream* includes flows from the smallest rivulet of water to the mightiest rivers on Earth. Depending on the geographic region, streams are also called rivers, brooks, runs, creeks, washes, wadis, and many other names.

Drainage Basins

Streams that are connected together form a drainage basin. A **drainage basin** (or *watershed*) is a geographic region drained by a single trunk stream and its tributaries. A **trunk stream** is a single large stream into which smaller tributaries merge. A **tributary** is a stream that joins with other streams to form a larger stream. **Figure 16.2** illustrates these concepts using the Amazon River.

Topography determines the boundaries of drainage basins. There is no set limit to their size: The size of a drainage basin depends on the

floodplain
The area of flat land near a stream that experiences flooding on a regular basis.

stream
A channel in which water flows downhill by the force of gravity.

drainage basin
A geographic region drained by a single trunk stream and the smaller tributaries that flow into it.

trunk stream
A single large stream into which smaller tributaries merge.

tributary
A stream that joins with other streams to form a larger stream.

FIGURE 16.2 **GEO-GRAPHIC: Amazon River drainage basin.** *Drainage basins are named after their trunk streams. The Amazon River drainage basin (the light area), which encompasses 6.1 million km² (2.4 million mi²), is the largest drainage basin in the world.* (NASA/SCIENCE PHOTO LIBRARY)

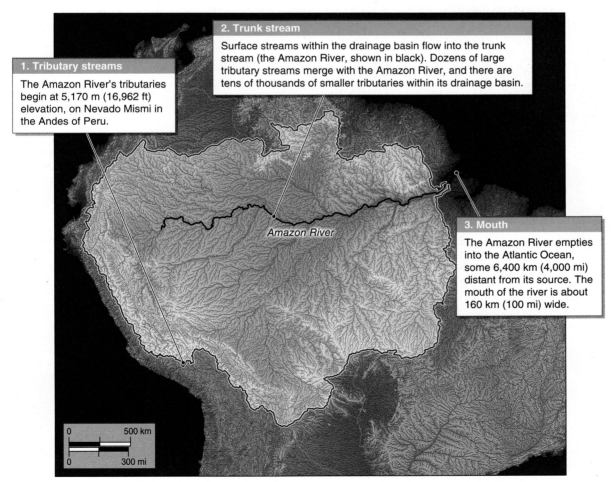

1. Tributary streams
The Amazon River's tributaries begin at 5,170 m (16,962 ft) elevation, on Nevado Mismi in the Andes of Peru.

2. Trunk stream
Surface streams within the drainage basin flow into the trunk stream (the Amazon River, shown in black). Dozens of large tributary streams merge with the Amazon River, and there are tens of thousands of smaller tributaries within its drainage basin.

Amazon River

3. Mouth
The Amazon River empties into the Atlantic Ocean, some 6,400 km (4,000 mi) distant from its source. The mouth of the river is about 160 km (100 mi) wide.

0   500 km
0   300 mi

drainage divide
A ridge or highland that separates drainage basins and defines their boundaries.

continental divide
A ridge or highland that separates drainage systems that empty into different ocean basins.

internal drainage
A drainage pattern in which streams terminate in a low-lying basin on land.

FIGURE 16.3 **Drainage basin hierarchy.**
The Mississippi River drainage basin is composed of six major sub-basins. Each is named after the trunk stream within the sub-basin.

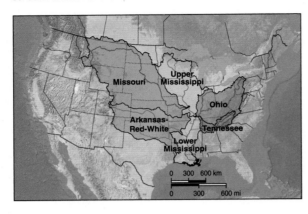

geographic scale used to define it, as illustrated in **Figure 16.3**. A single drainage basin can cover a small hillside or occupy much of a continent.

A ridge or highland that separates drainage basins and defines their boundaries is called a **drainage divide**. A ridge or highland that separates drainage systems that empty into different ocean basins is called a **continental divide** **(Figure 16.4)**.

Most streams drain into the oceans. But some do not. Some drainage basins have no outlet to the oceans. Instead, streams flow into a low-lying basin on land. Such regions are said to have an **internal drainage** system. As **Figure 16.5** shows, every continent has internal drainage systems, and a large portion of Eurasia has internal drainage.

FIGURE 16.4 **Drainage divides and continental divides.** *(A) Drainage divides separate different drainage basins. Both of these drainage basins empty into the same ocean. (B) Continental divides also separate different drainage basins, but in the case of continental divides, the separated drainage basins empty into different ocean basins.*

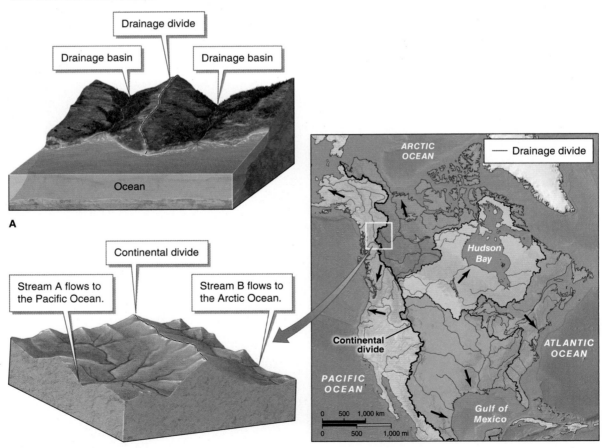

FIGURE **16.5** **Global drainage basins.** *Drainage basins for each of the world's oceans are grouped by color. For example, all drainage basins emptying into the Pacific Ocean are shown in blue. Internal drainage basins are shown in dark brown.*

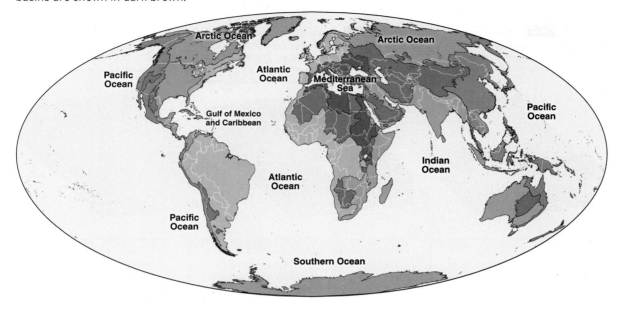

Internal drainage systems are located in arid regions where evaporation rates exceed precipitation. The water that collects in a large terrestrial basin can leave only through evaporation or infiltration into the ground. During evaporation, salts and other dissolved minerals remain behind in the standing water. For this reason, many internal drainage basins contain saline lakes **(Figure 16.6)**.

FIGURE **16.6** **The Dead Sea.** *The Dead Sea's water is nearly nine times more salty than ocean water. This high salinity makes the water very dense, allowing people to float on it easily. The sea's name reflects the fact that the water is too salty to support life, except for some salt-tolerant bacteria.* (Kord.com/Getty Images)

FIGURE 16.7 GEO-GRAPHIC: Stream drainage patterns.

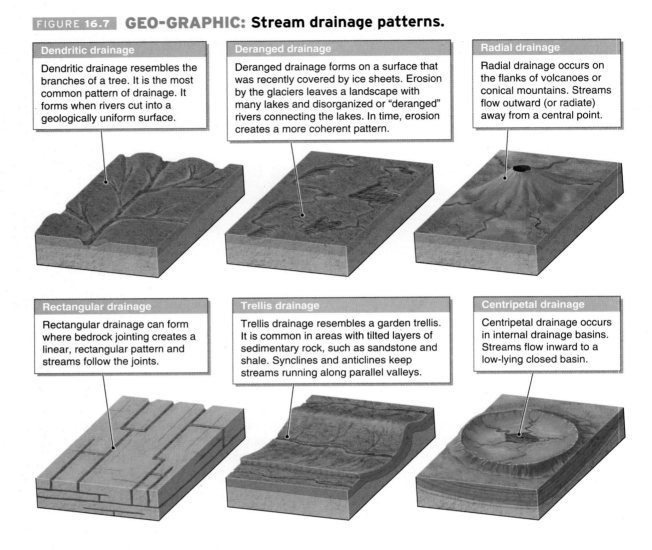

Dendritic drainage
Dendritic drainage resembles the branches of a tree. It is the most common pattern of drainage. It forms when rivers cut into a geologically uniform surface.

Deranged drainage
Deranged drainage forms on a surface that was recently covered by ice sheets. Erosion by the glaciers leaves a landscape with many lakes and disorganized or "deranged" rivers connecting the lakes. In time, erosion creates a more coherent pattern.

Radial drainage
Radial drainage occurs on the flanks of volcanoes or conical mountains. Streams flow outward (or radiate) away from a central point.

Rectangular drainage
Rectangular drainage can form where bedrock jointing creates a linear, rectangular pattern and streams follow the joints.

Trellis drainage
Trellis drainage resembles a garden trellis. It is common in areas with tilted layers of sedimentary rock, such as sandstone and shale. Synclines and anticlines keep streams running along parallel valleys.

Centripetal drainage
Centripetal drainage occurs in internal drainage basins. Streams flow inward to a low-lying closed basin.

dendritic drainage
A pattern of streams within a drainage basin that resembles the branching of a tree.

stream order
A numerical system used to rank stream size based on the number of tributaries flowing into a stream.

headwaters
The region where a stream originates.

intermittent stream
A stream that runs dry during part or most of the year.

Trunk streams and their tributaries form different drainage patterns within a drainage basin depending on the topography and the type of surface over which they are flowing. Although there are many different kinds of drainage patterns, six common ones are illustrated in **Figure 16.7**. The most common drainage pattern is **dendritic drainage**, in which the pattern of the streams resembles the branches of a tree.

Stream Order and Stream Permanence

Arthur Strahler (1918–2002) created a **stream order** system that is used to rank streams based on the number of tributaries flowing into them. The higher the stream order number, the larger the stream. The smallest streams are *first-order streams*, which have no tributaries, as is likely to be the case in the

headwaters of a drainage basin, where streams originate. A *second-order stream* is formed at the confluence (merging point) of two first-order streams. Stream order increases only when two streams of the same order join **(Figure 16.8)**.

About 80% of all streams are third-order streams or less. Very few streams are above the eighth order. The Mississippi River is a tenth-order stream, and the largest is the Amazon River, which is a twelfth-order stream.

What is the largest river in the world?

Stream Permanence

Stream order is related to stream permanence. A stream that runs dry during part or most of the year is an **intermittent stream**. Many first-order

FIGURE **16.8** **Stream order.** *Only when two streams of the same order unite does stream order increase.*

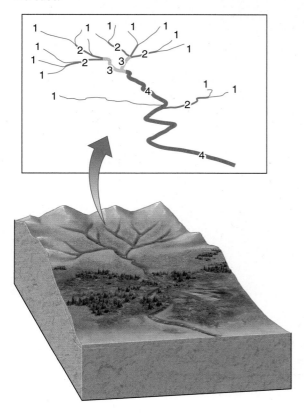

streams are intermittent streams. In contrast, an **ephemeral stream** flows briefly only after heavy rainstorms. **Permanent streams** flow year-round. Intermittent and permanent streams flow where and when the water table (see Section 9.3) is at or above the level of the ground, as illustrated in **Figure 16.9**.

Ephemeral streams are most common in arid regions, where thunderstorms bring sudden downpours. Ephemeral streams go by the informal names of *arroyos*, *dry washes*, or *wadis*, depending on the country in which they occur. Ephemeral streams are short-lived because their water evaporates and infiltrates the soil.

An **exotic stream** is a permanent stream that originates in a humid region and flows through an arid region where there is little precipitation. The Nile River, for example—which is the longest river in the world—begins in equatorial Africa, where there is ample rainfall. It then flows northward through the arid eastern Sahara in Sudan and Egypt as an exotic stream. By the time it reaches the Mediterranean Sea, its flow is much reduced because of evaporation, infiltration into the ground, and water diversions by people.

Anthropogenic Intermittent Streams

Diversions of water from streams by people have made many formerly permanent streams run low or

ephemeral stream
A stream that flows briefly after heavy rainstorms.

permanent stream
A stream that flows all year.

exotic stream
A permanent stream that originates in a humid region and flows through an arid region.

FIGURE **16.9** **Seasonal flow in intermittent streams.** *Intermittent streams flow seasonally when the water table is above the elevation of the stream channel.*

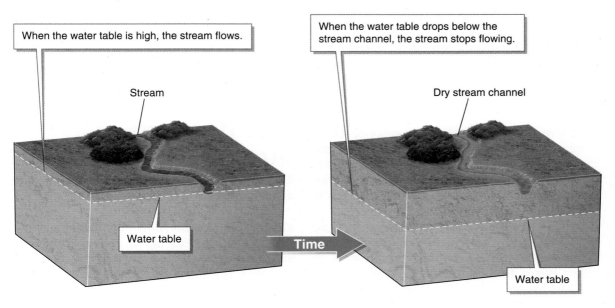

When the water table is high, the stream flows.

Stream

Water table

Time

When the water table drops below the stream channel, the stream stops flowing.

Dry stream channel

Water table

Picture This

(© Darryl Montgomery)

The Gila Reborn

This muddy trickle of water is the brief rebirth of the Gila River. Like the Colorado River, the Gila River is an exotic stream where it flows through the desert. The Gila River's headwaters are in the relatively wet highlands of western New Mexico. As it flows out of these mountains, several tributaries join it. In the past, the Gila flowed all the way to, and emptied into, the Colorado River near Yuma, Arizona. But water diversions now prevent the Gila from reaching the Colorado in all but the wettest years. Typically, the Gila runs dry downstream of Phoenix. In 2010, however, heavy rains in its headwaters allowed the Gila to fill its streambed downstream of Phoenix, if only for a little while, the first time it had done so in five years.

Consider This

1. Why does the Gila River run dry before it reaches the Colorado River? Has it always done so?

2. Is the Gila River a permanent stream, an intermittent stream, or an ephemeral stream, or all of these? Explain.

---

run dry. When this happens, human conflict may ensue, particularly where a stream crosses state or international borders. In the Middle East, for example, Turkey diverts water from the Tigris and Euphrates rivers near their headwaters, causing political friction with downstream neighbors such as Iraq.

The Colorado River and many of its tributaries in the southwestern United States provide water for 30 million people in seven western states. Water diversions are so extensive in this area that during dry periods, the Colorado River does not have enough water flowing in its channel to reach the Gulf of California in Mexico, where it emptied historically. **Picture This** highlights the Gila River, a tributary of the Colorado River, in this context.

fluvial erosion
Erosion by running water.

headward erosion
The process by which a stream channel migrates upslope by forming new rills through fluvial erosion.

stream discharge
The volume of water flowing past a fixed point within a stream channel; expressed in cubic meters or cubic feet per second.

16.2 Downcutting by Streams: Fluvial Erosion

◎ Explain how streams evolve through time as they erode Earth's surface.

Flowing water is the most important and widespread agent of erosion on Earth. Without the Sun's energy, fluvial erosion would not exist. As we have seen, the Sun provides heat energy to evaporate water and lift it into the atmosphere. The force of gravity is important as well: Water that condenses in the atmosphere falls to Earth as precipitation, and Earth's gravitational field pulls that water downslope. The kinetic energy of the stream's flowing water works to cut downward into Earth's surface (a process called *downcutting*) and transport rock fragments downslope toward the oceans.

As water flows back to the oceans, it forms stream channels. The force of water tumbles rocks in the channel and breaks them apart physically. At the same time, chemical weathering dissolves minerals in the rocks. Streams transport this broken and dissolved material downstream in the process of **fluvial erosion** (erosion by running water; from the Latin word *fluvius*, which means "river").

Fluvial erosion begins as rain falls on the ground. Some of the rainwater flows into and through the ground, where it contributes to soil moisture and groundwater. Where the ground surface is sloped, rainwater flows downslope in thin sheets called *sheet wash*.

As rainwater collects in low-lying areas, it begins to form shallow channels. Newly forming stream channels are called *rills*. Rills develop into *gullies* as they deepen. The flat areas between stream channels, where sheet wash occurs, are called *interfluves*. Stream channels are always lower than the interfluves.

As the amount of water and the speed of flow in a stream channel increase, the stream gains more energy to do the work of carrying soil particles and rock fragments downslope. **Figure 16.10** illustrates the process of **headward erosion**, by which a stream channel lengthens upslope through time, forming new rills and gullies by fluvial erosion. The spatial scale of headward erosion ranges from a few meters to hundreds of kilometers or more, and its time scale varies from weeks to thousands of years or longer, depending on the geographic setting, geology, and climate.

The Volume of Water: Stream Discharge

Stream discharge is the volume of water flowing past a fixed point within a stream channel. It is expressed in cubic meters per second (m³/s) or cubic feet per second (ft³/s). Discharge can be visualized as the number of 1 m (or 1 ft) cubes passing beneath a bridge every second. Discharge is often recorded on a *stream hydrograph* (see **Figure 16.11** on page 518).

Discharge is important because the more water is flowing through a stream channel, and the faster that water is flowing, the more energy the stream has to erode Earth's surface. **The discharge of a stream is influenced mainly by climate, stream order, season, and surface permeability (Table 16.1).**

Urbanization changes the permeability of the ground surface and therefore the discharge of streams. Paved surfaces are impermeable, and water flows from them quickly into nearby streams, rather than infiltrating the ground. As a result, streams in urbanized areas experience sudden spikes in discharge during heavy precipitation events, and discharge drops quickly after storms.

FIGURE 16.10 GEO-GRAPHIC: Headward erosion. (A) Headward erosion begins as rainwater collects in low-lying areas to form rills and gullies. (B) The process of headward erosion is visible in this photo of the Namib Desert in Namibia. Note the gemsbok in the top center for scale. (B. © Pete McBride/National Geographic Image Collection/Alamy)

Animation Headward erosion http://qrs.ly/lo49ed3

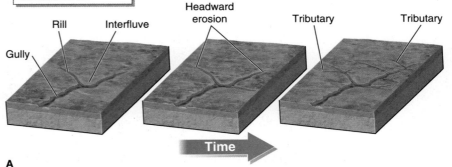

1. Rills, gullies, and interfluves
Stream flow occurs in the rills and gullies. Sheet wash occurs in the interfluves.

2. Headward erosion
Rills migrate upslope through headward erosion, which deepens and lengthens them.

3. New tributaries
New tributaries develop in the process of headward erosion.

Gully   Rill   Interfluve   Headward erosion   Tributary   Tributary

Time

A

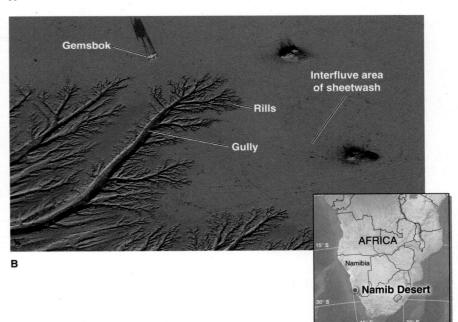

Gemsbok
Interfluve area of sheetwash
Rills
Gully
B

AFRICA
Namibia
15° S
30° S
Namib Desert
15° E   30° E

TABLE 16.1 AT A GLANCE: Stream Discharge Factors

1. Climate: Streams in wet regions have greater discharge than streams in arid regions.

2. Stream order: First-order streams are often intermittent or have little discharge, even in the wettest of climates.

3. Season: Streams experience peak flow periods that depend on the timing of precipitation or snowmelt. Heavy rainfall can increase stream discharge by several hundred times.

4. Surface permeability: Permeable soil and rock allow water to infiltrate the ground rather than flow over it in a stream channel. Greater permeability reduces surface stream discharge.

FIGURE **16.11** **Urbanization affects stream discharge.** *This stream hydrograph shows discharge in cubic feet per second for two streams of similar size in western Washington State from January 30 to February 7, 2000. On February 1, rainfall from a storm increased the discharge for both streams. Mercer Creek is in a paved, urbanized area near Bellevue, Washington. Its discharge peaked higher and faster than that of Newaukum Creek, which is in an undeveloped area.* (Source: USGS Fact Sheet 076-03.)

1. Pre-storm discharge
Before the storm, both creeks have a discharge of about 3 ft³/s.

2. Urbanized area post-storm discharge
Mercer Creek's discharge peaked at 24 ft³/s during the storm. The creek rose and fell within about 24 hours.

3. Undeveloped area post-storm discharge
Newaukum Creek's discharge peaked at about 10 ft³/s. Peak discharge was spread out over a 20-hour period. High flows continued for about a week as the saturated ground slowly released water back into the stream.

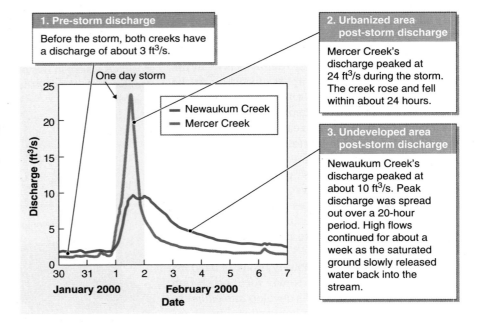

FIGURE **16.12** **SCIENTIFIC INQUIRY: How is stream discharge calculated?** *Calculating the discharge of streams is important for a number of applications, including water conservation, determination of water allocations among different regions and groups, and flood control.* (U.S. Geological Survey)

1. Measure the stream velocity
A *current meter* measures the velocity of the water. To account for varying flow velocities within the channel, many measurements are taken across the stream channel and averaged together.

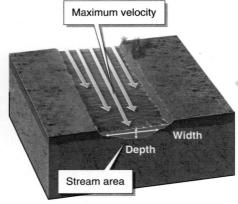

2. Measure the stream area
Stream area is calculated by multiplying average stream width by average stream depth. The average stream width and depth are calculated using many measurements across the channel.

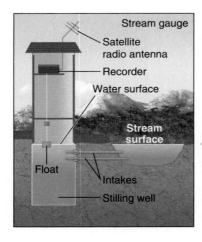

3. Measure stream height at a stream gauge
The relationship between stream area and flow velocity is strongly related to stream height, also called the *stream stage.* Stream stage can be measured in a *stilling well* connected to the stream with underwater pipes. The water's height is measured with floats or other digital instruments. The stage data are transmitted at regular intervals to ground or satellite receiving stations.

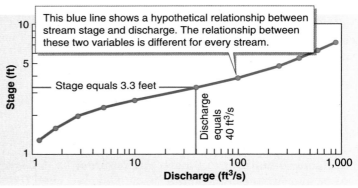

This blue line shows a hypothetical relationship between stream stage and discharge. The relationship between these two variables is different for every stream.

Stage equals 3.3 feet

Discharge equals 40 ft³/s

4. Calculate discharge
Every stream has a unique relationship between stream stage and stream discharge, due to variation in stream channel area with changing water levels. Once the relationship between stream stage, flow velocity, and area has been determined for a given stream, calculating that stream's discharge is only a matter of measuring stream stage.

CRUNCH THE NUMBERS: Calculating Stream Discharge

Using the discharge equation $Q = A \cdot v$, calculate the average discharge for the Amazon River and the Mississippi River. Give your answer in cubic meters per second.

Problem 1: At a given location, the Mississippi River is 1,670 m wide and an average of 12 m deep, with an average flow velocity of 0.91 m/s. What is the discharge for the Mississippi River at that location?

Problem 2: At a given location, the Amazon River is 15,200 m wide and an average of 15 m deep, with an average flow velocity of 1 m/s. What is the discharge for the Amazon River at that location?

Problem 3: Approximately how many Mississippi Rivers would fit into the Amazon River? To calculate this answer, divide the Amazon discharge by the Mississippi discharge.

abrasion
The process by which movement of one material wears away another material.

Figure 16.11 compares the discharge of an urbanized stream with that of a stream in a rural location.

In calculations, stream discharge is symbolized by Q. Discharge is measured by multiplying the stream channel area (A) by the speed of water flow, or *velocity* (v): $Q = A \cdot v$. Stream channel area is calculated by multiplying channel width by channel depth. The calculation of stream discharge takes into account the variations in flow velocity, stream channel area, and river height that are unique to each stream **(Figure 16.12)**.

The Amazon River has the highest average discharge in the world, about 200,000 m³/s, or 7 million ft³/s. The Amazon's flow constitutes nearly 20% of the world's total discharge by rivers into the oceans. **Crunch the Numbers** compares the flow of North America's largest river (in terms of discharge), the Mississippi River, with that of the Amazon River.

The Work of Water: Stream Load

Why are river rocks rounded?

The force of water, called *hydraulic action*, frees rock fragments and sets them in motion. The size of those fragments may range from tiny grains of sand and silt to large boulders.

Stream abrasion rounds and polishes rocks in a stream. **Abrasion** is the process by which movement of one material wears away another material. The continual tumbling of rocks in a streambed wears away other rocks and the channel bedrock **(Figure 16.13)**. Heavy rocks and boulders in a stream channel move only with high flows, however, such as those that follow heavy rains or snowmelt.

The material that moves within a stream channel is called the *stream load*. **The size of the particles that move within a stream is directly related to stream discharge and flow velocity.** There are three kinds of stream loads:

FIGURE 16.13 Stream abrasion. *The greatest discharge in streams draining the Himalayas occurs between May and September with the onset of the summer snowmelt season and warm monsoon rains. Stream abrasion, which rounds the rocks in the stream, occurs only during these peak flows. This photo was taken in July near Dharamsala, India, located in the foothills of the Himalayas. (© Roopaushree)*

FIGURE 16.14 **Variation in suspended loads.** *This photo shows the confluence of the Drava and Danube rivers near Osijek, Croatia. Arrows show the direction of flow. The Drava River has a comparatively low suspended load and thus runs clear compared with the Danube River.* (© Mario Romulić)

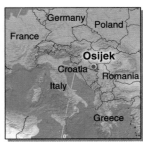

1. The **dissolved load** consists of soluble minerals that are carried in solution by a stream.

2. The **suspended load** consists of small particles of clay and silt that are light enough to remain suspended by turbulence (mixing) in the flowing water. The suspended load gives some streams their muddy appearance **(Figure 16.14)**.

3. A stream's **bed load** is the moving material in a stream channel (ranging from small sand grains to gravel, cobbles, and large boulders) that is too heavy to become suspended in the current. Sand grains are moved along in a bouncing or hopping motion called **saltation**. Larger rocks are moved by a dragging or tumbling motion called **traction**. Traction sufficient to move large rocks occurs only during peak flow periods. **Figure 16.15** illustrates the three types of stream loads.

Geomorphologists refer to the size of fragments a stream can transport as *stream competence*. Streams that can transport large fragments, such as boulders, have high stream competence. *Stream capacity* refers to the total amount of material (of all sizes) that a stream can transport. During periods of peak discharge, when the stream has more kinetic energy, stream capacity and competence increase.

FIGURE 16.15 **Three types of stream loads.**

dissolved load
Soluble minerals that are carried in solution by a stream.

suspended load
Small particles such as clay and silt that remain suspended in flowing water or wind.

bed load
Material in a stream channel such as sand, gravel, and rocks that is too heavy to become suspended in the current.

saltation
A bouncing or hopping motion of sediment in moving water (or air).

traction
The dragging and tumbling of large rocks in a stream channel.

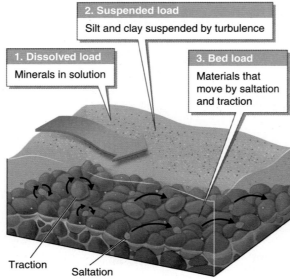

Stream Grading and Stream Gradient

Streams are referred to as *graded* if sediment transport within the stream equals the rate of sediment input from around the stream. In other words, in a graded stream, the channel is neither accruing nor losing sediments. Along the length of a graded stream, there is a dynamic equilibrium

FIGURE 16.16 **GEO-GRAPHIC:** Stream grading and stream gradient.

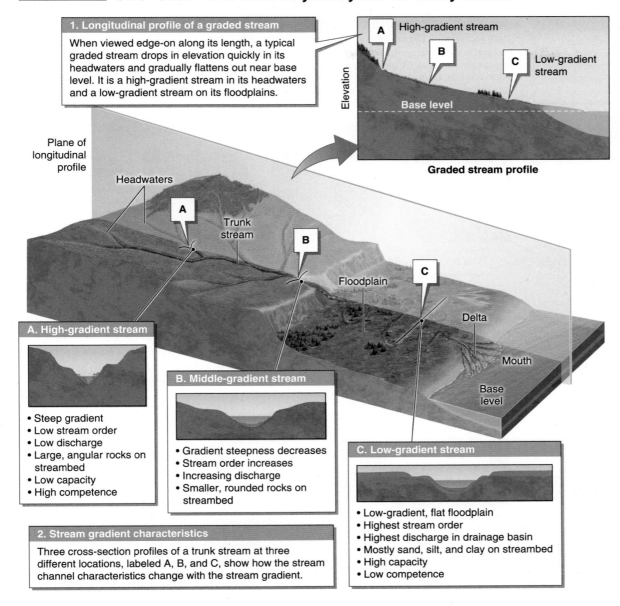

1. Longitudinal profile of a graded stream

When viewed edge-on along its length, a typical graded stream drops in elevation quickly in its headwaters and gradually flattens out near base level. It is a high-gradient stream in its headwaters and a low-gradient stream on its floodplains.

A   High-gradient stream

B

C   Low-gradient stream

Base level

Graded stream profile

Plane of longitudinal profile

Headwaters

A

Trunk stream

B

Floodplain

C

Delta

Mouth

Base level

A. High-gradient stream

- Steep gradient
- Low stream order
- Low discharge
- Large, angular rocks on streambed
- Low capacity
- High competence

B. Middle-gradient stream

- Gradient steepness decreases
- Stream order increases
- Increasing discharge
- Smaller, rounded rocks on streambed

C. Low-gradient stream

- Low-gradient, flat floodplain
- Highest stream order
- Highest discharge in drainage basin
- Mostly sand, silt, and clay on streambed
- High capacity
- Low competence

2. Stream gradient characteristics

Three cross-section profiles of a trunk stream at three different locations, labeled A, B, and C, show how the stream channel characteristics change with the stream gradient.

(or balance) between erosion, transportation, and deposition of sediments within the stream channel. A fully graded stream would have a smooth longitudinal profile like the one shown in **Figure 16.16**. Few streams, however, have such smoothly graded profiles because of the different rock types, geologic activity, and climates within any given drainage basin.

Similarly, stream *gradient* refers to the drop in elevation of the stream channel in the downstream direction. High-gradient streams drop quickly in elevation, and low-gradient streams are almost flat.

Carving Valleys and Canyons

Base level is the lowest level a stream can reach, usually sea level. A stream can erode Earth's surface only where it is above base level. The higher a stream is above base level, the more energy it will have to erode the land surface. At base level, a stream becomes standing water, loses its capacity and competence, and drops the sediments it is carrying.

The rate of stream downcutting and the resulting topography depend on the stream's elevation above base level, stream discharge, flow velocity, and the hardness and structure of the

base level
The lowest level a stream can reach, usually sea level; a stream becomes standing water at base level.

FIGURE 16.17 **GEO-GRAPHIC: Types of valleys and canyons.**

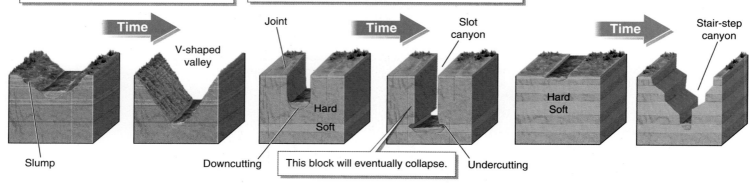

1. V-shaped valley

V-shaped valleys form when a stream downcuts into soft bedrock and soil. As rock and soil slide into the stream channel through mass movements, the stream develops sloping valley walls.

2. Slot canyon

Slot canyons form when a stream downcuts into bedrock with vertical joints. Erosion of soft sedimentary layers may undercut the canyon walls, causing large blocks to collapse and widen the canyon. Slot canyons form mostly in limestone and sandstone.

3. Stair-step canyon

Fluvial erosion of alternating layers of hard and soft bedrock forms stair-step canyons.

FIGURE 16.18 **Niagara Falls knickpoint.** *(A) A waterfall migrates upstream when the more resistant lip of rock that forms it is undercut and collapses into the plunge pool. (B) Niagara Falls, on the United States–Canada border, is one of the best-known waterfalls in the world. Niagara Falls consists of three waterfalls. The largest is Horseshoe Falls in Canada; American Falls and Bridal Veil Falls are in the United States. The Niagara knickpoint has retreated upstream (south) by almost 11 km (7 mi) during the last 10,000 years. (B. © Oleksiy Maksymenko/All Canada Photos/Getty Images)*

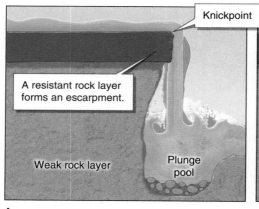
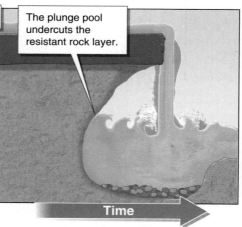
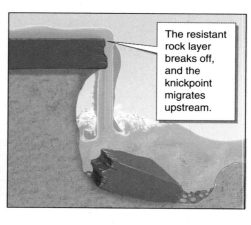

A

B

FIGURE 16.19 **GEO-GRAPHIC: Stream rejuvenation.**

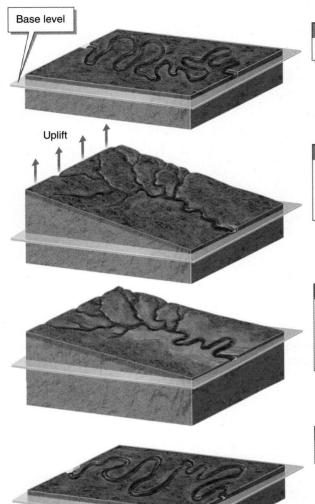

Base level

Uplift

Time 1: Flat floodplain

A low-gradient stream meanders on a floodplain.

Time 2: Steep slope with V-shaped canyons

As geologic uplift tilts a block of crust upward, the stream is rejuvenated. The stream forms V-shaped valleys, and a dendritic drainage pattern. Its tributaries migrate upslope through headward erosion.

Time 3: Widened valleys and floodplain development

As erosion transports material to sea level, the elevation of the block is gradually lowered. As the gradient decreases, the stream loses energy and deposits sediment, forming a flat floodplain. The stream begins meandering in the flat floodplain.

Time 4: Return to flat floodplain

A low-gradient stream meanders on a floodplain again.

bedrock the stream is cutting through. Harder rocks such as metamorphic rocks are more resistant to downcutting than softer rocks such as sandstone. Most streams cut V-shaped valleys in their headwaters, but this is not always the case, as shown in **Figure 16.17**.

Points of Resistance: Knickpoints

Knickpoints are locations where there is an abrupt increase in stream gradient over a short distance. All waterfalls, for example, form at knickpoints. They often form where a layer of rock that is resistant to erosion overlies a relatively weak and soft layer of rock. The resistant layer of rock creates an **escarpment**, a long cliff face or steep slope, over which the water flows. As the stream spills over the lip of the resistant rock layer, it may form a bowl at the base of the waterfall, called a **plunge pool**. Plunge pools are created by abrasion caused

by rocks circulating at the base of the waterfall. Eventually, a plunge pool can undercut the support of the resistant layer above, causing it to collapse. As a result, the knickpoint migrates upstream. This process is illustrated in **Figure 16.18**.

Lifting Streams: Stream Rejuvenation

Stream rejuvenation is a process in which a stream gains downcutting energy as its base level is lowered relative to its drainage basin. Stream rejuvenation is usually a consequence of geologic uplift, but lowered global sea level can also cause stream rejuvenation.

The higher above its base level a stream lies, the more it will cut into the sediments and bedrock beneath it. Eventually, barring further geologic uplift, the stream will return to its original gradient through weathering, mass wasting, erosion, and deposition **(Figure 16.19)**.

knickpoint
A location where there is an abrupt increase in stream gradient over a short distance.

escarpment
A long cliff face or steep slope.

plunge pool
A bowl at the base of a waterfall created by abrasion from circulating rocks.

stream rejuvenation
A process by which a stream gains downcutting energy as its base level is lowered relative to its drainage basin.

FIGURE 16.20 **Entrenched meanders.** *(A) Entrenched meander development requires geologic uplift. (B) The San Juan River in Utah has superb examples of entrenched meanders. These meanders formed long ago on a flat floodplain and were preserved as they cut through sedimentary rocks. This photo was taken at Goosenecks State Park in Utah, whose name refers to the similarity between the meanders and the curve of a goose's neck. (B. © Wild Horizon/UIG/Getty Images)*

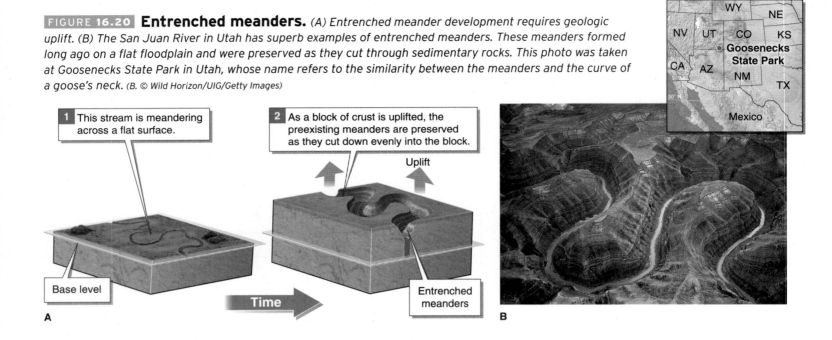

1 This stream is meandering across a flat surface.

2 As a block of crust is uplifted, the preexisting meanders are preserved as they cut down evenly into the block.

Uplift

Base level

Time

Entrenched meanders

A

B

FIGURE 16.21 **GEO-GRAPHIC: Formation of stream terraces.** *(A) Stream terraces form as a region is uplifted and a stream cuts into the sediments that have been deposited on a floodplain. (B) Cave Stream, in the Canterbury region of South Island, New Zealand, has cut into floodplain sediments, forming two terraces. (B. © G.R. "Dick" Roberts/Natural Sciences Image Library)*

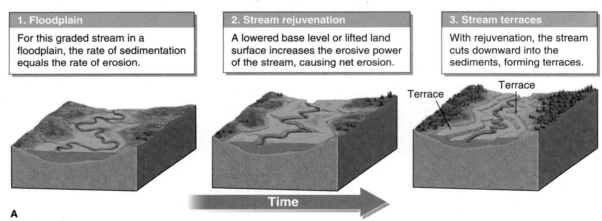

1. Floodplain

For this graded stream in a floodplain, the rate of sedimentation equals the rate of erosion.

2. Stream rejuvenation

A lowered base level or lifted land surface increases the erosive power of the stream, causing net erosion.

3. Stream terraces

With rejuvenation, the stream cuts downward into the sediments, forming terraces.

Terrace

Terrace

Time

A

Terrace

Terrace

Stream

AUSTRALIA

New Zealand

South Island

Canterbury Region

45° S

150° E

B

As we will see in Section 16.3, a stream that flows across a flat floodplain may form looping bends called meanders. If geologic uplift creates a level plateau, rather than a slope, stream meanders may be preserved as *entrenched meanders* as the stream erodes the plateau **(Figure 16.20)**. Entrenched meanders are found throughout the southwestern United States, where geologic uplift raised what was a large, flat floodplain and shallow sea to form today's Colorado Plateau. The uplift took place gradually and was slightly inclined toward the southwest.

Stream rejuvenation may also result in *stream terraces* where rivers flow through floodplains. **A rejuvenated stream can cut down into the floodplain sediments through headward erosion, creating stepped terraces (Figure 16.21).**

Antecedent and Superimposed Streams

Antecedent streams are streams that cut through bedrock ridges rather than flowing around them. Geologic uplift may allow a preexisting stream to cut through resistant ridges of rock as they are slowly lifted. If the rate of erosion is gradual, the stream can cut into the underlying ridge of bedrock while maintaining its original drainage pattern, resulting in a water gap **(Figure 16.22)**. A *water gap* is a place where a stream has cut through a resistant ridge of rock.

Superimposed streams are like antecedent streams in that they cut through resistant layers of rock and form water gaps. In the case of superimposed streams, however, the land surface is lowered through fluvial erosion rather than being lifted through tectonic forces.

Distinguishing a water gap caused by antecedence from one caused by superimposition is not possible with only a quick glance at the surface. The tectonic and erosional history of a region must be known before determining how the water gap formed. In some cases, streams with water gaps no longer flow in their former channels. When that occurs, a *wind gap* results.

FIGURE 16.22 Antecedent stream water gap. *(A) Antecedent streams cut through uplifting rocks. (B) Three hundred million years ago, the MacDonnell Ranges in central Australia were uplifted. This stream cut into them as they rose, forming this water gap, called* Simpsons Gap. *(B. © G.R. "Dick" Roberts/Natural Sciences Image Library)*

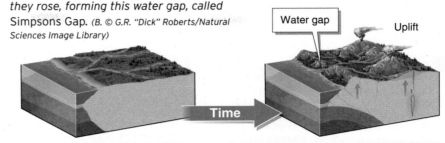

1. Before uplift
Before geologic uplift, this stream flows across a flat surface to the sea.

2. After uplift
If a mountain range is lifted slowly and it is composed of weak rock, the stream may cut through it and maintain its position, creating an antecedent stream and water gap.

A

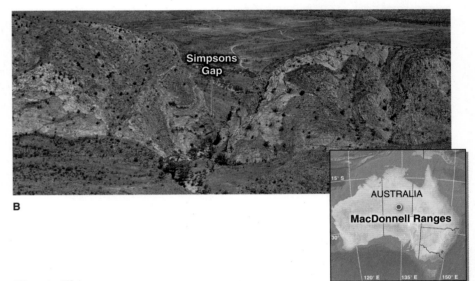

B

Stream Piracy

Stream piracy is the diversion of one stream into another as headward erosion merges the two streams. When a stream's tributaries migrate upslope and cut through the drainage divide of another drainage basin, streams within that drainage basin can be diverted into the new stream channel, as illustrated in **Figure 16.23**.

FIGURE 16.23 Stream piracy. *Stream piracy results in stream channel abandonment.*

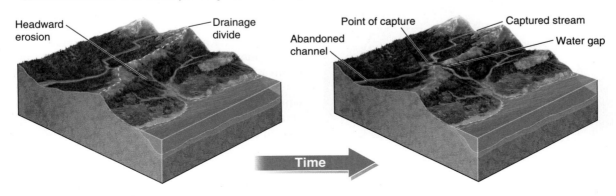

stream piracy
The diversion of one stream into another as headward erosion merges the two streams.

FIGURE 16.24 GEO-GRAPHIC:
Stream sorting. *Through abrasion and chemical weathering, rocks in a streambed are slowly broken down into smaller and smaller fragments. These fragments are sorted according to size along the stream's length.*

Animation
Stream
sorting
http://qrs.ly/qf49ed7

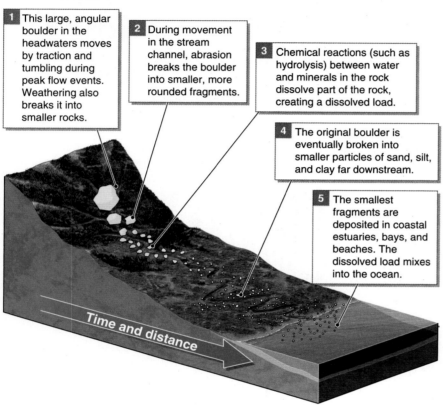

1 This large, angular boulder in the headwaters moves by traction and tumbling during peak flow events. Weathering also breaks it into smaller rocks.

2 During movement in the stream channel, abrasion breaks the boulder into smaller, more rounded fragments.

3 Chemical reactions (such as hydrolysis) between water and minerals in the rock dissolve part of the rock, creating a dissolved load.

4 The original boulder is eventually broken into smaller particles of sand, silt, and clay far downstream.

5 The smallest fragments are deposited in coastal estuaries, bays, and beaches. The dissolved load mixes into the ocean.

Time and distance

FIGURE 16.25 **Aggradation.** *Floodplains are formed through aggradation when sediment enters a stream faster than the stream can carry it away. Floodplains are composed of deep layers of alluvium.*

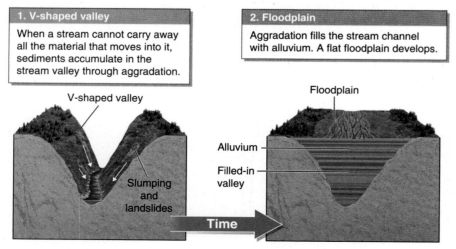

1. V-shaped valley

When a stream cannot carry away all the material that moves into it, sediments accumulate in the stream valley through aggradation.

2. Floodplain

Aggradation fills the stream channel with alluvium. A flat floodplain develops.

V-shaped valley

Slumping and landslides

Time

Floodplain

Alluvium

Filled-in valley

16.3 Building by Streams: Fluvial Deposition

◎ Discuss landforms resulting from the deposition of sediment by streams.

Streams shape Earth's surface not only by cutting into it, as we have seen, but also by transporting and depositing sediments downstream. Many important natural fluvial landforms are built by accumulations of stream-deposited sediments.

Dropping the Load: Stream Sorting

As long as stream capacity and stream competence are maintained, the stream load will continue to be transported. Where stream capacity or stream competence is reduced, material carried by the stream begins to settle out. **Where a stream stops flowing at base level, it loses all kinetic energy, and all the material it carries, except its dissolved load, settles out.**

Sediments are sorted by size as they are deposited by streams. The heaviest material in transport settles out first. The largest boulders are high in the drainage basin because they are too heavy to be carried very far. They eventually break into smaller and lighter fragments that will move more easily. Cobbles and pebbles will be moved farther downstream than boulders. Sand, silt, and clay settle out of the water still farther downstream.

To get a sense of how the sorting process works, imagine a white quartz boulder in a stream channel where all other rocks are dark. Because the boulder is white, we can easily see it and follow it from a high mountainous area and on downstream as it is broken into ever-smaller fragments over time. As the stream overflows its banks, these materials will be deposited along the course of the stream **(Figure 16.24)**. Sediments deposited on a floodplain by a stream are referred to as **alluvium**.

Places of Deposition

If a stream's capacity and competence become insufficient to carry all the sediments that enter the stream, the sediments will settle out in the stream channel and accumulate. The buildup of sediments in a streambed is called **aggradation**. Aggradation in the low-gradient sections of a stream forms a floodplain **(Figure 16.25)**.

Sediment input into a stream channel increases where vegetation is removed by fire or human activity. Sediments from unpaved roads in steep terrain can wash into streams as well. During the

FIGURE **16.26** **Hydraulic mining during the Gold Rush.** *Miners used water cannons called water monitors to loosen sediments, and the gold contained in them, from the foothills of the Sierra Nevada. Mining put more sediment into the streams than they could carry, resulting in aggradation in the stream channels. This photo shows mining operations in the 1860s in what is today Malakoff Diggins State Historic Park in California.* (U.S. Geological Survey/photo by Carlton Watkins)

alluvium
Sediments deposited on a floodplain by a stream.

aggradation
The buildup of sediments in a streambed.

braided stream
A stream that forms intertwining channels around sediments in the streambed.

alluvial fan
A gently sloping accumulation of sediment deposited at the base of a mountain by an ephemeral stream in arid regions.

Gold Rush in California in the middle 1800s, miners blasted the hillsides with water in search of gold. This *hydraulic mining* eroded the slopes and overwhelmed the streams with sediments (Figure 16.26).

Aggradation also occurs where streams flow out of glaciers. Glaciers flow downhill and grind the bedrock beneath them into rock fragments (see Section 17.3). The glacier's outlet stream can move this material only during peak summer flow periods. At most times, the stream occupies only a small portion of the streambed, flowing around elongated islands of gravel and sand. Such streams that form intertwining channels around sediments in the streambed are called **braided streams** (Figure 16.27).

Streams may also lose energy after they flow through a steep-walled, V-shaped canyon that abruptly opens up onto a flat valley floor. While in the canyon, the stream has a steep gradient and high velocity, but where the stream exits the canyon, its velocity slows, its capacity and compentency are reduced, and it drops its sediment into an alluvial fan. An **alluvial fan** is a gently sloping accumulation of sediment that is deposited at the

FIGURE **16.27** **A braided stream.** *This braided stream originates from Franz Josef Glacier in New Zealand.* (© David Wall/Alamy)

Sediment-filled valley

Braided stream channels

FIGURE **16.28** **An alluvial fan.** *This satellite image shows an alluvial fan (outlined with dotted line) in the Zagros Mountains of southern Iran. Here, an ephemeral stream emerges from a canyon and spills out onto the fan only after rare rainfall events. When flowing, the stream occupies only a small portion of the fan at any one time. Through time, the stream migrates across the fan. The green crops seen here get their water from pumped groundwater, not surface streams. (NASA image created by Jesse Allen, using data from NASA/GSFC/METI/ERSDAC/JAROS, and the U.S./Japan ASTER Science Team)*

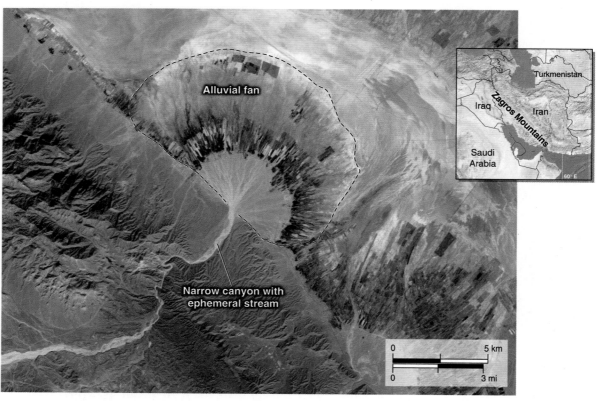

base of a mountain by an ephemeral stream in arid regions **(Figure 16.28)**.

Stream Meanders and Floodplains

A **meander** is a looping bend in a stream channel that forms on a floodplain. Meanders develop when the fastest-flowing portion of the stream, called the *thalweg*, erodes one bank more than the other. That bank, called a **cut bank**, where erosion exceeds deposition, becomes the outside edge of the meander. On the opposite bank, where the flow is slower, deposition exceeds erosion, and accumulations of silt, sand, and gravel, called a **point bar**, form.

Stream meanders are spatially dynamic features. Through time, stream channels shift across the floodplain, forming new meanders and abandoning old ones **(Figure 16.29)**. In places where a meander is cut off from the stream channel and the

channel is abandoned, a water-filled **oxbow lake** forms.

When a stream overflows its banks and floods, the standing sheet of water on the floodplain has no energy to carry its suspended load of silts and clays. These sediments settle out of the floodwaters and form deposits of alluvium. The smallest particles (clay and silt) are carried farthest away from the stream channel and accumulate on the floodplain. The largest particles (sand and gravel) accumulate near the stream channel in raised barriers that parallel the stream channel, called *natural levees* **(Figure 16.30** on page 530)**.

Tributaries entering a floodplain sometimes flow parallel to the trunk stream because they cannot flow over the higher floodplain and natural levees bordering the trunk stream channel. As a

meander
A looping bend in a stream channel on a floodplain.

cut bank
The outside edge of a meander, where erosion exceeds deposition.

point bar
An accumulation of silt, sand, and gravel that forms at the inside edge of a stream meander, where deposition exceeds erosion.

oxbow lake
A water-filled abandoned channel that results when a meander is cut off from the stream channel.

FIGURE 16.29 **Stream meanders.** *(A) Meanders develop on flat floodplains as the thalweg cuts into the outside edge of a meander. This process takes decades or longer. (B) This small stream near Cairns, Australia, developed its meanders and meander scars in the process outlined above. (C) Stream meanders are most common in low-gradient streams. But high-gradient streams, such as this small creek in the central Sierra Nevada in California, also develop meanders where the rivers flow through flat meadows. (B. © G.R. "Dick" Roberts/ Natural Sciences Image Library; C. Bruce Gervais)*

Animation
Stream
meanders
http://qrs.ly/8v49ed9

1. Before meanders

A straight stream channel on a flat floodplain will develop meanders when the fastest flow, called the *thalweg*, increases erosion on one bank.

2. Meanders

A cut bank forms on the outside bend of a meander where flow velocity is highest. On the inside of a meander, where flow velocity is lowest, sediments are deposited to form a point bar.

3. Meander neck

The meander loop deepens as erosion on the cut banks continues. As the meander deepens a meander neck forms.

4. Meander cutoff

At the meander neck, a cutoff forms as the two meanders join. The abandoned stream channel creates an oxbow lake if it is filled with water, or a meander scar if it becomes dry.

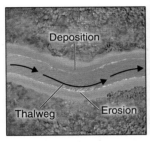
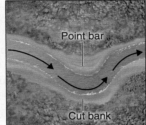
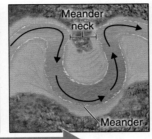
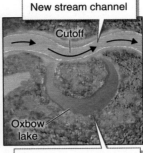

A

Time

B

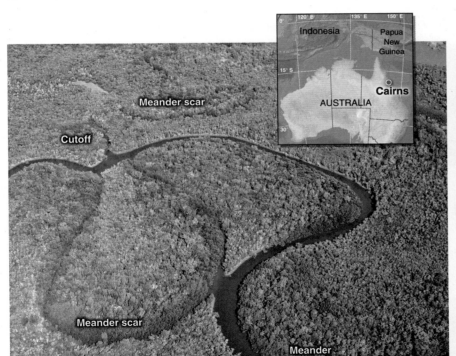

C

FIGURE 16.30
Formation of floodplains and natural levees. *Each flood event deposits sediments on the floodplain. Repeated flooding builds the natural levees over periods ranging from decades to centuries or more.*

Animation
Natural levees
http://qrs.ly/pt4brgp

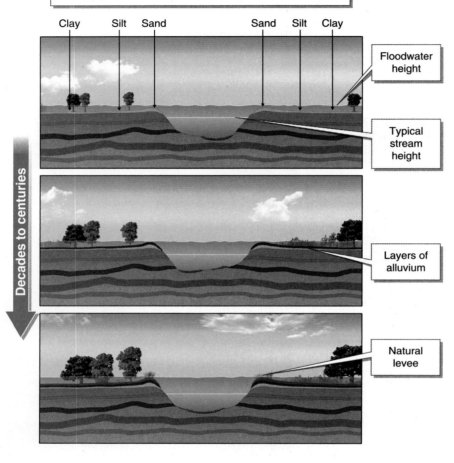

During flooding, particles are sorted by size and weight. The heaviest particles settle out closest to the stream channel.

Clay   Silt   Sand   Sand   Silt   Clay

Floodwater height

Typical stream height

Layers of alluvium

Natural levee

Decades to centuries

FIGURE 16.31 **Fluvial features of floodplains.**

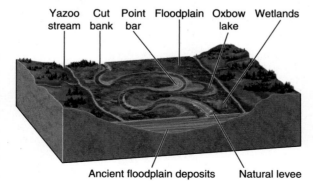

Yazoo stream   Cut bank   Point bar   Floodplain   Oxbow lake   Wetlands

Ancient floodplain deposits   Natural levee

reservoir
An artificial lake.

delta
An accumulation of sediment formed where a stream reaches base level.

distributary
One of a branching network of streams in a delta.

result, permanently flooded areas called *wetlands* (also called *swamps*, *backswamps*, or *bayous*) and *yazoo streams* form **(Figure 16.31)**.

What are swamps and bayous?

The End of the Line: Base Level

All streams stop flowing at base level. Water in all streams eventually finds the oceans, with the exception of those in internal drainage systems (see Section 16.1).

Along the way to the ocean, natural dams (such as beaver dams or landslide debris) may form a *temporary base level* (also called a *local base level*) as a pond or lake develops behind the obstruction. Over time, fluvial erosion will eventually cut through the obstruction, and the stream will flow freely again.

Streams are also dammed by people. Damming creates an artificial lake called a **reservoir**. Stream capacity and stream competence are zero in lakes and reservoirs, and as a result, all sediments settle out. At the end of this chapter, Geographic Perspectives further explores the problem of sedimentation in reservoirs.

GEOGRAPHIC PERSPECTIVES

A **delta** is an accumulation of sediments that forms where a stream reaches base level. Because of the amount of material deposited in deltas, the stream channel often becomes blocked, forcing the stream into a new channel around the sediments, as also occurs in a braided stream. In a delta, the trunk stream can shift and form a smaller branching network of streams called *distributary channels*, or **distributaries**. As shown in **Figure 16.32**, tributaries occur at the headwaters of a drainage basin, and distributaries occur in the delta.

Stream deltas are so named because the triangular shape of some deltas resembles that of the Greek letter delta (Δ), but not all deltas take this shape **(Figure 16.33)**. A delta's shape depends mainly on the stream's suspended load and on the influence of currents at the stream's mouth. Arcuate deltas are triangular and often have a braided or branching pattern of distributaries. The distributaries in a bird's foot delta resemble toes on a bird's foot.

The largest deltas form where coastal ocean currents are at a minimum and major streams carry a heavy load of suspended sediments. Where coastal currents are strong, however, river mouths have small or no deltas because the currents carry

FIGURE 16.32 **Features of a stream and its delta.** *The sediments visible on the surface of a delta are only a small fraction of the total sediment accumulations that make up the delta. Most of the sediments in a delta are hidden beneath the surface of the water.*

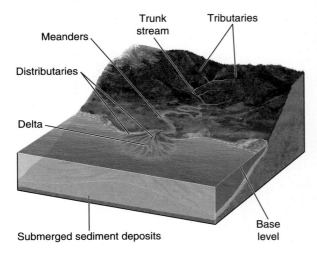

sediments away. The Columbia River, on the border of Oregon and Washington, the Congo River, in western Africa, and the Amazon River are examples of major streams with no coastal deltas.

In many deltas, the land elevation drops due to natural **subsidence**: the lowering of land elevation through the compaction of sediments. **Deltas keep pace with natural subsidence as their streams continually deposit new sediments that build up the land.** As long as sediments are renewed by fluvial deposition, there is an equilibrium between subsidence and sedimentation.

When artificial levees are built around a stream to control water flow, however, this equilibrium is disrupted. With levees in place, the river can no longer flood and form new meanders. The river's sediments are carried through and past the delta to the seaward edge and are deposited offshore, rather than in the delta. The interior delta becomes sediment starved, and as it sinks, the sea gradually encroaches on the land. **Picture This** (on page 532) highlights the effects of this process in New Orleans, which is built on the Mississippi River delta.

subsidence
Lowering of land elevation through compaction of sediments.

FIGURE 16.33 **Delta shapes.** *(A) The Yukon River originates in British Columbia, Canada, and empties into the Bering Sea in Alaska. Its delta has the classic arcuate shape with branching networks of distributaries. Notice the brown color of the sea where the river deposits its suspended load. (B) The Mississippi River forms a bird's foot delta (a portion of which is shown here).* (A. NASA Earth Observatory image created by Jesse Allen and Robert Simmon,using Landsat data provided by the United States Geological Survey; B. NASA/GSFC/METI/ERSDAC/JAROS, and U.S./Japan ASTER Science Team)

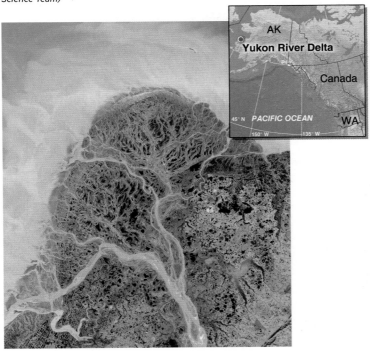

A

B

Picture This

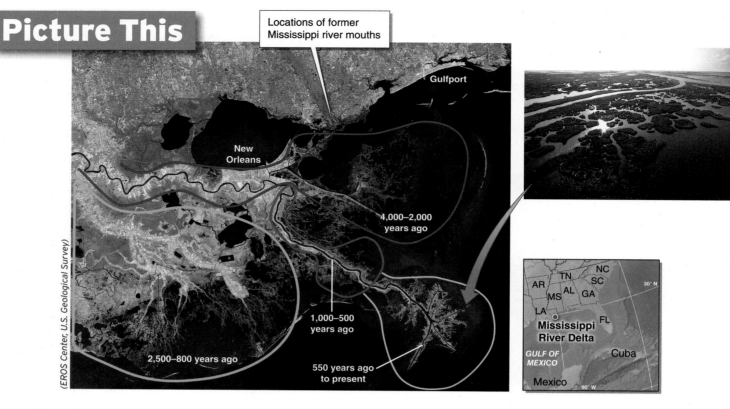

Locations of former Mississippi river mouths

Gulfport

New Orleans

4,000–2,000 years ago

1,000–500 years ago

2,500–800 years ago

550 years ago to present

(EROS Center, U.S. Geological Survey)

(© Jupiterimages/Stockbyte/Getty Images)

AR TN NC SC MS AL GA LA FL **Mississippi River Delta** GULF OF MEXICO Cuba Mexico 30° N 90° W

Vanishing Wetlands and a Sinking City

New Orleans is sinking. The past equilibrium between sedimentation and subsidence in the Mississippi River delta was disrupted when artificial levees were built around the river, mostly by the U.S. Army Corps of Engineers, in the 1930s and 1940s. In the past, the mouth and distributaries of the Mississippi River shifted every few hundred years to a new location, building the delta with new sediments. In this satellite image, the former positions of the river mouth are outlined in different colors, and their ages are given. Once the levees and upstream dams were in place, the trunk stream channel was stabilized to protect New Orleans. The river could no longer shift, flood, and build.

Some parts of New Orleans are now 2 to 6 m (3 to 12 ft) below sea level, and the coastal wetlands are riddled with holes and canals that were not present historically (inset). In many regions, the wetlands cannot grow fast enough to keep pace with subsidence. Because of the loss of coastal wetlands as well as rising sea level (see Section 19.3), New Orleans is increasingly vulnerable to flooding by hurricane storm surges.

Consider This

1. How did the Mississippi River's meandering process change after levees and upstream dams were put in place?
2. Why is New Orleans sinking?

16.4 Rising Waters: Stream Flooding

flood
Inundation by water in a region not normally covered by water, which results when stream discharge exceeds stream channel capacity.

flash flood
A flood that occurs with sudden, intense rainfall or dam collapse, often with little or no warning.

◎ Describe two modes of stream flooding and explain how people reduce their vulnerability to flooding.

A **flood** is inundation by water in a region not normally covered by water. **Flooding occurs when the volume of water moving through a stream exceeds the capacity of the stream channel.** Most low-gradient streams are naturally prone to flooding during periods of peak discharge. This is particularly true of streams in urbanized areas, where impermeable surfaces create rapid inflows of water into the stream channel (see Figure 16.11 above). There are two main types of flooding: flash floods and seasonal floods.

Flash Floods

A **flash flood** occurs with sudden, intense rainfall or the collapse of a dam. Flash floods are very dangerous because they often occur with little or no warning. Flash floods are most common in arid regions where rains come as sudden thunderstorm showers. Dry streambeds in deserts can become torrents of raging water within minutes following a thunderstorm.

The worst flash flood disaster in the United States was the Johnstown Flood in 1889. At about

FIGURE 16.34 **Thailand flooding.** *(A) The city of Ayutthaya, on the Chao Phraya River in southern Thailand, lies 60 km (40 mi) north of Bangkok. It sustained heavy flooding from tropical storm Nock-ten. The satellite image on the left, acquired July 11, 2011, shows normal conditions. The October 23, 2011, image on the right shows the city after it was inundated by floodwaters. (B) Standing floodwaters shut down the Don Muang International Airport, Bangkok's second largest airport. (A. NASA Earth Observatory image created by Jesse Allen and Robert Simmon, using EO-1 ALI data provided courtesy of the NASA EO-1 team and the United States Geological Survey; NASA Earth Observatory image created by Jesse Allen and Robert Simmon, using EO-1 ALI data provided courtesy of the NASA EO-1 team and the United States Geological Survey; B. © Pornchai Kittiwonsakul/AFP/Getty Images)*

A

B

3:00 p.m. on May 31, the South Fork Dam on the Conemaugh River in Pennsylvania collapsed. The earthen dam was poorly constructed and failed when torrential rains saturated and weakened it. Twenty million tons of water formed a wall 20 m (60 ft) high that raced down the valley leading to Johnstown. It took only 10 minutes for the water to destroy much of the town of 30,000 people. The flood left more than 2,000 people dead and caused $17 million in damage in the town.

Seasonal Floods

In contrast to flash floods, **seasonal floods** are predictable floods that occur with seasonally heavy rain or snowmelt. Seasonal floods follow prolonged rains that saturate the soil and inhibit more water from infiltrating the ground. If rains continue, their water must flow over land rather than into the ground. As a result, water spills out of the stream channel and inundates the surrounding floodplain. **Seasonal flooding poses less of a threat to human life than flash flooding because often the water rises slowly and there is ample time to evacuate.**

Seasonal flooding is common throughout South Asia because of its heavy monsoon rains (see Section 4.4) and tropical cyclones (see Section 5.3). In late July of 2011, the powerful tropical storm Nock-ten arrived during the summer monsoon. The storm brought extensive flooding to the Philippines, Hainan Province in China, northern Vietnam, Laos, and Thailand. Northern Thailand was one of the regions hit hardest by the storm **(Figure 16.34)**.

seasonal flood
A predictable period of flooding that occurs with seasonally heavy rain or snowmelt.

FIGURE 16.35 **GEO-GRAPHIC: Flood management structures.** *(A. © Akira Kaede/Photodisc/Getty Images; B. © Karl Johaentges/LOOK/Getty Images; C. © Matthew D. White/Photolibrary/Getty Images)*

Dam

What is it?
An earthen or concrete structure that blocks a stream and impounds water, forming a reservoir.
Advantages
1. Reduces peak flow by capturing water in the reservoir for later use, such as for agriculture or city use.
2. Generates mostly carbon-free hydroelectricity.
Disadvantages
1. Floods communities and reduces riparian wildlife habitat.
2. Sedimentation reduces the reservoir capacity.
3. Dams sometimes fail catastrophically.

Levee

What is it?
Earthen walls running parallel to a stream to keep water in its channel.
Advantages
1. Effectively controls flooding if built to withstand large flood events.
Disadvantages
1. May fail when built poorly or not properly maintained.
2. Levees built too close to the stream channel constrict the stream and reduce riparian habitat.
3. Deltas subside when levees prevent sediment deposition onto the floodplain, as in the case of New Orleans.

Stream bypass

What is it?
Outlet gates called *weirs* open at times of high flow to divert water out of the stream channel into a separate flood channel called a *stream bypass*.
Advantages
1. Effective means of reducing discharge within the main stream channel.
2. Periodically flooded land improves habitat for many organisms and renews alluvial soils for agriculture.
Disadvantages
1. Requires large amounts of undeveloped land that can be periodically flooded.

Controlling the Waters

The most effective tools to reduce the risk of flooding on floodplains are dams, levees, and stream bypasses. Engineers design these flood control structures so that they can handle the worst-case flood events. As Figure 16.35 discusses, each of these tools has advantages and disadvantages.

There are two ways to summarize the risk of flooding for a given location: the annual probability and the recurrence interval. The annual probability of flooding specifies the chances of a given discharge amount in a locality for any given year. For example, for a river that normally flows at 10,000 ft^3/s, the annual probability of a 50,000 ft^3/s flow might be calculated to be 1%. This probability means that in any given year, there is a 1% chance of a 50,000 ft^3/s discharge event. With each passing year, the probability increases arithmetically, such that after 100 years, there is a 100% chance of a 50,000 ft^3/s discharge event. Such calculations are based on historical climate and stream flow data.

The recurrence interval states how many years, on average, will pass between high-discharge events. In the case above, the recurrence interval for a 50,000 ft^3/s discharge event is once every 100 years. Such floods are called 100-year floods. A 500-year flood is a discharge event that happens once every 500 years, on average, and has an annual probability of 0.2%. Because recurrence intervals rely on averages, if a 500-year flood occurs, it does not mean that another 500 years will pass before such a flood happens again. Another 500-year flood could occur at any time. These rare and random events can be expected, on average, every 500 years.

GEOGRAPHIC PERSPECTIVES
16.5 Dam Pros and Cons

◎ Assess the benefits and drawbacks of dams.

According to the U.S. Army Corps of Engineers National Dams Inventory, there are more than 85,000 public and private dams in the United States. Most of these are small embankment dams (or earthen dams) that impound small reservoirs. Figure 16.36 shows the history of dam building in the United States. Canada has about 10,000 dams, and worldwide there are about 850,000 dams.

Dams are extremely important structures in most countries and provide many important benefits to society. But there are drawbacks to dams as well. In this section, the pros and cons of large dam projects are weighed.

The Pros of Dams

Water storage: Water is life, and dams provide water. **Dams deliver water by storing it in a reservoir and making it available at peak demand periods and in dry seasons.** In the United States, dams have played an essential role in the development of arid Western states, and they currently play a crucial role in development in many growing economies around the world. Most of the large cities of the arid western United States, including Phoenix, Las Vegas, Tucson, and Los Angeles, could not have developed to their current sizes without water from reservoirs. The agricultural heartland of California, the Central Valley, would not exist without the extensive series of dams that catch spring snowmelt from the Sierra Nevada and save it for the parched summer months.

Flood control: **Dams reduce flood risk by reducing the peak flows of streams during high-precipitation events.** The stream hydrograph in **Figure 16.37** shows the changes in stream hydrology that resulted from the installation of a dam.

Hydroelectricity: Carbon-free energy sources, such as wind power, solar power, and hydroelectricity, are essential to addressing the problem of climate change (see Section 6.5). **Many large dams generate carbon-free hydroelectricity by using the kinetic energy of the water rushing out of the base of the dam to spin steel turbines that produce electrical energy** (Figure 16.38).

Only about 6% of the energy demand in the United States is met by hydroelectricity. In contrast, over 98% of Norway's electricity is produced by hydroelectric power plants. Brazil produces 86% of its electricity from streams, and Canada produces over 60% of its electricity from streams. **Roughly half of the world's renewable energy comes from hydroelectricity.**

Transportation: Because of dams, many former rivers are now a series of long, narrow lakes that allow large vessels to safely navigate the waterway. The

FIGURE 16.36 **U.S. dams and reservoirs built since 1850.**
The history of dam building in the United States is shown in these four maps. Since 1850, the United States has seen exponential growth in the number of dams, reflecting the importance of these structures to human society. Most of the building of dams took place between 1950 and 2000; dam building has since decreased. (Courtesy of James Syvitski, University of Colorado at Boulder)

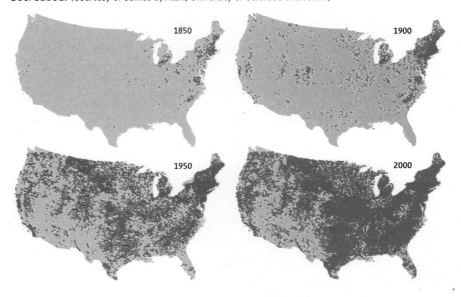

upper Mississippi River, from its headwaters to St. Louis, Missouri, has 43 dams and locks that slow stream flow, providing a transportation corridor essential to the region's economy.

FIGURE 16.37 **Pre- and post-dam stream hydrograph.** *This stream hydrograph shows flows in the Colorado River downstream of Glen Canyon Dam in 1942 and 1994. Before the dam was built, stream discharge peaked at over 90,000 ft³/s with the late spring snowmelt (1942 line), creating a major flood event. The 1994 levels represent typical flows after the dam was built. Peak discharge periods, such as the one seen in 1942, were eliminated.*

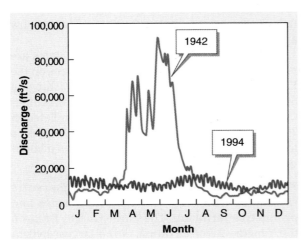

FIGURE 16.38 **Hydroelectricity generation.** *Water rushing from a reservoir spins large turbines that generate electricity in hydroelectric plants.*

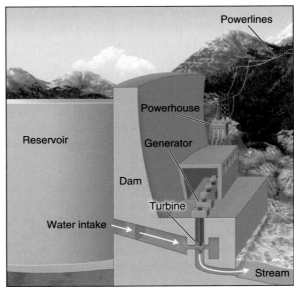

FIGURE 16.39   **Sediment-filled reservoir.** *Rindge Dam, built on Malibu Creek in Southern California over 50 years ago, is 30 m (100 ft) tall. There used to be a reservoir behind the dam, but the dam trapped sediment carried by the creek, which eventually filled the reservoir. Now vegetation grows on the former surface of the reservoir (shown with white line), and Malibu Creek runs over the top of the sediments and down a spillway.* (© AP Photo/Mark J. Terrill)

Recreation: Large reservoirs created by dams provide recreational opportunities for millions of people each year. Activities include water skiing, boating, fishing, swimming, and camping. Recreation on reservoirs is an important part of many local economies.

The Cons of Dams

Reservoirs behind dams provide water for thirsty cities and crops, but they may also destroy stream habitat or preexisting ecosystems and human communities. Other drawbacks of dams include the following:

Reservoir sedimentation: Reservoirs behind dams fill up with sediment because they form a temporary base level. The sediments that accumulate behind dams would have been deposited along coastal regions to help build and maintain coastal beaches. Without these sediments, the beaches erode (see Section 19.3). Furthermore, **as reservoirs fill with sediments, their** capacity to hold water decreases and sometimes disappears entirely, so that the useful life of the reservoir is limited, as shown in Figure 16.39.

The Aswan High Dam, on the Nile River in Egypt, was completed in 1970 and created artificial Lake Nasser. The Nile River carries a heavy suspended load as it runs through the desert of Sudan and Egypt. The river deposits 120 metric tons of sediment each year in Lake Nasser.

Before the emplacement of the dam, the clays and silts the river carried would settle out on the floodplain along the length of the river and build it up with nutrient-rich alluvium. The soils of the Nile floodplain had been sustainably farmed for over 5,000 years. In addition, a widespread and economically important brick-making industry relied on the sediments. Now, without the flooding and the addition of new sediments, synthetic (artificial) fertilizers are needed to maintain agricultural output along the Nile floodplain, and the brick-making industry in many areas is gone.

Loss of cultural sites and habitat: **When dams are built, the valleys upstream of the dam are flooded and the stream ecology is destroyed.** Lake Powell, the reservoir created by Glen Canyon Dam in Arizona, flooded extensive stretches of the lower Colorado River valley. Slot canyons, natural arches, wildlife habitat, and many active Native American communities and their archaeological sites were flooded, as shown in Figure 16.40.

Similarly, the Columbia River watershed has 46 major dams. These dams have been built in rivers in which salmon by the tens of millions once migrated from the Pacific Ocean to spawn in the gravels of small tributary streams. The dams now block the migration of salmon. "Fish ladders" and fish hatcheries were installed on some dam sites. Fish ladders are intended to allow salmon to bypass the structures, but have limited success. Fish hatcheries nurture domesticated (see Section 7.6) salmon, which scientists see as genetically less fit than wild salmon. As a result, and in conjunction with other factors such as commercial fishing, salmon populations throughout the Pacific Northwest are now a fraction of their former numbers.

In response to these problems, some dams are being removed. For example, the Elwha Dam, on the Elwha River in Olympic National Park, Washington State, was removed in 2012, and removal of the Glines Canyon Dam, on the same river, was completed in 2014. The Glines Canyon Dam, built in 1927, was 64 m (210 ft) high, making this the largest dam demolition project in U.S. history (Figure 16.41).

Flooded communities and farmland: **Reservoirs created by dams can destroy communities and productive farmland.** The Three Gorges Dam, on the Yangtze River in China, is the largest hydro-

FIGURE 16.40 **Glen Canyon Dam and Lake Powell.** *(A) Glen Canyon Dam was completed in 1966. At 216 m (710 ft), it is the fourth tallest dam in the United States. (B) Hundreds of archaeological sites, such as this submerged Puebloan structure at Doll Ruin in Moqui Canyon, now lie hidden beneath the waters of Lake Powell. (A. © Matthew Micah Wright/Lonely Planet Images/Getty Images; B. Photo courtesy of the NPS Submerged Resources Center)*

A

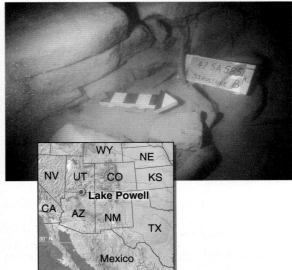

B

electric power station in the world. For many, the dam is a technological marvel and an important move away from reliance on energy from coal. To its critics, however, this dam has become symbolic of environmental sacrifice in the name of economic progress. The dam and reservoir forced the relocation of 1.5 million people, many of whom had lived in the area for generations. Some 1,300 archeological sites and 8,000 years of human history were erased when the waters rose.

The Chinese government has nineteen more dam construction projects slated for the upper Yangtze River in the coming decades, most of which will be for hydroelectric power. Similarly, eleven large hydroelectric dams will be built on the lower Mekong River by the governments of Laos, Vietnam, Thailand, and Cambodia in the coming decades. China has built five large hydroelectric projects on the upper Mekong and will have another three completed within the next few years.

Climate change: Reservoirs, particularly reservoirs located in the tropics, produce methane gas through anaerobic decomposition of underwater organic material. Methane is 21 times more potent as a greenhouse gas than carbon dioxide. Large reservoirs in the tropics can emit more greenhouse gases, in the form of methane, than coal-burning power plants that emit carbon dioxide. Midlatitude reservoirs also produce methane, but less than tropical reservoirs.

Taking the Good with the Bad

Although dams have provided many societal benefits, they have come at a cost. In some cases, the cost is relatively slight, while in others it is so steep that maintaining the dam no longer makes sense. Massive new hydroelectric projects in developed countries such as the United States are unlikely because the environmental and societal costs far outweigh the benefits. In developing countries, such as China, Brazil, and India, however, new large dam projects are on the upswing to meet the power and water needs of growing populations.

FIGURE 16.41 **Glines Canyon Dam removal.** *With the Glines Canyon Dam gone, an estimated half million salmon will have access to ancestral spawning grounds within the Elwha River watershed for the first time in 80 years. This photo shows the dam partially removed. (© Keith Thorpe/Peninsular Daily News, Port Angeles, WA)*

Video
Elwha River salmon
http://qrs.ly/aa49i1z

CHAPTER 16 Exploring with ◎ Google Earth

To complete these problems, first read the chapter. When you are finished, go to LaunchPad and open the Exploring with Google Earth file for this chapter. Click on the "Workbook Problems" folder to "fly" to each of the problems listed below and answer the questions. Be sure to keep your "Borders and Labels" layer activated. Refer to Appendix 4 if you need help using Google Earth.

PROBLEM 16.1 Drainage pattern identification: This drainage pattern, which resembles the branching network of a tree's limbs, is the most common one. (Hint: For help with this problem and Problems 16.2-16.4, see Figure 16.7.)

1. **What type of drainage pattern is this?**
   a. Dendritic   c. Deranged
   b. Radial   d. Trellis

2. **Zoom out. In what country is this placemark found?**
   a. Algeria   c. Chad
   b. Morocco   d. Tunisia

PROBLEM 16.2 Drainage pattern identification: This type of drainage pattern is common at high latitudes.

1. **What type of drainage pattern is this?**
   a. Dendritic   c. Deranged
   b. Radial   d. Trellis

2. **What formed this drainage pattern?**
   a. A volcano   c. Glacial erosion
   b. Tectonic folding   d. Bedrock jointing

PROBLEM 16.3 Drainage pattern identification: This type of drainage pattern is common on mountains. Notice that the circular dark green area is forested land protected by a nature reserve. The surrounding lighter green vegetation is agricultural land.

1. **What type of drainage pattern is this?**
   a. Dendritic   c. Deranged
   b. Radial   d. Trellis

2. **What formed this drainage pattern?**
   a. A volcano   c. Glacial erosion
   b. Tectonic folding   d. Bedrock jointing

PROBLEM 16.4 Drainage pattern identification: This type of drainage pattern occurs where layers of sedimentary rocks are compressed, creating structural basins and ridges.

1. **What type of drainage pattern is this?**
   a. Dendritic   c. Deranged
   b. Radial   d. Trellis

2. **What formed this drainage pattern?**
   a. A volcano   c. Glacial erosion
   b. Tectonic folding   d. Bedrock jointing

PROBLEM 16.5 This landform is the result of a stream cutting into the bedrock below. Zoom in close to the surface.

1. **What is the name of this landform?**
   a. A stair-step canyon   c. A slot canyon
   b. A V-shaped valley   d. A geologic fault

2. **Zoom out until you can see the drainage pattern of this stream system. What kind of drainage pattern is it?**
   a. Dendritic   c. Deranged
   b. Radial   d. Trellis

PROBLEM 16.6 This placemark lands on Victoria Falls in Africa. This spectacular feature formed where a stream flows over an escarpment. You can activate the 3D Buildings layer in the sidebar menu for greater relief.

1. **What is the name for this landform?**
   a. Slot canyon   c. Meander
   b. Knickpoint   d. Delta

2. **Zoom out. What country is this?**
   a. Zimbabwe   c. Botswana
   b. Zambia   d. Angola

PROBLEM 16.7 This placemark lands on Rio Juruá in Brazil, which will be the focus of Problems 16.7-16.10. Many streams, this one included, develop this looping, sinuous pattern on flat floodplains. (Hint: For help with these problems, see Figure 16.29.)

1. **What is the name of these bends in the stream?**
   a. Meander scars   c. Oxbow lakes
   b. Meanders   d. Alluvial fans

2. **What is the name for the crescent-shaped lakes seen here?**
   a. Alluvial fans   c. Meander scars
   b. Meanders   d. Oxbow lakes

3. **What is the name for the crescents not filled with water?**
   a. Meander scars   c. Alluvial fans
   b. Oxbow lakes   d. Meanders

PROBLEM 16.8 This placemark lands on Rio Juruá in Brazil.

1. **What is the inside bank of this meander called?**
   a. Point bar   c. Meander scar
   b. Oxbow lake   d. Cut bank

2. **What is the outside bank of this meander called?**
   a. Point bar   c. Meander scar
   b. Oxbow lake   d. Cut bank

3. **Which of these two channel locations experiences net deposition?**
   a. The inside of the bend   b. The outside of the bend

PROBLEM 16.9 This placemark lands on Rio Juruá in Brazil.

1. **What is the name for the relatively straight stream that follows the margin of the main stream?**
   a. Trunk stream   c. Exotic stream
   b. Yazoo stream   d. Intermittent stream

PROBLEM 16.10 This placemark lands on Rio Juruá in Brazil.

1. **What is likely to happen at this placemark in the near future?**
   a. The meander will be cut off.
   b. A new meander will form.
   c. A new tributary stream will form.
   d. Nothing is likely to happen.

2. **When that happens, what new feature will form?**
   a. A plunge pool   c. A cut bar
   b. A meander   d. An oxbow lake

PROBLEM 16.11 This placemark features the confluence of the Amazon River (to the south) and the Rio Negro (to the north) in Brazil. Use the compass in the upper right of the screen to note which way is north.

1. **Which river is the muddy one?**
   a. The Amazon River
   b. The Rio Negro

2. **What makes that river muddy?**
   a. Its bed load
   b. Its dissolved load
   c. Its suspended load
   d. Water pollution

3. **What city occurs at the confluence of these two rivers?**
   a. Iranduba
   b. Manaus
   c. Manaquiri
   d. New Delhi

4. **Zoom out. How far away is this city from the mouth of the Amazon?**
   a. 500 km
   b. 1,000 km
   c. 1,200 km
   d. 1,800 km

PROBLEM 16.12 This is Salmon Falls Creek. The surface bedrock in the region of this placemark is volcanic.

1. **What is the artificial structure that is visible?**
   a. A city
   b. Farm fields
   c. An airport
   d. A dam

2. **Is this a natural lake or an artificial reservoir?**
   a. Natural
   b. Artificial

PROBLEM 16.13 This is Salmon Falls Creek, the same water body featured in Problem 16.12. Notice that there are large meanders that are sunken into canyons. Within those large meanders, the active stream forms smaller meanders.

1. **What is the name for these sunken meanders?**
   a. Slot canyons
   b. Plunge pools
   c. Meander scars
   d. Entrenched meanders

2. **Are the larger sunken meanders still active and changing position?**
   a. Yes
   b. No

3. **Are the smaller stream meanders still active and changing position?**
   a. Yes
   b. No

PROBLEM 16.14 This placemark features Makgadikgadi Pans in southern Africa, among the world's largest salt flats. The pans are inhospitable in the dry season. In the rainy season, however, they become shallow, saline lakes that support plants and tens of thousands of migratory birds and animals such as zebras and wildebeests.

1. **What is the name of the pans' drainage system?**
   a. Dendritic drainage
   b. Internal drainage
   c. Cut bank
   d. Oxbow lake

PROBLEM 16.15 These branching canyons in the Namib Desert in Namibia are working their way northward.

1. **What is the name of the process by which these canyons are lengthening?**
   a. Headward erosion
   b. Abrasion
   c. Saltation
   d. Aggradation

PROBLEM 16.16 These landforms are found in Death Valley, California. They form as ephemeral streams emerge from steep-sided canyons and drop their sediments onto a flat plain or valley. Notice the two-lane highway that skirts around the contour of one of the landforms.

1. **What is the name of these landforms?**
   a. Tributaries
   b. Braided streams
   c. Alluvial fans
   d. Escarpments

2. **How wide is this feature?**
   a. 1 mi
   b. 2 mi
   c. 3 mi
   d. 4 mi

3. **What is the elevation at the base of the feature?**
   a. −270 ft
   b. 220 ft
   c. 1,200 ft
   d. 2,500 ft

PROBLEM 16.17 This placemark features the Kaskawulsh River in Kluane National Park and Reserve, Yukon Territory, Canada. The stream is choked with sediments from glacial erosion upstream from the placemark.

1. **What is the name of this type of stream?**
   a. Ephemeral stream
   b. Distributary
   c. Flooding stream
   d. Braided stream

PROBLEM 16.18 This is the Volga River delta in Russia, Europe's largest delta. It was set aside as a nature reserve in the early 1900s, and as a result, there is little human development.

1. **What kind of delta is this?**
   a. Arcuate delta
   b. Bird's foot delta

PROBLEM 16.19 This placemark lies in the center of a small drainage basin called Corral Canyon in Southern California. Fire activity is high in this area; as a result, many ridges are topped with firebreak roads that prevent the spread of fire by removing vegetation. Here, the firebreak roads coincide with the edges of the drainage basin and neatly outline the basin.

1. **What is the name of division between two drainage basins, as marked here by the firebreak roads?**
   a. Drainage divide
   b. Continental divide
   c. Base level
   d. Knickpoint

2. **What stream pattern occurs in this drainage basin?**
   a. Dendritic
   b. Radial
   c. Trellis
   d. Deranged

3. **Where does the trunk stream in this drainage basin end?**
   a. At a plunge pool
   b. At a tributary
   c. At base level
   d. At an escarpment

PROBLEM 16.20 This placemark is south of Provo, Utah. Be sure that the three markers in this problem's folder are active. Marker 1 marks the Price River, and marker 2 marks the San Rafael River. Both streams flow from west to east through a large anticlinal ridge called the San Rafael Swell, which formed about 60 million to 40 million years ago.

1. **Because these streams flow through this ridge rather than around it, they must be what type of streams?**
   a. Superimposed or antecedent
   b. Radial
   c. Braided
   d. Permanent

2. **Zoom in to marker 3 or double-click it. Note how the stream cuts through the ridge. What is the name of this landform?**
   a. Continental divide
   b. Cut bank
   c. Knickpoint
   d. Water gap

CHAPTER 16 **Study Guide**

Focus Points

16.1 Stream Patterns

Drainage basins: Drainage basins are composed of tributary streams and a trunk stream. They are delineated by topographic relief.

Drainage and continental divides: Drainage divides separate different drainage basins. Continental divides separate drainage basins that empty into different oceans.

Drainage patterns: Stream tributaries form different geographic patterns. The most common pattern is dendritic drainage.

Stream order: Most streams are third-order streams or smaller.

16.2 Downcutting by Streams: Fluvial Erosion

Fluvial erosion: Fluvial erosion is the most important and widespread agent of erosion on Earth.

Stream discharge: Stream discharge is determined by climate, stream order, season, and ground permeability. High-discharge streams have more energy to transport sediments than low-discharge streams.

Stream rejuvenation: Entrenched meanders, stream terraces, and antecedent streams all result when a stream is uplifted.

16.3 Building by Streams: Fluvial Deposition

Stream sorting: Streams drop large sediments first and the lightest materials last.

Aggradation landforms: Floodplains and braided streams are formed through aggradation.

Meanders: Streams migrate across their floodplains as they form meanders and meander cutoffs.

Flooding: Streams overflow their channels and cover the floodplain with a sheet of standing water. Sediments drop out of the still water.

Delta subsidence: The input of new sediments with flooding in a delta naturally keeps pace with the natural rate of subsidence through sediment compaction. Artificial levees prevent flooding and disrupt this equilibrium.

16.4 Rising Waters: Stream Flooding

Types of flooding: Flash floods and seasonal floods are the two modes of stream flooding.

Flood mitigation: Dams, levees, and stream bypasses help reduce flooding events.

16.5 Geographic Perspectives: Dam Pros and Cons

Dam pros: Dams provide many benefits to human society, including flood control, water availability, and hydroelectricity generation.

Dam cons: Dams create many problems for people, including destruction of habitat, farmland, and human communities and beach erosion resulting from sediment starvation.

Key Terms

abrasion, 519
aggradation, 526
alluvial fan, 527
alluvium, 526
base level, 521
bed load, 520
braided stream, 527
continental divide, 512
cut bank, 528
delta, 530
dendritic drainage, 514
dissolved load, 520
distributary, 530
drainage basin, 511
drainage divide, 512
ephemeral stream, 515
escarpment, 523
exotic stream, 515
flash flood, 532
flood, 532
floodplain, 510
fluvial erosion, 517
headward erosion, 517

headwaters, 514
intermittent stream, 514
internal drainage, 512
knickpoint, 523
meander, 528
oxbow lake, 528
permanent stream, 515
plunge pool, 523
point bar, 528
reservoir, 530
saltation, 520
seasonal flood, 533
stream, 511
stream discharge, 517
stream order, 514
stream piracy, 525
stream rejuvenation, 523
subsidence, 531
suspended load, 520
traction, 520
tributary, 511
trunk stream, 511

Concept Review

The Human Sphere: People and Floodplains

1. What are the benefits of locating a large city near a river on a floodplain? What problems arise for cities on floodplains?

16.1 Stream Patterns

2. What are tributaries and trunk streams? How do these phenomena fit into drainage basins?

3. What is the difference between a drainage divide and a continental divide?

4. What is an internal drainage basin? Why are lakes found there typically saline?

5. Compare the different types of drainage patterns. Which is the most common on Earth's surface?

6. What happens to stream order when a first-order stream merges with a second-order stream? What happens when two second-order streams merge? What order of stream is the Amazon River?

7. Compare and contrast intermittent, permanent, ephemeral, and exotic streams.

16.2 Downcutting by Streams: Fluvial Erosion

8. What is fluvial erosion? Why is it the most important agent of erosion?

9. What is headward erosion? How do rills and gullies relate to headward erosion?

10. What is downcutting? Where does it occur?

11. What is stream discharge? What four main factors determine stream discharge?

12. What is a stream hydrograph? Compare natural stream discharge with discharge of streams in urbanized areas.

13. What is abrasion? How does it relate to fluvial erosion?

14. What is a stream load? List three types of stream loads.

15. Compare stream capacity with stream competence. What factors increase each?

16. In what situations do stream capacity and stream competence decrease? What happens to the stream load when they decrease?

17. What does it mean to say that a stream is graded? Compare a graded stream with one that is not graded.

18. What is base level?

19. Why do some streams have V-shaped valley walls, while others form slot canyons?

20. What is a knickpoint? Why do knickpoints migrate upstream?

21. What is stream rejuvenation? What rejuvenates a stream? What do streams do once they are rejuvenated?

22. How do entrenched meanders and stream terraces form?

23 What is a water gap? Explain how this landform forms in the context of geologic uplift.

24. What is stream piracy? How does one stream divert another?

16.3 Building by Streams: Fluvial Deposition

25. What does it mean to say that streams "sort" their load? Why is it sorted? How is it sorted?

26. What is aggradation? Where does it occur? How does it relate to stream capacity and stream competence?

27. What are braided streams? Where do they form?

28. What are alluvial fans? Where do they form?

29. What is a stream meander? What is a thalweg, and how does it relate to stream meander

development? How are point bars and cut banks related to the development and migration of meanders?

30. Where do natural levees form? How do they form?

31. Identify several floodplain landforms.

32. Why do deltas form at base level? What are the two main delta shapes?

33. What are distributaries? Where are they found? How do they form?

34. What is subsidence? Why do deltas experience it? Explain how deltas maintain an equilibrium between sedimentation and subsidence.

35. How do artificial levees disrupt the equilibrium between sedimentation and subsidence?

16.4 Rising Waters: Stream Flooding

36. Why do floods happen? What two kinds of flooding are there?

37. What three major approaches are used to control floods? Explain how each works and the advantages and disadvantages of each.

16.5 Geographic Perspectives: Dam Pros and Cons

38. How do dams provide water?

39. How do dams generate hydroelectricity?

40. Why do sediments settle out in reservoirs?

41. How do dams create habitat loss? Relate your answer to the salmon runs of the Pacific Northwest.

42. How do dams relate to climate change?

Critical-Thinking Questions

1. Fluvial erosion cuts into mountains and reduces their height. Why haven't streams worn all of Earth's mountains flat?

2. Rocks are much harder than water. How does water carve valleys into mountains composed of solid bedrock?

3. Some stream channels naturally follow fault lines. Earthquakes make rocks there weak and easily eroded. How does this fact relate to problems with some dams on streams?

4. Do you live where it floods? What kinds of information would you need to answer this question if you do not know?

5. Which argument do you think is stronger, that for dam removal or that for dam building? Or does it depend on the circumstance? Explain your answer.

Test Yourself

Take this quiz to test your chapter knowledge.

1. **True or false:** Every drainage basin has a trunk stream.

2. **True or false:** Merging two second-order streams creates a fourth-order stream.

3. **True or false:** Flash floods are typically more dangerous than seasonal floods.

4. **True or false:** Exotic streams flow through arid regions and dry up before reaching the ocean.

5. **Multiple choice:** Which of the following features is not associated with stream meanders?
   a. Point bar
   b. Oxbow lake
   c. Knickpoint
   d. Alluvium

6. **Multiple choice:** Waterfalls migrate upstream through the process of _____.
   a. headward erosion.
   b. subsidence.
   c. stream meandering.
   d. stream aggradation.

7. **Multiple choice:** Internal drainage basins are most likely to have which one of the following?
   a. Escarpments   c. Plunge pools
   b. Permanent streams   d. Saline lakes

8. **Multiple choice:** Stream terraces are created when which of the following occurs?
   a. Flooding
   b. Geologic uplift
   c. The building of a new dam
   d. The merging of tributary streams

9. **Fill in the blank:** At _____, a stream stops flowing and becomes standing water.

10. **Fill in the blank:** A _____ separates two different drainage basins that flow into different oceans.

Further Reading

1. Heffernan, Olive. "Adapting to a Warmer World: No Going Back." *Nature* 491 (2012): 659-661.

2. Jefferson, Anne. "Levees and the Illusion of Flood Control." *Scientific American* Guest Blog, May 20, 2011. http://blogs.scientificamerican.com.

3. McPhee, John. *The Control of Nature*. New York: Farrar, Straus and Giroux, 1990.

Answers to Living Physical Geography Questions

1. **Why are major cities often located on rivers?** Rivers provide many societal benefits, including flat land for settlement, fertile soils, and access to inland areas from the coast.

2. **What is the largest river in the world?** The Nile River in Africa is the longest river. The largest river by volume is the Amazon River.

3. **Why are river rocks rounded?** River rocks are rounded by abrasion. As rocks move in a streambed, they grind against one another and are sanded smooth and round.

4. **What are swamps and bayous?** Swamps and bayous are informal names for permanently flooded lowlands. Scientists call these areas wetlands.

Picture This. YOUR TURN

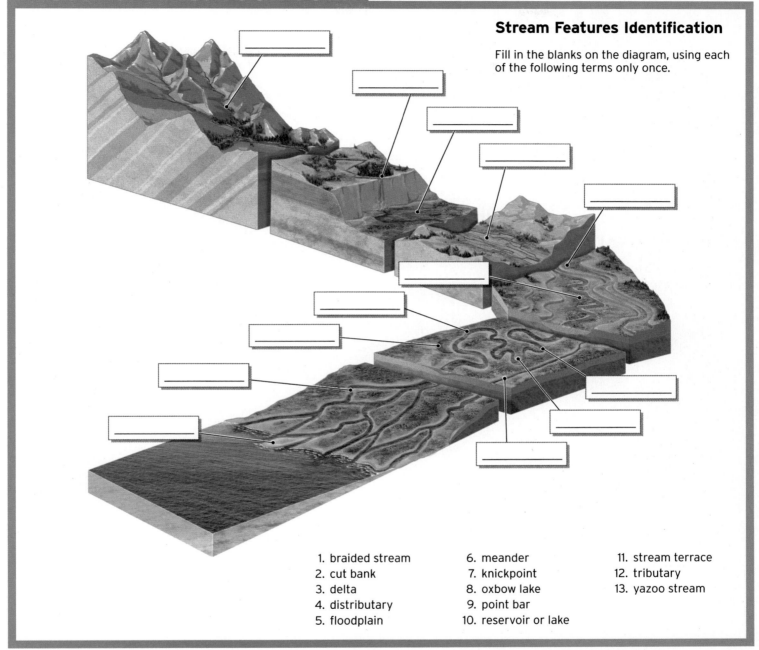

Stream Features Identification

Fill in the blanks on the diagram, using each of the following terms only once.

1. braided stream
2. cut bank
3. delta
4. distributary
5. floodplain
6. meander
7. knickpoint
8. oxbow lake
9. point bar
10. reservoir or lake
11. stream terrace
12. tributary
13. yazoo stream

17 THE WORK OF ICE: The Cryosphere and Glacial Landforms

These piedmont glaciers are spilling into a valley on Axel Heiberg Island in the Canadian Arctic. Glacial ice flows downhill, and as it does so, the ice carves into the bedrock below.

(© Dr. Juerg Alean/Science Source)

LIVING PHYSICAL GEOGRAPHY

➤ Why are bones and tusks of extinct mammoths appearing throughout Siberia?

➤ Why are explosive gases seeping from Arctic lakes?

➤ How do glaciers form?

➤ How does the soft ice of a glacier carve into solid bedrock?

➤ How did Yosemite Valley form?

To learn more about glacial erosion, turn to Section 17.3.

THE BIG PICTURE *Perpetually frozen ground and glaciers create unique landforms. The loss of ice on Greenland and Antarctica could cause significant sea-level rise.*

LEARNING GOALS *After reading this chapter, you will be able to:*

17.1 ◎ Identify features unique to areas with permanently frozen soils and explain environmental changes taking place in those areas.

17.2 ◎ Explain how glaciers form and move and describe different glacier types and their geographic settings.

17.3 ◎ Explain how glaciers cut into rocks and identify landforms caused by glacial erosion.

17.4 ◎ Identify landforms created from glacial sediments and explain how they formed.

17.5 ◎ Assess the role of polar ice sheets in current and future sea-level changes and explain why sea-level rise presents problems for human society.

THE HUMAN SPHERE: The Mammoth Hunters

FIGURE 17.1 **Mammoth remains.** *Preserved mammoth tusks, such as these found in Siberia, provide data for scientists studying these ancient animals, and they are prized for their ivory by collectors. Tusks of this size sell for about $100,000 each. An estimated 50 tons of mammoth bones are found each year in Russia. (© AP Photo/Francis Latreille/Nova Productions)*

FOR 5 MILLION YEARS, the woolly mammoth (*Mammuthus primigenius*)—a close relative of the modern African elephant—roamed across much of the Northern Hemisphere by the millions. By about 9,600 years ago, however, all mainland mammoth populations in North America and Eurasia were gone. The last remaining mammoth holdout was Wrangel Island, in northeastern Eurasia. That island's mammoth population disappeared about 4,000 years ago, right after humans colonized the island. Changing climate and human hunting pressure were the main causes of the extinction of the mammoth and many other large animals that also lived at that time.

> Why are bones and tusks of extinct mammoths appearing throughout Siberia?*

The remains of some mammoths have been preserved in the frozen northern soils. Now the cryosphere—the frozen portion of the hydrosphere—is rapidly changing. High latitudes are warming at twice the rate of the mid-latitudes because of the ice-albedo positive feedback (see Section 6.4). As the frozen soils thaw, the mammoth remains become exposed, and scientists and collectors can find them (Figure 17.1).

This chapter explores the cryosphere, in the context of both landforms and changing climate. We first explore periglacial landscapes, those that are unglaciated but perpetually frozen. We then examine how glaciers develop and begin moving, and we visit landforms resulting from the movement of glaciers. Finally, we explore Earth's two enormous ice sheets, on Greenland and on Antarctica, and their current and projected contributions to sea-level rise.

*Answers to the Living Physical Geography questions are found on page 576.

17.1 Frozen Ground: Periglacial Environments

◎ Identify features unique to areas with permanently frozen soils and explain environmental changes taking place in those areas.

Periglacial means "around glaciers," but the term refers to all unglaciated areas at high latitudes and high elevations subject to persistent and intense freezing. As a result of climate change, periglacial environments are one of the most rapidly changing physical systems on Earth. As they change, they are also capable of creating significant climate feedbacks that could further change the global climate system.

Permafrost

In many regions of Alaska, northern Canada, and Siberia, the ground just beneath the surface veneer of plants and seasonally thawed gelisol soils (see Section 9.1) is perpetually frozen, forming permafrost. **Permafrost** is ground that remains below freezing continuously for two years or more (Figure 17.2). Not all permafrost is composed of ice. If there is no water in the soil, there will be no ice, only unconsolidated rock fragments at a temperature below freezing. Loose frozen sand, for example, is also permafrost.

Although permafrost, by definition, remains frozen year-round, in most regions the topmost portion of the ground, called the **active layer**, thaws each summer and refreezes in fall. The depth of the active layer decreases farther north and at higher elevations in mountainous areas. When the active layer thaws, ice turns to liquid water, forming

FIGURE 17.2 **Permafrost.** *This exposure of permafrost is near Cherskii, Russia, in eastern Siberia. Note the person in the foreground for scale.* (© Katey M. Walter Anthony, University of Alaska Fairbanks (under NSF #0099113))

FIGURE 17.3 **Periglacial features.** *(A) Continuous permafrost occurs where the permafrost is 100 m (330 ft) thick or more. Permafrost that is thinner and interrupted by unfrozen ground, called talik, is discontinuous permafrost. (B) Permafrost is widely distributed throughout the Northern Hemisphere. This map shows discontinuous and continuous permafrost areas as well as areas with sporadic and isolated permafrost.*

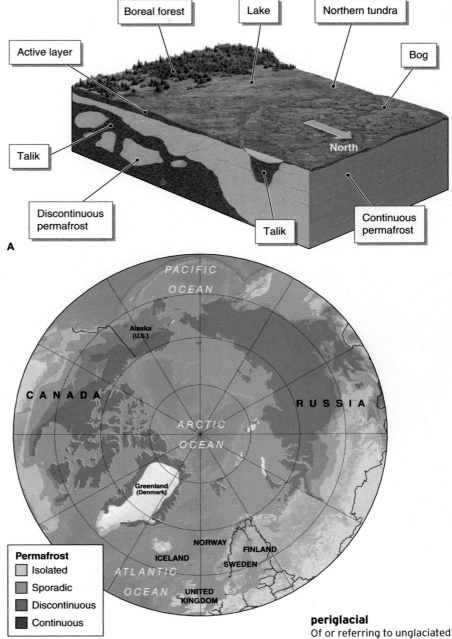

lakes and wetlands called *bogs* (Figure 17.3A). The boreal forest and northern tundra biomes (see Section 8.3) are found in areas with permafrost.

About 25% of the soils in the Northern Hemisphere have permafrost. At high latitudes, permafrost is typically unbroken, or *continuous*. Farther south, permafrost may become *isolated*, *sporadic*, or *discontinuous* (Figure 17.3B).

periglacial
Of or referring to unglaciated areas at high latitudes and high elevations subject to persistent and intense freezing.

permafrost
Ground that remains below freezing continuously for two years or more.

active layer
The top layer of permafrost that thaws each summer and refreezes in fall.

Picture This

(University of Alaska Fairbanks photo by Todd Paris)

Methane from Permafrost

This photo shows researcher Katey Walter Anthony lighting methane gas emerging from a frozen lake on the University of Alaska Fairbanks campus. As the permafrost beneath the lake thaws, anaerobic microorganisms (called *methanogens*) digest the organic carbon in the soils, producing methane gas as a by-product. The methane bubbles up from the lake bottom and is trapped beneath the frozen lake's cover of ice. If the ice is drilled through and the gas ignited, it forms a fireball. This process of permafrost thawing and *methanogenesis* (methane generation) is happening throughout the Northern Hemisphere's permafrost soils.

> Why are explosive gases seeping from Arctic lakes?

Two observations are becoming an increasing cause of concern for climate scientists. First, there are some 1.7 trillion metric tons of carbon stored in northern permafrost, twice as much as is currently in the atmosphere. Second, the Arctic is warming about twice as fast as the global average. This warming has the potential to thaw the permafrost and release the stored carbon in the form of methane and carbon dioxide.

A study published in 2012 in *Nature* finds that permafrost soils could release between 68 billion and 508 billion metric tons of carbon into the atmosphere by 2100. Because methane is such a potent greenhouse gas, scientists are concerned that permafrost thawing could create a positive feedback (see Section 3.6) that could accelerate the warming trend already under way.

Consider This

1. How are Arctic lakes becoming sources of methane?

2. Outline the positive feedback cycle that could result from permafrost methane production.

Most permafrost is found at 60 degrees north latitude and higher, but it can be found at all latitudes at high elevations. Near the equator permafrost is found at elevations higher than 5,000 m (16,400 ft). Mount Kilimanjaro in Kenya, for example, located at 3 degrees south latitude, has permafrost soil. The thickest permafrost, 1,650 m (5,445 ft) thick, is found in northeastern Russia. The permafrost there is over a half million years old.

The Southern Hemisphere has relatively little permafrost due to its lack of land at high latitudes.

Only 0.3% of Antarctica's land is not covered by the Antarctic ice sheet, and all of that exposed land is permafrost. The Patagonian ice fields in South America and the highlands of the Southern Alps in New Zealand have discontinuous permafrost.

As we saw in Section 6.4, the cryosphere is changing rapidly in response to warming of the atmosphere. **Rapid changes are occurring in periglacial environments, particularly in the active layer, as ground temperatures increase (Picture This).**

FIGURE 17.4 **Pingo and patterned ground.** *(A) Pingos can reach 50 m (160 ft) in height and range from the size of a car to the size of a large hill, like the one shown here. This pingo is in the McKenzie River delta in Canada. (B) This patterned ground is in the Farnell Valley, Antarctica. (A. Jason Pineau/All Canada Photos/Getty Images; B. © Maria Stenzel/National Geographic/Getty Images)*

A

B

Periglacial Features

Several landforms and phenomena are found only in periglacial environments. Two periglacial landforms are pingos and patterned ground. A *pingo* is a hill with a core of ice **(Figure 17.4A)**. Pingos form as liquid water from below is forced up through a layer of permafrost. As the water pushes through the permafrost, it forms a mound. Pingos grow at a rate of a few centimeters per year. *Patterned ground* is formed as freeze-thaw cycles slowly wedge soil apart. Over time, polygon shapes develop **(Figure 17.4B)**.

Trees growing on the active layer above permafrost are shallow-rooted and unstable because their roots cannot penetrate the permafrost just below. When the active layer deepens during particularly warm summers, the trees may become tilted, resulting in a *drunken forest* **(Figure 17.5)**.

Structures that radiate heat, such as railways and pipelines, thaw the permafrost beneath them. When permafrost thaws, it becomes unstable, and structures built on it sink into the ground. Such structures may therefore be elevated above the ground to avoid these problems.

FIGURE 17.5 **Drunken forest.** *This drunken forest is near Fairbanks, Alaska. (Tingjun Zhang, College of Earth and Environmental Science, Lanzhou University, China)*

FIGURE **17.6** **Engineering for permafrost.** *The Qinghai-Tibet railway, completed in 2006, has the highest elevation of any railway in the world. It is 1,956 km (1,215 mi) long and connects Xining, Qinghai Province, to Lhasa, Tibet Autonomous Region, China. Much of it is built on permafrost. If ice thaws beneath the tracks, the tracks will move, and such movements could derail a high-speed train. As a precaution, the tracks are raised above the permafrost, and in places vertical pipes circulate liquid nitrogen beneath the pilings to keep the soils around them frozen.* (© View Stock/Getty Images)

America far south of today's periglacial environments. These sediments range in size from massive boulders to tiny silt particles. In some places, large boulders seemed to have been placed randomly across the countryside. Many of them do not match the local bedrock, indicating that they came from far away **(Figure 17.7)**.

Originally, scientists thought water in streams created these sediments and transported these large boulders. But how could water have transported such massive boulders? Furthermore, the sediments that streams deposit are sorted by size (see Section 16.3). Why were these sediments unsorted? In 1837, the Swiss-American geologist Louis Agassiz proposed that the sediments and boulders were transported by now-melted glaciers. Originally, his "ice age theory" was subject to intense criticism by his colleagues in science, but within a decade or so, it was embraced because it is supported by the physical evidence.

Large boulders transported long distances by a glacier are called **glacial erratics**. Originally, glacial erratics and similar deposits of gravel and sand were attributed to the great biblical flood. It was thought

FIGURE **17.7** **Glacial erratic.** *This large, isolated boulder is on the coast of southern Sweden. Locally, it is called "Glumsten," and it served as a guidepost for sailors for hundreds of years, until a lighthouse was built. Note the picnic bench for scale.* (© Lars Wikander)

The 1,300 km (800 mi) Trans-Alaska Pipeline moves heated oil from the North Slope of Alaska all the way to the Pacific coast. Where it passes over permafrost, it has been elevated about 2 m (6.5 ft) above the ground to prevent melting of the permafrost, which would cause the pipe to rupture. China's Qinghai–Tibet railway is also engineered for permafrost conditions **(Figure 17.6)**.

17.2 About Glaciers

◎ **Explain how glaciers form and move and describe different glacier types and their geographic settings.**

In Section 6.2, we saw that Earth's climate was once much colder than it is today and that ice sheets once covered large areas of the Northern Hemisphere. Evidence of these colder conditions can be found in the form of sediments composed of unsorted rock fragments. Such sediments are commonplace throughout northern Eurasia and northern North

glacial erratic
A large boulder transported a long distance by a glacier.

that the boulders "drifted" into place, and they were therefore called *drift*. This term has persisted: Today, all deposits relating to glaciers and the streams flowing out of glaciers, from the largest boulders to the smallest silt particles, are collectively called *drift*.

What Is a Glacier?

A **glacier** is a large mass of ice that is formed from the accumulation of snow and that flows slowly downslope. Glaciers form one snowflake at a time,

over long periods. Glaciers form where snow accumulates and is compressed by gravity to granular snow, then firn, then glacial ice (Figure 17.8). **Glacial ice** is ice that has an air content of less than 20%. This process can take place only where snowfall does not melt completely in summer, so that snowfall accumulates year after year. Glaciers do not form in periglacial environments because snow melts

> **How do glaciers form?**

glacier
A large mass of ice that is formed from the accumulation of snow and flows slowly downslope.

glacial ice
Ice with an air content of less than 20%.

FIGURE 17.8   **GEO-GRAPHIC: Glacial ice.** *(A) Glacial ice forms as snowfall accumulates. (B) Hubbard Glacier, in southern Alaska, demonstrates some of the visual features of glacial ice. (© Accent Alaska.com/Alamy)*

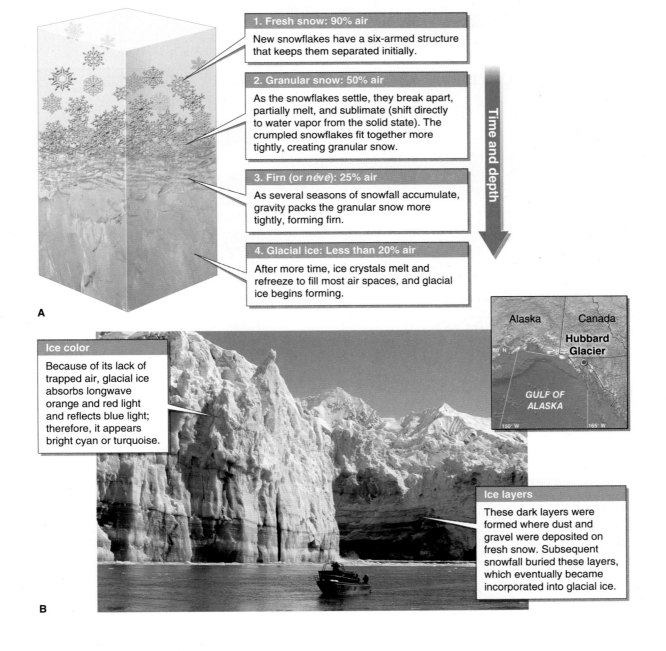

1. Fresh snow: 90% air
New snowflakes have a six-armed structure that keeps them separated initially.

2. Granular snow: 50% air
As the snowflakes settle, they break apart, partially melt, and sublimate (shift directly to water vapor from the solid state). The crumpled snowflakes fit together more tightly, creating granular snow.

3. Firn (or *névé*): 25% air
As several seasons of snowfall accumulate, gravity packs the granular snow more tightly, forming firn.

4. Glacial ice: Less than 20% air
After more time, ice crystals melt and refreeze to fill most air spaces, and glacial ice begins forming.

Time and depth

A

Ice color
Because of its lack of trapped air, glacial ice absorbs longwave orange and red light and reflects blue light; therefore, it appears bright cyan or turquoise.

Alaska   Canada
Hubbard Glacier
GULF OF ALASKA
150° W   165° W

Ice layers
These dark layers were formed where dust and gravel were deposited on fresh snow. Subsequent snowfall buried these layers, which eventually became incorporated into glacial ice.

B

FIGURE 17.9   **GEO-GRAPHIC: Plastic deformation and crevasses.** *(A) Crevasses form as ice flows over protrusions in the bedrock. (B) These crevasses have formed on Belcher Glacier as it flows toward the sea on Devon Island, Nunavut, Canada. (B. © Brad Danielson, University of Alberta)*

Animation
Crevasses
http://qrs.ly/t249s10

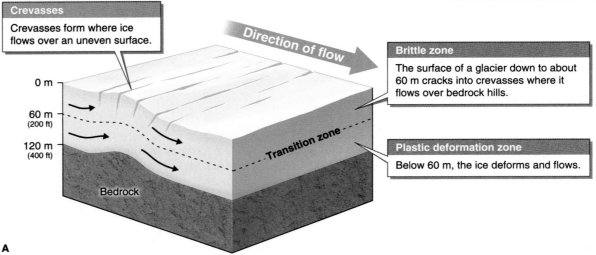

Crevasses
Crevasses form where ice flows over an uneven surface.

Direction of flow

Brittle zone
The surface of a glacier down to about 60 m cracks into crevasses where it flows over bedrock hills.

0 m
60 m (200 ft)
120 m (400 ft)

Transition zone

Plastic deformation zone
Below 60 m, the ice deforms and flows.

Bedrock

A

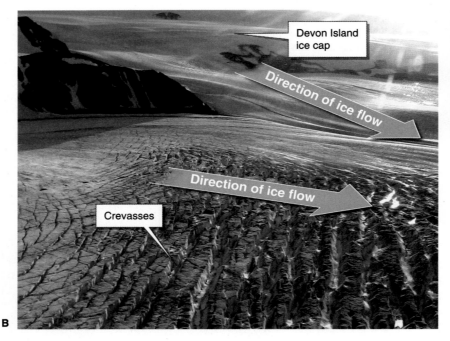

Devon Island ice cap

Direction of ice flow

Direction of ice flow

Crevasses

B

in summer or because there is insufficient snowfall. In addition, the slope where snow is accumulating cannot be too steep. If it is, the snow will slip downslope in avalanches rather than accumulate.

The time it takes for glacial ice to form ranges from decades to centuries, depending on snowfall rates. Heavy snowfall produces glaciers more quickly.

Flowing Ice

Glaciers move downslope by the processes of basal sliding and plastic deformation. Basal sliding is what causes a piece of ice to slide down the sloped hood of a car, for example, as liquid water lubricates the base of the ice. We discussed plastic deformation in Section 11.3 in the context of the solid rock of Earth's mantle, which slowly deforms

FIGURE 17.10 **Glacier flow rates.** *Ice flow in a glacier is fastest at its surface and center.*

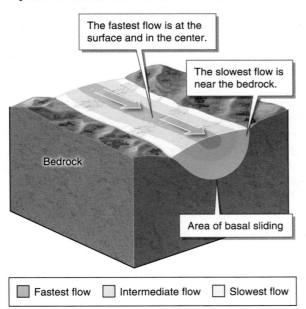

The fastest flow is at the surface and in the center.

The slowest flow is near the bedrock.

Bedrock

Area of basal sliding

| ■ Fastest flow | □ Intermediate flow | □ Slowest flow |

ice that decrease its volume. As a whole, a glacier with a neutral mass balance has inputs (snowfall) and outputs (melting, sublimation, and iceberg calving) that are equal. When snowfall is less than ice loss, a *negative mass balance* exists for the glacier. When snowfall exceeds ice loss, a glacier has a *positive mass balance*.

Along most of the length of a glacier, the mass balance is not neutral. At high elevations, more snow falls on the glacier than is lost through melting and sublimation. The area of a glacier where ice gain from snowfall exceeds ice loss is called the *zone of accumulation*. Below, in the *zone of ablation*, ice loss exceeds ice accumulation. At the terminus of a glacier, called the **toe**, more ice is lost than is gained through snowfall. The transition between the zone of accumulation and the zone of ablation is the **equilibrium line** (or snowline), the elevation at which a glacier's ice accumulation and ice loss are equal over a period of one year **(Figure 17.11).**

The forward movement of a glacier's toe, usually downslope, is called **glacial advance**; upslope movement of a glacier's toe is called **glacial retreat**.

crevasse
A crack that develops in the top 60 m of a glacier.

glacier mass balance
The difference between inputs to a glacier that increase its ice volume and losses of ice that decrease its ice volume.

toe
The leading edge and lowest elevation of a glacier.

equilibrium line
(or snowline) The elevation at which a glacier's ice accumulation and ice loss are equal over the period of one year.

glacial advance
The forward (usually downslope) movement of a glacier's toe.

glacial retreat
The upslope movement of the toe of a glacier.

and flows. Ice, too, is a solid, yet 60 m (200 ft) below the glacier's surface, ice can slowly deform and flow. From the glacier's surface down to 60 m, however, the ice is brittle. Cracks called **crevasses** form at the glacier's surface where it flows over uneven bedrock **(Figure 17.9).**

Glaciers flow downslope at an average rate of a few centimeters per day. They do not always move steadily downslope, however. Their speed varies depending on several factors, including air temperature, the topography over which they are flowing, and the amount of water lubricating their base. In a glacial surge, the speed of a glacier accelerates for a period of a few days to a month or more. Glacial surge speeds can be on the order of 30 m (100 ft) in a single day, or even faster.

Like the water in a stream, the ice within a glacier flows at different speeds. Friction with the bedrock slows down the ice at the margins. The areas of fastest flow are farthest from the bedrock; namely, near the surface and central portions of the glacier, as illustrated in **Figure 17.10.**

Inputs and Outputs: Glacier Mass Balance

A glacier's ice volume changes over time. **Glacier mass balance** is the difference between inputs to a glacier that increase its ice volume and losses of

FIGURE 17.11 **Glacier equilibrium line.** *The equilibrium line represents the elevation at which annual ice gain and ice loss are equal.*

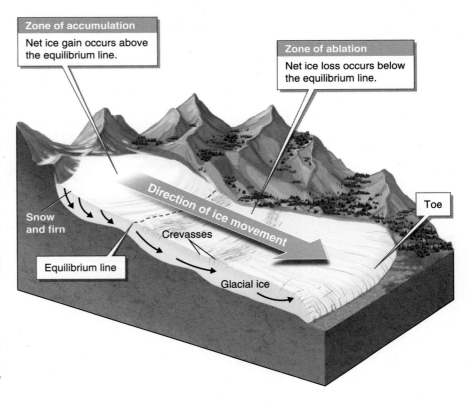

Zone of accumulation
Net ice gain occurs above the equilibrium line.

Zone of ablation
Net ice loss occurs below the equilibrium line.

Direction of ice movement

Toe

Snow and firn

Crevasses

Equilibrium line

Glacial ice

A glacier's toe is continually advancing and retreating in response to changes in glacier mass balance. As shown in **Figure 17.12**, however, the ice within a glacier is always flowing downslope even when the toe is retreating upslope.

Although the movement of a glacier's toe largely reflects the mass balance of a glacier, glaciers are complex systems, and other factors can cause the toe to advance or retreat. For example, increased basal sliding can cause the toe of a glacier to move downslope.

Glaciers are sensitive to changes in atmospheric temperature. Several glaciers on the coast of Norway are experiencing positive mass balance because snowfall in the zone of accumulation is exceeding ice loss in the zone of ablation, and the toes of these glaciers are advancing downslope. Ironically, these glaciers are advancing in response to climate change. Warming of the atmosphere and sea surface is increasing evaporation from the North Atlantic Ocean and producing more snowfall for the glaciers.

In mountains worldwide, most glaciers are in retreat in response to atmospheric warming. These glaciers are experiencing a negative mass balance because ice loss in the zone of ablation exceeds snowfall in the zone of accumulation. Scientists are carefully measuring the mass balance of glaciers around the world and monitoring them as Earth's climate changes (see Section 6.5). **Figure 17.13** explores how scientists monitor glaciers.

Animation
Glacier movement
http://qrs.ly/h149s11

FIGURE 17.12 **Movement of a glacier's toe.** *The position of a glacier's toe reflects the mass balance of the glacier. Like the glacier's toe, the equilibrium line also migrates in response to changes in mass balance.*

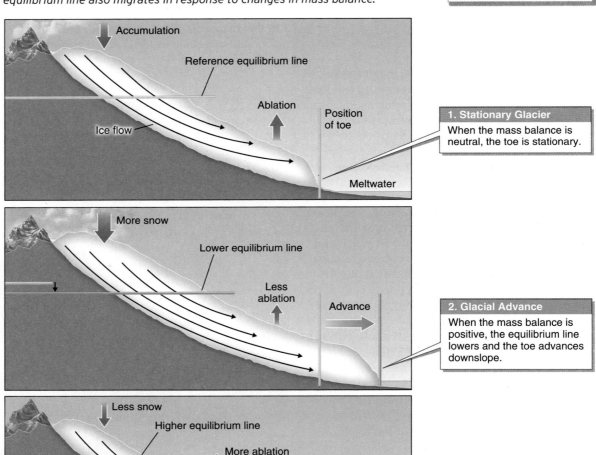

Accumulation
Reference equilibrium line
Ablation
Position of toe
Ice flow
Meltwater

1. Stationary Glacier
When the mass balance is neutral, the toe is stationary.

More snow
Lower equilibrium line
Less ablation
Advance

2. Glacial Advance
When the mass balance is positive, the equilibrium line lowers and the toe advances downslope.

Less snow
Higher equilibrium line
More ablation
Retreat

3. Glacial Retreat
When the mass balance is negative, the equilbrium line raises and the toe retreats upslope.

FIGURE 17.13 **SCIENTIFIC INQUIRY: How do scientists monitor glaciers?** *Monitoring of changes in glacier mass balance is essential for understanding the cryosphere's response to atmospheric warming. The loss of ice and snow allows the ground to absorb more sunlight and warm faster, creating an ice-albedo positive feedback (see Section 6.4). Melting glaciers also contribute to sea-level rise that threatens coastal populations.*

Photographic evidence

Historical photos provide important quantitative information about glacier mass balance over time. These photos show nearly a century of retreat of the South Cascade Glacier in Washington State. *(Top: Photo by L. Wernstedt, U.S. Forest Service; bottom three: Photos by U.S. Geological Survey)*

Field measurements

One means of measuring glacier mass balance is to place a network of marked stakes on the surface of a glacier. Measuring ice accumulation or loss at each stake allows scientists to determine the glacier's mass balance. These changes are compared with local temperature and precipitation data to see how the glacier is responding to climate change. Here, two researchers from the USGS are setting a measurement stake on the South Cascade Glacier. *(Photo by U.S. Geological Survey)*

Results

A graph of mass balance for the South Cascade Glacier shows that it has been losing ice since monitoring began in the late 1950s. Also shown here are mass balance graphs for the Wolverine and Gulkana glaciers, both in Alaska. The *y*-axis shows "meters water equivalence" (MWEQ): the depth of liquid water that has been lost from the glacier. Ninety-nine percent of Alaska's major glaciers are shrinking. This pattern of glacial retreat is being observed worldwide as a result of climate change.

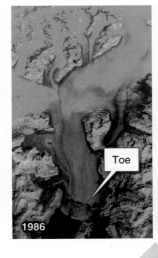

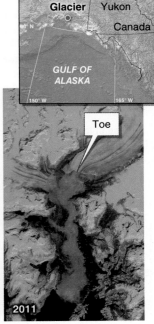

Toe

Toe

1986

2011

Satellite remote sensing

Satellites can be used to detect changes in glacier mass balance in many different ways, including sensing subtle changes in gravity around a glacier and detecting changes in the surface elevation of the glacier and in the position of its toe. These photos are false-color Landsat 5 images of the Columbia Glacier in the Chugach Mountains of southeastern Alaska. Snow and glacial ice are colored blue. Healthy vegetation is green; bare ground is brown; water is black. The distance across this image is about 22 km (13 mi). Since the 1980s, the Columbia Glacier has lost half its mass. At this rate, it will be gone by 2050. *(NASA images courtesy Landsat team)*

FIGURE 17.14 **Alpine glacier types.** *Cirque glaciers, valley glaciers, piedmont glaciers, and ice caps are the main types of glaciers found in mountainous areas. Cirques are the smallest alpine glacier type and ice caps are the most geographically extensive.*

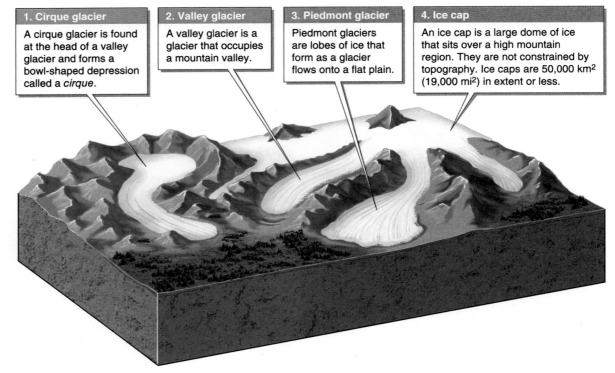

1. Cirque glacier
A cirque glacier is found at the head of a valley glacier and forms a bowl-shaped depression called a *cirque*.

2. Valley glacier
A valley glacier is a glacier that occupies a mountain valley.

3. Piedmont glacier
Piedmont glaciers are lobes of ice that form as a glacier flows onto a flat plain.

4. Ice cap
An ice cap is a large dome of ice that sits over a high mountain region. They are not constrained by topography. Ice caps are 50,000 km² (19,000 mi²) in extent or less.

alpine glacier
Any glacier found in a mountainous area.

cirque glacier
A glacier that forms at the head of a valley.

valley glacier
A glacier that occupies a mountain valley.

piedmont glacier
A lobe of ice that forms as a valley glacier flows onto a flat plain.

ice cap
A dome of ice that sits over a high mountain region and has an extent of 50,000 km² (19,300 m²) or less.

ice sheet
A flat sheet of ice that has an extent of 50,000 km² (19,300 mi²) or more.

nunatak
(pronounced nuh-nuh-TAK) Bedrock that protrudes above a glacier.

outlet glacier
A glacier that flows out of an ice sheet or ice cap through a constricted valley, usually into the ocean.

iceberg
A large block of ice that breaks from the toe of a glacier or an ice shelf and floats in the ocean or a lake.

ice shelf
The portion of an ice sheet or an outlet glacier that extends over the ocean.

Two Types of Glaciers

Today, glaciers occur on every continent except Australia. They are found from the equator at high elevations to the Arctic and Antarctica at sea level. **There are two basic types of glaciers: alpine glaciers and ice sheets. Alpine glaciers** (or mountain glaciers) are glaciers that are found in mountainous areas. There are four main types of alpine glaciers **(Figure 17.14)**.

Ice sheets, in contrast to alpine glaciers, are domed sheets of ice that cover a significant portion of a continent. They are larger than 50,000 km² (19,300 mi²). Only Greenland and Antarctica have ice sheets, and together they contain over 99% of all ice on Earth **(Figure 17.15A)**.

As ice sheets and ice caps flow slowly outward from their centers, they may surround an exposed high point of land, forming a **nunatak**: an area of bedrock that protrudes above the glacier. Large lobes of ice at the margins form outlet glaciers and piedmont glaciers. An **outlet glacier** is a glacier that flows out of an ice sheet or ice cap through a constricted valley, usually into the ocean. *Ice streams*

are areas where ice flow is accelerated, as when ice travels over steep terrain or through a constricted valley **(Figure 17.15B)**. The Geographic Perspectives, at the end of this chapter, examines outlet glacier flow speeds in Greenland and Antarctica in the context of climate change and global sea-level rise.

 GEOGRAPHIC PERSPECTIVES

Icebergs

On April 15, 1912, the maiden voyage of the "unsinkable" *Titanic* was brought to a tragic end when it struck an iceberg in the –2°C (28°F) waters of the North Atlantic Ocean about 650 km (400 mi) south of Newfoundland, Canada. The ship sank at approximately 2:20 a.m. local time. Because of a lack of lifeboats, more than 1,500 people were forced into the frigid water and died of exposure within minutes.

An **iceberg** is a large block of ice that breaks from the toe of a glacier or an ice shelf and floats in open water. When glaciers reach the sea (or a lake), they calve (release) icebergs as a result of stresses caused by the tides, ice buoyancy, and melt-

FIGURE 17.15 **Features of ice sheets.** *(A) As the contour lines show, the Greenland ice sheet reaches over 3,000 m (1.8 mi) above sea level in elevation, and the Antarctic ice sheet reaches over 4,000 m (2.4 mi) above sea level. Note that the two ice sheets are not shown at their relative sizes. (B) As an ice sheet or ice cap flows outward and downslope, several different types of glaciers and glacial features are formed.*

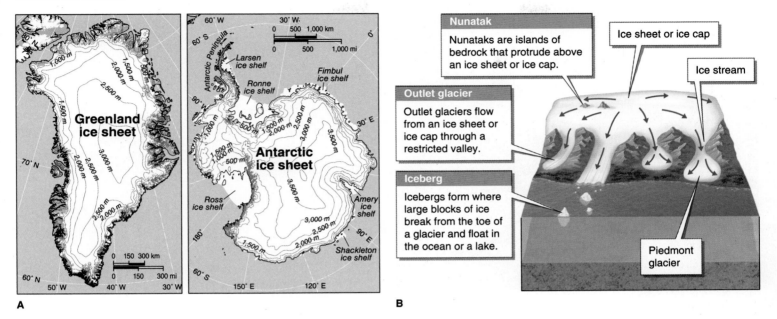

A   **B**

ing from beneath. Glaciers that reach sea level are called *tidewater glaciers*. Most tidewater glaciers are found above 55 degrees north and south latitude. The lowest-latitude tidewater glacier is San Rafael Glacier, found at 46.5 degrees south latitude in Chile.

Where ice sheets flow into the sea, they can form ice shelves. An **ice shelf** is the portion of an ice sheet or an outlet glacier that extends over the ocean. Icebergs that calve from ice shelves can be enormous **(Figure 17.16)**.

17.3 Carving by Ice: Glacial Erosion

◎ **Explain how glaciers cut into rocks and identify landforms caused by glacial erosion.**

Erosion by glaciers is less geographically widespread than erosion by streams. **Where they occur, however, glaciers exert a powerful erosive force and are capable of grinding down and wearing away even the hardest of bedrock.** Even in the tropics, as mountain ranges are uplifted through geologic time, they enter colder reaches of the troposphere where glaciers can form. As the glaciers begin flowing, they grind away at the mountains—the higher mountains are lifted, the more they are eroded by glaciers.

FIGURE 17.16 **Ice shelves.** *(A) Ice shelves form as ice sheets or outlet glaciers flow offshore and float on the water. When the ice shelf breaks, it calves icebergs. (B) This iceberg broke free from an ice shelf in Antarctica in 2002. It is about 220 m (720 ft) thick and rises about 20 m (65 ft) above the sea. It was photographed drifting in the Southern Ocean. (B. © Mlenny Photography/E+/Getty Images)*

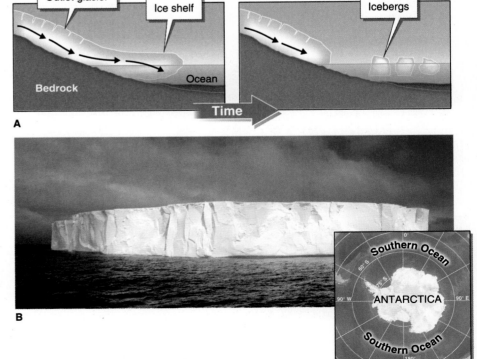

FIGURE 17.17 **Glacial abrasion and glacial flour.** *(A) This outcrop of Manhattan schist in Central Park, New York, has been smoothed by glacial erosion. Glacial striations are visible as parallel grooves in the rock. The faint shine of the rock comes from glacial polish. (B) Moraine Lake, Banff National Park, Canada, is famous for its brilliant blue water. The uniformly small particles of suspended glacial flour in the water reflect mostly blue wavelengths of light. (A. © Patti McConville/Alamy; B. © Philip and Karen Smith/The Image Bank/Getty Images)*

FIGURE 17.18 **Rock debris on glaciers.** *Valley glaciers typically accumulate a heavy load of rock debris as they flow through steep-walled valleys. These dark stripes on the Kaskawulsh Glacier in Kluane National Park, Yukon, Canada, are composed of rocks ranging in size from small particles of sand to large boulders. Arrows show the direction of ice flow. (© F. Barbagallo/De Agostini Picture Library/Getty Images)*

Many of Earth's most spectacular landforms were carved during the last glacial maximum (see Section 6.2). With natural climate warming, those glaciers have melted away, but they have left behind their mark of erosion.

Grinding Rocks: Plucking and Abrasion

Flowing glaciers cut into bedrock through plucking and abrasion. **Plucking** is the process by which a glacier pulls up and breaks off pieces of bedrock as it moves downslope. Abrasion, as we saw in Section 16.2, is the process by which movement of one material wears away another material.

When meltwater accumulates at the base of a glacier, then refreezes around protrusions in the bedrock, it allows the glacier to pull loose, or pluck, fragments of bedrock. The ice grabs the bedrock and pulls it up, much as you would pull a staple out of paper with a staple remover. Fragments of bedrock ranging from silt-sized particles to massive boulders become embedded in the base of the glacier as a result of glacial plucking.

> How does the soft ice of a glacier carve into solid bedrock?

As a glacier flows downslope, the rock fragments that have been plucked and embedded in its base grind against the bedrock much like sandpaper sanding wood. Grooves gouged into the surface of bedrock by glacial abrasion are called **glacial striations**. Often, a smoothed surface called **glacial polish** forms on the bedrock over which the glacier flows (**Figure 17.17 A**, facing page). Glacial abrasion pulverizes rock into a fine powder called *glacial flour*. When this powder is suspended in water, it can color the water bright turquoise or cyan (**Figure 17.17 B**).

Transporting Rocks: Ice and Glacial Streams

Most glaciers carry rock debris that has fallen on them through mass movement of overlying slopes as well as rock fragments they have picked up through plucking. As **Figure 17.18** on the facing page shows, rocks on glaciers and rocks embedded within them are transported downslope by the moving ice. **Flowing glaciers are like conveyor belts that move ice and rock debris downslope.** Rock material can be transported all the way to the toe of the glacier, where it is deposited in piles of unsorted sediments called *moraines* (see Section 17.4).

In summer, a glacier produces streams of meltwater that flow over the surface of the glacier (called *supraglacial streams*), inside the glacier in tunnels, and beneath the glacier between its base and bedrock (called *subglacial streams*) (**Figure 17.19**). Subglacial streams transport glacial sediments downslope. Much like streams

FIGURE 17.19 **Supraglacial and subglacial streams.** *(A) This supraglacial stream is flowing on top of the Greenland ice sheet. (B) This subglacial stream is an outlet for the Glacier du Mont Miné in the Alps of Switzerland. (A. © The Asahi Shimbun/Getty Images; B. © Scott Montross, Montana State University)*

A

B

FIGURE 17.20 **Proglacial lake and outwash plain.** *Bear Glacier in the Kenai Fjords Park in Alaska terminates in a proglacial lake filled with icebergs. The Pacific Ocean is in the foreground. (© Flyver/Alamy)*

that form deltas, subglacial streams exiting a glacier (called *outlet streams*) form a flat **outwash plain** as the sediments they carry accumulate (see Figure 17.20). Because of their heavy sediment loads, streams on outwash plains are typically braided (see Section 16.3). Outwash plains are examples of *glaciofluvial* landforms, meaning that both flowing ice and flowing water combine to create them.

Proglacial lakes (meaning lakes "in front of" the glacier) form at the toe of a glacier where a depression has been excavated by the ice or where sediments dam an outlet stream (**Figure 17.20**). Proglacial lakes are becoming more common as valley glaciers and outlet glaciers retreat upslope in response to the atmospheric warming of the last century.

plucking
The process by which a glacier pulls up and breaks off pieces of bedrock as it moves downslope.

glacial striation
A groove gouged into the surface of bedrock by glacial abrasion.

glacial polish
A smoothed bedrock surface resulting from glacial abrasion.

outwash plain
A flat area of sediments deposited by glacial outlet streams.

Picture This

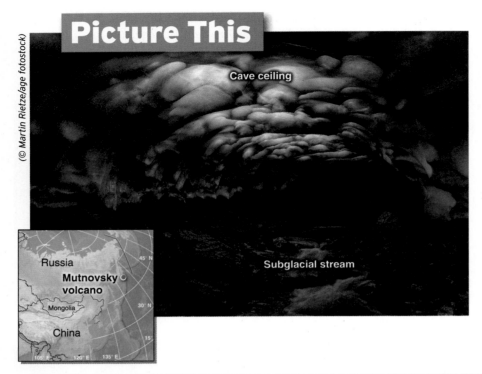

(© Martin Rietze/age fotostock)

Cave ceiling

Subglacial stream

Russia
Mutnovsky volcano
Mongolia
China
45° N
30° N
15°
105° E   120° E   135° E

A Lighted Ice Tunnel

This photo, taken in September 2012, shows a remarkable subglacial stream inside a glacier on Mutnovsky volcano on the Kamchatka Peninsula in Russia. Normally, subglacial stream tunnels are pitch black because light cannot pass through the thick glacial ice above. In this photo, however, the stream's ice tunnel is illuminated by outside light passing through the ceiling's thin ice. The patterns in the ceiling result from the way the ice has melted. Most of Kamchatka's glaciers have a negative mass balance and are thinning. If the ceiling of this subglacial tunnel continues thinning, the tunnel will eventually collapse.

Consider This

1. What is unusual about this subglacial stream's tunnel?

2. How does this tunnel relate to climate change?

Subglacial streams excavate tunnels through the ice. The ceilings of these tunnels sometimes become thin enough for light to pass through. As Picture This shows, when this happens, the interior of the glacier becomes illuminated, resembling stained glass.

Erosional Landforms

Glacial geomorphology is the study of landforms created by glaciers. Understanding how glaciers influence a landscape is important for understanding and describing the development of a region's topography and its climate history. In the remain-

Animation
Cirques and tarns
http://qrs.ly/4y49s17

FIGURE **17.21** **Cirques and tarns.** *This aerial photo shows four unnamed cirque glaciers and a tarn in the Chugach Mountains of southeastern Alaska. This landscape has been significantly shaped by glacial erosion.* (U.S. Geological Survey, photo by Bruce Molina)

Cirque headwall

Cirque

Cirque glacier

Outlet stream

Alaska
Canada
Chugash Mountains
GULF OF ALASKA
60° N
150° W   165° W

Tarn

FIGURE **17.22** **Arêtes, cols, and horns.** *(A) An aerial photo of the Himalayas in India shows many glacier types and glacial features, including arêtes and cols. (B) Shivling, also in India, which stands at 6,543 m (21,466 ft), is one among hundreds of horns in the Himalayas. (A. Image Science and Analysis Laboratory, NASA-Johnson Space Center (ISS027-E-005274); B. © Travel Ink/Gallo Images/Getty Images)*

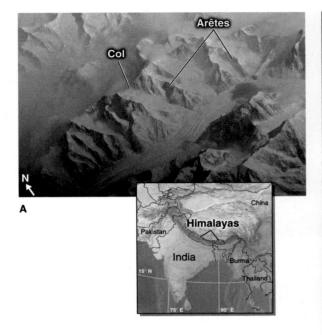

der of this section, we explore landforms created by glacial erosion, starting with those that form in high-elevation settings and concluding with those found at sea level.

Cirques and Tarns

Cirques and tarns are often found at the highest elevations in mountain ranges. A **cirque** is a bowl-shaped depression with steep walls, called *headwalls*, formed by a cirque glacier. A **tarn** is a mountain lake that forms within or just below a cirque. As a cirque glacier flows, it transports rockfall material downslope, rather than letting it accumulate in a talus cone and fill the cirque **(Figure 17.21)**.

Arêtes, Cols, and Horns

Where glaciers erode opposite sides of a mountain, a sharp, steep-sided ridge, called an **arête**, can form. A low area or pass over a ridge formed by two cirque glaciers positioned on opposite sides of the

ridge is called a **col**. Erosion by cirque glaciers can also form a pyramid-shaped mountain peak called a **horn**. The cirque glaciers do not reach the top of the horn; instead, the glaciers cut into and steepen the headwalls. These erosional features are shown in **Figure 17.22**.

Glacial Valleys and Paternoster Lakes

As we learned in Section 16.2, a stream's energy is focused on its narrow stream channel. As a result, streams cut V-shaped valleys. Glaciers, on the other hand, carve broad U-shaped **glacial valleys** (or glacial troughs), which often have steep or vertical valley walls. Because the base of a glacier is mostly flat, plucking and abrasion carve a flat valley. Where the sides of the valley are undercut by the glacier, rockfall often causes steep valley walls to develop.

Like trunk streams and tributary streams (see Section 16.1), trunk glaciers have a larger ice volume than tributary glaciers. As a result, they have more

cirque
A bowl-shaped depression with steep headwalls formed by a cirque glacier.

tarn
A mountain lake that forms within or just below a cirque.

arête
(pronounced ar-ET) A steep-sided, sharp ridge formed where glaciers erode opposite sides of a mountain.

col
A low area or pass over a ridge formed by two cirque glaciers.

horn
A steep, pyramid-shaped mountain peak formed by glaciers.

glacial valley
(or *glacial trough*) A U-shaped valley carved by a glacier.

FIGURE 17.23 **Glacial valley and hanging valley.** *(A) Yosemite Valley, in the Sierra Nevada of California, is a U-shaped valley formed by glaciers. (B) Bridalveil Creek flows through a hanging valley, then plunges over the vertical edge of Yosemite Valley to form Bridalveil Fall. (A. © Alice Cahill/Moment Open/Getty Images; B. © David Gomez/E+/Getty Images)*

How did Yosemite Valley form?

A

B

erosive power and cut deeper into the bedrock. The surface heights of trunk and tributary glaciers, however, are equal. After the glaciers have melted, a hanging valley is left where a tributary glacial valley feeds into a larger glacial valley with a deeper valley floor, as shown in **Figure 17.23**.

Relatively resistant portions of bedrock and ridges of debris called recessional moraines (discussed further in Section 17.4) sometimes form obstructions to stream flow, called *glacial steps*, along the floor of a glacial valley. A small lake may form behind each of these steps. Lakes that form in this way are called **paternoster lakes** (from Latin, meaning "our father," in reference to their similarity to religious rosary beads) **(Figure 17.24)**.

paternoster lake
One of a series of small lakes that form behind glacial steps in a glacial valley.

FIGURE 17.24 **Paternoster lakes.** *Glacier National Park, in Montana, has many glacial valleys with paternoster lakes. This photo was taken from the vantage point of Grinnell Glacier, overlooking Grinnell and Josephine lakes (in the foreground). Note the U-shaped valley. (© Robert Cable/Design Pics Inc./Alamy)*

FIGURE 17.25 **Roche moutonnée.** *A roche moutonnée is formed where glacial ice flows over a rock outcrop, abrades the upstream side of the outcrop, and plucks the downstream side, creating an asymmetrical hill. The blunt end points in the direction of the glacier's movement. This roche moutonnée near the town of Wanaka, on the South Island of New Zealand, is about 240 m (800 ft) high. (© Yvon Maurice)*

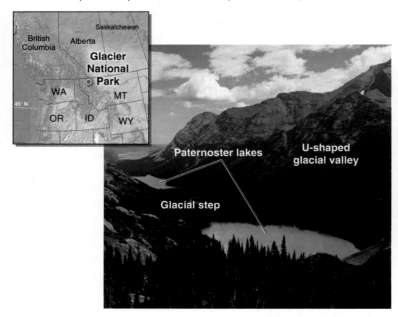

Also found on the floors of glacial valleys are protruding outcrops of bedrock called roches moutonnées (derived from the French *mouton*, for their resemblance to fleecy sheep). A **roche moutonnée** is an elongated and asymmetrical ridge of glacially carved bedrock (**Figure 17.25**, facing page).

Drowned Glacial Valleys: Fjords

Many high-latitude coastlines, such as those of southern Chile, southern Alaska, Norway, Iceland, and Greenland, look remarkably similar because they are dominated by fjords. **Fjords** are long U-shaped glacial valleys that have been flooded by the sea. Global sea level was drawn down by some 85 m (280 ft) during the last glacial maximum, when ice sheets covered much of North America and Eurasia (see Section 6.3). Outlet glaciers flowing from these ice sheets, as well as valley glaciers, eroded deep glacial valleys that reached below the present-day sea level. By roughly 10,000 years ago, most of this ice had melted. Sea level rose 85 m, and the glacial valleys were flooded, creating fjords (**Figure 17.26**).

Climate and Glacial Landforms

Latitude and elevation are important factors that determine whether glaciers will develop in a region and give rise to landforms like those we have explored in this section. Ultimately, climate controls the growth of glaciers in any given region. Like fluvial landforms (described in Chapter 16), glacial landforms develop through time as climate changes (**Figure 17.27**).

FIGURE 17.26 **Fjords.** *Preikestolen (Pulpit Rock) (note the people on the rock for scale) overlooks Lysefjordin, Norway. The vertical drop from Preikestolen to the fjord is 604 m (1,982 ft). The inset satellite image shows the many deep fjords of coastal Norway. (© Anders Blomqvist/Lonely Planet Images/Getty Images; inset, SeaWiFS Project, NASA/Goddard Space Flight Center, and DigitalGlobe™)*

FIGURE 17.27 **GEO-GRAPHIC: Climate change and glacial landform development.**

Animation
Glacial landform development
http://qrs.ly/z449sle

1. Preglacial landforms

Fluvial landforms, such as V-shaped valleys, dominate the preglacial topography. The mountains have rounded slopes.

2. Glaciation

With climate cooling, snow persists during the summer and glaciers develop. Glacial erosion forms glacial landforms, such as cirques, arêtes, and horns.

3. Postglacial landforms

With climate warming, the glaciers melt and leave behind a surface dominated by glacial landforms. If this glacial valley is flooded by rising seas, a fjord will form.

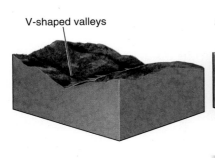

V-shaped valleys

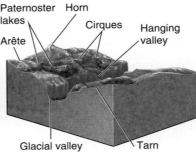

Horn
Arête — Cirques
Trunk glacier

Paternoster lakes — Horn
Arête — Cirques
Hanging valley
Glacial valley — Tarn

Time

roche moutonnée
(pronounced ROSH moo-ta-NAY) An elongated and asymmetrical ridge of glacially carved bedrock.

fjord
A U-shaped coastal glacial valley flooded by the sea.

17.4 Building by Ice: Glacial Deposition

◎ Identify landforms created from glacial sediments and explain how they formed.

Glaciers and streams have many aspects in common. Both are composed of water. Both flow downslope. Both carry sediments. And both deposit sediments where they stop flowing. This section examines landforms made by glacial sediments.

Deposits by Alpine Glaciers

Alpine glaciers transport material of all sizes and pile it into jumbled, unsorted moraines composed of till. A **moraine** is a heap of unsorted sediments deposited by a glacier. **Till** is any debris deposited by a glacier without the influence of running water. In most glaciated regions, moraines are prominent landforms. There are many kinds of moraines, each identified by where it forms with respect to the movement of the glacier. Moraine types include lateral moraines, medial moraines, recessional moraines, and terminal moraines.

A **recessional moraine** forms where the toe of the glacier pauses as it is retreating. A **terminal moraine** marks the farthest advance of the glacier's toe before it begins retreating. These moraine types are illustrated in **Figure 17.28**.

Moraines provide important information about the history of glaciation in a region and the history of an individual glacier. Once the age of a terminal moraine is known, estimating the average annual rate of glacial retreat is straightforward: Measure the distance between the toe of the glacier and the terminal moraine, and divide that distance by the age of the terminal moraine. **Crunch the Numbers** applies this method.

Deposits by Ice Sheets

We learned in Section 6.2 that Milankovitch cycles and the resulting orbital forcing cause glacial and interglacial cycles. The most recent glacial period, which is called the *Wisconsin glaciation*, ended about 12,000 years ago. During the Wisconsin glaciation, large ice sheets covered the high latitudes of the Northern Hemisphere **(Figure 17.29)**. These ice sheets scoured the landscape and deposited enormous amounts of glacial drift.

moraine
A heap of unsorted sediments deposited by a glacier.

till
Any debris deposited by a glacier without the influence of running water.

recessional moraine
A ridge of till that forms at the toe of a glacier; formed where the glacier pauses as it is gradually retreating upslope.

terminal moraine
A moraine that marks the farthest advance of a glacier's toe.

drumlin
An elongated hill formed by a moving ice sheet.

FIGURE 17.28 **GEO-GRAPHIC: Moraines.** *(A) This diagram illustrates how different types of moraines form. (B) An outlet stream from the Piedras Blancas glacier in Patagonia, in southern Argentina, has cut a V-shaped notch into the terminal moraine at the base of the glacier. The terminal moraine has formed a natural dam behind which a tarn has formed. A lateral moraine and a recessional moraine are also visible in this photo. (© Michael Schwab)*

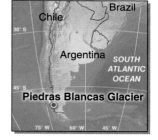

1. Lateral moraines
Rock fragments that break off from surrounding steep slopes, mainly through frost wedging, accumulate in ridges on the edge of the glacier and form a lateral moraine.

2. Medial moraines
Where two glaciers merge, their lateral moraines also merge, forming a single medial moraine. Trunk glaciers can develop several medial moraines as tributary glaciers merge.

3. Recessional moraines
Recessional moraines are ridges of till that form perpendicular to the length of the valley. Recessional moraines form as till on and in the glacier is deposited at the glacier's toe. They mark where the glacier temporarily paused as it retreated upslope.

4. Terminal moraine
The terminal moraine marks the farthest advance of the glacier's toe.

5. Outwash plain
Meltwater carries sediment downslope in braided streams.

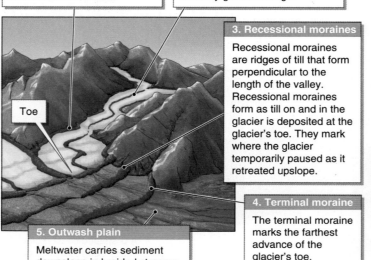

A

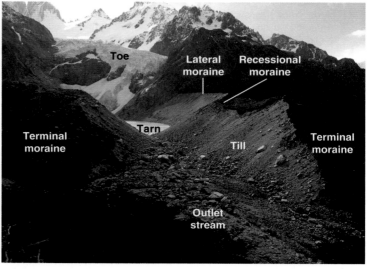

B

CRUNCH THE NUMBERS:
Calculating the Rate of Glacial Retreat

Calculate the average annual rate of retreat for the Exit Glacier in Alaska (see the opening photo in Chapter 6). It has retreated upslope 3,200 m (10,560 ft) from its terminal moraine, which has been determined by dendrochronology to be 200 years old.

1. Average annual rate of retreat in meters per year: _____

2. Average annual rate of retreat in feet per year: _____

Many areas of northern North America today are covered by nearly continuous layers of glacial sediments deposited by the Laurentide ice sheet. The sediments were deposited unevenly, resulting in an undulating, hummocky, and mounded surface called a *ground moraine*. In some places, these glacial deposits were molded into identifiable landforms by the moving ice sheet or by meltwater streams flowing beneath the glacier, or by a combination of ice and streams. Ice sheets produce many of the same kinds of depositional features that alpine glaciers create, such as terminal and recessional moraines. They also create landforms that are unique to ice sheets. **Drumlins** (Irish Gaelic for "hills"), for example, are elongated hills composed of till that was deposited by a moving ice sheet **(Figure 17.30)**.

FIGURE 17.29 **Ice sheets of the Wisconsin glaciation.** *During the Wisconsin glaciation, the Laurentide ice sheet and the Cordilleran ice sheet covered almost all of Canada and the northernmost United States. Northern Eurasia was covered by the Scandinavian ice sheet and the Siberian ice sheet. These ice sheets were up to 3 km (2 mi) thick. Because sea level was lower during the Wisconsin glaciation, Alaska was connected to Eurasia. This map does not show the changed shape of the continents at that time.*

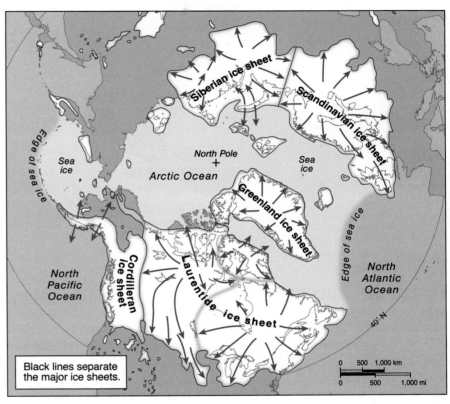

FIGURE 17.30 **Drumlins.** *(A) Drumlins are hills shaped by a moving ice sheet that are composed mostly of clays. They are no higher than 50 m (160 ft) and a few hundred meters in length. The tapering end of the drumlin points in the direction the ice was flowing. (B)* **Drumlin fields,** *such as this one in Dane County, in southern Wisconsin, cover portions of southern Canada and the northern United States. The ice sheet movement direction was toward the viewer.* (B. © Kevin Horan/The Image Bank/ Getty Images)

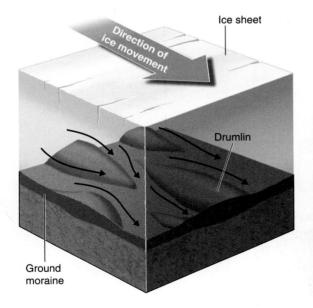

A

B

FIGURE **17.31** **Eskers.** *(A) Subglacial streams flow in tunnels beneath an ice sheet, depositing sand and gravel in their channels. After the ice sheet melts, these glacial sediments create eskers. Eskers are up to 50 m (160 ft) in height. (B) This esker is located in Manitoba, Canada. For scale, note the mature trees, which stand about 10 m (33 ft). (B. Grambo Photography/All Canada Photos/Getty Images)*

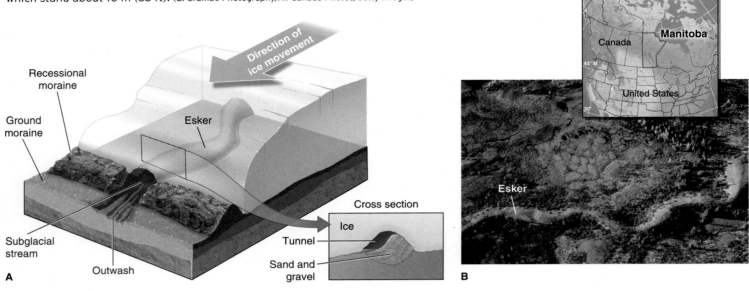

A

B

FIGURE **17.32** **GEO-GRAPHIC: Kame-and-kettle topography formation.** *(A) Kame-and-kettle topography forms as an ice sheet melts. (B) Kame-and-kettle topography is found throughout much of Canada. This photo is from the Northwest Territories. (B. © Thomas & Pat Leeson/Science Source)*

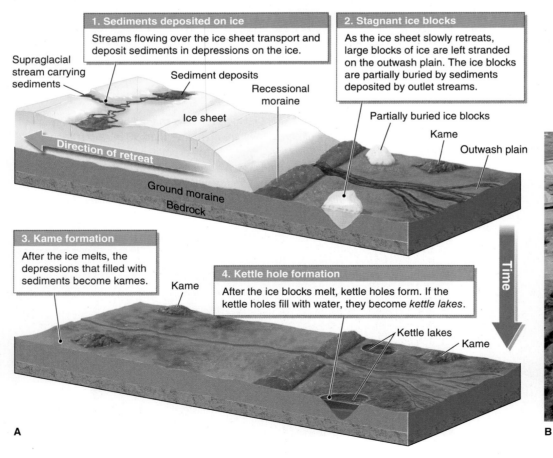

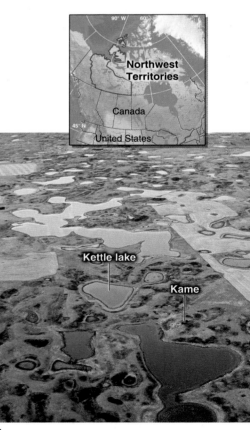

1. Sediments deposited on ice
Streams flowing over the ice sheet transport and deposit sediments in depressions on the ice.

2. Stagnant ice blocks
As the ice sheet slowly retreats, large blocks of ice are left stranded on the outwash plain. The ice blocks are partially buried by sediments deposited by outlet streams.

3. Kame formation
After the ice melts, the depressions that filled with sediments become kames.

4. Kettle hole formation
After the ice blocks melt, kettle holes form. If the kettle holes fill with water, they become *kettle lakes*.

A

B

FIGURE 17.33 **North American recessional moraines.** *There are many recessional moraines in the Great Lakes region. The moraines mapped in the dark blue area were formed by the Laurentide ice sheet some 15,000 years ago. Moraines in southern Illinois, Indiana, and Ohio (mapped in light blue) are from the previous glacial period, called the Illinoian glaciation, that occurred some 150,000 years ago. Southwestern Wisconsin does not have drift (or glaciofluvial deposits) and is called the "driftless area." Many scientists think the glaciofluvial deposits in the driftless area were washed away long ago in a large flood event caused by the sudden draining of one of the ancient lakes in the area.*

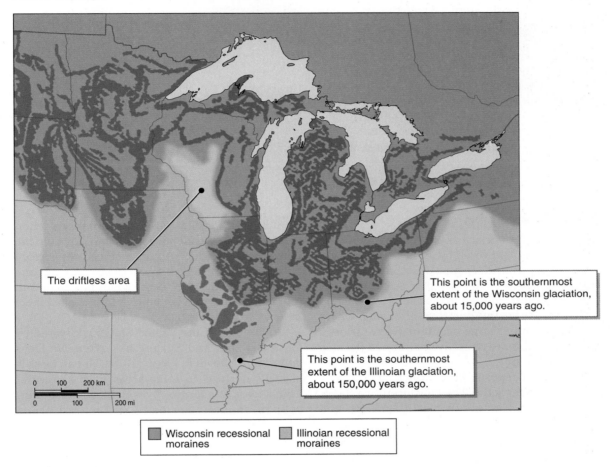

The driftless area

This point is the southernmost extent of the Wisconsin glaciation, about 15,000 years ago.

This point is the southernmost extent of the Illinoian glaciation, about 150,000 years ago.

0   100   200 km
0   100   200 mi

☐ Wisconsin recessional moraines   ☐ Illinoian recessional moraines

Another common landform deposited by ice sheets is an **esker** (meaning "ridge" in Irish Gaelic), a long ridge of sorted sand and gravel deposited by a subglacial stream. Eskers may run continuously for tens of kilometers in length parallel to the direction of ice sheet movement **(Figure 17.31)**.

Many areas across North America consist of rounded hills called *kames*, which are mounded accumulations of glaciofluvial sediments. The formation of kames is not well understood, but they are thought to be formed in part as sediments accumulate on top of depressions in a melting ice sheet. After the ice melts, the sediments are piled in mounds composed of sand and gravel.

Subglacial streams flowing beneath the Laurentide ice sheet deposited sediments on flat outwash plains where they exited the glacier. Large stagnant blocks of ice that broke from the retreating ice sheet were buried in these sediments. When the blocks eventually melted, they formed depressions called *kettle holes*. When kames and kettle holes form in the same area, the result is **kame-and-kettle topography**, a landscape dominated by irregular mounds and shallow depressions or lakes. **Figure 17.32** outlines the steps in the formation of kame-and-kettle topography.

In addition to creating kame-and-kettle topography, the retreat of the Laurentide ice sheet left a series of recessional moraines across much of the upper Midwest of the United States and the province of Ontario in Canada. From the ground, these recessional moraines are less easy to see than eskers, drumlins, and kettle holes. **Figure 17.33** maps their extent.

esker
A long ridge of sorted sand and gravel deposited by a subglacial stream.

kame-and-kettle topography
A glaciofluvial landscape dominated by irregular mounds and shallow depressions or lakes.

FIGURE 17.34 **Global loess deposits.** *Loess deposits are found mostly at midlatitudes. The inset photo shows a roadcut through the Loess Hills in the Missouri River valley in western Iowa. The holes have been excavated for nesting by bank swallows.* (© Lee Rentz/NHPA/Photoshot)

Loess deposits

Glacial Dust: Loess

About 10% of the surface of the continents, mostly at midlatitudes, is covered by loess deposits. **Loess** is made up of wind-deposited dust that often originates as glacial flour deposited on glacial outwash plains. Electrical charges on these tiny silt and clay particles cause the fine dust to stick together where it settles, forming large accumulations of loess. Deposits of loess are typically unstratified (lacking horizontal layers).

Many loess deposits were formed by processes that are no longer active. The Pleistocene ice sheets and mountain glaciers in North America and Scandinavia formed loess accumulations when summer meltwater deposited silt and clay onto the outwash plain. Cold winters reduced the stream flow, exposing the sediments to strong katabatic winds (see Section 4.4). These winds picked up and transported the fine sediments and deposited them in loess accumulations.

About 30% of the United States is covered by loess deposits, and Europe has extensive loess deposits, as shown in **Figure 17.34**. Not all loess is glacially derived. In some areas, such as central China, loess was formed by windblown dust originating in deserts rather than glacial outwash plains.

loess
(pronounced lehss) Wind-deposited silt and clay sediments that originate mostly from glacial outwash plains.

GEOGRAPHIC PERSPECTIVES
17.5 Polar Ice Sheets and Sea Level

◎ Assess the role of polar ice sheets in current and future sea-level changes and explain why sea-level rise presents problems for human society.

Alpine glaciers collectively contain enough water to raise sea level by nearly 0.5 m (1.6 ft) if they were to melt entirely. But this amount of water pales in comparison to that contained in the polar ice sheets, as **Table 17.1** shows.

Given the amount of ice that the ice sheets of Greenland and Antarctica contain, and the rise in global sea level they are capable of causing, scientists have been closely monitoring them for signs of change. Unfortunately, changes are being detected.

The Greenland Ice Sheet Is Changing

The current mass balance of the Greenland ice sheet is negative. Data from Europe's new CryoSat satellite indicate that as of 2014 Greenland is losing roughly 375 km³ (90 mi³) of ice each year. The ice sheet's mass is decreasing because its surface is melting and because more of its ice is flowing into the ocean.

Greenland's albedo has been steadily decreasing as the average temperature of the atmosphere increases and changes the snow cover on the ice

TABLE 17.1	Global Ice Volume			
ICE LOCATION	APPROXIMATE PERCENTAGE OF CRYOSPHERE	VOLUME (KM³)	POTENTIAL SEA-LEVEL RISE IN METERS	POTENTIAL SEA-LEVEL RISE IN FEET
Antarctica	91%	29,528,300	73.32	240.54
Greenland	8%	2,620,000	6.55	21.49
Alpine glaciers and all other ice	<1%	180,000	0.45	1.48
Total	100	32,328,300	80.32	263.51

Data from http://pubs.usgs.gov/fs/fs2-00/.

sheet's surface. Greenland's albedo has decreased in some areas by 18% relative to the 2000–2006 average. As temperatures rise, snow partially melts and clumps together. Angular, unmelted ice crystals reflect more sunlight than partially melted and rounded clumps. As a result of increased surface melting, the albedo of the ice sheet is lowered and the ice absorbs more solar energy.

The lowered surface albedo of Greenland and a warming atmosphere create conditions that could lengthen the brief summer melt period. Satellites that have been monitoring Greenland since 1979 have provided evidence that this trend is happening (Figure 17.35).

Albedo changes and increasing summer snowmelt days are not the full story of ice loss in Greenland. Some of Greenland's outlet glaciers have more than

FIGURE 17.35 **Changes in Greenland snowmelt.** *(A) The numbers of snowmelt days in 2011 are shown as departures from the 1979–2010 average number of snowmelt days. Orange shows areas with up to 25 days of melt above the average. White shows areas that do not depart from the average. The blue margins of the ice sheet were caused by erroneous satellite readings of bare rock. (B) For the first time, scientists have witnessed melting of nearly the entire surface of the ice sheet. In late July 2012, over a period of 4 days, 97% (shown in the area in red) of the topmost layer of the Greenland ice sheet briefly melted, then refroze. The ice beneath the surface layer did not melt. Such events are thought to occur only once every 150 years. (A. NOAA Climate.gov; B. Nicolo E. DiGirolamo, SSAI/NASA GSFC, and Jesse Allen, NASA)*

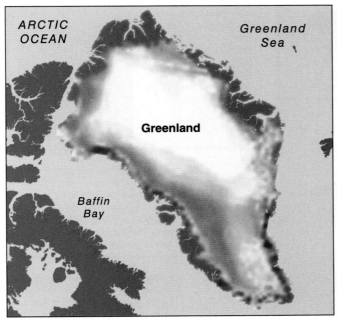

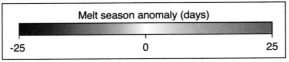

Melt season anomaly (days)

-25   0   25

A

B

moulin
(pronounced moo-LAN) A vertical shaft in a glacier through which meltwater flows.

doubled their rate of flow to the ocean during the last few decades. Scientists are not sure why this is happening, but suspect that supraglacial lakes and moulins that form during the summer snowmelt could play an important role **(Figure 17.36)**. A **moulin**, a vertical shaft in a glacier through which meltwater flows, may allow meltwater from a supraglacial lake to reach the base of the glacier.

Recent Changes in Antarctica

Until recently, most scientists assumed that it would take centuries before Antarctica's climate and ice would begin responding to the warming of the atmosphere. But scientific data are now challenging this assumption. Outlet glaciers that feed into the sea from the main ice sheets of Antarctica form floating ice shelves up to 250 m (800 ft) thick. These ice shelves appear to be sensitive barometers of climate change, as several of them have broken apart in the last several years. **Figure 17.37** shows the locations of Antarctica's ice shelves and recent changes in one of them, the Larsen B ice shelf.

Because ice shelves are already in the ocean, they do not cause a significant change in sea level when they break apart. The significance of their disintegration is that, once an ice shelf is gone, the outlet glaciers behind it flow to the sea faster because they are no longer slowed by the buttressing effects of the ice shelf. The glaciers that feed the Larsen B ice shelf began flowing about eight times faster after its breakup. Similar accelerated glacial flows have been documented in other regions after smaller ice shelves broke apart.

Research published in *Geophysical Research Letters* in March 2014 found that the rate of ice flow from six outlet glaciers on the West Antarctic ice sheet increased 75% between 1973 and 2013. These six outlet glaciers drain as much ice as all of Greenland's outlet glaciers combined. In addition, Europe's CryoSat shows that Greenland and Antarctica are now draining about 500 km³ (119 mi³) of ice into the ocean each year.

As outlet glaciers from Antarctica flow into the ocean, they cause sea-level rise because they displace seawater. The faster these outlet glaciers flow into the ocean, the more sea-level rise they cause.

FIGURE 17.36 **GEO-GRAPHIC: Influences on the flow of a Greenland outlet glacier.**
(Left, © The Asahi Shimbun/Getty Images; right, © Konrad Steffen)

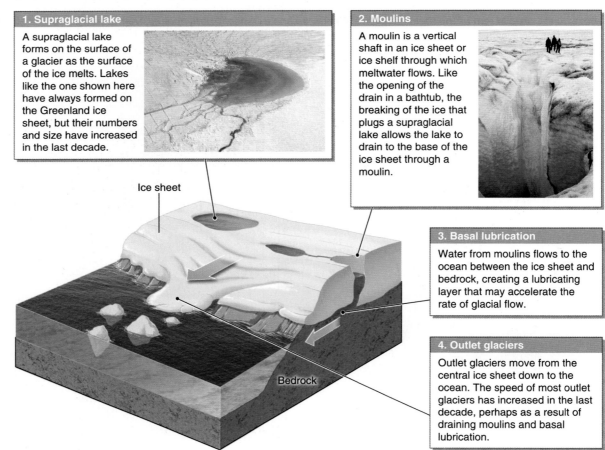

1. Supraglacial lake
A supraglacial lake forms on the surface of a glacier as the surface of the ice melts. Lakes like the one shown here have always formed on the Greenland ice sheet, but their numbers and size have increased in the last decade.

2. Moulins
A moulin is a vertical shaft in an ice sheet or ice shelf through which meltwater flows. Like the opening of the drain in a bathtub, the breaking of the ice that plugs a supraglacial lake allows the lake to drain to the base of the ice sheet through a moulin.

Ice sheet

3. Basal lubrication
Water from moulins flows to the ocean between the ice sheet and bedrock, creating a lubricating layer that may accelerate the rate of glacial flow.

4. Outlet glaciers
Outlet glaciers move from the central ice sheet down to the ocean. The speed of most outlet glaciers has increased in the last decade, perhaps as a result of draining moulins and basal lubrication.

Bedrock

FIGURE 17.37 **Antarctic ice shelves.** *(A) Ten large ice shelves flank the West and East Antarctic ice sheets. The largest is the Ross ice shelf. (B) It is extremely unusual for ice shelves to break apart as the Larsen B ice shelf did in 2002. The Larsen B ice shelf was at least 10,000 years old. These satellite images show the ice shelf before and after most of it broke apart. Scientists believe meltwater lakes weakened the ice shelf. (A. NASA/Goddard Space Flight Center, Scientific Visualization Studio; B. NASA/Goddard Space Flight Center, Scientific Visualization Studio)*

Video
Cryosphere tour
http://qrs.ly/zo49s1f

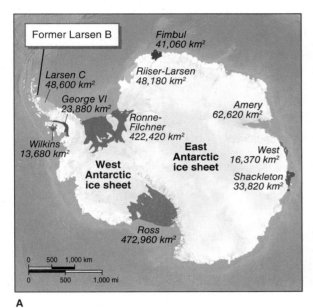

A

January 31, 2002

Larsen B ice shelf

Meltwater lakes on top of ice shelf

0 10 20 km
0 10   20 mi

1. Meltwater lakes

In late January 2002, large meltwater lakes formed on top of the Larsen B ice shelf. Moulins formed as the lakes drained and weakened the ice shelf. Warmer ocean water was also circulating beneath the ice shelf.

March 17, 2002

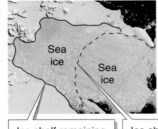

Sea ice

Sea ice

Ice shelf remaining after disintegration

Ice shelf extent before disintegration

2. Disintegration

Over the first half of March 2002, most of the Larsen B ice shelf disintegrated. In total, 3,250 km² (about 1,255 mi²) of ice broke apart, an area roughly the size of the state of Rhode Island.

B

How Much Will Sea Level Rise?

Between 1900 and 2000, sea level rose by about 20 cm (8 in), at an average rate of about 2 mm (0.08 in) per year. This rate has recently accelerated, and now sea level is rising at 3.2 mm (0.13 in) per year. Thermal expansion of ocean water and melting of alpine glaciers have contributed most to the observed sea-level rise. Greenland and Antarctica are now causing about one-third (1 mm, or 0.04 in) of sea-level rise.

How much do scientists think sea level will rise? It depends mainly on how these giant ice sheets respond to atmospheric warming. Predicting what they will do is difficult because their behavior is nonlinear, meaning that the rate at which they change can change. For example, if the surfaces of the ice sheets are lowered into warmer air because they are melting, they will melt even faster. Faster melting would lower their elevation even more, triggering a positive feedback. Estimates based on computer modeling indicate that warming of about 1.6°C (2.9°F) above the global pre-industrial temperature could be enough to trigger this positive feedback. If that happened, it would take about 2,000 years to melt both ice sheets entirely. By the end of this century, the annual rate of sea-level rise could reach some 6 mm (0.24 in) per year. Scientists anticipate that sea level will rise at least 1 m (3.3 ft) by the end of this century.

Worldwide, over 100 million people live in coastal areas at elevations within 1 m (3.3 ft) of the high-tide line. In the United States, 3.7 million people live within 1 m of the high-tide line. A 1 m rise in sea level would stress global societies. Given their sheer size and their potential to raise sea level, and given their potential sensitivity to warming, the polar ice sheets will be closely monitored as the global temperature continues to climb.

CHAPTER 17 **Exploring with ⊚ Google Earth**

To complete these problems, first read the chapter. When you are finished, go to LaunchPad and open the Exploring with Google Earth file for this chapter. Click on the "Workbook Problems" folder to "fly" to each of the problems listed below and answer the questions. Be sure to keep your "Borders and Labels" layer activated. Refer to Appendix 4 if you need help using Google Earth.

PROBLEM 17.1 Sharp, narrow ridges such as this one in Montana are common in mountainous areas that have been eroded by glaciers.

1. **What is the name of this landform?**
   a. Arête
   b. Col
   c. Horn
   d. Terminal moraine

2. **What is the name of the low saddle on the same ridge 800 m to the west?**
   a. Arête
   b. Col
   c. Horn
   d. Terminal moraine

3. **Pan around. Inspect the base of the landform on each side. What is the name of the two bowl-shaped amphitheaters carved on the north flank of this feature?**
   a. Cirque
   b. U-shaped valley
   c. Glacial step
   d. Hanging valley

PROBLEM 17.2 This boulder, named Yeager Rock, weighs some 400 tons. It lies on the Waterville Plateau, in eastern Washington State. The large boulders visible here are evidence of the ice sheet that covered this region as recently as 12,000 years ago.

1. **What is the name for large boulders such as these?**
   a. Drumlins
   b. Eskers
   c. Glacial erratics
   d. Glacial striations

PROBLEM 17.3 This landform consists of a long, winding ridge of glaciofluvial deposits. Notice at this placemark how the road jogs north as it crosses the landform.

1. **What is the name of this landform?**
   a. Esker
   b. Drumlin
   c. Cirque
   d. Fjord

2. **How was it formed?**
   a. By a subglacial stream
   b. By a valley glacier
   c. By icebergs
   d. By abrasion

3. **Why does the road jog north as it crosses the ridge?**
   a. To avoid a boulder
   b. To flatten the road
   c. To follow a county boundary
   d. Because an earthquake moved it

4. **How wide is this landform just north of the road?**
   a. 15 ft
   b. 30 ft
   c. 100 ft
   d. 130 ft

5. **About how long is it?**
   a. 2.5 mi
   b. 6 mi
   c. 13 mi
   d. 48 mi

PROBLEM 17.4 The glacier placemarked here is found at 80 degrees north latitude. This island belongs to Norway.

1. **What type of glacier is this?**
   a. Valley glacier
   b. Ice cap
   c. Piedmont glacier
   d. Ice sheet

2. **What is the name of this island?**
   a. Spitzbergen
   b. Svalbard
   c. Ellesmere Island
   d. Bylot Island

3. **How far away is this placemark from the North Pole? (To find the North Pole, pull down the View menu and activate Grid, or press Control-L.)**
   a. 175 km
   b. 480 km
   c. 1,100 km
   d. 1,750 km

PROBLEM 17.5 This type of glacier forms when a glacier spills onto a flat plain. This particular one is the largest of its kind in the world.

1. **What type of glacier is this?**
   a. Valley glacier
   b. Ice cap
   c. Piedmont glacier
   d. Ice sheet

2. **What is its maximum width?**
   a. 3 km
   b. 16 km
   c. 23 km
   d. 50 km

3. Zoom out. Where is this glacier?
a. British Columbia
b. Alaska
c. Svalbard
d. New Zealand

PROBLEM 17.6 At this placemark in Norway, many glaciers are growing because they are fed more snowfall by warmer (but still freezing) air.

1. What type of glacier is this?
a. Valley glacier
b. Ice cap
c. Piedmont glacier
d. Ice sheet

2. What type of lake is found at this glacier's toe?
a. A proglacial lake
b. An ephemeral lake
c. A pingo lake
d. A supraglacial lake

PROBLEM 17.7 The glaciers near the small village of Passu in Pakistan's Karakoram Range produce an enormous amount of till that forms moraines.

1. Why type of moraine does this placemark fall on?
a. Lateral moraine
b. Terminal moraine
c. Recessional moraine
d. Medial moraine

PROBLEM 17.8 This placemark falls on another moraine near Passu.

1. Why type of moraine does this placemark fall on?
a. Lateral moraine
b. Terminal moraine
c. Recessional moraine
d. Medial moraine

PROBLEM 17.9 This placemark falls on the village of Passu.

1. What glacial landform is the village of Passu built on?
a. Till
b. Patterned ground
c. Outwash plain
d. A tarn

PROBLEM 17.10 This is K2 in the Karakoram Range, the second highest point on Earth.

1. What type of glacial landform is K2?
a. Nunatak
b. Horn
c. Co
d. Arête

PROBLEM 17.11 This placemark features elongated landforms in Quebec, Canada.

1. What are these landforms?
a. Eskers
b. Drumlins
c. Loess
d. Pingos

PROBLEM 17.12 This placemark shows summer meltwater lakes and streams on the Greenland ice sheet.

1. What is the name for these lakes on the surface of the ice sheet?
a. Proglacial lakes
b. Ephemeral lakes
c. Pingo lakes
d. Supraglacial lakes

2. Through what feature can these surface lakes drain?
a. Eskers
b. Moulins
c. Glacial striations
d. Kettle holes

PROBLEM 17.13 This placemark is pinned to Milford Sound in the Southern Alps of New Zealand. This area was strongly modified by glacial erosion during the last glacial maximum, when sea level was some 85 m (280 ft) lower than today. Although it is not visible in Google Earth, Sterling Falls spills over the cliff face at the location of the placemark.

1. What is the name of this U-shaped valley that feeds into Milford Sound?
a. Fjord
b. Roche moutonnée
c. Hanging valley
d. Nunatak

2. Zoom out and tilt around to get a better sense of the scale of Milford Sound. What is the name for the U-shaped valley that has been flooded by seawater and now makes up Milford Sound?
a. Fjord
b. Roche moutonnée
c. Hanging valley
d. Nunatak

CHAPTER 17 **Study Guide**

Focus Points

17.1 Frozen Ground: Periglacial Environments

Permafrost: Permafrost covers about 25% of the Northern Hemisphere.

Release of carbon: Permafrost is thawing in response to climate change, releasing methane and carbon dioxide into the atmosphere.

17.2 About Glaciers

Glacier formation: Glaciers form through snow accumulation. Snow is compressed by gravity to form granular snow, then firn, and then glacial ice.

Glacier movement: Glaciers move downslope at an average rate of a few centimeters per day through basal sliding and plastic deformation. At times, they move faster in glacial surges.

Toe position: The position of a glacier's toe largely reflects the mass balance of the glacier.

Glacial retreat: Most alpine glaciers are retreating in response to atmospheric warming.

Types of glaciers: Glaciers can be categorized as alpine glaciers or ice sheets.

17.3 Carving by Ice: Glacial Erosion

Glacial erosion: Glaciers are important agents of erosion. They cut into bedrock by plucking it and abrading it with plucked rocks.

Glacial transport: Glaciers transport rock fragments downslope by means of ice flow and subglacial streams.

Glacial landforms: Glaciers make many unique landforms, including cirques, tarns, horns, and U-shaped valleys.

17.4 Building by Ice: Glacial Deposition

Glaciers and streams: Glaciers, like streams, deposit sediments where they stop flowing.

Moraines: Glaciers deposit till to form moraines.

Ice sheet deposits: Much of northern North America is covered by glacial sediments deposited by ice sheets of the Wisconsin glaciation.

Loess: Glacial sediments on outwash plains are an important source of loess deposits.

17.5 Geographic Perspectives. Polar Ice Sheets and Sea Level

Distribution of ice: About 99% of the cryosphere is found in the ice sheets of Greenland and Antarctica.

Ice loss: Greenland and Antarctica are losing about 344 billion tons of ice each year as a result of melting and an increased rate of outlet glacier flow to the sea.

Key Terms

active layer, 547
alpine glacier, 556
arête, 561
cirque, 561
cirque glacier, 556
col, 561
crevasse, 553
drumlin, 565
equilibrium line, 553
esker, 567
fjord, 563
glacial advance, 553
glacial erratic, 550
glacial ice, 551
glacial polish, 559
glacial retreat, 553
glacial striation, 559
glacial valley, 561
glacier, 551
glacier mass balance, 553
horn, 561
iceberg, 556
ice cap, 556

ice sheet, 556
ice shelf, 557
kame-and-kettle topography, 567
loess, 568
moraine, 564
moulin, 570
nunatak, 556
outlet glacier, 556
outwash plain, 559
paternoster lake, 562
periglacial, 547
permafrost, 547
piedmont glacier, 556
plucking, 558
recessional moraine, 564
roche moutonnée, 563
tarn, 561
terminal moraine, 564
till, 564
toe, 553
valley glacier, 556

Concept Review

The Human Sphere: The Mammoth Hunters

1. About when did the mainland mammoth populations in North America and Eurasia disappear? Why did the mammoth go extinct?

2. Why do people seek the remains of mammoths preserved in frozen ground?

17.1 Frozen Ground: Periglacial Environments

3. What does "periglacial" mean? Are there glaciers in periglacial environments?

4. What is permafrost, and how is it defined? Where does it occur?

5. Why are many Arctic lakes emitting methane?

6. What are pingos? What is patterned ground? Explain how they form.

7. In the context of the active layer, explain why "drunken forests" occur. Why might rail lines and pipelines sink into permafrost? How do engineers prevent sinking from happening?

17.2 About Glaciers

8. What is glacial drift? Give examples of drift.

9. What is a glacier? Where are glaciers found?

10. What are the three steps to glacier formation? What two requirements must first be met before a glacier can begin to form?

11. By what two processes do glaciers move?

12. What is glacier mass balance? Compare and contrast the zone of accumulation, the zone of ablation, and the equilibrium line.

13. What is a glacier's toe? Why does it move upslope and downslope?

14. What does it mean to say that a glacier is in retreat? What is retreating? What causes a glacier to retreat?

15. Compare and contrast the geographic settings of an alpine glacier and an ice sheet. How do their sizes compare?

16. What are the four types of alpine glaciers? Describe where each occurs.

17. What is an iceberg? How does one form?

17.3 Carving by Ice: Glacial Erosion

18. What effect does glacial erosion have on mountain height?

19. What are plucking and abrasion? How do these processes allow glacial ice to carve into hard bedrock?

20. What are glacial striations and glacial polish?

21. What is glacial flour? What effect does it have on the appearance of a lake?

22. By what two means are rock fragments moved downslope by glaciers?

23. What is an outwash plain? Where and how do they form?

24. What is a glaciofluvial process?

25. What is a proglacial lake? Where do they form?

26. Describe a cirque and explain how cirques form.

27. What are arêtes, horns, and cols, and how do they form?

28. Describe the shape of a glacial valley. What kind of glacier forms glacial valleys?

29. Compare a trunk glacier with a tributary glacier. Describe how a hanging valley forms from these glaciers.

30. What are paternoster lakes and how do they form?

31. What is a fjord? Why are there no fjords at middle and low latitudes?

17.4 Building by Ice: Glacial Deposition

32. Why are stream deposits sorted but glacial deposits unsorted?

33. What is till? What is the relationship of till to moraines?

34. Differentiate between lateral, medial, terminal, and recessional moraines.

35. Describe the formation of drumlins, eskers, and kettle holes in the context of ice sheet deposits.

36. What is loess and how does it form?

17.5 Geographic Perspectives: Polar Ice Sheets and Sea Level

37. On what continent is most of the cryosphere's ice stored? As a percentage, how much of the cryosphere is on that continent?

38. Describe Greenland's loss of ice in terms of the number of summer melt days, changing ice sheet albedo, and outlet glacier flow rates.

39. What is a supraglacial lake? How is it related to the speed of outflow glaciers on Greenland?

40. What large ice shelf recently broke apart? Explain the role of supraglacial lakes in causing it to break apart.

41. What happens to the speed of an outlet glacier when an ice shelf that supports it breaks apart?

42. How much has sea level risen in the last century? How much could sea level rise by the end of this century?

43. How many people worldwide live in coastal areas within 1 m of sea level?

Critical-Thinking Questions

1. If you were hiking outdoors and saw a large, isolated boulder, what information would help you to determine if it was a glacial erratic?

2. Why are the toes of some glaciers advancing rather than retreating upslope, even though the atmospheric temperature over those glaciers is increasing?

3. How would a 1 m rise in sea level affect you where you live? What information should you find to answer this question? How would you find that information?

4. What does it mean to say that ice sheets have "nonlinear" behavior in response to warming? Explain how nonlinear behavior works and why its effects are important.

Test Yourself

Take this quiz to test your chapter knowledge.

1. **True or false?** Glacier mass balance refers to the balance between ice gain and ice loss on a glacier.

2. **True or false?** For most glaciers, the zone of equilibrium is moving upslope with global warming.

3. **True or false?** Till is deposited by streams.

4. **True or false?** Melting of an ice shelf in itself does not cause significant sea-level rise.

5. **Multiple choice:** Which of the following is found below a cirque?

   a. Tarn   b. Horn   c. Col   d. Arête

6. **Multiple choice:** Which of the following indicates the maximum downslope position of a glacier in the past?
   a. Lateral moraine
   b. Medial moraine
   c. Terminal moraine
   d. Recessional moraine

7. **Multiple choice:** Which of the following is produced by a subglacial stream?
   a. Kettle hole
   b. Esker
   c. Ground moraine
   d. Loess

8. **Multiple choice:** Which of the following has the largest volume of ice?
   a. All alpine glaciers combined
   b. Greenland
   c. Antarctica
   d. Iceland

9. **Fill in the blank:** A(n) _____ forms U-shaped valleys in mountains.

10. **Fill in the blank:** A(n) _____ is a drowned U-shaped valley.

Further Reading

1. McClintock, James. *Lost Antarctica: Adventures in a Disappearing Land*. Basingstoke, U.K.: Palgrave Macmillan, 2012.

2. Mouginot, J., E. Rignot, and B. Scheuchl. "Sustained Increase in Ice Discharge from the Amundsen Sea Embayment, West Antarctica, from 1973 to 2013." *Geophysical Research Letters*, Published online March 5, 2014; DOI: 10.1002/2013GL59069.

3. NASA. Global Ice Viewer. http://climate.nasa.gov/GlobalIceViewer/index.cfm.

Answers to Living Physical Geography Questions

1. **Why are bones and tusks of extinct mammoths appearing throughout Siberia?** When ancient mammoths died, their bones were preserved in frozen northern soils. Now, as the soils thaw, the bones are being exposed.

2. **Why are explosive gases seeping from Arctic lakes?** As the permafrost beneath Arctic lakes thaws, microorganisms are digesting carbon in the soils and emitting methane, a flammable and potent greenhouse gas.

3. **How do glaciers form?** Glaciers form from the accumulation of snow. Where snow does not melt in summer and the slope is not too steep, a glacier may form.

4. **How does the soft ice of a glacier carve into solid bedrock?** With rock fragments frozen into its base, a flowing glacier can cut into the hardest of bedrock like rough sandpaper sanding soft wood.

5. **How did Yosemite Valley form?** Yosemite Valley was formed as a valley glacier cut into the granite bedrock, forming a deep U-shaped valley.

Picture This. YOUR TURN

Identifying Glacial Landforms

Fill in the blanks on the diagram, using each of the following terms only once.

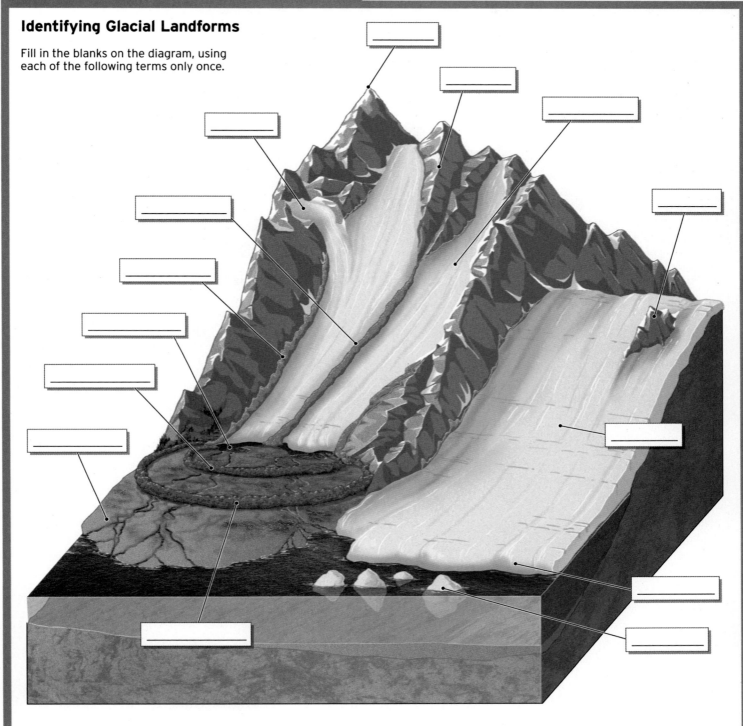

1. Arête
2. Cirque
3. Horn
4. Iceberg
5. Ice sheet
6. Ice shelf
7. Lateral moraine
8. Medial moraine
9. Nunatak
10. Outwash plain
11. Proglacial lake
12. Recessional moraines
13. Terminal moraine
14. Valley glacier

18 WATER, WIND, AND TIME: Desert Landforms

Chapter Outline

Uluru (or Ayers Rock) rises above a sea of sand in the Northern Territory in central Australia. It is a weathered mass of sandstone that is some 600 million years old.
(Per-Andre Hoffmann/Picture Press/Getty Images)

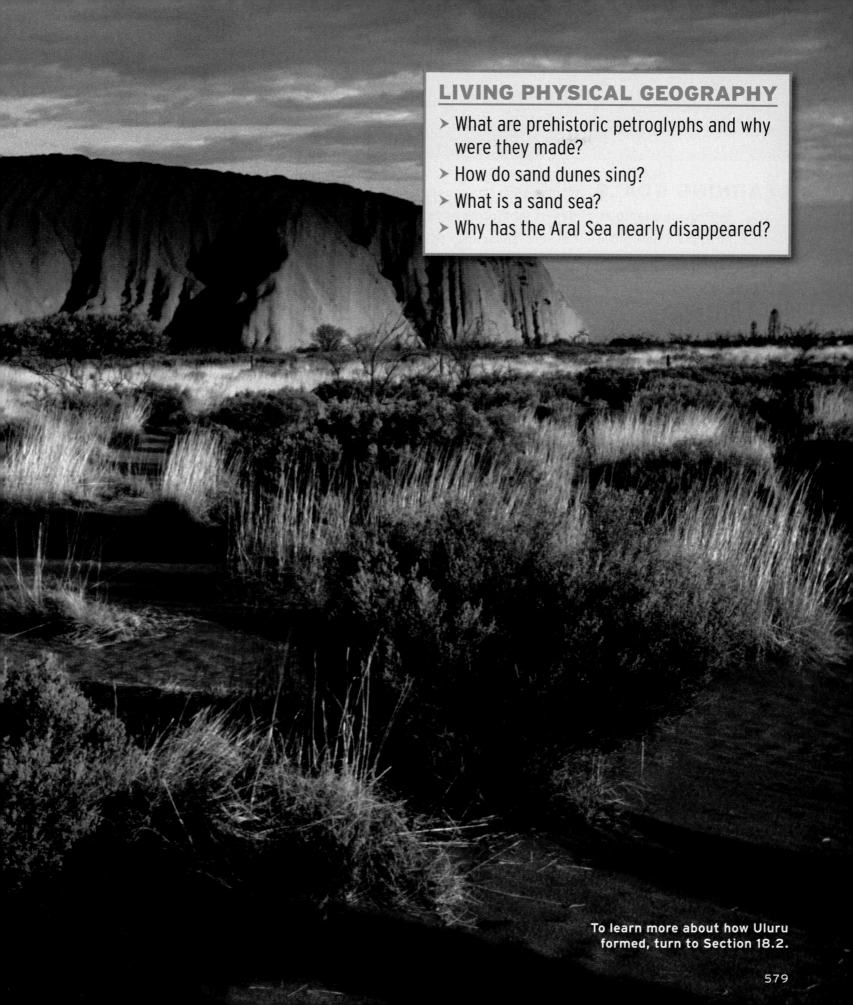

To learn more about how Uluru formed, turn to Section 18.2.

THE BIG PICTURE *Desert landforms are shaped by flowing water and wind. Desert lakes and their ecosystems are changed when people divert water from them.*

LEARNING GOALS *After reading this chapter, you will be able to:*

18.1 ◎ Provide examples of desert landforms and discuss the processes that form them.

18.2 ◎ Explain how different desert landscapes develop.

18.3 ◎ Assess the effect of water diversions on desert lakes.

THE HUMAN SPHERE: Flooding in the World's Driest Place

FIGURE 18.1 **Factors responsible for Antofagasta's aridity.** *The aridity of the Atacama Desert is a result of several factors. The desert is located in the subtropical high-pressure zone (see Section 4.3) as well as in the rain shadow created by the Andes (see Section 3.3). In addition, the cold Peru (Humboldt) Current is slow to evaporate, leaving little moisture in the air. (© Walter Bibikow/AWL Images/Getty Images)*

ANTOFAGASTA, A PORT CITY IN NORTHERN CHILE with a population of about 360,000, is the fourth largest city in Chile. It is located in the world's driest place, the Atacama Desert **(Figure 18.1)**.

Antofagasta receives only 4 mm (0.16 in) of rain each year, on average. Like most desert regions we will explore in this chapter, however, the city is built on a surface created by flowing water. Paradoxically, the citizens of Antofagasta must protect it against flooding and debris flows. On rare occasions during strong El Niño years, flooding rains fill the normally dry canyons to the east of the city with raging torrents of water. The bare hills have little to no vegetation to anchor soils, and the canyons turn into slurries of mud that flow down onto the alluvial fans on which the city is built. Such flooding has happened seven times in the city's history. The most recent flood event was in 1991, when more than 100 people died.

This chapter explores desert landforms and the processes that create them. We also turn our attention to different types of desert landscapes and see how each develops. Finally, we visit shrinking desert lakes and examine the anthropogenic factors that threaten them.

18.1 Desert Landforms and Processes

◎ Provide examples of desert landforms and discuss the processes that form them.

We usually think of deserts as hot, sandy places. For many desert regions, that image is accurate. But some deserts are cold and rocky, and the polar deserts are covered by ice sheets. What exactly is a desert? All deserts have severe moisture deficits for most or all of the year (see Section 8.4). Generally speaking, deserts occur where less than 25 cm (10 in) of precipitation falls annually. More humid regions can also be deserts if evapotranspiration rates are high and moisture loss exceeds precipitation.

Three main factors cause aridity: (1) the subtropical high-pressure zone found between about 20 and 30 degrees latitude north and south (see Section 4.3); (2) rain shadows on the leeward sides of major mountain ranges (see Section 3.3); and (3) inland locations at high latitudes or high elevations where the air is cold and its water vapor content is low. Between 20 and 30 degrees latitude, cold ocean currents may also contribute to aridity, as is the case for Antofagasta. Many deserts are caused by some combination of these three main factors, but the most geographically widespread cause of aridity is the influence of the subtropical high **(Figure 18.2)**.

Because of their aridity, all deserts have sparse plant cover and low biomass. As a result, no other environment on Earth is as exposed to the erosive

FIGURE 18.2 **World map of deserts.** *The Köppen climate system (see Section 8.1) classifies arid and semiarid regions as BWh and BWk climates. Arid climates are found on all continents. Deserts of about 500,000 km² (193,000 mi²) or greater, excluding those of Antarctica and the Arctic, are labeled on this map. The main causes of their aridity are given in the table.*

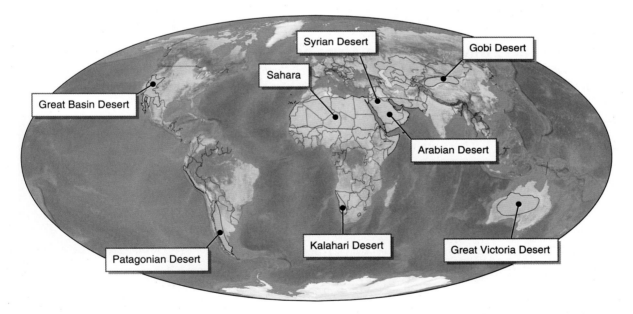

	AREA IN KM²	AREA IN MI²	MAIN CAUSE OF ARIDITY
Subtropical hot deserts			
Sahara (Africa)	9,100,000	3,500,000	Subtropical high
Arabian Desert (Middle East)	2,600,000	1,000,000	Subtropical high
Great Victoria Desert (Australia)	647,000	250,000	Subtropical high
Kalahari Desert (Africa)	570,000	220,000	Subtropical high
Syrian Desert (Middle East)	500,000	193,000	Subtropical high
Midlatitude cold deserts			
Gobi Desert (Asia)	1,300,000	500,000	Cold interior location
Patagonian Desert (South America)	670,000	260,000	Andes rain shadow
Great Basin (North America)	500,000	193,000	Sierra Nevada rain shadow

Picture This

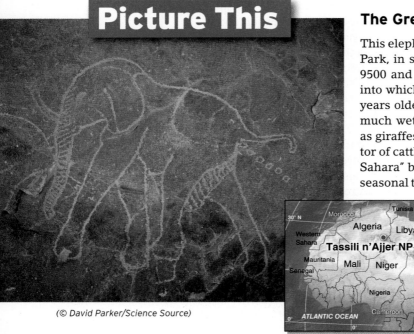

(© David Parker/Science Source)

The Green Sahara

This elephant petroglyph in Tassili n'Ajjer National Park, in southeastern Algeria, was made between 9500 and 6000 BCE, but the layer of rock varnish into which it was scratched is tens of thousands of years older. During the time when this petroglyph was made, the Sahara was much wetter. There was abundant permanent water, and large animals such as giraffes, crocodiles, elephants, hippopotamuses, and aurochs (a wild ancestor of cattle) lived throughout the region. This period is often called the "Green Sahara" because most of northern Africa consisted of savanna woodland and seasonal tropical forest. Natural climate change has since made northern Africa a desert, and these animals now live no closer than about 1,000 km (620 mi) to the south. The petroglyphs found throughout the Sahara (see also Figure GT.4) are a testament to how much northern Africa has changed in the last 8,000 years.

> **What are prehistoric petroglyphs and why were they made?***

Consider This

1. What is the Green Sahara? When did it occur?

2. The meanings of most petroglyphs in the Sahara are unknown. Why do you think people made them?

*Answers to the Living Physical Geography questions are found on page 605.

FIGURE 18.3 **SCIENTIFIC INQUIRY: Why did northern Africa become wetter, and how were people affected?** *Understanding Earth's natural history and how people have been affected by Earth's changing environments is one of the central themes in physical geography. Why was the Sahara so much wetter some 9,000 to 6,000 years ago? How were people affected by this episode of natural climate change?*

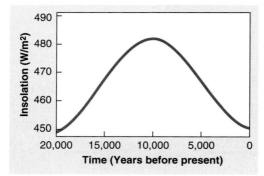

1. Why did northern Africa become wetter?
Changes in Earth-Sun orbital geometry caused increased summer insolation in the Northern Hemisphere (see Section 6.2). Summer insolation values were about 7% higher 10,000 years ago than they are today. Warmer summers in northern Africa created strong onshore flow of moist air and summer monsoon rains. Climate was wetter as a result.

(© Mike Hettwer)

3. How were people affected?
Petroglyphs in northern Africa show that the region was populated by nomadic hunting groups. Eventually, some of these groups began establishing semipermanent settlements and herding cattle, sheep, and goats. Bones, teeth, and artifacts have been preserved at human burial sites. These remains reveal the diet, health, and age of the people who left them. They also reveal where people moved. This information indicates that human settlements in the interior of northern Africa gradually disappeared as surface water became unavailable beginning about 6,000 years ago, as the region turned from savanna to desert.

2. What is the evidence for a wetter climate?
About 9,000 years ago, lake levels in northern Africa were at their highest. The map compares the levels of African lakes of 9,000 years ago with lake levels of the present. Some of those ancient lakes were large, and two were comparable in size to the Caspian Sea today. These lakes left behind beaches and fossils. Radiocarbon analysis (see Section 11.2) of organic material such as shells was used to determine the ages of the highest beaches, indicating when lake levels were highest. Other evidence comes from sediment cores (see Section 6.2) from various lakes in northern Africa as well as from the Mediterranean Sea and the Indian and Atlantic oceans.

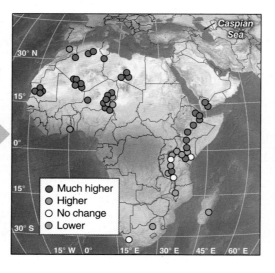

Legend:
- Much higher
- Higher
- No change
- Lower

effects of flowing water and wind, save perhaps coastal areas, as we will see in Section 19.2. We explored life in the desert biome in Section 8.4. In this chapter, we focus on the processes of desert geomorphology.

Weathering in the Desert

Physical weathering is more important than chemical weathering in deserts. Chemical weathering requires the presence of water, and water is only intermittently present in deserts. Chemical weathering therefore occurs very slowly in deserts compared with more humid regions. When water from rainfall or dew enters a rock, it gradually dissolves minerals within the rock. In sandstone, for example, calcite can hold quartz grains together. Quartz resists chemical weathering, but calcite does not. When calcite is dissolved through chemical weathering, the rock disintegrates and crumbles into quartz sand dunes. These grains can then be carried away by wind and water and deposited as quartz sand grains. Additionally, weak joints in rock cause the rock to fracture. If rocks tumble or fall down steep slopes, they are broken into smaller fragments.

The exposed surfaces of many desert rocks are covered with **rock varnish**: a thin, weathered, and darkened surface formed by the activities of bacteria and the accumulation of windblown clay particles. Rock varnish is a type of biochemical weathering found on rock surfaces almost exclusively in arid and semiarid climates. In more humid climates, rain washes away the clay particles too fast for rock varnish to form.

Scratching the surface of a rock removes the thin patina of rock varnish and reveals the lighter-colored rock beneath. People around the world have written or drawn on rock varnish for thousands of years. Many prehistoric rock carvings, called **petroglyphs**, have been made by scratching away rock varnish from a rock's surface. These images often record a history of animals and people that goes back many thousands of years, as discussed in **Picture This**.

The study of ancient environments such as those depicted in petroglyphs represents a line of scientific inquiry called *paleoecology*: the study of ancient ecosystems. **Figure 18.3** explores the paleoecology of the Sahara further.

Sculpting with Wind: Aeolian Processes

Aeolian (or *eolian*) means "of or relating to wind." Just as sediments are transported in a stream, aeolian erosion moves particles through traction, saltation, and suspension. The *surface load* of wind consists of particles moving by traction, rolling, and saltation. The *suspended load* consists of fine sediments of silt and clay that are suspended in the atmosphere. These particles can travel distances ranging from a few meters to thousands of kilometers as dust storms **(Figure 18.4)**.

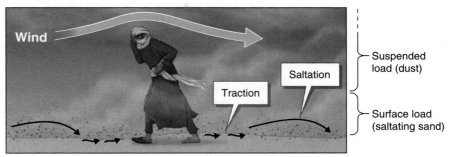

FIGURE 18.4 **Aeolian particle movement.** *(A) Sediments moved by wind are transported along the surface through traction and saltation and they are suspended in the air as dust. Only the lightest particles of clay and silt remain suspended in the air. (B) On March 25, 2011, this dust storm plunged Kuwait City into total darkness. (C) One day later, on March 26, 2011, NASA's satellite Terra captured the same dust storm as it moved south across the Arabian Peninsula. (B. © Surya Murali; C. NASA images courtesy Jeff Schmaltz, MODIS Rapid Response Team at NASA GSFC)*

A

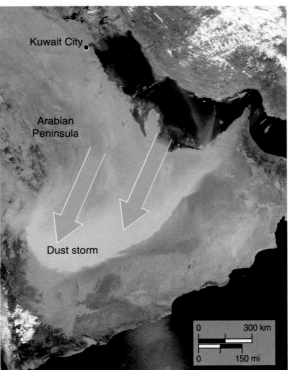

B

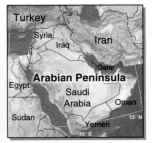

C

CRUNCH THE NUMBERS:
Dust Storm Movement
Using the scale bar in Figure 18.4B or Google Earth, measure the distance between Kuwait City and the southernmost tip of the Arabian Peninsula. Assuming that the March 2011 dust storm traveled at an average of 50 km/h (31 mph), how many hours did it take to travel the length of the peninsula?

Dust storms can travel rapidly. The March 2011 dust storm shown in Figure 18.4 moved about 50 km/h (31 mph) as it crossed the Arabian Peninsula. **Crunch the Numbers** calculates approximately how long it took the dust storm to cross the Arabian Peninsula.

Saltating sand grains hop over the ground within the first meter (3.3 ft) or so of the ground surface, abrading and sandblasting rock surfaces they collide with and creating ventifacts. A **ventifact** is a wind-sculpted desert rock shaped by abrasion by saltating sand **(Figure 18.5)**.

If enough fine-grained sediment is transported away from a region by the wind, the land surface will be lowered in the process of deflation. **Deflation** is the removal of sediments and lowering of the land surface by wind erosion.

Where the wind's speed increases as it flows around an obstruction, such as a large boulder, a blowout depression may occur. A *blowout depression* is a bowl-shaped depression formed in sand where wind flow becomes turbulent. Blowout depressions often form around pedestal rocks. A **pedestal rock** is a remnant of a layer of erosion-resistant cap rock supported by a slender column of less resistant rock **(Figure 18.6)**.

Yardangs are elongated ridges formed by deflation and sand abrasion in the desert. These ventifacts form where persistent winds move sand in the same direction for most of the year. They are generally two to three times longer than wide, and can be up to hundreds of meters high and several kilometers long **(Figure 18.7)**.

Pedestal rocks and yardangs are formed where there is net erosion by wind. The suspended material is often transported over the oceans, where it settles and slowly accumulates as sediment on the seafloor (see Section 13.3). Windblown dust from deserts plays important roles in Earth's physical systems, as **Picture This** explains.

rock varnish
A thin, weathered, and darkened surface on exposed rock surfaces formed by the activities of bacteria and the accumulation of windblown clay particles.

petroglyph
A prehistoric rock carving often made by scratching away rock varnish from a rock's surface.

aeolian
(or *eolian*) Of or relating to wind.

ventifact
A wind-sculpted desert rock shaped by abrasion by saltating sand.

deflation
The removal of sediments and lowering of the land surface by wind erosion.

pedestal rock
A remnant of a layer of erosion-resistant rock supported by a slender column of less resistant rock.

yardang
An elongated ridge formed by deflation and sand abrasion in a desert; generally, two to three times longer than it is wide.

FIGURE 18.5 **A ventifact.** *This sandstone ventifact, about 3 m (10 ft) high, in northern Chad has been pitted and scoured by many sandstorms.* (© Sinclair Stammers/Science Source)

FIGURE 18.6 **Pedestal rock.** *This large rock balances on a narrow pedestal in the Sahara in remote eastern Libya. The cap rock is more resistant to weathering and erosion than the rock forming the pedestal beneath it. As abrasion continues to thin the pedestal, the rock will eventually come crashing down. Note a blowout depression has formed at the base of the pedestal. (David Parker/Science Source)*

FIGURE 18.7 **Yardangs.** *Yardangs are formed through deflation and abrasion where winds blow persistently from the same direction. These yardangs are in the White Desert in western Egypt. Note the jeep for scale. (Raimund Linke/Getty Images)*

Picture This

Sahara Dust and Climate

One recurrent theme in physical geography is that of interacting physical systems. A good example is the dust plumes that move from the Sahara westward on the trade winds. This image developed from satellite data shows a dust plume stretching all the way from northern Africa to Florida on July 21, 2012. The darker the orange color, the higher the concentration of suspended material in the air.

The dust from northern Africa contains iron and phosphorus. Growth of phytoplankton (see Section 10.3) in the oceans is limited by a lack of iron and phosphorus. Therefore, the dust stimulates their growth as it settles on the ocean. Similarly, the soils of the Amazon rainforest are nutrient-poor (see Section 8.2), and the dust that settles there stimulates plant growth as well. Together, the marine phytoplankton and Amazon rainforest vegetation represent significant carbon sinks (see Section 6.3) and help slow the rate of increase of carbon dioxide in the atmosphere.

Climate models do not yet agree on whether precipitation in northern Africa will increase or decrease in the coming decades as the global temperature continues to climb. If climate change brings wetter conditions to the Sahara, less dust will be suspended in the air as vegetation grows and anchors the soils. If climate change brings drier conditions, more dust will be suspended as vegetation is diminished.

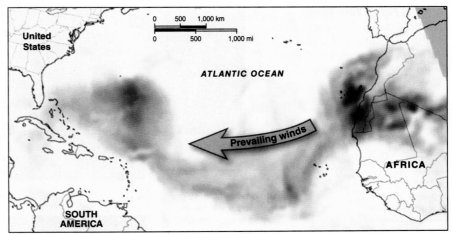

Consider This

1. Dust has a high albedo and reflects sunlight. What effect on temperature do dust storms have? In the context of Earth's albedo, what might happen to the atmosphere's temperature if more dust from the Sahara were suspended? What might happen if there were less dust in the air?

2. What might happen to the atmosphere's temperature if more dust from the Sahara increased the fertilization of phytoplankton and rainforests? What might happen if less dust decreased it?

sand dune
A hill or ridge formed by the accumulation of windblown sand.

slip face
The leeward side of a sand dune, where sand settles at its angle of repose.

barchan dune
(pronounced bar-KAHN) A crescent-shaped sand dune with the crescent tips pointing downwind.

star dune
A star-shaped dune formed as the prevailing wind changes direction through the year.

Sand Dunes

A **sand dune** is a hill or ridge formed by the accumulation of windblown sand. Only about 10% of deserts are covered by sand dunes. Where sand dunes do occur, they are prominent landforms. All sand dunes migrate in the direction of the prevailing wind, and they move across the desert floor more or less as a unit. Individual sand grains leave the windward side of the sand dune and accumulate at their angle of repose on the **slip face** on the leeward side of the dune. When viewed in cross section, sand dunes are composed of layers of deposited sand, creating a pattern called *cross-bedding*, as shown in **Figure 18.8**.

Three factors determine what kind of sand dune will form: (1) the amount of sand available,

(2) the strength of the wind, and (3) whether the wind changes direction over the year. The most common types of sand dune formations are barchan dunes, star dunes, and transverse dunes. **Barchan dunes** are crescent-shaped sand dunes with the crescent tips pointing downwind. **Star dunes** are star-shaped sand dunes that form as the prevailing wind changes direction through the year. **Transverse dunes** are long, narrow sand dunes with the ridge crest perpendicular (or transverse) to the prevailing wind. As **Figure 18.9** illustrates, wind direction plays an important role in sand dune formation.

How do sand dunes sing?

Singing Sand

About 30 sand dune locations around the world have been

FIGURE 18.8 GEO-GRAPHIC:

How sand migrates.
(A) All active sand dunes have a relatively gentle slope on the windward side (facing into the prevailing wind) and a steeper slope on the leeward side, called the slip face. This sand dune is in the southern Namib Desert in coastal Namibia. (B) A cross section of a sand dune reveals the cross-bedding structure created on its leeward side. (C) Cross-bedding can be seen in the Navajo sandstone formation in Zion National Park, Utah. These fossilized dunes are nearly 200 million years old. (A. © ALESSANDRO DELLA BELLA/Keystone/Corbis; C. Peter Carlson/Flickr RF/Getty Images)

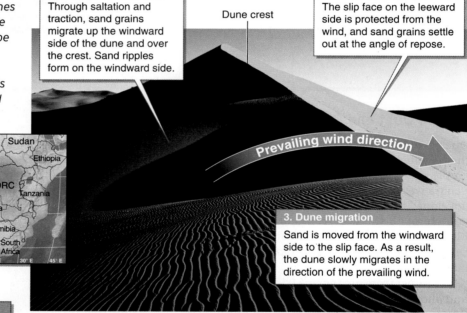

1. Windward side
Through saltation and traction, sand grains migrate up the windward side of the dune and over the crest. Sand ripples form on the windward side.

2. Slip face
The slip face on the leeward side is protected from the wind, and sand grains settle out at the angle of repose.

Dune crest

Prevailing wind direction

3. Dune migration
Sand is moved from the windward side to the slip face. As a result, the dune slowly migrates in the direction of the prevailing wind.

A

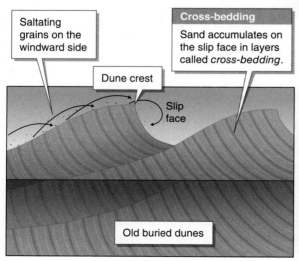

Saltating grains on the windward side

Dune crest

Cross-bedding
Sand accumulates on the slip face in layers called *cross-bedding*.

Slip face

Old buried dunes

B

C

FIGURE 18.9   **GEO-GRAPHIC: Kinds of sand dunes.** *Barchan dunes and star dunes form where sand does not completely cover the desert floor. Where sand is more plentiful, transverse, parabolic, or longitudinal dunes will form, depending on the strength of the wind.*

transverse dune
A long, narrow sand dune with the ridge crest perpendicular (or transverse) to the prevailing wind.

1. Barchan dunes
Where sand does not completely cover the desert floor and the prevailing wind consistently comes from the same direction, crescent-shaped barchan dunes can form. The crescent tips point downwind.

2. Star dunes
If the prevailing wind shifts direction over the year, barchans can join into star dunes.

3. Transverse dunes
Where sand completely covers the desert floor, linear dunes oriented perpendicularly (or transversely) to the prevailing wind may form.

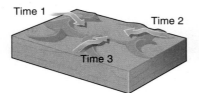

4. Parabolic dunes
Parabolic dunes can form from transverse dunes or other dune types when vegetation anchors the sand.

5. Longitudinal dunes
Longitudinal dunes have crests parallel to the prevailing wind direction. They may form where there is abundant sand and strong prevailing winds that vary only slightly in direction.

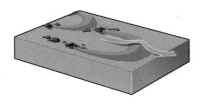

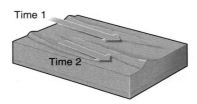

observed "singing" or "booming." As the grains of sand slide down the slip face, each grain vibrates when it encounters other grains. All together, billions of particles of sand vibrating at the same frequency can create an audible sound. The pitch of the sound depends on the size of the sand grains, their silica content, and how deep the sand dune is.

Desertification and Stabilizing Dunes

As we have seen, desertification is occurring in many arid regions where growing human populations put increasing pressure on already fragile semiarid environments. Arid western China has a growing problem with desertification. As human activities convert formerly vegetated regions to desert (see The Human Sphere in Chapter 4), dust storms develop and sweep eastward into populated areas.

One means of addressing desertification is to stabilize the sand so that vegetation can be reestablished. Plant roots anchor the sand and stop its movement. Where sand dunes are threatening human settlements, fences and netting can be used to slow the sand's movement so that vegetation can be planted **(Figure 18.10)**.

FIGURE 18.10   **Sand dune stabilization.** *These sand dunes in the Tengger Desert in Inner Mongolia of China are being stabilized with straw netting. The sand movement slows as it catches in the straw. (Bruce Dale/National Geographic/Getty Images)*

Active and unstable dunes

Netting

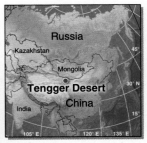

FIGURE 18.11 **Bajada.** *These alluvial fans have coalesced into a bajada in the Toiyabe Range in central Nevada. The slope of the bajada can be seen in relation to the level road.* (© Larry Workman)

Merged alluvial fans form a bajada

Sculpting with Water: Fluvial Processes

Deserts are by definition arid places, so it may seem odd that the most important agent of erosion in most desert areas is not wind, but flowing water. **Deserts are particularly vulnerable to erosion by water because they have little vegetation.** Plant roots anchor soil, and plants lessen the ero-sive effects of raindrops, sheet wash, and stream flow on the desert surface.

Fluvial Erosion

Many deserts receive summer thunderstorms and sudden flooding rains. The force of impact from raindrops dislodges particles. As water flows over the bare ground surface, these particles are picked up in the water and transported downslope. As trib-utaries merge, discharge increases, and streams gain erosive power. Desert streams are normally dry, but they run muddy brown from the suspended sedi-ments they carry after thunderstorms.

Each time rainfall fills the channel of an ephemeral desert stream with water, sediments move downstream in the channel. Once the rains cease, water infiltrates the ground, and the chan-nel goes dry again. The channel sediments will not move until the next time the channel fills with water. These ephemeral streams (see Section 16.1) go by many names, depending on the geographic locale. They are called *arroyos, dry washes,* or *coulees* in the United States. In the Middle East and northern Africa they are called *wadis,* in South Africa *dongas,* and in India they are *nullahs.*

Picture This

(Dennis Flaherty/Getty Images)

Sailing Stones

People have long known that rocks up to 300 kg (700 lb) in Death Valley's Racetrack Playa move across the playa floor, but it was unclear how the rocks moved. No one has ever actually witnessed the rocks in the act of moving, but their long trails are indisputable evidence that they do move. Time-lapse photography has been used in an attempt to capture a rock moving, but without success. This phenomenon has also been observed in nearby Bonnie Claire Playa in Nevada.

Gravity is not a factor because the playa floor is almost perfectly flat. Two separate rocks may start off with parallel trails, then diverge. The sizes of the rocks do not appear to influence their rate or direction of movement. Smooth rocks tend to travel in a less straight path than sharp-edged rocks.

Over the years, many hypotheses have been proposed to explain these rock movements. All involve a combination of strong wind, a slippery wetted-clay surface, and ice. In August 2014 a research paper published in PLOS ONE shed new light on this intriguing phenomenon. Researchers from Scripps Institution of Oceanography found that during winter, sheets of water on the playa floor freeze into thin panes of ice. The wind then breaks the ice into large pieces and moves them and the rocks embedded in them across the playa floor. Winds as slow as 16 km/h (10 mph) appear to be sufficient to move the ice and the rocks. Conditions necessary for rock movement are rare, and most rocks move at a rate of less than 6 m (20 ft) per minute for an hour or less once every ten years.

Consider This

1. Movement of rocks across playa floors such as Racetrack Playa is extremely rare. Why do you think that is?

2. Do you think the hypothesis presented here adequately explains how rocks of 300 kg move?

Fluvial Deposition

Where streams exit steep canyons, the stream gradient flattens out, stream velocity is reduced, and the kinetic energy of the stream is greatly reduced. As a result, the sediments carried by the stream are deposited, forming alluvial fans (see Section 16.3). Where alluvial fans emerge from adjacent valleys, they often coalesce to form a broad, sloping plain called a **bajada (Figure 18.11)**.

Where ephemeral desert streams empty into an internal drainage basin (see Section 16.1), they form a temporary shallow lake called a **playa lake**. Standing water in the playa lake typically evaporates within days to weeks. As the water evaporates, the dissolved minerals in the water form evaporite deposits as they precipitate out of the water (see Section 13.3). These deposits form a flat, dry lake bed called a **playa**. Playas are among the flattest and smoothest of all natural landforms on Earth. The world's fastest cars have set land speed records on the Bonneville Salt Flats, a playa in Utah. **Picture This** explores an unusual phenomenon that occurs in playas.

Some internal drainage basins in deserts develop saline lakes. A **saline lake** is a permanent body of salty water occupying a playa. Evaporation rates are high in these desert lakes, and as a result, dissolved minerals such as salt become concentrated in the water. Utah's Great Salt Lake and the Dead Sea in the Middle East are good examples of saline lakes. At the end of this chapter, Geographic

Perspectives explores the environmental effects of human activities on saline lakes.

18.2 Desert Landscapes

◎ Explain how different desert landscapes develop.

To many, deserts are among Earth's most beautiful and dramatic landscapes. In the desert, there is a contrast between the harsh, barren, and inhospitable nature of the place and its endless vistas, intriguing physical landforms, and sense of quiet timelessness. **Prominent desert landscapes include regs, ergs, mesa-and-butte terrain, inselbergs, basin-and-range topography, and badlands.** Each of these landscapes bears the signature of water, wind, and time.

Regs: Stony Plains

A flat, stony plain, or **reg**, may be formed by either of two different processes. The first is aeolian sorting, which results in accumulations of similarly sized particles, ranging in size from fields of boulders to sand dunes composed of quartz grains to loess deposits composed of fine silt. Small particles blow farthest, while heavier particles travel shorter distances.

Most rocks are not moved at all by the wind. As lighter particles, such as clay and silt, are transported away in the process of deflation, an accumulation of rocks, called a **lag deposit (Figure 18.12)**, may develop.

The second process forms regs consisting of stones that are tightly interlocked, as if they had been set in place by people. **Desert pavement** is a flat, rocky surface that resembles a cobblestone

bajada
(pronounced ba-HAH-da) A broad, sloping plain formed from merged alluvial fans.

playa lake
A shallow temporary lake that forms in an internal drainage basin.

playa
A flat, dry lake bed in a desert valley in an internal drainage basin.

saline lake
A permanent body of salty water occupying a playa.

reg
A flat stony plain.

lag deposit
A reg that results from the removal of smaller particles, such as clay and silt, by deflation.

desert pavement
A reg composed of tightly interlocked rocks that resembles a cobblestone street.

FIGURE 18.12 **GEO-GRAPHIC: Lag deposit reg.** *(A) A lag deposit forms when gravel and rocks are concentrated at the ground surface after smaller and lighter particles have blown away. (B) This lag deposit is southwest of Tamanrasset in southern Algeria. (B. Taghit/Flickr RF/Getty Images)*

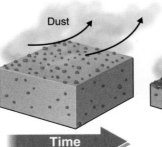

1. Original surface
The original surface is composed of a mixture of fine particles and large rocks.

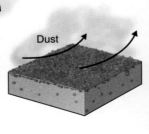

2. Lag deposit formation
Deflation removes only the fine particles. Over time, the larger rocks are concentrated on the surface, forming a lag deposit.

Dust

Dust

Time

A

B

FIGURE 18.13 **GEO-GRAPHIC: Desert pavement formation.** *(A) Desert pavement forms as desert soils are built up when clays and silts accumulate beneath rocks. (B) This reg in the desert of western Namibia is composed of desert pavement. (© Jean-Luc Manaud/Rapho Photo/Getty Images)*

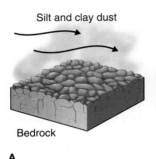

1. Weathered bedrock

Weathering forms rocky fragments on the surface of exposed bedrock.

2. Silt and clay accumulation

Silt and clay are blown in from far away and accumulate between the rocks. Rainwater causes the fine particles to percolate down beneath the rocks, while the rocks remain on the surface.

3. Pavement surface

Over time, the rocks break apart and form a tightly fitting, nearly flat stone surface.

Silt and clay dust

Bedrock

Time

A

B

erg

A desert landscape dominated by actively moving sand dunes.

street. Beneath desert pavement are aridisol soils composed of clay and silt. These soils often contain few or no stones. If deflation formed desert pavement, then one would expect to find stones within the soil that would later be brought to the surface by deflation. Recent research indicates, however, that desert pavement may form as desert soils are built up on bare bedrock **(Figure 18.13)**.

FIGURE 18.14 **Nazca geoglyphs.** *This aerial photograph shows a monkey (about 100 m, or 330 ft, across) carved into a reg in southern Peru. About two dozen strange figures and odd geometric shapes and patterns were etched into the Peruvian desert floor by the now-vanished Nazca civilization about 1,500 to 2,000 years ago. Although there are many hypotheses about these works, their purpose is not fully understood. (Aaron Oberlander/Flickr RF/Getty Images)*

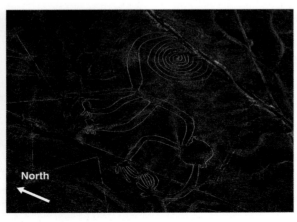

North

Regs, whether formed as lag deposits or desert pavement, occur in all deserts. They are also called *hamada* in the Sahara and *gibber plains* in Australia.

The top sides of the rocks in regs are often coated with rock varnish. Overturning or removing the rocks reveals a lighter surface. In some areas of southern Peru, the desert's surface was scraped and overturned by people of the ancient Nazca civilization to draw huge geoglyphs on the desert floor **(Figure 18.14)**.

Ergs: Sand Seas

What is a sand sea?

An **erg** (Arabic for "dune field") is a desert landscape that is dominated by actively moving sand dunes. Ergs, also called *sand seas*, are among Earth's most dramatic landscapes. They are devoid of vegetation and, by definition, are at least 125 km² (50 mi²) in extent. In all ergs, sand covers at least 20% of the desert floor. Any type of sand dune may form in an erg, and some ergs are flat sheets of sand with few dunes.

Ergs are most common where the subtropical high creates arid conditions. Ergs cannot develop in humid climates because vegetation will become established and stabilize the sand. The source of sand for ergs varies, but it is often derived from glacial outwash plains, dry lake beds, or river deltas. In much of the Middle East, such as Saudi Arabia, geologic uplift exposed marine sediments that were eroded to form ergs.

It takes hundreds of thousands to millions of years for large ergs to develop. Large ergs are found in the Namib Desert of Namibia, the Taklamakan Desert in China, the Gobi Desert in Mongolia, interior Australia, and portions of southwestern North America. Earth's largest erg is the Rub' al Khali (or the Empty Quarter) on the Arabian Peninsula. It is estimated to have been active for over a million years. It covers 583,000 km^2 (225,000 mi^2) and stretches from Saudi Arabia into Yemen, Oman, and the United Arab Emirates. After the Rub' al Khali, Earth's largest ergs are found in the Sahara, particularly in Algeria and Libya (Figure 18.15).

Mesa-and-Butte Terrain

Like sand seas, mesas and buttes come to mind for many when they picture a typical desert landscape. Mesa-and-butte terrain, however, is determined more by the composition and structure of the bedrock than by climate. Mesa-and-butte terrain also occurs in humid climates, but it is easiest to see in

FIGURE 18.15 **Ergs.** *(A) This astronaut photograph shows a small portion of the Rub' al Khali erg (or the Empty Quarter) in Oman. The sand dunes shown here, mainly longitudinal dunes, are about 100 m (330 ft) high (inset photo). Salt flats (or sabkhas) have formed between the dunes. (B) The Sahara has the greatest concentration of ergs of any region. The largest ones are mapped here. (A. © Felix Bleichenbacher; inset, NASA image created by Robert Simmon, using Landsat data provided by the United States Geological Survey)*

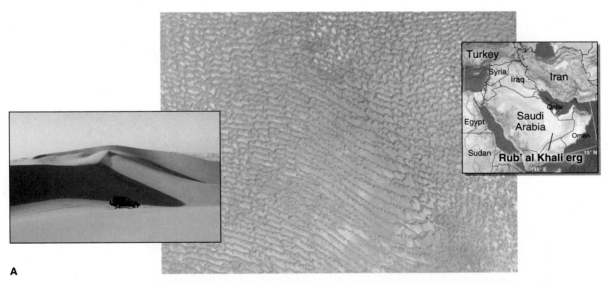

A

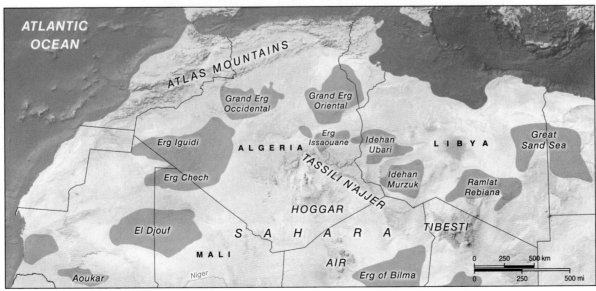

B

FIGURE 18.16 **GEO-GRAPHIC: Formation of mesas and buttes.** *(A) Mesa-and-butte terrain forms as a plateau consisting of sedimentary rock is eroded. (B) In Monument Valley, on the Colorado Plateau in northern Arizona and southern Utah, buttes and chimneys form as slabs of sandstone shear off along vertical joints and accumulate as talus on the slopes. The gentle slope at the base of the butte is composed of relatively soft shale that is too weak to develop a vertical cliff face. Where talus accumulates along the length of a mesa or linear escarpment, a talus apron results. (B. © Guido Alberto Rossi/Age Fotostock, Inc.)*

Animation
Mesa and butte formation
http://qrs.ly/ey4aets

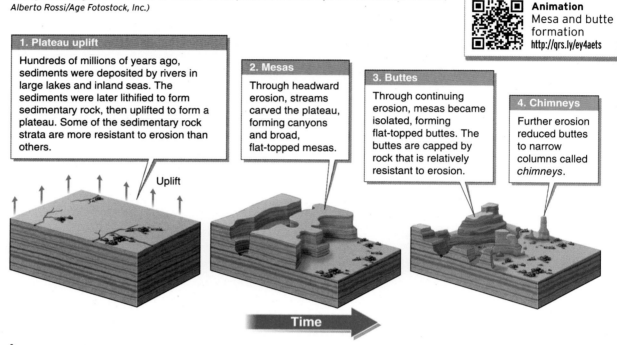

1. Plateau uplift

Hundreds of millions of years ago, sediments were deposited by rivers in large lakes and inland seas. The sediments were later lithified to form sedimentary rock, then uplifted to form a plateau. Some of the sedimentary rock strata are more resistant to erosion than others.

Uplift

2. Mesas

Through headward erosion, streams carved the plateau, forming canyons and broad, flat-topped mesas.

3. Buttes

Through continuing erosion, mesas became isolated, forming flat-topped buttes. The buttes are capped by rock that is relatively resistant to erosion.

4. Chimneys

Further erosion reduced buttes to narrow columns called *chimneys*.

Time

A

Mesa

Butte

Chimney

Resistant sandstone layers

Soft shale layers

Talus apron

WY
NE
NV UT CO KS
Monument Valley
CA AZ NM
TX
Mexico

B

FIGURE 18.17 **Cuestas and hogbacks.** *(A) Cuestas, such as the Bookcliffs near Grand Junction, Colorado, are formed where sedimentary rock dips less than 30° from horizontal. (B) Hogbacks are composed of erosion-resistant sedimentary rock layers with a dip of 30° or more from horizontal. This hogback is the San Rafael Reef, a steeply tilted layer of sandstone and limestone in eastern Utah.*
(A. © Jim Wark/airphotona.com; B. © Francois Gohier/Science Source)

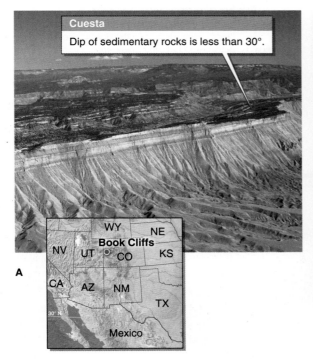

Cuesta
Dip of sedimentary rocks is less than 30°.

A

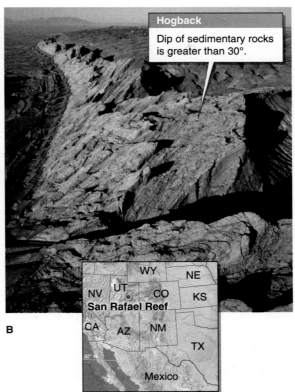

Hogback
Dip of sedimentary rocks is greater than 30°.

B

arid desert climates because it is not obscured by vegetation. The tepuis in Venezuela and western Guyana, for example, form mesa-and-butte terrain that is covered by tropical savanna and tropical rainforest.

Most mesas, buttes, and chimneys occur where a plateau has been uplifted, weathered, and eroded by flowing water. A **mesa** is flat-topped elevated area with one or more cliff-face sides and is wider than it is tall. A **butte** is a medium-sized flat-topped hill with cliff-face sides and is taller than it is wide. A **chimney** is a slender spire of rock with a flat top. Chimneys are far less common than mesas and buttes.

Although mesa-and-butte terrain can form on lava flows without geologic uplift, it is most common in sedimentary rocks that have been uplifted. Examples of mesa-and-butte terrain are found throughout the southwestern United States, particularly in Monument Valley on the Colorado Plateau. **Figure 18.16** illustrates how mesa-and-butte terrain develops.

The surface of a flat-topped mesa has little or no *dip* (or slope). Dipping occurs where sedimentary rock has been folded or tilted through faulting (see Section 12.4). Where sedimentary rock at the ground surface dips gently, a *cuesta* is formed **(Figure 18.17A)**. *Hogbacks* form where sedimentary rock at the ground surface dips steeply **(Figure 18.17B)**.

Inselbergs: Island Mountains

An **inselberg** (meaning "island mountain") is a large, weathered outcrop of bedrock surrounded by a flat plain. Inselbergs are exposed at the land surface through the process of exhumation (the removal

mesa
A flat-topped elevated area with one or more cliff-face sides that is wider than it is tall.

butte
A medium-sized flat-topped hill with cliff-face sides that is taller than it is wide.

chimney
A slender spire of rock with a flat top.

inselberg
A large, weathered outcrop of bedrock surrounded by a flat alluvium-filled plain.

FIGURE 18.18 **GEO-GRAPHIC: Inselbergs, Australia.** *(A) Kata Tjuta and Uluru were formed through differential erosion of sandstone. (B) Kata Tjuta (left) and Uluru (right) are about 30 km (18 mi) apart. They are composed of the same 600-million-year-old erosion-resistant arkose, a type of sandstone. (B. left: © Nigel Millett; right: Bildagentur-Online/McPhoto-Schultz/Science Photo Library/Science Source)*

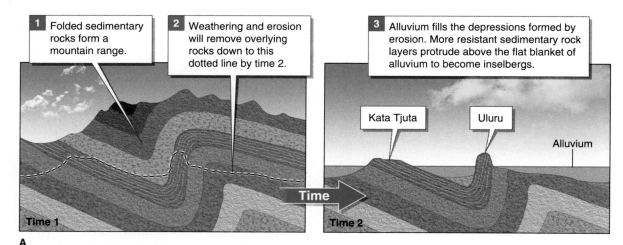

1 Folded sedimentary rocks form a mountain range.

2 Weathering and erosion will remove overlying rocks down to this dotted line by time 2.

3 Alluvium fills the depressions formed by erosion. More resistant sedimentary rock layers protrude above the flat blanket of alluvium to become inselbergs.

Kata Tjuta

Uluru

Alluvium

Time 1

Time

Time 2

A

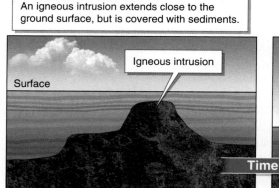

Kata Tjuta

Uluru

AUSTRALIA

Kata Tjuta and Uluru

B

FIGURE 18.19 **GEO-GRAPHIC: The making of a bornhardt.** *(A) Bornhardts are formed by exhumation of an igneous intrusion through erosion. Once the igneous intrusion is exposed, erosion begins to wear it down, but at a slower rate than the surrounding weaker sediments. (B) Spitzkoppe, in Namibia, is a bornhardt composed of granite. (David du Plessis/Gallo Images ROOTS Collection/Getty Images)*

1. Igneous intrusion

An igneous intrusion extends close to the ground surface, but is covered with sediments.

Igneous intrusion

Surface

2. Exhumation

Aeolian and fluvian erosion remove the overlying sediments, exposing the intrusion and forming a bornhardt.

Eroded bornhardt

Surface

Time

A

B

FIGURE 18.20 **GEO-GRAPHIC: Basin-and-range topography.** *(A) Basin-and-range topography has formed in the Great Basin, where the North American crust is being stretched, creating a series of parallel inselbergs (called horsts) surrounded by flat, alluvium-filled valleys (called grabens). (B) This map shows the geographic extent of the Great Basin.*

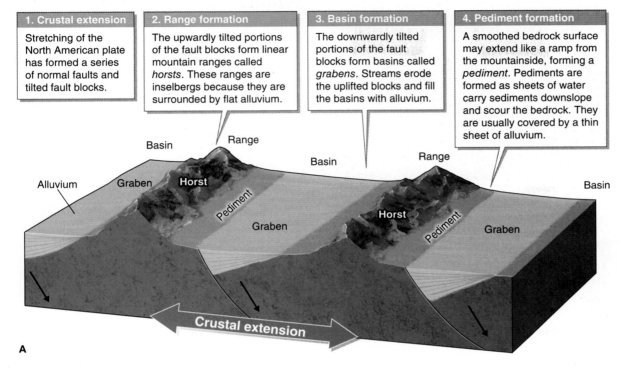

1. Crustal extension

Stretching of the North American plate has formed a series of normal faults and tilted fault blocks.

2. Range formation

The upwardly tilted portions of the fault blocks form linear mountain ranges called *horsts*. These ranges are inselbergs because they are surrounded by flat alluvium.

3. Basin formation

The downwardly tilted portions of the fault blocks form basins called *grabens*. Streams erode the uplifted blocks and fill the basins with alluvium.

4. Pediment formation

A smoothed bedrock surface may extend like a ramp from the mountainside, forming a *pediment*. Pediments are formed as sheets of water carry sediments downslope and scour the bedrock. They are usually covered by a thin sheet of alluvium.

A

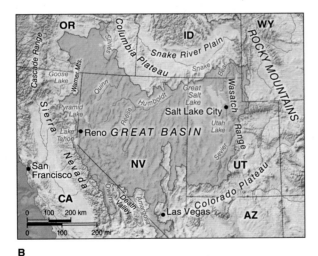

B

of overlying sediments and rock). **Inselbergs form because they are more resistant to erosion than the sediments and rocks surrounding them.** Like mesas and buttes, inselbergs are not restricted to desert climates, but they are easiest to observe there. Kata Tjuta (or the Olgas) and Uluru (or Ayers

Rock) in central Australia are two dramatic examples of inselbergs formed from sedimentary rocks **(Figure 18.18)**.

Bornhardts are inselbergs that take on a more rounded form and are usually derived from erosion-resistant crystalline rocks such as granite or gneiss. As the land surface is lowered through erosion, a crystalline rock body, such as a pluton, batholith, or laccolith (see Section 13.2), is exposed and rounded through weathering **(Figure 18.19)**.

Basin-and-Range Topography

The **Basin-and-Range Province** is located in the Great Basin of the western United States, where the crust is being stretched through rifting (see Figure 14.21), forming a large internal drainage basin containing a series of tilted fault blocks called horsts and a series of valleys called grabens. **Figure 18.20** illustrates the process that has created the Basin-and-Range Province.

Basin-and-range topography is not restricted to deserts. It is included in this section, however, because it is a prominent desert landscape in western

Basin-and-Range Province
A landscape located in the southwestern United States where the crust is being stretched apart through rifting, forming a large internal drainage basin with a series of tilted fault blocks.

FIGURE 18.21 **Badlands.** *These badlands are in the Qilian Mountains in China. They are composed of siltstone, mudstone, and shale. The high levels of minerals like iron and manganese in the rocks give them vibrant hues.* (ChinaFotoPress via Getty Images)

North America. The only comparable region of widespread extension of continental crust is in the East African rift zone.

Badlands

Badlands are landscapes riddled by rills and gullies **(Figure 18.21)**. They occur mostly in arid to semi-arid environments where slopes are largely unvegetated and weak rocks, such as shale, are eroded by infrequent but intense rainfall. They often have loose, dry, clay-rich soils. Badlands are "bad" because they cannot be farmed and because they are difficult to cross. They range in size from a few grouped hillsides to thousands of square kilometers. Badlands often have many fossils preserved in their sedimentary rocks.

GEOGRAPHIC PERSPECTIVES
18.3 Shrinking Desert Lakes
◎ Assess the effect of water diversions on desert lakes.

Some of the world's largest lakes (in surface area, but not in volume) are found in deserts. Desert lakes, as we have seen, are often located in internal drainage basins and are saline. Like the mass balance of a glacier, the hydrologic balance of many desert saline lakes is at an equilibrium between water entering the lake and water leaving the lake. In other words, the lake level is a result of the amount of water flowing into the lake in streams and the amount of water leaving the lake through evaporation and infiltration.

Many large desert lakes worldwide are shrinking as people divert the streams that flow into them. This section explores three lakes that have suffered similar effects as a result of water diversions.

Asia's Aral Sea

> Why has the Aral Sea nearly disappeared?

The Aral Sea, straddling Kazakhstan and Uzbekistan in western Asia, was once the fourth largest lake in the world in surface area. In the 1960s, the rivers flowing into the Aral Sea, shown in **Figure 18.22**, were diverted by large irrigation canals as part of a massive Soviet project to grow cotton.

From the standpoint of producing cotton for export to global markets, the program has been a success. But without the input of water from the rivers, the Aral Sea has shrunk over time. It is now less than 10% of its original size, having become a series of shallow, briny lakes that are ecologically dead **(Figure 18.23)**. The loss of the Aral Sea brought an end to the lucrative inland fishery that once existed there. At the peak of the harvest, more than 50,000 tons of fish were caught in the Aral Sea each year.

Even before the water diversions, the Amu Darya and Syr Darya carried agricultural fertilizers and sewage. As the streams emptied into the Aral Sea, this waste accumulated in the lake's sediments. After the lake bed was exposed and dried, winds stirred up toxic dust storms that poisoned the local communities. Rates of infant mortality, cancers, and respiratory disease among local people skyrocketed. The area has the highest rates of esophageal cancer in the world. Furthermore, without the moderating effects of the lake water, the local climate has become more extreme. Winters are colder, and summers are windier and hotter.

The Loss of Owens Lake

A story similar to that of the Aral Sea can be found in North America's Great Basin, where Owens and Mono lakes in eastern California have also suffered from water diversions.

FIGURE 18.22 **Aral Sea water diversions.** *(A) The Amu Darya and Syr Darya rivers, originating in the Tian Shan range to the southeast, once flowed into the Aral Sea basin, but are now diverted for agriculture. (B) Cotton fields in the Aral Sea basin. Cotton plants need a lot of water, and standing irrigation water evaporates rapidly in the desert sunlight. (B. © Martin Barlow/Art Directors & Trips Photo/age fotostock)*

A

FIGURE 18.23 **The shrinking Aral Sea.** *Satellite image of the Aral Sea in 2014. The remaining portions of the lake are dark green. The extent of the Aral Sea in 1960 is shown by the traced outline. The original lake bed was about 400 km (250 mi) in length and was roughly the size of Wisconsin. Hundreds of rusting boats (inset), now resting tens of kilometers from water, are a reminder of the fishery that once sustained local economies and people. (Right: NASA; inset: Kelly Cheng Travel Photography/ Flickr RF/Getty Images)*

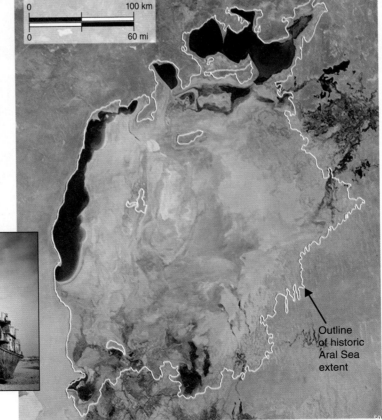

Outline of historic Aral Sea extent

Owens Lake was a 500 km² (200 mi²) body of water that formed where the Owens River terminated in the lower Owens Valley **(Figure 18.24)**. In the early 1900s, the city of Los Angeles needed water for its growing population and surreptitiously bought up land and water rights in the Owens Valley, some 266 km (165 mi) to the northeast of the city. Farmers who would not sell were coerced, sometimes under the threat of violence, to do so. Beginning in 1913, the lower Owens River was diverted to Los Angeles through a system of pipes called the Los Angeles Aqueduct, and by 1926, Owens Lake was gone.

Today, Owens Valley has the dubious distinction of being the dustiest place in North America. The dust in Owens Valley's dust storms is about 30% salt and includes the toxic elements chromium, cadmium, and arsenic. As in the case of the Aral Sea, the toxicity of the sediments arose chiefly from the use of agricultural chemicals that rivers carried into the lake and deposited on the lake bed.

FIGURE 18.24 **Owens and Mono lakes.** *(A) This map shows Mono Lake, Owens Valley, and the Los Angeles Aqueduct system. The inset photo shows the Los Angeles Aqueduct pipeline where it passes through Owens Valley. (B) An undated photograph of Owens Lake before water diversions is shown on the top. On the bottom, the playa lake bed is shown as it appears today.* (Top: © AP Photo/Eastern California Museum of Inyo County; bottom: Lieuwe Hofstra; inset: Jenna Cavelle)

A

B

Saving Mono Lake

Mono Lake (pronounced MOH-no), at 1 million to 3 million years old, may be the oldest lake in North America. Located 200 km (125 mi) north of Owens Lake, Mono Lake nearly shared its fate. Several streams flow from the high Sierra Nevada to the west of the lake and empty into the Mono Basin to form Mono Lake.

During the grab for Owens Lake water rights, the city of Los Angeles also acquired land in the Mono Basin and began sending water south. As stream inflow was reduced, the level of Mono Lake began dropping. The level dropped about 15 m (50 ft) between 1940 and 1980, as shown in **Figure 18.25**.

In the late 1970s, students and faculty from the University of California, Davis, started a "Save Mono Lake" campaign, and eventually, the issue of the lake's fate was brought to court. In 1994, legislation was passed to reduce water diversions and restore water to the Mono Basin. Since that time, the lake levels have become stable and are slowly rising, but they have not returned to their pre-1941 levels. Barring the onset of a long-term drought, the lake is on a course of recovery.

Desert lakes are sensitive systems that are easily lost. Both the Aral Sea and Owens Lake were lost due to water diversions. As the case of Mono Lake shows, reversing the loss of these lakes is possible with an organized and sustained effort.

FIGURE 18.25 **Mono Lake levels.** *(A) By the early 1980s, some 30% of Mono Lake's volume had been lost due to water diversions to Los Angeles. Mono Lake faced the same fate as the Aral Sea and Owens Lake. (B) Mono Lake is about 20 km (13 mi) across at its widest. The white ring surrounding the lake is the exposed lake bed, indicating the height of the lake before water diversions.* (B. © Christophe Lerouzo)

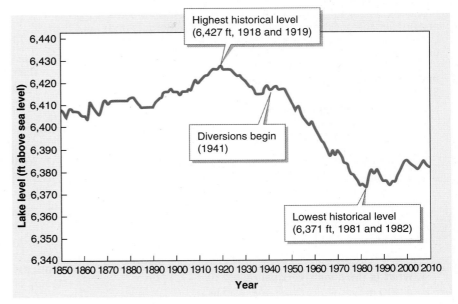

A

B

CHAPTER 18 Exploring with ☺ Google Earth

To complete these problems, first read the chapter. When you are finished, go to LaunchPad and open the Exploring with Google Earth file for this chapter. Click on the "Workbook Problems" folder to "fly" to each of the problems listed below and answer the questions. Be sure to keep your "Borders and Labels" layer activated. Refer to Appendix 4 if you need help using Google Earth.

PROBLEM 18.1 This placemark is pinned to a sand dune in the Sahara, in Algeria.

1. What type of sand dune is this?
a. Barchan
c. Transverse
b. Star
d. Parabolic

2. From which direction does the prevailing wind blow?
a. From the south
c. From the east
b. From the north
d. It changes depending on the season.

3. What is the dune's approximate diameter?
a. 0.5 km
c. 2 km
b. 1 km
d. 2.5 km

4. What is the dune's vertical relief?
a. 100 m
c. 600 m
b. 300 m
d. 900 m

5. Zoom out. You can see that these dunes extend for hundreds of kilometers. What is the name for a sea of sand such as this?
a. Reg
c. Playa
b. Erg
d. Yardang

6. What is the name of this particular sand sea?
a. Grand Erg Oriental Desert
b. Hamada de Tinrhert Desert
c. Grand Erg Occidental Desert
d. Erg Iquidi Desert

PROBLEM 18.2 These sand dunes clearly show the direction of the prevailing wind.

1. What kind of sand dunes are these?
a. Barchan
c. Transverse
b. Star
d. Parabolic

2. From which direction does the prevailing wind blow?
a. From the south
b. From the north
c. From the east
d. It changes depending on the season.

3. Notice the road running across the dunes. Was the road made before the dunes formed or after?
a. Before
b. After

4. Zoom out. What country is this?
a. Bolivia
c. Chile
b. Peru
d. Argentina

PROBLEM 18.3 This massive granite outcrop, called Ben Amera, rises out of the sand in Mauritania.

1. What is the name for this landform?
a. Ventifact
c. Bornhardt
b. Erg
d. Yardang

2. About how high does Ben Amera rise above the desert floor?
a. 100 m
c. 375 m
b. 250 m
d. 1,000 m

PROBLEM 18.4 Just to the east of Ben Amera, a gently tilting plateau rises from the desert floor.

1. What is the name for this gently tilting plateau?
a. Mesa
c. Hogback
b. Cuesta
d. Bajada

2. Zoom out. Where is this location?
a. Mauritania
c. Bolivia
b. Argentina
d. Peru

PROBLEM 18.5 This linear mountain ridge is composed of steeply tilting sedimentary rocks.

1. What is the name for this steeply tilting ridge?
a. Mesa
c. Hogback
b. Cuesta
d. Marine terrace

2. Zoom out. Where is this location?
a. Morocco
c. Algeria
b. Western Sahara
d. Mauritania

PROBLEM 18.6 This placemark lands on the Colorado Plateau.

1. What is the name for the placemarked landform?
a. Mesa
c. Chimney
b. Butte
d. Talus apron

PROBLEM 18.7 This placemark also lands on the Colorado Plateau.

1. What is the name for the placemarked landform?
a. Mesa
c. Chimney
b. Butte
d. Talus apron

PROBLEM 18.8 This placemark also lands on the Colorado Plateau.

1. What is the name for the placemarked landform?
a. Mesa
c. Chimney
b. Butte
d. Talus apron

PROBLEM 18.9 From 92 km in altitude, a significant portion of the western United States can be seen. Notice the north-south valleys and mountain ranges.

1. What is the name for this pattern of mountains and valleys?
a. Cuesta
c. Basin-and-range topography
b. Mesa-and-butte terrain
d. Desert pavement

2. **Notice that the placemark is in a dry depression, colored white in Google Earth. What is the name for this landform?**
   a. Playa
   b. Playa lake
   c. Saline lake
   d. Reg

PROBLEM 18.10 This placemark falls on several fan-shaped features that have merged together.

1. **What is the name for this landform?**
   a. Talus cone
   b. Alluvial fan
   c. Bajada
   d. Erg

2. **What is the distance from marker A to marker B?**
   a. 10 km
   b. 24 km
   c. 72 km
   d. 230 km

3. **What is the drop in elevation between marker A and marker B?**
   a. 50 m
   b. 200 m
   c. 350 m
   d. 700 m

4. **Zoom out. In what country is this placemark?**
   a. Mongolia
   b. China
   c. Russia
   d. Kazakhstan

PROBLEM 18.11 This lake is found in the Great Basin of Nevada, an internal drainage basin.

1. **What is the name for this kind of lake?**
   a. Playa
   b. Playa lake
   c. Saline lake
   d. Permanent lake

2. **What is the name of this particular lake?**
   a. Pyramid Lake
   b. Walker Lake
   c. Mono Lake
   d. Owens Lake

3. **What are the rings surrounding the lake?**
   a. Evidence of human effects on the lake
   b. Beaches at former lake levels
   c. Sedimentary rock layers
   d. Roads

4. **Based on your reading in this chapter, what factor most likely resulted in these rings?**
   a. Drought
   b. Bulldozers
   c. Water diversions
   d. Tectonic uplift

PROBLEM 18.12 This placemark visits a desert environment with little vegetation and brightly colored layers of deeply eroded rock.

1. **Why type of desert landscape is this?**
   a. An erg
   b. A reg
   c. Basin-and-range topography
   d. Badlands

2. **What kinds of rocks are these?**
   a. Igneous
   b. Sedimentary
   c. Metamorphic

3. **Zoom out. Where is this location?**
   a. Chile
   b. Argentina
   c. Bolivia
   d. Peru

CHAPTER 18 **Study Guide**

Focus Points

18.1 Desert Landforms and Processes

Weathering: Physical weathering is more prominent than chemical weathering in deserts.

Aeolian erosion: Erosion by wind is a significant factor in desert environments.

Sand dunes: Sand dune type is determined mostly by the amount of sand available and the direction of the prevailing wind.

Fluvial erosion: Fluvial erosion is more important than aeolian erosion in deserts. Fluvial erosion occurs mostly after heavy rainfall, when the channels of ephemeral streams are filled.

Fluvial deposition: Streams deposit sediments on alluvial fans and playas.

18.2 Desert Landscapes

Desert landscapes: Landscapes found in deserts include regs, ergs, mesa-and-butte terrain, inselbergs, basin-and-range topography, and badlands.

18.3 Geographic Perspectives: Shrinking Desert Lakes

Human diversions: Water diversions by people have caused desert lakes to shrink.

Hydrologic balance: The levels of desert lakes in internal drainage basins represent a balance between water flow into the lakes and water losses by evaporation and infiltration.

Shrinking lakes: The Aral Sea and the lakes of the Great Basin are examples of desert lakes that are shrinking due to water diversions.

Key Terms

aeolian (or *eolian*), 583
bajada, 589
barchan dune, 586
Basin-and-Range
    Province, 595
butte, 593
chimney, 593
deflation, 584
desert pavement, 589
erg, 590
inselberg, 593
lag deposit, 589
mesa, 593

pedestal rock, 584
petroglyph, 583
playa, 589
playa lake, 589
reg, 589
rock varnish, 583
saline lake, 589
sand dune, 586
slip face, 586
star dune, 586
transverse dune, 586
ventifact, 584
yardang, 584

Concept Review

The Human Sphere: Flooding in the World's Driest Place

1. Why must Antofagasta guard against flooding when it is in one of the driest places on Earth?

18.1 Desert Landforms and Processes

2. What single physical characteristic defines all deserts?

3. What three major physical factors create deserts?

4. Which is more important in deserts, physical or chemical weathering? Why?

5. What is rock varnish? How does it form?

6. What is a petroglyph? On what surface are petroglyphs often made?

7. What and when was the Green Sahara? What caused it? What is the evidence for it? How were people affected by it?

8. What is aeolian erosion? What similarities do aeolian erosion and fluvial erosion share?

9. What is a ventifact and how does it form? In this context, what are pedestal rocks and yardangs?

10. Describe the main physical aspects of a sand dune and describe how a sand dune migrates.

11. What are the major types of sand dunes?

12. Why do some sand dunes "sing"?

13. What is sand dune stabilization? How does it relate to reversing desertification?

14. Deserts are dry places. Why, then, is water the most important agent of erosion in deserts?

15. Give examples of local geographic names for ephemeral desert streams.

16. Where and how do bajadas form?

17. What is a playa lake? A playa? A saline lake? Explain how each forms.

18.2 Desert Landscapes

18. What is a reg? Compare the formation of lag deposits with the formation of desert pavement.

19. What is an erg? Where, geographically, are they most common?

20. What is mesa-and-butte terrain? Explain how it develops.

21. What are inselbergs? Explain how they develop.

22. What is basin-and-range topography? Explain how it develops.

23. What are badlands?

18.3 Geographic Perspectives: Shrinking Desert Lakes

24. Why do the levels of lakes in internal drainage basins fluctuate easily?

25. How are people causing large desert lakes worldwide to shrink?

26. Where was the Aral Sea? What happened to it?

27. Why are there now toxic dust storms in the Aral Sea Basin?

28. What do desert lakes in the Great Basin in the western United States have in common with the Aral Sea?

29. What happened to Owens Lake that nearly happened to Mono Lake? Why are there toxic dust storms in Owens Valley today?

30. Is Mono Lake's situation getting worse, stable, or improving? Explain.

Critical-Thinking Questions

1. Scraping the desert floor to make geoglyphs was no doubt a lot of work for the Nazca people. What purpose do you think these features served for the people who made them?

2. Regs composed of lag deposits and regs composed of desert pavement look alike on the surface. If you were in a desert and standing on a reg, what evidence would you look for to determine which process formed that particular reg?

3. What would happen to the great Saharan and Arabian ergs if the monsoon were to return to the interior desert, bringing summer rainfall?

4. What do you think would happen to the Aral Sea ecosystems and local economies if water diversions were stopped and the sea was allowed to refill?

Test Yourself

Take this quiz to test your chapter knowledge.

1. **True or false?** All deserts are arid.

2. **True or false?** Water is the most important agent of erosion in deserts.

3. **True or false?** Desertification means to turn to desert.

4. **True or false?** Barchan dunes form where the prevailing wind shifts direction throughout the year.

5. **Multiple choice:** Which of the following is a result of fluvial deposition?
   a. Bajadas
   b. Ergs
   c. Inselbergs
   d. Sand dunes

6. **Multiple choice:** Which of the following desert landscapes is most likely to have been produced on an uplifted plateau?
   a. Basin-and-range topography
   b. Regs
   c. Mesa-and-butte terrain
   d. Inselbergs

7. **Multiple choice:** Rifting results in which of the following landscapes?
   a. Badlands
   b. Mesa-and-butte terrain
   c. Basin-and-range topography
   d. Ergs

8. **Multiple choice:** Which of the following is not a factor that determines the type of sand dunes that will form?
   a. The amount of sand available
   b. The type of sand available
   c. The direction of the wind
   d. The strength of the wind

9. **Fill in the blank:** A _____ is a bowl-shaped depression formed in sand where the wind velocity increases.

10. **Fill in the blank:** The _____ is the leeward side of a sand dune where sand settles at the angle of repose.

Picture This. YOUR TURN

Desert Landform Identification

Fill in the blanks on the diagram, using each of the following terms only once.

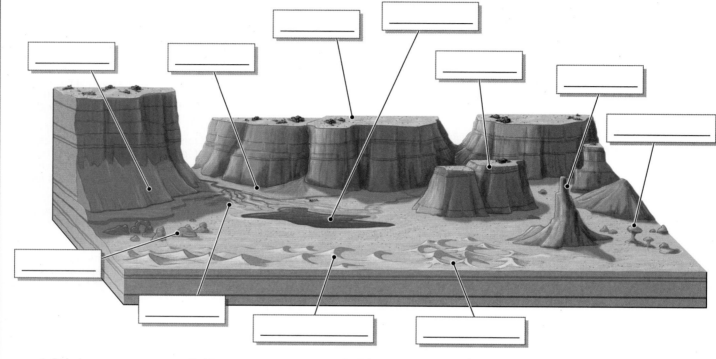

1. Bajada
2. Barchan dunes
3. Butte
4. Chimney
5. Mesa
6. Pedestal rock
7. Playa lake
8. Star dunes
9. Talus apron
10. Yardang
11. Wash

Further Reading

1. Abbey, Edward. *Desert Solitaire*. New York: McGraw-Hill, 1968.

2. Norris, Richard D., et al. "Sliding Rocks on Racetrack Playa, Death Valley National Park: First Observation of Rocks in Motion." *PLOS ONE*. August 27, 2014. DOI: 10.1371/journal. pone.0105948

3. Whitley, David. *Introduction to Rock Art Research*. 2nd ed. Walnut Grove, CA: Left Coast Press, 2011.

Answers to Living Physical Geography Questions

1. **What are prehistoric petroglyphs and why were they made?** Petroglyphs were a part of prehistoric desert cultures worldwide. The purpose of most of them is still unknown.

2. **How do sand dunes sing?** In some sand dunes, sand particles vibrate as they move, creating a "singing" sound.

3. **What is a sand sea?** A sand sea, or erg, is a desert region larger than 125 km^2 where sand covers at least 20% of the desert floor. Most ergs are in the northern Sahara.

4. **Why has the Aral Sea nearly disappeared?** Water diversions from the rivers flowing into the Aral Sea, mainly for growing cotton, shrank the sea to 10% of its former extent.

19 THE WORK OF WAVES: Coastal Landforms

Chapter Outline

These spherical boulders, called the *Moeraki Boulders*, lie on the beach near Hampden, South Island, New Zealand. The boulders are about 60 million years old and as large as 2 m (6.5 ft) across. They were embedded in sedimentary rocks on a coastal cliff until erosion freed them and they tumbled to the beach. *(Ben Pipe/Getty Images)*

LIVING PHYSICAL GEOGRAPHY

➤ What causes the tides?

➤ What are rip currents and why are they deadly?

➤ Why are some beaches black?

➤ Why is the sand on many beaches artificial?

To learn more about rocky shoreline erosion, turn to Section 19.2.

THE BIG PICTURE *Coastal beaches and rocky shores are shaped by wave energy. Human activities have contributed to the loss of sand from beaches through erosion.*

LEARNING GOALS *After reading this chapter, you will be able to:*

19.1 ◎ Discuss the role of tides and wave energy in coastal landform development.

19.2 ◎ Describe landforms on beaches and rocky coasts and explain how they form.

19.3 ◎ Assess and evaluate the practice of restoring eroded beaches by artificial replenishment of sand.

THE HUMAN SPHERE: Mavericks

FOR MOST OF THE YEAR, **the** world's professional-class surfers are scattered around the globe, working to hone their surfing skills. Once a year, between January and March, 24 preselected surfers may get the phone call telling them that the Mavericks Invitational surf competition is about to begin. They will have 24 hours to travel to Half Moon Bay, in Northern California, where they will surf some of Earth's largest and most powerful waves. The waves at Mavericks routinely reach heights of 10 m (33 ft), and waves as high as a six-story building, 24 m (80 ft), have been witnessed there **(Figure 19.1)**. These high coastal waves are the result of swells, waves that are generated in the open ocean. As the swells approach the coast, they encounter a gradually sloping seafloor at Mavericks that channels their energy into a focused area.

The waves of the ocean possess a considerable amount of energy, and they never rest. This chapter explores the ways in which wave energy shapes the coast and the landforms that result from it. Because waves are generated by wind, and wind is generated by solar heating, the erosional energy of coastal waves is ultimately derived from the Sun.

We begin this chapter by exploring tides, waves, and coastal currents. We next examine sandy and rocky shores and the landforms associated with each. Finally, we examine the problem of maintaining sand at popular coastal beaches.

FIGURE **19.1** **Riding wave energy.** *A surfer rides a large wave at the Mavericks Invitational in Northern California in 2012. (© Ezra Shaw/Getty Images)*

CA   NV

Half Moon
Bay

34° N

PACIFIC
OCEAN   120° W

19.1 Coastal Processes: Tides, Waves, and Longshore Currents

◎ Discuss the role of tides and wave energy in coastal landform development.

We begin our exploration of coastal landforms by examining the daily sea-level changes caused by tides. **Tides are important to the study of coastal processes because they allow the energy of waves to influence a greater vertical range of coastline than it would otherwise.**

Tidal Rhythms

If you have ever visited the ocean, you may have noticed the effects of tides. **Tides** are the rise and fall of sea level caused by the gravitational effects of the Moon and the Sun. At low tide, you may have seen algae and barnacles clinging to slippery rocks. At high tide, these organisms are submerged.

In a classical sense taken from astronomy, "tides" are distortions of the shape of one body by the gravitational pull of another body. The gravitational pull of the Moon and the Sun distorts Earth's atmosphere, its oceans, and the body of the planet itself. For our purposes, however, the term "tide" will be used to refer to the twice-daily changes of sea level in coastal areas.

Tides are caused by the *tide-generating force* created by the gravitational pull of the Moon and Sun as well as by the centrifugal force created by Earth's and the Moon's revolution around a common center of mass within the Sun-Earth-Moon system. These forces create two bulges of seawater on Earth. The tidal bulge beneath the Moon is larger than the one on the opposite side of the planet **(Figure 19.2)**.

> What causes the tides?*

The tide-generating force of the Moon is greater than that of the Sun because the Sun is nearly 400 times farther away from Earth than the Moon. *Lunar tides*, those caused by the Moon, are roughly twice as high as *solar tides*, those caused by the Sun.

Sometimes, tides are unusually high or low. When Earth, the Moon, and the Sun are aligned along the same axis, the tide-generating forces of the Moon and the Sun act together, and high tides called *spring tides* result. When the Moon is positioned at a right angle between Earth and the Sun, the Moon's pull acts perpendicularly to the Sun's, creating a lower *neap tide* **(Figure 19.3 on page 610)**. Other factors, such as windiness and how close the Moon is to Earth, also influence tide levels.

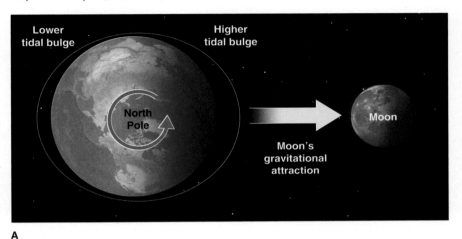

FIGURE 19.2 **Ocean tides.** *(A) Earth's two tidal bulges are greatly exaggerated here to be visible. The tidal bulge nearest the Moon is the larger of the two. Any location on Earth will pass through a tidal bulge approximately every 12 hours. (B) This tide graph shows the twice-daily tidal rhythm (in meters) in relation to the mean level of low water (MLLW) near Kodiak Island, Alaska, from July 28 to July 30, 2013.*

A

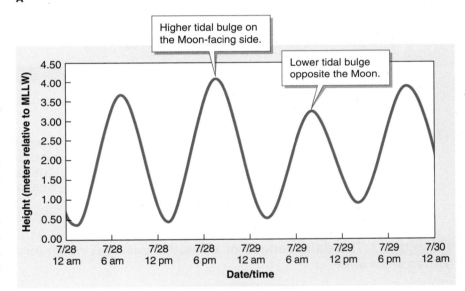

B

Because of Earth's rotation on its axis and the revolution of the Moon around Earth, the daily rhythm of the tides runs on a schedule of approximately 24 hours and 50 minutes. This means that for 6 hours and 13 minutes, the tide is coming in as a *flood tide*, and for the next 6 hours and 13 minutes the tide is going out as an *ebb tide*. This pattern repeats twice daily on most coastlines. *High tide* occurs when the flood tide has peaked, and *low tide* occurs when the ebb tide is at its lowest. The exposed shore area below the high-tide line is called the *intertidal zone*.

tide
The rise and fall of sea level caused by the gravitational effects of the Moon and the Sun.

FIGURE 19.3 **Spring and neap tides.** *The highest tides, called spring tides, occur when Earth, the Sun, and the Moon are aligned along the same axis (shown as a dotted line). Spring tides occur during a full moon or during a new moon. The lowest tides, called neap tides, occur when the Moon is in half-phase and at a right angle to the line between Earth and the Sun.*

Video
Tides
http://qrs.ly/tz4baj9

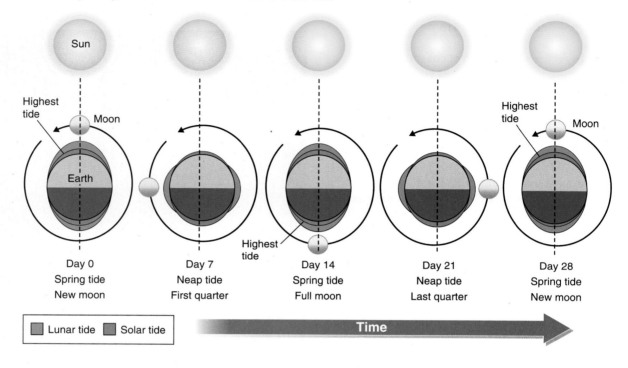

If Earth's surface were perfectly smooth, without wind, and covered only with water, the *tidal range*—the difference between low tide and high tide levels—would be the same for any given latitude at all locations. However, differences in bathymetry, windiness, and the positions and shapes of coastlines affect the height of tides and create uneven tidal ranges across the oceans **(Figure 19.4)**.

In some regions, tides are barely noticeable, while in others, their effects dominate the coastline. The average tidal range on Earth is 100 cm (36 in). The world's greatest tidal range occurs in the Bay of Fundy in eastern Canada **(Figure 19.5)**, where the maximum tidal range is 16.8 m (55 ft).

Coastal Waves

Waves result as wind energy is transferred to the ocean's surface by friction. If there were no wind, the oceans would be glassy smooth. Only infrequent wave-generating forces, such as earthquakes (see The Human Sphere in Chapter 14) and coastal landslides, would make waves.

As waves move across the surface of the open ocean, they give the appearance that the water is flowing, but that is not the case. A floating object on the ocean's surface, such as a bottle, moves in a circular pattern as the waves pass beneath it. The bottle does not move forward horizontally with the waves. Individual water molecules, like the bottle, trace a circular path. Waves that cause this circular movement are called **waves of oscillation**.

FIGURE 19.4 **The daily ranges of tides.** *This map shows average daily tidal ranges worldwide.*

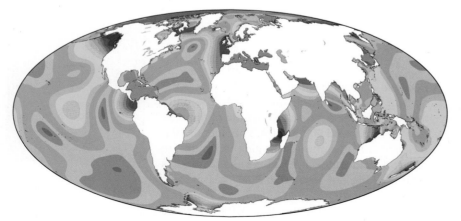

Average daily tidal range							
0	40	80	120	160	200	240	cm
0	16	32	47	63	79	94	in.

FIGURE **19.5** **The world's greatest tidal range.** *The unusually high tides in the Bay of Fundy are caused by the shape of the coastline. As water enters the bay, it is constricted and piles up in the narrow funnel of the bay. The inset photos show the same location at Hopewell Cape, in New Brunswick, at low tide (top) and at high tide (bottom). (Top, © Danita Delimont/Gallo Images/Getty Images; bottom: © Edward Kinsman/Photo Researchers/Getty Images)*

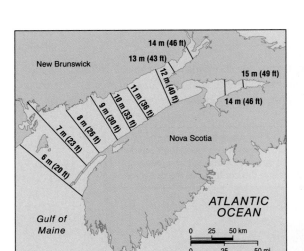

Because most waves are organized in long ridges, the rotating circles in a wave of oscillation are better pictured as connecting together to form long cylinders. The radius of the topmost cylinder at the surface is equal to the *wave height*. Waves are composed of a series of cylinders that are stacked vertically. With increasing depth, the diameter of the cylinders decreases. The movement of water ends at the *wave base*, at a depth equal to about three-quarters of the *wavelength* (the distance between wave crests) **(Figure 19.6)**.

In the open ocean, wave height depends on the speed of the wind, the duration of the wind, and the **fetch**: the distance of open water over which the

FIGURE **19.6** **GEO-GRAPHIC: Wave features.** *All wave motion ceases at the wave base. In shallow water, the wave base encounters the seafloor, creating waves of translation that form breakers.*

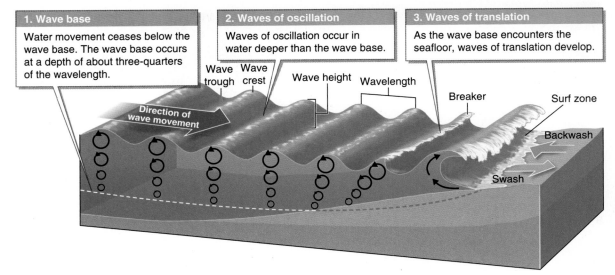

1. Wave base
Water movement ceases below the wave base. The wave base occurs at a depth of about three-quarters of the wavelength.

2. Waves of oscillation
Waves of oscillation occur in water deeper than the wave base.

3. Waves of translation
As the wave base encounters the seafloor, waves of translation develop.

Wave trough Wave crest Wave height Wavelength

Direction of wave movement

Breaker Surf zone Backwash Swash

waves of oscillation
Waves in which water moves in a circular path.

fetch
The distance of open water over which wind blows.

wave of translation
A wave in which water moves forward in the direction of wave movement.

swash
The rush of water up a beach following the collapse of a breaker.

backwash
The flow of water from breakers down the slope of a beach back toward the ocean.

wave refraction
The process in which waves approaching the shoreline bend and maintain a nearly parallel orientation to the shore.

wind blows. Slow winds over a short fetch, such as an inland lake, produce small waves. Fast and sustained winds blowing over the open ocean with a long fetch generate large waves with long wavelengths, called *swells*. Swells, which are generated only in the open ocean, can have wave heights of 2 to 10 m (6 to 33 ft) or more and wavelengths of 40 to 500 m (130 to 1,600 ft) or more.

As a wave approaches the coastline, the wave base comes in contact with the seafloor (see Figure 19.6). As the wave continues into shallower water, friction with the seafloor slows the base more than the top and as a result the wave crest grows higher. The wave crest also travels faster than the wave base, causing the wave to shear in an elliptical motion. In this type of wave, called a

FIGURE **19.7** **Wave refraction.** *(A) As a wave approaches the shoreline at an angle, it refracts around the contours of the coastline. (B) At Wharton Beach, an embayment on the southern coast of Western Australia, the waves are roughly parallel to the crescent-shaped shoreline. (B. Photo: mark_ncompass (Panoramio user #238632))*

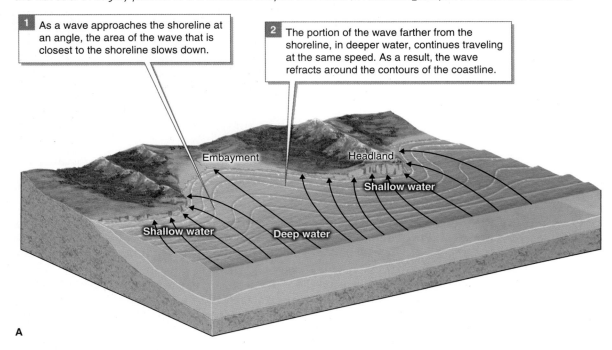

1 As a wave approaches the shoreline at an angle, the area of the wave that is closest to the shoreline slows down.

2 The portion of the wave farther from the shoreline, in deeper water, continues traveling at the same speed. As a result, the wave refracts around the contours of the coastline.

Embayment

Headland

Shallow water

Shallow water

Deep water

A

B

wave of translation, water does move forward horizontally in the direction of wave movement. Eventually, the wave crest collapses, forming a *breaker* (see Figure 19.6 on page 611).

On a beach, breakers form in the *surf zone*. As breakers collapse on themselves in their forward momentum, they create a **swash**: a rush of water up a beach. The slope of the beach will limit how far the swash can travel up the beach. The water flows back down the beach as **backwash** and returns to the ocean.

As waves approach the shoreline, they bend so that their orientation is roughly parallel to the shoreline. This process is called **wave refraction**. Even where the coast is uneven, with rocky prominences called **headlands** and concave sandy beaches called **embayments**, waves refract around the headlands and maintain a mostly parallel approach to the shoreline **(Figure 19.7)**.

Coastal Currents

Although wave refraction causes waves to approach a beach nearly parallel to the shoreline, most wash ashore at a slight angle. This angled approach of waves creates a **longshore current**, which flows parallel to the beach in the direction of wave movement. **Longshore drift** is the movement of sediment down the length of the beach in the direction of wave movement **(Figure 19.8)**. The longshore current and longshore drift transport sand, both on the beach and beneath the water in the surf zone. The surface layers of the sand are always moving down the length of the shore.

> What are rip currents and why are they deadly?

Picture This on page 614 discusses **rip currents**, short-lived jets of water that form as backwash from breakers flows back into the sea.

headland
A rocky prominence of coastal land.

embayment
A concave sandy beach between headlands.

longshore current
A current that flows parallel to the beach in the direction of wave movement.

longshore drift
The process by which sediment on a beach is moved down the length of the beach in the direction of wave movement.

rip current
A short-lived jet of backwash formed as water from breakers flows back into the sea.

FIGURE 19.8 **Longshore current and longshore drift.** *(A) Wave swash moves up the beach at an angle, but gravity pulls the backwash straight down the slope of the beach. As a result, sand follows a zigzag path down the beach in the process of longshore drift. (B) Along the Chandeleur Islands, off the coast of Louisiana, longshore current and longshore drift result as incoming waves approach the beach at an angle. The resulting movement of sand gradually lengthens the island. (B. © Annie Griffiths/National Geographic/Getty Images)*

Animation
Longshore drift
http://qrs.ly/1e4baj6

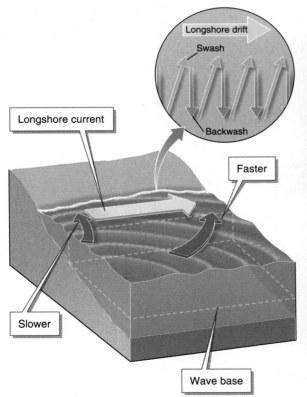

A

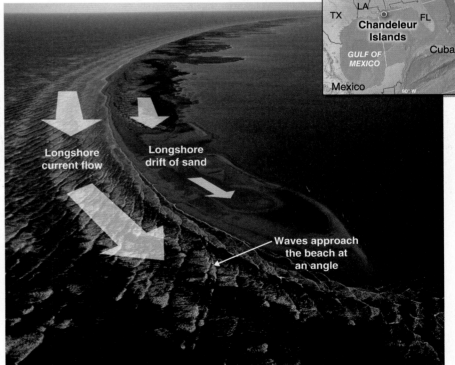

B

Picture This

(© Ron Niebrugge/Alamy)

Rip Currents

Hanakapi'ai Beach, on the island of Kaua'i, is marked with a sign warning visitors to avoid the water due to rip currents. An ominous running tally of fatalities is marked on the sign.

Rip currents are caused when breakers converge and the backwash flows into the sea at a focused point, usually where a trench occurs between submerged sandbars. Rip currents can form at any time, but they are most likely to form when wave heights are at a maximum. They range in width from a few meters to hundreds of meters. Some rip currents disappear at the breakers, but others may continue for hundreds of meters beyond the surf zone.

Rip currents do not pull people underwater. Instead, they carry people away from shore. Even the strongest swimmers may drown when they become too exhausted to swim back to safety. In the United States, about 150 people drown in rip currents each year. If you are caught in a rip current, the best strategy is to swim parallel to the beach to get out of the current, rather than trying to fight it by swimming toward the beach.

Consider This

1. What causes a rip current?

2. What is the best thing to do if caught in one?

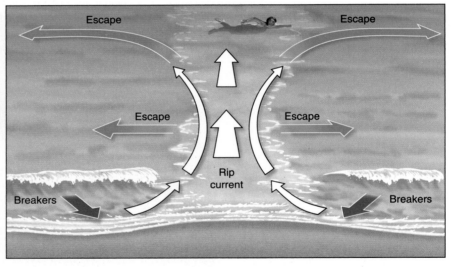

19.2 Coastal Landforms: Beaches and Rocky Coasts

◎ Describe landforms on beaches and rocky coasts and explain how they form.

The tectonic setting plays an important role in determining what kind of shoreline forms in any given region. Plate movements can lift or lower Earth's crust. At active continental margins near convergent plate boundaries (see Section 12.3), the converging plates compress the crust and raise it. Similarly, the weight of sediments or ice sheets (see Section 6.2) can depress the crust; if this weight is removed, the crust will rebound upward through isostasy. **Isostasy** is the gravitational equilibrium between the lithosphere and the support of the asthenosphere below.

When a coastline lifts to higher elevation, an emergent coast forms. An **emergent coast** is one where sea level is dropping or the land is rising.

isostasy
The gravitational equilibrium between the lithosphere and the support of the asthenosphere below.

emergent coast
A coast where sea level is dropping or the land is rising.

Emergent coasts are dominated by erosional landforms such as steep cliffs and rocky shorelines. The west coasts of North and South America, for example, are tectonically active emergent coasts with rocky shorelines. The emergent coast of eastern Canada is rising because the weight of the Laurentide ice sheet is gone.

Most plate boundaries do not coincide with continental margins. Instead, a single lithospheric plate holds both a continent and a *coastal plain* that extends beneath the sea as a flat, gently sloping continental shelf (see Section 10.1). These passive continental margins are often **submergent coasts**, where the land surface is subsiding. **Submergent coasts are dominated by depositional landforms such as beaches and coastal wetlands.** The southeastern United States and Gulf Coast, for example, have gentle slopes with sandy beaches and coastal wetlands.

Sea level can also change without raising or lowering of the lithosphere. About 15,000 years ago, during the most recent glacial period, sea level was 85 m (280 ft) lower than it is today because so much water was frozen on land in ice sheets (see Section 6.2). When the glacial period ended, the meltwater from these ice sheets raised sea level by 85 m. Change in global sea level as a result of change in the amount of water in the oceans is called **eustasy**.

Either way, an emergent coast occurs where sea level falls (through eustasy) or where the coast is lifted (through isostasy). Likewise, a submergent coast occurs where sea level rises (eustasy) or where the coast sinks (isostasy).

Other important factors that control the morphology of a coast are the amount of wave energy reaching it, the presence of biogenic structures such as coral reefs, the tidal range, and the amount and type of sediment that is available. **Table 19.1** groups coasts into five main categories. In this section, we discuss two of the most common types of coasts: beaches and rocky coasts.

submergent coast
A coast where sea level is rising or the land is sinking.

eustasy
A change in global sea level as a result of change in the amount of water in the oceans.

TABLE 19.1 Types of Coasts

TYPE OF COAST	DESCRIPTION	TEXT REFERENCE
1. Depositional coasts: Beaches and deltas		
Beach	Sand-dominated coast	Section 19.2
Barrier island	Sand-dominated coast, with a water body separating the island from the mainland	Section 19.2
Delta	Formed at river mouths	Section 16.3
2. Erosional coasts: Rocky shorelines		
Bedrock	Found anywhere bedrock is exposed to coastal wave energy	Section 19.2
Limestone karst	Various settings; common in Caribbean islands and in Croatia	Section 15.2
Lava flow	Various settings; found on Hawai'i	Section 12.4
3. Organic coasts		
Coral reef	Dominated by living reefs; restricted to the tropics and subtropics	Section 10.2
Mangrove	Dominated by mangroves; restricted to the tropics and subtropics	Section 10.2
Estuary	Formed where freshwater meets salt water at river mouths	Section 10.2
Anthropogenic	Includes any coast that has undergone significant modification by human activities	Chapter 10
4. Flooded coasts		
Ria	Drowned V-shaped river valley; found at the mouths of rivers and where estuaries form	Section 10.2
Fjord	Drowned U-shaped glacial valley at high latitudes	Section 17.3
5. Ice coasts		
Glaciers and ice shelves	Generally found at latitudes higher than 55 degrees	Chapter 17
Glacial sediments	Found where continental ice sheets deposited glacial sediments; common in northeastern Canada and northern British Isles	Section 17.4

FIGURE 19.9 **Beach zones.**

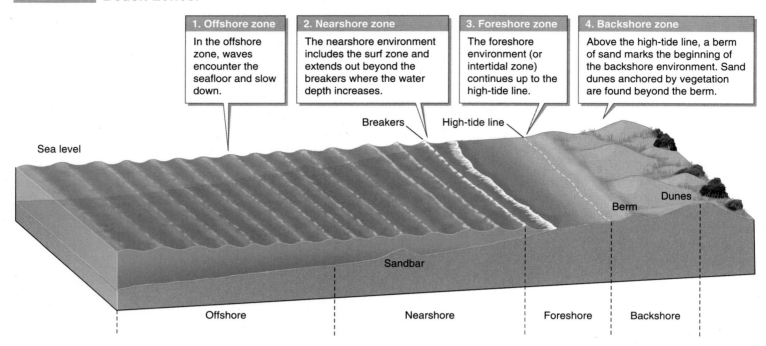

1. Offshore zone
In the offshore zone, waves encounter the seafloor and slow down.

2. Nearshore zone
The nearshore environment includes the surf zone and extends out beyond the breakers where the water depth increases.

3. Foreshore zone
The foreshore environment (or intertidal zone) continues up to the high-tide line.

4. Backshore zone
Above the high-tide line, a berm of sand marks the beginning of the backshore environment. Sand dunes anchored by vegetation are found beyond the berm.

Breakers   High-tide line

Sea level

Dunes

Berm

Sandbar

Offshore   Nearshore   Foreshore   Backshore

Beaches

Beaches consist of an *offshore zone, nearshore zone, foreshore zone* (or intertidal zone), and *backshore zone,* as illustrated in **Figure 19.9**. Waves that break on the gentle slope of a beach have less energy than those that break on a rocky coast. As waves move toward the beach, the base of each wave makes contact with the seafloor in the nearshore zone. As a result, the wave's energy is reduced as it works to transport sediments on the seafloor before encountering the foreshore zone.

> Why are some beaches black?

Beaches vary in the composition of their sediments, depending on the source of the sediments. Tan and beige beaches of quartz are the most common because quartz is particularly resistant to weathering and erosion and persists for a long time (see Section 15.1). Not all beaches are composed of quartz sand, however. Weathering and erosion of coral reefs results in brilliant white beaches consisting of broken fragments of reef- and shell-building organisms **(Figure 19.10A)**. Many volcanically active areas have black beaches made of basalt particles **(Figure 19.10B)**.

Nor are all beaches composed of sand. Where weathering and mass movement of nearby cliff faces are occurring, larger particles, such as gravel or cobbles, will form a **shingle beach (Figure 19.10C)**.

shingle beach
A beach composed of sediment particles larger than sand, such as gravel or cobbles.

sandspit
An elongated dry bar of sand that extends from a beach into the water; usually parallel with the shore.

Beach Landforms

Beaches are like rivers of sediment. **Sediment, usually sand, is continually entering the beach from the "upstream" end, and it is continually leaving the beach on the "downstream" end.** Longshore drift transports sediments down the length of the beach. Only the topmost meter or so of sand actively moves. Deeper layers move only during strong storms, or not at all. Typically, sand accumulates in summer, and the high waves of winter storms bring net erosion to the beach as they move the sand just offshore. Through time, most beaches are maintained by an equilibrium between erosion and deposition of sand. **Figure 19.11** on page 618 shows four beach landforms commonly created by the movement of sand:

- *Coastal sand dunes* are formed where prevailing winds blow sand inland. Vegetation traps the sand, allowing it to accumulate into dune formations. Through time, many coastal sand dunes become stabilized by vegetation through the process of ecological succession (see Section 7.4).

- A **sandspit** is an elongated dry bar of sand that extends from a beach out into the water, usually parallel with the shore.

FIGURE 19.10 **Three kinds of beaches.** *(A) The coral reefs surrounding the Galápagos Islands create white beaches composed of broken fragments of the reefs. (B) The beaches on Bioko Island in Equatorial Guinea are composed of black sand because the parent material is basalt. (C) Beaches that are composed of gravel, pebbles, cobbles, or some combination of these materials are called shingle beaches. This shingle beach with cobbles is located in Pembrokeshire, Wales. (A. © Ralph Lee Hopkins/National Geographic/Getty Images; B. © Tim Laman/National Geographic/Getty Images; C. © Tony Craddock/Science Source)*

A

B

C

- A **baymouth bar** is an unbroken sandspit that forms across the mouth of a river or an estuary. Baymouth bars create an enclosed brackish-water lagoon behind them and are formed by longshore drift.

- A **tombolo** is formed when a sandspit connects an island to the mainland. Sandspits, baymouth bars, and tombolos are all formed by longshore drift.

Another geographically widespread type of depositional coastal landform is a **barrier island**: an offshore sandbar that runs parallel to the coast. Worldwide, 2,149 barrier islands are recognized. These islands total more than 20,000 km (12,400 mi) in length, representing some 10% of all shorelines on Earth. Antarctica is the only continent without barrier islands. They range in size from a few meters wide and less than a kilometer in length, to several hundred meters wide and hundreds of

baymouth bar
A continuous sandspit formed by longshore drift that creates a lagoon of brackish water behind it.

tombolo
A landform consisting of an island and a sandspit that connects it to the mainland.

barrier island
An offshore sandbar that runs parallel to the coast.

FIGURE 19.11 **GEO-GRAPHIC:** **Beach landforms.** *(Top left, © Ben Visbeek; top right, Emich Szabolcs, www.emich.hu; bottom left, © Sakis Papadopoulos/Robert Harding World Imagery/Alamy; bottom right, © David Wall/Alamy)*

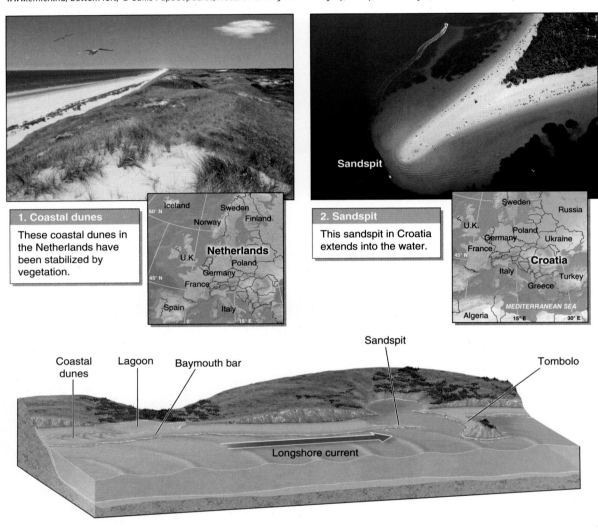

1. Coastal dunes
These coastal dunes in the Netherlands have been stabilized by vegetation.

2. Sandspit
This sandspit in Croatia extends into the water.

3. Baymouth bar
This baymouth bar encloses a lagoon in Dalyan, Turkey.

4. Tombolo
Mount Maunganui and the beach that connects it to North Island, New Zealand, form a tombolo.

kilometers in length. They are separated from the mainland by sounds, bays, estuaries, and lagoons (see Section 10.1).

Barrier-island formation requires an uninterrupted supply of sand, tectonically stable and flat coastal topography, and sufficient wave energy for longshore transport of sand. **Figure 19.12** provides several examples of barrier islands.

Barrier islands are particularly important to coastal communities because they absorb a significant amount of storm surge and wave energy from tropical cyclones (see Section 5.3). In so doing, they protect the mainland shoreline from the full force of storms.

FIGURE 19.12 **Barrier islands.** *(A) Some barrier islands are located far from the coast. This satellite image shows the barrier islands that make up the Outer Banks of North Carolina. Pamlico Sound is a lagoon created by these barrier islands. (B) This is an undeveloped barrier island located near Tampico, Mexico. (C) Ocean City, Maryland (shown here) is built on a barrier island. (A. EROS Center, U.S. Geological Survey; B. © Jim Wark/airphotona.com; C. © Chris Parypa/Alamy)*

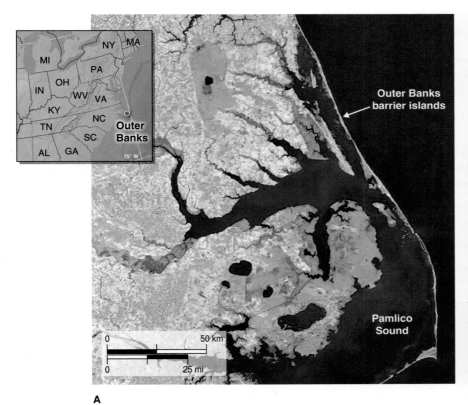

A

B

C

groin
A linear structure of concrete or stone that extends from a beach into the water, designed to slow the erosion of sand.

Human Modification of Beaches

Beaches can lose sand or gain sand overnight during powerful storms that pound them with wave energy. Sand not only drifts "downstream" to other coastal areas, but it also can be removed from the coastal system if it is carried to deeper waters.

Over time, longshore drift will return sand to the beach, assuming there is an adequate supply of sand feeding into the system from upstream. The sand will not return to a beach, however, if there is an inadequate supply of sand. Recall from Section 15.1 that sand is transported to the coast by streams. Streams flowing into artificial reservoirs drop their sediments in the inland reservoir rather than on the coast. As a result, **reservoirs become sediment traps that reduce the volume of sand flowing down a coast**, as diagrammed in **Figure 19.13**.

When streams do not supply a steady input of sediment, beaches become sediment starved, and their sand is lost to erosion. By some es-

timates, as much as 90% of the beaches in the United States are experiencing net erosion. These losses of sand present problems because beaches protect coastal development from the impact of storm energy, support local coastal economies, and provide habitat for many organisms, including shorebirds and nesting sea turtles. According to the Federal Emergency Management Agency (FEMA), beach erosion due to sea-level rise (see Section 17.5) and inland sediment traps is likely to destroy 25% of houses within 150 m (500 ft) of the coast in the United States in the next 60 years.

Given the extent of the problem of sand loss and the economic importance of beaches, scientists have developed several means of studying sediment flow on beaches so as to better manage beaches and reduce erosion **(Figure 19.14)**.

One method commonly employed to slow the erosion of sand is the use of groins. A **groin** is a linear structure made of concrete or stone that

FIGURE 19.13 GEO-GRAPHIC: Beach sediment starvation.

Coastal beaches are fed sand by streams. Reservoirs behind dams trap sediment, potentially diminishing the sand supply for coastal beaches.

Animation
Sand starvation
http://qrs.ly/d94baj5

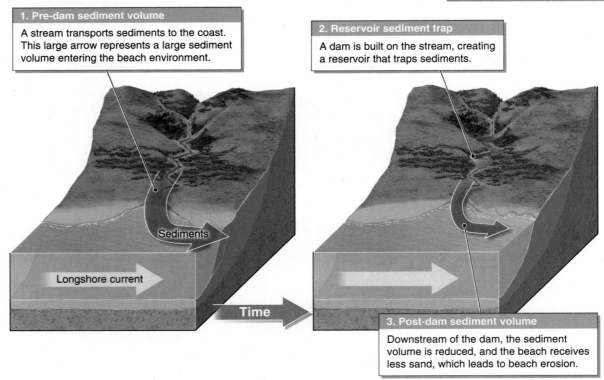

1. Pre-dam sediment volume
A stream transports sediments to the coast. This large arrow represents a large sediment volume entering the beach environment.

2. Reservoir sediment trap
A dam is built on the stream, creating a reservoir that traps sediments.

Sediments

Longshore current

Time

3. Post-dam sediment volume
Downstream of the dam, the sediment volume is reduced, and the beach receives less sand, which leads to beach erosion.

FIGURE 19.14 **SCIENTIFIC INQUIRY:**

How do scientists study beach erosion?

Understanding sediment flow on a beach is central to efforts to reduce erosion and preserve the beach. This USGS project is monitoring Cape Hatteras Beach in North Carolina. The findings of this research can be applied to other beaches as well. (All photos, U.S. Geological Survey, Coastal and Marine Geology Program)

Nearshore instrumentation

Long metal pipes are driven deep into the sediments just offshore. Scientific instruments will be secured to the anchored pipes. The instruments will measure many variables, including water movement and sediment transport.

Radar

A radar system mounted on the berm measures the speed and direction of the longshore current.

Photography

A camera is mounted on the railing of Cape Hatteras Lighthouse to provide additional information about longshore current and wave behavior.

Dye tracer

A green dye is dropped into the ocean to trace water movement in the nearshore environment. Movement of the dye is tracked from the air.

Truck-mounted LIDAR and radar

This truck carries LIDAR and radar equipment that is used to map changing beach topography and bathymetry.

FIGURE 19.15 **Groins and jetties.** *(A) Artificial means of managing sand movement include jetties and groins. (B) A groin field slows the rate of sand loss, and jetties keep the harbor clear of sediments, near Arles, France. (B. Ausloos Henry/Prisma/age fotostock)*

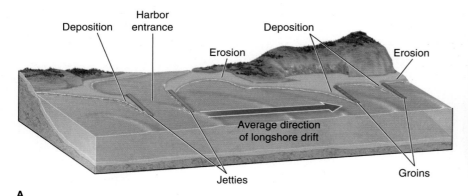

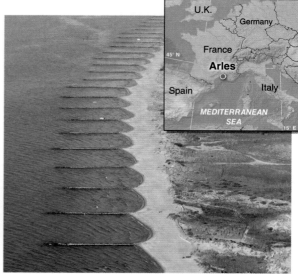

A

B

extends from a beach into the water **(Figure 19.15).** Sand moving down the beach will encounter the groin and accumulate against it. A series of groins in a row is called a *groin field*. Groin fields slow, but do not stop, the loss of sand from a beach.

One problem with the use of groins is that they are hard structures that mar the appearance and character of the beach. They also reduce the amount of sand transported downstream to other beaches, which, in turn, become sediment starved. This outcome can result in legal conflicts between beach landholders.

Jetties are artificial walls placed at the mouths of harbors, usually in pairs, to prevent sand from closing the harbor entrance (see Figure 19.15). Without

jetty
An artificial wall placed at the mouth of a harbor to prevent sand from closing the harbor entrance; usually placed in pairs.

seawall
An artificial hard structure designed to protect backshore environments from wave erosion during large storms.

jetties, frequent and costly dredging is required to keep a harbor deep and navigable by boats.

Seawalls are artificial hard structures designed to protect backshore environments from wave erosion during large storms. They are normally concrete or metal walls built parallel to the beach above the intertidal zone. Although they effectively reduce backshore erosion, they can increase the loss of beach sand by reflecting the energy of storm waves, which therefore erode more sand from the beach. They also prevent natural replenishment of backshore dunes with beach sand **(Figure 19.16).**

Another strategy for dealing with beach erosion is the artificial replenishment of sand. The pros and cons of this method are explored further in the Geographic Perspectives at the end of this chapter.

GEOGRAPHIC PERSPECTIVES

Rocky Coasts

Rocky coasts often have deeper water leading up to the coastline than beaches do. As a result, wave energy is not expended on the seafloor, as it is in most beach environments. Instead, the waves expend the full force of their energy against the rocks, which makes them a powerful and relentless force of erosion in these environments.

Water weighs 1 kg per liter (8.3 lb per gallon) and can be compressed very little. **The weight and force of crashing waves pry rocks apart as air and water are forced into even the tiniest joints.** In addition to headlands and embayments, described in Section 19.1, three other landforms are commonly found along rocky coastlines **(Figure 19.17):**

FIGURE 19.16 **A seawall in Honolulu, Hawai'i.** *This seawall has stabilized the position of the coastline, but at the expense of the beach. Seawalls usually accelerate beach erosion. (© Mark A. Johnson/Alamy)*

FIGURE 19.17 **GEO-GRAPHIC: Landforms of rocky coasts.** *(Clockwise from top left: © Christian Goupi/age fotostock/Getty Images; © Gareth Mccormack/Lonely Planet Images/Getty Images; © Christopher Biggs/Moment/Getty Images; © Reinhard Dirscherl/WaterFrame/age fotostock; © Skyscan Photolibrary/Alamy)*

Arch and sea stack

Arches are formed by differential erosion of a coastal cliff. When the arch collapses, a sea stack will form. Sea stacks are steep or vertical towers of rock separate from, but close to, a rocky coast. The coast pictured here is near Étretat, in northern France.

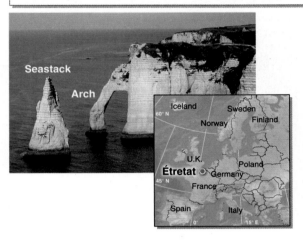

Headland and embayment

Headlands occur where resistant rock outcrops protrude into the sea. Embayments are concave shorelines where beaches form. This coastline is in County Kerry, Ireland.

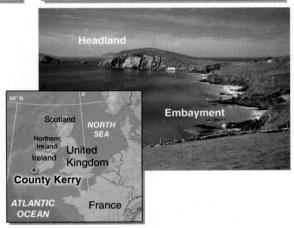

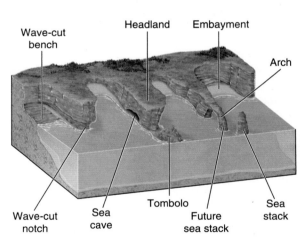

Sea cave

Sea caves, such as this one in Cabo San Lucas in Mexico, form where waves erode weaker areas of bedrock along joints.

Wave-cut notch

Weathering and erosion have formed a wave-cut notch at the base of this limestone island in the Republic of Palau.

Wave-cut bench

Wave-cut benches are flat coastal platforms created by erosion from waves and exposed at low tide. This wave-cut bench is near Bridgend in Southern Wales.

FIGURE 19.18 **Marine terrace.** *(A) This diagram illustrates the formation of a marine terrace by geologic uplift. Its formation is an example of isostasy because it results from uplift of the crust. (B) This photo shows a marine terrace on an emergent coastline in northern Scotland near the town of Durness. The flat terrace is a wave-cut bench that was exposed after the land was uplifted. (B. © Ian Gordon)*

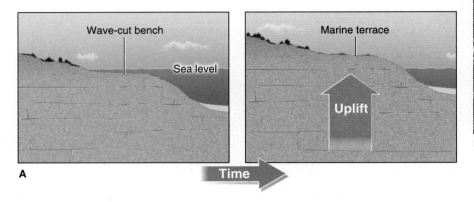

sea stack
A steep or vertical tower of rock separated from but near a rocky coastal cliff face.

wave-cut bench
A flat coastal platform resulting from wave erosion and exposed at low tide.

• A **sea stack** is a steep or vertical tower of rock separated from but near a rocky coastal cliff face.

• A **wave-cut bench** is a flat coastal platform resulting from wave erosion and exposed at low tide.

• A **wave-cut notch** is a notch formed at the base of a coastal cliff as a result of weathering and erosion.

On rocky shores, marine terraces indicate the presence of an emergent coastline. A **marine terrace** is a wave-cut bench that has been elevated above sea level (Figure 19.18). Either isostatic or eustatic changes can create a marine terrace.

Where a steep coastal cliff is composed of weak rock such as sandstone, the cliff may be undercut and break off in large pieces. Through time, the net result is that the cliff face retreats inland. The coastal cliffs in Big Sur, California, shown in Figure 19.19, have retreated at a rate of about 18 cm (7 in) per year over the last 50 years. Crunch the Numbers explores cliff retreat in Big Sur further.

FIGURE 19.19 **Cliff retreat.** *Highway 1 running through Big Sur is frequently closed as a result of landslides. In this March 2011 photo, a landslide followed several days of heavy rain that saturated and weakened the steep cliff. (© AP Photo/Monterey Herald, Orville Myers)*

Animation
Cliff retreat
http://qrs.ly/st4baj7

CRUNCH THE NUMBERS:
Calculating Cliff Retreat
Using 18 cm (7 in) as the average annual rate of cliff retreat in Big Sur, calculate how much total cliff retreat has occurred over the last 50 years.

To calculate the answer, multiply the annual rate of retreat by the number of years of retreat. If you use centimeters, divide by 100 to convert centimeters to meters. If you use inches, divide by 12 to get feet.

1. Answer in meters: _____

2. Answer in feet: _____

GEOGRAPHIC PERSPECTIVES
19.3 The Sisyphus Stone of Beach Nourishment

◎ Assess and evaluate the practice of restoring eroded beaches by artificial replenishment of sand.

Superstorm Sandy made landfall in New Jersey on October 22, 2012. About 94% of New Jersey's beaches and backshore dunes, as well as the structures on them, were damaged by the storm surge and waves that Sandy generated. Many of the beaches affected by the storm lost sand **(Figure 19.20)**. Some 60% of New Jersey's beaches were narrowed from 15 to 30 m (50 to 100 ft).

Beach erosion may occur in a single major storm event, but as we saw in Section 19.2, it may also be a gradual process in which sand is slowly lost over many years. There are three main options available to address the problem of beach erosion: (1) relocation of development away from the beachfront,

(2) hard structures such as the groins and seawalls discussed in Section 19.2, and (3) **beach nourishment** (or *beach replenishment*): the artificial replenishment of a beach with sand.

> Why is the sand on many beaches artificial?

Beach nourishment can be used after a single large storm, such as Sandy, has significantly eroded a beach. More often, however, beach nourishment is a routine maintenance process used to keep a beach from losing sand. The most common way to obtain sand is by offshore dredging. A large ship vacuums up sand from the seafloor and pumps it onshore through large metal pipes.

wave-cut notch
A notch formed at the base of a coastal cliff as a result of weathering and erosion.

marine terrace
A wave-cut bench that has been elevated above sea level.

beach nourishment
The artificial replenishment of a beach with sand.

FIGURE 19.20 **Superstorm Sandy accelerated beach erosion.** *Like many beaches on the East Coast, this section of beach in Mantoloking, New Jersey, was heavily eroded by the wave energy of Superstorm and many homes were destroyed. (Greg Thompson/U.S. Fish & Wildlife Service)*

FIGURE 19.21 **Beach nourishment.** *On this beach in Barcelona, Spain, sand is being siphoned off the seafloor by a ship and pumped to shore in a slurry of water. On the beach, bulldozers will shape the sand.* *(© Michael Weber/imageBROKER/ Alamy)*

Pipe leading to ship

Ship vacuuming up sand

Sand slurry pumped onto the beach

BAY OF BISCAY
France
Barcelona
Portugal
Spain
Morocco
Algeria
45° N

FIGURE 19.22 **Beach nourishment in Virginia.** *Virginia Beach has been nourished 49 times between 1951 and 2013. The sand seen here is a result of beach nourishment.* *(© Chris A. Crumley/Alamy)*

PA
MD
NJ
DE
VA
Virginia Beach
75° W

Bulldozers then push the sand into place **(Figure 19.21)**. Sand that is dredged off the coast and added to a beach is considered artificial sand.

The average lifetime for an artificial beach is five years. Sometimes, the sand lasts less than one year, and sometimes, it persists for a decade. On average, Virginia Beach, Virginia, has been nourished with sand every 1.3 years since 1951. The most recent beach nourishment, in 2013, cost taxpayers $9 million **(Figure 19.22)**.

As we have seen in this chapter, beaches are spatially dynamic landforms. Human activities have changed the dynamics of sand movement along coastlines, such that net erosion is now more common than net deposition for many beaches worldwide. Beach nourishment resets the clock on beach erosion by only a few years—it does not address the underlying problem.

Proponents of beach nourishment argue that just as the nation's roads and bridges must be maintained, so must the nation's beaches. Beaches are a public asset and an important part of the national economy. The U.S. Army Corps of Engineers oversees beach nourishment projects paid for by the federal government. The Corps sees beach nourishment as beach maintenance for the common good: The beaches have sand, and the hotels have tourists. The livelihoods of many people depend on vacationers attracted to beaches. The Corps estimates that it has saved $443 million in storm-related damages to hotels in Virginia Beach alone during the last decade.

Opponents of the practice claim that beach nourishment is an exercise in futility, a Sisyphean task. In Greek mythology, King Sisyphus was made to roll a huge stone up a hill repeatedly for eternity. Just as he was nearly at the top of the hill, the stone would slip and roll back down again, and he would then have to start over. By some estimates, the cost of maintaining beaches in the United States with beach nourishment will be about $6 billion per year by 2020. By the end of the century, the total costs could approach $90 billion. Given its costs, and given that it is only a temporary remedy, is beach nourishment a viable long-term strategy to address the problem of beach erosion?

At present, the answer appears to be yes. According to the Atlantic States Marine Fisheries Commission, the practice will increase in the coming decades. By 2050, southeastern Florida will have completed 100 beach nourishment projects and moved a total of 100 million cubic yards of sand. Many major tourist beaches around the world are experiencing erosion, including beaches in Australia, Hawai'i, Hong Kong, and Cancún, Mexico. All of them are relying on beach nourishment to maintain their beaches and keep the tourists coming.

CHAPTER 19 Exploring with ◎ Google Earth

To complete these problems, first read the chapter. When you are finished, go to LaunchPad and open the Exploring with Google Earth file for this chapter. Click on the "Workbook Problems" folder to "fly" to each of the problems listed below and answer the questions. Be sure to keep your "Borders and Labels" layer activated. Refer to Appendix 4 if you need help using Google Earth.

PROBLEM 19.1 These artificial structures near Venice, Italy, extend from the mouth of the harbor.

1. What are these artificial structures called?
   a. Groins
   b. Jetties
   c. Seawalls
   d. Headlands

2. What is their purpose?
   a. To keep the harbor channel open
   b. To reduce beach erosion
   c. To prevent inland flooding
   d. To protect against storms

PROBLEM 19.2 These artificial structures run down the length of the beach on Lido, an island near Venice, Italy.

1. What are these artificial structures called?
   a. Groins
   b. Jetties
   c. Seawalls
   d. Headlands

2. What is their purpose?
   a. To keep the harbor channel open
   b. To reduce beach erosion
   c. To prevent inland flooding
   d. To protect against storms

PROBLEM 19.3 These natural landforms consist of islands connected to the mainland.

1. What are these landforms called?
   a. Jetties
   b. Marine terraces
   c. Headlands
   d. Tombolos

2. What connects them to the mainland?
   a. A wave-cut notch
   b. A sandspit
   c. An embayment
   d. A butte

3. In what country is this placemark found?
   a. India
   b. Afghanistan
   c. Iran
   d. Pakistan

PROBLEM 19.4 This landform in Baja California, Mexico, is of a type that creates long, narrow beaches that sometimes seal off coastal bodies of water.

1. Does this landform seal off the water body behind it?
   a. Yes
   b. No

2. Based on your answer to question 1, what is the name of this landform?
   a. Sandspit
   b. Baymouth bar
   c. Transverse dune
   d. Embayment

3. About how long is this landform?
   a. 2 km
   b. 26 km
   c. 72 km
   d. 220 km

PROBLEM 19.5 These coastal water bodies are created by barrier islands or coral reefs.

1. What is the name of this type of water body?
   a. Saline lake
   b. Playa lake
   c. Longshore current
   d. Lagoon

2. Based on what you can see in Google Earth, does this water body contain fresh or salt water?
   a. Fresh
   b. Salt

3. If it is not already activated, activate your Photos layer and allow a few moments for icons for photos of this location to emerge. Click on a few of those icons. What large mammal uses this location as breeding grounds?
   a. Sea turtles
   b. Orcas
   c. Dolphins
   d. Gray whales

PROBLEM 19.6 This placemark falls on the rocky coast of Port Campbell National Park in southeastern Australia. Note that there are two red markers in the folder for this problem. Make sure both are activated.

1. What landform does this placemark pin?
   a. A barrier island
   b. A sea stack
   c. A tombolo
   d. A seawall

2. What landform does marker 1 pin?
   a. A jetty
   b. An embayment
   c. A headland
   d. A wave-cut bench

3. What landform does marker 2 pin?
   a. A jetty
   b. An embayment
   c. A headland
   d. A wave-cut bench

PROBLEM 19.7 To see the features at this placemark, you will have to tilt and pan around and carefully observe the surface of the coast. This island has a stair-step pattern notched into its coastline. (Hint: This island was tectonically lifted as recently as 120,000 years ago.)

1. What is the name of this feature?
   a. Marine terrace
   b. Headland
   c. Longshore current
   d. Embayment

2. About how many "stair-steps" can you see here?
   a. One
   b. Three
   c. About a dozen
   d. About thirty

3. Which one is the youngest?
a. The top one
b. The closest one to sea level

PROBLEM 19.8 This placemark lands on Dania Beach in Florida. In the lower left of your Google Earth screen, the date of the imagery is given when your cursor is over the Google Earth image. In this problem you will need to activate the Historical Imagery button in the top menu by clicking it. Drag the date-scroll button to December 30, 2005, to download the imagery for that date.

1. **Compared with the extent of Dania Beach after a beach nourishment project in February 2006, what is the relative state of the beach in the most recent image?**
   a. There is more sand.
   b. There is less sand.
   c. The beach has not changed during that time.

2. What do you see happening on the beach on February 28, 2006?
a. There is no beach.
b. The beach is far larger than it is today.
c. A beach nourishment project is under way.
d. People are sunbathing and relaxing.

PROBLEM 19.9 This placemark shows Dubai's "The World," an artificial chain of islands made of sand. The islands are intended to be developed commercially.

1. **Why is it unlikely that these islands will persist without artificial sand replenishment?**
   a. Because longshore currents will remove the sand
   b. Because tectonic subsidence will sink the islands
   c. Because seawalls will cause beach erosion
   d. Because the area is an emergent coastline

CHAPTER 19 **Study Guide**

Focus Points

19.1 Coastal Processes: Tides, Waves, and Longshore Currents

Tides: Tides increase the vertical range of wave erosion in coastal areas.

Waves: Ocean waves are generated by wind. As they approach the shore, they slow down, grow higher, and break on the shoreline.

Sediment transport: Wave energy creates longshore currents that move sediments along a coastline.

19.2 Coastal Landforms: Beaches and Rocky Coasts

Emergent coasts: Most emergent coasts have erosional landforms such as steep cliffs and rocky shorelines.

Submergent coasts: Most submergent coasts have depositional landforms such as beaches and wetlands.

Coast types: Beaches and rocky coasts are two common coast types.

Beach landforms: Beach landforms include coastal sand dunes, baymouth bars, sandspits, tombolos, and barrier islands.

Sand loss from beaches: Artificial reservoirs trap sediment transported by streams and prevent it from reaching coastal beaches downstream, starving the beaches of sand.

Solutions to sand loss: Groins, seawalls, and beach nourishment are solutions used to address sand loss on beaches.

Erosion of rocky coasts: The force and weight of crashing waves break rock apart, forming various rocky landforms. These landforms include sea stacks and arches, headlands and embayments, wave-cut notches, and wave-cut benches.

19.3 Geographic Perspectives: The Sisyphus Stone of Beach Nourishment

Beach erosion: Beach erosion is a widespread problem that threatens coastal development and economies.

Beach nourishment: Beach nourishment is a common response to beach erosion, but it has many drawbacks.

Key Terms

backwash, 613
barrier island, 617
baymouth bar, 617
beach nourishment, 625
embayment, 613
emergent coast, 614
eustasy, 615
fetch, 611

groin, 620
headland, 613
isostasy, 614
jetty, 622
longshore current, 613
longshore drift, 613
marine terrace, 624
rip current, 613

sandspit, 616
sea stack, 624
seawall, 622
shingle beach, 616
submergent coast, 615
swash, 613
tide, 609
tombolo, 617

wave-cut bench, 624
wave-cut notch, 624
wave of oscillation, 610
wave of translation, 613
wave refraction, 613

Concept Review

The Human Sphere: Mavericks

1. How do waves derive their energy from the Sun?

19.1 Coastal Processes: Tides, Waves, and Longshore Currents

2. What are tides? Why do they occur? Compare flood tides with ebb tides.

3. Compare neap tides with spring tides. Explain why each occurs.

4. How do waves form on the ocean's surface?

5. Compare a wave of oscillation with a wave of translation. Which one moves floating objects and water forward?

6. What factors contribute to wave height?

7. Why do waves approach nearly parallel to the coast?

8. What are longshore currents and longshore drift, and what causes them?

19.2 Coastal Landforms: Beaches and Rocky Coasts

9. What are emergent and submergent coastlines? What causes each? What landforms are most common in each?

10. What are eustasy and isostasy? What causes each?

11. What are the five major categories of coastlines?

12. Why are some beaches white and others black?

13. What is a shingle beach?

14. What is a barrier island?

15. How do inland dams and their reservoirs affect sediment transport to beaches?

16. How do scientists monitor movement of sand on a beach? What instruments do they use?

17. What physical structures are emplaced on a beach to slow the loss of sand?

18. What landforms are found along rocky coastlines?

19. What is a marine terrace? In what two ways do marine terraces form?

20. What is cliff retreat? What causes it?

19.3 Geographic Perspectives: The Sisyphus Stone of Beach Nourishment

21. Why is beach erosion a problem?

22. What is beach nourishment?

23. What are the underlying problems causing beach erosion around the world?

24. How well does beach nourishment address the problem of beach erosion? Give the pros and cons of this approach.

Critical-Thinking Questions

1. A recent study reports that ocean wave height is increasing worldwide. What effect, if any, do you think this increase will have on coastal erosion? Explain.

2. Think about the coast nearest to where you live. Is it an emergent or submergent coast? What information do you need to answer this question?

3. When was the last time you went to a beach? Do you think that beach has been nourished? How would you find out?

4. Critics argue that because places like Virginia Beach benefit from the tourism-related revenue, they should pay the entire bill for the cost of beach nourishment. The federal beach nourishment program has been criticized as "welfare for the rich," The critics believe that taxpayers from outside of the state where a beach is located, who will probably never visit that beach or benefit from it, should not pay for its maintenance. What is your opinion on this issue? How do you think beach erosion should be addressed?

Test Yourself

Take this quiz to test your chapter knowledge.

1. **True or false?** The lunar tide is higher than the solar tide.

2. **True or false?** Waves on the ocean form because of ocean currents.

3. **True or false?** Reservoirs supply sediments to coastal areas and help beaches grow.

4. **True or false?** Marine terraces form only on emergent coasts.

5. **True or false?** Seawalls are designed to protect sand on beaches.

6. **Multiple choice:** Which of the following is built to keep harbor entrances free of sediments?
   a. Groin   b. Jetty   c. Sea stack   d. Tombolo

7. **Multiple choice:** Which of the following is not a landform that results from deposition?
   a. Tombolo   c. Baymouth bar
   b. Sandspit   d. Headland

8. **Multiple choice:** Complete this sentence: Below the wave base, _____.
   a. wave motion ceases.
   b. waves of oscillation begin.
   c. baymouth bars form.
   d. wave refraction occurs.

9. **Fill in the blank:** If caught in a _____, you should swim parallel to shore until you are out of it.

10. **Fill in the blank:** Waves wrap around coastal contours because of _____.

Picture This. YOUR TURN

Coastal Landforms

Fill in the blanks on the diagram, using each of the following terms only once.

1. Arch
2. Sea stack
3. Tombolo
4. Embayment
5. Headland
6. Sandspit
7. Barrier island
8. Baymouth bar
9. Surf
10. Jetty
11. Groin
12. Marine terrace

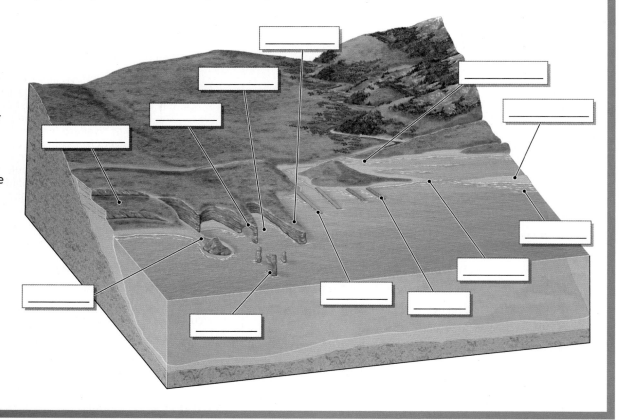

Further Reading

1. Hobbs, Carl. *The Beach Book: The Science of the Shore.* New York: Columbia University Press, 2012.

2. Hoefel, Fernanda, and Steve Elgar. "Wave-Induced Sediment Transport and Sandbar Migration." *Science* 299 (2003): 1885–1887.

3. Storrs, Carina. "Slip-Sliding Away: Myrtle Beach Erosion Could Explain Sand Loss along the U.S. East Coast." *Scientific American*, October 30, 2009. http://www.scientificamerican.com/article/myrtle-beach-south-carolina-coastline-erosion/.

Answers to Living Physical Geography Questions

1. **What causes the tides?** Tides are caused by the gravitational effects of the Moon and Sun.

2. **What are rip currents and why are they deadly?** A rip current is a narrow jet of backwash leaving the beach. Swimmers who get caught in a rip current can be swept out to sea.

3. **Why are some beaches black?** The color of a beach is determined by the type of sediments from which it forms. Most black beaches are composed of particles of basalt.

4. **Why is the sand on many beaches artificial?** Beach erosion requires the addition of sand. Sand that is dredged off the coast and added to a beach is considered artificial sand.

APPENDIX 1 Unit Conversions

Unit Conversions—Metric to U.S. Customary

METRIC	MULTIPLIER	U.S. CUSTOMARY
Length		
Millimeters (mm)	0.0394	Inches (in)
Meters (m)	3.28	Feet (ft)
Centimeters (cm)	0.394	Inches (in)
Kilometers (km)	0.621	Miles (mi)
Nautical mile	1.15	Statute mile
Area		
Square centimeters (cm^2)	0.155	Square inches (in^2)
Square meters (m^2)	10.8	Square feet (ft^2)
Square meters (m^2)	1.12	Square yards (yd^2)
Square kilometers (km^2)	0.386	Square miles (mi^2)
Hectares	2.47	Acres
Volume		
Cubic centimeters (cm^3)	0.061	Cubic inches (in^3)
Cubic meters (m^3)	35.3	Cubic feet (ft^3)
Cubic meters (m^3)	1.31	Cubic yards (yd^3)
Milliliters (ml)	0.0338	Fluid ounces (fl oz)
Liters (L)	1.06	Quarts (qt)
Liters (L)	0.264	Gallons (gal)
Cubic meters (m^3)	0.0008	Acre-feet (acre-ft)
Mass	0.0394	Inches (in)
Grams (g)	0.0353	Ounces (oz)
Kilograms (kg)	2.2	Pounds (lb)
Kilograms (kg)	0.0011	Tons (2,000 lb)
Metric ton (tonne) (t)	1.1	Short ton (tn)
Velocity		
Meters per second (m/s)	3.28	Feet per second (ft/s)
Kilometers per hour (km/h)	0.62	Miles per hour (mph)
Knots (kt) (nautical mph)	1.15	Miles per hour (mph)
Temperature		
Degrees Celsius (°C)	1.8 then add 32	Degrees Fahrenheit (°F)
Celsius degree (°C)	1.8	Fahrenheit degree (°F)

Unit Conversions—U.S. Customary to Metric

U.S. CUSTOMARY	MULTIPLIER	METRIC
Length		
Inches (in)	25.4	Millimeters (mm)
Inches (in)	2.54	Centimeters (cm)
Feet (ft)	0.305	Meters (m)
Miles (mi)	1.61	Kilometers (km)
Statute mile	0.8684	Nautical mile
Area		
Square inches (in^2)	6.45	Square centimeters (cm^2)
Square feet (ft^2)	0.0929	Square meters (m^2)
Square yards (yd^2)	0.836	Square meters (m^2)
Square miles (mi^2)	2.59	Square kilometers (km^2)
Acres	0.405	Hectares
Volume		
Cubic inches (in^3)	16.4	Cubic centimeters (cm^3)
Cubic feet (ft^3)	0.0283	Cubic meters (m^3)
Cubic yards (yd^3)	0.765	Cubic meters (m^3)
Fluid ounces (fl oz)	29.6	Milliliters (ml)
Quarts (qt)	0.946	Liters (L)
Gallons (gal)	3.79	Liters (L)
Acre-feet (acre-ft)	1,233.5	Cubic meters (m^3)
Mass		
Ounces (oz)	28.4	Grams (g)
Pounds (lb)	0.454	Kilograms (kg)
Tons (2,000 lb)	907.0	Kilograms (kg)
Short ton (tn)	0.907	Metric ton (tonne) (t)
Velocity		
Feet per second (ft/s)	0.3049	Meters per second (m/s)
Miles per hour (mph)	1.6	Kilometers per hour (km/h)
Miles per hour (mph)	0.8684	Knots (kt) (nautical mph)
Temperature		
Degrees Fahrenheit (°F)	0.556 after subtracting 32	Degrees Celsius (°C)
Fahrenheit degree (°F)	0.556	Celsius degree (°C)

APPENDIX 2 **Map Projections**

FIGURE **A.1** **A sphere converted to a flat map.** *When a sphere is forced onto flat paper, gaps result.*

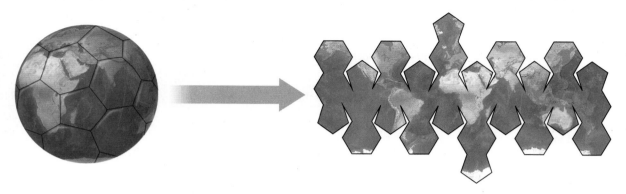

Maps are flat, two-dimensional representations of Earth's surface. A globe is a three-dimensional replica of the planet. World maps cannot portray the globe's curved surface without distorting the shapes and sizes of continents and ocean basins. To illustrate this distortion, imagine you have a soccer ball with Earth printed on it. A traditional soccer ball has 32 patches that are stitched together to make a sphere. It is impossible to lay these patches out on a flat piece of paper without causing gaps between the patches in the oceans or continents, as shown in Figure A.1.

Only a globe can keep the sizes and shapes of Earth's features accurate. But a globe has many limitations:

Only half a globe can be viewed at one time.

The edges of the visible half are distorted.

Globes are always at a small scale, and it is impossible to show details clearly.

Globes are more expensive to make than maps and less versatile in terms of creating new themes, such as vegetation cover or earthquake patterns.

Globes do not fit well into pockets or drawers.

Because of the limitations of globes, flat world maps will always be needed. But the problem of how to handle the gaps that result when the globe is transferred to a flat surface remains. Cartographers address that problem by using map projections.

Types of Map Projections

Cartographers use map projections to transfer the global surface onto a flat map surface. This process is called "projecting" because, before computers, cartographers used a light to project the outline of a wire globe onto a flat piece of paper, then traced the shadows onto the paper. The type of projection that resulted depended on how the paper was positioned in relation to the light. In all, there are three basic kinds of projections: cylindrical, conic, and azimuthal (Figure A.2).

FIGURE **A.2** **Map projections.** *Each projection type has a different application and use. The red line or dot represents the tangent where the map touches the globe. Map distortion increases with distance from the tangent.*

Cylindrical   Conic   Azimuthal

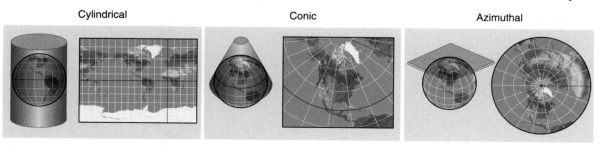

Equal-Area and Conformal Maps

There are two ways to address the gaps that result from stretching the global surface onto a flat piece of paper: preserve areas and sacrifice shapes, or preserve shapes and sacrifice areas. Equal-area projections preserve areas at the expense of shapes (Figure A.3).

A conformal projection preserves the shapes of continents at the expense of areas. Areas in a conformal map are distorted in different portions of the map. In the example shown in Figure A.4, high latitudes are stretched and expanded to preserve the true shapes of continents.

Only globes are both conformal and equal-area representations of Earth. Unlike a globe, no single world map projection can show both shapes and areas accurately.

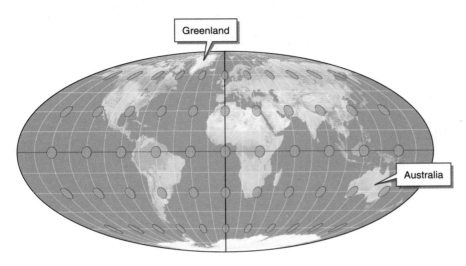

FIGURE A.3 **Mollweide equal-area projection.** *The orange circular areas are all approximately the same size and cover roughly the same geographic area no matter where on the map they are placed. This equalization of area is accomplished by compressing and distorting regions near the poles. Note that the orange areas at high latitudes become distorted ellipses compared with those at low latitudes. This equal-area map shows the true areas of Earth's surface: note, for example, that Australia is over three times larger than Greenland. The Mollweide projection is used throughout* Living Physical Geography. *(© 2012 Google, © 2012 Cnes/Spot image, U.S. Department of State Geographer, Image © 2012 GeoEye)*

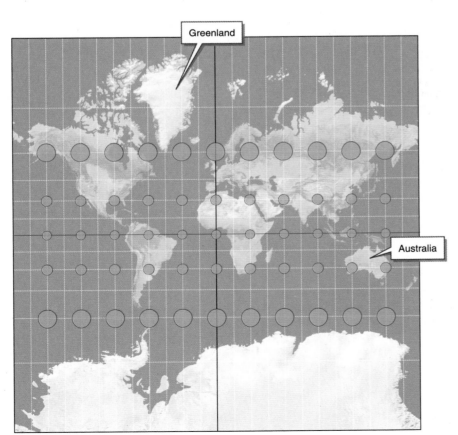

FIGURE A.4 **Mercator conformal projection.** *Even though they are of different sizes, all the orange areas on this map are perfect circles and cover the same amount of Earth's surface. Compared with those in the tropics, the circles at high latitudes are larger because those areas have been stretched. Notice that Greenland appears far larger than Australia in this projection. Antarctica's size is also greatly exaggerated. See the Mollweide projection in Figure A.3 to compare the relative areas of these landmasses.*

APPENDIX 3 Topographic Maps

Topographic maps, or "topo" (pronounced TOE-poe) maps, are often used by geographers when details of Earth's surface are needed. The U.S. Geological Survey (USGS) and other government agencies oversee the National Map program that makes topographic maps for the United States (available at http://nationalmap.gov).

Aerial photography and satellite imagery provide much of the data from which topographic maps are made. USGS topographic maps range in scale from 1:24,000 to 1:1,000,000 (see Section GT.3). The scale 1:24,000 is the most commonly used. Such maps represent 7.5 minutes of the geographic grid; they are therefore often referred to as 7.5 minute topos.

USGS topographic maps provide information about surface relief using contour lines. Human development, agriculture, waterways, glaciers, and vegetation are also shown on topographic maps. Figure A.5 shows a sample of a USGS topographic map of Crater Lake in Oregon, and provides some of the symbols commonly used on topo maps.

FIGURE A.5A **Topographic map.** *(National Map/USGS)*

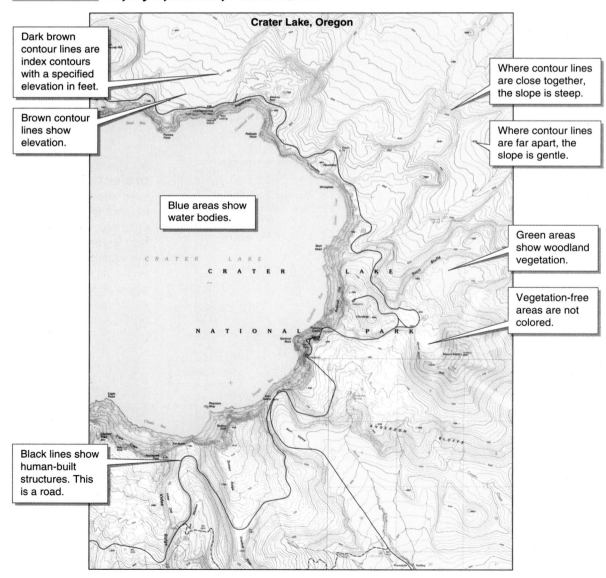

Crater Lake, Oregon

Dark brown contour lines are index contours with a specified elevation in feet.

Brown contour lines show elevation.

Where contour lines are close together, the slope is steep.

Where contour lines are far apart, the slope is gentle.

Blue areas show water bodies.

Green areas show woodland vegetation.

Vegetation-free areas are not colored.

Black lines show human-built structures. This is a road.

FIGURE A.5B **Topographic symbols.** *(National Map/USGS)*

BOUNDARY FEATURES

International	
State or territory	
County or equivalent	
Military Reservation	
National Reserve	

CONTOUR FEATURES

Index	8000
Intermediate	
Supplemental	
Depression Index	4000
Depression Intermediate	
Depression Supplemental	

HYDROGRAPHY POINT FEATURES

Dam/Weir (earthen/nonearthen)	
Gaging Station	
Gate	
Lock Chamber	
Rapids	
Rock (above water/underwater)	
Reservoir (earthen/nonearthen)	
Spring/Seep	
Waterfall	
Well	

HYDROGRAPHY LINEAR FEATURES

Canal/Ditch	
Coastline	
Dam/Weir (earthen)	
Dam/Weir (nonearthen)	
Flume	
Levee	
Nonearthen Shore	
Pipeline (underground)	
Rapids/Waterfall	
Reef	
Stream/River (intermittent)	
Stream/River (perennial)	
Tunnel	
Underground conduit	

HYDROGRAPHY AREA FEATURES

Area of complex channels	
Canal/Ditch	
Dam/Weir	
Flume	
Foreshore	
Glacier	
Innundation area	
Lake/Pond (intermittent)	
Lake/Pond (perennial)	
Lock Chamber/Spillway	
Playa	
Rapids	
Reservoir (nonearthen)	
Sea/Ocean	
Settling pond	
Stream/River (intermittent)	
Stream/River (perennial)	
Tailings pond	
Wash	

(National Map/USGS)

APPENDIX 4 **Using Google Earth**

Google Earth is a virtual, interactive globe that offers a unique spatial perspective on Earth's surface. Google Earth uses geo-referenced satellite imagery, aerial photography, and GIS to portray Earth's surface features in three dimensions.

Google Earth can be used with this book to enhance your understanding of key topics. *Living Physical Geography* offers a virtual tour and problem set with multiple-choice questions to strengthen your understanding of the text material. Digital ".kmz" files are provided at the LaunchPad website for this book: www.macmillanhighered.com/launchpad/gervais1e.

Getting Started

Google Earth is free to download on your personal electronic device and is often found installed on campus computers. It is not recommended that you use a smartphone to interface with Google Earth because the screen size is too small to discern many of the details that will be explored in this text and there is limited functionality. Once you have downloaded the program (at google.com/earth/download/ge/) or have accessed a device on which it is installed, find and double-click the program to get started.

Basic Functions and Practice Using Google Earth

PLACE SEARCHES: You can locate features by typing the location name, such as "Mount Everest," in the upper left search sidebar **(Figure A.6)**. The geographic coordinates of a feature, such as 27°59'8" N, 86°55'24" E, can also be entered. Doing either of these things allows you to "fly" to Mount Everest.

> *Practice: Type "Mount Everest" or "27°59'8" N, 86°55'24" E" in the search sidebar.*

TILTING: Notice in the Mount Everest view that it is initially very difficult to see the relief of the mountain. Tilting is an essential means of viewing and assessing vertical relief in a view. There are a number of ways to tilt your view:

Touch pad: Use the Tilt function in the upper right Navigation panel.

Keyboard: Hold the Shift key down and press the Up or Down arrow keys.

Computer mouse: Hold your mouse wheel down while moving the mouse toward or away from you.

> *Practice: Tilt your view so that you can see Mount Everest from the side (see Figure A.6).*

ZOOMING IN AND OUT (CHANGING "EYE ALTITUDE"): Zooming in closer or out farther from the surface provides different scales of view. The "eye altitude" indicator is located in the lower right of the screen. There are several ways to zoom in or out:

Touch pad: Use the Zoom slider tool in the upper right Navigation panel.

Keyboard: Use the Page Up key to zoom in and the Page Down key to zoom out.

Computer mouse: Double-click the left mouse button to zoom in and the right button to zoom out, or use the mouse scroll wheel.

> *Practice: With Mount Everest in view, zoom to 350 km (200 mi) above Earth's surface.*

MOVING: Moving can be done either by sliding your finger across the touchscreen or by holding a mouse button and dragging the view. There is also a Move tool in the Navigation panel in the upper right of the screen.

SIDEBAR LAYERS: In the bottom left of the screen are the sidebar layers. Here you can activate different data layers, such as roads and borders, political labels, georeferenced photos, current weather, and many other useful data.

> *Practice: Activate the "Borders and Labels" layer. You should see yellow international borders appear with the names of political bodies such as countries, territories, and cities.*

MEASURING DISTANCES: In the toolbar at the top of the screen there is a ruler icon that activates the measuring tool. Distance can be measured as a single line or as the cumulative distance along multiple points of a path. Different measurement units, such as kilometers or miles, are available in the pulldown menu.

> *Practice: Make sure that you are 350 km over Mount Everest with the "Borders and Labels" layer activated. Measure the distance between Mount Everest and the capital of Nepal, Kathmandu, in kilometers. (Your answer should be about 160 km.)*

DETERMINING ELEVATION: You can quickly determine the elevation of any location by moving the cursor over that location and reading the elevation indicator at the bottom of the screen. Locations beneath the oceans are given in negative values to indicate their depth below sea level. In the Tools menu, then the Options menu, you can change the units of display from kilometers to miles or vice versa.

> *Practice: Enter 19°59' N, 76°50' W to fly to southern Cuba. What is the elevation at this location? Your answer should be about 1,300 m (4,300 ft). Now move your cursor south by about 30 km (20 mi). What is the greatest depth of water you can find? Your answer should be about −6,700 m (−22,000 ft).*

ROTATING: North, by default, is at the top of the screen. Rotating provides different angles of view.

Touch pad: Touch and move the North arrow in the Navigation panel.

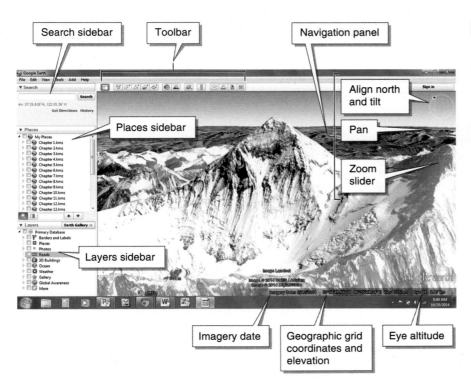

Search sidebar · **Toolbar** · **Navigation panel** · **Align north and tilt** · **Pan** · **Zoom slider** · **Places sidebar** · **Layers sidebar** · **Imagery date** · **Geographic grid coordinates and elevation** · **Eye altitude**

FIGURE A.6 **A Google Earth view of Mount Everest.** *Tilting makes it possible to see the topographic profile of a feature such as Mount Everest. Each of the functions shown here with callout bubbles will be used in the Exploring with Google Earth feature at the end of each chapter.* (Source: © 2014 Google, Image Landsat, © 2014 Cnes/Astrium, © 2014 DigitalGlobe)

Keyboard: Hold the Shift key down and press the Left or Right arrow keys.

Computer mouse: Hold your mouse wheel down while moving the mouse sideways.

Practice: Zoom in to an eye altitude of 20 km (12 mi) directly over Mount Everest. Rotate your view to examine all sides of the mountain.

THE GEOGRAPHIC GRID: You can turn the geographic grid on or off by pulling down the View menu and selecting or deselecting "Grid."

Practice: Turn the geographic grid on and go to the origin by entering "0, 0." Zoom out to an eye altitude of 4,000 km (2,400 mi). What country does the prime meridian first run through as it goes northward? Your answer should be Ghana. What country does the equator first run through as it goes eastward? Your answer should be Gabon.

Practice: Explore the geographic grid on your own by moving around the globe's surface and viewing the grid system. Type in your home address to see the coordinates of where you live. Zoom in to see your house or apartment.

GEOGRAPHIC COORDINATES: Slowly roll your cursor across the screen and note the changing geographic coordinates in the lower right of the screen.

Practice: Type "Dead Sea" in the search sidebar. What are the geographic coordinates in degrees and minutes? Your answer should be near 31°20' N, 35°30' E.

HISTORICAL IMAGERY: You can assess changes in a given region by activating historical imagery.

Practice: Examine deforestation in the Amazon Basin by typing in the coordinates 10°7' S, 63°32' W and zooming out to 40 km (25 mi) eye altitude. Click the Historical Imagery button found in the toolbar. The Historical Imagery icon will appear in the upper right of your screen. Drag the slider tool to the far left, to June 1975, and note the state of the forest. Next drag the slider tool to the right in increments, noting how the forest changes. You should be able to see a progression of deforestation through time.

VIEWING CONTOUR LINES: You can view contour lines in Google Earth by switching to Google Maps mode. Do this by clicking the Google Maps icon in the toolbar.

Practice: Enter "Mayon Volcano" in the search sidebar. Click the Google Maps icon in the toolbar. In the pulldown menu in the upper left corner, select "Terrain." You should be able to see the contour lines of the volcano. What is the interval between the index (dark) contours? Your answer should be 100 meters.

APPENDIX 5 Wind Chill and Heat-Index Charts

The air temperature that a person feels and the measured temperature are not always the same. Wind makes air feel colder because it removes heat from exposed skin. Humidity makes air feel warmer because it reduces evaporative cooling from exposed skin. Wind chill and heat-index charts (Figure A.7) can provide these apparent temperatures if wind speed or humidity and air temperature are known.

FIGURE A.7 **Wind chill and heat-index charts.** *(A) The wind chill temperature at a particular measured air temperature and wind speed can be determined by using this wind chill chart. A measured air temperature of 20°F (horizontal axis) and a 35 mph wind (vertical axis), for example, create a wind chill temperature of 0°F (circled in red). The chart also shows frostbite times for exposed skin. In the purple region, frostbite occurs within 5 minutes of exposure. (B) The heat-index temperature at a particular measured air temperature and relative humidity can be determined by using this heat-index chart. A measured air temperature of 84°F (horizontal axis) and a relative humidity of 60% (vertical axis) create a heat-index temperature of 88°F (circled in red).*

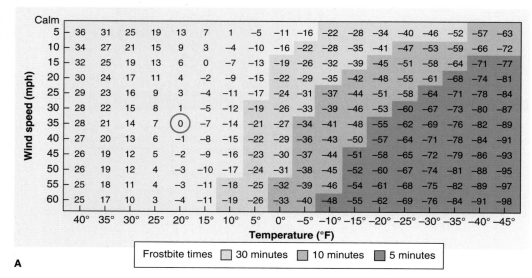

A

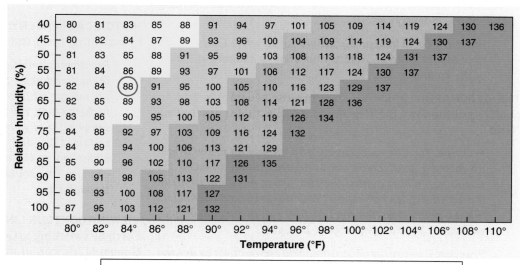

B

APPENDIX 6 The Köppen Climate Classification System

TABLE A.1 Köppen Climate Types

FIRST LETTERS	CHARACTERISTICS
A	• Tropical climates • Average monthly temperature above 18°C (64°F)
B	• Dry climates • Average annual precipitation below 76 cm (30 in)
C	• Mild midlatitude climates • The warmest month is above 10°C (50°F); the coldest month is between −3°C and 18°C (26°F and 64°F)
D	• Severe midlatitude climates • Average temperature is above 10°C (50°F) in the warmest month; average temperature is below 0°C (32°F) in the coldest month
E	• Polar climates • Warmest month is below 10°C (50°F)
H	• Highlands • Variable cold highland climates

SECOND LETTERS	CHARACTERISTICS
F	• Precipitation in all months
M	• Monsoon • Short winter dry season
S	• Summer dry • At least 70% of precipitation in winter
T	• Tundra • Warmest month 0°C to 10°C (32°F to 50°F)
W	• Winter drought

THIRD LETTERS	CHARACTERISTICS
A	• Hot summer • Warmest month above 22°C (72°F)
B	• Mild summer • Warmest month below 22°C (72°F)
C	• One to four months above 10°C (50°F)
D	• Bitter cold winter • Coldest month below −38°C (−36°F)
H	• Average yearly temperature above 18°C (64°F)
K	• Average yearly temperature below 18°C (64°F)

As we learned in Section 8.1, the Köppen climate classification system recognizes six basic climate types: A, B, C, D, E, and H. Except for B, each is identified by temperature characteristics. B climates are identified by aridity. Each of the major climate types is subdivided further based on temperature and precipitation characteristics. H climates are reserved for elevations above 1,500 m (4,920 ft). Table A.1 provides the specific characteristics for each climate type. For a map of these climate types and the biomes associated with them, see Figure 8.2.

Glossary

A

'A'ā (pronounced AH-ah) A mafic lava flow with a rough, blocky surface. (p. 447)

abrasion The process by which movement of one material wears away another material. (p. 519)

absolute age An age that is specified in years before the present. (p. 370)

abyssal plain A flat plain on the ocean floor at depths between 4,000 and 6,000 m (13,000 and 20,000 ft). (p. 335)

accreted terrane A mass of crust that is transported by plate movement and fused onto the margin of a continent. (p. 398)

acid rain Rainfall that has a lowered pH because it has mixed with sulfur compounds. (p. 46)

active continental margin A margin of a continent that follows a plate boundary, typically characterized by a deep-sea trench and a narrow continental shelf. (p. 402)

active layer The top layer of permafrost that thaws each summer and refreezes in fall. (p. 547)

active volcano A volcano that has erupted during the last 10,000 years and is likely to erupt again. (p. 445)

adiabatic cooling The cooling of an air parcel through expansion. (p. 105)

adiabatic warming The warming of an air parcel through compression. (p. 105)

advection fog Fog that results from moist air moving over a cold surface, such as a lake or a cold ocean current, that lowers its temperature to the dew point. (p. 111)

aeolian (or *eolian*) Of or relating to wind. (p. 583)

aerosols Microscopic solid or liquid particles suspended in the atmosphere. (p. 38)

aerovane A combination of an anemometer and a wind vane; measures wind speed and direction. (p. 127)

aftershock A small earthquake that follows the main earthquake. (p. 460)

aggradation The buildup of sediments in a streambed. (p. 526)

air mass A large region of air that is uniform in temperature and humidity. (p. 162)

air parcel A body of air of uniform humidity and temperature. (p. 101)

air pollution Harmful concentrations of gases or aerosols in the atmosphere. (p. 45)

air pressure The force exerted by molecules of air against a surface. (p. 39)

albedo The reflectivity of a surface, given as the percentage of incoming radiation that it reflects. (p. 78)

alluvial fan A gently sloping accumulation of sediment deposited at the base of a mountain by an ephemeral stream in arid regions. (p. 527)

alluvium Sediments deposited on a floodplain by a stream. (p. 526)

alpine glacier Any glacier found in a mountainous area. (p. 556)

alpine tree line The upper limit of trees in mountains, defined by low temperatures. (p. 281)

alpine tundra A cold, high-elevation treeless biome with herbaceous perennials. (p. 281)

anemometer (pronounced an-eh-MOM-eter) An instrument used to measure wind speed. (p. 127)

angle of repose The steepest angle at which loose sediments can settle. (p. 446)

Antarctic Circle The 66.5° south parallel. (p. 65)

Anthropocene (pronounced an-THROP-a-seen) The age of human transformation of Earth's physical systems; generally seen as starting in 1800. (p. 364)

anthropogenic Created or influenced by people. (p. 37)

anticline A fold in the crust with an archlike ridge. (p. 406)

anticyclone A meteorological system in which air flows away from a high-pressure region, creating clockwise circulation in the Northern Hemisphere and counterclockwise circulation in the Southern Hemisphere. (p. 133)

aquiclude A sediment or rock layer that lacks pores and cannot contain water. (p. 307)

aquifer A sediment or rock layer with pores that contain water. (p. 307)

Arctic Circle The 66.5° north parallel. (p. 65)

arête (pronounced ar-ET) A steep-sided, sharp ridge formed where glaciers erode opposite sides of a mountain. (p. 561)

artesian well A well that has been drilled through an aquiclude into a confined aquifer below and may gush water. (p. 310)

ash (volcanic) Fine volcanic powder consisting of pulverized rock particles and solidified droplets of lava. (p. 445)

asthenosphere The layer of the mantle, which deforms and flows, found between about 100 and 200 km (62 and 124 mi) in depth. (p. 375)

atmosphere The layer of gases surrounding Earth. (p. 10)

atoll A ring of coral reefs with an interior lagoon, formed around a sinking volcano. (p. 336)

aurora borealis/australis Displays of light (also called northern and southern lights) caused by energized molecules in the ionosphere. (p. 44)

avalanche A turbulent cloud of rock debris or snow that is mixed with air and races quickly down a steep slope. (p. 497)

B

backwash The flow of water from breakers down the slope of a beach back toward the ocean. (p. 613)

bajada (pronounced ba-HAH-da) A broad, sloping plain formed from merged alluvial fans. (p. 589)

barchan dune (pronounced bar-KAHN) A crescent-shaped sand dune with the crescent tips pointing downwind. (p. 586)

barometer An instrument used to measure air pressure. (p. 129)

barrier island An offshore sandbar that runs parallel to the coast. (p. 617)

barrier reef A coral reef that runs parallel to the shoreline and forms a deep-water lagoon behind it. (p. 336)

basalt A dark, heavy, fine-grained volcanic rock that constitutes oceanic crust. (p. 375)

base level The lowest level a stream can reach, usually sea level; a stream becomes standing water at base level. (p. 521)

Basin-and-Range Province A landscape located in the southwestern United States where the crust is being stretched apart through rifting, forming a large internal drainage basin with a series of tilted fault blocks. (p. 595)

batholith A body of intrusive igneous rock hundreds of kilometers in extent and formed by the movement and fusion of numerous plutons. (p. 423)

bathymetry Measurement of depth and topography beneath the surface of a body of water. (p. 334)

baymouth bar A continuous sandspit formed by longshore drift that creates a lagoon of brackish water behind it. (p. 617)

beach nourishment The artificial replenishment of a beach with sand. (p. 625)

bed load Material in a stream channel such as sand, gravel, and rocks that is too heavy to become suspended in the current. (p. 520)

bedrock Rock that is structurally part of and connected to Earth's crust. (p. 297)

biodiversity The number of living species in a specified region. (p. 225)

biogeographic region A continental-scale region that contains genetically similar groups of plants and animals. (p. 230)

biogeography The study of the geography of life and how it changes through space and time. (p. 225)

bioluminescence The production of light through chemical means by living organisms. (p. 346)

biomass The dried weight of living material. (p. 244)

biome An extensive geographic region with relatively uniform vegetation structure. (p. 257)

biosphere All life on Earth. (p. 11)

block (volcanic) A fragment of rock from the volcano's cone that is ejected during an explosive eruption. (p. 448)

bomb (volcanic) A streamlined fragment of lava ejected from a volcano that cooled and hardened as it moved through the air. (p. 448)

boreal forest A cold coniferous forest biome found in North America and Eurasia, with vegetation made up of needle-leaved evergreen trees and an understory of mosses, lichens, and herbaceous plants. (p. 277)

boundary layer The layer of the atmosphere where wind is slowed by friction with Earth's surface; extends about 1 km (3,280 ft) above the surface. (p. 133)

braided stream A stream that forms intertwining channels around sediments in the streambed. (p. 527)

butte A medium-sized flat-topped hill with cliff-face sides that is taller than it is wide. (p. 593)

bycatch Unwanted organisms caught by industrial fishing methods, which are usually thrown back to sea dead. (p. 350)

C

caldera A large depression that forms when a volcano's magma chamber empties and collapses after the volcano erupts. (p. 451)

capillary fringe The region of transition between the zone of aeration and the zone of saturation. (p. 308)

carbon cycle The movement of carbon through Earth's physical systems. (p. 202)

carbon footprint The amount of greenhouse gases (particularly carbon dioxide) any activity generates. (p. 216)

carbon monoxide (CO) A toxic odorless and invisible gas. (p. 45)

cartography The science and art of map making. (p. 19)

cementation A process in which minerals fill the spaces between loose particles and bind them together to form sedimentary rock. (p. 422)

Cenozoic era The last 66 million years of Earth history, marked by a persistent global cooling trend that began about 55 million years ago. (p. 196)

CFCs (chlorofluorocarbons) A class of ozone-degrading compounds used mainly as refrigerants, aerosol propellants, and fire retardants. (p. 50)

chemical energy Energy in a substance that can be released through a chemical reaction. (p. 8)

chemical sedimentary rock Sedimentary rock that forms as dissolved minerals are precipitated out of water. (p. 426)

chemical weathering A process that changes the minerals in a rock through chemical reactions involving water. (p. 482)

chimney A slender spire of rock with a flat top. (p. 593)

chinook wind A local downslope wind that forms on the leeward side of the Rocky Mountains. (p. 146)

cinder cone A small, cone-shaped volcano consisting of pyroclasts that settle at the angle of repose. (p. 446)

circle of illumination The line separating night from day, where sunrise and sunset are occurring. (p. 62)

cirque A bowl-shaped depression with steep headwalls formed by a cirque glacier. (p. 561)

cirque glacier A glacier that forms at the head of a valley. (p. 556)

cirrus A high cloud with a feathery appearance that is composed of ice crystals. (p. 109)

clastic sedimentary rock Sedimentary rock composed of broken pieces of other rocks. (p. 426)

climate The long-term average of weather and the average frequency of extreme weather events. (p. 193)

climate forcing factor A force that can change climate and is unaffected by the climate system. (p. 195)

cloud An aggregation of microscopic water droplets and ice crystals suspended in the air. (p. 108)

cloud droplets Microscopic drops of liquid water found in clouds. (p. 38)

coal An organic rock formed from the remains of terrestrial wetland forests and widely used today as a fuel source. (p. 428)

col A low area or pass over a ridge formed by two cirque glaciers. (p. 561)

cold front A region where cold air advances on relatively warm air; sometimes associated with severe weather. (p. 177)

collapse sinkhole A sinkhole formed where the ceiling of a cavern has collapsed. (p. 486)

collision Convergence of the continental crust of two different plates. (p. 398)

collision and coalescence The process by which cloud droplets merge to form raindrops. (p. 111)

colonization The successful establishment of a population in a new geographic region without the help of people. (p. 240)

columnar jointing A geometric pattern of angular columns that forms from joints in basaltic lava during cooling. (p. 451)

community The populations of organisms interacting in a geographic area. (p. 245)

competition An interaction between organisms that require the same resources. (p. 236)

condensation A change in the state of water from gas to liquid. (p. 95)

condensation nucleus A small particle in the atmosphere, about 0.2 μm in diameter, on which water vapor condenses. (p. 111)

conduction The process by which energy is transferred through a substance or between objects in direct contact. (p. 67)

cone of depression The cone-shaped lowering of the water table resulting from groundwater overdraft. (p. 312)

consumer An organism that cannot produce its own food through photosynthesis. (p. 243)

contaminant plume The cloud of pollution that migrates through an aquifer away from its source. (p. 316)

continental crust The crust that makes up the continents, composed mainly of granite. (p. 375)

continental divide A ridge or highland that separates drainage systems that empty into different ocean basins. (p. 512)

continental drift A theory proposed by Alfred Wegener stating that continents move slowly across Earth's surface. (p. 387)

continental effect The increase in seasonality with distance from the oceans. (p. 70)

continental shelf The shallow, sloping seafloor near continental margins. (p. 335)

continental volcanic arc A long chain of volcanoes formed on the margin of a continent above a subducting plate. (p. 397)

contour lines Lines of equal elevation in relation to sea level used on a topographic map. (p. 22)

convection The transfer of heat through movement of mass within a fluid (liquid or gas). (p. 68)

convective uplift The rising of an air parcel that is warmer and less dense than the surrounding air. (p. 107)

convergent evolution An evolutionary process in which two or more unrelated organisms that experience similar environmental conditions evolve similar adaptations. (p. 229)

convergent plate boundary A region where two lithospheric plates move toward each other. (p. 394)

convergent uplift The rising of air as a result of converging airflow. (p. 108)

coral bleaching The loss of coloration in corals caused by the absence of their mutualistic algae, which occurs when they have been stressed or have died. (p. 336)

Coriolis force (or *Coriolis effect*) The perceived deflection of moving objects in relation to Earth's surface. (p. 133)

crevasse A crack that develops in the top 60 m of a glacier. (p. 553)

crust The rigid outermost portion of Earth's surface. (p. 366)

cryosphere The frozen portion of the hydrosphere. (p. 194)

crystallization A process in which atoms or molecules come together in an orderly patterned structure. (p. 419)

cumulonimbus A cloud that extends high into the atmosphere and is capable of strong vertical development and of producing severe weather. (p. 109)

cumulus A dome-shaped, bunched cloud, with a flat base and billowy upper portions. (p. 109)

cut bank The outside edge of a meander, where erosion exceeds deposition. (p. 528)

cyanobacteria Photosynthetic bacteria that were among the first forms of life to evolve about 3.5 billion years ago. (p. 367)

cyclone A meteorological system in which air flows toward a low-pressure region, creating counterclockwise circulation in the Northern Hemisphere and clockwise circulation in the Southern Hemisphere. (p. 133)

D

debris flow A fast-flowing slurry of mud mixed with large objects, such as rocks and vegetation. (p. 494)

debris slide A landslide that consists of a mixture of rocks, soil, and vegetation. (p. 496)

December solstice A seasonal marker that occurs when the subsolar point is at 23.5° south, on about December 21. (p. 62)

decomposer An organism that breaks organic material down into simple compounds. (p. 243)

decompression melting The melting of hot mantle material into magma as a result of changes in pressure, which lower the melting point of the rock; occurs as mantle material rises to a shallow depth in the lithosphere. (p. 422)

deep-sea trench A long narrow valley on the seafloor; deep-sea trenches are the deepest parts of the oceans. (p. 336)

deflation The removal of sediments and lowering of the land surface by wind erosion. (p. 584)

delta An accumulation of sediment formed where a stream reaches base level. (p. 530)

dendritic drainage A pattern of streams within a drainage basin that resembles the branching of a tree. (p. 514)

denudation The lowering and wearing away of Earth's surface. (p. 481)

desert A biome with chronic moisture deficits and drought-adapted vegetation. (p. 283)

desert pavement A reg composed of tightly interlocked rocks that resembles a cobblestone street. (p. 589)

desertification The transformation of fertile land to desert, usually by overgrazing of livestock, deforestation, or natural drought. (p. 126)

dew point (or *dew-point temperature*) The temperature at which air becomes saturated. (p. 103)

differential weathering Unequal weathering across a rock surface. (p. 485)

digital elevation model (DEM) A digital representation of land surface or underwater topography. (p. 25)

dike A sheetlike vertical igneous rock formation. (p. 423)

disappearing stream A stream that leaves the ground surface and flows into subterranean channels. (p. 488)

dispersal The movement of an organism away from where it originated. (p. 230)

dissolved load Soluble minerals that are carried in solution by a stream. (p. 520)

distributary One of a branching network of streams in a delta. (p. 530)

divergent evolution An evolutionary process by which individuals in one reproductively isolated population evolve adaptations different from those of closely related individuals in another population. (p. 230)

divergent plate boundary A region where two lithospheric plates move apart. (p. 394)

doldrums A low-wind region near the equator, associated with the ITCZ. (p. 136)

Doppler radar An active remote sensing technology that uses microwave energy to measure the velocity and direction of movement of particles of precipitation within a cloud. (p. 25)

drainage basin A geographic region drained by a single trunk stream and the smaller tributaries that flow into it. (p. 511)

drainage divide A ridge or highland that separates drainage basins and defines their boundaries. (p. 512)

drift net fishing An industrial fishing method in which large nets are suspended in the upper reaches of the ocean. (p. 350)

drought A prolonged period of water shortage. (p. 306)

drumlin An elongated hill formed by a moving ice sheet. (p. 565)

dry adiabatic rate The rate of temperature change in an unsaturated parcel of air; 10°C/1,000 m (5.5°F/1,000 ft). (p. 105)

dynamic pressure Air pressure caused by air movement. (p. 130)

E

Earth system model A mathematical simulation of the behavior of the atmosphere, oceans, and biosphere; used to create long-term climate projections. (p. 213)

earthquake A sudden shaking of the ground caused by movements of Earth's crust. (p. 372)

ecological disturbance A sudden event that disrupts an ecosystem. (p. 240)

ecological succession The step-by-step series of changes in an ecosystem that follows a disturbance. (p. 240)

ecology The study of the interactions between organisms and their environment. (p. 225)

ecosystem The living organisms within a community and the nonliving components of the environment in which they live. (p. 225)

effusive eruption A nonexplosive eruption that produces mostly lava. (p. 452)

El Niño A periodic change in the state of Earth's climate caused by the slackening and temporary reversal of the Pacific equatorial trade winds and increased sea surface temperatures off coastal Peru. (p. 180)

electromagnetic spectrum (EMS) The full range of wavelengths of radiant energy. (p. 75)

eluviation The process by which rainwater carries soil particles downward. (p. 297)

embayment A concave sandy beach between headlands. (p. 613)

emergent coast A coast where sea level is dropping or the land is rising. (p. 614)

endemic Restricted to one geographic area. (p. 230)

energy The capacity to do work on or to change the state of matter. (p. 8)

enhanced Fujita scale (EF Scale) A system used to rank tornado strength based on damage done to the landscape. (p. 167)

environmental lapse rate The rate of cooling with increasing altitude in the troposphere. The average environmental lapse rate is 6.5°C per 1,000 m or 3.6°F per 1,000 ft. (p. 41)

ephemeral stream A stream that flows briefly after heavy rainstorms. (p. 515)

epicenter The location on the ground's surface immediately above the focus of an earthquake, where earthquake intensity is usually greatest. (p. 460)

epipelagic zone The sunlit surface of the ocean down to 200 m (650 ft). (p. 330)

epiphyte A plant that grows on the surface of another plant but does not take nutrients from that plant. (p. 260)

equator The line of latitude that divides Earth into two equal halves. The equator is exactly perpendicular to Earth's axis of rotation. (p. 16)

equilibrium line (or *snowline*) The elevation at which a glacier's ice accumulation and ice loss are equal over the period of one year. (p. 553)

erg A desert landscape dominated by actively moving sand dunes. (p. 590)

erosion The transport of rock fragments by moving water, ice, or air. (p. 481)

escarpment A long cliff face or steep slope. (p. 523)

esker A long ridge of sorted sand and gravel deposited by a subglacial stream. (p. 567)

estuary A brackish-water ecosystem found at the mouth of a river that is influenced by tides. (p. 341)

eustasy A change in global sea level as a result of change in the amount of water in the oceans. (p. 615)

evaporation A change in the state of water from liquid to gas. (p. 95)

evaporite A deposit of one or more minerals resulting from the repeated evaporation of water from a basin. (p. 430)

evapotranspiration The combined processes of evaporation and transpiration. (p. 99)

evolution The process of genetically driven change in a population caused by selection pressures in the environment. (p. 228)

exfoliation A physical weathering process in which joints form parallel to a rock surface, creating sheetlike slabs of rock. (p. 481)

exhumation The removal of overlying rock and sediment to expose deeper rocks at the surface. (p. 423)

exotic stream A permanent stream that originates in a humid region and flows through an arid region. (p. 515)

extinct volcano A volcano that has not erupted for tens of thousands of years and can never erupt again. (p. 445)

extinction The permanent and global loss of a species. (p. 232)

extrusive igneous rock (or *volcanic rock*) Rock that has cooled from lava on the crust's surface. (p. 423)

F

fault A fracture in the crust where movement and earthquakes occur. (p. 404)

fault scarp A cliff face resulting from the vertical movement of a reverse or normal fault. (p. 459)

fetch The distance of open water over which wind blows. (p. 611)

fishery A region where fish are caught for human consumption. (p. 349)

fjord A U-shaped coastal glacial valley flooded by the sea. (p. 563)

flash flood A flood that occurs with sudden, intense rainfall or dam collapse, often with little or no warning. (p. 532)

flood Inundation by water in a region not normally covered by water, which results when stream discharge exceeds stream channel capacity. (p. 532)

floodplain The area of flat land near a stream that experiences flooding on a regular basis. (p. 510)

fluvial erosion Erosion by running water. (p. 517)

flux melting The process by which subducted water lowers the melting point of mantle material and causes it to melt. (p. 423)

focus The location of initial movement along a fault during an earthquake. (p. 460)

foehn wind (pronounced FEH-rn) A downslope wind that forms on the leeward size of the European Alps. (p. 146)

fog A cloud at or near ground level that reduces visibility to less than 1 km (0.62 mi). (p. 111)

fold A wrinkle in the crust resulting from deformation caused by geologic stress. (p. 404)

food web The ecological interconnections among organisms occupying different trophic levels. (p. 242)

fossil The remains or the impression of an organism preserved in sedimentary rock. (p. 431)

fossil fuels The ancient remains of plants preserved in the lithosphere in the form of coal, oil, and natural gas. (p. 45)

fossil groundwater Water that entered an aquifer long ago and is no longer being replenished. (p. 314)

fracking (or *hydraulic fracturing*) The procedure by which water is pumped under high pressure into a shale formation to extract natural gas and oil. (p. 434)

fringing reef A coral reef that forms near and parallel to a coastline. (p. 336)

frontal uplift The rising of warm air masses where they meet relatively cold air masses. (p. 108)

frost wedging A physical weathering process in which water trapped in an opening in a rock freezes and expands, causing the opening to grow. (p. 482)

fulgurite A glassy hollow tube formed where lightning strikes sand. (p. 165)

G

geographic grid The coordinate system that uses latitude and longitude to identify locations on Earth's surface. (p. 16)

geographic information system (GIS) A system that uses computers to capture, store, analyze, and display spatial data. (p. 26)

geography The study of the spatial relationships among Earth's physical and cultural features and how they develop and change through time. (p. 4)

geohazard A hazard posed to people by the physical Earth. (p. 444)

geothermal energy Heat from Earth's interior. (p. 8)

glacial advance The forward (usually downslope) movement of a glacier's toe. (p. 553)

glacial erratic A large boulder transported a long distance by a glacier. (p. 550)

glacial ice Ice with an air content of less than 20%. (p. 551)

glacial period A cold interval within the Quaternary ice age. (p. 196)

glacial polish A smoothed bedrock surface resulting from glacial abrasion. (p. 559)

glacial retreat The upslope movement of the toe of a glacier. (p. 553)

glacial striation A groove gouged into the surface of bedrock by glacial abrasion. (p. 559)

glacial valley (or *glacial trough*) A U-shaped valley carved by a glacier. (p. 561)

glacier A large mass of ice that is formed from the accumulation of snow and flows slowly downslope. (p. 551)

glacier mass balance The difference between inputs to a glacier that increase its ice volume and losses of ice that decrease its ice volume. (p. 553)

global heat engine The movement of heat from low to high latitudes and low to high altitudes as a result of heating differences. (p. 83)

Global Positioning System (GPS) A global navigation system that uses satellites and ground-based receivers to determine the geographic coordinates of any location. (p. 19)

Gondwana A landmass that resulted when Pangaea split about 200 million years ago, which consisted of modern-day South America, Australia, Africa, India, and Antarctica. (p. 387)

granite A silica-rich rock composed of coarse grains. (p. 375)

great circle A continuous line that bisects the globe into two equal halves, such as the equator; it is the shortest distance between two points on Earth. (p. 20)

Great Pacific Garbage Patch A region of concentrated plastic litter formed by the North Pacific Gyre. (p. 351)

green economy A sustainable economic system that has a small environmental impact and is based on renewable energy sources. (p. 214)

greenhouse effect The process by which the atmosphere is warmed as greenhouse gases (such as water vapor, carbon dioxide, and methane) and clouds absorb and counterradiate heat. (p. 82)

greenhouse gas A gas that can absorb and emit thermal energy. (p. 37)

groin A linear structure of concrete or stone that extends from a beach into the water, designed to slow the erosion of sand. (p. 620)

groundwater Water found beneath Earth's surface in sediments and rocks. (p. 306)

groundwater discharge The movement of water out of an aquifer. 308

groundwater mining The process of extracting groundwater where there is little to no groundwater recharge. (p. 313)

groundwater overdraft Withdrawal of water from an aquifer faster than the aquifer is recharged at the site of a well. (p. 312)

groundwater recharge The movement of water into an aquifer. (p. 308)

groundwater remediation The process of cleaning a contaminated aquifer. (p. 316)

gyre A large, circular ocean current. (p. 334)

H

habitat The physical environment in which an organism lives. (p. 230)

habitat fragmentation The division and reduction of natural habitat into smaller pieces by human activity. (p. 285)

hail Hard, rounded pellets of ice that precipitate from cumulonimbus clouds with strong vertical airflow. (p. 113)

headland A rocky prominence of coastal land. (p. 613)

headward erosion The process by which a stream channel migrates upslope by forming new rills through fluvial erosion. (p. 517)

headwaters The region where a stream originates. (p. 514)

heat The internal energy transferred between materials or systems due to their temperature differences. (p. 67)

heat-index temperature The temperature perceived by people as a result of high atmospheric humidity coupled with high air temperatures. (p. 66)

herbivore An organism that eats only plants. (p. 242)

Holocene epoch The current interglacial period of warm and stable climate; the last 10,000 years of Earth history. (p. 197)

horn A steep, pyramid-shaped mountain peak formed by glaciers. (p. 561)

horse latitudes The low-wind regions centered on 30° north and south. (p. 136)

hot spot A location at the base of the lithosphere where high temperatures cause the overlying crust to melt. (p. 402)

humidity The amount of water vapor in the atmosphere. (p. 99)

humus (pronounced HYOU-mus) Organic material that makes up the topmost layers of soil (the O and A horizons). (p. 300)

hurricane The North American name for a tropical cyclone with sustained winds of 119 km/h (74 mph) or greater. (p. 169)

hydrogen bond The bond between water molecules that results from the attraction between one water molecule's positive end and another's negative end. (p. 96)

hydrologic cycle The movement of water within the atmosphere, biosphere, lithosphere, and hydrosphere. (p. 96)

hydrosphere All of Earth's water in its three phases: solid, liquid, and gas. (p. 11)

hydrothermal vent community A unique ecosystem found at volcanic hot springs that emit mineral-rich water onto the seafloor. (p. 348)

hygrometer An instrument used to measure humidity. (p. 99)

I

ice-albedo positive feedback A destabilizing positive feedback in the climate system in which the melting of ice and snow expose bare ground and ice-free water, which absorb more solar energy and cause more warming. (p. 195)

ice cap A dome of ice that sits over a high mountain region and has an extent of 50,000 km^2 (19,300 m^2) or less. (p. 556)

ice-crystal process (or *Bergeron process*) The process by which ice crystals grow within a cloud to form snow. (p. 111)

ice sheet A flat sheet of ice that has an extent of 50,000 km^2 (19,300 mi^2) or more. (p. 556)

ice shelf The portion of an ice sheet or an outlet glacier that extends over the ocean. (p. 556)

iceberg A large block of ice that breaks from the toe of a glacier or an ice shelf and floats in the ocean or a lake. (p. 556)

igneous rock Rock that has cooled from magma or lava. (p. 421)

infiltration The process by which water seeps into the ground through the force of gravity. (p. 308)

infrared radiation (IR) Electromagnetic radiation that has wavelengths longer than visible radiation. (p. 77)

inner core The innermost layer of Earth, composed of solid iron and nickel. (p. 373)

inselberg A large, weathered outcrop of bedrock surrounded by a flat alluvium-filled plain. (p. 593)

insolation (or *incoming solar radiation*) Solar radiation that reaches Earth. (p. 77)

interglacial period A warm interval that occurs between glacial periods. (p. 196)

intermittent stream A stream that runs dry during part or most of the year. (p. 514)

internal drainage A drainage pattern in which streams terminate in a low-lying basin on land. (p. 512)

intrusive igneous rock Rock that has cooled from magma below the crust's surface. (p. 423)

invasion The successful and unwanted establishment of a species in a new geographic area as a result of human activity. (p. 240)

ionosphere A region of the upper mesosphere and the thermosphere between about 80 and 500 km (50 to 310 mi) where gases are ionized by solar energy. (p. 44)

isobar A line drawn on a map connecting points of equal pressure. Isobars are quantitative representations of the changing molecular density of the air over a geographic region. (p. 131)

isostasy The gravitational equilibrium between the lithosphere and the support of the asthenosphere below. (p. 614)

ITCZ (or *intertropical convergence zone*) A global band of unstable, buoyant air parcels that tracks the migration of the subsolar point. (p. 134)

J

jetty An artificial wall placed at the mouth of a harbor to prevent sand from closing the harbor entrance; usually placed in pairs. (p. 622)

joint A crack or weak plane in rock. (p. 451)

June solstice A seasonal marker that occurs when the subsolar point is 23.5° north latitude, about June 21. (p. 63)

K

kame-and-kettle topography A glaciofluvial landscape dominated by irregular mounds and shallow depressions or lakes. (p. 567)

karst An area dominated by the weathering of carbonate rocks, usually limestone. (p. 485)

katabatic wind (or *gravity wind*) Wind that forms mainly over ice sheets or glaciers when intensely cold, dense, and heavy air spills downslope by the force of gravity. (p. 148)

Keeling curve A graph showing the change in atmospheric CO_2 concentrations since 1958. (p. 204)

kelp forest A coastal marine ecosystem dominated by kelp, found where ocean water is colder than 20°C (68°F). (p. 342)

keystone species A species whose effects support many other species within an ecosystem. (p. 235)

knickpoint A location where there is an abrupt increase in stream gradient over a short distance. (p. 523)

Köppen climate classification system (pronounced KUHR-pen) A system used to classify climate types by temperature and precipitation. (p. 257)

L

laccolith A shallow, dome-shaped igneous rock body. (p. 423)

lag deposit A reg that results from the removal of smaller particles, such as clay and silt, by deflation. (p. 589)

lagoon A fully or partly enclosed stretch of salt water formed by a coral reef or sand spit. (p. 336)

lahar A thick slurry of mud, ash, water, and other debris that flows rapidly down a snow-capped stratovolcano when it erupts. (p. 453)

lake-effect snow Heavy snowfall that results as cold air moves over large, relatively warm bodies of water, such as the Great Lakes. (p. 177)

land breeze A local offshore breeze created by heating and cooling differences between water and land. (p. 142)

landslide Rapid movement of rock or debris down a steep slope. (p. 494)

lapilli (pronounced la-PILL-eye) Marble- to golf ball–sized cooled fragments of lava. (p. 448)

large igneous province (LIP) An accumulation of flood basalts that covers an extensive geographic area. (p. 451)

large scale A geographic scale that pertains to a geographically restricted area and makes geographic features large to show more detail. (p. 6)

latent heat Energy that is absorbed or released during a change in the state of a substance, such as during evaporation or condensation of water. (p. 98)

latitude The angular distance as measured from Earth's center to a point north or south of the equator. (p. 16)

Laurasia A landmass that resulted when Pangaea split about 200 million years ago, which consisted of modern-day North America, Greenland, and Eurasia. (p. 387)

Laurentide ice sheet The large ice sheet that covered much of North America 20,000 years ago. (p. 200)

lava Hot molten rock that spills onto the surface of Earth's crust. (p. 375)

leaching The process by which rainwater carries dissolved nutrients downward. (p. 297)

liana A woody climbing vine. (p. 259)

lifting condensation level (LCL) The altitude at which an air parcel becomes saturated. (p. 105)

lightning An electrical discharge produced by thunderstorms. (p. 165)

limestone A chemical sedimentary rock composed mostly of calcite. (p. 427)

limestone column A cylindrical speleothem resulting when a stalactite joins with a stalagmite. (p. 491)

limiting factor Any factor that prevents an organism from reaching its reproductive or geographic potential. (p. 232)

liquefaction The transformation of solid sediments into an unstable slurry as a result of ground shaking during an earthquake. (p. 464)

lithification The formation of sedimentary rock through compaction and cementation of loose sediments. (p. 422)

lithosphere The layer of Earth that consists of the rigid crust and the rigid lithospheric mantle beneath it, extending to a depth of about 100 km (62 mi) on average. (p. 375)

Little Ice Age A natural cooling period from about 1350 to 1850 CE; felt mostly in the Northern Hemisphere. (p. 192)

loam Soil that consists of approximately 40% sand, 40% silt, and 20% clay and has a high organic content. (p. 299)

loess (pronounced lehss) Wind-deposited silt and clay sediments that originate mostly from glacial outwash plains. (p. 568)

longitude The angular distance as measured from Earth's center to a point east or west of the prime meridian. (p. 16)

longline fishing An industrial fishing method that employs thousands of baited hooks on lines up to 80 km (50 mi) in length. (p. 350)

longshore current A current that flows parallel to the beach in the direction of wave movement. (p. 613)

longshore drift The process by which sediment on a beach is moved down the length of the beach in the direction of wave movement. (p. 613)

longwave radiation (LWR) Radiation with wavelengths longer than 4 μm. (p. 76)

M

magma Melted rock that is below the surface of Earth's crust. (p. 375)

magnetosphere The outer edge of the magnetic field that surrounds Earth and shields it from the solar wind. (p. 377)

mangrove forest A coastal marine ecosystem dominated by saltwater-tolerant shrubs and trees, found in the tropics and subtropics. (p. 338)

mantle The layer of heated and slowly deforming solid rock between the base of the crust and the outer core. (p. 374)

mantle drag The dragging force between the asthenosphere and the overlying lithosphere. (p. 392)

mantle plume A mostly stationary column of hot rock that extends from deep in the mantle up to the base of the lithosphere. (p. 403)

map A flat two-dimensional representation of Earth's surface. (p. 6)

map scale A means of specifying how much the real world has been reduced on a map. (p. 20)

March equinox A seasonal marker that occurs when the subsolar point is over the equator about March 20. (p. 62)

marine terrace A wave-cut bench that has been elevated above sea level. (p. 624)

mass movement (or *mass wasting*) Downslope movement of rock, soil, snow, or ice caused by gravity. (p. 491)

matter Any material that occupies space and possesses mass. (p. 8)

meander A looping bend in a stream channel on a floodplain. (p. 528)

Medieval Warm Period A naturally warm period from about 950 to 1250 CE; felt mostly in the Northern Hemisphere. (p. 192)

Mediterranean biome A biome characterized by hot, dry summers and winter rainfall, with vegetation adapted to drought and fire. (p. 270)

meridian A line on the globe that runs from the North Pole to the South Pole and connects points of the same longitude. (p. 18)

mesa A flat-topped elevated area with one or more cliff-face sides that is wider than it is tall. (p. 593)

mesocyclone The rotating cylindrical updraft within a supercell thunderstorm. (p. 164)

mesosphere The layer of the atmosphere between 50 and 80 km (30 and 50 mi) above the surface. (p. 41)

metamorphic rock Rock formed by heat and pressure applied to preexisting rock. (p. 421)

mid-ocean ridge A submarine mountain range. (p. 335)

midlatitude cyclone (or *extratropical cyclone*) A large cyclonic storm at midlatitudes. (p. 177)

migration The seasonal movement of populations from one place to another, usually for feeding or breeding. (p. 227)

Milankovitch cycles Small changes in Earth-Sun orbital geometry that resulted in Quaternary glacial-interglacial cycles. (p. 197)

millibar (mb) A measure of atmospheric pressure; average sea level pressure is 1013.25 mb. (p. 100)

mineral A naturally occurring, crystalline, solid chemical element or compound with a uniform chemical composition. (p. 419)

modified Mercalli intensity (MMI) scale An earthquake ranking system based on the damage done to structures. (p. 462)

Moho The boundary that separates the crust from the lithospheric mantle, which lies about 35 km (22 mi) deep on average. (p. 375)

moist adiabatic rate The rate of cooling in a saturated air parcel; usually about 6°C/1,000 m (3.3°F/1,000 ft). (p. 105)

moment magnitude scale An earthquake ranking system based on the amount of ground movement produced. (p. 464)

monsoon A seasonal reversal of winds, characterized by summer onshore airflow and winter offshore airflow. (p. 142)

montane forest A forest biome composed of needle-leaved trees in the Northern Hemisphere and broad-leaved trees in the Southern Hemisphere; found on windward sides of mountains with abundant precipitation. (p. 277)

moraine A heap of unsorted sediments deposited by a glacier. (p. 564)

moulin (pronounced moo-LAN) A vertical shaft in a glacier through which meltwater flows. (p. 570)

mountain breeze A local downslope breeze produced by heating and cooling differences in mountainous areas. (p. 146)

mudflow A fast-moving flow composed mostly of mud. (p. 494)

multicell thunderstorm A type of thunderstorm that forms under conditions of moderate wind shear, is organized in squall lines or clusters, and often produces severe weather. (p. 163)

mutualism A relationship between two species from which both species benefit. (p. 236)

N

negative feedback A process in which interacting parts in a system stabilize the system. (p. 117)

niche The resources and environmental conditions that a species requires. (p. 230)

nimbostratus Rain-producing low-level sheets of clouds. (p. 109)

nitrogen dioxide (NO₂) A toxic reddish-brown gas produced mainly by vehicle tailpipe emissions. (p. 46)

non-native (or *exotic*) An organism that has been brought outside its original geographic range by people. (p. 225)

nor'easter A type of midlatitude cyclone that brings blizzard-like conditions to the Mid-Atlantic states and New England. (p. 177)

normal fault The result of tensional force as two fault blocks move apart, causing one fault block to slip downward in relation to the other fault block. (p. 459)

northern tree line The northernmost limit of the boreal forest. (p. 281)

northern tundra A cold, treeless high-latitude biome with vegetation consisting of shrubs and herbaceous perennials; found north of the boreal forest throughout northern Eurasia and North America (p. 281)

nunatak (pronounced nuh-nuh-TAK) Bedrock that protrudes above a glacier. (p. 556)

O

ocean conveyor belt The global system of surface and deep ocean currents that transfers heat toward the poles. (p. 199)

oceanic crust The crust beneath the oceans, composed mainly of basalt. (p. 375)

offshore wind A coastal wind flowing from land to sea. (p. 129)

omnivore An organism that eats both plants and animals. (p. 242)

onshore wind A coastal wind flowing from sea to land. (p. 129)

organic sedimentary rock Sedimentary rock composed mostly of organic material and derived from ancient organisms. (p. 426)

orogenesis Mountain building. (p. 407)

orogenic belt A linear mountain range. (p. 407)

orographic uplift The rising of air over mountains. (p. 107)

outcrop An exposed area of bedrock. (p. 421)

outer core The second innermost layer of Earth, composed of a liquid alloy of iron and nickel, which generates Earth's magnetic field. (p. 373)

outlet glacier A glacier that flows out of an ice sheet or ice cap through a constricted valley, usually into the ocean. (p. 556)

outwash plain A flat area of sediments deposited by glacial outlet streams. (p. 559)

oxbow lake A water-filled abandoned channel that results when a meander is cut off from the stream channel. (p. 528)

ozone (O₃) A molecule that is a pollutant in the lower atmosphere, but blocks harmful solar UV radiation in the stratosphere. (p. 47)

ozonosphere (pronounced oh-ZO-no-sphere) A region of the stratosphere with high concentrations of ozone molecules that block ultraviolet radiation. (p. 44)

P

Pacific Ring of Fire A zone of volcanically active mountain chains resulting from subduction on the margins of the Pacific Ocean. (p. 398)

pāhoehoe (pronounced pa-HOY-hoy) A lava flow with low viscosity and a smooth, glassy, or ropy surface. (p. 447)

paleoclimate Ancient climate. (p. 201)

Pangaea The supercontinent formed about 300 million years ago by the fusion of all continents. (p. 387)

Panthalassic Ocean The single large ocean that surrounded Pangaea 300 million years ago. (p. 387)

parallel A line that forms a circle on the globe by connecting points of the same latitude. (p. 16)

particulate matter (PM) Liquid and solid particles (aerosols) suspended in the atmosphere. (p. 47)

passive continental margin A margin of a continent that does not coincide with a plate boundary, typically characterized by a broad, sloping continental shelf. (p. 402)

paternoster lake One of a series of small lakes that form behind glacial steps in a glacial valley. (p. 562)

peat A brownish-black, heavy soil found in wetlands, formed from the partially decomposed remains of plants. (p. 428)

pedestal rock A remnant of a layer of erosion-resistant rock supported by a slender column of less resistant rock. (p. 584)

pedogenesis The process of soil formation. (p. 297)

pelagic Relating to the open sea. (p. 344)

perched water table A localized water table that lies above the regional water table. (p. 308)

percolation The process by which rainwater moves through the soil through narrow, meandering channels. (p. 307)

periglacial Of or referring to unglaciated areas at high latitudes and high elevations subject to persistent and intense freezing. (p. 547)

permafrost Ground that remains below freezing continuously for two years or more. (p. 547)

permanent stream A stream that flows all year. (p. 515)

permeability The ease with which water can flow through soil, sediments, or rocks. (p. 307)

petroglyph A prehistoric rock carving often made by scratching away rock varnish from a rock's surface. (p. 583)

photochemical smog Air pollution formed by the action of sunlight on tailpipe emissions. (p. 47)

photosynthesis The process by which plants, algae, and some bacteria convert the radiant energy of sunlight to chemical energy. (p. 8)

physical geography The study of Earth's living and nonliving physical systems and how they change naturally through space and time or are changed by human activity. (p. 4)

physical weathering The breakdown of rocks into smaller pieces, or clasts, without altering the chemical makeup of the rock. (p. 481)

phytoplankton Microscopic bacteria and algae that are suspended in the sunlit portions of water and photosynthesize. (p. 243)

piedmont glacier A lobe of ice that forms as a valley glacier flows onto a flat plain. (p. 556)

plane of the ecliptic The flat plane traced by the orbital paths of the planets in the solar system. (p. 61)

plate boundary The margin of a lithospheric plate. (p. 391)

plate tectonics A theory addressing the origin, movement, and recycling of lithospheric plates and the landforms that result. (p. 388)

playa A flat, dry lake bed in a desert valley in an internal drainage basin. (p. 589)

playa lake A shallow temporary lake that forms in an internal drainage basin. (p. 589)

plucking The process by which a glacier pulls up and breaks off pieces of bedrock as it moves downslope. (p. 558)

plunge pool A bowl at the base of a waterfall created by abrasion from circulating rocks. (p. 523)

pluton A dome-shaped igneous rock mass of no more than a few tens of kilometers in diameter. (p. 423)

point bar An accumulation of silt, sand, and gravel that forms at the inside edge of a stream meander, where deposition exceeds erosion. (p. 528)

polar easterlies Cold, dry winds originating near both poles and flowing south and east. (p. 137)

polar high An area of cold, dense air at each pole that forms a zone of thermal high pressure. (p. 134)

polar jet stream A discontinuous narrow band of fast-flowing air found at high altitudes between 30° and 60° latitude in the Northern Hemisphere. (p. 138)

population A group of organisms that interact and interbreed in the same geographic area. (p. 228)

porosity The available air space within sediments or rocks. (p. 307)

positive feedback A process in which interacting parts in a system destabilize the system. (p. 117)

potentiometric surface The elevation to which hydraulic pressure will push water in pipes or wells. (p. 310)

precipitation Solid or liquid water that falls from the atmosphere to the ground. (p. 95)

predation The consumption of one organism by another. (p. 234)

pressure-gradient force The force resulting from changes in barometric pressure across Earth's surface. (p. 130)

prevailing wind The direction the wind blows most frequently during a specified window of time. (p. 129)

primary forest Forest that has never been significantly modified by people. (p. 274)

primary pollutant A pollutant that enters the air or water directly from its source. (p. 45)

primary producer An organism that can convert sunlight into chemical energy through photosynthesis. (p. 241)

prime meridian Zero degrees longitude; the line of longitude that passes through Greenwich, England, and serves as the starting point from which all other lines of longitude are determined. (p. 16)

propagule Any material that is able to establish a new population. (p. 237)

protolith The parent or original rock from which metamorphic rock was formed. (p. 432)

pumice A lightweight, porous rock with at least 50% air content, formed from felsic lava. (p. 448)

pyroclast (or *pyroclastic materials*) Any fragment of solid material that is ejected from a volcano, ranging in size from ash to large boulders. (p. 445)

pyroclastic flow (or *nuée ardente*) A rapidly moving avalanche of searing hot gas and ash. (p. 454)

Q

Quaternary period The last 2.6 million years of Earth history; an ice age. (p. 196)

R

radiant energy (or *radiation*) Energy propagated in the form of electromagnetic waves, including visible light and heat. (p. 75)

radiation The process by which wave energy travels through the vacuum of space or through a physical medium such as air or water. (p. 68)

radiation fog (or *valley fog*) Fog that results when the ground radiates its heat away at night, cooling the air above it to the dew point. (p. 111)

radiative equilibrium temperature The temperature of an object resulting from the balance between incoming and outgoing energy. (p. 82)

radiometric dating A method of assigning absolute ages to Earth materials based on the radioactive decay of unstable elements in those materials. (p. 371)

rain shadow The dry, leeward side of a mountain range. (p. 106)

recessional moraine A ridge of till that forms at the toe of a glacier; formed where the glacier pauses as it is gradually retreating upslope. (p. 564)

reflection The process of returning a portion of the radiation striking a surface in the general direction from which it came. (p. 77)

reg A flat stony plain. (p. 589)

regolith Any loose, fragmented Earth material that covers bedrock. (p. 297)

relative age The age of one object or event in relation to the age of another without regard to how old either is. (p. 368)

relative humidity (RH) The ratio of water vapor content to water vapor capacity, expressed as a percentage. (p. 100)

relief The difference in elevation between two or more points on Earth's surface. (p. 10)

remote sensing Data collection from a distance. (p. 23)

renewable energy Energy that comes from sources that are not depleted when used, such as sunlight or wind. (p. 84)

reservoir An artificial lake. (p. 530)

reverse fault The result of compressional force as two fault blocks are pushed together, causing one block to move upward in relation to another block. (p. 459)

ridge push The process by which magma rising along a mid-ocean ridge forces oceanic crust of two separate plates apart. (p. 392)

rift A region where continental crust is stretching and splitting. (p. 394)

rift valley A linear valley with volcanoes formed by rifting of continental crust, sometimes filled with freshwater to form a deep lake. (p. 394)

rip current A short-lived jet of backwash formed as water from breakers flows back into the sea. (p. 613)

roche moutonnée (pronounced ROSH moo-ta-NAY) An elongated and asymmetrical ridge of glacially carved bedrock. (p. 563)

rock A solid mass composed of minerals or volcanic glass. (p. 420)

rock cycle A model of the processes by which rocks form, are transformed from one type to another, and are recycled into the mantle. (p. 421)

rock slide A landslide that consists of rocks and broken rock fragments. (p. 496)

rock varnish A thin, weathered, and darkened surface on exposed rock surfaces formed by the activities of bacteria and the accumulation of windblown clay particles. (p. 583)

rockfall A type of mass movement in which rocks tumble off a vertical or nearly vertical cliff face. (p. 499)

root wedging A physical weathering process in which plant roots break rocks apart. (p. 482)

Rossby wave (or *longwave*) A large undulation in the upper-level westerlies. (p. 138)

S

Saffir-Simpson scale A hurricane ranking system based on measured wind speeds. (p. 172)

saline lake A permanent body of salty water occupying a playa. (p. 589)

salinity The concentration of dissolved minerals in seawater. (p. 333)

salt wedging A physical weathering process in which salt crystals grow in pore spaces on a rock's surface and dislodge individual mineral grains within the rock. (p. 482)

saltation A bouncing or hopping motion of sediment in moving water (or air). (p. 520)

saltwater intrusion The contamination of a well by salt water as a result of groundwater overdraft. (p. 313)

sand dune A hill or ridge formed by the accumulation of windblown sand. (p. 586)

sandspit An elongated dry bar of sand that extends from a beach into the water; usually parallel with the shore. (p. 616)

sandstone A clastic sedimentary rock composed chiefly of quartz sand grains. (p. 427)

Santa Ana winds Winds that originate in the Great Basin and are heated adiabatically as they descend to sea level on the southern California coast and northern Baja California; often associated with major wildfires. (p. 147)

saturation The point at which an air parcel's water vapor content is equal to its water vapor capacity. (p. 99)

saturation vapor pressure The vapor pressure at which saturation occurs. (p. 100)

scattering The process of redirecting solar radiation in random directions as it strikes physical matter. (p. 77)

sclerophyllous Having stiff, leathery, and waxy leaves adapted to reduce water loss and herbivory. (p. 270)

sea breeze A local onshore breeze created by heating and cooling differences between water and land. (p. 142)

sea-level pressure Air pressure that has been adjusted to sea level. (p. 131)

sea stack A steep or vertical tower of rock separated from but near a rocky coastal cliff face. (p. 624)

seagrass meadow A shallow coastal ecosystem dominated by flowering plants that resemble grasses. (p. 340)

seamount A mountain rising from the seafloor, often a flat-topped inactive volcano. (p. 336)

seasonal flood A predictable period of flooding that occurs with seasonally heavy rain or snowmelt. (p. 533)

seawall An artificial hard structure designed to protect backshore environments from wave erosion during large storms. (p. 622)

secondary forest Forest that has regrown after being disturbed or cleared by people. (p. 274)

secondary pollutant A pollutant that is not directly emitted from a source, but forms through chemical reactions among primary pollutants in air or water. (p. 45)

sediment An accumulation of small fragments of rock and organic material that is not cemented together. (p. 421)

sedimentary rock Rock formed from compacted and cemented sediments. (p. 421)

seining An industrial fishing method that uses a large net to surround and catch fish. (p. 350)

seismic wave Energy released by an earthquake that travels through Earth's interior as a wave. (p. 372)

seismograph (or *seismometer*) An instrument used to detect, measure, and record ground shaking. (p. 461)

September equinox A seasonal marker that occurs when the subsolar point is over the equator about September 22. (p. 63)

sere A stage of ecological succession that follows ecological disturbance. (p. 241)

severe thunderstorm A thunderstorm that produces either hail sized 2.54 cm (1 in) in diameter, a tornado, or wind gusts of 93 km/h (58 mph) or greater. (p. 163)

shale A clastic sedimentary rock formed from clay. (p. 427)

shield volcano A broad, domed volcano formed from many layers of basaltic lava. (p. 445)

shingle beach A beach composed of sediment particles larger than sand, such as gravel or cobbles. (p. 616)

shortwave radiation (SWR) Solar radiation with wavelengths shorter than 4 μm; includes visible sunlight. (p. 76)

sill A horizontal sheet of igneous rock that was injected between layers of preexisting rock. (p. 423)

single-cell thunderstorm A type of thunderstorm that is short-lived and rarely severe. (p. 163)

sinkhole A depression in Earth's surface resulting from the weathering of carbonate rock underground. (p. 486)

sinkhole lake A sinkhole that has filled with water. (p. 486)

slab pull The process by which the weight of subducting oceanic lithosphere accelerates plate movement by pulling the plate deeper into the mantle. (p. 392)

slip face The leeward side of a sand dune, where sand settles at its angle of repose. (p. 586)

slump A type of mass movement in which regolith detaches and slides downslope along a spoon-shaped failure surface and comes to rest more or less as a unit. (p. 494)

small scale A geographic scale that makes geographic features small to cover a large area of Earth's surface. (p. 6)

soil The layer of sediment that has been modified by organisms and water; the region of the lithosphere into which plant roots extend. (p. 297)

soil creep The imperceptible downslope movement of soil and regolith as their volume changes in seasonal expansion-contraction cycles. (p. 493)

soil horizon A horizontal zone within the soil identified by its chemical and physical properties. (p. 297)

soil taxonomy A soil classification system that groups soils into 12 categories, or orders. (p. 305)

solar altitude The altitude of the Sun above the horizon in degrees. (p. 62)

solar irradiance The amount of solar energy that reaches Earth. (p. 199)

solifluction A type of soil creep in which freeze-thaw cycles cause the soil to flow slowly downslope in overlapping sheets. (p. 494)

spatial scale The physical size, length, distance, or area of an object or the physical space occupied by a process. (p. 5)

speciation The creation of new species through evolution. (p. 228)

species A group of individuals that naturally interact and can breed and produce fertile offspring. (p. 225)

specific heat The heat required to raise the temperature of any object or material by a given amount. (p. 72)

specific humidity The water vapor content of the atmosphere, expressed in grams of water per kilogram of air (g/kg). (p. 100)

speleothem A cavern formation that forms by precipitation of calcium carbonate. (p. 490)

spring A naturally occurring discharge of groundwater that is pushed to the ground surface by hydraulic pressure. (p. 308)

squall line A line of multicell thunderstorm cells that typically forms along a cold front. (p. 163)

stable atmosphere A condition in which air parcels are cooler and denser than the surrounding air and will not rise unless forced to do so. (p. 106)

stalactite A speleothem that grows from the ceiling of a cavern downward. (p. 491)

stalagmite A speleothem that grows from the floor of a cavern upward. (p. 491)

star dune A star-shaped dune formed as the prevailing wind changes direction through the year. (p. 586)

stepping-stone An island in an island chain that aids in the dispersal of organisms. (p. 238)

storm surge A rise in sea level caused by the strong winds and low atmospheric pressure of a hurricane. (p. 174)

stratosphere The atmospheric layer above the troposphere, which extends between about 12 and 50 km (7.5 and 30 mi) above Earth's surface and has a permanent temperature inversion. (p. 41)

stratovolcano (or *composite volcano*) A large, potentially explosive cone-shaped volcano composed of alternating layers of lava and pyroclast. (p. 445)

stratus A cloud type characterized by low, flat sheets of clouds. (p. 109)

stream A channel in which water flows downhill by the force of gravity. (p. 511)

stream discharge The volume of water flowing past a fixed point within a stream channel; expressed in cubic meters or cubic feet per second. (p. 517)

stream order A numerical system used to rank stream size based on the number of tributaries flowing into a stream. (p. 514)

stream piracy The diversion of one stream into another as headward erosion merges the two streams. (p. 525)

stream rejuvenation A process by which a stream gains downcutting energy as its base level is lowered relative to its drainage basin. (p. 523)

strike-slip fault The result of shearing force as one block moves horizontally in relation to another block. (p. 459)

subduction The process in which oceanic lithosphere bends and dives into the mantle beneath another lithospheric plate. (p. 391)

submergent coast A coast where sea level is rising or the land is sinking. (p. 615)

subpolar low A belt of low pressure roughly centered on 60° north and south and made up of cyclonic systems that bring frequent precipitation. (p. 135)

subsidence Lowering of land elevation through compaction of sediments. (p. 531)

subsolar point The single point at which the Sun's rays are perpendicular to Earth's surface at or near noon; restricted to between 23.5° north and south latitude. (p. 61)

subtropical high A discontinuous belt of aridity and high pressure made up of anticyclones roughly centered on 30° north and south latitude. (p. 135)

sulfur dioxide (SO$_2$) A pungent gas, produced by volcanic eruptions and by the burning of fossil fuels, that causes human health problems and acid rain. (p. 46)

supercell thunderstorm A thunderstorm with a rotating cylindrical updraft that usually produces severe weather. (p. 164)

superposition The principle that in a sequence of rock layers, the oldest rocks are always at the bottom and the youngest at the top. (p. 370)

suspended load Small particles such as clay and silt that remain suspended in flowing water or wind. (p. 520)

swash The rush of water up a beach following the collapse of a breaker. (p. 613)

sweepstakes dispersal Dispersal across an extensive region of inhospitable space. (p. 238)

syncline A fold in the crust with a U-shaped dip. (p. 406)

system A set of interacting parts or processes that function as a unit. (p. 4)

T

tafoni Pits or cavities on the surface of a rock that form through salt wedging. (p. 482)

talus (or *scree*) Pieces of angular broken rock that accumulate at the base of a steep slope or vertical cliff. (p. 499)

tarn A mountain lake that forms within or just below a cirque. (p. 561)

taxonomy The classification and naming of organisms based on their genetic similarities. (p. 243)

temperate deciduous forest A biome dominated by trees that shed their leaves in winter in response to low temperatures. (p. 271)

temperate grassland A grass-dominated biome characterized by significant moisture deficits, natural fires, and grazing herbivores. (p. 268)

temperate rainforest A forest biome found mostly on the west coasts of continents where annual precipitation is high; typically has large trees forming a dense canopy. (p. 274)

temperature The average kinetic movement of atoms and molecules of a substance. (p. 66)

temperature inversion A layer of the atmosphere in which air temperature increases with increased height. (p. 41)

temporal scale The window of time used to examine phenomena and processes or the length of time over which they develop or change. (p. 5)

terminal moraine A moraine that marks the farthest advance of a glacier's toe. (p. 564)

terraform To transform a planet to suit human needs. (p. 257)

thermal pressure Air pressure resulting from changes in temperature. (p. 129)

thermocline The transitional zone between warm surface water and cold water at depth. (p. 330)

thermosphere The atmospheric layer located from 80 to 600 km (50 to 370 mi) above the surface. (p. 41)

thunder An acoustic shock wave produced when lightning rapidly heats and expands the air around it. (p. 165)

thunderstorm A cumulonimbus cloud that produces lightning and thunder. (p. 161)

tide The rise and fall of sea level caused by the gravitational effects of the Moon and the Sun. (p. 609)

till Any debris deposited by a glacier without the influence of running water. (p. 564)

toe The leading edge and lowest elevation of a glacier. (p. 553)

tombolo A landform consisting of an island and a sandspit that connects it to the mainland. (p. 617)

topography The shape and physical character of Earth's surface. (p. 22)

tornado A violently rotating column of air that descends from a cumulonimbus cloud and touches ground. (p. 167)

tornado warning A warning issued by the National Weather Service after a tornado has been seen and called in to local authorities or when one is suggested by a Doppler radar hook echo signature. (p. 169)

tornado watch An alert issued by the National Weather service when conditions are favorable for tornadic thunderstorms. (p. 169)

traction The dragging and tumbling of large rocks in a stream channel. (p. 520)

trade winds Easterly surface winds found between the ITCZ and the subtropical high, between 0° and 30° north and south latitude. (p. 136)

transform plate boundary A plate boundary where one lithospheric plate slips laterally past another. (p. 394)

transmission The unimpeded movement of electromagnetic energy through a medium such as air, water, or glass. (p. 77)

transpiration The loss of water to the atmosphere by plants. (p. 96)

transverse dune A long, narrow sand dune with the ridge crest perpendicular (or transverse) to the prevailing wind. (p. 586)

trawling An industrial fishing method in which nets are dragged through the water column or along the seafloor. (p. 350)

tributary A stream that joins with other streams to form a larger stream. (p. 511)

trophic level One of the levels of an ecosystem through which energy and matter flow. (p. 242)

Tropic of Cancer The 23.5° north parallel; the maximum latitude of the subsolar point in the Northern Hemisphere. (p. 62)

Tropic of Capricorn The 23.5° south parallel; the maximum latitude of the subsolar point in the Southern Hemisphere. (p. 62)

tropical cyclone A tropical cyclonic storm with sustained winds of 119 km/h (74 mph) or greater. (p. 169)

tropical rainforest A forest biome in the humid lowland tropics; characterized by a multilayered forest structure and high biodiversity. (p. 259)

tropical savanna A woodland biome with a wet summer and dry winter climate pattern, characterized by widely spaced trees with a grass understory. (p. 264)

tropical seasonal forest A biome in the warm lowland tropics, characterized by high biodiversity and trees that are deciduous in response to winter drought. (p. 264)

tropical storm A tropical cyclonic storm with sustained winds between 63 and 118 km/h (39 to 73 mph). (p. 172)

tropics The geographic region located between 23.5 degrees north and south latitude. (p. 16)

tropopause The boundary between the troposphere and the stratosphere. (p. 42)

troposphere The lowest layer of the atmosphere, extending from Earth's surface up to about 12 km (7.5 mi), where all weather occurs. (p. 40)

trunk stream A single large stream into which smaller tributaries merge. (p. 511)

tsunami A large ocean wave triggered by an earthquake or other natural disturbance. (p. 444)

tundra A biome that occurs at any latitude where it is too cold for trees to grow. (p. 281)

typhoon A name used for tropical cyclones in Southeast Asia. (p. 170)

U

ultraviolet (UV) radiation Solar radiation that is shorter than visible wavelengths. (p. 44)

uniformitarianism The principle that the same imperceptible gradual processes are operating now and have operated in the past. (p. 368)

unstable atmosphere A condition in which air parcels rise on their own because they are warmer and less dense than the surrounding air. (p. 106)

upwelling The circulation of nutrient-rich water from the seafloor to the ocean surface. (p. 344)

urban heat island An urbanized region that is significantly warmer than surrounding rural areas. (p. 81)

V

valley breeze A local upslope breeze produced by heating and cooling differences in mountainous areas. (p. 146)

valley glacier A glacier that occupies a mountain valley. (p. 556)

vapor pressure The portion of air pressure exerted exclusively by molecules of water vapor. (p. 100)

ventifact A wind-sculpted desert rock shaped by abrasion by saltating sand. (p. 584)

virtual water The unseen water required to produce a manufactured item or food. (p. 319)

visible radiation (or *light*)The portion of the electromagnetic spectrum that people can see. (p. 76)

volatile organic compound (VOC) A toxic compound of hydrogen and carbon; also called a *hydrocarbon*. (p. 47)

volcanic explosivity index (VEI) An index used to rank volcanic eruptions based on the amount of material a volcano ejects during an eruption. (p. 453)

volcanic island arc A chain of islands formed where oceanic lithosphere of one plate is subducting beneath oceanic lithosphere of another plate. (p. 397)

volcano A mountain or hill formed by eruptions of lava and rock fragments. (p. 366)

W

Wadati-Benioff zone A sloping pattern of increasingly deep earthquake foci found in a subduction zone. (p. 396)

wall cloud A cylindrical cloud that protrudes from the base of a supercell thunderstorm. (p. 167)

warm front A region where warm air advances on and flows over cooler, heavier air; not associated with severe weather. (p. 177)

water footprint The amount of water required to produce a specific item, food, or service. (p. 318)

water table The top surface of an aquifer's zone of saturation. (p. 308)

water vapor Water in a gaseous state. (p. 11)

wave-cut bench A flat coastal platform resulting from wave erosion and exposed at low tide. (p. 624)

wave-cut notch A notch formed at the base of a coastal cliff as a result of weathering and erosion. (p. 624)

wave of translation A wave in which water moves forward in the direction of wave movement. (p. 613)

wave refraction The process in which waves approaching the shoreline bend and maintain a nearly parallel orientation to the shore. (p. 613)

waves of oscillation Waves in which water moves in a circular path. (p. 610)

weather The state of the atmosphere at any given moment, comprising ever-changing events on time scales ranging from minutes to weeks. (p. 193)

weathering The process by which solid rock is dissolved and broken apart into smaller fragments. (p. 481)

well A hole dug or drilled by people to gain access to groundwater. (p. 310)

westerlies Surface winds that come from the west and are found in both hemispheres between the subpolar low and the subtropical high. (p. 137)

wind shear Changes in wind speed and direction with altitude. (p. 163)

wind vane (or *weather vane*) An instrument used to measure wind direction. (p. 127)

Y

yardang An elongated ridge formed by deflation and sand abrasion in a desert; generally, two to three times longer than it is wide. (p. 584)

Younger Dryas A cold period that occurred 12,900 to 11,600 years ago. (p. 199)

Z

zone of aeration The layer of the ground not permanently saturated with water. (p. 308)

zone of saturation The layer of the ground that is usually saturated with water. (p. 308)

Further Readings

Geographer's Toolkit

1. Thomas, David S. G., and Andrew Goudie, eds. *The Dictionary of Physical Geography*, 3rd ed. Malden, MA: Blackwell Publishing, 2000.
2. de Blij, Harm. *Why Geography Matters: More Than Ever*. New York: Oxford University Press, 2012.
3. Jacobs, Frank. *Strange Maps: An Atlas of Cartographic Curiosities*. New York: Viking Studio, 2009.
4. Monmonier, Mark. *How to Lie with Maps*, 2nd ed. Chicago: University of Chicago Press, 1996.

Chapter 1

1. Molina, Mario, and Sherwood Rowland. "Stratospheric Sink for Chlorofluoromethanes: Chlorine Atom-Catalysed Destruction of Ozone." *Nature* 249 (1974): 810–812.
2. Murray, Christopher J. L., et al. "The State of U.S. Health, 1990–2010: Burden of Diseases, Injuries, and Risk Factors." *JAMA* 310 (2013): 591–606.
3. National Oceanic and Atmospheric Administration (NOAA). Stratospheric Ozone Monitoring and Research in NOAA. http://www.ozonelayer.noaa.gov/
4. Pasachoff, Jay, and Vincent Schaefer. *A Field Guide to the Atmosphere*. Peterson Field Guides. Boston: Houghton Mifflin Harcourt, 1998.
5. Wang, Yuan, Renyi Zhang, and R. Saravanan. "Asian Pollution Climatically Modulates Mid-Latitude Cyclones Following Hierarchical Modelling and Observational Analysis." *Nature Communications* 5 (2013): doi:10.1038/ncomms4098

Chapter 2

1. Malakoff, David, Jake Yeston, and Jesse Smith, "Getting Better to Get Bigger." Introduction to the special issue "Scaling Up Alternative Energy" of *Science* 329 (August 13, 2010).
2. Schiermeier, Quirin, Jeff Tollefson, Tony Scully, Alexandra Witze, and Oliver Morton, "Energy Alternatives: Electricity without Carbon." *Nature* 454 (2008): 816–823.
3. Wines, Michael. *A Push Away from Burning Coal as an Energy Source. New York Times*. November 14, 2013.
4. Yergin, Daniel. *The Quest: Energy, Security, and the Remaking of the Modern World*. New York: Penguin, 2011.

Chapter 3

1. Burt, Christopher. *Extreme Weather: A Guide and Record Book*. New York: W.W. Norton, 2007.
2. Fasullo, John T., and Kevin E. Trenberth. "A Less Cloudy Future: The Role of Subtropical Subsidence in Climate Sensitivity." *Science* 9 (2012): 792–794.
3. Koren, Ilan, Guy Dagan, and Orit Altaratz. "From Aerosol-Limited to Invigoration of Warm Convective Clouds." *Science* 344 (2014): 1143–1146.
4. Sherwood, Steven C., Sandrine Bony, and Jean-Louis Dufresne. "Spread in Model Climate Sensitivity Traced to Atmospheric Convective Mixing." *Nature* 505 (2014): 37–42.

5. World Meteorological Organization. *International Cloud Atlas: Manual on the Observation of Clouds and Other Meteors*. Geneva: World Meteorological Organization, 1975.

Chapter 4

1. Burton, Tony, et al. *The Wind Energy Handbook*. 2nd ed. Chichester: Wiley, 2011.
2. Carré, Matthieu, et al. "Holocene History of ENSO Variance and Asymmetry in the Eastern Tropical Pacific." *Science* 345 (August 7, 2014): 1045–1048.
3. Makani Power Airborne Wind Energy. http://www.makanipower.com/home/
4. Marvel, Kate, Ben Kravitz, and Ken Caldeira. "Geophysical Limits to Global Wind Power." *Nature Climate Change* 3 (2013): 118–121.
5. Subramanian, Meera. "The Trouble with Turbines: An Ill Wind." *Nature* 486 (2012): 310–311.

Chapter 5

1. Cullen, Heidi. *The Weather of the Future: Heat Waves, Extreme Storms, and Other Scenes from a Climate-Changed Planet*. New York: Harper, 2010.
2. Irfan, Umair. "El Niño Climate Pattern May Influence Disease Outbreaks Globally." *Scientific American*, January 30, 2012.
3. Trapp, Robert. "On the Significance of Multiple Consecutive Days of Tornado Activity." *Monthly Weather Review* 142 (2014): 1452–1459.
4. Yancheva, Gergana, et al. "Influence of the Intertropical Convergence Zone on the East Asian Monsoon." *Nature* 445 (2007): 74–77.

Chapter 6

1. Archer, David. *Global Warming: Understanding the Forecast*. Malden, MA: Blackwell Publishing, 2007.
2. Cullen, Heidi. *The Weather of the Future: Heat Waves, Extreme Storms, and Other Scenes from a Climate-Changed Planet*. New York: Harper, 2010.
3. DeConto, Robert M., et al. "Past Extreme Warming Events Linked to Massive Carbon Release from Thawing Permafrost." *Nature* 484 (2012): 87–91.
4. Diamond, Jared. *Collapse: How Societies Choose to Fail or Succeed*. New York: Viking Press, 2005.
5. Dow, Kirstin, and Thomas E. Downing. *The Atlas of Climate Change: Mapping the World's Greatest Challenge*, 3rd ed. Berkeley: University of California Press, 2011.
6. Heide-Jørgensen, Mads Peter, et al. "The Northwest Passage Opens for Bowhead Whales." *Biology Letters* 8 (2012): 270–273.
7. Mathez, Edmond A. *Climate Change: The Science of Global Warming and Our Energy Future*. New York: Columbia University Press, 2009.
8. Riser, Stephen, and M. Susan Lozier. "New Simulations Question the Gulf Stream's Role in Tempering Europe's Winters." *Scientific American* 308 (February 1, 2013): 50–55.
9. Zachos, James, et al. "Trends, Rhythms, and Aberrations in Global Climate 65 Ma to Present." *Science* 292 (2001): 886–993.

Chapter 7

1. Cox, C. Barry, and Peter D. Moore. *Biogeography: An Ecological and Evolutionary Approach*, 7th rf. Malden, MA: Blackwell Publishing, 2005.
2. Estes, James A., et al. "Trophic Downgrading of Planet Earth." *Science* 333 (2011): 301–306.
3. Hulme, Philip E. "Invasive Species Unchecked by Climate." *Science* 335 (2012): 538–539.
4. MacDonald, Glen. *Biogeography: Introduction to Space, Time, and Life*. Wiley, New York, 2003.
5. Quammen, David. *The Boilerplate Rhino: Nature in the Eye of the Beholder*. New York: Scribner, 2001.
6. Rull, Valentí. "Origins of Biodiversity." *Science* 331 (2011): 398–399.

Chapter 8

1. Lenzen, M., et al. "International Trade Drives Biodiversity Threats in Developing Nations." *Nature* 486 (2012): 109–112.
2. Little, Jane Braxton. "Regrowing Borneo's Rainforest—Tree by Tree." *Scientific American* (December 1, 2008).
3. Naidoo, R., et al. "A Newly Discovered Wildlife Migration in Namibia and Botswana is the Longest in Africa." *Oryx*, 2014. doi: 10.1017/S0030605314000222
4. Quammen, David. *The Song of the Dodo: Island Biogeography in an Age of Extinction*. New York: Scribner, 1997.
5. Sandom, Christopher J., et al. "High Herbivore Density Associated with Vegetation Diversity in Interglacial Ecosystems." *Proceedings of the National Academy of Sciences* 111 (2014): 4162–4167.

Chapter 9

1. Castle, Stephanie L., et al. "Groundwater Depletion During Drought Threatens Future Water Security of the Colorado River Basin." *Geophysical Research Letters* 31 (August 28, 2014): 5904–5911. doi: 10.1002/2014GL061055
2. Huggins, David R., and John P. Reganold. "No-Till: How Farmers Are Saving the Soil by Parking Their Plows." *Scientific American*, July 2008.
3. Kennett, Douglas, et al. "Development and Disintegration of Maya Political Systems in Response to Climate Change." *Science* 338 (November 9, 2012): 788–791.
4. Logan, William Bryant. *Dirt: The Ecstatic Skin of the Earth*. New York: W.W. Norton, 2007.
5. Petley, David. "Global Patterns of Loss of Life from Landslides." *Geology* 40 (2012): 927–930.
6. Reisner, Marc. *Cadillac Desert: The American Desert and Its Disappearing Water*. New York: Penguin Books, 1993.
7. Scholes, M. C., and R. J. Scholes. "Dust Unto Dust." *Science* 342 (November 1, 2013): 565–566.

Chapter 10

1. Crist, Darlene Trew, Gail Scowcroft, and James M. Harding. *World Ocean Census: A Global Survey of Marine Life*. Buffalo, New York: Firefly Books, 2009.
2. Dean, Cornelia. "Study Finds Hope in Saving Saltwater Fish." *New York Times*, July 30, 2009.
3. Earle, Sylvia A., and Linda K. Glover. *Ocean: An Illustrated Atlas*. Washington, D.C.: National Geographic Society, 2009.
4. Farndon, John. *Atlas of Oceans: An Ecological Survey of Underwater Life*. New Haven, Connecticut: Yale University Press, 2011.
5. Hinrichsen, Don. *The Atlas of Coasts and Oceans: Ecosystems, Threatened Resources, Marine Conservation*. Chicago: University of Chicago Press, 2011.
6. Maina, Joseph, et al. "Global Gradients of Coral Exposure to Environmental Stresses and Implications for Local Management." *PLoS ONE* 6 (August 10, 2011). doi: 10.1371/journal.pone.0023064

7. Pusceddu, A., et al. "Chronic and Intensive Bottom Trawling Impairs Deep-Sea Biodiversity and Ecosystem Functioning." *Proceedings of the National Academy of Sciences* 111 (June 17, 2014): 8861–8866.
8. Worm, Brian, et al. "Impacts of Biodiversity Loss on Ocean Ecosystem Services." *Science* 314 (2006): 787–790.

Chapter 11

1. Crowe, Sean A., et al. "Atmospheric Oxygenation Three Billion Years Ago." *Nature* 501 (2013): 535–538.
2. Crutzen, Paul. "Geology of Mankind." *Nature* 415 (2002): 23.
3. Hazen, Robert. *The Story of Earth: The First 4.5 Billion Years, from Stardust to Living Planet*. New York: Viking, 2012.
4. Kolbert, Elizabeth. "The Lost World." *The New Yorker*, December 23 and 30, 2013.
5. Vince, Gaia. "An Epoch Debate." *Science* 334 (October 7, 2011): 32–37.

Chapter 12

1. Hughes, Patrick. "Alfred Wegener (1880–1930): On the Shoulders of Giants." Earth Observatory, NASA, February 8, 2001. http://earthobservatory.nasa.gov/Features/Wegener/wegener.php
2. Kääb, Andreas, Etienne Berthier, Christopher Nuth, Julie Gardelle, and Yves Arnaud. "Contrasting Patterns of Early Twenty-First-Century Glacier Mass Change in the Himalayas." *Nature* 488 (August 23, 2012): 495–498.
3. Mitchell, Ross, Taylor Kilian, and David Evans. "Supercontinent Cycles and the Calculation of Absolute Palaeolongitude in Deep Time." *Nature* 482 (February 9, 2012): 208–211.
4. Redfern, Ron. *Origins: The Evolution of Continents, Oceans and Life*. Norman: University of Oklahoma Press, 2001.

Chapter 13

1. Eves, Robert L. *Water, Rock, and Time: The Geologic Story of Zion National Park*. Springdale, Utah: Zion Natural History Association, 2005.
2. Hand, Eric. "Injection Wells Blamed in Oklahoma Earthquakes." *Science* 345 (July 4, 2014): 13–14.
3. Hughes, David. "Energy: A Reality Check on the Shale Revolution." *Nature* 494 (2013): 307–308.
4. iLoveMountains.org. "The Human Cost of Coal: Mountaintop's Removal's Effect on Health and the Economy." Accessed 03/16/2013. http://ilovemountains.org/the-human-cost
5. McBrearty, Sally. "Palaeoanthropology: Sharpening the Mind." *Nature* 491 (November 7, 2012): 531–532.
6. Pellant, Chris. *Smithsonian Handbooks: Rocks and Minerals*. Washington, D.C.: Dorling Kindersley, 2002.

Chapter 14

1. Hall, Stephen. "Scientists on Trial: At Fault?" *Nature* 477 (2001): 264–269.
2. Klingaman, William. *The Year without Summer: 1816 and the Volcano That Darkened the World and Changed History*. New York: St. Martin's Press, 2013.
3. Revkin, Andrew. "With No Alert System, Indian Ocean Nations Were Vulnerable." *New York Times*, December 27, 2004.
4. Petersen, M.D., et al. "Documentation for the 2014 Update of the United States National Seismic Hazard Maps: U.S. Geological Survey Open-File Report 2014–1091." http://dx.doi.org/10.333/ofr20141091
5. Wignall, Paul. "Earth Science: Lethal Volcanism." *Nature* 477 (September 15, 2011): 285–286.

Chapter 15

1. Larsen, Isaac J., and David R. Montgomery. "Landslide Erosion Coupled to Tectonics and River Incision." *Nature Geoscience* 5 (2012): 468–473.
2. Parker, Robert N., et al. "Mass Wasting Triggered by the 2008 Wenchuan Earthquake Is Greater Than Orogenic Growth." *Nature Geoscience* 4 (2011): 449–452.
3. Perkins, Sid. "Death Toll from Landslides Vastly Underestimated." *Nature* (August 8, 2012). doi:10.1038/nature.2012.11140
4. Qiu, Jane. "Landslide Risks Rise Up Agenda." *Nature* 511 (July 15, 2014): 272–273.
5. Stone, Richard, and Robert Service. "Even for Slide-Prone Region, Landslide Was Off the Chart." *Science* 344 (April 4, 2014): 16–17.
6. Turner, Keith, and Robert Schuster. *Landslides: Investigation and Mitigation*. Washington, D.C.: Transportation Research Board, 1996.

Chapter 16

1. Egholm, David L., Mads F. Knudsen, and Mike Sandiford. "Lifespan of Mountain Ranges Scaled by Feedbacks Between Landsliding and Erosion by Rivers." *Nature* 498 (June 26, 2013): 475–478.
2. Frey, Philippe, and Michael Church. "How River Beds Move." *Science* 325 (September 18, 2009): 1509–1510.
3. Heffernan, Olive. "Adapting to a Warmer World: No Going Back." *Nature* 491 (2012): 659–661.
4. Jefferson, Anne. "Levees and the Illusion of Flood Control." *Scientific American Guest Blog*, May 20, 2011. http://blogs.scientificamerican.com
5. Kirwan, Matthew L., and J. Patrick Megonigal. "Tidal Wetland Stability in the Face of Human Impacts and Sea-Level Rise. *Nature* 504 (2013): 53–60.
6. Lovett, Richard. "Dam Removals: Rivers on the Run." *Nature* 511 (2014): 521–523.
7. McPhee, John. *The Control of Nature*. New York: Farrar, Straus and Giroux, 1990.
8. Nittrouer, Jeffrey A., et al. "Mitigating Land Loss in Coastal Louisiana by Controlled Diversion of Mississippi River Sand." *Nature Geoscience* 5 (August 2012): 534–537.

Chapter 17

1. Hanna, Edward, et al. "Ice-Sheet Mass Balance and Climate Change." *Nature* 498 (2013): 51–59.

2. Joughin, Ian, Benjamin E. Smith, and Brooke Medley. "Marine Ice Sheet Collapse Potentially Under Way for the Thwaites Glacier Basin, West Antarctica." *Science* 344 (May 16, 2014): 735–738.
3. Kerr, Richard. "Experts Agree Global Warming Is Melting the World Rapidly." *Science* 338 (November 30, 2012):1138.
4. McClintock, James. *Lost Antarctica: Adventures in a Disappearing Land*. Basingstoke, U.K.: Palgrave Macmillan, 2012.
5. NASA. Global Ice Viewer. http://climate.nasa.gov/GlobalIceViewer/index.cfm
6. Pokhrel, Yadu N., et al. "Model Estimates of Sea-Level Change Due to Anthropogenic Impacts on Terrestrial Water Storage." *Nature Geoscience* 5 (2012): 389–392.

Chapter 18

1. Abbey, Edward. *Desert Solitaire*. New York: McGraw-Hill, 1968.
2. Bray, Warwick. "Under the Skin of Nazca." *Nature* 358 (1992): 19.
3. Holmes, Jonathan A. "How the Sahara Became Dry." *Science* 320 (May 9, 2008): 752–753.
4. Norris, Richard D., et al. "Sliding Rocks on Racetrack Playa, Death Valley National Park: First Observation of Rocks in Motion." *PLoS One* 9 (August 27, 2014). doi: 10.1371/journal.pone.0105948
5. Thomas, David, Melanie Knight, and Giles Wiggs. "Remobilization of Southern African Desert Dune Systems by Twenty-First Century Global Warming." *Nature* 435 (June 30, 2005): 1218–1221.
6. Whitley, David. *Introduction to Rock Art Research*. 2nd ed. Walnut Grove, CA: Left Coast Press, 2011.

Chapter 19

1. Chu, M. L., et al. "A Simplified Approach for Simulating Changes in Beach Habitat Due to the Combined Effects of Long-Term Sea Level Rise, Storm Erosion, and Nourishment." *Environmental Modelling and Software* 52 (February 2014): 111–120.
2. Hobbs, Carl. *The Beach Book: The Science of the Shore*. New York: Columbia University Press, 2012.
3. Hoefel, Fernanda, and Steve Elgar. "Wave-Induced Sediment Transport and Sandbar Migration." *Science* 299 (2003): 1885–1887.
4. Storrs, Carina. "Slip-Sliding Away: Myrtle Beach Erosion Could Explain Sand Loss along the U.S. East Coast." *Scientific American* (October 30, 2009). http://www.scientificamerican.com/article/myrtle-beach-south-carolina-coastline-erosion/

Index

Note: Page numbers followed by the letter f indicate figures; page numbers followed by the letter t indicate tables; and page numbers in *italics* indicate photographs.

Index of Places Visited

WORLD POLITICAL MAP

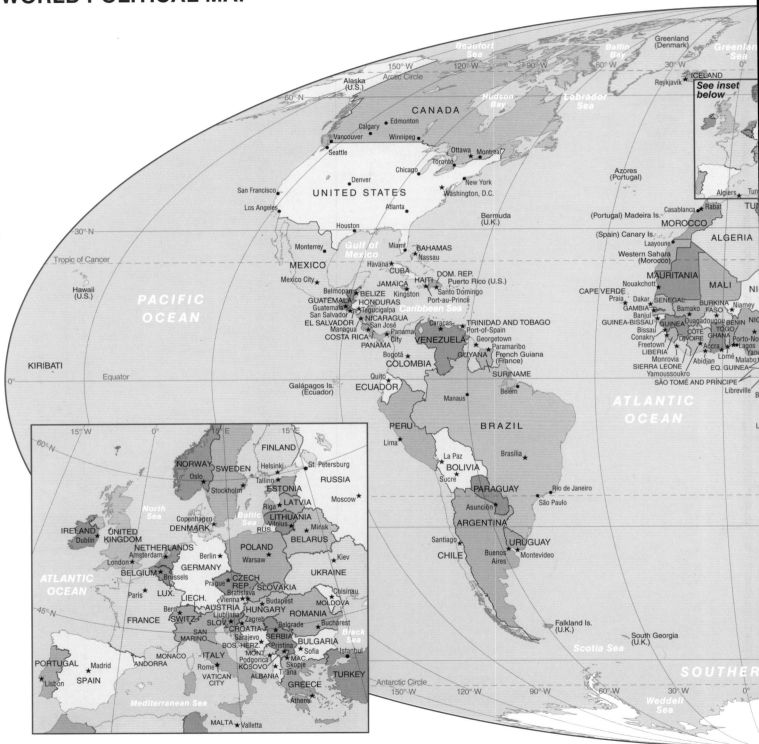

6, 169, 408

See inset below

Greenland (Denmark)

Beaufort Sea

Baffin Bay

Greenlan Sea

ICELAND
Reykjavík

Arctic Circle

Alaska (U.S.)

CANADA

Hudson Bay

Labrador Sea

Calgary • Edmonton
Vancouver • Winnipeg
Seattle
Ottawa ★ Montreal
Toronto
Chicago
Denver • New York
Washington, D.C.

San Francisco
UNITED STATES
Atlanta

Los Angeles

Houston

Azores (Portugal)

(Portugal) Madeira Is.
Casablanca ★ Rabat
(Spain) Canary Is.
MOROCCO

TUN

Laayoune

ALGERIA

Western Sahara (Morocco)

Monterrey
Gulf of Mexico
Miami BAHAMAS
Nassau
Havana CUBA
DOM. REP.
Santo Domingo
Puerto Rico (U.S.)

MAURITANIA
Nouakchott

MALI

NI

Mexico City
MEXICO

JAMAICA HAITI
Kingston
Port-au-Prince

CAPE VERDE
Praia • Dakar SENEGAL
GAMBIA Bamako
Banjul
GUINEA-BISSAU
Bissau
Conakry
Freetown

BURKINA
FASO Niamey
BENIN NIG
TOGO
GHANA
Porto-No
Lomé Lagos
Accra Yaou

Belmopan
GUATEMALA BELIZE
Guatemala HONDURAS
San Salvador Tegucigalpa
EL SALVADOR NICARAGUA
Managua San José
COSTA RICA Panama
PANAMA City

Caribbean Sea

TRINIDAD AND TOBAGO
Port-of-Spain
Georgetown
Paramaribo
GUYANA French Guiana (France)
SURINAME

Caracas
VENEZUELA

GUINEA Ouagadougou
CÔTE
D'IVOIRE
Abidjan
LIBERIA
Monrovia
SIERRA LEONE
Yamoussoukro

EQ. GUINEA
Malabo

SÃO TOMÉ AND PRÍNCIPE
Libreville

Tropic of Cancer

Hawaii (U.S.)

PACIFIC OCEAN

KIRIBATI

Equator

Galápagos Is. (Ecuador)

Bogotá
COLOMBIA
Quito
ECUADOR

Manaus

Belém

ATLANTIC OCEAN

L

PERU
Lima

BRAZIL

Brasília

30° N

0°

La Paz
BOLIVIA
Sucre

Rio de Janeiro
São Paulo

PARAGUAY
Asunción

ARGENTINA

Santiago
CHILE

Buenos Aires
URUGUAY
Montevideo

Falkland Is. (U.K.)

South Georgia (U.K.)

Scotia Sea

SOUTHER

Antarctic Circle

Weddell Sea

Europe inset

60° N

15° W   0°   15° E   15° E

FINLAND

NORWAY SWEDEN Helsinki
Oslo
Stockholm
Tallinn
ESTONIA
RIGA LATVIA
Riga
LITHUANIA
Vilnius
RUS.

St. Petersburg

RUSSIA

Moscow

North Sea

Copenhagen
DENMARK
Baltic Sea

Minsk
BELARUS

IRELAND UNITED KINGDOM
Dublin
NETHERLANDS
Amsterdam
London
BELGIUM
Brussels

POLAND
Berlin
Warsaw
GERMANY
Prague
CZECH REP.
SLOVAKIA
Bratislava
Vienna
LIECH. AUSTRIA HUNGARY
Budapest
Ljubljana
SLOV.
Zagreb
CROATIA
Belgrade

Kiev
UKRAINE

Chisinau
MOLDOVA

ATLANTIC OCEAN

Paris
LUX.

45° N

FRANCE SWITZ.
Bern

ROMANIA
Bucharest

San Marino
SAN MARINO
Sarajevo SERBIA
BOS.-HERZ. Pristina
MONT.
Podgorica KOSOVO
Tirana

BULGARIA
Sofia

Black Sea
Istanbul

PORTUGAL
Lisbon
SPAIN
Madrid

MONACO
ANDORRA
ITALY
Rome
VATICAN CITY

MAC.
Skopje
ALBANIA

TURKEY

GREECE
Athens

Mediterranean Sea

MALTA ★ Valletta